CONTINUUM & THE PUBLISHERS ASSOCIATION

DIRECTORY OF PUBLISHING
2009

UNITED KINGDOM AND THE REPUBLIC OF IRELAND

Continuum
The Tower Building
11 York Road
London SE1 7NX

80 Maiden Lane
Suite 704
New York, NY 10038

© Continuum 2008

All rights reserved. No part of this publication may
be reproduced, stored in a retrieval system, or transmitted,
in any form or by any means, electronic, mechanical,
photocopying, recording or otherwise, without the prior
permission in writing from the Publishers or their
appointed agents.

Thirty-fourth Edition 2008

British Library Cataloguing-in-Publication Data
A catalogue entry for this book is available from the British Library.

ISBN: 9781847065438

Research and editing by First Edition Translations, Cambridge
Text input, processing and typesetting by John Ainslie Consultancy
Printed and bound in the UK by MPG Books Ltd, Bodmin, Cornwall

Contents

1. Introduction
   - Foreword v
   - How to obtain British books vi
   - The Publishers Association viii
2. Publishers 1
3. Packagers 99
4. Authors' Agents 103
5. Trade & Allied Associations
   - 5.1 International 112
   - 5.2 United Kingdom & Republic of Ireland 112
6. Trade & Allied Services
   - 6.1 Editorial Services 121
   - 6.2 Design & Production Services 123
   - 6.3 Electronic Publishing Services 124
   - 6.4 Translation Services 125
   - 6.5 Sales & Marketing Services 126
   - 6.6 Distributors 129
   - 6.7 Remainder Merchants 136
   - 6.8 Main Wholesalers 136
   - 6.9 Main Library Suppliers 137
   - 6.10 Book Clubs 137
   - 6.11 Literary & Trade Events 138
   - 6.12 Publishing Reference Books & Periodicals 139
   - 6.13 Training 141
7. Appendices
   - 7.1 Publishers classified by Fields of Activity 143
   - 7.2 Index of ISBN Prefixes 158
   - 7.3 Index of Personal Names 162
   - 7.4 Index of Companies & Imprints 170
   - 7.5 UK Publishers by Postcode 184

1 Introduction

FOREWORD

The 34th edition of the *Directory of Publishing*, published by Continuum in association with The Publishers Association, provides an indispensable guide to book publishing in the United Kingdom and Republic of Ireland and contains details of nearly 900 publishers. In addition to the detailed entries on publishers, the *Directory* offers in depth coverage of the wider UK book trade, and lists over 500 organizations associated with the industry, including packagers, distributors, library suppliers, authors' agents and translation services. An appendix analyses publishers by field of speciality. Indexes include ISBN prefix numbers; names of key personnel and publishers' imprints; and a listing of UK publishers by postcode.

The directory is updated annually. Previous entrants are sent last year's entry and new entrants a questionnaire. We are grateful to all those who have provided information for this edition. We have done all we can to ensure accuracy and completeness, but cannot accept responsibility for errors or omissions that escaped us. New entrants either approached the publisher or were discovered by monitoring various sources – the trade press, publishers' catalogues, exhibitions, book fairs, and the files of the Publishers Association itself.

As in the previous edition we have not excluded all organizations which have failed to reply to our mailings. Instead we have re-run their 2008 entries (in abbreviated form) and marked them with an asterisk. However, such organizations will be deleted from the next edition if they fail to update their entries for the second year running.

We welcome all comments and suggestions from readers for improvements. We are also happy to receive details of possible new entries, but please note these must meet our criteria for inclusion. Publishers must either be a PA or CLÉ member or be of a certain size, publishing at least 5 new titles a year or employing at least 4 people.

All organizations are entered free of charge.

Continuum

ABBREVIATIONS

UK Book Trade Association Membership
Publishers Association
APD – Publishers Association: Academic & Professional Division
BA – Booksellers Association
EPC – Educational Publishers Council
IGSMTP – International Group of Scientific, Medical & Technical Publishers
IPG – Independent Publishers Guild

* Asterisked entries indicate 2007 data.
Underlined entries indicate members of the Publishers Association.

HOW TO OBTAIN BRITISH BOOKS

This introduction is particularly intended for booksellers ordering from a British publisher for the first time.

HOW TO ORDER
1 If you have not previously ordered from a publisher, you should write for details on:
   trade discounts;
   credit facilities;
   catalogue mailing.
Please enclose in your letter information including:
   name and address of your bank;
   names and addresses of one or two publishers, preferably British, with whom you already do business. In certain circumstances you may be directed to a local stockist, agent or representative.

2 When the publisher agrees to supply you, your order should include:
   your full name and address;
   order date and order number;
   dispatch instructions: where you want the books to be sent and where you want the invoice sent;
   carriage instructions:
      surface post
      special carrier (e.g. shipper)
      air freight
   invoicing instructions:
      if you want a separate invoice by airmail
      minimum number of copies you require
   full details of the book:
      number of copies you need
      title
      author/editor
      cased/limp/paperback
      international standard book number (ISBN)

3 Orders Clearing, Mardev Ltd, Quadrant House, The Quadrant, Sutton, Surrey SM2 5AS (tel: +44 (0)20 8652 3899, fax: +44 (0)20 8652 4597, email: enquiries@mardev.com, web site: http://www.mardevlists.com) have an Orders Clearing system: by sending all your orders for different publishers to the one address, you can save yourself money. Similarly, Orders Clearing operates a service for the payment of publishers' accounts, the Overseas Booksellers' Clearing House (OBCH). Booksellers may send one cheque for various accounts and OBCH will then distribute the payments to the different publishers.

4 An Orders Clearing Service is also offered by the Booksellers Order Distribution Ltd (BOD). Their address is 49 Victoria Road, Aldershot, Hampshire GU11 1SJ (tel: +44 (0)1252 20697, fax: +44 (0)1252 20697).

5 Nielsen BookNet provides a range of e-commerce services that allow electronic trading between booksellers, distributors, publishers, libraries and other suppliers, regardless of their size and location. Services include BookNet for booksellers and publishers/distributors, TeleOrdering and EDI messaging. Contact Nielsen BookData, 3rd Floor, Midas House, 62 Goldsworth Road, Woking, GU21 6LQ (tel: +44 (0)870 777 8710, fax: +44 (0)870 777 8711, email: sales@nielsenbookdata.co.uk, website: http://www.bookdata.co.uk).

FOR REFERENCE
1 **Nielsen BookData:**
Provides monthly and quarterly content-rich book information for English-language titles published internationally. Available on CD-ROM and online by subscription from Nielsen BookData, 3rd Floor, Midas House, 62 Goldsworth Road, Woking, GU21 6LQ (tel: +44 (0)870 777 8710, fax: +44 (0)870 777 8711, email: sales@nielsenbookdata.co.uk, website: http://www.bookdata.co.uk).

2 **The Bookseller:**
The British book trade journal, published weekly by Bookseller Publications, containing correspondence, articles, trade news, together with a list of books published each week (web site: http://www.theBookseller.com). See also section 6.12 for details of other periodicals and reference books of the trade.

3 **British National Bibliography:**
A subject list of new British books arranged by Dewey classification. Published weekly with interim cumulations and an annual cumulation by the British Library, National Bibliographic Service, Boston Spa, Wetherby, West Yorkshire LS23 7BQ (tel: +44 (0)1937 546585, fax: +44 (0)1937 546586, email: nbs-info@bl.uk, web site: http://www.bl.uk).

4 Individual publishers will normally provide catalogues of their own publications on request.

HOW TO PAY
You can pay by:
   cheque, bank draft or letter of credit
   bill of exchange drawn by the publisher on your giro or postal account
   international money order/postal order

IMPORTANT
Please make sure that:
   the publisher receives the *full amount* of the invoice value, free of all bank charges and transfer fees;
   you pay *promptly*;
   if you have any problems, raise them *promptly*;
   if you have any difficulty in paying, consult your local bank manager, or the British Embassy, Consulate or High Commission.

WHEN YOU HAVE DIFFICULTY IN OBTAINING BRITISH BOOKS
1   If you have a problem of a *general* nature, please write to the Publishers Association, 29b Montague Street, London WC1B 5BH (email: mail@publishers.org.uk, tel: +44 (0)20 7691 9191, fax: +44 (0)20 7691 9199). The Association cannot intervene in problems which may arise between individual booksellers and publishers.

2   **British Council**
Your nearest office may be able to help you with enquiries about UK publishing. Details of its network of offices are available from: British Council Information Centre, tel: +44 (0)161 957 7755, fax: +44 (0) 161 957 7762, email: general.enquiries@britishcouncil.org, minicom: +44 (0)161 957 7188, web site: http://www.britishcouncil.org.

PUBLISHERS' ABBREVIATED ANSWERS
Most publishers use one of the answers below when books are not available, and give an explanation of their answer codes at the bottom of the invoice.

NK	Not known, not ours, or so far in the future or so long out of print that it is unknown to the trade department
OO/TF	On order, to follow shortly
B8 *or* **BDG8**	Binding, will be available in August
B/ND	Binding (no date)
RP/June *or* **RP/6**	Reprint available in June
RP/2M	Reprint available in 2 months
NYP	Not yet published
NEP	New edition in preparation
RPUC	Reprint under consideration
OP	Out of print
OO/USA	On order, to be supplied by USA
TOP	Temporarily out of print
OS	Out of stock
RP/ND	Reprinting, no date

TECHNICAL TERMS
Firm
Books are normally supplied 'firm'. This means you will accept the books, pay for them, and will not be able to return them.

See-safe or **On approval**
Some publishers are prepared to supply books on the basis that they are paid for at normal credit terms, but if the books remain unsold they may be returned with the publisher's authorization for crediting against future orders. You will be expected to return the books at your own expense. You should always obtain in writing details from publishers of any such agreements they are prepared to offer to their customers.

Standing Orders
Some publishers operate a scheme which allows a bookseller automatically to receive books in given subjects as they are published. These are normally supplied 'on approval'. You should write to individual publishers for details of their schemes.

Continuation Orders
Continuation Orders can be placed for books published in series and multi-volume works. This means that each new volume that appears will be sent to you automatically.

Pro-forma Invoice
Some publishers may prefer to supply initial orders by means of a pro-forma invoice which has to be paid before the books are sent.

THE PUBLISHERS ASSOCIATION

29b Montague Street, London WC1B 5BW
Telephone: +44 (0)20 7691 9191 **Fax:** +44 (0)20 7691 9199
Email: mail@publishers.org.uk
Web site: http://www.publishers.org.uk

Chief Executive: Simon Juden
Director of Educational, Academic & Professional Publishing: Graham Taylor
Director of International Services: Simon Bell

Making the case for UK publishers

– The Publishers Association is the leading organisation working on the behalf of book, journal and electronic publishers based in the UK. We bring publishers together to discuss the critical issues facing the industry and to define the practical policies, which will drive our lobbying and campaigns in the UK and Internationally. The aim of The Publishers Association is to ensure a secure future for the UK publishing industry.

– Acting for the Industry: The PA's mission is to strengthen the trading environment for UK publishers by ensuring that the needs and concerns of the industry are heard at all levels of Government in the UK, in Europe and internationally. We are actively involved in issues such as: copyright legislation, the adaptation of legislation to digital technology, copyright licensing arrangements for education, business, and public bodies, legislation on VAT, e-commerce and other issues affecting publishers, funding for learning and information resources in schools, colleges and universities, the promotion of books and reading, export promotion of books and journals, anti-piracy campaigns (terrestrial and internet), efficiency in supply and marketing, the protection of freedom to publish.

– Front Line Information: PA posts front line information to our website and communicates with members through our regular e-mail bulletins. The Members Only section of the PA website contains detailed information prepared exclusively for members including: the latest market statistics, copyright law updates, comments on current government policy, PA briefs and reports on market concerns, anti-piracy action updates, digital rights information, updates on EU legislation.

Home and Export Markets

Market development is at the heart of the PA's activities, which include:

– International trade fairs, operating with UK Trade & Investment a subsidy scheme for companies wishing to exhibit. Additionally, our TurnKey Exhibition Services offer publishers a complete exhibition service for major fairs.

– Market intelligence, including free online access to the Global Publishing Information website (http://www.publishers.org.uk/gpi.nsf), and exclusive access to the Aid Digest.

– Trade delegations and seminars organised with UK Trade & Investment support, to gain knowledge of and exposure in growth markets such as China, Africa, Asia and Eastern Europe.

– Home trade initiatives, such as World Book Day, which result in a significant increase in sales, particularly of children's books, during the period of promotion.

Join the PA now – add your voice, have your say

As a PA member you can add your voice and have your say on the vital issues affecting our industry today. Membership is open to any company registered in the UK engaged in book, journal or electronic publishing as a bona fide and continuing operation. Subscription rates are based on turnover, with special introductory rates for new members and discounted rates for journal publishers.

The International Division

The International Division actively supports the international sales activities of PA members. We act against piracy, and on copyright and trade barrier issues, organise trade missions and UK representation at international trade fairs.

Trade Publishers Council

The Trade Publishers Council determines PA policy on consumer market matters, and acts on specific issues with the objectives of expanding the market and increasing efficiency. Other trade groups include our Children's Book Group and Religious Books Group.

Academic and Professional Publishing

The Academic and Professional Division provides a forum for higher education, monograph, journal and reference publishers. We represent publishers' concerns to key stakeholders, conduct market research and run a number of events.

The Educational Publishers Council (EPC)

The Educational Publishers Council provides a voice for school and college publishers. We campaign for better funding for learning resources and represent the industry in the development of the electronic market, as well as running seminars and compiling market statistics.

Digital Publishing Forum

Provides support for on-line and off-line electronic publishers, and organises a programme of seminars and meetings.

2 Publishers

2001

AA PUBLISHING
[trading as Automobile Association Developments Ltd]
Fanum House, Basingstoke, Hants
RG21 4EA
Telephone: 01256 491578
Fax: 01256 322575
Web Site: http://www.theAA.com

Distribution (UK):
Littlehampton Book Services Ltd,
Faraday Close, Durrington, Worthing,
West Sussex BN13 3RB

Directors: R. C. A. Miles *(Chief Executive)*
D. Watchus *(Publisher)*
T. A. Lee *(Sales & Marketing)*
R. Firth *(Production)*
B. Burkett *(Finance)*
S. Gold *(Human Resources)*

Atlases & Maps; Children's Books; Guide Books; Natural History; Transport; Travel & Topography; General Illustrated

ISBNs, Imprints & Series:
978 0 7495 Spiral Guides; Travel Series: Citypacks; Travel Series: Essentials; Travel Series: Explorers; Travel Series: Spirals 978 0 7495, 978 0 86145 Automobile Association

Distributor for:
AAA Road Maps of USA, Canada, Mexico; Footprint; Scottish Tourist Board

2002

ABSOLUTE PRESS
Scarborough House, 29 James Street West,
Bath BA1 2BT
Telephone: 01225 316013
Fax: 01225 445836
Email: sales@absolutepress.co.uk
Web Site: http://www.absolutepress.co.uk

Accounts, Warehouse, Trade Enquiries & Orders:
Central Books Ltd, 99 Wallis Road, London
E9 5LN
Telephone: (020) 8986 4854
Fax: (020) 8533 5821

Publisher & Editorial: Jon Croft
Art Director: Matt Inwood
Commissioning Editor: Meg Avent

Cookery, Wines & Spirits; Gardening; Guide Books; Illustrated & Fine Editions; Sports & Games; Travel & Topography

ISBNs, Imprints & Series: 978 0 948230

Overseas Representation:
Australia: Peribo Pty Ltd, Mount Kuring-Gai, NSW
South Africa: Stephan Phillips (Pty) Ltd, Umdloti Beach
USA (Outlines only): BHB International Inc, Seneca, SC, USA

2003

ACAIR LTD
Unit 7, 7 James Street, Stornoway,
Isle of Lewis HS1 2QN
Telephone: 01851 703020
Fax: 01851 703294
Email: info@acairbooks.com
Web Site: http://www.acairbooks.com

Distribution:
BookSource, 50 Cambuslang Road,
Glasgow G32 8NB
Telephone: 0845 370 0067
Fax: 0845 370 0068

Editor: Norma Macleod
Designer: Margaret Anne Macleod
Administrator: Margaret Martin

Children's Books; Educational & Textbooks; Fiction; History & Antiquarian; Poetry

Annual Turnover: £90,000

ISBNs, Imprints & Series: 978 0 86152

Book Trade Association Membership:
BA

2004

ACCENT PRESS LTD
The Old School, Upper High Street,
Bedlinog CF46 6SA
Telephone: 01443 710930
Fax: 01443 710940
Email: info@accentpress.co.uk
Web Site: http://www.accentpress.co.uk

Distribution:
Macmillan Distribution (MDL), Brunel Road,
Houndmills, Basingstoke, Hants RG21 6XS
Telephone: 01256 802692
Email: trade@macmillan.co.uk

Directors: Hazel Cushion *(Managing)*
Robert Cushion *(Finance)*
Administration: Karen Smart
Marketing: Cory Hughes
Production: Alison Stokes

Biography & Autobiography; Children's Books; Cookery, Wines & Spirits; Crafts & Hobbies; Crime; Educational & Textbooks; Fiction; Guide Books; Humour; Industry, Business & Management; Medical (incl. Self Help & Alternative Medicine); Poetry

New Titles: 45 (2007), 41 (2008)
No of Employees: 5
Annual Turnover: £350,000

Associated Companies:
Curriculum Concepts UK; Green Fuse; Wedding Bible Co; Xcite Books

Overseas Representation:
Australia, New Zealand, Papua New Guinea & Fiji: DA Information Services Pty Ltd, Mitcham, Vic, Australia
Austria, Switzerland, Benelux, Germany, France, Greece, Italy, Portugal, Spain, Gibraltar & Nordic Countries: Andrew Durnell Marketing Ltd, Tunbridge Wells, UK
Hong Kong: Katherine Lee, Asia Publishers Services Ltd
Singapore and all Asean countries: Ian Pringle, APD Singapore Pte Ltd, Singapore
South Africa: Shirley Cooksley, Quartet Sales & Marketing, Northcliffe
USA: National Book Network Inc, Blue Ridge Summit, PA

Book Trade Association Membership:
BA; IPG

2005

ACUMEN PUBLISHING LTD
Stocksfield Hall, Stocksfield,
Northumberland NE43 7TN
Telephone: 01661 844865
Fax: 01661 844865
Email: steven.gerrard@acumenpublishing.co.uk
Web Site: http://www.acumenpublishing.co.uk

Warehouse, Trade Enquiries, Orders & Distribution:
Marston Book Services, 160 Milton Park,
Abingdon, Oxon OX14 4YN
Telephone: 01235 465521
Fax: 01235 465555
Email: trade.orders@marston.co.uk
Web Site: http://www.marston.co.uk

Publisher: Steven Gerrard

Academic & Scholarly; Biography & Autobiography; Educational & Textbooks; History & Antiquarian; Philosophy; Politics & World Affairs; Sociology & Anthropology

New Titles: 16 (2007), 32 (2008)

ISBNs, Imprints & Series:
978 1 84465, 978 1 902683

Overseas Representation:
Australia & New Zealand: Palgrave Macmillan, South Yarra, Vic, Australia

Austria, Germany & Switzerland: Bernd Feldmann, Oranienburg, Germany
Belgium, Luxembourg & Netherlands: Kemper Conseil Publishing, De Star, Netherlands
Botswana, Lesotho, Namibia, South Africa, Swaziland & Zimbabwe: The African Moon Press, Kelvin, South Africa
Brunei, Cambodia, Indonesia, Laos, Philippines, Singapore, Thailand & Vietnam: APD Singapore Pte Ltd, Singapore
China, Hong Kong, Korea & Taiwan: Asia Publishers Services Ltd, Hong Kong
France, Italy, Portugal & Spain: Flavio Marcello Publishers' Agents & Consultants, Padua, Italy
Greece, Cyprus & Malta: Charles Gibbes Associates, Louslitges, France
India: Maya Publishers Pvt Ltd, New Delhi
Scandinavia: Colin Flint Ltd, Harlow, UK

Book Trade Association Membership:
IPG

2006

ADAM MATTHEW DIGITAL LTD
Pelham House, London Road,
Marlborough, Wiltshire SN8 2AA
Telephone: 01672 511921
Fax: 01672 511663
Email: david@amdigital.co.uk
Web Site: http://www.amdigital.co.uk

Publishers: William Pidduck
David Tyler
Khal Rudin *(Sales & Marketing Director)*

Electronic (Educational); Electronic (Professional & Academic)

New Titles: 7 (2007), 10 (2008)
No of Employees: 20

Parent Company:
Hanfrageo Holdings Ltd

Associated Companies:
Adam Matthew Publications Ltd

Overseas Representation:
Japan: Maruzen Co Ltd, Tokyo
Taiwan: Transmission Books & Microforms Co Ltd, Taipei

2007

ADAM MATTHEW PUBLICATIONS LTD
Pelham House, London Road,
Marlborough, Wiltshire SN8 2AA
Telephone: 01672 511921
Fax: 01672 511663
Email: david@ampltd.co.uk
Web Site: http://www.ampltd.co.uk

Publishers: William Pidduck
David Tyler
Khal Rudin *(Sales & Marketing Director)*

Academic & Scholarly; Economics; Gender Studies; History & Antiquarian; Literature & Criticism; Reference Books, Directories & Dictionaries

New Titles: 24 (2007), 14 (2008)
No of Employees: 20

ISBNs, Imprints & Series: 978 1 85711

Parent Company:
Hanfrageo Holdings Ltd

Associated Companies:
Adam Matthew Digital Ltd

Overseas Representation:
Japan: Maruzen Co Ltd, Tokyo
Taiwan: Transmission Books & Microforms Co Ltd, Taipei

2008

ADAMSON PUBLISHING LTD
8 The Moorings, Norwich NR3 3AX
Telephone: 01603 623336
Fax: 01603 624767
Email: stephen@adamsonbooks.com
Web Site: http://www.adamsonbooks.com

Chairman: Stephen Adamson

Educational & Textbooks; Reference Books, Directories & Dictionaries

New Titles: 4 (2007), 4 (2008)

ISBNs, Imprints & Series: 978 0 948543

2009

*ADLARD COLES NAUTICAL
38 Soho Square, London W1D 3HB
Telephone: (020) 7758 0200
Fax: (020) 7758 0333
Email: acn@acblack.com
Web Site: http://www.adlardcoles.com

Directors: Janet Murphy *(Editorial)*
David Wightman *(Sales)*
Jill Coleman *(Managing)*

Nautical

ISBNs, Imprints & Series:
978 0 7136, 978 0 85177

Parent Company:
A. & C. Black (Publishers) Ltd

Associated Companies:
Thomas Reed Publications; Reeds Almanac

Overseas Representation:
See: A. & C. Black (Publishers) Ltd, London, UK

2010

AGE CONCERN BOOKS
1268 London Road, Norbury, London SW16 4ER
Telephone: (020) 8765 7200
Fax: (020) 8765 7211
Email: books@ace.org.uk
Web Site: http://www.ageconcern.org.uk

Trade Distributor:
Orca Book Services, Stanley House,
3 Fleets Lane, Poole, Dorset BH15 3AJ
Telephone: 01202 665432
Fax: 01202 666219
Email: orders@orcabookservices.co.uk

Marketing Manager: (vacant)
Commissioning Editor: Peter Hooper
Production Controller: Keith Hawkins
Marketing Officer: Claire Milloy

Academic & Scholarly; Accountancy & Taxation; Computer Science; Educational & Textbooks; Gardening; Guide Books; Health & Beauty; Medical (incl. Self Help & Alternative Medicine); Reference Books, Directories & Dictionaries; Sociology & Anthropology

New Titles: 8 (2007), 10 (2008)

ISBNs, Imprints & Series:
Plan it! (series); Your Rights (series); Can do computing; We've Made It Easy
978 0 86242

Parent Company:
Age Concern

Book Trade Association Membership:
IPG

2011

AIR-BRITAIN (HISTORIANS) LTD
41 Penshurst Road, Leigh, Tonbridge, Kent TN11 8HL
Telephone: 01732 835637
Fax: 01732 835637
Email: mike@absales.demon.co.uk
Web Site: http://www.air-britain.com

Directors: Michael Graham Rice *(Sales)*
Howard Nash
Dr C. Chatfield
Treasurer: Don Schofield
Chairman: Peter Webber

Aviation; Military & War

New Titles: 15 (2007), 15 (2008)
Annual Turnover: £245,000

ISBNs, Imprints & Series: 978 0 85130

Overseas Representation:
Australia & New Zealand: Aviation Worldwide, Oamaru, New Zealand

2012

AKROS PUBLICATIONS
33 Lady Nairn Avenue, Kirkcaldy, Fife KY1 2AW
Telephone: 01592 651522
Web Site: http://www.akrospublications.co.uk

Sole Owner: Duncan Glen
Finance, Sales & Rights: Margaret Glen

Academic & Scholarly; Bibliography & Library Science; Fine Art & Art History; Guide Books; History & Antiquarian; Literature & Criticism; Photography; Poetry

ISBNs, Imprints & Series:
978 0 86142, 978 0 900036 Akros

2013

AL-FURQAN ISLAMIC HERITAGE FOUNDATION
Eagle House, High Street, Wimbledon, London SW19 5EF
Telephone: (020) 8944 1233
Fax: (020) 8944 1633
Email: info@al-furqan.com
Web Site: http://www.al-furqan.com

Office Manager: Susan John-Richards

Academic & Scholarly; History & Antiquarian; Mathematics & Statistics; Religion & Theology

ISBNs, Imprints & Series:
978 1 873992 Al-Furqan Publications

Book Trade Association Membership:
Publishers Association; BA

2014

ALBAN BOOKS LTD
14 Belford Road, Edinburgh EH4 3BL
Telephone: 0131 226 2217
Fax: 0131 225 5999
Email: sales@albanbooks.com
Web Site: http://www.albanbooks.com

Warehouse, Invoicing, Customer Services:
c/o Marston Book Services
Telephone: 01235 465500
Fax: 01235 465555

Managing Director: Jane Grounsell
Sales Manager: Nigel Parkinson
Marketing Executive: Elaine Reid
Accounts & Special Orders: Margaret Reid
Sales Representative: Kate Dennis

Academic & Scholarly; Children's Books; Educational & Textbooks; Philosophy; Reference Books, Directories & Dictionaries; Religion & Theology; Spirituality

Distributor for:
USA: Abingdon Press; Augsburg Fortress Publishers; Ave Maria Press; Baylor University Press; Wm B. Eerdmans Publishing Co; Hendrickson Publishers; Orbis Books; Templeton Foundation Press; Westminster John Knox Press

2015

ALBYN PRESS
2 Caversham Street, Chelsea, London SW3 4AH
Telephone: (020) 7351 4995
Fax: (020) 7351 4995
Email: leonard.holdsworth@btopenworld.com

Director: James Hughes *(Editorial)*
Production: Leonard Holdsworth
Sales: Margaret Fletcher

Fiction; Fine Art & Art History; Geography & Geology; Guide Books; History & Antiquarian; Illustrated & Fine Editions; Literature & Criticism; Poetry; Reference Books, Directories & Dictionaries; Transport; Scottish Books

ISBNs, Imprints & Series: 978 0 284

Parent Company:
Christchurch Publishers Ltd

Associated Companies:
Charles Skilton Publishing Group; Tallis Press

Book Trade Association Membership:
IPG

2016

IAN ALLAN PUBLISHING LTD
Riverdene Business Park, Molesey Road, Hersham, Surrey KT12 4RG
Telephone: 01932 266600
Fax: 01932 266601
Email: info@ianallanpublishing.co.uk
Web Site: http://www.ianallanpublishing.com

Distribution:
Littlehampton Book Services,
Faraday Close, Durrington, Worthing, West Sussex BN13 3RB
Telephone: 01903 828800 (trade orders)
Fax: 01903 828802
Email: orders@lbsltd.co.uk

Mail Order:
Midland Counties Publications,
4 Watling Drive, Hinckley, Leics LE10 3EY
Telephone: 01455 254450
Fax: 01455 233737

Email: orders@midlandcounties.com
Web Site: http://www.midlandcountiessuperstore.com

Representation (England & Wales):
Amalgamated Book Services, Suite 1, Royal Star Arcade, High Street, Maidstone, Kent ME14 1JL
Telephone: 01622 764555
Fax: 01622 763197

Representation (Scotland):
Alan Scollan, Earnockmuir Cottage, Meikle Earnock Road, Hamilton ML3 8RL
Telephone: 01698 459371

Chairman: David Allan
Directors: Tristan Hilderley *(Managing)*
Jonathan King *(Sales & Marketing)*
Managers: Nick Grant *(Publisher)*
Nigel Passmore *(Sales)*
Sue Frost *(Marketing)*
Alan Butcher *(Production)*

Atlases & Maps; Aviation; Biography & Autobiography; History & Antiquarian; Military & War; Nautical; Reference Books, Directories & Dictionaries; Sports & Games; Transport

New Titles: 120 (2007), 125 (2008)

ISBNs, Imprints & Series:
978 0 7110 Ian Allan
978 0 85318 Lewis; Lewis Masonic (only available from Midland Counties Publications)
978 0 86093 OPC
978 1 85780 Aerofax; Midland Publishing
978 1 903223 Classic Publications

Parent Company:
Ian Allan Group Ltd

Distributor for:
KRB (formerly Kestrel Railway Books); Millstream; Noodle Books; Pendragon; Polygon Press; Red Kite; Runpast; Specialty Press; John Sullivan

Overseas Representation:
Australia, New Zealand, New Guinea & Papua: DLS Australia (Pty) Ltd, Braeside, Vic, Australia
Austria, Belgium, France, Germany, Netherlands & Switzerland: European Marketing Services, London, UK
Canada: Vanwell Publishing Ltd, St Catharines, Ont
Central & Eastern Europe: Tony Moggach, InterMedia Americana (IMA) Ltd, London, UK
Middle & Far East: Julian Ashton, Ashton International Marketing Services, Sevenoaks, Kent, UK
Republic of Ireland & Northern Ireland: Sales Office, Ian Allan Publishing Ltd, Hersham, UK
Scandinavia: Gill Angell & Stewart Siddall, Angell Eurosales, Berwick-on-Tweed, UK
Spain, Portugal, Gibraltar, Italy, Malta, Greece, Slovenia, Croatia, Bosnia & Montenegro: Bookport Associates, Corsico (MI), Italy
USA (Aviation titles only): Specialty Press, North Branch, MN, USA
USA (Masonic titles only): Atlas Books (a division of BookMasters Inc), Ashland, OH, USA
USA (Military titles only): Casemate Publishers & Book Distributors LLC, Havertown, PA, USA

Book Trade Association Membership:
BA; IPG

2017

PHILIP ALLAN PUBLISHERS LTD
Market Place, Deddington, Oxon OX15 0SE
Telephone: 01869 338652
Fax: 01869 338803

Email: sales@philipallan.co.uk
Web Site: http://www.philipallan.co.uk

Editorial Director: Paul Cherry
Marketing Manager: Ceri Jenkins

Educational & Textbooks

New Titles: 200 (2008)
No of Employees: 36

ISBNs, Imprints & Series:
978 0 86003, 978 1 84489 Philip Allan Updates

Parent Company:
Hodder Education

Book Trade Association Membership:
EPC

2018

R. L. ALLAN & SON PUBLISHERS
[Ltd]
53 Bothwell Street, Glasgow G2 6TS
Telephone: 0141 204 1285
Fax: 0141 204 1285
Email: rlallan@btinternet.com
Web Site: http://www.bibles-direct.com

Managing Director: Nicholas Gray
Company Secretary: Wendy Gray
Administration: Margaret Milligan
Distribution: Eric Campbell

Religion & Theology

New Titles: 4 (2007), 5 (2008)
No of Employees: 4
Annual Turnover: £300,000

ISBNs, Imprints & Series: 978 0 948643

Parent Company:
Chapter House Ltd

2019

J. A. ALLEN
[an imprint of Robert Hale Ltd]
45–47 Clerkenwell Green, London EC1R 0HT
Telephone: (020) 7251 2661
Fax: (020) 7490 4958
Email: gj@halebooks.com
Web Site: http://www.halebooks.com

Warehouse & Shipping:
Combined Book Services Ltd, Units I/K, Paddock Wood Distribution Centre, Paddock Wood, Tonbridge, Kent TN12 6UU
Telephone: 01892 837171
Fax: 01892 837272
Email: orders@combook.co.uk

Commissioning Editor: Cassandra Campbell (*Publisher*)

Dogs; Equine & Equestrian

New Titles: 16 (2007), 15 (2008)

ISBNs, Imprints & Series: 978 0 85131

Parent Company:
Robert Hale Ltd

Overseas Representation:
See: Robert Hale Ltd, London, UK

2020

ALLIED MOUSE LTD
Mayfield, High Street, Dingwall IV15 9SS
Telephone: 01349 865400
Fax: 01349 866066

Directors: Sitakumari
Nick Sidle

Children's Books

ISBNs, Imprints & Series: 978 0 9513492

Book Trade Association Membership:
Publishers Association

2021

*****ALLIGATOR BOOKS LTD**
Gadd House, Arcadia Avenue, London N3 2JU
Telephone: (020) 8371 6622
Fax: (020) 8371 6633
Email: sales@alligatorbooks.co.uk
Web Site: http://www.alligatorbooks.co.uk

Children's Books; Reference Books, Directories & Dictionaries

ISBNs, Imprints & Series: 978 1 84239

Associated Companies:
UK: International Greetings PLC Group

2022

ALLISON & BUSBY
13 Charlotte Mews, London W1T 4EJ
Telephone: (020) 7580 1080
Fax: (020) 7580 1180
Email: susie@allisonandbusby.com
Web Site: http://www.allisonandbusby.com

Warehouse/Distribution:
Turnaround Publisher Services Ltd, Unit 3, Olympia Trading Estate, Coburg Road, London N22 6TZ
Telephone: (020) 8829 3000
Fax: (020) 8881 5088
Email: orders@turnaround-uk.com

Publishing Director: Susie Dunlop (*UK Sales*)
Managers: Chiara Priorelli (*Publicity*)
Lara Dafert (*Editorial*)
Finance: John Gardner
Editor: Louise Watson
Sales & Marketing Executive: Lesley Brown
Sales & Marketing Assistant: Christina Griffiths

Biography & Autobiography; Crime; Fiction; History & Antiquarian; Humour; Literature & Criticism

ISBNs, Imprints & Series:
978 0 7490, 978 0 85031 Allison & Busby

Parent Company:
Spain: Editorial Prensa Iberica SA

Overseas Representation:
Africa, Middle East & Gulf: InterMedia Americana (IMA) Ltd, London, UK
Australia & New Zealand: Keith Ainsworth (Pty) Ltd, Penrith, NSW, Australia
Canada: Georgetown Publications Inc, Toronto, Ont
France, Belgium & Netherlands: Michael Geoghegan, London, UK
Germany: Gabriele Kern Publishers Services, Frankfurt-am-Main
India: Maya Publishers Pvt Ltd, New Delhi
Italy: Ted Dougherty, London, UK
Scandinavia: Angell Eurosales, Berwick-on-Tweed, UK
South & Central America & Caribbean: InterMedia Americana (IMA) Ltd, London, UK
South & South East Europe, Eastern Europe & Egypt: IMA, Greece
South Africa: Trinity Books CC, Randburg
Spain, Portugal & Malta: Peter Prout Iberian Book Services, Madrid, Spain
USA: International Publishers Marketing Inc, Sterling, VA

Book Trade Association Membership:
IPG

2023

ALMA BOOKS LTD
London House,
243–253 Lower Mortlake Road, Richmond, Surrey TW9 2LL
Telephone: (020) 8948 9550
Fax: (020) 8948 5599
Email: info@almabooks.com
Web Site: http://www.almabooks.com

Directors: Alessandro Gallenzi (*Managing*)
Elisabetta Minervini (*Sales & Marketing*)

Biography & Autobiography; Crime; Fiction; Humour

New Titles: 15 (2007), 15 (2008)

ISBNs, Imprints & Series: 978 1 84688

Overseas Representation:
Australia: Tower Books Pty Ltd, Frenchs Forest, NSW
South Africa: Penguin Books South Africa (Pty) Ltd, Johannesburg
USA & Canada: Trafalgar Square Publishing / IPG, Chicago, IL, USA

2024

ALPHA SCIENCE INTERNATIONAL LTD
7200 The Quorum,
Oxford Business Park North,
Garsington Road, Oxford OX4 2JZ
Telephone: 01865 481433
Fax: 01865 481482
Email: alphascience@vsnl.net
Web Site: http://www.alphasci.com

Academic & Scholarly

Book Trade Association Membership:
Publishers Association

2025

AMBERWOOD PUBLISHING LTD
Unit 4, Stirling House, Sunderland Quay, Culpeper Close, Medway City Estate, Rochester, Kent ME2 4HN
Telephone: 01634 290115
Fax: 01634 290761
Email: books@amberwoodpublishing.com
Web Site: http://www.amberwoodpublishing.com

Warehouse:
Mulberry Court, Stour Road, Bournemouth, Dorset
Telephone: 01202 488333
Fax: 01202 476872

Managing Director: June Crisp
Co Secretary: Henry Crisp
Chairman: Victor Perfitt
Administration & Accounts, Dispatch:
Chris Derby
Yvonne James

Health & Beauty; Medical (incl. Self Help & Alternative Medicine)

ISBNs, Imprints & Series:
978 0 9517723, 978 1 899308

2026

AMERICAN PSYCHIATRIC PUBLISHING INC
5 Victoria House, 138 Watling Street East, Towcester NN12 6BT
Telephone: 01327 357770
Fax: 01327 359572
Email: appi@oppuk.co.uk
Web Site: http://www.appi.org

Warehouse & Distribution:
NBN International, Estover Road, Plymouth PL6 7PY
Telephone: 01752 202301
Fax: 01752 202331
Email: orders@nbninternational.com
Web Site: http://www.nbninternational.com

Manager: Gary Hall

Academic & Scholarly; Educational & Textbooks; Medical (incl. Self Help & Alternative Medicine); Psychology & Psychiatry; Reference Books, Directories & Dictionaries

New Titles: 20 (2007), 20 (2008)

ISBNs, Imprints & Series: 978 1 5856

Parent Company:
USA: American Psychiatric Publishing Inc

2027

AMNESTY INTERNATIONAL INTERNATIONAL SECRETARIAT
1 Easton Street, London WC1X 0DW
Telephone: (020) 7413 5500
Fax: (020) 7956 1157
Email: amnestyis@amnesty.org & orderpubs@amnesty.org
Web Site: http://www.amnesty.org

Secretary General: Irene Khan
Director, Publications Program: Sarah Wilbourne

Academic & Scholarly; Law; Politics & World Affairs; Human Rights

New Titles: 10 (2007), 16 (2008)
No of Employees: 350

ISBNs, Imprints & Series: 978 0 86210

2028

*****AMNESTY INTERNATIONAL UK**
Human Rights Action Centre,
17–25 New Inn Yard, London EC2A 3EA
Telephone: (020) 7033 1500
Fax: (020) 7033 1503
Email: nicky.parker@amnesty.org.uk
Web Site: http://www.amnesty.org.uk/

Trade Distribution UK & Europe:
Central Books, 99 Wallis Road, London E9 5LN
Telephone: 0845 458 9911
Fax: 0845 458 9912
Email: info@centralbooks.com

Managers: Nicky Parker (*Publisher*)
Maggie Paterson (*Head of Publishing & Design*)

Children's Books; Educational & Textbooks; Gay & Lesbian Studies; Gender Studies; Industry, Business & Management; Law; Mathematics & Statistics; Military & War; Politics & World Affairs

ISBNs, Imprints & Series:
978 0 86210, 978 1 873328

Distributor for:
Amnesty International, International Secretariat

Overseas Representation:
Canada: Amnesty International Canada, Vanier, Ont
USA: Amnesty International USA, New York, NY

Book Trade Association Membership:
IPG

2029

*****A.M.S. EDUCATIONAL LTD**
38 Parkside Road, Leeds LS6 4NB
Telephone: 0113 275 5500
Fax: 0113 275 7799

Email: admin@amseducational.co.uk

Directors: Stan Sharp *(Managing)*
  Margaret Sharp *(Finance)*
Manager: Victoria Keys *(Publishing)*

Children's Books; Educational & Textbooks; Military & War

ISBNs, Imprints & Series:
Educational Fun Factory; Propagator Press
978 0 946947 New Education Press (N.E.P.)
978 1 86029 A.M.S. Educational
978 1 899929 Leopard Learning
978 1 900899 Falconwood Series
978 1 902751 Senter Series

Distributor for:
Claire Publications; Desktop Publications; Prim-Ed Publishing

Book Trade Association Membership:
IPG

2030

ANDERSEN PRESS LTD
20 Vauxhall Bridge Road, London
SW1V 2SA
Telephone: (020) 7840 8701
Fax: (020) 7233 6263
Email:
  andersenpublicity@randomhouse.co.uk
Web Site: http://www.andersenpress.co.uk

Warehouse, Orders & Payments:
TBS Ltd, Colchester Road, Frating Green, Colchester, Essex CO7 7DW
Telephone: 01206 255678
Fax: 01206 255930

Address for Returns Requests:
Sales Department,
Random House Children's Books,
61-63 Uxbridge Road, London W5 5SA
Telephone: (020) 8231 6800
Fax: (020) 8231 6767
Web Site: http://www.andersenpress.co.uk

Directors: Klaus Flugge *(Managing & Publisher)*
  P. W. Durrance
  Rona Selby *(Editorial)*
Company Secretary: Mark Hendle
Editor: Liz Maude
Rights & Permissions: Sarah Pakenham
Marketing & Publicity: Anna Bowen

Children's Books

No of Employees: 9

ISBNs, Imprints & Series:
978 0 86264, 978 0 905478, 978 1 84270
Andersen Artists (greetings cards);
  Andersen Press; Andersen Young
  Readers' Library; Children's Picture Books

Associated Companies:
Random House

Overseas Representation:
Canada (Trade): Random House of Canada Ltd, Toronto, Ont, Canada
Other overseas markets See: Random House Group Ltd, London, UK

2031

PETER ANDREW PUBLISHING CO LTD
4 Charlecot Road, Droitwich, Worcs
WR9 7RP
Telephone: 01905 778543
Email: sales@peterandrew.com
Web Site: http://www.peterandrew.com

Directors: Philip Checkley
  Joan Checkley *(Sales)*

Academic & Scholarly; Accountancy & Taxation; Economics; Engineering; Health &
Beauty; Industry, Business & Management; Law; Sports & Games; Theatre, Drama & Dance

ISBNs, Imprints & Series: 978 0 946796

Book Trade Association Membership:
Book Data

2032

CHRIS ANDREWS PUBLICATIONS LTD
15 Curtis Yard, North Hinksey Lane, Oxford
OX2 0LX
Telephone: 01865 723404
Fax: 01865 725294
Email: chris.andrews1@btclick.com
Web Site: http://www.cap-ox.co.uk

Partners: Chris Andrews
  Virginia Andrews
Personal Assistant: Annabel Matthews

Travel & Topography

New Titles: 36 (2007), 30 (2008)
No of Employees: 3

ISBNs, Imprints & Series:
978 0 9509643, 978 0 9540331, 978 1 905385

Book Trade Association Membership:
IPG

2033

ANGLO-SAXON BOOKS
25 Brocks Road, Swaffham, Norfolk
PE37 7XG
Telephone: 0845 430 4200
Email: enq@asbooks.co.uk
Web Site: http://www.asbooks.co.uk

Contact: Tony Linsell

Academic & Scholarly; Educational & Textbooks; History & Antiquarian; Languages & Linguistics; Military & War; Poetry; Reference Books, Directories & Dictionaries

ISBNs, Imprints & Series:
978 1 898281 Anglo-Saxon Books
978 1 903313 Athelney

Overseas Representation:
USA & Canada: The David Brown Book Co, Oakville, CT, USA

2034

*ANN ARBOR PUBLISHERS LTD
PO Box 1, Belford, Northumberland
NE70 7JX
Telephone: 01668 214460
Fax: 01668 214484
Email: enquiries@annarbor.co.uk
Web Site: http://www.annarbor.co.uk

Managing Director: Peter D. Laverack

Children's Books; Educational & Textbooks; Psychology & Psychiatry; High Interest Low Reading Level Novels; Tests for Learning Difficulty; Work Books for Dyslexic Pupils

ISBNs, Imprints & Series:
978 0 87879, 978 0 931421, 978 1 900506

Distributor for:
Academic Therapy Publications; Ann Arbor Publishers; High Noon Books; PAR; Pearson Assessments

Book Trade Association Membership:
BEEA

2035

ANSHAN LTD
6 Newlands Road, Tunbridge Wells, Kent
TN4 9AT
Telephone: 01892 557767
Fax: 01892 530358
Email: info@anshan.co.uk
Web Site: http://www.anshan.co.uk

Warehouse:
CBS, Units I/K,
Paddock Wood Distribution Centre,
Paddock Wood, Tonbridge, Kent TN12 6UU
Telephone: 01892 837171
Fax: 01892 837272
Email: orders@combook.co.uk
Web Site: http://www.combook.co.uk

Directors: Shân White *(Managing)*
  Andrew White *(Sales)*
Marketing Assistant: Alison Dry

Academic & Scholarly; Chemistry; Computer Science; Educational & Textbooks; Engineering; Environment & Development Studies; Mathematics & Statistics; Medical (incl. Self Help & Alternative Medicine); Physics; Psychology & Psychiatry; Scientific & Technical

New Titles: 44 (2007), 63 (2008)

ISBNs, Imprints & Series:
978 1 848290, 978 1 904798, 978 1 905740

Overseas Representation:
Central Europe: Andrew Durnell Marketing Ltd, Tunbridge Wells, UK
China: Access Asia Media Services, Shanghai, P. R. of China
Japan (Science Titles): Nankodo Co Ltd, Tokyo, Japan; United Publishers Services Ltd, Tokyo, Japan
Republic of Ireland & Northern Ireland: Quantum Publishing Solutions Ltd, Paisley, UK
Scandinavia: Colin Flint Ltd, Harlow, UK
Taiwan: Unifacmanu Trading Co Ltd, Taipei
USA: Princeton Selling Group Inc, Philadelphia, PA

Book Trade Association Membership:
Publishers Association; IPG

2036

ANTIQUE COLLECTORS' CLUB LTD
Sandy Lane, Old Martlesham, Woodbridge, Suffolk IP12 4SD
Telephone: 01394 389950
Fax: 01394 389999
Email: sales@antique-acc.com
Web Site: http://www.antique-acc.com

Directors: Diana Steel *(Managing)*
  Sarah Smye *(Marketing)*
  Vanessa Shorten *(Financial)*
  James Smith *(Sales)*

Antiques & Collecting; Architecture & Design; Children's Books; Fine Art & Art History; Gardening; Humour; Natural History; Reference Books, Directories & Dictionaries

New Titles: 26 (2007), 30 (2008)
No of Employees: 32
Annual Turnover: £3.3M

ISBNs, Imprints & Series:
978 0 902028, 978 0 907462, 978 1 85149, 978 1 870673

Associated Companies:
ACC Books; Garden Art Press; Natural Wonders Press
UK: National Galleries of Scotland

Distributor for:
Acanthus Press; Adelson Galleries; Adler Planetarium and Astronomy; Umberto Allemandi; Architectura & Natura; Arnoldsche Verlagsanstalt; Arsenale Editrice; The Azur Corporation Ltd; Chris Beetles; Beta Plus; George Braziller; Brioni Books; Centro Di; The Chippendal Society; Christie's Books; Deben Gallery; Editions Vausor; Fine Arts Museum of San Francisco; Fine Arts Society; Fiske & Freeman; Fry Art Gallery; Gambero Rosso; GML Publishing; Grafiche Vianello; Alan & Simone Hartman; Heel Verlag; Hudson Hills Press LLC; Kew Publishing; Lannoo/Terra Publishers; Laynforah; Mandragora; Merrick & Day; David Messum; New Cavendish Books; Newark Museum; P. I. Global; Palace Editions; Pandora; Philadelphia Museum of Art; Pointed Leaf Press; Randall International; Ritika; Riverside Book Company; Royal Ontario Museum; Royal Pavilion Libraries & Museums; Scala Publishers; The Shoe String Book Co; J. & C. Smith; Sotheby's NY; Stichting Kunstboek; Storm King; M. T. Train; Verba Volant; Waanders Publishers; The Walters Art Museum
Australia: Images
France: Alain de Gourcuff Editeur

Overseas Representation:
All other territories: Antique Collectors' Club, Woodbridge, Suffolk, UK
Australia: Peribo Pty Ltd, Mount Kuring-Gai, NSW
Belgium & Luxembourg: Altera Diffusion, Belgium
Central Europe (excluding Russia): Csaba & Jackie Lengyel de Bagota, Budapest, Hungary
Far East (including Hong Kong, Taiwan, Philippines & China): Asia Publishers Services Ltd, Hong Kong
France: Interart SARL, Paris, UK
Germany, Austria & Switzerland: Michael Klein, Vilsbiburg, Germany
India: Timeless, The Art Book Studio, New Delhi
Iran: Jahan Adib Publishing, Tehran
Italy, Spain, Portugal & Greece: Penny Padovani, London, UK
Japan & South Korea: Ralph & Sheila Summers, Woodford Green, Essex, UK
Malaysia: APD Kuala Lumpur Pte Ltd, Selangor
Near & Middle East & Turkey: Avicenna Partnership, Dumfries, UK
Netherlands: Coen Sligting Bookimport, Amsterdam
New Zealand: Book Reps NZ Ltd, Auckland
Republic of Ireland & Northern Ireland: Robert Towers, Monkstown, Co Dublin, Republic of Ireland
Scandinavia & Iceland: Elisabeth Harder-Kreimann, Hamburg, Germany
South & Central America, Caribbean & Mexico: InterMedia Americana (IMA) Ltd, London, UK
South Africa: Peter Hyde Associates (Pty) Ltd, Cape Town
South East Asia (including Singapore, Thailand, Vietnam, Cambodia, Indonesia & Brunei): APD Singapore Pte Ltd, Singapore
USA: Antique Collectors Club Ltd, Easthampton, MA
West, Central & East Africa (excluding Sudan): InterMedia Africa Ltd (IMA), London, UK

Book Trade Association Membership:
IPG

2037

ANVIL PRESS POETRY LTD
Neptune House, 70 Royal Hill, London
SE10 8RF
Telephone: (020) 8469 3033
Fax: (020) 8469 3363
Email: anvil@anvilpresspoetry.com

Web Site: http://www.anvilpresspoetry.com

Distributors:
Littlehampton Book Services,
Columbia Building, Faraday Close,
Durrington, Worthing, West Sussex
BN13 3RB
Telephone: 01903 828800
Fax: 01903 828801 & 828802
Email: orders@lbsltd.co.uk
Web Site: http://www.lbsltd.co.uk

Editorial, Administration & Production:
Peter Jay (Managing Director)
Manager: Kit Yee Wong (Administrative)

Poetry

ISBNs, Imprints & Series:
978 0 85646, 978 0 900977 Anvil Editions; Poetica

Overseas Representation:
Australia: Eleanor Brasch Enterprises, Artarmon, NSW
Eastern Europe, Greece & Israel: Tony Moggach, InterMedia Americana (IMA) Ltd, London, UK
France, Benelux, Germany, Austria & Switzerland: Ted Dougherty, London, UK
Republic of Ireland: Robert Towers, Monkstown, Co Dublin
Spain: Peter Prout Iberian Book Services, Madrid
USA: Consortium Book Sales & Distribution Inc, St Paul, MN

Book Trade Association Membership:
IPG

2038

*AP INFORMATION SERVICES LTD
Marlborough House,
298 Regents Park Road, London N3 2UU
Telephone: (020) 8349 9988
Fax: (020) 8349 9797
Email: info@apinfo.co.uk
Web Site: http://www.apinfo.co.uk

Directors: Alan Philipp (Managing)
Gail Philipp (Finance & Human Resources)
Managers: Helen Irwin (Head - Business, Editorial)
Ed Gorman (Head - Sales & Marketing)
Sally Rodohan (Sales Administration)

Reference Books, Directories & Dictionaries

ISBNs, Imprints & Series:
978 1 86071, 978 1 902202, 978 1 905366

Associated Companies:
Aspire Publications Ltd

Overseas Representation:
USA: Money Market Directories, Charlottesville, VA

Book Trade Association Membership:
Data Publishers Association; European Directory Publishers Association

2039

APEX PUBLISHING LTD
PO Box 7086, Clacton-on-Sea, Essex
CO15 5WN
Telephone: 01255 428500
Email: mail@apexpublishing.co.uk
Web Site: http://www.apexpublishing.co.uk

Managers: Chris Cowlin (Production)
Jackie Bright (Marketing)
Managing Editor: Susan Kidby

Academic & Scholarly; Biography & Autobiography; Children's Books; Crafts & Hobbies; Crime; Fiction; Fine Art & Art History; Guide Books; Health & Beauty; Humour; Medical (incl. Self Help & Alternative Medicine); Military & War; Philosophy; Poetry; Politics & World Affairs; Reference Books, Directories & Dictionaries; Religion & Theology; Science Fiction; Sports & Games

ISBNs, Imprints & Series:
978 1 904444, 978 1 906358

Book Trade Association Membership:
IPG

2040

APPLETREE PRESS LTD
The Old Potato Station,
14 Howard Street South, Belfast BT7 1AP
Telephone: (028) 9024 3074
Fax: (028) 9024 6756
Email: reception@appletree.ie
Web Site: http://www.appletree.ie

Distribution:
BookSource, 50 Cambuslang Road,
Cambuslang, Glasgow G32 8NB
Telephone: 0141 642 9182
Fax: 0141 641 9181

Director: John Murphy (Managing)
Editor: Jean Brown
Managers: Paul McAvoy (Production)
Mark Elliott (Sales)

Biography & Autobiography; Cookery, Wines & Spirits; Guide Books; History & Antiquarian; Humour; Languages & Linguistics; Literature & Criticism; Military & War; Music; Politics & World Affairs; Reference Books, Directories & Dictionaries; Sports & Games; Travel & Topography; Irish Interest Non-Fiction

New Titles: 36 (2007) , 35 (2008)
No of Employees: 10

ISBNs, Imprints & Series:
978 0 86281, 978 0 904651

Overseas Representation:
Australia & New Zealand: Peribo Pty Ltd, Mount Kuring-Gai, NSW, Australia
France, Belgium, Scandinavia, Germany, Austria, Switzerland & Spain: Appletree Press, Belfast, UK
Greece, Cyprus, Israel, Russia, Eastern Europe & the Baltic States: IMA, Greece
Italy: Penguin Italia srl, Corsico, Milan
Netherlands: Novelty Books, Weesp
Republic of Ireland: CMD, Blackrock
USA & Canada: Independent Publishers Group (IPG), Chicago, IL, USA

Book Trade Association Membership:
CLÉ (Irish PA)

2041

ARC PUBLICATIONS LTD
Nanholme Mill, Shaw Wood Road,
Todmorden, Lancs OL14 6DA
Telephone: 01706 812338
Fax: 01706 818948
Email: arc.publications@btconnect.com
Web Site: http://www.arcpublications.co.uk

Directors: Tony Ward (Publishing)
Angela Jarman (Development)

Music; Poetry

New Titles: 15 (2007) , 18 (2008)
No of Employees: 2

ISBNs, Imprints & Series:
978 0 902771, 978 0 946407, 978 1 900072, 978 1 904614, 978 1 906570

Overseas Representation:
Australia & New Zealand: Eleanor Brasch Enterprises, Artarmon, NSW, Australia

Book Trade Association Membership:
IPG

2042

ARCADIA BOOKS LTD
15–16 Nassau Street, London W1W 7AB
Telephone: (020) 7436 9898
Email: info@arcadiabooks.co.uk
Web Site: http://www.arcadiabooks.co.uk

Distribution:
Turnaround, Unit 3, Olympia Trading Estate,
Coburg Road, London N22 6TZ
Telephone: (020) 8829 3000
Fax: (020) 8881 5088
Email: orders@turnaround-uk.com
Web Site: http://www.turnaround-uk.com

Publisher: Gary Pulsifer
Associate Publisher: Daniela de Groote
Editor: Angeline Rothermundt

Biography & Autobiography; Crime; Fiction; Gay & Lesbian Studies; Gender Studies; Photography; Politics & World Affairs; Travel & Topography; Translations

New Titles: 30 (2007) , 30 (2008)
No of Employees: 4

ISBNs, Imprints & Series:
Black Amber; Bliss Books; Euro Crime
978 1 900850
978 1 905147

Overseas Representation:
Australia: Tower Books Pty Ltd, Brookvale, NSW
Israel (selected titles only): Steimatzky Ltd, Bnei Brak, Israel
New Zealand: Addenda Ltd, Grey Lynn
North America: Independent Publishers Group (IPG), Chicago, IL, USA
South Africa: Quartet Sales & Marketing, Johannesburg

Book Trade Association Membership:
IPG; Hite Research Foundation; English PEN – Writers in Prison & Books to Prisoners Committee; BTBS (The Book Trade Charity)

2043

ARCHETYPE PUBLICATIONS LTD
6 Fitzroy Square, London W1T 5HJ
Telephone: (020) 7380 0800
Fax: (020) 7380 0500
Email: info@archetype.co.uk
Web Site: http://www.archetype.co.uk

Managing Director: James Black

Academic & Scholarly; Archaeology; Fine Art & Art History; Scientific & Technical

New Titles: 11 (2007) , 13 (2008)
No of Employees: 3
Annual Turnover: £250,000

ISBNs, Imprints & Series:
978 1 873132, 978 1 904982

Overseas Representation:
USA (All titles): Antique Collectors Club Ltd, Easthampton, MA, USA; JG Publishing Services, Los Angeles, CA, USA

2044

ARCHITECTURAL ASSOCIATION PUBLICATIONS
36 Bedford Square, London WC1B 3ES
Telephone: (020) 7887 4021
Fax: (020) 7414 0782
Email: publications@aaschool.ac.uk
Web Site: http://www.aaschool.ac.uk

Sales & Marketing Manager: Marilyn Sparrow
Publications Co-ordinator: Kirsten Morphet
Editor: Pamela Johnston

Architecture & Design

ISBNs, Imprints & Series:
978 1 870890, 978 1 902902

Parent Company:
Architectural Association Inc

Overseas Representation:
Australia: Robyn Ralton, Collingwood, Vic
France: Muriel Fischer, Paris
Germany & Austria: Kurt Salchli, Berlin, Germany
Netherlands & Belgium: Berend Bosch, Noordwijk, Netherlands
Southern Europe: Bookport Associates, Milan, Italy

Book Trade Association Membership:
Publishers Association

2045

ARCHIVE EDITIONS LTD
7 Ashley House, The Broadway,
Farnham Common, Slough SL2 3PQ
Telephone: 01753 646633
Fax: 01753 646746
Email: info@archiveeditions.co.uk
Web Site: http://www.archiveeditions.co.uk

Director: James M. Dening
Head of Customer Relations & Finance: Jeanette Wood
Managers: Ann Greenwood (Production)
Jessica Lagan (Marketing)

Academic & Scholarly; History & Antiquarian; Politics & World Affairs

New Titles: 1 (2007) , 3 (2008)

ISBNs, Imprints & Series:
978 1 84097, 978 1 85207

2046

ARCTURUS PUBLISHING LTD
26/27 Bickels Yard,
151–153 Bermondsey Street, London
SE1 2EJ
Telephone: (020) 7407 9400
Fax: (020) 7407 9444
Email: ian.mclellan@arcturuspublishing.com
Web Site: http://www.arcturuspublishing.com

Directors: Ian McLellan (Managing)
Roberta Bailey (Managing, Children's Books)
Mr Chok (Finance)
Tom Oakes (Marketing)
Tessa Rose (Editorial)
Peter Ridley (Design)
Managers: David Meads (Production)
Charlie Cooper (Rights)

Children's Books; Cookery, Wines & Spirits; Crafts & Hobbies; Crime; Educational & Textbooks; Fine Art & Art History; Gardening; History & Antiquarian; Humour; Magic & the Occult; Medical (incl. Self Help & Alternative Medicine); Military & War; Music; Natural History; Philosophy; Poetry; Reference Books, Directories & Dictionaries; Religion & Theology; Sports & Games

ISBNs, Imprints & Series:
978 1 84193 Arcturus; Capella

Overseas Representation:
Worldwide: Gunnar Lie & Associates Ltd, London, UK

2047

ARENA BOOKS (PUBLISHERS)
6 Southgate Green, Bury St Edmunds,
Suffolk IP33 2BL
Telephone: 01284 754123
Fax: 01284 754123
Email: arenabooks@tiscali.co.uk
Web Site: http://www.arenabooks.co.uk

Directors: James Farrell *(Managing)*
 Robert Corfe
Editor: Russell Corfe
Sales Manager: June Hardy

Academic & Scholarly; Economics; Fiction; History & Antiquarian; Industry, Business & Management; Literature & Criticism; Philosophy; Politics & World Affairs; Religion & Theology; Sociology & Anthropology; Travel & Topography

New Titles: 5 (2007), 7 (2008)
No of Employees: 4

ISBNs, Imprints & Series:
978 0 9538460, 978 0 9543161, 978 0 9556055

Overseas Representation:
Egypt: Abdul Radder Al-Bakkar, Cairo
Poland: Graal Sp, Warsaw
USA: Ingram Publisher Services, La Vergne, TN

Book Trade Association Membership:
IPG

2048

ARGYLL PUBLISHING
Glendaruel, Argyll PA22 3AE
Telephone: 01369 820229
Fax: 01369 820372
Email: argyll.publishing@virgin.net
Web Site: http://www.argyllpublishing.com

Publisher: Derek Rodger

Biography & Autobiography; Fiction; Guide Books; Health & Beauty; Medical (incl. Self Help & Alternative Medicine); Natural History

New Titles: 15 (2007), 15 (2008)

ISBNs, Imprints & Series:
Douglas Press; Thirsty Books
978 0 906938 West Dunbartonshire Libraries & Museums
978 1 874640, 978 1 902831, 978 1 906134

2049

ARRIS PUBLISHING LTD
12 Main Street, Adlestrop,
Moreton in Marsh, Glos GL56 0YN
Telephone: 01608 659328
Fax: 01608 659345
Email: gcs@arrisbooks.com
Web Site: http://www.arrisbooks.com

Distribution (for Arris titles):
Orca Book Distribution, Stanley House,
3 Fleets Lane, Poole, Dorset BH15 3AJ
Telephone: 01202 665432
Fax: 01202 666219

Distribution (for Chastleton titles – Travel):
Portfolio Books, Perivale, Middx UB6 7RL
Telephone: (020) 8997 9000
Fax: (020) 8997 9097
Email: info@portfoliobooks.com

Directors: Geoffrey Smith *(Joint Managing)*
 Victoria Huxley *(Editorial)*

Guide Books; History & Antiquarian; Natural History; Politics & World Affairs; Travel & Topography

New Titles: 15 (2007), 15 (2008)

ISBNs, Imprints & Series:
978 1 84437
978 1 905214 Chastleton Travel

Overseas Representation:
Germany, Eastern Europe, Switzerland, Austria, Italy & Greece: Portfolio Books, Perivale, UK
Spain & Portugal: Iberian Book Services, Madrid, Spain

2050

ASHGATE PUBLISHING LTD
Gower House, Croft Road, Aldershot, Hants GU11 3HR
Telephone: 01252 331551
Fax: 01252 344405
Email: info@ashgatepublishing.com
Web Site: http://www.ashgate.com

Warehouse & Mailing Shop, Orders:
Ashgate Publishing Direct Sales,
Bookpoint Ltd, 39 Milton Park, Abingdon, Oxon OX14 4TD
Telephone: 01235 400400
Fax: 01235 400454

Chairman: Nigel Farrow
Managing Director: Rachel Lynch
Publishers: John Smedley *(History (Variorum))*
 Jonathan Norman *(Business (Gower))*
Directors: Lucy Myers *(Managing – Lund Humphries)*
 Adrian Shanks *(Social Sciences)*
 Darren Wise *(Finance/Accounting)*
 Anne Nolan *(Ashgate Marketing)*
 Richard Dowling *(Sales)*
 Jo Burges *(Editorial & Production)*

Academic & Scholarly; Architecture & Design; Aviation; Bibliography & Library Science; Economics; Educational & Textbooks; Electronic (Professional & Academic); Environment & Development Studies; Fine Art & Art History; Gender Studies; Geography & Geology; History & Antiquarian; Illustrated & Fine Editions; Industry, Business & Management; Law; Literature & Criticism; Military & War; Music; Philosophy; Politics & World Affairs; Reference Books, Directories & Dictionaries; Religion & Theology; Sociology & Anthropology; Theatre, Drama & Dance; Transport

New Titles: 794 (2007), 742 (2008)
No of Employees: 109

ISBNs, Imprints & Series:
978 0 291, 978 1 85628, 978 1 85972 Avebury
978 0 566, 978 1 85904 Gower Publishing
978 0 576 Gregg International
978 0 7045 Wildwood House
978 0 7512 Gregg Revivals
978 0 7546, 978 1 84014 Ashgate Publishing
978 0 85331 Lund Humphries
978 0 85967, 978 1 85928 Scolar Press
978 0 86078 Variorum
978 1 85521 Dartmouth
978 1 85742 Arena

Parent Company:
Ashgate Publishing Group

Associated Companies:
Gower Publishing Co Ltd; Lund Humphries; Scolar Fine Art Ltd
USA: Ashgate Publishing Co

Overseas Representation:
Australia, South East Asia, Malaysia, Philippines, China, Hong Kong, Taiwan, Myanmar (Burma), & South Korea: Ashgate Publishing Asia-Pacific, Newport, NSW, Australia
India: Maya Publishers Pvt Ltd, New Delhi
Japan: United Publishers Services Ltd, Tokyo
USA: Ashgate Publishing Co, Burlington, VT

Book Trade Association Membership:
IPG

2051

ASHGROVE PUBLISHING
27 John Street, London WC1N 2BX
Telephone: (020) 7831 5013
Fax: (020) 7831 5011

Warehouse & Distribution:
Vine House Distribution Ltd, Waldenbury, North Common, Chailey, East Sussex BN8 4DR
Telephone: 01825 723398
Fax: 01825 724188

Managing Director: Brad Thompson

Audio Books; Cookery, Wines & Spirits; Fiction; Health & Beauty; Medical (incl. Self Help & Alternative Medicine); Psychology & Psychiatry

New Titles: 2 (2007), 3 (2008)
Annual Turnover: £30,000

ISBNs, Imprints & Series:
978 0 906798, 978 1 85398

Parent Company:
Hollydata Publishers Ltd

Associated Companies:
Childrens Corner Ltd

2052

ASHMOLEAN MUSEUM PUBLICATIONS
Ashmolean Museum, Beaumont Street, Oxford OX1 2PH
Telephone: 01865 278010
Fax: 01865 278106
Email: publications@ashmus.ox.ac.uk
Web Site: http://www.ashmolean.org

Warehouse, Trade Enquiries & Orders:
Gazelle Book Services Ltd,
White Cross Mills, Hightown, Lancaster LA1 4XS
Telephone: 01524 68765
Fax: 01524 63232

Publishing Managers: D. McCarthy *(Sales & Marketing)*
 E. Jolliffe *(Deputy, Editorial, Production, Web Editor)*
Photographic Services: A. Turner
 K. Wodehouse

Academic & Scholarly; Archaeology; Fine Art & Art History; History & Antiquarian; Numismatics

ISBNs, Imprints & Series:
978 0 900090, 978 0 907849, 978 1 85444

Parent Company:
Ashmolean Museum, University of Oxford

Overseas Representation:
Australia: Inbooks, c/o James Bennett Pty Ltd, Belrose, NSW
Europe: Gazelle Book Services Ltd, Lancaster, UK
USA: Antique Collectors Club Ltd, Easthampton, MA

Book Trade Association Membership:
BA; IPG; Museums & Galleries Publishing Group

2053

ASSOCIATION FOR LEARNING TECHNOLOGY
Gipsy Lane, Headington, Oxford OX3 0BP
Telephone: 01865 484125
Fax: 01865 484165
Email: admin@alt.ac.uk
Web Site: http://www.alt.ac.uk

Chief Executive: Seb Schmoller
Directors: Marion Samler *(Operations)*
 Mark van Harmelen *(Development)*

Academic & Scholarly

New Titles: 4 (2007), 6 (2008)
No of Employees: 7
Annual Turnover: £510,000

ISBNs, Imprints & Series:
978 0 9545870 Beyond Control (Research Proceeding)

2054

ASSOCIATION FOR SCOTTISH LITERARY STUDIES
c/o Dept of Scottish Literature,
University of Glasgow,
7 University Gardens, Glasgow G12 8QH
Telephone: 0141 330 5309
Fax: 0141 330 5309
Email: office@asls.org.uk
Web Site: http://www.asls.org.uk

Trade Enquiries:
BookSource, 50 Cambuslang Road,
Glasgow G32 8NB
Telephone: 0845 370 0063
Fax: 0845 370 0064
Email: orders@booksource.net
Web Site: http://www.booksource.net

General Manager: Duncan Jones

Academic & Scholarly; Educational & Textbooks; Languages & Linguistics; Literature & Criticism; Poetry; Theatre, Drama & Dance

New Titles: 6 (2007), 7 (2008)
No of Employees: 2
Annual Turnover: £80,000

ISBNs, Imprints & Series:
ASLS Annual Volumes (series); New Writing Scotland (series); Scotnotes (series)
978 0 948877

Overseas Representation:
USA & Canada: Independent Publishers Group (IPG), Chicago, IL, USA

Book Trade Association Membership:
Publishing Scotland

2055

ATLANTIC BOOKS
Ormond House, 26–27 Boswell Street, London WC1N 3JZ
Telephone: (020) 7269 1610
Fax: (020) 7430 0916
Email: enquiries@groveatlantic.co.uk
Web Site: http://www.groveatlantic.co.uk

Distribution:
TBS Ltd, Colchester Road, Frating Green, Colchester, Essex CO7 7DW
Telephone: 01206 255678
Fax: 01206 255930
Email: sales@tbs-ltd.co.uk
Web Site: http://www.thebookservice.co.uk

Company Secretary: Guy Newton
Directors: Toby Mundy *(Chief Executive Officer & Publisher)*
 Daniel Scott *(Managing)*
 Alan Craig *(Production)*
 Caroline Knight *(Editorial)*

Valerie Duff *(Rights)*
Karen Duffy *(Publicity)*
Ravi Mirchandoni *(Editor-in-Chief)*
Irina Stoyanova *(Financial Controller)*

Biography & Autobiography; Crime; Economics; Fiction; History & Antiquarian; Humour; Industry, Business & Management; Law; Literature & Criticism; Mathematics & Statistics; Military & War; Music; Natural History; Philosophy; Poetry; Politics & World Affairs; Psychology & Psychiatry; Reference Books, Directories & Dictionaries; Religion & Theology; Science Fiction; Transport

New Titles: 60 (2007), 65 (2008)
No of Employees: 23
Annual Turnover: £3.4M

ISBNs, Imprints & Series: 978 1 84354

Parent Company:
USA: Grove Atlantic Inc

Associated Companies:
USA: Grove/Atlantic Inc

Overseas Representation:
Australia: Penguin, Scoresby, Vic
Caribbean: David Willians, InterMedia Americana (IMA) Ltd, London, UK
Europe: Faber & Faber, London, UK
Far East: Julian Ashton, Ashton International Marketing Services, Sevenoaks, Kent, UK
New Zealand: Penguin Books (New Zealand) Ltd, Auckland
Republic of Ireland: Repforce Ireland, Irishtown, Dublin
South Africa: Penguin Group SA, Rosebank

Book Trade Association Membership:
IPG

2056

ATLANTIC EUROPE PUBLISHING CO LTD
Greys Court Farm, Greys Court,
Henley on Thames, Oxon RG9 4PG
Telephone: 01491 628188
Fax: 01491 628189
Email: e-mail addresses on website
Web Site: http://www.AtlanticEurope.com
& http://www.CurriculumVisions.com

Director: Dr B. J. Knapp

Chemistry; Children's Books; Educational & Textbooks; Electronic (Educational); Environment & Development Studies; Geography & Geology; History & Antiquarian; Mathematics & Statistics; Physics; Reference Books, Directories & Dictionaries; Religion & Theology; Scientific & Technical

ISBNs, Imprints & Series:
978 1 862140, 978 1 869860

2057

ATTIC PRESS
[an imprint of Cork University Press]
c/o Cork University Press,
Youngline Industrial Estate, Pailaduff Road,
Togher, Cork, Republic of Ireland
Telephone: +353 (021) 432 1725
Fax: +353 (021) 431 5329
Web Site: http://www.corkuniversitypress.com

Representation (Republic of Ireland & Northern Ireland):
Mullet Fitzpatrick, 58 New Vale Cottages, Shankhill, Dublin, Republic of Ireland

Orders & Distribution:
Gill & Macmillan, Hume Avenue, Park West, Dublin 12, Republic of Ireland

Publications Director: Mike Collins

Biography & Autobiography; Cookery, Wines & Spirits; Gender Studies; Music; Politics & World Affairs

New Titles: 2 (2007), 2 (2008)

ISBNs, Imprints & Series:
978 0 946211, 978 0 9535353, 978 1 85594

Parent Company:
Republic of Ireland: Cork University Press

Overseas Representation:
Netherlands & Germany: Brigitte Axster, Frankfurt, Germany
UK: Quantum Publishing Solutions Ltd, Paisley
UK (excluding Northern Ireland): Marston Book Services Ltd, Abingdon, UK
USA: Dufour Editions Inc, Chester Springs, PA

Book Trade Association Membership:
CLÉ (Irish PA)

2058

AUDIO-FORUM - THE LANGUAGE SOURCE
World Microfilms, PO Box 35488,
St John's Wood, London NW8 6WD
Telephone: (020) 7586 4499
Email: microworld@ndirect.co.uk
Web Site: http://www.microworld.uk.com

Director: S. C. Albert

Academic & Scholarly; Languages & Linguistics

ISBNs, Imprints & Series:
978 1 86013 with Sussex Pubs

Associated Companies:
Sussex Publications Ltd; World Microfilms Publications Ltd

Distributor for:
USA: Audio-Forum USA; Jeffrey Norton Publishing

2059

AURELIAN INFORMATION LTD
4(A) Alexandra Mansions, West End Lane,
London NW6 1LU
Telephone: (020) 7794 8609
Fax: (020) 7794 8609
Email: aurelian@dircon.co.uk
Web Site: http://www.dircon.co.uk/aurelian/

Distribution:
Wyvern DM Ltd, Harrier House,
Sedgeway Business Park, Witchford, Ely,
Cambs CB6 2HY
Telephone: Database enquiries: 01353 667733
Fax: 01353 669030 (Database enquiries)
Web Site: http://www.dircon.co.uk/aurelian/

Directors: Paul Petzold
Julia Kaufmann OBE *(Company Secretary)*

Industry, Business & Management; Reference Books, Directories & Dictionaries; Charities & Voluntary Organizations; Internet for Business; Internet for Charity Sector

ISBNs, Imprints & Series:
978 1 899247 Aurelian; National Charities Database

2060

AUREUS PUBLISHING LTD
Castle Court, Castle-upon-Alun,
St Bride's Major, Vale of Glamorgan
CF32 0TN
Telephone: 01656 880033
Fax: 01656 880033
Email: info@aureus.co.uk
Web Site: http://www.aureus.co.uk

Director: Meuryn Hughes

Biography & Autobiography; Music; Sports & Games

New Titles: 14 (2007), 10 (2008)

ISBNs, Imprints & Series: 978 1 899750

2061

AURORA METRO PUBLICATIONS LTD
67 Grove Avenue, Twickenham, London
TW1 4HX
Telephone: (020) 3261 0000
Fax: (020) 3261 0000
Email: info@aurorametro.com
Web Site: http://www.aurorametro.com

Distribution:
Central Books, 99 Wallis Road, Hackney,
London E9 5LN
Telephone: (020) 8986 4854
Fax: (020) 8533 5821
Email: info@centralbooks.com & orders@centralbooks.com
Web Site: http://www.centralbooks.com

Publisher: Cheryl Robson
Sales & Marketing: Steve Robson
Aidan Jenkins

Academic & Scholarly; Children's Books; Cinema, Video, TV & Radio; Cookery, Wines & Spirits; Educational & Textbooks; Fiction; Gay & Lesbian Studies; Gender Studies; Humour; Reference Books, Directories & Dictionaries; Theatre, Drama & Dance; Travel & Topography

ISBNs, Imprints & Series:
978 0 9515877, 978 0 9536757, 978 0 9542330, 978 0 9546912, 978 0 9551566, 978 1 906582 Aurora Metro Press

Overseas Representation:
Canada: Playwrights Press Canada, Toronto, Ont
South Africa: Quartet Sales & Marketing, Johannesburg
USA: TCG/Consortium, St Paul, MN

Book Trade Association Membership:
IPG

2062

AURUM PRESS
7 Greenland Street, London NW1 0ND
Telephone: (020) 7284 7160
Fax: (020) 7485 4902
Email: firstname.secondname@aurumpress.co.uk
Web Site: http://www.aurumpress.co.uk

Distribution & Warehouse:
Littlehampton Book Services,
Columbia Building, Faraday Close,
Durrington, Worthing, West Sussex
BN13 3RB
Telephone: 01903 828800
Fax: 01903 828801

Directors: W. J. McCreadie *(Managing)*
Piers Burnett *(Managing Deputy)*
Graham Eames *(Sales)*
Graham Coster *(Editorial)*

Architecture & Design; Biography & Autobiography; Cinema, Video, TV & Radio; Cookery, Wines & Spirits; Crafts & Hobbies; Fashion & Costume; Gardening; Health & Beauty; Humour; Military & War; Music; Natural History; Photography; Sports & Games; Travel & Topography

New Titles: 70 (2007), 75 (2008)
No of Employees: 18
Annual Turnover: £4.5M

ISBNs, Imprints & Series:
978 1 84513, 978 1 85410, 978 1 902538, 978 1 903221

Parent Company:
Quarto Group Plc

Overseas Representation:
Africa (excluding South Africa) & Eastern Europe: InterMedia Americana (IMA) Ltd, London, UK
Australia: Bookwise International, Adelaide, SA
Canada: Fitzhenry & Whiteside Ltd, Markham, Ont
Europe: Bill Bailey Publishers Representatives, Newton Abbot, Devon, UK
Far East: Ashton International Marketing Services, Sevenoaks, Kent, UK
Latin America & Caribbean: Humphrys Roberts Associates, London, UK
New Zealand: Hachette Livre New Zealand, Auckland
Scandinavia: McNeish Publishing Services, East Sussex, UK
South Africa: Trinity Books CC, Randburg
USA: IPG Trafalgar Square, Chicago, IL

Book Trade Association Membership:
IPG

2063

AUSTIN & MACAULEY PUBLISHERS LTD
CGC-33-01 Canada Square, Canary Wharf,
London E14 5LB
Telephone: (020) 7038 8212
Fax: (020) 7038 8100
Email: mail@austinmacauley.com
Web Site: http://www.austinmacauley.com

Editors: Annette Longman *(Chief)*
David Calvert *(Executive)*
Marketing Executive: Ross Malik

Academic & Scholarly; Animal Care & Breeding; Antiques & Collecting; Audio Books; Biography & Autobiography; Biology & Zoology; Children's Books; Cinema, Video, TV & Radio; Computer Science; Cookery, Wines & Spirits; Crime; Educational & Textbooks; English as a Foreign Language; Environment & Development Studies; Fashion & Costume; Fiction; Gardening; Gay & Lesbian Studies; Health & Beauty; Humour; Literature & Criticism; Magic & the Occult; Medical (incl. Self Help & Alternative Medicine); Military & War; Natural History; Nautical; Philosophy; Politics & World Affairs; Psychology & Psychiatry; Religion & Theology; Science Fiction; Sociology & Anthropology; Sports & Games; Theatre, Drama & Dance; Travel & Topography; Vocational Training & Careers

New Titles: 7 (2007), 30 (2008)
No of Employees: 25
Annual Turnover: £250,000

2064

AUSTRALIAN CONSOLIDATED PRESS UK
10 Scirocco Close,
Moulton Park Office Village, Northampton
NN3 6AP
Telephone: 01604 642200

Fax: 01604 642300
Email: books@acpuk.com

Directors: Jean Gardiner *(Managing)*
Linda Ayres *(Sales)*
Laura Bamford
Office Manager: Anna Pisani

Children's Books; Cookery, Wines & Spirits; Crafts & Hobbies

New Titles: 46 (2007), 41 (2008)
No of Employees: 6

ISBNs, Imprints & Series:
978 0 94989, 978 1 86396, 978 1 90377 Australian Women's Weekly Home Library

Parent Company:
Australia: ACP Publishing Pty Ltd

Overseas Representation:
Germany, Austria & Switzerland: Gabriele Kern Publishers Services, Frankfurt-am-Main, Germany
Hungary, Poland, Slovakia, Czech Republic, Romania, Albania, Yugoslavia, Croatia Slovenia, Bosnia & Herzegovina, Macedonia & Bulgaria: Csaba Lengyel, Pendragon Trading Bt, Budapest, Hungary
Lebanon, Egypt, Jordan, Dubai, Saudi Arabia & United Arab Emirates: Michael Morris Associates, Saffron Walden, UK

2065

AUTHENTIC MEDIA
9 Holdom Avenue, Bletchley,
Milton Keynes, Bucks
Telephone: 01908 364205
Fax: 01908 648592
Email: donna.harris@authenticmedia.co.uk
Web Site: http://www.authenticmedia.co.uk

Head Office:
IBS-STL UK, PO Box 300,
Kingstown Broadway, Carlisle, Cumbria
CA3 0HA
Telephone: 01228 512512
Fax: 01228 514949
Web Site: http://www.stldistribution.co.uk

Publishers: Mark Finnie
Malcolm Down *(Fiction & Children)*
Manager: Pete Barnsley *(Marketing)*
Editorial: Robin Parry *(Paternoster (Academic))*
Kath Williams *(Authentic (General) – Administration)*
Liz Williams *(Authentic (General) – Supervisor)*
Production Controller: Peter Little

Academic & Scholarly; Biography & Autobiography; Children's Books; Religion & Theology

New Titles: 175 (2007), 170 (2008)

ISBNs, Imprints & Series:
978 0 8500 Authentic Bibles
978 1 84227, 978 1 85364 Paternoster
978 1 85078, 978 1 86024 Authentic Lifestyle
978 1 93406 Authentic US Lifestyle

Parent Company:
IBS-STL UK

Overseas Representation:
India: OM Book Services, Delhi
USA: STL Inc, Waynesboro, GA

2066

AUTHORHOUSE UK LTD
500 Avebury Boulevard, Milton Keynes,
Bucks MK9 2BE
Telephone: 01908 309250
Fax: 01908 309259
Email: tdavies@authorhouse.co.uk
Web Site: http://www.authorhouse.co.uk

Directors: Tim Davies *(Managing)*
Daniel Cooke *(Business Development)*

Biography & Autobiography; Children's Books; Cookery, Wines & Spirits; Crime; Fiction; Humour; Poetry; Religion & Theology; Science Fiction

New Titles: 750 (2007), 900 (2008)
No of Employees: 12
Annual Turnover: £1.5M

ISBNs, Imprints & Series:
978 1 4208, 978 1 4259, 978 1 4343

Parent Company:
USA: Author Solutions Inc

Associated Companies:
USA: Authorhouse (USA); Inkubook; Inkubuzz; iUniverse; Wordclay

2067

AVA PUBLISHING (UK) LTD
56A Chapel Road, Worthing, West Sussex
BN11 1BE
Telephone: 01903 204455
Fax: 01903 237346
Email: sturner@avabooks.co.uk
Web Site: http://www.avabooks.ch

Publisher: Brian Morris
Managers: Terry Hancock *(Finance)*
Sarah Turner *(Marketing)*
Editor in Chief: Caroline Walmsley

Architecture & Design; Educational & Textbooks; Electronic (Educational); Fashion & Costume; Industry, Business & Management; Photography; Reference Books, Directories & Dictionaries

New Titles: 21 (2007), 23 (2008)
No of Employees: 12

ISBNs, Imprints & Series:
978 2 88479, 978 2 940373, 978 2 940411

Overseas Representation:
Rest of Europe: Thames & Hudson Ltd, London, UK
USA & Canada (General only): Sterling Publishing Co Inc, New York, NY, USA
USA & Canada (Photography Design titles & textbooks): Watson-Guptill Publications, New York, NY, USA

2068

AWARD PUBLICATIONS LTD
The Old Riding School, Welbeck Estate,
Worksop, Notts S80 3LR
Telephone: 01909 478170
Fax: 01909 484632
Email: info@awardpublications.co.uk
Web Site: http://www.awardpublications.co.uk

Directors: Anna Wilkinson *(Managing)*
David King *(International Sales)*
David Meggs *(UK Sales)*

Children's Books

New Titles: 50 (2007), 45 (2008)

ISBNs, Imprints & Series:
978 0 86163, 978 1 84135, 978 1 89976

2069

B SMALL PUBLISHING LTD
The Book Shed, 36 Leyborne Park, Kew,
Richmond, Surrey TW9 3HA
Telephone: (020) 8948 2884
Fax: (020) 8948 6458
Email: books@bsmall.co.uk
Web Site: http://www.bsmall.co.uk

Sales Representation, UK Trade Enquiries & Orders:
Bounce! Sales & Marketing Ltd,
14 Greville Street, London EC1N 8SB
Telephone: (020) 7138 3650
Fax: (020) 7138 3658
Email: sales@bouncemarketing.co.uk
Web Site: http://www.bouncemarketing.co.uk

Foreign Rights:
Anne Murray
Telephone: (020) 8877 9040
Fax: (020) 8877 9040
Email: annemurray@goody.org.uk

Editorial: Catherine Bruzzone *(Publisher)*
UK Sales & Marketing Manager: Caroline MacMillan

Children's Books; Languages & Linguistics

New Titles: 15 (2007), 12 (2008)

ISBNs, Imprints & Series:
978 1 874735, 978 1 902915, 978 1 905710

Overseas Representation:
Australia (languages only): Intext Book Co Pty Ltd, Hawthorn, Vic, Australia
Hong Kong: Stanford House
South Africa: Phambili Agencies CC, Johannesburg

Book Trade Association Membership:
IPG

2070

B SQUARED
4c Vulcan Close, Sandhurst, Berks
GU47 9DD
Telephone: 0845 466 0141
Fax: 0845 466 0191
Email: info@bsquared.co.uk
Web Site: http://www.bsquared.co.uk

Executives: Brenda Byrom
Brian Pickles
Dale Pickles

Academic & Scholarly; Educational & Textbooks

No of Employees: 4
Annual Turnover: £400,000

2071

BERNARD BABANI (PUBLISHING) LTD
The Grampians, Shepherds Bush Road,
London W6 7NF
Telephone: (020) 7603 2581/7296
Fax: (020) 7603 8203
Email: enquiries@babanibooks.com
Web Site: http://www.babanibooks.com

Director: Michael H. Babani *(Sales, Production, Managing)*

Computer Science; Crafts & Hobbies; Educational & Textbooks; Electronic (Educational); Electronic (Entertainment); Electronic (Professional & Academic); Engineering; Mathematics & Statistics; Scientific & Technical; Radio & Electronics

New Titles: 20 (2007), 18 (2008)

ISBNs, Imprints & Series:
978 0 85934, 978 0 900162 Babani Press

Associated Companies:
Bernards (Publishers) Ltd

Book Trade Association Membership:
IPG

2072

BACK-IN-PRINT BOOKS LTD
PO Box 47057, London SW18 1YW
Telephone: (020) 8637 0975
Email: rolf@backinprint.co.uk
Web Site: http://www.backinprint.co.uk

Orders:
Gardners Books, 1 Whittle Drive,
Eastbourne BN23 6QH

Orders:
Bertrams, Norwich

Directors: Rolf Stricker
Gillian Cutress

Biography & Autobiography; Crime; Educational & Textbooks; Fiction; Guide Books; Literature & Criticism; Military & War

New Titles: 1 (2007)

ISBNs, Imprints & Series: 978 1 903552

Associated Companies:
Italy: Editoriale Shopping Italia srl

2073

BADGER PUBLISHING LTD
15 Wedgwood Gate,
Pin Green Industrial Estate, Stevenage
SG1 4SU
Telephone: 01438 356907
Fax: 01438 747015
Email: enquiries@badger-publishing.co.uk
Web Site: http://www.badger-publishing.co.uk

Managers: David Jamieson *(General & Publisher)*
Jean Constantine *(Sales & Marketing)*
Accountant: Melanie Forder

Educational & Textbooks

New Titles: 50 (2007), 44 (2008)
No of Employees: 14

ISBNs, Imprints & Series:
978 1 84424, 978 1 84691, 978 1 85880

Parent Company:
Republic of Ireland: Educational Company of Ireland

Book Trade Association Membership:
Publishers Association; EPC

2074

DUNCAN BAIRD PUBLISHERS
29 Jewry Street, Winchester, Hants
SO23 8RY
Telephone: 01962 841411
Fax: 01962 841413
Email: enquiries@dbp.co.uk
Web Site: http://www.dbp.co.uk

Directors: Duncan Baird *(Managing)*
Alex Mitchell *(Sales)*
Bob Saxton *(Editorial)*
Roger Walton *(Art)*
Adela Cory *(Production)*
Ryan Tring *(Finance)*

Architecture & Design; Cookery, Wines & Spirits; Fine Art & Art History; Health & Beauty; Magic & the Occult; Medical (incl. Self Help & Alternative Medicine); Natural History; Philosophy; Reference Books, Directories & Dictionaries; Religion & Theology

New Titles: 70 (2007), 76 (2008)

ISBNs, Imprints & Series:
978 1 84483, 978 1 90585

Associated Companies:
Watkins Publishing

Overseas Representation:
Australia: Simon & Schuster (Australia) Pty Ltd, Pymble, NSW
Canada: Raincoast Book Distribution Ltd, Vancouver, BC
New Zealand: HarperCollins (NZ) Ltd, Glenfield, Auckland

2075

THE BANNER OF TRUTH TRUST
3 Murrayfield Road, Edinburgh EH12 6EL
Telephone: 0131 337 7310
Fax: 0131 346 7484
Email: info@banneroftruth.co.uk
Web Site: http://www.banneroftruth.co.uk

Warehouse:
17 Bankhead Drive,
Sighthill Industrial Estate, Edinburgh EH11 4DW
Telephone: 0131 442 2945
Fax: 0131 442 2945

General Manager: John Rawlinson
Editor: Jonathan Watson

Religion & Theology

ISBNs, Imprints & Series: 978 0 85151

Associated Companies:
USA: The Banner of Truth

Overseas Representation:
New Zealand: Sovereign Grace Books, Auckland
Nigeria: Amazing Grace Ltd, Kano
Philippines: Evangelical Outreach Inc, Quezon City
South Africa: Barnabas Book Room, Durban North; Farel Distributors (Pty) Ltd, North Riding
USA: The Banner of Truth, Carlisle, PA

2076

THE BANTON PRESS
Dippin Cottage, Kildonan, Isle of Arran KA27 8SB
Telephone: 01770 820231
Fax: 01770 820231
Email: bantonpress@ndo.co.uk
Web Site: http://www.bantonpress.co.uk

Managing Director: Mark Brown

Magic & the Occult; Religion & Theology

New Titles: 2 (2008)

ISBNs, Imprints & Series: 978 1 85652

2077

BARDDAS
Pen-Rhiw, 71 Pentrepoeth Road, Morriston, Swansea SA6 6AE
Telephone: 01792 792829
Fax: 01792 792829
Email: alan.llwyd@googlemail.com

Assistant Officer:
Bod Aeron, Heol Pen-Sarn, Y Bala, Gwynedd LL23 7SR
Telephone: 01678 521051
Fax: 01678 521051
Email: elwyn@barddas.fsnet.co.uk
Web Site: http://www.barddas.com

Administrative Officer: Alan Llwyd
Assistant Officer: Elwyn Edwards

Poetry

New Titles: 11 (2007), 11 (2008)
No of Employees: 2
Annual Turnover: £100,000

ISBNs, Imprints & Series: 978 1 900437

2078

BAREFOOT BOOKS
124 Walcot Street, Bath BA1 5BG
Telephone: 01225 322400
Fax: 01225 322499
Email: info@barefootbooks.com
Web Site: http://www.barefootbooks.com

Trade Sales (Orders):
Littlehampton Book Services Ltd, Faraday Close, Durrington, Worthing, West Sussex BN13 3RB
Telephone: 01903 828800
Fax: 01903 828801

Publisher: Tessa Strickland *(Editorial)*
Director: Nancy Traversy *(Managing)*
Managers: Claire Dowling *(UK Trade Sales)*
   Libby Putman *(US Trade Sales)*
   Melisa Schulman *(US Trade Sales)*
   Jose Lorenzo *(Foreign Rights)*
   Jeanne Nicholson *(Marketing)*
   Silvana Tann *(UK Trade Sales)*
   Suzanne Gaved *(UK Marketing)*

Audio Books; Children's Books; Gift Books

Annual Turnover: £7M

ISBNs, Imprints & Series:
978 1 84148, 978 1 84686, 978 1 898000, 978 1 901223, 978 1 902283, 978 1 905236

Overseas Representation:
Australia: Willow Connection Pty Ltd, Brookvale, NSW
East Africa: A–Z Africa Book Services, Rotterdam, Netherlands
Europe (Trade), Indian Sub-Continent & Middle East: Gabriele Kern Publishers Services, Frankfurt-am-Main, Germany; Penny Padovani, Montanare di Cortona, Italy; Jenny Padovani, Barcelona, Spain
Latin America & Caribbean: David Williams, InterMedia Americana (IMA) Ltd, London, UK
New Zealand: Addenda Ltd, Grey Lynn
Republic of Ireland & Northern Ireland: Conor Hackett, Dublin, Republic of Ireland
South Africa: Phambili Agencies CC, Germiston; Salmonberry Press
South East Asia, Far East, North Asia, Hong Kong, Singapore, Brunei & Malaysia (Libraries), Singapore, Brunei & Malaysia (Trade & Special Sales): Chris Ashdown, Publishers Marketing Services Pte Ltd, Singapore
South East, Far East & North Asia: Publishers International Marketing, London, UK
USA: Barefoot Books Inc, Cambridge, MA

2079

BARNY BOOKS
Hough on the Hill, Grantham NG32 2BB
Telephone: 01400 250246 & 01522 790009
Fax: 01400 251737
Email: barnybooks@hotmail.co.uk
Web Site: http://www.barnybooks.biz

Editor: Molly Burkett
Business Manager: Jayne Thompson

Biography & Autobiography; Children's Books; Fiction; History & Antiquarian; Humour; Industry, Business & Management; Medical (incl. Self Help & Alternative Medicine); Military & War; Transport

New Titles: 15 (2007), 15 (2008)
No of Employees: 2

ISBNs, Imprints & Series:
Events, People to be Remembered (Joseph Banks – Sir John Hawrins)
978 0 948204
978 1 903172 Once upon a Wartime (Series)
978 1 906542

2080

BARTSKY LTD
39A Welbeck Street, London W1G 8DH
Email: email@bartsky.com

Contact: Richard Astor

Law; Medical (incl. Self Help & Alternative Medicine)

ISBNs, Imprints & Series:
978 1 873994 Bartsky Law; Bartsky Medicine; JurisPrudent

2081

BATSFORD
[an imprint of Chrysalis Books Group]
10 Southcombe Street, London W14 0RA
Telephone: (020) 7605 1400
Fax: (020) 7605 1401
Email: tpersaud@anovabooks.com
Web Site: http://www.anovabooks.com

Distribution, Warehouse & Enquiries:
HarperCollins Distribution, Campsie View, Westerhill Road, Bishopbriggs, Glasgow G64 2QT
Telephone: 0141 306 3100
Fax: 0141 306 3767

Publisher: Tina Persaud
Marketing Manager: Komal Patel
Head of International Rights: Sinead Hurley

Archaeology; Architecture & Design; Crafts & Hobbies; Fashion & Costume; Gardening; History & Antiquarian

ISBNs, Imprints & Series: 978 0 7134

Parent Company:
Anova Books

Overseas Representation:
Australia: Capricorn Link (Australia) Pty Ltd, Windsor, NSW
Canada: Sterling Publishing Co Inc, New York, NY, USA
Eastern Europe: Tony Moggach, InterMedia Americana (IMA) Ltd, London, UK
Far East: Ashton International Marketing Services, Sevenoaks, Kent, UK
France, Netherlands & Luxembourg: Ted Dougherty, London, UK
Germany, Switzerland & Austria: Gabriele Kern Publishers Services, Frankfurt-am-Main, Germany
Mexico & Central America: Christopher Humphrys, Humphrys Roberts Associates, London, UK
New Zealand: HarperCollins (NZ) Ltd, Glenfield, Auckland
Scandinavia & Italy: McNeish Publishing Services, East Sussex, UK
Singapore: Pansing Distribution Sdn Bhd
South Africa: Trinity Books CC, Randburg
South America: Terry Roberts, Cotia SP, Brazil
Spain, Portugal, Malta & Greece: Penny Padovani, London, UK

Book Trade Association Membership:
IPG

2082

BBC ACTIVE
80 Strand, London WC2R 0RL
Telephone: (020) 7010 2731
Fax: (020) 7010 6965

Email: jonathan.scott@pearson.com
Web Site: http://www.bbcactive.com

Customer Services:
Edinburgh Gate, Harlow, Essex CM20 2JE
Telephone: 01279 623623
Web Site: http://www.bbcactive.com

Head: Susan Ross
Head of Digital & Brand Development: Julia King
Head of Sales & Marketing: Valerie de la Rochette *(Product Development)*
Publisher: Maureen Gallagher

Chemistry; Children's Books; Computer Science; Educational & Textbooks; Electronic (Educational); English as a Foreign Language; Geography & Geology; History & Antiquarian; Languages & Linguistics; Mathematics & Statistics; Physics; Religion & Theology; Audio & Video Cassettes; CD-ROMs; DVDs

New Titles: 40 (2007), 50 (2008)

ISBNs, Imprints & Series:
978 0 563, 978 1 4066

Parent Company:
Pearson Education

Book Trade Association Membership:
EPC

2083

BBC AUDIOBOOKS LTD
St James House, The Square,
Lower Bristol Road, Bath BA2 3BH
Telephone: 01225 878000
Fax: 01225 310771
Email: jan.paterson.01@bbc.com
Web Site: http://www.bbcaudiobooks.com

Directors: Paul Dempsey *(Managing)*
   Jan Paterson *(Publishing & Marketing)*
   Mike Bowen *(Commercial)*
   Sam Newman *(Sales)*
   Tracy Leeming *(Operations)*

Audio Books

New Titles: 157 (2007), 174 (2008)
No of Employees: 75

ISBNs, Imprints & Series:
978 0 563, 978 1 8460 Radio Collection (Audio Cassettes, CDs & MP3 CDs)
978 0 754 Word for Word (Audio Cassettes & CDs)
978 1 85549 Cover to Cover Cassettes (Audio Cassettes & CDs)

Parent Company:
BBC Worldwide

Overseas Representation:
USA: BBC Audiobooks America

2084

BCR PUBLISHING LTD
3 Cobden Court, Wimpole Close, Bromley, Kent BR2 9JF
Telephone: (020) 8466 6987
Fax: (020) 8466 0654
Email: info@bcrpub.co.uk
Web Site: http://www.bcrpub.co.uk

Managing Director: Michael Bickers
Editor: Roopi Makkar
Marketing Manager: Anya Tatyanchenko

Industry, Business & Management

ISBNs, Imprints & Series:
978 0 9522351, 978 0 9539877

2085

B & D PUBLISHING
PO Box 4658, Stratford upon Avon,
Warwickshire CV37 1EP
Telephone: 01789 417824
Fax: 01789 417826
Email: postmaster@banddpublishing.co.uk
Web Site: http://
www.banddpublishing.co.uk

Academic & Scholarly; Educational & Textbooks

Book Trade Association Membership:
Publishers Association

2086

BEAM EDUCATION
Maze Workshops, 72A Southgate Road,
London N1 3JT
Telephone: (020) 7684 3323
Fax: (020) 7684 3334
Email: info@beam.co.uk
Web Site: http://www.beam.co.uk

Directors: Sheila Ebbutt *(Managing)*
Graham Barker *(Sales & Marketing)*
Product Development: Carole Skinner
Production Manager: Gary Hayes
Senior Editor: Marion Dill

Educational & Textbooks; Mathematics & Statistics

New Titles: 15 (2007), 30 (2008)
No of Employees: 14

ISBNs, Imprints & Series:
978 1 874099, 978 1 903142, 978 1 906224

Parent Company:
Nelson Thornes Ltd

2087

BEAUTIFUL BOOKS LTD
36–38 Glasshouse Street, London W1B 5DL
Telephone: (020) 7734 4448
Fax: (020) 3070 0764
Email: simon@beautiful-books.co.uk
Web Site: http://www.beautiful-books.co.uk

Sales & Distribution:
Turnaround Publisher Services, Unit 3,
Olympia Trading Estate, Coburg Road,
London N22 6TZ
Telephone: (020) 8829 3000
Fax: (020) 8881 5088
Email: claire@turnaround-uk.com
Web Site: http://www.turnaround-uk.com

Publisher: Simon Petherick
Production Manager: Tamsin Griffiths
Editor: Anthony Nott
Publicity: Katherine Josselyn

Audio Books; Fiction; Humour; Literature & Criticism; Music; Psychology & Psychiatry; Travel & Topography

New Titles: 10 (2007), 23 (2008)
No of Employees: 4
Annual Turnover: £500,000

ISBNs, Imprints & Series:
978 0 95494, 978 1 905636 Beautiful
Books; Bloody Books; Burning House

Overseas Representation:
Australia & New Zealand: Peribo Pty Ltd,
Mount Kuring-Gai, NSW, Australia
Europe (including Ireland): Turnaround
Publisher Services Ltd, London, UK
Worldwide (foreign rights): The Marsh
Agency, London, UK

2088

*BEDFORD FREEMAN WORTH (BFW)
at Palgrave Macmillan, Houndmills,
Basingstoke, Hants RG21 6XS
Telephone: 01256 302983

Trade Orders & Warehouse:
Macmillan Direct, Customer Services,
Brunel Road, Houndmills, Basingstoke,
Hants RG21 6XS
Telephone: 01256 302699
Fax: 01256 364733
Email: mdl@macmillan.co.uk
Web Site: http://www.macmillan-mdl.co.uk

Publisher: Margaret Hewinson

Academic & Scholarly; Biology & Zoology; Chemistry; Geography & Geology; Mathematics & Statistics; Physics; Psychology & Psychiatry; Astronomy/Cosmology

ISBNs, Imprints & Series: 978 0 7167

Parent Company:
USA: W. H. Freeman & Co

Distributor for:
Palgrave Macmillan; University Science
Books; Worth Publishers
USA: Sinauer Associates

Overseas Representation:
Australia & New Zealand: Macmillan
Education Australia, South Yarra, Vic,
Australia
USA: W. H. Freeman & Co, New York

Book Trade Association Membership:
IGSMTP; CAPP

2089

THE BELMONT PRESS
29 Tenby Avenue, Harrow HA3 8RU
Telephone: (020) 8907 4700
Fax: (020) 8907 7354
Web Site: http://www.waterways.co.uk &
http://www.belmont1948.co.uk

Directors: John Lawes *(Managing)*
Mark Lawes *(Technical)*

Atlases & Maps; History & Antiquarian; Nautical; Transport; Travel & Topography; Inland Waterways

New Titles: 6 (2007), 6 (2008)
No of Employees: 5

ISBNs, Imprints & Series:
978 0 905366 Belmont series of books;
Navigator series of maps; Working
Waterways series

Parent Company:
Belmont (1948) Ltd

Associated Companies:
Belmont Books; Waterway Books;
Waterways Book Service

Distributor for:
Enigma Publishing; Remus Publishing; W.H.
Walker & Bros; Robert Wilson Designs;
Working Waterways Series

2090

BENE FACTUM PUBLISHING LTD
PO Box 58122, London SW8 5WZ
Telephone: (020) 7720 6767
Email: inquiries@bene-factum.co.uk

Representation:
John Wilson (Booksales) Ltd, 1 High Street,
Princes Risborough, Berks HP27 0AG
Telephone: 01844 275927
Fax: 01844 274402

Distribution:
Marston Book Services, PO Box 269,
Abingdon, Oxon OX14 4YN
Telephone: 01235 465500
Fax: 01235 465555

Managing Director: Anthony Weldon

Biography & Autobiography; Children's Books; Gardening; History & Antiquarian; Industry, Business & Management; Law; Medical (incl. Self Help & Alternative Medicine); Military & War; Reference Books, Directories & Dictionaries; Vocational Training & Careers

New Titles: 10 (2007), 10 (2008)

ISBNs, Imprints & Series:
978 0 9522754, 978 1 903071

Book Trade Association Membership:
IPG

2091

BERG PUBLISHERS
1st Floor, Angel Court,
81 St Clements Street, Oxford OX4 1AW
Telephone: 01865 245104
Fax: 01865 791165
Email: kearle@bergpublishers.com
Web Site: http://www.bergpublishers.com

Distribution & Returns:
Orca Book Services, Stanley House,
3 Fleets Lane, Poole, Dorset BH15 3AJ
Telephone: 01202 665432
Fax: 01202 666219
Email: orders@orca-book-services.co.uk

Trade Enquiries & Orders:
Quantum Publishing Solutions,
2 Cheviot Road, Paisley PA2 8AN
Telephone: 0141 884 1398

Directors: Kathryn Earle *(Managing & Editorial)*
Tristan Palmer *(Editorial)*
Managers: Veruschka Selbach *(Marketing & Sales)*
Ken Bruce *(Production)*

Academic & Scholarly; Architecture & Design; Cinema, Video, TV & Radio; Educational & Textbooks; Fashion & Costume; Sociology & Anthropology

New Titles: 50 (2008)

ISBNs, Imprints & Series:
978 0 485 19, 978 0 85496, 978 1 84520,
978 1 84788, 978 1 85973

Parent Company:
Oxford International Publishers Ltd

Overseas Representation:
Australia & New Zealand: Footprint Books
Pty, Mona Vale, NSW, Australia
China & Hong Kong: Access Asia Media
Services, Shanghai, P. R. of China
*Europe, Republic of Ireland & Northern
Ireland:* Andrew Durnell Marketing Ltd,
Tunbridge Wells, UK
India: Maya Publishers Pvt Ltd, New Delhi
Japan: United Publishers Services Ltd, Tokyo
Korea: Information & Culture Korea (ICK),
Seoul, Korea, South
Latin America & Caribbean: InterMedia
Americana (IMA) Ltd, London, UK
Middle East & Africa: International
Publishing Services (IPS) Middle East Ltd,
Dubai, UAE
Pakistan: World Press, Lahore
Russia: Knigi Graniz
Taiwan: Unifacmanu Trading Co Ltd, Taipei
USA: Palgrave Macmillan, New York, NY

Book Trade Association Membership:
IPG

2092

BERGHAHN BOOKS
3 Newtec Place, Magdalen Road, Oxford
OX4 1RE
Telephone: 01865 250011
Fax: 01865 250056
Email: publisher@berghahnbooks.com
Web Site: http://
www.berghahnbooks.com

Warehouse & Orders:
Marston Book Services, PO Box 269,
Abingdon, Oxon OX14 4YN
Telephone: 01235 465500
Fax: 01235 465555
Email: enquiries@marston.co.uk

Representation (UK):
Compass Academic Ltd,
The Barley Mow Centre,
10 Barley Mow Passage, Chiswick, London
W4 4PH
Telephone: (020) 8994 6477
Fax: (020) 8400 6132

Managing Director: Marion Berghahn
(Publisher)
Managers: Mark Stanton *(Production)*
David Crabtree *(Publicity)*
Lore Cortis *(Rights)*
Rupert Jones-Parry *(Sales)*

Academic & Scholarly; Biography & Autobiography; Cinema, Video, TV & Radio; Economics; Electronic (Professional & Academic); Environment & Development Studies; Gender Studies; History & Antiquarian; Languages & Linguistics; Literature & Criticism; Military & War; Politics & World Affairs; Religion & Theology; Sociology & Anthropology; Theatre, Drama & Dance; Travel & Topography

New Titles: 122 (2007), 100 (2008)
No of Employees: 12
Annual Turnover: $1.8M

ISBNs, Imprints & Series:
978 1 57181, 978 1 84545

Associated Companies:
USA: Berghahn Books Inc

Distributor for:
Durkheim Press; Yad Vashem [English
language titles only]
India: Social Science Press

Overseas Representation:
Australia & New Zealand: Woodslane Pty
Ltd, Warriewood, NSW, Australia
Benelux: Jos de Jong, Belgium
Canada: Renouf Books, Ottawa, Ont
China & Hong Kong: Access Asia Media
Services, Malaysia
Eastern Europe: Dr László Horváth
Publishers Representative, Budapest,
Hungary
Europe: Berghahn Books, Oxford, UK
Germany (stockholding): Missing Link
International Booksellers, Bremen,
Germany
Greece & Cyprus: Charles Gibbes
Associates, London, UK
India: Julian Russ, Oxford, UK
Italy & France: Flavio Marcello Publishers'
Agents & Consultants, Padua, Italy
Japan (stockholding): United Publishers
Services Ltd, Tokyo, Japan
Latin/Central America: Cranbury
International LLC, Montpelier, VT, USA
Middle East & Turkey: Avicenna Partnership,
Oxford, UK
North America & Rest of the World:
Berghahn Books, New York, NY, USA
Scandinavia: David Towle International,
Stockholm, Sweden

South Africa: Nigel Doyle
Spain & Portugal: Iberian Book Services, Madrid, Spain

2093

BIBLE READING FELLOWSHIP
15 The Chambers, Vineyard, Abingdon, Oxon OX14 3FE
Telephone: 01865 319700
Fax: 01865 319701
Email: enquiries@brf.org.uk
Web Site: http://www.brf.org.uk

Distribution:
STL Distribution, Kingstown, Broadway, Carlisle CA3 0HA
Telephone: 01228 512512
Fax: 01228 514949
Email: info@stl.org
Web Site: http://www.stldistribution.co.uk

Chief Executive Officer: R. Fisher
General Manager: Karen Laister
Commissioning Editors: Sue Doggett
   Naomi Starkey

Children's Books; Educational & Textbooks; Religion & Theology

New Titles: 42 (2007), 42 (2008)
No of Employees: 24

ISBNs, Imprints & Series:
Barnabas; Day by Day with God; Guidelines; New Daylight; People's Bible Commentary Series; Quiet Spaces
978 0 7459, 978 1 84101

Overseas Representation:
Australia: Willow Connection Pty Ltd, Brookvale, NSW
Canada: Anglican Book Centre, Toronto, Ont
New Zealand: Scripture Union Wholesale, Wellington
USA: The Bible Reading Fellowship, Winter Park, FL

2094

JOSEPH BIDDULPH PUBLISHER
32 Strŷd Ebeneser, Pontypridd CF37 5PB
Telephone: 01443 662559

Sole Proprietor: Joseph Biddulph

Academic & Scholarly; Architecture & Design; Languages & Linguistics; Law; Poetry; Reference Books, Directories & Dictionaries; Heraldry

New Titles: 2 (2007), 4 (2008)

ISBNs, Imprints & Series:
978 0 948565 Languages Information Centre
978 1 897999 Joseph Biddulph Publisher

2095

BIRLINN LTD
West Newington House,
10 Newington Road, Edinburgh EH9 1QS
Telephone: 0131 668 4371
Fax: 0131 668 4466
Email: info@birlinn.co.uk
Web Site: http://www.birlinn.co.uk

Distribution:
BookSource, 50 Cambuslang Road, Glasgow G32 8NB
Telephone: 0845 370 0067
Fax: 0845 370 0068
Email: info@booksource.net

Managing Director: Hugh Andrew
Finance: Rona Stewart
Production: Liz Short
Publisher: Neville Moir
Editorial: Andrew Simmons
Sales: Helen Stanton

Rights: Maria White
Publicity: Jan Rutherford
Key Accounts Manager: Bob Smith *(Sales)*

Fiction; Guide Books; History & Antiquarian; Humour; Illustrated & Fine Editions; Military & War; Adventure; Local Interest

New Titles: 150 (2007), 150 (2008)
No of Employees: 18
Annual Turnover: £2.9M

ISBNs, Imprints & Series:
978 0 7486, 978 0 9544075, 978 1 84697, 978 1 904598 Polygon
978 0 85976 John Donald
978 1 84158, 978 1 874744 Birlinn
978 1 84183, 978 1 87364 Mercat
978 1 84341 Birlinn General (Military & Adventure titles)
978 1 904607 John Donald (Print on demand titles)

Associated Companies:
John Donald Publishers Ltd; Polygon

Distributor for:
Clar; Maclean Press

Overseas Representation:
Australia: UNIREPS University and Reference Publishers' Services, Sydney, NSW
Austria, Belgium, France, Germany, Greece, Italy, Luxembourg, Netherlands & Switzerland: Ted Dougherty, London, UK
Canada: Vanwell Publishing Ltd, St Catharines, Ont
Denmark, Finland, Iceland, Norway, Portugal, Spain, Sweden & Eastern Europe: Bill Bailey Publishers Representatives, Newton Abbot, Devon, UK
South East Asia: CKK Ltd, Northwood, Middx, UK
USA (academic): Interlink Publishing Group Inc, Northampton, MA, USA
USA (for military & adventure titles only): Casemate Publishers & Book Distributors LLC, Havertown, PA, USA

Book Trade Association Membership:
IPG; Publishing Scotland

2096

BITTER LEMON PRESS
37 Arundel Gardens, London W11 2LW
Telephone: (020) 7727 7927
Fax: (020) 7460 2164
Email: books@bitterlemonpress.com
Web Site: http://www.bitterlemonpress.com

Crime; Fiction

New Titles: 8 (2007), 8 (2008)

ISBNs, Imprints & Series: 978 1 94738

Book Trade Association Membership:
IPG

2097

BLACK ACE BOOKS
PO Box 7547, Perth PH2 1AU
Telephone: 01821 642822
Fax: 01821 642101
Web Site: http://www.blackacebooks.com

Publisher & Rights: Hunter Steele
Publicity & Sales: Boo Wood

Academic & Scholarly; Biography & Autobiography; Fiction; History & Antiquarian; Philosophy

ISBNs, Imprints & Series: 978 1 872 988

Overseas Representation:
Italy: Piergiorgio Nicolazzini Literary Agency, Milan
Japan: The English Agency (Japan) Ltd, Tokyo

2098

*BLACK DOG PUBLISHING LTD
Unit 4.4 Tea Building,
56 Shoreditch High Street, London E1 6JJ
Telephone: (020) 7613 1922
Fax: (020) 7613 1944
Email: sales@blackdogonline.com
Web Site: http://www.blackdogonline.com

Warehouse & Distribution:
Marston Book Services, PO Box 269, Abingdon, Oxon OX14 4YN
Telephone: 01235 465500
Fax: 01235 465555
Email: direct.orders@marston.co.uk

Editorial: Safiya Waley
Sales: Andrius Juknys
Office Manager: Irene Amore
Press: Alex Bratt

Architecture & Design; Cinema, Video, TV & Radio; Fashion & Costume; Fine Art & Art History; Gender Studies; History & Antiquarian; Music; Philosophy; Photography; Theatre, Drama & Dance; Transport; Travel & Topography

ISBNs, Imprints & Series:
Labels Unlimited
978 1 901033 Architecture & Urbanism (Serial books); -De, -Dis, -Ex; Revisions; Serial Books Design
978 1 904772, 978 1 906155

Overseas Representation:
Australia: Bam Books @ Manic, Carlton North, Vic
Canada & USA: Client Distribution Services, Jackson, TN, USA
Europe, Asia & New Zealand: Marston Book Services Ltd, Abingdon, UK

2099

BLACK SPRING PRESS LTD
Curtain House, 134–146 Curtain Road, London EC2A 3AR
Telephone: (020) 7613 3066
Fax: (020) 7613 0028
Email: general@blackspringpress.co.uk
Web Site: http://www.blackspringpress.co.uk

Distribution:
Turnaround Publisher Services Ltd, Unit 3, Olympia Trading Estate, Coburg Road, London N22 6TZ
Telephone: (020) 8829 3000
Fax: (020) 8881 5088
Email: orders@turnaround-uk.com
Web Site: http://www.turnaround-psl.com

Publisher: Robert Hastings

Biography & Autobiography; Cinema, Video, TV & Radio; Fiction; Music

New Titles: 4 (2007), 6 (2008)
No of Employees: 2
Annual Turnover: £50,000

ISBNs, Imprints & Series: 978 0 948238

Overseas Representation:
Europe, Middle East & Far East: Turnaround Publisher Services Ltd, London, UK

2100

A. & C. BLACK (PUBLISHERS) LTD
37 Soho Square, London W1D 3QZ
Telephone: (020) 7758 0200
Fax: (020) 7758 0222
Email: publicity@acblack.com

Distribution:
Macmillan Distribution (MDL), Brunel Road, Houndmills, Basingstoke, Hants RG21 6XS
Telephone: 01256 329242

Directors: Nigel Newton *(Chairman)*
   Jill Coleman *(Managing)*
   Jonathan Glasspool *(Deputy Managing)*
   Janet Murphy *(Adlard Coles Nautical)*
   Oscar Heini *(Production)*
   David Wightman *(Rights, Sales & Marketing)*
   Colin Adams *(Group Finance)*
   Chris Facey *(Finance)*
   Jayne Parsons *(Children's Books)*
Head of Publicity & Marketing: Rosanna Bortoli

Architecture & Design; Children's Books; Crafts & Hobbies; Educational & Textbooks; Fashion & Costume; Fine Art & Art History; Health & Beauty; Music; Natural History; Nautical; Reference Books, Directories & Dictionaries; Sports & Games; Theatre, Drama & Dance; Ornithology

ISBNs, Imprints & Series:
Adlard Coles Nautical; Andrew Brodie Publications; Draw Books; Featherstone Education; Know the Game; New Mermaids; Thomas Reeds; Whitaker's Almanacks
978 0 7136 A. & C. Black
978 0 7470 Christopher Helm (incorporating Pica Press); T & AD Poyser
978 1 871569 The Herbert Press

Parent Company:
Bloomsbury Plc

Distributor for:
Guardian Books; Little Tiger Press; V & A Publications; Wisden

Overseas Representation:
Africa, Middle East, Greece, Turkey, Israel & Cyprus: Grant Hartley, International Sales Dept Penguin UK, London, UK
Australia & New Zealand: Allen & Unwin Pty Ltd, Sydney, NSW, Australia
Canada: Raincoast Books, Vancouver, BC
France, Morocco, Tunisia & Algeria: Helen Woodeson, Penguin France SA, Blagnac, France
Germany & Austria: Edith Strommen, Penguin Books Deutschland GmbH, Frankfurt am Main, Germany
Hong Kong, Macau, Thailand, Indonesia, Philippines, China, Brunei, Cambodia, Vietnam, Laos & Burma: Adrian Greenwood, International Sales Dept Penguin UK, London, UK
India: Maya Publishers Pvt Ltd, New Delhi
Italy: Umberto Vigoni, Penguin Italia srl, Corsico, Milan
Malaysia & Singapore: Pansing Distribution Sdn Bhd, Singapore
Malta: Melanee Winder, International Sales Dept Penguin UK, London, UK
Netherlands, Belgium & Luxembourg: Feico Deutekom, Penguin Books Benelux BV, Amsterdam, Netherlands
Poland, Slovakia, Ukraine, Baltic States, Eastern & Central Europe: Grazyna Soszynska, Poznan-Baranowo, Poland
Portugal: Mario A. Iotti, Penguin Books SA, Madrid, Spain
Republic of Ireland: Brian Blennerhassett, Butler Sims Ltd, Dublin 14
Scandinavia: Sarah Watkins, International Sales Dept Penguin UK, London, UK
South America & Caribbean: David Williams, InterMedia Americana (IMA) Ltd, London, UK
South Korea, Taiwan & Japan: Yvonne Francis, International Sales Dept Penguin UK, London, UK
Southern Africa: Book Promotions (Pty)/ Horizon Books (Pty) Ltd, Cape Town, South Africa
Spain: Javier Riveira, Penguin Books SA, Madrid

Switzerland: Kathy John, International Sales Dept Penguin UK, London, UK
USA: Consortium Book Sales & Distribution Inc, St Paul, MN

Book Trade Association Membership:
EPC; Music Publishers Association

2101

BLACKHALL PUBLISHING
33 Carysfort Avenue, Blackrock, Co Dublin, Republic of Ireland
Telephone: +353 (01) 278 5090
Fax: +353 (01) 278 4446
Email: blackhall@eircom.net
Web Site: http://www.blackhallpublishing.com

Managing Director: Gerard O'Connor
Commissioning Editor: Elizabeth Brennan
Financial Controller: Conor O'Mahony
Editor: Eileen O'Brien
Marketing: Sarah Franklin
Production Assistant: Susan Gaigher

Academic & Scholarly; Accountancy & Taxation; Economics; Industry, Business & Management; Law; Medical (incl. Self Help & Alternative Medicine); Psychology & Psychiatry; Sociology & Anthropology

New Titles: 20 (2007), 25 (2008)
No of Employees: 5

ISBNs, Imprints & Series:
978 1 842180, 978 1 901657

Overseas Representation:
UK: Columba Mercier Distribution, Dublin, Republic of Ireland

2102

BLACKSTAFF PRESS
4C Heron Wharf, Sydenham Business Park, Belfast BT3 9LE
Telephone: 028 9045 5006
Fax: 028 9046 6237
Email: info@blackstaffpress.com
Web Site: http://www.blackstaffpress.com

Distribution (UK & Northern Ireland):
Gill & Macmillan, Hume Avenue, Park West, Dublin 12, Republic of Ireland
Telephone: +353 (01) 5009 500
Fax: +353 (01) 5009 599
Email: sales@gillmacmillan.ie
Web Site: http//www.gillmacmillan.ie

Editors: Patricia Horton *(Managing)*
  Helen Wright
  Janice Smith *(Production)*
Publicist: Cormac Austin

Academic & Scholarly; Agriculture; Archaeology; Biography & Autobiography; Cinema, Video, TV & Radio; Cookery, Wines & Spirits; Crime; Fiction; Geography & Geology; Guide Books; Health & Beauty; History & Antiquarian; Humour; Illustrated & Fine Editions; Literature & Criticism; Mathematics & Statistics; Medical (incl. Self Help & Alternative Medicine); Military & War; Music; Natural History; Photography; Poetry; Politics & World Affairs; Reference Books, Directories & Dictionaries; Religion & Theology; Sports & Games; Theatre, Drama & Dance; Travel & Topography

ISBNs, Imprints & Series:
978 0 85640 The Blackstaff Press

Parent Company:
W. G. Baird (Holdings) Ltd

Overseas Representation:
All other areas: Blackstaff Press, Belfast, UK
USA: Dufour Editions Inc, Chester Springs, PA

Book Trade Association Membership:
BA; IPG; CLÉ (Irish PA)

2103

BLACKTHORN PRESS
Blackthorn House, Middleton Road, Pickering, North Yorks YO18 8AL
Telephone: 01751 474043
Email: blackthornpress@yahoo.com
Web Site: http://www.blackthornpress.com

Proprietor: Alan Avery

Fine Art & Art History; History & Antiquarian; Literature & Criticism

New Titles: 6 (2007), 6 (2008)
Annual Turnover: £30,000

ISBNs, Imprints & Series: 978 0 9540535

2104

BLACKWELL PUBLISHING
see: Wiley-Blackwell

2105

JOHN BLAKE PUBLISHING LTD
[incorp. Smith Gryphon Publishers Ltd & Metro Publishing Ltd]
3 Bramber Court, 2 Bramber Road, London W14 9PB
Telephone: (020) 7381 0666
Fax: (020) 7381 6868
Email: rosie@blake.co.uk

Distributors:
Littlehampton Book Services, Faraday Close, Durrington, Worthing, West Sussex BN13 3RB
Telephone: 01903 828800
Fax: 01903 828802
Email: orders@lbsltd.co.uk
Web Site: http://www.lbsltd.co.uk

Directors: John Blake *(Managing)*
  Rosie Ries *(Deputy Managing)*
  Ray Mudie *(Sales)*
Editor-in-Chief: Michelle Signore
Accounts Executive: Joanna Kennedy
Senior Editors: Clive Hebard
  Stuart Robertson
Head of Marketing: Clare Tillyer
Sales & Logistics Manager: Stuart Finglass

Audio Books; Biography & Autobiography; Cookery, Wines & Spirits; Crime; Humour; Music; Sports & Games

New Titles: 100 (2007), 110 (2008)
No of Employees: 13

ISBNs, Imprints & Series:
978 1 84358, 978 1 84454, 978 1 85782

Associated Companies:
Metro Books; Smith Gryphon Publishers Ltd

Overseas Representation:
Australia & New Zealand: Bookwise International, Adelaide, SA, Australia
Germany: Michael Mellor, Munich
South Africa: Peter Hyde Associates (Pty) Ltd, Cape Town
USA: Trafalgar Publishing, Chicago, IL

Book Trade Association Membership:
BA

2106

BLOODAXE BOOKS LTD
Highgreen, Tarset, Northumberland NE48 1RP
Telephone: 01434 240500 (editorial) 01678 521550 (sales)
Fax: 01434 240505 (editorial) 01678 521544 (sales)
Email: editor@bloodaxebooks.com (editorial), sales@bloodaxebooks.com
Web Site: http://www.bloodaxebooks.com

Warehouse, Trade Enquiries & Orders:
Littlehampton Book Services, Faraday Close, Durrington, Worthing, West Sussex BN13 3RB
Telephone: 01903 828800
Fax: 01903 828802
Email: orders@lbsltd.co.uk

Chairman: Simon Thirsk
Managing Director: Neil Astley *(Editorial)*
Company Secretary: Nansi Thirsk
Finance Officer: Bethan Jones
Permissions & Foreign Rights: Suzanne Fairless-Aitken
Sales Assistant: Rita Black
Publicity: Christine Macgregor
Prizes & Administration: Rebecca Hodkinson

Literature & Criticism; Poetry

New Titles: 35 (2007), 35 (2008)
No of Employees: 6

ISBNs, Imprints & Series:
978 0 906427, 978 1 85224 Bloodaxe Books
978 1 85557 Pandon Press

Associated Companies:
Pandon Press Ltd

Overseas Representation:
Australia: John Reed Book Distribution, Tea Gardens, NSW
Caribbean: Hugh Dunphy, Kingston, Jamaica
Europe: Michael Geoghegan, London, UK
India: Surit Mitra, New Delhi
Italy, Spain & Portugal: Penny Padovani, London, UK
North America: Dufour Editions Inc, Chester Springs, PA, USA
Republic of Ireland: Repforce Ireland, Irishtown, Dublin
South & Central America, Africa (excluding South Africa), Eastern Europe, Middle East, Turkey, Israel, Greece & Cyprus: InterMedia Americana (IMA) Ltd, London, UK

2107

BLOOMSBURY PUBLISHING PLC
36 Soho Square, London W1D 3QY
Telephone: (020) 7494 2111
Fax: (020) 7434 0151
Web Site: http://www.bloomsbury.com

Distributor:
Macmillan Distribution (MDL), Houndmills, Basingstoke, Hants RG21 6XS
Telephone: 01256 329242
Fax: 01256 364733

Directors: Nigel Newton *(Chief Executive)*
  Richard Charkin *(Executive)*
  Alexandra Pringle *(Editor-in-Chief)*
  Liz Calder *(Editorial)*
  Kathleen Farrul *(Marketing)*
  Colin Adams *(Finance)*
  Ruth Logan *(Rights)*
  Colin Midson *(Publicity)*
  Penny Edwards *(Production)*
  David Ward *(Sales)*
  Sarah Odedina *(Children's)*

Audio Books; Biography & Autobiography; Children's Books; Cinema, Video, TV & Radio; Cookery, Wines & Spirits; Fiction; Health & Beauty; Politics & World Affairs

No of Employees: 300
Annual Turnover: £150M

ISBNs, Imprints & Series: 978 0 7475

Parent Company:
USA: Bloomsbury

Associated Companies:
A & C Black
Germany: Berlin Verlag

Overseas Representation:
Africa & Middle East: Grant Hartley, Penguin International Sales, London, UK
Australia & New Zealand: Allen & Unwin Pty Ltd, Sydney, NSW, Australia
Canada: Penguin Books Canada, Toronto, Ont
Central & Eastern Europe: Grazyna Soszynska, Penguin Poland, Poznan-Baranowo, Poland
France, Morocco, Tunisia & Algeria: Jean-Luc Morel, Penguin Group, Roissy, France
Germany & Austria: Uli Hoernemann, Berlin Verlag, Berlin, Germany
Hong Kong, Macau, China, Philippines, Thailand, Indonesia, Vietnam, Cambodia, Taiwan & Korea: Yvonne Francis, Penguin International Sales, London, UK
India: Penguin Books India, New Delhi
Italy: Penguin Italia srl, Corsico, Milan
Japan: Lisa Finch, Bloomsbury International Sales, Bloomsbury Publishing, London, UK
Netherlands, Belgium & Luxembourg: Penguin Books Benelux BV, Amsterdam, Netherlands
Pakistan: Julian Russ, Tula Publishing Ltd, Oxford, UK
Republic of Ireland & Northern Ireland: Louise Dobbin, Repforce Ireland, Irishtown, Dublin, Republic of Ireland
Scandinavia: Sarah Davison-Aitkens, Penguin International Sales, London, UK
Singapore & Malaysia: Penguin Books Malaysia, c/o Pearson Malaysia Sdn Bhd, Selangor Darul Ehsan, Malaysia; Penguin Books Singapore, c/o Pearson Education South Asia Pte Ltd, Singapore
South Africa: Jonathan Ball Publishers (Pty) Ltd, Johannesburg
South East Europe, Cyprus, Greece, Gibraltar, Turkey, Israel, Caribbean & Latin America: Tamsin Pagella, Penguin International Sales, London, UK
Spain & Portugal: Geraldine Kilpatrick, Penguin Books SA, Madrid, Spain
Sri Lanka: Shan Rajaguru, Colombo
Switzerland & Malta: Kathy John, Penguin International Sales, London, UK

Book Trade Association Membership:
Publishers Association

2108

BLUE SKY PRESS
57 Longfield Avenue, Fareham, Hants PO14 1BU
Telephone: 07816 411341
Fax: 01329 221969
Email: press@mrbluesky.net
Web Site: http://www.mrbluesky.net

Executive Assistant: Victoria Stone
Managing Editor: Cfyn Markwick-Day

Fiction; Music; Poetry

ISBNs, Imprints & Series: 978 9 544983

Parent Company:
Mr Blue Sky Ltd

2109

BODLEIAN LIBRARY PUBLISHING
Bodleian Library, Broad Street, Oxford OX1 3BG
Telephone: 01865 277626
Fax: 01865 277187
Email: publishing@bodley.ox.ac.uk
Web Site: http://www.bodleianbookshop.co.uk

Trade Enquiries & Orders:
Turpin Distribution Ltd,
Stratton Business Park, Pegasus Drive,
Biggleswade, Beds SG18 8QS
Telephone: 01767 604968
Fax: 01767 601640
Email: custserve@turpin-distribution.com
Web Site: http://www.turpin-distribution.com

Representation (UK Book Trade):
Yale University Press

Publisher: Samuel Fanous
Project Manager: Deborah Susman

Academic & Scholarly; Antiques & Collecting; Architecture & Design; Biography & Autobiography; Children's Books; Fine Art & Art History; History & Antiquarian; Humour; Literature & Criticism; Military & War; Reference Books, Directories & Dictionaries

New Titles: 8 (2007), 13 (2008)
No of Employees: 4
Annual Turnover: £300,000

ISBNs, Imprints & Series:
Postcards from...; Treasures of the Bodleian Library
978 1 85124

Parent Company:
University of Oxford

Overseas Representation:
North America & Canada: Chicago University Press, Chicago, IL, USA

Book Trade Association Membership:
IPG; Association of Cultural Enterprises

2110

BOOK CASTLE PUBLISHING LTD
12 Church Street, Dunstable, Beds LU5 4RU
Telephone: 01582 605670
Fax: 01582 662431
Email: bc@book-castle.co.uk
Web Site: http://www.book-castle.co.uk

Publisher, Manager: Paul Bowes
Production Manager: Sally Siddons
(External Sales & Marketing)

Biography & Autobiography; History & Antiquarian; Travel & Topography

New Titles: 10 (2007), 12 (2008)
No of Employees: 11

ISBNs, Imprints & Series:
978 0 950 9773, 978 1 871199, 978 1 903747, 978 1 906632

Parent Company:
Book Castle (Deltastar Ltd)

Book Trade Association Membership:
BA

2111

BOOK MARKETING LTD
7 John Street, London WC1N 2ES
Telephone: (020) 7440 8930
Fax: (020) 7242 7485
Email: bml@bookmarketing.co.uk
Web Site: http://www.bookmarketing.co.uk

Academic & Scholarly; Children's Books; Educational & Textbooks; Religion & Theology; Trade

Book Trade Association Membership:
Publishers Association

2112

BORTHWICK PUBLICATIONS
Borthwick Institute, University of York,
Heslington, York YO10 5DD
Telephone: 01904 321160
Web Site: http://www.york.ac.uk/borthwick

Publications Manager: Sara Slinn

Academic & Scholarly; Archaeology; Educational & Textbooks; History & Antiquarian; Law; Religion & Theology

New Titles: 4 (2007), 5 (2008)

ISBNs, Imprints & Series:
978 0 903857 Borthwick List & Indexes;
Borthwick Papers; Borthwick Studies in History; Borthwick Texts & Calendars; Borthwick Wallets; Monastic Research Bulletin
978 1 094497 Borthwick Publications

Parent Company:
University of York

2113

BOSSINEY BOOKS LTD
Hillside, Langore, Launceston, Cornwall PL15 8LD
Telephone: 01566 774176
Email: bossineybooks@btinternet.com
Web Site: http://www.bossineybooks.com

Distribution:
Tor Mark Press, PO Box 4, Redruth, Cornwall TR16 5YX
Telephone: 01209 822101
Fax: 01209 822035
Email: office@tormark.co.uk
Web Site: http://www.tormark.co.uk

Directors: Jane White
Paul White

Cookery, Wines & Spirits; Guide Books; History & Antiquarian; Magic & the Occult; Local Interest Books

ISBNs, Imprints & Series:
Tamar Books
978 1 899383, 978 1 906474

Book Trade Association Membership:
IPG

2114

BOWKER (UK) LTD
1st Floor, Medway House, Cantelupe Road, East Grinstead, West Sussex RH19 3BJ
Telephone: 01342 310450
Fax: 01342 310486
Email: sales@bowker.co.uk
Web Site: http://www.bowker.co.uk

Directors: Doug McMillan *(Managing)*
Pam Roud *(Sales)*
Marketing Manager: Jo Grange

Academic & Scholarly; Bibliography & Library Science; Electronic (Educational); Electronic (Professional & Academic); Reference Books, Directories & Dictionaries

No of Employees: 16

ISBNs, Imprints & Series: 978 0 8352

Associated Companies:
USA: Cambridge Information Group

Overseas Representation:
see: http://www.bowker.co.uk, UK

Book Trade Association Membership:
BA; Data Publishers Association

2115

MARION BOYARS PUBLISHERS LTD
24 Lacy Road, London SW15 1NL
Telephone: (020) 8788 9522
Fax: (020) 8789 8122
Email: catheryn@marionboyars.com
Web Site: http://www.marionboyars.co.uk

Distribution:
Central Books, 99 Wallis Road, London E9 5LN
Telephone: (020) 8986 4854
Fax: (020) 8533 5821
Email: orders@centralbooks.com

Managing Director: Catheryn Kilgarriff
(Publicity, Rights & Permissions, Production)
Managers: Rebecca Gillieron *(Editorial)*
Katharine Bright-Holmes *(Editorial)*
Kit Maude *(Sales Co-ordinator)*

Biography & Autobiography; Children's Books; Cinema, Video, TV & Radio; Fiction; Literature & Criticism; Music; Philosophy; Theatre, Drama & Dance

New Titles: 15 (2007), 12 (2008)
No of Employees: 4
Annual Turnover: £300,000

ISBNs, Imprints & Series:
978 0 7145 Marion Boyars

Associated Companies:
USA: Marion Boyars Publishers Inc

Overseas Representation:
Australia & New Zealand: Peribo Pty Ltd, Mount Kuring-Gai, NSW, Australia
France, Germany & Switzerland: Michael Geoghegan, London, UK
Italy, Spain, Portugal & Greece: Penny Padovani, London, UK
South Africa: Stephan Phillips (Pty) Ltd, Cape Town
USA: Consortium Book Sales & Distribution Inc, St Paul, MN

Book Trade Association Membership:
IPG

2116

BOYDELL & BREWER LTD
PO Box 9, Woodbridge, Suffolk IP12 3DF
Telephone: 01394 610615
Fax: 01394 610316
Email: sandersson@boydell.co.uk
Web Site: http://www.boydell.co.uk

Directors: R. W. Barber *(Group Managing)*
P. Clifford *(Managing)*
M. J. Richards *(Sales)*
C. L. Palmer *(Editorial)*
W. Ellis *(Accounts)*
Managers: J. M. Jordan *(Customer Orders)*
M. L. Webb *(Production)*

Academic & Scholarly; Archaeology; History & Antiquarian; Literature & Criticism; Military & War; Music; Philosophy; Reference Books, Directories & Dictionaries; Travel & Topography

New Titles: 200 (2008)

ISBNs, Imprints & Series:
978 0 85115 Boydell Press
978 0 85991 D. S. Brewer
978 1 57113 Camden House
978 1 85566 Tamesis
978 1 900639 Companion Guides

Associated Companies:
USA: Boydell & Brewer Inc; University of Rochester Press

Distributor for:
Almenach de Gotha; Bedfordshire Historical Record Society; Henry Bradshaw Society; Burke's Peerage; Canterbury & York Society; Church of England Record Society; Early English Text Society; Ecclesiastical History Society; Lincoln Records Society; Plumbago Books; Royal Society of Literature; Suffolk Records Society; Surtees Society; Victoria County History; Yorkshire Archaeological Society
USA: University of Rochester Press

Overseas Representation:
Australia: DA Information Services Pty Ltd, Mitcham, Vic
Belgium, Luxembourg & Netherlands: Kemper Conseil Publishing, Leidschendam, Netherlands
Eastern Europe: Marek Lewinson, Warsaw, Poland
France: Mare Nostrum, Paris
Germany, Austria & Switzerland: Bernd Feldmann, Oranienburg, Germany
Greece & Cyprus: Charles Gibbes Associates, Louslitges, France
India & Sri Lanka: Viva Group, New Delhi, India
Italy: David Pickering, Mare Nostrum Publishing Consultants, Rome
Middle East & North Africa: Publishers International Marketing, Storrington, UK
Pakistan: T.M.L. Publishers' Consultants & Representatives, Lahore
Philippines: Edwin Makabenta, Quezon City
Republic of Ireland: Mullett Fitzpatrick, Shankill, Co Dublin
Scandinavia: Colin Flint Ltd, Publishers Scandinavian Consultancy, Cambridge, UK
South East Asia & Korea: Publishers International Marketing, London, UK
Spain & Portugal: Iberian Book Services, Madrid, Spain

2117

BRADT TRAVEL GUIDES LTD
23 High Street, Chalfont St Peter, Bucks SL9 9QE
Telephone: 01753 893444
Fax: 01753 892333
Email: info@bradtguides.com
Web Site: http://www.bradtguides.com

British Orders (Distributor):
Portfolio, Suite 3 & 4, 2nd Floor, Great West House, Great West Road, Brentford, Middx TW8 9DF
Telephone: (020) 8326 5620
Fax: (020) 8326 5621
Email: sales@portfoliobooks.com

Directors: Donald Greig *(Executive)*
Peter Jay *(Finance)*
Adrian Phillips *(Editorial)*
Managers: Mrs Debbie Hunter *(Finance)*
Debbie Everson *(Export)*
Helen Anjomshoaa *(Rights & Publishing Services)*
Helen Calderon *(Sales)*
Deborah Gerrard *(Advertising)*
Assistant – Editorial/Production: Anna Moores
Emma Thomson
Elsepth Beidas
Book Keeper: Julie May

Guide Books; Travel & Topography

New Titles: 42 (2007), 42 (2008)
No of Employees: 14

ISBNs, Imprints & Series:
978 1 84162 Mini Guide Series
978 1 84162, 978 1 898323 Backpacking Guide Series; Eccentric Series; Guide to Series; Rail Guide Series; Wildlife Series

Overseas Representation:
Africa (excluding South Africa, Namibia, & Zimbabwe): A–Z Africa Book Services, Rotterdam, Netherlands

Australia: Woodslane Pty Ltd, Warriewood, NSW
Austria: Freytag & Berndt, Vienna
Belgium: Craenen bvba, Herent (Winksele)
Denmark: Scanvik Books ApS, Copenhagen
Eastern Europe: CLB Marketing Services, Budapest, Hungary
Ecuador: Libri Mundi, Quito
France: Cartothèque EGG, Notre Dame D'Oé
Germany: GeoCenter ILH, Stuttgart
Italy: Librimport, Milan
Middle East: Peter Ward Book Exports, London, UK
Netherlands: Nilsson & Lamm BV, Weesp
Russia: CenterCom, Moscow
Singapore: Pansing Distribution Pte Ltd, Singapore
South & Central America: David Williams, InterMedia Americana (IMA) Ltd, London, UK
South Africa: Wild Dog Press, Johannesburg
Spain: Altair, Barcelona
Sweden: Platypus Platypus Dyk & Resebocker, Helsingborg
Switzerland: Distribution OLF SA, Fribourg
USA: Globe Pequot Press, Guilford, CT

Book Trade Association Membership:
IPG

2118 ▬

BRANDON/MOUNT EAGLE PUBLICATIONS
PO Box 32, Dingle, Co Kerry, Republic of Ireland
Telephone: +353 (066) 915 1463
Fax: +353 (066) 915 1234
Web Site: http://www.brandonbooks.com

Warehouse, Trade Orders:
Gill & Macmillan, Hume Avenue, Park West, Dublin 12, Republic of Ireland
Telephone: +353 (01) 500 9500
Fax: +353 (01) 500 9599
Email: sales@gillmacmillan.ie

Publisher & Managing Director: Steve MacDonogh

Biography & Autobiography; Fiction; Literature & Criticism; Politics & World Affairs; Travel & Topography

ISBNs, Imprints & Series:
978 0 86322 Brandon
978 1 902011 Mount Eagle

Associated Companies:
Republic of Ireland: Brandon Book Publishers Ltd

Overseas Representation:
UK (excluding Northern Ireland): Turnaround Publisher Services Ltd, London, UK
USA: Dufour Editions Inc, Chester Springs, PA

Book Trade Association Membership:
CLÉ (Irish PA)

2119 ▬

NICHOLAS BREALEY PUBLISHING
3–5 Spafield Street, London EC1R 4QB
Telephone: (020) 7239 0360
Fax: (020) 7239 0370
Email: rights@nicholasbrealey.com
Web Site: http://www.nicholasbrealey.com

Orders & Warehouse:
TBS Ltd, Colchester Road, Frating Green, Colchester, Essex CO7 7DW
Telephone: 01206 256000
Fax: 01206 819587

Managing Director: Nicholas Brealey *(Editorial & Rights)*
Managers: Angie Tainsh *(Sales/Office)*
Sally Lansdell *(Publishing)*

Biography & Autobiography; Economics; Industry, Business & Management; Psychology & Psychiatry; Travel & Topography; Vocational Training & Careers

New Titles: 25 (2007), 25 (2008)
No of Employees: 4

ISBNs, Imprints & Series:
978 0 85290 Industrial Society (acquired titles)
978 1 85788 Nicholas Brealey
978 1 877864, 978 1 93193 Intercultural Press
978 1 90483 Nicholas Brealey International

Associated Companies:
USA: Intercultural Press Inc

Overseas Representation:
Asia (excluding Hong Kong, Singapore & Malaysia): Sales East, UK
Australia: Allen & Unwin Pty Ltd, Sydney, NSW
Europe (excluding Scandinavia) & Switzerland: Michael Geoghegan, London, UK
India: Research Press, New Delhi
Republic of Ireland: Gill Simpson, Dublin
Scandinavia: Angell Eurosales, Berwick-on-Tweed, UK
Singapore & Malaysia: Horizon Books Pte Ltd, Singapore
South Africa: Wild Dog Press, Highlands North
USA: Nicholas Brealey Publishing North America, Boston, MA; National Book Network, Blue Ridge Summit, PA & Lanham, MD

Book Trade Association Membership:
IPG

2120 ▬

BREEDON BOOKS PUBLISHING CO LTD
3 The Parker Centre, Derby DE21 4SZ
Telephone: 01332 384235
Fax: 01332 292755
Email: steve.caron@breedonpublishing.co.uk
Web Site: http://www.breedonbooks.co.uk

Directors: Stephen Caron *(Chairman & Managing)*
Jane Caron *(Finance)*
Marketing: Claire Lynes
Editorial: Michelle Grainger *(Publishing Manager)*

Biography & Autobiography; Sports & Games; Transport

New Titles: 45 (2007), 60 (2008)

ISBNs, Imprints & Series:
978 0 907969, 978 1 85983, 978 1 873626

2121 ▬

BREWIN BOOKS LTD
Doric House, 56 Alcester Road, Studley, Warwickshire B80 7LG
Telephone: 01527 854228
Fax: 01527 852746
Email: admin@brewinbooks.com
Web Site: http://www.brewinbooks.com

Warehouse:
Supaprint Works, Unit 19, Enfield Industrial Estate, Redditch, Worcs B97 6BZ
Telephone: 01527 62212
Fax: 01527 60451
Email: admin@supaprint.com
Web Site: http://www.supaprint.com

Directors: Alan Brewin *(Managing)*
Alistair Brewin *(Art, Book design and production)*
Company Secretary: Julie Brewin

Biography & Autobiography; History & Antiquarian; Military & War; Transport

New Titles: 25 (2007), 30 (2008)
No of Employees: 6

ISBNs, Imprints & Series:
978 0 947731, 978 0 9505570, 978 1 85858 Brewin Books
978 1 85858 Alton Douglas Books; History-into-Print

Distributor for:
City of Birmingham Libraries [Local History]; Hereford County Council [Trail Path Guides]; Hunt End Books [Local History (Worcs)]

2122 ▬

BRIDGE BOOKS
61 Park Avenue, Wrexham LL12 7AW
Telephone: 01978 358661 & 0845 166 2851
Email: enquiries@bridgebooks.co.uk

Partners: W. Alister Williams
Susan A. Williams

Aviation; History & Antiquarian; Military & War; Travel & Topography

New Titles: 18 (2007), 18 (2008)

ISBNs, Imprints & Series:
978 0 9508285, 978 1 84494, 978 1 872424

Associated Companies:
Maelor Interactive Publishing

2123 ▬

BRILLIANT PUBLICATIONS
Unit 10, Sparrow Hall Farm, Edlesborough, Dunstable LU6 2ES
Telephone: 01525 222292
Fax: 01525 222720
Email: info@brilliantpublications.co.uk
Web Site: http://www.brilliantpublications.co.uk

Sales & Distribution:
BEBC Distribution, Albion Close, Parkstone, Poole, Dorset BH12 3LL
Telephone: 01202 712910
Fax: 0845 130 9300
Email: brilliant@bebc.co.uk

Publisher: Priscilla Hannaford
Finance Director: Richard Dorrance
Marketing: Alison Marshall

Educational & Textbooks; Languages & Linguistics

New Titles: 10 (2007), 16 (2008)
No of Employees: 4

ISBNs, Imprints & Series:
978 1 897675
978 1 903853
978 1 905780

Book Trade Association Membership:
Publishers Association; EPC; IPG

2124 ▬

BRITISH ASSOCIATION FOR ADOPTION & FOSTERING
[BAAF]
Saffron House, 6–10 Kirby Street, London EC1N 8TS
Telephone: (020) 7421 2602
Fax: (020) 7421 2601
Email: shaila.shah@baaf.org.uk
Web Site: http://www.baaf.org.uk

Trade Enquiries:
Turnaround Distribution, Unit 3, Olympia Trading Estate, Coburg Road, London N22 6TZ
Telephone: (020) 8829 3000
Fax: (020) 8881 5088
Email: orders@turnaround-uk.com

Chief Executive: David Holmes
Director of Publications: Shaila Shah *(Editorial, Production, Sales & Rights)*

Academic & Scholarly; Children's Books; Psychology & Psychiatry; Reference Books, Directories & Dictionaries; Sociology & Anthropology

New Titles: 25 (2007), 35 (2008)
No of Employees: 110

ISBNs, Imprints & Series:
978 0 903534, 978 1 873868, 978 1 903699, 978 1 905664

Overseas Representation:
Australia (selected titles): Innovative Resources, Bendigo, Vic, Australia

Book Trade Association Membership:
The Publishers Forum for the Voluntary Sector

2125 ▬

BRITISH GEOLOGICAL SURVEY
Keyworth, Nottingham NG12 5GG
Telephone: 0115 936 3241 (Sales)
Fax: 0115 936 3488
Email: sales@bgs.ac.uk
Web Site: http://www.bgs.ac.uk & http://www.geologyshop.com (online shop)

Distribution & Representation:
Cordee Ltd, 3a de Montfort Street, Leicester LE1 7HD
Telephone: 0116 254 3579

Director: Dr John Ludden
Head of Graphics Communications: Jim Rayner
Copyright & IPR: Dr Jean Alexander
Head of Sales: Ms Elaine Johnston

Atlases & Maps; Geography & Geology; Guide Books; Scientific & Technical

New Titles: 55 (2007), 60 (2008)
No of Employees: 850

ISBNs, Imprints & Series:
978 0 7518 British Geological Survey (Maps)
978 0 85272 British Geological Survey (Books & Reports)

Parent Company:
Natural Environment Research Council

Distributor for:
Durham County Council; Journal of Mines & Minerals

2126 ▬

BRITISH LIBRARY
96 Euston Road, London NW1 2DB
Telephone: (020) 7412 7535
Fax: (020) 7412 7768
Email: blpublications@bl.uk
Web Site: http://www.bl.uk

Orders:
The British Library, Turpin Distribution Ltd, Stratton Business Park, Pegasus Drive, Biggleswade, Beds SG18 8QB
Telephone: 01767 604955
Fax: 01767 601640
Email: custserv@turpin-distribution.com
Web Site: http://www.turpin-distribution.com

Head of Publishing: David Way

Editorial & Rights: Lara Speicher *(Managing Editor)*
Publishing Manager: Catherine Britton

Academic & Scholarly; Bibliography & Library Science; Biography & Autobiography; Fine Art & Art History; History & Antiquarian; Illustrated & Fine Editions

New Titles: 40 (2007), 40 (2008)

ISBNs, Imprints & Series:
978 0 7123 Bibliography of British Newspapers; The British Library; British Library Guides; British Library Occasional Papers; The British Library Studies in Medieval Culture; The British Library Studies in the History of the Book; Corpus of British Medieval Library Catalogues; The Panizzi Lectures

Parent Company:
The British Library

Overseas Representation:
Australia: InBooks, Belrose, NSW
Canada: University of Toronto Press, North York, Ont
USA: University of Chicago Press, Chicago, IL

Book Trade Association Membership:
Publishers Association; BA; CAPP

2127

BRITISH LIBRARY, PUBLISHING OFFICE
96 Euston Road, St Pancras, London NW1 2DB
Telephone: (020) 7412 7704
Fax: (020) 7412 7768
Email: david.way@bl.uk
Web Site: http://www.bl.uk

Distribution:
Turpin Ltd, Stratton Business Park, Pegasus Drive, Biggleswade, Beds SG18 8QB
Telephone: 01767 604955
Fax: 01767 604800
Email: custserv@turpin-distribution.com
Web Site: http://www.turpin-distribution.com

Managers: David Way *(Publishing)*
Catherine Britton

Audio Books; Bibliography & Library Science; Biography & Autobiography; Electronic (Educational); Fine Art & Art History; History & Antiquarian; Illustrated & Fine Editions; Music; Natural History; Reference Books, Directories & Dictionaries

New Titles: 40 (2007), 40 (2008)

ISBNs, Imprints & Series: 978 0 7123

Overseas Representation:
Canada: University of Toronto Press, North York, Ont
Europe: Books for Europe, Massagno, Switzerland
USA: University of Chicago Press, Chicago, IL

Book Trade Association Membership:
Publishers Association; BA; CAPP

2128

BRITISH MUSEUM PRESS
38 Russell Square, London WC1B 3QQ
Telephone: (020) 7323 1234
Fax: (020) 7436 7315
Email: rbradley@britishmuseum.co.uk
Web Site: http://www.britishmuseum.org

Trade Distributor:
Thames & Hudson Ltd,
44 Clockhouse Road, Farnborough, Hants GU14 7QZ
Telephone: 01252 541602
Fax: 01252 377380
Email: customerservices@thameshudson.co.uk

Directors: Brian Oldman *(Managing)*
Helen Watts *(Finance & Administration)*
Rosemary Bradley *(Publishing)*
Editorial: Teresa Francis
Production: Susan Walby
Rights: Louise Fletcher
Marketing/Publicity: Margaret Robe

Academic & Scholarly; Antiques & Collecting; Archaeology; Children's Books; Fine Art & Art History; Natural History; Reference Books, Directories & Dictionaries; Sociology & Anthropology

New Titles: 42 (2008)
No of Employees: 14

ISBNs, Imprints & Series: 978 0 7141

Parent Company:
The British Museum Co Ltd

Overseas Representation:
USA (Trade orders): British Museum Press, London, UK
Worldwide (excluding USA): Thames & Hudson (Distributors) Ltd, Farnborough, Hants, UK

Book Trade Association Membership:
Publishers Association

2129

BROOKLANDS BOOKS LTD
PO Box 146, Cobham, Surrey KT11 1LG
Telephone: 01932 865051
Fax: 01932 868803
Email: sales@brooklands-books.com
Web Site: http://www.brooklands-books.com

Directors: I. Dowdeswell
J. Powell
Sales Manager: B. Cleveland

Aviation; Military & War; Transport

ISBNs, Imprints & Series: 978 1 85520

Parent Company:
USA: Robert Bentley Publishers; Cartech; SA Design

Distributor for:
USA: Robert Bentley Inc; SA Design

Overseas Representation:
Southern Europe: Bookport Associates, Corsico (MI), Italy

Book Trade Association Membership:
IPG

2130

BROWN DOG BOOKS
6 The Old Dairy, Melcombe Road, Bath BA2 3LR
Telephone: 01225 478444
Fax: 01225 478440
Email: sales@manning-partnership.co.uk
Web Site: http://www.manning-partnership.co.uk

Directors: Garry Manning *(Managing)*
Roger Hibbert *(Sales & Marketing)*
Heather Morris *(Editorial)*
Managers: Karen Twissell *(Office)*
James Wheeler *(Sales)*

Children's Books; Humour; Sports & Games

ISBNs, Imprints & Series:
978 1 903056 Brown Dog Books
978 1 903222 Nightingale

Parent Company:
Manning Partnership Ltd

Distributor for:
Brimax; Carroll & Brown; Five Mile Press; Interpet Publishing; Lorenz; Nightingale Press; Peter Pauper; Powerfresh; Mathew Price; Search Press; Southwater

2131

BROWN, SON & FERGUSON, LTD
4–10 Darnley Street, Glasgow G41 2SD
Telephone: 0141 429 1234/5922
Fax: 0141 420 1694
Email: info@skipper.co.uk
Web Site: http://www.skipper.co.uk

Chairman & Production Director: T. Nigel Brown
Company Secretary & Editorial Director: L. Ingram-Brown
Sales Manager: D. H. Provan

Nautical; Theatre, Drama & Dance

New Titles: 5 (2007), 4 (2008)
No of Employees: 12

ISBNs, Imprints & Series: 978 0 85174

Associated Companies:
James Munro & Co

Book Trade Association Membership:
Publishing Scotland

2132

BROWN & WHITTAKER PUBLISHING
Stronsaule, Tobermory, Isle of Mull PA75 6PR
Telephone: 01688 302381
Fax: 01688 302454
Email: olivebrown@msn.com
Web Site: http://www.brown-whittaker.co.uk

Partners: Olive Brown
Jean Whittaker

Archaeology; Biography & Autobiography; Biology & Zoology; Cookery, Wines & Spirits; Guide Books; History & Antiquarian; Natural History; Poetry

New Titles: 1 (2007), 1 (2008)
Annual Turnover: £17,000

ISBNs, Imprints & Series:
978 0 9528428, 978 0 9532775, 978 1 9043530

Book Trade Association Membership:
Publishing Scotland

2133

BRYNTIRION PRESS
Bryntirion, Bridgend, Mid Glamorgan CF31 4DX
Telephone: 01656 655886
Fax: 01656 665919

Representation:
Evangelical Press, Faverdale North, Darlington DL3 0PH
Telephone: 01325 380232
Fax: 01325 466153
Email: sales@evangelical-press.org

Press Officer: Huw Kinsey

Religion & Theology

New Titles: 4 (2007), 4 (2008)
No of Employees: 2

ISBNs, Imprints & Series:
978 0 900898, 978 0 9502686, 978 1 85049 Evangelical Library of Wales
978 0 900898, 978 1 85049 Evangelical Movement of Wales; Evangelical Press of Wales

Parent Company:
Evangelical Movement of Wales

Distributor for:
Association of Christian Teachers of Wales; Evangelical Library (London); Yr Undeb Cristnogol

Book Trade Association Membership:
BA; Undeb Cyhoeddwyr a Llyfrwerthwyr Cymru; (The Union of Welsh Publishers and Booksellers)

2134

*BURALL FLORAPRINT
[a trading brand of Floramedia UK Ltd]
PO Box 29, Oldfield Lane, Wisbech, Cambridgeshire PE13 2TH
Telephone: 0870 728 7222
Fax: 0870 728 7277
Email: floraprint@burall.com
Web Site: http://www.bflora.com

Head Office:
Floramedia UK Ltd, Global House, Global Park, Moorside, Eastgates, Colchester CO1 2TW
Telephone: 01206 877800
Fax: 01206 877855
Email: info@floramedia.co.uk
Web Site: http://www.floramedia.co.uk

Managing Director: B. Pinker

Gardening

ISBNs, Imprints & Series:
978 0 903001 Floramedia; Floraprint

Parent Company:
Netherlands: Floramedia Group BV

Overseas Representation:
Australia: Macbird Floraprint Pty Ltd, Scoresby, Vic
Austria: Floramedia GmbH, Vienna
Belgium: Floramedia NV, Antwerp
Canada: John Markham Associates, Sidney, BC
France: Maurylfor SA, Malesherbes
Germany: Verlagsgesellschaft Grun ist Leben mbH, Pinneberg
Liechtenstein: Floramedia Group AG, Vaduz
New Zealand: Floramedia New Zealand, Wellington
Republic of Ireland: Carleys Bridge Potteries Ltd, Enniscorthy
South Africa: Floramedia Southern Africa, Florida
Spain: Floramedia España, Valencia
Switzerland: Floramedia AG, Rapperswil-Jona

2135

BURNS & OATES
The Tower Building, 11 York Road, London SE1 7NX
Telephone: (020) 7922 0880
Fax: (020) 7922 0881
Web Site: http://www.continuumbooks.com

Distribution, Orders, Credit Control:
Orca Book Services Ltd, Stanley House, 3 Fleets Lane, Poole, Dorset BH15 3AJ
Telephone: 01202 665432
Fax: 01202 666219
Web Site: http://www.orcabookservices.co.uk

Chief Executive: Oliver Gadsby
Directors: Robin Baird-Smith *(Publishing)*
Bob Marsh *(Finance)*

Benn Linfield *(Production)*
Ken Rhodes *(Sales & Marketing)*
Rights Manager: Elizabeth White

Academic & Scholarly; Reference Books, Directories & Dictionaries; Religion & Theology

ISBNs, Imprints & Series: 978 0 86012

Parent Company:
The Continuum International Publishing Group Ltd

Overseas Representation:
see: The Continuum International Publishing Group Ltd, London, UK

Book Trade Association Membership:
IPG

2136

BUSINESS EDUCATION PUBLISHERS
evolve Business Centre, Cygnet Way,
Rainton Bridge Business Park,
Houghton-le-Spring, Tyne & Wear
DH4 5QY
Telephone: 0191 305 5160
Fax: 0191 305 5506
Email: info@bepl.com
Web Site: http://www.bepl.com

Warehouse:
Unit 18, Hartlepool Workshops,
Usworth Road Industrial Estate,
Usworth Road, Hartlepool, Cleveland
TS25 1PD
Telephone: 01429 234153
Fax: 01429 234153

Managing Director: Paul Callaghan
Managers: Andrea Murphy *(Publications)*
Joe McQuilling *(Warehouse)*

Academic & Scholarly; Biography & Autobiography; Computer Science; Educational & Textbooks; History & Antiquarian; Industry, Business & Management; Law; Military & War

ISBNs, Imprints & Series:
978 0 907679, 978 1 901888

Book Trade Association Membership:
BA; Book Data

2137

BUTTERFINGERS BOOKS
Unit 4, Greystone Yard, Notting Hill Way,
Lower Weare, Axbridge, Somerset
BS26 2JU
Telephone: 01458 851520
Email: laurie@butterfingersbooks.co.uk
Web Site: http://www.butterfingers.co.uk

Director: L. H. R. Collard *(Rights)*

Educational & Textbooks; Sports & Games

Annual Turnover: £30,000

ISBNs, Imprints & Series:
978 0 9513240, 978 1 898591

Distributor for:
Circustuff
Germany: Die Jonglerie
USA: Brian Dubé Inc; Finesse Press; Renegade Juggling

Overseas Representation:
North America: Brian Dube Inc, New York, NY, USA

2138

CABI
Nosworthy Way, Wallingford, Oxon
OX10 8DE
Telephone: 01491 832111

Fax: 01491 833508 & 829292 (order fulfilment)
Email: publishing@cabi.org
Web Site: http://www.cabi.org/

Directors: Ms Caroline McNamara *(Executive, Commercial)*
Ms Andrea Powell *(Executive, Publishing)*
Shaun Hobbs *(Database Publishing)*
Elizabeth Dodsworth *(Knowledge for Development)*
Nigel Farrar *(Books Publishing)*

Academic & Scholarly; Agriculture; Animal Care & Breeding; Biology & Zoology; Environment & Development Studies; Medical (incl. Self Help & Alternative Medicine); Scientific & Technical; Veterinary Science

ISBNs, Imprints & Series:
978 0 85198, 978 0 85199, 978 1 84593

Parent Company:
CAB International

Distributor for:
International Food Information Service;
Royal Society of Edinburgh

Overseas Representation:
Africa: CABI Africa, Nairobi, Kenya
All other areas: Commercial Department, Wallingford, UK
Asia: CABI South East & East Asia, Serdang, Malaysia
Australia, New Zealand & Papua New Guinea: DA Information Services Pty Ltd, Mitcham, Vic, Australia
Canada: CABI North America, Cambridge, MA, USA
Caribbean: CABI Caribbean & Latin America, Curepe, Trinidad
Denmark, Finland, Iceland, Norway & Sweden: Colin Flint Ltd, Harlow, UK
Germany, Austria & Switzerland: Missing Link International Booksellers, Bremen, Germany
India: Book Marketing Services, Chennai
Middle East (excluding Iran): James & Lorin Watt Ltd, Publishing Consultants, Oxford, UK
South Africa: Academic Marketing Services (Pty) Ltd, Craighall
USA, Central America, Caribbean, Mexico, Puerto Rico & Guam: Oxford University Press, Cary, NC, USA

Book Trade Association Membership:
BA

2139

CALYPSO PUBLICATIONS
2 Gatcombe Road, London N19 4PT
Telephone: (020) 7281 4948
Fax: (020) 7281 4948
Email: Gerald@calypso.org.uk
Web Site: http://www.calypso.org.uk/ourbooks

Proprietor: G. H. Jennings

Academic & Scholarly; Animal Care & Breeding; Biology & Zoology; Crafts & Hobbies; Educational & Textbooks; Natural History; Reference Books, Directories & Dictionaries; Scientific & Technical; Travel & Topography

ISBNs, Imprints & Series:
978 0 906301, 978 1 902788

Parent Company:
The Calypso Organization

Overseas Representation:
Australia: Andrew Isles Bookshop, Melbourne, Vic
Cyprus: Soloneion Book Centre, Nicosia
USA: The Aquatic Bookshop, Placerville, CA

2140

CAMBRIDGE UNIVERSITY PRESS
The Edinburgh Building, Shaftesbury Road,
Cambridge CB2 8RU
Telephone: 01223 312393
Fax: 01223 315052
Email: information@cambridge.org
Web Site: http://www.cambridge.org

Orders:
Telephone: 01223 325577
Fax: 01223 325151
Email: intcustserve@cambridge.org
Web Site: http://www.cambridge.org

Chief Executive of the Press: Stephen R. R. Bourne
Press Board: Christopher Boughton *(Managing Director, Asia-Pacific)*
Andrew Brown *(Managing Director, Academic)*
Hanri Pieterse *(Managing Director, Cambridge Learning)*
Andrew Gilfillan *(Managing Director, Europe, Middle East & Africa)*
Steven Miller *(Chief Financial Officer)*
Richard Ziemacki *(President, Americas)*
Directors: Ron Bennett *(Legal Services)*
Peter Davison *(Corporate Affairs)*
Richard Fisher *(Academic & Professional)*
David Harrison *(ELT Sales & Marketing)*
Ron Ragsdale *(ELT Editorial)*
Maralyn Johnson *(Chief Technology Officer)*
Simon Ross *(Journals)*
Pete Shemilt *(Academic Sales & Marketing)*
Simon Read *(Education)*
Howard Buckley *(Chief Financial Officer, EH)*
Cheryl Park *(Human Resources)*
Andy Williams *(Academic & Professional)*
Geoff Staff *(Cambridge Learning)*

Academic & Scholarly; Accountancy & Taxation; Agriculture; Archaeology; Architecture & Design; Bibliography & Library Science; Biography & Autobiography; Biology & Zoology; Chemistry; Children's Books; Computer Science; Economics; Educational & Textbooks; Electronic (Educational); Electronic (Professional & Academic); Engineering; English as a Foreign Language; Environment & Development Studies; Fine Art & Art History; Gender Studies; Geography & Geology; History & Antiquarian; Industry, Business & Management; Languages & Linguistics; Law; Literature & Criticism; Mathematics & Statistics; Medical (incl. Self Help & Alternative Medicine); Music; Natural History; Philosophy; Physics; Politics & World Affairs; Psychology & Psychiatry; Reference Books, Directories & Dictionaries; Religion & Theology; Scientific & Technical; Sociology & Anthropology; Theatre, Drama & Dance; Animal Behaviour; Astronomy; Biotechnology; Classics; Ecology; History & Philosophy of Science

New Titles: 2500 (2007), 2500 (2008)
No of Employees: 1848
Annual Turnover: £177M

ISBNs, Imprints & Series: 978 0 521

Associated Companies:
Greece: Cambridge University Press (Greece) EPE
Hong Kong: Cambridge Knowledge (China) Ltd; United Publishers Services Ltd
India: Cambridge University Press India (Pvt) Ltd
Japan: Cambridge University Press Japan KK; Kabushiki Kaisha Phoenic
Mexico: ELT Trading SA de CV
South Africa: Cambridge University Press South Africa (Pty) Ltd
UK: Cambridge Global Grid for Learning; Cambridge Hitachisoft Educational Solutions PLC; Cambridge Printing Services Ltd; Cambridge University Press (Holdings) Ltd; Greenwich Medical Media Ltd; Oncoweb Ltd

Overseas Representation:
Contact: Chris Boughton, Managing Director, Asia-Pacific, Cambridge University Press, Cambridge, UK; Peter Langworth, Cambridge University Press, Cambridge, UK; Richard Ziemacki, President, The Americas, Cambridge University Press, Cambridge, UK

Book Trade Association Membership:
Publishers Association; BA; EPC; IGSMTP; CAPP; IPG; Association of Learned & Professional Society Publishers; BML; IBD; PIRA

2141

*****CAMERON & HOLLIS**
PO Box 1, Moffat, Dumfriesshire DG10 9SU
Telephone: 01683 220808
Fax: 01683 220012
Email: mail@cameronbooks.co.uk
Web Site: http://www.cameronbooks.co.uk

Directors: Ian Cameron
Jill Hollis

Antiques & Collecting; Architecture & Design; Cinema, Video, TV & Radio; Fine Art & Art History

ISBNs, Imprints & Series: 978 0 906506

Parent Company:
Cameron Books

2142

*****CAMRA BOOKS**
230 Hatfield Road, St Albans, Herts
AL1 4LW
Telephone: 01604 832149
Fax: 01727 848795
Email: camra@camra.org.uk
Web Site: http://www.camra.org.uk

UK Sales:
Compass, Barley Mow Centre,
10 Barley Mow Passage, Chiswick, London
W4 4PH
Telephone: (020) 8994 6477
Fax: (020) 8400 6132
Email: sales@compass-ibs.co.uk

Distribution:
Littlehampton Book Services,
Faraday Close, Durrington, Worthing,
West Sussex BN13 3RB
Telephone: 01903 828500
Email: orders@lbsltd.co.uk
Web Site: http://www.lbsltd.co.uk

Head of Marketing: Louise Ashworth
Senior Marketing Manager: Georgina Rudman
Managing Editor: Simon Hall

Cookery, Wines & Spirits; Guide Books; Reference Books, Directories & Dictionaries; Travel & Topography

ISBNs, Imprints & Series: 978 1 85249

Parent Company:
Campaign for Real Ale Ltd

2143

CANONGATE BOOKS
14 High Street, Edinburgh EH1 1TE
Telephone: 0131 557 5111
Fax: 0131 557 5211
Email: info@canongate.co.uk
Web Site: http://www.meetatthegate.com

Warehouse & Orders:
The Book Service Ltd, Distribution Centre, Colchester Road, Frating Green, Colchester, Essex CO7 7DW
Telephone: 01206 256000
Fax: 01206 255715
Email: helpdesk@tbs-ltd.co.uk
Web Site: http://www.thebookservice.co.uk

Publisher: Jamie Byng
Directors: Kathleen Anderson (Finance)
Caroline Gorham (Production)
Polly Collingridge (Rights)
Jenny Todd (Sales & Marketing)
Anya Serota (Publishing (Fiction))
Nick Davies (Editorial (Non-Fiction))
Managing Editor: Stephanie Gorton

Biography & Autobiography; Crime; Fiction; Fine Art & Art History; Guide Books; History & Antiquarian; Humour; Illustrated & Fine Editions; Literature & Criticism; Music; Philosophy; Poetry; Politics & World Affairs; Scottish

New Titles: 35 (2007), 40 (2008)
No of Employees: 28
Annual Turnover: £8.8M

ISBNs, Imprints & Series:
978 0 86241, 978 1 84195 Canongate; Canongate Classics; Myths

Associated Companies:
Australia: Text Publishing
USA: Canongate US

Overseas Representation:
Australia: Penguin Books Australia Ltd, Camberwell, Vic
Eastern Europe, Cyprus, Israel & Turkey: Csaba & Jackie Lengyel de Bagota, Budapest, Hungary
Latin America & Caribbean: InterMedia Americana (IMA) Ltd, London, UK
New Zealand: Archetype Books, Wellington
Scandinavia, Benelux, France, Germany, Austria, Switzerland, Greece, Italy, Spain & Portugal: Export Sales Department, Canongate Books, Edinburgh, UK
South Africa: Penguin Books South Africa, Gardenview
USA: Publishers Group West, Berkeley, CA

Book Trade Association Membership:
IPG; Publishing Scotland

2144

CANOPUS PUBLISHING LTD
27 Queen Square, Bristol BS1 4ND
Telephone: 0117 972 6660
Email: robin@canopusbooks.com
Web Site: http://www.canopusbooks.com

Managing Director: Robin Rees
Publisher, Physical Science: Tom Spicer

Academic & Scholarly; Physics; Reference Books, Directories & Dictionaries; Scientific & Technical

New Titles: 5 (2007), 5 (2008)
No of Employees: 4
Annual Turnover: £150,000

ISBNs, Imprints & Series: 978 0 9549846

Overseas Representation:
Europe: Andrew Durnell Marketing Ltd, Tunbridge Wells, UK

2145

CAPALL BANN PUBLISHING
Auton Farm, Milverton, Somerset TA4 1NE
Telephone: 01823 401528
Fax: 01823 401529
Email: enquiries@capallbann.co.uk
Web Site: http://www.capallbann.co.uk

Publishers: Jon Day (Sales & Rights)
Julia Day (Administration & Editorial)

Animal Care & Breeding; Archaeology; Cookery, Wines & Spirits; Crafts & Hobbies; Educational & Textbooks; Environment & Development Studies; Gardening; Gender Studies; Guide Books; Health & Beauty; History & Antiquarian; Magic & the Occult; Medical (incl. Self Help & Alternative Medicine); Music; Natural History; Philosophy; Psychology & Psychiatry; Religion & Theology; Theatre, Drama & Dance

New Titles: 24 (2007), 30 (2008)

ISBNs, Imprints & Series:
978 1 86163, 978 1 898307

Overseas Representation:
Australia (New Age): Brumby Books Holdings Pty Ltd, Kilsyth South, Vic, Australia
South Africa: Bacchus Books, Cresta
USA: Holmes Publishing Group, Edmunds, WA; New Leaf Distributing Co, Lithia Springs, GA

2146

CAPITAL TRANSPORT PUBLISHING
PO Box 250, Harrow, Middlesex HA3 5ZH
Email: info@capitaltransport.com
Web Site: http://www.capitaltransport.com

Trade Orders:
The Trade Counter, Mendlesham Industrial Estate, Norwich Road, Mendlesham, Norfolk IP14 5NA
Telephone: 01449 766629
Fax: 01449 767122
Email: orders@tradecounter.co.uk

Publisher: James Whiting

Transport

New Titles: 10 (2007), 12 (2008)
Annual Turnover: £350,000

ISBNs, Imprints & Series:
978 1 85414 Capital History; Capital Transport

Book Trade Association Membership:
IPG

2147

CAPUCHIN CLASSICS
128 Kensington Church Street, London W8 4BH
Telephone: (020) 7221 7166
Fax: (020) 7792 9288
Email: info@capuchin-classics.co.uk
Web Site: http://www.capuchin-classics.co.uk

Director: Max Scott
Editor-at-Large: Emma Howard
Editor: Christopher Ind

Fiction

New Titles: 20 (2008)
No of Employees: 6

Parent Company:
Stacey Arts Ltd

Book Trade Association Membership:
IPG

2148

CAREERS EUROPE
72–74 Godwin Street, Bradford BD1 3PT
Telephone: 01274 829600
Fax: 01274 829610

Email: europe@careersb.co.uk
Web Site: http://www.careerseurope.co.uk

Managers: Michael Carey
Leila Proud (Sales & Research)

Educational & Textbooks

ISBNs, Imprints & Series: 978 1 899483

Associated Companies:
UK: Careers Bradford Ltd

2149

CAREL PRESS
4 Hewson Street, Carlisle, Cumbria CA2 5AU
Telephone: 01228 538928
Fax: 01228 591816
Email: info@carelpress.com
Web Site: http://www.carelpress.com & http://www.shortershakespeare.com

Publisher: Chas White

Atlases & Maps; Educational & Textbooks; Electronic (Educational); Languages & Linguistics; Literature & Criticism; Mathematics & Statistics; Reference Books, Directories & Dictionaries; Sports & Games; Theatre, Drama & Dance

ISBNs, Imprints & Series:
978 1 872365, 978 1 905600, 978 1 905600

Distributor for:
Arc Theatre Co; ODT Inc (Maps); One Page Book Co

Book Trade Association Membership:
IPG

2150

CARLTON PUBLISHING GROUP
20 Mortimer Street, London W1T 3JW
Telephone: (020) 7612 0400
Fax: (020) 7612 0408
Email: sales@carltonbooks.co.uk & editorial@carltonbooks.co.uk

Distribution:
HarperCollins Publishers, PO Box Glasgow G4 0NB
Telephone: 0141 306 3100
Fax: 0141 306 3767
Email: uk.orders@harpercollins.co.uk

Directors: J. Goodman (Managing)
D. Inman (Deputy Managing)
P. Murray Hill (Publishing)
R. Porter (Design)
A. Whitton (Financial)
J. Greenhough (Sales)

Antiques & Collecting; Architecture & Design; Children's Books; Cinema, Video, TV & Radio; Computer Science; Cookery, Wines & Spirits; Crafts & Hobbies; Crime; Fashion & Costume; Health & Beauty; History & Antiquarian; Humour; Military & War; Music; Natural History; Science Fiction; Sports & Games; Transport

New Titles: 150 (2007), 150 (2008)
No of Employees: 75
Annual Turnover: £17.2M

ISBNs, Imprints & Series:
978 0 233 Andre Deutsch
978 1 84222 Carlton Books
978 1 85375 Prion
978 1 85868

Overseas Representation:
All Other Markets: Gunnar Lie & Associates Ltd, London, UK
Australia & New Zealand: c/o Jonathan Goodman, Carlton Publishing Group, London, UK

North America & Foreign Language: c/o David Inman, Carlton Publishing Group, London, UK

2151

CARNEGIE PUBLISHING LTD
Carnegie House, Chatsworth Road, Lancaster LA1 4SL
Telephone: 01524 840111
Fax: 01524 840222
Email: anna@carnegiepublishing.com
Web Site: http://www.carnegiepublishing.com

Directors: Alistair Hodge (Managing)
Anna Goddard (Production)

Academic & Scholarly; Agriculture; Archaeology; History & Antiquarian; Industry, Business & Management; Natural History

New Titles: 14 (2007), 20 (2008)
No of Employees: 7
Annual Turnover: £450,000

ISBNs, Imprints & Series:
978 1 85936 Carnegie Publishing Ltd
978 1 874181 Palatine Books
978 1 904244 Scotforth Books
978 1 905472 Crucible Books

Book Trade Association Membership:
IPG

2152

JON CARPENTER PUBLISHING
Alder House, Market Street, Charlbury OX7 3PH
Telephone: 01608 811969
Fax: 01608 811969
Email: jon@joncarpenter.co.uk

Trade Orders:
Central Books, 99 Wallis Road, London E9 5LN
Telephone: (020) 8986 4854
Fax: (020) 8533 5821
Email: orders@centralbooks.com

Contact: Jon Carpenter

Academic & Scholarly; Cookery, Wines & Spirits; Economics; Environment & Development Studies; History & Antiquarian; Medical (incl. Self Help & Alternative Medicine); Philosophy; Politics & World Affairs; Sociology & Anthropology

New Titles: 8 (2007), 8 (2008)

ISBNs, Imprints & Series:
978 0 9549727, 978 1 897766, 978 1 906067 Jon Carpenter
978 1 902279 Wychwood Press

Distributor for:
Australia: Envirobook Pty

Overseas Representation:
Australia: Envirobook, Annandale, NSW
South Africa: New Horizon Distributors, Claremont
USA: Independent Publishers Group (IPG), Chicago, IL

Book Trade Association Membership:
BA

2153

CARROLL & BROWN LTD
20 Lonsdale Road, London NW6 6RD
Telephone: (020) 7372 0900
Fax: (020) 7372 0460
Email: mail@carrollandbrown.co.uk

Directors: Amy Carroll (Managing)
Chrissie Lloyd (Art)
Rights: Simonne Waud

UK Sales: Derek Thornhill
Production: Amanda Mackie

Animal Care & Breeding; Cookery, Wines & Spirits; Crafts & Hobbies; Health & Beauty; Medical (incl. Self Help & Alternative Medicine); Mind, Body, Spirit; Parenting & Pregnancy

New Titles: 8 (2007), 5 (2008)
No of Employees: 10

ISBNs, Imprints & Series:
978 90 3258, 978 90 4760

Associated Companies:
Carroll & Brown Publishers Ltd

Overseas Representation:
Worldwide: Derek Thornhill, Carroll & Brown Ltd, London, UK

Book Trade Association Membership:
Book Packagers Association

2154

THE CATHOLIC TRUTH SOCIETY
40–46 Harleyford Road, London SE11 5AY
Telephone: (020) 7640 0042
Fax: (020) 7640 0046
Email: info@cts-online.org.uk
Web Site: http://www.cts-online.org.uk

Retail Bookshop & Mail Order:
25 Ashley Place, London SW1P 1LT
Telephone: (020) 7834 1363
Fax: (020) 7821 7398
Email: bookshop@cts-online.org.uk
Web Site: http://www.cts-online.org.uk

Directors: Rt Rev Paul Hendricks (*Chairman*)
Fergal Martin (*General Secretary, Publisher, Rights & Permissions, Accounts, Editorial*)
John Dilger (*Hon Treasurer*)
Production: Stephen Campbell
Sales: Richard Brown
Systems: Carlo Boi

Biography & Autobiography; Children's Books; Educational & Textbooks; Guide Books; History & Antiquarian; Religion & Theology

New Titles: 70 (2007), 80 (2008)
No of Employees: 22
Annual Turnover: £1.2M

ISBNs, Imprints & Series:
978 1 86082 The Incorporated Catholic Truth Society; CTS Publications

Distributor for:
Vatican City: Osservatore Romano

Overseas Representation:
Australia & New Zealand: St Pauls Publications, Strathfield, NSW, Australia

Book Trade Association Membership:
BA

2155

*CATNIP PUBLISHING LTD
Islington Business Centre,
3–5 Islington High Street, London N1 9LQ
Telephone: (020) 7745 2370
Fax: (020) 7745 2372
Email: martin@catnippublishing.co.uk

Sales:
Bounce Sales & Marketing Ltd (address as above)
Telephone: (as above)
Fax: (as above)

Directors: Robert Snuggs (*Managing*)
M. West (*Editorial*)
Andrea Reece (*Publishing*)

Children's Books

ISBNs, Imprints & Series:
978 1 846470, 978 1 903207
978 1 899248, 978 1 903285, 978 1 905117 Catnip Publishing; Happy Cat Books

Book Trade Association Membership:
IPG

2156

JOHN CATT EDUCATIONAL LTD
Great Glemham, Saxmundham, Suffolk
IP17 2HD
Telephone: 01728 663666
Fax: 01728 663415
Email: DerekBingham@johncatt.co.uk
Web Site: http://www.johncatt.com

Directors: Jonathan Evans (*Managing*)
Christine Evans (*Information*)
General Manager: David Ahier (*Business Development*)
Editor-in-Chief & Publisher: Derek Bingham
Editor: Wendy Bosberry-Scott

Educational & Textbooks

ISBNs, Imprints & Series:
978 1 901577, 978 1 904724

Book Trade Association Membership:
Periodical Publishers' Association

2157

CAXTON PUBLISHING GROUP LTD
20 Bloomsbury Street, London WC1B 3JH
Telephone: (020) 7636 7171
Fax: (020) 7636 1922
Email: office@caxtonpublishing.com
Web Site: http://www.caxtonpublishing.com

Directors: Finbarr McCabe (*Managing*)
James Birney (*Sales & Marketing, Operations*)

Antiques & Collecting; Architecture & Design; Atlases & Maps; Aviation; Children's Books; Cookery, Wines & Spirits; Crafts & Hobbies; Crime; Do-It-Yourself; Fiction; Fine Art & Art History; Gardening; Magic & the Occult; Medical (incl. Self Help & Alternative Medicine); Military & War; Natural History; Reference Books, Directories & Dictionaries; Transport

No of Employees: 6

ISBNs, Imprints & Series:
978 1 84067 Caxton Editions; Knight Paperbacks
978 1 84186 Brockhampton Press
978 1 84447 TimeLife
978 1 904449 Chaucer Press
978 1 904668 Mercury Books

2158

CBD RESEARCH LTD
Chancery House, 15 Wickham Road, Beckenham, Kent BR3 5JS
Telephone: (020) 8650 7745
Fax: (020) 8650 0768
Email: cbd@cbdresearch.com
Web Site: http://www.cbdresearch.com

Crime; Reference Books, Directories & Dictionaries

New Titles: 3 (2007), 4 (2008)

ISBNs, Imprints & Series:
978 0 900 246 CBD Research; Chancery House Press
978 0 9554514

Book Trade Association Membership:
IPG; Data Publishers Association

2159

CENGAGE LEARNING EMEA
50–51 Bedford Row, London WC1R 4LR
Telephone: (020) 7067 2500
Fax: (020) 7067 2600
Web Site: http://www.CengageLearning.co.uk

Directors: Tom Davy (*Managing, Chief Executive Officer*)
Ross Clayton (*Finance, Chief Financial Officer*)
Andrew Robinson (*Sales*)
Diane Thomas (*Sales*)
Rossella Proscia (*Marketing*)
John Yates (*Publishing*)
Production: Kay Larkin

Academic & Scholarly; Educational & Textbooks; English as a Foreign Language; Industry, Business & Management; Vocational Training & Careers

Distributor for:
Arden Shakespeare; Brooks/Cole; Cengage Learning; Delmar Learning; Gale; Heinle; South Western; Wadsworth

Book Trade Association Membership:
Publishers Association

2160

CENTRE FOR ALTERNATIVE TECHNOLOGY PUBLICATIONS
Machynlleth, Powys SY20 9AZ
Telephone: 01654 705980
Fax: 01654 702782
Email: caroline.oakley@cat.org.uk
Web Site: http://www.ecobooks.co.uk

Production Manager: Graham Preston
Publisher: Caroline Oakley
Marketing Officer: Allan Shepherd

Architecture & Design; Do-It-Yourself; Educational & Textbooks; Environment & Development Studies; Gardening; Travel & Topography

New Titles: 2 (2008)
No of Employees: 3
Annual Turnover: £150,000

ISBNs, Imprints & Series:
978 1 898049, 978 1 902175 New Futures

Overseas Representation:
USA & Canada: New Society Publishers, Gabriola Island, BC, Canada

Book Trade Association Membership:
IPG

2161

CENTRE FOR ECONOMIC POLICY RESEARCH
53–56 Great Sutton Strreet, London, EC1V 0DG
Telephone: (020) 7183 8801
Fax: (020) 7183 8820
Email: cepr@cepr.org
Web Site: http://www.cepr.org

Chief Executive Officer: Stephen Yeo
Publications Manager: Anil Shamdasani

Academic & Scholarly; Economics; Industry, Business & Management; Politics & World Affairs

New Titles: 3 (2007), 5 (2008)
No of Employees: 16

ISBNs, Imprints & Series: 978 1 898128

Overseas Representation:
USA & Canada: The Brookings Institution, Washington, DC, USA

2162

CENTRE FOR POLICY ON AGEING
25–31 Ironmonger Row, London EC1V 3QP
Telephone: (020) 7553 6500
Fax: (020) 7553 6501
Email: cpa@cpa.org.uk
Web Site: http://www.cpa.org.uk/

Warehouse, Trade Enquiries & Orders:
Central Books, 99 Wallis Road, London E9 5LN
Telephone: 0845 458 9911
Fax: 0845 458 9912
Email: orders@centralbooks.com
Web Site: http://www.centralbooks.co.uk

Director: Gillian Crosby

Academic & Scholarly; Electronic (Professional & Academic); Sociology & Anthropology

New Titles: 4 (2007), 4 (2008)
No of Employees: 6

ISBNs, Imprints & Series:
978 0 904139, 978 1 901097

Book Trade Association Membership:
IPG

2163

CHALKSOFT LTD
PO Box 49, Spalding, Lincs PE11 1NZ
Telephone: 01775 769518
Fax: 01775 762618
Email: chalksoft@clara.co.uk
Web Site: http://www.chalksoft.clara.co.uk

Managing Director: David Baldwin
Office Manager: Mrs Gillian Baldwin (*Sales & Rights*)

Academic & Scholarly; Animal Care & Breeding; Children's Books; Educational & Textbooks; Electronic (Educational); Gardening; Geography & Geology; Mathematics & Statistics; Music; Natural History; Scientific & Technical

New Titles: 16 (2007), 18 (2008)
No of Employees: 4

ISBNs, Imprints & Series:
978 1 85116 Chalksoft; Nene Valley Publishing; School Garden Co; SGC Books

Associated Companies:
Nene Valley Publishing; School Garden Co

Book Trade Association Membership:
IPG

2164

CHAMBERS HARRAP PUBLISHERS LTD
7 Hopetoun Crescent, Edinburgh EH7 4AY
Telephone: 0131 556 5929
Fax: 0131 556 5313
Email: admin@chambersharrap.co.uk
Web Site: http://www.chambersharrap.com

Distributor:
Bookpoint, 130 Milton Park, Abingdon, Oxon OX14 4SB
Telephone: 01235 400400
Fax: 01235 400401

Managing Director & Publisher: Patrick White
Managers: Jane Camillin (*Sales & Marketing*)

Ian Scott (Production)
Vivian Marr (Editorial)

Reference Books, Directories & Dictionaries

New Titles: 70 (2007), 65 (2008)
No of Employees: 30

ISBNs, Imprints & Series:
978 0 245 Harrap
978 0 550 Chambers

Parent Company:
France: Hachette Livre

Overseas Representation:
Africa: Anita Zih, A–Z Africa Book Services, Rotterdam, Netherlands
All other international enquiries: Hema Shah, Export Sales Dept, Hodder, London, UK
Australia: Hachette Livre Australia, Sydney, NSW
Caribbean: Christopher Humphrys, Humphrys Roberts Associates, London, UK
China: Ian Taylor Associates Ltd, London, UK
Eastern Europe: Jacek Lewinson, Warsaw, Poland
Europe & Middle East (schools enquiries): Gill Dee, International Schools Sales Manager, Hodder, London, UK
France & French-speaking countries: Larousse, Paris, France
Germany, Austria & Switzerland: Giana Elyea, Hodder, London, UK
Greece, Malta & Cyprus: Zitsa Seraphimidi, J & L Watt, Paleo Faliro, Greece
Hong Kong, Taiwan & Japan: Andrew White, The White Partnership, Tunbridge Wells, UK
India: Sunil Sachdev, Allied Publishers Ltd, New Delhi
Italy, Spain & Portugal: Anna Kelsall, Hodder, London, UK
Korea: Information & Culture Korea (ICK), Seoul, Korea, South
Middle East: James & Lorin Watt Ltd, Publishing Consultants, Oxford, UK
New Zealand: Hachette Livre New Zealand, Auckland
Pakistan: Salahuddin Iqbal, Paramount Books (Pvt) Ltd, Karachi
Scandinavia & Benelux: Jack Tipping, Hodder, London, UK
Singapore, Malaysia & Brunei (schools only): APD Malaysia, Malaysia; APD Singapore Pte Ltd, Singapore
Singapore, Malaysia & Brunei (trade): MPH Distributors, Singapore
South Africa: Pan Macmillan SA Pty Ltd, Hyde Park
South America: Terry Roberts, Humphrys Roberts Associates, Cotia SP, Brazil
USA: Katrina Kruse, Houghton Mifflin, Boston, MA

Book Trade Association Membership:
Publishing Scotland

2165

CHANNEL VIEW PUBLICATIONS LTD
Frankfurt Lodge, Clevedon Hall, Victoria Road, Clevedon, North Somerset BS21 7HH
Telephone: 01275 876519
Fax: 01275 871673
Email: info@multilingual-matters.com
Web Site: http://www.multilingual-matters.com

Distribution:
Marston Distributors, PO Box 269, Unit 160, Milton Park, Abingdon OX14 4YN
Telephone: 01235 465500
Fax: 01235 465555
Email: trade.order@marston.co.uk
Web Site: http://www.marston.co.uk

Directors: Mike Grover (Chair)
T. Grover (Managing)
Editors: Anna Roderick (Commissioning, Permissions & Foreign Rights)
Elinor Robertson (Marketing)
Production Manager: Sarah Williams

Academic & Scholarly; Educational & Textbooks; Environment & Development Studies; Languages & Linguistics; Psychology & Psychiatry; Sociology & Anthropology; Travel & Topography

New Titles: 40 (2007), 40 (2008)
No of Employees: 4
Annual Turnover: £700,000

ISBNs, Imprints & Series:
978 0 905028, 978 1 85359 Bilingual Education & Bilingualism; Child Language and Child Development; Communication Disorders Across Languages; Critical Language and Literary Studies; Language & Education Library; Language Planning and Policy; Languages for Intercultural Communication and Education; Linguistic Diversity & Language Rights; Modern Languages in Practice; Multilingual Matters; New Perspectives on Language and Education; Non Writing Viewpoints; Parents' and Teachers' Guides; Professional Interpreting in the Real World; Second Language Acquisition; Topics in Translation; Translating Europe
978 1 84541, 978 1 873150 Aspects of Tourism; Channel View Publication; Tourism & Cultural Change
978 1 84769 New Multilingual Matters

Associated Companies:
Multilingual Matters

Overseas Representation:
Australia: DA Information Services Pty Ltd, Mitcham, Vic
Canada: University of Toronto Press, North York, Ont
China: Access Asia Media Services, Shanghai, P. R. of China
Hong Kong: Aromix Books
India: Viva Books, New Delhi
Iran: Kowkab Publishers, Tehran
Japan: Koro Komori
Korea: Se-Jun Jung, Seoul, Korea, South
Malaysia: PMS Marketing Services, Selangor
Pakistan: Book Bird Publishers Representatives, Lahore
Singapore: Publishers Marketing Services Pte Ltd
USA: UTP, Tonawanda, NY

Book Trade Association Membership:
IPG; Association of Learned & Professional Society Publishers; UK Serials Group

2166

CHARTERED INSTITUTE OF PERSONNEL & DEVELOPMENT
151 The Broadway, London SW19 1JQ
Telephone: (020) 8612 6570
Fax: (020) 8543 4371
Email: publish@cipd.co.uk
Web Site: http://www.cipd.co.uk/bookstore

Distribution:
McGraw-Hill Education, McGraw-Hill House, Shoppenhangers Road, Maidenhead, Berks SL6 2QL
Telephone: 01628 502700
Fax: 01628 770224
Web Site: http://www.cipd.co.uk/bookstore

Managers: Ruth Lake (Publishing/Commissioning)
Margaret Marriott (Business Development)
Dawn Wood (Sales & Marketing)
Nathan Harris (Operations)
Senior Sales & Marketing Executive: Sinead Burke
Marketing Executive: Roger Dickens
Operations Executives: Caroline Windle
Robert Williams
Editors: Andrea Blue (Commissioning)
Kirsty Smy (Development)
Lindsay Anderson (Online Content)
Publishing Administrator: Christine Oelschlaeger

Academic & Scholarly; Educational & Textbooks; Industry, Business & Management; Personnel Management

New Titles: 36 (2007), 26 (2008)
No of Employees: 14
Annual Turnover: £3.3M

ISBNs, Imprints & Series:
978 0 85292, 978 1 84398

2167

THE CHARTERED INSTITUTE OF PUBLIC FINANCE & ACCOUNTANCY
3 Robert Street, London WC2N 6RL
Telephone: (020) 7543 5600
Fax: (020) 7543 5607
Email: steve.wilkins@cipfa.org
Web Site: http://www.cipfa.org.uk/shop

Managers: Stephen Wilkins (Publications, Assistant Director (Courses, Conferences & Publications))
Sara Hackwood (Publications, Production & Promotion)

Accountancy & Taxation; Economics

New Titles: 23 (2007), 25 (2008)
No of Employees: 7
Annual Turnover: £2M

ISBNs, Imprints & Series:
978 0 85299, 978 1 84508

Book Trade Association Membership:
Association of Learned & Professional Society Publishers

2168

CHATHAM PUBLISHING
3 Barham Avenue, Elstree, Herts WD6 3PW
Telephone: (020) 8953 4969
Fax: (020) 8953 4969
Email: l.leventhal@hotmail.co.uk
Web Site: http://www.chathampublishing.com

Trade Enquiries & Orders:
Bookpoint Ltd, 39 Milton Park, Abingdon, Oxon OX14 4TD
Telephone: 01235 400400

Publisher: Lionel Leventhal

Military & War; Nautical; Transport; Maritime and Naval History

ISBNs, Imprints & Series: 978 1 86176

Parent Company:
Lionel Leventhal Ltd

Overseas Representation:
Australia & New Zealand: Peribo Pty Ltd, Mount Kuring-Gai, NSW, Australia
Austria, Switzerland, Czech & Slovak Republics, Hungary, Poland, Croatia, Slovenia, Spain (including Gibraltar) & Portugal: Sandro Salucci, Florence, Italy
Belgium: De Krijger, Erps
Canada: Vanwell Publishing Ltd, St Catharines, Ont
France & Netherlands: Casemate Books, Newbury, UK
Germany: Robbert J. Pleysier, Heerde, Netherlands
India: Knowledge World International, Delhi
Middle East & Far East: Publishers International Marketing, Burmarsh, UK
New Zealand: South Pacific Books (Imports) Ltd, Auckland
South Africa: Peter Renew, Titles SA, Johannesburg
USA: MBI Publishing Co, St Paul, MN

2169

*CHAUCER PRESS
20 Bloomsbury Street, London WC1B 3JH
Telephone: (020) 7636 7171
Fax: (020) 7636 1922
Web Site: http://www.chaucerpress.com

Warehouse & Trade Enquiries:
Littlehampton Book Services, Faraday Close, Durrington, Worthing, West Sussex BN13 3RB
Telephone: 01903 828800
Fax: 01903 828802
Email: orders@lbsltd.co.uk
Web Site: http://www.lbsltd.co.uk

Chief Executive Officer: John Maxwell
Directors: Finbarr McCabe (Sales)
Terry Price (Operations)

Fine Art & Art History; Literature & Criticism

ISBNs, Imprints & Series: 978 1 904449

Parent Company:
Caxton Publishing Group

Overseas Representation:
Australia & New Zealand: Bookwise International, Wingfield, SA, Australia
Europe: Bill Bailey Publishers Representatives, Newton Abbot, Devon, UK
Far East: Bookwise Asia, Singapore, Singapore
South Africa: Peter Matthews Agencies, Alberton
USA & Canada: International Publishers Marketing Inc, Herndon, VA, USA

2170

CHEMCORD LTD
16 Inch Keith, St Leonards, East Kilbride, Glasgow G74 2JZ
Telephone: 01355 235447
Fax: 01355 235447
Email: office@chemcord.co.uk
Web Site: http://www.chemcord.co.uk

Directors: Jim Melrose
Douglas Buchanan
Sales Manager & Company Secretary: Pat Buchanan

Educational & Textbooks

No of Employees: 1

2171

CHICKEN HOUSE PUBLISHING LTD
2 Palmer Street, Frome, Somerset BA11 1DS
Telephone: 01373 454488
Fax: 01373 454499
Email: chickenhouse@doublecluck.com
Web Site: http://www.doublecluck.com

Warehouse, Trade Enquiries & Orders:
Scholastic Ltd, Westfield Road, Southam, Warwickshire CV47 0RA
Telephone: 0845 850 1144
Email: tradeorders@scholastic.co.uk

Directors: Barry Cunningham (Managing)
Rachel Hickman (Deputy Managing)
Fiction Editor: Imogen Cooper
Managers: Elinor Bagenal (Rights)
Esther Waller (Publishing)

Children's Books

New Titles: 21 (2007), 19 (2008)
No of Employees: 8

ISBNs, Imprints & Series:
978 1 903434, 978 1 904442, 978 1 905294

Parent Company:
USA: Scholastic

Overseas Representation:
Bermuda: Mary Winchell, Flatts
Central & Eastern Europe & Israel: Vincent Walsh, Yellow Brick Media, Scarborough, UK
Hong Kong & China: Jolie Li, Scholastic Asia, Causeway Bay, Hong Kong
Jamaica & other Caribbean Islands: Sharon Neita, The Book Merchant Ltd, Kingston, Jamaica
Japan: Keiko Niwano, Scholastic, Saitama
Korea: Helen Yang, Scholastic Asia, Seoul, Korea, South
Latin America: Janine Kelly, Scholastic, Buenos Aires, Argentina
Middle East & Northern Africa: Michelle Alwan & Bassem Badran, Bab Idriss, Beirut, Lebanon
Philippines: Henry Chua, Scholastic, Makati City
Puerto Rico: Darlene Vazquez, Caribe Grolier/Scholastic Inc, Santurce
Singapore, Malaysia & Indonesia: Selina Lee, Scholastic, Kuala Lumpur, Malaysia
Southern & East Africa: Brian Mey, Scholastic, Cape Town, South Africa
Taiwan: Sonia Dung, Scholastic, Taipei
Thailand: Maneerat Kurdmanee, Scholastic Asia, Bangkok
West Africa: Joyce Agyare, Scholastic, Tema, Ghana

2172

*CHILD'S PLAY (INTERNATIONAL) LTD
Ashworth Road, Bridgemead, Swindon, Wilts SN5 7YD
Telephone: 01793 616286
Fax: 01793 512795
Email: allday@childs-play.com
Web Site: http://www.childs-play.com

Publisher, Chief Executive: Neil Burden
Sales Director: Paul Gerrish
Managers: Peter Constable (Distribution)
Alan Johnson (Production)
Beth Cox (Education)
Chair: Adriana Twinn

Children's Books

ISBNs, Imprints & Series:
978 0 85953, 978 1 84643, 978 1 904550 Child's Play

Overseas Representation:
Australia: Child's Play Australia, Terrey Hills, NSW
Canada: Monarch Books of Canada Ltd, Downsview, Ont
Malta: Grimand Co Ltd, Lija
New Zealand: Educational Equipment Wholesale Ltd, Auckland
South Africa: Phambili Agencies CC, Germiston
United Arab Emirates: Child's Play Dubai, Dubai, UAE
USA: Child's Play Inc, Auburn, ME

Book Trade Association Membership:
EPC; IPG

2173

CHRISTIAN EDUCATION
1020 Bristol Road, Selly Oak, Birmingham B29 6LB
Telephone: 0121 472 4242
Fax: 0121 472 7575
Email: enquiries@christianeducation.org.uk
Web Site: http://www.christianeducation.org.uk

Director: Peter Fishpool (Chief Executive Officer)
Editors: Azhar Lodhi (Design & Production)
Anstice Hughes (Publications Team Leader)
Finance Officer: Brenda Holyoake
Managers: Diane Horton (Office, Sales & Administration)
Jennifer Smith (Marketing)
Sales Administrator: Pete Johnson

Academic & Scholarly; Children's Books; Educational & Textbooks; Religion & Theology

New Titles: 12 (2007), 12 (2008)
No of Employees: 13
Annual Turnover: £1M

ISBNs, Imprints & Series:
978 1 904024 International Bible Reading Association; RE Today Services
978 1 904024, 978 1 905893 Christian Education Publications

Associated Companies:
Christian Education Publications; RE Today Services

Book Trade Association Membership:
Publishers Association; EPC; Christian Booksellers Convention

2174

CHRISTIAN FOCUS PUBLICATIONS
Geanies House, Fearn, Tain, Ross-shire IV20 1TW
Telephone: 01862 871005
Fax: 01862 871699
Email: info@christianfocus.com
Web Site: http://www.christianfocus.com

Managing Director: William MacKenzie
Managers: Ian Thompson (General & Sales)
Willie Mackenzie (Editorial (Adult))
Jonathan Dunbar (Production)
Catherine Mackenzie (Editorial (Child))
Danie van Straaten (Design)
Philip Magee (Marketing)

Biography & Autobiography; Children's Books; Educational & Textbooks; History & Antiquarian; Religion & Theology; Sports & Games

New Titles: 64 (2007), 87 (2008)
No of Employees: 20

ISBNs, Imprints & Series:
Christian Focus; Christian Focus 4 Kids; Christian Heritage; Mentor
978 0 906731, 978 1 84550, 978 1 85792, 978 1 871676

Parent Company:
UK: Balintore Holdings

Overseas Representation:
Australia: Family Reading, Ballarat, Vic
Canada: R. G. Mitchell Family Books Inc, Kitchener, Ont
New Zealand: Soul Distributors, Auckland
South Africa: Struik Christian Books, Cape Town
USA: STL Inc, Johnson City, TN

Book Trade Association Membership:
Evangelical Christian Publishers Association (USA); Christian Booksellers Association (USA)

2175

*CHRISTIAN RESEARCH ASSOCIATION
Vision Building, 4 Footscray Road, Eltham, London SE9 2TZ
Telephone: (020) 8294 1989
Fax: (020) 8294 0014
Email: admin@christian-research.org.uk
Web Site: http://www.christian-research.org.uk & www.ukchristianbook.org.uk

Publishing Director: Dr Peter Brierley (Rights & Permissions)

Reference Books, Directories & Dictionaries; Religion & Theology

ISBNs, Imprints & Series:
978 0 947697, 978 1 85321

Distributor for:
Australia: Christian Research Association

Overseas Representation:
Australia: Christian Research Association, Kew

2176

THE CHRYSALIS PRESS
7 Lower Ladyes Hills, Kenilworth, Warks CV8 2GN
Telephone: 01926 855223
Email: brian@margaretbuckley.com
Web Site: http://www.margaretbuckley.com

Director: Brian Boyd
Editor: Jane Buckley
Officers: B. R. Buckley (Finance)
Stephen Mackey (Marketing)

Academic & Scholarly; Biography & Autobiography; Fiction; History & Antiquarian; Literature & Criticism; Travel & Topography

New Titles: 3 (2007), 2 (2008)

ISBNs, Imprints & Series: 978 1 897765

Book Trade Association Membership:
IPG

2177

CHURCH HOUSE PUBLISHING
The Archbishops' Council, Church House, Great Smith Street, London SW1P 3AZ
Telephone: (020) 7898 1451
Fax: (020) 7898 1449
Email: publishing@c-of-e.org.uk
Web Site: http://www.chpublishing.co.uk

Sales, Customer Service & Warehouse:
Norwich Books & Music, St Mary's Works, St Mary's Plain, Norwich NR3 3BH
Telephone: 01603 612914
Fax: 01603 624483
Email: orders@norwichbooksandmusic.co.uk
Web Site: http://www.chpublishing.co.uk

Head of Publishing: Thomas Allain-Chapman
Managers: Cynthia Hamilton (Sales)
Tracy Somorjay (Marketing)
Kathryn Pritchard (Product Development)
Katherine Allenby (Production)
Andrew Sweeney (New Media)
Commissioning Editor: Tracey Messenger
Copyright Administrator: Linda Foster

Reference Books, Directories & Dictionaries; Religion & Theology

New Titles: 40 (2007), 45 (2008)
No of Employees: 11
Annual Turnover: £1.1M

ISBNs, Imprints & Series: 978 0 7151

Parent Company:
UK: The Archbishops' Council

Overseas Representation:
Africa, Caribbean, Hong Kong, Korea, Malaysia, Singapore, Taiwan & Thailand: Kelvin van Hasselt Publishing Services, Briningham, Norfolk, UK
Australia & New Zealand: Willow Connection Pty Ltd, Brookvale, NSW, Australia
Canada: Bayard/Novalis Distribution, Toronto, Ont
USA: Church Publishing Inc, New York, NY

Book Trade Association Membership:
Publishers Association; Christian Suppliers' Group

2178

CHURCH OF IRELAND PUBLISHING
Church of Ireland House, Church Avenue, Rathmines, Dublin 6, Republic of Ireland
Telephone: +353 (01) 492 3979
Fax: +353 (01) 492 4770
Email: susan.hood@rcbdub.org
Web Site: http://www.cip.ireland.anglican.org

Publications Officer: Susan Hood

Academic & Scholarly; History & Antiquarian; Religion & Theology

New Titles: 5 (2007), 5 (2008)

ISBNs, Imprints & Series: 978 1 904884

Book Trade Association Membership:
CLÉ (Irish PA); Church Publishers Network (UK & Ireland)

2179

CICERONE PRESS LTD
2 Police Square, Milnthorpe, Cumbria LA7 7PY
Telephone: 015395 62069
Fax: 015395 63417
Email: info@cicerone.co.uk
Web Site: http://www.cicerone.co.uk

Directors: Jonathan Williams (Managing)
Lesley Williams (Sales & Marketing)

Guide Books; Sports & Games; Travel & Topography

New Titles: 28 (2007), 30 (2008)
No of Employees: 7

ISBNs, Imprints & Series:
978 0 902363, 978 1 85284

Overseas Representation:
Europe: Bill Bailey Publishers Representatives, Newton Abbot, Devon, UK
France: Editeur, Vaison la Romaine
Netherlands: Nilsson & Lamm BV, Weesp
Spain: Map Iberia FeB SL, Avila
USA: Midpoint Trade Books Inc, New York

Book Trade Association Membership:
IPG

2180

*CILT, THE NATIONAL CENTRE FOR LANGUAGES
20 Bedfordbury, London WC2N 4LB
Telephone: (020) 7379 5101
Fax: (020) 7379 5082
Email: emma.rees@cilt.org.uk
Web Site: http://www.cilt.org.uk

Distribution & Orders:
Central Books Ltd, 99 Wallis Road, London E9 5LN
Telephone: 0845 458 9911
Fax: 0845 458 9912
Email: mo@centralbooks.com
Web Site: http://www.centralbooks.com

Publishing Manager: Isabelle Almeida
Assistant Director, Communications:
Teresa Tinsley

Academic & Scholarly; Educational & Textbooks; Languages & Linguistics; Vocational Training & Careers

ISBNs, Imprints & Series:
Advanced Pathfinder; Classic Pathfinder; Info Tech; New Pathfinder; Pathfinder; Reflections on Practice; Resource File; Young Pathfinder
978 1 874016, 978 1 902031, 978 1 904243

Book Trade Association Membership:
EPC; CAPP

2181

CLAIRE PUBLICATIONS
Unit 8, Tey Brook Centre, Great Tey, Colchester, Essex CO6 1JE
Telephone: 01206 211020
Fax: 01206 212755
Email: mail@clairepublications.com
Web Site: http://www.clairepublications.com

Managing Director: Noel Graham
Finance: Elaine Hayward
Production: Michelle Ripton
Rights: Dorcas Smith

Educational & Textbooks; Mathematics & Statistics

New Titles: 10 (2007), 10 (2008)
No of Employees: 6
Annual Turnover: £200,000

ISBNs, Imprints & Series: 978 0 904572

Book Trade Association Membership:
British Educational Supplies Association

2182

T. & T. CLARK
The Tower Building, 11 York Road, London SE1 7NX
Telephone: (020) 7922 0880
Fax: (020) 7922 0881
Web Site: http://www.continuumbooks.com

Warehouse, Trade Enquiries & Orders:
Orca Book Services, Stanley House, 3 Fleets Lane, Poole, Dorset BH15 3AJ
Telephone: 01202 665432
Fax: 01202 666219
Web Site: http://www.orcabookservices.co.uk

Chief Executive: Oliver Gadsby
Directors: Robin Baird-Smith *(Editorial)*
Bob Marsh *(Finance)*
Ken Rhodes *(Sales & Marketing)*
Benn Linfield *(Production)*

Academic & Scholarly; Philosophy; Reference Books, Directories & Dictionaries; Religion & Theology

ISBNs, Imprints & Series:
978 0 567, 978 1 84127, 978 1 85075

Parent Company:
The Continuum International Publishing Group Ltd

Overseas Representation:
see: The Continuum International Publishing Group Ltd, London, UK

Book Trade Association Membership:
IPG

2183

JAMES CLARKE & CO
PO Box 60, Cambridge CB1 2NT
Telephone: 01223 350865
Fax: 01223 366951
Email: publishing@jamesclarke.co.uk & orders@jamesclarke.co.uk
Web Site: http://www.james.clarke.co.uk

Managing Director: Adrian Brink
Customer Service: Mudasir Gul
Accounts Department: Penny Bull
Sales & Publicity: Lucia Perez
Antoaneta Ouzuonova
Editorial: Aidan van de Weyer

Academic & Scholarly; Bibliography & Library Science; Biography & Autobiography; History & Antiquarian; Philosophy; Reference Books, Directories & Dictionaries; Religion & Theology

New Titles: 3 (2007), 20 (2008)
No of Employees: 6

ISBNs, Imprints & Series: 978 0 227

Associated Companies:
The Lutterworth Press

Overseas Representation:
Asia: Access Asia Media Services, Shanghai, P. R. of China
Philippines: Edwin Makabenta, Quezon City
Spain & Portugal: Iberian Book Services, Madrid, Spain
USA: Ingram Publisher Services Inc, Chambersburg, PA

Book Trade Association Membership:
EPC; CAPP; IPG

2184

CLASS PUBLISHING
Barb House, Barb Mews, London W6 7PA
Telephone: (020) 7371 2119
Fax: (020) 7371 2878
Email: post@class.co.uk
Web Site: http://www.class.co.uk

Trade Enquiries & Orders & Distribution:
Macmillan Distribution (MDL), Brunel Road, Houndmills, Basingstoke, Hants RG21 6XS
Telephone: 01256 329242
Fax: 01256 331413
Email: mdl@macmillan.co.uk
Web Site: http://www.macmillan-mdl.co.uk

Managers: Richard Warner
Judith Wise *(Healthcare Marketing)*
Rebecca Hirst *(Healthcare Special Sales)*
Sylvia Hotchin *(Legal Customer Services)*
Editor: Melissa Chapman *(Legal Publisher)*

Health & Beauty; Law; Medical (incl. Self Help & Alternative Medicine)

New Titles: 25 (2007), 25 (2008)

ISBNs, Imprints & Series:
978 1 85959, 978 1 872362

Book Trade Association Membership:
IPG

2185

CLASSICAL COMICS LTD
PO Box 7280, Litchborough, Towcester, Northants NN12 9AR
Telephone: 0845 812 3000
Web Site: http://www.classicalcomics.com

Chairman: Clive Bryant
Creative Director: Jo Wheeler

Children's Books; Educational & Textbooks; Fiction; Literature & Criticism; Theatre, Drama & Dance

New Titles: 4 (2007), 12 (2008)
No of Employees: 4

ISBNs, Imprints & Series: 978 1 906332

Parent Company:
UK: Providence Press

Overseas Representation:
Australia, New Zealand & Fiji: Book & Volume, Birregurra, Vic, Australia
USA & Canada: Publishers Group West, Berkeley, CA, USA

Book Trade Association Membership:
IPG

2186

CLÓ IAR-CHONNACHTA
Indreabhán, Conamara, Co Galway, Republic of Ireland
Telephone: +353 (091) 593307
Fax: +353 (091) 593362
Email: cic@iol.ie
Web Site: http://www.cic.ie

Representation:
AIS, 31 Fenian Street, Dublin 2, Republic of Ireland
Telephone: +353 (01) 661 6522
Fax: +353 (01) 661 2378

Managing Director: Micheal Ó Conghaile
Sales & Marketing: Caitriona Ní Bhaoill
General Manager: Deirdre Ní Thuathail
Rights: Toner Quinn

Audio Books; Biography & Autobiography; Children's Books; Educational & Textbooks; Fiction; Gay & Lesbian Studies; History & Antiquarian; Languages & Linguistics; Literature & Criticism; Music; Photography; Poetry; Theatre, Drama & Dance; Travel & Topography

New Titles: 12 (2007), 12 (2008)
No of Employees: 5

ISBNs, Imprints & Series:
978 1 874700, 978 1 900693, 978 1 902420, 978 1 905560

Overseas Representation:
USA: Dufour Editions Inc, Chester Springs, PA; Galway Traders, Seattle, WA

Book Trade Association Membership:
CLÉ (Irish PA)

2187

COACHWISE LTD
Chelsea Close, off Amberley Road, Armley, Leeds LS12 4HP
Telephone: 0113 231 1310
Fax: 0113 203 8826
Email: enquiries@coachwisesolutions.co.uk
Web Site: http://www.coachwisesolutions.co.uk

Directors: Kath Leonard *(Commercial)*
Melanie Drake *(Marketing & Mail Order)*
Head of Publications & Design: Martin Betts

Academic & Scholarly; Audio Books; Children's Books; Educational & Textbooks; Electronic (Educational); Sports & Games

ISBNs, Imprints & Series:
978 1 905540, 978 1 902523

Parent Company:
UK: The National Coaching Foundation

Distributor for:
UK: The Association for Physical Education; The National Coaching Foundation [Sports Coach UK]

Overseas Representation:
USA: Soccer Learning Systems, Pleasanton, CA

Book Trade Association Membership:
Publishers Association

2188

COASTAL PUBLISHING
The Studio, Puddletown Road, Wareham, Dorset BH20 6AE
Telephone: 01929 554195
Fax: 01929 554502
Email: enquiries@coastalpublishing.co.uk
Web Site: http://www.coastalpublishing.co.uk

Academic & Scholarly; Trade

Book Trade Association Membership:
Publishers Association

2189

COIS LIFE
62 Páirc na Rós, Ascaill na Cille, Dún Laoghaire, Co Dublin, Republic of Ireland
Telephone: +353 (01) 280 7951
Fax: +353 (01) 280 7951
Email: eolas@coislife.ie
Web Site: http://www.coislife.ie

Trade - Wholesaler
Áis, 31 Fenian Street, Dublin 2, Republic of Ireland
Telephone: +353 (01) 661 6522

Directors: C. Nic Pháidín *(Company Secretary)*
S. Ó Cearnaigh *(Chairman)*

Academic & Scholarly; Children's Books; Educational & Textbooks; Fiction; Languages & Linguistics; Literature & Criticism; Poetry; Theatre, Drama & Dance

New Titles: 9 (2007), 10 (2008)
No of Employees: 2
Annual Turnover: £150,000

ISBNs, Imprints & Series: 978 1 901176

Book Trade Association Membership:
CLÉ (Irish PA)

2190

COLLINS & BROWN
Anova Books, 10 Southcombe Street, London W14 0RA
Telephone: (020) 7605 1400
Fax: (020) 7605 1401
Email: lbrudenell@anovabooks.com
Web Site: http://www.anovabooks.com

Warehouse & Trade Orders:
HarperCollins, Glasgow
Telephone: 0141 306 3100
Fax: 0141 306 1401

Associate Publisher: Katie Cowan
Marketing & Publicity Manager: Laura Brudenell

Animal Care & Breeding; Cookery, Wines & Spirits; Crafts & Hobbies; Do-It-Yourself; Fashion & Costume; Fiction; Health & Beauty; Magic & the Occult; Medical (incl. Self Help & Alternative Medicine); Music; Photography; Reference Books, Directories & Dictionaries; Sports & Games; Theatre, Drama & Dance

New Titles: 40 (2007), 41 (2008)

ISBNs, Imprints & Series: 978 1 84340

Parent Company:
Anova Books

Overseas Representation:
Australia: HarperCollins Publishers, Pymble, NSW
Belgium, France, Netherlands & Luxembourg: Anova Books, London, UK
Caribbean, Mexico & Central America: Christopher Humphrys, Humphrys Roberts Associates, London, UK
Eastern Europe: Csaba Lengyel de Bagota, CLB Marketing Services, Budapest, Hungary
Far East: Julian Ashton, Ashton International Marketing Services, Sevenoaks, Kent, UK
Germany, Switzerland & Austria: Gabriele Kern Publishers Services, Frankfurt-am-Main, Germany
India: Mr Seshadri, Overleaf, New Delhi
Italy, Spain, Portugal & Greece: Padovani Books Ltd, London, UK
New Zealand: HarperCollins (NZ) Ltd, Glenfield, Auckland
Pakistan: Tahir M. Lodhi, Lahore
Russia & Baltic States: Tony Moggach, InterMedia Americana (IMA) Ltd, London, UK
Scandinavia: Katie McNeish, McNeish Publishing Services, East Sussex, UK
Singapore & Malaysia: Pansing Distribution Sdn Bhd, Singapore
South Africa: Trinity Books CC, Randburg
South America: Terry Roberts, Humphrys Roberts Associates, Cotia SP, Brazil
USA & Canada: Sterling Publishing Co Inc, New York, NY, USA

Book Trade Association Membership:
IPG

2191

*COLLINS GEO
[a division of HarperCollins Publishers]
Westerhill Road, Bishopbriggs, Glasgow G64 2QT
Telephone: 0141 306 3576
Fax: (020) 8237 4209
Email: sheena.barclay@harpercollins.co.uk
Web Site: http://www.collinsbartholomew.com

Directors: Thomas Webster *(Managing)*
Sarah Bailey *(Managing)*
James Graves *(Production)*
Sheena Barclay *(Collins Geo)*
Jamie Moore *(Marketing)*
Financial Controller: Suzanne Blake
Manager: Helen Gordon *(General)*

Atlases & Maps; Educational & Textbooks; Electronic (Educational); Guide Books; Travel & Topography

ISBNs, Imprints & Series:
978 0 00 360 Collins Longman
978 0 00 447 Collins Cartographic
978 0 7028 Bartholomew; Nicholson
978 0 7230 Times Books

Parent Company:
HarperCollins

Overseas Representation:
Australia: HarperCollins Publishers, Pymble, NSW
Canada: HarperCollins Publishers, Toronto & Scarborough, Ont
Denmark: Scanvik Books ApS, Copenhagen
France: Editions Geographiques Generales, Paris
Germany & Austria: Internationales Landkartenhaus Geocenter, Stuttgart, Germany
India: Maya Publishers Pvt Ltd, New Delhi; Rupa, New Delhi
Italy: InterOrbis Media Distribution srl Ed, Corsico (Milan)
Japan: Maruzen Co Ltd, Tokyo
Netherlands: Nilsson & Lamm BV, Weesp
New Zealand: HarperCollins (NZ) Ltd, Glenfield, Auckland
Singapore & Malaysia: MPH Distributors, Singapore
South Africa: Jonathan Ball, HarperCollins Publishers, Johannesburg & Jeppestown
Sweden: Lantmateriet Kartbutiken, Stockholm & Vällingby
Thailand: Asia Book Co Ltd, Bangkok
USA: Hammond Inc, Maplewood, NJ

Book Trade Association Membership:
Publishers Association; Publishing Scotland

2192

COLOURPOINT BOOKS
Colourpoint House, Jubilee Business Park, 21 Jubilee Road, Newtownards, Co Down BT23 4YH
Telephone: (028) 9182 6339
Fax: (028) 9182 1900
Email: info@colourpoint.co.uk
Web Site: http://www.colourpoint.co.uk

Representation:
Bookworld, Unit 10, Hodfar Road, Sandy Lane Industrial Estate, Stourport on Severn, Worcs DY13 9QB
Telephone: 01299 823330

Distribution:
MIMO Distribution (as principal address)
Telephone: (028) 9182 0505
Email: sales@mimodistribution.co.uk

Partners: Norman Johnston *(Editorial)*
Sheila Johnston *(Editorial)*
Wesley Johnston *(Editorial)*
Malcolm Johnston *(Finance)*
Company Administrator: Denise Martin *(Administration & Marketing Manager)*

Educational & Textbooks; Fiction; History & Antiquarian; Transport

New Titles: 11 (2007), 30 (2008)
No of Employees: 6
Annual Turnover: £260,000

ISBNs, Imprints & Series:

978 1 898392, 978 1 904242, 978 1 906578

Distributor for:
MIMO Distribution

Book Trade Association Membership:
Irish Educational PA

2193

*COLUMBA
55A Spruce Avenue,
Stillorgan Industrial Park, Blackrock,
Co Dublin, Republic of Ireland
Telephone: +353 (01) 294 2556
Fax: +353 (01) 294 2564
Email: info@columba.ie
Web Site: http://www.columba.ie

Managing Director & Publisher: Séan O Boyle
Sales Director: Cecilia West

History & Antiquarian; Medical (incl. Self Help & Alternative Medicine); Psychology & Psychiatry; Religion & Theology

ISBNs, Imprints & Series:
978 0 948183, 978 1 85607 The Columba Press
978 1 85607 Currach Press

Overseas Representation:
Australia: Rainbow Books, Melbourne, Vic
Canada: Anglican Book Centre, Toronto, Ont; Bayard Distribution, Toronto, Ont
New Zealand: Catholic Supplies, Auckland
USA: Dufour Editions Inc, Chester Springs, PA

Book Trade Association Membership:
CLÉ (Irish PA); Booksellers Association

2194

COMMONWEALTH SECRETARIAT
Marlborough House, Pall Mall, London SW1Y 5HX
Telephone: (020) 7747 6342
Fax: (020) 7839 9081
Email: g.bentham@commonwealth.int
Web Site: http://www.thecommonwealth.org

Orders:
York Publishing Services, 64 Hallfield Road, Layerthorpe, York
Telephone: 01904 431213
Fax: 01904 430868
Email: orders@yps-publishing.co.uk
Web Site: http://www.yps-publishing.co.uk

Publications Manager: Guy Bentham

Academic & Scholarly; Agriculture; Economics; Electronic (Educational); Environment & Development Studies; Gender Studies; Industry, Business & Management; Law; Politics & World Affairs; Reference Books, Directories & Dictionaries; Scientific & Technical

New Titles: 29 (2007), 32 (2008)

ISBNs, Imprints & Series:
978 0 85092, 978 1 84859

Overseas Representation:
Canada: Renouf Publishing Co Ltd, Ottawa, Ont
Ghana: F. Reimmer Book Services, Accra
Hong Kong: Transglobal Publishers Services Ltd
Iberia: Iberian Book Services, Madrid, Spain
India: Parrot Reads Publishers, New Delhi
Malawi & Zambia: Anglia Book Distributors Ltd, Blantyre, Malawi
Malaysia: Globe Enterprise, Selangor; MDC Publishers, Kuala Lumpur
Middle East, Mediterranean & North Africa: Avicenna Partnership, Oxford, UK
Nigeria: Mosuro The Booksellers Ltd, Ibadan
Pakistan: Book Bird Publishers Representatives, Lahore
Singapore: Horizon Books Pte Ltd; Select Books Pte Ltd
South Africa: Anglia Book & Freight Pty Ltd, Knysna; Hargraves Library Service, Claremont & Cape Town
USA: Stylus Publishing Inc, Sterling, VA

Book Trade Association Membership:
Publishers Association; IPG

2195

CONRAN OCTOPUS
2–4 Heron Quays, London E14 4JP
Telephone: (020) 7531 8400
Fax: (020) 7531 8627
Web Site: http://www.conran-octopus.co.uk

Distribution:
Littlehampton Book Services Ltd, Faraday Close, Durrington, Worthing, West Sussex BN13 3TG
Telephone: 01903 828500
Fax: 01903 828802

Directors: Lorraine Dickey *(Publisher)*
Jonathan Christie *(Art)*
Steven Edney *(UK Sales & Marketing)*

Antiques & Collecting; Architecture & Design; Cookery, Wines & Spirits; Crafts & Hobbies; Do-It-Yourself; Gardening

ISBNs, Imprints & Series:
978 1 84091, 978 1 85029

Parent Company:
Octopus Publishing Group

Overseas Representation:
Australia: Hachette Livre Australia, Sydney, NSW
Canada: McArthur & Co Publishers Ltd, Toronto, Ont
Central America & Caribbean: Ethan Atkin, Cranbury International LLC, Montpelier, VT, USA
China: GCMC, Guangzhou, P. R. of China
France, Netherlands, Belgium, Scandinavia, Iceland, Lithuania, Estonia & Latvia: Bill Bailey Publishers Representatives, Newton Abbot, Devon, UK
Germany, Austria & Switzerland: Gabriele Kern Publishers Services, Frankfurt-am-Main, Germany
Hong Kong & Taiwan: Asia Publishers Services Ltd, Hong Kong
Hungary, Croatia, Slovenia, Czech Republic, Slovakia & Poland: Csaba & Jackie Lengyel de Bagota, Budapest, Hungary
India & Sri Lanka: Ajay Parmar, New Delhi, India
Italy, Spain, Portugal, Greece & Gibraltar: Penny Padovani, London, UK
Middle East, Turkey, Israel, Cyprus & Malta: Peter Ward Book Exports, London, UK
New Zealand: Hachette Livre New Zealand, Auckland
Philippines & Korea: Benjie Ocampo, Marketing Services for Publishers, Pasig City, Philippines
Republic of Ireland: Mullett Fitzpatrick, Shankill, Co Dublin
Russia & CIS, & North Africa: Tony Moggach, InterMedia Americana (IMA) Ltd, London, UK
Singapore, Indonesia, Vietnam, Burma, Laos & Thailand: APD Singapore Pte Ltd, Singapore
South Africa: Quartet Sales & Marketing, Johannesburg
South America: Humphrys Roberts Associates, Cotia SP, Brazil

2196

CONSTABLE & ROBINSON LTD
3 The Lanchesters,
162 Fulham Palace Road, London W6 9ER
Telephone: (020) 8741 3663
Fax: (020) 8748 7562
Email: enquiries@constablerobinson.com
Web Site: http://www.constablerobinson.com

Warehouse & Distribution:
TBS Ltd, Colchester Road, Frating Green, Colchester, Essex CO7 7DW
Telephone: 01206 256000
Fax: 01206 819587

Directors: Nick Robinson *(Managing)*
Jan Chamier *(Publishing)*
Nova Jayne Heath *(Publishing)*
Adrian Andrews *(Finance)*
Andrew Hayward *(Sales & Marketing)*
Leo Hollis *(Editorial - History)*
Eryl Humphrey Jones *(Rights)*
Sam Evans *(Publicity)*
Senior Commissioning Editor: Krystyna Green *(Robinson - Crime - Fiction & Non-Fiction)*
Editors: Pete Duncan *(Non-Fiction)*
Becky Hardie *(General Non-Fiction)*
Andreas Campomar *(General Non-Fiction)*
Sales Manager: Haydn Jones

Biography & Autobiography; Children's Books; Crime; Fiction; Health & Beauty; Humour; Medical (incl. Self Help & Alternative Medicine); Military & War; Psychology & Psychiatry; Science Fiction; Travel & Topography

New Titles: 150 (2007), 150 (2008)
No of Employees: 30
Annual Turnover: £5.75M

ISBNs, Imprints & Series:
978 0 094, 978 1 84119, 978 1 84529, 978 1 85487 Constable
978 0 094, 978 1 84119, 978 1 85487 Magpie Books
978 0 094, 978 1 84119, 978 1 84529, 978 1 85487 Robinson

Overseas Representation:
Australia (Constable & Robinson - Library Supplies): DLS Australia (Pty) Ltd, Braeside, Vic, Australia
Australia (Constable & Robinson - Retail): Peribo Pty Ltd, Mount Kuring-Gai, NSW, Australia
Central & Eastern Europe, Russia, CIS, Middle East, North & Central America: Tony Moggach, IMA, London, UK
France: Anselm Robinson, London, UK
India: Maya Publishers Pvt Ltd, New Delhi
Italy & Greece: Ted Dougherty, London, UK
Japan & China: Publishers International Marketing, London, UK
New Zealand: Southern Publishers Group, Auckland
Republic of Ireland: Vivienne Lavery, Blackrock, Co Dublin
Scandinavia & Iceland: McNeish Publishing Services, East Sussex, UK
South Africa: Penguin Books South Africa, Parklands
South East Asia: CKK Ltd, Northwood, Middx, UK
Spain & Portugal: Iberian Book Services, Madrid, Spain
Western Europe: Michael Geoghegan, London, UK

Book Trade Association Membership:
Publishers Association; IPG

2197

CONSTRUCTION INDUSTRY RESEARCH & INFORMATION ASSOCIATION (CIRIA)
Classic House, 174–180 Old Street, London EC1V 9BP
Telephone: (020) 7549 3300
Fax: (020) 7253 0523
Email: enquiries@ciria.org
Web Site: http://www.ciria.org

Publishing Director: John Tomlin
Publishing Executive: Clare Drake

Academic & Scholarly; Archaeology; Architecture & Design; Engineering; Environment & Development Studies; Industry, Business & Management; Scientific & Technical

New Titles: 14 (2007), 20 (2008)
No of Employees: 45

ISBNs, Imprints & Series:
978 0 86017 CIRIA Publications

Overseas Representation:
Hong Kong: Wardell Armstrong China Ltd
USA (non exclusive distributors): Balogh International Inc, Champaign, IL, USA

Book Trade Association Membership:
IPG; PIRA

2198

THE CONTINUUM INTERNATIONAL PUBLISHING GROUP LTD
The Tower Building, 11 York Road, London SE1 7NX
Telephone: (020) 7922 0880
Fax: (020) 7922 0881
Web Site: http://www.continuumbooks.com

Distribution:
Orca Book Services, Stanley House, 3 Fleets Lane, Poole, Dorset BH15 3AJ
Telephone: 01202 665432
Fax: 01202 666219
Web Site: http://www.orcabookservices.co.uk

Chief Executive: Oliver Gadsby
Directors: Bob Marsh *(Finance)*
Robin Baird-Smith *(Publishing)*
Vivien Ward *(Publishing)*
Ken Rhodes *(Sales & Marketing)*
Benn Linfield *(Production)*
Rights Manager: Elizabeth White *(Special Sales & Rights)*

Academic & Scholarly; Bibliography & Library Science; Biography & Autobiography; Cinema, Video, TV & Radio; Economics; Educational & Textbooks; Electronic (Educational); Electronic (Professional & Academic); Environment & Development Studies; Gay & Lesbian Studies; Gender Studies; History & Antiquarian; Languages & Linguistics; Literature & Criticism; Music; Philosophy; Politics & World Affairs; Reference Books, Directories & Dictionaries; Religion & Theology; Sociology & Anthropology; Theatre, Drama & Dance; Vocational Training & Careers

New Titles: 600 (2007), 650 (2008)
No of Employees: 160
Annual Turnover: £10M

ISBNs, Imprints & Series:
978 0 225 Geoffrey Chapman
978 0 264 Mowbray
978 0 304 Cassell Academic; Cassell Reference
978 0 485 Athlone
978 0 567 T. & T. Clark International
978 0 5829 Claridge Press
978 0 7136 A. & C. Black (New Testament Commentaries)
978 0 7185 Leicester University Press
978 0 7201 Mansell
978 0 7220 Sheed & Ward
978 0 8264 Continuum
978 0 8601 Burns & Oates
978 0 8618, 978 1 8556 Pinter
978 1 56338 Trinity Press International
978 1 84127, 978 1 85075 Sheffield Academic Press
978 1 84371, 978 1 85506 Thoemmes Continuum
978 1 84714 Continuum Collection
978 1 84725 Hambledon Continuum
978 1 85539 Network Continuum Education
978 1 87062, 978 1 90051 Claridge Press

Associated Companies:
USA: The Continuum International Publishing Group Inc

Overseas Representation:
Australia: Palgrave Macmillan, Melbourne, Vic
Australia (Religion titles only): Rainbow Books, Melbourne, Vic, Australia
Austria, Greece, Cyprus & Eastern Europe: Tyers Book Sales, UK
Hong Kong, China, Taiwan & Philippines: Asia Publishers Services Ltd, Hong Kong
India & Sri Lanka: Viva Books, New Delhi, India
Japan: United Publishers Services Ltd, Tokyo
Korea: Information & Culture Korea (ICK), Seoul, Korea, South
Mexico, Central & South America: Cranbury International LLC, Montpelier, VT, USA
Middle East, North Africa & Malta: International Publishing Services (IPS) Middle East Ltd, Dubai, UAE
Netherlands, Germany, France, Switzerland, Italy, Israel & Caribbean: The Continuum International Publishing Group Ltd, London, UK
Nigeria: Bounty Press Ltd, Ibadan
Pakistan: T.M.L. Publishers' Consultants & Representatives, Lahore
Scandinavia: Colin Flint Ltd, Publishers Scandinavian Consultancy, Cambridge, UK
Singapore, Malaysia, Indonesia & Thailand: APD Singapore Pte Ltd, Singapore
Southern Africa: Book Promotions (Pty) Ltd/ Horizon Books (Pty) Ltd, Cape Town, South Africa
Spain, Portugal & Gibraltar: Iberian Book Services, Madrid, Spain

Book Trade Association Membership:
IPG

2199

*CONWAY
10 Southcombe Street, London W14 0RA
Telephone: (020) 7605 1400
Fax: (020) 7605 1401
Email: jlee@anovabooks.com
Web Site: http://www.anovabooks.com

Distribution:
HarperCollins, Campsie View, Westerhill Road, Bishopbriggs, Glasgow G64 2QT
Telephone: 0141 306 3100
Fax: 0141 306 3767

Associate Publisher: John Lee *(Editorial)*
Publicity & Marketing Manager: Komal Patel

Aviation; Engineering; History & Antiquarian; Military & War; Nautical; Politics & World Affairs; Transport

ISBNs, Imprints & Series:
978 0 85177 Conway Maritime Press; Putnam Aeronautical Books
978 1 84486
978 1 85753 Brassey's (UK)

Overseas Representation:
Australia: Capricorn Link (Australia) Pty Ltd, Windsor, NSW
Canada: Vanwell Publishing Ltd, St Catharines, Ont
Caribbean: Humphrys Roberts Associates, London, UK
Eastern Europe: CLB Marketing Services, Budapest, Hungary
Far East: Ashton International Marketing Services, Sevenoaks, Kent, UK
France, Netherlands & Luxembourg: Anova Books, London, UK
Germany, Austria & Switzerland: Gabriele Kern Publishers Services, Frankfurt-am-Main, Germany
New Zealand: HarperCollins (NZ) Ltd, Glenfield, Auckland
Russia & Baltic States: Tony Moggach, InterMedia Americana (IMA) Ltd, London, UK
Scandinavia: McNeish Publishing Services, East Sussex, UK
Singapore & Malaysia: Pansing Distribution Sdn Bhd, Singapore
South Africa: Trinity Books CC, Randburg
South America: Terry Roberts, Cotia SP, Brazil
Spain, Portugal, Malta, Greece & Italy: Padovani Books Ltd, London, UK
USA: Casemate Publishers & Book Distributors LLC, Havertown, PA

2200

*COORDINATION GROUP PUBLICATIONS LTD (CGP LTD)
Broughton House, Griffin Street, Broughton-in-Furness, Cumbria LA20 6HH
Telephone: 01229 715700
Fax: 01229 716958
Email: moragdean@cgpbooks.co.uk
Web Site: http://www.cgpbooks.co.uk

Academic & Scholarly

ISBNs, Imprints & Series:
978 1 84146, 978 1 84762

Associated Companies:
USA: CGP Study; Coordination Group Publications Inc [trading as CGP Education]

2201

COPPER BEECH PUBLISHING LTD
PO Box 159, East Grinstead, Sussex RH19 4FS
Telephone: 01342 314734
Fax: 01342 312196
Email: sales@copperbeechpublishing.co.uk
Web Site: http://www.copperbeechpublishing.co.uk

Rights: Jan Barnes
Editorial: Julie Hird
Finance: Elizabeth Moreira

Cookery, Wines & Spirits; Fashion & Costume; Gardening; History & Antiquarian; Sports & Games; Transport

ISBNs, Imprints & Series:
English Eccentricities; The Etiquette Collection
978 0 9516295, 978 1 898617

Book Trade Association Membership:
IPG

2202

CORK UNIVERSITY PRESS
Youngline Industrial Estate, Pailaduff Road, Togher, Cork, Republic of Ireland
Telephone: +353 (021) 490 2980
Fax: +353 (021) 431 5329
Email: corkuniversitypress@ucc.ie
Web Site: http://www.corkuniversitypress.com

Orders & Distribution (Republic of Ireland, Northern Ireland & Europe):
Gill & Macmillan Distribution, Hume Avenue, Park West, Dublin 12, Republic of Ireland
Telephone: +353 (01) 500 9500
Fax: +353 (01) 500 9596

Representation (Republic of Ireland & Northern Ireland):
Robert Towers, 2 The Crescent, Monkstown, Co Dublin, Republic of Ireland
Telephone: +353 (01) 280 6532
Fax: +353 (01) 280 6020

Publications Director: Mike Collins
Editors: Sophie Watson *(Commissioning)*
Moria O'Donovan *(Production)*

Academic & Scholarly; Archaeology; Architecture & Design; Atlases & Maps; Environment & Development Studies; Fine Art & Art History; Gay & Lesbian Studies; Gender Studies; History & Antiquarian; Literature & Criticism; Music; Philosophy; Photography

ISBNs, Imprints & Series:
Atrium; Attic Press
978 0 902561, 978 1 85918 Field Day Essays; Irish Narratives; Undercurrents

Overseas Representation:
Germany, Austria & Switzerland (Rights only): Brigitte Axster, Frankfurt, Germany
Japan: United Publishers Services Ltd, Tokyo
North America: Stylus Publishing LLC, Herndon, VA, USA
UK & Europe: Quantum Publishing Solutions Ltd, Paisley, UK
UK (excluding Northern Ireland) (Distribution): Marston Book Services Ltd, Abingdon, UK

Book Trade Association Membership:
CLÉ (Irish PA)

2203

CORNWALL EDITIONS LTD
8 Langurtho Road, Fowey, Cornwall
PL23 1EQ
Telephone: 01726 832483
Fax: 01726 832483
Email: info@cornwalleditions.co.uk
Web Site: http://www.cornwalleditions.co.uk

Publisher: Ian Grant
Manager: Judy Martin (Customer Services)

Archaeology; Children's Books; Fiction; History & Antiquarian; Natural History

New Titles: 1 (2007), 2 (2008)
Annual Turnover: £10,000

ISBNs, Imprints & Series:
978 1 904880 Cornwall Editions; Ian Grant Publishers

Book Trade Association Membership:
IPG

2204

COUNCIL FOR BRITISH ARCHAEOLOGY
St Mary's House, 66 Bootham, York
YO30 7BZ
Telephone: 01904 671417
Fax: 01904 671384
Email: books@britarch.ac.uk
Web Site: http://www.britarch.ac.uk

Distribution:
Central Books Ltd, 99 Wallis Road, London
E9 5LN
Telephone: 0845 458 9910
Fax: 0845 458 9912
Email: mo@centralbooks.com
Web Site: http://www.centralbooks.com

Directors: Michael Heyworth
Peter Olver (Finance)
Senior Officers: Gill Chitty (Conservation Co-ordinator)
Donald Henson (Education)
Officers: Lynne Walker (Listed Buildings)
Dan Hull (Head of Information & Communication)
Marcus Smith (Information)
Sophie Cringle (Marketing & Events)
Nicky Milsted (Young Archaeologists' Club Magazine)
Mike Pitts (Magazine Editor)
Catrina Appleby (Publications)

Archaeology

New Titles: 8 (2007), 9 (2008)
No of Employees: 23
Annual Turnover: £1.1M

ISBNs, Imprints & Series:
Archaeology of York; British and Irish Archaeological Bibliography; CBA Research Reports
978 1 902771 Practical Handbooks in Archaeology

Book Trade Association Membership:
Association of Learned & Professional Society Publishers

2205

COUNCIL OF MORTGAGE LENDERS
Bush House, Aldwych, London WC2B 4PJ
Telephone: (020) 7438 8908
Email: pat.gauntlett@cml.org.uk
Web Site: http://www.cml.org.uk

Director General: Michael Coogan
Chief Economist: Bob Pannell
Head of External Affairs: Sue Anderson
Senior Legal Advisor: Samantha Barnett
Publication Officer: Pat Gauntlett

Economics; Housing

New Titles: 3 (2007), 4 (2008)
No of Employees: 37

ISBNs, Imprints & Series:
978 0 954457, 978 1 872423, 978 1 905257

2206

COUNTRYSIDE BOOKS
2 Highfield Avenue, Newbury, Berks
RG14 5DS
Telephone: 01635 43816
Fax: 01635 551004
Email: info@countrysidebooks.co.uk
Web Site: http://www.countrysidebooks.co.uk

Publisher: Nicholas Battle
Partner: Suzanne Battle
Sales Manager: Jackie Arrowsmith
Managing Editor: Paula Leigh

Aviation; Guide Books; History & Antiquarian; Humour; Reference Books, Directories & Dictionaries; Travel & Topography; Local History

New Titles: 56 (2007), 52 (2008)

ISBNs, Imprints & Series:
978 0 86368, 978 0 905392, 978 1 85306, 978 1 85455

Parent Company:
Countryside Book UK

Distributor for:
Cube Publications Ltd; The Dovecote Press; Kent County Council; Meridian Books; Power Publications

Overseas Representation:
USA & Canada: The David Brown Book Co, Oakville, CT, USA

Book Trade Association Membership:
IPG

2207

COUNTYVISE LTD
14 Appin Road, Birkenhead CH41 9HH
Telephone: 0151 647 3333
Fax: 0151 647 8286
Email: info@countyvise.co.uk
Web Site: http://www.countyvise.co.uk

Directors: John Emmerson (Managing)
Jean Emmerson

Biography & Autobiography; Crime; History & Antiquarian; Humour; Natural History; Poetry; Religion & Theology; Sports & Games; Transport

New Titles: 15 (2007), 15 (2008)

ISBNs, Imprints & Series:
978 0 907768, 978 1 901231
978 0 9516129 Merseyside Port Folios
978 1 871201 Liver Press
978 1 873245 Picton Press (Liverpool)
978 1 906205 Appin Press

2208

CQ PRESS
PO Box 317, Oxford OX2 9RU
Telephone: 01865 861669
Email: smiller@cqpress.com
Web Site: http://www.cqpress.com

Distribution:
Marston Book Services, PO Box 269, Milton Park, Abingdon, Oxon OX14 4YN
Telephone: 01235 465521
Fax: 01235 465555
Email: direct.orders@marston.co.uk

Representation:
Quantum Publishing Solutions,
2 Cheviot Road, Paisley PA2 8AN
Telephone: 0141 884 1398
Fax: 0141 884 5322
Email: quantumjim@btopenworld.com

Contact: Sue Miller

Academic & Scholarly; Educational & Textbooks; Environment & Development Studies; Politics & World Affairs; Reference Books, Directories & Dictionaries

ISBNs, Imprints & Series:
978 0 87187, 978 0 87289, 978 1 56643, 978 1 56802, 978 1 933116

Overseas Representation:
Europe: Andrew Durnell Marketing Ltd, Tunbridge Wells, UK

2209

CRÉCY PUBLISHING LTD
Unit 1A, Ringway Trading Estate, Shadowmoss Road, Manchester M22 5LH
Telephone: 0161 499 0024
Fax: 0161 499 0298
Email: books@crecy.co.uk
Web Site: http://www.crecy.co.uk

Managing Director: Jeremy M. Pratt
Managers: Gill Richardson (Customer Services)
Julia Nash (Financial)
Chris Tordoff (Marketing)

Aviation; History & Antiquarian; Military & War; Nautical; Transport

New Titles: 2 (2007), 8 (2008)
No of Employees: 11

ISBNs, Imprints & Series:
978 0 85979 Airdata Publications
978 0 907579 Goodall Publications
978 0 947554 Crécy
978 1 874783 Airplan Flight Equipment Ltd
978 1 902109 Hikoki Publications

Distributor for:
Air Research Publications; Airplan Flight Equipment Ltd; Airtime Publishing; Aviation Publications Inc; Camber Publications Ltd; Independent Books; Old Sausage Publishers; Pacific Century

Overseas Representation:
Australia: J. B. Wholesalers, Bibra Lake, WA
Canada: Vanwell Publishing Ltd, St Catharines, Ont
Europe: Bookport Associates, Corsico (MI), Italy
New Zealand: South Pacific Books (Imports) Ltd, Auckland
USA: Motorbooks, St Paul, MN; Specialty Press, North Branch, MN

2210

CRESCENT MOON PUBLISHING
PO Box 393, Maidstone, Kent ME14 5XU
Telephone: 01622 729593
Email: cresmopub@yahoo.co.uk
Web Site: http://www.crescentmoon.org.uk

Director: Jeremy Robinson
Editors: C. Hughes
C. Hellawell
Design: Jean Kazan

Academic & Scholarly; Biography & Autobiography; Cinema, Video, TV & Radio; Fine Art & Art History; Gardening; Gender Studies; Literature & Criticism; Magic & the Occult; Music; Philosophy; Photography; Poetry; Religion & Theology; Sociology & Anthropology; Theatre, Drama & Dance; Travel & Topography

ISBNs, Imprints & Series:
Art in Close-Up Series; British Poets Series; European Writers Series; Thomas Hardy Studies Series; Painters Series; John Cowper Powys Studies Series; Sculptors Series
978 1 86171, 978 1 871846 Crescent Moon
978 1 898283 Joe's Press

Overseas Representation:
USA: State Mutual Book & Periodical Service Ltd, New York

Book Trade Association Membership:
Small Press Group

2211

CRESSRELLES PUBLISHING CO LTD
10 Station Road Industrial Estate, Colwall, Malvern WR13 6RN
Telephone: 01684 540154
Fax: 01684 540154
Email: simon@cressrelles.co.uk
Web Site: http://www.cressrelles.co.uk

Directors: Simon Smith (Sales)
Leslie Smith

Theatre, Drama & Dance

New Titles: 2 (2007), 2 (2008)

ISBNs, Imprints & Series:
978 0 7155 Kenyon-Deane
978 0 85343 J. Garnet Miller
978 0 85956 Cressrelles
978 0 90002 Actinic Press

Associated Companies:
New Playwrights' Network

Distributor for:
USA: Anchorage Press Inc

Overseas Representation:
Australia: Origin Theatrical, Sydney, NSW
New Zealand: Play Bureau of New Zealand Ltd, New Plymouth
Republic of Ireland: Drama League of Ireland, Dublin
South Africa: Dalro (Pty) Ltd, Braamfontein
USA: Bakers Plays, Quincy, MA

2212

CRIMSON PUBLISHING
2nd Floor, Westminster House, Kew Road, Richmond, Surrey TW9 2ND
Telephone: (020) 8334 1600
Fax: (020) 8334 1601
Email: info@crimsonpublishing.co.uk
Web Site: http://www.crimsonpublishing.co.uk

Bookshop Orders:
Portfolio Books
Telephone: (020) 8997 9000
Fax: (020) 8997 9097

Director: David Lester
Accounts: Allison Harper
Production: Jo Jacomb
Marketing: Lucy Smith

Biography & Autobiography; Educational & Textbooks; Guide Books; Industry, Business & Management; Reference Books, Directories & Dictionaries; Travel & Topography; Vocational Training & Careers

New Titles: 40 (2008)

ISBNs, Imprints & Series:
Crimson Publishing; Trotman; Vacation Work; White Ladder Press
978 0 901205, 978 0 907638, 978 1 85458

Distributor for:
Italy: Green Volunteers

Overseas Representation:
Australia: Woodslane Pty Ltd, Warriewood, NSW
Benelux: Nilsson & Lamm BV, Weesp, Netherlands
South Africa: Trinity Books CC, Randburg
USA: Globe Pequot Press, Guilford, CT

2213

PAUL H. CROMPTON LTD
94 Felsham Road, London SW15 1DQ
Telephone: (020) 8780 1063 & 8788 9130
Fax: (020) 8780 1063
Email: cromptonph@aol.com

Distribution:
Airlift Book Co, 8 The Arena, Mollison Avenue, Enfield EN3 7NJ
Telephone: (020) 8804 0400
Fax: (020) 8804 0044

Editorial, Production: Paul Crompton (Information Co-ordination)
Sales: Rosalie Brookhouse
  Peter Howcroft
Artistic, Design Director: Richard Batchelor
Administration, Office: Tirzah Christian

Health & Beauty; Medical (incl. Self Help & Alternative Medicine); Religion & Theology; Sports & Games; Martial Arts; Survival

ISBNs, Imprints & Series:
978 0 901764, 978 1 874250

Distributor for:
USA: Ryukyu Imports; Smiling Tiger Publications; Unique Publications; YMAA

Overseas Representation:
Australia: Banyan Tree Book Distributors, Darra, Qld
USA & Canada: Ryukyu Imports, USA; Unique Publications, USA

2214

CROSSBOW EDUCATION LTD
41 Sawpit Lane, Brocton, Staffs ST17 0TE
Telephone: 01785 660902
Fax: 01785 661431
Email: sales@crossboweducation.co.uk
Web Site: http://www.crossboweducation.co.uk

Chief Executive Officer: Robert Hext (Sales & Research UK & USA)
General Director: Anne Hext (UK & USA)
Manager: Pelle Johansson (UK Sales & Production)
Finance & Wages: Ruth Johansson (UK)

Academic & Scholarly; Educational & Textbooks

New Titles: 1 (2007), 3 (2008)
No of Employees: 7
Annual Turnover: £300,000

ISBNs, Imprints & Series: 978 1 900891

Overseas Representation:
USA: Crossbow Education Corp, Cornelius, NC

Book Trade Association Membership:
EPC

2215

THE CROWOOD PRESS LTD
The Stable Block, Crowood Lane, Ramsbury, Marlborough, Wiltshire SN8 2HR
Telephone: 01672 520320
Fax: 01672 520280
Email: enquiries@crowood.com
Web Site: http://www.crowood.com

Distributors:
Grantham Book Services, Isaac Newton Way, Alma Park Industrial Estate, Grantham, Lincs NG31 9SD
Telephone: 01476 541000
Fax: 01476 541060
Email: orders@gbs.tbs-ltd.co.uk
Web Site: http://www.crowood.com

Chairman: John Dennis (Publisher)
Director: Ken Hathaway (Managing)
Sales & Marketing: Julie Sankey

Agriculture; Animal Care & Breeding; Antiques & Collecting; Aviation; Crafts & Hobbies; Do-It-Yourself; Gardening; Military & War; Natural History; Nautical; Sports & Games; Theatre, Drama & Dance; Transport

New Titles: 70 (2007), 70 (2008)
No of Employees: 8

ISBNs, Imprints & Series:
978 0 946284, 978 1 84797, 978 1 85223, 978 1 86126

Overseas Representation:
Australia: Peribo Pty Ltd, Mount Kuring-Gai, NSW
Canada: Vanwell Publishing Ltd, St Catharines, Ont
Scandinavia: Angell Eurosales, Berwick-on-Tweed, UK
Singapore, Malaysia & Brunei: Publishers Marketing Services Pte Ltd, Singapore
South Africa: Peter Hyde Associates (Pty) Ltd, Cape Town
Southern Europe: Bookport Associates, Corsico (MI), Italy
USA: Trafalgar Square Publishing, North Pomfret, VT
Western Europe: Anselm Robinson, London, UK

2216

G. L. CROWTHER
224 South Meadow Lane, Preston PR1 8JP
Telephone: 01772 257126

Sole Proprietor: G. L. Crowther

Atlases & Maps; Geography & Geology; Transport

New Titles: 30 (2007), 15 (2008)

ISBNs, Imprints & Series:
978 1 85615 National Series of Waterway Tramway and Railway Atlases

2217

CRW PUBLISHING LTD
6 Turville Barns, Eastleach, Cirencester, Glos GL7 3QB
Telephone: 01367 850448
Fax: 0870 751 7073
Email: clive.reynard@btinternet.com
Web Site: http://www.collectors-library.com

Trade Orders:
Macmillan Distribution (MDL), Brunel Road, Basingstoke, Hants RG21 6XS
Telephone: 01256 302692 & 0845 070 5656 (automated line – orders & availability)
Fax: 01256 812558
Email: orders@macmillan.co.uk

Directors: Ken Webb (Chairman & Production)
  Marus Clapham (Editorial)
  Clive Reynard (Sales)
  Cameron Brown (Non-Executive)

Children's Books; Fiction; Humour

New Titles: 14 (2007), 14 (2008)
No of Employees: 5

Annual Turnover: £500,000

ISBNs, Imprints & Series:
978 1 904633, 978 1 904919, 978 1 905716 Collector's Library; Collector's Library Editions/Cases
978 1 904633, 978 1 905716 Book Blocks

Overseas Representation:
Australia: Gary Allen Pty Ltd, Wetherill Park BC, NSW
New Zealand: David Bateman Ltd, Auckland
South Africa: Alternative Books CC, Ferndale

2218

CSA WORD
[the trading name for CSA Telltapes Ltd]
6a Archway Mews, London SW15 2PE
Telephone: (020) 8871 0220
Fax: (020) 8877 0712
Email: info@csaword.co.uk
Web Site: http://www.csaword.co.uk

Distribution:
Orca Book Services, Stanley House, 3 Fleets Lane, Poole, Dorset BH15 3AJ
Telephone: 01202 665432
Fax: 01202 666219
Email: orders@orca-book-services.co.uk

Managing Director: Clive Stanhope
Managers: Victoria Williams (Sales)
  Rebecca Fenton (Digital Rights)

Audio Books

New Titles: 27 (2007), 30 (2008)

ISBNs, Imprints & Series:
978 1 873859, 978 1 901768, 978 1 904605, 978 1 906147

Overseas Representation:
USA & Canada: Publishers Group West, Jackson, TN, USA

Book Trade Association Membership:
Audiobook Publishers Association (APA)

2219

CUALANN PRESS LTD
6 Corpach Drive, Dunfermline, Fife KY12 7XG
Telephone: 01383 733724
Fax: 01383 733724
Email: info@cualann.com & cualann@btinternet.com
Web Site: http://www.cualann.com

Director: Brid Hetherington

Biography & Autobiography; History & Antiquarian; Military & War; Sports & Games; Travel & Topography

New Titles: 4 (2007)

ISBNs, Imprints & Series:
978 0 9535036, 978 0 9544416, 978 0 9554273

Book Trade Association Membership:
Publishing Scotland

2220

CURRACH PRESS
55A Spruce Avenue, Stillorgan Industrial Park, Blackrock, Co Dublin, Republic of Ireland
Telephone: +353 (01) 294 2556
Fax: +353 (01) 294 2564
Email: info@currach.ie
Web Site: http://www.currach.ie

Trade Enquiries & Orders:
Columba Mercier Distribution (address as above)
Telephone: +353 (01) 294 2560

Fax: +353 (01) 294 2564
Email: cmd@columba.ie

Publisher: Jo O'Donoghue
Publicity Officer: Teresa Daly
Sales Manager: Michael Brennan

Biography & Autobiography; Cinema, Video, TV & Radio; Cookery, Wines & Spirits; History & Antiquarian; Music; Photography; Sports & Games; Transport; Travel & Topography

New Titles: 12 (2007), 18 (2008)
No of Employees: 4

ISBNs, Imprints & Series: 978 1 85607

Parent Company:
Republic of Ireland: The Columba Bookservice Ltd

Overseas Representation:
Australia: Rainbow Books, Fairfield, Vic
Europe: Andrew Durnell Marketing Ltd, Tunbridge Wells, UK
New Zealand: Pleroma Christian Supplies, Otane, Central Hawkes Bay
USA & Canada: Dufour Editions Inc, Chester Springs, PA, USA

Book Trade Association Membership:
CLÉ (Irish PA)

2221

*JAMES CURREY PUBLISHERS
73 Botley Road, Oxford OX2 0BS
Telephone: 01865 244111
Fax: 01865 246454
Email: vanessa.hinkley@jamescurrey.co.uk
Web Site: http://www.jamescurrey.co.uk

Trade Enquiries & Orders:
Marston Book Services Ltd, PO Box 269, Abingdon, Oxon OX14 4YN
Telephone: 01235 465500
Fax: 01235 465555
Email: enquiries@marston.co.uk

Chairman: James Currey
Administration: Vanessa Hinkley
Managing Director: Douglas H. Johnson
Editorial: Lynn Taylor

Academic & Scholarly; Archaeology; Bibliography & Library Science; Economics; Environment & Development Studies; Gender Studies; Geography & Geology; History & Antiquarian; Literature & Criticism; Politics & World Affairs; Religion & Theology; Sociology & Anthropology; Studies of Africa; Studies of Third World

ISBNs, Imprints & Series:
978 0 85255 James Currey; Hans Zell

Overseas Representation:
Africa (excluding South Africa): InterMedia Africa Ltd (IMA), London, UK
Australia: Bushbooks, Gosford, NSW
Kenya: East African Educational Publishers Ltd, Nairobi
South Africa: David Philip Publishers Pty Ltd, Claremont
Uganda: Fountain Publishers Ltd, Kampala

Book Trade Association Membership:
IPG

2222

CYHOEDDIADAU'R GAIR
Ael y Bryn, Chwilog, Pwllheli, Gwynedd LL53 6SH
Telephone: 01766 819120
Fax: 01766 819120
Email: aled@ysgolsul.com

Director: Aled Davies

Children's Books; Religion & Theology

ISBNs, Imprints & Series: 978 1 85994

Parent Company:
Welsh Sunday School Council

Overseas Representation:
Worldwide: Welsh Books Council, Aberystwyth, UK

Book Trade Association Membership:
IPG

2223

DANCE BOOKS LTD
The Old Bakery, 4 Lenten Street, Alton, Hants GU34 1HG
Telephone: 01420 86138
Fax: 01420 86142
Email: dwl@dancebooks.co.uk
Web Site: http://www.dancebooks.co.uk

Warehouse, Trade Enquiries & Orders:
Vine House Distribution, Waldenbury, North Common, Chailey, East Sussex BN8 4DR
Telephone: 01825 723398
Fax: 01825 724188
Email: sales@vinehouseuk.co.uk
Web Site: http://www.vinehouseuk.co.uk

Chairman: John O'Brien
Directors: David Leonard *(Managing, Editorial & Production)*
Richard Holland *(Sales)*

Academic & Scholarly; Music; Theatre, Drama & Dance

New Titles: 12 (2007), 6 (2008)
No of Employees: 6

ISBNs, Imprints & Series:
978 0 903102, 978 1 85273

Distributor for:
USA: Dance Horizons; Princeton Book Co

Overseas Representation:
Australia: Footprint Books Pty Ltd, Warriewood, NSW
USA: Princeton Book Company, Hightstown, NJ

Book Trade Association Membership:
BA

2224

DARTON, LONGMAN & TODD LTD
1 Spencer Court,
140–142 Wandsworth High Street, London SW18 4JJ
Telephone: (020) 8875 0155
Fax: (020) 8875 0133
Email: tradesales@darton-longman-todd.co.uk
Web Site: http://www.dltbooks.com

Warehouse (Authorised Returns) & Shipping:
Unit 9, Amor Way, Dunhams Lane, Letchworth Garden City, Herts SG6 1UG
Telephone: 01462 673470
Fax: 01462 482742

Directors: T. K. Lee *(Accounts)*
Brendan Walsh *(Editorial)*
Trevor Price *(Distribution, Warehouse Manager)*
Helen Porter *(Managing Editor)*
Leslie Kay *(Production & Company Secretary)*
Aude Pasquier *(Sales & Marketing)*
Jackie Hawkins *(Trade)*
Georgina Lord *(Publicity)*

Academic & Scholarly; Biography & Autobiography; Educational & Textbooks; Environment & Development Studies; Philosophy; Psychology & Psychiatry; Religion & Theology

ISBNs, Imprints & Series: 978 0 232

Overseas Representation:
Africa, Caribbean Commonwealth, Far East & South Africa: Kelvin van Hasselt Publishing Services, Briningham, Norfolk, UK
Australia: Rainbow Books, Fairfield, Vic
Canada: Novalis Inc, Toronto, Ont
Malta: Preca Library, Societas Doctrinae Christianae, M.U.S.E.U.M., Bajda
New Zealand: Pleroma Christian Supplies, Otane, Central Hawkes Bay

Book Trade Association Membership:
Publishers Association; BA

2225

THE DAVENANT PRESS
PO Box 323, Burford OX18 4XN
Telephone: 01993 824754
Fax: 01993 824129
Email: judith@history.u-net.com
Web Site: http://www.davenantpress.co.uk

Proprietor: Judith Ann Loades

Academic & Scholarly; Animal Care & Breeding; Archaeology; Biography & Autobiography; Educational & Textbooks; History & Antiquarian; Religion & Theology

New Titles: 40 (2008)

ISBNs, Imprints & Series:
978 1 85944 Davenant Press General Academic Titles; Notes on English Literature; Notes on History; Notes on Politics

Book Trade Association Membership:
BA; IPG

2226

DAVID & CHARLES LTD
Brunel House, Newton Abbot, Devon TQ12 4PU
Telephone: 01626 323200
Fax: 01626 323317
Web Site: http://www.davidandcharles.co.uk

Directors: Sara Domville *(Managing)*
Richard Dodman *(UK Sales & Marketing)*
James Gaisford *(Finance)*
Roger Lane *(Production)*

Animal Care & Breeding; Antiques & Collecting; Cookery, Wines & Spirits; Crafts & Hobbies; Do-It-Yourself; Humour; Military & War; Natural History; Photography; Sports & Games; Equestrian

New Titles: 70 (2007), 70 (2008)
No of Employees: 150

ISBNs, Imprints & Series:
978 0 7153 David & Charles
978 0 907115 Pevensey Press

Parent Company:
USA: F & W Publications

Distributor for:
Dover Books; F & W Publications (North Light Books, Writer's Digest Books, Betterway Books); Reader's Digest Books
USA: Adams Media; Krause Publications

Overseas Representation:
Asia, Middle East & Caribbean: Michelle Morrow Curreri, Beverly, MA, USA
Australia: Capricorn Link (Australia) Pty Ltd, Windsor, NSW
Belgium, France & Netherlands: Ted Dougherty, London, UK
Denmark, Finland, Norway, Sweden & Netherlands (Foreign Rights Agent): Candida Buckley, Leeds, Kent, UK
Denmark, Sweden, Norway & Finland: Angell Eurosales, Berwick-on-Tweed, UK
France (Foreign Rights Agent): Lora Fountain Literary Agent, Paris, France
Germany, Austria & Switzerland: Gabriele Kern Publishers Services, Frankfurt-am-Main, Germany
India, Bangladesh, Nepal & Sri Lanka: Maya Publishers Pvt Ltd, New Delhi, India
Italy, Spain, Portugal, Greece & Gibraltar: Penny Padovani, London, UK
Mauritius, Kenya, Gambia, Botswana & Zimbabwe: Pat Bence, Export Sales Manager, David & Charles Ltd, Newton Abbot, UK
New Zealand: David Bateman Ltd, Auckland
Poland, Croatia, Hungary, Czech Republic, Romania, Slovak Republic, Yugoslavia, Bulgaria, Slovenia & Bosnia: Casba & Jackie Lengyel de Bagota, CLB Marketing Services, Budapest, Hungary
South Africa: Trinity Books CC, Randburg
USA & Canada: F & W Publications Ltd, Cincinnati, USA

2227

DAY ONE PUBLICATIONS
Ryelands Road, Leominster HR6 8NZ
Telephone: 01568 613740
Fax: 01568 611473
Email: info@dayone.co.uk
Web Site: http://www.dayone.co.uk

Director: John Roberts
Managers: Mark Roberts
Jim Holmes *(Marketing & Sales)*

Biography & Autobiography; Children's Books; Guide Books; Religion & Theology; Travel & Topography

New Titles: 32 (2007), 40 (2008)

ISBNs, Imprints & Series:
978 0 902548, 978 1 846250, 978 1 903087

Parent Company:
Day One Christian Ministries

Overseas Representation:
Canada: Sola Scriptura Ministries, Guelph, Ont
USA: Day One Christian Ministries (Inc), Greenville, SC

Book Trade Association Membership:
Christian Booksellers Convention (UK); CBA (USA)

2228

DEDALUS LTD
Langford Lodge, St Judith's Lane, Sawtry, Cambs PE28 5XE
Telephone: 01487 832382
Email: info@dedalusbooks.com
Web Site: http://www.dedalusbooks.com

Distribution, Warehouse & Invoicing:
Central Books Ltd, 99 Wallis Road, London E9 5LN
Telephone: 0845 458 9911
Fax: 0845 458 9912
Email: orders@centralbooks.com

UK Sales:
Turnaround Publisher Services Ltd, Unit 3, Olympia Trading Estate, Coburg Road, London N22 6TZ
Telephone: (020) 8829 3000

Directors: Robert Irwin *(Editorial)*
Juri Gabriel *(Chairman & Rights)*
Eric Lane *(Managing)*
Lindsay Thomas *(Marketing)*
Mike Mitchell *(Translations)*

Cookery, Wines & Spirits; Fiction; Gardening; Literature & Criticism

New Titles: 13 (2007), 14 (2008)
No of Employees: 2
Annual Turnover: £70,000

ISBNs, Imprints & Series:
Dedalus Euro Shorts
978 0 946626, 978 1 873982 Dedalus European Classics; Empire of the Senses; Europe 1992–2010; Modern English Fiction
978 1 903517 Dedalus Concept Books

Overseas Representation:
Australia & New Zealand: Peribo Pty Ltd, Mount Kuring-Gai, NSW, Australia
Canada: Disticor Book Division, Toronto, Ont
France, Belgium, Germany, Switzerland, Austria & Netherlands: Michael Geoghegan, London, UK
Spain, Portugal, Greece & Italy: Penny Padovani, London, UK
USA: SCB Distributors, Gardena, CA

Book Trade Association Membership:
IPG

2229

DELANCEY PRESS LTD
23 Berkeley Square, London W1J 6HE
Telephone: (020) 7665 6605
Email: delanceypress@aol.com
Web Site: http://www.delanceypress.co.uk

Managing Director: Tatiana Wilson *(Marketing)*
Finance: Jackie Naish
Sales & Marketing Manager: Amanda Rutherfurd
Editor: Alexandra Shelly

Children's Books; Fiction; Humour; Psychology & Psychiatry

New Titles: 1 (2007), 2 (2008)

ISBNs, Imprints & Series: 978 0 9539119

Book Trade Association Membership:
Publishers Association; BA; IPG

2230

DELTA ALPHA PUBLISHING LTD
19H John Spencer Square, London N1 2LZ
Telephone: (020) 7359 1822
Fax: (020) 7359 1822
Email: dap@deltaalpha.com
Web Site: http://www.deltaalpha.com

Director: Damien Abbott
Marketing Managers: Deborah Lloyd
John Knox

Law; Reference Books, Directories & Dictionaries

New Titles: 3 (2007), 1 (2008)
No of Employees: 3
Annual Turnover: £25,000

ISBNs, Imprints & Series: 978 0 9668946

Associated Companies:
USA: Delta Alpha Publishing

Overseas Representation:
Australia: Delta Alpha, Scarborough, Qld
USA: Port City Fulfilment, Kimball, MI

Book Trade Association Membership:
IPG; Publisher Marketing Association, USA; Australian PA

2231

RICHARD DENNIS PUBLICATIONS
The Old Chapel, Shepton Beauchamp, Ilminster, Somerset TA19 0LE
Telephone: 01460 240044
Fax: 01460 242009

Email:
books@richarddennispublications.com
Web Site: http://www.richarddennispublications.com

Production: Richard Dennis
Administration: Sharon Pearce
Accounts: Tracie Welch
Photographer: Magnus Dennis
Marketing: Buchan Dennis

Academic & Scholarly; Antiques & Collecting; Architecture & Design; Biography & Autobiography; Fine Art & Art History; History & Antiquarian; Illustrated & Fine Editions

New Titles: 2 (2007), 4 (2008)
No of Employees: 5

ISBNs, Imprints & Series:
978 0 903685, 978 0 9553741

Overseas Representation:
USA: Antique Collectors Club Ltd, Easthampton, MA

2232

DENOR PRESS LTD
PO Box 12913, London N12 8ZR
Telephone: (020) 8343 7368
Fax: (020) 8446 4504
Email: denor@dial.pipex.com
Web Site: http://www.denorpress.com

Directors: Lucille Leader *(Production & Editorial)*
  Dr Geoffrey Leader
Consultant/Accountant: Philip Woolfson
Marketing/Administration: Felicia Beder

Biography & Autobiography; Fiction; Medical (incl. Self Help & Alternative Medicine)

New Titles: 4 (2008)
No of Employees: 2

ISBNs, Imprints & Series: 978 0 9526056

Overseas Representation:
USA: Lightning Source

2233

J M DENT
[Imprint of The Orion Publishing Group Ltd]
Orion House, 5 Upper St Martins Lane, London WC2H 9EA
Telephone: (020) 7240 3444
Fax: (020) 7240 4822

Trade Counter & Warehouse:
Littlehampton Book Services Ltd,
Faraday Close, Durrington, Worthing,
West Sussex BN13 3RB
Telephone: 01903 828500
Fax: 01903 828625

Academic & Scholarly; Biography & Autobiography; Children's Books; Economics; Fiction; Gardening; History & Antiquarian; Law; Literature & Criticism; Music; Reference Books, Directories & Dictionaries; Scientific & Technical; Everyman classics

ISBNs, Imprints & Series:
978 0 460 J M Dent; Everyman Paperbacks

Parent Company:
The Orion Publishing Group Ltd

Overseas Representation:
see: The Orion Publishing Group Ltd, London, UK

2234

DIONYSIA PRESS LTD
7 Duddingston House Courtyard,
127 Milton Road West, Edinburgh
EH15 1JG

Director: Eve Smith
Marketing: Denise Smith *(Secretary)*
Editor: Thom Nairn

Literature & Criticism

New Titles: 5 (2007), 5 (2008)
No of Employees: 6

ISBNs, Imprints & Series: 978 1 903171

Distributor for:
Greece: Dionysia Press

Overseas Representation:
Greece: Dionysia Zervanou, Athens

Book Trade Association Membership:
Publishing Scotland

2235

DISCOVERY WALKING GUIDES LTD
10 Tennyson Close, Dallington,
Northampton NN5 7HJ
Web Site: http://www.walking.demon.co.uk

Company Secretary: David Brawn
Director: Ros Brawn

Atlases & Maps; Guide Books; Travel & Topography

New Titles: 6 (2007), 10 (2008)

ISBNs, Imprints & Series:
978 1 904946 Drive! Touring Maps; Tour & Trail Maps; Walk! Guide Books

Overseas Representation:
Canary Islands (Western): Garcia y Correa, Canary Islands, Spain
Madeira: J. R. Barata Su Lda, Madeira, Portugal
Spain: Map Iberia FeB SL, Avila

2236

*DONHEAD PUBLISHING LTD
Lower Coombe, Donhead St Mary,
Shaftesbury, Dorset SP7 9LY
Telephone: 01747 828422
Fax: 01747 828522
Email: enquiries@donhead.com
Web Site: http://www.donhead.com

Directors: Jill Pearce
  Chris Hall

Architecture & Design; Scientific & Technical; Building Conservation; Heritage & Museum Studies

ISBNs, Imprints & Series: 978 1 873394

Overseas Representation:
USA: Port City Fulfilment, Kimball, MI

Book Trade Association Membership:
IPG

2237

ASHLEY DRAKE PUBLISHING LTD
PO Box 733, Cardiff CF14 7ZY
Telephone: 07803 940867
Fax: 0870 705 2582
Email: post@ashleydrake.com
Web Site: http://www.ashleydrake.com

Distribution:
Gazelle Book Services, White Cross Mills, Hightown, Lancaster LA1 4XS
Telephone: 01524 68765
Fax: 01524 63232
Email: sales@gazellebooks.co.uk

Directors: Ashley Drake *(Managing)*
  Siwan Drake *(Company Secretary)*

Academic & Scholarly; Biography & Autobiography; Children's Books; Cookery, Wines & Spirits; History & Antiquarian; Languages & Linguistics; Literature & Criticism; Politics & World Affairs; Psychology & Psychiatry; Sports & Games; Theatre, Drama & Dance

New Titles: 3 (2008)
Annual Turnover: £30,000

ISBNs, Imprints & Series:
978 1 86057 Welsh Academic Press
978 1 874312 Hisarlik Press
978 1 899869 Gwasg Addysgol Cymru
978 1 899877 Y Ddraig Fach
978 1 902719 St David's Press (formerly Ashley Drake Publishing)
978 1 903532 Morgan Publishing
978 1 904609 Scandinavian Academic Press

Overseas Representation:
USA: International Specialized Book Services Inc, Portland, OR
Worldwide: Gazelle Drake Book Services, UK

2238

DRAMATIC LINES
PO Box 201, Twickenham TW2 5RQ
Telephone: (020) 8296 9502
Fax: (020) 8296 9503
Email: mail@dramaticlinespublishers.co.uk
Web Site: http://www.dramaticlines.co.uk

Managing Editor: John Nicholas
Sales, Marketing & Production: Heather Stephens
Development: Irene Palko

Children's Books; Educational & Textbooks; History & Antiquarian; Theatre, Drama & Dance

New Titles: 2 (2007), 3 (2008)

ISBNs, Imprints & Series:
978 0 952222, 978 0 953777

Book Trade Association Membership:
Publishers Association

2239

DREAMCATCHER PUBLISHING LTD
Honeysuckle Cottage,
4 Weaverhead Close, Thaxted, Essex
CM6 2PP
Telephone: 01371 831087
Email: juliaheron@btinternet.com
Web Site: http://www.dreamcatcherpublishing.com

Directors: Julia Heron *(Managing)*
  Jamie Musialek *(IT)*
  Caroline Hooper *(Publishing)*

Biography & Autobiography; Children's Books; Educational & Textbooks; Electronic (Educational); Fiction; Poetry; Science Fiction

ISBNs, Imprints & Series:
978 0 9544619 Storycatcher Books / children's fiction
978 0 9554992 Memorycatcher Books

Overseas Representation:
Canada: Martine Jacquot
China: David Zou / CNN, P. R. of China
USA: Pinnock & Co

2240

DREF WEN CYF/LTD
28 Church Road, Whitchurch, Cardiff
CF14 2EA
Telephone: (029) 2061 7860
Fax: (029) 2061 0507
Email: gwil@drefwen.com
Web Site: http://www.drefwen.com

Directors: Roger Boore
  Anne Boore
  Gwilym Boore
  Alun Boore
  Rhys Boore

Audio Books; Children's Books; Educational & Textbooks; Fiction; Welsh Language Learners

New Titles: 36 (2007), 50 (2008)
No of Employees: 4

ISBNs, Imprints & Series:
978 0 85596, 978 0 946962

Book Trade Association Membership:
Cwlwm Cyhoeddwyr Cymru (Union of Welsh Publishers)

2241

GERALD DUCKWORTH & CO LTD
90–93 Cowcross Street, London EC1M 6BF
Telephone: (020) 7490 7300
Fax: (020) 7490 0080
Email: info@duckworth-publishers.co.uk
Web Site: http://www.ducknet.co.uk

Distribution:
Grantham Book Services,
Isaac Newton Way,
Alma Park Industrial Estate, Grantham
NG31 9SD

Directors: Peter Mayer *(Owner & Managing)*
  Ray Davies *(Production)*
  Deborah Blake *(Editorial)*
Editor: Mary Morris *(Editorial)*
Manager: Suzannah Rich *(Publicity)*

Academic & Scholarly; Archaeology; Biography & Autobiography; Fiction; Fine Art & Art History; History & Antiquarian; Humour; Literature & Criticism; Politics & World Affairs; Religion & Theology; Science Fiction; Travel & Topography

ISBNs, Imprints & Series:
Ardis
978 0 7156
978 1 85399 Bristol Classical Press

Associated Companies:
Bristol Classical Press

Overseas Representation:
Australia & New Zealand (Duckworth): Tower Books Pty Ltd, Frenchs Forest, NSW, Australia
Canada: Publishers International Marketing, Dulles, VA, USA
Europe & Scandinavia: Bill Bailey Publishers Representatives, Newton Abbot, Devon, UK
Middle East & Indian Subcontinent: Publishers International Marketing, Storrington, UK
South Africa: Book Promotions Pty Ltd, Diep River
South East Asia & North East Asia: Publishers International Marketing, London, UK
USA: Books International Inc, Dulles, VA

2242

DUNEDIN ACADEMIC PRESS
Hudson House, 8 Albany Street, Edinburgh
EH1 3QB
Telephone: 0131 473 2397

Fax: 01250 870920
Email: mail@dunedinacademicpress.co.uk
Web Site: http://www.dunedinacademicpress.co.uk

Representation (UK):
Compass Academic Ltd,
The Barley Mow Centre,
10 Barley Mow Passage, Chiswick, London
W4 4PH
Telephone: (020) 8994 6477
Fax: (020) 8400 6132
Email: AS@compass-academic.co.uk

Distribution (excluding North America & Australasia):
Dunedin Academic Press, c/
o Turpin Distribution, Pegasus Drive,
Stratton Business Park, Biggleswade, Beds
SG18 8TQ
Telephone: 01767 604951
Fax: 01767 601640
Email: books@turpin-distribution.com

Consultant Editor: Dr Douglas Grant
Directors: Anthony Kinahan
 Norman Steven

Academic & Scholarly; Geography & Geology; History & Antiquarian; Music; Philosophy; Politics & World Affairs; Religion & Theology; Sociology & Anthropology

New Titles: 18 (2007), 20 (2008)

ISBNs, Imprints & Series: 978 1 903765

Overseas Representation:
Arab World & Iran: Dar Kreidieh, Beirut, Lebanon
Australasia: Inbooks, c/o James Bennett Pty Ltd, Belrose, NSW, Australia
Hong Kong & Macau: Transglobal Publishers Services Ltd, Hong Kong
India: Overseas Press India Pvt Ltd, New Delhi
Korea South, Taiwan & Philippines: Edwin Makabenta, Quezon City, Philippines
Malaysia, Singapore & Thailand: Inthanon Publishing, Bangkok, Thailand
North America: International Specialized Book Services Inc, Portland, OR, USA
Republic of Ireland (including Northern Ireland): Brookside Publishing Services, Dublin, Republic of Ireland
Scandinavia: Jan Norbye, Ølstykke, Denmark
Spain & Portugal: Chris Humphrys, Gaucin, Spain

Book Trade Association Membership:
Publishing Scotland

2243

*EAGLE PUBLISHING LTD
Unit 2, Atworth Business Estate, Atworth,
Wilts SN12 8SB
Telephone: 01225 899141
Fax: 01225 768811
Email: eaglepublishing@btconnect.com

Distributors:
IVP Books, Norton Street, Nottingham
NG7 3HR
Telephone: 0115 978 1054
Fax: 0115 942 2694
Web Site: http://www.ivpbooks.com

Distributors:
Airlift Book Co, 8 The Arena,
Mollison Avenue, Enfield, Middx EN3 7NL
Telephone: (020) 8804 0400

Managing Director: David Wavre

Religion & Theology; Colour gift book; Self-Help

ISBNs, Imprints & Series:
978 0 86347 Eagle

Overseas Representation:
Australia & South Africa: IVP Books, Nottingham, UK
New Zealand: Scripture Union Wholesale, Wellington
Republic of Ireland: Columba Book Service, Blackrock, Co Dublin

2244

EARTHSCAN
Dunstan House, 14A St Cross Street,
London EC1N 8XA
Telephone: (020) 7841 1930
Fax: (020) 7242 1474
Email: earthinfo@earthscan.co.uk
Web Site: http://www.earthscan.co.uk

Distribution:
Macmillan Distribution (MDL), Brunel Road,
Houndmills, Basingstoke, Hants RG21 6XS
Telephone: 01256 329242
Fax: 01256 842084
Email: orders@macmillan.co.uk

Executive Chairman: Edward Milford
Managing Director: Jonathan Sinclair Wilson
Production: Gina Mance
Head of Sales & Marketing: Veruschka Selbach

Academic & Scholarly; Agriculture; Architecture & Design; Atlases & Maps; Biology & Zoology; Economics; Educational & Textbooks; Electronic (Professional & Academic); Engineering; Environment & Development Studies; Geography & Geology; Industry, Business & Management; Law; Politics & World Affairs; Reference Books, Directories & Dictionaries; Scientific & Technical; Sociology & Anthropology; Transport

New Titles: 75 (2007), 95 (2008)
No of Employees: 18

ISBNs, Imprints & Series:
978 0 907383, 978 1 873936, 978 1 902916 James & James
978 1 84407, 978 1 85383 Earthscan

Overseas Representation:
Africa (excluding North & South Africa): Tony Moggach, InterMedia Africa Ltd (IMA), London, UK
Australia, New Zealand & Papua New Guinea: DA Information Services Pty Ltd, Mitcham, Vic, Australia
Canada: UBC Press, Georgetown, Ont
China & Hong Kong: Nicola Everitt, Access Asia Media Services, Shanghai, P. R. of China
India: Vinod Vasishtha, Viva Books, New Delhi
Japan: United Publishers Services Ltd, Tokyo
Korea: Se-Yung Jun, Information & Culture Korea (ICK), Seoul, Korea, South
Latin America & Caribbean: Ethan Atkin, Cranbury International LLC, Montpelier, VT, USA
Malaysia & Brunei: UBSD, Selangor, Malaysia
Middle East & North Africa: Zoe Kaviani, International Publishing Services (IPS) Middle East Ltd, Dubai, UAE
Pakistan, Afghanistan & Tajikistan: Book Bird Publishers Representatives, Lahore, Pakistan
Philippines: Megatexts Phil Inc, Cebu City
South Africa: Book Promotions (Pty) Ltd, Plumstead
Taiwan: Unifacmanu Trading Co Ltd, Taipei
USA: Stylus Publishing LLC, Herndon, VA

Book Trade Association Membership:
IPG

2245

ECO-LOGIC BOOKS
Mulberry House, 19 Maple Grove, Bath
BA2 3AF
Telephone: 01225 484472
Fax: 0871 522 7054
Email: books@eco-logicbooks.com
Web Site: http://www.eco-logicbooks.com

Senior Executive: Peter Andrews

Agriculture; Architecture & Design; Crafts & Hobbies; Environment & Development Studies; Gardening

New Titles: 2 (2007), 4 (2008)

ISBNs, Imprints & Series: 978 1 899233

Distributor for:
Common Ground; Verey & von Kanitz Rural Classics
Australia: Holmgren Design Services
USA: Alan C. Hood & Co Inc; Mole Publishing Co; Oasis Design; Post Carbon Publishing; Trucking Turtle Publishing

2246

*ECONOMIC & SOCIAL RESEARCH INSTITUTE
Whitaker Square, Sir John Rogerson's Quay,
Dublin 1, Republic of Ireland
Telephone: +353 (01) 863 2000
Fax: +353 (01) 863 2100
Email: admin@esri.ie
Web Site: http://www.esri.ie

Director: Prof. F. Ruane
Secretary: Gillian Davidson
Research Professors: J. D. Fitz Gerald (*Economics*)
 C. T. Whelan (*Sociology & Social Policy*)
 T. Callan (*Economics*)
 M. Wiley (*Health Services Research*)
 J. Williams (*Head of Survey Unit*)
 P. O'Connell (*Sociology*)
 B. Whelan (*Economics*)

Academic & Scholarly; Economics; Educational & Textbooks; Environment & Development Studies; Gender Studies; Mathematics & Statistics; Medical (incl. Self Help & Alternative Medicine); Sociology & Anthropology

ISBNs, Imprints & Series:
978 0 7070 Research Series

Book Trade Association Membership:
Association of Irish Learned Journals

2247

EDINBURGH UNIVERSITY PRESS
22 George Square, Edinburgh EH8 9LF
Telephone: 0131 650 4218
Fax: 0131 662 0053
Email: university.press@ed.ac.uk
Web Site: http://www.eup.ed.ac.uk

Trade Enquiries:
Marston Book Services, PO Box 269,
Abingdon, Oxon OX14 4SP
Telephone: 01235 465500
Fax: 01235 465555
Web Site: http://www.marston.co.uk

Chairman (Non-Executive): Ivon Asquith
Executive Board: Timothy Wright (*Chief Executive*)
 Jackie Jones (*Head of Publishing*)
 Ian Davidson (*Head of Production*)
 Jan Thomson (*Head of Finance*)
 Catriona Murray (*Head of Sales & Marketing*)
Managers: Claire Abel (*Rights & Co-Publications*)
 Wendy Gardner (*Marketing*)
 Anna Skinner (*Marketing*)
Sales Administrator & Digital Print Co-ordinator: Rebecca Mackenzie

Academic & Scholarly; Archaeology; Educational & Textbooks; Gender Studies; History & Antiquarian; Languages & Linguistics; Law; Literature & Criticism; Philosophy; Politics & World Affairs; Reference Books, Directories & Dictionaries; Religion & Theology; Sociology & Anthropology; American Studies; Botany & Environment; Celtic Studies; Cultural Studies, Media Studies; Islamic Studies; Scottish Studies

ISBNs, Imprints & Series:
978 0 7486, 978 0 85224 Edinburgh University Press
978 1 85331 Keele University Press
978 1 902930 Polygon @ Edinburgh

Parent Company:
University of Edinburgh

Overseas Representation:
Albania, Bosnia, Bulgaria, Croatia, Czech & Slovak Republics, Herzegovina, Hungary, Macedonia, Romania, Serbia, Slovenia, Yugoslav Republics & Israel: Contact Sales Department, Edinburgh, UK
Australia & New Zealand: UNIREPS University and Reference Publishers' Services, Sydney, NSW, Australia
Benelux: Kemper Conseil Publishing, Voorburg, Netherlands
Germany, Austria & Switzerland: SHS Publishers' Consultants and Representatives, Oranienberg, Germany
Greece: Charles Gibbes Associates, Louslitges, France
Hong Kong, Taiwan, Korea, Malaysia & Singapore: Taylor & Francis Asia Pacific, Singapore
India: Maya Publishers Pvt Ltd, New Delhi
Japan: United Publishers Services Ltd, Tokyo
Middle East: James & Lorin Watt Ltd, Publishing Consultants, Oxford, UK
Pakistan: Mohammad Dahir, Karachi
Scandinavia: Colin Flint Ltd, Harlow, UK
South Africa: Academic Marketing Services (Pty) Ltd, Craighall
Southern Europe (including Spain): Charles Gibbes Associates, London, UK
USA & Canada (most titles, enquiries): Columbia University Press, New York, USA
USA & Canada (most titles, orders): Columbia University Press, New York, USA

Book Trade Association Membership:
Publishers Association; CAPP; IPG; Publishing Scotland

2248

EDUCATIONAL PLANNING BOOKS LTD
PO Box 63, Hathersage, Hope Valley,
Derbyshire S32 1DJ
Telephone: 01433 651010
Fax: 01433 650000
Email: sales@epb-ltd.co.uk

Warehouse:
Bamford Works, Bamford, Hope Valley,
Derbyshire S33 0BH
Telephone: 01433 651010
Fax: 01433 650000
Email: sales@epb-ltd.co.uk
Web Site: http://www.edplanbooks.com

Managing Director: G. N. S. Garner

Educational & Textbooks

No of Employees: 8
Annual Turnover: £850,000

Book Trade Association Membership:
Publishers Association; EPC

2249

EGMONT UK LTD
239 Kensington High Street, London
W8 6SA
Telephone: (020) 7761 3500
Fax: (020) 7761 3510
Email: info@euk.egmont.com
Web Site: http://www.egmont.co.uk

Egmont Press & Sales Departments:
3rd Floor, Beaumont House,
Kensington Village, Avonmore Road,
London W14 8TS
Telephone: (020) 7605 6600
Fax: (020) 7605 6601

Senior Vice-President & UK Managing Director: Rob McMenemy
Chief Financial Officer: Carsten Moller
Directors: Gillian Laskier (Group Sales)
Cally Poplak (Press)
David Riley (Publishing)
Debbie Cook (Magazines)

Children's Books

New Titles: 535 (2007), 454 (2008)
No of Employees: 198
Annual Turnover: £45M

ISBNs, Imprints & Series:
978 0 416 Methuen
978 0 6035 Dean
978 0 7497 Mammoth
978 1 4052 Egmont

Parent Company:
Denmark: Egmont Fonden

Book Trade Association Membership:
Publishers Association; BA

2250

*ELAND PUBLISHING LTD
3rd Floor, 61 Exmouth Market, London
EC1R 4QL
Telephone: (020) 7833 0762
Fax: (020) 7833 4434
Email: info@travelbooks.co.uk
Web Site: http://www.travelbooks.co.uk

Trade Distribution:
Grantham Book Services,
Isaac Newton Way,
Alma Park Industrial Estate, Grantham,
Lincs NG31 9SD
Telephone: 01476 541080
Fax: 01476 541061
Email: orders@gbs.tbs-ltd.co.uk

Trade Representation (UK):
Publishers Group UK, 8 The Arena,
Mollison Avenue, Enfield, Middx EN3 7NL
Web Site: http://www.pguk.co.uk

Travel & Topography

ISBNs, Imprints & Series:
978 0 907871, 978 0 955010

Associated Companies:
UK: Baring & Rogerson; Sickle Moon Books

Overseas Representation:
Australia & New Zealand: UNIREPS
University and Reference Publishers'
Services, Sydney, NSW, Australia
Eastern Europe, Russia & Sub-Saharan
Africa: Tony Moggach, London, UK
France, Benelux, Scandinavia & Iceland:
Angell Eurosales, Berwick-on-Tweed, UK
Germany, Austria & Switzerland: Ted
Dougherty, London, UK
Italy, Spain, Portugal, Greece & Gibraltar:
Penny Padovani, London, UK
Mexico, Central & Southern America: David
Williams, InterMedia Americana (IMA)
Ltd, London, UK
Middle East, North Africa, Turkey & Iran:
Peter Ward Book Exports, London, UK

Thailand, Burma, Laos & Vietnam: Orchid
Press, Bangkok, Thailand
USA & Canada: Dufour Editions Inc, Chester
Springs, PA, USA

Book Trade Association Membership:
IPG

2251

EDWARD ELGAR PUBLISHING LTD
Glensanda House, Montpellier Parade,
Cheltenham, Glos GL50 1UA
Telephone: 01242 226934
Fax: 01242 262111
Email: info@e-elgar.co.uk
Web Site: http://www.e-elgar.co.uk

Distribution:
Marston Book Services Ltd, PO Box 269,
Abingdon, Oxon OX14 4YN
Telephone: 01235 465500
Fax: 01235 465555
Email: client@marston.co.uk
Web Site: http://www.marston.co.uk

Personnel Director & Secretary: Sandy Elgar
Managing Director: Edward Elgar
Senior Commissioning Editor: Francine O'Sullivan
Rights & Permissions: Jennie Hawden
Head of Editorial & Production Services: Julie Leppard
Marketing, Publicity & Sales: Hilary Quinn

Academic & Scholarly; Agriculture;
Economics; Educational & Textbooks;
Environment & Development Studies;
Industry, Business & Management; Law;
Reference Books, Directories & Dictionaries;
Transport

New Titles: 306 (2007), 280 (2008)
No of Employees: 50

ISBNs, Imprints & Series:
978 1 84064, 978 1 84376, 978 1 84542,
978 1 84720, 978 1 84844, 978 1 85278
978 1 85898

Associated Companies:
USA: Edward Elgar Publishing Inc

Overseas Representation:
Japan: United Publishers Services Ltd, Tokyo
North & South America: Edward Elgar
Publishing Inc, Northampton, MA, USA
Singapore, Malaysia, Thailand, Indonesia,
Philippines, Brunei, Vietnam, Myanmar,
Laos & Cambodia: Taylor & Francis Asia
Pacific, Singapore

2252

ELLIOTT & THOMPSON
27 John Street, London WC1N 2BX
Telephone: (020) 7831 5011
Fax: (020) 7831 5011
Email: gmo73@dial.pipex.com
Web Site: http://www.elliottthompson.com

Directors: Brad Thompson
Lorne Forsyth
Anna Navidski

Children's Books; Fiction; Fine Art & Art
History; History & Antiquarian; Humour;
Literature & Criticism; Military & War;
Music; Poetry; Travel & Topography

New Titles: 6 (2007), 8 (2008)
No of Employees: 2
Annual Turnover: £75,000

ISBNs, Imprints & Series:
978 1 904027 Gold Editions; Spitfire;
Young Spitfire

Distributor for:
Al Madad Foundation

Book Trade Association Membership:
IPG

2253

ELM PUBLICATIONS
Seaton House, Kings Ripton, Huntingdon
PE28 2NJ
Telephone: 01487 773238
Fax: 01487 773359
Email: elm@elm-training.co.uk
Web Site: http://www.elm-training.co.uk

Managing Director: Sheila Ritchie (Home & Export Sales)
Managers: Duncan Ritchie (IT Director/ Secretary)
Jacqueline Wieczovek (Sales)

Educational & Textbooks; Electronic
(Educational); Industry, Business &
Management; Transport; Travel &
Topography; Training

New Titles: 12 (2007), 10 (2008)
No of Employees: 4

ISBNs, Imprints & Series:
978 0 946139, 978 0 9505828, 978 1 85450

Parent Company:
Elm Consulting Ltd

Book Trade Association Membership:
BA

2254

ELSEVIER LTD
The Boulevard, Langford Lane, Kidlington,
Oxford OX5 1GB
Telephone: 01865 843000
Fax: 01865 853010
Email: initial.surname@elsevier.com
Web Site: http://www.elsevier.com

Also at:
Elsevier, Trends,
Current Opinion and Academic Press
imprints, 84 Theobald's Road, London
WC1X 8RR
Telephone: (020) 7611 4000
Fax: (020) 7611 4501

Also at:
Mosby & W. B. Saunders imprints,
32 Jamestown Road, London NW1 7BY
Telephone: (020) 7424 4200
Fax: (020) 7424 4431

Also at:
Churchill Livingstone imprint,
20–22 East Street, Edinburgh EH7 4BQ
Telephone: 0131 524 1700
Fax: 0131 524 1800

Managing Directors: A. F. Moon
(International Director, Global Real Estate
& Corporate Services)
Jim Donohue (Book Publishing (S & T))
Jose Wehnes (Health Sciences
International)
Directors: L. Pierce (Production)
L. Waite (Marketing)
Helen Gainford (Global Rights)

Academic & Scholarly; Chemistry;
Educational & Textbooks; Medical (incl. Self
Help & Alternative Medicine); Scientific &
Technical

ISBNs, Imprints & Series:
Harcourt Ltd; Harcourt Health Sciences;
Harcourt Publishers Ltd; Scutari Press
978 0 08 Elsevier Advanced Technology;
Elsevier Applied Science; Elsevier Trends
Journals; Pergamon
978 0 12 Academic Press

978 0 443 Churchill-Livingstone
978 0 7020 W. B. Saunders
978 0 7243 Mosby

Parent Company:
Netherlands: Elsevier BV

Associated Companies:
USA: Elsevier Inc

Overseas Representation:
Australia: Elsevier Australia, Marrickville, NSW
Brazil: Editora Campus Ltda, Rio de Janeiro
India: Elsevier India, New Delhi
Japan: Elsevier Japan, Tokyo
Korea: Elsevier, Seoul, Korea, South
Pakistan: Rae & Sons Publishers
Representatives, Lahore

Book Trade Association Membership:
Publishers Association; IGSMTP; STM

2255

EMERALD GROUP PUBLISHING LTD
Howard House, Wagon Lane, Bingley,
West Yorkshire BD16 1WA
Telephone: 01274 777700
Web Site: http://www.emeraldinsight.com

Chairman: Martin Fojt
Chief Executive Officer: John Peters
Head of Editorial: Niki Haunch
Head of Strategic Marketing: Moyna Keenan

Academic & Scholarly; Accountancy &
Taxation; Archaeology; Computer Science;
Economics; Educational & Textbooks;
Electronic (Educational); Electronic
(Professional & Academic); Engineering;
Environment & Development Studies;
Industry, Business & Management;
Languages & Linguistics; Philosophy;
Psychology & Psychiatry; Sociology &
Anthropology; Vocational Training &
Careers

New Titles: 8 (2007), 9 (2008)
No of Employees: 200
Annual Turnover: £24M

2256

ENCYCLOPAEDIA BRITANNICA (UK) LTD
2nd Floor, Unity Wharf, 13 Mill Street,
London SE1 2BH
Telephone: (020) 7500 7800
Fax: (020) 7500 7578
Email: pmcguire@britannica.co.uk
Web Site: http://www.britannica.co.uk

Distributors:
Encyclopaedia Britannica (UK) Ltd, Units I/
K, Paddock Wood Distribution Centre,
Paddock Wood, Tonbridge, Kent TN12 6UU
Telephone: 01892 839814
Fax: 01892 837272
Email: britannica@combook.co.uk

Director: Ian Grant (Managing)
Vice-President: Jane Helps (Operations)
Managers: Patrick McGuire (Print Sales)
Lotta Farley (CD Sales)
Christine Hodgson (Direct Marketing)
Nick Harris (Online Sales)
Chrysandra Halstead (Marketing Co-ordinator)

Atlases & Maps; Children's Books;
Electronic (Educational); Reference Books,
Directories & Dictionaries

ISBNs, Imprints & Series:
978 0 85229, 978 1 59339

Parent Company:
USA: Encyclopaedia Britannica Inc

Distributor for:
France: Encyclopaedia Universalis

Overseas Representation:
Germany, Austria, Switzerland & Netherlands: Ted Dougherty, London, UK
Italy: Mare Nostrum Publishing Consultants, Rome
Scandinavia: Colin Flint Ltd, Harlow, UK
South-East Europe, North Africa & Middle East (excluding GCC): Avicenna Partnership, Oxford, UK
Spain & Portgual: Iberian Book Services, Madrid, Spain
Sub-Saharan Africa (excluding South Africa), Eastern Europe (excluding Russia): InterMedia Americana (IMA) Ltd, London, UK

Book Trade Association Membership:
IPG

2257

ENERGY INSTITUTE
61 New Cavendish Street, London
W1G 7AR
Telephone: (020) 7467 7100

Publishing Manager: Erica Sciolti

Academic & Scholarly; Chemistry; Electronic (Professional & Academic); Engineering; Environment & Development Studies; Industry, Business & Management; Reference Books, Directories & Dictionaries; Scientific & Technical

ISBNs, Imprints & Series: 978 0 85293

Book Trade Association Membership:
Association of Learned & Professional Society Publishers

2258

ENGLISH HERITAGE
Kemble Drive, Swindon SN2 2GZ
Telephone: 01793 414619
Fax: 01793 414769
Email: robin.taylor@english-heritage.org.uk
Web Site: http://www.english-heritage.org.uk

Distributor:
Central Books, 99 Wallis Road, London
E9 5LN
Telephone: (020) 8986 4854
Fax: (020) 8533 5821
Email: bill@centralbooks.com

Postal Sales:
c/o Gillards, Trident Works, Temple Cloud, Bristol BS39 5AZ
Telephone: 01761 452966
Fax: 01761 453408
Email: ehsales@gillards.com

Managing Editor: Robin Taylor
Head of Publishing: John Hudson
Sales & Publicity Manager: Clare Blick

Academic & Scholarly; Archaeology; Architecture & Design; Children's Books; Educational & Textbooks; Guide Books; History & Antiquarian; Military & War; Scientific & Technical; Travel & Topography; Conservation (UK)

New Titles: 20 (2007)

ISBNs, Imprints & Series:
978 1 84802, 978 1 85074, 978 1 873592, 978 1 905624

Overseas Representation:
Australia: James Bennett Pty Ltd, Belrose, NSW
USA: The David Brown Book Co, Oakville, CT

Book Trade Association Membership:
Associated of Learned & Professional Society Publishers

2259

ENITHARMON PRESS
26B Caversham Road, London NW5 2DU
Telephone: (020) 7482 5967
Fax: (020) 7284 1787
Email: books@enitharmon.co.uk
Web Site: http://www.enitharmon.co.uk

Warehouse:
Central Books, 99 Wallis Road, London
E9 5LN
Telephone: (020) 8986 4854
Fax: (020) 8533 5821

Director: Stephen Stuart-Smith
Managers: Jacqueline Gabbitas *(Marketing)*
Satnam Kanvar *(Finance)*
Isabel Britten *(Editorial)*

Fiction; Illustrated & Fine Editions; Literature & Criticism; Poetry

ISBNs, Imprints & Series:
978 1 870612, 978 1 900564, 978 1 904634

Associated Companies:
Enitharmon Editions Ltd

Overseas Representation:
USA & Canada: Dufour Editions Inc, Chester Springs, PA, USA

Book Trade Association Membership:
IPG

2260

EQUINOX PUBLISHING LTD
Unit 6, The Village, 101 Amies Street, London SW11 2JW
Telephone: (020) 7350 2836
Fax: (020) 7350 2836
Email: jjoyce@equinoxpub.com
Web Site: http://www.equinoxpub.com

Distribution:
Marston Book Services Ltd, PO Box 269, Abingdon, Oxon OX14 4YN
Telephone: 01235 465521
Fax: 01235 465555
Email: trade.orders@marston.co.uk

Publisher: Janet Joyce
Editorial & Rights: Valerie Hall

Academic & Scholarly; Archaeology; Biography & Autobiography; Cookery, Wines & Spirits; Educational & Textbooks; Electronic (Professional & Academic); Gender Studies; History & Antiquarian; Languages & Linguistics; Music; Philosophy; Reference Books, Directories & Dictionaries; Religion & Theology; Sociology & Anthropology

New Titles: 35 (2007), 40 (2008)
No of Employees: 2
Annual Turnover: £360,000

ISBNs, Imprints & Series:
978 1 84553, 978 1 904768

Distributor for:
J R Collis Publications; Contact Pastoral Trust

Overseas Representation:
Australia & New Zealand: Eleanor Brasch Enterprises, Artarmon, NSW, Australia
China, Hong Kong & Taiwan: Ian Taylor & Associates, P. R. of China
Europe: Andrew Durnell Marketing Ltd, Tunbridge Wells, UK
India: Maya Publishers Pvt Ltd, New Delhi
Japan: United Publishers Services Ltd, Tokyo
North America: The David Brown Book Co, Oakville, CT, USA
Singapore, Malaysia & Brunei: Publishers Marketing Services Pte Ltd, Singapore
South Africa, Botswana, Lesotho, Namibia, Swaziland & Zimbabwe: Chris Reinders, The African Moon Press, Kelvin, South Africa

Book Trade Association Membership:
IPG; Association of Learned & Professional Society Publishers (UK Serials Interest Group)

2261

THE ERSKINE PRESS
The White House, Sandfield Lane, Eccles, Norwich, Norfolk NR16 2PB
Telephone: 01953 887277
Fax: 01953 888361
Email: erskpres@aol.com
Web Site: http://www.erskine-press.com

Director: Crispin de Boos
Commissioning Editor: Lesley de Boos

Academic & Scholarly; Biography & Autobiography; History & Antiquarian; Illustrated & Fine Editions; Medical (incl. Self Help & Alternative Medicine); Military & War; Natural History; Travel & Topography

New Titles: 4 (2007), 9 (2008)
Annual Turnover: £70,000

ISBNs, Imprints & Series:
978 0 948285, 978 1 85297 Archival Facsimiles; Erskine Press

Parent Company:
jack afrika Publishing Ltd

Book Trade Association Membership:
IPG

2262

ETHICS INTERNATIONAL PRESS LTD
[publishes for Centre for Business & Public Sector Ethics]
St Andrews Castle,
St Andrews Street South, Bury St Edmunds, Suffolk IP33 3PH
Telephone: 01223 357458
Fax: 01223 303598
Email: info@ethicspress.com
Web Site: http://www.ethicspress.com

Director: Dr Rosamund Thomas
Managers: Robert Willis *(Marketing)*
Christopher Thomas *(General)*

Academic & Scholarly; Educational & Textbooks; Electronic (Educational); Electronic (Professional & Academic); Environment & Development Studies; Industry, Business & Management; Politics & World Affairs; Vocational Training & Careers

ISBNs, Imprints & Series:
978 1 871891 Teaching Ethics (Book series)

Associated Companies:
Ethics International MultiMedia Ltd

Book Trade Association Membership:
Publishers Association

2263

EUROMONITOR INTERNATIONAL PLC
60–61 Britton Street, London EC1M 5UX
Telephone: (020) 7251 8024
Fax: (020) 7608 3149
Email: info@euromonitor.com
Web Site: http://www.euromonitor.com

Directors: Trevor Fenwick *(Managing)*
Robert Senior *(Chairman)*
David Gudgin

Economics; Industry, Business & Management; Reference Books, Directories & Dictionaries

ISBNs, Imprints & Series:
978 0 86338, 978 1 84264

Associated Companies:
Dubai: Euromonitor International
Lithuania: Euromonitor International
P. R. of China: Euromonitor International (Shanghai) Co Ltd
Singapore: Euromonitor International (Asia) Pte Ltd
USA: Euromonitor International Inc

Book Trade Association Membership:
Data Publishers Association; European Association of Directory Publishers

2264

EVANGELICAL PRESS & SERVICES LTD
Grange Close, Faverdale,
North Industrial Estate, Darlington DL3 0PH
Telephone: 01325 380232
Fax: 01325 466153
Email: sales@evangelicalpress.org
Web Site: http://www.evangelicalpress.org

Managers: A. L. Gosling *(General)*
P. Cooper *(Production)*
A. Williamson *(Senior Editor)*

Academic & Scholarly; Archaeology; Biography & Autobiography; History & Antiquarian; Reference Books, Directories & Dictionaries; Religion & Theology

New Titles: 24 (2007), 24 (2008)
No of Employees: 15
Annual Turnover: £950,000

ISBNs, Imprints & Series:
978 0 85234 Evangelical Press
978 0 946462 Grace Publications
978 0 95279 Carey Publications
978 1 85049 Bryntirion Press

Associated Companies:
France: Europresse SARL

Distributor for:
Bryntirion Press; Carey Publications; Free Presbyterian Publishing; Gospel Standard Publications; Knox Press; Sovereign Publications
Canada: Joshua Press
USA: Baker Book House; Calvary Press; Hendricksen Publishers; P & R Publishing; Pilgrim Publications; Reformation Heritage Books; Reformation Trust; Solid Ground Publications

Book Trade Association Membership:
Christian Booksellers Association; Evangelical Christian Publishers Association

2265

EVANS PUBLISHING GROUP
2A Portman Mansions, Chiltern Street, London W1U 6NR
Telephone: (020) 7487 0920
Fax: (020) 7487 0921
Email: sales@evansbrothers.co.uk
Web Site: http://www.evansbooks.co.uk

Trade Office:
Zero to Ten, Suite 1.3, Coomb House,
7 St John's Road, Isleworth, Middx
TW7 6NH
Telephone: (020) 8758 9777
Fax: (020) 8758 9888
Web Site: http://www.evansbooks.co.uk

Directors: Stephen Pawley *(Managing)*

Brian Jones *(International)*
Andrew Macmillan *(UK Sales)*
UK Publisher: Ms Su Swallow
Accountant: Danny Daly
Managers: Ms Alex Evans *(Marketing)*
Ms Jenny Mulvanny *(Production)*
Ms Britta Martins-Simon *(Foreign Rights)*
Jason McGovern *(Export Sales)*

Children's Books; Educational & Textbooks

ISBNs, Imprints & Series:
978 0 237 Evans
978 1 84089 Zero to Ten
978 1 84234 Cherrytree

Associated Companies:
Kenya: Evans Brothers (Kenya) Ltd
Nigeria: Evans Brothers (Nigeria Publishers) Ltd
Sierra Leone: Evans Brothers (Sierra Leone) Ltd

Book Trade Association Membership:
Publishers Association; EPC

2266

EVERYMAN'S LIBRARY
Northburgh House, 10 Northburgh Street, London EC1V 0AT
Telephone: (020) 7566 6350
Fax: (020) 7490 3708
Email: books@everyman.uk.com

Trade Orders & Enquiries:
GBS, Isaac Newton Way,
Alma Park Industrial Estate, Grantham
NG31 9SD
Telephone: 01476 541000
Fax: 01476 541061

Directors: David Campbell *(Managing)*
Managers: Clémence Jacquinet *(Editorial (Travel Guides))*
Jane Holloway *(Editorial (Classics))*

Academic & Scholarly; Children's Books; Fiction; Guide Books; Illustrated & Fine Editions; Literature & Criticism; Philosophy; Travel & Topography

New Titles: 18 (2007), 15 (2008)

ISBNs, Imprints & Series:
Everyman Children's Classics; Everyman Classics; Everyman Guides; Everyman Pocket Classics; Everyman Pocket Poets; Everyman Wodehouse

Parent Company:
USA: Alfred A. Knopf [(a division of Random House US)]

Overseas Representation:
Worldwide (excluding North America): Random House International (Everyman's Library), UK

2267

EX LIBRIS PRESS
16A New St John's Road, St Helier, Jersey JE2 3LD
Telephone: 01534 780488
Fax: 01534 780488
Email: roger.jones@ex-librisbooks.co.uk
Web Site: http://www.ex-librisbooks.co.uk

Stockists:
Gardners Books, 1 Whittle Drive,
Willingdon Drove, Eastbourne, East Sussex
BN23 6QH
Telephone: 01323 521777
Fax: 01323 521666

Proprietor: Roger Jones

Archaeology; Biography & Autobiography; Cookery, Wines & Spirits; Gardening; Geography & Geology; Guide Books; History & Antiquarian; Natural History; Nautical; Poetry; Transport; Travel & Topography

New Titles: 4 (2007), 4 (2008)

ISBNs, Imprints & Series:
ELSP (Ex Libris Self Publishing)
978 0 948578, 978 0 9506563, 978 1 903341 Seaflower Books
978 1 906641

2268

*EXECUTIVE GRAPEVINE INTERNATIONAL LTD
New Barnes Mill, Cottonmill Lane,
St Albans AL1 2HA
Telephone: 01727 844335
Fax: 01727 844779
Email: a.dalby@executive-grapevine.co.uk
Web Site: http://www.askgrapevine.com

Chief Executive Officer: Helen Barrett
Managing Director: Anna Weston
Head of Sales & Marketing: Sabrina Ponte
Head of Business Services: Andrew Dalby

Industry, Business & Management; Reference Books, Directories & Dictionaries; Human Resources; Talent Management

ISBNs, Imprints & Series:
978 1 903530, 978 1 903550

Book Trade Association Membership:
Data Publishers Association

2269

EXLEY PUBLICATIONS LTD
16 Chalk Hill, Watford, Herts WD19 4BG
Telephone: 01923 250505 & 248328
Fax: 01923 818733
Email: sales@exleypublications.co.uk
Web Site: http://www.helenexleygiftbooks.com

Warehouse:
Trade Counter, The Airfield, Norwich Road,
Mendlesham, Suffolk IP14 5NA
Telephone: 01449 766629
Fax: 01449 767122

Directors: Helen M. Exley *(Managing & Editorial)*
Richard A. Exley *(Finance & Production)*
Lincoln Exley *(Associate)*
Sonya Greenhough *(Foreign Rights)*
Managers: Charlotte Markey *(Head of UK Sales)*
Michael Illingworth *(Export Sales)*
Keith Allen-Jones *(Foreign Rights)*

Educational & Textbooks; Humour; Gift Books

ISBNs, Imprints & Series:
978 1 84634, 978 1 85015, 978 1 86187, 978 1 90513

Associated Companies:
France: Exley SA
USA: Exley Giftbooks

Overseas Representation:
Australia: Card & Paper House; New Holland Publishers Pty Ltd, French's Forest, NSW
Canada: Pierre Belvedere, Montreal
Hong Kong: Pacific Century Distribution Ltd
India: Maya Publishers Pvt Ltd, New Delhi
Israel: Astra Agency, Jerusalem
Korea: Union Enterprise Co Ltd, Seoul, Korea, South
Lebanon: Librarie Samir Editeur, Beirut
Malta: Audio Visual Centre Ltd, Sliema
New Zealand: David Bateman Ltd, Auckland

Pakistan: Mackwin & Co, Karachi
Philippines: Balatbat & Sons International, Filinvest
Republic of Ireland: Island Publications Ltd, Dublin
Singapore: Cards n Such Pte Ltd
Southern Africa: Struik Book Distributors, Johannesburg, South Africa
Spain: Editorial Edaf SA, Madrid
Vietnam: Fahasa Companie, Ho Chi Minh City

Book Trade Association Membership:
IPG

2270

EXPRESS NEWSPAPERS
The Northern and Shell Building,
10 Lower Thames Street, London EC3R 6AE
Telephone: 0871 520 7887
Fax: 0871 434 7966
Email: fiona.tucker@express.co.uk
Web Site: http://www.express.co.uk

Head of Books Publishing: Fiona Tucker

Atlases & Maps; Biography & Autobiography; Crime; Do-It-Yourself; Gardening; Guide Books; Health & Beauty; Humour; Illustrated & Fine Editions; Poetry; Reference Books, Directories & Dictionaries; Sports & Games; Transport; Travel & Topography

New Titles: 16 (2007), 15 (2008)

ISBNs, Imprints & Series: 978 0 85079

Parent Company:
Northern and Shell Media

Overseas Representation:
Canada: Canadian Manda Group, Toronto, Ont
India: Wilco International

2271

*EYE BOOKS LTD
8 Peacock Yard, Iliffe Street, London SE17 3LH
Telephone: 0845 450 8870
Email: books @ eye-books.com
Web Site: http://www.eye-books.com

Finance:
Colemore Farm, Colemore Green,
Bridgnorth, Shropshire WV16 4ST
Telephone: 01746 766665
Fax: 01746 766665
Email: books@eye-books.com

Directors: D. Hiscocks *(Managing)*
W. B. Hiscocks *(Finance)*

Biography & Autobiography; Humour; Military & War; Photography; Travel & Topography; Mind Body Spirit

ISBNs, Imprints & Series:
978 0 9530575, 978 1 9030700, 978 1 9030701, 978 1 9030702, 978 1 9030703, 978 1 9030704

Overseas Representation:
Africa: Zytek, Johannesburg, South Africa
Australia & New Zealand: Bookwise International, Adelaide, SA, Australia

Book Trade Association Membership:
IPG

2272

*FABER & FABER LTD
3 Queen Square, London WC1N 3AU
Telephone: (020) 7465 0045
Fax: (020) 7465 0034
Email: mailbox@faber.co.uk
Web Site: http://www.faber.co.uk

Accounts:
16 Burnt Mill, Elizabeth Way, Harlow, Essex CM20 2HX
Fax: 01279 417366
Web Site: http://www.faber.co.uk

Distribution & Orders:
TBS Ltd, Colchester Road, Frating Green, Colchester, Essex CO7 7DW
Telephone: 01206 256004
Fax: 01206 255912

Chief Executive: Stephen Page
Directors: Walter Donohue *(Publisher & Film)*
Valerie Eliot
Julian Loose *(Editorial, Fiction & Non-Fiction)*
Lee Brackstone
David Tebbutt *(Finance)*
Nigel Marsh *(Production)*
Jason Cooper *(Rights)*
Will Atkinson *(Sales)*
Rachel Alexander *(Publicity)*
Editorial: Paul Keegan *(Poetry)*
Julia Wells *(Children's)*
Dinah Wood *(Plays)*
Belinda Matthews *(Music)*

Biography & Autobiography; Children's Books; Cinema, Video, TV & Radio; Cookery, Wines & Spirits; Fiction; Literature & Criticism; Music; Poetry; Politics & World Affairs; Theatre, Drama & Dance

ISBNs, Imprints & Series: 978 0 571

Associated Companies:
USA: Faber & Faber Inc

Distributor for:
De la Mare Publishing Ltd; Sanctuary Publishing; Screenpress Publishing
USA: Faber & Faber Inc

Overseas Representation:
Argentina, Bermuda, Bolivia, Brazil, Central America, Chile, Columbia, Ecuador, French West Indies, Jamaica, Mexico, Paraguay, Peru, Uruguay & Venezuela: InterMedia Americana (IMA) Ltd, London, UK
Asia (including Japan, Korea, Taiwan & Hong Kong): Julian Ashton, Sevenoaks, Kent, UK
Australia: Allen & Unwin Pty Ltd, Crows Nest, NSW
Canada: Penguin Books Canada, Toronto, Ont
Central Europe, Netherlands, Belgium, Luxembourg, Switzerland & Scandinavia: Bunmi Oke, Faber & Faber, London, UK
Eastern Europe (excluding Russia & Baltic States): Csaba Lengyel de Bagota, Budapest, Hungary
France, Germany & Austria: Patrick Keogh, Faber & Faber, London, UK
India: Penguin Books India, New Delhi
Italy: Penguin Italia srl, Corsico, Milan
Middle East (including Israel & Iran), North Africa, Malta & Turkey: Peter Ward Book Exports, London, UK
New Zealand: Allen & Unwin Pty Ltd, Auckland
Pakistan: Faber & Faber, London, UK
Republic of Ireland: Gill Hess Ltd, Skerries, Co Dublin
Singapore & Malaysia: Penguin Singapore, Singapore
Southern Africa: Book Promotions Pty Ltd, Cape Town, South Africa
Spain & Portugal: Penguin Spain, Madrid, Spain
Thailand, Cambodia, Laos, Vietnam & Myanmar: Keith Hardy, Hardy Bigfoss International Co Ltd, Bangkok, Thailand
USA: Faber & Faber Inc, A Division of Farrer, Strauss & Giroux, New York

Book Trade Association Membership:
Publishers Association

2273

FABIAN SOCIETY
11 Dartmouth Street, London SW1H 9BN
Telephone: (020) 7227 4900
Fax: (020) 7976 7153
Email: info@fabian-society.org.uk
Web Site: http://www.fabian-society.org.uk

General Secretary: Sunder Katwala
Sales: Margaret McGillen
Editorial Director: Tom Hampson

Academic & Scholarly; Economics; Environment & Development Studies; Philosophy; Politics & World Affairs

ISBNs, Imprints & Series:
978 0 7163 Fabian Pamphlet

Associated Companies:
NCLC Publishers Ltd

Distributor for:
NCLC Publishers Ltd

Book Trade Association Membership:
BA

2274

FACET PUBLISHING
7 Ridgmount Street, London WC1E 7AE
Telephone: (020) 7255 0590
Fax: (020) 7255 0591
Email: info@facetpublishing.co.uk
Web Site: http://www.facetpublishing.co.uk

Warehouse:
Bookpoint Ltd, 130 Milton Park, Abingdon, Oxon OX14 4SB
Telephone: 01235 827702
Fax: 01235 827703
Email: orders@bookpoint.co.uk

Managing Director: John Woolley
Managers: Kathryn Beecroft *(Production)*
Rohini Ramachandran *(Sales)*
Lena Stuart *(Marketing)*
Publisher: Helen Carley
Typesetter: June York
Commissioning Editor: Louise Le Bas

Academic & Scholarly; Bibliography & Library Science; Educational & Textbooks; Electronic (Professional & Academic); Reference Books, Directories & Dictionaries

ISBNs, Imprints & Series:
978 0 85365, 978 1 85604 Clive Bingley; Facet Publishing; Library Association Publishing

Parent Company:
CILIP [Chartered Institute of Library and Information Professionals]

Overseas Representation:
Australia & New Zealand: Inbooks, c/o James Bennett Pty Ltd, Belrose, NSW, Australia
Canada & USA: Neal-Schuman Publishers Inc, New York, NY, USA
India: Book Marketing Services, Chennai
Japan: United Publishers Services Ltd, Tokyo
Middle East: International Publishing Services (IPS) Middle East Ltd, Dubai, UAE
South East Asia: Taylor & Francis Asia Pacific, Singapore
Spain & Portugal: Iberian Book Services, Madrid, Spain

Book Trade Association Membership:
Publishers Association; CAPP; IPG

2275

FAMILY PUBLICATIONS
Denis Riches House, 66 Sandford Lane, Kennington, Oxford OX1 5RP
Telephone: 0845 0500 879
Fax: 01865 321325
Email: sales@familypublications.co.uk
Web Site: http://www.familypublications.co.uk

Managing Director: Colin Mason

Biography & Autobiography; Religion & Theology

New Titles: 11 (2007), 12 (2008)
No of Employees: 8
Annual Turnover: £330,000

ISBNs, Imprints & Series: 978 1 871217

Distributor for:
USA: Ascension Press; Bethlehem Books; Ignatius Press; William H. Sadlier Inc

Overseas Representation:
Australia: Freedom Publishing, North Melbourne, Vic

Book Trade Association Membership:
BA

2276

A. & A. FARMAR
78 Ranelagh Village, Dublin 6, Republic of Ireland
Telephone: +353 (01) 496 3625
Fax: +353 (01) 497 0107
Email: afarmar@iol.ie
Web Site: http://www.farmarbooks.com

Trade Orders (Republic of Ireland):
Columba Mercier Distribution Ltd, 55a Spruce Avenue, Stillorgan Industrial Park, Blackrock, Co Dublin, Republic of Ireland
Telephone: +353 (01) 294 2560
Fax: +353 (01) 294 2564

Editorial: Anna Farmar
Production: Tony Farmar

Cookery, Wines & Spirits; History & Antiquarian; Irish business & organisational histories

ISBNs, Imprints & Series:
978 1 899047, 978 1 906353

Overseas Representation:
UK (Trade Orders): Central Books Ltd, London, UK

Book Trade Association Membership:
CLÉ (Irish PA)

2277

FEATHER BOOKS
P O Box 438, Shrewsbury SY3 0WN
Telephone: 01743 872177
Fax: 01743 872177
Email: john@waddysweb.freeuk.com
Web Site: http://www.waddysweb.freeuk.com

Director: Revd John Waddington-Feather *(Sales & Marketing)*
Managers: Sheila Waddington-Feather *(Production)*
Paul Evans *(Sub-Editor, Production)*
Tony Reavill *(Recording & Drama Producer)*
David Grundy *(Music Director & Editor)*
Anna Waddington-Feather *(Public Relations & Sub-Editor)*
Janet Evans *(Sub-Editor)*

Academic & Scholarly; Audio Books; Children's Books; Crime; Fiction; Humour; Literature & Criticism; Music; Poetry; Religion & Theology; Theatre, Drama & Dance

New Titles: 33 (2007), 30 (2008)

ISBNs, Imprints & Series:
978 0 947718, 978 1 84175 Feather Books Drama Series
978 1 84175 Christianity & Literature Series; Feather Books Biography Series; Feather Books Poetry Series

Associated Companies:
Moorside Words & Music

2278

FHG GUIDES LTD
Abbey Mill Business Centre, Seedhill, Paisley PA1 1TJ
Telephone: 0141 887 0428
Fax: 0141 889 7204
Email: admin@fhguides.co.uk
Web Site: http://www.holidayguides.com

Book Trade Representative:
Christopher Halliday, Kuperard Publishers, 59 Hutton Grove, London N12 8DS
Telephone: (020) 8446 2440
Fax: (020) 8446 2441
Email: christopher@kuperard.co.uk

Publishing Director: G. Pratt

Guide Books; Sports & Games

New Titles: 11 (2007), 10 (2008)

ISBNs, Imprints & Series: 978 1 85055

Parent Company:
Kuperard Publishers

Book Trade Association Membership:
Periodical Publishers Association

2279

FINDHORN PRESS LTD
305a The Park, Findhorn, Forres, Moray IV36 3TE
Telephone: 01309 690582
Fax: 01309 690036
Email: info@findhornpress.com
Web Site: http://www.findhornpress/

Publisher: Thierry Bogliolo
Managers: Carol Shaw *(Marketing & Publicity)*
Sabine Weeke *(Rights, Editorial)*

Animal Care & Breeding; Cookery, Wines & Spirits; Guide Books; Health & Beauty; Medical (incl. Self Help & Alternative Medicine); Religion & Theology; Ecology; Metaphysical; Mind, Body, Spirit; New Age

New Titles: 24 (2007), 24 (2008)
No of Employees: 3

ISBNs, Imprints & Series:
978 0 905249, 978 1 84409, 978 1 899171

Overseas Representation:
Australia: Brumby Books Holdings Pty Ltd, Kilsyth South, Vic
New Zealand: Ceres Books, Ellerslie
North America: Independent Publishers Group (IPG), Chicago, IL, USA
Republic of Ireland & Europe: Deep Books Ltd, London, UK
Singapore: Pen International Ltd, Singapore
South Africa: Blue Weaver Marketing, Tokai
USA: New Leaf Distributing Co, Lithia Springs, GA

Book Trade Association Membership:
IPG; Publishing Scotland

2280

FIRST & BEST IN EDUCATION LTD
Earlstrees Court, Earlstrees Road, Corby, Northants NN17 4HH
Telephone: 01536 399005 (Orders & Accounts), 399004 (Editorial)
Fax: 01536 399012
Email: sales@firstandbest.co.uk
Web Site: http://www.shop.firstandbest.co.uk

Finance Manager: Jane Edmonds
Managing Director: Tony Attwood
Senior Editor: Anne Cockburn

Educational & Textbooks; Electronic (Educational)

Book Trade Association Membership:
EPC

2281

FIVE LEAVES PUBLICATIONS
PO Box 8786, Nottingham NG1 9AW
Telephone: 0115 969 3597
Email: info@fiveleaves.co.uk
Web Site: http://www.fiveleaves.co.uk

Publisher: Ross Bradshaw

Academic & Scholarly; Children's Books; Crime; Fiction; History & Antiquarian; Poetry; Theatre, Drama & Dance; Jewish

New Titles: 18 (2007), 18 (2008)
No of Employees: 1

ISBNs, Imprints & Series:
Crime Express
978 0 907123, 978 1 905512 Five Leaves Publications

Overseas Representation:
Spain & Portugal: Iberian Book Services, Madrid, Spain

2282

FLAMBARD PRESS
Stable Cottage, East Fourstones, Hexham, Northumberland NE47 5DX
Telephone: 01434 674360
Fax: 01434 674178
Email: flambardpress@btinternet.com
Web Site: http://www.flambardpress.co.uk

Managing Editor: Peter Lewis
Marketing Manager: Margaret Lewis
Editor: Will Mackie

Biography & Autobiography; Crime; Fiction; Photography; Poetry

New Titles: 8 (2007), 8 (2008)
No of Employees: 2

ISBNs, Imprints & Series:
978 1 873226, 978 1 906601

Book Trade Association Membership:
IPG

2283

FLORIS BOOKS
15 Harrison Gardens, Edinburgh EH11 1SH
Telephone: 0131 337 2372
Fax: 0131 347 9919
Email: floris@florisbooks.co.uk
Web Site: http://www.florisbooks.co.uk

Warehouse & Orders:
BookSource, 50 Cambuslang Road, Glasgow G32 8NB
Telephone: 0845 370 0067
Fax: 0845 370 0068
Email: orders@booksource.net

Chief Executive: Christian Maclean
Marketing: Katy Lockwood-Holmes

Academic & Scholarly; Children's Books; Crafts & Hobbies; Gardening; Health & Beauty; Medical (incl. Self Help & Alternative Medicine); Philosophy; Religion & Theology

New Titles: 40 (2007), 40 (2008)

No of Employees: 7

ISBNs, Imprints & Series:
978 0 86315, 978 0 903540, 978 0 906155

Distributor for:
Lindisfarne Press

Overseas Representation:
Australia: Footprint Books Pty Ltd, Warriewood, NSW
New Zealand: Ceres Books, Ellerslie
USA (34 Children's & Parents' titles): Gryphon House Inc, Beltsville, MD, USA
USA (all titles): Steiner Books Inc, Herndon, VA, USA

Book Trade Association Membership:
Publishing Scotland

2284

FOLENS LTD
Waterslade House, Thame Road, Haddenham, Bucks HP17 8NT
Telephone: 0870 609 1235 (order hotline), 1237 (customer services)
Fax: 0870 609 1236 (order hotline)
Email: folens@folens.com
Web Site: http://www.folens.com

Chairman: Dirk Folens
Directors: Adrian Cockell *(Managing)*
Peter Burton *(Publishing)*
Jacqui Dilley *(Marketing)*

Atlases & Maps; Educational & Textbooks; Electronic (Educational); English as a Foreign Language; Reference Books, Directories & Dictionaries

New Titles: 62 (2007), 108 (2008)
No of Employees: 45
Annual Turnover: £5M

ISBNs, Imprints & Series:
978 0 94788, 978 1 84163, 978 1 84191, 978 1 84303, 978 1 85008, 978 1 85276
Belair Publications
978 1 86202 Belair Publications

Overseas Representation:
Australia: Educational Supplies Pty Ltd
Bahrain: The Bookcase, Manama
Canada: Bacon & Hughes Ltd, Ottawa, Ont
Egypt: International Language Bookshop
Hong Kong: Transglobal Publishers Services Ltd
Jamaica: The Book Merchant Ltd, Kingston
Jordan: Al-Kashkool Bookshop, Amman; Philadelphia Book Gallery
Kuwait: Saeed & Samir Bookstore Co Ltd
Malaysia: Extrazeal; University Book Store (M) Sdn Bhd
Malta: Agius & Agius Ltd, Valletta
New Zealand: South Pacific Books (Imports) Ltd, Auckland
Oman: Al Manahil Educational Consultancy
Saudi Arabia: Elmia Bookstores, Al Khobar
Singapore: September 21 Enterprise Pte Ltd
South Africa: Everybody's Books, Durban
Spain: TEK Books (Bookworld Espana)
United Arab Emirates: All Prints Distributors & Publishers, UAE; Jashanmal National, UAE; Magrudy Enterprises, Dubai, UAE
USA: Social Studies School Service (USA)

Book Trade Association Membership:
Publishers Association; EPC

2285

FOOD TRADE PRESS LTD
Station House, Hortons Way, Westerham, Kent TN16 1BZ
Telephone: 01959 563944
Fax: 01959 561285
Email: books@foodtradepress.com
Web Site: http://www.foodtradepress.com

Director: Adrian Binsted *(Publishing)*

Agriculture; Chemistry; Reference Books, Directories & Dictionaries; Food Science & Technology

New Titles: 11 (2007), 12 (2008)

ISBNs, Imprints & Series:
978 0 900379, 978 0 903962

Associated Companies:
Attwood & Binsted Ltd

Distributor for:
Campden & Chorleywood Research Association; Leatherhead Food Research Association
Denmark: Mercantila Publishing AS
Italy: Chiriotti Editori Srl
Spain: Montagud Editores SA
Switzerland: Binsted Frères SA
USA: American Association of Cereal Chemists; American Institute of Baking; Chemical Publishing Co Inc; CTI Publications Inc; Food & Nutrition Press Inc; Food Processors Institute; Edward E. Judge & Sons

2286

FOOTPRINT HANDBOOKS
6 Riverside Court, Lower Bristol Road, Bath BA2 3DZ
Telephone: 01225 469141
Fax: 01225 469461
Email: discover@footprintbooks.com
Web Site: http://www.footprintbooks.com

Directors: Andy Riddle *(Managing)*
Patrick Dawson *(Editorial & Operations)*
Managers: Alan Murphy *(Commissioning Editor)*
Zoë Jackson *(Business Development)*

Guide Books; Sports & Games; Travel & Topography

New Titles: 20 (2007), 40 (2008)
No of Employees: 18

ISBNs, Imprints & Series:
978 0 900751 Footprint Handbooks/Trade & Travel Handbooks
978 1 900949, 978 1 903471, 978 1 904777, 978 1 906098 Footprint Handbooks

Distributor for:
Authentik Guides; Insiders' Guides; Travellers Handbook; Wexas International
France: Les Editions du Mont Tonnerre
USA: Globe Pequot Press

Overseas Representation:
Australia & New Zealand: Woodslane Pty Ltd, Warriewood, NSW, Australia
Belgium: Craenen bvba, Herent (Winksele)
Canada: Manda Group, Toronto, Ont
Europe: Bill Bailey Publishers Representatives, Newton Abbot, Devon, UK
Israel: SKP, Tel Aviv
Latin America: InterMedia Americana (IMA) Ltd, London, UK
Netherlands: Nilsson & Lamm BV, Weesp
Republic of Ireland: Fitzmull Books, Dublin
South Africa: Faradawn CC, Saxonwold
South East Asia: Pansing Distribution Pte Ltd, Singapore, Singapore
USA & Latin America: Globe Pequot Press, Guilford, CT, USA

2287

FORENSIC SCIENCE SOCIETY
Clarke House, 18A Mount Parade, Harrogate HG1 1BX
Telephone: 01423 506068
Fax: 01423 566391
Email: journal@forensic-science-society.org.uk
Web Site: http://www.forensic-science-society.org.uk

Hon. Editor: Niamh Nic Daéid

Scientific & Technical

2288

THE FOSTERING NETWORK
87 Blackfriars Road, London SE1 8HA
Telephone: (020) 7620 6400
Fax: (020) 7620 6401

Director: Robert Tapsfield
Head of External Affairs: Lucy Peake
Publishing: David McConnell

Children's Books; Educational & Textbooks; Psychology & Psychiatry; Sociology & Anthropology; Vocational Training & Careers; Child Care

New Titles: 16 (2007), 4 (2008)
No of Employees: 2

ISBNs, Imprints & Series: 978 0 946015

2289

W. FOULSHAM & CO LTD
The Publishing House, Bennetts Close, Cippenham, Berks SL1 5AP
Telephone: 01753 526769
Fax: 01753 535003
Email: hardwick@foulsham.com
Web Site: http://www.foulsham.com

Distribution:
Macmillan Distribution (MDL), Houndmills, Basingstoke RG21 2XS
Telephone: 01256 329242
Fax: 01256 812558
Email: mdl@macmillan.co.uk
Web Site: http://www.mdl.macmillan.co.uk

Directors: Barry Belasco *(Managing)*
Graham Kitchen *(Financial)*
Roy Mantel *(Production)*
Wendy Hobson *(Editorial)*

Accountancy & Taxation; Antiques & Collecting; Children's Books; Cookery, Wines & Spirits; Crafts & Hobbies; Crime; Educational & Textbooks; Gardening; Guide Books; Health & Beauty; Humour; Industry, Business & Management; Magic & the Occult; Medical (incl. Self Help & Alternative Medicine); Military & War; Poetry; Reference Books, Directories & Dictionaries; Religion & Theology; Travel & Topography

New Titles: 60 (2007), 60 (2008)
No of Employees: 12

ISBNs, Imprints & Series:
978 0 572 Arcturus; Foulsham; Quantum

Overseas Representation:
Australia: Capricorn Link (Australia) Pty Ltd, Windsor, NSW
Belgium, Germany, Luxembourg, Netherlands, Switzerland & Austria: Robbert J. Pleysier, Heerde, Netherlands
Cambodia, Laos, Myanmar, Thailand, Philippines & Vietnam: Ashton International Marketing Services, Sevenoaks, Kent, UK
Canada: Codasat, Vancouver, BC
Caribbean: Macmillan Caribbean Ltd, Oxford, UK
Central & Eastern Europe: Dr László Horváth Publishers Representative, Budapest, Hungary
Central & South America: InterMedia Americana (IMA) Ltd, London, UK
Far East, Singapore & Malaysia: Ashton International Marketing Services, Sevenoaks, Kent, UK
France, Gibraltar, Greece, Italy, Spain & Portugal: Sandro Salucci, Florence, Italy
India: Maya Publishers Pvt Ltd, New Delhi
Middle East: Richard Carman Associates, Northwich, UK
New Zealand: Southern Publishers Group, Auckland
South Africa: Alternative Books CC, Ferndale
Sub Saharan Africa: InterMedia Africa Ltd (IMA), London, UK
USA: Associated Publishers Group, Nashville, TN

2290

FOUR COURTS PRESS
7 Malpas Street, Dublin 8, Republic of Ireland
Telephone: +353 (01) 453 4668
Fax: +353 (01) 453 4672
Email: info@four-courts-press.ie
Web Site: http://www.four-courts-press.ie

Distributor:
Gill & Macmillan, Hume Avenue, Park West, Dublin 12, Republic of Ireland
Telephone: +353 (01) 500 9555
Fax: +353 (01) 500 9599
Email: info@four-courts-press.ie
Web Site: http://www.four-courts-press.ie

Managing Director: Michael Adams
Marketing: Anthony Tierney
Production: Martin Healy
Editorial: Martin Fanning
Sales: Jessica Breen
Editorial Assistant: Aoife Walsh

Academic & Scholarly; Archaeology; Fine Art & Art History; History & Antiquarian; Law; Philosophy; Religion & Theology

New Titles: 62 (2007), 65 (2008)
No of Employees: 6

ISBNs, Imprints & Series:
Four Courts Press; Open Air
978 0 906127, 978 1 85182

Overseas Representation:
USA: International Specialized Book Services Inc, Portland, OR

2291

*FREE ASSOCIATION BOOKS
PO Box 37664, London NW7 2XU
Email: info@fabooks.com
Web Site: http://www.fabooks.com

Trade Distribution:
NBN International Ltd, Estover Road, Plymouth PL6 7PZ
Telephone: 01752 202301
Fax: 01752 202333
Email: orders@nbninternational.com

Rights & Permissions:
The Cathy Miller Foreign Rights Agency, 18 The Quadrangle, 49 Atalanta Street, London SW6 6TU
Telephone: (020) 7385 9098
Fax: (020) 7385 1774

Managing Director: Trevor E. Brown
Home & Export Sales: Nicola Vinall
Elisabeth Pavey

Academic & Scholarly; Computer Science; Economics; History & Antiquarian; Medical (incl. Self Help & Alternative Medicine); Philosophy; Psychology & Psychiatry; Religion & Theology; Scientific & Technical; Cultural Studies; Psychoanalysis; Psychotherapy

ISBNs, Imprints & Series:
978 0 7134, 978 0 946960, 978 1 85343

Overseas Representation:
Australasia: Astam Books Pty Ltd, Leichhardt, NSW, Australia
Israel: Bookworm, Tel Aviv

Japan: Kay Kato Associates, Kanagawa
USA & Canada: International Specialized Book Services Inc, Portland, OR, USA

Book Trade Association Membership: IPG

2292

SAMUEL FRENCH LTD
52 Fitzroy Street, London W1T 5JR
Telephone: (020) 7387 9373
Fax: (020) 7387 2161
Email: theatre@samuelfrench-london.co.uk
Web Site: http://www.samuelfrench-london.co.uk

Directors: Leon F. Embry *(Chairman)*
Vivien Goodwin *(Managing)*
Amanda Smith
Paul Taylor

Theatre, Drama & Dance

New Titles: 35 (2007), 35 (2008)
No of Employees: 40

ISBNs, Imprints & Series: 978 0 573

Parent Company:
Samuel French Inc

Distributor for:
USA: Samuel French Inc

Overseas Representation:
Australia: The Dominie Group, Brookvale, NSW
East Africa: Phoenix Players Ltd, Nairobi, Kenya
Malta: Dingli Co International, Valletta
New Zealand: Play Bureau of New Zealand Ltd, New Plymouth
Republic of Ireland: Drama League of Ireland, Dublin
South Africa, Namibia, Swaziland, Botswana & Lesotho: Dalro (Pty) Ltd, Braamfontein, South Africa
Zimbabwe: National Theatre Organization, Harare

Book Trade Association Membership: Publishers Association; BA

2293

FRIENDS OF THE EARTH
26–28 Underwood Street, London N1 7JQ
Telephone: (020) 7490 1555
Fax: (020) 7490 0881
Web Site: http://www.foe.co.uk & http://community.foe.co.uk

Manager: Adam Bradbury *(Publications)*

Academic & Scholarly; Educational & Textbooks; Environment & Development Studies; Gardening; Reference Books, Directories & Dictionaries; Transport

New Titles: 1 (2008)
No of Employees: 150
Annual Turnover: £11M

ISBNs, Imprints & Series: 978 1 85750

2294

GALACTIC CENTRAL PUBLICATIONS
25a Copgrove Road, Leeds, West Yorkshire LS8 2SP
Telephone: 0113 248 8124
Email: philsp@philsp.com
Web Site: http://www.philsp.com

Publisher: Phil Stephensen-Payne

Bibliography & Library Science

ISBNs, Imprints & Series: 978 1 871133

Overseas Representation:
USA: Chris Drumm, Polk City, IA

2295

*THE GALLERY PRESS
Loughcrew, Oldcastle, Co Meath, Republic of Ireland
Telephone: +353 (049) 854 1779
Fax: +353 (049) 854 1779
Email: gallery@indigo.ie
Web Site: http://www.gallerypress.com

Director: Peter Fallon *(Editorial, Production)*
Administration: Jean Barry
Suella Wynne
Sales & Accounts: Anne Duggan

Fiction; Poetry; Theatre, Drama & Dance

ISBNs, Imprints & Series:
978 0 902996, 978 0 904011, 978 1 85235

2296

GALORE PARK PUBLISHING LTD
19–21 Sayers Lane, Tenterden, Kent TN30 6BW
Telephone: 01580 764242
Fax: 01580 764142
Email: info@galorepark.co.uk
Web Site: http://www.galorepark.co.uk

Directors: Nicholas Oulton *(Managing)*
Louise Martine *(Production)*
Marketing Manager / Public Relations: Natalie Friend
Financial Controller: Steve Jones

Children's Books; Educational & Textbooks

New Titles: 11 (2007), 11 (2008)
No of Employees: 12
Annual Turnover: £1M

ISBNs, Imprints & Series:
978 1 902984 Galore Park Publishing; Iseb Publications

Book Trade Association Membership: Publishers Association; BA; IPG

2297

GARNET PUBLISHING LTD
8 Southern Court, South Street, Reading RG1 4QS
Telephone: 0118 959 7847
Fax: 0118 959 7356 (Trade Enquiries & Orders)
Email: dan@garnetpublishing.co.uk
Web Site: http://www.garnetpublishing.co.uk

Managers: Dan Nunn *(Permissions, Rights & Editorial)*
Nick Holroyd *(Office, Production & Finance)*
Val Eve *(Sales)*

Academic & Scholarly; Architecture & Design; Cookery, Wines & Spirits; Economics; Electronic (Professional & Academic); Fiction; Gender Studies; Guide Books; History & Antiquarian; Literature & Criticism; Photography; Politics & World Affairs; Religion & Theology; Sociology & Anthropology; Travel & Topography

New Titles: 20 (2007), 24 (2008)
No of Employees: 5

ISBNs, Imprints & Series:
978 1 85964, 978 1 873938, 978 1 902932 Garnet Publishing; Ithaca Press; South Street Press

Associated Companies:
Garnet Education; Ithaca Press; South Street Press

Overseas Representation:
Australia: InBooks, Frenchs Forest, NSW
Europe: Andrew Durnell Marketing Ltd, Tunbridge Wells, UK
USA (Academic): International Specialized Book Services Inc, Portland, OR, USA
USA (Trade): IPM, Dulles, VA, USA

Book Trade Association Membership: IPG

2298

GATEHOUSE MEDIA LTD
PO Box 965, Warrington, Cheshire WA4 9DE
Telephone: 01925 267778
Fax: 01925 267778
Email: info@gatehousebooks.com
Web Site: http://www.gatehousebooks.com

Directors: Catherine White *(Managing)*
Mark White

Audio Books; Educational & Textbooks; English as a Foreign Language

ISBNs, Imprints & Series:
978 1 84231 Gatehouse Books

Overseas Representation:
Canada: Grass Roots Press, Edmonton, Alb
USA: Peppercorn Books Press, Snow Camp, NC

Book Trade Association Membership: Publishers Association

2299

GEDDES & GROSSET
David Dale House, New Lanark ML11 9DJ
Telephone: 01555 665000
Fax: 01555 665694
Email: info@gandg.sol.co.uk

Sales:
David Dale House, New Lanark ML11 9DJ
Telephone: 01555 665000
Fax: 01555 665694
Email: info@gandg.sol.co.uk

Warehouse:
Peter Haddock Ltd, Industrial Estate, Pinfold Lane, Bridlington YO16 5BT
Telephone: 01262 678121
Fax: 01262 400043

Executives: Ron Grosset *(Publisher)*
Mike Miller *(Publisher)*

Atlases & Maps; Children's Books; Cookery, Wines & Spirits; History & Antiquarian; Magic & the Occult; Medical (incl. Self Help & Alternative Medicine); Reference Books, Directories & Dictionaries

New Titles: 35 (2007), 35 (2008)
No of Employees: 6
Annual Turnover: £2.5M

ISBNs, Imprints & Series: 978 1 85534

Parent Company:
D. C. Thomson & Co Ltd

Associated Companies:
Waverley Books Ltd

Overseas Representation:
Africa & Caribbean: Kelvin van Hasselt Publishing Services, Briningham, Norfolk, UK
Central & South America: InterMedia Americana Ltd (IMA), Gibraltar
Southern Africa: Book Promotions Pty Ltd, Cape Town, South Africa

Book Trade Association Membership: Publishing Scotland

2300

GEOCENTER INTERNATIONAL LTD
Meridian House, Churchill Way West, Basingstoke, Hants RG21 6YR
Telephone: 01256 817987
Fax: 01256 817988
Email: sales@geocenter.co.uk

Distribution:
Grantham Book Services,
Isaac Newton Way,
Alma Park Industrial Estate, Grantham, Lincs NG31 9SD
Telephone: 01476 541080
Fax: 01476 541061

Public Relations:
Julia Spence, 29 St Mary's Street, Wallingford, Oxon OX10 0ET
Telephone: 01491 824524
Fax: 01491 824694
Email: juliaspence@ukonline.co.uk

Sales & Marketing Director: Ian MacDonald
Managers: Andy Casey *(Sales)*
Petra Hourd *(Marketing – Insight)*
Donna Burridge *(Marketing – Cartographic)*
Sam Bufton *(Marketing – Berlitz Language)*
Diane McEntee *(Marketing – Berlitz Travel)*
Hayley Whitlock *(Marketing – Ullmann)*

Academic & Scholarly; Architecture & Design; Atlases & Maps; Cookery, Wines & Spirits; Gardening; Guide Books; Languages & Linguistics; Music; Photography; Reference Books, Directories & Dictionaries; Transport; Travel & Topography

New Titles: 60 (2007), 40 (2008)
No of Employees: 18
Annual Turnover: £7.5M

ISBNs, Imprints & Series:
978 0 84165 AMC Maps & Atlases
978 2 8315, 978 981 246 Berlitz
978 3 468 Langenscheidt Dictionaries
978 3 575 GeoCenter Maps
978 3 8331 Ullmann
978 3 88618 Nelles Maps
978 962 421, 978 981 234, 978 981 258 Insight Guides
978 962 593 Periplus Maps

Parent Company:
Germany: Langenscheidt KG

Distributor for:
AMC [AMC Maps & Atlases]; Apa Guides [Insight Guides]; Langenscheidt [Dictionaries]; Nelles Verlag [Nelles Guides & Maps]; Periplus Editions [Guides, Maps & Cookery Books]; RV Verlag [GeoCenter Maps]; Ullmann [Art & Architecture, Lifestyle, Reference]

Overseas Representation:
Europe: Bill Bailey Publishers Representatives, Newton Abbot, Devon, UK
South America: InterMedia Americana Ltd (IMA), Gibraltar

Book Trade Association Membership: Book Data Subscriber

2301

THE GEOGRAPHICAL ASSOCIATION
160 Solly Street, Sheffield S1 4BF
Telephone: 0114 296 0088
Fax: 0114 296 7176
Email: info@geography.org.uk
Web Site: http://www.geography.org.uk

Chief Executive: David Lambert
Programme Director: John Lyon

Managers: Richard Gill *(Business)*
Fran Royle *(Publications)*
Assistant Editor: Dorcas Turner

Atlases & Maps; Educational & Textbooks; Electronic (Educational); Geography & Geology; Guide Books; Travel & Topography

New Titles: 12 (2007), 10 (2008)
No of Employees: 24

ISBNs, Imprints & Series:
978 0 900395, 978 0 948512, 978 1 84377, 978 1 899085, 978 1 903448

Book Trade Association Membership:
EPC

2302

GEOGRAPHY PUBLICATIONS
24 Kennington Road, Templeogue, Dublin 6W, Republic of Ireland
Telephone: +353 (01) 456 6085
Fax: +353 (01) 456 6085
Email: books@geographypublications.com
Web Site: http://www.geographypublications.com

Contact: William Nolan

Academic & Scholarly; Archaeology; Atlases & Maps; Biography & Autobiography; Educational & Textbooks; Geography & Geology; History & Antiquarian; Languages & Linguistics; Reference Books, Directories & Dictionaries

New Titles: 2 (2007), 3 (2008)

ISBNs, Imprints & Series:
978 0 906602 History & Society Series

2303

GEOLOGICAL SOCIETY PUBLISHING HOUSE
Unit 7, Brassmill Enterprise Centre, Brassmill Lane, Bath BA1 3JN
Telephone: 01225 445046
Fax: 01225 442836
Email: neal.marriott@geolsoc.org.uk & dawn.angel@geolsoc.org.uk (sales enquiries)
Web Site: http://www.geolsoc.org.uk/bookshop

Director of Publishing: Neal Marriott
Marketing Co-ordinator: Alison Tucker
Editors: Angharad Hills *(Commissioning)*
Sarah Gibbs *(Senior Production)*
Sales & Customer Service Supervisor: Dawn Angel

Academic & Scholarly; Engineering; Environment & Development Studies; Geography & Geology; Scientific & Technical

New Titles: 25 (2007), 25 (2008)
No of Employees: 13

ISBNs, Imprints & Series:
978 0 903317, 978 1 86239, 978 1 897799 Geological Society

Distributor for:
USA: American Association of Petroleum Geologists; Geological Society of America; SEPM

Overseas Representation:
India: EWP, New Delhi
Spain & Portugal: Iberian Book Services, Madrid, Spain
USA: AAPG, Tulsa; Princeton Selling Group Inc, Philadelphia, PA

Book Trade Association Membership:
Association of Learned & Professional Society Publishers

2304

GIBSON SQUARE
47 Lonsdale Square, London N1 1EW
Telephone: (020) 7096 1100
Fax: (020) 7993 2214
Email: info@gibsonsquare.com
Web Site: http://www.gibsonsquare.com

Warehouse:
Littlehampton Book Services, Faraday Close, Durrington, Worthing, West Sussex BN13 3RB
Telephone: 01903 828500
Fax: 01903 828802
Email: orders@lbsltd.co.uk
Web Site: http://www.lbsltd.co.uk

Publisher: Martin Rynja

Biography & Autobiography; Cinema, Video, TV & Radio; Fine Art & Art History; Gay & Lesbian Studies; History & Antiquarian; Humour; Philosophy; Politics & World Affairs; Travel & Topography

ISBNs, Imprints & Series:
978 1 903933, 978 1 906142

Overseas Representation:
Australia: Tower Books Pty Ltd, Frenchs Forest, NSW
Canada: Raincoast Book Distribution Ltd, Vancouver, BC
New Zealand: Addenda Ltd, Grey Lynn

Book Trade Association Membership:
IPG

2305

GILL & MACMILLAN LTD
Hume Avenue, Park West, Dublin 12, Republic of Ireland
Telephone: +353 (01) 500 9500
Fax: +353 (01) 500 9599
Email: ftobin@gillmacmillan.ie
Web Site: http://www.gillmacmillan.ie

Chairman: M. H. Gill
Directors: M. D. O'Dwyer *(Managing)*
A. Murray *(Educational Publishing)*
P. A. Thew *(Marketing & Sales)*
B. D. Curtin *(Company Secretary/Financial)*
M. O'Keeffe *(Production)*
F. M. Tobin *(General Publishing)*
J. Manning *(Distribution)*

Academic & Scholarly; Biography & Autobiography; Children's Books; Cookery, Wines & Spirits; Economics; Educational & Textbooks; Guide Books; History & Antiquarian; Humour; Literature & Criticism; Politics & World Affairs; Psychology & Psychiatry; Reference Books, Directories & Dictionaries; Travel & Topography

New Titles: 152 (2007), 113 (2008)
No of Employees: 75
Annual Turnover: £9.64M

ISBNs, Imprints & Series:
978 0 7171 Newleaf; RíRá
978 0 946551, 978 1 858600 Gateway

Overseas Representation:
Australia: Brumby Books Holdings Pty Ltd, Kilsyth South, Vic
India, Pakistan & Sri Lanka: Pan Macmillan, New Delhi, India
Middle East, South East & North Asia: Pan Macmillan Asia, Hong Kong
New Zealand: New Holland Publishers (New Zealand), Auckland
South Africa: Pan Macmillan SA Pty Ltd, Johannesburg
UK: Bounce! Sales & Marketing Ltd, London

Book Trade Association Membership:
CLÉ (Irish PA)

2306

GLASGOW MUSEUMS
Martyrs' School, Parson Street, Glasgow G4 0PX
Telephone: 0141 271 8307
Fax: 0141 271 8354
Email: susan.pacitti@csglasgow.org
Web Site: http://www.glasgowmuseums.com

Managing Editor: Susan Pacitti

Archaeology; Fashion & Costume; Fine Art & Art History; History & Antiquarian; Transport

New Titles: 5 (2007), 5 (2008)
No of Employees: 2

ISBNs, Imprints & Series: 978 0 902752

Parent Company:
Culture & Sport Glasgow

Book Trade Association Membership:
Publishing Scotland

2307

GLOBAL ORIENTAL LTD
PO Box 219, Folkestone CT20 2WP
Telephone: 01303 226799
Fax: 01303 243087
Email: info@globaloriental.co.uk
Web Site: http://www.globaloriental.co.uk

Distribution (UK):
Orca Book Services Ltd, Stanley House, 3 Fleets Lane, Poole, Dorset BH15 3AJ
Telephone: 01202 665432
Fax: 01202 666219

Managing Director & Publisher: Paul Norbury
Assistant Editor: David Blakeley

Academic & Scholarly; Biography & Autobiography; Fashion & Costume; Gender Studies; Geography & Geology; History & Antiquarian; Illustrated & Fine Editions; Languages & Linguistics; Literature & Criticism; Philosophy; Politics & World Affairs; Psychology & Psychiatry; Religion & Theology; Sociology & Anthropology; Travel & Topography; Oriental

New Titles: 25 (2007), 40 (2008)

ISBNs, Imprints & Series:
978 1 86034 (selected)
978 1 874267 (selected)
978 1 901903, 978 1 905246

Overseas Representation:
Australia: Asia Bookroom, Canberra
China: Access Asia Media Services, Shanghai, P. R. of China
India: Maya Publishers Pvt Ltd, New Delhi
Japan: United Publishers Services Ltd, Tokyo
Korea: Impact Korea, Seoul, Korea, South
Singapore & Malaysia: P. C. Tham, Singapore
Taiwan: Unifacmanu Trading Co Ltd, Taipei
USA: University of Hawai'i Press, Honolulu

2308

GLOBAL PROFESSIONAL PUBLISHING
Random Acres, Slip Mill Lane, Hawkhurst, Kent TN18 5AD
Telephone: 01580 753387
Fax: 01580 753201
Email: publishing@gppbooks.com
Web Site: http://www.financialworldpublishing.com

Distribution:
Publishers Group UK, 8 The Arena, Mollison Avenue, Enfield, Middx EN3 7NL
Telephone: (020) 8804 0400

Fax: (020) 8804 0044
Web Site: http://www.pguk.co.uk

Executive: Nick Lockett
Sales & Rights: Eric Dobby

Academic & Scholarly; Accountancy & Taxation; Computer Science; Economics; Educational & Textbooks; Electronic (Educational); Electronic (Professional & Academic); Law; Mathematics & Statistics; Reference Books, Directories & Dictionaries

New Titles: 8 (2007), 45 (2008)
No of Employees: 4
Annual Turnover: £300,000

Parent Company:
Global Professional Publishing Holdings

Overseas Representation:
Australia: Woodslane, Mona Vale, NSW
Benelux: Jos de Jong, Just in Time Promotions, Heenstal, Netherlands
Eastern Europe: Dr László Horváth Publishers Representative, Budapest, Hungary
Italy, Greece & Cyprus: Charles Gibbes Associates, London, UK
Middle East & Malta: Avicenna Partnership, Oxford, UK
South East Asia: Asia Publishers Services Ltd, Hong Kong
South West Asia: APD Singapore Pte Ltd, Singapore
Spain, Portugal & Gibraltar: Iberian Book Services, Madrid, Spain
USA & Canada: Stylus Publishing Inc, Sterling, VA, USA

2309

GLOWWORM BOOKS & GIFTS LTD
Unit 4, Bishopsgate Business Park, Broxburn EH52 5LH
Telephone: 01506 857570
Fax: 01506 858100
Web Site: http://www.glowwormbooks.co.uk

Directors: Katrena Allan *(Managing)*
Gordon Allan *(Production)*

Children's Books

New Titles: 1 (2008)

ISBNs, Imprints & Series:
978 0 955755, 978 1 871512

Book Trade Association Membership:
BSA

2310

GLYNDWR PUBLISHING
PO Box 68, Cowbridge, Vale of Glamorgan CF71 9AY
Telephone: 01446 775516
Email: breverton@hotmail.co.uk
Web Site: http://www.glyndwrpublishing.co.uk

Principal: T. Breverton

Academic & Scholarly; Biography & Autobiography; History & Antiquarian; Military & War; Nautical; Reference Books, Directories & Dictionaries

New Titles: 1 (2007), 1 (2008)

ISBNs, Imprints & Series:
978 1 903529 Wales Books - Glyndwr Publishing

Associated Companies:
USA: Pelican Publishing Co

2311

ALAN GODFREY MAPS
Prospect Business Park, Leadgate, Consett
DH8 7PW
Telephone: 01207 583388
Fax: 01207 583399
Email: godfreyedition@btinternet.com
Web Site: http://
www.alangodfreymaps.co.uk

Contact: Alan Godfrey

Atlases & Maps; History & Antiquarian

New Titles: 120 (2007), 120 (2008)
No of Employees: 3

ISBNs, Imprints & Series:
978 0 85054, 978 0 907554, 978 1 84151,
978 1 84784

Overseas Representation:
Australia: Mapworks, North Essendon, Vic

Book Trade Association Membership:
IPG; British Cartographic Society;
International Map Trade Association

2312

GODSFIELD PRESS LTD
2–4 Heron Quays, London E14 4JP
Telephone: (020) 7531 8400
Fax: (020) 7531 8562
Email: enquiries@godsfieldpress.com
Web Site: http://www.godsfieldpress.com

Publisher: Jane Birch
UK Sales & Marketing: Steven Edney
Director: Tracy Killick *(Creative)*

Magic & the Occult; Medical (incl. Self Help & Alternative Medicine); Religion & Theology

ISBNs, Imprints & Series:
978 1 84181, 978 1 899434

Parent Company:
Octopus Publishing Group

2313

THE GOLDSMITH PRESS LTD
Newbridge, Co Kildare, Republic of Ireland
Telephone: +353 (045) 433613
Fax: +353 (045) 434648
Email: de@iol.ie

Director: Vivienne Abbott
Secretary: Breda Ennis

Academic & Scholarly; Biography & Autobiography; Cookery, Wines & Spirits; English as a Foreign Language; Fine Art & Art History; Literature & Criticism; Poetry

New Titles: 4 (2007), 4 (2008)
No of Employees: 2

ISBNs, Imprints & Series: 978 1 870491

Book Trade Association Membership:
CLÉ (Irish PA)

2314

VICTOR GOLLANCZ LTD
Orion House, 5 Upper St Martins Lane,
London WC2H 9EA
Telephone: (020) 7240 3444
Fax: (020) 7240 5822
Web Site: http://www.orionbooks.co.uk

Warehouse, Trade Enquiries & Orders:
see The Orion Publishing Group Ltd

Directors: Lisa Milton *(Managing)*
Dallas Manderson *(Group Sales)*
Mark Streatfeild *(Export Sales)*
Mark Prior *(Finance)*
Linda Gawley *(UK Sales)*
Simon Spanton *(Editorial)*
Jo Fletcher *(Editorial)*

Fiction; Science Fiction

ISBNs, Imprints & Series:
978 0 575 Victor Gollancz Ltd; VGSF

Parent Company:
The Orion Publishing Group Ltd

Overseas Representation:
see: The Orion Publishing Group Ltd,
London, UK

2315

GOMER
Llandysul, Ceredigion SA44 4JL
Telephone: 01559 363090
Fax: 01559 363758
Email: meinir@gomer.co.uk
Web Site: http://www.gomer.co.uk

Directors: J. H. Lewis *(Executive)*
Jonathan Lewis *(Managing)*
Mairwen Prys Jones *(Publishing)*
Accounts: Carol Bignell
Sales: Meinir James *(Head of Marketing)*

Biography & Autobiography; Children's Books; Fine Art & Art History; History & Antiquarian; Languages & Linguistics; Literature & Criticism; Photography; Poetry; Reference Books, Directories & Dictionaries; Sports & Games; Transport; Welsh Language Publications

ISBNs, Imprints & Series:
978 0 85088, 978 0 86383, 978 1 84323,
978 1 85902 Pont (English language publications for children)

Parent Company:
J. D. Lewis & Sons Ltd

Book Trade Association Membership:
BA; IPG; Union of Welsh Publishers & Booksellers

2316

GOTHIC IMAGE PUBLICATIONS
PO Box 2568, Glastonbury, Somerset
BA6 8XR
Telephone: 01458 831281
Fax: 01458 833385
Email: publications@gothicimage.co.uk
Web Site: http://www.gothicimage.co.uk

Trade Orders:
PGUK, Mollison Avenue, Enfield, Middx
EN3 7NJ
Telephone: (020) 8804 0400
Fax: (020) 8804 0044

Also:
Counter Culture, The Long Barn,
Sutton Mallet, Somerset TA7 9AD
Telephone: 01278 722888
Fax: 01278 722888
Web Site: http://www.counterculture-books.co.uk

Directors: Frances Howard-Gordon *(All titles - Editorial & Commissioning)*
Jamie George *(Export Sales)*
Diana Macleash *(Financial Controller)*

Biography & Autobiography; Fine Art & Art History; Guide Books; Humour; Magic & the Occult; Philosophy; Photography; Politics & World Affairs; Psychology & Psychiatry; Religion & Theology; Travel & Topography

New Titles: 3 (2007), 3 (2008)
No of Employees: 3

ISBNs, Imprints & Series:
978 0 906362 Traveller's Guide Series

Overseas Representation:
Europe: PGUK, Enfield, UK
USA: SCB Distributors, Gardena, CA

2317

GOWER PUBLISHING CO LTD
Gower House, Croft Road, Aldershot, Hants
GU11 3HR
Telephone: 01252 331551
Fax: 01252 344405
Email: info@gowerpub.com
Web Site: http://www.gowerpub.com

Customer Service Department/World Distribution:
Bookpoint Ltd, 39 Milton Park, Abingdon,
Oxon OX14 4TD
Telephone: 01235 400400
Fax: 01235 400454
Email: gower@bookpoint.co.uk
Web Site: http://www.gowerpub.com

Management: N. A. E. Farrow *(Chairman)*
Rachel Lynch *(Managing Director)*
Darren Wise *(Finance Director)*
Richard Dowling *(Sales Director)*
Josephine Gooderham *(Director - Publishing Systems)*
Jonathan Norman *(Publishing Director - Training Resources & Business Books)*
Susan White *(Marketing Manager)*
Foreign Rights: E. Vartto

Accountancy & Taxation; Architecture & Design; Educational & Textbooks; Engineering; Industry, Business & Management; Law; Vocational Training & Careers

New Titles: 28 (2007), 38 (2008)
No of Employees: 120

ISBNs, Imprints & Series:
978 0 566 Gower
978 0 7546 Ashgate
978 0 85331 Lund Humphries

Parent Company:
Ashgate Publishing Co Ltd

Associated Companies:
USA: Ashgate Publishing Co

Overseas Representation:
Africa (excluding South Africa & North Africa): InterMedia Africa Ltd (IMA),
London, UK
Central & Eastern Europe: Dr László Horváth Publishers Representative, Budapest, Hungary
India: Maya Publishers Pvt Ltd, New Delhi
Iran: Kowkab Publishers, Tehran
Japan: United Publishers Services Ltd, Tokyo
Korea: Information & Culture Korea (ICK), Seoul, Korea, South
Middle East: Publishers International Marketing, Burmarsh, UK
North & South America: Ashgate Publishing Co, Burlington, VT, USA
Pakistan: Book Bird Publishers Representatives, Lahore
South East Asia, Myanmar (Burma), China, Hong Kong, South Korea, Australia & New Zealand: Ashgate Publishing Asia-Pacific, Newport, NSW, Australia

Book Trade Association Membership:
IPG

2318

GRACEWING PUBLISHING
Gracewing House, 2 Southern Avenue,
Leominster, Herefordshire HR6 0QF
Telephone: 01568 616835
Fax: 01568 613289
Email: gracewingx@aol.com
Web Site: http://www.gracewing.co.uk

Managing Director: Tom Longford *(Sales, Editorial)*
Managers: Jo Ashworth *(Publishing)*
Adrian Hodnett *(Customer Service)*
Mary Clewer *(Accounts)*
Monica Manwaring *(Publicity)*

Academic & Scholarly; Architecture & Design; Biography & Autobiography; Guide Books; History & Antiquarian; Philosophy; Religion & Theology

New Titles: 36 (2007), 39 (2008)

ISBNs, Imprints & Series: 978 0 85244

Distributor for:
Mercer University Press; Newman House;
OSV; Smyth & Helwys; St Bedes;
Templegate

Overseas Representation:
Australia: Freedom Publishing, North Melbourne, Vic
Canada: Novalis Inc, Toronto, Ont
USA: Liturgy Training Publications, Chicago, IL; Morehouse, Harrisburg, PA

2319

GRAFFEG
2 Radnor Court, 256 Cowbridge Road East,
Cardiff CF5 1GZ
Telephone: (029) 2037 7312
Fax: (029) 2039 8101
Email: info@graffeg.com
Web Site: http://www.graffeg.com

Managing Director: Peter Gill
Marketing Manager: Vanessa Kilcoyne

Architecture & Design; Cookery, Wines & Spirits; Gardening; Geography & Geology; Guide Books; Natural History; Photography; Travel & Topography

New Titles: 8 (2007), 5 (2008)
No of Employees: 3

ISBNs, Imprints & Series:
978 0 9544334, 978 1 905582

Overseas Representation:
Worldwide: Welsh Books Council,
Aberystwyth, UK

Book Trade Association Membership:
IPG

2320

W. F. GRAHAM (NORTHAMPTON) LTD
2 Pondwood Close, Moulton Park,
Northampton NN3 6RT
Telephone: 01604 645537
Fax: 01604 648414
Email: books@wfgraham.co.uk
Web Site: http://www.wfgraham.co.uk

Managing Director: Tim Graham
Manager: Ian Wilson *(General)*

Children's Books

ISBNs, Imprints & Series: 978 1 85128

Overseas Representation:
Far East: CKK Ltd, Northwood, Middx, UK
West Indies: Humphrys Roberts Associates,
London, UK

2321

GRANADA LEARNING
The Chiswick Centre,
414 Chiswick High Road, London W4 5TF
Telephone: (020) 8996 3363
Fax: (020) 8742 8546
Email: mail@granadalearning.co.uk
Web Site: http://www.gl-assessment.co.uk

Educational & Textbooks

Book Trade Association Membership: Publishers Association

2322

GRANTA BOOKS
12 Addison Avenue, London W11 4QR
Telephone: (020) 7605 1360
Fax: (020) 7605 1361
Email: rights@granta.com
Web Site: http://www.granta.com

Trade Orders:
TBS Ltd, Distribution Centre, Colchester Road, Frating Green, Colchester, Essex CO7 7DW
Telephone: 01206 255678
Fax: 01206 255715
Email: mdl@macmillan.co.uk

Sales: Brigid Macleod
Publicity: Pru Rowlandson
Production: Sarah Wasley
Rights: Angela Rose
Editorial: Sara Holloway

Biography & Autobiography; Fiction; Politics & World Affairs; Travel & Topography

ISBNs, Imprints & Series:
978 0 90314 Granta Magazine
978 1 86207 Granta Books

Parent Company:
Granta Publications

Associated Companies:
Granta Magazine

Overseas Representation:
Australia & New Zealand: Allen & Unwin Pty Ltd, Sydney, NSW, Australia
Canada: Raincoast Book Distribution Ltd, Vancouver, BC
Caribbean: Rob Thompson, Pan Macmillan, Oxford, UK
Europe, Scandinavia & Middle East: Aimee Roche, Pan Macmillan, Basingstoke, UK
Germany, Austria, Central & Eastern Europe: Chris Geoghegan, Pan Macmillan, Basingstoke, UK
Hong Kong, Thailand, Indonesia, Philippines & China: Daniel Watts, Macmillan Publishers (China) Ltd, Hong Kong
Indian Subcontinent: Rajdeep Mukherjee, Pan Macmillan, New Delhi, India
Latin America: James Papworth, Pan Macmillan, Basingstoke, UK
Netherlands: Nilsson & Lamm BV, Weesp
Republic of Ireland: Repforce Ireland Ltd, Monkstown
Singapore & Malaysia: Horizon Books Pte Ltd, Singapore
South Africa: Jonathan Ball Publishers (Pty) Ltd, Jeppestown
Southern Europe: Megan Lea, Pan Macmillan, Basingstoke, UK

2323

GRANTA EDITIONS
25–27 High Street, Chesterton, Cambridge CB4 1ND
Telephone: 01223 352790
Fax: 01223 460718
Email: bpc@bpccam.co.uk
Web Site: http://www.bpccam.co.uk

Warehouse:
CED, Over Industrial Park, 2 Norman Way, Over, Cambridge CB24 5QE
Telephone: 01954 231957
Fax: 01954 230041

London Office:
The Baltic Exchange, St Mary Axe, London EC3A 8EX
Telephone: (020) 7623 2308
Fax: (020) 7623 2309
Email: bpc@bpccam.co.uk
Web Site: http://www.bpccam.co.uk

Managing Director: Colin Walsh
Managers: Susan Buck *(Accounts)*
Jo Littlechild *(Marketing)*
Jo'e Coleby *(Editorial Project)*

Academic & Scholarly; Accountancy & Taxation; Agriculture; Antiques & Collecting; Aviation; Biography & Autobiography; Cookery, Wines & Spirits; Do-It-Yourself; Educational & Textbooks; Environment & Development Studies; Fashion & Costume; Fine Art & Art History; Guide Books; Health & Beauty; Illustrated & Fine Editions; Law; Medical (incl. Self Help & Alternative Medicine); Music; Natural History; Nautical; Reference Books, Directories & Dictionaries; Scientific & Technical; Sports & Games; Theatre, Drama & Dance; Travel & Topography

New Titles: 14 (2007), 15 (2008)
No of Employees: 3
Annual Turnover: £250,000

ISBNs, Imprints & Series:
978 0 906782, 978 1 857570

Parent Company:
Book Production Consultants Ltd

Associated Companies:
Book Connections Ltd

2324

GREEN BOOKS
Foxhole, Dartington, Totnes, Devon TQ9 6EB
Telephone: 01803 863843 & 863260
Fax: 01803 863843
Email: sales@greenbooks.co.uk
Web Site: http://www.greenbooks.co.uk

UK Trade Distributor:
Central Books, 99 Wallis Road, London E9 5LN

Publisher: John Elford
Sales & Marketing: Bee West
Editorial: Amanda Cuthbert

Architecture & Design; Biography & Autobiography; Do-It-Yourself; Economics; Environment & Development Studies; Fine Art & Art History; Gardening; Guide Books; Health & Beauty; Literature & Criticism; Natural History; Philosophy; Politics & World Affairs; Reference Books, Directories & Dictionaries; Travel & Topography

New Titles: 15 (2007), 15 (2008)
No of Employees: 6

ISBNs, Imprints & Series:
978 0 9527302 Themis Books
978 1 870098 Green Books & Resurgence Books
978 1 900322 Green Earth Books
978 1 903998 Green Books

Distributor for:
USA: Chelsea Green Publishing Co [selected titles]

Overseas Representation:
Australia: Brumby Books Holdings Pty Ltd, Kilsyth South, Vic
New Zealand: Ceres Books, Ellerslie
USA: Chelsea Green Publishing Co, White River Junction, VT

2325

GREEN MAGIC
The Long Barn, Sutton Mallet, Somerset TA7 9AR
Telephone: 01278 722888
Fax: 01278 722565
Email: petergotto@aol.com
Web Site: http://www.greenmagicpublishing.com

Representation (UK):
Counter Culture, (address as above)
Telephone: (as above)
Fax: (as above)

Representation:
Bookspeed, 16 Salamander Yards, Edinburgh EH6 7DD

Owner: Pete Gotto

Archaeology; Magic & the Occult; Medical (incl. Self Help & Alternative Medicine); Religion & Theology; Travel & Topography

ISBNs, Imprints & Series:
978 0 9536631, 978 0 9542963, 978 0 9547230

Overseas Representation:
Australia: Brumby Books Holdings Pty Ltd, Kilsyth South, Vic
Canada: Marginal Distribution, Peterborough
New Zealand: Peaceful Living Publications, Auckland
South Africa: Bacchus Books, Gauteng
USA: SCB Distributors, Gardena, CA

Book Trade Association Membership:
BA

2326

W. GREEN THE SCOTTISH LAW PUBLISHER
[a Thomson Company]
21 Alva Street, Edinburgh EH2 4PS
Telephone: 0131 225 4879
Fax: 0131 225 2104
Email: Alan.Bett@thomson.com
Web Site: http://www.wgreen.thomson.com

Director: Mrs Gilly Grant
Marketing Manager: Alan Bett
Publisher: Mrs Jill Hyslop

Law

New Titles: 28 (2007), 28 (2008)
No of Employees: 25

ISBNs, Imprints & Series: 978 0 414

Parent Company:
International Thomson Corporation

Overseas Representation:
Australia: The Law Book Co Ltd, North Ryde
Bangladesh: Karim International, Dhaka
Botswana: Kerrison Book Services, Gabarone
Canada: Carswell Publishing Ltd, Scarborough, Ont
Ghana: J. A. Amoah, Accra
India: N. M. Tripathi Pte Ltd, Bombay
Israel: Steimatzky Ltd, Bnei Brak
Japan: Macmillan Shuppan KK, Tokyo
Kenya, Tanzania, Uganda & Mauritius: Kelvin van Hasselt Publishing Services, Briningham, Norfolk, UK
Malawi, Zambia & Zimbabwe: Barbie Keene, Harare, Zimbabwe
Malaysia, Singapore & Brunei: Malayan Law Journal Pte Ltd, Singapore
Pakistan: Pakistan Law House, Karachi

Book Trade Association Membership:
Publishing Scotland

2327

GREENHILL BOOKS / LIONEL LEVENTHAL LTD
3 Barham Avenue, Elstree, Herts WD6 3PW
Telephone: (020) 8953 4969
Fax: (020) 8953 4969
Email: l.leventhal@hotmail.co.uk
Web Site: http://www.greenhillbooks.com

Warehouse:
Bookpoint Ltd, 39 Milton Park, Abingdon, Oxon OX14 4TD
Telephone: 01235 400400
Fax: 01235 832068

Director: Lionel Leventhal

Aviation; History & Antiquarian; Military & War

Overseas Representation:
Australia & New Zealand: Peribo Pty Ltd, Mount Kuring-Gai, NSW, Australia
Austria, Switzerland, Czech & Slovak Republics, Hungary, Poland, Croatia, Slovenia, Spain (including Gibraltar) & Portugal: Sandro Salucci, Florence, Italy
Belgium: De Krijger, Erps
Canada: Vanwell Publishing Ltd, St Catharines, Ont
France & Netherlands: Casemate Books, Newbury, UK
Germany: Robbert J. Pleysier, Heerde, Netherlands
India: Knowledge World International, Delhi
Middle East & Far East: Publishers International Marketing, Burmarsh, UK
New Zealand: South Pacific Books (Imports) Ltd, Auckland
South Africa: Peter Renew, Titles SA, Johannesburg
USA: MBI Publishing Co, St Paul, MN

2328

GREENLEAF PUBLISHING
Aizlewood's Mill, Nursery Street, Sheffield S3 8GG
Telephone: 0114 282 3475
Fax: 0114 282 3476
Email: sales@greenleaf-publishing.com
Web Site: http://www.greenleaf-publishing.com

Office Manager: Jayney Bown
Directors: Dean Bargh *(Editorial)*
John Stuart *(Managing)*

Academic & Scholarly; Educational & Textbooks; Environment & Development Studies; Industry, Business & Management; Scientific & Technical

New Titles: 8 (2007), 9 (2008)

ISBNs, Imprints & Series:
978 1 874719, 978 1 906093

Overseas Representation:
Australia: DA Information Services Pty Ltd, Mitcham, Vic
India: Viva Books, New Delhi
Taiwan: Unifacmanu Trading Co Ltd, Taipei
USA & Canada: Renouf Publishing Co Ltd, Ottawa, Ont, Canada

2329

GREENLIGHT PUBLISHING
119 Newland Street, Witham, Essex CM8 1WF
Telephone: 01376 521900
Fax: 01376 521901
Email: alan@acguk.com
Web Site: http://www.greenlightpublishing.co.uk

Managing Director: Alan Golbourn
IT Manager: Daniel Golbourn

Antiques & Collecting; Archaeology; Crafts & Hobbies

No of Employees: 15

ISBNs, Imprints & Series: 978 1 897738

Parent Company:
UK: Ace Publications Ltd

2330

GREENWOOD PUBLISHING GROUP
Wilkinson House, Jordan Hill, Oxford
OX2 8DP
Telephone: 01865 314201
Fax: 01865 314657
Email: suzanne.wheatley@harcourt.co.uk
Web Site: http://www.greenwood.com &
http://www.heineman.com

Customer Service:
Linacre House, Jordan Hill, Oxford OX2 8DP
Telephone: 01865 888181
Fax: 01865 314091
Email:
greenwood.enquiries@harcourt.co.uk

Representation:
Roundhouse Group, Millstone, Limers Lane,
Northam, Devon EX39 2RG
Telephone: 01237 474474
Fax: 01237 474774
Email: roundhouse.group@ukgateway.net

Director: Tony Sloggett
Marketing Manager: Suzanne Wheatley
Senior Acquisitions Editor: Simon Mason

*Academic & Scholarly; Bibliography &
Library Science; Biography &
Autobiography; Cinema, Video, TV &
Radio; Economics; Educational &
Textbooks; Gender Studies; History &
Antiquarian; Industry, Business &
Management; Law; Literature & Criticism;
Medical (incl. Self Help & Alternative
Medicine); Military & War; Music;
Philosophy; Politics & World Affairs;
Psychology & Psychiatry; Reference Books,
Directories & Dictionaries; Religion &
Theology; Science Fiction; Sociology &
Anthropology; Sports & Games; Theatre,
Drama & Dance*

ISBNs, Imprints & Series:
978 0 275 Praeger Publishers
978 0 313, 978 0 8371 Greenwood Press
978 0 325 Heinemann USA
978 0 86569 Auburn House
978 0 86709 Boynton/Cook
978 0 89789 Bergin & Garvey
978 0 89930, 978 1 56720 Quorum Books
978 1 56750 Ablex Publishing
978 1 57356 Oryx Press
978 1 84645 Greenwood World Publishing

Parent Company:
Houghton Mifflin Harcourt

Overseas Representation:
Africa: Kelvin van Hasselt Publishing
Services, Briningham, Norfolk, UK
Australia & New Zealand: DA Information
Services Pty Ltd, Mitcham, Vic, Australia
Canada (Institutional orders only): Edu
Reference Publishers Direct Inc, Toronto,
Ont, Canada
*Cyprus, Malta, Turkey, Jordan, Palestine,
Morocco, Tunisia & Algeria:* Claire de
Gruchy, Avicenna Partnership, Oxford,
UK
*Egypt, Gulf States, Iran, Iraq, Lebanon, Libya
& Syria:* Bill Kennedy, Avicenna
Partnership, Oxford, UK
Europe: Andrew Durnell Marketing Ltd,
Tunbridge Wells, UK
Hong Kong, Taiwan, China & Korea: Asia
Publishers Services Ltd, Hong Kong
India, Sri Lanka, Bangladesh & Pakistan:
Overleaf, New Delhi, India
Israel: Franklins International, Tel Aviv
Japan: Yushodo Co Ltd, Tokyo
*Mexico, Central & South America &
Caribbean (including Puerto Rico):*
Cranbury International LLC, Montpelier,
VT, USA
*Singapore, Malaysia, Thailand, Indonesia,
Philippines, Brunei, Vietnam, Camabodia
& Laos:* APD Singapore Pte Ltd,
Singapore

South Africa: Heinemann International
South Africa, Sandton

2331

GRESHAM BOOKS LTD
46 Victoria Road, Summertown, Oxford
OX2 7QD
Telephone: 01865 513582
Fax: 01865 512718
Email: info@gresham-books.co.uk
Web Site: http://www.gresham-books.co.uk

Directors: Paul Lewis *(Managing)*
Mary Lewis *(Sales)*

*History & Antiquarian; Music; Religion &
Theology*

New Titles: 35 (2007), 30 (2008)
No of Employees: 2

ISBNs, Imprints & Series:
978 0 905418, 978 0 946095, 978 0
9502121

2332

GRUB STREET
4 Rainham Close, London SW11 6SS
Telephone: (020) 7924 3966 & 7738 1008
Fax: (020) 7738 1009
Email: post@grubstreet.co.uk
Web Site: http://www.grubstreet.co.uk

Distribution:
Littlehampton Book Services Ltd,
Faraday Close, Durrington, Worthing,
West Sussex BN13 3RB
Telephone: 01903 828500
Fax: 01903 828802
Email: ...@lbsltd.co.uk
Web Site: http://www.lbsltd.co.uk

Director: John Davies
Sales & Marketing: Anne Dolamore

*Aviation; Cookery, Wines & Spirits; Military
& War*

New Titles: 35 (2007), 36 (2008)
No of Employees: 4
Annual Turnover: £900,000

ISBNs, Imprints & Series:
978 0 948817, 978 1 898697, 978 1
902304, 978 1 904010, 978 1 904943,
978 1 906502

Overseas Representation:
Asia & Middle East: Grub Street, London,
UK
Australia: Capricorn Link (Australia) Pty Ltd,
Windsor, NSW
Canada: Vanwell Publishing Ltd, St
Catharines, Ont
Germany, Austria & Switzerland: EMS
(Anselm Robinson), London, UK
*North West Europe (including France,
Belgium, Netherlands & Scandinavia):*
Angell Eurosales, Berwick-on-Tweed, UK
Republic of Ireland: Vivienne Lavery,
Blackrock, Co Dublin
South Africa: Penguin Books South Africa
(Pty) Ltd, Johannesburg
Southern Europe: Penny Padovani, London,
UK
USA: Casemate Publishers & Book
Distributors LLC, Havertown, PA

Book Trade Association Membership:
IPG; BA (Associate Member)

2333

GUILDHALL PRESS
Unit 15, Rath Mor Centre, Bligh's Lane,
Derry BT48 0LZ
Telephone: (028) 7136 4413
Fax: (028) 7137 2949
Email: info@ghpress.com

Web Site: http://www.ghpress.com

Manager: Paul Hippsley *(Project &
Managing Editor, Marketing)*

*Academic & Scholarly; Biography &
Autobiography; Children's Books; Crime;
Educational & Textbooks; Fiction; Gay &
Lesbian Studies; Guide Books; History &
Antiquarian; Humour; Literature &
Criticism; Music; Photography; Poetry;
Politics & World Affairs; Theatre, Drama &
Dance*

New Titles: 12 (2007), 12 (2008)
No of Employees: 5

ISBNs, Imprints & Series: 978 0 946451

Overseas Representation:
Australia: Irish Book Centre, Melbourne
USA: Irish Books & Media Inc, Minneapolis,
MN

Book Trade Association Membership:
CLÉ (Irish PA)

2334

GWASG CARREG GWALCH
12 Iard yr Orsaf, Llanrwst, Conwy LL26 0EH
Telephone: 01492 642031
Fax: 01492 641502
Email: llyfrau@carreg-gwalch.com
Web Site: http://www.carreg-gwalch.com

Manager: Myrddin ap Dafydd
Editor: Gordon Jones

Folklore; Welsh Interest

New Titles: 55 (2007), 55 (2008)

ISBNs, Imprints & Series:
978 0 86381, 978 1 84524, 978 1 84527

Overseas Representation:
Worldwide: Welsh Book Centre,
Aberystwyth, UK

Book Trade Association Membership:
Welsh PA

2335

GWASG GWENFFRWD
PO Box 21, Corwen LL21 9WZ
Telephone: 0845 330 6754

Director of Research: Dr H. G. A. Hughes

*Academic & Scholarly; Bibliography &
Library Science; Biography &
Autobiography; Children's Books;
Educational & Textbooks; Electronic
(Professional & Academic); History &
Antiquarian; Languages & Linguistics;
Literature & Criticism; Poetry; Politics &
World Affairs; Reference Books, Directories
& Dictionaries; Religion & Theology;
Sociology & Anthropology; Travel &
Topography*

New Titles: 6 (2007), 6 (2008)
No of Employees: 2

ISBNs, Imprints & Series:
978 0 9501861, 978 1 85651

2336

GWASG GWYNEDD
Cibyn, Caernarfon, Gwynedd LL55 2BD
Telephone: 01286 674486
Fax: 01286 678489

Managing Director: Alwyn Elis
Administration: Alwena Owen
Editor: Nan Elis

Biography & Autobiography; Children's

Books; Welsh Interest

New Titles: 10 (2007), 10 (2008)

ISBNs, Imprints & Series: 978 0 86074

2337

HACHETTE CHILDREN'S BOOKS
338 Euston Road, London NW1 3BH
Telephone: (020) 7873 6000
Fax: (020) 7873 6024
Email: gm@hachettechildrens.co.uk

Distribution Centre:
Bookpoint Ltd, 130 Milton Park, Abingdon,
Oxon OX14 4SB
Telephone: 01235 400400
Fax: 01235 400445

Directors: Marlene Johnson *(Managing)*
Catherine Newman *(Chief Operating
Officer)*
Les Phipps *(Group Sales)*
Andrew Sharp *(Group Rights)*
Charmian Allwright *(Group Production)*
Margaret Conroy *(Publishing (Audio &
Licensed))*
Anne McNeil *(Publishing (Picture Books &
Fiction))*
Susan Barry *(Marketing)*
Rachel Cooke *(Franklin Watts)*
Managers: Anne Marimuthu *(Finance)*
Paul Litherland *(Trade Sales)*

*Audio Books; Children's Books; Educational
& Textbooks; Fiction; Fine Art & Art History;
Poetry; Reference Books, Directories &
Dictionaries; Books for Babies; Novelty
Books*

New Titles: 1363 (2007), 1500 (2008)
No of Employees: 110

ISBNs, Imprints & Series:
Aladdin/Watts; Animal Ark Series; Felicity
Wishes range; Franklin Watts; Hodder
Home Learning Series; Orchard Books;
Rainbow Magic
978 0 340 Hodder Children's Books; Kipper
range
978 0 750 Hodder Wayland

Parent Company:
Hachette Livre UK

Distributor for:
Aladdin

Overseas Representation:
*Africa, West Indies, South & Central
America:* Tony Moggach, InterMedia
Americana (IMA) Ltd, London, UK
Australia: Hachette Livre Australia, Sydney,
NSW
Australia & New Zealand: Watts ANZ,
Sydney, NSW, Australia
Brazil (paperbacks): Agencia Siciliano de
Livros, São Paulo, Brazil
Canada (trade & paperbacks): McArthur &
Co Publishers Ltd, Toronto, Ont, Canada
Eastern Europe: David Williams, InterMedia
Americana (IMA) Ltd, London, UK
Germany, Switzerland & Austria: Gabriele
Kern Publishers Services, Frankfurt-am-
Main, Germany
Hong Kong: Publishers' Associates Ltd
India: Ajay Parmar, New Delhi
Israel: Steimatzky Ltd, Bnei Brak
Italy, Spain, Portugal & Gibraltar: Penny
Padovani, London, UK
Japan & Korea: Yasy Murayama, Ageo,
Japan
Netherlands (trade): Nilsson & Lamm BV,
Weesp, Netherlands
New Zealand: Hachette Livre New Zealand,
Auckland
*Norway, Sweden, Finland, Denmark,
Iceland, Netherlands & France:* Angell
Eurosales, Berwick-on-Tweed, UK
Pakistan (paperbacks): Liberty Books (Pvt)
Ltd, Karachi, Pakistan

Republic of Ireland & Northern Ireland:
Repforce Ireland Ltd, Monkstown, Republic of Ireland
Singapore & Malaysia: APD Singapore Pte Ltd, Singapore
South Africa: Jonathan Ball Publishers (Pty) Ltd, Jeppestown; Pan Macmillan SA Pty Ltd, Hyde Park
South Africa & Southern Africa (Wayland): Pan Macmillan SA Pty Ltd, Hyde Park, South Africa
Southern Africa (trade): Jonathan Ball Publishers (Pty) Ltd, Johannesburg, South Africa

Book Trade Association Membership:
Publishers Association; EPC

2338

HACHETTE LIVRE UK LTD
338 Euston Road, London NW1 3BH
Telephone: (020) 7873 6000
Fax: (020) 7873 6024
Web Site: http://www.hachettelivre.co.uk

Academic & Scholarly; Children's Books; Educational & Textbooks; Electronic (Professional & Academic); Law; Medical (incl. Self Help & Alternative Medicine); Religion & Theology; Trade

Associated Companies:
UK: Philip Allan; Chambers Harrap Publishers Ltd; Hachette Children's Books; Hodder & Stoughton; Hodder Education Group; Little, Brown Group UK; John Murray; Octopus Publishing Group; Orion Publishing Group; Piatkus Books

Book Trade Association Membership:
Publishers Association

2339

PETER HADDOCK PUBLISHING
Pinfold Lane, Bridlington, East Yorkshire YO16 6BT
Telephone: 01262 678121
Fax: 01262 400043
Email: sales@phpublishing.co.uk
Web Site: http://www.phpublishing.co.uk

Directors: Rodney Noon *(Managing)*
David Haddock
Pat Hornby
Managers: Peter Thornton *(Shipping)*
Brian Pannhausen *(Warehouse)*
Jason Hickey *(Customer Services)*

Children's Books; Reference Books, Directories & Dictionaries

ISBNs, Imprints & Series:
Big Time
978 0 7105

Parent Company:
D. C. Thomson & Co Ltd

Book Trade Association Membership:
BA

2340

HALBAN PUBLISHERS
22 Golden Square, Piccadilly, London W1F 9JW
Telephone: (020) 7437 9300
Fax: (020) 7437 9512
Email: books@halbanpublishers.com
Web Site: http://www.halbanpublishers.com

Distribution:
Littlehampton Book Services, Faraday Close, Durrington, Worthing, West Sussex BN13 3RB
Telephone: 01903 828842
Fax: 01903 828621
Email: rose.mellish@lbsltd.co.uk

Directors: Peter Halban
Martine Halban

Biography & Autobiography; Fiction; History & Antiquarian; Literature & Criticism; Philosophy; Politics & World Affairs; Religion & Theology

ISBNs, Imprints & Series:
978 1 870015, 978 1 905559

Overseas Representation:
Australia: Allen & Unwin Pty Ltd, Crows Nest, NSW
Canada: McArthur & Co Publishers Ltd, Toronto, Ont
Caribbean: Humphrys Roberts Associates, London, UK
East & West Africa: Richard Carman Associates, Northwich, UK
Europe (excluding Scandinavia & Netherlands): c/o Florence Chatelain, The Orion Publishing Group Ltd, London, UK
India, Sri Lanka & Bangladesh: Maya Publishers Pvt Ltd, New Delhi, India
Japan, South East Asia, Far East & Pakistan: Ralph & Sheila Summers, Woodford Green, Essex, UK
Middle East & North Africa: Peter Ward Book Exports, London, UK
Netherlands: Consul Books, Blaricum
New Zealand: Hodder Moa Beckett Publishers (NZ) Ltd, Auckland
Republic of Ireland: Gill Hess Ltd, Skerries, Co Dublin
Russia, Baltic States & former USSR: Tony Moggach, IMA, London, UK
Scandinavia: Pernille Larsen (Books for Europe), Roskilde, Denmark
South Africa: Jonathan Ball Publishers (Pty) Ltd, Johannesburg
South America: Humphrys Roberts Associates, Cotia SP, Brazil
USA & other territories: Export Department, The Orion Publishing Group Ltd, London, UK
Yugoslavia, Bosnia, Romania, Poland, Bulgaria, Hungary, Czech Republic, Slovakia, Slovenia & Croatia: Csaba & Jackie Lengyel de Bagota, Budapest, Hungary

Book Trade Association Membership:
IPG

2341

HALDANE MASON LTD
PO Box 34196, London NW10 3YB
Telephone: (020) 8459 2131
Fax: (020) 8728 1216
Email: info@haldanemason.com
Web Site: http://www.haldanemason.com

Warehouse, Trade Enquiries & Orders:
Vine House Distribution Ltd, The Old Mill House, Mill Lane, Uckfield, East Sussex TN22 5AA
Telephone: 01825 767396
Fax: 01825 765649
Email: sales@vinehouseuk.co.uk

Directors: Ron Samuel
Ms Sydney Francis

Children's Books; Cookery, Wines & Spirits; Crafts & Hobbies; Educational & Textbooks; Health & Beauty; Medical (incl. Self Help & Alternative Medicine); Natural History; Sports & Games

ISBNs, Imprints & Series:
Haldane Mason; Red Kite Books
978 1 902463
978 1 905339

Book Trade Association Membership:
IPG

2342

ROBERT HALE LTD
Clerkenwell House,
45–47 Clerkenwell Green, London EC1R 0HT
Telephone: (020) 7251 2661
Fax: (020) 7490 4958
Email: gj@halebooks.com
Web Site: http://www.halebooks.com

Warehouse & Returns:
Combined Book Services, Units I/K, Paddock Wood Distribution Centre, Paddock Wood, Tonbridge, Kent TN12 6UU
Telephone: 01892 837171
Fax: 01892 837272
Email: orders@combook.co.uk

Directors: John Hale *(Managing)*
Robert Kynaston *(Finance)*
Managers: Elizabeth Robson *(Rights)*
Gill Jackson *(General)*
Robert Hale *(Production)*
Susan Hale *(Editorial)*

Animal Care & Breeding; Antiques & Collecting; Biography & Autobiography; Cinema, Video, TV & Radio; Crafts & Hobbies; Crime; Fiction; Humour; Magic & the Occult; Military & War; Music; Natural History; Photography; Politics & World Affairs; Travel & Topography

New Titles: 258 (2007), 240 (2008)
No of Employees: 19

ISBNs, Imprints & Series:
978 0 7090, 978 0 7091, 978 0 7198 NAG Press
978 0 85131 J. A. Allen

Distributor for:
Phoenix

Overseas Representation:
Australia: DLS Australia (Pty) Ltd, Braeside, Vic
France, Germany, Netherlands, Austria & Switzerland: Ted Dougherty, London, UK
Italy, Spain, Portugal, Greece & Gibraltar: Penny Padovani, London, UK
New Zealand: South Pacific Books (Imports) Ltd, Auckland
South Africa: Trinity Books CC, Randburg
USA: Trafalgar Square Publishing, North Pomfret, VT

2343

HALSGROVE
Halsgrove House, Ryelands Estate, Bagley Road, Wellington, Somerset TA21 9PZ
Telephone: 01823 653777
Fax: 01823 665294
Email: sales@halsgrove.com
Web Site: http://www.halsgrove.com

Managing Director: Julian Davidson
Chairman: Steven Pugsley
Publisher: Simon Butler

Archaeology; Aviation; Biography & Autobiography; Fine Art & Art History; Guide Books; History & Antiquarian; Illustrated & Fine Editions; Military & War; Natural History; Travel & Topography

New Titles: 110 (2007), 160 (2008)
No of Employees: 15
Annual Turnover: £2M

ISBNs, Imprints & Series:
978 0 906551 Rylands
978 0 906690 Halstar
978 1 84114 Halsgrove

Parent Company:
UK: D. A. A. Halsgrove Ltd

Associated Companies:
UK: Halstar Ltd

Distributor for:
UK: Halsgrove; Halstar; Ryelands

2344

HAMBLEDON CONTINUUM LTD
The Tower Building, 11 York Road, London SE1 7NX
Telephone: (020) 7922 0880
Fax: (020) 7922 0881
Web Site: http://www.continuumbooks.com

Distribution, Orders, Credit Control:
Orca Book Services, Stanley House, 3 Fleets Lane, Poole, Dorset BH15 3AJ
Telephone: 01202 665432
Fax: 01202 666219
Web Site: http://www.orcabookservices.co.uk

Chief Executive: Oliver Gadsby
Directors: Robin Baird-Smith *(Publishing)*
Bob Marsh *(Financial)*
Ken Rhodes *(Sales & Marketing)*
Benn Linfield *(Production)*
Managers: Ben Hayes *(Editorial)*
Elizabeth White *(Rights)*

Academic & Scholarly; Archaeology; Architecture & Design; Fine Art & Art History; History & Antiquarian; Military & War; Politics & World Affairs; Reference Books, Directories & Dictionaries

New Titles: 40 (2007), 40 (2008)

ISBNs, Imprints & Series:
978 0 907628, 978 0 9506882, 978 1 85285

Parent Company:
The Continuum International Publishing Group Ltd

Overseas Representation:
see: The Continuum International Publishing Group Ltd, London, UK

Book Trade Association Membership:
IPG

2345

HANBURY PLAYS
Keeper's Lodge, Broughton Green, Droitwich, Worcs WR9 7EE
Telephone: 01527 821564
Email: hanburyplays@tiscali.co.uk
Web Site: http://www.hanburyplays.co.uk

Proprietor: Brian J. Burton

Theatre, Drama & Dance; Plays

New Titles: 4 (2007), 4 (2008)

ISBNs, Imprints & Series:
978 0 85197, 978 0 907926, 978 1 85205

Distributor for:
USA: Contemporary Drama Service; Pioneer Drama Service

Overseas Representation:
Australia: The Dominie Group, Brookvale, NSW
Malta: Dingli Co International, Valletta
New Zealand: Play Bureau of New Zealand Ltd, New Plymouth

2346

HARDEN'S LTD
14 Buckingham Street, London WC2N 6DF
Telephone: (020) 7839 4763
Fax: (020) 7839 7561
Email: rh@hardens.com
Web Site: http://www.hardens.com

2347

Directors: Richard Harden
Peter Harden

Guide Books; Reference Books, Directories & Dictionaries

ISBNs, Imprints & Series: 978 1 873721

2347

HARLEQUIN MILLS & BOON LTD
Eton House, 18–24 Paradise Road, Richmond, Surrey TW9 1SR
Telephone: (020) 8288 2800
Fax: (020) 8288 2899
Web Site: http://www.millsandboon.co.uk

Electronic (Professional & Academic); Trade

Book Trade Association Membership:
Publishers Association

2348

HARPERCOLLINS PUBLISHERS LTD
77–85 Fulham Palace Road, London W6 8JB
Telephone: (020) 8741 7070
Fax: (020) 8307 4440
Web Site: http://www.harpercollins.co.uk

Registered Office (Warehouse, Trade Orders & Distribution, Finance):
Westerhill Road, Bishopbriggs, Glasgow G64 2QR
Telephone: 0141 772 3200
Fax: 0141 772 3200 x3119

Chief Executive Officer: Victoria Barnsley *(Publisher)*
Chief Operating Officer: Keith Mullock *(Executive)*
Managing Directors: Amanda Ridout *(HarperCollins)*
Katie Fulford *(Acting, Collins)*
Robert Scriven *(Languages)*
Mario Santos *(Children's)*
Belinda Budge *(Harper Non-Fiction)*
John Bond *(Press Books)*
David Swarbick *(Group Sales & Marketing)*
Nigel Ward *(Education)*
Directors: James Graves *(Group Production)*
Lucy Vanderbilt *(Rights, General Books)*
Sylvia May *(International Sales, General Books)*
Myles Archbald *(Rights & Associate Publisher - Collins Reference)*
Helen Ellis *(Publicity)*
Executive Directors: Julian Thomas *(Business Systems & Services)*
Sean Plunkett *(Supply Chain)*
Ed Kielbasiewicz *(Finance)*
Siobhan Kerry *(Communications)*
Publishing Directors: Paul Baggaley *(Perennial)*
Juliet Lawler *(World Atlases)*
Denise Bates *(Illustrated Reference)*
Julia Wisdom *(Harper Fiction, Crime)*
Susan Watt *(Harper Fiction)*
Jonathan Taylor *(Harper Sport)*
Jane Johnson *(Harper Fiction, Voyager)*
Gillie Russell *(Children's Fiction)*
Sally Potter *(Harper Thorsons/Harper Element)*
Nick Pearson *(Fourth Estate)*
David Brawn *(Tolkien & Estates)*
Sue Buswell *(Children's Picture Books)*
Clare Smith *(Harper Press Fiction)*
Arabella Pike *(Harper Press Non-Fiction)*
Lynne Drew *(Harper Fiction)*

Animal Care & Breeding; Antiques & Collecting; Architecture & Design; Atlases & Maps; Audio Books; Biography & Autobiography; Biology & Zoology; Chemistry; Children's Books; Cinema, Video, TV & Radio; Cookery, Wines & Spirits; Crafts & Hobbies; Crime; Do-It-Yourself; Economics; Educational & Textbooks; Electronic (Educational); Electronic (Professional & Academic); English as a Foreign Language; Fiction; Fine Art & Art History; Gardening; Gender Studies; Geography & Geology; Guide Books; Health & Beauty; History & Antiquarian; Humour; Illustrated & Fine Editions; Industry, Business & Management; Languages & Linguistics; Literature & Criticism; Magic & the Occult; Medical (incl. Self Help & Alternative Medicine); Military & War; Natural History; Photography; Physics; Poetry; Politics & World Affairs; Psychology & Psychiatry; Reference Books, Directories & Dictionaries; Religion & Theology; Science Fiction; Scientific & Technical; Sports & Games; Travel & Topography

ISBNs, Imprints & Series:
Collins; Collins Classics; Collins Crime; Collins Dictionaries COBUILD; Collins New Naturalist Library; Collins Teacher; Collins/Times Maps & Atlases; CollinsEducation; CollinsGems; Fourth Estate; Harper Perennial; Harper Sport; Harper Thorsons/Harper Element; HarperCollins; HarperCollins Audio; HarperCollins Children's Books; HarperCollins Entertainment; HarperCollins Non-Fiction; Janes; Times Books; Tolkien; Voyager

Parent Company:
News Corporation

Overseas Representation:
Australia: HarperCollins Publishers, Pymble, NSW
Canada: HarperCollins Publishers, Toronto & Scarborough, Ont
India: HarperCollins Publishers India Pvt Ltd, New Delhi
New Zealand: HarperCollins (NZ) Ltd, Glenfield, Auckland
USA: HarperCollins Publishers, New York
Worldwide (except countries listed): HarperCollins Publishers Ltd, Glasgow & London, UK

Book Trade Association Membership:
Publishers Association

2349

HART PUBLISHING
16C Worcester Place, Oxford OX1 2JW
Telephone: 01865 517530
Fax: 01865 510710
Email: mail@hartpub.co.uk
Web Site: http://www.hartpub.co.uk

Warehouse:
Hoddle, Doyle, Meadows, Station Road, Linton, Cambridge CB1 6UX

Joint Owners: Richard Hart
Jane Parker

Academic & Scholarly; Law

New Titles: 84 (2007), 90 (2008)

ISBNs, Imprints & Series:
978 1 84113, 978 1 901362

Distributor for:
Belgium: Intersentia

Overseas Representation:
Benelux: Intersentia, Antwerp, Belgium
Canada: Codasat, c/o University Toronto Press Distribution, Downsview, Ont
Central & Eastern Europe: Dr László Horváth Publishers Representative, Budapest, Hungary
Greece, Turkey, Arab Middle East & North Africa: James & Lorin Watt Ltd, Publishing Consultants, Oxford, UK
India: Ravindra Saxena, Sara Books Pvt Ltd, New Delhi
Italy & France: Mare Nostrum Publishing Consultants, Rome, Italy
Scandinavia: Colin Flint Ltd, Harlow, UK
South East Asia: STM Publisher Services Pte Ltd, Singapore
Spain & Portugal: Peter Prout Iberian Book Services, Madrid, Spain
USA: International Specialized Book Services Inc, Portland, OR

Book Trade Association Membership:
IPG

2350

HARVARD UNIVERSITY PRESS
Fitzroy House, Chenies Street, London WC1E 7EY
Telephone: (020) 7306 0603
Fax: (020) 7306 0604
Email: info@HUP-MITpress.co.uk
Web Site: http://www.hup.harvard.edu

Orders & Warehouse:
c/o John Wiley & Sons, Southern Cross Trading Estate, 1 Oldlands Way, Bognor Regis, West Sussex PO22 9SA
Telephone: 01243 779777
Fax: 01243 829121
Email: cs-books@wiley.co.uk

Managing Director: Ann Sexsmith
Publicity & Promotion Manager: Fiona Wyatt

Academic & Scholarly; Biography & Autobiography; Biology & Zoology; Cinema, Video, TV & Radio; Economics; Fine Art & Art History; Gender Studies; Health & Beauty; History & Antiquarian; Law; Literature & Criticism; Military & War; Music; Natural History; Philosophy; Politics & World Affairs; Psychology & Psychiatry; Reference Books, Directories & Dictionaries; Religion & Theology; Sociology & Anthropology

ISBNs, Imprints & Series:
Beknap
978 0 674 Harvard University Press
978 0 67499 Loeb Classical Library

Parent Company:
USA: Harvard University Press

Overseas Representation:
China: Everest International Publishing Services, Beijing, P. R. of China
Germany, Austria, Switzerland & Italy: Uwe Lüdemann, Berlin, Germany
Hong Kong: Jane Lam, Aromix Books
India: Mediamatics, Calcutta
Israel: Rodney Franklin Agency, Tel Aviv
Japan: Rockbook, Yokohama
Malaysia: Simon Tay, Apex Knowledge, Selangor
Middle East (excluding Greece & Israel): Avicenna Partnership, Oxford, UK
North America, Mexico & Central America: Harvard University Press, Cambridge, MA, USA
Poland, Hungary, Croatia, Slovenia, Slovakia, Czech Republic, Russia, Lithuania, Latvia, Estonia, Romania, Serbia, Albania & Bosnia Herzegovina: Ewa Ledóchowicz, Konstancin-Jeziorna, Poland
Scandinavia, Netherlands, Luxembourg, Belgium & France: Fred Hermans, Bovenkarspel, Netherlands
South Africa: Cory Voigt Associates, Braamfontein
South America: Julio E. Emod, São Paulo, Brazil
South East Asia: Joseph Goh, IGP Services, Singapore
South Korea: Se-Yung Jun, Seoul, Korea, South
Spain & Portugal: Chris Humphrys, Gaucin, Spain
Taiwan: B. K. Norton, Taipei

Book Trade Association Membership:
IPG

2351

HARVEY MAP SERVICES LTD
12–22 Main Street, Doune, Perthshire FK16 6BJ
Telephone: 01786 841202
Fax: 01786 841098
Email: sh@harveymaps.co.uk
Web Site: http://www.harveymaps.co.uk

Managing Director: Susan Harvey
Office Manager: Jacci Cameron

Atlases & Maps; Sports & Games

New Titles: 12 (2007), 11 (2008)
No of Employees: 7
Annual Turnover: £500,000

ISBNs, Imprints & Series: 978 1 85137

Distributor for:
Canada: Chrismar Inc
Denmark: Compukort
South Africa: Jacana Media [Maps]

Book Trade Association Membership:
International Map Trade Association

2352

HAWKER PUBLICATIONS
Culvert House, Culvert Road, London SW11 5DH
Telephone: (020) 7720 2108
Fax: (020) 7498 3023
Web Site: http://www.careinfo.com

Distribution:
NBN Plymbridge Ltd, Estover Road, Plymouth, Devon PL6 7PZ
Telephone: 01752 202300

Directors: Dr R. Hawkins *(Managing)*
P. Petker *(Sales)*

Health & Beauty; Medical (incl. Self Help & Alternative Medicine); Vocational Training & Careers

No of Employees: 23

ISBNs, Imprints & Series:
978 1 874790 Better Care Guides; Hawker Publications

Overseas Representation:
Australia: Basing House Books, Hammondville, NSW

Book Trade Association Membership:
IPG

2353

HAWTHORN PRESS
Hawthorn House, 1 Lansdown Lane, Stroud, Glos GL5 1BJ
Telephone: 01453 757040
Fax: 01453 751138
Email: info@hawthornpress.com
Web Site: http://www.hawthornpress.com

Distribution & Sales:
BookSource, 50 Cambuslang Road, Glasgow G32 8NB
Telephone: 0845 370 0063
Fax: 0845 370 0064
Email: orders@booksource.net

Directors: Martin Large
Judy Large
Managers: Alan Lord *(Finance)*
Frances Fineran *(IT & Typesetter)*
Carole Richards *(Marketing)*
Rachel Jenkins *(Publishing)*

Academic & Scholarly; Children's Books; Crafts & Hobbies; Educational & Textbooks; Gardening; Gender Studies; Industry, Business & Management; Music; Psychology & Psychiatry; Religion & Theology

New Titles: 7 (2007) , 7 (2008)
No of Employees: 3
Annual Turnover: £300,000

ISBNs, Imprints & Series:
978 0 950706, 978 1 903458
978 1 869890 Conflict & Peace Building; Early Years; Family Activities & Crafts; Parenting & Relationships; Psychology & Self Help; Rudolf Steiner Education

Overseas Representation:
Australia: Footprint Books Pty Ltd, Warriewood, NSW
Canada: Tri-fold Books, Guelph, Ont
New Zealand: Ceres Books, Ellerslie
South Africa: Peter Hyde Associates (Pty) Ltd, Cape Town; Rudolf Steiner Publications, Bryanston
USA (All titles): Steiner Books Inc, Herndon, VA, USA

Book Trade Association Membership:
IPG

2354

HAYNES PUBLISHING
Sparkford, Nr Yeovil, Somerset BA22 7JJ
Telephone: 01963 440635 & 442080 (Customer Services)
Fax: 01963 440825 & 440001 (Customer Services)
Email: sales@haynes.co.uk
Web Site: http://www.haynes.co.uk

Directors: J. Haynes *(Managing)*
James Bunkum *(Finance)*
Jeremy Yates-Round *(Sales & Marketing, UK & Europe)*
Michael Webb *(Automotive Sales)*
Nigel Clements *(Production)*
Matthew Minter *(Motor Trade, Editorial)*
Mark Hughes *(Book Division, Editorial)*
Graham Cook *(Overseas Sales & Rights)*

Animal Care & Breeding; Architecture & Design; Atlases & Maps; Aviation; Biography & Autobiography; Children's Books; Computer Science; Crafts & Hobbies; Do-It-Yourself; Electronic (Educational); Gardening; Guide Books; Health & Beauty; Medical (incl. Self Help & Alternative Medicine); Military & War; Music; Nautical; Photography; Reference Books, Directories & Dictionaries; Scientific & Technical; Sports & Games; Transport; Travel & Topography

New Titles: 82 (2007) , 90 (2008)
No of Employees: 129
Annual Turnover: £29.2M

ISBNs, Imprints & Series:
978 0 85059, 978 1 85260 Patrick Stephens Ltd
978 0 85429 G. T. Foulis
978 0 85696, 978 0 900550 J. H. Haynes & Co Ltd
978 0 902280, 978 0 946609, 978 1 85509 Oxford Illustrated Press
978 1 84425, 978 1 85010, 978 1 85960 Haynes

Parent Company:
Haynes Publishing Group Plc

Distributor for:
Duke Video; The Stationery Office
Italy: Giorgio Nada Editore
USA: David Bull Publishing

Overseas Representation:
Australia: Haynes Manuals Inc, Padstow, NSW
New Zealand: Pace Publications, Wanganui
Sweden: Haynes Publishing Nordiska AB, Uppsala
USA: Haynes Manuals Inc, Newbury Park, CA
USA (non-Manual titles only): MBI Publishing Co, St Paul, MN, USA

Book Trade Association Membership:
BA

2355

HAYWARD PUBLISHING
Southbank Centre, Belvedere Road, London SE1 8XX
Telephone: (020) 7921 0826
Fax: (020) 7921 0700
Email: deborah.power@southbankcentre.co.uk
Web Site: http://www.southbankcentre.co.uk

Sales Manager: Deborah C. Power
Publications Co-ordinator: Giselle Osborne
Art Publisher: Caroline Wetherilt

Architecture & Design; Fine Art & Art History; Photography

New Titles: 6 (2007) , 9 (2008)
No of Employees: 3

ISBNs, Imprints & Series: 978 1 85332

Book Trade Association Membership:
BA

2356

HEART OF ALBION PRESS
2 Cross Hill Close, Wymeswold, Loughborough LE12 6UJ
Telephone: 01509 880725
Fax: 01509 881715
Email: albion@indigogroup.co.uk
Web Site: http://www.hoap.co.uk

Owner: R. N. Trubshaw

Archaeology; Electronic (Educational); Guide Books; History & Antiquarian; Magic & the Occult; Philosophy; Psychology & Psychiatry; Religion & Theology; Sociology & Anthropology

New Titles: 9 (2007) , 6 (2008)
Annual Turnover: £30,000

ISBNs, Imprints & Series:
978 1 872883, 978 1 905646 Alternative Albion; Explore Books; Heart of Albion

2357

ROGER HEAVENS
2 Lowfields, Little Eversden, Cambridge CB23 1HJ
Telephone: 01223 262839
Fax: 01223 262033
Email: roger@ahaygarth.fsnet.co.uk
Web Site: http://www.booksoncricket.net

Proprietor: Roger Heavens
Editors: Sally Heavens
Roger Packham

Academic & Scholarly; Sports & Games

New Titles: 4 (2007) , 5 (2008)
Annual Turnover: £25,000

ISBNs, Imprints & Series:
978 1 900592 Roger Heavens; RH Business Books

Overseas Representation:
Australia: Roger Page, Yallambe, Vic

Book Trade Association Membership:
IPG

2358

HELION & CO LTD
26 Willow Road, Solihull, West Midlands B91 1UE
Telephone: 0121 705 3393
Fax: 0121 711 4075
Email: books@helion.co.uk
Web Site: http://www.helion.co.uk

Managing Director: Duncan Rogers
General Manager: Wilfrid Rogers

Academic & Scholarly; History & Antiquarian; Military & War

New Titles: 15 (2007) , 30 (2008)
No of Employees: 3

ISBNs, Imprints & Series:
978 1 874622, 978 1 906033 Helion & Co Ltd
978 1 905756 Unveiled Publishing

Distributor for:
Aegis Consulting/Aberjona Press; Eagle Editions; Vanwell Publishing

Overseas Representation:
Australia & New Zealand: Crusader Trading Pty Ltd, Weston, ACT, Australia
Austria, France, Switzerland, Benelux, Germany, Eastern Europe, Greece, Italy, Portugal, Spain, Gibraltar, Slovenia & Croatia: Casemate Publishing UK, Newbury, UK
Canada: Vanwell Publishing Ltd, St Catharines, Ont
USA: Casemate Publishers & Book Distributors LLC, Havertown, PA

2359

HEMMING INFORMATION SERVICES
32 Vauxhall Bridge Road, London SW1V 2SS
Telephone: (020) 7973 6604
Fax: (020) 7233 5053
Email: l.alderson@hgluk.com
Web Site: http://www.hgluk.com

Also at:
8 The Old Yarn Mills, Sherborne, Dorset DT9 3RQ
Telephone: 01935 816030
Fax: 01935 817200
Email: info@hisdorset.com

Directors: Graham Bond *(Managing)*
Linda Alderson *(Production)*
Mike Burton *(Editorial (Local Government titles))*
Emma Sabin *(Sales)*
Senior Editor: Dean Wanless

Reference Books, Directories & Dictionaries

No of Employees: 125

ISBNs, Imprints & Series: 978 0 7079

Parent Company:
Hemming Group Ltd

Book Trade Association Membership:
Data Publishers Association; European Directory Publishers Association

2360

IAN HENRY PUBLICATIONS LTD
20 Park Drive, Romford, Essex RM1 4LH
Telephone: 01708 749119
Fax: 01708 736213
Email: info@ian-henry.com
Web Site: http://www.ian-henry.com

Managing Director: Ian Wilkes

Cookery, Wines & Spirits; Educational & Textbooks; Fiction; History & Antiquarian; Humour; Medical (incl. Self Help & Alternative Medicine); Theatre, Drama & Dance; Transport

New Titles: 4 (2007) , 7 (2008)

ISBNs, Imprints & Series: 978 0 86025

Distributor for:
UK: Havering Museum

2361

THE HERBERT PRESS
[an imprint of A. & C. Black]
38 Soho Square, London W1D 3HB
Telephone: (020) 7758 0320
Fax: (020) 7758 0222
Email: llambert@acblack.com

Chairman: Nigel Newton
Managing Director: Jill Coleman
Publisher: Linda Lambert

Architecture & Design; Crafts & Hobbies; Fashion & Costume; Fine Art & Art History; Illustrated & Fine Editions

New Titles: 10 (2007) , 10 (2008)
Annual Turnover: £170,000

ISBNs, Imprints & Series:
978 0 7136, 978 0 906969, 978 1 871569 Design Handbooks; The Herbert History of Art & Architecture

Parent Company:
A. C. Black Plc

Associated Companies:
Bloomsbury

Overseas Representation:
Australia: Allen & Unwin Pty Ltd, Sydney, NSW
Europe: Penguin Group, London, UK

2362

NICK HERN BOOKS
The Glasshouse, 49a Goldhawk Road, London W12 8QP
Telephone: (020) 8749 4953
Fax: (020) 8735 0250
Email: info@nickhernbooks.demon.co.uk
Web Site: http://www.nickhernbooks.co.uk

Distributor:
Grantham Book Services Ltd,
Isaac Newton Way,
Alma Park Industrial Estate, Grantham,
Lincs NG31 9SD
Telephone: 01476 541000
Fax: 01476 541060
Email: orders@gbs.tbs-ltd.co.uk

Managing Director: Nick Hern
Production Editor: Matt Applewhite
Managers: Robin Booth *(Sales & Marketing)*

Cinema, Video, TV & Radio; Theatre, Drama & Dance

ISBNs, Imprints & Series: 978 1 85459

Distributor for:
Canada: Playwrights Press Canada
USA: Drama Book Publishers; Theatre Communications Group

Overseas Representation:
Australia: Currency Press, Sydney
Canada: Playwrights Press Canada, Toronto, Ont
USA: Theatre Communications Group, New York

Book Trade Association Membership:
IPG

2363

HIGHLAND BOOKS
Two High Pines, Knoll Road, Godalming, Surrey GU7 2EP
Telephone: 01483 424560
Fax: 01483 424388
Email: info@highlandbks.com
Web Site: http://www.highlandbks.com

Distribution / Trade Orders:
STL, PO Box 300, Kingstown Broadway, Carlisle, Cumbria CA3 0QS
Telephone: 01228 512512
Fax: 01228 514949
Web Site: http://www.stl.org

Director: Philip Ralli

Biography & Autobiography; Children's Books; Religion & Theology

New Titles: 4 (2007), 12 (2008)
No of Employees: 2
Annual Turnover: £30,000

ISBNs, Imprints & Series:
978 0 946616, 978 1 897913 Highland
978 1 905496 Usharp

Overseas Representation:
New Zealand: Scripture Union Wholesale, Wellington
South Africa: Methodist Wholesale, Cape Town

2364

*HILMARTON MANOR PRESS
Calne, Wilts SN11 8SB
Telephone: 0124 976 0208
Fax: 0124 976 0379
Email: mailorder@hilmartonpress.co.uk
Web Site: http://www.hilmartonpress.co.uk

Directors: C. Baile de Laperriere
S. Baile de Laperriere

Antiques & Collecting; Architecture & Design; Fine Art & Art History; Reference Books, Directories & Dictionaries

ISBNs, Imprints & Series:
978 0 904722, 978 0 9500508

Distributor for:
Art Trade Press
France: ACR Edition; Henri Addor & Associates; ADEC; Bibliotheque des Arts; Edition de l' Amateur; Editions de l'Echelle de Jacob; Editions Van Wilder; Editions Vial; GRUND; Mayer Edition; Servedit-Acatos; Tardy
Germany: Art & Antiques Editions; Art Address Verlag
Switzerland: Bibliotheque des Arts; Editions Acatos; Ides et Calendes
USA: Sound View Press

2365

HINTON HOUSE PUBLISHERS
Lincoln Park, Borough Road, Brackley, Northants NN13 7BE
Telephone: 01280 706706
Fax: 01280 706333
Email: similes@aol.com

Educational & Textbooks

Book Trade Association Membership:
Publishers Association

2366

HIPPOPOTAMUS PRESS
22 Whitewell Road, Frome, Somerset BA11 4EL
Telephone: 01373 466653
Fax: 01373 466653
Email: rjhippopress@aol.com

Publisher: R. John
Editor: M. Pargitter
Editorial Assistant: Anna Martin

Literature & Criticism; Poetry

New Titles: 4 (2007), 6 (2008)
Annual Turnover: £16,000

ISBNs, Imprints & Series: 978 0 904179

Distributor for:
Austria: University of Salzburg Press

2367

HISTORICAL PUBLICATIONS LTD
32 Ellington Street, London N7 8PL
Telephone: (020) 7607 1628
Fax: (020) 7609 6451
Email: richardson@historicalpublications.co.uk

Distribution:
Countryside Books, 2 Highfield Avenue, Newbury, Berks RG14 5DS
Telephone: 01635 43816
Fax: 01635 551004
Email: info@countrysidebooks.co.uk
Web Site: http://www.countrysidebooks.co.uk

Managing Director: John Richardson
Secretary: Helen English

Architecture & Design; History & Antiquarian; Travel & Topography

New Titles: 6 (2007), 6 (2008)
No of Employees: 3

ISBNs, Imprints & Series:
978 0 948667, 978 1 905286

2368

HOBNOB PRESS
PO Box 1838, East Knoyle, Salisbury SP3 6FA
Telephone: 01747 830015
Email: john@hobnobpress.co.uk
Web Site: http://www.hobnobpress.co.uk

Sole Trader: John Chandler

Academic & Scholarly; Archaeology; Guide Books; History & Antiquarian; Literature & Criticism; Travel & Topography

New Titles: 12 (2007), 11 (2008)
Annual Turnover: £42,000

ISBNs, Imprints & Series: 978 0 946418

Distributor for:
Ex Libris Press; Wiltshire Buildings Record; Wiltshire Record Society

2369

HODDER EDUCATION
338 Euston Road, London NW1 3BH
Telephone: (020) 7873 6000
Fax: (020) 7873 6299 & 6325
Web Site: http://www.hoddereducation.co.uk

Distribution Centre:
Bookpoint Ltd, 130 Milton Park, Abingdon, Oxon OX14 4SB
Telephone: 01235 400400
Fax: 01235 400445

Directors: Philip Walters *(Managing)*
C. P. Shaw *(Tertiary)*
Alyssum Ross *(Production & Design)*
Elisabeth Tribe *(Schools Publishing)*
Katie Roden *(Consumer Education)*
John Mitchell *(Scotland – Hodder Gibson)*
Philip Walters *(Sales & Marketing (acting))*
Robert Sulley *(Schools Business Development & International)*
Tim Mahar *(Consumer Education Sales & Marketing)*
Janice Tolan *(School Sales & Marketing)*
Alexia Chan *(FE/HE Editorial)*
Jo Koster *(Health Sciences Editorial)*
Martin Davies *(Schools (Maths, Science & English))*
Jim Belben *(Schools (Humanities & Modern Languages))*
Sam Eardley *(Tertiary Sales & Marketing)*
Steve Connolly *(Editorial Digital Publishing)*
Patrick White *(Managing, Chambers Harrap)*

Academic & Scholarly; Accountancy & Taxation; Animal Care & Breeding; Antiques & Collecting; Archaeology; Atlases & Maps; Audio Books; Aviation; Biology & Zoology; Chemistry; Cinema, Video, TV & Radio; Computer Science; Cookery, Wines & Spirits; Crafts & Hobbies; Do-It-Yourself; Economics; Educational & Textbooks; Electronic (Educational); Electronic (Professional & Academic); English as a Foreign Language; Environment & Development Studies; Gardening; Gender Studies; Geography & Geology; Health & Beauty; History & Antiquarian; Industry, Business & Management; Languages & Linguistics; Law; Literature & Criticism; Mathematics & Statistics; Medical (incl. Self Help & Alternative Medicine); Natural History; Philosophy; Physics; Politics & World Affairs; Psychology & Psychiatry; Reference Books, Directories & Dictionaries; Religion & Theology; Scientific & Technical; Sociology & Anthropology; Sports & Games; Vocational Training & Careers

New Titles: 777 (2007), 836 (2008)
No of Employees: 222
Annual Turnover: £45M

ISBNs, Imprints & Series:
978 0 245 Harrap
978 0 340 Hodder & Stoughton; Hodder & Stoughton Educational; Hodder Arnold; Hodder Murray; Teach Yourself
978 0 550 Chambers
978 0 7131 Arnold
978 0 7169 Hodder Gibson
978 0 7195 John Murray
978 0 86003, 978 1 84489 Philip Allan

Parent Company:
Hodder Headline Plc/Hachette Livre

Associated Companies:
Headline Book Publishing Ltd; Hodder & Stoughton

Overseas Representation:
All other international queries: Scipio Stringer, Head of International Services, Hodder, London, UK
Australia (FE/Medical/Trade): Hachette Livre Australia, Sydney, NSW, Australia
Australia (Livewires): Cambridge University Press, Australia
Australia (School – excluding Livewires): Thomson Learning (Australia), NSW, Australia
Bangladesh (School/FE/Medical/Trade): Ansania Mission Book Distribution House, Bangladesh
Barbados, St Lucia, Grenada, St Vincent & Grenadines (School/FE/Medical/Trade): Louis A. Forde, St Michael, Barbados
Cameroon (School/FE/Medical/Trade): Macmillan Publishers Cameroon Ltd, Limbe, Cameroon
Canada (FE/Medical/Trade, excluding Teach Yourself): Oxford University Press Canadian Branch, Don Mills, Ont, Canada
Canada (School – excluding Modern Languages): Bacon & Hughes Ltd, Ottawa, Ont, Canada
Canada (School – Modern Languages only): The Resource Centre, Waterloo, Canada
Canada (Teach Yourself): McGraw-Hill, Canada
Caribbean (Trade) & South America (School/FE/Medical/Trade): Humphrys Roberts Associates, London, UK
China (School/FE/Medical/Trade): Ian Taylor Associates Ltd, London, UK
Egypt (School): Macmillan Publishers Egypt Ltd, Cairo, Egypt
Ethiopia (School/FE/Medical/Trade): Etcon Ltd, Ethiopia
Europe (School): Gill Dee, International Schools Sales Manager, Hodder, London, UK
France, Italy, Spain & Portugal (FE/Medical/Trade): Anne Kelsall, Hodder, London, UK
Germany, Austria & Switzerland (School/FE/Medical/Trade): Giana Elyea, Hodder, London, UK
Ghana (School/FE/Medical/Trade): EPP Book Services Ltd, Accra, Ghana
Greece & Cyprus (School/FE/Medical/Trade): Zitsa Seraphimidi, J & L Watt, Paleo Faliro, Greece
Hong Kong (School/FE/Medical/Trade) & Taiwan (School/FE/Medical/Trade): Asia Publishers Services Ltd, Hong Kong
Hong Kong (School): Pilot Publishers Services Ltd, Kowloon, Hong Kong
India (School/FE/Medical/Trade, excluding Teach Yourself): Viva Group, New Delhi, India
India (Medical): Jaypee Brothers Medical Publishers (Pte) Ltd, New Delhi, India
India (Teach Yourself): Rupa, New Delhi, India
Iran (FE/Medical/Trade): Farhad Maftoon, Tehran, Iran
Israel (FE/Medical/Trade): Rodney Franklin Agency, Tel Aviv, Israel
Jamaica, Bahamas & Belize (School/FE/Medical/Trade): Kingston Bookshop, Kingston, Jamaica
Japan (School/FE/Trade): United Publishers Services Ltd, Tokyo, Japan
Japan (Medical): Nankodo Co Ltd, Tokyo, Japan
Kenya (School/FE/Medical/Trade): Book Distributors Ltd, Nairobi, Kenya; Textbook Centre, Nairobi, Kenya
Korea (School/FE/Medical/Trade): Information & Culture Korea (ICK), Seoul, Korea, South
Leeward Islands, St Kitts & Dominica (School/FE/Medical): R. J. Laws & Sons, Basseterre, St Kitts
Malawi (School/FE/Medical/Trade): Macmillan Malawi Ltd, Blantyre, Malawi
Maldives (School/FE/Medical/Trade): Asrafee Bookshop, Maldives
Mauritius (School/FE/Medical/Trade): Editions le Printemps, Vacoas, Mauritius
Middle East (FE/Medical/Trade): James & Lorin Watt Ltd, Publishing Consultants, Oxford, UK
Middle East (School); Africa, Caribbean & Middle East (all other international queries): Rebecca Duprey, Hodder, London, UK
Namibia, Swaziland, Botswana, Lesotho & South Africa (School/FE/Medical): Book Promotions Pty Ltd, Diep River, South Africa
Namibia, Swaziland, Botswana, Lesotho, South Africa & Zimbabwe (Trade): Pan Macmillan SA Pty Ltd, Hyde Park, South Africa
New Zealand (School/FE/Medical/Trade): Hachette Livre New Zealand, Auckland, New Zealand
Nigeria (School/FE/Medical/Trade): Bounty Press Ltd, Ibadan, Nigeria
Pakistan ((School/FE/Medical/Trade): Andrew White, The White Partnership, Tunbridge Wells, UK
Republic of Ireland (School/FE/Medical/Trade): Vivienne Lavery, Blackrock, Co Dublin, Republic of Ireland
Scandinavia, Benelux & Eastern Europe (FE/Medical/Trade): Jacek Lewinson, Warsaw, Poland

Singapore, Indonesia, Brunei, Malaysia, Thailand & Philippines (School/FE/Medical): APD Malaysia, Malaysia; APD Singapore Pte Ltd, Singapore
Singapore, Indonesia, Brunei, Malaysia, Thailand & Philippines (Trade): Pansing Distribution Pte Ltd, Singapore, Singapore
Tanzania (School/FE/Medical/Trade): Macmillan Aidan Ltd, Dar es Salaam, Tanzania
Trinidad, Tobago & Guyana (School/FE/Medical/Trade): RIK Services Ltd, San Fernando, Trinidad
Turkey (Medical): Nobel Tip Kitabevlen, Turkey
Uganda (School/FE/Medical/Trade): Macmillan Uganda Ltd, Kampala, Uganda
USA (FE/Medical): Oxford University Press Inc USA, New York, NY, USA
USA (Teach Yourself): McGraw-Hill, Chicago, IL, USA
USA (Trade – excluding Teach Yourself): Trafalgar Square Publishing / IPG, Chicago, IL, USA
Zambia (School/FE/Medical/Trade): Macmillan Zambia, Lusaka, Zambia

Book Trade Association Membership:
EPC; IGSMTP; CAPP

2370

HODDER GIBSON
2A Christie Street, Paisley PA1 1NB
Telephone: 0141 848 1609
Fax: 0141 889 6315
Email: hoddergibson@hodder.co.uk
Web Site: http://www.hoddereducation.co.uk

Distribution:
Bookpoint, 130 Milton Park, Abingdon, Oxon OX14 4SB
Telephone: 01235 400400

Managing Director: John Mitchell
Sales Manager: Jim Donnelly

Academic & Scholarly; Educational & Textbooks

New Titles: 30 (2007), 35 (2008)

ISBNs, Imprints & Series:
978 0 340 Hodder
978 0 7169 formerly Robert Gibson & Sons

Parent Company:
Hodder Headline

Book Trade Association Membership:
EPC; Publishing Scotland

2371

HODDER & STOUGHTON FAITH
338 Euston Road, London NW1 3BH
Telephone: (020) 7873 6000
Fax: (020) 7873 6059
Email: religious-sales@hodder.co.uk
Web Site: http://www.hodderreligious.co.uk

Distribution Centre:
Bookpoint Ltd, 130 Milton Park, Abingdon, Oxon OX14 4SB
Telephone: 01235 400400
Fax: 01235 400445

Directors: Wendy Grisham *(Publishing)*
Jean Whitnall *(Sales & Marketing)*
Elizabeth Hallett *(Design & Production)*
Publisher, Bibles & Digital Media: Ian Metcalfe

Biography & Autobiography; Humour; Medical (incl. Self Help & Alternative Medicine); Religion & Theology

ISBNs, Imprints & Series:
978 0 340 Hodder & Stoughton; Hodder Christian Books; New International Version; New Light Bibles

Parent Company:
Hachette Livre UK Ltd

Associated Companies:
Edward Arnold Ltd; Hachette Livre; Headline Book Publishing Ltd

Overseas Representation:
Australia: Hachette Livre Australia, Sydney, NSW
Canada (Christian trade): R. G. Mitchell Family Books Inc, Kitchener, Ont, Canada
Canada (General trade): McArthur & Co Publishers Ltd, Toronto, Ont, Canada
New Zealand: Hachette Livre New Zealand, Auckland
Pakistan (paperbacks): Liberty Books (Pvt) Ltd, Karachi, Pakistan
Singapore: Pansing Distribution Sdn Bhd
Southern Africa: Jonathan Ball Publishers (Pty) Ltd, Johannesburg, South Africa
USA: Trafalgar Square Publishing, North Pomfret, VT

2372

HODDER & STOUGHTON GENERAL
338 Euston Road, London NW1 3BH
Telephone: (020) 7873 6000
Fax: (020) 7873 6195

Distribution Centre:
Bookpoint Ltd, 130 Milton Park, Abingdon, Oxon OX14 4SB
Telephone: 01235 400400
Fax: 01235 400445

Directors: Jamie Hodder-Williams *(Managing)*
Lisa Highton *(Deputy Managing)*
Lucy Hale *(Sales)*
Karen Geary *(Publicity)*
Auriol Bishop *(Paperback Fiction)*
Elizabeth Hallett *(Production)*
Carolyn Mays *(Fiction)*
Rowena Webb *(Non-Fiction)*
Rupert Lancaster *(Audio)*
Carole Welch *(Sceptre)*
Subsidiary Rights: Jason Bartholomew *(Rights)*

Audio Books; Biography & Autobiography; Cinema, Video, TV & Radio; Cookery, Wines & Spirits; Crime; Fiction; History & Antiquarian; Humour; Military & War; Politics & World Affairs; Science Fiction; Sports & Games

New Titles: 300 (2007), 300 (2008)

ISBNs, Imprints & Series:
978 0 340 Hodder & Stoughton; Mobius; Sceptre

Parent Company:
Hachette Livre UK Ltd

Associated Companies:
Headline Book Publishing Ltd
France: Hachette Livre

Overseas Representation:
Australia: Hachette Livre Australia, Sydney, NSW
Canada (trade & paperbacks): McArthur & Co Publishers Ltd, Toronto, Ont, Canada
New Zealand: Hachette Livre New Zealand, Auckland
Pakistan (paperbacks): Liberty Books (Pvt) Ltd, Karachi, Pakistan
Singapore: Pansing Distribution Sdn Bhd
Southern Africa (trade): Jonathan Ball Publishers (Pty) Ltd, Jeppestown, South Africa

2373

ALISON HODGE PUBLISHERS
2 Clarence Place, Penzance, Cornwall TR20 8XA
Telephone: 01736 368093
Email: info@alison-hodge.co.uk
Web Site: http://www.alison-hodge.co.uk

Distribution:
Tormark, Redruth, Cornwall TR16 5HY
Telephone: 01209 822101
Fax: 01209 822035
Email: sales@tormark.co.uk

Publisher: Alison Hodge

Biography & Autobiography; Cookery, Wines & Spirits; Fine Art & Art History; Gardening; Natural History; Photography; Sports & Games; Travel & Topography

New Titles: 5 (2007), 6 (2008)

ISBNs, Imprints & Series:
The County Gardens Guides Inspirations Series; Pocket Cornwall
978 0 906720

Overseas Representation:
Europe: Bill Bailey Publishers Representatives, Newton Abbot, Devon, UK

2374

HOLLAND PUBLISHING PLC
18 Bourne Court, Southend Road, Woodford Green, Essex IG8 8HD
Telephone: (020) 8551 7711
Fax: (020) 8551 1266
Email: sales@holland-publishing.co.uk
Web Site: http://www.holland-publishing.co.uk

Directors: J. W. Holland *(Managing)*
T. C. Railton *(Sales)*
Mrs S. M. Holland *(Company Secretary)*

Children's Books; Educational & Textbooks

No of Employees: 16
Annual Turnover: £4M

ISBNs, Imprints & Series:
Christmas is Fun; Colouring is Fun; Creative Colouring; Doodle Design; Halloween is Fun; Learning is Fun; Phonics is Fun; Puzzle Zone
978 1 85038

2375

HOLO BOOKS
Clarendon House, 52 Cornmarket, Oxford OX1 3HJ
Telephone: 01865 513681
Fax: 01865 554199
Email: holobooks@yahoo.co.uk
Web Site: http://www.holobooks.co.uk

Orders:
Central Books, 99 Wallis Road, London E9 5LN
Telephone: (020) 8986 4854
Fax: (020) 8533 5821
Email: orders@centralbooks.com
Web Site: http://www.centralbooks.co.uk

Partners: Susanna Hoe
Derek Roebuck
Manager: Leonie Harries

Academic & Scholarly; Archaeology; Biography & Autobiography; Gender Studies; Guide Books; History & Antiquarian; Humour; Law; Travel & Topography

New Titles: 1 (2007), 2 (2008)

ISBNs, Imprints & Series:
The Arbitration Press; Of Islands and Women Series; The Women's History Press

Distributor for:
Hong Kong: Roundhouse Publications (Asia)
USA: Bear Creek Books

Overseas Representation:
Hong Kong: Far East Media
USA: Wm. W. Gaunt & Sons Inc, Holmes Beach, FL

2376

HONNO (WELSH WOMEN'S PRESS)
c/o MyW Centre, Vulcan Street, Aberystwyth SY23 1JH
Telephone: 01970 623150
Fax: 01970 623150
Email: post@honno.co.uk
Web Site: http://www.honno.co.uk

Secretary (Honorary):
Ailsa Craig, Heol y Cawl, Dinas Powys, Vale of Glamorgan CF6 4AH
Telephone: (029) 2051 5014
Fax: (029) 2051 5014
Email: (as above)
Web Site: (as above)

Secretary: Rosanne Reeves
Marketing & Information Officer: Helena Earnshaw
Editor: Caroline Oakley

Biography & Autobiography; Fiction

New Titles: 7 (2007), 7 (2008)
No of Employees: 4
Annual Turnover: £60,000

ISBNs, Imprints & Series:
978 1 870206 Honno Autobiography; Honno Children's Fiction; Honno Classic Fiction; Honno Historical Fiction; Honno Modern Fiction; Honno Poetry

Book Trade Association Membership:
Union of Welsh Booksellers & Publishers

2377

HOPSCOTCH EDUCATIONAL PUBLISHING
St Jude's Church, Dulwich Road, Herne Hill, London SE24 0PB
Telephone: (020) 7738 5454
Fax: (020) 7778 8317
Email: rebecca.h@markallengroup.com
Web Site: http://www.hopscotchbooks.com

Manager: Angela Shaw *(Publishing)*
Assistant: Rebecca Haworth *(Publishing)*

Educational & Textbooks

ISBNs, Imprints & Series:
978 1 902239, 978 1 904307, 978 1 905390

Parent Company:
UK: Mark Allen Group

Book Trade Association Membership:
BESA

2378

*HOUSE OF LOCHAR
Isle of Colonsay, Argyll PA61 7YR
Telephone: 01951 200232
Fax: 01951 200232
Email: lochar@colonsay.org.uk
Web Site: http://www.houseoflochar.com

Distribution:
BookSource, 50 Cambuslang Road, Glasgow G32 8NB

Principal: Kevin Byrne
Manager: Georgina Hobhouse *(Manager)*

Fiction; History & Antiquarian; Transport; Travel & Topography; Scottish Non-Fiction

ISBNs, Imprints & Series:
West Highland Series (Walking Booklets)
978 1 899863

Book Trade Association Membership:
Publishing Scotland

2379

HOW TO BOOKS LTD
Spring Hill House, Spring Hill Road,
Begbroke, Oxford OX5 1RX
Telephone: 01865 375794
Fax: 01865 379162
Email: info@howtobooks.co.uk
Web Site: http://www.howtobooks.co.uk

Customer Services:
Grantham Book Services,
Isaac Newton Way,
Alma Park Industrial Estate, Grantham,
Lincs NG31 9SG
Telephone: 01476 541080
Fax: 01476 541061
Email: orders@gbs.tbs-ltd.co.uk
Web Site: http://www.howtobooks.co.uk

Managing Director: Giles Lewis
Editorial: Nikki Read
Rights: Ros Loten
Production: Bill Antrobus
Finance: Martin Wilkinson

Accountancy & Taxation; Antiques & Collecting; Educational & Textbooks; Gardening; Guide Books; Industry, Business & Management; Languages & Linguistics; Law; Literature & Criticism; Medical (incl. Self Help & Alternative Medicine); Reference Books, Directories & Dictionaries; Travel & Topography; Vocational Training & Careers; Creative Writing; Home & Family; Living & Working Abroad; Property

New Titles: 76 (2007), 80 (2008)

ISBNs, Imprints & Series:
978 1 84528, 978 1 85703

Parent Company:
UK: How To Ltd

Overseas Representation:
Africa: Kelvin van Hasselt Publishing Services, Briningham, Norfolk, UK
Australia & New Zealand: Footprint Books Pty Ltd, Sydney, NSW, Australia
East Asia: STP Distributors Pte Ltd, Singapore
Germany & Benelux: Robbert J. Pleysier, Heerde, Netherlands
Latin America & West Indies: InterMedia Americana (IMA) Ltd, London, UK
Middle East & Turkey: Publishers International Marketing, Sutton St Nicholas, Herefordshire, UK
Republic of Ireland: Slemish, Ballymena, Northern Ireland, UK
South Africa: Phambili CC, Kensington
Spain & Portugal: Peter Prout Iberian Book Services, Madrid, Spain
USA: Parkwest Publications Inc, Jersey City, NJ

Book Trade Association Membership:
IPG

2380

HUMAN KINETICS EUROPE LTD
107 Bradford Road, Stanningley, Leeds LS28 6AT
Telephone: 0113 255 5665
Fax: 0113 255 5885
Email: hk@hkeurope.com
Web Site: http://www.humankinetics.com/

Managing Director: Sara Cooper
Managers: Phil Carter *(Sales)*
Sian Partridge *(Sales)*
Graham Wilson *(Finance)*
Karen Ingram *(Customer Services)*
Rory Aspell *(Marketing)*
John Dickinson *(Editorial)*

Academic & Scholarly; Educational & Textbooks; Electronic (Educational); Electronic (Professional & Academic); Health & Beauty; Medical (incl. Self Help & Alternative Medicine); Psychology & Psychiatry; Scientific & Technical; Sports & Games; Theatre, Drama & Dance

New Titles: 150 (2007), 150 (2008)
No of Employees: 15
Annual Turnover: £1.8M

ISBNs, Imprints & Series:
978 0 73600, 978 0 87322, 978 0 88011, 978 0 918438, 978 0 931250

Parent Company:
USA: Human Kinetics Inc

Associated Companies:
Australia: Human Kinetics
Canada: Human Kinetics
New Zealand: Human Kinetics

Overseas Representation:
Australia: Human Kinetics (Australia), Torrens Park, SA
Brazil (academic): Tecmedd, São Paulo, Brazil
Canada: Human Kinetics (Canada), Windsor, Ont
China (including Hong Kong): AA Media Services, Shanghai, P. R. of China
India: Disvan Enterprises, New Delhi
Iran: Kowkab Publishers, Tehran
Japan: Eureka Press, Kyoto
Korea: Daehan Media Co Ltd, Seoul, Korea, South
Middle East: Amin Al-Abini, Cairo, Egypt
New Zealand: Human Kinetics (New Zealand), Auckland
Singapore & Malaysia: Icon Books Singapore Pte Ltd, Singapore
South Africa (academic): Academic & Professional Book Distributor, Johannesburg, South Africa
South Africa (trade): Real Books CC, Johannesburg, South Africa
Taiwan: Unifacmanu Trading Co Ltd, Taipei
Thailand, Indonesia, Bangladesh, Brunei & Philippines: Alkem Co (S) Pte Ltd, Singapore
USA: Human Kinetics, Champaign, IL

Book Trade Association Membership:
IPG

2381

JOHN HUNT PUBLISHING LTD
c/o O Books, The Bothy, Deershot Lodge, Park Lane, Ropley, Hants SO24 0BE
Fax: 01962 773769
Email: john.hunt@0-books.net
Web Site: http://www.johnhunt-publishing.com & http://www.o-books.net

Directors: John Hunt *(Editorial)*
Kate Rowlandson *(Sales)*
Manager: Ros Baynes *(Accounts)*

Children's Books; Magic & the Occult; Philosophy; Religion & Theology

New Titles: 70 (2007), 100 (2008)
No of Employees: 3
Annual Turnover: £1M

ISBNs, Imprints & Series:
978 1 84298 John Hunt
978 1 903816 O-Books

Overseas Representation:
Australia: Brumby Books Holdings Pty Ltd, Kilsyth South, Vic
New Zealand: Peaceful Living Publications, Auckland
Singapore: STP Distributors Pte Ltd
South Africa: Alternative Books CC, Ferndale
USA & Canada: NBN, Blue Ridge Summit, PA, USA

Book Trade Association Membership:
IPG

2382

C. HURST & CO (PUBLISHERS) LTD
41 Great Russell Street, London WC1B 3PL
Telephone: (020) 7255 2201
Email: hurst@atlas.co.uk
Web Site: http://www.hurstpub.co.uk

Distributor:
Marston Book Services, PO Box 269, Abingdon, Oxon OX14 4YN
Telephone: 01235 465500
Fax: 01235 465555

Managing Director: Michael Dwyer

Academic & Scholarly; Economics; Gender Studies; Politics & World Affairs; Religion & Theology; Sociology & Anthropology

New Titles: 40 (2007), 50 (2008)
No of Employees: 3

ISBNs, Imprints & Series:
978 0 903983, 978 0 905838, 978 1 85065

Distributor for:
Signal Books

Overseas Representation:
Australia: UNIREPS University and Reference Publishers' Services, Sydney, NSW
Benelux, France & Suisse Romande: Michael Geoghegan, London, UK
China & Hong Kong: Access Asia Media Services, Beijing, P. R. of China
Eastern Europe: Ewa Ledóchowicz, Konstancin-Jeziorna, Poland
Greece, Malta, Italy & Cyprus: Charles Gibbes Associates, Louslitges, France
Japan: United Publishers Services Ltd, Tokyo
Middle East: Avicenna Partnership, Oxford, UK
Nordic countries: Colin Flint Ltd, Harlow, UK
Republic of Ireland: Geoff Bryan, Dublin
South East Asia: Horizon Books Pte Ltd, Singapore
Southern Africa: Bacchus Books, Johannesburg, South Africa
Spain & Portugal: Iberian Book Services, Madrid, Spain

2383

HYPATIA PUBLICATIONS
[including Patten Press]
Trevelyan House, 16 Chapel Street, Penzance, Cornwall TR18 4AW
Telephone: 01736 366597
Fax: 01736 333307
Email: info@hypatia-trust.org.uk
Web Site: http://www.hypatia-trust.org.uk

Warehouse:
Jamieson Library, Old Post Office, Newmill, Penzance, Cornwall TR20 8XN
Telephone: 01736 360549
Email: budden@lineone.net

Directors: Dr Melissa Hardie
Dr Phil Budden *(Finance)*
Donna Anton *(IT)*
P/A: Peter Waverly

Academic & Scholarly; Bibliography & Library Science; Biography & Autobiography; Educational & Textbooks; Fine Art & Art History

New Titles: 4 (2007), 3 (2008)
Annual Turnover: £40,000

ISBNs, Imprints & Series: 978 1 872229

Parent Company:
UK: The Hypatia Trust

Associated Companies:
UK: Jamieson Library; Patten Press

Overseas Representation:
USA: Malcolm Summers, VT

2384

ICHEME
165–189 Railway Terrace, Rugby CV21 3HQ
Telephone: 01788 578214
Fax: 01788 560833
Email: jcressey@icheme.org
Web Site: http://www.icheme.org

Marketing Executive: Jo Cheshire
Marketing Manager: Jacqueline Cressey

Engineering; Scientific & Technical

New Titles: 8 (2007), 6 (2008)
No of Employees: 60
Annual Turnover: £300,000

ISBNs, Imprints & Series: 978 0 85295

Distributor for:
USA: Princeton Selling Group Inc

Overseas Representation:
Asia: Clarke Associates Ltd, Bristol, UK
Australia & New Zealand: DA Information Services Pty Ltd, Mitcham, Vic, Australia
Europe: Momenta Publishing Ltd, Hindhead, Surrey, UK
USA & Canada: Princeton Selling Group Inc, Philadelphia, PA, USA

2385

ICON BOOKS LTD
Omnibus Business Centre,
39–41 North Road, London N7 9DP
Telephone: (020) 7700 9964
Fax: 01763 208080
Email: info@iconbooks.co.uk

Distribution:
TBS Distribution Centre, Colchester Road, Frating Green, Colchester, Essex CO7 7DW
Telephone: 01206 255678 (UK trade) & 255644 (Export)
Fax: 01206 255930 (UK trade) & 255916 (Export)
Email: sales@tbs-ltd.co.uk & export@tbs-ltd.co.uk

UK Rights (Icon & Wizard titles):
The Marsh Agency, 50 Albemarle Street, London W1S 4BD
Telephone: (020) 7493 4361
Fax: (020) 7495 8961
Email: steph@patersonmarsh.co.uk

Sales Representation (UK):
Faber & Faber, 3 Queen Square, London WC1N 3AU
Telephone: (020) 7465 0045
Fax: (020) 7465 0034
Email: sales@faber.co.uk

Directors: Peter Pugh *(Managing)*
Simon Flynn *(Publishing)*
Duncan Heath *(Editorial)*
Andrew Furlow *(Marketing)*
Najma Finlay *(Publicity)*

Academic & Scholarly; Aviation; Biography & Autobiography; Chemistry; Children's Books; Crime; Economics; Educational & Textbooks; Fiction; Gender Studies; Geography & Geology; Health & Beauty; History & Antiquarian; Humour; Languages

& Linguistics; Literature & Criticism; Mathematics & Statistics; Military & War; Natural History; Philosophy; Physics; Poetry; Politics & World Affairs; Psychology & Psychiatry; Reference Books, Directories & Dictionaries; Religion & Theology; Science Fiction; Scientific & Technical; Sociology & Anthropology; Sports & Games

New Titles: 39 (2007), 40 (2008)
No of Employees: 12

ISBNs, Imprints & Series:
978 1 84046, 978 1 84831

Associated Companies:
Wizard Books

Overseas Representation:
Australasia: Allen & Unwin Pty Ltd, Sydney, NSW, Australia
Canada: Penguin Books Canada, Toronto, Ont
Singapore & Malaysia: Penguin Books Singapore, Jurong, Singapore
South Africa: Book Promotions Ltd, Johannesburg
USA (Rights - Icon & Wizard titles): Carol Mann Agency, New York, NY, USA
USA (Totem Books): National Book Network Inc, Blue Ridge Summit, PA, USA

2386

ICSA INFORMATION & TRAINING LTD
16 Park Crescent, London W1B 1AH
Telephone: (020) 7612 7020
Fax: (020) 7323 1132
Email: publishing@icsa.co.uk
Web Site: http://www.icsabookshop.co.uk

Distribution, Orders, Customer Service & Accounts:
Marston Book Services Ltd, PO Box 269, Abingdon, Oxon OX14 4YN
Telephone: 01235 465500
Fax: 01235 465555
Email: direct.order@marston.co.uk

Joint Managing Directors: Clare Grist Taylor
Susan Richards
Sales & Marketing: Kate Murphy
New Business Development: Isabel Gillies

Industry, Business & Management

New Titles: 15 (2007), 20 (2008)
No of Employees: 11

ISBNs, Imprints & Series:
978 0 902197, 978 1 85418, 978 1 86072, 978 1 87286

Book Trade Association Membership:
IPG

2387

THE ILEX PRESS LTD
The Old Candlemakers, West Street, Lewes, East Sussex BN7 2NZ
Telephone: 01273 487440
Fax: 01273 487441
Web Site: http://www.ilex-press.com

Sales & Distribution, Trade Enquiries & Orders:
Trade Distribution & Accounts,
Thames & Hudson (Distributors),
44 Clockhouse Road, Farnborough, Hants GU14 7QZ
Telephone: 01252 541602
Fax: 01252 541602
Email: customerservices@thameshudson.co.uk

Directors: Alastair Campbell *(Publisher)*
Stephen Paul *(Managing)*
Peter Bridgewater *(Creative)*

Crafts & Hobbies; Electronic (Entertainment); Fine Art & Art History; Industry, Business & Management; Photography

New Titles: 27 (2007), 40 (2008)
No of Employees: 21

ISBNs, Imprints & Series: 978 1 904705

2388

IMMUNISATION INFORMATION
Department of Health, Skipton House, 80 London Road, London SE1 6LH
Telephone: (020) 7972 3809
Fax: (020) 7972 5240
Email: Chris.Owen@doh.gsi.gov.uk
Web Site: http://www.dh.gov.uk

Academic & Scholarly; Educational & Textbooks; Medical (incl. Self Help & Alternative Medicine)

Book Trade Association Membership:
Publishers Association

2389

IMPERIAL COLLEGE PRESS
57 Shelton Street, Covent Garden, London WC2H 9HE
Telephone: (020) 7836 3954
Fax: (020) 7836 2002
Email: edit@icpress.co.uk
Web Site: http://www.icpress.co.uk

Trade Enquiries & Orders:
World Scientific Publishing,
57 Shelton Street, Covent Garden, London WC2H 9HE
Telephone: (020) 7836 0888
Fax: (020) 7836 2020
Email: sales@wspc.co.uk
Web Site: http://www.wspc.co.uk

Chairman: Prof K. K. Phua
Publisher: Laurent Chaminade
Editors: Lance Bucharov *(Senior Commissioning)*
Lizzie Bennett *(Senior)*

Academic & Scholarly; Biology & Zoology; Chemistry; Computer Science; Economics; Electronic (Educational); Electronic (Professional & Academic); Engineering; Environment & Development Studies; Industry, Business & Management; Mathematics & Statistics; Medical (incl. Self Help & Alternative Medicine); Physics; Scientific & Technical

ISBNs, Imprints & Series: 978 1 86094

Parent Company:
Singapore: World Scientific

Overseas Representation:
Hong Kong: World Scientific Publishing (HK) Co Ltd
India: World Scientific Publishing Co Pte Ltd, Bangalore
Singapore: World Scientific Publishing Co Pte Ltd
Taiwan: World Scientific Publishing Co Pte Ltd, Taipei
USA: World Scientific Publishing Co Inc, River Edge, NJ

2390

IMPRINT ACADEMIC
PO Box 200, Exeter, Devon EX5 5HY
Telephone: 01392 851550
Fax: 01392 851178
Email: sandra@imprint.co.uk
Web Site: http://www.imprint.co.uk

Partners: J. K. B. Sutherland
K. A. Sutherland
Managing Editor: A. Freeman

Administrator: S. Good
Print Manager: D. Hall

Academic & Scholarly; Philosophy; Politics & World Affairs; Psychology & Psychiatry; Religion & Theology; Scientific & Technical; Sociology & Anthropology

New Titles: 30 (2007), 30 (2008)

ISBNs, Imprints & Series:
978 0 907845, 978 1 84540 Idealist Studies; Imprint Art; Societas

Overseas Representation:
USA: Ingram Publisher Services Inc, Chambersburg, PA; Philosophy Documentation Center, Charlottesville, VA

2391

IMRAY LAURIE NORIE & WILSON LTD
Wych House, The Broadway, St Ives, Huntingdon PE27 5BT
Telephone: 01480 462114
Fax: 01480 496109
Email: ilnw@imray.com
Web Site: http://www.imray.com

Directors: William Wilson *(Managing)*
Mrs E. N. Wilson
Ian Rippington *(Sales)*
Accountant: Emma Woodfield

Geography & Geology; Nautical; Sports & Games; Transport; Travel & Topography

New Titles: 12 (2007), 12 (2008)
No of Employees: 24

ISBNs, Imprints & Series:
978 0 85288, 978 1 84623

Associated Companies:
Stanfords Charts

Distributor for:
Ordnance Survey; J. M. Pearson & Sons; RCC Pilotage Foundation; United Kingdom Hydrographic Office
France: Editions du Briel; Editions Vagnon; Euromapping; Navicarte
Netherlands: ANWB; Hydrographic Office
Norway: Hydrographic Office
Republic of Ireland: Irish Cruising Club
USA: Cruising Guide Publications; University of Hawaii Press

Overseas Representation:
Australia: Boat Books (Australia) Pty Ltd, Sydney, NSW; Boating Books and Charts (Australia) Pty Ltd, Melbourne, Vic
Belgium: The Boathouse, Nieuwpoort
France: Les Editions du Plaisancier, Neyron
Greece: Contract Yacht Services, Lerkas; Tecrep Marine SA, Piraeus
Netherlands: Vrolijk Watersport BV, Scheveningen
New Zealand: Trans-Pacific Marine Ltd, Auckland
USA: C. Plath, Annapolis, MD
USA (Imray books only): Bluewater Books and Charts, Fort Lauderdale, FL, USA
USA (Imray-Iolaire charts only): Weems & Plath, Annapolis, MD, USA

Book Trade Association Membership:
International Map Trade Association

2392

IN EASY STEPS LTD
5C Southfield Road, Southam, Warks CV47 0FB
Telephone: 01926 817999
Fax: 01926 817005
Email: sevanti@ineasysteps.com
Web Site: http://www.ineasysteps.com

Distribution:
Bookpoint Ltd, 130 Milton Park, Abingdon, Oxon OX14 4SB
Telephone: 01235 400400
Fax: 01235 832068

Directors: Sevanti Kotecha *(Business Development)*
Harshad Kotecha *(Publishing)*

Accountancy & Taxation; Computer Science; Crafts & Hobbies; Educational & Textbooks; Electronic (Professional & Academic); Photography; Reference Books, Directories & Dictionaries; Scientific & Technical; Vocational Training & Careers

New Titles: 25 (2007), 25 (2008)

ISBNs, Imprints & Series:
978 1 84078 In easy steps
978 1 874029 Complete Guides; In easy steps

Overseas Representation:
Australia & New Zealand: Woodslane Pty Ltd, Warriewood, NSW, Australia
South Africa: Intersoft Simon (Pty) Ltd, Johannesburg
South East Asia: STP Distributors Pte Ltd, Singapore
USA: Publishers Group West, Berkeley, CA

Book Trade Association Membership:
IPG

2393

INCORPORATED COUNCIL OF LAW REPORTING FOR ENGLAND AND WALES
Megarry House, 119 Chancery Lane, London WC2A 1PP
Telephone: (020) 7242 6471
Fax: (020) 7831 5247
Email: postmaster@iclr.co.uk
Web Site: http://www.lawreports.co.uk

Binding Dept & Warehouse:
3 Star Yard, London WC2A 2JL
Telephone: (020) 7242 8632
Fax: (020) 7405 4898
Email: postmaster@iclr.co.uk
Web Site: http://www.lawreports.co.uk

Secretary: John Cobbett
Managers: Graham Chapman *(Office)*
Stephen Mitchell *(Binding)*
Editor: Robert Williams
Permissions Secretary: Helen Yates *(Assistant to Secretary)*
Administrators: Louise Carlin *(Marketing)*
Claire Kingsnorth *(Subscription)*
Rebecca Perks *(Assistant to Editor)*

Law

No of Employees: 55
Annual Turnover: £5M

Overseas Representation:
Australia: LBC Information Services, Rozelle, NSW
Canada: Carswell Publishing Ltd, Scarborough, Ont

2394

INSTANT-BOOKS UK LTD
10 Tennyson Close, Dallington, Northampton NN5 7HJ
Email: instant.books@ntlworld.com
Web Site: http://www.instant-books.org

Directors: David Brawn *(Company Secretary)*
Ros Brawn
P. Tomlinson
J. Cawley
N. Robbins-Cherry
G. Robbins-Cherry

Atlases & Maps; Guide Books; Travel & Topography

New Titles: 20 (2007), 20 (2008)

ISBNs, Imprints & Series:
978 1 84834 Instant-Book Editions; Tour & Trail Maps; Walk! Guidebooks

2395

INSTITUTE FOR EMPLOYMENT STUDIES
Mantell Building, University of Sussex, Brighton BN1 9RF
Telephone: 01273 873694
Fax: 01273 690430
Email: iesbooks@employment-studies.co.uk
Web Site: http://www.employment-studies.co.uk

Distributors:
Gardners Books Ltd, 1 Whittle Drive, Eastbourne BN23 6QH
Telephone: 01323 521555
Fax: 01323 521666
Email: sales@gardners.com
Web Site: http://www.gardners.com

Publications & Marketing Manager: Richard James

Industry, Business & Management

New Titles: 10 (2007), 10 (2008)
No of Employees: 40

ISBNs, Imprints & Series:
978 1 85184 IES Report Series

2396

INSTITUTE FOR FISCAL STUDIES
Third Floor, 7 Ridgmount Street, London WC1E 7AE
Telephone: (020) 7291 4800
Fax: (020) 7323 4780
Email: mailbox@ifs.org.uk
Web Site: http://www.ifs.org.uk/

Director: Robert Chote
Executive Administrator: Robert Markless
Research Director: Richard Blundell
External Relations Manager: Emma Hyman

Academic & Scholarly; Accountancy & Taxation; Economics; Law

New Titles: 15 (2007), 15 (2008)
No of Employees: 40
Annual Turnover: £4.2M

ISBNs, Imprints & Series:
978 0 902992, 978 1 873357
Commentary; Report; Working Paper

2397

INSTITUTE OF ACOUSTICS
77A St Peter's Street, St Albans, Herts AL1 3BN
Telephone: 01727 848195
Fax: 01727 850553
Email: ioa@ioa.org.uk
Web Site: http://www.ioa.org.uk

Chief Executive: Kevin Macan-Lind
Editor: Ian Bennett
Managers: Dennis Baylis *(Advertising)*
Judy Edrich *(Public Relations)*

Academic & Scholarly; Scientific & Technical

2398

INSTITUTE OF CLINICAL RESEARCH
Institute House, Boston Drive, Bourne End, Bucks SL8 5YS
Telephone: 01628 536960

Fax: 01628 530641
Email: info@icr-global.org
Web Site: http://www.icr-global.org

General Manager: Anne Hewitt
Financial Controller: Mervin Foulds
Head of Information Services: Helena Korjonen
Sales: Marguerita Best *(Administration Assistant)*

Scientific & Technical

New Titles: 4 (2007), 5 (2008)

ISBNs, Imprints & Series:
978 0 9549345, 978 1 905238

Overseas Representation:
India: Institute of Clinical Research Professionals

Book Trade Association Membership:
Publishers Association

2399

INSTITUTE OF DEVELOPMENT STUDIES
University of Sussex, Brighton, Sussex BN1 9RE
Telephone: 01273 678269
Fax: 01273 621202
Email: bookshop@ids.ac.uk & g.edwards@ids.ac.uk (Subscription enquiries)
Web Site: http://www.ids.ac.uk/go/bookshop/

Head of Information: Geoff Barnard
Communications Manager: Nick Perkins
Assistants: Alison Norwood *(Production)*
Gary Edwards *(Sales & Marketing)*

Academic & Scholarly; Agriculture; Bibliography & Library Science; Economics; Educational & Textbooks; Environment & Development Studies; Gender Studies; Industry, Business & Management; Politics & World Affairs; Sociology & Anthropology

ISBNs, Imprints & Series:
978 0 903354, 978 1 85864 Institute of Development Studies
978 0 903715 Bridge Reports; Bulletin; Development Bibliographies; Discussion Papers; IDS Commisioned Studies; Research Reports; Working Papers

2400

INSTITUTE OF EDUCATION (PUBLICATIONS), UNIVERSITY OF LONDON
20 Bedford Way, London WC1H 0AL
Telephone: (020) 7612 6000
Web Site: http://www.ioe.ac.uk/publications

Trade Enquiries, Orders & Distribution:
Central Books Ltd, 99 Wallis Road, London E9 5LN
Telephone: 0845 458 9911
Fax: 0845 458 9912
Email: info@centralbooks.com
Web Site: http://www.centralbooks.com

Academic & Scholarly; Educational & Textbooks; Sociology & Anthropology

New Titles: 15 (2007), 15 (2008)
No of Employees: 4

Overseas Representation:
North America: Stylus Publishing Inc, Sterling, VA, USA

Book Trade Association Membership:
IPG

2401

INSTITUTE OF EMPLOYMENT RIGHTS
The People's Centre,
50–54 Mount Pleasant, Liverpool L3 5SD
Telephone: 0151 702 6925
Fax: 0151 702 6935
Email: office@ier.org.uk
Web Site: http://www.ier.org.uk

Brighton Office:
Phelim MacCafferty,
Projects & Events Officer,
179 Preston Road, Brighton BN1 6AG
Telephone: 01273 330819
Email: phelim@ier.org.uk

Director: Carolyn Jones
Administration & Publications Officer: Treena Johnson
Projects & Events Officer: Phelim MacCafferty

Academic & Scholarly; Economics; Law; Politics & World Affairs

New Titles: 6 (2007), 8 (2008)
No of Employees: 3
Annual Turnover: £140,000

ISBNs, Imprints & Series:
978 0 9543781, 978 0 9551795, 978 1 873271

2402

*INSTITUTE OF FOOD SCIENCE & TECHNOLOGY
5 Cambridge Court,
210 Shepherds Bush Road, London W6 7NJ
Telephone: (020) 7603 6316
Fax: (020) 7602 9936
Email: info@ifst.org
Web Site: http://www.ifst.org

Chief Executive: Helen Wild
Team Executive: Angela Winchester

Scientific & Technical

ISBNs, Imprints & Series: 978 0 905367

Book Trade Association Membership:
Association of Learned Society Publishers

2403

THE INSTITUTE OF MATHEMATICS AND ITS APPLICATIONS
Catherine Richards House,
16 Nelson Street, Southend-on-Sea, Essex SS1 1EF
Telephone: 01702 354020
Fax: 01702 354111
Email: post@ima.org.uk
Web Site: http://www.ima.org.uk

Director: David Youdan *(Executive)*

Mathematics & Statistics

New Titles: 2 (2007)
No of Employees: 16

ISBNs, Imprints & Series: 978 0 905091

Book Trade Association Membership:
Association of Learned & Professional Society Publishers

2404

INSTITUTE OF PHYSICS & ENGINEERING IN MEDICINE
Fairmount House, 230 Tadcaster Road, York YO24 1ES
Telephone: 01904 610821
Fax: 01904 612279
Email: office@ipem.ac.uk
Web Site: http://www.ipem.ac.uk

General Secretary: R. W. Neilson
Publications Co-ordinator: M. Goodall

Engineering; Medical (incl. Self Help & Alternative Medicine); Physics; Scientific & Technical

New Titles: 1 (2007), 4 (2008)
No of Employees: 12

ISBNs, Imprints & Series:
978 1 903613 IPEM Report Series

Book Trade Association Membership:
Association of Learned & Professional Society Publishers

2405

INSTITUTION OF ENGINEERING AND TECHNOLOGY (IET)
Michael Faraday House, Six Hills Way, Stevenage, Herts SG1 2AY
Telephone: 01438 767328
Fax: 01438 765515
Email: books@theiet.org
Web Site: http://www.theiet.org

Trade Enquiries & Orders:
PO Box 96, Stevenage, Herts SG1 2SD
Telephone: 01438 767328
Fax: 01438 767375
Email: sales@theiet.org
Web Site: http://www.theiet.org

Warehouse:
7 Fulton Close, Argyle Way, Stevenage, Herts
Telephone: 01438 355029
Fax: 01438 355034

Directors: Steven Mair *(Managing)*
Nick Canty *(Publishing)*
Sales Manager: Bianca Campbell

Academic & Scholarly; Computer Science; Electronic (Professional & Academic); Engineering; Scientific & Technical

ISBNs, Imprints & Series:
978 0 85296, 978 0 86341, 978 0 901223, 978 0 906048

Associated Companies:
Peter Peregrinus Ltd
USA: INSPEC Inc

Overseas Representation:
Far East: Clarke Associates Ltd, Bristol, UK
Middle East: Amin Al-Abini, Cairo, Egypt
USA & Canada: INSPEC Inc, Edison, NJ, USA

Book Trade Association Membership:
BA; IGSMTP; Association of Learned & Professional Society Publishers

2406

INTELLECT LTD
PO Box 862, Bristol BS99 1DE
Telephone: 0117 958 9910
Fax: 0117 958 9911
Email: mail@intellectbooks.com
Web Site: http://www.intellectbooks.com/

Distribution:
Gardners Books, 1 Whittle Drive, Eastbourne BN23 6QH
Telephone: 01323 521777
Fax: 01323 521666
Email: custcare@gardners.com
Web Site: http://www.gardners.com

Chairman: Masoud Yazdani *(Editor-in-Chief)*
Publisher: May Yao *(Books)*

Academic & Scholarly; Architecture & Design; Cinema, Video, TV & Radio; Computer Science; Educational &

Textbooks; Electronic (Educational); Electronic (Professional & Academic); Environment & Development Studies; Gender Studies; History & Antiquarian; Languages & Linguistics; Literature & Criticism; Philosophy; Scientific & Technical; Sociology & Anthropology; Theatre, Drama & Dance

New Titles: 22 (2007), 35 (2008)
No of Employees: 8

ISBNs, Imprints & Series:
Advances in Art & Urban Futures; Advances in Human Computer Interaction; Elm Bank Publications; European Studies Series; Intellect Play Series; Progress in Neural Networks; Trends in Functional Programming; Venton
978 0 89391, 978 1 56750, 978 1 84150, 978 1 871516

Overseas Representation:
Australasia: UNIREPS University and Reference Publishers' Services, Sydney, NSW, Australia
North America: University of Chicago Press, Chicago, IL, USA

Book Trade Association Membership:
IPG

2407

INTERACTYX
[formerly The Enterprise Library]
2 Aboyne Castle Business Centre, Aboyne, Aberdeenshire AB34 5LP
Telephone: 01339 386282
Fax: 01339 887787
Email: info@ent-lib.co.uk
Web Site: http://www.livecon.com

Academic & Scholarly

Book Trade Association Membership:
Publishers Association

2408

INTERNATIONAL MEDICAL PRESS
2–4 Idol Lane, London EC3R 5DD
Telephone: (020) 7398 0500
Fax: (020) 7398 0501
Email: info@intmedpress.com
Web Site: http://www.intmedpress.com

Academic & Scholarly; Electronic (Professional & Academic); Medical (incl. Self Help & Alternative Medicine)

Book Trade Association Membership:
Publishers Association

2409

INTERNATIONAL NETWORK FOR THE AVAILABILITY OF SCIENTIFIC PUBLICATIONS (INASP)
58 St Aldates, Oxford OX1 1ST
Telephone: 01865 249909
Fax: 01865 251060
Email: inasp@inasp.info
Web Site: http://www.inasp.info/

Director: Tag McEntegart *(Executive)*
Senior Programme Manager: Julie Walker *(Head, Publishing Training & INASP Publications)*
Programme Officer: Sioux Cumming

Academic & Scholarly; Bibliography & Library Science; Electronic (Professional & Academic); Reference Books, Directories & Dictionaries

ISBNs, Imprints & Series: 978 1 902928

Book Trade Association Membership:
Association of Learned & Professional Society Publishers

2410

IOP PUBLISHING
Dirac House, Temple Back, Bristol BS1 6BE
Telephone: 0117 929 7481
Fax: 0117 929 4318
Email: custserv@iop.org
Web Site: http://www.iop.org

Directors: Jerry Cowhig *(Managing)*
Michael Bray *(Financial)*
Ken Lillywhite *(Business Development & Journals Sales & Marketing)*
Marco Vinaccia *(Group IT & Production)*
Karen O'Flaherty *(Group Human Resources)*

Computer Science; Electronic (Professional & Academic); Mathematics & Statistics; Physics; Scientific & Technical

New Titles: 13 (2007), 4 (2008)
No of Employees: 250
Annual Turnover: £30.7M

Parent Company:
The Institute of Physics

Associated Companies:
USA: IOP Publishing Inc

Overseas Representation:
Japan (books): Eastern Book Service Inc, Tokyo, Japan
Japan (journals): Maruzen Co Ltd, Tokyo, Japan
Other Territories (books): Enquiries, Institute of Physics Publishing, Bristol, UK
Pakistan (books): Pak Book Corporation, Lahore, Pakistan
South East Asia, New Zealand & Australia (books): Hemisphere Publication Services, Singapore
USA & Canada (books): IOP Publishing, Williston, VT, USA
USA, Canada & Mexico (journals): American Institute of Physics, Melville, NY, USA

Book Trade Association Membership:
Publishers Association; IGSMTP; Association of Learned & Professional Society Publishers

2411

IRWELL PRESS LTD
59A High Street, Clophill, Beds MK45 4BE
Telephone: 01525 861888
Fax: 01525 862044
Email: George@irwellpress.co.uk
Web Site: http://www.irwellpress.co.uk

Directors: George Reeve
Chris Hawkins

Transport

New Titles: 12 (2007), 12 (2008)
Annual Turnover: £50,000

ISBNs, Imprints & Series:
978 1 871608, 978 1 903266

Overseas Representation:
Australia: Train World Property, East Brighton, Vic

2412

ISIS PUBLISHING LTD
Unit 7, Centremead, Osney Mead, Oxford OX2 0ES
Telephone: 01865 250333
Fax: 01865 790358
Email: pauline.horne@isis-publishing.co.uk
Web Site: http://www.isis-publishing.co.uk

Distribution:
Ulverscroft Large Print Books Ltd, The Green, Bradgate Road, Anstey, Leicester LE7 7FU
Telephone: 0116 236 4325
Fax: 0116 234 0205
Email: sales@ulverscroft.co.uk
Web Site: http://www.ulverscroft.co.uk

Director: Robert Thirlby *(Chief Executive)*
Managers: Pauline Horne *(Distribution, General, Sales & Marketing)*
Lorna Dubose *(Finance)*
Becky Curtis *(Editorial – General Books)*

Audio Books; Biography & Autobiography; Crime; Fiction; Humour; Poetry; Science Fiction; Large Print Publications

New Titles: 360 (2007), 360 (2008)
No of Employees: 20

ISBNs, Imprints & Series:
978 0 7531, 978 1 84559, 978 1 85089, 978 1 85695

Parent Company:
Ulverscroft Group Ltd

Overseas Representation:
Australia: Ulverscroft Large Print Books (Australia) Pty Ltd, Crows Nest, NSW
Canada: Stricker Books, Toronto, Ont
Denmark: Bierman & Bierman A/S, Grindsted
Japan: PIC, Tokyo
New Zealand: Ulverscroft Large Print Books Ltd, Fielding
Norway: Lydlitteratur, Nesoya
Republic of Ireland: Ulverscroft Large Print Books Ltd, Dublin
South Africa (Audio): Book Talk Pty Ltd, Parkhurst, South Africa
Sweden: Bibliotekstjanst AB, Lund
USA (Audio & Large print): Ulverscroft Large Print Books (USA) Inc, West Seneca, NY, USA

2413

THE ISLAMIC TEXTS SOCIETY
35 Parkside, Cambridge CB1 1JE
Telephone: 01223 314387
Fax: 01223 324342
Email: mail@its.org.uk
Web Site: http://www.its.org.uk

Distribution:
Orca Book Services Ltd, Unit A3, Fleets Corner, Poole, Dorset BH17 0HL
Telephone: 01202 665432
Fax: 01202 666219
Email: orders@orcabookservices.co.uk

Trust Secretary: Fatima Azzam

Academic & Scholarly; Law; Religion & Theology; Islam

New Titles: 1 (2007), 3 (2008)

ISBNs, Imprints & Series:
Al-Ghazali Series
978 0 946621, 978 1 903682 Fundamental Rights & Liberties Series: Principles & Applications

Overseas Representation:
USA: Independent Publishers Group (IPG), Chicago, IL

Book Trade Association Membership:
Publishers Association

2414

ISTE LTD
6 Fitzroy Square, London W1T 5DX
Telephone: (020) 7387 7333
Fax: (020) 7380 1051
Email: info@iste.co.uk
Web Site: http://www.iste.co.uk

Book Trade Association Membership:
Publishers Association

2415

ITHACA PRESS
[Books on The Middle East]
8 Southern Court, South Street, Reading RG1 4QS
Telephone: 0118 959 7847
Fax: 0118 959 7356 *(Trade Enquiries & Orders)*
Email: enquiries@garnetpublishing.co.uk
Web Site: http://www.garnetpublishing.co.uk

Representation (UK):
Compass Academic,
The Barley Mow Centre,
10 Barley Mow Passage, Chiswick, London W4 4PH
Telephone: (020) 8994 6477

Managing Director: Khalil Abu Shawareb
Managers: Dan Nunn *(Editorial, Rights & Permissions)*
Nick Holroyd *(Production Controller)*

Academic & Scholarly; Economics; Fiction; Gender Studies; History & Antiquarian; Languages & Linguistics; Law; Literature & Criticism; Politics & World Affairs; Religion & Theology; Sociology & Anthropology

New Titles: 20 (2007), 20 (2008)
No of Employees: 4

ISBNs, Imprints & Series:
978 0 86372, 978 0 903729

Parent Company:
Garnet Publishing Ltd

Overseas Representation:
Australia: InBooks, Frenchs Forest, NSW
Europe: Andrew Durnell Marketing Ltd, Tunbridge Wells, UK
USA (academic): International Specialized Book Services Inc, Portland, OR, USA
USA (trade): International Publishers Marketing Inc, Sterling, VA, USA

Book Trade Association Membership:
IPG

2416

IVP
IVP Book Centre, Norton Street, Nottingham NG7 3HR
Telephone: 0115 978 1054
Fax: 0115 942 2694
Email: ivp@ivpbooks.com
Web Site: http://www.ivpbooks.com

Chief Executive Officer: Brian Wilson
Finance & Operations: George Russell

Academic & Scholarly; Reference Books, Directories & Dictionaries; Religion & Theology

New Titles: 46 (2007), 47 (2008)
No of Employees: 35

ISBNs, Imprints & Series:
978 0 85110, 978 0 85111, 978 1 84474 Apollos; IVP
978 0 85684 Crossway Books

Distributor for:
Bible Society; Christian Medical Fellowship; Dorling Kindersley Religious; Eagle Publishing; Good Book Company; Matthias Media; Piquant
USA: Crossway Books; IVP; Youthworks

Overseas Representation:
Australia: Family Reading, Ballarat, Vic
East Africa: Keswick Book Society, Nairobi, Kenya
Netherlands: ASAF Import 3, Westervoort
New Zealand: Soul Distributors, Auckland
Philippines: Evangelical Outreach Inc,

Quezon City; Overseas Missionary Fellowship, Manila
Singapore: Bethesda Book Centre
South Africa: Protestant Book Centre, Cape Town
Sweden: Din Bok - Formsamlingsbokhandeln, Goteborg
USA: InterVarsity Press, Downers Grove, IL

Book Trade Association Membership:
Christian Suppliers' Group; Evangelical Christian Publishers Association

2417

IWA PUBLISHING
Alliance House, 12 Caxton Street, London SW1H 0QS
Telephone: (020) 7654 5500
Fax: (020) 7654 5555
Email: publications@iwap.co.uk
Web Site: http://www.iwapublishing.com

Orders:
Portland Customer Services, Commerce Way, Whitehall Industrial Estate, Colchester CO2 8HP
Telephone: 01206 796351
Fax: 01206 799331
Email: sales@portland-services.com

Publisher, Managing Director & Commissioning Editor: Michael Dunn
Managers: Michelle Jones *(Publications)*
Ian Morgan *(Marketing)*

Academic & Scholarly; Electronic (Professional & Academic); Engineering; Industry, Business & Management; Reference Books, Directories & Dictionaries; Scientific & Technical

ISBNs, Imprints & Series:
978 1 84339, 978 1 900222

Parent Company:
International Water Association

Overseas Representation:
Australia & New Zealand: Australian Water Association, Artarmon, NSW, Australia; DA Information Services Pty Ltd, Mitcham, Vic, Australia
India: Surinder K. Lijhara, Overseas Media, Faridabad
Japan: Kay Kato Associates, Kanagawa
Malaysia: Tony Poh, STM Publisher Services Pte Ltd, Singapore
North America: Martin P. Hill Consulting, New York, NY, USA
Taiwan: Ta Tong Book Co Ltd, Taipei

Book Trade Association Membership:
Association of Learned & Professional Society Publishers

2418

JAMES & JAMES (PUBLISHERS) LTD
2–5 Benjamin Street, London E1M 5QL
Email: mj@tmiltd.com
Web Site: http://www.tmiltd.com

Chairman: Hamish MacGibbon

Academic & Scholarly; History & Antiquarian; Industry, Business & Management

New Titles: 6 (2007), 10 (2008)
Annual Turnover: £200,000

ISBNs, Imprints & Series: 978 0 907383

Parent Company:
Third Millennium Information Ltd

2419

JANE'S INFORMATION GROUP LTD
163 Brighton Road, Coulsdon, Surrey CR5 2YH
Telephone: (020) 8700 3745
Fax: (020) 8763 1006
Email: info.uk@janes.com
Web Site: http://www.janes.com

Directors: Scott Key *(Managing)*
Ian Kay *(Reference)*
Steve Cannon *(Finance)*
Michael Dell *(Deputy Chief Executive Officer)*
Public Relations: Amanda Castle

Aviation; Electronic (Professional & Academic); Industry, Business & Management; Military & War; Nautical; Politics & World Affairs; Reference Books, Directories & Dictionaries; Transport

ISBNs, Imprints & Series: 978 0 7106

Parent Company:
HIS

Associated Companies:
The Woodbridge Co Ltd

Overseas Representation:
Australia & New Zealand: Jane's Information Group Australia, Rozelle, NSW, Australia
Egypt: Middle East Agency, Cairo
India: Jane's Information Group, New Delhi
Indonesia, Korea, Malaysia, Singapore & Taiwan: Jane's Information Group Asia, Singapore
Japan: Jane's Information Group, Tokyo
Kuwait & Saudi Arabia: Jane's Information Group, Dubai, UAE
North & South America: Jane's Information Group Inc, Alexandria, VA, USA
Worldwide (excluding countries listed): Jane's Information Group, UK

Book Trade Association Membership:
Data Publishers Association

2420

JANUS PUBLISHING CO LTD
105–107 Gloucester Place, London W1U 6BY
Telephone: (020) 7486 6633
Fax: (020) 7486 6090
Email: publisher@januspublishing.co.uk
Web Site: http://www.januspublishing.co.uk

Distribution/Sales:
25 Winnock Road, Colchester, Essex CO1 2BG
Telephone: 01206 578856
Fax: 01206 573221
Email: sales@januspublishing.co.uk

Representation (UK):
Impulse Sales & Marketing, The Mount, Burton Road, Elford, Nr Tamworth, Staffordshire B79 9BN

Directors: J. A. Leung *(Managing, Rights & Permissions)*
Tina Brand *(Sales)*

Academic & Scholarly; Biography & Autobiography; Children's Books; Crime; Do-It-Yourself; Economics; Educational & Textbooks; Fashion & Costume; Fiction; Fine Art & Art History; History & Antiquarian; Humour; Literature & Criticism; Magic & the Occult; Medical (incl. Self Help & Alternative Medicine); Military & War; Nautical; Philosophy; Poetry; Politics & World Affairs; Religion & Theology; Science Fiction; Sociology & Anthropology; Sports & Games

New Titles: 16 (2007), 20 (2008)
No of Employees: 6

ISBNs, Imprints & Series:
978 1 85756 Janus Books
978 1 90283 Empiricus Books

Parent Company:
Junction Books Ltd

Overseas Representation:
Malaysia, Singapore & Brunei: Proof Line (M) Sdn Bhd, Petaling Jaya, Malaysia
Scandinavia: Richard Bowen c/o Janus Publishing Co Ltd, London, UK
USA & Canada: IPG, Concord, MA, USA

Book Trade Association Membership:
BA; IPG

2421

JARNDYCE BOOKSELLERS
46 Great Russell Street, London WC1B 3PA
Telephone: (020) 7631 4220
Fax: (020) 7631 4220
Email: books@jarndyce.co.uk
Web Site: http://www.jarndyce.co.uk

Partners: Brian Lake
Janet Nassau

Academic & Scholarly; Bibliography & Library Science; Economics; Fiction; Languages & Linguistics; Literature & Criticism; Poetry; Reference Books, Directories & Dictionaries; Sociology & Anthropology

New Titles: 6 (2007), 8 (2008)

ISBNs, Imprints & Series: 978 1 900718

Book Trade Association Membership:
Antiquarian Booksellers' Association; Provincial Booksellers' Fairs Association

2422

JOLLY LEARNING LTD
Tailours House, High Road, Chigwell, Essex IG7 6DL
Telephone: (020) 8501 0405
Fax: (020) 8500 1696
Email: chris@jollylearning.co.uk
Web Site: http://www.jollylearning.co.uk

Managing Director: Christopher Jolly
Managers: Diane Harding *(Accounts)*
Androula Stratton *(Marketing)*
Angela Hockley *(Editorial)*

Educational & Textbooks; Electronic (Educational)

No of Employees: 11
Annual Turnover: £3M

ISBNs, Imprints & Series:
978 1 84414, 978 1 870946, 978 1 903619

Overseas Representation:
USA: Jolly Learning Ltd, c/o American International Distribution Corporation, Williston, VT

Book Trade Association Membership:
IPG

2423

JONES & BARTLETT INTERNATIONAL
Barb House, Barb Mews, London W6 7PA
Telephone: 01278 723553
Fax: 01278 723554
Email: ldowning@jbpub.com
Web Site: http://www.jbpub.com

Warehouse, Trade Enquiries & Orders:
Macmillan Distribution (MDL), Brunel Road, Houndmills, Basingstoke RG21 6XS
Telephone: 01256 329242
Fax: 01256 331413
Email: mdl@macmillan.co.uk
Web Site: http://www.macmillan-mdl.co.uk

Managers: Richard Warner
Lorna Downing *(Product)*
Chris Gribble *(Sales)*

Biology & Zoology; Chemistry; Computer Science; Educational & Textbooks; Geography & Geology; Law; Mathematics & Statistics; Medical (incl. Self Help & Alternative Medicine); Physics; Psychology & Psychiatry; Scientific & Technical; Sports & Games; Vocational Training & Careers

ISBNs, Imprints & Series:
978 0 7637, 978 0 86729

Parent Company:
USA: Jones & Bartlett Inc

2424

JORDAN PUBLISHING LTD
21 St Thomas Street, Bristol BS1 6JS
Telephone: 0117 918 1228
Fax: 0117 925 0486
Email: ann.vowles@jordanpublishing.co.uk
Web Site: http://www.jordanpublishing.co.uk

Directors: Caroline Vandridge-Ames *(Managing)*
Deborah Saunders *(Publishing)*
Head of Marketing & Sales: Ann-Marie Vowles
Editorial Manager: Achim Bosse

Accountancy & Taxation; Electronic (Professional & Academic); Industry, Business & Management; Law

ISBNs, Imprints & Series:
978 0 85308 Family Law; Jordans

Parent Company:
West of England Trust

2425

RICHARD JOSEPH PUBLISHERS LTD
PO Box 15, Torrington, Devon EX38 8ZJ
Telephone: 01805 625750
Fax: 01805 625376
Email: office@sheppardsworld.co.uk
Web Site: http://www.sheppardsworld.co.uk

Managing Director: Richard Joseph
Compiler: (to be appointed)
Production Manager: Claire Brumham

Reference Books, Directories & Dictionaries

ISBNs, Imprints & Series:
978 1 872699 Sheppard

2426

S. KARGER AG
c/o London Liaison Office, 4 Rickett Street, London SW6 1RU
Telephone: (020) 7386 0500
Fax: (020) 7610 3337
Email: uk@karger.ch
Web Site: http://www.karger.com

President: Dr Thomas Karger
Finance: Rolf Zurlinden
Sales & Marketing: Moritz Thommen
Production: Hermann Vonlanthen
Editorial & Rights: Thomas Nold

Mathematics & Statistics; Medical (incl. Self Help & Alternative Medicine); Psychology & Psychiatry

New Titles: 60 (2007), 60 (2008)
No of Employees: 250

ISBNs, Imprints & Series: 978 3 8055

Parent Company:
Switzerland: S. Karger AG

Overseas Representation:
Australia: DA Information Services Pty Ltd, Mitcham, Vic
Baltic States: Bookshop Krisostomus, Tartu, Estonia
China: Karger China, Shanghai, P. R. of China
France: Librairie Médi-Sciences SARL, Paris
Germany: S. Karger GmbH, Freiburg
Gulf Council countries, Iran, Middle East, North Africa & Turkey: Trans Middle East International Distribution Co Ltd, Amman, Jordan
India, Bangladesh & Sri Lanka: Panther Publishers Private Ltd, Bangalore, India
Japan: Karger Japan Inc, Tokyo
Pakistan: Tahir M. Lodhi, Lahore
Republic of Ireland: S. Karger AG, London, UK
Singapore: APAC Publishers Services Pte Ltd
South & Central America: Cranbury International LLC, Montpelier, VT, USA
South Africa: Academic Marketing Services (Pty) Ltd, Craighall
Switzerland (Head Office): S. Karger AG, Basel, Switzerland
USA: S. Karger Publishers Inc, Unionville

2427

KARNAC BOOKS LTD
118 Finchley Road, London NW3 5HT
Telephone: (020) 7431 1075
Fax: (020) 7435 9076
Email: shop@karnacbooks.com
Web Site: http://www.karnacbooks.com

Directors: Oliver Rathbone *(Managing)*
Alex Massey *(Sales)*

Gender Studies; Psychology & Psychiatry

New Titles: 55 (2007), 58 (2008)
No of Employees: 12

ISBNs, Imprints & Series:
978 0 946439, 978 1 85575 Clunie Press; Institute of Psycho-Analysis, London; Karnac Books; Library of Analytical Psychology; Maresfield Library; Systemic Thinking Theory & Practice Series; Tavistock Institute of Marital Studies (TIMS); Winnicott Studies (Series)

Distributor for:
Apex One; Carl Auer International; Rebus Press; Tavistock Institute of Marital Studies; Zeig Tucker & Co

Overseas Representation:
Europe: Andrew Durnell Marketing Ltd, Tunbridge Wells, UK

Book Trade Association Membership:
BA; IPG

2428

RICHARD KAY PUBLICATIONS
80 Sleaford Road, Boston, Lincs PE21 8EU
Telephone: 01205 353231
Email: rebecca@richardkay.freeserve.co.uk

Proprietor: Richard K. Allday

Academic & Scholarly; Biography & Autobiography; History & Antiquarian; Medical (incl. Self Help & Alternative Medicine); Military & War; Politics & World Affairs; Reference Books, Directories & Dictionaries

New Titles: 3 (2007), 3 (2008)

ISBNs, Imprints & Series:
978 0 902662, 978 1 902882

Distributor for:
History of Boston Project

2429

*KEGAN PAUL LTD
PO Box 256, London WC1B 3SW
Telephone: (020) 7580 5511
Fax: (020) 7436 0899
Email: books@keganpaul.com
Web Site: http://www.keganpaul.com

Distribution:
Marston Book Services Ltd,
160 Milton Park, Abingdon, Oxon
OX14 4SD
Telephone: 01235 465500
Fax: 01235 465555
Email: direct.orders@marston.co.uk
Web Site: http://www.marston.co.uk

Directors: Peter Hopkins *(Chairman & Managing)*
Kaori O'Connor *(Editorial)*

Academic & Scholarly; Antiques & Collecting; Archaeology; Architecture & Design; Bibliography & Library Science; Biography & Autobiography; Cookery, Wines & Spirits; Crafts & Hobbies; Economics; Environment & Development Studies; Fashion & Costume; Fiction; Fine Art & Art History; Gardening; Geography & Geology; Guide Books; Health & Beauty; History & Antiquarian; Illustrated & Fine Editions; Languages & Linguistics; Law; Magic & the Occult; Medical (incl. Self Help & Alternative Medicine); Natural History; Philosophy; Poetry; Politics & World Affairs; Reference Books, Directories & Dictionaries; Religion & Theology; Sociology & Anthropology; Travel & Topography

ISBNs, Imprints & Series: 978 0 7103

Overseas Representation:
USA, Canada & South America: Columbia University Press, New York, USA

2430

KENYON-DEANE
10 Station Road Industrial Estate, Colwall, Malvern, Herefordshire WR13 6RN
Telephone: 01684 540154
Fax: 01684 540154
Email: simon@cressrelles.co.uk
Web Site: http://www.cressrelles.co.uk

Managers: Leslie Smith *(Finance, Production, Editorial & Rights)*
Simon Smith *(Sales & Marketing)*

Theatre, Drama & Dance

New Titles: 6 (2007), 6 (2008)

ISBNs, Imprints & Series: 978 0 7155

Parent Company:
Cressrelles Publishing Co Ltd

Distributor for:
USA: Anchorage Press

Overseas Representation:
Australia: Origin Theatrical, Sydney, NSW
New Zealand: Play Bureau of New Zealand Ltd, New Plymouth
Republic of Ireland: Drama League of Ireland, Dublin
South Africa: Dalro (Pty) Ltd, Braamfontein
USA: Bakers Plays, Quincy, MA

2431

KEW PUBLISHING
Sir Joseph Banks Building,
Royal Botanic Gardens, Kew, Richmond, Surrey TW9 3AE
Telephone: (020) 8332 5751 & 5219 (trade enquiries)
Fax: (020) 8332 5646
Email: publishing@kew.org & kewbooks@kew.org
Web Site: http://www.kew.org @ http://www.kewbooks.org

Head of Publishing: Gina Fullerlove
Sales, Marketing & Business Development: John Harris
Production Controller: Lloyd Kirton

Academic & Scholarly; Biology & Zoology; Fine Art & Art History; Scientific & Technical

New Titles: 30 (2007), 30 (2008)
No of Employees: 13

ISBNs, Imprints & Series: 978 1 84246

Parent Company:
UK: Royal Botanic Gardens

Book Trade Association Membership:
IPG

2432

HILDA KING EDUCATIONAL
Ashwells Manor Drive, Penn, Bucks
HP10 8EU
Telephone: 01494 813947 & 817947
Fax: 01494 813947
Email: rkinged@aol.com
Web Site: http://www.hildaking.co.uk

Director: Hilda King
Executive: R. E. King

Educational & Textbooks

ISBNs, Imprints & Series: 978 1 873533

2433

LAURENCE KING PUBLISHING LTD
361–373 City Road, London EC1V 1LR
Telephone: (020) 7841 6900
Fax: (020) 7841 6939
Email: enquiries@laurenceking.co.uk
Web Site: http://www.laurenceking.co.uk

Chairman: Nick Perren
Directors: Laurence King *(Managing)*
John Stoddart *(Financial)*
Felicity Awdry *(Production)*
Philip Cooper *(Editorial)*
Lee Ripley *(Editorial–College & Fine Art)*
Managers: Janet Pilch *(Rights)*
Lewis Gill *(Marketing)*

Architecture & Design; Fashion & Costume; Fine Art & Art History

ISBNs, Imprints & Series:
Portfolio (series)

Book Trade Association Membership:
Publishers Association

2434

THE KING'S ENGLAND PRESS
Cambertown House, Commercial Road,
Goldthorpe, Rotherham S63 9BL
Telephone: 01484 663790
Fax: 01484 663790
Email: steve@kingsengland.com
Web Site: http://www.kingsengland.com & http://www.pottypoets.com

Managing Director: Steve Rudd
Company Secretary: Debbie Nunn

Archaeology; Children's Books; History & Antiquarian; Poetry; Travel & Topography

New Titles: 2 (2007), 2 (2008)
No of Employees: 2

ISBNs, Imprints & Series: 978 1 872438

2435

JESSICA KINGSLEY PUBLISHERS
116 Pentonville Road, London N1 9JB
Telephone: (020) 7833 2307
Fax: (020) 7837 2917
Email: post@jkp.com
Web Site: http://www.jkp.com

Trade Enquiries & Orders:
Macmillan Distribution (MDL), Brunel Road, Houndmills, Basingstoke, Hants RG21 6XS
Telephone: 01256 302985
Fax: 01256 841426
Email: trade@macmillan.co.uk
Web Site: http://www.macmillandistribution.co.uk

Managing Director: Jessica Kingsley
Finance: Dee Brigham
Marketing: Helen Longmate
Electronic Media: Jemima Kingsley
Sales: Bill Goodall

Academic & Scholarly; Children's Books; Educational & Textbooks; Health & Beauty; Law; Medical (incl. Self Help & Alternative Medicine); Psychology & Psychiatry; Religion & Theology; Sociology & Anthropology; Sports & Games; Vocational Training & Careers

New Titles: 128 (2007), 150 (2008)
No of Employees: 30

ISBNs, Imprints & Series:
978 1 84310 Community, Culture and Change
978 1 84310, 978 1 85302 Jessica Kingsley Publishers
978 1 84819 Singing Dragon
978 1 85302 Children in Charge; Forensic Focus; Research Highlights in Social Work

Associated Companies:
USA: Jessica Kingsley Publishers Inc

Overseas Representation:
Australia & New Zealand: Footprint Books Pty, Mona Vale, NSW, Australia
Canada: University of British Columbia Press, Vancouver, BC
Europe: Andrew Durnell Marketing Ltd, Tunbridge Wells, UK
Hong Kong, Taiwan, China, Philippines & Korea: Asia Publishers Services Ltd, Hong Kong
Japan: United Publishers Services Ltd, Tokyo
Singapore, Malaysia, Brunei & Indonesia: Publishers Marketing Services, Petaling Jaya, Malaysia; Publishers Marketing Services Pte Ltd, Singapore
Thailand: STM Publisher Services Pte Ltd, Singapore
USA: Jessica Kingsley Publishers Inc, Philadelphia

Book Trade Association Membership:
Publishers Association; EPC; CAPP

2436

KINGSWAY PUBLICATIONS
[a division of Kingsway Communications Ltd]
Lottbridge Drove, Eastbourne, East Sussex
BN23 6NT
Telephone: 01323 437751
Fax: 01323 411970
Email: books@kingsway.co.uk
Web Site: http://www.kingsway.co.uk

Distribution & Warehouse:
STL Wholesale, PO Box 300,
Kingstown Broadway, Carlisle, Cumbria
CA3 0QS
Telephone: 01228 512512
Fax: 01228 514949

Chief Executive Officer: John Paculabo
Managers: Adrian Willard *(Marketing)*
Richard Herkes *(Publishing)*
Bill Owen *(Finance & Administration)*
Chris Jackson *(International Rights)*
Miriam Doherty *(Trade Books)*
Sue Price *(Church Resources)*

Biography & Autobiography; Children's Books; Fiction; Humour; Medical (incl. Self Help & Alternative Medicine); Religion & Theology; Theatre, Drama & Dance

ISBNs, Imprints & Series:
Great Ideas; Honor; Life Journey; Nexgen; Riveroak; Survivor; Victor
978 0 85476, 978 0 85491, 978 0 86065, 978 0 86239, 978 0 902088, 978 1 84291 Kingsway

Parent Company:
David C. Cook

Distributor for:
Barbour; Charisma House; Harrison House; Lifeway, Broodman & Holmon; New Leaf Press; Regal

Overseas Representation:
Australia: Kennedy International, NSW
Canada: David C. Cook Distribution Canada, Paris, Ont
Hong Kong: Cross Communications Ltd
Japan: Christian Literature Crusade, Tokyo
New Zealand: Scripture Union, Wellington
Singapore: Aenon International Pte Ltd; SKS Books Warehouse
South Africa: Struik Christian Books Pty Ltd, Maitland, Cape Town

2437

CHRIS KINGTON PUBLISHING
33–41 Dallington Street, London EC1V 0BB
Telephone: (020) 7954 3474
Fax: 0845 450 6410
Email: enquiries@chriskingtonpublishing.co.uk
Web Site: http://www.chriskingtonpublishing.co.uk

Educational & Textbooks; Electronic (Professional & Academic)

Book Trade Association Membership:
Publishers Association

2438

KOGAN PAGE LTD
120 Pentonville Road, London N1 9JN
Telephone: (020) 7278 0433
Fax: (020) 7837 6348
Email: kpinfo@koganpage.com or kpsales@koganpage.com
Web Site: http://www.koganpage.com

Warehouse:
Littlehampton Book Services, PO Box 4264, Worthing BN 13 3T
Telephone: 01903 828800

Directors: Philip Kogan *(Chairman)*
Helen Kogan *(Managing)*
Gordon Watts *(Financial)*
Louise Cameron *(Publishing Services)*
Ben Glover *(Sales)*
Michael Smith *(Marketing)*

Academic & Scholarly; Accountancy & Taxation; Educational & Textbooks; Electronic (Educational); Electronic (Professional & Academic); Industry, Business & Management; Reference Books, Directories & Dictionaries; Transport; Vocational Training & Careers

New Titles: 150 (2007), 150 (2008)
Annual Turnover: £6M

ISBNs, Imprints & Series: 978 0 7494

Distributor for:
Bloomberg Press [excluding Americas]; GMB Publishing

Overseas Representation:
Australia & New Zealand: Woodslane Pty Ltd, Warriewood, NSW, Australia
Burma, China, Vietnam, Hong Kong,
Taiwan, Middle East & Thailand: Publishers International Marketing, London, UK
Canada: Renouf Publishing Co Ltd, Ottawa, Ont
Caribbean: InterMedia Americana (IMA) Ltd, London, UK
India: Viva Books, New Delhi
Singapore, Malaysia & Brunei: Penguin Books Singapore, Jurong, Singapore
South Africa: Book Promotions Pty Ltd, Diep River
USA: Ingram Publisher Services, La Vergne, TN

Book Trade Association Membership:
Publishers Association; Data Publishers Association

2439

KUBE PUBLISHING LTD
Ratby Lane, Markfield, Leicester LE67 9SY
Telephone: 01530 249230
Fax: 01530 249656
Email: info@kubepublishing.com
Web Site: http://www.kubepublishing.com

Director: Haris Ahmad
Executives: Anwar Cara *(Production)*
Khalid Manzoor *(Distribution & Sales)*
Administration Co-ordinator: Miss Rufeedah Cara
Commissioning Editor: Yahya Birt

Academic & Scholarly; Audio Books; Children's Books; Economics; Educational & Textbooks; Law; Religion & Theology

New Titles: 12 (2007), 10 (2008)
No of Employees: 8

ISBNs, Imprints & Series:
978 0 86037 Islamic Foundation
978 0 9536768 Revival
978 1 84774 Kube

Distributor for:
Pakistan: Institute of Policy Studies; Islamic Book Publishers
USA: Foundation for Islamic Knowledge; Institute of Islamic Thought

2440

*LAGOON BOOKS
42 Glentham Road, Barnes, London SW13 9JJ
Telephone: (020) 8563 6520
Fax: (020) 8563 6522
Email: books@lagoongames.com
Web Site: http://www.lagoongames.com

Directors: Simon Melhuish
Heather Watherston *(Managing)*
Book Development Manager: Nikole Bamford
Sales & Marketing Executive: Alastair Cronin

Children's Books; Cookery, Wines & Spirits; Electronic (Educational); Electronic (Entertainment); Humour; Sports & Games; Puzzle Books

ISBNs, Imprints & Series:
978 1 89971, 978 1 902813

Parent Company:
Lagoon Trading Co Ltd

Overseas Representation:
Australia: Independence Studios, Sydney, NSW; Tower Books Pty Ltd, Frenchs Forest, NSW
Canada: Concepts 401 Inc, North York, Ont
USA: The Lagoon Group, Boston

2441

*JAY LANDESMAN
8 Duncan Terrace, London N1 8BZ
Telephone: (020) 7837 7290
Email: jay@landesman.freeserve.co.uk
Web Site: http://www.franlandesman.com

Rights: Jay Landesman
Executive & Editorial: Mary Rose Storey
Production: Simon Wallace

Bibliography & Library Science; Biography & Autobiography; Humour; Literature & Criticism; Music; Poetry; Theatre, Drama & Dance

ISBNs, Imprints & Series:
978 0 905150 Golden Handshake; Jay Landesman Ltd; Polytantric Press

Associated Companies:
Golden Handshake; Polytantric Press

2442

LANDMARK PUBLISHING LTD
Ashbourne Hall, Cokayne Avenue, Ashbourne, Derbyshire DE6 1EJ
Telephone: 01335 347349
Fax: 01335 347303
Email: landmark@clara.net
Web Site: http://www.landmarkpublishing.co.uk

Trade Enquiries:
Grantham Book Services,
Isaac Newton Way,
Alma Park Industrial Estate, Grantham, Lincs NG31 9SD

Trade Enquiries (alternative):
Tiptree Book Services

Managing Director: C. L. M. Porter
Managers: C. Gilbert *(Sales & Marketing)*
S. Porter *(Office)*

History & Antiquarian; Transport; Travel & Topography

New Titles: 36 (2007), 36 (2008)
No of Employees: 6

ISBNs, Imprints & Series:
978 1 84306 Landmark Collectors Library; Landmark Countryside Collection; Landmark Visitors Guides

2443

PETER LANG LTD
Evenlode Court, Main Road,
Long Hanborough, Witney, Oxon OX29 8SZ
Telephone: 01993 880088
Fax: 01993 882040
Email: oxford@peterlang.com
Web Site: http://www.peterlang.net

Publishing Director: Graham Speake
Commissioning Editors: Hannah Godfrey
Nick Reynolds
Production Controlller: Mette Bundgaard

Academic & Scholarly

New Titles: 165 (2007), 130 (2008)
No of Employees: 6
Annual Turnover: £500,000

ISBNs, Imprints & Series: 978 3 03911

Parent Company:
Switzerland: Peter Lang

Associated Companies:
Belgium: P. I. E. – Peter Lang SA
Germany: Peter Lang GmbH
USA: Peter Lang Publishing Inc

Overseas Representation:
Worldwide: Peter Lang, Pieterlen, Switzerland

Book Trade Association Membership:
IPG

2444

*LAW SOCIETY PUBLISHING
113 Chancery Lane, London WC2A 1PL
Telephone: (020) 7841 5470
Fax: (020) 7841 5507
Email: publishing@lawsociety.org.uk
Web Site: http://www.publishing.lawsociety.org.uk

Distribution:
Marston Book Services Ltd, PO Box 312, Abingdon, Oxon OX14 4YH
Telephone: 01235 465656
Fax: 01235 465660

Financial Controller: Chris Wright
Managers: Stephen Honey *(Publishing)*
Sarah Foulkes *(Production)*
Claire Baumforth *(Group Marketing)*
Millie Patel *(Marketing)*
Commissioning Editors: Janet Noble
Ben Mullane
Simon Blackett

Law

ISBNs, Imprints & Series:
978 1 85328 The Law Society

Parent Company:
The Law Society

Book Trade Association Membership:
Data Publishers Association

2445

LAWPACK PUBLISHING LTD
76–89 Alscot Road, London SE1 3AW
Telephone: (020) 7394 4040
Fax: (020) 7394 4041
Email: enquiries@lawpack.co.uk
Web Site: http://www.lawpack.co.uk

Managing Director: Thomas Coles
Editor: Jamie Ross
Sales Manager: Russell Roworth

Computer Science; Do-It-Yourself; Law; Reference Books, Directories & Dictionaries; Vocational Training & Careers

New Titles: 12 (2007), 12 (2008)

ISBNs, Imprints & Series:
978 1 898217, 978 1 902646, 978 1 904053, 978 1 905261

2446

LDA
Hyde Buildings, Ashton Road, Hyde, Cheshire SK14 4SH
Telephone: 0161 367 2000
Fax: 0161 367 2094
Email: katy.james@findel-education.co.uk
Web Site: http://www.idalearning.com

Managing Director: Emma Markey *(Brand)*
Marketing Manager: Katy James

Children's Books; Educational & Textbooks

New Titles: 20 (2007), 60 (2008)

ISBNs, Imprints & Series:
978 0 905114, 978 1 85503

Parent Company:
Findel Education

Overseas Representation:
Australia: The Educational Experience Pty Ltd, Newcastle, NSW
Austria: Der Spielzeugmacher, St Georgen
Barbados: Quest, Christ Church
Belgium: Baert Sprl, Brussels
Canada: Louise Kool & Galt Ltd, Scarborough, Ont; Louise Kool & Galt Ltd, Scarborough, Ont

Denmark: Gonge, Egå
Finland: Early Learning OY, Helsinki
France: Mot a Mot, Paris
Germany: Verlag An Der Ruhr, Mülheim
Greece: Ed Toys, Athens; Andreas Leon, Athens
Hong Kong: Artsberg Enterprises Ltd
Iceland: Namsgagnastofnun, Reykjavik
Israel: Shaked Education Games & Learning Materials, Holon
Italy: Edizioni Centro Studio Erickson, Trento; La Favelliana, Milan
Malaysia: Young Learners Educational Centre, Kuala Lumpur
Malta: Royal Trading Agency, Valletta
Netherlands: Dalcomtext, Paterswolde; Pro Special, Zutphen; Swets & Zeitlinger BV, Lisse
Norway: Okani Laermidler, Bergen
Portugal: ABACO, Lisbon; PSICO, Lisbon
Republic of Ireland: Carrol Educational Supplies, Dublin; K. & M. Evans, Dublin; Surgisales Teaching Aids, Dublin
Singapore: International Quality Toys
South Africa: Educational Toy Centre, Johannesburg; Play & Schoolroom Pty, Parklands
Spain: Eductrade, Madrid
Sweden: Beta Pedagog, Skällinge; Playing & Learning, Danderyd
Thailand: Productivity Corp Ltd, Bangkok
USA: Living & Learning Inc, Bethlehem, PA

Book Trade Association Membership:
IPG; BESA

2447

LEARNING MATTERS LTD
33 Southernhay East, Exeter EX1 1NX
Telephone: 01392 215560
Fax: 01392 215561
Email: info@learningmatters.co.uk
Web Site: http://www.learningmatters.co.uk

Distribution:
BEBC Distribution, Albion Close, Parkstone, Poole BH12 3LL
Telephone: 0845 230 9000
Fax: 01202 715556
Email: learningmatters@bebc.co.uk
Web Site: http://www.bebc.co.uk

Managing Director: Jonathan Harris
Sales & Marketing Manager: Zoe Engert

Academic & Scholarly; Educational & Textbooks; Sociology & Anthropology

New Titles: 40 (2007), 50 (2008)
No of Employees: 10

ISBNs, Imprints & Series:
978 1 84445, 978 1 903300 Learning Matters
978 1 903337 Crucial

Overseas Representation:
Barbados: Days Bookstore, Bridgetown
Ghana: EPP Books Services Ltd, Accra
Hong Kong: Asia Publishers Services Ltd
Jamaica: The Book Merchant Ltd, Kingston
Malaysia: APD Kuala Lumpur Pte Ltd, Selangor
Mauritius: Editions le Printemps, Vacoas
Pakistan: Publishers Marketing Associates, Karachi
Singapore: APD Singapore Pte Ltd

Book Trade Association Membership:
IPG

2448

LEARNING TOGETHER
18 Shandon Park, Belfast BT5 6NW
Telephone: (028) 9040 2086
Fax: (028) 9040 2086
Email: info@learningtogether.co.uk
Web Site: http://www.learningtogether.co.uk

Distribution:
Orca Book Services, Unit A3, Fleets Corner, Poole, Dorset BH17 0HL
Telephone: 01202 665432
Fax: 01202 666219
Email: mail@orcabookservices.co.uk

Representation:
c/o Alan Goodworth, Roundhouse Group, Millstone, Limers Lane, Northam, North Devon EX39 2RG
Telephone: 01237 474474
Fax: 01237 474774
Email: roundhouse.group@ukgateway.net

Managing Director: Janet McConkey
Author/Publisher: Stephen McConkey

Educational & Textbooks

Annual Turnover: £70,000

ISBNs, Imprints & Series:
978 1 873385 Practice Tests In Series

Book Trade Association Membership:
Publishers Association; EPC

2449

LEATHERHEAD FOOD INTERNATIONAL
Randalls Road, Leatherhead, Surrey KT22 7RY
Telephone: 01372 822556 & 822241 (Sales)
Fax: 01372 822272
Email: chill@leatherheadfood.com
Web Site: http://www.leatherheadfood.com

Deputy Chief Executive Officer: Ann Fry
Business Manager, Market & Technical Services: Catherine Hill

Law; Scientific & Technical

New Titles: 18 (2007), 20 (2008)

ISBNs, Imprints & Series:
978 0 905748, 978 1 904007, 978 1 905224

Overseas Representation:
Australia & New Zealand: DA Information Services Pty Ltd, Mitcham, Vic, Australia
North America: Publications Resource Group, North Adams, MA, USA

2450

*LEGAL ACTION GROUP
242 Pentonville Road, London N1 9UN
Telephone: (020) 7833 2931
Fax: (020) 7837 6094
Email: lag@lag.org.uk
Web Site: http://www.lag.org.uk

Director: (t.b.a.)
Managers: Esther Pilger *(Publisher)*
Nim Moorlhy *(Marketing)*
Customer Services Executives: Adam Wilson
Andrew Troszok

Law

ISBNs, Imprints & Series:
978 0 905099, 978 1 903307

Book Trade Association Membership:
IPG

2451

LEGEND PRESS
Unit 11, 63 Clerkenwell Road, London EC1M 5NP
Telephone: (020) 7253 7019
Email: info@legendpress.co.uk
Web Site: http://www.legendpress.co.uk

Managing Director: Tom Chalmers

Fiction

New Titles: 5 (2007), 10 (2008)
No of Employees: 2
Annual Turnover: £60,000

ISBNs, Imprints & Series:
978 0 9551032, 978 1 906558

Book Trade Association Membership:
IPG

2452

LETTERLAND INTERNATIONAL LTD
33 New Road, Barton, Cambridge CB23 7AY
Telephone: 0870 766 2629
Fax: 01223 264126
Email: info@letterland.com
Web Site: http://www.letterland.com

Distribution:
Trade Counter Distribution, Mendlesham Industrial Estate, Norwich Road, Mendlesham, Suffolk IP14 5NA
Telephone: 01449 766629
Email: support@tradecounter.co.uk

Directors: Mark Wendon
Karen Halliday *(Marketing)*
Production Manager: Jonathan Wendon

Children's Books; Educational & Textbooks; Electronic (Educational); English as a Foreign Language

ISBNs, Imprints & Series:
978 0 907345, 978 1 86209

Overseas Representation:
Australia: Ed Source, Bassendean, WA
Canada: Educan, Weston, Ont
Colombia: Paula Perez, Bogota
Hong Kong: ETC Educational Technology Connection (HK) Ltd, Tai Koo Shing
Japan: J & N English Club, Shizuoka-ken
Korea: Infobooks, Seoul, Korea, South
New Zealand: Wakelin Educational Services, Ashburton
Nigeria: Kcxploits, Lagos
Singapore, Malaysia, Thailand & Indonesia: Tumble Tots (Asia) Pty Ltd, Singapore, Singapore
South Africa: Educational Ideas, Johannesburg
Taiwan: Hello! Book Club, Taipei County
USA: Letterland International, Enfield, NH

Book Trade Association Membership:
Publishers Association; EPC; IPG; International Reading Association

2453

LETTS AND LONSDALE
4 Grosvenor Place, London SW1X 7DL
Telephone: (020) 7096 2900
Fax: (020) 7096 2945
Email: orders@lettsandlonsdale.co.uk
Web Site: http://www.lettsandlonsdale.com

Warehouse, Distribution:
HarperCollins, Campsie View, Westerhill Road, Bishopbriggs, Glasgow G64 2QT

Directors: Andrew Ware *(Managing)*
Peter Stafford *(Sales & Marketing)*
Christopher Glennie *(Publishing)*

Biology & Zoology; Chemistry; Children's Books; Educational & Textbooks; Geography & Geology; History & Antiquarian; Languages & Linguistics; Mathematics & Statistics; Philosophy; Physics; Psychology & Psychiatry; Reference Books, Directories & Dictionaries; Scientific & Technical; Sociology & Anthropology; Sports & Games; Vocational Training & Careers

ISBNs, Imprints & Series:
978 1 84085, 978 1 84315, 978 1 85758, 978 1 85805, 978 1 90589, 978 1 90641

Associated Companies:
Leckie & Leckie

Overseas Representation:
Botswana: Book Promotions Pty Ltd, Diep River, South Africa
Caribbean: The Book Merchant Ltd, Kingston, Jamaica
Ghana: EPP Books Services Ltd, Accra
Malaysia: APD Kuala Lumpur Pte Ltd, Selangor
Middle East: Peter Ward Book Exports, London, UK
New Zealand: Addenda, Auckland
Pakistan: Publishers Marketing Associates, Karachi
Philippines: CRW Books, Rizal
Singapore: APD Singapore Pte Ltd
Tanzania, Uganda & Seychelles: A–Z Africa Book Services, Rotterdam, Netherlands

Book Trade Association Membership:
EPC

2454

DEWI LEWIS PUBLISHING
8 Broomfield Road, Heaton Moor, Stockport SK4 4ND
Telephone: 0161 442 9450
Fax: 0161 442 9450
Email: mail@dewilewispublishing.com
Web Site: http://www.dewilewispublishing.com

Trade Enquiries & Orders:
Turnaround, Unit 3 Olympia Trading Estate, Coburg Road, London N22 6TZ
Telephone: (020) 8829 3000
Fax: (020) 8881 5088
Email: orders@turnaround-uk.com
Web Site: http://www.turnaround-uk.com

Publisher: Dewi Lewis
Sales & Marketing Director: Caroline Warhurst

Architecture & Design; Fine Art & Art History; Illustrated & Fine Editions; Photography; Reference Books, Directories & Dictionaries

New Titles: 15 (2007), 18 (2008)
No of Employees: 2

ISBNs, Imprints & Series:
978 1 899235, 978 1 904587

Overseas Representation:
Australia: Tower Books Pty Ltd, Frenchs Forest, NSW
Germany: Visual Books Sales Agency, Berlin
New Zealand: Southern Publishers Group, Auckland
North America: Consortium Book Sales & Distribution Inc, St Paul, MN, USA

2455

LEXUS LTD
60 Brook Street, Glasgow G40 2AB
Telephone: 0141 556 0440
Fax: 0141 556 2202
Email: peterterrell@lexusforlanguages.co.uk
Web Site: http://www.lexusforlanguages.co.uk

Publisher: Peter Terrell
Typesetter & Designer: Elfreda Crehan

Educational & Textbooks; Languages & Linguistics; Reference Books, Directories & Dictionaries

New Titles: 3 (2007), 4 (2008)
No of Employees: 3
Annual Turnover: £100,000

ISBNs, Imprints & Series:
978 1 904737 Chinese Classroom; Travelmates

2456

LIBERTIES PRESS
Guinness Enterprise Centre, Taylor's Lane, Dublin 8, Republic of Ireland
Telephone: +353 (01) 402 0805
Email: sean@libertiespress.com
Web Site: http://www.libertiespress.com

Directors: Sean O'Keeffe
Peter O'Connell

Architecture & Design; Cookery, Wines & Spirits; Health & Beauty; History & Antiquarian; Literature & Criticism; Politics & World Affairs; Religion & Theology; Sports & Games

New Titles: 15 (2007), 20 (2008)
No of Employees: 4

ISBNs, Imprints & Series:
978 0 9545335, 978 1 905483

Parent Company:
Republic of Ireland: Liberties Media Ltd

Book Trade Association Membership:
CLÉ (Irish PA)

2457

LIBRIS LTD
26 Lady Margaret Road, London NW5 2XL
Telephone: (020) 7482 2390
Email: libris@onetel.com
Web Site: http://www.librislondon.co.uk

Orders:
Central Books Ltd, 99 Wallis Road, London E9 5LN
Telephone: (020) 8986 4854
Fax: (020) 8533 5821
Email: orders@centralbooks.com

Directors: N. M. Jacobs
S. A. Kitzinger

Academic & Scholarly; Biography & Autobiography; Fiction; Languages & Linguistics; Literature & Criticism; Music; Photography; Poetry; Travel & Topography

New Titles: 2 (2008)

ISBNs, Imprints & Series:
978 1 870352, 978 1 870352

2458

THE LILLIPUT PRESS LTD
62–63 Sitric Road, Arbour Hill, Dublin 7, Republic of Ireland
Telephone: +353 (01) 671 1647
Fax: +353 (01) 671 1233
Email: info@lilliputpress.ie
Web Site: http://www.lilliputpress.ie

Distributors (Trade Orders):
Gill & Macmillan, Hume Avenue, Park West, Dublin 12, Republic of Ireland
Telephone: +353 (01) 500 9500
Fax: +353 (01) 500 9599

Directors: Antony Farrell (*Managing & Publisher*)
David Dickson
Vincent Hurley
Terence Brown
Vivienne Guinness
Kathy Gilfillan

Academic & Scholarly; Architecture & Design; Biography & Autobiography; Fiction; Fine Art & Art History; History & Antiquarian; Illustrated & Fine Editions; Literature & Criticism; Music; Photography; Reference Books, Directories & Dictionaries

New Titles: 20 (2008)
No of Employees: 4
Annual Turnover: £400,000

ISBNs, Imprints & Series:
978 0 946640, 978 1 84351, 978 1 874675, 978 1 901866

Associated Companies:
Republic of Ireland: Sitric Books Ltd

Overseas Representation:
France: Lora Fountain Literary Agent, Paris
UK: Central Books Ltd, London

Book Trade Association Membership:
CLÉ (Irish PA)

2459

*FRANCES LINCOLN LTD
4 Torriano Mews, Torriano Avenue, London NW5 2RZ
Telephone: (020) 7284 4009
Fax: (020) 7485 0490
Email: reception@frances-lincoln.com
Web Site: http://www.franceslincoln.com

Warehouse, Trade Enquiries & Orders:
Bookpoint Ltd, 130 Milton Park, Abingdon, Oxon OX14 4SB
Telephone: 01235 400400
Fax: 01235 400500

Directors: John Nicoll (*Managing*)
Jon Rippon (*Finance*)
Martin Oestreicher (*Sales & Marketing*)
Janetta Otter-Barry (*Editorial - Children's Books*)
Andrew Dunn (*Foreign Rights*)
Managers: Sara Borthwick (*Business*)
Jo Christian (*Editorial - Adult Books*)
Sarah Roberts (*Publicity & Marketing*)
Laura Grandi (*Production*)

Architecture & Design; Children's Books; Cookery, Wines & Spirits; Fine Art & Art History; Gardening; Guide Books; Health & Beauty; Illustrated & Fine Editions; Religion & Theology; Sports & Games; Travel & Topography; Art & Mythology; Design & Decoration; Mind Body Spirit; Parenting

ISBNs, Imprints & Series:
978 0 7112, 978 1 84507

Distributor for:
Allen & Unwin [Children's Books]; Barn Owl Books Ltd; Boxer Books; Tamarind; Tara Publishing

Overseas Representation:
All countries other than those listed: Frances Lincoln, London, UK
Australia (Adult Books) & New Zealand: Bookwise International, Adelaide, SA, Australia
Australia (Children's Books): Walker Books Australia, Newtown, NSW, Australia
Canada: Raincoast Book Distribution Ltd, Vancouver, BC
South Africa: Pan Macmillan SA Pty Ltd, Hyde Park
USA (Adult Books): Antique Collectors Club Ltd, Easthampton, MA, USA
USA (Children's Books): Publishers Group West, Berkeley, CA, USA

Book Trade Association Membership:
IPG

2460

LION HUDSON PLC
Wilkinson House, Jordan Hill Road, Oxford OX2 7DR
Telephone: 01865 302750
Fax: 01865 302757
Email: info@lionhudson.com
Web Site: http://www.lionhudson.com

Directors: Denis Cole (*Chairman*)
Paul Clifford (*Managing*)
Nicholas Jones (*Deputy Managing*)
Rodney Shepherd (*Publishing - Monarch*)
John O'Nions (*Sales & Marketing*)
Roy McCloughry
Stephen Price (*Production*)
Sales Manager: Robert Wendover (*Export*)
International & Subsidiary Rights: Paul Whitton
Financial Controller: Vicky Pulley

Biography & Autobiography; Children's Books; Educational & Textbooks; Religion & Theology

New Titles: 160 (2007), 160 (2008)
No of Employees: 60
Annual Turnover: £9M

ISBNs, Imprints & Series:
978 0 7459, 978 0 85648 Aslan; Lion; Lion Children's
978 1 85424 Monarch
978 1 85985 Candle

Overseas Representation:
Australia: Bookwise International, Adelaide, SA
New Zealand: New Holland Publishers (New Zealand), Auckland
South Africa: Pearson Education, Cape Town

Book Trade Association Membership:
Publishers Association; EPC

2461

LISU
Loughborough University, Loughborough, Leics LE11 3TU
Telephone: 01509 635680
Fax: 01509 635699
Email: lisu@lboro.ac.uk
Web Site: http://www.lboro.ac.uk/departments/dis/lisu

Director: Claire Creaser

Bibliography & Library Science; Reference Books, Directories & Dictionaries

New Titles: 7 (2007), 7 (2008)

ISBNs, Imprints & Series:
978 0 948848, 978 1 905499
978 1 901786 LISU Reports

Parent Company:
Loughborough University

2462

LITTLE, BROWN BOOK GROUP
100 Victoria Embankment, London EC4Y 0DY
Telephone: (020) 7911 8000
Fax: (020) 7911 8100
Email: firstname.surname@littlebrown.co.uk
Web Site: http://www.littlebrown.co.uk & http://www.orbitbooks.co.uk

Distribution Centre:
TBS Ltd, Colchester Road, Frating Green, Colchester, Essex CO7 7DW
Telephone: 01206 255678 (orders)
Fax: 01206 255930 (orders)
Email: exportmanagement@tbs-ltd.co.uk

Directors: Ursula Mackenzie (*Chief Executive Officer & Publisher*)
David Kent (*Chief Operating Officer*)
Diane Spivey (*Rights*)
Roger Cazalet (*Group Marketing*)
Peter Cotton (*Art*)
Rosalie MacFarlane (*Publicity*)
Robert Manser (*Group Sales*)
Richard Beswick (*Publisher – Little Brown & Abacus*)
Tim Holman (*Publisher – Orbit*)
Lennie Goodings (*Publisher – Virago*)
Antonia Hodgson (*Publisher – Sphere & Piatkus*)
Nick Ross (*Production*)
Siobhan Hughes (*Legal*)

Audio Books; Biography & Autobiography; Cookery, Wines & Spirits; Crime; Fiction; History & Antiquarian; Humour; Literature & Criticism; Medical (incl. Self Help & Alternative Medicine); Military & War; Music; Poetry; Politics & World Affairs; Psychology & Psychiatry; Science Fiction; Sports & Games; Travel & Topography

New Titles: 350 (2007), 530 (2008)
No of Employees: 147
Annual Turnover: £60M

ISBNs, Imprints & Series:
978 0 316, 978 1 4087 Little, Brown
978 0 349 Abacus
978 0 7499 Piatkus
978 0 7515 Sphere Paperbacks
978 0 8212 Bulfinch
978 1 4055 Audio Books
978 1 84149, 978 1 85723 Orbit
978 1 84408, 978 1 85381, 978 1 86049 Virago
978 1 84744 Sphere Hardbacks
978 1 904233 Atom

Parent Company:
Hachette Livre Group of Companies

Overseas Representation:
Africa: A–Z Africa Book Services, Rotterdam, Netherlands
Australia: Hachette Livre Australia, Sydney, NSW
Canada: Penguin Books Canada, Toronto, Ont
Caribbean, Central & South America: Jerry Carrillo Inc, USA
China: Wei Zhao, New York, NY, USA
France & Scandinavia: Melanie Boesen, Hachette US, Denmark
Germany, Sweden & Middle East: Simon McArt, Little, Brown Book Group, London, UK
India: Penguin Books India, New Delhi
Italy: Penguin Italia srl, Corsico, Milan
Japan, Thailand, Indonesia, Hong Kong, Korea & Taiwan: Gilles Fauveau, Japan
New Zealand: Hachette Livre New Zealand, Auckland
Singapore & Malaysia: Penguin Books Singapore, Jurong, Singapore
South Africa: Penguin Books SA (Pty) Ltd, Denver Ext 4
Spain & Portugal: Penguin Books SA, Madrid, Spain
Switzerland, Belgium, Netherlands, Gibraltar, Malta & Cyprus: Sarah Humphreys, Little, Brown Book Group, London, UK

Book Trade Association Membership:
BA; Book Marketing Ltd

2463

*LITTLE TIGER PRESS
[an imprint of Magi Publications]
1 The Coda Centre, 189 Munster Road, London SW6 6AW
Telephone: (020) 7385 6333
Fax: (020) 7385 7333
Email: info@littletiger.co.uk
Web Site: http://www.littletigerpress.com

Distribution:
Macmillan Distribution (MDL), Brunel Road, Houndmills, Basingstoke, Hants RG21 6XS
Telephone: 01256 302692
Fax: 01256 812521
Email: mdl@macmillan.co.uk

Proprietor: Monty Bhatia
Directors: David Bucknor (Sales)
Aude Lavielle (Rights)
Yolande Denny (Production)
Publisher: Jude Evans
Commissioning Editor: Stephanie Stansbie

Children's Books

ISBNs, Imprints & Series:
978 1 84506, 978 1 85430 Little Tiger Press
978 1 84715 Stripes Publishing

Parent Company:
Magi Publications

Overseas Representation:
Australia: Global Language Books, Toongabbie, NSW
Hong Kong: Publishers' Associates Ltd
Malaysia: Pansing Distributors (M) Sdn Bhd, Shah Alam
Singapore & Brunei: STP Distributors Pte Ltd, Singapore
Southern Africa: Titles SA, Johannesburg, South Africa

2464

THE LITTMAN LIBRARY OF JEWISH CIVILIZATION
PO Box 645, Oxford OX2 0UJ
Telephone: 01865 790740
Fax: 01865 722964
Email: info@littman.co.uk
Web Site: http://www.littman.co.uk

Distribution:
NBN International, Estover Road, Plymouth PL6 7PY
Telephone: 01752 202300
Fax: 01752 202333
Email: orders@nbninternational.com
Web Site: http://www.nbninternational.com

Managing Editor: Connie Webber
Chief Executive Officer: Ludo Craddock
Directors: Colette Littman
Robert Littman

Academic & Scholarly; Biography & Autobiography; Educational & Textbooks; Fine Art & Art History; History & Antiquarian; Literature & Criticism; Music; Philosophy; Politics & World Affairs; Religion & Theology; Sociology & Anthropology; Theatre, Drama & Dance

New Titles: 7 (2007), 7 (2008)

ISBNs, Imprints & Series:
978 0 631 Polin Series
978 1 874774, 978 1 904113 Littman Library of Jewish Civilization

Overseas Representation:
Australia & New Zealand: Peribo Pty Ltd, Mount Kuring-Gai, NSW, Australia
USA & Canada: International Specialized Book Services Inc, Portland, OR, USA

Book Trade Association Membership:
IPG

2465

LIVERPOOL UNIVERSITY PRESS
4 Cambridge Street, Liverpool L69 7ZU
Telephone: 0151 794 2233
Fax: 0151 794 2235
Email: lup@liv.ac.uk
Web Site: http://www.liverpool-unipress.co.uk

Sales & Distribution:
Marston Book Services, PO Box 269, Abingdon, Oxon OX14 4YN
Telephone: 01235 465500
Fax: 01235 465555

Email: trade.order@marston.co.uk
Web Site: http://www.marston.co.uk

Publisher: Robin Bloxsidge
Editorial Director: Anthony Cond
Managers: Simon Bell (Sales & Marketing)
Tracey Mooney (Finance)
Andrew Kirk (Production)
Editor: Helen Tookey (Journals Production)
Journals Publishing Executive: Clare Hooper

Academic & Scholarly; Architecture & Design; Educational & Textbooks; Fine Art & Art History; History & Antiquarian; Languages & Linguistics; Literature & Criticism; Politics & World Affairs; Science Fiction; Sociology & Anthropology

New Titles: 55 (2008)

ISBNs, Imprints & Series:
978 0 85323, 978 1 84631

Overseas Representation:
Africa & Middle East: International Publishing Services (IPS) Middle East Ltd, Dubai, UAE
Benelux & Germany: Roy de Boo, Hooge Mierde, Netherlands
Central & Latin America: InterMedia Americana (IMA) Ltd, London, UK
Far East (excluding Japan): STM Publisher Services Pte Ltd, Singapore
France & Italy: Flavio Marcello Publishers' Agents & Consultants, Padua, Italy
India: Viva Group, New Delhi
Malaysia: Yuha Associates, Selangor Darul Ehsan
North America: International Specialized Book Services Inc, Portland, OR, USA
Republic of Ireland: John Fitzpatrick, Dublin
Scandinavia: Jan Norbye, Ølstykke, Denmark
Spain & Portugal: Iberian Book Services, Madrid, Spain

Book Trade Association Membership:
CAPP; IPG

2466

LIVING TIME® MEDIA INTERNATIONAL
Units 18c–19c, Wem Business Park, New Street, Wem, Shropshire SY4 5JX
Telephone: 01939 236623
Fax: 01939 234324
Email: info@livingtime.co.uk
Web Site: http://www.livingtime.co.uk

International Rights Centre (IRC):
5 Tite Street, Chelsea, London SW3 4JU
Telephone: 07877 851410
Fax: (020) 7351 5722 (rights)
Email: rights@livingtime.co.uk
Web Site: http://www.livingtimemedia.com

Head of Publishing/Chief Executive: Alderson Smith
Editor-in-Chief: Edouard d'Araille
International Sales Executive: John Hargreaves
Rights Executives: James Hartley (Foreign & Subsidiary)
Anthony Nevill (Film)
Children's Book Rights Licensor: Carolyn Eden

Academic & Scholarly; Biography & Autobiography; Children's Books; Cinema, Video, TV & Radio; Crime; Educational & Textbooks; English as a Foreign Language; Fiction; Literature & Criticism; Philosophy; Poetry; Psychology & Psychiatry; Science Fiction

New Titles: 24 (2007), 50 (2008)
No of Employees: 6
Annual Turnover: £250,000

ISBNs, Imprints & Series:
978 1 903331 Living Time® Press
978 1 905820 Living Time® Media International

Parent Company:
Living Time®

Associated Companies:
The Academy of the 3rd Millennium; Fortune Street®; Living Time Vision (LTV); Living Time® Design; Living Time® Films Ltd; Living Time® Music

Overseas Representation:
Worldwide: Hubert Janssen, Living Time® Europe, Amsterdam, Netherlands

Book Trade Association Membership:
Publishers Association

2467

LOGASTON PRESS
Little Logaston, Woonton, Almeley, Herefordshire HR3 6QH
Telephone: 01544 327344
Email: logastonp@aol.com
Web Site: http://www.logastonpress.co.uk

Proprietor: Andy Johnson
Executive: Karen Stout

Archaeology; Architecture & Design; Fine Art & Art History; Guide Books; History & Antiquarian; Natural History; Reference Books, Directories & Dictionaries; Rural Interest

New Titles: 20 (2007), 15 (2008)
No of Employees: 2
Annual Turnover: £120,000

ISBNs, Imprints & Series:
978 0 9510242, 978 1 873827, 978 1 904396, 978 1 906663 Monuments in the Landscape Series

2468

LOMOND BOOKS LTD
14 Freskyn Place,
East Mains Industrial Estate, Broxburn EH52 5NF
Telephone: 01506 855955
Fax: 01506 855965
Email: sales@lomondbooks.co.uk

Directors: Trevor Maher
Duncan Baxter (Sales)
Jackie Brown (Operations)
Michael Burke

Children's Books; Cookery, Wines & Spirits; Crafts & Hobbies; Guide Books; History & Antiquarian; Humour; Illustrated & Fine Editions; Natural History; Reference Books, Directories & Dictionaries

New Titles: 10 (2007), 10 (2008)
No of Employees: 11

ISBNs, Imprints & Series:
978 0 94778, 978 1 84204

Book Trade Association Membership:
BA

2469

LUATH PRESS LTD
543/2 Castlehill, The Royal Mile, Edinburgh EH1 2ND
Telephone: 0131 225 4326
Fax: 0131 225 4324
Email: gavin.macdougall@luath.co.uk
Web Site: http://www.luath.co.uk

Distribution:
HarperCollins, Westerhill Road, Bishopbriggs, Glasgow G64 2QR
Telephone: 0870 787 1722

Fax: 0870 787 1723
Email: enquiries@harpercollins.co.uk
Web Site: http://b2b.harpercollins.co.uk

Director: Gavin MacDougall
Rights & Overseas Distribution: Nele Andersch
Production & Editorial: Leila Cruickshank
Sales & Marketing: Chani McDain
Press & Events: Angela Aldretsch

Biography & Autobiography; Children's Books; Cinema, Video, TV & Radio; Cookery, Wines & Spirits; Crime; Fiction; Gardening; Geography & Geology; Guide Books; History & Antiquarian; Humour; Languages & Linguistics; Literature & Criticism; Magic & the Occult; Medical (incl. Self Help & Alternative Medicine); Military & War; Music; Natural History; Photography; Poetry; Politics & World Affairs; Sports & Games; Theatre, Drama & Dance; Travel & Topography; Veterinary Science; Walking

New Titles: 40 (2007), 40 (2008)

ISBNs, Imprints & Series:
Scots in; Viewpoints
978 0 946487 Luath Guides to Scotland; Walk with Luath; Wild Lives
978 0 946487, 978 1 84282 Let's Explore
978 0 946487, 978 1 84282, 978 1 906307 Luath
978 0 946487, 978 1 84282 On the Trail of; The Quest for
978 1 84282, 978 1 905222 Luath Storyteller

Overseas Representation:
Australia & New Zealand: Luath Press Ltd, Edinburgh, UK
USA & Canada: Ingram Publisher Services, Nashville, TN, USA

Book Trade Association Membership:
Publishing Scotland

2470

LUND HUMPHRIES
Gower House, Croft Road, Aldershot, Hants GU11 3HR
Telephone: 01252 331551
Fax: 01252 344405
Email: info@lundhumphries.com
Web Site: http://www.lundhumphries.com

Trade Distribution:
Bookpoint Ltd, 39 Milton Park, Abingdon, Oxon OX14 4TD
Telephone: 01235 400400
Fax: 01235 400413
Email: orders@bookpoint.co.uk

Directors: Nigel Farrow (Chairman, Ashgate Publishing)
Lucy Myers (Managing)

Academic & Scholarly; Antiques & Collecting; Architecture & Design; Fine Art & Art History; Photography

ISBNs, Imprints & Series: 978 0 85331

Parent Company:
Ashgate Publishing

Distributor for:
Australia: Powerhouse Museum

Overseas Representation:
Australia & Far East: Ashgate Publishing Asia-Pacific, Newport, NSW, Australia
Central & Eastern Europe: Dr László Horváth Publishers Representative, Budapest, Hungary
Finland, Sweden, Norway, Denmark & Iceland: Andrew Durnell Marketing Ltd, Tunbridge Wells, UK
France & Netherlands: Casemate Books, Newbury, UK

Germany, Austria, Switzerland, Italy, Greece, Luxembourg & Belgium: Ted Dougherty, London, UK
India: Maya Publishers Pvt Ltd, New Delhi
Japan (stockholding agents): United Publishers Services Ltd, Tokyo, Japan
Korea: Information & Culture Korea (ICK), Seoul, Korea, South
Middle East: Publishers International Marketing, Sutton St Nicholas, Herefordshire, UK
New Zealand: South Pacific Books (Imports) Ltd, Auckland
South Africa: Peter Hyde Associates (Pty) Ltd, Cape Town
South America & Africa (excluding South Africa): InterMedia Americana (IMA) Ltd, London, UK
Spain & Portugal: Penny Padovani, London, UK
USA & Canada: Lund Humphries, Burlington, VT, USA

2471

THE LUTTERWORTH PRESS
PO Box 60, Cambridge CB1 2NT
Telephone: 01223 350865
Fax: 01223 366951
Email: publishing@lutterworth.com
Web Site: http://www.lutterworth.com

Trade Enquiries & Orders:
James Clarke & Co, PO Box 60, Cambridge CB1 2NT
Telephone: (as above)
Fax: (as above)
Email: orders@jamesclarke.co.uk
Web Site: (as above)

Managing Director: Adrian Brink
Customer Service: Mudasir Gul
Accounts Department: Penny Bull
Sales & Publicity: Lucia Perez
 Antoaneta Ouzuonova
Editorial: Aidan van de Weyer

Academic & Scholarly; Antiques & Collecting; Architecture & Design; Biography & Autobiography; Children's Books; Crafts & Hobbies; Educational & Textbooks; Fine Art & Art History; History & Antiquarian; Illustrated & Fine Editions; Literature & Criticism; Military & War; Natural History; Philosophy; Politics & World Affairs; Reference Books, Directories & Dictionaries; Religion & Theology; Sports & Games

New Titles: 19 (2007) , 15 (2008)
No of Employees: 6

ISBNs, Imprints & Series:
978 0 7188 The Lutterworth Press
978 0 7444 Patrick Hardy
978 0 906554 Acorn Editions

Parent Company:
James Clarke & Co Ltd

Overseas Representation:
China & Asia: AA Media Services, Shanghai, P. R. of China
Philippines: Edwin Makabenta, Quezon City
Spain & Portugal: Iberian Book Services, Madrid, Spain
USA: Ingram Publisher Services Inc, Chambersburg, PA

Book Trade Association Membership:
EPC; CAPP; IPG

2472

McCRIMMON PUBLISHING CO LTD
10–12 High Street, Great Wakering, Essex SS3 0EQ
Telephone: 01702 218956
Fax: 01702 216082
Email: info@mccrimmons.com
Web Site: http://www.mccrimmons.com

Bookshop:
All Saints Pastoral Centre, London Colney, St Albans, Herts
Telephone: 01727 827612
Fax: 01727 827612
Email: (as above)
Web Site: (as above)

Secretary: Joan McCrimmon
Director: Don McCrimmon *(Sales)*
Graphic Designer: Nick Snode
Accounts: Sue Anderson
Bookshop Manager: Louise Madden
Sales Ledger: Caroline Lee
Warehouse: Robert Mossop
Music: Richard Dawson

Children's Books; Educational & Textbooks; Electronic (Educational); Music; Religion & Theology

No of Employees: 10
Annual Turnover: £850,000

ISBNs, Imprints & Series: 978 0 85597

Distributor for:
USA: Harcourt Brace & Co; Harcourt Religion Publishers (RE division); LTP Publications; Printery House Inc

Overseas Representation:
Australia: John Garrett Publishing, Mulgrave, Vic
Hong Kong: Catholic Truth Society
New Zealand: Pleroma Christian Supplies, Otane, Central Hawkes Bay
South Africa: The Catholic Bookshop, Cape Town

2473

McGRAW-HILL EDUCATION
Shoppenhangers Road, Maidenhead, Berks SL6 2QL
Telephone: 01628 502500
Fax: 01628 770224
Web Site: http://www.mcgraw-hill.co.uk

Vice-Presidents: Simon Allen *(Senior International, English Language Publishing)*
 Derek Stordahl *(Market Development, MH.Prop.)*
Director Operations Europe: Alan Martin

Academic & Scholarly; Accountancy & Taxation; Architecture & Design; Aviation; Biology & Zoology; Chemistry; Computer Science; Economics; Educational & Textbooks; Electronic (Educational); Electronic (Professional & Academic); Engineering; English as a Foreign Language; Geography & Geology; Industry, Business & Management; Law; Mathematics & Statistics; Medical (incl. Self Help & Alternative Medicine); Philosophy; Physics; Politics & World Affairs; Psychology & Psychiatry; Reference Books, Directories & Dictionaries; Scientific & Technical; Sociology & Anthropology; Transport; Vocational Training & Careers

ISBNs, Imprints & Series: 978 0 07

Parent Company:
USA: McGraw-Hill Inc

Associated Companies:
Open University Press
Australia: McGraw-Hill Book Co Australia Pty Ltd
Canada: McGraw-Hill Ryerson Ltd
Colombia: McGraw-Hill/InterAmericana (Colombia) SA
India: Tata-McGraw-Hill Publishing Co Ltd
Italy: McGraw-Hill Libri Italia srl
Japan: McGraw-Hill Book Co
Mexico: Libros McGraw-Hill de Mexico SA de CV
Portugal: McGraw-Hill/Interamericana de Portugal Ltda

Singapore: McGraw-Hill International Book Co
Spain: McGraw-Hill/Interamericana de España SA
USA: Wm. C. Brown; Brown & Benchmark; Irwin; Irwin Professional; Osborne/McGraw-Hill
Venezuela: McGraw-Hill/InterAmericana (Venezuela) SA

Distributor for:
Canada: B. C. Decker
USA: Amacom; Berrett-Koehler; Harvard Business School Press; R & D Books

Book Trade Association Membership:
Publishers Association; BA

2474

McGRAW-HILL PUBLISHING COMPANY
McGraw-Hill House,
Shoppenhangers Road, Maidenhead, Berks SL6 2QL
Telephone: 01628 502500
Fax: 01628 773932
Email: uk_queries@mcgraw-hill.com
Web Site: http://www.mcgraw-hill.co.uk

Academic & Scholarly; Educational & Textbooks; Trade

Associated Companies:
UK: Kingscourt / McGraw-Hill; Open University Press

Book Trade Association Membership:
Publishers Association

2475

MACMILLAN CHILDREN'S BOOKS LTD
20 New Wharf Road, London N1 9RR
Telephone: (020) 7014 6000
Fax: (020) 7014 6001
Web Site: http://www.panmacmillan.com

Trade Enquiries:
Macmillan Distribution (MDL), Houndmills, Basingstoke, Hants RG21 6XS
Telephone: 01256 329242
Fax: 01256 840154
Email: mdl@macmillan.co.uk

Directors: Emma Hopkin *(Managing)*
 Tracy Florance *(Production)*
 Tracy Phillips *(Group Rights)*
 Vanessa Clarke *(UK Deputy Sales)*
 Kate Mackenzie *(Rights)*
 Anne Glenn *(Art)*
 Rebecca McNally *(Publishing)*
 Suzanne Carnell *(Editorial, Picture & Gift Books)*
 Sarah Fabiny *(Editorial, Campbell Books)*
 Gaby Morgan *(Editorial, Poetry & Non-Fiction)*
 Sarah Dudman *(Editorial, Fiction)*
 Melissa Fairley *(Editorial, Kingfisher)*
 Mike Buckley *(Art, Kingfisher)*

Audio Books; Children's Books; Poetry

New Titles: 220 (2007) , 320 (2008)

ISBNs, Imprints & Series:
978 0 330, 978 0 333 Campbell Books; Macmillan Children's Books; Young Picador
978 0 7534 Kingfisher

Parent Company:
Macmillan Ltd

Associated Companies:
Macmillan Education Ltd; Macmillan Publishers Ltd; Palgrave Macmillan Ltd; Pan Macmillan Ltd

Book Trade Association Membership:
Publishers Association; Children's Book Circle; PA Children's Book Group

2476

MACMILLAN EDUCATION
Macmillan Oxford, Between Towns Road, Oxford OX4 3PP
Telephone: 01865 405700
Fax: 01865 405701
Web Site: http://www.mhelt.com

Distribution:
Macmillan Distribution (MDL), Houndmills, Basingstoke, Hants RG21 6XS
Telephone: 01256 329242
Fax: 01256 840154
Email: mdl@macmillan.co.uk

Chairman: Julian Drinkall *(Chief Executive)*
Directors: Jeremy Dieguez *(Managing, Europe)*
 Paul Emmett *(Finance)*
 John Peacock *(Technology, Digital & Operations)*
 Flavio Centofanti *(Regional, Middle East)*
 Steven Tweed *(Regional Sales, Africa)*
 Cathy Smith *(International ELT Sales & Marketing)*
 Steven Maginn *(Regional, East Asia)*
 Alison Hubert *(Africa & Caribbean, International Curriculum)*
 Angela Lilley *(International ELT Publishing)*
 Sue Bale *(Dictionary Publishing)*
Company Secretary: Martin Powter

Atlases & Maps; Children's Books; Educational & Textbooks; English as a Foreign Language; Environment & Development Studies; Languages & Linguistics; Reference Books, Directories & Dictionaries

ISBNs, Imprints & Series:
Macmillan Education; Macmillan Heinemann ELT
978 0 333

Parent Company:
Macmillan Ltd

Associated Companies:
Macmillan Children's Books; Macmillan Publishers Ltd; Palgrave Macmillan; Pan Macmillan

Overseas Representation:
See: Macmillan Publishers Ltd, Basingstoke, UK

Book Trade Association Membership:
Publishers Association

2477

MACMILLAN PRESS LTD
see: Palgrave Macmillan

2478

MACMILLAN PUBLISHERS LTD
The Macmillan Building, 4 Crinan Street, London N1 9XW
Telephone: (020) 7833 4000
Fax: (020) 7843 4640
Web Site: http://www.macmillan.co.uk

Trade Enquiries, Warehouse, Orders & Registered Office:
Macmillan Distribution (MDL), Brunel Road, Houndmills, Basingstoke, Hants RG21 6XS
Telephone: 01256 329242
Fax: 01256 840154
Email: mdl@macmillan.co.uk

Directors: Dr A. Thomas *(Chief Executive)*
 D. J. G. Knight
 W. H. Farries *(Finance)*
 S. C. Inchcombe
 J. Drinkall
Company Secretary: C. E. Fleming

Parent Company:
Germany: Georg von Holtzbrinck GmbH

Associated Companies:
Boxtree Ltd; Campbell Books Ltd; Macmillan Children's Books; Macmillan Distribution Ltd; Macmillan Education; Nature Publishing Group Ltd; Palgrave Macmillan; Pan Macmillan; Sidgwick & Jackson Ltd; Stockton Press Ltd
Argentina: Editorial Estrada SA; Editorial Puerto de Palos SA; Macmillan Publishers SA
Armenia: Macmillan Armenia CJS
Australia: Macmillan Publishers Australia Pty Ltd; Macquarie Library Pty Ltd; Macquarie Online Pty Ltd; Pan Macmillan Australia Pty Ltd; Sun Books Pty Ltd
Botswana: Macmillan Botswana Publishing Co (Pty) Ltd
Brazil: Macmillan do Brasil
Cameroon: Macmillan Publishers Cameroon Ltd
Egypt: Macmillan Publishers Egypt Ltd
Ghana: Unimax Macmillan Ltd
Greece: Macmillan Hellas SA
Hong Kong: Macmillan Publishers (China) Ltd; Peninsula Production & Distribution Ltd
India: Macmillan India Ltd; MPS Technologies Ltd
Japan: Macmillan Language House Ltd; Nature Japan KK
Kenya: Macmillan Kenya (Publishers) Ltd
Korea, South: Macmillan Korea Publishers Ltd
Malawi: Macmillan Malawi Ltd
Mexico: Ediciones Castillo SA de CV; Editorial Macmillan de Mexico SA de CV
Mozambique: Macmillan Mozambique Lda
Namibia: Gamsberg Macmillan Publishers (Pty) Ltd
New Zealand: Macmillan Publishers New Zealand Ltd
Nigeria: Macmillan Nigeria Publishers Ltd; Northern Nigerian Publishing Co Ltd
Peru: Macmillan Publishers SA
Poland: Macmillan Polska Sp.Z.O.O.
Republic of Ireland: Gill & Macmillan Ltd
Romania: Macmillan Romania SRL
Rwanda: Macmillan Rwanda Publishers Ltd
South Africa: Clever Books (Pty) Ltd; Hodder & Stoughton Ed SA (Pty) Ltd; Macmillan South Africa Publishers (Pty) Ltd; Pan Macmillan South Africa Publishers (Pty) Ltd
Spain: Macmillan Iberia SA
Swaziland: Macmillan Boleswa Publishers Pty Ltd; Macmillan Swaziland National Publishing Co (Pty) Ltd
Tanzania: Macmillan Aidan Ltd
Uganda: Macmillan Uganda Ltd
USA: Bedford, Freeman & Worth Publishing Group LLC; Tom Doherty Associates LLC; Farrar, Straus & Giroux LLC; Henry Holt and Co LLC; Holtzbrinck Publishers LLC; Macmillan Academic Publishing Inc; Macmillan Publishers Inc; Nature America Inc; St Martin's Press LLC; Stockton Press Inc
Zambia: Macmillan Publishers (Zambia) Ltd
Zimbabwe: College Press Publishers (Pvt) Ltd
Hong Kong: Macmillan New Asia Publishers Ltd

Distributor for:
see: Macmillan Children's Books; Macmillan Education; Palgrave Macmillan; Pan Macmillan

Overseas Representation:
Armenia: Macmillan Armenia JV CJSC, Yerevan
Australia: Macmillan Education Australia, South Yarra, Vic; Pan Macmillan (Australia) Pty Ltd, Sydney, NSW
Botswana: Macmillan Botswana Publishing Co Ltd, Gaborone
Brazil: Macmillan do Brasil, São Paulo
Cameroon: Macmillan Publishers Cameroon Ltd, Limbe
Canada: The Resource Centre, Waterloo
China: Macmillan Publishers (China) Ltd, Hong Kong; Pan Macmillan Asia, Hong Kong
Cyprus: Char. J. Philippides & Son Ltd, Nicosia
Dubai: Macmillan Education Dubai, Dubai, UAE
East & Central Africa: Macmillan Kenya (Publishers) Ltd, Nairobi, Kenya
Egypt: Macmillan Publishers Egypt Ltd, Cairo
Ethiopia: Macmillan Publishers Ltd, Addis Ababa
France & Netherlands: Anne Georges, Brussels, Belgium
Gambia: Macmillan Publishers Ltd, Banjul
Ghana: Unimax Macmillan Ltd, Accra
Greece: Macmillan Hellas LLC, Athens
Hungary: Edit Szabo, Budapest
India: Books India Pvt Ltd, New Delhi; Macmillan India Ltd, Bangalore; Palgrave Macmillan, New Delhi
Italy: Macmillan Publishers Ltd, Milan
Japan: Macmillan Language House, Tokyo
Kenya: Macmillan Kenya (Publishers) Ltd, Nairobi
Korea: Macmillan Korea Publishers Ltd, Seoul, Korea, South
Malawi: Macmillan Malawi Ltd, Blantyre
Malta: Agius & Agius Ltd, Valletta
Mexico & Central America: Editorial Macmillan de Mexico SA de CV, Mexico DF, Mexico
Mozambique: Macmillan Mozambique Lda
Namibia: Gamsberg Macmillan Publishers (Pty) Ltd, Windhoek
New Zealand: Macmillan Publishers New Zealand Ltd, Albany, Auckland
Nigeria: Macmillan Nigeria Publishers Ltd, Yaba - Lagos
Pakistan: Book Bird Publishers Representatives, Lahore
Peru: Macmillan Publishers SA, Lima
Poland: Macmillan Polska, Warsaw
Republic of Ireland: Gill & Macmillan Ltd, Dublin
Romania: Macmillan Romania SRL, Bucharest
Rwanda: Macmillan Publishers Rwanda Ltd, Kigali
Saudi Arabia: Al-Dar Al-Sawlatia, Riyadh
Sierra Leone: Macmillan Publishers Ltd, Freetown
Singapore: Pansing Distribution Sdn Bhd
South Africa: Macmillan South Africa Publishers (Pty) Ltd, Braamfontein; Pan Macmillan SA Pty Ltd, Hyde Park
Swaziland: Macmillan Boleswa Publishers (Pty) Ltd, Manzini
Taiwan: Macmillan Education, Taipei
Tanzania: Macmillan Aidan Ltd, Dar es Salaam
Turkey: Dilyay, Istanbul
Uganda: Macmillan Uganda Ltd, Kampala
Zambia: Macmillan Zambia, Lusaka
Zimbabwe: College Press Publishers (Pvt) Ltd, Harare

Book Trade Association Membership:
Publishers Association; IPG

2479

MAGNA LARGE PRINT BOOKS
Magna House, Long Preston, Skipton, North Yorks BD23 4ND
Telephone: 01729 840225 & 840526
Fax: 01729 840683
Email: dallen@magnaprint.co.uk

Director: Robert Thirlby *(Chairman)*
General Manager: Diane Allen
Accounts: David Mellin

Audio Books; Fiction; Large Print Books; Story Sound Audio Cassettes & CDs

New Titles: 312 (2007), 312 (2008)

ISBNs, Imprints & Series:
978 0 7505, 978 1 84262 Large Print
978 1 85903 Audio

Parent Company:
Ulverscroft Large Print Books

Distributor for:
Mills & Boon Large Print

Overseas Representation:
Worldwide: Ulverscroft Large Print Books, UK

2480

THE MAIA PRESS LTD
82 Forest Road, London E8 3BH
Telephone: (020) 7683 8141
Fax: (020) 7683 8141
Email: maggie@maiapress.com
Web Site: http://www.maiapress.com

Trade Enquiries, Distributor:
Central Books, 99 Wallis Road, London E9 5LN
Telephone: (020) 8986 4854
Fax: (020) 8533 5821
Email: bill@centralbooks.com
Web Site: http://www.centralbooks.com

Representation (UK):
Turnaround Publisher Services Ltd, Unit 3, Olympia Trading Estate, Coburg Road, London N22 6TZ
Telephone: (020) 8829 3000
Fax: (020) 8881 5088
Email: andy@turnaround-uk.com
Web Site: http://www.turnaround-uk.com

Directors: Maggie Hamand
Jane Havell

Fiction

New Titles: 3 (2007), 7 (2008)
No of Employees: 2
Annual Turnover: £66,000

ISBNs, Imprints & Series: 978 1 904559

Overseas Representation:
Australia: Tower Books Pty Ltd, Frenchs Forest, NSW
Far East: Ashton International Marketing Services, Sevenoaks, Kent, UK
France, Belgium, Netherlands, Germany, Austria, Switzerland, Croatia, Slovenia, Hungary, Czech Republic, Slovakia & Poland: Michael Geoghegan, London, UK
Scandinavia: Angell Eurosales, Berwick-on-Tweed, UK
Singapore & Malaysia: Pansing Distribution Pte Ltd, Singapore, Singapore
Southern Europe: Padovani Books Ltd, London, UK
USA: Dufour Editions Inc, Chester Springs, PA

Book Trade Association Membership:
IPG

2481

MAINSTREAM PUBLISHING CO (EDINBURGH) LTD
7 Albany Street, Edinburgh EH1 3UG
Telephone: 0131 557 2959
Fax: 0131 556 8720
Email: enquiries@mainstreampublishing.com
Web Site: http://www.mainstreampublishing.com

Distribution, Trade Enquiries & Orders:
TBS Ltd, Colchester Road, Frating Green, Colchester, Essex CO7 7DW
Telephone: 01206 255600
Fax: 01206 255930

Directors: Bill Campbell *(Joint Managing, Editorial)*
Peter MacKenzie *(Joint Managing, Sales)*
Fiona Brownlee *(Marketing & Rights, Publicity)*
Ailsa Bathgate *(Editorial)*
Company Accountant: Douglas Nicoll
Production Manager: Neil Graham *(Production & Design)*

Biography & Autobiography; Cinema, Video, TV & Radio; Cookery, Wines & Spirits; Crime; Fine Art & Art History; Guide Books; Health & Beauty; History & Antiquarian; Humour; Illustrated & Fine Editions; Literature & Criticism; Medical (incl. Self Help & Alternative Medicine); Military & War; Music; Photography; Politics & World Affairs; Sports & Games

New Titles: 60 (2007), 66 (2008)
No of Employees: 19
Annual Turnover: £3.8M

ISBNs, Imprints & Series:
978 0 906391, 978 1 84018, 978 1 84596, 978 1 85158

Associated Companies:
Random House UK [Partner]

Overseas Representation:
Australia: Random House Australia Pty Ltd, Sydney, NSW
Canada: Random House of Canada Ltd, Mississauga, Ont
Caribbean & Latin America: Random House Inc, New York, NY, USA
Germany, Switzerland, Austria, Belgium, Denmark, Finland & Luxembourg: Jörg Riekenbrauk, Cologne, Germany
Hong Kong, Taiwan, South Korea & China: Stanson Yeung, Random House of Canada Ltd, Toronto, Ont, Canada
India, Sri Lanka & Bangladesh: N. S. Krishna, Random House Publishers India Pte Ltd, New Delhi, India
New Zealand: Random House New Zealand Ltd, Auckland
Norway, Sweden, Spain, France, Italy, Portugal, Cyprus, Greece, Malta, Middle East, Pakistan & Africa (excluding South Africa): Random House Group Ltd, London, UK
South Africa: Random House (SA) Pty Ltd, Parktown
USA: Trafalgar Square Publishing / IPG, Chicago, IL

Book Trade Association Membership:
BA; Publishing Scotland

2482

MANAGEMENT POCKETBOOKS LTD
Laurel House, Station Approach, Alresford, Hants SO24 9JH
Telephone: 01962 735573
Fax: 01962 733637
Email: sales@pocketbook.co.uk
Web Site: http://www.pocketbook.co.uk

Directors: Ros Baynes *(Managing)*
Adrian Hunt

Educational & Textbooks; Industry, Business & Management

New Titles: 10 (2007), 8 (2008)

ISBNs, Imprints & Series:

978 1 870471, 978 1 903776
Management Pocketbooks; Teachers' Pocketbooks

Overseas Representation:
Australia: Training Solutions Group, Mudgeeraba, Qld
Caribbean: InterMedia Americana (IMA) Ltd, London, UK
Far East: Publishers International Marketing, Ferndown, Dorset, UK
India: Research Press, New Delhi
South Africa: Learning Resources Pty Ltd, Johannesburg

2483

MANDRAKE OF OXFORD
PO Box 250, Oxford OX1 1AP
Telephone: 01865 243671
Fax: 01865 432929
Email: mandrake@mandrake.uk.net
Web Site: http://www.mandrake.uk.net

Directors: Mogg Morgan
Kim Morgan

Children's Books; Crime; Fiction; Fine Art & Art History; Literature & Criticism; Magic & the Occult; Medical (incl. Self Help & Alternative Medicine); Philosophy; Poetry; Religion & Theology; Sociology & Anthropology; New Science

New Titles: 10 (2007), 10 (2008)

ISBNs, Imprints & Series:
978 1 869928 Golden Dawn; Mandrake of Oxford

Overseas Representation:
USA: Ingram Publisher Services, Nashville, TN; New Leaf Distributing Co, Lithia Springs, GA

Book Trade Association Membership:
IPG

2484

MANEY PUBLISHING
Suite 1C, Joseph's Well, Hanover Walk, Leeds LS3 1AB
Telephone: 0113 386 8154
Fax: 0113 386 8178
Email: maney@maney.co.uk
Web Site: http://www.maney.co.uk

Also at:
1 Carlton House Terrace, London SW1Y 5DB
Telephone: (020) 7451 7300
Fax: (020) 7451 7307

Directors: Michael Gallico (Managing)
Mark Simon (Publishing)
Shelly Lynds (Sales & Marketing)
Managers: Liz Rosindale (Editorial)
Mark Hull (Managing Editor)
Lynne Medhurst (Head of Marketing & Promotions)

Academic & Scholarly; Archaeology; Architecture & Design; Electronic (Professional & Academic); Engineering; Fashion & Costume; Geography & Geology; History & Antiquarian; Illustrated & Fine Editions; Languages & Linguistics; Literature & Criticism; Medical (incl. Self Help & Alternative Medicine); Scientific & Technical

New Titles: 41 (2007), 33 (2008)
No of Employees: 33

ISBNs, Imprints & Series:
Legenda
978 0 901286 Northern Universities Press
978 0 901286, 978 1 902653 Maney Publishing

Distributor for:
European Respiratory Society; Modern Humanities Research Association; Pasold Research Fund; Society for Italian Studies; Society for Medieval Archaeology

Overseas Representation:
USA: Publishers Communication Group, Boston, MA

Book Trade Association Membership:
IGSMTP; Association of Learned & Professional Society Publishers

2485

MANSON PUBLISHING LTD
73 Corringham Road, London NW11 7DL
Telephone: (020) 8905 5150
Fax: (020) 8201 9233
Email: manson@mansonpublishing.com
Web Site: http://www.mansonpublishing.com

Distribution:
John Wiley & Sons Ltd,
Customer Services Dept, 1 Oldlands Way, Bognor Regis, West Sussex PO22 9SA
Telephone: 01243 843294
Fax: 01243 843303
Email: cs-books@wiley.com
Web Site: http://www.wiley.co.uk

Managing Director: Michael Manson

Agriculture; Animal Care & Breeding; Biology & Zoology; Geography & Geology; Medical (incl. Self Help & Alternative Medicine); Scientific & Technical; Veterinary Science

New Titles: 15 (2007), 15 (2008)
No of Employees: 3

ISBNs, Imprints & Series:
978 1 84076, 978 1 874545

Associated Companies:
The Veterinary Press Ltd

Overseas Representation:
All other areas: Wiley-Blackwell, Oxford, UK
Australia & New Zealand (Medical & Veterinary titles): All things Medical, Sydney University, Sydney, NSW, Australia
Australia & New Zealand (Science titles): CSIRO Publishing, Collingwood, Vic, Australia
Japan (Medical & Veterinary titles): Nankodo Co Ltd, Tokyo, Japan

Book Trade Association Membership:
Publishers Association; IPG

2486

MARITIME BOOKS
Lodge Hill, Liskeard, Cornwall PL14 4EL
Telephone: 01579 343663
Fax: 01579 346747
Email: sales@navybooks.com
Web Site: http://www.navybooks.com

Managing Director: M. Critchley
Editor: S. Bush
Manager: P. Garnett

Military & War; Transport

New Titles: 5 (2007), 6 (2008)
No of Employees: 3

ISBNs, Imprints & Series:
978 0 907771, 978 1 904459

2487

MARSHALL CAVENDISH PARTWORKS LTD
32–38 Saffron Hill, London EC1N 8FN
Telephone: (020) 7421 8120
Fax: (020) 7421 8121
Email: mcelt@marshallcavendish.co.uk
Web Site: http://www.mcelt.co.uk

Educational & Textbooks

Book Trade Association Membership:
Publishers Association

2488

MAVERICK HOUSE PUBLISHERS
Office 19, Dunboyne Business Park, Dunboyne, Co Meath, Republic of Ireland
Telephone: +353 (01) 825 5717
Fax: +353 (01) 686 5036
Email: info@maverickhouse.com
Web Site: http://www.maverickhouse.com

Managing Director: Jean Harrington

Biography & Autobiography; Crime; Humour; Military & War; Politics & World Affairs; Sports & Games

New Titles: 11 (2007), 12 (2008)
No of Employees: 5

ISBNs, Imprints & Series:
978 0 9542945, 978 0 9548707, 978 0 9548708, 978 1 905379

Overseas Representation:
Australia: Tower Books Pty Ltd, Frenchs Forest, NSW
Singapore & Malaysia: Paperclip, Singapore
UK: Turnaround Publisher Services Ltd, London

Book Trade Association Membership:
CLÉ (Irish PA)

2489

*KEVIN MAYHEW LTD
Buxhall, Stowmarket IP14 3BW
Telephone: 01449 737978
Fax: 01449 737834
Email: info@kevinmayhewltd.com
Web Site: http://www.kevinmayhewltd.com

Chairman: Kevin Mayhew
Managing Director: Kevin Whomes
Sales & Marketing Manager: Tim Messinger

Educational & Textbooks; Music; Religion & Theology

ISBNs, Imprints & Series:
978 0 86208, 978 0 86209, 978 1 84003, 978 1 84417

Associated Companies:
Anglicanshop.com

Overseas Representation:
USA: Brodt Music Inc, Charlotte, NC

2490

MEADOWSIDE CHILDREN'S BOOKS
185 Fleet Street, London EC4A 2HS
Telephone: (020) 7400 1092
Fax: (020) 7400 1037
Email: info@meadowsidebooks.com
Web Site: http://www.meadowsidebooks.com

Publisher: Simon Rosenheim
Sales Director: Rupert Harbour

Children's Books

New Titles: 80 (2007), 80 (2008)

ISBNs, Imprints & Series: 978 1 84539

Parent Company:
UK: D. C. Thomson

Overseas Representation:
Australia & New Zealand: Bookwise International, Wingfield, SA, Australia

2491

*THE MEDICI SOCIETY LTD
Grafton House, Hyde Estate Road, London NW9 6JZ
Telephone: (020) 8205 2500
Fax: (020) 8205 2552
Email: sales@medici.co.uk
Web Site: http://www.medici.co.uk

Chief Executive: Graeme Derby
Managers: Catriona Mitchell (Export)
David Hardstaff (Operations)
Jo Oldridge (Design)
David Rametta (Marketing)
National Sales: Lee Hartley
Senior Production: Steven Greer

Children's Books; Fine Art & Art History

ISBNs, Imprints & Series: 978 0 85503

Overseas Representation:
Argentina: Empredin SA, Buenos Aires
Australia: McMillan Cards & Paper Pty Ltd, Dee Why, NSW
Canada: Jannex Enterprises (1980), Markham, Ont
New Zealand: Oxted Resources Ltd, Auckland
Republic of Ireland: Maple Leaf Agencies, Dublin
South Africa: H. R. & L. Shapiro, Cape Town
Sweden: Papeterie, Savedahlen
USA: Kensington Cards Inc, Los Angeles, CA

2492

*MEHRING BOOKS
PO Box 3978, Sheffield S1 2BS
Telephone: 0114 213 0191
Email: sales@mehringbooks.co.uk
Web Site: http://www.mehringbooks.co.uk

Contact: Richard Turner

Economics; History & Antiquarian; Literature & Criticism; Politics & World Affairs

ISBNs, Imprints & Series:
978 0 929087, 978 1 873045

Distributor for:
Australia: Mehring Books
Germany: Arbeiterpresse Verlag
USA: Mehring Books

Overseas Representation:
Australia: Mehring Books, Marrickville, NSW
Germany: Arbeiterpresse Verlag, Essen
USA: Mehring Books, Oak Park, MI

Book Trade Association Membership:
IPG

2493

MELISENDE PUBLISHING LTD
Pennine Way Office, 87–89 Saffron Hill, London EC1N 8QU
Telephone: (020) 7269 9870
Email: melisende@btinternet.com
Web Site: http://www.melisende.com

Directors: Leonard Harrow (Editorial)
Alan Ball (Sales & Marketing)

Academic & Scholarly; Archaeology; Architecture & Design; Crafts & Hobbies; Fine Art & Art History; History & Antiquarian; Illustrated & Fine Editions; Politics & World Affairs; Religion & Theology; Travel & Topography

ISBNs, Imprints & Series: 978 1 901764

Distributor for:
Altajir World of Islam Trust; Sangam Books Ltd
Cyprus: Rimal Publications

Overseas Representation:
Middle East: Rimal Publications, Cyprus

2494

MENTOR BOOKS
43 Furze Road, Sandyford Industrial Estate,
Dublin 18, Republic of Ireland
Telephone: +353 (01) 295 2112/3
Fax: +353 (01) 295 2114
Email: all@mentorbooks.ie
Web Site: http://www.mentorbooks.ie

General Manager: Daniel C. McCarthy

Academic & Scholarly; Biography & Autobiography; Biology & Zoology; Cinema, Video, TV & Radio; Crime; Economics; Educational & Textbooks; Fiction; Geography & Geology; Guide Books; Health & Beauty; History & Antiquarian; Humour; Industry, Business & Management; Languages & Linguistics; Mathematics & Statistics; Photography; Poetry; Politics & World Affairs; Reference Books, Directories & Dictionaries; Scientific & Technical; Sports & Games; Travel & Topography

New Titles: 54 (2007), 61 (2008)
No of Employees: 20

ISBNs, Imprints & Series:
978 0 947548, 978 1 902586, 978 1 84210

Book Trade Association Membership:
CLÉ (Irish PA)

2495

MERCIER PRESS LTD
Unit 3, Oak House, Riverview Business Park,
Bessboro Road, Blackrock, Cork,
Republic of Ireland
Telephone: +353 (021) 461 4700
Fax: +353 (021) 461 4802
Email: info@mercierpress.ie
Web Site: http://www.mercierpress.ie

Managing Director: Clodagh Feehan
Commissioning Editors: Mary Feehan
  Eoin Purcell
Rights & Permissions: Sharon O'Donovan
Managing Editor: Brian Ronan
Sales Executive: Niamh Hatton
Marketing Co-ordinator: Patrick Crowley
Design: Catherine Twibill

Academic & Scholarly; Archaeology; Biography & Autobiography; Children's Books; Fiction; History & Antiquarian; Humour; Literature & Criticism; Poetry; Politics & World Affairs; Religion & Theology; Theatre, Drama & Dance

New Titles: 33 (2007), 37 (2008)

ISBNs, Imprints & Series:
978 0 85342, 978 1 85635 Mercier Press
978 1 86023 Marino Books

Overseas Representation:
Australia: Tower Books Pty Ltd, Frenchs Forest, NSW
USA: James Trading Group, Nanuet, NY

Book Trade Association Membership:
CLÉ (Irish PA); Independent Publishers Guild

2496

MERCURY BOOKS
20 Bloomsbury Street, London WC1B 3JH
Telephone: (020) 7636 7171
Fax: (020) 7636 1922

Warehouse & Trade Enquiries:
Littlehampton Book Services,
Faraday Close, Durrington, Worthing,
West Sussex BN13 3RB
Telephone: 01903 828800
Fax: 01903 828802
Email: orders@lbsltd.co.uk
Web Site: http://www.lbsltd.co.uk

Director: Finbarr McCabe *(Sales)*

Archaeology; Atlases & Maps; Geography & Geology; History & Antiquarian; Literature & Criticism; Military & War; Reference Books, Directories & Dictionaries

New Titles: 10 (2008)
No of Employees: 7

ISBNs, Imprints & Series:
978 1 84560, 978 1 904668

Parent Company:
Caxton Publishing Group

Overseas Representation:
Australia & New Zealand: Bookwise International, Wingfield, SA, Australia
Europe: Bill Bailey Publishers Representatives, Newton Abbot, Devon, UK
Far East: Bookwise Asia, Singapore, Singapore
South Africa: Peter Matthews Agencies, Alberton
USA & Canada: International Publishers Marketing Inc, Herndon, VA, USA

2497

MERCURY JUNIOR
20 Bloomsbury Street, London WC1B 3JH
Telephone: (020) 7636 7171
Fax: (020) 7636 1922

Warehouse, Trade Enquiries & Orders:
Littlehampton Book Services,
Faraday Close, Durrington, Worthing,
West Sussex BN13 3RB
Telephone: 01903 828800
Fax: 01903 828802
Email: orders@lbsltd.co.uk
Web Site: http://www.lbsltd.co.uk

Director: Finbarr McCabe *(Sales & Marketing)*

Children's Books

New Titles: 10 (2008)
No of Employees: 7

ISBNs, Imprints & Series:
978 1 84560, 978 1 904668

Parent Company:
Caxton Publishing Group

Overseas Representation:
Australia & New Zealand: Bookwise International, Wingfield, SA, Australia
Europe: Bill Bailey Publishers Representatives, Newton Abbot, Devon, UK
Far East: Bookwise Asia, Singapore, Singapore
South Africa: Peter Matthews Agencies, Alberton
USA & Canada: International Publishers Marketing Inc, Herndon, VA, USA

2498

THE MERLIN PRESS LTD
99b Wallis Road, London E9 5LN
Telephone: (020) 8533 5800
Email: info@merlinpress.co.uk
Web Site: http://www.merlinpress.co.uk

Distribution:
Central Books Ltd, 99 Wallis Road, London E9 5LN
Telephone: (020) 8986 4854
Fax: (020) 8533 5821
Email: orders@centralbooks.com

Managing Director: Anthony Zurbrugg
Manager: Adrian Howe

Academic & Scholarly; Biography & Autobiography; Economics; Gender Studies; History & Antiquarian; Politics & World Affairs; Sociology & Anthropology

ISBNs, Imprints & Series:
978 0 85036 The Merlin Press Ltd
978 1 85284 Green Print

Parent Company:
Africa Book Centre Ltd

Overseas Representation:
Australia: Eleanor Brasch Enterprises, Artarmon, NSW
Canada: Fernwood Books, Black Point, NS
South Africa: Blue Weaver Marketing, Tokai
USA: Independent Publishers Group (IPG), Chicago, IL

2499

*MERLIN PUBLISHING/ WOLFHOUND PRESS
Newmarket Hall, Cork Street, Dublin 8,
Republic of Ireland
Telephone: +353 (01) 453 5866
Fax: +353 (01) 453 5930
Email: publishing@merlin.ie
Web Site: http://www.merlinwolfhound.com

Distribution:
Gill & Macmillan, Hume Avenue,
Park West, Dublin 12, Republic of Ireland
Telephone: +353 (01) 500 9500
Fax: +353 (01) 500 9599
Email: info@gillmacmillan.ie
Web Site: http://www.gillmacmillan.ie

Managing Director: Chenile Keogh *(Publisher)*
Managers: Aoife Barrett *(Editorial)*
  Julie Dobson *(Sales & Marketing)*
Sales Representative: Tony Hayes

Academic & Scholarly; Biography & Autobiography; Children's Books; Cinema, Video, TV & Radio; Cookery, Wines & Spirits; Crime; Educational & Textbooks; Fiction; Fine Art & Art History; Gender Studies; Guide Books; Health & Beauty; History & Antiquarian; Humour; Law; Literature & Criticism; Music; Photography; Poetry; Politics & World Affairs; Reference Books, Directories & Dictionaries; Religion & Theology; Sports & Games; Travel & Topography

ISBNs, Imprints & Series:
Wolfhound Press
978 0 86327
978 1 903582 Merlin Publishing

Parent Company:
Republic of Ireland: Merlin Media Ltd

Overseas Representation:
Australia: Tower Books Pty Ltd, Frenchs Forest, NSW
New Zealand: Forrester Books (NZ) Ltd, Albany
UK: Bounce! Sales & Marketing Ltd, London
USA (Wolfhound & Merlin): Interlink Publishing Group Inc, Northampton, MA, USA

Book Trade Association Membership:
CLÉ (Irish PA)

2500

MERRELL PUBLISHERS LTD
81 Southwark Street, London SE1 0HX
Telephone: (020) 7928 8880
Fax: (020) 7928 1199
Email: mail@merrellpublishers.com
Web Site: http://www.merrellpublishers.com

Trade & Credit Orders, Returns:
Marston Book Services, PO Box 269,
Abingdon, Oxon OX14 4YN
Telephone: 01235 465500
Fax: 01235 465555
Email: trade.order@marston.co.uk

Directors: Hugh Merrell *(Rights)*
  Julian Honer *(Editorial)*
  Nicola Bailey *(Art)*
  Joan Brookbank *(US)*
  Kim Cope *(Sales & Marketing)*
Production Manager: Michelle Draycott
Managing Editor: Claire Chandler

Academic & Scholarly; Architecture & Design; Fine Art & Art History; Illustrated & Fine Editions; Photography

ISBNs, Imprints & Series: 978 1 85894

Overseas Representation:
All other territories: Kim Cope, Merrell Publishers, London, UK
Australia & New Zealand: Bookwise International, Wingfield, SA, Australia
Canada: Canadian Manda Group, Toronto, Ont
Central America & Caribbean: Chris Humphrys, Humphrys Roberts Associates, London, UK
Eastern Europe: Csaba & Jackie Lengyel de Bagota, CLB Marketing Services, Budapest, Hungary
Estonia, Latvia & Lithuania: Tony Moggach, InterMedia Americana (IMA) Ltd, London, UK
France: Critiques Livres Distribution, Bagnolet
Germany, Austria & Switzerland: Gabriele Kern Publishers Services, Frankfurt-am-Main, Germany
Hong Kong, Taiwan, China, Korea, Japan, Indonesia, Philippines & Thailand: Julian Ashton, Ashton International Marketing Services, Sevenoaks, Kent, UK
India, Bangladesh, Nepal, Bhutan & Sri Lanka: Surit Mitra, Maya Publishers Pvt Ltd, New Delhi, India
Italy, Greece, Spain & Portugal: Padovani Books Ltd, Montanare di Cortona, Italy; Padovani Books Ltd, London, UK
Malaysia, Singapore & Brunei: Pansing Distribution Pte Ltd, Singapore, Singapore
Middle East, Turkey, Israel, Cyprus & Malta: Peter Ward Book Exports, London, UK
Netherlands, Belgium & Luxembourg: Nilsson & Lamm BV, Weesp, Netherlands
Republic of Ireland & Northern Ireland: Robert Towers, Monkstown, Co Dublin, Republic of Ireland
Scandinavia: Elisabeth Harder-Kreimann, Hamburg, Germany
South America: Terry Roberts, Humphrys Roberts Associates, Cotia SP, Brazil
Southern Africa: Shirley Cooksley, Quartet Books, Sunningdale, South Africa
USA: Perseus Group, Jackson, TN

2501

MERTON PRIORY PRESS LTD
9 Owen Falls Avenue, Chesterfield S41 0FR
Telephone: 01246 554026
Email: mertonpriory@btinternet.com
Web Site: http://www.merton.dircon.co.uk

Owner: Philip Riden

Academic & Scholarly; Archaeology; Biography & Autobiography; History & Antiquarian; Transport

New Titles: 4 (2007), 4 (2008)
Annual Turnover: £20,000

ISBNs, Imprints & Series: 978 1 898937

2502

METHODIST PUBLISHING HOUSE
4 John Wesley Road, Werrington,
Peterborough PE4 6ZP
Telephone: 01733 325002
Fax: 01733 384180

2503 / PUBLISHERS

Web Site: http://www.mph.org.uk

Chair: Eric Jarvis
Heads of Department: Jane McClean (Accounts)
Karen Kendall (Customer Services)

Academic & Scholarly; Educational & Textbooks; Electronic (Professional & Academic); Poetry; Religion & Theology

New Titles: 24 (2007), 18 (2008)
No of Employees: 13

ISBNs, Imprints & Series:
978 0 716204 Epworth
978 1 85852 Inspire; Methodist Publishing House

Parent Company:
The Methodist Church

Overseas Representation:
USA (Epworth titles only): Westminster John Knox Press, Louisville, KY, USA

Book Trade Association Membership:
BA

2503

MEYRICK MARKETING LTD
[trading as The Francis Frith Collection]
Frith's Barn, Teffont, Salisbury, Wilts SP3 5QP
Telephone: 01722 716376
Fax: 01722 716881
Email: sales@francisfrith.co.uk
Web Site: http://www.francisfrith.co.uk

Directors: John Buck (Managing)
Jason Buck (Development)
John Brewer (Finance)
Managing Editor: Julia Skinner
IP Rights Manager: Isobel Hall

History & Antiquarian; Photography; Travel & Topography

New Titles: 6 (2007), 12 (2008)
No of Employees: 16
Annual Turnover: £1M

ISBNs, Imprints & Series:
978 1 84589, 978 1 85937

Book Trade Association Membership:
IPG

2504

MICHELIN MAPS & GUIDES
Hannay House, 39 Clarendon Road, Watford WD17 1JA
Telephone: 01923 205240
Fax: 01923 205241
Web Site: http://www.michelin.co.uk/travel

Warehouse/Returns:
Michelin Tyre Plc, Maps & Guides,
Building 82 Campbell Road,
Stoke on Trent, Staffs ST4 4EY
Telephone: 01923 205242
Fax: 01923 205241

Commercial Director, Head of Travel Publications: I. Murray
Trade Marketing Manager: J. Khawam

Atlases & Maps; Guide Books; Travel & Topography

ISBNs, Imprints & Series:
978 2 06, 978 3 92107 The Green Guide Series; Local Map Series; National Map Series; The Red Guide Series; Regional Map Series; Zoom Map Series

Parent Company:
France: Manufacture Française des Pneumatiques Michelin

Overseas Representation:
Belgium & Luxembourg: Michelin Belux, Brussels, Belgium
Italy: Michelin Italiana SPA, Milan
Spain: Michelin Espana Portugal SA, Madrid
USA: Michelin Travel Publications, Greenville, SC

Book Trade Association Membership:
BA

2505

MICROFORM ACADEMIC PUBLISHERS
Main Street, East Ardsley, Wakefield, West Yorkshire WF3 2AP
Telephone: 01924 825700
Fax: 01924 871005
Email: map@microform.co.uk
Web Site: http://www.microform.co.uk/academic

Managing Director: Nigel Le Page
Head of Publishing: Roderic Vassie

Academic & Scholarly; Biography & Autobiography; Economics; History & Antiquarian; Literature & Criticism; Military & War; Politics & World Affairs; Religion & Theology; Sociology & Anthropology

ISBNs, Imprints & Series:
British Records Relating to America in Microform (BRRAM) (series); Records of the Raj (series)

Overseas Representation:
Japan: Far Eastern Booksellers, Tokyo
USA & Canada: PraXess, New York, NY, USA

2506

MIDDLETON PRESS
Easebourne Lane, Midhurst, Sussex GU29 9AZ
Telephone: 01730 813169
Fax: 01730 812601
Web Site: http://www.middletonpress.co.uk

Author & Proprietor: Dr J. C. V. Mitchell

Military & War; Nautical; Transport

ISBNs, Imprints & Series:
978 0 906520, 978 1 873793, 978 1 901706, 978 1 904474, 978 1 906008

2507

*MILESTONE PUBLICATIONS
62 Murray Road, Horndean, Waterlooville, Hants PO8 9JL
Telephone: 023 9259 7440
Fax: 023 9259 1975
Email: info@gosschinaclub.co.uk
Web Site: http://www.gosscrestedchina.co.uk

Managing Director: Lynda Pine (Publishing)
Manageress: Debbie Webb

Antiques & Collecting

ISBNs, Imprints & Series:
978 1 85265, 978 1 903852

Parent Company:
Goss & Crested China Ltd

2508

MILET PUBLISHING LTD
c/o Turnaround Publisher Services Ltd,
Unit 3, Olympia Trading Estate,
Coburg Road, Wood Green, London N22 6TZ
Telephone: (020) 8829 3000
Fax: (020) 8881 5088
Email: info@milet.com

Web Site: http://www.milet.com

Directors: Patricia A. Billings
Sedat Turhan

Children's Books; English as a Foreign Language; Fiction; Languages & Linguistics; Reference Books, Directories & Dictionaries

ISBNs, Imprints & Series: 978 1 84059

Distributor for:
Turkey: Engin; Fono; Net; Redhouse/Sev; A. Turizm

Overseas Representation:
Australia & New Zealand (Distributors): Global Language Books, Toongabbie, NSW, Australia; Tower Books Pty Ltd, Frenchs Forest, NSW, Australia
USA & Canada (Distributors): Tuttle Publishing, North Clarendon, VT, USA

2509

J. GARNET MILLER
10 Station Road Industrial Estate, Colwall, Malvern, Worcs WR13 6RN
Telephone: 01684 540154
Fax: 01684 540154
Email: simon@cressrelles.co.uk
Web Site: http://www.cressrelles.co.uk

Managers: Leslie Smith
Simon Smith

Theatre, Drama & Dance

New Titles: 6 (2007), 6 (2008)

Parent Company:
Cressrelles Publishing Co Ltd

Overseas Representation:
Australia: Origin Theatrical, Sydney, NSW
New Zealand: Play Bureau of New Zealand Ltd, New Plymouth
Republic of Ireland: Drama League of Ireland, Dublin
South Africa: Dalro (Pty) Ltd, Braamfontein
USA: Bakers Plays, Quincy, MA

2510

MILLER'S
2–4 Heron Quays, London E14 4JP
Telephone: (020) 7531 8400
Fax: (020) 7531 8650
Email: info-mb@mitchell-beazley.co.uk
Web Site: http://www.mitchell-beazley.co.uk

Distributor:
Littlehampton Book Services Ltd,
Faraday Close, Durrington, Worthing,
West Sussex BN13 3RB
Telephone: 01903 828500
Fax: 01903 828625

Directors: Judith Miller (Publisher/Managing)
Sarah Harrigan (Finance)
Steven Edney (Sales & Marketing, UK)
Andrew Welham (Sales & Marketing, International)

Antiques & Collecting

ISBNs, Imprints & Series:
978 0 85533, 978 1 84000, 978 1 84533, 978 1 85732

Parent Company:
Hachette

Associated Companies:
Mitchell Beazley; Octopus Publishing Group

Overseas Representation:
Australia: Hachette Livre Australia, Sydney, NSW

China, Hong Kong & Taiwan: Asia Publishers Services Ltd, Hong Kong
Cyprus, Malta, Israel, Middle East & North Africa: Peter Ward Book Exports, London, UK
Germany, Austria & Switzerland: Gabriele Kern Publishers Services, Frankfurt-am-Main, Germany
Hungary, Czech & Slovak Republics & Slovenia: Csaba & Jackie Lengyel de Bagota, Budapest, Hungary
Indonesia, Thailand, Vietnam, Brunei, Laos & Cambodia: APD Singapore Pte Ltd, Singapore
Italy, Spain, Portugal & Greece: Penny Padovani, London, UK
New Zealand: Hachette Livre New Zealand, Auckland
Philippines: Marketing Services for Publishers, Pasig City
South Africa: Penguin Books South Africa (Pty) Ltd, Johannesburg
South America: Terry Roberts, Cotia SP, Brazil

Book Trade Association Membership:
BA

2511

THE MIT PRESS LTD
Fitzroy House, 11 Chenies Street, London WC1E 7EY
Telephone: (020) 7306 0603
Fax: (020) 7306 0604
Email: info@HUP-MITpress.co.uk
Web Site: http://www-mitpress.mit.edu

Trade & Warehouse:
John Wiley & Sons Ltd, Distribution Centre,
Southern Cross Trading Estate,
1 Oldlands Way, Bognor Regis, West Sussex PO22 9SA
Telephone: 01243 779777
Fax: 01243 820250
Email: cs-books@wiley.co.uk

Managers: Ann Sexsmith (General)
Ann Twiselton (Publicity)
Judith Bullent (Texts/Exhibitions)

Academic & Scholarly; Architecture & Design; Bibliography & Library Science; Biography & Autobiography; Biology & Zoology; Computer Science; Economics; Environment & Development Studies; Fine Art & Art History; Gay & Lesbian Studies; Gender Studies; Industry, Business & Management; Languages & Linguistics; Music; Natural History; Philosophy; Photography; Politics & World Affairs; Psychology & Psychiatry; Reference Books, Directories & Dictionaries; Scientific & Technical

ISBNs, Imprints & Series:
978 0 262 American Association for Artificial Intelligence Press; Bradford Books; MIT Press
978 0 936756, 978 1 57027, 978 1 58435 Semiotext(e)
978 0 942299, 978 1 890951 Zone Books

Parent Company:
USA: MIT Press

Distributor for:
Afterall; Zone Books (Urzone Publishing Ltd)
USA: Semiotext(e)

Overseas Representation:
Australia & New Zealand: Footprint Books Pty Ltd, Warriewood, NSW, Australia
Belgium, France, Iceland, Netherlands, Norway, Sweden, Finland & Denmark: Fred Hermans, Bovenkarspel, Netherlands
Canada & Australia: David Stimpson, Toronto, Ont, Canada
China: Wei Zhao, Everest International Publishing Services, Beijing, P. R. of China

Germany, Austria, Switzerland & Italy: Uwe Lüdemann, Berlin, Germany
Hong Kong: Jane Lam, Kowloon
India: Mediamatics, Calcutta
Iran: Farhad Maftoon, Tehran
Israel: Rodney Franklin Agency, Tel Aviv
Japan: Rockbook, Yokohama
Malaysia & Brunei: Simon Tay, Apex Knowledge, Selangor, Malaysia
Mexico, Central America & Caribbean: Cynthia Zimpfer, Maplewood, NJ, USA
Middle East (excluding Greece, Iran & Israel): Avicenna Partnership, Oxford, UK
Pakistan: Saleem Malik, World Press, Lahore
Philippines: Jean Lim, Megatexts Phil, Makati City
Poland, Hungary, Croatia, Slovenia, Slovakia & Czech Republic: Ewa Ledóchowicz, Konstancin-Jeziorna, Poland
Singapore, Indonesia, Vietnam, Laos, Cambodia & Myanmar: Evelyn Soh, IGP Services, Singapore
South Africa: Cory Voigt Associates, Braamfontein
South America: Terry Roberts, Cotia SP, Brazil
South Korea: Se-Yung Jun, Seoul, Korea, South
Spain & Portugal: Chris Humphrys, Gaucin, Spain
Taiwan: B. K. Norton, Taipei

2512

MITCHELL BEAZLEY
2–4 Heron Quays, London E14 4JP
Telephone: (020) 7531 8502
Fax: (020) 7537 0773
Web Site: http://www.mitchell-beazley.com

Distribution:
Littlehampton Book Services, Faraday Close, Durrington, Worthing, West Sussex BN13 3RB
Telephone: 01903 828801
Fax: 01903 828802
Web Site: http://www.pubeasy.books.lbsltd.co.uk

Directors: David Lamb *(Publisher/Managing)*
Sarah Harrigan *(Finance)*
Steven Edney *(Sales & Marketing - UK)*
Andrew Welham *(Sales & Marketing - International)*

Antiques & Collecting; Archaeology; Architecture & Design; Cookery, Wines & Spirits; Crafts & Hobbies; Fashion & Costume; Fine Art & Art History; Gardening; Health & Beauty; History & Antiquarian; Illustrated & Fine Editions; Medical (incl. Self Help & Alternative Medicine); Music; Natural History; Photography; Reference Books, Directories & Dictionaries; Sports & Games; Travel & Topography

ISBNs, Imprints & Series:
978 0 85533, 978 1 84000, 978 1 85732

Parent Company:
Octopus Publishing Group Ltd

Overseas Representation:
All other territories: Sarah Daniels, Mitchell Beazley, London, UK
Australia: Hachette Livre Australia, Sydney, NSW
Belgium, Netherlands, France, Iceland, Scandinavia & Baltics: Bill Bailey Publishers Representatives, Newton Abbot, Devon, UK
Central America & Caribbean: Ethan Atkin, Cranbury International LLC, Montpelier, VT, USA
China, Hong Kong, Taiwan & Korea: Asia Publishers Services Ltd, Hong Kong
Cyprus, Malta, Israel, Middle East & North Africa: Peter Ward Book Exports, London, UK

Germany, Austria & Switzerland: Gabriele Kern Publishers Services, Frankfurt-am-Main, Germany
Hungary, Czech & Slovak Republics, Slovenia, Romania & Poland: Csaba & Jackie Lengyel de Bagota, CLB Marketing Services, Budapest, Hungary
India: Ajay Parmar, New Delhi
Indonesia, Thailand, Vietnam, Brunei, Laos, Cambodia & Singapore: APD Singapore Pte Ltd, Singapore
Italy, Spain, Portugal, Greece & Gibraltar: Penny Padovani, London, UK
Malaysia: APD Kuala Lumpur Pte Ltd, Selangor
New Zealand: Hachette Livre New Zealand, Auckland
Philippines: Marketing Services for Publishers, Pasig City
South Africa: Penguin Books South Africa (Pty) Ltd, Johannesburg
South America: Terry Roberts, Humphrys Roberts Associates, Cotia SP, Brazil
Sub-Saharan Africa (excluding South Africa): Kelvin van Hasselt Publishing Services, Briningham, Norfolk, UK

Book Trade Association Membership:
BA

2513

M & K UPDATE
The Old Bakery, St John's Street, Keswick, Cumbria CA12 5AS
Telephone: 01768 773030
Fax: 01768 781099
Email: enquiries@mkupdate.co.uk
Web Site: http://www.mkupdate.co.uk

Academic & Scholarly

Book Trade Association Membership:
Publishers Association

2514

MOONLIGHT PUBLISHING LTD
King's Manor, East Hendred, Oxon OX12 8JY
Telephone: 01235 821821
Fax: 01235 821155
Email: moonlight.publishing@virgin.net
Web Site: http://www.moonlightpublishing.co.uk

Children's Books; Trade

Book Trade Association Membership:
Publishers Association

2515

MOORLEY'S PRINT & PUBLISHING LTD
23 Park Road, Ilkeston, Derbyshire DE7 5DA
Telephone: 0115 932 0643
Fax: 0115 932 0643
Email: info@moorleys.co.uk
Web Site: http://www.moorleys.co.uk

Directors: Peter R. Newberry *(Joint Managing, Financial)*
Patrick Mancini *(Joint Managing, Production)*

Music; Poetry; Religion & Theology; Theatre, Drama & Dance

New Titles: 10 (2007), 5 (2008)
No of Employees: 6
Annual Turnover: £15,000

ISBNs, Imprints & Series:
978 0 86071, 978 0 901495

Associated Companies:
Truedata Computer Services

Distributor for:
Cliff College Publishing; Darby Publications; Mainstream Baptists for Life & Growth; Met Specials; Nimbus Press; Social Work Christian Fellowship
Malaysia: Pustaka Sufes SDN BHD

Book Trade Association Membership:
Christian Booksellers Association; Publishing Licensing Society

2516

MOTOR RACING PUBLICATIONS LTD
PO Box 1318, Croydon, Surrey CR9 5YP
Telephone: (020) 8654 2711
Fax: (020) 8407 0339
Email: john@mrpbooks.co.uk
Web Site: http://www.mrpbooks.co.uk

Orders:
Vine House Distribution Ltd,
The Old Mill House, Mill Lane, Uckfield, East Sussex TN22 5AA
Telephone: 01825 767396
Fax: 01825 765649
Email: sales@vinehouseuk.co.uk
Web Site: http://www.vinehouseuk.co.uk

Managing Director: John Blunsden

Biography & Autobiography; Sports & Games; Transport

New Titles: 2 (2008)

ISBNs, Imprints & Series:
978 0 900549, 978 0 947981, 978 1 899870 Motor Racing Publications; MRP Publishing
978 0 948358 The Fitzjames Press

Associated Companies:
The Fitzjames Press

Overseas Representation:
Austria, Benelux & Germany: Robbert J. Pleysier, Books for Europe, Heerde, Netherlands
Eastern Europe: Tony Moggach, London, UK
France & Greece: Sandro Salucci, Florence, Italy
Italy, Malta, Spain, Gibraltar & Portugal: Joe Portelli, Bookport Associates, Corsico (MI), Italy
Scandinavia & Iceland: Angell Eurosales, Berwick-on-Tweed, UK
USA: MBI Distribution Services, Osceola, WI

2517

MULTI SCIENCE PUBLISHING CO LTD
5 Wates Way, Brentwood, Essex CM15 9TB
Telephone: 01277 224632
Fax: 01277 223453
Email: mscience@globalnet.co.uk
Web Site: http://www.multi-science.co.uk

Academic & Scholarly; Architecture & Design; Aviation; Computer Science; Electronic (Professional & Academic); Engineering; Environment & Development Studies; Physics; Reference Books, Directories & Dictionaries; Scientific & Technical; Sports & Games

New Titles: 5 (2007), 5 (2008)
No of Employees: 10

ISBNs, Imprints & Series: 978 0 906522

Book Trade Association Membership:
IGSMTP

2518

MURDOCH BOOKS UK LTD
6th Floor, Erico House,
93–99 Upper Richmond Road, London SW15 2TG
Telephone: (020) 8785 5995
Fax: (020) 8785 5985

Distribution & Invoicing:
Macmillan Distribution Ltd, Brunel Road, Houndmills, Basingstoke, Hants RG21 2XS
Telephone: 01256 329242
Fax: 01256 327961

Group Chief Executive: Juliet Rogers
International Rights & Export: Cathy Slater
UK Sales & Marketing: Carrie Boyes
UK Finance Director: John Sprinks

Biography & Autobiography; Cookery, Wines & Spirits; Crafts & Hobbies; Do-It-Yourself; Gardening; Health & Beauty; History & Antiquarian; Travel & Topography

ISBNs, Imprints & Series:
978 1 74045 Murdoch Books
978 1 74045, 978 1 74196, 978 1 92120, 978 1 92125 Pier 9

Parent Company:
Australia: Murdoch Books Pty Ltd

Overseas Representation:
Asia: Pan Macmillan Asia, Hong Kong
Australia & New Zealand: Murdoch Books Pty Ltd, Sydney, NSW, Australia
Europe: Gabriele Kern Publishers Services, Frankfurt-am-Main, Germany; Angell Eurosales, Berwick-on-Tweed, UK; Penny Padovani, London, UK
Middle East: Peter Ward Book Exports, London, UK
South America & Caribbean: Humphrys Roberts Associates, London, UK

2519

JOHN MURRAY PUBLISHERS
[a division of Hachette Livre UK]
338 Euston Road, London NW1 3BH
Telephone: (020) 7873 6000
Fax: (020) 7873 6446

UK Orders & Invoicing, Payments & Credit Control & Warehouse:
Bookpoint, 130 Milton Park, Abingdon, Oxon OX14 4SB
Telephone: 01235 400400
Fax: 01235 821511

Directors: Roland Philipps *(Managing)*
James Spackman *(Sales & Marketing)*
Nikki Barrow *(Publicity)*
Jason Bartholomew *(Rights)*
Eleanor Birne *(Publishing)*

Biography & Autobiography; Fiction; Fine Art & Art History; History & Antiquarian; Humour; Military & War; Travel & Topography

New Titles: 50 (2007), 50 (2008)

ISBNs, Imprints & Series: 978 0 7195

Parent Company:
Hachette Livre UK

Overseas Representation:
Australia: Alliance Distribution Services Pty Ltd, Tuggerah, NSW; Hachette Livre Australia, Sydney, NSW
Canada: McArthur & Co Publishers Ltd, Toronto, Ont
Hong Kong: Asia Publishers Services Ltd
India: Hachette Book Publishing India, New Delhi
Netherlands (Hardbacks and Trade Paperbacks): Nilsson & Lamm BV, Weesp, Netherlands
Netherlands (Paperbacks): Van Ditmar BV, Amsterdam, Netherlands
New Zealand: Hachette Livre New Zealand, Auckland
Pakistan: Oxford University Press Pakistan Branch, Karachi
Singapore & Malaysia: Pansing Distribution Sdn Bhd, Singapore

South Africa: Jonathan Ball Publishers (Pty) Ltd, Johannesburg
USA: Trafalgar Square Publishing, North Pomfret, VT

Book Trade Association Membership:
IPG

2520

MW EDUCATIONAL
Westcliff Drive, Leigh-on-Sea, Essex SS9 2LB
Telephone: 01702 715282
Fax: 01702 715172
Email: mweducational@yahoo.co.uk
Web Site: http://www.mweducational.com

Distribution:
Gardners Books Ltd, 1 Whittle Drive, Eastbourne, East Sussex BN23 6QH
Telephone: 01323 521555

Chief Executive Officer: Mark Chatterton

Children's Books; Educational & Textbooks

ISBNs, Imprints & Series:
978 1 901146 The A Plus Series of 11+ Practice Papers; The Advantage Series of SATs Practice Papers

2521

MYRIAD EDITIONS
59 Lansdowne Place, Brighton BN3 1FL
Telephone: 01273 720000
Email: candida@MyriadEditions.com
Web Site: http://www.MyriadEditions.com

Directors: Candida Lacey *(Managing)*
Robert Benewick
Judith Mackay
Design: Corinne Pearlman
Production: Isabelle Lewis
Editorial: Jannet King
Rights: Sadie Mayne

Academic & Scholarly; Atlases & Maps; Electronic (Professional & Academic); Environment & Development Studies; Fiction; Gender Studies; Military & War; Politics & World Affairs

Overseas Representation:
China & Taiwan: Big Apple Tuttle-Mori Agency Inc, Taipei, Taiwan
Japan: Tuttle-Mori Agency Inc, Tokyo
Spain, Portugal & South America: Ilustrata Empresariale SL, Barcelona, Spain

Book Trade Association Membership:
IPG

2522

MYRMIDON BOOKS LTD
Rotterdam House, 116 Quayside, Newcastle upon Tyne NE1 3DY
Telephone: 0191 206 4005
Email: enquiries@myrmidonbooks.com
Web Site: http://www.myrmidonbooks.com

Distribution:
Littlehampton Book Services, Faraday Close, Durrington, Worthing, West Sussex TN13 3RB
Telephone: 01903 828500
Email: enquiries@lbsltd.co.uk
Web Site: http://www.lbsltd.co.uk

Directors: Ed Handyside *(Publishing)*
Anne Westgarth *(Editorial)*

Fiction

New Titles: 3 (2007), 9 (2008)
No of Employees: 3
Annual Turnover: £120,000

ISBNs, Imprints & Series: 978 1 905802

Overseas Representation:
Australia & New Zealand: Bookwise International, Wingfield, SA, Australia
Singapore, Malaysia & neighbouring territories: Pansing Distribution Pte Ltd, Singapore, Singapore
South Africa & neighbouring territories: Zytek Publishing (Pty) Ltd, Bedfordview, South Africa

Book Trade Association Membership:
Publishers Association; IPG

2523

*NATE (NATIONAL ASSOCIATION FOR THE TEACHING OF ENGLISH)
50 Broadfield Road, Sheffield S8 0XJ
Telephone: 01142 555419
Fax: 01142 555296
Email: info@nate.org.uk
Web Site: http://www.nate.org.uk

Publications Manager: A. Fairhall
Company Secretary: L. Fairfax
Communications Director: I. McNeilly
Publications Co-ordinator: J. Selwood

Academic & Scholarly; Educational & Textbooks; Literature & Criticism; Theatre, Drama & Dance

ISBNs, Imprints & Series:
Cracking KS3 Scripts; Critical Reading at post 16; Guided Reading Packs; NATE Drama Packs
978 0 901291 Classic Reading
978 0 904709 Perspectives in Education

Distributor for:
Australia: Phoenix Books

Book Trade Association Membership:
EPC

2524

THE NATIONAL ACADEMIES PRESS
5 Victoria House, 138 Watling Street East, Towcester NN12 6BT
Telephone: 01327 357770
Fax: 01327 359572
Email: nap@oppuk.co.uk
Web Site: http://www.nap.edu

Warehouse & Distribution:
Marston Book Services, 160 Milton Park, PO Box 169, Abingdon, Oxon OX14 4YN
Telephone: 01235 465521
Email: direct.orders@marston.co.uk
Web Site: http://www.marston.co.uk

Marketing Manager: Gary Hall

Academic & Scholarly; Agriculture; Animal Care & Breeding; Biology & Zoology; Chemistry; Educational & Textbooks; Engineering; Environment & Development Studies; Geography & Geology; Industry, Business & Management; Mathematics & Statistics; Medical (incl. Self Help & Alternative Medicine); Natural History; Nautical; Physics; Psychology & Psychiatry; Scientific & Technical; Veterinary Science

New Titles: 300 (2007), 300 (2008)

ISBNs, Imprints & Series:
978 0 309 Joseph Henry Press; National Academies Press

Parent Company:
USA: National Academies Press

2525

NATIONAL ARCHIVES OF SCOTLAND
HM General Register House, Edinburgh EH1 3YY
Telephone: 0131 535 1314
Fax: 0131 535 1360
Email: enquiries@nas.gov.uk
Web Site: http://www.nas.gov.uk

Keeper of the Records of Scotland:
George P. MacKenzie
Head of Outreach Services: David Brown

History & Antiquarian

New Titles: 2 (2007), 2 (2008)
No of Employees: 150
Annual Turnover: £5,000

ISBNs, Imprints & Series: 978 1 870874

Book Trade Association Membership:
Publishing Scotland

2526

THE NATIONAL AUTISTIC SOCIETY (NAS)
393 City Road, London EC1V 1NG
Telephone: (020) 7833 2299
Fax: (020) 7833 9666
Email: nas@nas.org.uk
Web Site: http://www.autism.org.uk

Trade Enquiries & Orders:
Central Books, 99 Wallis Road, London E9 5LN
Telephone: 0845 458 9911
Fax: 0845 458 9912
Email: nas@centralbooks.com
Web Site: http://www.autism.org.uk/pubs

Publications Sales: Cathy Mercer
Publications Marketing: Alex Tyla
Communications: Kathryn Quinton

Educational & Textbooks; Psychology & Psychiatry

New Titles: 10 (2007), 12 (2008)
No of Employees: 2500

ISBNs, Imprints & Series:
978 1 899280
978 1 905722

Book Trade Association Membership:
Publishers Form, NCVO

2527

*NATIONAL CHILDREN'S BUREAU
Book Sales, 8 Wakley Street, London EC1V 7QE
Telephone: (020) 7843 6000
Fax: (020) 7843 6087
Email: booksales@ncb.org.uk
Web Site: http://www.ncb.org.uk

Head of Publishing: Shirley Norrie
Marketing & PR Manager: Sarah Thorne
Publishing Co-ordinator: Paula McMahon
Publishing Assistant: Rebecca Mason

Academic & Scholarly; Educational & Textbooks; Electronic (Professional & Academic); Reference Books, Directories & Dictionaries

ISBNs, Imprints & Series:
978 0 902817, 978 1 870985, 978 1 874579, 978 1 900990, 978 1 904787

2528

NATIONAL EXTENSION COLLEGE TRUST LTD
The Michael Young Centre, Purbeck Road, Cambridge CB2 8HN
Telephone: 01223 400200 or 2528
Fax: 01223 400399
Email: info@nec.ac.uk
Web Site: http://www.nec.ac.uk

Directors: Alison West *(Chief Executive)*
Jorgen Clausen *(Finance)*
Andrew Herne *(IT)*
Tim Burton *(Publishing)*
Tony Hopwood *(Sales & Marketing)*

Educational & Textbooks; Electronic (Educational); Languages & Linguistics; Law; Mathematics & Statistics; Medical (incl. Self Help & Alternative Medicine); Physics; Psychology & Psychiatry; Religion & Theology; Sociology & Anthropology; Vocational Training & Careers

New Titles: 30 (2007), 9 (2008)
No of Employees: 43

ISBNs, Imprints & Series:
978 0 86082, 978 1 85356

Book Trade Association Membership:
IPG

2529

NATIONAL GALLERIES OF SCOTLAND
Belford Road, Edinburgh EH4 3DS
Telephone: 0131 624 6257 & 6261
Fax: 0131 623 7135
Email: publications@nationalgalleries.org
Web Site: http://www.nationalgalleries.org

Head of Publishing: Janis Adams
Publishing Manager: Christine Thompson
Editorial Assistant: David Simpson

Fine Art & Art History; Photography

New Titles: 20 (2007), 15 (2008)

ISBNs, Imprints & Series:
978 0 903148, 978 0 903598, 978 1 903278

Overseas Representation:
North America: Antique Collectors Club Ltd, Easthampton, MA, USA

2530

NATIONAL GALLERY CO LTD
St Vincent House, 30 Orange Street, London WC2H 7HH
Telephone: (020) 7747 5950
Fax: (020) 7747 5951
Email: admin@nationalgallery.co.uk
Web Site: http://www.nationalgallery.co.uk

Distribution:
Yale University Press, 47 Bedford Square, London WC1B 3DP
Telephone: (020) 7079 4900
Fax: (020) 7079 4901
Email: sales@yaleup.co.uk
Web Site: http://www.yalebooks.co.uk

Publisher: Louise Rice *(Publishing & Logistics Director)*
Editors: J. Green *(Senior Project)*
Tom Windross *(Project)*
Claire Young *(Project)*
Publishing Administrator: Davida Saunders
Production Manager: Jane Hyne
Production Controller: Penny Le Tissier
Picture Researchers: Suzanne Bosman *(Senior)*
Maria Ranauro

Academic & Scholarly; Children's Books; Cookery, Wines & Spirits; Electronic (Educational); Electronic (Professional & Academic); Fine Art & Art History; Guide Books

New Titles: 10 (2007), 20 (2008)

ISBNs, Imprints & Series:
978 0 901791, 978 0 947645, 978 1 85709

Parent Company:
The National Gallery Trust

Overseas Representation:
Africa (excluding Southern Africa & Nigeria): Kelvin van Hasselt Publishing Services, Briningham, Norfolk, UK
Austria, Germany, Italy & Switzerland: Uwe Lüdemann, Berlin, Germany
Benelux, Denmark, Finland, France, Iceland, Norway & Sweden: Fred Hermans, Bovenkarspel, Netherlands
Hong Kong, China & Philippines: Ed Summerson, Asia Publishers Services Ltd, Hong Kong
India: S. Janakiraman, Book Marketing Services, Chennai
Iran: Farhad Maftoon, Tehran
Middle East: International Publishers Representatives (IPR) Ltd, Nicosia, Cyprus
Nigeria: Bounty Press Ltd, Ibadan
Pakistan: Anwer Iqbal, Book Bird Publishers Representatives, Lahore
Poland, Czech Republic, Hungary & Slovenia: Ewa Ledóchowicz, Konstancin-Jeziorna, Poland
Republic of Ireland & Northern Ireland: Robert Towers, Monkstown, Co Dublin, Republic of Ireland
Singapore, Malaysia, Brunei & Indonesia: APD Singapore Pte Ltd, Singapore
Southern Africa: Book Promotions Pty Ltd, Diep River, South Africa
Spain & Portugal: Chris Humphrys, Provincia de Malaga, Spain
USA, Canada, Mexico, Central & South America, Australia, New Zealand, Japan, Korea & Taiwan: Yale University Press, New Haven, CT, USA

2531

NATIONAL GALLERY OF IRELAND
National Gallery Bookshop,
Merrion Square, Dublin 2,
Republic of Ireland
Telephone: +353 (01) 663 3518
Fax: +353 (01) 661 9898
Email: bookshop@ngi.ie
Web Site: http://www.nationalgallery.ie

Bookshop Accounts: Kate Brown
Manager: Lydia Furlong
Rights & Reproduction: Marie McFeely

Fine Art & Art History

New Titles: 2 (2007), 4 (2008)
No of Employees: 10

ISBNs, Imprints & Series: 978 0 903162

Overseas Representation:
Worldwide: Art Books International Ltd, London, UK; Paul Holberton Ltd, UK

Book Trade Association Membership: Booksellers Association; CLÉ (Irish PA)

2532

NATIONAL HOUSING FEDERATION
Lion Court, 25 Procter Street, Holborn,
London WC1V 6NY
Telephone: (020) 7067 1010
Fax: (020) 7067 1011
Email: info@housing.org.uk
Web Site: http://www.housing.co.uk

Publishing Manager: Bev Markham
Production Editor: Fiona Shand
Publishing Co-ordinator: Rick Lloyd

Accountancy & Taxation; Educational & Textbooks; Law; Reference Books, Directories & Dictionaries; Vocational Training & Careers

ISBNs, Imprints & Series: 978 0 86297

2533

NATIONAL PORTRAIT GALLERY PUBLICATIONS
National Portrait Gallery, St Martin's Place,
London WC2H 0HE
Telephone: (020) 7306 0055 ext 266 & (020) 7312 2482 (direct line)
Fax: (020) 7321 6657
Email: pvadhia@npg.org.uk
Web Site: http://www.npg.org.uk/publications

Distribution:
Grantham Book Services,
Isaac Newton Way,
Alma Park Industrial Estate, Grantham,
Lincs NG31 9SD
Telephone: 01476 541080
Fax: 01476 541061
Email: orders@gbs.tbs_ltd.co.uk (UK only)
Web Site: http://www.granthambookservices.co.uk

Representation (UK):
Casemate Books, 17 Cheap Street,
Newbury, Berks RG14 5DD
Telephone: 01635 231091
Fax: 01635 41619
Web Site: http://www.casematepublishing.co.uk

Head of Trading: Robert Carr-Archer
Head of Rights & Reproductions: Tom Morgan
Managers: Celia Joicey (Publishing)
Ruth Müller-Wirth (Production)
Pallavi Vadhia (Sales & Marketing)
Editors: Beka Cohen (Project)
Claudia Bloch (Assistant)

Academic & Scholarly; Biography & Autobiography; Fashion & Costume; Fine Art & Art History; Gender Studies; History & Antiquarian; Illustrated & Fine Editions; Literature & Criticism; Photography

New Titles: 16 (2007), 13 (2008)

ISBNs, Imprints & Series:
978 0 904017, 978 1 85514

Overseas Representation:
Australia: Peribo Pty Ltd, Mount Kuring-Gai, NSW
France: Casemate Books, Newbury, UK
Germany, Austria, Switzerland, Belgium & Luxembourg: Exhibitions International, Leuven, Belgium
Italy, Spain, Portugal & Greece: Penny Padovani, London, UK
Netherlands: Amsterdam University Press, Amsterdam
Republic of Ireland & Northern Ireland: Robert Towers, Monkstown, Co Dublin, Republic of Ireland
South America: David Williams, InterMedia Americana (IMA) Ltd, London, UK
USA: Antique Collectors Club Ltd, Easthampton, MA

Book Trade Association Membership: BA; IPG

2534

THE NATIONAL TRUST
Heelis, Kemble Drive, Swindon, Wilts
SN2 2NA
Telephone: 01793 817400
Fax: 01793 817401
Email: grant.berry@nationaltrust.org.uk
Web Site: http://www.nationaltrust.org.uk

Also at:
Anova Books, 10 Southcombe Street,
London W14 0RA
Telephone: (020) 7605 1400
Web Site: http://www.anovabooks.com

Publisher & Commercial Manager: John Stachiewicz
Publishing Co-ordinator: Grant Berry
Editors: Oliver Garrett
Anna Groves

Academic & Scholarly; Agriculture; Antiques & Collecting; Archaeology; Architecture & Design; Biography & Autobiography; Children's Books; Cookery, Wines & Spirits; Fashion & Costume; Fine Art & Art History; Gardening; Guide Books; History & Antiquarian; Humour; Natural History; Reference Books, Directories & Dictionaries; Travel & Topography

New Titles: 24 (2007), 24 (2008)
No of Employees: 4

ISBNs, Imprints & Series:
978 0 7078, 978 1 8435

Parent Company:
Anova Books [books]; Tempus Publishing [guide books]

2535

THE NATIONAL YOUTH AGENCY
Eastgate House,
19–23 Humberstone Road, Leicester
LE5 3GJ
Telephone: 0116 242 7350
Fax: 0116 242 7444
Email: nya@nya.org.uk
Web Site: http://www.nya.org.uk

Head of Media Services: Andy Hopkinson

Academic & Scholarly; Educational & Textbooks

New Titles: 15 (2007)
No of Employees: 6
Annual Turnover: £100,000

ISBNs, Imprints & Series: 978 0 86155

2536

NATURAL HISTORY MUSEUM PUBLISHING
The Natural History Museum,
Cromwell Road, London SW7 5BD
Telephone: (020) 7942 5060
Fax: (020) 7942 5291
Email: publishing@nhm.ac.uk
Web Site: http://www.nhm.ac.uk/publishing

Warehouse & Distribution:
Bookpoint Ltd, 130 Milton Park, Abingdon,
Oxon OX14 4SB
Telephone: 01235 400400
Fax: 01235 400500
Email: mailorder@bookpoint.co.uk

Managers: Lynn Millhouse (Production)
Trudy Brannan (Editorial)
Colin Ziegler (Head of Publishing)
Marketing Executive: Howard Trent

Academic & Scholarly; Archaeology; Biography & Autobiography; Biology & Zoology; Children's Books; Educational & Textbooks; Fine Art & Art History; Geography & Geology; Natural History; Reference Books, Directories & Dictionaries; Scientific & Technical

New Titles: 7 (2007), 9 (2008)
No of Employees: 6

ISBNs, Imprints & Series: 978 0 565

2537

NAXOS AUDIOBOOKS
40A High Street, Welwyn, Herts AL6 9EQ
Telephone: 01438 717808
Fax: 01438 717809
Email: naxos_audiobooks@compuserve.com
Web Site: http://www.naxos.co.uk/audiobooks/

Distribution:
Select Music & Video,
34A Holmethorpe Avenue, Redhill, Surrey
RH1 2NN
Telephone: 01737 645600
Fax: 01737 766316

Director: Nicolas Soames
Sales Manager: Mark Scott

Audio Books

ISBNs, Imprints & Series: 978 962634

Parent Company:
Hong Kong: HNH International

Associated Companies:
Naxos Classical Music
Hong Kong: Naxos Classical Music

Overseas Representation:
Australia: Select, Sydney
Austria: Gramola Co, Vienna, Australia
Brazil: RKR Musical, Sao Paulo
Canada: Naxos of Canada Ltd, Scarborough, Ont
Czech Republic: Classic Music Distribution, Prague
Denmark: Olga Musik, Ry
Finland: FG Distribution, Helsinki
France: Naxos of France, Paris
Germany: MVD, Munich; Naxos Deutschland, Münster
Greece: Greek Record Club, Athens
Hungary: Phoenix Studio, Budapest
Iceland: JAPIS, Reykjavik
Israel: MCI Records, Tel Aviv
Japan: Naxos Japan, Nagoya & Tokyo
Korea: Hae Dong Co Ltd, Seoul, Korea, South
Malaysia: AV Masters Sdn Bhd, Kuala Lumpur
Netherlands: Vanguard Classics, Nieuwegein
New Zealand: Triton Music Ltd, Auckland
Norway: Musikkdistribusjon AS, Oslo
Philippines: Universal Records, Kalookan City
Republic of Ireland: Cosmic Sounds Ltd, Dublin
Singapore: Naxos Pte Ltd
Slovak Republic: Slovart Music, Bratislava, Slovakia
South Africa: Booktalk (Pty) Ltd, Craighall
Spain: FERYSA, Madrid
Sri Lanka: Titus Stores, Columbo
Sweden: Naxos Sweden, Orebro
Switzerland: FAME, Meggen (Lucerne)
Taiwan: Rock Records & Tapes, Taipei
Thailand: Media Plus & Broadcasting Network Ltd, Bangkok
Turkey: Haci Emin Elendi Sokak, Istanbul
USA: Naxos of America Inc, Pennsauken, NJ

Book Trade Association Membership: Spoken Word Publishers' Association

2538

NEED2KNOW
Remus House, Coltsfoot Drive, Woodston,
Peterborough PE2 9JX
Telephone: 01733 898103
Fax: 01733 313524
Email: sales@n2kbooks.com
Web Site: http://www.n2kbooks.com

Imprint Manager: Kate Gibbard

Cookery, Wines & Spirits; Health & Beauty; Medical (incl. Self Help & Alternative Medicine); Vocational Training & Careers

New Titles: 3 (2007), 20 (2008)

ISBNs, Imprints & Series:
afterschoolclub.net; Anchor Books; New Fiction; Poetry Now; Pond View; Triumph

House; Writers' Bookshop; Young Writers
978 1 86144 Need2Know

Parent Company:
Forward Press Ltd

Book Trade Association Membership:
BA

2539

*NELSON THORNES LTD
[formerly Stanley Thornes Ltd & Thomas Nelson & Sons Ltd]
Delta Place, 27 Bath Road, Cheltenham GL53 7TH
Telephone: 01242 267100
Fax: 01242 221914 (General) & 253695 (Orders)
Email: nelsonthornes.com
Web Site: http://www.nelsonthornes.com

Distribution:
Alexandra Way, Ashchurch, Tewkesbury, Glos GL20 8PE

Directors: Linden Harris (Managing)
Jacqui Millar (Finance)
Jonathan Bunce (Sales & Marketing)
Roland Nicholas (Operations)
Emma Bourne (International)
Head of Customer Services & Distribution: M. van de Weijer

Accountancy & Taxation; Biology & Zoology; Chemistry; Children's Books; Computer Science; Economics; Educational & Textbooks; Electronic (Educational); Engineering; Environment & Development Studies; Fashion & Costume; Geography & Geology; Health & Beauty; History & Antiquarian; Industry, Business & Management; Languages & Linguistics; Literature & Criticism; Mathematics & Statistics; Medical (incl. Self Help & Alternative Medicine); Physics; Politics & World Affairs; Psychology & Psychiatry; Religion & Theology; Scientific & Technical; Sociology & Anthropology; Sports & Games; Theatre, Drama & Dance; Vocational Training & Careers

ISBNs, Imprints & Series:
978 0 17, 978 0 7487

Parent Company:
Netherlands: Wolters Kluwer NV

Distributor for:
Australia: Nelson

Overseas Representation:
Antigua & Montserrat: The Best of Books, St John's, Antigua
Argentina: Kel Ediciones SA (Agents), Buenos Aires
Australia (Primary & Secondary): Thomson Learning (Australia), NSW, Australia
Bahamas: Media Enterprises Ltd, Nassau
Barbados: Days Bookstore, Bridgetown
Belize: The Book Center, Belize City
Botswana: REP Agencies Ltd, Gaborone
Canada (Primary & Secondary, excluding Modern Languages, & Further Education): Bacon & Hughes Ltd, Ottawa, Ont, Canada
Canada (Secondary Modern Languages only): The Resource Centre, Waterloo, Canada
Chile: Books and Bits, Santiago
China: Ian Taylor Associates Ltd, London, UK
Colombia: The English Book Centre, Bogota
Denmark, Finland, Norway & Sweden: Charlotte Svensson, Onsala, Sweden
Dominica: Jays Ltd, Roseau
Egypt: Galaxy Trade, Giza
Fiji & Pacific Islands: Premier Book Centre, Ba, Fiji
Ghana: EPP Book Services Ltd, Accra
Grenada: Grenada Teachers School Supplies, St George's
Gulf States, Iran, Syria, Libya, Jordan, Lebanon, Cyprus, Yemen, Tunis, Turkey, Morocco & Algeria (Further & Higher Education only): International Publishing Services (IPS) Middle East Ltd, Dubai, UAE
Guyana: Austin's Book Services, Georgetown
Hong Kong & Macao: Transglobal Publishers Services Ltd, Hong Kong
India: Overleaf, New Delhi
Jamaica: Kingston Bookshop, Kingston
Kenya: Savani's Book Centre, Nairobi
Malawi & Zambia: Anglia Book Distributors Ltd, Blantyre, Malawi
Malaysia: APD Kuala Lumpur Pte Ltd, Selangor
Malta: Miller Distributors Ltd, Luqa
Malta (Primary): Audio Visual Centre Ltd, Sliema, Malta
Mauritius: Editions le Printemps, Vacoas
New Zealand: Opus Textbooks, Auckland
Nigeria: Chelis Bookazine, Lagos
North America & Canada (Higher Education titles only): International Specialized Book Services Inc, Portland, OR, USA
Pakistan: Publishers Marketing Associates, Karachi
Republic of Ireland (Modern Languages only): Modern Languages, Dublin, Republic of Ireland
Republic of Ireland (Primary, Secondary & Further Education): Carrol Educational Supplies, Dublin, Republic of Ireland
Singapore & Brunei: APD Singapore Pte Ltd, Singapore
South Africa, Lesotho, Swaziland & Mozambique (New Way, Sound Start & Primary Literacy Programme): Macmillan Boleswa, Braamfontein, South Africa
South Africa, Lesotho, Swaziland & Namibia (excluding New Way, Sound Start & Primary Literacy Programme): Penguin Books South Africa, Parklands, South Africa
South Pacific: Premier Book Centre, Ba, Fiji
Sri Lanka: Zubair Makeen & Sons, Colombo
St Kitts & Nevis, Anguilla, St Maarten & BVI: Walls Deluxe Record & Bookshop, Basseterre, St Kitts
St Lucia: Leonise Francois, Morna Fortune
St Vincent & The Grenadines: Gaymes Book Centre, St Vincent
Sweden, Denmark, Norway, Finland, Iceland, Estonia, Latvia & Lithuania (Health Science & Science & Engineering titles only): David Towle International, Stockholm, Sweden
Tanzania: A Novel Idea, Dar es Salaam
Thailand: Book Link, Bangkok
Trinidad & Tobago: Books Etc, San Fernando, Trinidad
Vietnam: Fahasa Companie, Ho Chi Minh City
Zimbabwe: Prestige Books, Harare

Book Trade Association Membership:
Publishers Association; BA; EPC

2540

NETWORK CONTINUUM EDUCATION LTD
The Tower Building, 11 York Road, London SE1 7NX
Telephone: (020) 7922 0880
Fax: (020) 7922 0881
Web Site: http://www.continuumbooks.com

Distribution, Orders, Credit Control:
Orca Book Services Ltd, Stanley House, 3 Fleets Lane, Poole, Dorset BH15 3AJ
Telephone: 01202 665432
Fax: 01202 666219
Web Site: http://www.orcabookservices.co.uk

Chief Executive: Oliver Gadsby
Directors: Bob Marsh (Finance)
Ken Rhodes (Sales & Marketing)
Benn Linfield (Production)
Vivien Ward (Publishing)
Rights Manager: Elizabeth White (Special Sales & Rights)

Academic & Scholarly; Educational & Textbooks; Electronic (Professional & Academic); Reference Books, Directories & Dictionaries

ISBNs, Imprints & Series: 978 1 85539

Parent Company:
The Continuum International Publishing Group Ltd

Overseas Representation:
see: The Continuum International Publishing Group Ltd, London, UK

Book Trade Association Membership:
IPG

2541

NEW INTERNATIONALIST PUBLICATIONS LTD
55 Rectory Road, Oxford OX4 1BW
Telephone: 01865 728181
Fax: 01865 793152
Email: hi@newint.org
Web Site: http://www.newint.org/

Representation (UK):
Turnaround Publisher Services Ltd, Unit 3, Olympia Trading Estate, Coburg Road, London N22 6TZ
Telephone: (020) 8829 3000
Fax: (020) 8881 5088

Company Accountant: Anne Maxfield
Managers: Fran Harvey (Production)
Dan Raymond Barker (Publications Marketing)
Publications Editor: Troth Wells
Magazine Marketing: Michael York
Amanda Synnott

Atlases & Maps; Cookery, Wines & Spirits; Electronic (Educational); Environment & Development Studies; Fiction; Photography; Politics & World Affairs; Reference Books, Directories & Dictionaries

No of Employees: 20
Annual Turnover: £3M

ISBNs, Imprints & Series:
978 0 9540499, 978 1 869847, 978 1 904456, 978 1 906523 No-Nonsense Series

Parent Company:
New Internationalist Trust Ltd

Overseas Representation:
Australia: Palgrave Macmillan, South Yarra, Vic
Australia & Papua New Guinea: New Internationalist Publications Ltd, Adelaide, SA, Australia
Canada: New Internationalist Publications Ltd, Toronto, Ont
New Zealand & Aotearoa: New Internationalist Publications Ltd, Christchurch, New Zealand
South Africa: Stephan Phillips (Pty) Ltd, Cape Town
USA: Consortium Book Sales & Distribution Inc, St Paul, MN

Book Trade Association Membership:
IPG; Periodical Publishers Association

2542

NEW ISLAND BOOKS LTD
2 Brookside, Dundrum Road, Dublin 14, Republic of Ireland
Telephone: +353 (01) 298 3411
Fax: +353 (01) 298 7912
Email: inka.hagen@newisland.ie
Web Site: http://www.newisland.ie

Distribution:
Gill & Macmillan, Hume Avenue, Park West, Dublin 12, Republic of Ireland
Telephone: +353 (01) 500 9555
Fax: +353 (01) 294 2564

Representation (Republic of Ireland & Northern Ireland):
Compass Ireland, 39 Craddockstown Way, Naas, Co Kildare, Republic of Ireland
Telephone: +353 (045) 889314
Fax: +353 (045) 889450
Email: alasdair@compassireland.ie

Publisher: Edwin Higel
Managers: Deirdre Nolan (Editorial)
Inka Hagen (Production & Design)
Aisling Glynn (Accounts)
Mariel Deegan (Marketing)
Thomas Cooney (Publicity & Marketing)

Biography & Autobiography; Crime; English as a Foreign Language; Fiction; Gardening; Guide Books; Humour; Literature & Criticism; Poetry; Politics & World Affairs; Theatre, Drama & Dance

New Titles: 25 (2007), 25 (2008)
No of Employees: 6

ISBNs, Imprints & Series:
978 1 874597, 978 1 902602, 978 1 904301, 978 1 905494

Overseas Representation:
UK: Compass Independent Book Sales, London
USA & Canada: Dufour Editions Inc, Chester Springs, PA, USA; Irish Books & Media Inc, Minneapolis, MN, USA

Book Trade Association Membership:
CLÉ (Irish PA)

2543

NEW PLAYWRIGHTS' NETWORK
10 Station Road Industrial Estate, Colwall, Malvern, Worcs WR13 6RN
Telephone: 01684 540154
Fax: 01684 540154
Email: simon@cressrelles.co.uk
Web Site: http://www.cressrelles.co.uk

Contact: L. G. Smith

Theatre, Drama & Dance

New Titles: 8 (2007), 8 (2008)

ISBNs, Imprints & Series: 978 0 86319

Overseas Representation:
Australia: Origin Theatrical, Sydney, NSW
New Zealand: Play Bureau of New Zealand Ltd, New Plymouth
Republic of Ireland: Drama League of Ireland, Dublin
South Africa: Dalro (Pty) Ltd, Braamfontein
USA: Bakers Plays, Quincy, MA

2544

NEWPRO UK LTD
Old Sawmills Road, Faringdon, Oxon SN7 7DS
Telephone: 01367 242411
Fax: 01367 241124
Email: sales@newprouk.co.uk
Web Site: http://www.newprouk.co.uk

Managing Director & Publisher:
Christopher J. Coleman
Company Secretary: Beryl L. Coleman

Antiques & Collecting; Natural History; Photography

New Titles: 2 (2007), 2 (2008)

ISBNs, Imprints & Series:
Fountain Press; Hove Foto Books
978 0 86343, 978 0 906447, 978 1 87403

Distributor for:
Classic Collection; Fountain Press; Hove Foto Books; Van Hasbroeck
Italy: Editrice Reflex
USA: Centennial Photo Service; Marling Menu Masters; McKeown's Price Guides

Overseas Representation:
Far East, Near East & Middle East: Publishers International Marketing, Storrington, UK
South Africa: Zytek Publishing (Pty) Ltd, Bedfordview

2545

NIELSEN BOOK
3rd Floor, Midas House,
62 Goldsworth Road, Woking, Surrey
GU21 6LQ
Telephone: 0870 777 8710
Fax: 0870 777 8711
Email: info.book@nielsen.com
Web Site: http://www.nielsenbook.co.uk

Editorial:
89–95 Queensway, Stevenage, Herts
SG1 1EA
Telephone: 0845 450 0016
Fax: 01438 745578
Email: newtitles.book@nielsen.com & pubhelp.book@nielsen.com
Web Site: http://www.nielsenbook.co.uk

President: Jonathan Nowell
Directors: Richard Knight *(Operations)*
Ann Betts *(Commercial)*
Jon Windus *(Product Development)*
Andrew Sugden *(Financial)*
Leonie Dorkins *(Human Resources)*
Simon Skinner *(Sales)*
Julie Meynink *(Business Development)*
Head of Marketing: Mo Siewcharran
Senior Managers: Peter Mathews *(Publishing Services)*
Howard Willows *(Data Development)*
Gwyneth Morgan *(Editorial Systems)*
Samantha Watson *(Quality Assurance)*
Manager: Vesna Nall *(Publisher Subscriptions)*
Head of Data Sales: Paul Dibble
Head of BookNet Sales: Stephen Long

Bibliography & Library Science; Information Services

New Titles: 1 (2007) , 1 (2008)
No of Employees: 120
Annual Turnover: £15M

Associated Companies:
BDS; Bookseller Publications; Nielsen BookData Asia Pacific; Nielsen BookNet; Nielsen BookScan; The Nielsen Company; UK DOI Agency; UK ISBN Agency; UK SAN Agency

Overseas Representation:
South Africa: Publications Network (Pty) Ltd (trading as SAPNet)

Book Trade Association Membership:
BA; IPG; Data Publishers Association

2546

NMS ENTERPRISES LIMITED - PUBLISHING
National Museums Scotland,
Chambers Street, Edinburgh EH1 1JF
Telephone: 0131 247 4026
Fax: 0131 247 4012
Email: publishing@nms.ac.uk
Web Site: http://www.nms.ac.uk/books

Representation:
CPR, SPCK Head Office, 36 Causton Street, London SW1P 4ST

Telephone: (020) 7592 3900
Email: sales@spck.org.uk

Distribution (UK):
BookSource, 50 Cambuslang Road,
Glasgow G32 8NB
Telephone: 0845 370 0067
Fax: 0845 370 0068
Email: orders@booksource.net

Director of Publishing: Lesley A. Taylor
Marketing Manager: Kate Blackadder
Administration & Sales: Maggie Wilson

Academic & Scholarly; Antiques & Collecting; Archaeology; Architecture & Design; Biography & Autobiography; Biology & Zoology; Children's Books; Cookery, Wines & Spirits; Educational & Textbooks; Fine Art & Art History; Geography & Geology; Guide Books; History & Antiquarian; Military & War; Natural History; Poetry; Scientific & Technical; Sociology & Anthropology; Transport

New Titles: 10 (2007) , 11 (2008)
No of Employees: 3

ISBNs, Imprints & Series:
978 0 948636, 978 1 901663, 978 1 905267

Parent Company:
National Museums Scotland

Overseas Representation:
USA: Antique Collectors Club Ltd, Easthampton, MA

Book Trade Association Membership:
Publishing Scotland

2547

NORTH YORK MOORS NATIONAL PARK
The Old Vicarage, Bondgate, Helmsley,
Yorks YO62 5BP
Telephone: 01439 770657
Fax: 01439 770691
Email: J.Renney@northyorkmoors-npa.gov.uk
Web Site: http://www.moors.uk.net

Head of Information Services: Julie Lawrence
Finance Officer: Pat Waters-Marsh
Sales & Marketing Assistant: Darren Sims
Information & Interpretation Manager: Jill Renney

Archaeology; Biology & Zoology; Children's Books; Educational & Textbooks; Environment & Development Studies; Geography & Geology; Guide Books; History & Antiquarian; Natural History

New Titles: 5 (2007) , 4 (2008)

ISBNs, Imprints & Series:
978 0 907480, 978 1 904622

2548

NORTHCOTE HOUSE PUBLISHERS LTD
Horndon House, Horndon, Tavistock, Devon
PL19 9NQ
Telephone: 01822 810066
Fax: 01822 810034
Email: northcote.house@virgin.net
Web Site: http://www.northcotehouse.co.uk

Distributors:
Combined Book Services,
Paddock Wood Distribution Centre,
Paddock Wood, Tonbridge, Kent TN12 6UU
Telephone: 01892 837171
Fax: 01892 837372

Email: orders@combook.co.uk
Web Site: http://www.combook.co.uk

Managing Director: Brian Hulme *(Publisher)*
Marketing Manager: Sarah Piper

Educational & Textbooks; Literature & Criticism; Theatre, Drama & Dance

New Titles: 25 (2007) , 35 (2008)
No of Employees: 2
Annual Turnover: £100,000

ISBNs, Imprints & Series:
978 0 7463 Northcote House; Resources in Education; Starting Out....; Writers and Their Work

Overseas Representation:
Africa (excluding South Africa) & Eastern Europe: Tony Moggach, IMA, London, UK
Australia & New Zealand: Book & Volume, Birregurra, Vic, Australia
Caribbean: Hugh Dunphy, Kingston, Jamaica
Germany, Austria, Switzerland, France, Italy & Benelux: Ted Dougherty, London, UK
India: Maya Publishers Pvt Ltd, New Delhi
Middle East: Hani Kreidieh, Beirut, Lebanon
Pakistan: Book Bird Publishers Representatives, Lahore
Scandinavia: David Towle International, Stockholm, Sweden
Spain & Portugal: Peter Prout Iberian Book Services, Madrid, Spain
USA & Canada: Ashgate Publishing Co, Burlington, VT, USA

Book Trade Association Membership:
IPG

2549

W. W. NORTON & COMPANY LTD
Castle House, 75–76 Wells Street, London
W1T 3QT
Telephone: (020) 7323 1579
Fax: (020) 7436 4553
Email: office@wwnorton.co.uk
Web Site: http://www.wwnorton.co.uk

Distribution:
John Wiley & Sons Ltd, 1 Oldlands Way,
Shripney, Bognor Regis, Sussex PO22 9SA
Telephone: 01243 779777
Fax: 01243 820250
Email: cs-books@wiley.co.uk

Directors: R. A. Cameron *(Managing)*
S. King
W. D. McFeely *(USA)*
S. R. Lawrence *(USA)*
G. Luciano *(USA)*
Patrick Wright
R. Harrington *(USA)*
Robert Kiernan
Judith Pamplin *(Sales)*

Architecture & Design; Biology & Zoology; Chemistry; Cinema, Video, TV & Radio; Computer Science; Cookery, Wines & Spirits; Economics; Fine Art & Art History; Gardening; Gender Studies; Geography & Geology; History & Antiquarian; Literature & Criticism; Mathematics & Statistics; Military & War; Music; Natural History; Nautical; Philosophy; Physics; Poetry; Politics & World Affairs; Psychology & Psychiatry; Sports & Games; Theatre, Drama & Dance

ISBNs, Imprints & Series:
978 0 393 Norton
978 0 87140 Liveright
978 0 88150 Countryman Press

Parent Company:
USA: W. W. Norton & Company

Distributor for:
USA: New Directions Publishing Corporation

Overseas Representation:
Africa & Caribbean: Kelvin van Hasselt Publishing Services, Briningham, Norfolk, UK
India: Viva Group, New Delhi
Middle East & North Africa: International Publishers Representatives (IPR) Ltd, Nicosia, Cyprus
Pakistan: World Press, Lahore
Republic of Ireland: Andrew Russell Book Representation, Co Cork
South Africa: Chris Reinders, The African Moon Press, Kelvin

2550

NORWOOD PUBLISHERS LTD
3 Chapel Street, Norwood Green, Halifax,
West Yorkshire HR3 8QU
Telephone: 01274 602454
Fax: 01274 676665
Email: enquiries@norwoodpublishers.co.uk
Web Site: http://www.norwoodpublishers.co.uk

Partners: M. H. Wolfenden
Mrs A. M. Wolfenden

Educational & Textbooks

ISBNs, Imprints & Series: 978 1 873784

2551

*THE NOSTALGIA COLLECTION
Silver Link Publishing Ltd, The Trundle,
Ringstead Road, Great Addington,
Kettering, Northants NN14 4BW
Telephone: 01536 330543 & 330588
Fax: 01536 330588
Email: sales@nostalgiacollection.com
Web Site: http://www.nostalgiacollection.com

Directors: Peter Townsend *(Managing, Publisher)*
Frances Townsend *(Company Secretary)*
Managers: Michael Sanders *(Production)*
David Walshaw *(Mail Order & Advertising)*

History & Antiquarian; Military & War; Nautical; Transport; Nostalgia

ISBNs, Imprints & Series:
978 0 947971, 978 1 85794 Silver Link Publishing Ltd
978 1 85895 Past & Present Publishing Ltd

Associated Companies:
Past & Present Publishing Ltd; Silver Link Publishing Ltd

Distributor for:
Past & Present Publishing Ltd; Silver Link Publishing Ltd

Book Trade Association Membership:
BA

2552

OAK TREE PRESS
19 Rutland Street, Cork, Republic of Ireland
Telephone: +353 (021) 431 3855
Fax: +353 (021) 431 3496
Email: info@oaktreepress.com
Web Site: http://www.oaktreepress.com

Directors: Brian O'Kane *(Managing)*
Rita O'Kane *(Sales)*

Academic & Scholarly; Accountancy & Taxation; Educational & Textbooks; Industry, Business & Management; Law

New Titles: 3 (2007) , 8 (2008)
No of Employees: 3

ISBNs, Imprints & Series:
978 1 84621 Oak Tree eWare
978 1 86076, 978 1 872853, 978 1 904887 Oak Tree Press

Parent Company:
Republic of Ireland: Cork Publishing Ltd

2553

THE O'BRIEN PRESS LTD
12 Terenure Road East, Rathgar, Dublin 6, Republic of Ireland
Telephone: +353 (01) 492 3333
Fax: +353 (01) 492 2777
Email: books@obrien.ie
Web Site: http://www.obrien.ie

Publisher: Michael O'Brien
Directors: Ivan O'Brien *(Managing)*
Mary Web *(Editorial)*
Rights Manager: Kunak McGann

Architecture & Design; Biography & Autobiography; Children's Books; Cookery, Wines & Spirits; Guide Books; Humour; Politics & World Affairs; Sports & Games; Travel & Topography

New Titles: 52 (2007), 48 (2008)
No of Employees: 17
Annual Turnover: £2M

ISBNs, Imprints & Series:
978 0 86278, 978 0 905140, 978 1 84717

Associated Companies:
Republic of Ireland: O'Brien Educational

Overseas Representation:
Australia: Tower Books Pty Ltd, Frenchs Forest, NSW
Britain: Compass DSA, Slough, UK
USA & Canada: James Trading Group, Nanuet, NY, USA

Book Trade Association Membership:
IPG

2554

*OCTAGON PRESS LTD
78 York Street, London W1H 1PD
Telephone: (020) 7168 5308
Email: admin@octagonpress.com
Web Site: http://www.octagonpress.com

Manager: Anna Murphy

Biography & Autobiography; Environment & Development Studies; Humour; Magic & the Occult; Philosophy; Poetry; Psychology & Psychiatry; Religion & Theology; Sociology & Anthropology; Travel & Topography

ISBNs, Imprints & Series:
978 0 863040, 978 0 900860

Distributor for:
Institute for Cultural Research

Overseas Representation:
USA: I.S.H.K. Books, Cambridge, MA

2555

OCTOPUS PUBLISHING GROUP
2–4 Heron Quays, London E14 4JP
Telephone: (020) 7531 8400
Fax: (020) 7531 8650
Email: info-ho@hamlyn.co.uk
Web Site: http://www.octopusbooks.co.uk

Distribution:
Littlehampton Book Services Ltd, Faraday Close, Durrington, Worthing, West Sussex BN13 3PB
Telephone: 01903 828500
Fax: 01903 828625
Email: orders@lbsltd.co.uk
Web Site: http://www.lbsltd.co.uk

Directors: Alison Goff *(Chief Executive Officer)*
Andrew Welham *(Deputy Chief Executive Officer)*
Angela Luxton *(Divisional Finance)*
Steven Edney *(Group Sales & Marketing)*
Jane Smith *(Marketing & Publicity)*
Frances Johnson *(Operations)*

Animal Care & Breeding; Antiques & Collecting; Architecture & Design; Atlases & Maps; Cookery, Wines & Spirits; Crafts & Hobbies; Do-It-Yourself; Fine Art & Art History; Gardening; Health & Beauty; History & Antiquarian; Natural History; Sports & Games

ISBNs, Imprints & Series:
978 0 600 Cassell Illustrated; Conran Octopus; Gaia; Godsfield Press; Hamlyn; Mitchell Beazley; Philips

Parent Company:
Octopus Publishing Group

Overseas Representation:
Australia: Bookwise International, Adelaide, SA
Central America & Caribbean: Humphrys Roberts Associates, London, UK
Eastern Europe & Africa: InterMedia Americana (IMA) Ltd, London, UK
France, Belgium & Luxembourg: Ted Dougherty, London, UK
Germany, Switzerland & Austria: Gabriele Kern Publishers Services, Frankfurt-am-Main, Germany
Hong Kong & Taiwan: Asia Publishers Services Ltd, Hong Kong
India, Bangladesh & Sri Lanka: Viva Group, New Delhi, India
Israel: Steimatzky Ltd, Bnei Brak
Italy, Greece, Spain & Portugal: Penny Padovani, London, UK
Japan: Noriko Sakai, Tokyo
Malaysia: APD Kuala Lumpur Pte Ltd, Selangor
Middle East & North Africa: Peter Ward Book Exports, London, UK
Netherlands: Nilsson & Lamm BV, Weesp
New Zealand: Reed Publishing (NZ) Ltd, Auckland
Philippines: Marketing Services for Publishers, Pasig City
Republic of Ireland & Northern Ireland: Brookside Publishing Services, Dublin, Republic of Ireland
Scandinavia: Anglo-Nordic Books, Godalming, UK
Singapore & Thailand: APD Singapore Pte Ltd, Singapore
South Africa & Sub-Sahara: Penguin Books South Africa, Parklands, South Africa
South America: Terry Roberts, Cotia SP, Brazil

2556

*OICA INTERNATIONAL (UK) LTD
35 Farrow Lane, Avonley Village, London SE14 5DB
Telephone: (020) 7635 6487
Email: info@oicainternational.co.uk
Web Site: http://www.oicainternational.co.uk

Director: Okezie I. Aruoma

Academic & Scholarly; Biology & Zoology; Chemistry; Educational & Textbooks; Health & Beauty; Industry, Business & Management; Medical (incl. Self Help & Alternative Medicine); Reference Books, Directories & Dictionaries; Scientific & Technical

ISBNs, Imprints & Series: 978 1 903063

2557

OLD HOUSE BOOKS
The Old Police Station, Moretonhampstead, Devon TQ13 8PA
Telephone: 01647 440707
Fax: 01647 440202
Email: edward@allhusen.co.uk
Web Site: http://www.oldhousebooks.co.uk

Managing Director: Edward Allhusen

Atlases & Maps; Crafts & Hobbies; Geography & Geology; Guide Books; History & Antiquarian; Natural History; Reference Books, Directories & Dictionaries; Sports & Games; Transport; Travel & Topography

New Titles: 6 (2007), 5 (2008)
No of Employees: 3

ISBNs, Imprints & Series: 978 1 873590

Overseas Representation:
USA: Parkwest, Miami, FL

2558

OLD POND PUBLISHING
Dencora Business Centre, 36 White House Road, Ipswich IP1 5LT
Telephone: 01473 238200
Fax: 01473 238201
Email: sales@oldpond.com
Web Site: http://www.oldpond.com

Director: Roger Smith
Marketing: Heather Jarrold

Agriculture; Transport; Veterinary Science

New Titles: 20 (2007), 20 (2008)
No of Employees: 4

ISBNs, Imprints & Series:
978 0 9533651, 978 1 903366, 978 1 905523

Book Trade Association Membership:
IPG

2559

THE OLD STILE PRESS
Catchmays Court, Llandogo, Monmouthshire NP25 4TN
Telephone: 01291 689226
Email: oldstile@dircon.co.uk
Web Site: http://www.oldstilepress.com

Partners: Nicolas McDowall
Frances McDowall

Illustrated & Fine Editions; Poetry

New Titles: 3 (2007), 2 (2008)

ISBNs, Imprints & Series: 978 0 907664

Book Trade Association Membership:
Fine Press Book Association

2560

*OLDCASTLE BOOKS LTD
18 Coleswood Road, Harpenden, Herts AL5 1EQ
Telephone: 01582 761264
Fax: 01582 761264
Web Site: http://www.noexit.co.uk

Distributor:
Turnaround Distribution

Director: Ion Mills *(Home & Export Sales)*

Cinema, Video, TV & Radio; Fiction; History & Antiquarian; Literature & Criticism; Music; Sports & Games; Crime & Noir Fiction; Gambling Books

ISBNs, Imprints & Series:
978 0 948353, 978 1 84243, 978 1 874061, 978 1 901982 No Exit Press (Crime & Noir Fiction); Oldcastle Books Gambling Books
978 1 84344 High Stakes Gambling Books
978 1 903042, 978 1 904048 Pocket Essentials

Overseas Representation:
Australia: Tower Books Pty Ltd, Frenchs Forest, NSW
Canada (Pocket Essentials only): Codasat, Vancouver, BC, Canada
New Zealand: Southern Publishers Group, Auckland
USA (Pocket Essentials only): Trafalgar Square Publishing, North Pomfret, VT, USA

2561

THE OLEANDER PRESS
16 Orchard Street, Cambridge CB1 1JT
Telephone: 01223 350898
Email: editor@oleanderpress.com
Web Site: http://www.oleanderpress.com

Managing Director: Jon Gifford *(Publisher)*
Managers: Jane Doyle *(Sales)*
Will Marston *(Rights)*

Biography & Autobiography; History & Antiquarian; Humour; Languages & Linguistics; Literature & Criticism; Poetry; Reference Books, Directories & Dictionaries; Sports & Games; Travel & Topography

ISBNs, Imprints & Series:
978 0 900891, 978 0 902675, 978 0 906672

2562

OMNIBUS PRESS
14–15 Berners Street, London W1T 3LJ
Telephone: (020) 7612 7400
Fax: (020) 7612 7545
Email: lucy.grant@musicsales.co.uk
Web Site: http://www.omnibuspress.co.uk

Warehouse:
Book Sales Ltd, Newmarket Road, Bury St Edmunds, Suffolk IP33 3YB
Telephone: 01284 702600
Fax: 01284 768301
Email: music@musicsales.co.uk
Web Site: http://www.musicsales.co.uk

Directors: Robert Wise *(Managing)*
Tony Latham *(Financial)*
Managers: Lucy Grant *(Sales & Marketing)*
Susan Currie *(Production)*
Editor: Chris Charlesworth

Biography & Autobiography; Music

New Titles: 50 (2008)

ISBNs, Imprints & Series:
Sanctuary
978 0 7119 Music Sales; Wise Publications
978 0 7119, 978 1 84609, 978 1 84772 Omnibus Press
978 1 8444 Omnibus Press

Parent Company:
Music Sales Ltd

Associated Companies:
Australia: Music Sales (Pty) Ltd
USA: Music Sales Corp

Distributor for:
Dover Books; IMP; Parker Mead Ltd; Retail Entertainment Data; Rogan House; Schirmer Books

Overseas Representation:
Australia: Macmillan Distribution, South Yarra, Vic

Australia (for Music Shops): Music Sales (Australia), Rosebery, NSW, Australia
Belgium: Exhibitions International, Leuven
Central America, Mexico & Caribbean: Humphrys Roberts Associates, London, UK
Eastern Europe: Tony Moggach, InterMedia Americana (IMA) Ltd, London, UK
France: Music Sales Ltd, UK
Germany, Austria & Switzerland: Gabriele Kern Publishers Services, Frankfurt-am-Main, Germany
Greece, Turkey, Cyprus, Malta & Middle East: Peter Ward Book Exports, London, UK
Indian Sub Continent: Publishers International Marketing, Storrington, UK
Netherlands & Luxembourg: Nilsson & Lamm BV, Weesp, Netherlands
New Zealand: Macmillan Publishers New Zealand Ltd, Albany, Auckland
Scandinavia: McNeish Publishing Services, East Sussex, UK
South Africa: Trinity Books CC, Randburg
South America: Humphrys Roberts Associates, Cotia SP, Brazil
South East & North Asia: Chris Ashdown Publishers International Marketing, London, UK
Spain, Portugal, Gibraltar & Italy: Penny Padovani, London, UK
USA & Canada: Music Sales Corporation, Chester, NY, USA

Book Trade Association Membership:
BA (Associate Member)

2563

ON STREAM PUBLICATIONS LTD
Currabaha, Cloghroe, Co Cork, Republic of Ireland
Telephone: +353 (021) 438 5798
Email: info@onstream.ie
Web Site: http://www.onstream.ie

Managing Director & Editor: Roz Crowley

Academic & Scholarly; Biography & Autobiography; Cookery, Wines & Spirits; Environment & Development Studies; Health & Beauty; Reference Books, Directories & Dictionaries

New Titles: 3 (2007), 4 (2008)

ISBNs, Imprints & Series: 978 1 897685

Book Trade Association Membership:
CLÉ (Irish PA)

2564

ONEWORLD CLASSICS
London House,
243–253 Lower Mortlake Road, Richmond, Surrey TW9 2LL
Telephone: (020) 8948 9550
Fax: (020) 8948 5599
Email: info@oneworldclassics.com
Web Site: http://www.oneworldclassics.com

Publishing Director: Alessandro Gallenzi
Associate Publisher: Elisabetta Minervini

Fiction; Literature & Criticism; Poetry

New Titles: 30 (2007), 50 (2008)

ISBNs, Imprints & Series:
978 0 7145 Calder Publications
978 1 84749 One World Classics

Associated Companies:
UK: Calder Publications Ltd

Overseas Representation:
Australia: Tower Books Pty Ltd, Frenchs Forest, NSW
South Africa: Penguin Books South Africa (Pty) Ltd, Johannesburg
USA & Canada: Trafalgar Square Publishing / IPG, Chicago, IL, USA

2565

*ONEWORLD PUBLICATIONS
185 Banbury Road, Oxford OX2 7AR
Telephone: 01865 310597
Fax: 01865 310598
Email: info@oneworld.publications.com
Web Site: http://www.oneworld-publications.com

Trade Enquiries & Orders:
Grantham Book Services,
Isaac Newton Way,
Alma Park Industrial Estate, Grantham, Lincs NG31 9SD
Telephone: 01476 541080
Fax: 01476 541061
Email: orders@gbs.tbs-ltd.co.uk

Partners: Novin Doostdar
Juliet Mabey

Academic & Scholarly; History & Antiquarian; Literature & Criticism; Military & War; Philosophy; Politics & World Affairs; Psychology & Psychiatry; Religion & Theology; Scientific & Technical; Sociology & Anthropology; Inspirational

ISBNs, Imprints & Series: 978 1 85168

Overseas Representation:
USA & Canada: National Book Network, Blue Ridge Summit, PA & Lanham, MD, USA

2566

*ONLYWOMEN PRESS LTD
40 St Lawrence Terrace, London W10 5ST
Telephone: (020) 8354 0796
Fax: (020) 8960 2817
Email: onlywomenpress@btconnect.com
Web Site: http://www.onlywomenpress.com

Trade Distribution:
Central Books Ltd, 99 Wallis Road, London E9 5LN
Telephone: 0845 458 9911
Fax: 0845 458 9912
Web Site: http://www.centralbooks.com

Directors: L. Mohin *(Managing)*
V. J. Lee

Academic & Scholarly; Biography & Autobiography; Children's Books; Crime; Fiction; Gay & Lesbian Studies; Gender Studies; Literature & Criticism

ISBNs, Imprints & Series: 978 0 906500

Overseas Representation:
Australia: Bulldog Books, Beaconsfield, NSW
North America: Alamo Square Distribution, USA

Book Trade Association Membership:
IPG

2567

THE OPEN BIBLE TRUST
Fordland Mount, Upper Basildon, Reading RG8 8LU
Telephone: 01491 671357
Email: admin@obt.org.uk
Web Site: http://www.obt.org.uk

Editor: Michael Penny *(Administrator)*
Treasurer: Sylvia Penny

Religion & Theology

New Titles: 7 (2007), 8 (2008)
No of Employees: 2
Annual Turnover: £34,000

ISBNs, Imprints & Series:
978 0 947778, 978 1 902859

Associated Companies:
USA: Bible Search Publications Inc

Overseas Representation:
Australia: Benean Bible Fellowship of Australia, Glendale, NSW
Canada: Lloyd Allen, Scarborough, Ont
New Zealand: Graeme Abbott, Hamilton
USA: Bible Search Publications, Brookfield, WI

2568

OPEN GATE PRESS
[incorporating Centaur Press (1954)]
51 Achilles Road, London NW6 1DZ
Telephone: (020) 7431 4391
Fax: (020) 7431 5129
Email: books@opengatepress.co.uk
Web Site: http://www.opengatepress.co.uk

Trade Enquiries & Orders:
Central Books Ltd, 99 Wallis Road, London E9 5LN
Telephone: 0845 458 9911
Fax: 0845 458 9912
Email: sales@centralbooks.com
Web Site: http://www.centralbooks.com

Editorial: Jeannie Cohen
Production: Elisabeth Petersdorff

Academic & Scholarly; Environment & Development Studies; Philosophy; Politics & World Affairs; Psychology & Psychiatry; Religion & Theology

New Titles: 4 (2008)
No of Employees: 3

ISBNs, Imprints & Series:
978 0 900001, 978 1 871871

Associated Companies:
Centaur Press; Linden Press [imprint of Centaur Press]

Book Trade Association Membership:
Publishers Association; IPG

2569

OPEN UNIVERSITY WORLDWIDE
Michael Young Building, Walton Hall, Milton Keynes, Bucks MK7 6AA
Telephone: 01604 858785
Web Site: http://www.ouw.co.uk

Academic & Scholarly; Biology & Zoology; Chemistry; Computer Science; Economics; Educational & Textbooks; Electronic (Educational); Engineering; English as a Foreign Language; Environment & Development Studies; Fine Art & Art History; Geography & Geology; History & Antiquarian; Industry, Business & Management; Languages & Linguistics; Literature & Criticism; Mathematics & Statistics; Medical (incl. Self Help & Alternative Medicine); Natural History; Physics; Politics & World Affairs; Psychology & Psychiatry; Religion & Theology; Scientific & Technical; Sociology & Anthropology; Theatre, Drama & Dance

New Titles: 120 (2007), 120 (2008)

ISBNs, Imprints & Series: 978 0 7492

2570

OPTIMUS PROFESSIONAL PUBLISHING
33–41 Dallington Street, London EC1V 0BB
Telephone: 0845 450 6404
Fax: 0845 450 6410
Email: info@teachingexpertise.com
Web Site: http://www.teachingexpertise.com

Managing Director: Emma Rogers

Educational & Textbooks; Electronic (Educational); Geography & Geology; History & Antiquarian; Natural History; Vocational Training & Careers

ISBNs, Imprints & Series:
978 1 899857, 978 1 904677, 978 1 905538, 978 1 906517

Parent Company:
Electric Word PLC

Book Trade Association Membership:
EPC; IPG

2571

ORCHARD PUBLISHING
43–47 Mill Way, Grantchester, Cambs CB3 9ND
Telephone: 01223 845788
Fax: 01223 845862
Email: opl@callan.co.uk
Web Site: http://www.callan.co.uk

Academic & Scholarly; Educational & Textbooks

Book Trade Association Membership:
Publishers Association

2572

O'REILLY UK LTD
4 Castle Street, Farnham, Surrey GU9 7HS
Telephone: 01252 711776
Fax: 01252 734211
Email: information@oreilly.co.uk
Web Site: http://www.oreilly.co.uk

Distributors:
John Wiley, 1 Oldlands Way, Bognor Regis PO22 9SA
Telephone: 01243 779777
Fax: 01243 843303
Email: cs-books@wiley.co.uk

Managing Director: Graham Cameron
Managers: Josette Garcia *(Public Relations)*
Simon Chappell *(Sales)*

Computer Science

New Titles: 140 (2007), 30 (2008)

ISBNs, Imprints & Series:
978 0 59600, 978 1 56592

Parent Company:
USA: O'Reilly Media Inc

Book Trade Association Membership:
IPG

2573

ORION BOOKS LTD
Orion House, 5 Upper St Martins Lane, London WC2H 9EA
Telephone: (020) 7240 3444
Fax: (020) 7240 4822

Trade Counter & Warehouse:
Littlehampton Book Services Ltd,
Faraday Close, Durrington, Worthing, West Sussex BN13 3RB
Telephone: 01903 828500
Fax: 01903 828625
Web Site: http://www.orionbooks.co.uk

Managing Directors: Lisa Milton *(Orion Books)*
Susan Lamb *(Orion Paperbacks)*
Publishing Directors: Jon Wood *(Orion Fiction)*

2574 / PUBLISHERS

Ian Marshall (Orion Non-Fiction)
Publisher: Fiona Kennedy (Orion Children's)

Biography & Autobiography; Children's Books; Fiction; Science Fiction; Fantasy

ISBNs, Imprints & Series:
978 1 84255, 978 1 85881 Orion Children's
978 1 85797 Orion; Orion Paperbacks
978 1 85798 Gollancz
978 1 85799 Phoenix
978 1 89758 Phoenix House

Parent Company:
The Orion Publishing Group Ltd

Overseas Representation:
see: The Orion Publishing Group Ltd, London, UK

2574

THE ORION PUBLISHING GROUP LTD
Orion House, 5 Upper St Martins Lane, London WC2H 9EA
Telephone: (020) 7240 3444
Fax: (020) 7240 4822

Trade Counter & Warehouse:
Littlehampton Book Services Ltd, Faraday Close, Durrington, Worthing, West Sussex BN13 3RB
Telephone: 01903 828500
Fax: 01903 828625
Email: ...@lbsltd.co.uk
Web Site: http://www.lbsltd.co.uk

Chairman: Arnaud Nourry
Chief Executives: Peter Roche
  Malcolm Edwards (Deputy & Publisher)
Directors: Susan Lamb (Managing – Mass Market)
  Lisa Milton (Managing – Orion Books)
  Dallas Manderson (Group Sales)
  Linda Gawley (Home Sales)
  Mark Streatfeild (Export Sales)
  Fiona McIntosh (Production)
  Mark Prior (Finance)
  Martin Evans (Distribution)
  Lord Weidenfeld
  Susan Howe (Group Rights)

Antiques & Collecting; Archaeology; Audio Books; Biography & Autobiography; Children's Books; Cinema, Video, TV & Radio; Cookery, Wines & Spirits; Crafts & Hobbies; Crime; Fashion & Costume; Fiction; Fine Art & Art History; Gardening; Guide Books; Health & Beauty; History & Antiquarian; Humour; Illustrated & Fine Editions; Military & War; Natural History; Nautical; Philosophy; Politics & World Affairs; Reference Books, Directories & Dictionaries; Science Fiction; Sports & Games; Travel & Topography

ISBNs, Imprints & Series:
978 0 297 W & N Illustrated; Weidenfeld & Nicolson
978 0 304 Cassell
978 0 460 J M Dent; Everyman Paperbacks
978 0 460, 978 0 7528, 978 1 85797 Orion Paperbacks
978 0 575, 978 1 85797, 978 1 85798 Gollancz
978 0 752 First Time Authors Fiction; Oriel
978 0 7528 Orion Fiction; Orion Media
978 0 7538 Phoenix Mass Market
978 1 84212 Phoenix Press
978 1 84255, 978 1 85881 Orion Children's
978 1 85797 Orion
978 1 89758 Phoenix House

Parent Company:
France: Hachette Livre

Associated Companies:
Cassell plc; J M Dent Ltd; Victor Gollancz; Littlehampton Book Services Ltd; Orion Books Ltd; George Weidenfeld and Nicolson Ltd

Distributor for:
Peter Halban Publishers

Overseas Representation:
Australia: Hachette Livre Australia (Orion Division), Sydney, NSW
Austria, Belgium, Cyprus, France, Germany, Greece, Italy, Luxembourg, Netherlands, Portugal, Spain & Switzerland: Kim Tyler, The Orion Publishing Group Ltd, London, UK
Canada: McArthur & Co Publishers Ltd, Toronto, Ont
Caribbean: Chris Humphrys, Humphrys Roberts Associates, London, UK
Eastern Europe: Csaba & Jackie Lengyel de Bagota, Budapest, Hungary
India: Hachette Livre India, New Delhi
New Zealand: Hachette Livre New Zealand (Orion Division), Auckland
Philippines, Korea & Taiwan: Ralph & Sheila Summers, Woodford Green, Essex, UK
Scandinavia, Middle East, Turkey, Malta & Russia: Jennie McCann, The Orion Publishing Group Ltd, London, UK
South Africa: Jonathan Ball Publishers (Pty) Ltd, Johannesburg
South Africa, USA, Far East, South East Asia, India & Pakistan: Michael Goff, The Orion Publishing Group Ltd, London, UK
South America: Terry Roberts, Humphrys Roberts Associates, Cotia SP, Brazil

2575

OSPREY PUBLISHING LTD
Midland House, West Way, Botley, Oxford OX2 0PH
Telephone: 01865 727022
Fax: 01865 727017
Email: info@ospreypublishing.com
Web Site: http://www.ospreypublishing.com

Distribution:
Grantham Book Services,
Isaac Newton Way,
Alma Park Industrial Estate, Grantham, Lincs NG31 9SD
Telephone: 01476 541080
Fax: 01476 541061
Email: orders@gbs-tbs-ltd.co.uk

Directors: Rebecca Smart (Managing)
  Chris Tinsley (Financial Controller)
  Joanna Sharland (Rights)
Chairman: Philip Sturrock

Aviation; History & Antiquarian; Military & War

New Titles: 125 (2007) , 125 (2008)
Annual Turnover: £5.6M

ISBNs, Imprints & Series:
978 0 85045, 978 1 84176, 978 1 84603, 978 1 85532

Overseas Representation:
Australia: Capricorn Link (Australia) Pty Ltd, Windsor, NSW
Benelux, Austria, Germany & Switzerland: Robbert J. Pleysier, Heerde, Netherlands
Caribbean & Latin America: Humphrys Roberts Associates, London, UK
Eastern Europe: Tony Moggach, London, UK
Far East: Ashton International Marketing Services, Sevenoaks, Kent, UK
Greece, Italy & France: Sandro Salucci, Florence, Italy
Middle East: Peter Ward Book Exports, London, UK
New Zealand: David Bateman Ltd, Auckland
Scandinavia: Katie McNeish, East Sussex, UK
Spain, Portugal & Gibraltar: Iberian Book Services, Madrid, Spain
USA: Random House Publishing Services, New York, NY

2576

OUTSELL INC / EPS
[formerly Electronic Publishing Services]
26 Rosebery Avenue, London EC1R 4SX
Telephone: (020) 7837 3345
Fax: (020) 7837 8901
Email: dworlock@outsellinc.com
Web Site: http://www.outsellinc.com

Electronic (Professional & Academic)

Book Trade Association Membership:
Publishers Association

2577

OVOLO PUBLISHING LTD
1 The Granary, Brook Farm, Ellington, Huntingdon, Cambs PE28 0AE
Telephone: 01480 891777
Fax: 01480 893836
Email: info@ovolobooks.co.uk
Web Site: http://www.ovolobooks.co.uk

Managing Director: Mark Neeter
Marketing Manager: Michelle Thorn

Architecture & Design; Do-It-Yourself; Music

New Titles: 7 (2007) , 8 (2008)
No of Employees: 6
Annual Turnover: £600,000

Distributor for:
UK: Centaur Books; Waterways World Books

Book Trade Association Membership:
IPG

2578

*PETER OWEN PUBLISHERS
73 Kenway Road, London SW5 0RE
Telephone: (020) 7373 5628 & 7370 6093
Fax: (020) 7373 6760
Email: admin@peterowen.com
Web Site: http://www.peterowen.com

Trade Counter & Warehouse:
Central Books, 99 Wallis Road, London E9 5LN
Telephone: (020) 8986 4854
Fax: (020) 8533 5821
Email: orders@centralbooks.com
Web Site: http://www.centralbooks.com

Directors: Peter Owen (Managing)
  Antonia Owen (Editorial)
Managers: Nick Pearson (Production)
  Michael O'Connell (Sales & Publicity)
  Simon Smith (Rights & Editorial)
Marketing Co-ordinator: Kit Maude (Publicity)

Biography & Autobiography; Cinema, Video, TV & Radio; Fashion & Costume; Fiction; Gay & Lesbian Studies; History & Antiquarian; Literature & Criticism; Music; Theatre, Drama & Dance

ISBNs, Imprints & Series:
978 0 7206 Peter Owen Modern Classics

Overseas Representation:
Australia: Peribo Pty Ltd, Mount Kuring-Gai, NSW
Canada: Scholarly Book Services Inc, Toronto
Europe, Scandinavia & Iceland: Books for Europe, Massagno, Switzerland
New Zealand: Addenda Ltd, Grey Lynn
South Africa: Stephan Phillips (Pty) Ltd, Cape Town
USA: Dufour Editions Inc, Chester Springs, PA

Book Trade Association Membership:
IPG

2579

OXBOW BOOKS
10 Hythe Bridge Street, Oxford OX1 2EW
Telephone: 01865 241249
Fax: 01865 794449
Email: oxbow@oxbowbooks.com
Web Site: http://www.oxbowbooks.com

Managing Director: David Brown
Finance: Jane Lovell
Editorial: Clare Litt
Marketing: Eleanor Hooker
Sales: James Dickson
Production: Val Lamb

Academic & Scholarly; Archaeology; Biography & Autobiography; Fashion & Costume; History & Antiquarian; Literature & Criticism; Natural History; Nautical; Sociology & Anthropology; Classical Studies; Egyptology; Medieval Studies

New Titles: 70 (2007) , 50 (2008)

ISBNs, Imprints & Series:
978 0 85668 Aris & Phillips
978 0 946897, 978 1 84217, 978 1 900188 Oxbow Books
978 0 9545575, 978 1 905119 Windgather Press

Distributor for:
American Numismatic Society; American School of Classical Studies in Athens; American School of Prehistoric Research; American Schools of Oriental Research; American Society of Papyrologists; Antiquity Publications; Archaeological Institute of America; Aris and Phillips; Armatura Press; Association for Study of Travel in Egypt & the Near East; Australian Centre for Egyptology; British Academy [Backlist titles]; British Institute in East Africa; The British Institute of Archaeology at Ankara; British Museum Press Scholarly Titles; The British School at Rome; British School of Archaeology in Iraq; Francis Cairns Publications; Cambridge Philological Society; Celtic Studies Publications; Center for Old World Archaeology & Art; Classical Press of Wales; Cotsen Institute of Archaeology at UCLA; Council for British Research in the Levant; Czech Institute of Archaeology; Edinburgh University, Dept of Archaeology; Egypt Exploration Society; Gibb Memorial Trust; Griffith Institute of Oxford University; Halgo; Illuminata Publishers; Institute for Aegean Prehistory Academic Press; Institute for Mesoamerican Studies; Institute of Classical Archaeology; International Monographs in Prehistory; Journal of Juristic Papyrology; Kelsey Museum of Archaeology; The Khalili Collections; Legenda; Maney Publishing [heritage titles]; McDonald Institute for Archaeological Research; Museum of Fine Arts, Boston; Museum of London Archaeology Service; National Heritage Board of Sweden; Ocarina Books; Orcadian Books [archaeology titles]; Oriental Institute Chicago; Oxford Archaeology; Oxford Centre for Maritime Archaeology; Oxford University School of Archaeology; Society of Antiquaries of London; Spire Books; St George's Chapel, Windsor; University of Iceland Press; Wessex Archaeology; Western Academic & Specialist Press; Windgather Press; Yale Egyptological Seminar; York University, Dept of Archaeology
Albania: Centre for Albanian Archaeology
Australia: Macmillan Art Publishers
Belgium: Citeaux
Colombia: Pro Calima Foundation
Denmark: Viking Ship Museum, Roskilde

Greece: Ekdotike Athenon; Institute for Philosophical Research
Israel: Israel Antiquities Authority
Poland: Akanthina
Sweden: Riksantikvarieambetet; Societas Archaeologica Upsaliensis
Turkey: Homer Kitabevi
USA: Eliot Werner Publications; Gorgias Press; Regatta Press

Overseas Representation:
Far East (excluding Japan) & South East Asia: Chris Ashdown, Publishers International Marketing, Los Angeles, CA, USA
Germany, Netherlands & Belgium: Roy de Boo, Continental Contacts, Hooge Mierde, Netherlands
Italy & Greece: Flavio Marcello Publishers' Agents & Consultants, Padua, Italy
Middle East: Ray Potts, Publishers International Marketing, Sutton St Nicholas, Herefordshire, UK
Scandinavia: Jan Norbye, Ølstykke, Denmark
Spain, Portugal & Gibraltar: Peter Prout, Iberian Book Services, Madrid, Spain
USA & Canada: The David Brown Book Co, Oakville, CT, USA

Book Trade Association Membership:
BA; IPG; American Booksellers Association

2580

OXFAM PUBLISHING
Oxfam House, John Smith Drive, Cowley, Oxford OX4 2JY
Telephone: 01865 473727
Fax: 01865 472393
Email: publish@oxfam.org.uk
Web Site: http://www.oxfam.org.uk/publications.html

Warehouse:
BEBC Distribution, PO Box 1496, Parkstone, Dorset BH12 3YD
Telephone: 01202 712933
Fax: 01202 712930
Email: oxfam@bebc.co.uk

Sales & Marketing Manager: Robert Cornford
Promotions Executive: Jennie Morant
Managing Editor: Claire Harvey

Academic & Scholarly; Agriculture; Children's Books; Economics; Educational & Textbooks; Electronic (Educational); Environment & Development Studies; Gender Studies; Politics & World Affairs

New Titles: 12 (2007), 12 (2008)
No of Employees: 15
Annual Turnover: £400,000

ISBNs, Imprints & Series:
978 0 85598 Oxfam Publications
978 1 870727 Oxfam Education

Overseas Representation:
All other territories: BEBC Distribution, Parkstone, UK
Australia & New Zealand: InBooks, Frenchs Forest, NSW, Australia
Bangladesh: Midas, Dhaka
Canada: Renouf Publishing Co Ltd, Ottawa, Ont
Caribbean: Ian Randle Publishers Ltd, Kingston, Jamaica
Egypt: The Middle East Readers Information Center, Cairo
Eritrea: The Red Sea Press Inc, Asmara
Ethiopia: T.G.B. Roman Trading Enterprise, Addis Ababa
Germany: Missing Link International Booksellers, Bremen; Triops - Tropical Scientific Books, Darmstadt
Ghana: EPP Books Services Ltd, Accra
India: Maya Publishers Pvt Ltd, New Delhi
Kenya: Legacy Books & Distributors, Nairobi
Lebanon: Co-operative for Research & Training on Development, Beirut
Malawi: Anglia Book Distributors Ltd, Blantyre
Malaysia: MDC Book Distribution, Kuala Lumpur
Mongolia: Nomin House Co Ltd, Ulaanbaatar
Nepal: Everest Media International, Kathmandu
Nigeria: EPP Books, Lagos
Rwanda: Bookshop Ikirezi, Kigali
Singapore: Select Books Pte Ltd
South Africa, Botswana, Swaziland, Lesotho, Mozambique & Namibia: Anglia Book & Freight Consolidator, Knysna, South Africa
Switzerland: Münstergass-Buchhandlung, Berne
Tanzania: Mkuki na Nyota Publishers, Dar es Salaam
Thailand: Booknet Co Ltd, Bangkok
Uganda: Fountain Publishers Ltd, Kampala
USA: Stylus Publishing LLC, Herndon, VA
Zambia: Prestige Books, Lusaka
Zimbabwe: Prestige Books, Harare

Book Trade Association Membership:
IPG

2581

OXFORD UNIVERSITY PRESS
Great Clarendon Street, Oxford OX2 6DP
Telephone: 01865 556767
Fax: 01865 267746
Email: webenquiry@oup.com
Web Site: http://www.oup.com

Academic & Scholarly; Children's Books; Educational & Textbooks; Electronic (Professional & Academic); Law; Medical (incl. Self Help & Alternative Medicine); Religion & Theology; Trade

Book Trade Association Membership:
Publishers Association

2582

PACKARD PUBLISHING LTD
Forum House, Stirling Road, Chichester, West Sussex PO19 7DN
Telephone: 01243 537977
Fax: 01243 537977
Email: info@packardpublishing.co.uk
Web Site: http://www.packardpublishing.com

Director: Michael Packard *(Managing, Sales, Rights & Permissions)*

Academic & Scholarly; Agriculture; Architecture & Design; Biology & Zoology; Educational & Textbooks; Environment & Development Studies; Gardening; Geography & Geology; Languages & Linguistics; Music; Natural History; Reference Books, Directories & Dictionaries; Scientific & Technical; Sports & Games

New Titles: 2 (2007), 8 (2008)

ISBNs, Imprints & Series:
978 0 906527, 978 1 85341 Packard
978 0 948690 Packard (Arabic titles)

Distributor for:
Lebanon: Librairie du Liban
USA: Carolina Biological Supply Co Inc (Biology Readers only); Stipes Publishing LLC

Overseas Representation:
North America: Stipes Publishing LLC, Champaign, IL, USA

2583

PALGRAVE MACMILLAN
Houndmills, Basingstoke, Hants RG21 6XS
Telephone: 01256 329242
Fax: 01256 479476
Web Site: http://www.palgrave.com

Warehouse, Trade Enquiries & Orders:
Macmillan Distribution (MDL), Brunel Road, Houndmills, Basingstoke, Hants RG21 6XS
Telephone: 01256 329242
Fax: 01256 840154
Email: mdl@macmillan.co.uk

Chairman: Annette Thomas
Directors: D. J. G. Knight *(Managing)*
S. Burridge *(Publishing, Scholarly & Reference)*
M. Hewinson *(Publishing, College)*
D. Bull *(Publishing, Journals)*
L. Keelan *(Sales)*
V. Capstick *(Marketing)*
Finance: R. H. Hartgill
Operations: J. W. Peacock

Academic & Scholarly; Accountancy & Taxation; Biology & Zoology; Chemistry; Computer Science; Economics; Educational & Textbooks; Electronic (Educational); Engineering; Environment & Development Studies; Gender Studies; Geography & Geology; History & Antiquarian; Industry, Business & Management; Languages & Linguistics; Law; Literature & Criticism; Mathematics & Statistics; Medical (incl. Self Help & Alternative Medicine); Philosophy; Physics; Politics & World Affairs; Psychology & Psychiatry; Reference Books, Directories & Dictionaries; Religion & Theology; Scientific & Technical; Sociology & Anthropology; Theatre, Drama & Dance; Vocational Training & Careers

New Titles: 1068 (2007), 1125 (2008)

ISBNs, Imprints & Series:
978 0 333, 978 1 4039

Parent Company:
Macmillan Ltd

Associated Companies:
Macmillan Children's Books; Macmillan Education; Macmillan Publishers Ltd; Pan Macmillan Ltd; Stockton Press Ltd
USA: Stockton Press Inc

Distributor for:
Bedford; W. H. Freeman; Sinauer Associates; Spectrum; University Science Books; Worth Publishers

Overseas Representation:
Africa (excluding areas listed): Africa Dept, Palgrave Macmillan Ltd, Basingstoke, Hants, UK
Australia: Palgrave Macmillan, South Yarra, Vic
Austria & Germany: Katrin Lilienthal, Frankfurt-am-Main, Germany
China: Frank Xu, Macmillan c/o FLTRP, Beijing, P. R. of China
Colombia: Grupo K-T-Dra Ltda, Santa Fe de Bogota
Denmark, Norway, Finland, Sweden & Iceland: Steve Haslemere, Colin Flint Ltd, Publishers Scandinavian Consultancy, Cambridge, UK
East Asia (including Hong Kong, Philippines, Thailand, Vietnam & Indonesia): Steve Maginn, Palgrave Macmillan, Macmillan Publishers (China) Ltd, Hong Kong
Eastern Europe: Janet Levinson, Warsaw, Poland
Egypt: Ali Abdul Wahab, Macmillan Publishers Egypt Ltd, Cairo
Ethiopia: Meskerem Demeke, Addis Ababa
Europe (excluding areas listed): European Dept, Palgrave Macmillan Ltd, Basingstoke, Hants, UK
Ghana: Unimax Publishers Ltd, Accra-North
Greece & Cyprus: Zitsa Seraphimidi, Faliro, Greece
India: Ajit De, Calcutta; Kalpana Shukla, Palgrave Macmillan, New Delhi; V. Ravi, Palgrave Macmillan, Chennai; Sunil Sharma, New Delhi; Anand Vithalkar, Mumbai
Iran: Sepehr Bookshop, Tehran
Italy: David Pickering, Mare Nostrum Publishing Consultants, Rome
Japan: Palgrave Macmillan Ltd, Basingstoke, Hants, UK
Jordan: Jaqueline Sabri, Amman
Kenya: Macmillan Kenya (Publishers) Ltd, Nairobi
Korea: Jinsoo Yoon, Macmillan Publishers, Jongro-Gu, Seoul, Korea, South
Latin America, Caribbean & all other areas: Palgrave Macmillan Ltd, Basingstoke, Hants, UK
Lebanon: Faisal Mreish, Beirut
Malaysia: UBSD Distribution Sdn Bhd, Selangor
Middle East (excluding areas listed): Middle Eastern Dept, Palgrave Macmillan Ltd, Basingstoke, Hants, UK
Netherlands, Belgium, Luxembourg, France & Switzerland: Anne Georges, Brussels, Belgium
New Zealand: Vicki Johnson, Macmillan Publishers New Zealand Ltd, Albany, Auckland
Nigeria: Macmillan Nigeria Publishers Ltd, Yaba - Lagos
Pakistan: Book Bird Publishers Representatives, Lahore
Singapore & Brunei: Pansing Distribution Sdn Bhd, Singapore
Southern Africa (including Botswana, Lesotho & Swaziland): Cory Voigt, Palgrave Macmillan, Johannesburg, South Africa
Spain: Trinidad Lopez, Madrid
Taiwan: Wendy Wu, Macmillan Education, Taipei
Tanzania: Macmillan Aidan Ltd, Dar es Salaam
Uganda: Macmillan Uganda Ltd, Kampala
United Arab Emirates: Ali Basim, Macmillan Education Dubai, Dubai, UAE
USA: Palgrave Macmillan, New York, NY

Book Trade Association Membership:
Publishers Association; CAPP; BDPA; STM

2584

*PALLAS ATHENE
42 Spencer Rise, London NW5 1AP
Telephone: (020) 7692 9984
Email: afw@pallasathene.co.uk
Web Site: http://www.pallasathene.co.uk

Trade Enquiries & Orders:
Marston Book Services, 160 Milton Park, Abingdon, Oxon OX14 9SD

President & Publisher: Alexander Fyjis-Walker

Architecture & Design; Fine Art & Art History; Gardening; Guide Books; Travel & Topography

ISBNs, Imprints & Series:
978 0 9529986 Pallas Athene Arts
978 1 84368
978 1 873429 Pallas Guides

Overseas Representation:
USA: Trafalgar Square Publishing / IPG, Chicago, IL

2585

PAN MACMILLAN
20 New Wharf Road, London N1 9RR
Telephone: (020) 7014 6000
Fax: (020) 7014 6001
Email: books@macmillan.co.uk
Web Site: http://www.panmacmillan.com

Warehouse, Trade Enquiries & Orders:
Macmillan Distribution (MDL), Houndmills, Basingstoke, Hants RG21 6XS
Telephone: 01256 329242

Fax: 01256 840154
Email: mdl@macmillan.co.uk

Directors: Anthony Forbes Watson
(Managing)
Annette Thomas *(Chief Executive Officer, Macmillan Publishers Ltd)*
Emma Hopkin *(Managing, Macmillan Children's Books)*
Ian Metcalfe *(Financial)*
Anna Bond *(UK Sales)*
Aimee Roche *(International Sales)*
Chris Gibson *(Production)*
Geoff Duffield *(Sales & Marketing)*
Camilla Elworthy *(Publicity)*
Fiona Carpenter *(Art & Design)*
Imogen Taylor *(Editorial, Fiction)*
Peter Lavery *(Editorial, Fiction)*
Ursula Doyle *(Editorial, Picador)*
Maria Rejt *(Publishing - Macmillan, Pan, Picador)*
Jeremy Trevathan *(Publishing - Macmillan, Pan)*
Georgina Morley *(Editorial, Non-Fiction)*
Margaret Halton *(Rights)*

Biography & Autobiography; Children's Books; Cinema, Video, TV & Radio; Fiction; Gardening; Guide Books; Health & Beauty; History & Antiquarian; Literature & Criticism; Science Fiction; Sports & Games; Travel & Topography

New Titles: 772 (2007), 839 (2008)

ISBNs, Imprints & Series:
978 0 230 Macmillan Children's Books; Tor; Macmillan
978 0 283 Sidgwick & Jackson
978 0 330 Pan; Picador
978 0 333 Campbell
978 0 752 Boxtree

Parent Company:
Macmillan Ltd

Associated Companies:
Boxtree Ltd; Macmillan Children's Books; Macmillan Education; Macmillan Publishers Ltd; Palgrave Macmillan; Pan Books Ltd; Sidgwick & Jackson Ltd

Overseas Representation:
All other areas - send orders to: International Department, Pan Macmillan, Basingstoke, UK
Australia: Pan Macmillan (Australia) Pty Ltd, Sydney, NSW
Canada: H. B. Fenn & Co Ltd, Bolton, Ont
Hong Kong: Publishers' Associates Ltd
India: Pan Macmillan, New Delhi
Japan: Shino Yasuda, Tokyo
New Zealand: Macmillan Publishers New Zealand Ltd, Albany, Auckland
Republic of Ireland: David Adamson, Dublin
South Africa, Botswana, Lesotho, Swaziland, Namibia & Zimbabwe: Pan Macmillan SA Pty Ltd, Hyde Park, South Africa
South East Asia: Pansing Distribution Sdn Bhd, Singapore
West Indies & Caribbean: Macmillan Education Ltd, Oxford, UK

Book Trade Association Membership:
Publishers Association

2586

PANAF BOOKS
75 Weston Street, London SE1 3RS
Telephone: 01234 340430
Fax: 0870 333 1196
Email: zakakembo@yahoo.co.uk
Web Site: http://www.panafbooks.com

Distribution:
Central Books, 99 Wallis Road, London E9 5LN
Telephone: (020) 8986 5463 & 0845 458 9911
Fax: 0845 458 9912

Distribution & Stockist:
Gardners Books, 1 Whittle Drive, Eastbourne BN23 6QH
Telephone: 01323 521555
Fax: 01323 525502 & 521666
Email: customercare@gardners.com

Production & Marketing:
19 Muirfield, Gt Denham, Bedford MK40 4FB
Telephone: 0870 333 1192 & 1194
Fax: 0870 333 1196
Email: zakakembo@yahoo.co.uk
Web Site: http://www.panafbooks.com

Publisher: S. S. Kakembo
Group Financial Adviser: Andrew Upton
Director: E. R. Kakembo
Sales: E. Nani-Kofi
Consultant: J. Milne

Academic & Scholarly; Biography & Autobiography; Politics & World Affairs; Sociology & Anthropology

ISBNs, Imprints & Series:
978 0 901787 Panaf; PGL – Autobiographies & Biographies Series

Parent Company:
Panaf Ltd

Overseas Representation:
East Africa (including Uganda, Kenya & Tanzania): Crane Publishers Ltd, Kampala, Uganda
Ghana: Hensteve Publications Ltd, Accra

2587

PAPADAKIS PUBLISHER
11 Shepherd Market, Mayfair, London W1J 7PG
Telephone: (020) 7823 2323
Email: alex@papadakis.net
Web Site: http://www.papadakis.net

Managing Director: Andreas Papadakis
Editors: Alexandra Papadakis
Sheila de Vallee

Architecture & Design; Cookery, Wines & Spirits; Fashion & Costume; Gardening; Natural History; Photography

ISBNs, Imprints & Series:
978 1 901092 New Architecture; Papadakis

Parent Company:
New Architecture Group Ltd

Overseas Representation:
Rest of World: John Rule Sales & Marketing, London, UK
USA: Antique Collectors Club, Wappinger Falls, NY

Book Trade Association Membership:
Publishers Association

2588

PATHFINDER BOOKS
120 Bethnal Green Road, London E2 6DG
Telephone: (020) 7613 3855
Fax: (020) 7613 3855
Email: admin@pathfinderbooks.co.uk
Web Site: http://www.pathfinderpress.com

Manager: J. Silberman

Academic & Scholarly; Economics; Gender Studies; History & Antiquarian; Military & War; Philosophy; Politics & World Affairs; Sociology & Anthropology

ISBNs, Imprints & Series:
978 0 87348 Pathfinder

Distributor for:
USA: Pathfinder Press

Overseas Representation:
Australia, Asia & Pacific: Pathfinder Press, Haymarket, NSW, Australia
Canada: Pathfinder Press Distribution, Toronto, Ont
Iceland: Pathfinder, Reykjavik
New Zealand: Pathfinder, Auckland
Sweden: Pathfinder, Hägersten
USA, Caribbean & Latin America: Pathfinder Press, New York, USA

2589

PAVILION
Anova Books, 10 Southcombe Street, London W14 0RA
Telephone: (020) 7605 1400
Fax: (020) 7605 1401
Email: lbrudenell@anovabooks.com
Web Site: http://www.anovabooks.com

Warehouse, Trade Orders & Enquiries:
HarperCollins, Glasgow
Telephone: 0141 306 3100
Fax: 0141 306 3767

Associate Publisher: Anna Cheifetz
Marketing & Publicity Manager: Laura Brudenell

Architecture & Design; Biography & Autobiography; Children's Books; Cinema, Video, TV & Radio; Cookery, Wines & Spirits; Fashion & Costume; Gardening; Health & Beauty; Music; Photography; Theatre, Drama & Dance; Travel & Topography

New Titles: 20 (2007), 20 (2008)

ISBNs, Imprints & Series: 978 1 86205

Parent Company:
Anova Books

Overseas Representation:
Australia: HarperCollins Publishers, Pymble, NSW
Belgium, France, Netherlands & Luxembourg: Anova Books, London, UK
Canada: Raincoast Books, Vancouver, BC
Caribbean, Mexico & Central America: Christopher Humphrys, Humphrys Roberts Associates, London, UK
Eastern Europe: Csaba Lengyel de Bagota, CLB Marketing Services, Budapest, Hungary
Far East: Julian Ashton, Ashton International Marketing Services, Sevenoaks, Kent, UK
Germany, Switzerland & Austria: Gabriele Kern Publishers Services, Frankfurt-am-Main, Germany
India: Mr Seshadri, Overleaf, New Delhi
Italy, Spain, Portugal & Greece: Penny Padovani, London, UK
New Zealand: HarperCollins (NZ) Ltd, Glenfield, Auckland
Pakistan: Tahir M. Lodhi, Lahore
Russia & Baltic States: Tony Moggach, InterMedia Americana (IMA) Ltd, London, UK
Scandinavia: Katie McNeish, McNeish Publishing Services, East Sussex, UK
Singapore & Malaysia: Pansing Distribution Sdn Bhd, Singapore
South Africa: Quartet Sales & Marketing, Northcliffe
South America: Terry Roberts, Humphrys Roberts Associates, Cotia SP, Brazil
USA: Independent Publishers Group (IPG), Chicago, IL

Book Trade Association Membership:
IPG

2590

*PAVILION CHILDREN'S BOOKS
Anova Books Ltd, 10 Southcombe Street, London W1Y 0RA
Telephone: (020) 7610 5291

Fax: (020) 7314 1598
Email: childrens@anovabooks.com
Web Site: http://www.anovabooks.com

Trade Enquiries:
HarperCollins Distribution, Campsie View, Westerhill Road, Bishopbriggs, Glasgow G64 2QT
Telephone: 0141 772 3200
Email: orders@harpercollins.co.uk

Publisher: Ben Cameron
Sales Director: Jonathan White
Rights Manager: Paul Fraser

Children's Books

ISBNs, Imprints & Series:
978 1 84138, 978 1 85561 Belitha Press
978 1 84347, 978 1 903174 Big Fish
978 1 84365, 978 1 85145, 978 1 85793, 978 1 86205 Pavilion Children's Books
978 1 84458 Chrysalis Children's Books
978 1 85602 David Bennett Books
978 1 903370 Learning World
978 1 903954, 978 1 904516 Zigzag

Parent Company:
Anova Books Ltd

Associated Companies:
Belitha Press; David Bennett Books; Big Fish; Learning World; Pavilion Books; Zigzag

2591

PAVILION PUBLISHING (BRIGHTON) LTD
Richmond House, Richmond Road, Brighton BN2 3RL
Telephone: 01273 623222
Fax: 01273 625526
Email: info@pavpub.com
Web Site: http://www.pavpub.com

Managers: Jo Sharrocks *(Publishing)*
Paul Somerville *(Marketing)*

Academic & Scholarly; Educational & Textbooks; Electronic (Professional & Academic); Medical (incl. Self Help & Alternative Medicine); Psychology & Psychiatry; Sociology & Anthropology; Health & Social Care

New Titles: 20 (2007), 25 (2008)
No of Employees: 30

ISBNs, Imprints & Series: 978 1 84196

2592

PC PUBLISHING
Keeper's House, Merton, Thetford, Norfolk IP25 6QH
Telephone: 01953 889900
Email: info@pc-publishing.com
Web Site: http://www.pc-publishing.com

Distribution:
Littlehampton Book Services, Faraday Close, Durrington, Worthing, West Sussex BN13 3RB
Telephone: 01903 828500
Fax: 01903 828625

Director: Philip Chapman *(Publisher)*

Music; Scientific & Technical; Computers

ISBNs, Imprints & Series:
978 1 870775, 978 1 906005

Parent Company:
UK: Music Technology Books Ltd

Overseas Representation:
Australia: Woodslane Pty Ltd, Warriewood, NSW
USA: O'Reilly Associates, Sebastopol, CA

2593

PCCS BOOKS LTD
2 Cropper Row, Alton Road, Ross-on-Wye
HR9 5LA
Telephone: 01989 763900
Fax: 01989 763901
Email: contact@pccs-books.co.uk
Web Site: http://www.pccs-books.co.uk

Editorial:
The Old Police House, Llangarron,
Ross-on-Wye HR9 6PT
Telephone: 01989 770270
Fax: 01989 770700
Email: pete@pccs-books.co.uk
Web Site: http://www.pccs-books.co.uk

Directors: Maggie Taylor-Sanders
Peter J. Sanders

*Academic & Scholarly; Gender Studies;
Medical (incl. Self Help & Alternative
Medicine); Psychology & Psychiatry;
Religion & Theology*

New Titles: 7 (2007), 10 (2008)
No of Employees: 7
Annual Turnover: £300,000

ISBNs, Imprints & Series:
978 1 898059 Critical Psychology Division
(Series); Incomplete Guides (Series);
PCCS Books; Person-Centred Approach
& Client-Centred Therapy Essential
Readers (Series); Primers Series; Rogers'
Therapeutic Conditions Series (Vols 1–4);
Steps in Counselling Series
978 1 906254

Book Trade Association Membership:
IPG

2594

PEARSON EDUCATION LTD
Edinburgh Gate, Harlow, Essex CM20 2JE
Telephone: 01279 623623
Fax: 01279 431059
Web Site: http://www.pearsoned.co.uk

*Academic & Scholarly; Educational &
Textbooks; Electronic (Professional &
Academic); Law*

Parent Company:
UK: Pearson Group

Book Trade Association Membership:
Publishers Association

2595

PEARSON EDUCATION OXFORD
[formerly Harcourt Education]
Halley Court, Jordan Hill, Oxford OX2 8EJ
Telephone: 01865 311366
Fax: 01865 314641
Email: enquiries@pearson.com
Web Site: http://www.heinemann.co.uk

*Educational & Textbooks; Electronic
(Professional & Academic)*

Parent Company:
UK: Pearson Group

Associated Companies:
UK: Ginn; Heinemann; Payne-Gallway;
Raintree; Rigby

Book Trade Association Membership:
Publishers Association

2596

PEN PRESS PUBLISHERS LTD
25 Eastern Place, Brighton BN2 1GJ
Telephone: 0845 108 0530
Fax: 01273 261434
Email: info@penpress.co.uk
Web Site: http://www.penpress.co.uk

Directors: Lynn Ashman
Grace Rafael
Arts Design: Jacqueline Abromet
Senior Editor: Linda Lloyd

*Biography & Autobiography; Children's
Books; Cookery, Wines & Spirits; Crime; Do-
It-Yourself; Educational & Textbooks;
Fiction; Gay & Lesbian Studies; Health &
Beauty; Humour; Industry, Business &
Management; Literature & Criticism; Magic
& the Occult; Medical (incl. Self Help &
Alternative Medicine); Military & War;
Music; Philosophy; Poetry; Politics & World
Affairs; Reference Books, Directories &
Dictionaries; Religion & Theology; Science
Fiction; Sports & Games; Theatre, Drama &
Dance; Travel & Topography*

New Titles: 97 (2007), 100 (2008)
No of Employees: 6

ISBNs, Imprints & Series:
978 1 900796, 978 1 904018, 978 1
904754, 978 1 905203, 978 1 906206,
978 1 906710

Book Trade Association Membership:
IPG; The Guild of Master Craftsmen

2597

THE PENGUIN GROUP (UK) LTD
80 Strand, London WC2R 0RL
Telephone: (020) 7010 3000
Fax: (020) 7010 6060
Email: ...@uk.penguingroup.com
Web Site: http://www.penguin.co.uk

Distribution Centre:
Penguin UK, Central Park, Rugby,
Warwickshire CV23 0WB
Telephone: 01788 514300

Also at:
Pearson Shared Services/Pearson Education,
Edinburgh Gate, Harlow, Essex CM20 2JE
Telephone: 01279 623102
Fax: 0870 850 5255
Email: veronica.reeve@pearsontc.co.uk

Chief Executive: John Makinson
Managing Directors: Helen Fraser
(Penguin)
Gary June *(Dorling Kindersley)*
Francesca Dow *(Puffin)*
Sally Floyer *(Frederick Warne)*
Tom Weldon *(Penguin General)*
Directors: Brian Landers *(Finance)*
Susan Taylor *(Human Resources)*
Peter Bowron *(Group Sales &
Distribution)*
Helena Peacock *(Legal)*
Simon Prosser *(Publishing – Hamish
Hamilton)*
Liz Allen *(Production)*
Tony Lacey *(Publishing – Viking)*
Juliet Annan *(Publishing – Fig Tree)*
Louise Moore *(Publishing – Michael
Joseph)*
Chantal Noel *(Rights – Penguin)*

*Academic & Scholarly; Antiques &
Collecting; Archaeology; Atlases & Maps;
Audio Books; Biography & Autobiography;
Children's Books; Cinema, Video, TV &
Radio; Cookery, Wines & Spirits; Crafts &
Hobbies; Crime; Do-It-Yourself; Fiction;
Gardening; Guide Books; Health & Beauty;
History & Antiquarian; Humour; Industry,
Business & Management; Literature &
Criticism; Medical (incl. Self Help &
Alternative Medicine); Military & War;
Music; Natural History; Philosophy;
Photography; Poetry; Politics & World
Affairs; Psychology & Psychiatry; Reference
Books, Directories & Dictionaries; Religion &
Theology; Travel & Topography*

ISBNs, Imprints & Series:
Joint ventures with BBC Paperbacks

978 0 14 Arkana; Ladybird; Penguin;
Penguin Audiobooks; Puffin
978 0 140 Allen Lane; Penguin Classics;
Penguin Music Classics; The Penguin
Press; Frederick Warne
978 0 241 Hamish Hamilton
978 0 670 Viking
978 0 7181 Michael Joseph

Associated Companies:
Dorling Kindersley Ltd; Hamish Hamilton
Ltd; Michael Joseph Ltd; Ladybird Books
Ltd [subsidiary of Penguin]; Rough
Guides; Ventura Publishing Ltd; Viking
Ltd; Frederick Warne (& Co) Ltd
Australia: Penguin Books Australia Ltd
Canada: Penguin Books Canada Ltd
New Zealand: Penguin Books (NZ) Ltd
USA: Penguin Putnam Inc

Distributor for:
Which; Wisden

Overseas Representation:
All other areas: Penguin International Sales,
London, UK
Australia: Penguin Books Australia Ltd,
Camberwell, Vic
Canada: Penguin Books Canada, Toronto,
Ont
France: Penguin France SA, Blagnac
Germany & Austria: Penguin Books
Deutschland GmbH, Frankfurt am Main,
Germany
India, Bangladesh, Sri Lanka & Nepal:
Penguin Books India, New Delhi, India
Italy: Penguin Italia srl, Corsico, Milan
Netherlands: Penguin Books Benelux BV,
Amsterdam
New Zealand: Penguin Books (New
Zealand) Ltd, Auckland
*Poland, Baltic States, Slovenia, Slovakia &
Ukraine:* Grazyna Soszynska, Poznan-
Baranowo, Poland
Singapore & Malaysia: Penguin Books
Singapore & Malaysia, Singapore
South Africa: Penguin Group SA, Rosebank
Spain & Portugal: Penguin Books SA,
Madrid, Spain
USA: Penguin Group USA, New York, NY

2598

PENTATHOL PUBLISHING
40 Gibson Street, Wrexham,
Wrexham County LL13 7NS

Owner/Chief Executive: Athol E. Cowen

Poetry

ISBNs, Imprints & Series: 978 1 8730

Book Trade Association Membership:
Publishers Association; BA

2599

*PHAIDON PRESS LTD
18 Regent's Wharf, All Saints Street,
London N1 9PA
Telephone: (020) 7843 1000
Fax: (020) 7843 1010
Web Site: http://www.phaidon.com

Orders:
Phaidon Customer Services
Telephone: (020) 7843 1234
Fax: (020) 7843 1111
Email: sales@phaidon.com
Web Site: http://www.phaidon.com

Warehouse:
Grove Lane, Marston Trading Estate, Frome,
Somerset BA11 4AT
Telephone: 01373 474710
Fax: 01373 474711
Web Site: http://www.phaidon.com

Directors: Andrew Price *(Chairman)*
James Booth-Clibborn *(International
Sales & Marketing)*

Amanda Renshaw *(Editorial)*
Paul Foster *(UK Sales)*
Emilia Terragni *(Editorial)*
Sue Medlicott *(Production)*
Jonathan Feinmesser *(Financial)*

*Academic & Scholarly; Architecture &
Design; Children's Books; Cinema, Video,
TV & Radio; Cookery, Wines & Spirits;
Fashion & Costume; Fine Art & Art History;
Illustrated & Fine Editions; Music;
Photography*

ISBNs, Imprints & Series: 978 0 7148

Associated Companies:
France: Phaidon Sarl
Germany: Phaidon Verlag
Japan: Phaidon KK
USA: Phaidon Press Inc

Distributor for:
Electa Architecture

Overseas Representation:
Australia & New Zealand: Bookwise
International, Adelaide, SA, Australia
France: Phaidon SARL, Paris
Germany: Phaidon Verlag GmbH, Berlin
Other Territories: Phaidon Press Ltd,
London, UK
South Africa: Real Books CC, Auckland Park
USA: Phaidon Press Inc, New York, NY

2600

THE PHARMACEUTICAL PRESS
1 Lambeth High Street, London SE1 7JN
Telephone: (020) 7735 9141
Fax: (020) 7572 2509
Email: pharmpress@rpsgb.org
Web Site: http://www.pharmpress.com

Orders:
The Pharmaceutical Press, c/
o Turpin Distribution,
Stratton Business Park, Pegasus Drive,
Biggleswade, Beds SG18 8TQ
Telephone: 01767 604971
Fax: 01767 601640
Email: rps@turpin-distribution.com
Web Site: http://www.pharmpress.com

Representation (UK):
Compass Academic Ltd,
Barley Mow Centre,
10 Barley Mow Passage, London W4 4PH
Telephone: (020) 8994 6477
Fax: (020) 8400 6132
Email: ca@compass-academic.co.uk

Directors: C. Fry *(Managing, Publications)*
P. J. Weller *(Development)*
Managers: J. Wilson *(Production)*
J. Mulholland *(Licensing)*
J. Dargan *(Marketing)*
C. Watling *(Sales)*

*Academic & Scholarly; Electronic
(Professional & Academic); Medical (incl.
Self Help & Alternative Medicine); Scientific
& Technical; Veterinary Science*

New Titles: 29 (2007), 30 (2008)
No of Employees: 125
Annual Turnover: £20M

ISBNs, Imprints & Series: 978 0 85369

Parent Company:
The Royal Pharmaceutical Society of Great
Britain

Overseas Representation:
Australia: Australian Pharmaceutical
Publishing Co Ltd, Hawthorn;
Pharmaceutical Society of Australia,
Curtin
Canada: Login Bros Canada, Winnipeg,
Man
Germany, Austria & Switzerland: Deutscher
Apotheker Verlag, Stuttgart, Germany

Greece: J & L Watt, Paleo Faliro
Israel: Probook, Tel Aviv
Italy: David Pickering, Rome
Japan: Maruzen Co Ltd, Tokyo
Middle East: James & Lorin Watt Ltd, Publishing Consultants, Oxford, UK
New Zealand: Pharmaceutical Society of New Zealand, Wellington
Republic of Ireland: Brookside Publishing Services, Dublin
Scandinavia, Finland, Iceland & Baltic States: David Towle International, Stockholm, Sweden
South Africa: Pharmaceutical Society of South Africa, Pretoria
Spain & Portugal: Christina de Lara Ruiz, Madrid, Spain
USA: Pharmaceutical Press, Grayslake, IL

Book Trade Association Membership:
IGSMTP; Association of Learned & Professional Society Publishers

2601

PHILIP'S
2–4 Heron Quays, London E14 4JP
Telephone: (020) 7531 8427
Fax: (020) 7531 8474
Web Site: http://www.philips-maps.co.uk

Distribution:
Littlehampton Book Services,
Faraday Close, Durrington, West Sussex BN13 3RP
Telephone: 01903 828500
Fax: 01903 828625
Email: orders@lbsltd.co.uk
Web Site: http://www.lbsltd.co.uk

International Sales Department:
(as principal address)
Telephone: (020) 7644 6937
Fax: (020) 7644 6986
Email: wendy.graham@philips-maps.co.uk
Web Site: http://www.philips-maps.co.uk

Directors: Steven Edney *(UK Sales & Marketing)*
Victoria Dawbarn *(Rights & Contract Sales)*
Katherine Knowler *(Production)*
David Gaylard *(Mapping)*

Atlases & Maps; Educational & Textbooks; Natural History; Reference Books; Directories & Dictionaries; Astronomy; Globes

ISBNs, Imprints & Series: 978 0 540

Parent Company:
Octopus Publishing Group [part of Hachette Livre, France]

Overseas Representation:
Australia: Hachette Livre Australia, Sydney, NSW
Canada & USA: Scholarly Book Services Inc, Toronto, Canada
Caribbean & South America: David Williams, InterMedia Americana (IMA) Ltd, London, UK
Hong Kong: Asia Publishers Services Ltd
India: Octopus Publishing Group, New Delhi
Korea: Se-Yung Jun, Seoul, Korea, South
Middle East: Peter Ward Book Exports, London, UK
New Zealand: Hachette Livre New Zealand, Auckland
Philippines: Benjie Ocampo, Pasig City
Singapore & Malaysia: APD Singapore Pte Ltd, Singapore
South Africa: Penguin Books South Africa, Parklands

Book Trade Association Membership:
International Map Traders Association

2602

PIATKUS BOOKS
Little, Brown Book Group,
100 Victoria Embankment, London EC4Y 0DY
Telephone: (020) 7911 8030
Fax: (020) 7911 8100
Email: info@littlebrown.co.uk
Web Site: http://www.littlebrown.co.uk & http://www.piatkus.co.uk

Distribution:
Grantham Book Services,
Isaac Newton Way, Alma Industrial Estate, Grantham, Lincs NG31 9SD
Telephone: 01476 541000
Fax: 01476 541060

Directors: Gill Bailey *(Non-Fiction Editorial)*
Robert Manser *(UK Sales)*
Simon Colverson *(Production)*
Emma Dunford *(Fiction)*

Biography & Autobiography; Cookery, Wines & Spirits; Crime; Fiction; Gender Studies; Health & Beauty; History & Antiquarian; Humour; Industry, Business & Management; Magic & the Occult; Medical (incl. Self Help & Alternative Medicine); Military & War; Music; Psychology & Psychiatry; Sociology & Anthropology

ISBNs, Imprints & Series:
978 0 7499 Portrait Books
978 0 7499, 978 0 86188 Piatkus Books

Parent Company:
France: Hachette Livre
UK: Little, Brown Book Group

Overseas Representation:
Australia: Hachette Livre Australia, Sydney, NSW
Canada: Georgetown Warehouse, Toronto, Ont
New Zealand: Hachette Livre New Zealand, Auckland
Singapore & Malaysia: Pansing Distribution Sdn Bhd, Singapore
South Africa: Penguin Books SA (Pty) Ltd, Denver Ext 4

2603

PICCADILLY PRESS
5 Castle Road, London NW1 8PR
Telephone: (020) 7267 4492
Fax: (020) 7267 4493
Email: books@piccadillypress.co.uk
Web Site: http://www.piccadillypress.co.uk

Warehouse & Distribution:
Grantham Book Services,
Isaac Newton Way,
Alma Park Industrial Estate, Grantham, Lincs NG31 9SD
Telephone: 01476 541000
Fax: 01476 541060

Publisher & Managing Director: Brenda Gardner
UK Rights & Book Clubs: Lea Garton
Editorial/Commissioning: Ruth Williams
Anne Clark
Rights: Margot Edwards
Financial Controller: Geoffrey Lill
Publicity: Mary Byrne
Managers: Geoff Barlow *(Production)*
Robert Snuggs *(Sales)*
Assistant Editor: Melissa Patey
Publishing Assistant: Vivien Tesseras

Children's Books; Books for Parents

New Titles: 30 (2007), 30 (2008)

ISBNs, Imprints & Series:
978 1 84812, 978 1 85340

Overseas Representation:
Australia: Peribo Pty Ltd, Mount Kuring-Gai, NSW
Malaysia: Publishers Marketing Services, Petaling Jaya
New Zealand: c/o Piccadilly Press, London, UK
Singapore: Publishers Marketing Services Pte Ltd
Southern Africa: Trinity Books CC, Randburg, South Africa

Book Trade Association Membership:
IPG

2604

PICKERING & CHATTO (PUBLISHERS) LTD
21 Bloomsbury Way, London WC1A 2TH
Telephone: (020) 7405 1005
Fax: (020) 7405 6216
Email: info@pickeringchatto.co.uk
Web Site: http://www.pickeringchatto.com

Distribution & Orders:
Turpin Distribution Ltd,
Stratton Business Park, Pegasus Drive, Biggleswade, Beds SG18 8QT
Telephone: 01767 604800
Fax: 01767 601640
Web Site: http://www.turpin-distribution.com

Directors: James Powell
Lord Rees-Mogg *(Chairman)*
Editorial & Rights: Mark Pollard
David Heaton *(Production)*
Finance: Stephen Warren

Academic & Scholarly; Economics; History & Antiquarian; Literature & Criticism; Religion & Theology; Scientific & Technical

New Titles: 50 (2007), 60 (2008)
No of Employees: 11
Annual Turnover: £1.1M

ISBNs, Imprints & Series: 978 1 85196

Overseas Representation:
India: Applied Media, New Delhi
Japan: Japan Book Associates, Kyoto
Spain & Portugal: Iberian Book Services, Madrid, Spain
Taiwan: Unifacmanu Trading Co Ltd, Taipei
USA: Ashgate Publishing Co, Burlington, VT

Book Trade Association Membership:
IPG

2605

PIPERS' ASH LTD
Church Road, Christian Malford, Chippenham, Wiltshire SN15 4BW
Telephone: 01249 720563
Fax: 0870 056 8916
Email: pipersash@supamasu.com
Web Site: http://www.supamasu.com

Managing Director: A. Tyson
Secretary: Mrs A. M. Tyson

Biography & Autobiography; Children's Books; Fiction; Literature & Criticism; Philosophy; Poetry; Psychology & Psychiatry; Religion & Theology; Science Fiction; Sports & Games; Theatre, Drama & Dance

New Titles: 12 (2007), 15 (2008)

ISBNs, Imprints & Series:
978 1 902628, 978 1 904494 Biographies; Children's Libraries; Cornucopia; Kickstarters; Stagecraft; Trinity Collections

Overseas Representation:
Australia: Stephen Tyson, Sydney

New Zealand: Dr Yvonne Eve Walus, Auckland

2606

PIQUANT EDITIONS
4 Thornton Road, Carlisle, Cumbria CA3 9HZ
Telephone: 01228 525075
Email: info@piquant.net
Web Site: http://www.piquant.net

Representation (UK):
IVP, Norton Street, Nottingham NG7 3HR

Director: Pieter Kwant
Publisher & Editor: Elria Kwant
Sales & Operations Manager: Luke Lewis

Biography & Autobiography; Illustrated & Fine Editions; Religion & Theology

New Titles: 7 (2007), 7 (2008)
No of Employees: 2
Annual Turnover: £101,000

ISBNs, Imprints & Series:
978 1 903689 Fire and Blood series; Piquant Editions; Visibilia series

Overseas Representation:
USA: STL Inc, Waynesboro, GA

Book Trade Association Membership:
Publishers Association

2607

THE PLAYWRIGHTS PUBLISHING CO
70 Nottingham Road, Burton Joyce, Notts NG14 5AL
Telephone: 01159 313356
Email: playwrightspublishing@yahoo.com
Web Site: http://www.geocities.com/playwrightspublishingco

Proprietor: Liz Breeze
Consultant: Tony Breeze

Theatre, Drama & Dance

New Titles: 6 (2007), 6 (2008)
No of Employees: 2

ISBNs, Imprints & Series:
978 1 872758 Ventus Books
978 1 873130 Playwrights Publishing Co

Associated Companies:
Ventus Books

Distributor for:
Ventus Books

2608

PLOWRIGHT PRESS
PO Box 66, Warwick CV34 4XE
Telephone: 01926 499433
Fax: 01926 499433
Web Site: http://www.plowrightpress.co.uk

Director: Ruth Johns

Biography & Autobiography; Environment & Development Studies; Gender Studies; History & Antiquarian; Sociology & Anthropology

ISBNs, Imprints & Series:
978 0 907895, 978 0 951696, 978 0 954312, 978 0 955094 'Ordinary' Lives Series

Distributor for:
Family First Ltd; Ruth's Archive

Book Trade Association Membership:
IPG; Society of Authors

2609

PLUTO BOOKS LTD
345 Archway Road, London N6 5AA
Telephone: (020) 8374 2193
Fax: (020) 8348 9133
Email: pluto@plutobooks.com
Web Site: http://www.plutobooks.com

Trade Enquiries & Orders:
Marston Book Services,
Unit 160 Milton Park, Abingdon, Oxon
OX14 4SD
Telephone: 01235 465500
Fax: 01235 465555
Email: trade.orders@marston.co.uk
Web Site: http://www.marston.co.uk

Directors: Anne Beech *(Managing)*
Roger Van Zwanenberg *(Chair)*
Simon Liebesny *(Sales)*
Rights & Permissions: Gilly Duff
Managing Editor: Robert Webb
Marketing Manager: Melanie Patrick

Academic & Scholarly; Cinema, Video, TV & Radio; Economics; Environment & Development Studies; Gender Studies; Law; Literature & Criticism; Philosophy; Politics & World Affairs; Sociology & Anthropology

New Titles: 55 (2007), 55 (2008)
No of Employees: 12

ISBNs, Imprints & Series:
978 0 7453, 978 0 86104 Pluto Press
978 1 85172 Journeyman Press

Distributor for:
Autonomedia; Paradigm Publishers

Overseas Representation:
Australia: Palgrave Macmillan, Melbourne, Vic
Canada: Fernwood Books, Toronto, Ont
Germany (stock-holding distributor): Missing Link International Booksellers, Bremen, Germany
Germany, Austria, Switzerland, Scandinavia, Benelux, France, Italy, Greece, Malta, Central Europe & Baltic States: Andrew Durnell Marketing Ltd, Tunbridge Wells, UK
India: Maya Publishers Pvt Ltd, New Delhi
Japan: United Publishers Services Ltd, Tokyo
Middle East: International Publishers Representatives (IPR) Ltd, Nicosia, Cyprus
Republic of Ireland & Northern Ireland: Brookside Publishing Services, Dublin, Republic of Ireland
South Africa: Horizon Books, Plumstead
South East Asia: Taylor & Francis Asia Pacific, Kowloon, Hong Kong; Taylor & Francis Asia Pacific, Petaling Jaya, Malaysia; Taylor & Francis Asia Pacific, Beijing, P. R. of China; Taylor & Francis Asia Pacific, Singapore
Spain & Portugal: Iberian Book Services, Madrid, Spain
USA: University of Michigan Press, Ann Arbor, MI
USA (Orders): Perseus Distribution, Jackson, TN, USA

Book Trade Association Membership:
IPG

2610

THE POLICY PRESS
University of Bristol, Fourth Floor,
Beacon House, Queen's Road, Bristol
BS8 1QU
Telephone: 0117 331 4054
Fax: 0117 331 4093
Email: tpp-info@bris.ac.uk
Web Site: http://www.policypress.org.uk

Distribution:
Marston Book Services, PO Box 269,
Abingdon, Oxon OX14 4YN
Telephone: 01235 465500
Fax: 01235 465556
Email: direct.orders@marston.co.uk
Web Site: http://www.marston.co.uk/

UK Representation:
Compass Academic Ltd,
Barley Mow Centre,
10 Barley Mow Passage, Chiswick, London
W4 4PH
Telephone: (020) 8944 6477
Fax: (020) 8400 6132
Email: ca@compass-academic.co.uk
Web Site: http://www.academic.compass-booksales.co.uk

Directors: Alison Shaw
Julia Mortimer *(Assistant)*

Academic & Scholarly; Economics; Educational & Textbooks; Gender Studies; Politics & World Affairs; Sociology & Anthropology

ISBNs, Imprints & Series: 978 1 86134

Parent Company:
University of Bristol

Overseas Representation:
Australia, New Zealand & Papua New Guinea: DA Information Services Pty Ltd, Mitcham, Vic, Australia
Belgium, France, Netherlands & Luxembourg: Kemper Conseil Publishing, Voorburg, Netherlands
Germany, Switzerland & Austria: Missing Link International Booksellers, Bremen, Germany
India, Sri Lanka, Nepal, Bangladesh & Bhutan: Surit Mitra, Maya Publishers Pvt Ltd, New Delhi, India
Japan: Kinokuniya Co Ltd, Tokyo; Maruzen Co Ltd, Tokyo
Malaysia & Brunei: UBSD Distribution Sdn Bhd, Selangor, Malaysia
Norway, Denmark, Sweden, Finland & Iceland: Helena Svojsikova, University Presses Marketing, Bristol, UK
Republic of Ireland: Troika Independent Publishers' Services, London, UK
South Africa: Blue Weaver Marketing, Tokai
Spain, Portugal & Gibraltar: Iberian Book Services, Madrid, Spain
Taiwan: Unifacmanu Trading Co Ltd, Taipei
Thailand, Taiwan, Hong Kong, Korea, China, Singapore, Malaysia, Philippines & Vietnam: Tony Poh Leong Wah, Singapore, Singapore
USA & Canada: International Specialized Book Services Inc, Portland, OR, USA

Book Trade Association Membership:
IPG

2611

POLITY PRESS
65 Bridge Street, Cambridge CB2 1UR
Telephone: 01223 324315
Fax: 01223 461385
Email: editorial@polity.co.uk
Web Site: http://www.polity.co.uk

Distribution Warehouse:
John Wiley & Sons Ltd, 1 Oldlands Way,
Bognor Regis, Wrst Sussex PO22 9SA
Telephone: 01243 843294
Fax: 01243 843303
Email: cs-books@wiley.co.uk

Publicity:
Polity Press, 9600 Garsington Road, Oxford
OX4 2DQ
Telephone: 01865 476711
Fax: 01865 471711
Email: boconnor@wiley.com
Web Site: http://www.polity.co.uk

Directors: Anthony Giddens *(Editorial)*
David Held *(Editorial)*
John Thompson *(Editorial)*

Academic & Scholarly; Cinema, Video, TV & Radio; Educational & Textbooks; Gender Studies; History & Antiquarian; Literature & Criticism; Philosophy; Politics & World Affairs; Sociology & Anthropology

New Titles: 105 (2007), 77 (2008)
No of Employees: 17

ISBNs, Imprints & Series: 978 0 7456

Overseas Representation:
Australia: John Wiley & Sons Australia Ltd, Milton, Qld
Canada: John Wiley & Sons Canada Ltd, Etobicoke, Ont
Europe, Middle East & Africa: Karen Wootton, John Wiley & Sons Ltd, Chichester, UK
Germany: Wiley-VCH, Weinheim
Japan: Wiley Japan, Tokyo
Singapore: John Wiley & Sons (Asia) Pte Ltd
USA: John Wiley & Sons Inc, Hoboken, NJ

Book Trade Association Membership:
IPG

2612

PORTHILL PUBLISHERS
PO Box 311, Edgware, Middx HA9 9EA
Telephone: (020) 8958 6783
Fax: (020) 8905 4516

Director: Radomir Putnikovich
Secretary: Penelope Putnikovich

Children's Books; Fine Art & Art History; Humour

New Titles: 2 (2007), 2 (2008)
No of Employees: 4

ISBNs, Imprints & Series: 978 1 870732

2613

PORTICO
10 Southcombe Street, London W14 0RA
Telephone: (020) 7605 1400
Fax: (020) 7605 1401
Web Site: http://www.anovabooks.com

Warehouse, Trade Orders & Enquiries:
HarperCollins, Glasgow G64 2QT
Telephone: 0141 306 3100
Fax: 0141 306 3767

Associate Publisher: Tom Bromley
Marketing & Publicity: Helen Ponting

Humour; Languages & Linguistics; Music; Reference Books, Directories & Dictionaries; Sports & Games

New Titles: 25 (2007), 25 (2008)
No of Employees: 70

ISBNs, Imprints & Series: 978 1 9063

Parent Company:
Anova Books

Overseas Representation:
Australia: HarperCollins Publishers, Pymble, NSW
Belgium, France, Netherlands & Luxembourg: Ted Dougherty, London, UK
Caribbean, Mexico & Central America: Christopher Humphrys, Lynda Hopkins, Humphrys Roberts Associates, London, UK
Eastern Europe: Csaba Lengyel de Bagota, Jackie Lengyel de Bagota, CLB Marketing Services, Budapest, Hungary
Far East: Julian Ashton, Ashton International Marketing Services, Sevenoaks, Kent, UK
Germany, Switzerland & Austria: Gabriele Kern Publishers Services, Frankfurt-am-Main, Germany
India: Anova Books, London, UK
Italy, Spain, Portugal & Greece: Penny Padovani, Padovani Books Ltd, London, UK
Middle East: Peter Ward Book Exports, London, UK
New Zealand: HarperCollins (NZ) Ltd, Glenfield, Auckland
Pakistan: Tahir M. Lodhi, Lahore
Russia, Baltic States, Israel & Sub-Saharan Africa: Tony Moggach, InterMedia Americana (IMA) Ltd, London, UK
Scandinavia: Katie McNeish, McNeish Publishing Services, East Sussex, UK
Singapore: Pansing Distribution Sdn Bhd
South Africa: Quartet Sales & Marketing, Northcliffe
South America: Terry Roberts, Humphrys Roberts Associates, Cotia SP, Brazil
USA & Canada: Trafalgar Square Publishing, distributed by Independent Publishers Group, Chicago, IL, USA

Book Trade Association Membership:
IPG

2614

PORTLAND PRESS LTD
Commerce Way, Colchester CO2 8HP
Telephone: 01206 796351
Fax: 01206 799331
Email: editorial@portlandpress.com &
sales@portland-services.com
Web Site: http://www.portlandpress.com
& http://www.portland-services.com

Directors: Rhonda Oliver *(Managing)*
John Misselbrook *(Financial)*
Adam Marshall *(Marketing & Sales)*
John Day *(IT)*

Academic & Scholarly; Biology & Zoology; Educational & Textbooks; Electronic (Professional & Academic); Medical (incl. Self Help & Alternative Medicine); Reference Books, Directories & Dictionaries; Scientific & Technical

New Titles: 3 (2007), 3 (2008)
No of Employees: 55
Annual Turnover: £4.3M

ISBNs, Imprints & Series:
978 0 904498 Biochemical Society
978 1 85578, 978 1 85578 Portland Press

Parent Company:
The Biochemical Society

Distributor for:
Antiquity Publications Ltd; Bioscientifica Ltd; Channel View Publications; Earthscan; Energy Institute; Expert Information; International Water Association Publishing; The Policy Press; Practical Action Publishing; Professional Engineering Publishing; The Royal Society; Royal Society of Chemistry; Royal Society of Medicine; SCR Publishing; The Society for Endocrinology; Vathek Publishing; WEF Publishing

Overseas Representation:
Australia: DA Information Services Pty Ltd, Mitcham, Vic
India: Affiliated East-West Press Pvt Ltd, New Delhi
Japan: USACO Corporation, Tokyo

Book Trade Association Membership:
IGSMTP; IPG; Association of Learned & Professional Society Publishers; UK Serials Group

2615

PORTOBELLO BOOKS LTD
12 Addison Avenue, Holland Park, London
W11 4QR
Telephone: (020) 7605 1380

Fax: (020) 7605 1361
Email: mail@portobellobooks.com
Web Site: http://www.portobellobooks.com

Directors: David Graham *(Managing)*
Laura Barber *(Editorial)*
Tasja Dorkofikis *(Serial Rights)*
Pru Rowlandson *(Publicity)*
Brigid Macleod *(Sales)*
Publisher: Philip Gwyn Jones

Biography & Autobiography; Fiction; History & Antiquarian; Politics & World Affairs; Travel & Topography

New Titles: 23 (2007), 29 (2008)
No of Employees: 7
Annual Turnover: £600,000

ISBNs, Imprints & Series: 978 1 84627

Associated Companies:
UK: Granta

Overseas Representation:
Australia & New Zealand: Penguin Books Australia Ltd, Camberwell, Vic, Australia
Canada: PGC, Toronto, Ont
European Union & Far East: Pan Macmillan, London, UK
Netherlands: Nilsson & Lamm BV, Weesp
South Africa: Penguin Books South Africa (Pty) Ltd, Johannesburg

Book Trade Association Membership:
IPG; Independent Alliance

2616

POSITIVE PRESS LTD
28a Gloucester Road, Trowbridge, Wilts BA14 0AA
Telephone: 01225 719204
Fax: 01225 712187
Email: dankat@jennymosley.co.uk
Web Site: http://www.circle-time.co.uk

Managing Director: Jenny Mosley
Sales Account Manager: Danka Tadd

Children's Books; Educational & Textbooks

New Titles: 4 (2008)

ISBNs, Imprints & Series:
978 0 09540, 978 0 09545, 978 0 95301, 978 1 90460, 978 1 90486

Book Trade Association Membership:
BA

2617

PRESTEL PUBLISHING LTD
4 Bloomsbury Place, London WC1A 2QA
Telephone: (020) 7323 5004
Fax: (020) 7636 8004
Email: sales@prestel-uk.co.uk
Web Site: http://www.prestel.com

Warehouse, Trade Enquiries & Orders:
Macmillan Distribution Ltd, Brunel Road, Houndmills, Basingstoke, Hants RG21 6XS
Telephone: 01256 302692
Fax: 01256 812588
Email: orders@macmillan.co.uk

Managing Director: Andrew Hansen
Commissioning Editor (London): Philippa Hurd
Sales, Marketing & Publicity Executive: Anna Kenning
Key Accounts Manager: Oliver Barter

Antiques & Collecting; Archaeology; Architecture & Design; Children's Books; Cinema, Video, TV & Radio; Fashion & Costume; Fine Art & Art History; Gardening; Guide Books; Music; Photography; Sports & Games; Theatre, Drama & Dance; Travel & Topography

New Titles: 78 (2007), 94 (2008)

ISBNs, Imprints & Series:
978 0 9542079, 978 1 904563 Trolley
978 1 934772 Periscope Publishing Ltd
978 3 7658 Bucher
978 3 7913 Adventures in Art Series; Pegasus Series

Parent Company:
Germany: Prestel Verlag GmbH & Co KG

Associated Companies:
USA: Prestel Publishing

Overseas Representation:
Africa (excluding South Africa): Tony Moggach, InterMedia Americana (IMA) Ltd, London, UK
Asia (including China, Hong Kong, Korea, Philippines & Taiwan): Ed Summerson, Asia Publishers Services Ltd, Hong Kong
Australia: Peribo Pty Ltd, Mount Kuring-Gai, NSW
Canada: Canadian Manda Group, Toronto, Ont
France: Interart SARL, Paris
Iran: Book City, Tehran
Israel: Lonnie Kahn & Co Ltd, Rishon Lezion
Malta, Cyprus, Turkey, Middle East & North Africa: Peter Ward Book Exports, London, UK
Netherlands & Belgium: Nilsson & Lamm BV, Weesp, Netherlands
Scandinavia: Elisabeth Harder-Kreimann, Hamburg, Germany
South & Central America: David Williams, InterMedia Americana (IMA) Ltd, London, UK
South Africa, South East Asia & Japan: Andrew Hansen, Prestel, London, UK
Southern Europe: Books for Europe, Massagno, Switzerland
Switzerland: Buchzentrum AG, Hägendorf
USA: Prestel Publishing, New York, NY

2618

*MATHEW PRICE LTD
The Old Glove Factory, Bristol Road, Sherborne, Dorset DT9 4HP
Telephone: 01935 816010
Fax: 01935 816310
Email: mathewp@mathewprice.com

UK Sales:
The Manning Partnership, 6 The Old Dairy, Melcombe Road, Bath BA2 3LR
Telephone: 01225 478444
Fax: 01225 478440
Email: sales@manning-partnership.co.uk

Chairman: Mathew Price

Children's Books; Philosophy

ISBNs, Imprints & Series:
978 0 84248 Mathew Price Ltd
978 0 948867 Meher Baba Books

2619

PRINCETON UNIVERSITY PRESS
6 Oxford Street, Woodstock, Oxon OX20 1TW
Telephone: 01993 814500
Fax: 01993 814504
Email: admin@pupress.co.uk
Web Site: http://www.pup.princeton.edu

Publishing Director - Europe: Richard Baggaley
Publicity & Marketing Manager: Caroline Priday
Senior Editor: Ian Malcolm

Academic & Scholarly; Economics; Industry, Business & Management; Philosophy; Politics & World Affairs; Sociology & Anthropology

ISBNs, Imprints & Series: 978 0 691

Parent Company:
USA: Princeton University Press

Overseas Representation:
All other countries: Export Department, Princeton University Press, Ewing, NJ, USA
Continental Europe & Israel: Customer Service Operations, Princeton University Press, c/o John Wiley & Sons Ltd, Bognor Regis, UK

Book Trade Association Membership:
IPG

2620

PROFESSIONAL ENGINEERING PUBLISHING
1 Birdcage Walk, London SW1H 9JJ
Telephone: (020) 7304 6852
Fax: (020) 7304 6852
Email: peterw@pepublishing.com
Web Site: http://www.pepublishing.com

Directors: A. Singleton *(Publishing)*
Peter Williams *(Academic)*
Paul Williams *(Commercial)*
John Pullin *(Editorial)*
Managers: D. Fidler *(Systems Finance)*
M. Spencer *(Production)*
M. Lord *(Marketing & Development)*
R. Grimes *(Journals Publisher)*

Academic & Scholarly; Aviation; Computer Science; Engineering; Medical (incl. Self Help & Alternative Medicine); Nautical; Scientific & Technical; Transport

Parent Company:
Institution of Mechanical Engineers

Overseas Representation:
India: Allied Publishers Ltd, New Delhi
North, Central & South America: PP&F, Birmingham, AL, USA

Book Trade Association Membership:
Association of Learned & Professional Society Publishers; UK Serials Group (UKSG)

2621

*PROFILE BOOKS
3A Exmouth House, Pine Street, London EC1R 0JH
Telephone: (020) 7841 6300
Fax: (020) 7841 3969
Email: info@profilebooks.com
Web Site: http://www.profilebooks.com

Directors: Andrew Franklin *(Managing)*
Stephen Brough *(Editorial)*
Kate Griffin *(Marketing)*
Claire Beaumont *(Sales)*
Ruth Killick *(Publicity)*
Rights Manager: Penny Daniel *(Editorial & Rights)*
Publisher: Pete Ayrton
Publicity: Rebecca Gray

Biography & Autobiography; Fiction; History & Antiquarian; Industry, Business & Management; Politics & World Affairs

ISBNs, Imprints & Series:
The Economist Books; Profile Books; Serpent's Tail
978 1 86197

Overseas Representation:
Australia: Allen & Unwin Pty Ltd, Sydney, NSW
Canada: Renouf Publishing Co Ltd, Ottawa, Ont
Europe: Faber & Faber, London, UK
Hong Kong, China, Taiwan & Philippines: Asia Publishers Services Ltd, Hong Kong
India & Pakistan: Viva Books, New Delhi, India
Middle East, North Africa & Turkey: Peter Ward Book Exports, London, UK
Singapore, Malaysia, Thailand & Vietnam: APD Singapore Pte Ltd, Singapore
South Africa: Jonathan Ball Publishers (Pty) Ltd, Johannesburg
USA: Trafalgar Square Press

Book Trade Association Membership:
IPG

2622

PROQUEST
International Office, The Quorum, Barnwell Road, Cambridge CB5 8SW
Telephone: 01223 215512
Fax: 01223 215514
Email: marketing@proquest.co.uk
Web Site: http://www.proquest.co.uk

Sales: T. Robinson
General Manager & Vice-President Technology & Operations: J. Taylor
Marketing: S. Tilley

Academic & Scholarly; Accountancy & Taxation; Agriculture; Bibliography & Library Science; Biology & Zoology; Economics; Electronic (Educational); Electronic (Professional & Academic); History & Antiquarian; Literature & Criticism; Mathematics & Statistics; Medical (incl. Self Help & Alternative Medicine); Music; Physics; Poetry; Politics & World Affairs; Psychology & Psychiatry; Reference Books, Directories & Dictionaries; Religion & Theology; Scientific & Technical; Theatre, Drama & Dance

ISBNs, Imprints & Series: 978 0 85964

Parent Company:
USA: ProQuest

Overseas Representation:
Australia & New Zealand: ProQuest, Melbourne, Vic, Australia
China: ProQuest, Beijing, P. R. of China
Dubai: ProQuest, Dubai Media City, UAE
Europe: ProQuest, Cambridge, UK
Germany: ProQuest, Friedberg
Hong Kong: ProQuest, Wanchai
Italy: ProQuest, Florence
Japan: ProQuest, Yokohama
Korea, Taiwan, Philippines & Vietnam: ProQuest, Seoul, Korea, South
Latin America: ProQuest, Rio de Janeiro, Brazil
North America: ProQuest, Ann Arbor, MI, USA
South East Asia & Far East: ProQuest, Petaling Jaya, Malaysia
Spain: ProQuest España, Madrid

Book Trade Association Membership:
Publishers Association

2623

PROSPECT BOOKS
Allaleigh House, Blackawton, Totnes, Devon TQ9 7DL
Telephone: 01803 712269
Fax: 01803 712311
Email: tom.jaine@prospectbooks.co.uk
Web Site: http://www.prospectbooks.co.uk

Distribution:
Central Books, 99 Wallis Road, London E9 5LN
Telephone: (020) 8986 4854

Owner: Tom Jaine

Cookery, Wines & Spirits

New Titles: 8 (2007), 8 (2008)

2624

PUBLISHING HOUSE
Trinity Place, Barnstaple EX32 9HG

Telephone: 01271 328892
Fax: 01271 328768
Email: mail@vernoncoleman.com
Web Site: http://www.vernoncoleman.com

Publishing Director: Sue Ward

Fiction; Medical (incl. Self Help & Alternative Medicine); Politics & World Affairs

New Titles: 4 (2008)

ISBNs, Imprints & Series:
978 0 9503527, 978 1 898146 Chilton Designs
978 0 9521492, 978 1 898947 European Medical Journal
978 1 899726 Blue Books
978 1 904001 Great Fiction

2625

PUNK PUBLISHING LTD
3 The Yard, Pegasus Place, London SE11 5SD
Telephone: (020) 7820 9333
Email: sophie@punkpublishing.co.uk
Web Site: http://www.punkpublishing.com

Publisher: Jonathan Knight
Editor: Keith Didcock

Travel & Topography

New Titles: 4 (2007), 3 (2008)
No of Employees: 4

ISBNs, Imprints & Series: 978 0 9552036

Book Trade Association Membership:
IPG

2626

QUADRILLE PUBLISHING LTD
5th Floor, Alhambra House, 27–31 Charing Cross Road, London WC2H 0LS
Telephone: (020) 7839 7117
Fax: (020) 7839 7118
Email: enquiries@quadrille.co.uk

Directors: Alison Cathie *(Managing)*
Jane O'Shea *(Publishing)*
Vincent Smith *(Deputy Managing)*
Helen Lewis *(Creative)*
Managers: Ian West *(Sales)*
Clare Lattin *(Publicity)*
Melanie Gray *(International Sales)*

Cookery, Wines & Spirits; Crafts & Hobbies; Do-It-Yourself; Fashion & Costume; Gardening; Health & Beauty; Humour; Magic & the Occult; Medical (incl. Self Help & Alternative Medicine); Photography

New Titles: 33 (2008)
No of Employees: 35

ISBNs, Imprints & Series:
978 1 844000, 978 1 899988, 978 1 902757, 978 1 903845

Book Trade Association Membership:
BA

2627

QUARTET BOOKS
27 Goodge Street, London W1T 2LD
Telephone: (020) 7636 3992
Fax: (020) 7637 1866
Email: quartetbooks@easynet.co.uk

Warehouse:
NBN International, Estover Road, Plymouth PL6 7PZ
Telephone: 01752 202300
Fax: 01752 202330
Web Site: http://www.nbninternational.com

Director: David Elliott

Biography & Autobiography; Fiction; History & Antiquarian; Music

New Titles: 3 (2007), 20 (2008)
No of Employees: 3
Annual Turnover: £250,000

ISBNs, Imprints & Series:
978 0 86072 Robin Clark

Parent Company:
Namara Group

Associated Companies:
Robin Clark; The Women's Press

Overseas Representation:
Australia: Tower Books Pty Ltd, Frenchs Forest, NSW
Caribbean & South America: InterMedia Americana (IMA) Ltd, London, UK
France, Belgium, Germany, Austria, Switzerland, Italy & Greece: Ted Dougherty, London, UK
India, Denmark, Finland, Norway & Sweden: Quartet Books Ltd, London, UK
Japan: Japan/English Service Inc, Chiba-ken
Middle East: Peter Ward Book Exports, London, UK
Netherlands: Nilsson & Lamm BV, Weesp
New Zealand: Southern Publishers Group, Auckland
South Africa: Trinity Books CC, Randburg
Spain & Portugal: Iberian Book Services, Madrid, Spain
Sub-Saharan Africa (excluding South Africa) & Eastern Europe: InterMedia Americana (IMA) Ltd, London, UK
USA: Interlink Publishing Group Inc, Northampton, MA

2628

QUILLER PUBLISHING LTD
Wykey House, Wykey, Shrewsbury SY4 1JA
Telephone: 01939 261616
Fax: 01939 261606
Email: info@quillerbooks.com
Web Site: http:// www.countrybooksdirect.com

Warehouse, Distribution, Orders & Sales Enquiries:
Grantham Book Services, Isaac Newton Way, Alma Park Industrial Estate, Grantham, Lincolnshire NG31 9SD
Telephone: 01476 541080
Fax: 01476 541061
Email: orders@gbs.tbs-ltd.co.uk

Directors: Andrew Johnston *(Managing)*
John Beaton *(Editorial)*
Managers: Belle Cowie *(Marketing)*
Jonathan Heath *(Sales)*
Lesley Gowers *(Editorial)*

Animal Care & Breeding; Antiques & Collecting; Biography & Autobiography; Cookery, Wines & Spirits; Crafts & Hobbies; Fine Art & Art History; Gardening; Humour; Illustrated & Fine Editions; Military & War; Natural History; Nautical; Reference Books, Directories & Dictionaries; Sports & Games; Transport; Travel & Topography; Veterinary Science

New Titles: 35 (2008)

ISBNs, Imprints & Series:
978 0 901366, 978 1 872082, 978 1 872119, 978 1 905693 Kenilworth Press
978 0 907621, 978 1 84689, 978 1 904057 Quiller Press
978 0 948253 The Sportsman's Press
978 1 84037, 978 1 85310 Swan Hill Press

Distributor for:
USA: Half Halt Press; Stackpole Books [Hunting & Fishing Titles only]

Overseas Representation:
Australia: Peribo Pty Ltd, Mount Kuring-Gai, NSW
Europe & Scandinavia: Books for Europe, London, UK
Singapore: Fathima News Enterprise
South Africa: Trinity Books CC, Randburg
USA & Canada: Half Halt Press, Boonsboro, MD, USA; Stackpole Books Inc, Mechanicsburg, PA, USA

Book Trade Association Membership:
IPG

2629

QUINTESSENCE PUBLISHING CO LTD
Quintessence House, Grafton Road, New Malden, Surrey KT3 3AB
Telephone: (020) 8949 6087
Fax: (020) 8336 1484
Email: info@quintpub.co.uk
Web Site: http://www.quintpub.co.uk

Finance Manager: Mrs Susan Newbury

Medical (incl. Self Help & Alternative Medicine)

New Titles: 27 (2007), 30 (2008)
No of Employees: 8

ISBNs, Imprints & Series:
978 0 86715, 978 1 85097, 978 3 87632, 978 4 87417

Parent Company:
Germany: Quintessenz Verlag

Associated Companies:
Japan: Quintessence Publishing Co Ltd
USA: Quintessence Publishing Co Inc

Distributor for:
Germany: Quintessenz Verlags GmbH
Japan: Quintessence Publishing Co Ltd
USA: Quintessence Publishing Co Inc

Overseas Representation:
Australia: Martin Halas Dental Co Pty Ltd, Sydney
Brazil: Quintessence Editora Ltda, São Paulo

Book Trade Association Membership:
BA

2630

RACEFORM LTD
RFM House, Compton, Newbury, Berks RG20 6NL
Telephone: 01635 578080
Fax: 01635 578101
Email: julian.brown@racingpost.co.uk
Web Site: http://www.racingpost.co.uk/shop

Book Publishing Manager: Julian Brown

Sports & Games

New Titles: 35 (2007), 38 (2008)
No of Employees: 18

ISBNs, Imprints & Series:
978 1 904317, 978 1 905153 Raceform
978 1 905156 Highdown Books

Parent Company:
Racing Post

2631

*THE RADCLIFFE PRESS
6 Salem Road, London W2 4BU
Telephone: (020) 7243 1225
Fax: (020) 7243 1226

Distributor:
Macmillan Distribution Ltd, Brunel Road, Houndmills, Basingstoke, Hants RG21 6XS

Publisher: Lester Crook
Managers: Liz Stuckey *(Finance)*
Stuart Weir *(Production)*
Isabella Steer *(Rights)*
Martin Ashworth *(Sales)*
Paul Davighi *(Marketing)*
Nicole Ettinger *(Publicity)*
Liz Friend Smith *(Editor)*

Biography & Autobiography; History & Antiquarian; Military & War; Politics & World Affairs; Travel & Topography

ISBNs, Imprints & Series:
978 1 84511, 978 1 85043, 978 1 86064

Overseas Representation:
Australia: Palgrave Macmillan, South Yarra, Vic
USA: Palgrave Macmillan, New York, NY

2632

*RADCLIFFE PUBLISHING LTD
18 Marcham Road, Abingdon, Oxon OX14 1AA
Telephone: 01235 528820
Fax: 01235 528830
Email: contact.us@radcliffemed.com
Web Site: http://www.radcliffe-oxford.com

Directors: Andrew Bax *(Managing)*
Gillian Nineham *(Editorial)*
Margaret McKeown *(Financial)*
Managers: Jamie Etherington *(Editorial)*
Steve Bonner *(Production)*
Gregory Moxon *(Marketing)*

Educational & Textbooks; Electronic (Educational); Electronic (Professional & Academic); Industry, Business & Management; Medical (incl. Self Help & Alternative Medicine); Reference Books, Directories & Dictionaries; Scientific & Technical; Vocational Training & Careers

ISBNs, Imprints & Series:
978 1 84619, 978 1 85775, 978 1 870905

Overseas Representation:
Australia: Elsevier Australia, Marrickville, NSW
Eastern Europe: Dr László Horváth Publishers Representative, Budapest, Hungary
India, Bangladesh, Sri Lanka, Nepal & Pakistan: Jaypee Brothers Medical Publishers (Pte) Ltd, New Delhi, India
Middle East: International Publishing Services (IPS) Middle East Ltd, Dubai, UAE
Scandinavia: David Towle International, Stockholm, Sweden
Singapore, Malaysia, Thailand, Vietnam, Cambodia, Laos, Myanmar, Brunei, Indonesia, Philippines & Taiwan: Alkem Co (S) Pte Ltd, Singapore
USA: Martin P. Hill Consulting, New York, NY

2633

RAND PUBLICATIONS
5 Victoria House, 138 Watling Street East, Towcester NN12 6BT
Telephone: 01327 357770
Fax: 01327 359572
Email: rand@oppuk.co.uk
Web Site: http://www.rand.org

Warehouse & Distribution:
NBN International, Estover Road, Plymouth PL6 7PY
Telephone: 01752 202301
Fax: 01752 202331
Email: orders@nbninternational.com
Web Site: http:// www.nbninternational.com

Manager: Gary Hall

Academic & Scholarly; Economics; Educational & Textbooks; Military & War; Politics & World Affairs

New Titles: 100 (2007), 100 (2008)

ISBNs, Imprints & Series: 978 0 8330

Parent Company:
USA: Rand Publications

2634

RANDOM HOUSE CHILDREN'S BOOKS
61–63 Uxbridge Road, London W5 5SA
Telephone: (020) 8231 6800
Fax: (020) 8231 6767
Web Site: http://www.kidsatrandomhouse.co.uk

Children's Books

Book Trade Association Membership:
Publishers Association

2635

RANDOM HOUSE UK LTD
20 Vauxhall Bridge Road, London SW1V 2SA
Telephone: (020) 7840 8400
Fax: (020) 7233 8791
Web Site: http://www.randomhouse.co.uk

Children's Books; Trade

Parent Company:
UK: Random House Group Ltd

Associated Companies:
UK: Arrow; Jonathan Cape; Century; Chatto & Windus; Ebury; Everyman; Harvill Secker; William Heinemann; Hutchinson; Mainstream; Pimlico; Rider; Vermilion; Vintage; Yellow Jersey

Book Trade Association Membership:
Publishers Association

2636

RANSOM PUBLISHING LTD
51 Southgate Street, Winchester SO23 9EH
Email: jenny@ransom.co.uk
Web Site: http://www.ransom.co.uk

Directors: Jenny Ertle *(Managing)*
Stephen Rickard *(Publishing)*
Marketing Manager: Rebecca Pash

Children's Books; Educational & Textbooks; Electronic (Educational); Geography & Geology

New Titles: 41 (2007), 98 (2008)
No of Employees: 6
Annual Turnover: £250,000

ISBNs, Imprints & Series:
978 1 84167, 978 1 900127 321 Go!; Backstreet; Boffin Boy; Cutting Edge; Dark Man; Goal!; Siti's Sisters; Starchasers; Trailblazers

Book Trade Association Membership:
IPG

2637

RAVETTE PUBLISHING LTD
Unit 3, Tristar Centre, Star Road, Partridge Green, West Sussex RH13 8RA
Telephone: 01403 711443
Fax: 01403 711554
Email: ravettepub@aol.com

Warehouse, Invoicing & Accounts:
Orca Book Services, Stanley House, 3 Fleets Lane, Poole, Dorset BH15 3AJ
Telephone: 01202 665432

Fax: 01202 666219
Email: mail@orcabookservices.co.uk
Web Site: http://www.orcabookservices.co.uk

Managing Director: Mrs M. Lamb
Production Manager: R. Lamb
Company Secretary: Miss I. Parris

Children's Books; Humour

New Titles: 28 (2007), 21 (2008)
No of Employees: 4

ISBNs, Imprints & Series:
978 1 84161 Born to Shop; Juicy Lucy; Odd Streak; Peanuts; Garfield; Hackman 978 1 84161, 978 1 85304 The Odd Squad

Overseas Representation:
Australia: Peribo Pty Ltd, Mount Kuring-Gai, NSW
Europe: Walton Marketing Services, Chislehurst, UK
Middle East: Peter Ward Book Exports, London, UK
Philippines, Korea, Taiwan, Thailand & Indonesia: Ashton International Marketing Services, Sevenoaks, Kent, UK
Singapore & Malaysia: Pansing Distribution Sdn Bhd, Singapore
South Africa: Peter Matthews Sales Agency, Brackenhurst

Book Trade Association Membership:
IPG; Bookdata

2638

REARDON PUBLISHING
[also known as Reardon and Son Publishers]
PO Box 919, Cheltenham, Glos GL50 9AN
Telephone: 01242 231800
Email: reardon@bigfoot.com
Web Site: http://www.reardon.co.uk & http://www.cotswoldbookshop.com

Director: Nicholas Reardon

Archaeology; Atlases & Maps; Audio Books; Children's Books; Cinema, Video, TV & Radio; Guide Books; History & Antiquarian; Humour; Magic & the Occult; Military & War; Natural History; Nautical; Travel & Topography

ISBNs, Imprints & Series:
Walkcards (series)
978 0 9508674 Rideabout Series
978 1 873877 Walkabout Series
978 1 874192 Driveabout Series

Distributor for:
Cheltenham Tourism; Cicerone Press; Cordee; Corinium Publications; Estate Publications; Flukes UK; Harvey Maps; OS Maps; Philips Maps; Rambler Association; Video Ex

Book Trade Association Membership:
Outdoor Writers Guild

2639

REDCLIFFE PRESS LTD
81g Pembroke Road, Bristol BS8 3EA
Telephone: 0117 973 7207
Fax: 0117 923 8991
Email: info@redcliffepress.co.uk
Web Site: http://www.redcliffepress.co.uk

Trade Orders:
NBN International, Estover Road, Plymouth PL6 7PY
Telephone: 01752 202349
Fax: 01752 202333
Email: orders@nbninternational.com

Directors: A. N. Sansom *(Sales)*
John Sansom *(Publishing)*
Clara Sansom *(Production)*

Architecture & Design; Fine Art & Art History; History & Antiquarian; Literature & Criticism; Poetry; West Country History

New Titles: 4 (2007), 10 (2008)
No of Employees: 3

ISBNs, Imprints & Series:
978 1 900178, 978 1 904537

Associated Companies:
Art Dictionaries Ltd; Sansom & Co Ltd

Overseas Representation:
USA: Antique Collectors Club Ltd, Easthampton, MA

2640

REDEMPTORIST PUBLICATIONS
Alphonsus House, Chawton, Hants GU34 3HQ
Telephone: 01420 88222
Fax: 01420 88805
Email: rp@rpbooks.co.uk
Web Site: http://www.rpbooks.co.uk

Director: Rev Denis McBride *(Publishing)*
Head of Operations: Andrew Lane
Managers: Michael Roberts *(Sales & Service)*
Christine Thirkell *(Financial Controller)*
Patricia Wilson *(Marketing)*
Commissioning Editor: M. Hutchinson

Religion & Theology

ISBNs, Imprints & Series: 978 0 85231

Distributor for:
USA: Abbey Press; Creative Communications; Dimension Books; HarperCollins; ICS Publications; Liguori/Triumph; Loyola Press; Peter Pauper Press; RCL (Resources for Christian Living); Regina Press (Malhame); Resurrection Press; Servant Publications; Sophia Institute; St Anthony Messenger Press/Franciscan Catholic Book Publishing Co

Book Trade Association Membership:
BA

2641

REFLECTIONS OF A BYGONE AGE
15 Debdale Lane, Keyworth, Notts NG12 5HT
Telephone: 0115 937 4079
Fax: 0115 937 6197
Email: reflections@postcardcollecting.co.uk

Contacts: Brian Lund
F. Mary Lund

History & Antiquarian; Transport

New Titles: 8 (2007), 10 (2008)
No of Employees: 2

ISBNs, Imprints & Series:
978 0 946245, 978 1 900138, 978 1 905408

2642

THE RICHMOND PUBLISHING CO
[Ltd]
PO Box 963, Slough SL2 3RS
Telephone: 01753 643104
Fax: 01753 646553

Managing Director: Mrs S. J. Davie

Academic & Scholarly; Biology & Zoology; Educational & Textbooks; Natural History; Scientific & Technical

No of Employees: 2

Annual Turnover: £50,000

ISBNs, Imprints & Series:
978 0 85546 Richmond Publishing
978 1 85153 Field Studies Council
978 3 85604 Mykologia Lucerne

Distributor for:
Field Studies Council; WWF United Kingdom
Switzerland: Mykologia Lucerne

2643

RIPLEY PUBLISHING LTD
17–18 Bardfield Centre, Great Bardfield, Essex CM7 4SL
Telephone: 01371 812542
Fax: 01371 811393
Email: miles@ripleys.com
Web Site: http://www.ripleys.com

Publisher: Anne Marshall
Managing Editor: Becky Miles
Foreign Rights Manager: Amanda Dula

Children's Books

New Titles: 12 (2007), 12 (2008)
No of Employees: 6

Parent Company:
Canada: The Jim Pattison Group

2644

*RIPPING YARNS.COM
5 Old Inn Road, Findon, Aberdeenshire AB12 3RT
Telephone: 01224 783197
Email: admin@rippingyarns.com
Web Site: http://www.rippingyarns.com

Director: Ian Robertson
Sales & Marketing, Editorial: Krystina Lotoczko

Military & War; Sports & Games; Travel & Topography

ISBNs, Imprints & Series:
978 0 9541794, 978 1 904466

Parent Company:
Rockbuy Ltd

Overseas Representation:
Europe: Cordee, Leicester, UK

2645

RISING STARS UK LTD
22 Grafton Street, London W1S 4EX
Telephone: (020) 7495 6793
Fax: (020) 7495 6796
Email: info@risingstars-uk.com
Web Site: http://www.risingstars-uk.com

Customer Service, Trade Enquiries & Warehouse:
Macmillan Distribution (MDL), Brunel Road, Houndmills, Basingstoke, Hants RG21 6XS

Directors: Andrea Carr *(Managing)*
Ben Barton *(Publishing)*
Tim Pearce *(Production)*

Children's Books; Educational & Textbooks; Electronic (Educational); Fiction

ISBNs, Imprints & Series:
978 1 84680, 978 1 905056

Overseas Representation:
Contact: English Language International, Dunstable, UK

Book Trade Association Membership:
Publishers Association; EPC; IPG

2646

***RISK BOOKS**
Incisive Media Management Ltd,
Haymarket House, 28–29 Haymarket,
London SW1Y 4RX
Telephone: (020) 7484 9700
Fax: (020) 7930 2238
Email: books@incisivemedia.com
Web Site: http://www.riskbooks.com

Managing Director: Matthew Crabbe

Academic & Scholarly; Finance; Professional

ISBNs, Imprints & Series: 978 1 904339

2647

ROADMASTER PUBLISHING
PO Box 176, Chatham, Kent ME5 9AQ
Telephone: 01634 862843
Fax: 01634 201555
Email: info@roadmasterpublishing.co.uk

Sales Manager: Malcolm Wright

*Geography & Geology; Guide Books;
Nautical; Transport; Travel & Topography*

ISBNs, Imprints & Series: 978 1 871814

Distributor for:
Nostalgia Road Publications; Trans-Pennine
Publishing

2648

ROBINSWOOD PRESS LTD
30 South Avenue, Stourbridge,
West Midlands DY8 3XY
Telephone: 01384 397475
Fax: 01384 440443
Email: cjm@robinswoodpress.com
Web Site: http://
www.robinswoodpress.com

Managing Director: C. J. Marshall
Company Secretary: S. M. Marshall
Editor: S. Connolly

*Academic & Scholarly; Children's Books;
Educational & Textbooks; Electronic
(Educational); English as a Foreign
Language; Fiction*

New Titles: 68 (2007), 6 (2008)
No of Employees: 5
Annual Turnover: £150,000

ISBNs, Imprints & Series:
978 1 869981, 978 1 906053

Associated Companies:
Republic of Ireland: Robinswood Press
(Dublin) Ltd

Overseas Representation:
Republic of Ireland: STA Ltd, Dublin

2649

ROBSON BOOKS
The Old Magistrates Court,
10 Southcombe Street, London W14 0RA
Telephone: (020) 7605 1400
Fax: (020) 7605 1401
Email: tbromley@anovabooks.com
Web Site: http://www.anovabooks.com

Distributors:
HarperCollins Distribution, Campsie View,
Westerhill Road, Bishopbriggs, Glasgow
G64 2QT
Telephone: 0141 306 3100
Fax: 0141 306 3767

Publisher: Tom Bromley
Publicity & Marketing Manager: Helen
Ponting

*Biography & Autobiography; Cinema,
Video, TV & Radio; Cookery, Wines &
Spirits; Crime; Health & Beauty; Humour;
Music; Sports & Games; Theatre, Drama &
Dance; Travel & Topography*

ISBNs, Imprints & Series: 978 1 86105

Parent Company:
Anova Books Group Ltd

Overseas Representation:
Asia: Ashton International Marketing
Services, Sevenoaks, Kent, UK
Australia: HarperCollins Publishers, Pymble,
NSW
Canada: Raincoast Books, Vancouver, BC
France & Benelux: Ted Dougherty, London,
UK
Germany, Switzerland & Austria: Gabriele
Kern Publishers Services, Frankfurt-am-
Main, Germany
Italy, Spain & Portugal: Penny Padovani,
Padovani Books Ltd, London, UK
New Zealand: HarperCollins (NZ) Ltd,
Glenfield, Auckland
Scandinavia: McNeish Publishing Services,
East Sussex, UK
Singapore & Malaysia: Pansing Distribution
Sdn Bhd, Singapore
South Africa: Trinity Books CC, Randburg
USA: Trafalgar Square Publishing,
distributed by Independent Publishers
Group, Chicago, IL

Book Trade Association Membership:
IPG

2650

ALAN ROGERS GUIDES LTD
Spelmonden Old Oast, Goudhurst,
Cranbrook, Kent TN17 1HE
Telephone: 01580 214000
Email: susie@alanrogers.com
Web Site: http://www.alanrogers.com

Publishing Manager: Susie Smart

Travel & Topography

New Titles: 13 (2007), 11 (2008)

ISBNs, Imprints & Series:
978 0 954527, 978 0 955048, 978 1
906215

Parent Company:
Mark Hammerton Group

2651

ROTOVISION SA
Sheridan House, 114 Western Road, Hove,
East Sussex BN3 1DD
Telephone: 01273 727268 & 716010/11/
12 (Customer Services)
Fax: 01273 727269
Email: sales@rotovision.com
Web Site: http://www.rotovision.com

Directors: Piers Spence *(Managing)*
Nicole Kemble *(Rights)*
Financial Controller: Mari Ahlfeld-Smith
Publisher: April Sankey

*Architecture & Design; Cinema, Video, TV &
Radio; Fashion & Costume; Fine Art & Art
History; Music; Photography; Reference
Books, Directories & Dictionaries; Theatre,
Drama & Dance*

New Titles: 26 (2007), 28 (2008)
No of Employees: 20

ISBNs, Imprints & Series: 978 2 88046

Parent Company:
Quarto Group

Overseas Representation:
Australia: Thames & Hudson (Australia) Pty
Ltd, Fishermans Bend, Vic
France: Interart SARL, Paris
Germany, Switzerland & Austria: Michael
Klein, Vilsburg, Germany
Middle East: International Publishing
Services (IPS) Middle East Ltd, Dubai, UAE
South East Asia: APD Singapore Pte Ltd,
Singapore

Book Trade Association Membership:
BA

2652

ROUND HALL LTD
43 Fitzwilliam Place, Dublin 2,
Republic of Ireland
Telephone: +353 (01) 662 5301
Fax: +353 (01) 662 5302
Email: roundhall.info@thomson.com
Web Site: http://
www.roundhall.thomson.com

Distribution:
Gill & Macmillan, Hume Avenue,
Park West, Dublin 12, Republic of Ireland
Telephone: +353 (01) 500 9500

Director: Julie Clarke
Managers: Anne Waters *(Finance)*
Terri McDonnell *(Production)*
Martin McCann *(Editorial)*
Catherine Dolan *(Commercial)*
Brendan Reid *(Sales)*
Pauline Ward *(Sales)*
Maura Smyth *(Marketing)*

*Academic & Scholarly; Accountancy &
Taxation; Educational & Textbooks;
Electronic (Professional & Academic);
Industry, Business & Management; Law;
Medical (incl. Self Help & Alternative
Medicine); Reference Books, Directories &
Dictionaries*

ISBNs, Imprints & Series:
978 1 85800, 978 1 899738 Thomson
Round Hall
978 1 86089 Round Hall Professional

Parent Company:
USA: Thomson Corp

Associated Companies:
Australia: LBC
Canada: Carswell
New Zealand: Brookers
UK: Sweet & Maxwell
USA: West Group

2653

ROUNDHOUSE PUBLISHING LTD
Roundhouse Group, Maritime House,
Basin Road North, Hove, East Sussex
BN41 1WR
Telephone: 01273 704962
Fax: 01273 704963
Email: sales@roundhousegroup.co.uk
Web Site: http://
www.roundhousegroup.co.uk

Warehouse & Distribution:
Orca Book Services, Stanley House,
Fleets Lane, Poole, Dorset BH15 3AJ
Telephone: 01202 665432
Fax: 01202 666219
Email: orders@orca-book-services.co.uk

Managing Director: Alan Goodworth
(Publisher)
Marketing Manager: Matt Goodworth

*Academic & Scholarly; Architecture &
Design; Atlases & Maps; Biography &
Autobiography; Children's Books; Cinema,
Video, TV & Radio; Cookery, Wines &
Spirits; Crafts & Hobbies; Fine Art & Art
History; Guide Books; Health & Beauty;
History & Antiquarian; Industry, Business &
Management; Literature & Criticism;
Medical (incl. Self Help & Alternative
Medicine); Military & War; Music; Natural
History; Philosophy; Photography; Politics &
World Affairs; Reference Books, Directories
& Dictionaries; Religion & Theology; Sports
& Games; Theatre, Drama & Dance; Travel
& Topography*

ISBNs, Imprints & Series:
978 1 85710 Roundabout - Books for
Young Readers; Roundhouse Publishing

Associated Companies:
Roundabout Books; Roundhouse Reference
Books; Roundtrip Travel; Windsor Books
International

Distributor for:
Georgina Campbell; Learning Together; O-
Books; Angela Patchell Books; Sea Squirt
Books; Sinclair-Stevenson; Thalamus
Publishing; Michael Wilcox School of
Colour; Worth Books
Australia: Allen & Unwin; Explore Australia;
Global Exchange; Hale & Iremonger;
Hardie Grant Books; Health Directions;
National Gallery of Victoria; University of
Queensland Press; Watermark Press
Austria: Strokes International
Belgium: Editions l'Octogone
Canada: Key Porter Books; Self-Counsel
Press; Ulysses Travel Guides
France: Petit Futé Guides; Sisyphe Editions
Germany: Meyer & Meyer
Hong Kong: PPP Co
India: Marg Publications
Italy: Arkivia Books
Netherlands: New in Chess
New Zealand: Awa Press
Singapore: Archipelago Press; C-Licence
Spain: Ebiz Guides; Santana Books
USA: Allworth Press; AM Editores;
Applause Books; Black Sparrow Press;
Boyds Mills Press; Breckling Press; C & T
Publications; Capstone; Creative
Homeowner; Cumberland House;
Fairview Press; Free Spirit; Getty
Publications; David R. Godine; Graphic
Arts Center; Gryphon House; Home
Planners; Hunter Publishing; Interlink
Publishing; Knock Knock Books;
Landauer; Listen & Live; Martingale &
Co; Open Road; Paragon House; Pelican
Publishing; Portland Press; Quality
Medical Pub.; RDR Books; Robins Lane
Press; J Ross Publishing; Seven Locks
Press; Soundprints; Triumph Books;
University Press of Mississippi; Vanguard
Press; Westholme; Writings of Mary
Baker Eddy

Overseas Representation:
Europe (East) & Scandinavia: Bill Bailey
Publishers Representatives, Totnes, UK
Europe (Spain & Portugal only): Iberian
Book Services, Madrid, Spain
Europe (West) (excluding Scandinavia): Ted
Dougherty, London, UK

2654

ROUTE PUBLISHING LTD
PO Box 167, Pontefract WF8 4WW
Telephone: 01977 797695
Email: info@route-online.com
Web Site: http://www.route-online.com

Distribution:
Central Books, 99 Wallis Road, London
E9 5LN
Telephone: (020) 8986 4854
Fax: (020) 8533 5821
Email: bill@centralbooks.com
Web Site: http://www.centralbooks.com

Directors: Ian Daley *(Artistic)*
Isabel Galan *(Public Relations)*

Biography & Autobiography; Fiction; Poetry

ISBNs, Imprints & Series: 978 1 901927

Parent Company:
ID Publishing

2655

Overseas Representation:
USA: Dufour Editions Inc, Chester Springs, PA

2655

ROUTLEDGE-CAVENDISH
2 Park Square, Milton Park, Abingdon, Oxon OX14 4RN
Telephone: (020) 7017 6000
Fax: (020) 7017 6336
Email: law@routledge.com
Web Site: http://www.routledgecavendish.com

Publisher: Fiona Kinnear

Academic & Scholarly; Educational & Textbooks; Electronic (Professional & Academic); Environment & Development Studies; Gay & Lesbian Studies; Gender Studies; Law; Medical (incl. Self Help & Alternative Medicine); Philosophy; Politics & World Affairs

New Titles: 184 (2007), 180 (2008)

ISBNs, Imprints & Series:
Birkbeck Law Press; The Glasshouse Press; UCL Press
978 1 85941, 978 1 874241, 978 1 876213

Parent Company:
Taylor & Francis Group

Book Trade Association Membership:
BA; IGSMTP; CAPP; IPG

2656

JOSEPH ROWNTREE FOUNDATION
The Homestead, 40 Water End, York YO30 6WP
Telephone: 01904 629241
Fax: 01904 620072
Email: julia.lewis@jrf.org.uk
Web Site: http://www.jrf.org.uk

Distribution:
York Publishing Services, 64 Hallfield Road, Layerthorpe, York YO31 7ZQ
Telephone: 01904 430033
Fax: 01904 430868
Email: orders@yps.ymn.co.uk

Directors: Julia Unwin CBE
Julia Lewis *(Communications)*
Paul Dack *(Finance)*

Academic & Scholarly; Architecture & Design; Economics; Politics & World Affairs; Sociology & Anthropology

2657

ROYAL COLLECTION PUBLICATIONS
St James's Palace, London SW1A 1BQ
Telephone: (020) 7024 5584
Fax: (020) 7839 8168
Email: jacky.collissharvey@royalcollection.org.uk
Web Site: http://www.royalcollection.org.uk

Distributor:
Thames & Hudson Ltd, 181a High Holborn, London WC1V 7QX
Telephone: (020) 7845 5000
Fax: (020) 7845 5055
Web Site: http://www.thamesandhudson.com

Publisher: Jacky Colliss Harvey
Commissioning Editor: Kate Owen
Publishing Assistant: Debbie Bogard

Academic & Scholarly; Antiques & Collecting; Architecture & Design; Biography & Autobiography; Fine Art & Art History; Guide Books; History &
Antiquarian; Illustrated & Fine Editions; Natural History; Photography

New Titles: 10 (2007), 10 (2008)
No of Employees: 3

ISBNs, Imprints & Series:
978 1 902163, 978 1 902163, 978 1 905686, 978 1 905686

Overseas Representation:
Rest of World: Thames & Hudson Ltd, London, UK
USA & Canada: Antique Collectors Club Ltd, Easthampton, MA, USA

2658

ROYAL COLLEGE OF GENERAL PRACTITIONERS
14 Princes Gate, Hyde Park, London SW7 1PU
Telephone: (020) 7581 3232
Fax: (020) 7225 3047
Email: hfarrelly@rcgp.org.uk
Web Site: http://www.rcgp.org.uk

Publishing & Sales Manager: Ms Helen Farrelly

Academic & Scholarly; Electronic (Professional & Academic); Medical (incl. Self Help & Alternative Medicine); Psychology & Psychiatry; Vocational Training & Careers

ISBNs, Imprints & Series: 978 0 85084

Book Trade Association Membership:
Association of Learned & Professional Society Publishers

2659

ROYAL COLLEGE OF PSYCHIATRISTS
17 Belgrave Square, London SW1X 8PG
Telephone: (020) 7235 2351
Fax: (020) 7259 6507
Email: publications@rcpsych.ac.uk
Web Site: http://www.rcpsych.ac.uk

Warehouse:
Turpin Distribution, Customer Services, Pegasus Drive, Stratton Business Park, Biggleswade, Beds SG18 8TQ
Telephone: 01767 604951
Fax: 01767 601640
Email: custserv@turpin-distribution.com
Web Site: http://www.turpin-distribution.com

Head of Publications: Dave Jago
Sales & Marketing Manager: Daniel Tomkins

Academic & Scholarly; Medical (incl. Self Help & Alternative Medicine); Psychology & Psychiatry

New Titles: 9 (2007), 9 (2008)

ISBNs, Imprints & Series:
978 0 902241, 978 1 901242 Gaskell; RCPsych Publications

Overseas Representation:
Australia & New Zealand: All things Medical, Sydney University, Sydney, NSW, Australia
Republic of Ireland: Compass Academic, London, UK
Scandinavia (including Iceland & Estonia): David Towle International, Stockholm, Sweden
USA & Canada: Balogh International Inc, Champaign, IL, USA

Book Trade Association Membership:
IPG; Association of Learned & Professional Society Publishers

2660

ROYAL GEOGRAPHICAL SOCIETY (WITH INSTITUTE OF BRITISH GEOGRAPHERS)
1 Kensington Gore, London SW7 2AR
Telephone: (020) 7591 3022
Fax: (020) 7591 3001
Email: rhed@rgs.org
Web Site: http://www.rgs.org

Head of Finance & Services: David Riviere
Managing Editor: Journals: Amy Swann

Academic & Scholarly; Electronic (Educational); Electronic (Professional & Academic); Environment & Development Studies; Geography & Geology

ISBNs, Imprints & Series:
RGS-IBG Book Series (academic/scholarly texts only)

2661

ROYAL IRISH ACADEMY
Academy House, 19 Dawson Street, Dublin 2, Republic of Ireland
Telephone: +353 (01) 676 2570 & 676 4222
Fax: +353 (01) 676 2346
Email: publications@ria.ie
Web Site: http://www.ria.ie

Executive Secretary: Patrick Buckley *(Rights & Permissions)*
Managing Editor: Ruth Hegarty *(Production & Sales)*

Academic & Scholarly; Archaeology; Atlases & Maps; Biology & Zoology; History & Antiquarian; Languages & Linguistics; Reference Books, Directories & Dictionaries

New Titles: 19 (2007), 19 (2008)
No of Employees: 6

ISBNs, Imprints & Series:
978 0 901714, 978 0 9543855, 978 1 874045

Overseas Representation:
North America: International Specialized Book Services Inc, Portland, OR, USA

Book Trade Association Membership:
CLÉ (Irish PA); Association of Learned & Professional Society Publishers

2662

THE ROYAL SOCIETY OF CHEMISTRY
Sales & Customer Care, Thomas Graham House, Science Park, Milton Road, Cambridge CB4 0WF
Telephone: 01223 420066
Fax: 01223 426017
Email: sales@rsc.org
Web Site: http://www.rsc.org

Warehouse:
Portland Customer Services, Portland Press, Commerce Way, Colchester CO2 8HP
Telephone: 01206 226050
Fax: 01206 799331
Email: sales@portland-services.com
Web Site: http://www.portlandpress.com

Director: Robert Parker *(Publishing)*
Managers: Barry Anderson *(Home & Export Sales & Customer Care)*
Nichole Gibson *(Production Operations)*

Academic & Scholarly; Chemistry; Educational & Textbooks; Electronic (Educational); Electronic (Professional & Academic); Reference Books, Directories & Dictionaries; Scientific & Technical

New Titles: 53 (2007), 55 (2008)
No of Employees: 300

ISBNs, Imprints & Series:
978 0 85186, 978 0 85404

Overseas Representation:
Asia, Australia & New Zealand: Clarke Associates Ltd, Bristol, UK
Australia, New Zealand & Papua New Guinea: DA Information Services Pty Ltd, Mitcham, Vic, Australia
Hungary: Dr László Horváth Publishers Representative, Budapest
India: S. Janakiraman, Book Marketing Services, Chennai
Italy: Flavio Marcello Publishers' Agents & Consultants, Padua
Japan: Aiko Hoyosa, Tokyo
Middle East, Malta, Greece, Turkey, Cyprus & Iran: Farhad Maftoon, Tehran, Iran; Anthony Rudkin Associates, Oxford, UK
Nigeria: Olu Anulopo, Bounty Books, Ibadan
North America & Mexico: Springer-Verlag New York Inc, Secaucus, NJ, USA
Scandinavia & Iceland: Colin Flint Ltd, Harlow, UK
South America: Terry Roberts, Humphrys Roberts Associates, Cotia SP, Brazil
Spain & Portugal: Arie Ruitenbeek, Madrid, Spain

Book Trade Association Membership:
Association of Learned Society Publishers; STM (European Group)

2663

*ROYAL SOCIETY OF MEDICINE PRESS LTD
1 Wimpole Street, London W1G 0AE
Telephone: (020) 7290 3945
Fax: (020) 7290 2929
Email: ian.jones@rsm.ac.uk
Web Site: http://www.rsmpress.co.uk

Warehousing & Distribution:
Marston Book Services, PO Box 269, Abingdon, Oxon OX14 4YN
Telephone: 01235 465500
Fax: 01235 465555

Managing Director: Peter Richardson
Production Manager: Mark Sanderson
Head of Sales & Marketing: Ian Jones
Finance: Micky Sandell
Journals Publisher: Delia Siedle
Editors: Alison Campbell *(Managing)*
Sarah Burrows *(Commissioning)*

Medical (incl. Self Help & Alternative Medicine)

ISBNs, Imprints & Series:
978 1 85315 Controversies and Dilemmas Series; Eponymists in Medicine Series; Get Through Series; In Practice Series; International Congress and Symposium Series; Key Advances Series; Key Paper Conferences Series; Recent Advances Series; Round Table Series

Parent Company:
Royal Society of Medicine

Overseas Representation:
USA: Bookmasters Inc, Ashland, OH

Book Trade Association Membership:
Association of Learned & Professional Society Publishers

2664

RUSSELL HOUSE PUBLISHING LTD
4 St George's House,
Uplyme Road Business Park, Lyme Regis DT7 3LS
Telephone: 01297 443948
Fax: 01297 442722
Email: help@russellhouse.co.uk
Web Site: http://www.russellhouse.co.uk

Directors: Geoffrey Mann *(Managing)*

Martin Jones
Terry Nemko

Academic & Scholarly; Educational & Textbooks; Law; Psychology & Psychiatry; Sociology & Anthropology; Sports & Games; Vocational Training & Careers

New Titles: 19 (2007) , 25 (2008)
No of Employees: 6

ISBNs, Imprints & Series:
978 1 898924, 978 1 903855, 978 1 905541

Overseas Representation:
North America: International Specialized Book Services Inc, Portland, OR, USA

2665

SAGE PUBLICATIONS LTD
1 Oliver's Yard, 55 City Road, London EC1Y 1SP
Telephone: (020) 7324 8500
Fax: (020) 7324 8600
Email: info@sagepub.co.uk
Web Site: http://www.sagepub.co.uk

Warehouse:
Unit 11, Keirbeck Business Centre, North Woolwich Road, Silvertown, London E16 2BG

Directors: Stephen Barr *(Managing)*
Katherine Jackson *(Financial & Deputy Managing)*
Ziyad Marar *(Deputy Managing)*
Clive Parry *(Marketing & Sales)*
Phil Denvir *(IT)*
Richard Fidczuk *(Production)*
Sara Miller McCune
Blaise Simqu
Paul Chapman
Tony Histed *(Associate, Sales)*
Anne Farlow *(Non-Executive)*
Brenda Gowley *(Non-Executive)*
Managers: Alison Browne *(Customer Service (Books))*
Huw Alexander *(Rights & Permissions)*

Academic & Scholarly; Bibliography & Library Science; Economics; Educational & Textbooks; Electronic (Educational); Gender Studies; Industry, Business & Management; Mathematics & Statistics; Politics & World Affairs; Psychology & Psychiatry; Reference Books, Directories & Dictionaries; Religion & Theology; Scientific & Technical; Sociology & Anthropology

New Titles: 695 (2007)

ISBNs, Imprints & Series:
978 0 7619, 978 0 8039, 978 1 4129

Parent Company:
USA: SAGE Publications Inc

Associated Companies:
Paul Chapman Publishing Ltd
India: SAGE Publications Pvt Ltd
USA: Corwin Press Inc; Pine Forge Press Inc; Sage Publications Inc

Overseas Representation:
Australia & New Zealand: Footprint Books Pty Ltd, Sydney, NSW, Australia
South Africa: Academic Marketing Services (Pty) Ltd, Craighall

Book Trade Association Membership:
Publishers Association; IPG

2666

SAINT ALBERT'S PRESS
[British Province of Carmelites]
Carmelite Projects & Publications Office, More House, Heslington, York YO10 5DX
Telephone: 01904 411521
Fax: 01904 410664

Email: projects@carmelites.org.uk
Web Site: http://www.carmelite.org/sap/

Orders & Book Deposit:
Saint Albert's Press Book Distribution, Carmelite Friars, 34 Tanners Street, Faversham, Kent ME13 7JN
Telephone: 01795 537038
Fax: 01795 539511
Email: saintalbertspress@carmelites.org.uk
Web Site: http://www.carmelite.org/sap/

Director: Johan Bergström-Allen
Sales: Gloria Carey
Bursar: Richard Copsey

Academic & Scholarly; History & Antiquarian; Poetry; Religion & Theology

New Titles: 4 (2007) , 7 (2008)
No of Employees: 2
Annual Turnover: £10,000

ISBNs, Imprints & Series: 978 0 904849

Parent Company:
UK: Carmelite Charitable Trust

Associated Companies:
UK: The Carmelite Press; Whitefriars Press

Distributor for:
Italy: Edizioni Carmelitane
USA: Carmelite Institute

Book Trade Association Membership:
IPG

2667

ST JEROME PUBLISHING LTD
2 Maple Road West, Brooklands, Manchester M23 9HH
Telephone: 0161 973 9856
Fax: 0161 905 3498
Email: stjerome@compuserve.com
Web Site: http://www.stjerome.co.uk

Academic & Scholarly; Electronic (Professional & Academic)

Book Trade Association Membership:
Publishers Association

2668

ST PAULS PUBLISHING
187 Battersea Bridge Road, London SW11 3AS
Telephone: (020) 7978 4300
Fax: (020) 7978 4370
Email: editions@stpauls.org.uk
Web Site: http://www.stpauls.ie

Director: Celso Godilano
Commissioning Editor: Annabel Robson
Sales: Eugene Priante
Marketing: Alexander Anandam
Permissions & Foreign Rights: Pamela Tamburini

Biography & Autobiography; Philosophy; Religion & Theology

New Titles: 12 (2007) , 18 (2008)
No of Employees: 3

ISBNs, Imprints & Series: 978 0 85439

Associated Companies:
Argentina: Ediciones San Pablo
Australia: St Pauls Publications
Brazil: Edições San Pablo
Canada: Medias Paul
Colombia: Ediciones San Pablo
France: Editions Mediaspaul
India: Better Yourself Books; St Pauls
Italy: Edizioni San Paolo
Japan: Chuoshuppan-Sha
Kenya: St Pauls Publications
Korea, South: St Pauls
Mexico: Ediciones San Pablo

Philippines: St Pauls
Portugal: Edições San Pablo
Republic of Ireland: St Pauls
Spain: Ediciones San Pablo
USA: Alba House
Venezuela: Ediciones San Pablo

Distributor for:
St Pauls

Overseas Representation:
Australia: St Pauls Publications, Homebush
Kenya: St Paul Book Centre, Nairobi
Nigeria: St Paul Book Centre, Oke-Padi
Tanzania: St Paul Book Centre, Dar-es-Salaam
Uganda: St Paul Book Centre, Kampala

Book Trade Association Membership:
BA

2669

SALT PUBLISHING LTD
PO Box 937, Great Wilbraham, Cambridge CB1 5JX
Telephone: 01223 882220
Fax: 01223 882260
Email: enquiries@saltpublishing.com
Web Site: http://www.saltpublishing.com

Editor: Chris Hamilton-Emery
General Manager: Jennifer Hamilton-Emery

Biography & Autobiography; Fiction; Literature & Criticism; Poetry

New Titles: 70 (2007) , 70 (2008)
No of Employees: 2
Annual Turnover: £130,000

ISBNs, Imprints & Series:
978 0 646 Folio (Salt)
978 1 84471, 978 1 876857 Salt Publishing

Overseas Representation:
Australia: Inbooks, c/o James Bennett Pty Ltd, Belrose, NSW
USA: Small Press Distribution Inc, Berkeley, CA

Book Trade Association Membership:
IPG

2670

SANDSTONE PRESS LTD
PO Box 5725, 1 High Street, Dingwall, Ross-shire IV15 9WJ
Telephone: 01349 862583
Fax: 01349 862583
Email: info@sandstonepress.com
Web Site: http://www.sandstonepress.com

Directors: Robert Davidson *(Managing)*
Iain Gordon *(Company Secretary)*
Moira Forsyth

Academic & Scholarly; Biography & Autobiography; Crime; English as a Foreign Language; Environment & Development Studies; Fiction; Humour; Illustrated & Fine Editions; Literature & Criticism; Politics & World Affairs; Science Fiction; Sports & Games

New Titles: 5 (2007) , 10 (2008)
Annual Turnover: £40,000

ISBNs, Imprints & Series:
978 1 905207 Sandstone Highliner Series; Sandstone Meanmnach Series; Sandstone Vista Series

Book Trade Association Membership:
Publishing Scotland

2671

SANSOM & CO LTD
81g Pembroke Road, Clifton, Bristol BS8 3EA
Telephone: 0117 973 7207
Fax: 0117 923 8991
Email: johnsansom@aol.com & info@sansomandcompany.co.uk
Web Site: http://www.sansomandcompany.co.uk

Trade Orders:
NBN International, Estover Road, Plymouth PL6 7PZ
Telephone: 01752 202349
Fax: 01752 202333
Email: orders@nbninternational.com

Directors: A. N. Sansom *(Sales)*
John Sansom *(Publishing)*
Clara Sansom *(Production)*

Architecture & Design; Fine Art & Art History; Literature & Criticism

New Titles: 6 (2007) , 11 (2008)
No of Employees: 3

ISBNs, Imprints & Series:
978 1 900178, 978 1 904537

Associated Companies:
Art Dictionaries Ltd; Redcliffe Press Ltd

Overseas Representation:
USA: Antique Collectors' Club, Woodbridge, Suffolk, UK

2672

SAQI BOOKS
26 Westbourne Grove, London W2 5RH
Telephone: (020) 7221 9347
Fax: (020) 7229 7492
Email: enquiries@saqibooks.com
Web Site: http://www.saqibooks.com

Distribution:
Gazelle Book Services, White Cross Mills, Hightown, South Road, Lancaster LA1 4XS
Telephone: 01524 68765
Fax: 01524 63232
Email: ian@gazellebooks.co.uk

Director: André Gaspard
Editor: Lara Frankena
Publisher: André Gaspard
Publicity & Marketing: Ashley Biles
Rights: Anna Wilson

Academic & Scholarly; Architecture & Design; Biography & Autobiography; Cookery, Wines & Spirits; Fiction; Fine Art & Art History; Gender Studies; History & Antiquarian; Humour; Literature & Criticism; Philosophy; Photography; Poetry; Politics & World Affairs; Religion & Theology; Sociology & Anthropology; Arab World; Islam; Middle East

New Titles: 25 (2007) , 25 (2008)

ISBNs, Imprints & Series:
Saqi Essentials
978 0 86356

Associated Companies:
Lebanon: Dar Al Saqi Sarl

Overseas Representation:
Australia: Palgrave Macmillan, South Yarra, Vic
USA: Consortium Publishers, St Paul, MN

Book Trade Association Membership:
BA; CAPP; IPG

2673

SAVE THE CHILDREN
1 St John's Lane, London EC1M 4AR

2674 / PUBLISHERS

Telephone: (020) 7012 6400
Fax: (020) 7012 6963
Email: f.ellery@savethechildren.org.uk
Web Site: http://www.savethechildren.org.uk

Distributor:
NBN International, Estover Road, Estover, Plymouth PL6 7PY
Telephone: 01752 202301
Fax: 01752 202333
Email: orders@nbninternational.com
Web Site: http://www.nbninternational.com

Managers: Frances Ellery (Publications, Editorial)
Sue Macpherson (Planning & Production)

Academic & Scholarly; Children's Books; Educational & Textbooks; Politics & World Affairs; Sociology & Anthropology

New Titles: 15 (2007), 15 (2008)

ISBNs, Imprints & Series:
978 1 841870, 978 1 870322, 978 1 899120

Book Trade Association Membership:
IPG

2674

ALASTAIR SAWDAY PUBLISHING
The Old Farmyard, Yanley Lane, Long Ashton, Bristol BS41 9LR
Telephone: 01275 395430
Fax: 01275 393388
Email: info@sawdays.co.uk
Web Site: http://www.sawdays.co.uk/bookshop

Distribution & Sales:
Penguin (UK), 80 The Strand, London WC2R 0RL
Telephone: (020) 7010 3000
Fax: (020) 7010 3198
Email: sales@penguin.co.uk

Editorial Director: Annie Shillito
Publisher/Chairman: Alastair Sawday
Managers: Julia Richardson (Production)
Bridget Bishop (Finance)
Rob Richardson (Sales & Marketing)
Sue Bourner (Editorial)
Joe Green (Web/IT)

Environment & Development Studies; Guide Books; Travel & Topography

New Titles: 10 (2007), 12 (2008)
No of Employees: 31

ISBNs, Imprints & Series:
978 1 901970, 978 1 906136 Alastair Sawday's Special Places to Stay; Fragile Earth

Overseas Representation:
USA & Canada: Globe Pequot Press, Guilford, CT, USA
Worldwide (excluding USA & Canada): Penguin Books Ltd, London, UK

Book Trade Association Membership:
IPG

2675

S. B. PUBLICATIONS
14 Bishopstone Road, Seaford, East Sussex BN25 2UB
Telephone: 01323 893498
Fax: 01323 893860
Email: sbpublications@tiscali.co.uk
Web Site: http://www.sbpublications.co.uk

Owner/Manager: Mrs L. S. Woods
Finance: Mrs D. Quick
Sales Manager: Lindsay Woods
Editorial: Ms E. Howe

Proofreader: C. Howden
Sales & Administration: Miss C. Gillett

Guide Books; History & Antiquarian; Natural History; Travel & Topography; Local History (S. E. England); Walking

New Titles: 6 (2007), 12 (2008)

ISBNs, Imprints & Series: 978 1 85770

2676

SCALA PUBLISHERS LTD
Northburgh House, 10 Northburgh Street, London EC1V 0AT
Telephone: (020) 7490 9900
Fax: (020) 7336 6870
Email: jmckinley@scalapublishers.com
Web Site: http://www.scalapublishers.com

Directors: David Campbell (Chairman)
Jennifer Wright (Museum Publications (USA))
Jenny McKinley (Marketing & Publications (excl. USA))
Oliver Craske (Editorial)
Tim Clark (Production)
Mark Bicknell (Finance)

Antiques & Collecting; Architecture & Design; Children's Books; Fine Art & Art History; Guide Books; Illustrated & Fine Editions; Travel & Topography

New Titles: 30 (2007), 30 (2008)

ISBNs, Imprints & Series: 978 1 85759

Associated Companies:
France: Editions Scala

Overseas Representation:
Australia (Sales): Bookwise International, Adelaide, SA, Australia
Worldwide: Antique Collectors' Club, Woodbridge, Suffolk, UK

Book Trade Association Membership:
IPG

2677

SCHOLASTIC UK LTD
Euston House, 24 Eversholt Street, London NW1 1DB
Telephone: (020) 7756 7756
Web Site: http://www.scholastic.co.uk

School Book Clubs:
(as above)

Scholastic Children's Books:
(as above)

School Book Fairs:
(as above)

Scholastic Education:
Villiers House, Clarendon Avenue, Leamington Spa, Warks CV32 5PR

Directors: Elaine McQuade (Scholastic Children's Books – Managing)
Kate Wilson (Group Managing)
Denise Cripps (Education – Managing)
Alan Hurcombe (Finance)

Children's Books; Educational & Textbooks

Parent Company:
USA: Scholastic Inc

Associated Companies:
Australia: Scholastic Australia Pty Ltd
Canada: Scholastic Canada Ltd
New Zealand: Scholastic New Zealand Ltd
UK: Chicken House Publishing

Overseas Representation:
Australia: Scholastic Australia Ltd, Gosford, NSW
Canada: Scholastic Canada Ltd, Markham, Ont
Far East (excluding Singapore, Malaysia & Indonesia): Scholastic Hong Kong, Hong Kong
New Zealand: Scholastic NZ, Auckland

Book Trade Association Membership:
Publishers Association; EPC; Periodical Publishers Association

2678

SCHOOLPLAY PRODUCTIONS LTD
15 Inglis Road, Colchester, Essex CO3 3HU
Telephone: 01206 540111
Fax: 01206 766944
Email: schoolplay@inglis-house.demon.co.uk
Web Site: http://www.schoolplayproductions.co.uk

Directors: J. R. Lucas (Managing)
W. Baker
Administrators: Mrs C. S. Wenden
Mrs B. M. Sparkes

Educational & Textbooks; Music; Theatre, Drama & Dance

New Titles: 5 (2007), 5 (2008)

ISBNs, Imprints & Series:
978 1 872475, 978 1 902472

Book Trade Association Membership:
Publishers Association

2679

SCHOTT MUSIC LTD
48 Great Marlborough Street, London W1F 7BB
Telephone: (020) 7534 0700
Fax: (020) 7534 0719
Email: info@schott-music.com
Web Site: http://www.schott-music.com

Trade Enquiries & Orders:
MDS Service Centre,
5–6 Raywood Office Complex,
Leacon Lane, Charing, Ashford, Kent TN27 0EN
Telephone: 01233 712233
Fax: 01233 714948
Email: orders.uk@mds-partner.com
Web Site: http://www.smdextranet.schott-extranet.de

Directors: Judith Webb (Joint Managing)
Roberto Garcia (Sales)
Managers: Guy Thomas (Buying)
Nicola Mather (Marketing)
Head of International Publishing:
Wendy Lampa

Academic & Scholarly; Music

New Titles: 40 (2007), 50 (2008)

ISBNs, Imprints & Series:
978 0 85162 Boosey & Hawkes Music Publishers Ltd
978 0 901938, 978 0 946535, 978 1 902455 Schott London
978 0 930448 Schott USA
978 3 254 Atlantis Musikbuch-Verlag AG
978 3 7931, 978 3 87090 Bote & Bock GmbH & Co KG
978 3 7957 Schott Music GmbH & Co KG
978 3 901974 Richard Strauss GmbH & Co KG
978 3 920030 Apollo-Verlag Paul Lincke GmbH
978 3 920045 Ars-Viva-Verlag
978 3 920201 Cranz GmbH
978 3 920468, 978 3 937315 Matth. Hohner AG
978 3 923051 Anton J. Benjamin GmbH
978 3 932398 Schott Music & Media GmbH (Intuition)

Parent Company:
Germany: Schott Music GmbH & Co KG

Associated Companies:
Ernst Eulenburg Ltd

Distributor for:
A piacere; Ars viva; Bardic Edition; Boosey & Hawkes Music Publishers Ltd; Delius Trust; Edition HH; Finzi Trust; Hyperion; Itchy Fingers Publications; Universal Edition Ltd
Austria: Amadeus; Apollo-Verlag Paul Lincke GmbH; Ars-Viva-Verlag; Atlantis-Musikbuch-Verlag; Anton J. Benjamin GmbH; Boosey & Hawkes GmbH; Bote & Bock GmbH & Co KG; Cranz GmbH; G. Henle Verlag; Matth. Hohner AG; Möseler Verlag; Musikverlag Doblinger; Musikverlag Zimmermann; Ries & Erler; Schott Music GmbH & Co KG; Sikorski; Richard Strauss GmbH & Co KG
Canada: Bartok Records; European American Music Distributors LLC; Carl Fischer Music; Hal Leonard Corporation; Musica Russica; Theodore Presser Company; Schott Music Corporation
Czech Republic: Panton
Finland: Fennica Gehrmann
Germany: Amadeus; Apollo-Verlag Paul Lincke GmbH; Ars-Viva-Verlag; Atlantis-Musikbuch-Verlag; Anton J. Benjamin GmbH; Boosey & Hawkes GmbH; Bote & Bock GmbH & Co KG; Cranz GmbH; G. Henle Verlag; Matth. Hohner AG; Möseler Verlag; Musikverlag Doblinger; Musikverlag Zimmermann; Ries & Erler; Schott Music GmbH & Co KG; Sikorski; Richard Strauss GmbH & Co KG
Japan: Zen On Music Company
Poland: PWM
Russia: DSCH; Russian Music Publishing
Singapore: Classical Spectrum
Slovakia: Panton
USA: Bartok Records; European American Music Distributors LLC; Carl Fischer Music; Hal Leonard Corporation; Musica Russica; Theodore Presser Company; Schott Music Corporation

Overseas Representation:
Europe: Schott Music GmbH & Co KG, Mainz, Germany
Japan: Schott Japan Co Ltd, Tokyo
USA: Hal Leonard Corporation, Milwaukee, WI

2680

SCION PUBLISHING LTD
Bloxham Mill, Barford Road, Bloxham, Oxon OX15 4FF
Telephone: 01295 722873
Fax: 01295 722875
Web Site: http://www.scionpublishing.com

Distribution:
NBN International, Estover Road, Plymouth PL6 7PZ

Directors: Dr Jonathan Ray (Managing)
Simon Watkins (Sales & Marketing)

Academic & Scholarly; Biology & Zoology; Chemistry; Medical (incl. Self Help & Alternative Medicine); Scientific & Technical

New Titles: 12 (2007), 12 (2008)
No of Employees: 3
Annual Turnover: £600,000

ISBNs, Imprints & Series: 978 1 904842

Distributor for:
UK: Medical Partners Publishing; The Ray Society
USA: Cold Spring Harbor Laboratory Press; DNA Press; Roberts & Co

Overseas Representation:
Americas (North & South): Cold Spring Harbor Laboratory Press, Woodbury, NY, USA
Australia & New Zealand: Macmillan Education Australia, South Yarra, Vic, Australia
Europe (excluding France, Italy, Spain & Portugal): Andrew Durnell Marketing Ltd, Tunbridge Wells, UK
Far East: The White Partnership, Tunbridge Wells, UK
France, Italy, Spain & Portugal: Flavio Marcello Publishers' Agents & Consultants, Padua, Italy
South Africa: Mike Brightmore, Academic Marketing Services, Johannesburg

Book Trade Association Membership:
IPG

2681

SCM-CANTERBURY PRESS LTD
13–17 Long Lane, London EC1A 9PN
Telephone: (020) 7776 7551
Fax: (020) 7776 7556
Email: office@scm-canterburypress.co.uk
Web Site: http://www.scm-canterburypress.co.uk

Warehouse & Distribution:
St Mary's Works, St Mary's Plain, Norwich NR3 3BH
Telephone: 01603 612914
Fax: 01603 624483
Email: admin@SCM-CanterburyPress.co.uk

UK Representation (Bookshops):
Christian Publishers Representatives, Holy Trinity Church, Marylebone Road, London
Telephone: (020) 7387 5282
Fax: (020) 7388 2352

Directors: Dominic Vaughan *(Managing)*
Valerie Bingham *(RMEP)*
Brenda Medhurst *(Financial Controller)*
Kevin Allard *(Customer Services, Key Account & UK Sales)*
Michael Addison *(Sales & Marketing)*
Managers: Stephen Rogers *(Production)*
Clive Edwards *(RMEP, Rights & Permissions)*
Commissioning Director: Christine Smith *(Canterbury Press)*
Editor: Natalie Watson *(SCM Press)*

Academic & Scholarly; Biography & Autobiography; Educational & Textbooks; Gender Studies; Music; Philosophy; Reference Books, Directories & Dictionaries; Religion & Theology; Travel & Topography; Judaica

ISBNs, Imprints & Series:
978 0 334 SCM Press
978 0 900274, 978 1 85175 Religious and Moral Education Press
978 0 907547 Hymns Ancient & Modern
978 1 85311 Canterbury Press, Norwich

Parent Company:
Hymns Ancient and Modern Ltd

Associated Companies:
G. J. Palmer & Sons Ltd

Distributor for:
Acora [Canterbury Press]; Australian Theological Forum [SCM Press]; James Clarke [Canterbury Press]; DEO Publishing [SCM Press]; Epworth Press; Lutterworth Press (Religion & Theology titles only) [Canterbury Press]; SLG Press [Canterbury Press]; Tufton Books [Canterbury Press]
Canada: Anglican Book Centre
USA: Trinity Press International

Overseas Representation:
Africa & South East Asia (Canterbury Press): Publishers International Marketing, London, UK
Australia & New Zealand (SCM Press): Openbook Publishers, Adelaide, SA, Australia
Australia (Canterbury Press, Norwich): Rainbow Books, Fairfield, Vic, Australia
Canada (SCM Press & Canterbury Press, Norwich): Novalis Inc, Toronto, Ont, Canada
New Zealand (Canterbury Press, Norwich): Church Book Stores, Auckland, New Zealand
South Africa (SCM Press): Tech Materials International Inc, Herndon, VA, South Africa
USA (Canterbury Press, Norwich): Morehouse, Harrisburg, PA, USA
USA (SCM Press): International Publishers Marketing Inc, Sterling, VA, USA
West Indies (Canterbury Press, Norwich): Hugh Dunphy, Kingston, Jamaica

Book Trade Association Membership:
Publishers Association; IPG

2682

SCOTTISH CHILDREN'S PRESS
Unit 6, Newbattle Abbey Business Park, Newbattle Road, Dalkeith EH22 3LJ
Telephone: 0131 660 4757 (Editorial)
Fax: 0870 285 4846
Email: info@scottishbooks.com
Web Site: http://www.scottishbooks.com

Warehouse, Trade Enquiries & Orders:
Telephone: 0131 660 4666 (Orders)
Fax: 0131 660 4666
Email: orders@scottishbooks.com

Directors: Brian Pugh *(Company Secretary)*
Avril Gray

Archaeology; Biography & Autobiography; Children's Books; Cookery, Wines & Spirits; Fiction; History & Antiquarian; Languages & Linguistics; Natural History; Poetry; Religion & Theology; Sports & Games

ISBNs, Imprints & Series: 978 1 899827

Associated Companies:
S.C.P. Publishers Ltd [trading as Scottish Cultural Press]

2683

*SCOTTISH CULTURAL PRESS
Unit 6, Newbattle Abbey Business Park, Newbattle Road, Dalkeith EH22 3LJ
Telephone: 0131 660 6366 (Editorial) & 4666 (Orders)
Fax: 0870 285 4846
Email: info@scottishbooks.com & orders@scottishbooks.com
Web Site: http://www.scottishbooks.com

Directors: Brian Pugh *(Company Secretary)*
Avril Gray

Archaeology; Audio Books; Biography & Autobiography; Cookery, Wines & Spirits; Environment & Development Studies; Geography & Geology; History & Antiquarian; Languages & Linguistics; Literature & Criticism; Military & War; Natural History; Nautical; Poetry; Reference Books, Directories & Dictionaries; Religion & Theology; Sociology & Anthropology; Theatre, Drama & Dance; Scottish Culture

ISBNs, Imprints & Series:
978 1 84017, 978 1 898218 Scottish Cultural Press (S.C.P. Publishers Ltd)
978 1 899827 Scottish Children's Press (S.C.P. Childrens Ltd)

Associated Companies:
S.C.P. Childrens Ltd [trading as Scottish Children's Press]

2684

SCOTTISH TEXT SOCIETY
School of English Studies, University of Nottingham, Nottingham NG7 2RD
Telephone: 0115 951 5922
Fax: 0115 951 5924
Email: editorialsecretary@scottishtextsociety.org
Web Site: http://www.scottishtextsociety.org

Registered Office:
27 George Square, Edinburgh EH8 9LD

President: Sally Mapstone
Editorial Secretary: Nicola Royan

Academic & Scholarly; History & Antiquarian; Literature & Criticism; Poetry

ISBNs, Imprints & Series: 978 1 897976

Overseas Representation:
Worldwide: Boydell & Brewer Ltd, Woodbridge, Suffolk, UK

Book Trade Association Membership:
Publishing Scotland

2685

SCRIPTURE UNION PUBLISHING
Scripture Union, 207–209 Queensway, Bletchley, Milton Keynes, Bucks MK2 2EB
Telephone: 01908 856000
Fax: 01908 856111
Email: info@scriptureunion.org.uk
Web Site: http://www.scripture.org.uk/

Warehouse:
STL, Carlisle

Mail Order:
PO Box 5148, Milton Keynes MLO MK2 2YX
Telephone: 01908 856006
Fax: 01908 856020
Email: subs@scriptureunion.org.uk

Publishing Director: Terry Clutterham
Accounts: Dave Parsons
Rights: Rosemary North
Promotions: Michael Welch
Production: Clive Cornelius

Children's Books; Educational & Textbooks; Music; Religion & Theology

New Titles: 48 (2007), 45 (2008)

ISBNs, Imprints & Series:
978 0 85421, 978 0 86201 Scripture Union

Overseas Representation:
Australasia, East Asia & Pacific: Resources for Ministry, Gosford, NSW, Australia
Canada: Scripture Union, Pickering
New Zealand: Scripture Union Wholesale, Wellington
USA: Scripture Union, Wayne, PA

Book Trade Association Membership:
BA; EPC

2686

SEARCH PRESS LTD
Wellwood, North Farm Road, Tunbridge Wells, Kent TN2 3DR
Telephone: 01892 510850
Fax: 01892 515903
Email: sales@searchpress.com
Web Site: http://www.searchpress.com

Directors: Martin de la Bédoyère *(Managing)*
Caroline de la Bédoyère
Rosalind Dace *(Editorial)*
Editors: Katie Chester
Heather Scott
Sophie Kersey
Designer: Juan Hayward
Production Manager: Inger Arthur

Children's Books; Crafts & Hobbies; Do-It-Yourself; Gardening

ISBNs, Imprints & Series:
978 0 85532 Beginner's Guide to Needlecrafts; Children's Crafts; Design Source Books; Leisure Arts; Search Press
978 1 84448, 978 1 903975

Distributor for:
Akacia; Ashby & Woolsey; Country Bumpkins; Forté Uitgevers; Interweave Press; Kangaroo Press; Sally Milner Publishing; Peel Productions; David Porteous Editions; School of Colour Publishing; Scrapbook Storytelling; Traplet Publications; XRX Books

Overseas Representation:
Africa & Caribbean: Kelvin van Hasselt Publishing Services, Briningham, Norfolk, UK
Asia, Japan & Pacific Islands: Publishers International Marketing, Dulles, VA, USA
Australia: Keith Ainsworth (Pty) Ltd, Penrith, NSW
Canada: Fitzhenry & Whiteside Ltd, Markham, Ont
Eastern Europe: Tony Moggach, InterMedia Americana (IMA) Ltd, London, UK
Germany, Austria & Switzerland: PS Publishers' Services, Frankfurt, Germany
India: Maya Publishers Pvt Ltd, New Delhi
Iran: Samin Far Qeshm Co, Tehran
Italy, Spain, Portugal, Gibraltar & Greece: Penny Padovani, London, UK
Malta: Hobbyworld, Mosta, UK
New Zealand: David Bateman Ltd, Auckland
Pakistan: Tahir M. Lodhi, Lahore
Scandinavia: Angell Eurosales, Berwick-on-Tweed, UK
Singapore & Malaysia: Mark Kuo, Selangor Darul Ehsan, Malaysia
Southern Africa: Trinity Books CC, Randburg, South Africa
Turkey: Belsu Ic Ve Dis Tic Ltd, STI, Istanbul
USA & Canada (book trade): Independent Publishers Group (IPG), Chicago, IL, USA
USA (craft industry): Search Press USA, Petaluma, CA, USA

2687

SEASQUIRT PUBLICATIONS
18d Church Gate, Loughborough, Leics LE11 1UD
Telephone: 01509 219633
Fax: 01509 264441
Email: info@seasquirtbooks.com
Web Site: http://www.jimjazzmouse.com & http://www.infestedwaters.co.uk

Children's Books; Trade

Book Trade Association Membership:
Publishers Association

2688

*SEDA PUBLICATIONS
[Staff & Educational Development Association]
Woburn House, 20–24 Tavistock Square, London WC1H 9HF
Telephone: (020) 7380 6767
Fax: (020) 7387 2655
Email: office@seda.ac.uk
Web Site: http://www.seda.ac.uk

Co-chair of SEDA: James Wisdom

Academic & Scholarly

Book Trade Association Membership:
Association of Learned & Professional Society Publishers

2689

SEREN
57 Nolton Street, Bridgend CF31 3AE
Telephone: 01656 663018
Email: seren@seren-books.com
Web Site: http://www.seren-books.com

Distribution:
Central Books, 99 Wallis Road, London E9 5LN
Telephone: (020) 8986 4854
Fax: (020) 8533 5821
Email: orders@centralbooks.com
Web Site: http://www.centralbooks.com

Managing Director: Mick Felton
Marketing Officer: Simon Hicks
Editors: Amy Wack *(Poetry)*
 Penny Thomas *(Fiction)*

Biography & Autobiography; Fiction; Fine Art & Art History; Literature & Criticism; Poetry; Politics & World Affairs; Theatre, Drama & Dance

New Titles: 22 (2007) , 22 (2008)
No of Employees: 5
Annual Turnover: £160,000

ISBNs, Imprints & Series:
978 0 907476, 978 1 85411

Parent Company:
Poetry Wales Press Ltd

Overseas Representation:
Australia: Eleanor Brasch Enterprises, Artarmon, NSW
USA & Canada: Independent Publishers Group (IPG), Chicago, IL, USA

2690

SESSIONS OF YORK
The Ebor Press, Huntington Road, York YO31 9HS
Telephone: 01904 659224
Fax: 01904 637068
Email: ebor.info@sessionsofyork.co.uk
Web Site: http://www.sessionsofyork.co.uk

Chairman & Managing Director: W. Mark Sessions
Publishing Manager: Bob Jarrett

Archaeology; Biography & Autobiography; Children's Books; History & Antiquarian; Industry, Business & Management; Natural History; Poetry; Politics & World Affairs; Religion & Theology

New Titles: 20 (2007) , 20 (2008)
No of Employees: 150

ISBNs, Imprints & Series: 978 1 85072

Parent Company:
William Sessions Holdings Ltd

Book Trade Association Membership:
Quakers Uniting in Publishing

2691

SEVERN HOUSE PUBLISHERS LTD
9–15 High Street, Sutton, Surrey SM1 1DF
Telephone: (020) 8770 3930
Fax: (020) 8770 3850
Email: editorial@severnhouse.com
Web Site: http://www.severnhouse.com

Distribution:
Grantham Book Services Ltd,
Isaac Newton Way,
Alma Park Industrial Estate, Grantham, Lincs NG31 9SD

Telephone: 01476 541080
Fax: 01476 541061

Chairman: Edwin Buckhalter
Publishing Director: Amanda Stewart
Sales Manager: Michelle Duff

Crime; Fiction; Science Fiction

ISBNs, Imprints & Series:
978 0 7278 Severn House Large Print
978 1 84751 Trade Paperbacks

Parent Company:
Severn House Books (Holdings) Ltd

Associated Companies:
USA: Severn House Publishers

Overseas Representation:
Australia: DLS Australia (Pty) Ltd, Braeside, Vic
USA: Ingram Publisher Services, Nashville, TN

Book Trade Association Membership:
Crime Writers Association; Romantic Novelists Association

2692

SGC BOOKS
PO Box 49, Spalding, Lincs PE11 1NZ
Telephone: 01775 712424
Fax: 01775 762618
Email: chalksoft@clara.co.uk
Web Site: http://www.chalksoft.clara.co.uk

Directors: David Baldwin *(Managing)*
 Gillian Baldwin *(Home Sales, Rights)*

Children's Books; Gardening; Health & Beauty; Natural History

New Titles: 4 (2007) , 4 (2008)
No of Employees: 3

ISBNs, Imprints & Series: 978 1 85116

Parent Company:
Chalksoft Ltd

Associated Companies:
Nene Valley Publishing

Book Trade Association Membership:
IPG

2693

SHARON HOUSE PUBLISHING
152 Wakefield Road, Onset, West Yorkshire WF5 9AQ
Telephone: 01924 279966
Fax: 01924 279966
Email: sharonhousepublishing@yahoo.co.uk
Web Site: http://www.sharonhousepublishing.com

Trade

Book Trade Association Membership:
Publishers Association

2694

SHAW & SONS LTD
21 Bourne Park, Bourne Road, Crayford, Kent DA1 4BZ
Telephone: 01322 621100
Fax: 01322 550553
Email: sales@shaws.co.uk
Web Site: http://www.shaws.co.uk

Directors: R. H. Smith *(Finance)*
 Crispin Williams *(Publications)*

Academic & Scholarly; Educational & Textbooks; Law; Reference Books, Directories & Dictionaries

New Titles: 12 (2007) , 10 (2008)
ISBNs, Imprints & Series:
978 0 7219 R. Hazell & Co; Shaw & Sons
978 0 9045 Owen Wells Publishing

Parent Company:
Shaw & Sons Group Ltd

Book Trade Association Membership:
Law Services Association

2695

SHEAF PUBLISHING
Beehive Works, Milton Street, Sheffield S3 7WL
Telephone: 0114 273 9067
Fax: 0114 270 6888

Managers: T. Cooper
 I. Irvine *(Works)*
Book-keeper: L. Haywood

History & Antiquarian; Transport

New Titles: 3 (2007) , 5 (2008)
No of Employees: 5
Annual Turnover: £400,000

ISBNs, Imprints & Series:
978 0 9505458, 978 1 85048

2696

SHELDON PRESS
36 Causton Street, London SW1P 4ST
Telephone: (020) 7592 3900
Fax: (020) 7592 3939
Email: jmoriarty@spck.org.uk
Web Site: http://www.sheldonpress.co.uk

Directors: Joanna Moriarty *(Publishing)*
 Alan Mordue *(Sales & Marketing)*
Editor: Fiona Marshall
Rights: Sophie Dean *(Sales Co-ordinator)*

Gender Studies; Health & Beauty; Medical (incl. Self Help & Alternative Medicine); Psychology & Psychiatry

ISBNs, Imprints & Series:
978 0 85969 Sheldon Press
978 1 902694 Azure Books

Parent Company:
The Society for Promoting Christian Knowledge (SPCK)

Overseas Representation:
Australia: Willow Connection Pty Ltd, Brookvale, NSW
India: ISPCK, Delhi
Middle East: Family Bookshop Group Co Ltd, Limassol, Cyprus
South Africa: Alternative Books CC, Ferndale

2697

SHELDRAKE PRESS
188 Cavendish Road, London SW12 0DA
Telephone: (020) 8675 1767
Fax: (020) 8675 7736
Email: enquiries@sheldrakepress.co.uk
Web Site: http://www.sheldrakepress.co.uk

Distribution:
NBN International Ltd, Estover Road, Plymouth PL6 7PY
Telephone: 01752 202300
Fax: 01752 202330
Email: enquiries@nbninternational.com
Web Site: http://www.nbninternational.com

Director: Simon Rigge *(Publisher)*
Company Secretary: Roger Rigge

Architecture & Design; Children's Books; Cookery, Wines & Spirits; Guide Books; History & Antiquarian; Humour; Transport; Travel & Topography

New Titles: 1 (2007) , 1 (2008)

ISBNs, Imprints & Series: 978 1 873329

Parent Company:
Sheldrake Holdings Ltd

Overseas Representation:
USA: Interlink Publishing Group Inc, Northampton, MA

2698

SHEPHEARD-WALWYN (PUBLISHERS) LTD
15 Alder Road, London SW14 8ER
Telephone: (020) 8241 5927
Email: books@shepheard-walwyn.co.uk
Web Site: http://www.shepheard-walwyn.co.uk

Orders:
NBN International, Plymbridge House, Estover Road, Plymouth PL6 7PY
Telephone: 01752 202301
Fax: 01752 202330
Email: orders@nbninternational.com
Web Site: http://www.nbninternational.com

Managing Director: Anthony R. A. Werner

Academic & Scholarly; Biography & Autobiography; Economics; History & Antiquarian; Illustrated & Fine Editions; Philosophy; Politics & World Affairs; Religion & Theology; Scottish Interest

New Titles: 7 (2007) , 7 (2008)
No of Employees: 2
Annual Turnover: £100,000

ISBNs, Imprints & Series:
The Letters of Marsilio Ficino; Marsilio Ficino's Commentaries on Plato's Writings; Who's Who in British History series
978 0 85683

Overseas Representation:
Australia: John Reed Book Distribution, Brookvale, NSW
USA & Canada: Independent Publishers Group (IPG), Chicago, IL, USA

Book Trade Association Membership:
IPG

2699

SHERWOOD PUBLISHING
Wild Hill, Broadoak End, Hertford SG14 2JA
Telephone: 01992 550246
Fax: 01992 535283
Email: sherwood@adinternational.com
Web Site: http://www.sherwoodpublishing.com

Chief Executive: Mrs Julie Hay

Industry, Business & Management; Psychology & Psychiatry

New Titles: 2 (2008)

ISBNs, Imprints & Series:
978 0 9521964, 978 0 9539852

Overseas Representation:
India: Creative Communication and Management Center, Bombay

Book Trade Association Membership:
IPG

2700

THE SHETLAND TIMES LTD
Gremista, Lerwick, Shetland ZE1 0PX
Telephone: 01595 693622
Fax: 01595 694637
Email: publishing@shetland-times.co.uk
Web Site: http://www.shetland-books.co.uk

Scottish Agent:
BookSource, 50 Cambuslang Road, Glasgow G32 8NB

Publications Manager: Charlotte Black

Biography & Autobiography; Guide Books; Music; Natural History

New Titles: 6 (2007), 7 (2008)
No of Employees: 2

ISBNs, Imprints & Series:
978 0 900662, 978 1 898852, 978 1 904746

Book Trade Association Membership:
BA; Publishing Scotland

2701

SHIRE PUBLICATIONS LTD
Midland House, West Way, Botley, Oxford OX2 0PH
Email: shire@shirebooks.co.uk
Web Site: http://www.shirebooks.co.uk

Director: Rebecca Smart *(Managing)*
Managers: Sue Ross *(Home & Export Sales)*
Nicholas Wright *(Publisher)*

Antiques & Collecting; Archaeology; Architecture & Design; Biography & Autobiography; Gardening; Guide Books; History & Antiquarian; Military & War; Natural History; Sociology & Anthropology; Transport; Travel & Topography

New Titles: 32 (2008)
No of Employees: 4
Annual Turnover: £765,000

ISBNs, Imprints & Series:
978 0 7478, 978 0 85263

2702

SHORT BOOKS LTD
34 Exmouth House, Pine Street, London EC1R 0JH
Telephone: (020) 7833 9429
Fax: (020) 7833 9500
Email: Rebecca@shortbooks.biz
Web Site: http://www.theshortbookco.com

Distribution:
TBS, Colchester Road, Frating Green, Colchester CO7 7DW
Telephone: 01206 255678
Fax: 01206 255930

Publisher: Rebecca Nicolson
Managing Director: Catherine Gibbs
Editor: Aurea Carpenter

Biography & Autobiography; Children's Books; Fiction; History & Antiquarian; Humour; Philosophy; Sports & Games

New Titles: 12 (2007), 14 (2008)
No of Employees: 4

ISBNs, Imprints & Series:
978 1 904095, 978 1 904977, 978 1 906021

Book Trade Association Membership:
IPG

2703

SIGEL PRESS
51A Victoria Road, Cambridge CB4 3BW
Telephone: 01223 303303
Fax: 01223 303303
Email: info@sigelpress.com
Web Site: http://www.sigelpress.com

Directors: Thomas Sigel *(Managing & Publisher)*
Andrew Hogbin *(Operations)*

Academic & Scholarly; Accountancy & Taxation; Audio Books; Children's Books; Educational & Textbooks; Environment & Development Studies; Fiction; Military & War; Science Fiction

New Titles: 6 (2007), 2 (2008)
No of Employees: 2
Annual Turnover: £50,000

ISBNs, Imprints & Series: 978 1 905941

Associated Companies:
USA: Sigel Press

Book Trade Association Membership:
IPG

2704

SIGMA PRESS
5 Alton Road, Wilmslow, Cheshire SK9 5DY
Telephone: 01625 531035
Fax: 01625 531035
Email: info@sigmapress.co.uk
Web Site: http://www.sigmapress.co.uk

Warehouse:
NBN International, Estover Road, Plymouth PL6 7PY
Telephone: 01752 202303
Fax: 01752 202334

Senior Editor: Graham Beech
Assistant Editor: Diana Beech

Crafts & Hobbies; Guide Books; Sports & Games; Travel & Topography

New Titles: 6 (2007), 4 (2008)

ISBNs, Imprints & Series:
978 0 905104, 978 1 85058 Sigma Leisure; Sigma Press

Overseas Representation:
USA: Barnes & Noble Distribution, Jamesburg, NJ

2705

SILVER MOON BOOKS
108c Goldhurst Terrace, London NW6 3HR
Telephone: (020) 7625 7592

Trade Enquiries & Orders:
Turnaround Publisher Services, Unit 3, Olympia Trading Estate, Coburg Road, London N22 6TZ
Telephone: (020) 8829 3000
Fax: (020) 8881 5088

Director: Jane Cholmeley

Fiction; Gay & Lesbian Studies

ISBNs, Imprints & Series: 978 1 872642

2706

SIMON & SCHUSTER (UK) LTD
1st Floor, 222 Gray's Inn Road, London WC1X 8HB
Telephone: (020) 7316 1900
Fax: (020) 7316 0331
Email: @simonandschuster.co.uk
Web Site: http://www.simonsays.co.uk

Customer Services & Distribution Centre:
HarperCollins, Customer Service Centre, Westerhill Road, Bishopbriggs, Glasgow G64 2QT
Telephone: 0141 306 3100
Fax: 0141 306 3767

Directors: Ian Stewart Chapman *(Managing)*
Suzanne Baboneau *(Adult Publishing)*
Julie Wright *(Pocket Books Publisher)*
Mike Jones *(Editorial – Non-Fiction)*
Ingrid Selberg *(Children's Publishing)*
Charlotte Robertson *(Group Sales)*
Hannah Corbett *(Publicity – Adult Trade)*
Jonathan Atkins *(International Publishing & Sales)*
David Hyde *(Production)*
Sarah Birdsey *(Rights)*

Audio Books; Biography & Autobiography; Children's Books; Cookery, Wines & Spirits; Crime; Fiction; Guide Books; Health & Beauty; Humour; Industry, Business & Management; Medical (incl. Self Help & Alternative Medicine); Music; Politics & World Affairs; Science Fiction; Sports & Games; Travel & Topography

ISBNs, Imprints & Series:
978 0 671, 978 0 684, 978 0 7432, 978 1 4165 Free Press; Scribner
978 0 671, 978 0 684, 978 0 7432, 978 1 4165, 978 1 84737 Simon & Schuster
978 0 671, 978 0 7434, 978 1 4165, 978 1 84739 Pocket
978 0 6898, 978 1 4169, 978 1 84738 Simon & Schuster Children's
978 0 7435 Simon & Schuster Audio

Parent Company:
USA: Simon & Schuster Inc

Distributor for:
UK: Duncan Baird; BL Publishing; Long Barn Books
USA: Andrews McMeel; Atria; Fireside; Free Press; Pocket; Scribner; Simon & Schuster Inc; Simon & Schuster Audio; Touchstone; VIZ Media; Zagat

Overseas Representation:
Australia: Simon & Schuster (Australia) Pty Ltd, Pymble, NSW
Canada: Simon & Schuster (Canada), Markham, Ont
New Zealand: HarperCollins (NZ) Ltd, Glenfield, Auckland
Singapore: Penguin Books Singapore, Jurong
South Africa: Jonathan Ball Publishers (Pty) Ltd, Johannesburg
USA: Trafalgar Square Publishing / IPG, Chicago, IL

Book Trade Association Membership:
Publishers Association

2707

CHARLES SKILTON LTD
2 Caversham Street, London SW3 4AH
Telephone: (020) 7351 4995
Fax: (020) 7351 4995
Email: leonard.holdsworth@btopenworld.com

Directors: James Hughes *(Managing)*
Margaret Fletcher *(Sales)*
Editor: Leonard Holdsworth

Cinema, Video, TV & Radio; Cookery, Wines & Spirits; Fashion & Costume; Fiction; Fine Art & Art History; Gay & Lesbian Studies; Guide Books; Illustrated & Fine Editions; Literature & Criticism; Military & War; Poetry; Theatre, Drama & Dance; Transport; Travel & Topography

ISBNs, Imprints & Series:
978 0 284 Skilton

978 1 901846 Christchurch

Parent Company:
Christchurch Publishers Ltd

Associated Companies:
Caversham Communications Ltd; Christchurch Publishers Ltd; Luxor Press

Book Trade Association Membership:
IPG

2708

SLIGHTLY FOXED
67 Dickinson Court, 15 Brewhouse Yard, London EC1V 4JX
Telephone: (020) 7549 2121
Fax: 0870 199 1245
Email: all@foxedquarterly.com
Web Site: http://www.foxedquarterly.com

Managing Director: Gail Pirkis
Co-Editor: Hazel Wood
Marketing Manager: Stephanie Allen
Administrator: Jennie Paterson

Academic & Scholarly; Biography & Autobiography; Children's Books; Fiction; Gardening; History & Antiquarian; Illustrated & Fine Editions; Travel & Topography

New Titles: 4 (2007), 8 (2008)
No of Employees: 2
Annual Turnover: £200,000

ISBNs, Imprints & Series: 978 1 906562

Book Trade Association Membership:
IPG

2709

SLS LEGAL PUBLICATIONS (NI)
Lansdowne House, 50 Malone Road, Belfast BT9 5BS
Telephone: (028) 9066 7711
Fax: (028) 9066 7733
Email: s.gamble@qub.ac.uk
Web Site: http://www.sls.qub.ac.uk

Director: Miss M. Dudley
Publications Editor: Mrs S. Gamble

Academic & Scholarly; Law

ISBNs, Imprints & Series: 978 0 85389

Book Trade Association Membership:
Publishers Association; CAPP

2710

SMITH SETTLE PRINTING & BOOKBINDING LTD
Gateway Drive, Yeadon, West Yorkshire LS19 7XY
Telephone: 0113 250 9201
Fax: 0113 250 9223
Email: sales@smithsettle.com
Web Site: http://www.smith-settle.co.uk

Directors: Donald Waters *(Managing)*
Tracey Daly *(Finance)*

Academic & Scholarly; Agriculture; Archaeology; Biography & Autobiography; History & Antiquarian; Illustrated & Fine Editions; Sports & Games; Travel & Topography

No of Employees: 2

ISBNs, Imprints & Series: 978 1 84103

Associated Companies:
Westbury

Distributor for:
Ken Smith Publishing Ltd; Woodstock Books Ltd

Book Trade Association Membership:
IPG

2711

ADAM SMITH INSTITUTE
23 Great Smith Street, London SW1P 3BL
Telephone: (020) 7222 4995
Fax: (020) 7222 1436
Email: info@adamsmith.org.uk
Web Site: http://www.adamsmith.org.uk

Director: Dr Eamonn Butler
President: Dr Madsen Pirie

Accountancy & Taxation; Economics; Politics & World Affairs

New Titles: 2 (2007), 12 (2008)

ISBNs, Imprints & Series:
978 0 906517, 978 1 870109, 978 1 873712, 978 1 902737

Parent Company:
ASI (Research) Ltd

2712

COLIN SMYTHE LTD
PO Box 6, Gerrards Cross, Bucks SL9 8XA
Telephone: 01753 886000
Fax: 01753 886469
Email: sales@colinsmythe.co.uk
Web Site: http://www.colinsmythe.co.uk

Warehouse & Despatch only:
Clipper Distribution Services Ltd, Windmill Grove, Portchester, Hants PO16 9HT
Telephone: (023) 9220 0080
Fax: (023) 9220 0090

Managing Director: Colin Smythe *(Sales, Editorial, Rights & Production)*

Academic & Scholarly; Bibliography & Library Science; Biography & Autobiography; Literature & Criticism; Theatre, Drama & Dance; Heraldry; Orders of Knighthood

New Titles: 3 (2007), 3 (2008)
No of Employees: 2
Annual Turnover: £2.5M

ISBNs, Imprints & Series:
978 0 85105 Dolmen Press
978 0 86140, 978 0 900675, 978 0 901072
978 0 905715 Van Duren

Distributor for:
Republic of Ireland: Tir Eolas
USA: ELT Press

Overseas Representation:
Ireland: Hibernian Book Services, Dublin, Republic of Ireland
USA & Canada: Dufour Editions Inc, Chester Springs, PA, USA
USA & Canada (recent academic titles): Oxford University Press Inc USA, New York, NY, USA

Book Trade Association Membership:
Publishers Association; IPG; Booksellers' Association Associate Member

2713

SNOWBOOKS
120 Pentonville Road, London N1 9JN
Telephone: 0790 406 2414
Email: emma@snowbooks.com
Web Site: http://www.snowbooks.com

Distribution:
Littlehampton Book Services, Faraday Close, Durrington, Worthing, West Sussex BN13 3RB
Telephone: 01903 828511
Fax: 01903 828801

Email: orders@lbsltd.co.uk
Web Site: http://www.lbsltd.co.uk

Managing Director: Emma Barnes
Chairman: Rob Jones
Publisher: Anna Torborg

Cookery, Wines & Spirits; Crafts & Hobbies; Crime; Fiction; Humour; Illustrated & Fine Editions; Science Fiction; Sports & Games; Transport

New Titles: 27 (2007), 25 (2008)
No of Employees: 2
Annual Turnover: £400,000

ISBNs, Imprints & Series:
978 0 954575, 978 1 905005, 978 1 906727

Overseas Representation:
Australia: Julie Pinkham, Hardie Grant Books, Prahran, Vic
Europe & Ireland: Andrew Durnell, Durnell Marketing Ltd, Tunbridge Wells, UK
Far East: Peter Couzens, Sales East, Bangkok, Thailand
USA & Canada: Consortium Publishers, St Paul, MN, USA

Book Trade Association Membership:
IPG

2714

SOCCER BOOKS LTD
72 St Peter's Avenue, Cleethorpes, Lincs DN35 8HU
Telephone: 01472 696226
Fax: 01472 698546
Email: info@soccer-books.co.uk
Web Site: http://www.soccer-books.co.uk

Directors: John Robinson *(Managing)*
Michael Robinson

Sports & Games; Transport

New Titles: 9 (2007), 10 (2008)
No of Employees: 5

ISBNs, Imprints & Series:
978 1 86223 Complete Results & Line-ups (Series); Football In (Series); Supporters' Guide (Series)

2715

SOCIAL AFFAIRS UNIT
10/11 Morley House,
314–322 Regent Street, London W1B 5SA
Telephone: (020) 7637 4356
Fax: (020) 7436 8530
Email: mosbacher@socialaffairsunit.org.uk
Web Site: http://www.socialaffairsunit.org.uk

Director: Michael Mosbacher

Academic & Scholarly; Crime; Economics; Educational & Textbooks; Environment & Development Studies; Industry, Business & Management; Medical (incl. Self Help & Alternative Medicine); Politics & World Affairs; Reference Books, Directories & Dictionaries; Sociology & Anthropology

New Titles: 7 (2007), 10 (2008)
No of Employees: 4
Annual Turnover: £250,000

ISBNs, Imprints & Series:
978 0 907631, 978 1 904863

2716

THE SOCIETY FOR PROMOTING CHRISTIAN KNOWLEDGE (SPCK)
36 Causton Street, London SW1P 4ST
Telephone: (020) 7592 3900
Fax: (020) 7592 3939
Email: publishing@spck.org.uk

Web Site: http://www.spck.org.uk

Warehouse & Distribution:
Marston Book Services, Unit 160, Milton Park, Abingdon, Oxon OX14 4SD
Telephone: 01235 465500
Fax: 01235 465555

Directors: Simon Kingston *(Chief Executive Officer)*
Joanna Moriarty *(Publishing)*
Alan Mordue *(Sales & Marketing)*
Barry Finch *(Production)*
Editors: Alison Barr
Fiona Marshall
Ruth McCurry
Rights: Sophie Dean *(Sales Co-ordinator)*

Academic & Scholarly; Illustrated & Fine Editions; Medical (incl. Self Help & Alternative Medicine); Psychology & Psychiatry; Religion & Theology

ISBNs, Imprints & Series:
978 0 281 SPCK; Triangle Books
978 0 7459 Lynx Communication
978 0 85969, 978 1 84709 Sheldon Press
978 1 902694 Azure Books

Overseas Representation:
Australia: Willow Connection Pty Ltd, Brookvale, NSW
Canada: Bayard Distribution, Toronto, Ont
Far East (Sheldon): CKK Ltd, Northwood, Middx, UK
Far East (SPCK, Triangle, Azure): Publishers International Marketing, London, UK
India: ISPCK, Delhi
Middle East (Sheldon): Family Bookshop Group Co Ltd, Limassol, Cyprus
New Zealand (SPCK, Triangle, Azure): Omega Distributors Ltd, Auckland, New Zealand
Northern Europe: Ted Dougherty, London, UK
South Africa (Sheldon): Alternative Books CC, Ferndale, South Africa
USA (SPCK, Triangle, Azure): Westminster John Knox Press, Louisville, KY, USA

Book Trade Association Membership:
Publishers Association

2717

*SOCIETY OF ANTIQUARIES OF SCOTLAND
NMS, Chambers Street, Edinburgh EH1 4JF
Telephone: 0131 247 4145
Fax: 0131 247 4163
Email: sales@socantscot.org
Web Site: http://www.socantscot.org

Director: Dr Simon Gilmour
Sales & Publicity Manager: Erin Osborne-Martin

Academic & Scholarly; Archaeology; History & Antiquarian

ISBNs, Imprints & Series: 978 0 903903

2718

SOCIETY OF GENEALOGISTS ENTERPRISES LTD
14 Charterhouse Buildings, London EC1M 7BA
Telephone: (020) 7251 8799
Fax: (020) 7250 1800
Email: sales@sog.org.uk
Web Site: http://www.sog.org.uk/

Chief Executive: June Perrin
Retail Manager: Anthony Mortimer

History & Antiquarian

New Titles: 1 (2007), 2 (2008)
No of Employees: 3

ISBNs, Imprints & Series: 978 1 903462

Parent Company:
Society of Genealogists

Book Trade Association Membership:
BA

2719

THE SOCIETY OF METAPHYSICIANS LTD
Archers' Court, Stonestile Lane, The Ridge, Hastings, East Sussex TN35 4PG
Telephone: 01424 751577
Fax: 01424 751577
Email: newmeta@btinternet.com
Web Site: http://www.metaphysicians.org.uk

Managing Director: Dr J. J. Williamson
General Secretary: Ms C. Yuen
Scientific & Literary Research: D. Cumberland
Tutor: Mervin Gould

Academic & Scholarly; Educational & Textbooks; Electronic (Educational); Environment & Development Studies; Magic & the Occult; Medical (incl. Self Help & Alternative Medicine); Philosophy; Scientific & Technical; Esoteric; Neometaphysics; Paraphysics; Parapsychology

New Titles: 8 (2007), 6 (2008)
No of Employees: 5

ISBNs, Imprints & Series:
978 0 900680, 978 1 85228, 978 1 85810

Associated Companies:
Metaphysical Research Group
Argentina: Sociedad de Metafisica Inglesa
Belgium: Society of Metaphysicians
Italy: Istituto Italiano di Ricerche Metafisiche
Nigeria: Society of Metaphysicians (Nigeria) Ltd

Distributor for:
USA: Ars Obscura [Archival Reproductions]; Health Research [Rare reprints]

Overseas Representation:
Australia: Magic Circle Bookshop, Perth
Belgium: Ignoramus, As; L' Univers Particulier, Brussels
Netherlands: Boekhandel Synthese, 's Gravenhage
New Zealand: Bennet's Bookshop, Palmerston North
Spain: Eyras Editorial, Madrid
Tenerife: Soluciones, Spain
USA: H.R., Pomeroy, WA

2720

SOLIDUS
Hope Springs, Far End, Sheepscombe, Stroud, Glos GL6 7RL
Telephone: 01452 812886
Email: info@soliduspress.com
Web Site: http://www.soliduspress.com

Manager: Helen Miles

Children's Books; Fiction

New Titles: 4 (2007), 2 (2008)

ISBNs, Imprints & Series:
978 0 954337 Solidus
978 1 904529 Back to Front

Book Trade Association Membership:
IPG

2721

SOUTHGATE PUBLISHERS
The Square, Sandford, Crediton, Devon EX17 4LW
Telephone: 01363 776888
Fax: 01363 776889

Email: info@southgatepublishers.co.uk
Web Site: http://www.southgatepublishers.co.uk

Managing Director: Drummond Johnstone
Production Manager: Marlene Buckland

Educational & Textbooks; Environment & Development Studies; Vocational Training & Careers

New Titles: 14 (2007), 14 (2008)

ISBNs, Imprints & Series: 978 1 85741

Associated Companies:
Mosaic Educational Publications

Distributor for:
Campaign for Learning; Learning Through Landscapes Trust

Overseas Representation:
Canada: Bacon & Hughes Ltd, Ottawa, Ont

Book Trade Association Membership:
IPG

2722

SOUVENIR PRESS LTD
43 Great Russell Street, London WC1B 3PA
Telephone: (020) 7580 9307/8 & 7637 5711/2/3
Fax: (020) 7580 5064
Email: souvenirpress@ukonline.co.uk

Distributors & Warehouse:
Bookpoint Ltd, 130 Milton Trading Estate, Abingdon, Oxon OX14 4SB
Telephone: 01235 400400
Fax: 01235 400413

Managing Director & Chairman: Ernest Hecht

Academic & Scholarly; Animal Care & Breeding; Antiques & Collecting; Archaeology; Biography & Autobiography; Crafts & Hobbies; Gardening; Gender Studies; Health & Beauty; Humour; Industry, Business & Management; Literature & Criticism; Magic & the Occult; Medical (incl. Self Help & Alternative Medicine); Military & War; Music; Natural History; Philosophy; Psychology & Psychiatry; Religion & Theology; Sociology & Anthropology; Sports & Games; Theatre, Drama & Dance; Travel & Topography; Veterinary Science

ISBNs, Imprints & Series:
978 0 285 Condor Books; Human Horizons; Souvenir Press (Educational & Academic) Ltd; Souvenir Press Ltd

Associated Companies:
Pictorial Presentations Ltd; Pop Universal Ltd; Souvenir Press (Educational & Academic) Ltd

Overseas Representation:
Australia: Tower Books Pty Ltd, Brookvale, NSW
Austria, Benelux, France, Germany, Switzerland, Greece & Italy: Ted Dougherty, London, UK
India: Rupa, New Delhi
Middle East: Peter Ward Book Exports, London, UK
New Zealand: Addenda, Auckland
Scandinavia: John Edgeler, London, UK
South Africa: Trinity Books CC, Randburg

2723

SPARTAN PRESS MUSIC PUBLISHERS LTD
Strathmashie House, Laggan, Inverness-shire PH20 1BU
Telephone: 01528 544770
Fax: 01528 544771
Email: sales@spartanpress.co.uk
Web Site: http://www.spartanpress.co.uk

Directors: Mark Goddard *(Managing)*
Pat Goddard
Managers: Sandra Grant *(Sales)*
Ian Stevenson *(IT)*
Finishing: Sharon Curtis
Pat Haines

Music

New Titles: 36 (2007), 36 (2008)

ISBNs, Imprints & Series:
ISMN: 57 999

Distributor for:
Netherlands: European Music Centre
UK: Camden Music; Colne Edition; G. S. Music; Hunt Edition; Múzicas Editions; Nova Music; Pan Educational Music; Queen's Temple Publications; Sunshine Music Co; Useful Music; Yorke Edition

Overseas Representation:
Netherlands: European Music Centre, Huizen
USA & Canada: Theodore Presser Co, King of Prussia, PA, USA

2724

SPECIAL INTEREST MODEL BOOKS LTD
50a Willis Way, Poole, Dorset BH15 3SY
Telephone: 01202 649930
Fax: 01202 649950
Email: chrlloyd@globalnet.co.uk
Web Site: http://www.specialinterestmodelbooks.co.uk

Managing Director: Chris Lloyd

Aviation; Cookery, Wines & Spirits; Crafts & Hobbies; Engineering; Nautical; Transport

ISBNs, Imprints & Series:
978 0 85242 Workshop Practice Series
978 0 900841 Amateur Winemaker Books
978 1 85486 formerly Argus Books; formerly MAP (Model & Allied Publications); formerly Nexus Special Interest Books

Overseas Representation:
Australia: Capricorn Link (Australia) Pty Ltd, Windsor, NSW
Eastern Europe, East & West Africa: Anthony Moggach, InterMedia Americana (IMA) Ltd, London, UK
New Zealand: South Pacific Books (Imports) Ltd, Auckland
Scandinavia (including Denmark, Sweden, Norway, Finland & Iceland) & Netherlands: Angell Eurosales, Berwick-on-Tweed, UK
South Africa: Everybody's Books, Kwa Zulu Natal, South Africa
South & Central America & Caribbean: David Williams, InterMedia Americana (IMA) Ltd, London, UK
South East Asia (including Singapore, Malaysia, Brunei, Indonesia, Hong Kong, Taiwan, China, Philippines, Thailand & Japan): Ashton International Marketing Services, Sevenoaks, Kent, UK
Southern Europe (including Spain, Portugal, Italy, Malta & Greece): Joe Portelli, Bookport Associates, Corsico (MI), Italy
Western Europe (including France, Belgium, Germany, Switzerland & Austria): Anselm Robinson, European Marketing Services, London, UK

2725

SPEECHMARK PUBLISHING LTD
70 Alston Drive, Bradwell Abbey, Milton Keynes MK13 9HG
Telephone: 0845 034 4610
Fax: 0845 034 4649
Email: info@speechmark.net
Web Site: http://www.speechmark.net

Customer Service:
(as above)
Telephone: 0800 243755 & 0845 034 4610
Fax: 0845 034 4649
Email: sales@speechmark.net
Web Site: http://www.speechmark.net

Directors: Catherine McAllister *(Managing)*
Liz Lane *(Sales & Marketing)*
Publishing Manager: Sue Christelow

Children's Books; Educational & Textbooks; English as a Foreign Language; Health & Beauty; Languages & Linguistics; Medical (incl. Self Help & Alternative Medicine); Psychology & Psychiatry; Care of the Elderly; Occupational Therapy; Speech Therapy

New Titles: 23 (2007)

ISBNs, Imprints & Series:
ColorCards; Helping Children with Feelings; Speechmark Editions
978 0 86388

Parent Company:
UK: Electric Word Plc

2726

SPOKESMAN
Russell House, Bulwell Lane, Nottingham NG6 0BT
Telephone: 0115 978 4504 & 970 8318
Fax: 0115 942 0433
Email: elfeuro@compuserve.com
Web Site: http://www.spokesmanbooks.com

Managers: Ken Fleet *(General)*
Tony Simpson *(Publications)*
Editor: Ken Coates

Economics; Fiction; History & Antiquarian; Military & War; Philosophy; Poetry; Politics & World Affairs; Sociology & Anthropology; Theatre, Drama & Dance; Europe; Works of Bertrand Russell

New Titles: 17 (2007), 10 (2008)
No of Employees: 5

ISBNs, Imprints & Series:
978 0 85124 Socialist Renewal; The Spokesman

Associated Companies:
Bertrand Russell Peace Foundation Ltd

2727

SPORTSBOOKS LTD
1 Evelyn Court, Malvern Road, Cheltenham GL50 2JR
Telephone: 01242 256755
Fax: 01242 254694
Email: randall@sportsbooks.ltd.uk
Web Site: http://www.sportsbooks.ltd.uk

Distribution:
Turnaround Publisher Services Ltd, Unit 3, Olympia Industrial Estate, Coburg Road, London N22 6TZ
Telephone: (020) 8829 3000
Fax: (020) 8881 5088
Email: orders@turnaround-uk.com
Web Site: http://www.turnaround-psl.com

Chairman: Randall Northam
Director: Veronica Northam

Fiction; History & Antiquarian; Sports & Games

New Titles: 12 (2007), 12 (2008)

ISBNs, Imprints & Series:
978 0 9541544, 978 1 899807 BMM; Sportsbooks

Overseas Representation:
Australia & New Zealand: Landmark Press, Drovin, Vic, Australia
South Africa: Zytek Publishing (Pty) Ltd, Bedfordview

2728

SPRINGER VERLAG LONDON
Ashbourne House, The Guildway, Old Portsmouth Road, Guildford GU3 1LP
Telephone: 01483 734433
Fax: 01483 734411
Email: ken.derham@springer-sbm.com
Web Site: http://www.springer.com

Academic & Scholarly; Medical (incl. Self Help & Alternative Medicine)

Book Trade Association Membership:
Publishers Association

2729

STACEY INTERNATIONAL
128 Kensington Church Street, London W8 4BH
Telephone: (020) 7221 7166
Fax: (020) 7792 9288
Email: info@stacey-international.co.uk
Web Site: http://www.stacey-international.co.uk

Distribution:
Central Books, 99 Wallis Road, Hackney Wick, London E9 5LN
Telephone: 0845 458 9911
Fax: 0845 458 9912
Email: orders@centralbooks.com
Web Site: http://www.centralbooks.com

Chairman: T. C. G. Stacey
Director: Max Scott

Academic & Scholarly; Archaeology; Architecture & Design; Biography & Autobiography; Children's Books; Educational & Textbooks; Fine Art & Art History; Geography & Geology; Guide Books; History & Antiquarian; Illustrated & Fine Editions; Languages & Linguistics; Military & War; Natural History; Photography; Politics & World Affairs; Reference Books, Directories & Dictionaries; Religion & Theology; Travel & Topography

ISBNs, Imprints & Series:
978 0 905743, 978 1 900988, 978 1 903185

Parent Company:
Stacey Arts Ltd

Associated Companies:
Gorilla Guides; Rubicon Press

Book Trade Association Membership:
IPG

2730

STAINER & BELL LTD
PO Box 110, 23 Gruneisen Road, London N3 1DZ
Telephone: (020) 8343 3303
Fax: (020) 8343 3024
Email: post@stainer.co.uk
Web Site: http://www.stainer.co.uk

Directors: Keith Wakefield *(Joint Managing, Marketing, Permissions, Accounts & Distribution)*
Carol Wakefield *(Joint Managing)*
Antony Kearns *(Deputy Managing)*
Nicholas Williams *(Publishing)*
Amanda Aknai *(Production)*

Academic & Scholarly; Biography & Autobiography; History & Antiquarian; Music; Reference Books, Directories & Dictionaries; Religion & Theology; Theatre, Drama & Dance

New Titles: 29 (2007), 30 (2008)
No of Employees: 8
Annual Turnover: £774,349

ISBNs, Imprints & Series:
978 0 85249 Augener; Early English Church Music; Galliard; Music for London Entertainment; Musica Britannica; Stainer & Bell; Weekes; Joseph Williams

Associated Companies:
Galliard Ltd

Distributor for:
USA: ECS Publishing Co [Rental Library]

Overseas Representation:
USA (hymn copyrights & selected titles): Hope Publishing, Carol Stream, IL, USA
USA (Rental Library): ECS Publishing Co, Boston, MA, USA

Book Trade Association Membership:
The Music Publishers Association Ltd

2731

RUDOLF STEINER PRESS
Hillside House, The Square, Forest Row, East Sussex RH18 5ES
Telephone: 01342 824433
Fax: 01342 826437
Email: office@rudolfsteinerpress.com
Web Site: http://www.rudolfsteinerpress.com

Trade Enquiries & Orders:
BookSource, 50 Cambuslang Road, Glasgow G32 8NB
Telephone: 0845 370 0063
Fax: 0845 370 0064
Email: orders@booksource.net
Web Site: http://www.booksource.net

Manager: Sevak Gulbekian (Chief Editor)

Biography & Autobiography; Educational & Textbooks; Fine Art & Art History; Magic & the Occult; Medical (incl. Self Help & Alternative Medicine); Music; Philosophy; Politics & World Affairs; Religion & Theology; Sociology & Anthropology; Theatre, Drama & Dance

New Titles: 20 (2007), 20 (2008)
Annual Turnover: £160,000

ISBNs, Imprints & Series:
978 0 85440, 978 1 85584 Mercury Arts Publications; New Knowledge Books; Sophia Books; Rudolf Steiner Press
978 0 88010, 978 0 091014 Steiner Books
978 0 88010, 978 0 91014 Anthroposophic Press

Distributor for:
Mercury Arts Publications; New Knowledge Books
Australia: Completion Press
USA: Steinerbooks

Overseas Representation:
Australia: Rudolf Steiner Book Centre, Sydney, NSW
Canada: Tri-fold Books, Guelph, Ont
New Zealand: Ceres Books, Ellerslie
South Africa: Rudolf Steiner Publications, Bryanston
USA: Steiner Books Inc, Herndon, VA

Book Trade Association Membership:
IPG

2732

STENLAKE PUBLISHING LTD
54–58 Mill Square, Catrine, Ayrshire KA5 6RD
Telephone: 01290 551122
Fax: 01290 551122
Email: enquiries@stenlake.co.uk
Web Site: http://www.stenlake.co.uk

Editorial: David Pettigrew
Managing Director: Richard Stenlake
Sales: Alex F. Young

Antiques & Collecting; Aviation; Cinema, Video, TV & Radio; Crafts & Hobbies; History & Antiquarian; Literature & Criticism; Nautical; Poetry; Transport

New Titles: 30 (2007), 40 (2008)

ISBNs, Imprints & Series:
978 0 907526 Alloway Publishing
978 1 84033, 978 1 872074

2733

STEP FORWARD PUBLISHING LTD
St Jude's Church, Dulwich Road, Herne Hill, London SE24 0PB
Telephone: (020) 7738 5454
Fax: (020) 7733 2325
Email: enquiries@practicalpreschool.com
Web Site: http://www.practicalpreschool.com

Directors: Rebecca Linssen (Group Editorial)
Mark Allen (Managing)
Manager: Angela Shaw (Publishing)
Assistant: Rebecca Haworth (Publishing)

Educational & Textbooks

New Titles: 15 (2008)

ISBNs, Imprints & Series:
978 1 902438, 978 1 904575

Parent Company:
UK: Mark Allen Group

Book Trade Association Membership:
EPC; IPG

2734

STOBART DAVIES LTD
Stobart House, Pontyclerc, Penybanc Road, Ammanford, Carmarthenshire SA18 3HP
Telephone: 01269 593100
Fax: 01269 596116
Email: sales@stobartdavies.com
Web Site: http://www.stobartdavies.com

Directors: Jane Evans
Nigel Evans

Crafts & Hobbies; Do-It-Yourself; Natural History; Scientific & Technical

New Titles: 7 (2007), 8 (2008)
No of Employees: 6
Annual Turnover: £260,000

ISBNs, Imprints & Series: 978 0 85442

Parent Company:
Stobart Davis (2002) Ltd

Distributor for:
India: International Book Distributors

Overseas Representation:
Australia & New Zealand: Footprint Books Pty Ltd, Warriewood, NSW, Australia
Europe: Ted Dougherty, London, UK
Far East: Sales East, Bangkok, Thailand
New Zealand: David Bateman Ltd, Auckland
South Africa: Peter Hyde Associates (Pty) Ltd, Cape Town

Book Trade Association Membership:
BA; IPG

2735

STOKESBY HOUSE PUBLICATIONS
Stokesby, Norfolk NR29 3ET
Telephone: 01493 750645
Email: pamela.minett@waitrose.com
Web Site: http://www.stokesbyhouse.co.uk

Publisher & Marketing: Pamela Minett

Educational & Textbooks; Environment & Development Studies; Medical (incl. Self Help & Alternative Medicine)

ISBNs, Imprints & Series:
978 0 9514490, 978 1 873600

2736

STOTT'S CORRESPONDENCE COLLEGE
PO Box 35488, St John's Wood, London NW8 6WD
Telephone: (020) 7586 4499
Email: microworld@ndirect.co.uk
Web Site: http://www.microworld.uk.com

Director: S. C. Albert

Academic & Scholarly; Crafts & Hobbies; Fashion & Costume; Health & Beauty

Distributor for:
Australia: Stott's Correspondence College

2737

STRI (SPORTS TURF RESEARCH INSTITUTE)
St Ives Estate, Bingley, West Yorks BD16 1AU
Telephone: 01274 565131
Fax: 01274 561891
Email: info@stri.co.uk
Web Site: http://www.stri.co.uk/bookshop

Chief Executive: Dr Gordon McKillop
Financial Director: Mark Godfrey
Head of External Affairs: Anne Wilson

Educational & Textbooks; Environment & Development Studies; Reference Books, Directories & Dictionaries; Scientific & Technical; Sports & Games

New Titles: 2 (2007), 2 (2008)
No of Employees: 70
Annual Turnover: £300,000

ISBNs, Imprints & Series:
978 0 9503647, 978 1 873431

Overseas Representation:
Australia & New Zealand: Johima Pty Ltd, Parramatta, NSW, Australia
Netherlands: Prograss BV, Harderwijk

2738

STRONG OAK PRESS
PO Box 728, Crawley, West Sussex RH10 7WD
Telephone: 01293 552727
Email: strongoakpress@hotmail.com

Managing Director: Steven Apps

Biography & Autobiography; Fine Art & Art History; History & Antiquarian; Military & War; Travel & Topography; List of Books on Scotland (History, Art)

ISBNs, Imprints & Series:
978 0 907590, 978 1 871048 Spa Books

Distributor for:
The Strong Oak Press Ltd

South Africa: William Waterman Publications [including Ashanti Publishing & Justified Press]

2739

STUDYMATES LTD
Studymates House, PO Box 225, Abergele, Conwy County LL18 9AY
Telephone: 01745 832863
Fax: 01745 826606
Email: manager@studymates.co.uk
Web Site: http://www.studymates.co.uk

Warehouse, Trade Enquiries & Orders:
Central Books Ltd, 99 Wallis Road, London E9 5LN
Telephone: 0845 458 9911
Email: sales@centralbooks.com

Representation (UK):
Compass Academic Ltd,
The Barley Mow Centre,
10 Barley Mow Passage, Chiswick, London W4 4PH
Telephone: (020) 8994 6477
Fax: (020) 8400 6132

Directors: Graham Lawler (Managing)
Judith Lawler (Finance)

Academic & Scholarly; Audio Books; Biology & Zoology; Chemistry; Educational & Textbooks; Electronic (Educational); English as a Foreign Language; History & Antiquarian; Industry, Business & Management; Languages & Linguistics; Law; Literature & Criticism; Mathematics & Statistics; Medical (incl. Self Help & Alternative Medicine); Military & War; Physics; Poetry; Politics & World Affairs; Religion & Theology; Scientific & Technical; Sociology & Anthropology; Theatre, Drama & Dance

ISBNs, Imprints & Series:
978 1 84285 Aber-Torchlight Books; Studymates Professional

Parent Company:
Serveonline Ltd

Overseas Representation:
Asia: The White Partnership, Tunbridge Wells, UK
Australia & New Zealand: Footprint Books Pty Ltd, Sydney, NSW, Australia
Caribbean: Humphrys Roberts Associates, London, UK
Europe: Andrew Durnell Marketing Ltd, Tunbridge Wells, UK
Middle East: International Publishing Services (IPS) Middle East Ltd, Dubai, UAE

Book Trade Association Membership:
IPG

2740

SUMMER PALACE PRESS
31 Stranmillis Park, Belfast BT9 5AU
Telephone: (028) 9066 7759
Email: clednageeragh@eircom.net

Co-Directors: Joan Newmann
Kate Newmann

Poetry

New Titles: 1 (2007), 8 (2008)

ISBNs, Imprints & Series:
978 0 9535912, 978 0 9544752, 978 0 9552122

Book Trade Association Membership:
CLÉ (Irish PA)

2741

SUMMERSDALE PUBLISHERS LTD
46 West Street, Chichester, West Sussex
PO19 1RP
Telephone: 01243 771107
Fax: 01243 786300
Email: enquiries@summersdale.com
Web Site: http://www.summersdale.com

Warehouse, Trade Enquiries & Orders:
Littlehampton Book Services,
Faraday Close, Durrington, Worthing,
West Sussex BN13 3RB
Telephone: 01903 828500
Fax: 01903 828625
Email: orders@lbsltd.co.uk
Web Site: http://www.lbsltd.co.uk

Directors: Alastair Williams (Joint Managing)
Stewart Ferris (Joint Managing)
Nicky Douglas (Sales)
Jennifer Barclay (Editorial)

Audio Books; Cookery, Wines & Spirits; Crafts & Hobbies; Do-It-Yourself; Electronic (Educational); Electronic (Entertainment); Electronic (Professional & Academic); Guide Books; History & Antiquarian; Humour; Law; Sports & Games; Travel & Topography

New Titles: 63 (2007), 80 (2008)
No of Employees: 12
Annual Turnover: £2M

ISBNs, Imprints & Series:
978 1 84024, 978 1 873475

Distributor for:
Protection Publications

Overseas Representation:
Australia & New Zealand: Peribo Pty Ltd, Mount Kuring-Gai, NSW, Australia
Canada: Ben Kooter, Vanwell Publishing Ltd, St Catharines, Ont
India: Surit Mitra, New Delhi
Northern Europe: Michael Geoghegan, London, UK
Scandinavia: McNeish Publishing Services, East Sussex, UK
Southern Africa: Zytek Publishing (Pty) Ltd, Bedfordview, South Africa
Southern Europe: Bookport Associates, Milan, Italy

Book Trade Association Membership:
IPG

2742

SUNFLOWER BOOKS
12 Kendrick Mews, London SW7 3HG
Telephone: (020) 7589 1862
Fax: (020) 7589 1862
Email: mail@sunflowerbooks.co.uk
Web Site: http://www.sunflowerbooks.co.uk

Distribution:
Portfolio Books Ltd, Suite 3/4,
Great West House, Great West Road,
Brentford, Middx TW8 9DF
Telephone: (020) 8326 5620
Fax: (020) 8326 5621

Joint Managing Directors: Pat Underwood
John Seccombe

Travel & Topography

ISBNs, Imprints & Series:
978 0 948513, 978 1 85691 Landscapes Series
978 1 85691 Sunflower Complete Guides; Walk & Eat Series

Parent Company:
P. A. Underwood Ltd

2743

***SUPPORTIVE LEARNING PUBLICATIONS (SLP)**
23 West View, Chirk, Wrexham LL14 5HL
Telephone: 01691 774778
Fax: 01691 774849
Email: @slpuk.demon.co.uk
Web Site: http://www.slpeducation.co.uk

Director: Phil Roberts

Educational & Textbooks; Geography & Geology; History & Antiquarian; Humour; Mathematics & Statistics; Sports & Games; Theatre, Drama & Dance

ISBNs, Imprints & Series: 978 1 871585

Overseas Representation:
All other areas: Blackwell Publishing Ltd, Oxford, UK
USA, Canada & Puerto Rico: Blackwell Publishing Inc, Malden, MA, USA; Blackwell Publishing Professional, Ames, IA, USA

Book Trade Association Membership:
EPC

2744

SUSSEX ACADEMIC PRESS
PO Box 139, Eastbourne, East Sussex
BN24 9BP
Telephone: 01323 479220
Fax: 01323 478185
Email: edit@sussex-academic.co.uk
Web Site: http://www.sussex-academic.co.uk

Warehouse, Trade Enquiries & Orders:
Gazelle Book Services, White Cross Mills,
Hightown, Lancaster LA1 4XS
Telephone: 01524 68765
Fax: 01524 63232

Directors: Anthony Grahame (Editorial)
Anita Grahame (Finance)

Academic & Scholarly; Archaeology; Bibliography & Library Science; Biography & Autobiography; Economics; Educational & Textbooks; Environment & Development Studies; Fine Art & Art History; Gender Studies; Geography & Geology; History & Antiquarian; Industry, Business & Management; Law; Literature & Criticism; Military & War; Music; Philosophy; Politics & World Affairs; Psychology & Psychiatry; Religion & Theology; Sociology & Anthropology; Sports & Games; Theatre, Drama & Dance

New Titles: 35 (2007), 35 (2008)
No of Employees: 4
Annual Turnover: £185,000

ISBNs, Imprints & Series:
978 1 84519, 978 1 898723, 978 1 902210, 978 1 903900 Sussex Academic
978 1 898595 The Alpha Press

Parent Company:
The Alpha Press

Overseas Representation:
North America: International Specialized Book Services Inc, Portland, OR, USA
Rest of the World: Gazelle Book Services Ltd, Lancaster, UK

2745

SUSSEX PUBLICATIONS
World Microfilms, PO Box 35488,
St John's Wood, London NW8 6WD
Telephone: (020) 7586 4499
Email: microworld@ndirect.co.uk
Web Site: http://www.microworld.uk.com

Director: S. C. Albert

Academic & Scholarly; Audio Books; Cinema, Video, TV & Radio; Fine Art & Art History; History & Antiquarian; Literature & Criticism; Music

ISBNs, Imprints & Series:
978 0 905272, 978 1 86013

2746

THE SWEDENBORG SOCIETY
20–21 Bloomsbury Way, London
WC1A 2TH
Telephone: (020) 7405 7986
Fax: (020) 7831 5848
Email: richard@swedenborg.org.uk
Web Site: http://www.swedenborg.org.uk

Company Secretary: Richard Lines
Publications Manager: Stephen McNeilly

Academic & Scholarly; Literature & Criticism; Religion & Theology

New Titles: 5 (2007), 3 (2008)
No of Employees: 4
Annual Turnover: £250,000

2747

SYMPOSIUM PUBLICATIONS LITERARY & ART
37 Chepstow Road, London W2 5BP
Telephone: (020) 7792 3762
Email: sympo@sympo.fsworld.co.uk
Web Site: http://www.sympo.co.uk

Director: Mrs L. A. Melech
Editorial Consultant: J. Wheeler-Melech

Academic & Scholarly; Children's Books; Educational & Textbooks; English as a Foreign Language; Fine Art & Art History; Literature & Criticism; Poetry

New Titles: 2 (2008)

ISBNs, Imprints & Series:
978 0 9524749 Symposium Brush-Up Shakespeare Series; Symposium Gem Art Series
978 0 9547757 Sympo Sunrise (Children's Stories)

Overseas Representation:
Spain: Débora Vázquez Padín, Pontevedra

2748

***TA HA PUBLISHERS LTD**
1 Wynne Road, London SW9 0BB
Telephone: (020) 7737 7266
Fax: (020) 7737 7267
Email: sales@taha.co.uk
Web Site: http://www.taha.co.uk

Directors: A. Siddiqui
Dr Abia A. Siddiqui
Rights: Dr J. U. N. Ratai

Children's Books; Languages & Linguistics; Religion & Theology

ISBNs, Imprints & Series:
978 0 907461, 978 1 842000, 978 1 897940

2749

TABB HOUSE
7 Church Street, Padstow, Cornwall
PL28 8BG
Telephone: 01841 532316
Fax: 01841 532316

Distributor (for West Country titles in Cornwall, Devon & Somerset):
Tor Mark Press, PO Box 4, Redruth,
Cornwall TR16 5YX
Telephone: 01209 822101
Fax: 01209 822035

Email: sales@tormarkpress.prestel.co.uk
Web Site: http://www.willowbooks.co.uk

Wholesaler (for all titles for Waterstone's):
Gardners Books Ltd, 1 Whittle Drive,
Willingdon Drove, Eastbourne, Sussex
BN23 6QH
Telephone: 01323 521555
Fax: 01323 521666
Email: sales@gardners.com
Web Site: http://www.gardners.com

Director: Caroline White (Editorial)
Promotion & Marketing Manager: K. Bickmore

Biography & Autobiography; Children's Books; Fiction; Literature & Criticism; Poetry; Local History & Factual

New Titles: 2 (2007), 2 (2008)

ISBNs, Imprints & Series:
978 0 907018, 978 1 873951
978 0 953951 Tabb House Originals

Book Trade Association Membership:
IPG

2750

TAIGH NA TEUD MUSIC PUBLISHERS
13 Upper Breakish, Isle of Skye IV42 8PY
Telephone: 01471 822528
Fax: 01471 822811
Email: sales@scotlandsmusic.com
Web Site: http://www.scotlandsmusic.com
& http://www.playscottishmusic.com

Sales Manager: Alasdair Martin
Music Editor: Christine Martin

Languages & Linguistics; Music

New Titles: 6 (2007), 6 (2008)
No of Employees: 3

ISBNs, Imprints & Series:
978 1 871931 Taigh na Teud

Overseas Representation:
Australia: Celtic Southern Cross, Bracknell, Tasmania
North America: Music Sales Corporation, Chester, NY, USA

2751

***TAMARIND LTD**
PO Box 52, Northwood, Middx HA6 1UN
Telephone: (020) 8866 8808
Fax: (020) 8866 5627
Email: info@tamarindbooks.co.uk
Web Site: http://www.tamarindbooks.co.uk

Managing Director: Verna Wilkins
Accountant: Margaret Crush

Children's Books; Educational & Textbooks

ISBNs, Imprints & Series: 978 1 870516

Book Trade Association Membership:
IPG

2752

***TANGERINE DESIGNS LTD**
2 High Street, Freshford, Bath BA2 7WE
Telephone: 01225 720001
Email: enquiries@tangerinedesigns.co.uk
Web Site: http://www.tangerinedesigns.co.uk

Managing Director: Christine Swift
Global English Sales: Cathy Power
Northern Territories Rights: Trish Pugsley

Children's Books; Electronic (Entertainment)

2753

TARQUIN PUBLICATIONS
99 Hatfield Road, St Albans, Herts AL1 4JL
Telephone: 0870 143 2568
Fax: 0845 456 6385
Email: sales@tarquinbooks.com
Web Site: http://www.tarquinbooks.com

Editorial: Andrew Griffin *(Rights & Permissions)*
Sales & Promotion: Barry Graystone
Financial: Kevin Tubridy

Atlases & Maps; Children's Books; Crafts & Hobbies; Educational & Textbooks; Mathematics & Statistics; Do-it-Yourself Pop-up Books

New Titles: 2 (2007), 4 (2008)

ISBNs, Imprints & Series:
978 0 906212, 978 1 899618

Parent Company:
Richard Griffin (1820) Ltd

Overseas Representation:
Australia: W & G Education Pty Ltd, Berwick, Vic; H. E. Wootton & Sons, Toorak, Vic
New Zealand: Eton Press (Auckland) Ltd, Auckland; Mahobe Resources (NZ), Newmarket
Portugal: Editôra Replicação, Lisbon
Singapore: Nature Craft Pte Ltd
USA: Parkwest Publications Inc, Jersey City, NJ

Book Trade Association Membership:
IPG

2754

TARTARUS PRESS
Coverley House, Carlton-in-Coverdale, Leyburn, North Yorks DL8 4AY
Telephone: 01969 640399
Fax: 01969 640399
Email: tartarus@pavilion.co.uk
Web Site: http://www.tartaruspress.com

Co-Proprietors: R. B. Russell
Rosalie Parker

Antiques & Collecting; Fiction; Illustrated & Fine Editions; Literature & Criticism; Reference Books, Directories & Dictionaries

New Titles: 8 (2007), 10 (2008)

ISBNs, Imprints & Series: 978 1 872621

2755

TATE PUBLISHING
[a division of Tate Enterprises Ltd]
Millbank, London SW1P 4RG
Telephone: (020) 7887 8869/70/71
Fax: (020) 7887 8878

Warehouse, Trade Enquiries & Orders:
Telephone: (020) 7887 8869 (5 lines)
Fax: (020) 7887 8878
Email: tgpl@tate.org.uk
Web Site: http://www.tate.org.uk

Managers: Celia Clear *(Chief Executive)*
James Attlee *(Sales & Marketing)*
Sarah Rogers *(Finance)*
Sarah Tucker *(Production)*
Roger Thorp *(Publishing)*

Children's Books; Fine Art & Art History; Photography

New Titles: 35 (2007), 33 (2008)
Annual Turnover: £2.8M

ISBNs, Imprints & Series:
British Artists Series; Movements in Modern Art Series; St Ives Artists Series
978 0 905005, 978 0 946590, 978 1 85437 Essential Artists Series
978 1 85437 Modern Artists Series

Parent Company:
Tate Enterprises Ltd

Overseas Representation:
Asia (including Hong Kong, Taiwan, China, Korea & Philippines): Asia Publishers Services Ltd, Hong Kong
Australia: Thames & Hudson (Australia) Pty Ltd, Fishermans Bend, Vic
Austria, Belgium, Germany, Netherlands & Switzerland: Exhibitions International, Leuven, Belgium
Denmark, Finland, Iceland, Norway & Sweden: Elisabeth Harder-Kreimann, Hamburg, Germany
Eastern Europe: Phil Tyers, Athens, Greece
Far East (including Japan, Vietnam, Singapore, Malaysia, Indonesia & Thailand): Andrew Hansen, London, UK
France: Interart SARL, Paris
Italy, Greece, Spain & Portugal: Penny Padovani, London, UK
Mexico, Central America & Caribbean: Chris Humphrys, Humphrys Roberts Associates, London, UK
Middle East: Ray Potts, Villanton, France
North & South America & Canada: Harry N. Abrams Inc, New York, NY, USA
Republic of Ireland & Northern Ireland: Gabrielle Redmond, Dublin, Republic of Ireland
South Africa: David Krut Publishing, Johannesburg
South America: Terry Roberts, Humphrys Roberts Associates, São Paulo, Brazil

Book Trade Association Membership:
BA

2756

*I. B. TAURIS & CO LTD
6 Salem Road, London W2 4BU
Telephone: (020) 7243 1225
Fax: (020) 7243 1226
Email: mail@ibtauris.com
Web Site: http://www.ibtauris.com

Distribution:
Macmillan Distribution Ltd, Brunel Road, Houndmills, Basingstoke, Hants RG21 6XS

Directors: Iradj Bagherzade *(Chairman & Publisher)*
Jonathan McDonnell *(Managing)*
Isabella Steer *(Rights)*
Managers: Stuart Weir *(Production)*
Liz Stuckey *(Financial)*
Martin Ashworth *(Sales)*
Paul Davighi *(Marketing)*
Nicole Ettinger *(Publicity)*

Academic & Scholarly; Archaeology; Architecture & Design; Biography & Autobiography; Cinema, Video, TV & Radio; Fine Art & Art History; Gender Studies; Geography & Geology; Guide Books; History & Antiquarian; Military & War; Politics & World Affairs; Reference Books, Directories & Dictionaries; Religion & Theology; Sociology & Anthropology

ISBNs, Imprints & Series:
978 1 84511, 978 1 85043, 978 1 86064 International Library of African Studies; International Library of Historical Studies; International Library of Human Geography; International Library of Political Studies; Isma'ili Heritage Series; Library of International Relations; Library of Middle East History; Library of Modern Middle East Studies; Library of Ottoman Studies; Tauris Parke Paperbacks

Associated Companies:
British Academic Press; Tauris Academic Studies; Tauris Parke Books

Distributor for:
UAE: The Emirates Center for Strategic Studies & Research
The Khalili Collection; Libri Publications; The Radcliffe Press; Philip Wilson Publishers

Overseas Representation:
Africa (excluding South Africa & Zimbabwe): InterMedia Americana (IMA) Ltd, London, UK
Australia: Palgrave Macmillan, South Yarra, Vic
India: Viva Group, New Delhi
Iran: Behruz Neirami, Tehran
Japan: United Publishers Services Ltd, Tokyo
Korea, China, Hong Kong & Taiwan: Taylor & Francis Asia Pacific, Singapore
Middle East & North Africa: International Publishers Representatives (IPR) Ltd, Nicosia, Cyprus
New Zealand: Forrester Books (NZ) Ltd, Albany
Northern Europe: Andrew Durnell Marketing Ltd, Tunbridge Wells, UK
South America & Caribbean: InterMedia Americana (IMA) Ltd, London, UK
South East Asia: Horizon Books Pte Ltd, Singapore
USA & Canada: Palgrave Macmillan, New York, NY, USA

Book Trade Association Membership:
IPG

2757

TAYLOR & FRANCIS
2 & 4 Park Square, Milton Park, Abingdon, Oxford OX14 4RN
Telephone: (020) 7017 6000
Fax: (020) 7017 6336
Email: jackie.benoist@tandf.co.uk
Web Site: http://www.taylorandfrancis.com

Warehouse, Trade Enquiries & Orders:
Bookpoint, 130 Milton Park, Abingdon, Oxon OX14 4SB
Telephone: 01235 400400

Chief Executive: Roger Horton
Directors: Jeremy North *(Managing – Books)*
Christoph Chesher *(Sales)*
Stuart Dawson *(Finance)*
Ian Bannerman *(Managing – Journals)*
Mark Majurey *(Digital Development – Books)*
David Green *(Publishing – Journals)*
Beverley Acreman *(Marketing – Journals)*
Matt Howells *(Production – Journals)*
Claire L'Infant *(Humanities – Books)*
Alan Jarvis *(Social Sciences – Books)*
Nigel Eyre *(Production – Books)*
Jackie Harbor *(Marketing – Books)*
Rights Managers: Adele Parker *(Books)*
Paulette Dooler *(Journals)*

Academic & Scholarly; Archaeology; Architecture & Design; Biology & Zoology; Chemistry; Economics; Educational & Textbooks; Electronic (Professional & Academic); Engineering; Environment & Development Studies; Gay & Lesbian Studies; Gender Studies; Geography &
Geology; History & Antiquarian; Industry, Business & Management; Languages & Linguistics; Law; Literature & Criticism; Mathematics & Statistics; Medical (incl. Self Help & Alternative Medicine); Military & War; Music; Philosophy; Physics; Politics & World Affairs; Psychology & Psychiatry; Reference Books, Directories & Dictionaries; Religion & Theology; Scientific & Technical; Sociology & Anthropology; Sports & Games; Theatre, Drama & Dance

New Titles: 2700 (2007), 2700 (2008)
No of Employees: 800

ISBNs, Imprints & Series:
978 0 415 Psychology Press; Routledge; Routledge-Cavendish; Taylor & Francis
978 0 8058 Lawrence Erlbaum Associates
978 0 8247 Dekker
978 0 8493 CRC

Parent Company:
Informa Plc

Associated Companies:
India: Routledge India Office
Norway: Taylor & Francis AS
Singapore: Taylor & Francis Asia Pacific
Sweden: Taylor & Francis AB
USA: Garland Science; Taylor & Francis Books Inc

Distributor for:
Guildford Press; Swedish Pharmaceutical Press

Overseas Representation:
Australasia: Palgrave Macmillan, South Yarra, Vic, Australia
Austria, Switzerland & Germany: Gabriela Mauch, Area Sales Manager, Central Europe, Stuttgart, Germany
Belgium, Netherlands, France & Luxembourg: Liza Walraven, Sales Representative, Amsterdam, Netherlands
Botswana: Carlson Moilwa, Book Promotions/Horizon Books
Eastern Europe: Marek Lewinson, Warsaw, Poland
Greece: Ryan Cooper, Taylor & Francis Group, Abingdon, UK
Israel: Franklins International, Tel Aviv
Japan: United Publishers Services Ltd, Tokyo
Korea: Information & Culture Korea (ICK), Seoul, Korea, South
Mexico, Central & South America: Cranbury International LLC, Montpelier, VT, USA
Middle East & North Africa: International Publishing Services (IPS) Middle East Ltd, Dubai, UAE
New Zealand: Victoria Johnson, Macmillan Publishers New Zealand Ltd, Albany, Auckland
Nigeria: Publisher Support Services Ltd, Ikeja
North America: Taylor & Francis Inc, Boca Raton, FL, USA
Norway, Denmark & Faroe Islands: Keith Gray, Sales Representative, Copenhagen, Denmark
Pakistan: M. Anwer Iqbal, Book Bird Publishers Representatives, Lahore
Republic of Ireland: Brookside Publishing Services, Dublin
South Africa, Namibia, Lesotho & Swaziland: Book Promotions Pty Ltd, Diep River, South Africa
Sweden, Finland & Iceland: Sara Pellijeff, Sales Representative, Stockholm, Sweden
West Indies & Caribbean: Jasmina Basic, Taylor & Francis Group, Abingdon, UK

Book Trade Association Membership:
IGSMTP; CAPP

2758

TAYLOR GRAHAM PUBLISHING
29 Church Street, Southport PR9 0QT
Web Site: http://www.taylorgraham.com

Distributor for:
UK: Alligator Books [foreign rights agent]; Funkkia [publishing licensor]; Rockpool Children's Books [foreign rights agent]

Overseas Representation:
Australia, New Zealand, Canada & USA: Cathy Power, Tangerine Designs Ltd, Bath, UK

Book Trade Association Membership:
Publishers Association

Director: Peter J. Taylor

Academic & Scholarly; Bibliography & Library Science; Computer Science; Scientific & Technical

ISBNs, Imprints & Series: 978 0 947568

Overseas Representation:
USA & Canada: Taylor Graham Publishing, Los Angeles, CA, USA

Book Trade Association Membership:
UK Serials Group

2759

TEACHIT (UK) LTD
1 Widsombe Parade, Bath BA2 4JT
Telephone: 01225 788850
Email: mail@teachit.co.uk
Web Site: http://www.teachit.co.uk

Educational & Textbooks; Electronic (Professional & Academic)

Book Trade Association Membership:
Publishers Association

2760

TELEGRAM
26 Westbourne Grove, London W2 5RH
Telephone: (020) 7229 2911
Fax: (020) 7229 7492
Email: rebecca@telegrambooks.com
Web Site: http://www.telegrambooks.com

Distribution (UK):
Marston Book Services Ltd,
160 Milton Park, Abingdon, Oxon
OX14 4SD
Telephone: 01235 465500
Fax: 01235 465555
Web Site: http://www.marston.co.uk

Sales (UK):
Compass, The Barley Mow Centre,
10 Barley Mow Passage, Chiswick W4 4PH
Telephone: (020) 8994 6477
Fax: (020) 8400 6132
Web Site: http://www.compass-booksales.co.uk

Director: André Gaspard
Commissioning Editor: Rebecca O'Connor
Managers: Anna Wilson *(Rights)*
Ashley Biles *(Sales)*
Rob Fakes *(Publicity)*
Rights Assistant: Lynn Gaspard
Production Editor: Shikha Sethi

Biography & Autobiography; Fiction

New Titles: 17 (2007), 15 (2008)
No of Employees: 7

ISBNs, Imprints & Series: 978 1 84659

Parent Company:
Saqi Books

Overseas Representation:
Australia & New Zealand: Palgrave Macmillan, South Yarra, Vic, Australia
Europe: Andrew Durnell, Andrew Durnell Marketing Ltd, Tunbridge Wells, UK
India: Pradeep Kumar, Viva Marketing, New Delhi
Italy: Agnese Incisa, Letteraria Agnese Incisa, Turin
Middle East: Dar al Saqi SARL, Beirut, Lebanon
Netherlands & Scandinavia: Jan Michael, Amsterdam, Netherlands
Pakistan: Mohammad Eusoph, Mr Books, Islamabad
Singapore: Nelson Koh, Horizon Books Pte Ltd
South Africa: Stephan Phillips (Pty) Ltd, Cape Town
Spain, Portugal & Germany: Anna Soler-Pont, Pontas Literary & Film Agency, Barcelona, Spain
USA & Canada: Consortium Publishers, St Paul, MN, USA

Book Trade Association Membership:
IPG

2761

THOMAS TELFORD LTD
Thomas Telford House, 1 Heron Quay, London E14 4JD
Telephone: (020) 7987 6999
Fax: (020) 7538 4101
Email: leon.heward-mills@thomastelford.com
Web Site: http://www.thomastelford.com

Warehouse:
c/o Combined Book Services, Unit 1/K, Paddock Wood Distribution Centre, Paddock Wood, Kent TN12 6UU
Telephone: 01892 837171
Fax: 01892 837272

Retail Bookshop:
1 Great George Street, London SW1P 3AA
Telephone: (020) 7665 2464
Fax: (020) 7665 2245

Representation (UK & Northern Ireland):
Momenta Publishing Ltd,
2 Moorlands Close, Hindhead, Surrey
GU26 6SY

Managers: Leon Heward-Mills *(Publisher)*
David Atkins *(Editorial & Production)*
Richard Oldershaw *(Sales)*

Architecture & Design; Engineering; Scientific & Technical

ISBNs, Imprints & Series: 978 0 7277

Parent Company:
Institution of Civil Engineers

Distributor for:
British Geotechnical Society

Overseas Representation:
Australia & New Zealand: DA Information Services Pty Ltd, Mitcham, Vic, Australia
Germany: Bernd Feldmann, Oranienburg
Italy, France, Spain, Portugal & Greece: AMS Europe Ltd, Farnham, UK
Japan: Maruzen Co Ltd, Tokyo
Republic of Ireland, Netherlands & Belgium: Momenta Publishing Ltd, Hindhead, Surrey, UK
South Africa: South African Institution of Civil Engineers, Midrand
USA: American Society of Civil Engineers, Reston, VA

Book Trade Association Membership:
Association of Learned & Professional Society Publishers

2762

TELOS PUBLISHING LTD
61 Elgar Avenue, Tolworth, Surrey KT5 9SP
Telephone: (020) 8399 1921
Email: david@telos.co.uk
Web Site: http://www.telos.co.uk

Business/Accounts:
5a Church Road, Shortlands, Bromley, Kent BR2 0HP
Telephone: (020) 8466 1115
Email: stephen@telos.co.uk

Publishers: David J. Howe
Stephen James Walker

Cinema, Video, TV & Radio; Crime; Fiction

New Titles: 9 (2007), 8 (2008)

ISBNs, Imprints & Series:
978 1 84583, 978 1 903889

Overseas Representation:
Australia & New Zealand: Bookwise International, Wingfield, SA, Australia
USA & Canada: Fitzhenry & Whiteside Ltd, Markham, Ont, Canada

2763

TEMPLAR PUBLISHING
The Granary, North Street, Dorking, Surrey RH4 1DN
Telephone: 01306 876361
Fax: 01306 889097
Email: info@templarco.co.uk
Web Site: http://www.templarco.co.uk

Sales & Marketing:
Bounce Sales & Marketing,
14 Greville Street, London EC1N 8SB

Distribution:
Grantham Book Services,
Isaac Newton Way,
Alma Park Industrial Estate, Grantham,
Lincs NG31 9SD

Directors: Michael Freedman *(Chairman)*
Amanda Wood *(Managing)*
Elaine Hunt *(Financial)*
Ruth Huddleston *(Sales)*
Karen Ellison *(Production)*
Mike Jolley *(Art)*
Odile Louis-Sidney *(Rights)*
Richard Scrivener *(Commercial & Operations)*

Children's Books; Fiction

New Titles: 87 (2007), 123 (2008)
No of Employees: 40
Annual Turnover: £15M

ISBNs, Imprints & Series:
978 1 84011, 978 1 898784
978 1 904513 Amazing Baby

Parent Company:
The Templar Co Plc

Overseas Representation:
Australia: Karlov Marketing Services Pty Ltd, Castle Hill, NSW

Book Trade Association Membership:
BA; IPG

2764

TEMPLE LODGE PUBLISHING
Hillside House, The Square, Forest Row, East Sussex RH18 5ES
Telephone: 01342 824000
Fax: 01342 826437
Email: office@templelodge.com
Web Site: http://www.templelodge.com

Distribution:
BookSource, 50 Cambuslang Road, Glasgow G32 8NB
Telephone: 0141 643 3955
Fax: 0845 370 0068
Email: orders@booksource.net
Web Site: http://www.booksource.net

Chief Editor: S.E. Gulbekian

Health & Beauty; Magic & the Occult; Medical (incl. Self Help & Alternative Medicine); Philosophy; Politics & World Affairs; Religion & Theology

New Titles: 10 (2007), 10 (2008)
Annual Turnover: £60,000

ISBNs, Imprints & Series:
978 0 904693, 978 1 902636

Overseas Representation:
Australia: Rudolf Steiner Book Centre, Sydney, NSW
Canada: Tri-fold Books, Guelph, Ont
New Zealand: Steinerbooks, Auckland
South Africa: Rudolf Steiner Publications, Bryanston
USA: Steiner Books Inc, Herndon, VA

Book Trade Association Membership:
IPG

2765

*TENEUES PUBLISHING UK LTD
PO Box 402, West Byfleet KT14 7ZF
Telephone: 01932 403509
Fax: 01932 403514
Email: amcdonald@teneues.co.uk
Web Site: http://www.teneues.com

Trade Enquiries & Orders:
Grantham Book Services Ltd,
Isaac Newton Way, Grantham, Lincs
NG31 9SD
Telephone: 01476 541080
Fax: 01476 541061
Email: orders@gbs.tbs-ltd.co.uk

Chairman: Hendrik Teneues
Managers: Alexandra McDonald *(Sales & Marketing)*
Bridget Clark *(Sales)*
Administrator: Elaine Hyde

Architecture & Design; Photography; Travel & Topography

ISBNs, Imprints & Series:
978 3 57091 Stern Portfolios
978 3 8238, 978 3 8327 Teneues

Book Trade Association Membership:
IPG

2766

*TENTMAKER PUBLICATIONS
121 Hartshill Road, Stoke-on-Trent, Staffs ST4 7LU
Telephone: 01782 746879
Fax: 01782 414805
Email: sales@tentmaker.org.uk
Web Site: http://www.tentmaker.org.uk

Production Manager: Phil Roberts
Owner: Joy Roberts

History & Antiquarian; Religion & Theology; Transport

ISBNs, Imprints & Series:
978 1 899003, 978 1 901670 Tentmaker Publications
978 1 901670 Berith Publications

Distributor for:
UK: K & M Books

2767

THAMES & HUDSON LTD
181A High Holborn, London WC1V 7QX
Telephone: (020) 7845 5000
Fax: (020) 7845 5050
Email: l.willis@thamesandhudson.co.uk
Web Site: http://www.thamesandhudson.com

Warehouse, Accounts & Returns:
Thames & Hudson (Distributors) Ltd,
44 Clockhouse Road, Farnborough, Hants
GU14 7QZ
Telephone: 01252 541602
Fax: 01252 377380
Email: customerservices@thameshudson.co.uk

Directors: Thomas Neurath *(Chairman)*
Constance Kaine *(Deputy Chairman)*
Jamie Camplin *(Managing)*
Trevor Naylor *(Sales & Marketing)*

Peter Meades (Financial)
Christopher Ferguson (Operations)
Neil Palfreyman (Production)
Brian Meek (Company Secretary)
Johanna Neurath (Design)
Christian Frederking (Rights)
Export Area Managers: Stephen Embrey
Sara Ticci
Scipio Stringer
Managers: Laura Willis (Marketing)
Melanie Stacey (UK Sales)
Marketing & Media: Kate Burvill
Sales: Jonathan Earl
Export Sales: Ian Bartley

Academic & Scholarly; Antiques & Collecting; Archaeology; Architecture & Design; Biography & Autobiography; Crafts & Hobbies; Educational & Textbooks; Environment & Development Studies; Fashion & Costume; Fine Art & Art History; Gardening; Gay & Lesbian Studies; Guide Books; History & Antiquarian; Illustrated & Fine Editions; Literature & Criticism; Magic & the Occult; Military & War; Music; Natural History; Philosophy; Photography; Reference Books, Directories & Dictionaries; Religion & Theology; Sociology & Anthropology; Theatre, Drama & Dance; Travel & Topography

ISBNs, Imprints & Series:
978 0 500 Thames & Hudson
978 0 642 National Gallery of Australia
978 0 7141 British Museum Press
978 0 784763 Art Gallery of NSW
978 0 86565 Vendome
978 0 87070 Museum of Modern Art, New York
978 0 89207 Guggenheim Museum Publications
978 0 89381, 978 1 597110, 978 1 931788 Aperture
978 0 900946, 978 1 903973 The Royal Academy of Arts
978 0 906183 Institute for Archaeo-Metallurgical Studies
978 0 952741 Frieze
978 0 952766, 978 1 900826, 978 1 902686 Scriptum
978 0 953703 Dakini
978 0 9542813, 978 0 9546894, 978 1 9057120 Chris Boot
978 0 977985, 978 0 979048 Mark Batty Publisher
978 1 85669 Laurence King
978 1 86154 Booth-Clibborn
978 1 900828 Violette Editions
978 1 902163 The Royal Collection
978 1 904705 Ilex Press
978 2 0801, 978 2 08030 Flammarion SA, France
978 2 884790, 978 2 940373 Ava Publishing
978 3 86521, 978 3 88243, 978 3 905509, 978 3 931141 Steidl
978 3 87624, 978 8 88118, 978 8 88491 Skira Editore
978 3 938780 Braun Verlagshaus
978 9 748225, 978 9 749863 River Books

Parent Company:
T & H Holdings Ltd

Associated Companies:
Thames & Hudson (Distributors) Ltd
Australia: Thames & Hudson (Australia) Pty Ltd
France: Editions Thames & Hudson sarl
P. R. of China: Thames & Hudson China Ltd
Singapore: Thames & Hudson (S) Pte Ltd
USA: Thames & Hudson Inc

Distributor for:
British Museum Press; Laurence King
Australia: National Gallery of Australia
France: Flammarion SA
Germany: Braun Verlagshaus
Israel: Institute for Archaeo-Metallurgical Studies
Italy: Skira Editore

USA: Mark Batty Publisher; Museum of Modern Art, New York

Overseas Representation:
Africa, Caribbean, Central America, Eastern Europe, Eastern Mediterranean, India, Italy, Japan, Mexico, Middle East, Pakistan, Portugal & Spain: Export Sales Department, Thames & Hudson Ltd, London, UK
Australia, New Zealand, Papua New Guinea & Pacific Islands: Thames & Hudson (Australia) Pty Ltd, Fishermans Bend, Vic, Australia
Austria, Switzerland & Germany (excluding South): Michael Klein, Vilsbiburg, Germany
Bangladesh: Zeenat Book Supply Ltd, Dhaka
Brazil & South America: Terry Roberts, Cotia SP, Brazil
China, Hong Kong & Macau: Thames & Hudson China Ltd, Aberdeen, Hong Kong
France: Interart SARL, Paris
Germany (South): Wolfgang Willmann & Susanne Sieger, Frankfurt, Germany
Iran: Book City, Tehran
Israel: Lonnie Kahn & Co Ltd, Rishon Lezion
Korea & Taiwan: Asia Publishers Services Ltd, Hong Kong
Lebanon: Levant Distributors, Beirut
Malaysia: Thames & Hudson (S) Pte Ltd, Petaling Jaya
Netherlands: Menno Visser, Utrecht
Republic of Ireland: UK Sales Department, Thames & Hudson Ltd, London, UK
Scandinavia & Baltic States: Per Burell, Stocksund, Sweden
Singapore & South East Asia: Thames & Hudson (S) Pte Ltd, Singapore
South Africa, Swaziland, Lesotho, Namibia, Botswana & Zimbabwe: Peter Hyde Associates (Pty) Ltd, Cape Town, South Africa
Thailand: Asia Book Co Ltd, Bangkok

Book Trade Association Membership:
Publishers Association

2768

*THARPA PUBLICATIONS
Conishead Priory, Ulverston, Cumbria LA12 9QQ
Telephone: 01229 588599
Fax: 01229 483919
Email: tharpa@tharpa.com
Web Site: http://www.tharpa.com

Director: Peter Davis
Accounts: Kelsang Gakyi
Distribution Manager: Murdo McNab

Religion & Theology; Mind Body Spirit

ISBNs, Imprints & Series:
978 0 948006, 978 0 9548790

Parent Company:
New Kadampa Tradition

Overseas Representation:
Australia: Gary Allen Pty Ltd, Smithfield, NSW
Canada: Tharpa Canada, Toronto, Ont
Singapore & Malaysia: MPH Distributors, Singapore
South Africa: Bacchus Books, Gauteng
USA (Office): Tharpa Publications, New York, NY, USA

Book Trade Association Membership:
IPG

2769

*THINK BOOKS
Think Publishing, Pall Mall Deposit, Barlby Road, London W10 6BL
Telephone: (020) 8962 3020
Fax: (020) 8962 8689

Email: mark@thinkpublishing.co.uk
Web Site: http://www.think-books.com

Distributors:
Macmillan Distribution, Brunel Road, Houndmills, Basingstoke, Hants RG21 6XS
Telephone: 01256 302699

Publisher: Mark Searle

Biology & Zoology; Children's Books; Environment & Development Studies; Gardening; Guide Books; Humour; Illustrated & Fine Editions; Natural History; Reference Books, Directories & Dictionaries

ISBNs, Imprints & Series: 978 1 84525

Parent Company:
UK: Pan Macmillan; Think Publishing

Overseas Representation:
North America: Sterling Publishing Co Inc, New York, NY, USA
Worldwide (excluding North America): Pan Macmillan, London, UK

Book Trade Association Membership:
IPG

2770

THIRD MILLENNIUM PUBLISHING LTD
2–5 Benjamin Street, London EC1M 5QL
Telephone: (020) 7336 0144
Fax: (020) 7608 1188
Email: info@tmltd.com
Web Site: http://www.tmltd.com

Chairman: Julian Platt
Publisher: Christopher Fagg
Directors: Joel Burden (Business Development)
David Burt
Managers: Michael D. Jackson (Marketing)
Bonnie Murray (Production)

Antiques & Collecting; Educational & Textbooks; Fine Art & Art History; Guide Books; Military & War; Photography

New Titles: 15 (2007), 20 (2008)
No of Employees: 9
Annual Turnover: £1.1M

ISBNs, Imprints & Series: 978 1 903942

Distributor for:
UK: Pardoe Blacker Design

Overseas Representation:
USA & Canada: Dan Farrell, Antique Collectors Club Ltd, Easthampton, MA, USA

2771

THOMSON INTERNATIONAL LEGAL & REGULATORY
100 Avenue Road, Swiss Cottage, London NW3 3PF
Telephone: (020) 7393 7000
Fax: (020) 7393 7010
Web Site: http://www.thomson.com/solutions/legal

Law

Associated Companies:
UK: Current Law Publishers; ESC Publishing; Gee Publishing; W. Green & Son; Information for Industry; Legal Information Resources; Morgan Hill; Pensions Research; Professional Publishing; Steven & Sons; Sweet & Maxwell; Thomson Tax; Westlaw UK

Book Trade Association Membership:
Publishers Association

2772

THOROGOOD PUBLISHING LTD
10–12 Rivington Street, London EC2A 3DU
Telephone: (020) 7749 4748
Fax: (020) 7720 6110
Email: info@thorogoodpublishing.co.uk
Web Site: http://www.thorogoodpublishing.co.uk

Trade Orders:
Marston Book Services, 160 Milton Park, Abingdon, Oxon OX14 4SD
Telephone: 01235 465500
Fax: 01235 465655
Email: trade.enq@marston.co.uk
Web Site: http://www.marston.co.uk

Directors: Neil Thomas (Chairman)
Neill Ross (Managing)
Nina Rossey (Finance)
Angela Spall (Editorial, Production)
Marketing Manager: Matthew Harris (Rights)
Marketing Executive: Geeta Chambers

Accountancy & Taxation; Biography & Autobiography; Industry, Business & Management; Law; Military & War; Travel & Topography

New Titles: 18 (2007), 18 (2008)
No of Employees: 8

ISBNs, Imprints & Series: 978 1 85418

Associated Companies:
UK: Falconbury Ltd

Overseas Representation:
Australia & New Zealand: Woodslane Pty Ltd, Warriewood, NSW, Australia
Europe: Andrew Durnell Marketing Ltd, Tunbridge Wells, UK
Hong Kong, Taiwan, China & Korea: Asia Publishers Services Ltd, Hong Kong
India: Viva Group, New Delhi
Latin America: InterMedia Americana (IMA) Ltd, London, UK
Middle East, Greece & Cyprus: Ray Potts, Publishers International Marketing, Aude, France
Singapore, Malaysia & South East Asia: APD Singapore Pte Ltd, Singapore

Book Trade Association Membership:
IPG

2773

F. A. THORPE PUBLISHING
The Green, Bradgate Road, Anstey, Leicester LE7 7FU
Telephone: 0116 236 4325
Fax: 0116 234 0205
Email: ulverscroft@dial.pipex.com
Web Site: http://dspace.dial.pipex.com/town/plaza/hf33/

Chief Executive: Robert Thirlby

Biography & Autobiography; Fiction; Travel & Topography; Large Print Leisure

New Titles: 456 (2007), 456 (2008)

ISBNs, Imprints & Series:
978 0 7089, 978 1 84395, 978 1 84617, 978 1 84782 Charnwood Hardback Series; Linford Softcover Series; Ulverscroft Hardcover Series

Associated Companies:
Isis Publishing; Magna Large Print Books; Ulverscroft Large Print Books Ltd

Distributor for:
Soundings Audio Books

Overseas Representation:
Australia: Sandra Lavender, Crows Nest

Canada: Mrs Diane Van Veen, Burlington, Ont
New Zealand: John Gregory, Feilding
USA: Ulverscroft Large Print Books (USA) Inc, West Seneca, NY

2774

THOTH PUBLICATIONS
64 Leopold Street, Loughborough, Leics LE11 5DN
Telephone: 01509 210626
Fax: 01509 238034
Email: enquiries@thoth.co.uk
Web Site: http://www.thoth.co.uk

Senior Partner: Tom Clarke
Partner: Susan Attwood

Biography & Autobiography; Magic & the Occult; Religion & Theology

New Titles: 16 (2007), 8 (2008)

ISBNs, Imprints & Series: 978 1 870450

Distributor for:
Sun Chalice

Book Trade Association Membership:
BA

2775

THRASS (UK) LTD
Units 1–3 Tarvin Sands, Barrow Lane, Tarvin, Chester CH3 8JF
Telephone: 01829 741413
Fax: 01829 741419
Email: enquiries@thrass.demon.co.uk
Web Site: http://www.thrass.co.uk

Director: Alan Davies
Consultant: Hilary Davies
Office Manager: Rachel Woodward

Educational & Textbooks; Electronic (Educational)

New Titles: 5 (2007), 5 (2008)

ISBNs, Imprints & Series:
978 1 904912, 978 1 906295

2776

TINDAL STREET PRESS
217 The Custard Factory, Gibb Street, Birmingham B9 4AA
Telephone: 0121 773 8157
Email: emma@tindalstreet.co.uk
Web Site: http://www.tindalstreet.co.uk

Distribution (UK):
Turnaround, Unit 3, Olympia Trading Estate, Coburg Road, London N22 6TZ
Telephone: (020) 8829 3000
Email: orders@turnaround-uk.com
Web Site: http://www.turnaround-uk.com

Publishing Director: Alan Mahar
Editor/Publicist: Luke Brown

Fiction

New Titles: 5 (2007), 6 (2008)
No of Employees: 3
Annual Turnover: £200,000

ISBNs, Imprints & Series:
978 0 9535895, 978 0 9541303, 978 0 9547913, 978 0 9551384, 978 0 9556476

Overseas Representation:
Australia: Tower Books Pty Ltd, Frenchs Forest, NSW; Tower Books Pty Ltd, Brookvale, NSW
New Zealand: Addenda, Auckland

USA & Canada: Dufour Editions Inc, Chester Springs, PA, USA

Book Trade Association Membership:
IPG

2777

TITAN PUBLISHING GROUP
144 Southwark Street, London SE1 0UP
Telephone: (020) 7620 0200
Fax: (020) 7803 1990
Email: editorial@titanemail.com
Web Site: http://www.titanbooks.com

Trade Enquiries & Orders:
Grantham Book Services,
Isaac Newton Way,
Alma Park Industrial Estate, Grantham, Lincs NG31 9SD
Telephone: 01476 541000
Fax: 01476 541061
Email: orders@gbs.tbs-ltd.co.uk

Directors: Nick Landau *(Managing)*
Vivian Cheung *(Executive)*
Tim Whale *(Global Sales)*
Katy Wild *(Editorial)*
Head of Finance: Chris Horn
Marketing Manager: Erin Monahan
Print & Paper Buyer: Kevin Woolf
Rights Executive: Jenny Boyce

Children's Books; Cinema, Video, TV & Radio; Graphic Novels

New Titles: 198 (2007), 311 (2008)
No of Employees: 147

ISBNs, Imprints & Series: 978 1 84576

Overseas Representation:
All other countries: Titan Books, Sales & Marketing Department, London, UK
Central & Eastern Europe (including Poland): Csaba Lengyel de Bagota, Budapest, Hungary
Far East: Ralph & Sheila Summers, Formtone Ltd, London, UK
France, Belgium, Netherlands, Greece, Malta, Israel & South Africa: Paul Walton, Chislehurst, UK
Germany, Switzerland & Austria: Gabriele Kern Publishers Services, Frankfurt-am-Main, Germany
Middle East: Peter Ward Book Exports, London, UK
Republic of Ireland: Gill Hess Ltd, Skerries, Co Dublin
Scandinavia & Italy: Katie McNeish, McNeish Publishing Services, East Sussex, UK
Spain, Portugal & Gibraltar: Peter Prout, Iberian Book Services, Madrid, Spain

2778

TOP THAT! PUBLISHING PLC
Marine House, Tide Mill Way, Woodbridge, Suffolk IP12 1AP
Telephone: 01394 386651
Fax: 01394 386011
Email: barrie@topthatpublishing.com
Web Site: http://www.topthatpublishing.com

Directors: Barrie Henderson *(Managing)*
Dave Greggor *(Sales)*
Simon Couchman *(Creative)*
Douglas Eadie *(Finance)*
Daniel Graham *(Editorial)*
Stuart Buck *(Production)*
Head of European Sales: Anja Scaife
Business Development Manager: Rachel Ford

Children's Books; Cookery, Wines & Spirits; Crafts & Hobbies; Gardening; Guide Books; Health & Beauty; Humour; Natural History; Reference Books, Directories & Dictionaries

No of Employees: 47
Annual Turnover: £11M

ISBNs, Imprints & Series:
Pocket Money Press; Tide Mill Press
978 1 84229 Kudos
978 1 902973 Art Rom; Art Tricks; Cool Kits; Explorasaws; file-online.com; Fun Kits; I-Quiz; Know How Know Why; Magic Bookshop Bears; Megatastic; Mini Maestro; Paper Magic; Play Pals; Puzzle Zone; Stickertastic; Teachers Pets; Top That!

Associated Companies:
USA: Top That! Publishing

Overseas Representation:
USA: Top That! Publishing, Valencia, CA

Book Trade Association Membership:
IPG

2779

TOPICAL RESOURCES
Jumps Farm, Durton Lane, Broughton, Preston, Lancs PR3 5LE
Telephone: 01772 863158
Fax: 01772 866153
Email: sales@topical-resources.co.uk
Web Site: http://www.topical-resources.co.uk

Partners: Peter Bell
Heather Bell
Sales Assistants: Kath Cope
Sue Concill

Audio Books; Children's Books; Educational & Textbooks

ISBNs, Imprints & Series:
978 1 872977, 978 1 905509

Overseas Representation:
Republic of Ireland: Martin Pender, Primary Educational Resources, Enniscorthy, Co Wexford

Book Trade Association Membership:
IPG

2780

*TRANS-PENNINE PUBLISHING LTD
PO Box 10, Appleby-in-Westmorland, Cumbria CA16 6FA
Telephone: 01768 351053
Fax: 01768 353558
Email: admin@transpenninepublishing.co.uk
Web Site: http://www.transpenninepublishing.co.uk

Warehouse:
Nostalgia Road Publications, Chancel Place, Kendal LA9 5NZ
Telephone: 01539 738832
Fax: 01539 730075
Email: sales@nostalgiaroad.co.uk
Web Site: http://www.nostalgiaroad.co.uk

Director: Larraine Earnshaw
Managing Editor: Alan Earnshaw
Managers: Matthew Richardson *(Production)*
Bryony Richardson *(Office)*
Peter Earnshaw *(Sales & Marketing)*
Editorial: Louise Tarn

Geography & Geology; History & Antiquarian; Military & War; Transport; Travel & Topography

ISBNs, Imprints & Series:
978 1 903016 British Railways in Colour; Buses in Colour; Classic Marques; Cumbria Heritage; Famous Fleets; Fare Stage; Nostalgia Road; Railway Preservation; Rural Railways

2781

TRANSITA LTD
Spring Hill House, Spring Hill Road, Begbroke, Oxon OX5 1RX
Telephone: 01865 375796
Fax: 01865 379162
Email: info@transita.co.uk
Web Site: http://www.transita.co.uk

Customer Services:
Grantham Book Services,
Isaac Newton Way,
Alma Park Industrial Estate, Grantham, Lincs NG31 9SG
Telephone: 01476 541080
Fax: 01476 541061
Email: orders@gbs.tbs-ltd.co.uk
Web Site: http://www.transita.co.uk

Managing Director: Giles Lewis
Editorial: Nikki Read
Rights: Ros Loten
Production: Bill Antrobus
Finance: Martin Wilkinson

Fiction

New Titles: 2 (2007), 2 (2008)

ISBNs, Imprints & Series: 978 1 905175

Associated Companies:
How To Books Ltd

Overseas Representation:
Africa: Kelvin van Hasselt Publishing Services, Briningham, Norfolk, UK
East Asia: STP Distributors Pte Ltd, Singapore
Germany & Benelux: Robbert J. Pleysier, Heerde, Netherlands
Latin America & West Indies: InterMedia Americana (IMA) Ltd, London, UK
Middle East & Turkey: Publishers International Marketing, Sutton St Nicholas, Herefordshire, UK
Republic of Ireland: Slemish, Ballymena, Northern Ireland, UK
South Africa: Phambili CC, Kensington
Spain & Portugal: Peter Prout Iberian Book Services, Madrid, Spain

2782

TRANSWORLD PUBLISHERS LTD
[a division of the Random House Group Ltd]
61–63 Uxbridge Road, London W5 5SA
Telephone: (020) 8579 2652
Fax: (020) 8579 5479
Email: info@transworld-publishers.co.uk
Web Site: http://www.booksattransworld.co.uk

Warehouse & Distribution:
PO Box 17, Wellingborough, Northants NN8 4BU
Telephone: 01933 225761
Fax: 01933 271235
Email: warehouse@transworld-publishers.co.uk

Directors: Larry Finlay *(Managing)*
Bill Scott-Kerr *(Publisher)*
Francesca Liversidge *(Senior Publishing – Bantam Books)*
Sally Gaminara *(Publishing – Bantam Press)*
Marianne Velmans *(Publishing – Doubleday)*
Nigel Waters *(Finance)*
Ed Christie *(Sales & Marketing)*
Martin Higgins *(UK Sales)*
Janine Giovanni *(UK Marketing)*
Diana Jones *(International Sales)*
Alison Martin *(Production)*
Patsy Irwin *(Publicity)*
Andy Lay *(Operations Manager)*
Claire Ward *(Art)*
Helen Edwards *(Rights)*

Audio Books; Biography & Autobiography; Cinema, Video, TV & Radio; Cookery, Wines & Spirits; Crime; Fiction; Gardening; Health & Beauty; History & Antiquarian; Humour; Military & War; Music; Politics & World Affairs; Science Fiction; Sports & Games; Travel & Topography; New Age

ISBNs, Imprints & Series:
Channel 4 Books
978 0 385 Doubleday
978 0 552 Black Swan; Corgi
978 0 553 Bantam
978 0 593 Bantam Press; Eden Project
978 0 903 Expert Gardening Books

Parent Company:
USA: Random House Inc

Associated Companies:
Random House Children's Books; Random House UK Ltd
Australia: Random House Australia Pty Ltd
Canada: Random House of Canada Ltd
New Zealand: Random House New Zealand Ltd
South Africa: Random House (Pty) Ltd

Overseas Representation:
Australia: Random House Australia Pty Ltd, Sydney, NSW
Canada: Random House of Canada Ltd, Toronto, Ont
New Zealand: Random House New Zealand Ltd, Auckland
South Africa: Random House (SA) Pty Ltd, Parktown

Book Trade Association Membership:
BA (Associate Member)

2783

TRAVEL PUBLISHING LTD
Airport Business Centre,
10 Thornbury Road, Estover, Plymouth
PL6 7PP
Telephone: 01752 697280
Fax: 01752 697299
Email: info@travelpublishing.co.uk
Web Site: http://www.travelpublishing.co.uk

Sales & Distribution:
Portfolio, Suite 3 & 4, Great West House, Great West Road, Brentford, Middx
TW8 9DF
Telephone: (020) 8326 5620
Fax: (020) 8326 5621
Email: e-mail@portfoliobooks.com

Directors: Peter Robinson (Chairman)
Chris Day (Company Secretary)

Guide Books; Travel & Topography

ISBNs, Imprints & Series:
978 1 902007, 978 1 904434 Country Living Rural Guides; Golfers Guides; Hidden Inns; Hidden Places; Off the Motorway
978 1 904434 Country Pubs & Inns

Overseas Representation:
USA & Canada: Casemate Publishers & Book Distributors LLC, Havertown, PA, USA

Book Trade Association Membership:
IPG

2784

TRENTHAM BOOKS
Westview House, 734 London Road, Oakhill, Stoke on Trent ST4 5NP
Telephone: 01782 745567 & 844699
Fax: 01782 745553
Email: tb@trentham-books.co.uk
Web Site: http://www.trentham-books.co.uk

Editorial:
28 Hillside Gardens, Highgate, London
N6 5ST
Telephone: (020) 8348 2174
Email: gillian@trentham-books.co.uk

Directors: Gillian Klein (Chairman, Rights & Permissions, Editor)
Barbara Wiggins (Business Manager)

Academic & Scholarly; Educational & Textbooks; Gender Studies; Law; Politics & World Affairs; Theatre, Drama & Dance

New Titles: 29 (2007), 27 (2008)
No of Employees: 5

ISBNs, Imprints & Series:
978 0 948080, 978 0 9507735, 978 1 85856

Associated Companies:
Trentham Print Design Ltd

Distributor for:
Arts Council [selected titles]; Commission for Racial Equality [selected titles]; Design and Technology Association [selected titles]; Open University [selected titles]
France: European Institute of Education & Social Policy [selected titles]; UNESCO Institute for Educational Planning [selected titles]

Overseas Representation:
Australia, New Zealand & South East Asia: DA Information Services Pty Ltd, Mitcham, Vic, Australia
Canada: Bacon & Hughes Ltd, Ottawa, Ont
China, Taiwan, Hong Kong & South East Asia: Tony Poh Leong Wah, Singapore, Singapore
Malaysia: UBSD Distribution Sdn Bhd, Selangor
Philippines: Megatexts Phil Inc, Cebu City
Spain & Portugal: Iberian Book Services, Madrid, Spain
Taiwan: Unifacmanu Trading Co Ltd, Taipei
USA: Stylus Publishing Inc, Sterling, VA

Book Trade Association Membership:
IPG

2785

TRINITARIAN BIBLE SOCIETY
Tyndale House, Dorset Road, London
SW19 3NN
Telephone: (020) 8543 7857
Fax: (020) 8543 6370
Email: TBS@trinitarianbiblesociety.org
Web Site: http://www.trinitarianbiblesociety.org

Online Sales:
Web Site: http://www.TBS-sales.org

General Secretary: D. P. Rowland
Assistant General Secretary: D. Larlham
Consultant Accountant: D. C. S. Cooke

Religion & Theology

No of Employees: 27

ISBNs, Imprints & Series:
978 0 907861, 978 1 86228

Overseas Representation:
Australia: Trinitarian Bible Society (Australia), Grafton, NSW
Brazil: Sociedade Bíblica Trinitariana do Brasil, São Paulo
Canada: Trinitarian Bible Society, Chilliwack, BC
New Zealand: Trinitarian Bible Society (New Zealand), Gisborne
USA: Trinitarian Bible Society (USA), Grand Rapids, MI

2786

TRIUMPH HOUSE
Remus House, Coltsfoot Drive, Woodston, Peterborough PE2 9JX
Telephone: 01733 898102
Fax: 01733 313524
Email: triumphhouse@forwardpress.co.uk
Web Site: http://www.forwardpress.co.uk

Communications Assistant: Sharon Spencer (Marketing)

Poetry; Religion & Theology

ISBNs, Imprints & Series:
afterschoolclub.net; Anchor Books; Need2Know; New Fiction; Poetry Now; Pond View; Spotlight Poets; Writers' Bookshop; Young Writers
978 1 86161, 978 1 90422 Triumph House

Parent Company:
Forward Press

Book Trade Association Membership:
BA

2787

TROTMAN PUBLISHING
[an imprint of Crimson Publishing Ltd]
Crimson Publishing Ltd,
Westminster House, Kew Road, Richmond
TW9 2ND
Telephone: (020) 8334 1786
Fax: (020) 8334 1601
Email: jessicas@crimsonpublishing.co.uk
Web Site: http://www.trotman.co.uk

Warehouse:
NBN International Ltd, Estover Road, Plymouth PL6 7PY
Telephone: 01752 202301
Fax: 01752 202333

Directors: David Lester (Managing)
Thomas Lee (Commercial)
Commissioning Editor: Jessica Spencer

Educational & Textbooks; Industry, Business & Management; Reference Books, Directories & Dictionaries; Travel & Topography; Vocational Training & Careers

New Titles: 48 (2007), 48 (2008)
No of Employees: 55

ISBNs, Imprints & Series:
978 0 85660, 978 1 84455 Trotman; Trotman Education

Parent Company:
UK: Crimson Publishing Ltd

Book Trade Association Membership:
IPG; Data Publishers Association

2788

TROUBADOR PUBLISHING LTD
9 De Montfort Mews, Leicester LE1 7FW
Telephone: 0116 255 9311
Fax: 0116 255 9323
Email: books@troubador.co.uk
Web Site: http://www.troubador.co.uk

Warehouse:
Tipac Leicester Ltd, Disraeli Street, Leicester LE2 8LX
Telephone: 0116 244 0220
Fax: 0116 244 0620

Directors: Jeremy Thompson (Managing)
Jane Rowland (Academic Publishing)
Managers: Julia Fuller (Marketing)
Terry Compton (Production)

Academic & Scholarly; Biography & Autobiography; Children's Books; Cookery, Wines & Spirits; Crime; Economics; Fiction; Guide Books; History & Antiquarian; Humour; Industry, Business & Management; Languages & Linguistics; Literature & Criticism; Magic & the Occult; Medical (incl. Self Help & Alternative Medicine); Military & War; Natural History; Philosophy; Poetry; Politics & World Affairs; Psychology & Psychiatry; Science Fiction; Theatre, Drama & Dance; Transport; Travel & Topography

New Titles: 152 (2007), 180 (2008)
No of Employees: 5
Annual Turnover: £600,000

ISBNs, Imprints & Series:
978 1 899293, 978 1 905886, 978 1 906221, 978 1 906510 Matador
978 1 904744 T2
978 1 905237 Italian Studies

Book Trade Association Membership:
IPG

2789

*TRU-EST LTD
22 Buckingham Gate, London SW1E 6LB
Telephone: (020) 7674 0400
Fax: (020) 7674 0404
Web Site: http://www.tru-est.com

Chief Executive Officer: J. Anderson
Director: I. Orton (Editorial)
Production: Lee Stinton (Chief Designer)
Managers: W. Marston (Circulation)
James Rawes (Group Business Development)

Accountancy & Taxation; Economics; Industry, Business & Management; Law; Reference Books, Directories & Dictionaries

Associated Companies:
Wealth Management Information Services Ltd

Book Trade Association Membership:
Data Publishers Association

2790

TRURAN
Croft Prince, Mount Hawke, Truro TR4 8EE
Telephone: 01209 891287
Fax: 01209 891134
Email: info@truranbooks.co.uk
Web Site: http://www.truranbooks.co.uk

Trade Enquiries:
Tor Mark Press,
United Downs Industrial Estate, St Day, Redruth, Cornwall TR16 5HY
Telephone: 01209 822101
Fax: 01209 822035
Email: sales@tormarkpress.prestel.co.uk

Directors: Ivan Corbett
Heather Corbett

Aviation; Biography & Autobiography; Cookery, Wines & Spirits; Fiction; Fine Art & Art History; Gardening; Geography & Geology; Guide Books; History & Antiquarian; Languages & Linguistics; Military & War; Natural History; Nautical; Photography; Reference Books, Directories & Dictionaries

New Titles: 12 (2007), 9 (2008)
Annual Turnover: £25,000

ISBNs, Imprints & Series:
Cornish Classics; Truran
978 0 9506431, 978 0 907566, 978 1 85022

Book Trade Association Membership:
IPG

2791

*TSO (THE STATIONERY OFFICE LTD)
St Crispins, Duke Street, Norwich NR3 1PD
Telephone: 01603 622211
Fax: 01603 696506
Email: tsoservices@tso.co.uk
Web Site: http://www.tso.co.uk

Warehouse & Offices:
51 Nine Elms Lane, London SW8 5DR
Telephone: (020) 7873 8787
Email: tsoservices@tso.co.uk
Web Site: http://www.tso.co.uk

Press & Offices:
Mandela Way, London SE1 5SS
Telephone: (020) 7394 4200
Email: tsoservices@tso.co.uk
Web Site: http://www.tso.co.uk

Directors: Jeremy Hook *(Commercial)*
Richard South *(Official Publishing)*
Richard Dell *(Chief Executive Officer)*
Richard Coward *(Finance)*

Academic & Scholarly; Accountancy & Taxation; Aviation; Computer Science; Economics; Educational & Textbooks; Electronic (Professional & Academic); Engineering; Geography & Geology; Industry, Business & Management; Law; Mathematics & Statistics; Medical (incl. Self Help & Alternative Medicine); Nautical; Politics & World Affairs; Reference Books, Directories & Dictionaries; Scientific & Technical; Transport; Veterinary Science

ISBNs, Imprints & Series:
International Organisations
978 0 10 Parliamentary Publications
978 0 11 Non-Parliamentary Publications
978 0 337 Northern Ireland Publications
978 0 8213 World Bank
978 1 55 International Monetary Fund

Distributor for:
Construction Industry Publications; English Heritage [selected back-list titles only]; International Labour Organisation
Austria: International Atomic Energy Agency
France: Council of Europe; European Pharmacopoeia Commission; Organisation for Economic Co-operation and Development; United Nations Educational, Scientific and Cultural Organisation
Germany: Deutscher Apotheker Verlag; G. Thieme Verlag
Italy: Food and Agriculture Organisation of the United Nations
Japan: Japanese Pharmacopoeia; United Nations University
Luxembourg: European Communities/Union
Spain: World Tourism Organisation
Switzerland: United Nations; World Health Organisation; World Trade Organisation
USA: Bernan Press [selected USA Government publications]; Facts & Comparisons; International Monetary Fund; Kluwer Law; United Nations; US Pharmacopoeia Convention; World Bank; World Trade Press

Overseas Representation:
Australia: DA Information Services Pty Ltd, Mitcham, Vic
Austria: Universitats Buchhandlung, Graben
Belgium & Luxembourg: Jean de Lannoy, Brussels, Belgium
Canada: Carswell Publishing Ltd, Scarborough, Ont; Renouf Publishing Co Ltd, Ottawa, Ont
Cyprus: Soloneion Book Centre, Nicosia
Denmark: Arnold Busck, Copenhagen
Finland: Akateeminen Kirjakauppa, Helsinki
Germany: Alexander Horn, Wiesbaden
Greece: G C Eleftherondakis SA, Athens; Papasotiriou, Athens
Hong Kong: Swindon Book Co Ltd
Iceland: Boksala Studenta, Reykjavik
India: Viva Books, New Delhi
Italy: Libreria Internazionale, Milan; Licosa SPA, Florence
Japan: Maruzen Co Ltd, Tokyo
Jordan: Jordan Book Centre, Amman
Kuwait: The Kuwait Bookshop Co Ltd, Safat
Netherlands: Kooyker Ginsberg, Leiden
Norway: Academic Book Centre, Oslo
Singapore: Alkem Co (S) Pte Ltd
South Africa: Pharma Books cc, Pretoria
Spain: Diaz de Santos SA, Madrid
Sweden: Longus Book Imports, Stockholm
Switzerland: Buchhandlung Hans Huber, Berne; Stheli International Booksellers, Zurich; Wepf & Co, Basel
United Arab Emirates: Al Mutanabbi Bookshop, Abu Dhabi, UAE; Elcome International LLC, Dubai, UAE
USA: Balogh International Inc, Champaign, IL; Bernan Associates, Lanham, MD; Dream Catchers, San Antonio, TX; Judith Marx Golub, Los Altos, CA

Book Trade Association Membership:
BA; EPC; CAPP; Data Publishers Association

2792

TTS GROUP
Nunn Brook Road, Huthwaite, Sutton-in-Ashfield, Notts NG17 2HU
Telephone: 01623 447878
Fax: 01623 440543
Web Site: http://www.tts-group.co.uk

Book Trade Association Membership:
Publishers Association

2793

TWELVEHEADS PRESS
PO Box 59, Chacewater, Truro, Cornwall TR4 8ZJ
Email: enquiries@twelveheads.com
Web Site: http://www.twelveheads.com

Partners: Alan Kittridge
Michael Messenger
John Stengelhofen

Archaeology; Guide Books; History & Antiquarian; Nautical; Transport

New Titles: 3 (2007), 4 (2008)

ISBNs, Imprints & Series: 978 0 906294

2794

TYNE BRIDGE PUBLISHING
Newcastle Libraries, PO Box 88, Newcastle upon Tyne NE99 1DX
Telephone: 0191 277 4174
Fax: 0191 277 4137
Email: anna.flowers@newcastle.gov.uk
Web Site: http://www.newcastle.gov.uk/tynebridgepublishing

Publications Manager: Anna Flowers
Marketing Officer: Vanessa Histon

Architecture & Design; Biography & Autobiography; Engineering; Fine Art & Art History; History & Antiquarian; Military & War; Nautical

New Titles: 4 (2007), 5 (2008)
No of Employees: 2
Annual Turnover: £140,000

ISBNs, Imprints & Series:
978 1 85795 Newcastle Libraries and Information Service; Tyne Bridge Publishing

Parent Company:
City & Council of Newcastle upon Tyne

2795

UCAS
Rosehill, New Barn Lane, Cheltenham, Glos GL52 3LZ
Telephone: 01242 222444
Fax: 01242 544960
Email: publicationservices@ucas.ac.uk
Web Site: http://www.ucas.com

Trade Enquiries & Orders:
Publication Services, UCAS, PO Box 130, Cheltenham, Glos GL52 3ZF
Telephone: 01242 544610
Fax: 01242 544806
Email: publicationservices@ucas.ac.uk
Web Site: http://www.ucasbooks.com

Head of Communications: Chris Dry
Publications Co-ordinator: Steven Matthews
Senior Management Accountant: Amruta Hiremath
Publication Services Manager: Joanne Voysey

Academic & Scholarly; Educational & Textbooks; Reference Books, Directories & Dictionaries; Vocational Training & Careers

New Titles: 12 (2007), 13 (2008)

ISBNs, Imprints & Series: 978 1 84361

2796

ULVERSCROFT LARGE PRINT BOOKS LTD
The Green, Bradgate Road, Anstey, Leics LE7 7FU
Telephone: 0116 236 4325
Fax: 0116 234 0205
Email: sales@ulverscroft.co.uk
Web Site: http://www.ulverscroft.co.uk

Trade

Book Trade Association Membership:
Publishers Association

2797

UNICORN PRESS
76 Great Suffolk Street, London SE1 0BL
Telephone: (020) 7928 1191
Email: unicornpress@btinternet.com
Web Site: http://www.unicornpress.org

Trade Distributor:
Marston Book Services, 160 Milton Park, PO Box 269, Abingdon, Oxford OX14 4YN
Telephone: 01235 465604
Fax: 01235 465655
Email: nichola.kidd@marston.co.uk

Proprietor: Hugh Tempest-Radford
Sales: Emma Farrell

Antiques & Collecting; Architecture & Design; Biography & Autobiography; Fashion & Costume; Fine Art & Art History; History & Antiquarian; Military & War; Nautical; Photography; Reference Books, Directories & Dictionaries

New Titles: 6 (2007), 9 (2008)

ISBNs, Imprints & Series:
978 0 906290, 978 1 906509

Overseas Representation:
All other areas: Unicorn Press, London, UK
USA: Antique Collectors Club Ltd, Easthampton, MA

2798

UNITED WRITERS PUBLICATIONS LTD
Ailsa, Castle Gate, Penzance, Cornwall TR20 8BG
Telephone: 01736 365954
Fax: 01736 365954
Email: sales@unitedwriters.co.uk
Web Site: http://www.unitedwriters.co.uk

Editorial & Sales: M. Sheppard
Production: T. Sully

Biography & Autobiography; Children's Books; Cinema, Video, TV & Radio; Educational & Textbooks; Fiction; Humour; Industry, Business & Management; Military & War; Nautical; Psychology & Psychiatry; Science Fiction; Sports & Games; Travel & Topography

New Titles: 4 (2007), 7 (2008)

ISBNs, Imprints & Series:
978 0 901976, 978 1 85200

2799

UNIVERSITY COLLEGE DUBLIN PRESS
Newman House, 86 St Stephen's Green, Dublin 2, Republic of Ireland
Telephone: +353 (01) 477 9812 & 9813
Fax: +353 (01) 477 9821
Email: ucdpress@ucd.ie
Web Site: http://www.ucdpress.ie

Distribution (Republic of Ireland):
Columba Mercier Distribution,
55A Spruce Avenue,
Stillorgan Industrial Park, Blackrock,
Co Dublin, Republic of Ireland
Fax: +353 (01) 294 2564

Representation (Republic of Ireland):
Hibernian Book Services,
93 Longwood Park, Rathfarnham,
Dublin 14, Republic of Ireland
Telephone: +353 (01) 493 6043
Fax: +353 (01) 493 7833

Executive Editor: Barbara Mennell
Assistant Editor: Noelle Moran

Academic & Scholarly

New Titles: 15 (2007), 16 (2008)
No of Employees: 2

ISBNs, Imprints & Series:
978 1 900621, 978 1 904558, 978 1 906359

Overseas Representation:
Australia & New Zealand: Eleanor Brasch Enterprises, Artarmon, NSW, Australia
Germany, Austria & Switzerland: SHS Publishers' Consultants and Representatives, Oranienberg, Germany
North America: Dufour Editions Inc, Chester Springs, PA, USA
Spain & Portugal: Iberian Book Services, Madrid, Spain
UK & Benelux countries: Theo Van de Bilt Sales and Marketing, Sawbridgeworth, UK
UK, Europe & all other countries (distribution): Central Books Ltd, London, UK

Book Trade Association Membership:
CLÉ (Irish PA)

2800

UNIVERSITY OF EXETER PRESS
Reed Hall, Streatham Drive, Exeter EX4 4QR
Telephone: 01392 263066
Fax: 01392 263064
Email: uep@exeterpress.co.uk
Web Site: http://www.exeterpress.co.uk

Distribution:
NBN International, Estover Road, Plymouth PL6 7PY
Telephone: 01752 202301
Fax: 01752 202331

Email: cservs@nbninternational.com
Web Site: http://www.nbninternational.com

Publisher: Simon Baker
Sales: Anna Henderson

Academic & Scholarly; Archaeology; Cinema, Video, TV & Radio; History & Antiquarian; Literature & Criticism; Theatre, Drama & Dance; Classical Studies; Film History; Maritime History; Medieval English Texts & Studies; Performance Studies

New Titles: 25 (2007), 25 (2008)

ISBNs, Imprints & Series:
978 0 85989 University of Exeter Press
978 1 904675 Bristol Phoenix Press
978 1 905816 The Exeter Press

Parent Company:
The Exeter Press Ltd

Overseas Representation:
Australia & New Zealand: Footprint Books Pty, Mona Vale, NSW, Australia
Benelux: Roy de Boo, Hooge Mierde, Netherlands
China, Hong Kong, Taiwan & South East Asia: Tony Poh, Singapore
France & Italy: Flavio Marcello Publishers' Agents & Consultants, Padua, Italy
Germany, Austria & Switzerland: SHS Publishers' Consultants and Representatives, Oranienberg, Germany
Greece & Cyprus: Charles Gibbes Associates, Louslitges, France
Japan: United Publishers Services Ltd, Tokyo
Republic of Ireland: Gabrielle Redmond, Dublin
Scandinavia: Jan Norbye, Ølstykke, Denmark
Spain & Portugal: Iberian Book Services, Madrid, Spain
USA & Canada: University of Chicago Press, Chicago, IL, USA

Book Trade Association Membership:
IPG

2801

UNIVERSITY OF HERTFORDSHIRE PRESS
University of Hertfordshire,
Learning & Information Services, LRC,
College Lane, Hatfield AL10 9AB
Telephone: 01707 284681
Fax: 01707 284666
Email: UHPress@herts.ac.uk
Web Site: http://www.herts.ac.uk/UHPress

Trade Enquiries & Orders:
Central Books Ltd, 99 Wallis Road, London E9 5LN
Telephone: 0845 458 9911
Fax: 0845 458 9912
Email: info@centralbooks.com
Web Site: http://www.centralbooks.com

Manager: Jane Housham
Assistant: Sue Mariscal *(Administration)*
Marketing Executive: Helen Miller
Production Editor: Sarah Elvins

Academic & Scholarly; Educational & Textbooks; History & Antiquarian; Literature & Criticism; Mathematics & Statistics; Psychology & Psychiatry; Scientific & Technical; Sociology & Anthropology; Theatre, Drama & Dance

New Titles: 15 (2007), 15 (2008)

ISBNs, Imprints & Series:
978 0 900458, 978 1 905313 Guidelines for Research in Parapsychology; The Interface Collection; Regional and Local History
978 0 9542189, 978 1 905313 Hertfordshire Publications
978 1 898543, 978 1 905313 University of Hertfordshire (Faculties)
978 1 902806, 978 1 905313 University of Hertfordshire Press

Parent Company:
University of Hertfordshire

Overseas Representation:
Spain & Portugal: Iberian Book Services, Madrid, Spain
USA: Independent Publishers Group (IPG), Chicago, IL

Book Trade Association Membership:
IPG

2802

UNIVERSITY OF WALES PRESS
10 Columbus Walk, Brigantine Place, Cardiff CF10 4UP
Telephone: (029) 2049 6899
Fax: (029) 2049 6108
Email: press@press.wales.ac.uk
Web Site: http://uwp.co.uk

Distribution (UK):
NBN International Ltd, Estover Road, Plymouth PL6 7PY
Telephone: 01752 202300
Fax: 01752 202330

Director: Ashley Drake
Managers: Sian Chapman *(Production)*
Victoria Nickerson *(Sales & Marketing)*
Commissioning Editor: Sarah Lewis
Finance: Paul Folland

Academic & Scholarly; Archaeology; Biography & Autobiography; Educational & Textbooks; Gender Studies; History & Antiquarian; Illustrated & Fine Editions; Languages & Linguistics; Literature & Criticism; Military & War; Music; Philosophy; Poetry; Politics & World Affairs; Reference Books, Directories & Dictionaries; Religion & Theology; Sociology & Anthropology; Sports & Games

New Titles: 60 (2007), 70 (2008)
No of Employees: 14
Annual Turnover: £500,000

ISBNs, Imprints & Series:
978 0 7083, 978 0 900768 GPC Books; Gwasg Prifysgol Cymru; University of Wales Press

Parent Company:
University of Wales

Distributor for:
The Glamorgan County History Trust; Zena Publications [one title]

Overseas Representation:
Australia: UNIREPS University and Reference Publishers' Services, Sydney, NSW
India: Maya Publishers Pvt Ltd, New Delhi
Japan: United Publishers Services Ltd, Tokyo
South East Asia: STM Publisher Services Pte Ltd, Singapore
USA & Canada: Chicago University Press, Chicago, IL, USA

Book Trade Association Membership:
IPG; Literary Publishers (Wales) Ltd

2803

MERLIN UNWIN BOOKS LTD
7 Corve Street, Ludlow, Shropshire SY8 1DB
Telephone: 01584 877456
Fax: 01584 877457
Email: books@merlinunwin.co.uk
Web Site: http://www.merlinunwin.co.uk

Warehouse & Returns:
Merlin Unwin Books Warehouse, c/o Wow Distribution, The Yard, Woofferton Grange, Brimfield, Ludlow SY8 4NP

Directors: Merlin Unwin *(Management, Design)*
Karen McCall *(Managing, Editorial)*
Finance: Gillian Bissell
Marketing & Production: Joanne Potter

Agriculture; Biography & Autobiography; Cookery, Wines & Spirits; Humour; Illustrated & Fine Editions; Medical (incl. Self Help & Alternative Medicine); Military & War; Natural History; Philosophy; Photography; Reference Books, Directories & Dictionaries; Sports & Games

New Titles: 10 (2007), 7 (2008)
No of Employees: 4

ISBNs, Imprints & Series:
978 1 873674, 978 1 90612

Distributor for:
LPPHA (London Police Pensioner Housing Association)

Book Trade Association Membership:
IPG

2804

UPFRONT PUBLISHING
9 Culley Court, Bakewell Road, Orton Southgate, Peterborough PE2 6XP
Telephone: 01733 311124
Fax: 01733 352933
Email: info@upfrontpublishing.com
Web Site: http://www.upfrontpublishing.com

Managing Director: Andy Cork
Publishing Manager: Simon Potter

Biography & Autobiography; Fiction; Poetry

New Titles: 50 (2007), 75 (2008)
No of Employees: 2

ISBNs, Imprints & Series: 978 1 84426

Parent Company:
Print on Demand – Worldwide [formerly Copytech Digital]

2805

LAURENCE URDANG INC
PO Box 156, Chearsley, Aylesbury, Bucks HP18 0DQ
Telephone: 01844 208474
Email: verbatim.uk@tesco.net
Web Site: http://www.verbatimbooks.com

President: Laurence Urdang *(Editorial)*
Administration: Mrs Hazel Hall *(Assistant to the President)*

Languages & Linguistics; Reference Books, Directories & Dictionaries

ISBNs, Imprints & Series:
Verbatim Books
978 0 930454

Parent Company:
USA: Laurence Urdang Inc

Overseas Representation:
USA: Laurence Urdang Inc, Old Lyme, CT

2806

USBORNE PUBLISHING LTD
Usborne House, 83–85 Saffron Hill, London EC1N 8RT
Telephone: (020) 7430 2800
Fax: (020) 7242 0974 & 7430 1562
Email: mail@usborne.co.uk
Web Site: http://www.usborne.com

Warehouse:
HarperCollins, Westerhill Road, Bishopsbriggs, Glasgow G64 2QT
Telephone: 0141 306 3100
Fax: 0141 306 3767

Directors: T. P. Usborne *(Managing)*
R. Jones *(General Manager)*
J. Tyler *(Editorial)*
D. Harte
L. Hunt
K. M. Ball *(Company Secretary)*
Rights Controller: E. Wright
UK Marketing: C. Herisson
Editorial: M. Larkin *(Fiction)*
G. Lewis

Children's Books; Computer Science; Crafts & Hobbies; Fiction; Languages & Linguistics; Music; Natural History; Reference Books, Directories & Dictionaries; Scientific & Technical; Sports & Games

New Titles: 384 (2007), 352 (2008)
No of Employees: 150
Annual Turnover: £32.5M

ISBNs, Imprints & Series:
978 0 7460, 978 0 86020

2807

VALLENTINE MITCHELL PUBLISHERS
Suite 314, Premier House,
112–114 Station Road, Edgware, Middx HA8 7BJ
Telephone: (020) 8952 9526
Fax: (020) 8952 9242
Email: info@vmbooks.com
Web Site: http://www.vmbooks.com

Managing Director: Stewart Cass
Editor & Production: Jenni Tinson
Sales & Marketing, Publicity: Toby Harris

Academic & Scholarly; Biography & Autobiography; History & Antiquarian; Politics & World Affairs; Religion & Theology

ISBNs, Imprints & Series: 978 0 85303

Book Trade Association Membership:
IPG

2808

VELOCE PUBLISHING LTD
33 Trinity Street, Dorchester, Dorset DT1 1TT
Telephone: 01305 260068
Fax: 01305 268864
Email: veloce@veloce.co.uk
Web Site: http://www.veloce.co.uk

Directors: Rod Grainger *(Publisher)*
Judith Brooks *(Company Secretary)*

Biography & Autobiography; Illustrated & Fine Editions; Reference Books, Directories & Dictionaries; Sports & Games; Transport

New Titles: 48 (2007), 55 (2008)
No of Employees: 12

ISBNs, Imprints & Series:
978 1 84584, 978 1 874105, 978 1 901295, 978 1 903706, 978 1 904788

Overseas Representation:
Australia & New Zealand: Capricorn Link (Australia) Pty Ltd, Windsor, NSW, Australia
France: Editions du Palmier, Nîmes; Librairie du Collectionneur, Paris
Germany: Heel-Verlag, Konigswinter
Germany, Austria & Benelux: Anselm Robinson, London, UK
Japan: Shimada & Co Inc, Tokyo; Takahara Bookstore Co Ltd, Aichi-ken
New Zealand: South Pacific Books (Imports)

Ltd, Auckland; TechBooks, Auckland
Scandinavia: MarGie Bookshop, Stockholm, Sweden; Angell Eurosales, Berwick-on-Tweed, UK
South Africa: Motor Books, Johannesburg
South East Asia: Ashton International Marketing Services, Sevenoaks, Kent, UK
Spain & Italy: Bookport Associates, Corsico (MI), Italy; Libro Motor SI, Madrid, Spain
USA: Motorbooks International Inc, Osceola, WI

2809

VERITAS PUBLICATIONS
Veritas House, 7–8 Lower Abbey Street, Dublin 1, Republic of Ireland
Telephone: +353 (01) 878 8177
Fax: +353 (01) 878 6507
Email: publications@veritas.ie
Web Site: http://www.veritas.ie

Editors: Ruth Kennedy *(Managing)*
  Donna Doherty *(Commissioning)*
Commercial Manager: Maureen Sanders
Publicity & Marketing: Amanda Conlon-McKenna
Director: Maura Hyland
Sales Representatives: Ann O'Neill
  Sheila McMacken
Financial Controller: Eamonn Connelly

Academic & Scholarly; Biography & Autobiography; Children's Books; Educational & Textbooks; Philosophy; Religion & Theology; Social Issues

New Titles: 45 (2007), 45 (2008)
No of Employees: 94
Annual Turnover: £6.1M

ISBNs, Imprints & Series:
978 0 85390, 978 0 86217, 978 1 84730, 978 1 85390

Parent Company:
Republic of Ireland: Veritas Communications

Overseas Representation:
Australia: John Garrett Publishing, Mulgrave, Vic
Malta: Libreria Taghlim Nisrani, Sliema
New Zealand: Catholic Supplies (NZ) Ltd, Wellington
South Africa: The Catholic Bookshop, Cape Town; St Augustine's Catholic Bookshop, Port Elizabeth
USA: Acta, Chicago, IL; Dufour Editions Inc, Chester Springs, PA; Ignatius Press, San Francisco, CA

Book Trade Association Membership:
CLÉ (Irish PA)

2810

VERTICAL EDITIONS
7 Bell Busk, Skipton, North Yorkshire BD23 4DT
Telephone: 01729 830787
Fax: 01729 830979
Email: custserv@verticaleditions.com
Web Site: http://www.verticaleditions.com

Publisher: Karl Waddicor

Biography & Autobiography; Sports & Games

New Titles: 5 (2007), 7 (2008)
No of Employees: 1
Annual Turnover: £90,000

ISBNs, Imprints & Series: 978 1 904091

Book Trade Association Membership:
IPG

2811

VICTORIA & ALBERT MUSEUM PUBLISHING
Victoria & Albert Museum, South Kensington, London SW7 2RL
Telephone: (020) 7942 2966
Fax: (020) 7942 2967
Email: vapubs.info@vam.ac.uk
Web Site: http://www.vandabooks.com

Distribution:
Macmillan Distribution (MDL), Houndmills, Basingstoke RG21 6XS
Telephone: 01256 302692
Fax: 01256 812558 (UK orders) & 842084 (Export orders)
Email: mdl@macmillan.co.uk
Web Site: http://www.macmillandistribution.co.uk

Managing Editor: Anjali Bulley
Managers: Clare Davis *(Production)*
  Clare Taylor *(Marketing)*
  Nina Jacobson *(Rights)*
Assistant Editor: Frances Ambler

Academic & Scholarly; Antiques & Collecting; Architecture & Design; Biography & Autobiography; Fashion & Costume; Fine Art & Art History; Photography; Theatre, Drama & Dance

New Titles: 22 (2007), 19 (2008)
No of Employees: 10

ISBNs, Imprints & Series:
978 0 905209, 978 0 948107, 978 1 85177

Parent Company:
Victoria & Albert Museum

Overseas Representation:
Australia & New Zealand: Allen & Unwin Pty Ltd, Sydney, NSW, Australia
Central & Eastern Europe: Grazyna Soszynska, Poznan-Baranowo, Poland
France: Critiques Livres Distribution, Bagnolet
Germany & Austria: Penguin Books Deutschland GmbH, Frankfurt am Main, Germany
India: Maya Publishers Pvt Ltd, New Delhi
Italy: Penguin Italia srl, Corsico, Milan
Netherlands, Belgium & Luxembourg: Penguin Books Benelux BV, Amsterdam, Netherlands
Singapore, Indonesia & Thailand: APD Singapore Pte Ltd, Singapore
South America & Central America: David Williams, InterMedia Americana (IMA) Ltd, London, UK
Southern Africa: Book Promotions Pty Ltd, Cape Town, South Africa
Spain & Portugal: Penguin Books SA, Madrid, Spain
Turkey, Africa, Middle East, Japan, Hong Kong, Taiwan, Korea, Scandinavia, Switzerland, Malta, Greece, Cyprus, Israel, China & Philippines: International Sales Department, Penguin Books Ltd, London, UK
USA: Harry N. Abrams Inc, New York, NY

Book Trade Association Membership:
IPG; International Association of Museum Publishers

2812

VIRGIN BOOKS LTD
20 Vauxhall bridge Road, London SW1V 2SA
Telephone: (020) 7840 8400
Email: info@virgin-books.co.uk
Web Site: http://www.virgin.com

Directors: John Sadler *(Managing)*
  Clare Pierotti *(Publicity)*
  Han Ismail *(Home Sales)*
Managers: Gill Woolcott *(Production)*
  Vickie Boff *(Marketing)*

Editors: Carolyn Thorne *(Editorial Director – Illustrated Books, Travel, Health & Wellbeing)*
  Ed Faulkner *(Editorial Director – Non-Fiction)*
  Adam Nevill *(Commissioning – Erotic Fiction, Horror)*
  Louisa Joyner *(Editorial Director – non-fiction)*

Biography & Autobiography; Cinema, Video, TV & Radio; Gay & Lesbian Studies; Health & Beauty; Illustrated & Fine Editions; Military & War; Music; Reference Books, Directories & Dictionaries; Sports & Games

ISBNs, Imprints & Series:
978 0 352 Black Lace (heteroerotic fiction by women); Nexus (heteroerotic fiction)
978 0 86369 Virgin (paperback)
978 1 85227 Virgin (hardback)

Parent Company:
Virgin Group Ltd

Overseas Representation:
Australia: Random House Australia Pty Ltd, Sydney, NSW
Canada: H. B. Fenn & Co Ltd, Bolton, Ont
Caribbean, South & Central America, Middle East, Pakistan & Africa (excluding South Africa): Felicity Smith, Random House Group Ltd, London, UK
Eastern Europe, Baltic States, Israel, Belarus, Russia, Turkey & Ukraine: Mariann Kenedi, Budapest, Hungary
Germany, Austria, Norway, Denmark, Finland: Jörg Riekenbrauk, Cologne, Germany
India: Random House Publishers India Pte Ltd, New Delhi
Japan: Akiko Iwamoto, Tokyo
Netherlands, Belgium, Luxembourg, France, Switzerland: Pauline Konink, Hilversum, Netherlands
New Zealand: Random House New Zealand Ltd, Auckland
Philippines, Guam, Thailand, Indonesia, Singapore, Malaysia, Hong Kong, Taiwan, South Korea & China: Transworld Publishers Ltd, London, UK
South Africa: Random House South Africa Pty Ltd, Houghton
Sweden, Iceland, Spain, Portugal, Gibraltar, Italy, Malta, Cyprus, Greece: Andrew Wyman, Random House Group Ltd, London, UK
USA: Macmillan, New York, NY

Book Trade Association Membership:
BA

2813

VISION
101 Southwark Street, London SE1 0JF
Telephone: (020) 7928 5599
Fax: (020) 7928 8822
Email: info@visionpaperbacks.co.uk
Web Site: http://www.visionpaperbacks.co.uk

Warehouse:
Littlehampton Book Services, Faraday Close, Durrington, Worthing, West Sussex BN13 3RB
Telephone: 01903 828500
Fax: 01903 828625

Directors: Sheena Dewan *(Managing)*
  Paul Swallow *(Sales)*

Biography & Autobiography; Crime; Gay & Lesbian Studies; Gender Studies; Military & War; Politics & World Affairs; Sociology & Anthropology

New Titles: 23 (2007), 15 (2008)

ISBNs, Imprints & Series:
978 1 901250, 978 1 904132, 978 1 905745 Fusion Press; Vision Paperbacks

978 1 904132, 978 1 905745 Vision

Parent Company:
Satin Publications Ltd

Overseas Representation:
All other export territories: Vision, London, UK
Australia: Bookwise International, Adelaide, SA
Singapore, Malaysia & Brunei: Horizon Books Pte Ltd, Singapore
South Africa: Quartet Sales & Marketing, Johannesburg
USA & Canada: Independent Publishers Group (IPG), Chicago, IL, USA

Book Trade Association Membership:
IPG

2814

VOLTAIRE FOUNDATION LTD
University of Oxford, 99 Banbury Road, Oxford OX2 6JX
Telephone: 01865 284600
Fax: 01865 284610
Email: email@voltaire.ox.ac.uk
Web Site: http://www.voltaire.ox.ac.uk

Distribution:
Marston Book Services, 160 Milton Park, Abingdon, Oxon OX14 4YN
Telephone: 01235 465521 (Trade) & 465500 (Direct Sales)
Fax: 01235 465555 (Trade) & 465556 (Direct Sales)
Email: trade.orders@marston.co.uk & direct.orders@marston.co.uk
Web Site: http://www.marston.co.uk

Director: Dr Nicholas Cronk
Publisher: Clare Fletcher *(Sales, Marketing)*
Managers: Janet Godden *(Editorial)*
  Dr Robert McNamee *(Electronic Publishing)*
Administrator: Liz Hancock *(Sales, Marketing, Rights & Permissions, Admin Support)*
Managing Editor, SVEC: Lyn Roberts

Academic & Scholarly; Bibliography & Library Science; Biography & Autobiography; Electronic (Professional & Academic); Fiction; History & Antiquarian; Languages & Linguistics; Literature & Criticism; Philosophy; Reference Books, Directories & Dictionaries; Religion & Theology

New Titles: 26 (2007), 26 (2008)
No of Employees: 20

ISBNs, Imprints & Series:
978 0 7294 Correspondance complète de Françoise de Graffigny; Correspondance complète de Jean Jacques Rousseau; Correspondance complète de Pierre Bayle, Correspondance générale de La Beaumelle; Œuvres complètes de Montesquieu; Œuvres complètes de Voltaire; SVEC (Studies on Voltaire and the Eighteenth Century); Vif Une nouvelle collection en livre de poche

Parent Company:
University of Oxford

Overseas Representation:
France: Aux Amateurs de Livres, Paris

2815

WALLFLOWER PRESS
6 Market Place, London W1W 8AF
Telephone: (020) 7436 9494
Email: yoram@wallflowerpress.co.uk
Web Site: http://www.wallflowerpress.co.uk

Representation (UK):
Signature Book Representation, PO Box 12, York YO1 7WD
Telephone: 01904 631320
Fax: 01904 675445
Email: admin@signaturebooks.co.uk

Commissioning Editor: Yoram Allon
Managers: Amanda O'Boyle *(Sales & Marketing)*
Tom Cabot *(Production)*
Jackie Downs *(Editorial)*

Academic & Scholarly; Cinema, Video, TV & Radio

New Titles: 25 (2007), 30 (2008)
No of Employees: 6
Annual Turnover: £350,000

ISBNs, Imprints & Series:
978 1 903364, 978 1 904764, 978 1 905674

Overseas Representation:
Australia & New Zealand: Woodslane Pty Ltd, Warriewood, NSW, Australia
Europe: Andrew Durnell Marketing Ltd, Tunbridge Wells, UK
USA & Canada: Columbia University Press, Irvington, NY, USA

2816

WARBURG INSTITUTE
University of London, Woburn Square, London WC1H 0AB
Telephone: (020) 7862 8949
Fax: (020) 7862 8955
Email: warburg.books@sas.ac.uk
Web Site: http://warburg.sas.ac.uk

Administrative Assistant: E. Witchell

Academic & Scholarly; Archaeology; Architecture & Design; Bibliography & Library Science; Biography & Autobiography; Fine Art & Art History; History & Antiquarian; Magic & the Occult; Philosophy; Religion & Theology

New Titles: 2 (2007), 2 (2008)

ISBNs, Imprints & Series:
978 0 85481 Special Publications (Warburg); Studies of the Warburg Institute; Warburg Institute Colloquia; Warburg Institute Surveys and Texts; Warburg Studies and Texts

Overseas Representation:
Italy: Nino Aragno Editore, Savigliano

2817

WARD LOCK EDUCATIONAL CO LTD
Bic Ling Kee House, 1 Christopher Road, East Grinstead, West Sussex RH19 3BT
Telephone: 01342 318980
Fax: 01342 410980
Email: wle@lingkee.com
Web Site: http://www.wardlockeducational.com

Director: Au Bak Ling *(Chairman - Hong Kong)*
Sales, Rights & Permissions: Eileen Parsons *(Company Secretary)*

Biology & Zoology; Chemistry; Educational & Textbooks; Geography & Geology; Mathematics & Statistics; Music; Physics; Religion & Theology; English

No of Employees: 2

ISBNs, Imprints & Series: 978 0 7062

Parent Company:
Ling Kee (UK) Ltd

Associated Companies:
BLA Publishing Ltd

Overseas Representation:
Australia (KMP only): Concept Mathematics Pty Ltd, Frankston, Vic, Australia
Canada: Bacon & Hughes Ltd, Ottawa, Ont
Republic of Ireland: International Educational Services, Leixlip

2818

WATERSIDE PRESS
Sherfield Gables, Reading Road, Sherfield-on-Loddon, Hook, Hants RG27 0JG
Telephone: 01256 882250
Fax: 0845 230 0744
Email: enquiries@watersidepress.co.uk
Web Site: http://www.watersidepress.co.uk

Proprietor: Bryan Gibson
Editor: Jane Green
Administrator: Alex Gibson

Academic & Scholarly; Biography & Autobiography; Crime; Educational & Textbooks; History & Antiquarian; Law; Reference Books, Directories & Dictionaries; Sociology & Anthropology; Theatre, Drama & Dance

New Titles: 20 (2007), 20 (2008)

ISBNs, Imprints & Series:
978 1 872870, 978 1 904380

Overseas Representation:
USA: International Specialized Book Services Inc, Portland, OR

2819

PAUL WATKINS PUBLISHING
1 High Street, Donington, Lincs PE11 4TA
Telephone: 01775 821542
Email: pwatkins@pwatkinspublishing.fsnet.co.uk

Proprietor: Shaun Tyas

Academic & Scholarly; Architecture & Design; Fine Art & Art History; History & Antiquarian; Languages & Linguistics; Nautical

New Titles: 9 (2007), 8 (2008)

ISBNs, Imprints & Series:
978 1 871615 Paul Watkins
978 1 900289 Shaun Tyas

Distributor for:
Caedmon of Whitby; English Place-Name Society; Richard III and Yorkist History Trust; Society for Name Studies in Britain and Ireland

Book Trade Association Membership:
Small Press Centre

2820

WEIDENFELD & NICOLSON
[Imprint of The Orion Publishing Group Ltd]
Orion House, 5 Upper St Martin's Lane, London WC2H 9EA
Telephone: (020) 7240 3444
Fax: (020) 7240 4822

Trade Counter & Warehouse:
Littlehampton Book Services Ltd, Faraday Close, Durrington, Worthing, West Sussex BN13 3RB
Telephone: 01903 828500
Fax: 01903 828802

Managing Director: Malcolm Edwards
Publishing: Alan Samson

Kirsty Dunseath
Editor-in-Chief: Michael Dover

Biography & Autobiography; Fiction; Humour; Illustrated & Fine Editions; Industry, Business & Management; Law; Philosophy; Photography; Politics & World Affairs; Sports & Games; Travel & Topography

ISBNs, Imprints & Series: 978 0 297

Parent Company:
The Orion Publishing Group Ltd

Overseas Representation:
see: The Orion Publishing Group Ltd, London, UK

2821

JOSEPH WEINBERGER LTD
12–14 Mortimer Street, London W1T 3JJ
Telephone: (020) 7580 2827
Fax: (020) 7436 9616
Email: general.info@jwmail.co.uk
Web Site: http://www.josef-weinberger.com

Directors: John Schofield *(Managing)*
Robert Heath *(Financial)*
Plays Division Manager: Michael Callahan

Theatre, Drama & Dance

New Titles: 15 (2007), 20 (2008)

ISBNs, Imprints & Series:
978 0 8222 Dramatists Play Service Inc
978 0 85676 Josef Weinberger Plays

Distributor for:
USA: Dramatists Play Service Inc

Overseas Representation:
Australia: Hal Leonard (Australia), Melbourne, Vic
New Zealand: Play Bureau of New Zealand Ltd, New Plymouth
Republic of Ireland & Northern Ireland: Drama League of Ireland, Dublin, Republic of Ireland
South Africa: Dalro (Pty) Ltd, Braamfontein
USA: Dramatists Play Service Inc, New York, NY

2822

WHICH? BOOKS
2 Marylebone Road, London NW1 4DF
Telephone: (020) 7770 7000
Fax: (020) 7770 7660
Email: books@which.co.uk
Web Site: http://www.which.co.uk

Head of Book Publishing: Angela Newton
Head of Lifestyle Marketing: Suzie Stevens
Press Manager: Nicola Frame
Senior Editor of 'The Good Food Guide': Caroline Blake

Accountancy & Taxation; Guide Books; Law; Reference Books, Directories & Dictionaries; Vocational Training & Careers; Legal, Financial & Practical Advice; Personal Finance

New Titles: 11 (2007), 11 (2008)

ISBNs, Imprints & Series:
978 1 84490 The Good Food Guide; Which? Essential Guides

Parent Company:
Which? Ltd [part of Consumers' Association]

2823

*****WHITE LADDER PRESS**
Great Ambrook, near Ipplepen, Devon TQ12 5UL
Telephone: 01803 813343
Fax: 01803 813928
Email: enquiries@whiteladderpress.com
Web Site: http://www.whiteladderpress.com

Trade Sales:
Virgin Books Ltd, Thames Wharf Studios, Rainville Road, London W6 9HA
Telephone: (020) 7386 3300
Fax: (020) 7386 3360
Email: sales@virgin-books.co.uk
Web Site: http://www.virgin-books.co.uk

Managing Editor: Roni Jay

Cookery, Wines & Spirits; Gardening; Health & Beauty; Natural History; Travel & Topography; Family

ISBNs, Imprints & Series:
978 0 9543914, 978 0 9548219, 978 1 905410

Overseas Representation:
Worldwide: Miller Rights Agency, London, UK

Book Trade Association Membership:
BA; IPG

2824

WHITING & BIRCH LTD
90 Dartmouth Road, London SE23 3HZ
Telephone: (020) 8244 2421
Fax: (020) 8244 2448
Email: enquiries@whitingbirch.net
Web Site: http://www.whitingbirch.net

Directors: David Whiting
Diana Birch

Academic & Scholarly; Medical (incl. Self Help & Alternative Medicine); Psychology & Psychiatry; Sociology & Anthropology

New Titles: 18 (2007), 47 (2008)
No of Employees: 2

ISBNs, Imprints & Series:
978 1 86177, 978 1 871177

Overseas Representation:
USA: Ingram Publisher Services Inc, Chambersburg, PA; Lightning Source

2825

WHITTET BOOKS LTD
South House, Yatesbury Manor, Yatesbury, Wilts SN11 8YE
Telephone: 01672 539004
Fax: 01672 555555
Email: annabel@whittet.dircon.co.uk
Web Site: http://www.whittetbooks.com

Warehouse:
BSP, BSP House, Station Road, Linton, Cambs CB1 6NW
Telephone: 01223 894870
Fax: 01223 894871

Managing Director: Annabel Whittet

Agriculture; Animal Care & Breeding; Biology & Zoology; Gardening; Illustrated & Fine Editions; Natural History; Veterinary Science

New Titles: 3 (2008)

ISBNs, Imprints & Series:
978 0 905483, 978 1 873580

Parent Company:
A. Whittet & Co Ltd

Overseas Representation:
USA & Canada: Diamond Farm Book Publishers, Brighton, Canada

2826

WHITTLES PUBLISHING
Dunbeath Mains Cottages, Dunbeath, Caithness KW6 6EY
Telephone: 01593 731333
Fax: 01593 731400
Email: info@whittlespublishing.com
Web Site: http://www.whittlespublishing.com

Warehouse/Distributor:
BookSource, 50 Cambuslang Road, Glasgow G32 8NB
Telephone: 0845 370 0063
Fax: 0845 370 0064
Email: customerservice@booksource.net
Web Site: http://www.booksource.net

Publisher: Dr Keith Whittles
Sales & Promotions Manager: Mrs Sue Steven

Academic & Scholarly; Biography & Autobiography; Educational & Textbooks; Engineering; Fiction; Geography & Geology; Military & War; Natural History; Nautical; Scientific & Technical; General

New Titles: 20 (2007), 25 (2008)

ISBNs, Imprints & Series:
978 1 870325, 978 1 904445

Overseas Representation:
Australia, New Zealand & Papua New Guinea: James Bennett Pty Ltd, Belrose, NSW, Australia
Germany, Austria & Switzerland: Missing Link International Booksellers, Bremen, Germany
Hong Kong, China, Taiwan & Korea: Asia Publishers Services Ltd, Hong Kong
India: Sara Books Pvt Ltd, New Delhi
Italy, Spain, Portugal & France: Flavio Marcello Publishers' Agents & Consultants, Padua, Italy
Latin America, Caribbean & Sub-Saharan Africa: InterMedia Americana (IMA) Ltd, London, UK
Middle East (including Greece, Turkey & Iran): Avicenna Partnership, Dumfries, UK
Singapore, Malaysia, Brunei, Philippines, Indonesia, Thailand, Laos, Cambodia & Vietnam: APD Singapore Pte Ltd, Singapore
South Africa: Book Promotions (Pty) Ltd, Plumstead

Book Trade Association Membership:
Publishing Scotland

2827

WILD GOOSE PUBLICATIONS
4th Floor, Savoy House,
140 Sauchiehall Street, Glasgow G2 3DH
Telephone: 0141 332 6292
Fax: 0141 332 1090
Email: admin@ionabooks.com
Web Site: http://www.ionabooks.com

Trade Orders:
BookSource, 50 Cambuslang Road, Glasgow G32 8NB
Email: orders@booksource.net
Web Site: http://www.booksource.net

Publishing Managers: Sandra Kramer
Alex O'Neill *(Assistant & Marketing Officer)*
Production: Jane Riley
Office Administrator: Tri Ta
Project Editor: Neil Paynter
Publishing Assistant: Lorna Rae Sutton

Music; Religion & Theology

New Titles: 12 (2007), 10 (2008)
No of Employees: 6
Annual Turnover: £280,000

ISBNs, Imprints & Series:
978 0 947988, 978 1 901557, 978 1 905010

Parent Company:
The Iona Community

Overseas Representation:
Australia & New Zealand: Willow Connection Pty Ltd, Brookvale, NSW, Australia
Canada: Novalis Inc, Toronto, Ont
New Zealand: Pleroma Christian Supplies, Otane, Central Hawkes Bay
USA: GIA Publications, Chicago, IL

Book Trade Association Membership:
IPG

2828

JOHN WILEY & SONS LTD
The Atrium, Southern Gate, Chichester, West Sussex PO19 8SQ
Telephone: 01243 779777
Fax: 01243 775878
Email: europe@wiley.co.uk
Web Site: http://www.wiley.com

European Distribution Centre:
Southern Cross Trading Estate,
1 Oldlands Way, Bognor Regis, West Sussex PO22 9SA
Telephone: 01243 779777
Fax: 01243 820250
Email: csbooks@wiley.co.uk

Senior Vice-President, Europe & International Development: S. Smith
Directors: C. J. Dicks *(Chief Financial & Operations Officer)*
P. Kisray *(Sales, Professional/Trade & Educational Publishing)*
C. Nobbs *(Distribution)*

Academic & Scholarly; Accountancy & Taxation; Agriculture; Animal Care & Breeding; Antiques & Collecting; Archaeology; Architecture & Design; Atlases & Maps; Aviation; Biography & Autobiography; Biology & Zoology; Chemistry; Children's Books; Computer Science; Cookery, Wines & Spirits; Do-It-Yourself; Economics; Educational & Textbooks; Electronic (Educational); Electronic (Professional & Academic); Engineering; Environment & Development Studies; Gardening; Geography & Geology; Guide Books; Health & Beauty; History & Antiquarian; Humour; Industry, Business & Management; Languages & Linguistics; Literature & Criticism; Magic & the Occult; Mathematics & Statistics; Medical (incl. Self Help & Alternative Medicine); Military & War; Music; Natural History; Philosophy; Photography; Physics; Poetry; Politics & World Affairs; Psychology & Psychiatry; Reference Books, Directories & Dictionaries; Religion & Theology; Scientific & Technical; Sociology & Anthropology; Sports & Games; Travel & Topography; Veterinary Science; Vocational Training & Careers

ISBNs, Imprints & Series:
978 0 470, 978 0 471

Parent Company:
USA: John Wiley & Sons Inc

Associated Companies:
Capstone Publishing Ltd; Whurr Publishers Ltd; Wiley Distribution Services Ltd; Wiley Heyden Ltd; Wiley-Blackwell Ltd
Germany: Wiley-VCH Verlag GmbH
Inpharm-Internet Services Ltd; Wiley Interface Ltd; Wiley Pharmafile Ltd

Distributor for:
USA: California University Press; Columbia University Press; Harvard University Press; Johns Hopkins University Press; Loeb Classical Library; The MIT Press; W. W. Norton & Co Ltd; O'Reilly UK Ltd; Princeton University Press; Sybex International Corp; The University of Chicago Press; Yale University Press

Overseas Representation:
Australia: John Wiley & Sons Australia Ltd, Milton, Qld
Canada: John Wiley & Sons Canada Ltd, Etobicoke, Ont
Japan: John Wiley & Sons Ltd, Tokyo
Mexico & Latin America, Pakistan & North Africa: John Wiley & Sons Inc, Hoboken, NJ, USA
Singapore & Asia: John Wiley & Sons (Asia) Pte Ltd, Singapore

Book Trade Association Membership:
Publishers Association; BA; EPC; IGSMTP; CAPP; IEPRC

2829

WILLOW ISLAND EDITIONS
41 Water Lane, Middlestown, Wakefield, West Yorkshire WF4 4PX
Telephone: 01924 270723
Email: richard@willowisland.co.uk
Web Site: http://www.willowisland.co.uk

Contact: Richard Bell

Crafts & Hobbies; Gardening; Guide Books; Natural History; Travel & Topography

ISBNs, Imprints & Series: 978 1 902467

2830

NEIL WILSON PUBLISHING LTD
O/2 19 Netherton Avenue, Glasgow G13 1BQ
Telephone: 0141 954 8007
Fax: 0141 954 8007
Email: info@nwp.co.uk
Web Site: http://www.nwp.co.uk

Distributor, Sales Ledger & Trade Orders:
BookSource, 50 Cambuslang Road, Glasgow G32 5NB
Telephone: 0845 370 0067
Fax: 0845 370 0068
Email: orders@booksource.net
Web Site: http://www.booksource.net

Managing Director: Neil Wilson *(Sales, Rights & Permissions)*

Biography & Autobiography; Cookery, Wines & Spirits; Crime; Guide Books; History & Antiquarian; Humour; Military & War; Music; Nautical; Photography; Travel & Topography; Irish Interest; Scottish Interest

New Titles: 10 (2007), 8 (2008)
Annual Turnover: £110,000

ISBNs, Imprints & Series:
11:9; The Angel's Share; The In Pinn; The Vital Spark
978 1 897784, 978 1 903238, 978 1 906476

Overseas Representation:
USA: Interlink Publishing Group Inc, Northampton, MA

Book Trade Association Membership:
Publishing Scotland

2831

PHILIP WILSON PUBLISHERS
109 Drysdale Street, The Timber Yard, London N1 6ND

Telephone: (020) 7033 9900
Fax: (020) 7033 9922
Email: sales@philip-wilson.co.uk
Web Site: http://www.philip-wilson.co.uk

Antiques & Collecting; Architecture & Design; Fine Art & Art History

New Titles: 10 (2007), 10 (2008)
No of Employees: 5

ISBNs, Imprints & Series: 978 0 85667

Distributor for:
India: Niyogi Books

Overseas Representation:
USA: Palgrave Macmillan, New York, NY
Worldwide: I. B. Tauris & Co Ltd, London, UK

2832

WINDHORSE PUBLICATIONS
38 Newmarket Road, Cambridge CB5 8DT
Telephone: (020) 7617 7514
Email: info@windhorsepublications.com
Web Site: http://www.windhorsepublications.com

UK Trade Orders:
Wisdom Books, 25 Stanley Road, Ilford, Essex IG1 1RW
Telephone: (020) 8553 5020
Fax: (020) 8553 5122
Email: sales@wisdom-books.com
Web Site: http://www.wisdom-books.com

General Manager: Caroline Jestaz *(Editorial & Rights)*
Publishing Assistant: Sarah Ryan *(Sales & Marketing, Production)*

Biography & Autobiography; Philosophy; Religion & Theology

New Titles: 8 (2007), 5 (2008)
No of Employees: 2

ISBNs, Imprints & Series:
978 0 904766, 978 1 899579

Overseas Representation:
Australia & New Zealand: Windhorse Books, Newtown, NSW, Australia
USA: Consortium Book Sales & Distribution Inc, St Paul, MN

Book Trade Association Membership:
IPG

2833

WIT PRESS
Ashurst Lodge, Ashurst, Southampton, Hampshire SO40 7AA
Telephone: (023) 8029 3223
Fax: (023) 8029 2853
Email: witpress@witpress.com
Web Site: http://www.witpress.com

Chairman: Prof. C. A. Brebbia
Production Manager: B. Privett
Sales Co-ordinator: Ms Lorraine Carter

Academic & Scholarly; Archaeology; Architecture & Design; Biology & Zoology; Computer Science; Electronic (Professional & Academic); Engineering; Environment & Development Studies; Geography & Geology; Industry, Business & Management; Mathematics & Statistics; Medical (incl. Self Help & Alternative Medicine); Scientific & Technical; Transport

New Titles: 47 (2007), 53 (2008)
No of Employees: 11
Annual Turnover: £450,000

ISBNs, Imprints & Series:
978 0 905451, 978 1 84564, 978 1 85312

Parent Company:
Computational Mechanics International Ltd

Overseas Representation:
Australia & New Zealand: DA Information Services Pty Ltd, Mitcham, Vic, Australia
France: Librairie Lavoisier, Paris
Germany: Dietmar Dreier, Duisburg
India: Shankar's Book Agency Pvt Ltd, New Delhi; Shankar's Book Agency Pvt Ltd, Calcutta
Italy: DEA srl, Rome
Japan: Maruzen Co Ltd, Tokyo
Korea: Kumi Trading Co Ltd, Seoul, Korea, South
Kuwait: The Kuwait Bookshop Co Ltd, Safat
Malaysia: Koop Book Centre, Johor
Norway: Tapir International Booksellers, Trondheim
Poland: Press Import Wydawnictw Naukowych, Warsaw
Portugal: Julio de Figueiredo Lda, Lisbon
Spain: Diaz de Santos SA, Madrid; Libreria Pons SL, Zaragoza
Sweden: Longus Book Imports, Stockholm
Taiwan: Ta Tong Book Co Ltd, Taipei
USA, Canada & Mexico: WIT Press, Billerica, MA, USA

Book Trade Association Membership:
LAPSLD

2834

WITHERBY SEAMANSHIP INTERNATIONAL
4 Dunlop Square, Deans, Livingston, West Lothian EH54 8SB
Telephone: 01506 463227
Fax: 01506 468999
Email: kat@emailws.com
Web Site: http://www.witherbyseamanship.com & http://www.witherbyinsurance.com

Directors: Iain Macneil *(Managing)*
Kat Heathcote
General Manager: Stewart Heney

Audio Books; Educational & Textbooks; Electronic (Professional & Academic); Industry, Business & Management; Law; Nautical; Reference Books, Directories & Dictionaries; Scientific & Technical; Transport

ISBNs, Imprints & Series:
978 0 900886, 978 0 948691, 978 1 85609

Distributor for:
Chartered Institute of Loss Adjustors; Institute of Chartered Shipbrokers; Institute of Risk Management; Intercargo; International Association of Classification Societies; International Chamber of Shipping; International Tanker Owners' Pollution Federation; INTERTANKO; Oil Companies International Marine Forum; The Society of Consulting Marine Engineers and Ship Surveyors; Society of International Gas Tanker & Terminal Operators; Tanker Structure Co-operative Forum

Overseas Representation:
Australia: Boat Books, St Kilda, Vic
Hong Kong: Hong Kong Ships Supplies Co
Japan: Cornes & Co, Tokyo
Singapore: Motion Smith
USA: New York Nautical, New York

Book Trade Association Membership:
BA; IPG

2835

WOLTERS KLUWER HEALTH (P & E) LTD
250 Waterloo Road, London SE1 8RD
Telephone: (020) 7981 0500
Fax: (020) 7981 0501
Email: enquiry@lww.co.uk
Web Site: http://www.lww.co.uk

Academic & Scholarly; Electronic (Professional & Academic); Medical (incl. Self Help & Alternative Medicine)

Book Trade Association Membership:
Publishers Association

2836

THE WOMEN'S PRESS
27 Goodge Street, London W1T 2LD
Telephone: (020) 7636 3992
Fax: (020) 7637 1866
Web Site: http://www.the-womens-press.com

Warehouse:
NBN International Ltd, Estover Road, Plymouth PL6 7PY
Telephone: 01752 202300
Fax: 01752 202330
Email: control@nbninternational.com
Web Site: http://www.nbninternational.com

Director: David Elliott

Biography & Autobiography; Crime; Fiction; Gay & Lesbian Studies; Gender Studies; Health & Beauty; Literature & Criticism; Politics & World Affairs; Psychology & Psychiatry; Reference Books, Directories & Dictionaries; Teenage

New Titles: 2 (2008)
No of Employees: 2
Annual Turnover: £150,000

ISBNs, Imprints & Series:
Livewire Books for Young Adults
978 0 7043

Overseas Representation:
Africa, Eastern Europe, Caribbean & South America: InterMedia Americana (IMA) Ltd, London, UK
Australia: Tower Books Pty Ltd, Frenchs Forest, NSW
Europe: Ted Dougherty, London, UK
New Zealand: Southern Publishers Group, Auckland
Republic of Ireland: Fergus Corcoran, Ennisherry
South Africa: Quartet Sales & Marketing, Johannesburg
Spain & Portugal: Iberian Book Services, Madrid, Spain
USA: Interlink Publishing Group Inc, Northampton, MA

Book Trade Association Membership:
IPG

2837

WOODHEAD PUBLISHING LTD
Abington Hall, Granta Park, Great Abington, Cambridge CB21 6AH
Telephone: 01223 891358
Fax: 01223 893694
Email: custserv@woodhead-publishing.com
Web Site: http://www.woodheadpublishing.com

Warehouse & Distribution:
Combined Book Services, Units I/K, Paddock Wood Distribution Centre, Paddock Wood, Tonbridge, Kent TN12 6UU
Telephone: 01892 837171
Fax: 01892 837272
Email: (as above)

Directors: Martin Woodhead *(Managing)*
R. Burleigh *(Finance)*
Francis Dodds *(Editorial)*
Managers: Neil MacLeod *(Marketing)*
Mary Campbell *(Production)*
Commissioning Editors: Sarah Whitworth
Kathryn Wickett
Rob Sitton
Sheril Leich
Cliff Elwell
Laura Bunney
Ian Borthwick

Electronic (Professional & Academic); Engineering; Environment & Development Studies; Industry, Business & Management; Law; Scientific & Technical

New Titles: 65 (2007), 70 (2008)
No of Employees: 27
Annual Turnover: £2.5M

ISBNs, Imprints & Series:
978 1 84569, 978 1 85573 Woodhead Publishing
978 1 85573 Abington Publishing; Gresham Books

Distributor for:
Germany: Beuth (The German Standards Institute); Stahleisen (The German Iron & Steel Institute); VDI (The Association of German Engineers)
USA: CRC LLC Press Ltd

Overseas Representation:
China: Ian Taylor & Associates, P. R. of China
Eastern Europe & Russia: Dr László Horváth Publishers Representative, Budapest, Hungary
Germany, Austria & Switzerland: Bernd Feldmann, Oranienburg, Germany
Greece, Middle East, Turkey, Cyprus & Malta: Avicenna Partnership, Oxford, UK
India: Sara Books Pvt Ltd, New Delhi
Iran: Farhad Maftoon, Tehran
Italy, Spain, Portugal & France: Flavio Marcello Publishers' Agents & Consultants, Padua, Italy
Japan: Ben Kato, Tokyo; United Publishers Services Ltd, Tokyo
Mexico, Central & South America: Cranbury International LLC, Montpelier, VT, USA
Netherlands, Belgium & Luxembourg: Netwerk Academic Book Agency, Rotterdam, Netherlands
Nigeria: Bounty Books, Ibadan
Pakistan: Tahir M. Lodhi, Lahore
Scandinavia: Jan Norbye, Ølstykke, Denmark
South Africa: Academic Marketing Services, Johannesburg
South East Asia: APAC Publishers Services Pte Ltd, Singapore
South Korea: Information & Culture Korea (ICK), Seoul, Korea, South

Book Trade Association Membership:
IGSMTP; IPG

2838

*WORD FOR LIFE TRUST
The House of Bread, Ross Road, Christchurch, Coleford, Glos GL16 7NS
Telephone: 01594 837744
Fax: 01594 837742
Email: hwflt@wflt.org
Web Site: http://www.wflt.org

Directors: Denis Brazell *(Development - Resources)*
Keith Hawkins *(Development - Trust)*
Frances Hawkins *(Assistant)*
Resources Co-ordinator: Audrey Ashton

Gender Studies; Magic & the Occult; Medical (incl. Self Help & Alternative Medicine); Reference Books, Directories & Dictionaries; Religion & Theology

ISBNs, Imprints & Series:
978 1 903577 Living Word Series

Book Trade Association Membership:
Association of Christian Writers

2839

WORDSWORTH EDITIONS LTD
8b East Street, Ware, Herts SG12 9HJ
Telephone: 01920 465167
Fax: 01920 462267
Email: enquiries@wordsworth-editions.com
Web Site: http://www.wordsworth-editions.com

Directors: Helen Trayler *(Managing)*
Derek Wright *(Finance)*

Children's Books; Fiction; Literature & Criticism; Poetry; Reference Books, Directories & Dictionaries

New Titles: 73 (2007), 82 (2008)
No of Employees: 3
Annual Turnover: £2M

ISBNs, Imprints & Series:
978 1 84022, 978 1 85326

Overseas Representation:
Australia & Papua New Guinea: Peribo Pty Ltd, Mount Kuring-Gai, NSW, Australia
Czech Republic: Bohemian Ventures sro, Prague
Germany & Austria: Buchvertrieb Blank GmbH, Vierkirchen, Germany
India: OM Book Services, Delhi
Malta & Gozo: Audio Visual Centre Ltd, Sliema, Malta
New Zealand & South Pacific: Allphy Book Distributors Ltd, Auckland, New Zealand
Poland: Top Mark Centre, Warsaw
Romania: Noi Distributie SA, Bucharest
Slovak Republic: Slovak Ventures sro, Nitra, Slovakia
South Africa: Alternative Books CC, Ferndale
Spain: Ribera Libros, SL, Arrigorriaga
USA: L. B. May & Associates, Knoxville, TN

2840

WORLD MICROFILMS
PO Box 35488, St John's Wood, London NW8 6WD
Telephone: (020) 7586 4499
Email: microworld@ndirect.co.uk
Web Site: http://www.microworld.uk.com, http://www.pidgeondigital.com

Director: S. C. Albert

Academic & Scholarly; Architecture & Design; Cinema, Video, TV & Radio; History & Antiquarian

ISBNs, Imprints & Series: 978 1 85035

Distributor for:
USA: Norman Ross Publishing Inc

2841

WORTH PRESS LTD
34 South End, Bassingbourn, Herts SG8 5NJ
Telephone: 01763 248075
Fax: 01763 248155
Email: info@worthpress.co.uk
Web Site: http://www.worthpress.co.uk

Warehouse:
Antony Rowe Ltd, Units 3 & 4, Pegasus Way, Bowerhill, Melksham SN12 6TR
Telephone: 01225 703691
Fax: 01225 704518

Contacts: Ken Webb
Rupert Webb

Architecture & Design; Aviation; Fiction; Military & War; Religion & Theology

New Titles: 10 (2008)

ISBNs, Imprints & Series: 978 1 903025

Overseas Representation:
Asia: Publishers International Marketing, Sutton St Nicholas, Herefordshire, UK
Scandinavia: Anglo-Nordic Books, Godalming, UK

2842

XPL PUBLISHING
99 Hatfield Road, St Albans, Herts AL1 4EG
Telephone: 0870 143 2569
Fax: 0845 456 6385
Email: sales@xplpublishing.com
Web Site: http://www.xplpublishing.com

Managing Director: Andrew Griffin

Academic & Scholarly; Accountancy & Taxation; Industry, Business & Management; Law; Medical (incl. Self Help & Alternative Medicine)

New Titles: 8 (2007), 10 (2008)
No of Employees: 3

ISBNs, Imprints & Series: 978 1 85811

Parent Company:
Richard Griffin (1820) Ltd

Overseas Representation:
Hong Kong: Bloomsbury Books Ltd
Republic of Ireland: Brookside Publishing Services, Dublin
USA: International Specialized Book Services Inc, Portland, OR

Book Trade Association Membership:
IPG

2843

Y LOLFA CYF
Hen Swyddfa'r Heddlu, Talybont, Ceredigion SY24 5HE
Telephone: 01970 832304
Fax: 01970 832782
Email: ylolfa@ylolfa.com
Web Site: http://www.ylolfa.com

Director: Garmon Gruffudd
Administrator: Sonia Hughes
Editor: Lefi Gruffudd
Marketing: Morgan Tomos
Projects Editor: Mared Roberts
Production: Paul Williams

Biography & Autobiography; Children's Books; Cookery, Wines & Spirits; Fiction; Guide Books; Humour; Languages & Linguistics; Music; Politics & World Affairs; Sports & Games; Welsh Language Books

New Titles: 60 (2007), 65 (2008)

ISBNs, Imprints & Series:
Alcemi; Dinas
978 0 86243, 978 0 904864 Y Lolfa

Book Trade Association Membership:
Union of Welsh Publishers & Booksellers

2844

YALE UNIVERSITY PRESS LONDON
47 Bedford Square, London WC1B 3DP
Telephone: (020) 7079 4900
Fax: (020) 7079 4901
Email: firstname.lastname@yaleup.co.uk
Web Site: http://www.yalebooks.co.uk

Warehouse & Fulfilment:
John Wiley & Sons Ltd, Distribution Centre, Shripney Road, Bognor Regis, West Sussex PO22 9SA
Telephone: 01243 829121
Fax: 01243 82050

Directors: Robert Baldock *(Managing)*
Kate Pocock *(Sales & Marketing)*

Publishers: Gillian Malpass *(Art & Architecture)*
Sally Salvesen *(Decorative Arts)*
Heather McCallum *(Trade Books)*
Managers: Katie Harris *(Publicity)*
Charlotte Stafford *(Promotion & Direct Mail)*
Anne Bihan *(Rights)*
Andrew Jarmain *(Sales)*
Stephen Kent *(Production & Design)*
Accountant: Donal Burke

Academic & Scholarly; Archaeology; Architecture & Design; Biography & Autobiography; Economics; Fashion & Costume; Fine Art & Art History; Gender Studies; History & Antiquarian; Illustrated & Fine Editions; Languages & Linguistics; Military & War; Music; Natural History; Philosophy; Photography; Politics & World Affairs; Religion & Theology; Theatre, Drama & Dance

ISBNs, Imprints & Series: 978 0 300

Parent Company:
USA: Yale University Press

Associated Companies:
Yale Representation Ltd

Overseas Representation:
Africa (excluding Southern Africa & Nigeria): Kelvin van Hasselt Publishing Services, Briningham, Norfolk, UK
Austria, Germany, Italy & Switzerland: Uwe Lüdemann, Berlin, Germany
Benelux, Denmark, Finland, France, Iceland, Norway & Sweden: Fred Hermans, Bovenkarspel, Netherlands
Hong Kong, China & Philippines: Asia Publishers Services Ltd, Hong Kong
India: S. Janakiraman, Book Marketing Services, Chennai
Iran: Farhad Maftoon, Tehran
Middle East: International Publishers Representatives (IPR) Ltd, Nicosia, Cyprus
Nigeria: Bounty Books, Ibadan
Pakistan: Anwer Iqbal, Book Bird Publishers Representatives, Lahore
Poland, Czech Republic, Croatia, Hungary, Slovakia & Slovenia: Ewa Ledóchowicz, Konstancin-Jeziorna, Poland
Republic of Ireland & Northern Ireland: Robert Towers, Monkstown, Co Dublin, Republic of Ireland
Singapore, Malaysia, Brunei & Indonesia: APD Singapore Pte Ltd, Singapore
Southern Africa: Book Promotions Pty Ltd, Diep River, South Africa
Spain & Portugal: Chris Humphrys, Gaucin, Spain
USA, Central & South America, Mexico, Canada, Australia, New Zealand, Japan, Korea & Taiwan: Yale University Press, New Haven, CT, USA

Book Trade Association Membership:
Publishers Association; CAPP; IPG

2845

YORE PUBLICATIONS
12 The Furrows, Harefield, Middx UB9 6AT
Telephone: 01895 823404
Fax: 01895 823404r2865
Email: fay.twydell@blueyonder.co.uk
Web Site: http://www.yore.demon.co.uk/index.html

Partners: Dave Twydell
Fay Twydell
Typist/Secretary: Kara Matthews

Sports & Games

New Titles: 7 (2007), 8 (2008)

ISBNs, Imprints & Series:
978 0 954163, 978 0 954783, 978 0 955788, 978 1 874427

2846

ZAMBEZI PUBLISHING LTD
22 Second Avenue, Camels Head, Plymouth, Devon PL2 2EQ
Telephone: 01752 367300
Fax: 01752 350453
Email: info@zampub.com
Web Site: http://www.zampub.com

Business:
PO Box 221, Plymouth, Devon PL2 2YJ
Telephone: 01752 367300
Fax: 01752 350453
Email: (as above)
Web Site: (as above)

Directors: Sasha Fenton *(Chief Executive Officer)*
Jan Budkowski *(Managing)*

Industry, Business & Management; Magic & the Occult; Medical (incl. Self Help & Alternative Medicine); Mind, Body, Spirit

New Titles: 5 (2007), 9 (2008)
Annual Turnover: £30,000

ISBNs, Imprints & Series:
978 0 9533478, 978 1 90306501

Overseas Representation:
Europe: Gardners Books Ltd, Eastbourne, UK
USA & Rest of the World: Sterling Publishing Co Inc, New York, NY, USA

Book Trade Association Membership:
PMA (USA)

2847

ZED BOOKS LTD
7 Cynthia Street, London N1 9JF
Telephone: (020) 7837 4014 & 8466
Fax: (020) 7833 3960
Email: zed@zedbooks.net
Web Site: http://www.zedbooks.co.uk

Distribution:
NBN International Ltd, Estover, Plymouth PL6 7PZ
Telephone: 01752 202301
Fax: 01752 202331

Trade Representation - UK & Republic of Ireland:
Compass Academic
Telephone: (020) 8994 6477
Email: ca@compass-academic.co.uk
Web Site: http://www.academic.compass-booksales.co.uk/academic

Directors: Julian Hosie *(Marketing)*
Margaret Ling *(Finance & Company Secretary)*
Commissioning Editors: Tamsine O'Riordan
Ellen McKinlay
Publicity Officer: Rosemary Taylorson
Sales Executive: Ruben Mootoosamy
Production Editor: Nikhil Bhoopal
Managers: David Birkett *(Sales)*
Dan Och *(Production)*

Academic & Scholarly; Economics; Environment & Development Studies; Gender Studies; Politics & World Affairs; Sociology & Anthropology

New Titles: 48 (2007), 50 (2008)
No of Employees: 10
Annual Turnover: £1.14M

ISBNs, Imprints & Series:
978 0 86232, 978 0 905762, 978 1 84277, 978 1 84813, 978 1 85649

Overseas Representation:
Australia & New Zealand: Palgrave Macmillan, South Yarra, Vic, Australia
Bangladesh: The University Press Ltd, Dhaka

Canada: Fernwood Books Ltd, Halifax, NS
Egypt: MERIC, Cairo
Fiji: University Book Centre, Suva
Germany: Missing Link International Booksellers, Bremen
Ghana: EPP Books Services Ltd, Accra
Hong Kong: Hong Kong University Press
India: Madhyam International, New Delhi
Iran: Book City, Tehran
Japan: Far Eastern Booksellers, Tokyo
Lebanon: Levant Distributors, Beirut
Malaysia: Gerakbudaya Enterprise, Selangor
Nepal: Everest Media International, Kathmandu
Pakistan: Vanguard Books Pvt Ltd, Lahore
Singapore: Publishers Marketing Services Pte Ltd
South Africa: New Africa Books Pty Ltd, Claremont
Tanzania: Tema Publishers Co Ltd, Dar es Salaam
Thailand: White Lotus, Bangkok
Uganda: Aristoc Booklex Ltd, Kampala
USA: Palgrave Macmillan, New York, NY
West Africa: EPP Books Services Ltd, Accra, Ghana

Book Trade Association Membership:
IPG

2848

ZERO TO TEN
Evans Publishing Group, Suite 1.3, Coomb House, 7 St John's Road, Isleworth, Middx TW7 6NH
Telephone: (020) 8758 9777
Fax: (020) 8758 9888
Web Site: http://www.evansbooks.co.uk

Sales Director: Andrew Macmillan

Children's Books

ISBNs, Imprints & Series:
978 0 237 Evans
978 1 84089 Zero to Ten
978 1 84234 Cherrytree

Associated Companies:
Kenya: Evans Brothers (Kenya) Ltd
Nigeria: Evans Brothers (Nigeria Publishers) Ltd
Sierra Leone: Evans Brothers (Sierra Leone) Ltd

Book Trade Association Membership:
EPC

2849

*ZETICULA
57 St Vincent Crescent, Glasgow G3 8NQ
Telephone: 07967 646044

Distribution:
Gardners Books, 1 Whittle Drive, Eastbourne BN23 6QH

Manager: Stuart Johnston

Academic & Scholarly; Bibliography & Library Science; Biography & Autobiography; Educational & Textbooks; Environment & Development Studies; Fiction; Geography & Geology; History & Antiquarian; Humour; Military & War; Reference Books, Directories & Dictionaries; Religion & Theology; Transport; Travel & Topography

ISBNs, Imprints & Series:
978 0 902664 The Grimsay Press
978 1 84622 humming earth
978 1 900369 Parker
978 1 904999 Kennedy & Boyd
978 1 905021 Mansion Field
978 1 905022 Covenanters Press

Book Trade Association Membership:
IPG

2850

ZYMURGY PUBLISHING
Houlton Estate, Walker Road,
Newcastle upon Tyne NE6 2HL
Telephone: 0191 276 2425

Fax: 0191 276 2425
Email: martin.ellis@ablibris.com

Publisher: Martin Ellis

Biography & Autobiography; Cookery, Wines & Spirits; Crime; Humour; Illustrated & Fine Editions; Natural History; Photography; Travel & Topography

New Titles: 4 (2007), 3 (2008)

ISBNs, Imprints & Series: 978 1 903506

Book Trade Association Membership:
IPG; Publishers Publicity Circle

3 Packagers

3001

ALADDIN BOOKS LTD
2–3 Fitzroy Mews, London W1T 6DF
Telephone: (020) 7383 2084
Fax: (020) 7388 6391
Email: sales@aladdinbooks.co.uk
Web Site: http://www.aladdinbooks.co.uk

Directors: Charles V. Nicholas
Mrs E. Whittaker
Production: Alexandra Mew
Finance: Emma Rowley
Foreign Rights: Maria Laverty
Editorial: Katie Harker

Children's Books; Educational & Textbooks

ISBNs, Imprints & Series:
978 0 7496 Aladdin/Watts
978 1 59604, 978 1 932799 Creative
  Company/Stargazer

Associated Companies:
Archon Press Ltd; Learning Factory;
Nicholas Enterprises Ltd
Denmark: Margit Schaleck Agency

Overseas Representation:
China & Taiwan: Andrew Nurnberg
  Associates Ltd, Beijing, P. R. of China
Denmark: Margit Schaleck Agency
Germany: Harry Olechnowitz
Korea: Imprima Agency, Korea, South

3002

*ALBION PRESS LTD
Spring Hill, Idbury, Oxon OX7 6RU
Telephone: 01993 831094
Fax: 01993 831982

Directors: Emma Bradford *(Managing)*
Neil Philip *(Editorial)*

Children's Books

3003

AMBER BOOKS LTD
Bradley's Close, 74–77 White Lion Street,
London N1 9PF
Telephone: (020) 7520 7600
Fax: (020) 7520 7606 & 7607
Email: enquiries@amberbooks.co.uk
Web Site: http://www.amberbooks.co.uk

Directors: Stasz Gnych *(Managing)*
Sara Ballard *(Rights)*
Peter Thompson *(Head of Production)*
Publishing Manager: Charles Catton

*Animal Care & Breeding; Atlases & Maps;
Aviation; Crafts & Hobbies; Crime; Fashion
& Costume; History & Antiquarian; Military
& War; Nautical; Reference Books,
Directories & Dictionaries; Sports & Games;
Transport*

New Titles: 60 (2007), 60 (2008)
No of Employees: 18
Annual Turnover: £5M

ISBNs, Imprints & Series: 978 1 904687

Book Trade Association Membership:
Book Packagers Association

3004

AMOLIBROS
Loundshay Manor Cottage,
Preston Bowyer, Milverton, Taunton,
Somerset TA4 1QF
Telephone: 01823 401527
Fax: 01823 401527
Email: amolibros@aol.com
Web Site: http://www.amolibros.co.uk

Trade Enquiries & Orders:
Gardners Books, 1 Whittle Drive,
Eastbourne BN23 6QH
Telephone: 01323 521555
Fax: 01323 521666

Managing Consultant: Jane Tatam

*Academic & Scholarly; Animal Care &
Breeding; Biography & Autobiography;
Children's Books; Fiction; Gardening;
Geography & Geology; History &
Antiquarian; Literature & Criticism; Magic &
the Occult; Music; Nautical; Philosophy;
Poetry; Politics & World Affairs; Sports &
Games; Theatre, Drama & Dance; Travel &
Topography*

New Titles: 30 (2008)

3005

NICOLA BAXTER LTD
PO Box 215, The Brew House,
Framingham Earl Road, Yelverton, Norwich
NR14 7UR
Telephone: 01508 491111
Email: nb@nicolabaxter.co.uk
Web Site: http://www.nicolabaxter.co.uk

Proprietor: Nicola Baxter

Children's Books; Educational & Textbooks

New Titles: 30 (2007), 30 (2008)
No of Employees: 3

Book Trade Association Membership:
Association of Book Packagers

3006

BENDER RICHARDSON WHITE
PO Box 266, Uxbridge UB9 5NX
Telephone: 01895 832444
Fax: 01895 835213
Email: brw@brw.co.uk

Directors: Lionel Bender *(Editorial)*
Kim Richardson *(Sales & Production)*
Ben White *(Art & Design)*

*Biology & Zoology; Children's Books;
Educational & Textbooks; Natural History;
Reference Books, Directories & Dictionaries;
Religion & Theology*

3007

BLA PUBLISHING LTD
1 Christopher Road, East Grinstead,
West Sussex RH19 3BT
Telephone: 01342 318980
Fax: 01342 410980
Email: eileen@wleducat.freeserve.co.uk

Chairman: Au Bak Ling
Contact: Eileen Parsons *(Company
Secretary, Sales, Rights & Permissions)*

*Antiques & Collecting; Aviation; Biology &
Zoology; Chemistry; Children's Books;
Computer Science; Medical (incl. Self Help
& Alternative Medicine); Military & War;
Music; Natural History; Nautical; Physics;
Reference Books, Directories & Dictionaries;
Religion & Theology*

No of Employees: 2

ISBNs, Imprints & Series:
Thames Head

Parent Company:
Ling Kee (UK) Ltd

Associated Companies:
Ward Lock Educational Co Ltd

3008

*BLUE BEYOND BOOKS
1 Paget Road, Ipswich IP1 3RP
Telephone: 01473 423247
Fax: 01473 214096
Email: martin.spettigue@virgin.net

Manager: Martin Spettigue
Sales Representatives: Mark Thomas
Nelly Coudoa
Ms Hita
Ms Spence
Darrel Lewis

*Magic & the Occult; Music; Philosophy;
Poetry; Religion & Theology; Mind Body
Spirit/New Age*

Associated Companies:
USA: Aum Publications; McKeever
Publishing

Distributor for:
USA: Aum Publications; McKeever
Publishing

Overseas Representation:
Australia: Wisdom's Delight, Brisbane, Qld
Canada: Peace Publishing, Ottawa, Ont
France: Editions Sri Chinmey, Paris
Germany: The Golden Shore, Nurnberg
USA: Heart-Light Distributors, Seattle, WA

3009

BOOK STREET LTD
Foresters Hall, 25–27 Westow Street,
London SE19 3RY
Telephone: (020) 8771 5115
Fax: (020) 8771 9994
Email: graham@bwj-ltd.com

Directors: Graham Brown *(Managing)*
Michael Morris

Children's Books; Crafts & Hobbies

New Titles: 6 (2007)

3010

BOOKPOWER
[formerly ELST]
120 Pentonville Road, London N1 9JN
Telephone: (020) 7843 1938
Fax: (020) 7837 6348
Email: BookPower@mistral.co.uk
Web Site: http://www.BookPower.org

Head, Administration: Valerie Teague

*Academic & Scholarly; Accountancy &
Taxation; Animal Care & Breeding; Biology
& Zoology; Computer Science; Economics;
Educational & Textbooks; Engineering;
Industry, Business & Management; Medical
(incl. Self Help & Alternative Medicine);
Scientific & Technical; Veterinary Science;
Vocational Training & Careers*

New Titles: 4 (2007), 3 (2008)
No of Employees: 1

ISBNs, Imprints & Series:
BookPower (formerly ELST); ELST

Associated Companies:
ELST (Educational Low-Priced Sponsored
Textbooks)

PACKAGERS

Overseas Representation:
Ghana: Gibrine Adam, EPP Book Services Ltd, Accra
India: Vinod Vasishtha, Viva Group, New Delhi
Kenya: Jimmi Makotsi, Acacia Publishers, Nairobi
Nigeria: L. Adesuyi, Harilah Books, Ikeja; Kolade Mosuro, Mosuro The Booksellers Ltd, Ibadan
Pakistan: British Council, Karachi
Sri Lanka: Pitraban Books, Colombo
Zimbabwe: Maureen Stewart, British Council, Bulawayo

3011

BRIDGEWATER BOOK CO
The Old Candlemakers, West Street, Lewes, East Sussex BN7 2NZ
Telephone: 01273 403120
Fax: 01273 487441
Email: (surname)@bridgewaterbooks.co.uk
Web Site: http://www.bridgewaterbooks.co.uk

Directors: Stephen Paul *(Managing)*
Peter Bridgewater *(Creative)*
Jenny Manstead *(Sales)*

Academic & Scholarly; Architecture & Design; Atlases & Maps; Children's Books; Cinema, Video, TV & Radio; Cookery, Wines & Spirits; Crafts & Hobbies; Do-It-Yourself; Educational & Textbooks; Fashion & Costume; Fine Art & Art History; Gardening; Guide Books; Health & Beauty; History & Antiquarian; Humour; Illustrated & Fine Editions; Magic & the Occult; Medical (incl. Self Help & Alternative Medicine); Music; Natural History; Photography; Reference Books, Directories & Dictionaries; Religion & Theology; Sports & Games; Theatre, Drama & Dance; Travel & Topography

New Titles: 50 (2007), 50 (2008)
No of Employees: 23

Parent Company:
The Ivy Publishing Group

Associated Companies:
Ilex Press; The Ivy Press

3012

BROWN WELLS & JACOBS LTD
Foresters Hall, 25–27 Westow Street, London SE19 3RY
Telephone: (020) 8771 5115
Fax: (020) 8771 9994
Email: graham@bwj-ltd.com
Web Site: http://www.bwj.org

Director: Graham Brown *(Managing, Design, Sales & Production)*
Production Manager: Jenny Broom

Children's Books; Crafts & Hobbies

New Titles: 28 (2007), 30 (2008)
No of Employees: 5

ISBNs, Imprints & Series: 978 1 873829

Distributor for:
Brown Wells & Jacobs Ltd (Packaging)

3013

CAMBRIDGE PUBLISHING MANAGEMENT LTD
Burr Elm Court, Main Street, Caldecote, Cambs CB3 7NU
Telephone: 01954 214006
Fax: 01954 214001
Email: j.dobbyne@cambridgepm.co.uk
Web Site: http://www.cambridgepm.co.uk

Directors: Jackie Dobbyne *(Managing)*
Tim Newton *(Production)*
Editorial: Karen Beaulah

Academic & Scholarly; Archaeology; Architecture & Design; Biography & Autobiography; Children's Books; Cinema, Video, TV & Radio; Cookery, Wines & Spirits; Crafts & Hobbies; Educational & Textbooks; English as a Foreign Language; Fashion & Costume; Fine Art & Art History; Gardening; Industry, Business & Management; Medical (incl. Self Help & Alternative Medicine); Military & War; Natural History; Reference Books, Directories & Dictionaries; Religion & Theology; Sports & Games; Travel & Topography; Vocational Training & Careers

No of Employees: 18
Annual Turnover: £1.3M

3014

*CAMERON BOOKS
PO Box 1, Moffat, Dumfriesshire DG10 9SU
Telephone: 01683 220808
Fax: 01683 220012
Email: mail@cameronbooks.co.uk
Web Site: http://www.cameronbooks.co.uk

Directors: Ian A. Cameron
Jill Hollis

Antiques & Collecting; Architecture & Design; Cinema, Video, TV & Radio; Cookery, Wines & Spirits; Environment & Development Studies; Fine Art & Art History; Natural History

ISBNs, Imprints & Series:
978 0 906506 Cameron & Hollis

3015

*CORPUS PUBLISHING LTD
PO Box 8, Lydney, Glos GL15 6YD
Telephone: 01594 560600
Fax: 01594 560550
Email: info@firststonepub.co.uk

Publisher: John Sellers

Accountancy & Taxation; Animal Care & Breeding; Children's Books; Medical (incl. Self Help & Alternative Medicine); Sports & Games

ISBNs, Imprints & Series:
978 1 903333 Corpus Publishing
978 1 904439 First Stone Publishing

3016

COWLEY ROBINSON PUBLISHING LTD
8 Belmont, Bath BA1 5DZ
Telephone: 01225 339999
Fax: 01225 339995
Email: stewart.cowley@cowleyrobinson.com

Directors: Stewart Cowley
D. Hawcock
P. Fleming
Managers: Leanne Down *(Production)*
Anna Sainaghi *(Senior Sales)*

Children's Books

New Titles: 28 (2007), 30 (2008)
No of Employees: 13
Annual Turnover: £2M

Parent Company:
Allcloud Ltd

3017

D & N PUBLISHING
Unit 3C, Lowesden Business Park, Lambourn Woodlands, Hungerford, Berkshire RG17 7RU
Telephone: 01488 73657
Email: d@dnpublishing.co.uk

Manager/Owner: David Price-Goodfellow
Designer/Owner: Namrita Price-Goodfellow

Animal Care & Breeding; Antiques & Collecting; Aviation; Biology & Zoology; Crafts & Hobbies; Do-It-Yourself; Fashion & Costume; Fine Art & Art History; Gardening; Geography & Geology; Guide Books; History & Antiquarian; Medical (incl. Self Help & Alternative Medicine); Military & War; Natural History; Photography; Reference Books, Directories & Dictionaries; Sports & Games; Theatre, Drama & Dance; Transport; Travel & Topography

No of Employees: 2

3018

*DIAGRAM VISUAL INFORMATION LTD
195 Kentish Town Road, London NW5 2JU
Telephone: (020) 7482 3633
Fax: (020) 7482 4932
Email: info@diagramgroup.com
Web Site: http://www.diagramgroup.com

Managing Director: Bruce Robertson

Educational & Textbooks; Geography & Geology; Health & Beauty; Reference Books, Directories & Dictionaries; Sports & Games

Overseas Representation:
Bulgaria: Nika Literary Agency, Sofia
Eastern Europe: DS Druck- und Verlagsservice, Stuttgart, Germany
Hungary: DS Budapest Kft, Budapest
Japan: Tuttle-Mori Agency Inc, Tokyo
Korea: KCC, Seoul, Korea, South
Lithuania: Musa Knyga, Vilnius
Netherlands & Scandinavia: Jan Michael, Amsterdam, Netherlands
Poland: DS Druck Warszawa, Warsaw
Romania: Mast Publishing, Bucharest
Russia: ICSTI, Moscow
Thailand: Big Apple Tuttle-Mori Agency (Thailand) Co Ltd, Bangkok

3019

EDDISON SADD EDITIONS LTD
St Chad's House, 148 King's Cross Road, London WC1X 9DH
Telephone: (020) 7837 1968
Fax: (020) 7837 2025
Email: info@eddisonsadd.co.uk
Web Site: http://www.eddisonsadd.com

Accounts:
Facts & Figures
Telephone: 01280 813111
Fax: 01280 817229

Directors: Nick Eddison *(Managing)*
Ian Jackson *(Editorial)*
Susan Cole *(Rights)*
David Owen *(Financial)*
Elaine Partington *(Art)*
Sarah Rooney *(Production)*

Children's Books; Cookery, Wines & Spirits; Health & Beauty; Magic & the Occult; Medical (incl. Self Help & Alternative Medicine); Mind, Body, Spirit; Puzzles

New Titles: 15 (2007), 15 (2008)
No of Employees: 11
Annual Turnover: £2.4M

ISBNs, Imprints & Series:
Bookinabox

Associated Companies:
Connections Book Publishing

Overseas Representation:
Worldwide: Melia Publishing Services, UK

3020

*ELM GROVE BOOKS LTD
Elm Grove, Marsh Lane, Henstridge, Somerset BA8 0TQ
Telephone: 01963 362498
Email: Hugh@elmgrovebooks.com

Directors: Hugh Elwes *(Managing)*
Susie Elwes *(Editorial)*

Children's Books; Reference Books, Directories & Dictionaries

3021

EMMA TREEHOUSE LTD
The Studio, Church Street, Nunney, Frome, Somerset BA11 4LW
Telephone: 01373 836233
Fax: 01373 836299
Email: sales@emmatreehouse.com

Directors: David Bailey
Richard Powell
Hilary Allom
Managers: Christine Barham
Margret Heilegenstadt

Children's Books

New Titles: 36 (2007), 36 (2008)
No of Employees: 6

ISBNs, Imprints & Series:
Treehouse Children's Books
978 1 85576

Distributor for:
Macmillan Distribution

Book Trade Association Membership:
Book Packagers Association

3022

ESSENTIAL WORKS LTD
168A Camden Street, London NW1 9PT
Telephone: (020) 7485 1341
Email: info@essentialworks.co.uk

Directors: John Conway *(Managing)*
Mal Peachey *(Publishing)*
Rights & Co-Editions: Jackie Strachan
Jane Moseley

Biography & Autobiography; Cinema, Video, TV & Radio; Cookery, Wines & Spirits; Crafts & Hobbies; Crime; Do-It-Yourself; Fashion & Costume; Fine Art & Art History; Health & Beauty; Humour; Illustrated & Fine Editions; Medical (incl. Self Help & Alternative Medicine); Military & War; Music; Photography; Reference Books, Directories & Dictionaries; Sports & Games; Theatre, Drama & Dance; Transport

Associated Companies:
Conspiracy Books Ltd

3023

FOCUS PUBLISHING (SEVENOAKS) LTD
11A St Botolph's Road, Sevenoaks, Kent TN13 3AJ
Telephone: 01732 742456
Fax: 01732 743381
Email: info@focus-publishing.co.uk
Web Site: http://www.focus-publishing.co.uk

Directors: Guy Croton *(Managing)*

Caroline Watson (Publishing)
Designer: Heather McMillan
Editor: Vicky Hales-Dutton

Animal Care & Breeding; Aviation; Biology & Zoology; Cookery, Wines & Spirits; Crafts & Hobbies; Crime; Do-It-Yourself; Gardening; Geography & Geology; Magic & the Occult; Mathematics & Statistics; Medical (incl. Self Help & Alternative Medicine); Military & War; Music; Natural History; Nautical; Photography; Sports & Games; Theatre, Drama & Dance; Transport

3024

FREELANCE MARKET NEWS
Sevendale House, 7 Dale Street,
Manchester M1 1JB
Telephone: 0161 228 2362
Fax: 0161 228 3533
Email: fmn@writersbureau.com
Web Site: http://www.writersbureau.com

Editorial & Circulation: Miss Angela Cox

Educational & Textbooks; Fiction; Literature & Criticism; Photography; Poetry

Parent Company:
The Writers Bureau Ltd

3025

GRAHAM-CAMERON PUBLISHING & ILLUSTRATION
The Studio, 23 Holt Road, Sheringham,
Norfolk NR26 8NB
Telephone: 01263 821333
Fax: 01263 821334
Email: mike@graham-cameron-illustration.com

Marketing & Sales:
Duncan Graham-Cameron,
59 Hertford Road, Brighton BN1 7GG
Telephone: 01273 385890
Email: duncan@graham-cameron-illustration.com
Web Site: http://www.graham-cameron-illustration.com

Partners: Mike Graham-Cameron *(Managing & Editorial)*
Helen Graham-Cameron *(Executive, Art & Editorial)*
Duncan Graham-Cameron *(Executive, Marketing & Sales)*

Architecture & Design; Children's Books; Educational & Textbooks; English as a Foreign Language; Military & War; Natural History

ISBNs, Imprints & Series: 978 0 947672

Associated Companies:
Graham-Cameron Illustration

Book Trade Association Membership:
IPG; Cambridge Book Association; Pica Club; The Paternosters

3026

HART MCLEOD LTD
14A Greenside, Waterbeach, Cambridge
CB5 9HP
Telephone: 01223 861495
Fax: 01223 862902
Email: inhouse@hartmcleod.co.uk
Web Site: http://www.hartmcleod.co.uk

Directors: Graham Hart *(Editorial)*
Chris McLeod *(Design)*
Joanne Barker *(Design)*

Academic & Scholarly; Educational & Textbooks; Sports & Games

3027

THE IVY PRESS LTD
The Old Candlemakers, West Street, Lewes,
East Sussex BN7 2NZ
Telephone: 01273 487440
Fax: 01273 487441
Web Site: http://www.ivy-group.co.uk

Directors: Stephen Paul *(Managing)*
Nikki Tilbury *(Rights)*
Peter Bridgewater *(Creative)*

Crafts & Hobbies; Fashion & Costume; Health & Beauty; Illustrated & Fine Editions

New Titles: 27 (2007), 40 (2008)
No of Employees: 26

3028

LITTLE PEOPLE BOOKS
The Home of BookBod, Knighton,
Radnorshire LD7 1UP
Telephone: 01547 520925
Email: littlepeoplebooks@thehobb.tv
Web Site: http://www.thehobb.tv/littlepeoplebooks

Directors: Grant Jessé *(Production, Managing Editor)*
Helen Wallis *(Rights, Finance)*

Audio Books; Children's Books; Educational & Textbooks; Digital Publications; Water Environment

ISBNs, Imprints & Series: 978 1 899573

Parent Company:
Grant Jessé

Associated Companies:
Karavadra: Multimedia

Book Trade Association Membership:
IPG; Book Packagers Association

3029

MARKET HOUSE BOOKS LTD
Suite B, Elsinore House,
43 Buckingham Street, Aylesbury, Bucks
HP20 2NQ
Telephone: 01296 484911
Fax: 01296 338934
Email: dainthth@mhbref.com

Directors: Dr John Daintith
Peter Sapsed
Chief Editor: Elizabeth Martin
Production: Anne Stibbs

Computer Science; Industry, Business & Management; Law; Medical (incl. Self Help & Alternative Medicine); Music; Psychology & Psychiatry; Reference Books, Directories & Dictionaries; Scientific & Technical; Theatre, Drama & Dance

3030

MONKEY PUZZLE MEDIA LTD
The Rectory, Eyke, Woodbridge, Suffolk
IP12 2QW
Telephone: 01394 460100

Directors: Roger Goddard-Coote *(Managing)*
Paul Mason *(Editorial)*
Picture Manager: Lynda Lines

Atlases & Maps; Children's Books; Educational & Textbooks; Fine Art & Art History; Geography & Geology; Health & Beauty; History & Antiquarian; Natural History; Politics & World Affairs; Scientific & Technical; Sports & Games; Travel & Topography

3031

ORPHEUS BOOKS LTD
6 Church Green, Witney, Oxon OX28 4AW
Telephone: 01993 774949
Fax: 01993 700330
Email: nicholas@orpheusbooks.com
Web Site: http://www.orpheusbooks.com

Directors: Nicholas Harris
Sarah Hartley

Children's Books

ISBNs, Imprints & Series:
978 1 901323, 978 1 905473

3032

PARAGON PUBLISHING
4 North Street, Rothersthorpe, Northants
NN7 3JB
Telephone: 01604 832149
Email: mark.webb@tesco.net
Web Site: http://www.intoprint.net

Proprietor: Mark Webb

Academic & Scholarly; Architecture & Design; Computer Science; Educational & Textbooks; Electronic (Educational); Electronic (Professional & Academic); English as a Foreign Language; Environment & Development Studies; Fiction; Languages & Linguistics; Poetry; Religion & Theology; Science Fiction; Scientific & Technical; Sports & Games; Theatre, Drama & Dance

New Titles: 8 (2007), 8 (2008)

ISBNs, Imprints & Series:
KinderKlub; Primary Modern Language; Stadium & Arena
978 1 899820 Into Print

3033

PLAYNE BOOKS LTD
Park Court Barn, Trefin, Haverfordwest,
Pembrokeshire SA62 5AU
Telephone: 01348 837073
Fax: 01348 837063
Email: playne.books@virgin.net

Editorial Director: Gill Davies
Production: David Playne

Children's Books; History & Antiquarian; Theatre, Drama & Dance; Travel & Topography

New Titles: 4 (2007), 10 (2008)
No of Employees: 2

Associated Companies:
Playne Design; Playne Plays; Spinfolds

Book Trade Association Membership:
IPG

3034

TONY POTTER PUBLISHING
1 Stairbridge Court,
Bolney Grange Business Park,
Stairbridge Lane, Bolney, Haywards Heath,
West Sussex RH17 5PA
Telephone: 01444 232889
Fax: 01444 232142
Email: pat@tonypotter.com
Web Site: http://www.tonypotter.com

Managing Director: Dr Tony Potter
Managing Editor: Pat Hegarty
Rights Consultant: Susannah Moore
Production Manager: Liz Baird

Children's Books; Humour

New Titles: 50 (2007), 50 (2008)
No of Employees: 14

ISBNs, Imprints & Series:
978 1 905288 Over the Moon
978 1 906013 Teapot Press

Book Trade Association Membership:
IPG

3035

QUANTUM PUBLISHING
6 Blundell Street, London N7 9BH
Telephone: (020) 7700 6700
Fax: (020) 7700 4191
Email: quantum@quarto.com
Web Site: http://www.quarto.com

Publisher: Anastasia Cavouras

Antiques & Collecting; Archaeology; Architecture & Design; Atlases & Maps; Aviation; Children's Books; Cookery, Wines & Spirits; Crafts & Hobbies; Do-It-Yourself; Fashion & Costume; Fine Art & Art History; Gardening; Health & Beauty; History & Antiquarian; Magic & the Occult; Medical (incl. Self Help & Alternative Medicine); Military & War; Music; Natural History; Nautical; Photography; Sports & Games; Transport

New Titles: 30 (2007), 30 (2008)

ISBNs, Imprints & Series:
Cartographica Press; Oceana; Quantum

Parent Company:
Quarto Publishing Plc

3036

READER'S DIGEST CHILDREN'S PUBLISHING LTD
The Ice House, 124–126 Walcot Street,
Bath BA1 5BG
Telephone: 01225 473200
Fax: 01225 460942
Email: customercare@readersdigest.co.uk
Web Site: http://www.rd.com

Directors: Paul E. Stuart *(Commercial)*
Jennifer Fifield *(International Sales)*

Children's Books; Novelty Books

New Titles: 15 (2007), 20 (2008)
No of Employees: 12
Annual Turnover: £6M

ISBNs, Imprints & Series:
978 1 84880, 978 1 85724

Parent Company:
USA: The Reader's Digest Association Inc

Associated Companies:
USA: Reader's Digest Children's Publishing Inc

3037

*REGENCY HOUSE PUBLISHING LTD
Niall House, 24–26 Boulton Road,
Stevenage, Herts SG1 4QX
Telephone: 01438 314488
Fax: 01438 311303
Email: regency-house@btconnect.com

Managing Director: Miss N. Trodd
Managers: B. H. Trodd
Annabel Trodd

Architecture & Design; Aviation; Children's Books; Crafts & Hobbies; Magic & the Occult; Military & War

ISBNs, Imprints & Series: 978 1 85361

3038

*TANGERINE DESIGNS LTD
2 High Street, Freshford, Bath BA2 7WE
Telephone: 01225 720001

Email: enquiries@tangerinedesigns.co.uk
Web Site: http://www.tangerinedesigns.co.uk

Managing Director: Christine Swift
Co-edition Sales Agent: Trish Pugsley
English Sales: Cathy Power

Children's Books

Distributor for:
Alligator Books Ltd [Foreign Rights Agents];
Funkkia Ltd [Publishing Licensors];
Rockpool Children's Books [Foreign Rights Agents]

Book Trade Association Membership:
Publishers Association

3039

TOUCAN BOOKS LTD
Third Floor, 89 Charterhouse Street,
London EC1M 6PE
Telephone: (020) 7250 3388
Fax: (020) 7250 3123
Email: ellen@toucanbooks.co.uk

Directors: Ellen Dupont *(Managing)*
Robert Sackville-West

Architecture & Design; Atlases & Maps; Children's Books; Crafts & Hobbies; Fine Art & Art History; Gardening; History &
Antiquarian; Natural History; Reference Books, Directories & Dictionaries

Book Trade Association Membership:
Book Packagers Association

3040

TRUST FOR THE STUDY OF ADOLESCENCE
23 New Road, Brighton, East Sussex
BN1 1WZ
Telephone: 01273 693311
Fax: 01273 647322
Email: publications@tsa.uk.com
Web Site: http://www.tsa.uk.com

Educational & Textbooks; Professionals Working with Parents; Research in Adolescence; Teenagers in Foster Care

New Titles: 4 (2007), 2 (2008)
No of Employees: 18

ISBNs, Imprints & Series: 978 1 871504

Book Trade Association Membership:
BA

3041

TUCKER SLINGSBY LTD
Fifth Floor, Regal House, 70 London Road,
Twickenham TW1 3QS
Telephone: (020) 8744 1007
Fax: (020) 8744 0041
Email: info@tuckerslingsby.co.uk

Directors: Del Tucker
Janet Slingsby

Children's Books; Cookery, Wines & Spirits; Crafts & Hobbies; Gardening; Health & Beauty; Humour

New Titles: 25 (2007), 35 (2008)

ISBNs, Imprints & Series: 978 1 902272

3042

WATERSIDE PRESS
Sherfield Gables, Sherfield-on-Loddon,
Hook RG27 0JG
Telephone: 01256 882250
Fax: 01256 882250
Email: bryangibson@watersidepress.co.uk
Web Site: http://www.watersidepress.co.uk

Managing Editor: Bryan Gibson

Academic & Scholarly; Biography & Autobiography; Crime; Educational & Textbooks; Fiction; History & Antiquarian; Languages & Linguistics; Law; Literature & Criticism; Reference Books, Directories & Dictionaries; Sociology & Anthropology; Theatre, Drama & Dance

New Titles: 10 (2007), 12 (2008)

ISBNs, Imprints & Series:
978 1 872870, 978 1 904380, 978 1 906534

Associated Companies:
Bryan Gibson Publications

Overseas Representation:
North America: International Specialized Book Services Inc, Portland, OR, USA

3043

DAVID WEST CHILDREN'S BOOKS
7 Princeton Court, 55 Felsham Road,
London SW15 1AZ
Telephone: (020) 8780 3836
Fax: (020) 8780 9313
Email: dww@btinternet.com
Web Site: http://www.davidwestchildrensbooks.com

Proprietor/Publisher: David West
Publisher: Lynn Lockett

Architecture & Design; Children's Books; Cinema, Video, TV & Radio; Crafts & Hobbies; Fashion & Costume; Geography & Geology; History & Antiquarian; Military & War; Music; Natural History; Scientific & Technical; Sports & Games; Transport

4 Authors' Agents

4001

AITKEN ALEXANDER ASSOCIATES
18–21 Cavaye Place, London SW10 9PT
Telephone: (020) 7373 8672
Fax: (020) 7373 6002
Email: reception@gillonaitken.co.uk
Web Site: http://
www.aitkenalexander.co.uk

Directors: Gillon Aitken *(Chairman)*
Clare Alexander *(Joint Managing)*
Sally Riley *(Joint Managing)*
Andrew Kidd
Joaquim Fernandes *(Company Secretary)*
Foreign Rights: Sally Riley
Film/TV: Lesley Shaw

All MSS except plays, film & TV scripts, short stories & articles if not by existing clients.

Specialization: quality full-length fiction & non-fiction.

Associated Companies:
Hughes Massie Ltd

4002

THE AMPERSAND AGENCY LTD
Ryman's Cottages, Little Tew, Oxon OX7 4JJ
Telephone: 01608 683677 & 683898
Fax: 01608 683449
Email: peter@theampersandagency.co.uk
Web Site: http://
www.theampersandagency.co.uk

Directors: Peter Buckman *(Managing)*
Anne-Marie Doulton *(Editor)*
Consultants: Peter Janson-Smith
Patrick Neale

All MSS except poetry, science fiction, fantasy or illustrated children's books.

Specialization: literary and commercial fiction and non-fiction for all markets. A full range of services including foreign and media rights is offered. Member of the Association of Authors' Agents.

Overseas Representation:
Worldwide: The Buckman Agency, Oxford

4003

DARLEY ANDERSON LITERARY, TV & FILM AGENCY
Estelle House, 11 Eustace Road, London SW6 1JB
Telephone: (020) 7385 6652
Fax: (020) 7386 5571
Email: enquiries@darleyanderson.com
Web Site: http://www.darleyanderson.com

Sole Proprietor: Darley Anderson

Associate Agents: Zoë King
Camilla Bolton
Film & TV: Steve Fisher
Managers: Madeleine Buston *(Rights)*
Ella Andrews *(Agency)*

All MSS except short stories, academic or poetry.

Specialization: fiction: all types of thrillers & all types of fiction including contemporary, 20th century romantic sagas, women in jeopardy; also crime (cosy/hard-boiled/historical), horror, comedy & Irish novels; popular culture; non-fiction: celebrity autobiographies, biographies, 'true life' women in jeopardy, popular psychology, self-improvement, diet, health, beauty & fashion, gardening, cookery, inspirational & religious, and children's fiction.

Overseas Representation:
Bulgaria: Anthea Literary Agency, Sofia
China & Taiwan: Jia-Xi Books
Czech & Slovak Republics: Andrew Nurnberg Associates, Prague
Germany: Thomas Schlück Literary Agency, Garbsen
Greece: O A Literary Agency, Markopoulo, Athens
Hungary: Kàtai & Bolza Literary Agents, Budapest
Israel: I. Pikarski Literary Agency, Tel Aviv
Italy: Natoli, Stefan & Oliva Agenzia Letteraria, Milan
Japan: The English Agency Japan Ltd, Tokyo; Japan Uni Agency, Tokyo; Tuttle-Mori Agency Inc, Tokyo
Korea: EYA, Seoul
Netherlands: Jan Michael, Amsterdam
Poland: Graal Ltd, Warsaw
Romania: International Copyright Agency, Bucharest
Russia: Synopsis Literary Agency, Moscow
Scandinavia: Jan Michael, Amsterdam
Turkey: Akcali Copyright Agency, Istanbul; ONK Agency Ltd, Istanbul
USA: Darley Anderson Books, London; Helen Breitwieser, Cornerstone Literary Agency, Los Angeles, CA; Liza Dawson Associates, New York, NY
USA (for film): Steve Fisher APA Talent & Literary Agency, Los Angeles, CA

4004

ANNETTE GREEN AUTHORS' AGENCY
1 East Cliff Road, Tunbridge Wells, Kent TN4 9AD
Telephone: 01892 514275
Fax: 01892 558262
Email: david@annettegreenagency.co.uk
Web Site: http://
www.annettegreenagency.co.uk

Partners: Annette Green
David Smith

All MSS except sci-fi or fantasy, young children's, poetry or dramatic scripts.

Specialization: literary and commercial fiction, general non-fiction & young adult.

Rights Representative in UK for:
USA: Laura Langlie Literary Agent, Brooklyn, New York, NY

Overseas Representation:
USA: Laura Langlie Literary Agent, Brooklyn, New York, NY

4005

AQUARIUS LIBRARY
[a division of SPM London Ltd]
PO Box 5, 136 Emmanuel Road, Hastings TN34 3ZY
Telephone: 01424 721196
Fax: 01424 717704
Email: aquarius.lib@clara.net
Web Site: http://
www.aquariuscollection.com

Postal Address:
PO Box 5, Hastings, East Sussex TN34 1HR
Telephone: 01424 721196
Fax: 01424 717704
Email: aquarius.lib@clara.net
Web Site: http://
www.aquariuscollection.com

Directors: Gilbert Gibson *(Managing)*
David Corkill *(Picture Library)*

Specialization: Hollywood candid photography, film stills (old & new, colour & b/w), showbusiness personalities and all other aspects of international showbusiness and mass entertainment.

Parent Company:
Sun-Pacific Music (London) Ltd

Associated Companies:
UK: Aquarius Collection Ltd

4006

ARTELLUS LTD
30 Dorset House, Gloucester Place, London NW1 5AD
Telephone: (020) 7935 6972
Fax: (020) 7487 5957
Web Site: http://www.artellusltd.co.uk

Director: Leslie Gardner
Associate: Darryl Samaraweera *(Company Secretary)*
Chair: Gabriele Pantucci

All MSS except film scripts.

Specialization: speculative fiction, thrillers, non-fiction – commercial and literary, self-help, history, science. Selective readers service on request.

Rights Representative in UK for:
Eastern Europe: Prava i Prevodi, Belgrade
Far East: Big Apple Tuttle-Mori Agency Inc, Shanghai
Spain & Portugal: Carmen Balcells Agencia Literaria SA, Barcelona

4007

TASSY BARHAM ASSOCIATES
23 Elgin Crescent, London W11 2JD
Telephone: (020) 7229 8667
Fax: (020) 7229 8667
Email: tassy@tassybarham.com

Agent: Tassy Barham

Specialization: Brazil. Representing European and American agencies and publishers in Brazil, and Portuguese-language writers into the UK.

4008

LORELLA BELLI LITERARY AGENCY (LBLA)
54 Hartford House, 35 Tavistock Crescent, Notting Hill, London W11 1AY
Telephone: (020) 7727 8547
Fax: 0870 787 4194
Email: info@lorellabelliagency.com
Web Site: http://
www.lorellabelliagency.com

Proprietor: Lorella Belli

All MSS except children's books, science fiction, fantasy, academic, poetry, original scripts. No reading fee. May suggest revision.

Specialization: general fiction and non-fiction (particularly interested in first-time writers, commercial women's fiction, crime/thrillers, international and multicultural writing, journalists, books on/about Italy). Clients range from commercial fiction to literary fiction to a number of non-fiction writers and journalists. Also represents European, Canadian, Australian and American agencies in the UK and abroad. Commission: 15% home; 20% overseas and dramatic rights. Works with co-agents abroad; film & TV rights handled by an associate agency.

Rights Representative in UK for:
Australia: Calidris Literary Agency, Goulburn, NSW

4009 / AUTHORS' AGENTS

USA: Paula Balzer Literary Agency, New York, NY; Imprint Agency, New York, NY; Sarah Lazin Books, New York, NY; Mildred Marmur Associates, Larchmont, NY

4009

BLAKE FRIEDMANN LITERARY AGENCY LTD
122 Arlington Road, London NW1 7HP
Telephone: (020) 7284 0408
Fax: (020) 7284 0442
Email: "firstname"@blakefriedmann.co.uk
Web Site: http://www.blakefriedmann.co.uk

Directors & Agents: Carole Blake *(Book Sales)*
Julian Friedmann *(Film & TV)*
Isobel Dixon *(Book Sales)*
Film, TV & Radio Sales: Conrad Williams
Accounts Manager: Adrian Clark
Agent: Oli Munson *(Book Sales)*

All MSS except science fiction, plays, poetry & short stories (excluding existing clients).

Specialization: placing book rights internationally; film, television & radio rights.

Overseas Representation:
Bulgaria: Anthea Literary Agency, Sofia
China, Taiwan & Hong Kong: Andrew Nurnberg Literary Agency, Taipei; Andrew Nurnberg Associates, Beijing
Czech Republic: Dilia (Czechoslovak Theatrical & Literary Agency), Prague
France: La Nouvelle Agence, Paris
Germany: Liepman AG, Zurich
Hungary: Kàtai & Bolza, Literary Agents, Budapest
Italy: Natoli, Stefan & Oliva Agenzia Letteraria, Milan
Japan: The English Agency Japan Ltd, Tokyo
Korea: KCC International Ltd, Seoul
Poland: Graal Ltd, Warsaw
Romania: S. Kessler International Copyright Agency, Bucharest
Russia: Andrew Nurnberg Associates, Moscow
Scandinavia: Leonhardt & Hoier Literary Agency, Copenhagen
Spain, Brazil & Portugal: MB Associates
USA, Canada, Greece & Turkey: Blake Friedmann Literary Agency, London

4010

LUIGI BONOMI ASSOCIATES LTD
91 Great Russell Street, London WC1B 3PS
Telephone: (020) 7637 1234
Fax: (020) 7637 2111
Email: info@bonomiassociates.co.uk
Web Site: http://www.bonomiassociates.co.uk

Directors: Luigi Bonomi
Amanda Preston
Literary Agent: Molly Stirling
Administration Assistant: Ajda Vucicevic

All MSS except poetry, children's stories or adult science fiction/fantasy.

Specialization: fiction: commercial and literary fiction, thrillers, crime, women's fiction. Non-fiction: history, science, parenting, lifestyle, diet, health, TV tie-ins. Keen to find new authors and help them develop their careers. Send preliminary letter, synopsis and first three chapters. No reading fee. Will suggest revision. Works with foreign agencies and has links with TV presenters' agencies and production companies. Authors include James Barrington, Chris Beardshaw, Gennaro Contaldo, Nick Foulkes, David Gibbins, Richard Hammond, Jane Hill, John Humphrys, Graham Joyce, Simon Kernick, Colin McDowell, Dr Gillian McKeith, Richard Madeley and Judy Finnigan, James May, Nicola Monaghan, Mike Morley, Sue Palmer, Andrew Pepper, Melanie Phillips, Jem Poster, Esther Rantzen, John Rickards, Mike Rossiter, Catherine Sampson, Prof Bryan Sykes, Mitch Symons, Alan Titchmarsh, Martin Townsend, Sir Terry Wogan, Sally Worboyes. Founded 2005. Fiction and non-fiction (home 15%, overseas 20%).

Overseas Representation:
Worldwide: Intercontinental Literary Agency, London

4011

*ALAN BRODIE REPRESENTATION LTD
6th Floor, Fairgate House,
78 New Oxford Street, London WC1A 1HB
Telephone: (020) 7079 7990
Fax: (020) 7079 7999
Email: info@alanbrodie.com
Web Site: http://www.alanbrodie.com

Directors: Alan Brodie
Sarah McNair
Alison Lee
Agent: Lisa Foster

All MSS except unsolicited MSS - must have recommendation from a professional. No novels, short stories, etc.

Specialization: plays & dramatic works.

4012

JENNY BROWN ASSOCIATES
33 Argyle Place, Edinburgh EH9 1JT
Telephone: 0131 229 5334
Email: jenny@jennybrownassociates.com
Web Site: http://www.jennybrownassociates.com

Agents: Jenny Brown
Mark Stanton
Lucy Juckes *(Children's)*
Allan Guthrie

All MSS except academic, poetry, science fiction, horror & fantasy. Submissions: send letter, synopsis, CV, sample chapters and SAE.

Specialization: non-fiction (including sport & music) and literary fiction (including crime & thrillers). Most of the agency's clients are based in Scotland, but the company represents writers from all over the UK, and sells their work worldwide.

Overseas Representation:
Worldwide: The Marsh Agency, London

4013

FELICITY BRYAN
2a North Parade, Banbury Road, Oxford OX2 6LX
Telephone: 01865 513816
Fax: 01865 310055
Email: agency@felicitybryan.com
Web Site: http://www.felicitybryan.com

Directors: Felicity Bryan
Catherine Clarke

All MSS except science fiction, fantasy, romance.

Specialization: adult fiction & general non-fiction, history & popular science, children 8–12 upwards.

Overseas Representation:
China: Big Apple Tuttle-Mori Agency Inc, Shanghai
Europe, Russia & China: Andrew Nurnberg Associates, London
Japan: Japan Uni Agency, Tokyo; Tuttle-Mori Agency Inc, Tokyo
Korea: EYA, Seoul

4014

THE BUCKMAN AGENCY
Ryman's Cottage, Little Tew, Oxford OX7 4JJ
Telephone: 01608 683677
Fax: 01608 683449
Email: r.buckman@talk21.com & j.buckman@talk21.com

Also at:
Jessica Buckman, 118 Effra Road, Wimbledon, London SW19 8PR
Telephone: (020) 8544 2674
Fax: (020) 8543 9653

Partners: Rosemarie Buckman *(Literary Agent)*
Jessica Buckman *(Literary Agent)*

Specialization: handling of translation rights in all foreign rights markets for fiction and non-fiction, working on behalf of UK and US agencies.

4015

BRIE BURKEMAN
14 Neville Court, Abbey Road, London NW8 9DD
Telephone: 0870 199 5002
Fax: 0870 199 1029
Email: brie.burkeman@mail.com

Proprietor: Brie Burkeman
Agent: Isabel White

All MSS except academic, text, poetry, short stories, musicals or short films. No reading fee but return postage essential. Unsolicited e-mail attachments will be deleted without opening.

Specialization: commercial and literary full-length fiction and non-fiction books, as well as full length scripts for film and theatre. Worldwide representation, works with sub-agents where necessary. Also associated with Serafina Clarke Ltd and independent film and TV consultant to literary agents and publishers. Commission: 15% home, 20% overseas. Member of AAA and PMA.

Overseas Representation:
Worldwide: The Buckman Agency, Oxford

4016

CAMPBELL THOMSON & MCLAUGHLIN LTD
50 Albermarle Street, London W1S 4BD
Telephone: (020) 7493 4361
Fax: (020) 7495 8961
Email: cbruton@ctmcl.co.uk
Web Site: http://www.ctmcl.co.uk

Director: Paul Marsh *(Managing)*
Agent: Charlotte Bruton
Consultant: John McLaughlin

All MSS except children's, poetry, SF; book length MSS only.

Associated Companies:
Peter Janson-Smith Ltd

Rights Representative in UK for:
USA: The Fox Chase Agency Inc, Chesterbrook, PA; Raines & Raines Agency, Medusa, NY

Overseas Representation:
Worldwide (all translation rights): The Marsh Agency, London

4017

CASAROTTO RAMSAY & ASSOCIATES LTD
Waverley House, 7–12 Noel Street, London W1F 8GQ
Telephone: (020) 7287 4450
Fax: (020) 7287 9128
Email: agents@casarotto.co.uk
Web Site: http://www.casarotto.uk.com

Directors: Giorgio Casarotto
Tom Erhardt
Jenne Casarotto
Mel Kenyon
Sara Pritchard
Charlotte Kelly
Jodi Shields
Rachel Holroyd

Specialization: film scripts, TV scripts, play scripts, radio scripts only after preliminary letter. No books.

4018

CHAPMAN & VINCENT
7 Dilke Street, London SW3 4JE
Telephone: (020) 7352 5582
Fax: 01763 243033
Email: chapmanvincent@hotmail.co.uk

Directors: Jennifer Chapman
Gilly Vincent

Specialization: non-fiction only. Please do not submit by fax. Write with two sample chapters and SAE. E-mail submissions without attachments can be considered. A small agency whose clients come mainly from personal recommendation. The agency aims to look after only a small number of writers and is not actively seeking clients but happy to consider really original work. Clients include George Carter, Leslie Geddes-Brown, Lucinda Lambton, Rowley Leigh and Eve Pollard. Commission: Home 15%; US & Europe 20%. Member of the Association of Authors' Agents.

Overseas Representation:
USA: Elaine Markson Literary Agency, New York, NY

4019

MARY CLEMMEY LITERARY AGENCY
6 Dunollie Road, London NW5 2XP
Telephone: (020) 7267 1290
Fax: (020) 7813 9757
Email: mcwords@googlemail.com

Literary Agent: Mary Clemmey

All MSS except science fiction, horror, fantasy, poetry or children's books. No unsolicited e-mail submissions.

Specialization: fiction and non-fiction, high quality work with an international market. TV, film, radio and theatre scripts from existing clients only. Please approach only by preliminary letter and synopsis (SAE essential for response).

Rights Representative in UK for:
USA: Betsy Amster Literary Enterprises, Los Angeles, CA; Lynn C. Franklin Associates Ltd, New York, NY; Frederick Hill Bonnie Nadell Associates Literary Agency, San Francisco, CA; The Miller Agency, New York, NY; Roslyn Targ Literary Agency Inc, New York, NY; The Weingel Fidel Agency, New York, NY

Overseas Representation:
USA: Elaine Markson Literary Agency, New York, NY

4020

ELSPETH COCHRANE PERSONAL MANAGEMENT
16 Trinity Close, The Pavement, London SW4 0JD
Telephone: (020) 7622 3566
Email: elspethcochrane@talktalk.net

Directors: Elspeth Cochrane *(Managing)*
Tony Barlow

Specialization: fiction, non-fiction, biographies, screenplays. Subjects have included Richard Burton, Marlon Brando, Sean Connery, Clint Eastwood, Lord Olivier. Also scripts for all media, with special interest in drama. No unsolicited MSS. Preliminary letter, synopsis and SAE are essential in the first instance. Clients include Royce Ryton, Robert Tanitch. Commission: 12.5%.

4021

ROSICA COLIN LTD
1 Clareville Grove Mews, London SW7 5AH
Telephone: (020) 7370 1080
Fax: (020) 7244 6441

All MSS except poetry. No unsolicited submissions please.

Specialization: theatre, film, television, radio & foreign rights.

4022

JANE CONWAY-GORDON LTD
1 Old Compton Street, London W1D 5JA
Telephone: (020) 7494 0148
Fax: (020) 7287 9264
Email: jconway_gordon@dsl.pipex.com

Company Director: Jane Conway-Gordon

All MSS except science fiction, poetry, children's, short pieces; return postage essential.

Overseas Representation:
Europe (excluding Germany & France): Intercontinental Literary Agency, London
France: La Nouvelle Agence, Paris
Germany: Liepman AG, Zurich
USA: Lyons Literary LLC, New York, NY

4023

COOMBS MOYLETT LITERARY AGENCY
3 Askew Road, London W12 9AA
Telephone: (020) 8740 0454
Email: lisa.moylett@btopenworld.com

Proprietor: Lisa Moylett
Editor: Juliet van Oss
Submissions: Victoria Ross

All MSS except science fiction, poetry or children's.

Specialization: commercial and literary fiction and non-fiction. Special interests in fiction are thrillers, crime/mystery; women's literary and contemporary and in non-fiction: biography; history and current affairs. The agency is particularly interested in finding and developing new talent. Services include the selling of subsidiary rights such as film & TV and translation. The agency has good relations with US publishers and is represented in both Japan by Tuttle Mori and in Germany by the Michael Meller Literary Agency. Guidelines for submission: first three chapters, a short synopsis and SAE (essential for the return of material). No e-mail or disc submissions.

Overseas Representation:
Germany: Michael Meller Literary Agency, Munich
Japan: Tuttle-Mori Agency Inc, Tokyo

4024

RUPERT CREW LTD
[International Literary Representation]
1a King's Mews, London WC1N 2JA
Telephone: (020) 7242 8586
Fax: (020) 7831 7914
Email: info@rupertcrew.co.uk
Web Site: http://www.rupertcrew.co.uk

Founder: F. Rupert Crew
Joint Managing Directors: Doreen Montgomery *(Chairman)*
Caroline Montgomery *(Company Secretary)*

All MSS except science fiction, fantasy, short stories, poetry, film & TV scripts.

Specialization: international business management for authors desiring world representation. Preliminary letter with SAE required. Also acts as publishers' consultants.

Overseas Representation:
China: Big Apple Tuttle-Mori Agency Inc, Shanghai
Eastern Europe: Andrew Nurnberg Associates, London
France: Eliane Benisti, Paris
Germany: Paul & Peter Fritz AG Literary Agency, Zurich
Hungary: Kàtai & Bolza Literary Agents, Budapest
Italy: Agenzia Letteraria Internazionale srl, Milan
Japan: The English Agency Japan Ltd, Tokyo; Tuttle-Mori Agency Inc, Tokyo
Scandinavia & Spain: Sane Töregård Agency, Karlshamn
Taiwan: Big Apple Tuttle-Mori Associates, Shin-Juang
USA: The Martell Agency, New York, NY
Worldwide (Film/TV): MBA Literary Agents, London

4025

*CURTIS BROWN
Haymarket House, 28–29 Haymarket, London SW1Y 4SP
Telephone: (020) 7393 4400
Fax: (020) 7393 4401/2
Email: cb@curtisbrown.co.uk
Web Site: http://www.curtisbrown.co.uk

Directors: Jonathan Lloyd *(Chief Executive Officer)*
Fiona Inglis *(Australia)*
Jonny Geller *(Managing – Book Division)*
Nick Marston *(Managing – Media Division)*
Ben Hall *(Operations)*
Jacquie Drewe
Agents: Carol Jackson *(Rights)*
Camilla Hornby
Vivienne Schuster
Gordon Wise
Elizabeth Scheinkman
Jonny Pegg
Janice Swanson

All MSS except short stories & poetry.

Specialization: negotiation in all publishing markets; and television, film & dramatic writing, directing, presenting & acting.

Associated Companies:
Australia: Curtis Brown (Australia) Pty Ltd

Rights Representative in UK for:
USA: Gelfman Schneider Literary Agents Inc, New York, NY

4026

FELIX DE WOLFE LTD
Kingsway House, 103 Kingsway, London WC2B 6QX
Telephone: (020) 7242 5066
Fax: (020) 7242 8119
Email: info@felixdewolfe.com

Director: Caroline de Wolfe

All MSS except non-fiction, children's.

Overseas Representation:
France: Michelle Lapautre, Paris
Italy: Liepman AG, Zurich

4027

DORIAN LITERARY AGENCY
Upper Thornehill, 27 Church Road, St Marychurch, Torquay, Devon TQ1 4QY
Telephone: 01803 312095

Proprietor: Dorothy Lumley

All MSS except children's, poetry, plays or technical.

Specialization: all types of fiction for adults.

Rights Representative in UK for:
USA: Fedogan & Bremer Publishers, Minneapolis, MN

Overseas Representation:
China: Big Apple Tuttle-Mori Agency Inc, Shanghai
France: Agence Litteraire Lenclud, Paris
Germany: Thomas Schlück Literary Agency, Garbsen
Hungary: Prava i Prevodi, Budapest
Italy: Agenzia Letteraria Internazionale Srl, Milan
Japan (non-exclusive): The English Agency Japan Ltd, Tokyo; Japan Uni Agency Inc, Tokyo; Tuttle-Mori Agency Inc, Tokyo
Korea: EYA, Seoul
Netherlands: Dorian Literary Agency, Devon
Poland & East Europe: Prava i Prevodi, Belgrade
Russia: Projex International, Moscow
Scandinavia: A/S Bookman Literary Agency, Copenhagen
South Africa: International Press Agency Pty Ltd, Ndabeni
Spain: Raquel de la Concha, Madrid
Taiwan: Big Apple Tuttle-Mori Agency, Taipei
Turkey: Asli Karasuil Agency, Istanbul

4028

ROBERT DUDLEY AGENCY
8 Abbotstone Road, London SW15 1QR
Telephone: (020) 8788 0938
Fax: (020) 8780 3586
Email: rdudley@btinternet.com
Web Site: http://www.robertdudleyagency.co.uk

Agent: Robert Dudley

All MSS except film scripts.

Specialization: Robert Dudley Agency looks after a variety of authors of both fiction and non-fiction. Non-fiction subjects include sport, management, history, militaria, politics, health and well-being, travel, biography, film and archaeology.

Parent Company:
Bowerdean Publishing Co Ltd

4029

EDWARDS FUGLEWICZ
49 Great Ormond Street, London WC1N 3HZ
Telephone: (020) 7405 6725
Fax: (020) 7405 6726
Email: info@efla.co.uk

Partners: Ros Edwards
Helenka Fuglewicz

All MSS except children's books, science fiction, fantasy or horror. No unsolicited MSS.

Specialization: fiction and non-fiction: biography, history, and popular culture. Founded in 1996.

Rights Representative in UK for:
Republic of Ireland: Poolbeg Press, Dublin
UK: The Bodleian Library, Oxford

4030

FAITH EVANS ASSOCIATES
27 Park Avenue North, London N8 7RU
Telephone: (020) 8340 9920
Fax: (020) 8340 9410
Email: faith@faith-evans.co.uk

Specialization: Small agency. No phone calls or unsolicited MSS.

4031

FOX & HOWARD LITERARY AGENCY
4 Bramerton Street, Chelsea, London SW3 5JX
Telephone: (020) 7352 8691
Fax: (020) 7352 8691

Agents: Chelsey Fox
Charlotte Howard

Specialization: general non-fiction: biography, history and popular culture, reference, business, mind, body and spirit, health (home 15%, overseas 20%). No reading fee, but preliminary letter and synopsis with SAE essential. Founded 1992.

4032

FRASER ROSS ASSOCIATES
6 Wellington Place, Edinburgh EH6 7EQ
Telephone: 0131 553 2759
Email: lindsey.fraser@tiscali.co.uk
Web Site: http://www.fraserross.co.uk

Also at:
Telephone: 0131 657 4412
Email: kjross@tiscali.co.uk

Partners: Lindsey Fraser
Kathryn Ross

All MSS except poetry, short stories & science fiction.

Specialization: representing writers and illustrators for children's books, and writers for adults (home 10–15%, overseas 20%). Send the first three chapters (or equivalent), a synopsis, CV and covering letter. Return postage is essential. Current clients include Thomas Bloor, Chris Fisher, Tanya Landman, Vivian French, Dugald Steer and Jamie Rix.

4033

JÜRI GABRIEL
35 Camberwell Grove, London SE5 8JA
Telephone: (020) 7703 6186
Email: Juri@JuriGabriel.com

Proprietor: Jüri Gabriel

All MSS except screenplays, tele or radio scripts (only handles performance rights in existing works for existing clients); science fantasy; children's books, poetry, short stories or articles.

Specialization: literary fiction, popular academic and anything that combines intellect, originality and wit. In first instance please send a two page synopsis, three sample chapters, a brief c.v. and return postage if you want the material back. No submissions by fax or e-mail. Clients include Maurice Caldera, Diana Constance, Miriam Dunne, Matt Fox, Paul Genney, Pat Gray, Mikka Haugaard, Robert Irwin, John Lucas, David Madsen, Richard Mankiewicz, Karina Mellinger, David Miller, Andy Oakes, John Outram, Phil Roberts, Roger Storey, Dr Stefan Szymanski, Dr Terence White, Dr Robert Youngson. Commission: home 10%, US & translation 20%.

4034 ∎

DAVID GODWIN ASSOCIATES
55 Monmouth Street, London WC2H 9DG
Telephone: (020) 7240 9992
Fax: (020) 7395 6110
Web Site: http://
www.davidgodwinassociates.co.uk

Literary Agent: David Godwin
Company Secretary: Heather Godwin
Managers: Kirsty McLachlan *(Film & TV Rights)*
Kerry Glencourse *(Foreign & US Rights)*

All MSS except science fiction & children's.

Specialization: UK, US and translation rights, TV & film.

4035 ∎

GRAHAM MAW CHRISTIE
19 Thornhill Crescent, London N1 1BJ
Telephone: (020) 7737 4766
Email: enquiries@grahammawchristie.com
Web Site: http://
www.grahammawchristie.com

Directors: Jane Graham Maw
Jennifer Christie

All MSS except fiction, children's or poetry.

Specialization: literary agents for general non-fiction: autobiography/memoir, business, web-to-book, food and drink, health, lifestyle, parenting, personal development, popular culture, reference, TV tie-in. No reading fee. Will suggest revision. See website for guidance on submissions.

4036 ∎

LOUISE GREENBERG BOOKS LTD
The End House, Church Crescent, London N3 1BG
Telephone: (020) 8349 1179
Fax: (020) 8343 4559
Email: louisegreenberg@msn.com

All MSS except sport, leisure, poetry, children's. No telephone approaches from authors.

Specialization: full length literary fiction and serious non-fiction. Screen work for book clients only.

Associated Companies:
UK: Sarah Manson Literary Agents [Children's Books]

Rights Representative in UK for:
USA: Rosalie Siegel International Literary Agent, Penington, NJ

4037 ∎

GREENE & HEATON LTD
37 Goldhawk Road, London W12 8QQ
Telephone: (020) 8749 0315
Fax: (020) 8749 0318
Email: info@greeneheaton.co.uk
Web Site: http://www.greeneheaton.co.uk

Directors: Carol Heaton
Charles Elliott *(Company Secretary)*
Judith Murray
Antony Topping

All MSS except plays, TV & film-scripts, articles & poetry, stories (other than from existing clients), science fiction or fantasy. Preliminary letter and return postage required.

Rights Representative in UK for:
Canada: The Cooke Agency, Toronto, Ont
USA: Jean V. Naggar Literary Agency, New York, NY; The Sagalyn Literary Agency, Bethesda, MD; Denise Shannon Literary Agency, New York, NY

Overseas Representation:
Canada: The Cooke Agency, Toronto, Ont
France: VVV Agency, Paris
German-speaking countries: Paul & Peter Fritz AG Literary Agency, Zurich; Liepman AG, Zurich
Italy: Antonella Antonelli Agenzia Letteraria, Milan
Japan: Tuttle-Mori Agency Inc, Tokyo
Netherlands, Eastern Europe & Russia: Andrew Nurnberg Associates, London
Scandinavia: The Buckman Agency, Oxford
Spain: Carmen Balcells Agencia Literaria SA, Barcelona
USA: Jean V. Naggar Literary Agency, New York, NY; Denise Shannon Literary Agency, New York, NY

4038 ∎

GREGORY & COMPANY AUTHORS' AGENTS
3 Barb Mews, London W6 7PA
Telephone: (020) 7610 4676
Fax: (020) 7610 4686
Email: info@gregoryandcompany.co.uk
Web Site: http://
www.gregoryandcompany.co.uk

Proprietor: Jane Gregory
Editorial: Stephanie Glencross
Rights: Claire Morris
Jemma McDonagh
Accounts: Terry Bland

All MSS except children's, juvenile, academic & technical books, poetry & plays, TV & film scripts, science fiction, short stories. Preliminary letter with synopsis, first three chapters and SAE essential.

Specialization: fiction: commercial, crime, literary, suspense and thrillers. Editorial advice given to own authors. Film & TV rights for own published authors only, no original scripts.

Associated Companies:
The Jane Gregory Agency

Overseas Representation:
Brazil: Tassy Barham Associates, London
Bulgaria: Interrights Literary & Translation Agency, Sofia
China: Big Apple Tuttle-Mori Associates, Shin-Juang
Croatia: Zvonimir Majdak, Zagreb
Czech Republic & Slovakia: Andrew Nurnberg Associates, Prague
France: La Nouvelle Agence, Paris
Hungary: Lex Copyright, Budapest
Israel: Ilana Pikarski, Tel Aviv
Japan: Japan Uni Agency Inc, Tokyo; Tuttle-Mori Agency Inc, Tokyo
Korea: EYA, Seoul
Poland: Andrew Nurnberg Associates, Warsaw
Romania: Simona Kessler International Copyright Agency Ltd, Bucharest
Russia: Andrew Nurnberg Associates, Moscow
Scandinavia: Leonhardt & Hoier Literary Agency, Copenhagen
Spain: Carmen Balcells Agencia Literaria SA, Barcelona
Turkey: Akcali Copyright Trade & Tourism Co Ltd, Istanbul

4039 ∎

ANTONY HARWOOD LTD
103 Walton Street, Oxford OX2 6EB
Telephone: 01865 559615
Fax: 01865 310660
Email: mail@antonyharwood.com
Web Site: http://
www.antonyharwood.com

Agents: Antony Harwood
James MacDonald Lockhart

All MSS except screenwriting, poetry or children's fiction for readers aged 10 or younger.

Specialization: handles fiction and non-fiction. Founded 2000.

4040 ∎

A. M. HEATH & CO LTD
6 Warwick Court, London WC1R 5DJ
Telephone: (020) 7242 2811
Fax: (020) 7242 2711
Web Site: http://www.amheath.com

Directors: William Hamilton *(Managing)*
Sara Fisher *(Company Secretary)*
Victoria Hobbs
Agents: Sarah Molloy *(Children's)*
Euan Thorneycroft

All MSS except plays, scripts, poetry, scientific, technical for the layman only.

Rights Representative in UK for:
USA: Miriam Altshuler Literary Agency, Red Hook, NY; Brandt & Hochman Inc, New York, NY; Jane Chelius Literary Agency, Brooklyn, NY; Lescher & Lescher Ltd, New York, NY; Gina Maccoby Literary Agency, New York, NY; Russell & Volkening Inc, New York, NY

Overseas Representation:
Brazil: Tassy Barham, London
Bulgaria & Serbia: Andrew Nurnberg Literary Agency, Sofia
China & Taiwan: Andrew Nurnberg Literary Agency, Shanghai; Andrew Nurnberg Literary Agency, Taipei
Czech & Slovak Republics & Slovenia: Andrew Nurnberg Associates, Prague
France: La Nouvelle Agence, Paris
Germany, Switzerland & Austria: Mohrbooks Literary Agency, Zurich
Hungary & Croatia: Andrew Nurnberg Ltd, Budapest
Israel: Deborah Harris Agency, Jerusalem
Italy: Luigi Bernabó Associates Srl, Milan
Japan: Tuttle-Mori Agency Inc, Tokyo
Korea: EYA, Seoul
Netherlands: Van Gelderen Literary Agency, Amsterdam
Poland: ANAW Literary Agency, Warsaw
Romania: Simona Kessler International Copyright Agency Ltd, Bucharest
Russia: Andrew Nurnberg Associates, Moscow
Scandinavia: Licht & Burr Literary Agency, Copenhagen
Spain: MB Agency, Barcelona
Thailand: Big Apple Tuttle Mori Agency (Thailand) Co Ltd, Bangkok
Turkey, Greece, Indonesia, Portugal, Latvia, Lithuania & Estonia: A. M. Heath & Co Ltd, London

4041 ∎

DAVID HIGHAM ASSOCIATES
5–8 Lower John Street, Golden Square, London W1F 9HA
Telephone: (020) 7434 5900
Fax: (020) 7437 1072
Email: dha@davidhigham.co.uk
Web Site: http://www.davidhigham.co.uk

Specialization: agents for the negotiation of all rights in fiction, general non-fiction, children's fiction and picture books, plays, film and TV scripts. Represented in all foreign markets. Preliminary letter and return postage essential. No reading fee. Founded 1935.

4042 ∎

KATE HORDERN LITERARY AGENCY
18 Mortimer Road, Clifton, Bristol BS8 4EY
Telephone: 0117 923 9368
Email: katehordern@blueyonder.co.uk

Proprietor: Kate Hordern

All MSS except children's books.

Specialization: quality literary and commercial fiction, including women's fiction, suspense and genre fiction, and general non-fiction. Clients include Jeff Dawson, Richard Bassett, J. T. Lees, Will Randall, Leigh Eduardo, Duncan Hewitt, Kylie Fitzpatrick.

4043 ∎

VALERIE HOSKINS ASSOCIATES
20 Charlotte Street, London W1T 2NA
Telephone: (020) 7637 4490
Fax: (020) 7637 4493
Email: vha@vhassociates.co.uk

Managing Director: Valerie Hoskins
Agent: Rebecca Watson
Assistant: Georgina Paget

Specialization: film & television rights for published work. The company is not a publishing agency.

4044 ∎

*ICM BOOKS
4–6 Soho Square, London W1D 3PZ
Telephone: (020) 7432 0800
Fax: (020) 7432 0808
Web Site: http://www.icmtalent.com

Literary Agents: Kate Jones
Karolina Sutton

All MSS except plays or scripts. Submissions must include sample chapters and letter. No reading fee.

Parent Company:
USA: International Creative Management Inc

Rights Representative in UK for:
USA: International Creative Management Inc (ICM), New York, NY

4045 ∎

IMG UK LTD
McCormack House, Burlington Lane, London W4 2TH
Telephone: (020) 8233 5300
Fax: (020) 8233 5268
Email: sarah.wooldridge@imgworld.com
Web Site: http://www.imgworld.com

Consultant: Sarah Wooldridge
Accountant: Sally Matthews

All MSS except science fiction, fiction, children's, short stories and poetry.

Specialization: non-fiction. No reading fee. Please send synopsis with sample chapter and SAE. Also handle IMG speakers. 20% commission.

Associated Companies:
Worldwide: IMG

4046

THE INSPIRA GROUP
5 Bradley Road, Enfield, Middx EN3 6ES
Telephone: (020) 8292 5163
Fax: 0870 139 3057
Email: darin@theinspiragroup.com
Web Site: http://www.theinspiragroup.com

Managing Director: Darin Jewell
Rights: Shaun Ebelthite
Administration: Charlene Webber

Specialization: children's books, fantasy/sci-fi, and general fiction. Manuscripts in all genres are considered. Clients include Michael Tolkien, Simon Hall, John Wilson and Simon Brown. Authors should e-mail their full MSS, synopsis and short literary CV (with their postal address and landline tel. no.) to darin@theinspiragroup.com

4047

*INTERCONTINENTAL LITERARY AGENCY
Centric House, 390 Strand, London WC2R 0LT
Telephone: (020) 7379 6611
Fax: (020) 7240 4724
Email: ila@ila-agency.co.uk
Web Site: http://www.ila-agency.co.uk

Agents: Nicki Kennedy
  Sam Edenborough
  Mary Esdaile
  Tessa Girvan

Specialization: translation rights exclusively.

Rights Representative in UK for:
UK (translation): Peters Fraser & Dunlop Group
USA (translation): Harold Matson Co

4048

JANKLOW & NESBIT (UK) LTD
33 Drayson Mews, London W8 4LY
Telephone: (020) 7376 2733
Fax: (020) 7376 2915
Email: queries@janklow.co.uk

Literary Agents: Tif Loehnis
  Claire Paterson
  Jenny McVeigh
Foreign Rights: Rebecca Folland

All MSS except poetry, plays, film & TV scripts.

Specialization: fiction and non-fiction; commercial and literary. Send full outline (non-fiction), synopsis and first three sample chapters (fiction) plus informative covering letter and return postage.

Overseas Representation:
USA: Janklow & Nesbit Associates, New York, NY

4049

JOHNSON & ALCOCK LTD
Clerkenwell House,
45–47 Clerkenwell Green, London EC1R 0HT
Telephone: (020) 7251 0125
Fax: (020) 7251 2172
Email: info@johnsonandalcock.co.uk
Web Site: http://www.johnsonandalcock.co.uk

Directors: Andrew Hewson
  Michael Alcock
Agents: Anna Power
  Ed Wilson

All MSS except technical or academic material, poetry, plays, fantasy, horror. No unsolicited manuscripts; please send synopsis, full CV, sample opening chapters and SAE in the first instance. No reading fee.

Specialization: fiction and non-fiction. General non-fiction, mainly biography, history, current affairs, health and lifestyle; literary and commercial fiction; graphic novels.

Rights Representative in UK for:
USA: Soho Press, New York, NY

Overseas Representation:
Worldwide - contact: Johnson & Alcock Ltd, London

4050

JANE JUDD LITERARY AGENCY
18 Belitha Villas, London N1 1PD
Telephone: (020) 7607 0273
Fax: (020) 7607 0623
Web Site: http://www.janejudd.com

Proprietor: Jane C. Judd

All MSS except plays, poetry and short stories.

Specialization: general non-fiction & fiction.

Rights Representative in UK for:
USA: Mercury House, San Francisco, CA; Permanent Press, Sag Harbor, NY; RLR Associates, New York, NY; Chris Tomasino, New York, NY; Marian Young, New York, NY

Overseas Representation:
France: La Nouvelle Agence, Paris
Germany: Thomas Schlück Literary Agency, Garbsen
Italy: Stefania Fietta ALI, Milan
Netherlands & Scandinavia: Jan Michael, Amsterdam
Spain & Portugal: Julio F Yañez Literary Agency, Barcelona
USA: RLR Associates, New York, NY

4051

MICHELLE KASS ASSOCIATES
85 Charing Cross Road, London WC2H 0AA
Telephone: (020) 7439 1624
Fax: (020) 7734 3394
Email: office@michellekass.co.uk

Specialization: an agency representing novelists, writers and directors for film, TV and theatre.

4052

THE FRANCES KELLY AGENCY
111 Clifton Road, Kingston-upon-Thames, Surrey KT2 6PL
Telephone: (020) 8549 7830
Fax: (020) 8547 0051

Proprietor: Frances Kelly

Specialization: general non-fiction, all academic & professional disciplines; return postage & preliminary letter requested.

4053

KNIGHT FEATURES
20 Crescent Grove, London SW4 7AH
Telephone: (020) 7622 1467
Fax: (020) 7622 1522
Email: peter@knightfeatures.co.uk

Proprietor: Peter Knight
Associates: Gaby Martin
  Andrew Knight
  Samantha Ferris

All MSS except short stories, poetry & unsolicited MSS (reading fee). No e-mail submissions.

Specialization: worldwide selling of strip cartoons, major features and serializations. Exclusive syndication agent in UK & Irish Republic for United Feature Syndicate (Peanuts, Dilbert, etc.) & Newspaper Enterprise Association (Frank & Ernest, Born Loser, King Baloo, etc.), also Paws Inc (Garfield), Creators Syndicate (The Far Side).

Rights Representative in UK for:
New Zealand: The Puzzle Co
USA: Paws Inc; United Media Inc, New York, NY

4054

LENZ-MULLIGAN RIGHTS & CO-EDITIONS
15 Sandbourne Avenue, London SW19 3EW
Telephone: (020) 8543 7846
Email: lenzmulligan@btconnect.com

Rights Manager: Gundhild Lenz-Mulligan

All MSS except poetry and film scripts.

Specialization: sale of co-editions and rights in the Nordic countries and Dutch, English and German-speaking markets. Particularly interested in children's books. Also offers proofreading and translation services of German language material. Represents European, American and Australian publishers, packagers and authors.

Rights Representative in UK for:
Australia: Tracy Marsh Publications, West Beach, SA
Germany: Ars Edition
Netherlands: Forte Uitgevers, Utrecht; Image Books Factory, Eindhoven

4055

BARBARA LEVY LITERARY AGENCY
64 Greenhill, Hampstead High Street, London NW3 5TZ
Telephone: (020) 7435 9046
Fax: (020) 7431 2063

Associate: John F. Selby *(Solicitor)*

Specialization: general fiction & non-fiction, and TV presenters.

Rights Representative in UK for:
USA: Arcadia, Danbury, CT; Richard Parks, New York, NY

Overseas Representation:
Foreign Language Markets: The Buckman Agency, London
USA: Marshall Rights, London

4056

LIMELIGHT MANAGEMENT
33 Newman Street, London W1T 1PY
Telephone: (020) 7637 2529
Fax: (020) 7637 2538
Email: limelight.management@virgin.net
Web Site: http://www.limelightmanagement.com

Owner/Founder: Fiona Lindsay *(Managing Director)*
Agent: Mary Bekhait

Specialization: full-length and short MSS. Fiction and non-fiction. Food, wine, health, crafts, gardening, biography/memoirs, popular culture, travel, women's interest (home 15%, overseas 20%), TV and radio rights (15–20%); will suggest revision where appropriate. No reading fee.

4057

CHRISTOPHER LITTLE LITERARY AGENCY
10 Eel Brook Studios,
125 Moore Park Road, London SW6 4PS
Telephone: (020) 7736 4455
Fax: (020) 7736 4490
Email: info@christopherlittle.net
Web Site: http://www.christopherlittle.net

Proprietor: Christopher Little *(Agent)*
Agent: Patrick Janson-Smith

All MSS except poetry, plays, science fiction, fantasy, textbooks, illustrated children's or short stories. Film scripts for established clients only.

Specialization: full length commercial fiction and non-fiction. No reading fee. Send detailed letter plus synopsis and three sample chapters, and SAE in first instance.

4058

LONDON INDEPENDENT BOOKS
26 Chalcot Crescent, London NW1 8YD
Telephone: (020) 7706 0486
Fax: (020) 7724 3122

Literary Agent: Carolyn Whitaker

All MSS except computers & young children's.

Specialization: fiction & non-fiction, particularly travel & fantasy.

4059

ANDREW LOWNIE LITERARY AGENCY LTD
36 Great Smith Street, London SW1P 3BU
Telephone: (020) 7222 7574
Fax: (020) 7222 7576
Email: lownie@globalnet.co.uk
Web Site: http://www.andrewlownie.co.uk

Proprietor: Andrew Lownie

Specialization: non-fiction only. History, biography, packaging celebrities for book market and representing book projects for journalists. Titles agented include the Oxford Classical Dictionary, Cambridge Guide to Literature in English, Norma Major's books on Joan Sutherland and Chequers, Juliet Barker, Duncan Falconer, Laurence Gardner, Lawrence James, Damien Lewis, David Stafford, Alan Whicker, Sir John Mills, authorized lives of Sir Henry Cooper and Dick Emery, Desmond Seward, Daniel Tammet, Cathy Glass, Joyce Cary and Julian Maclaren - Ross Estates, numerous books about the SAS. Return postage essential. No reading fee. Commission 15% worldwide.

Overseas Representation:
Worldwide (excluding USA & Japan): The Marsh Agency, London

4060

LUTYENS & RUBINSTEIN
231 Westbourne Park Road, London W11 1EB
Telephone: (020) 7792 4855
Fax: (020) 7792 4833
Email: submissions@lutyensrubinstein.co.uk

Partners: Felicity Rubinstein
  Sarah Lutyens

All MSS except childrens' books, science fiction, fantasy, poetry, screenplays, scripts for theatre and/or TV and radio.

Specialization: general adult non-fiction and fiction.

Rights Representative in UK for:
Australia: Jenny Darling Associates, Vic; Text Publishing, Melbourne, Vic
USA: Rosenstone/Wender, New York, NY; Emma Sweeney Harold Ober Associates, New York, NY

Overseas Representation:
France: La Nouvelle Agence, Paris
Germany: Eggers & Landwehr, Berlin
Italy: Grandi & Associates, Milan
USA: Witherspoon Associates, New York, NY

4061

DUNCAN MCARA
28 Beresford Gardens, Edinburgh EH5 3ES
Telephone: 0131 552 1558
Email: duncanmcara@mac.com

All MSS except 'genre' fiction, educational & children's.

Specialization: literary fiction; non-fiction: art, architecture, archaeology, biography, history, military, Scottish. Home: 10%; Overseas: 20%. Preliminary letter with SAE essential. No reading fee. Also acts as editorial consultant on all aspects of general trade publishing. Editing, re-writing, copy-editing, proof correction for wide range of UK publishers.

4062

THE MCKERNAN LITERARY AGENCY & CONSULTANCY
5 Gayfield Square, Edinburgh EH1 3NW
Telephone: 0131 557 1771
Email: maggie@mckernanagency.co.uk
Web Site: http://www.mckernanagency.co.uk

Agent: Maggie McKernan

All MSS except film scripts, screenplays, picture books for children.

Specialization: assisting and developing writers, as well as representing their interests in their dealings with publishers, selling rights and handling negotiations of contracts. Handle fiction and non-fiction (commercial and literary novels of all kinds, including crime, historical, contemporary). Consideration will be given to novels for children over the age of 10, but not picture books.

Overseas Representation:
USA & Worldwide (translation rights): Capel & Land Ltd, London

4063

EUNICE MCMULLEN LTD
Low Ibbotsholme Cottage, off Bridge Lane, Troutbeck Bridge, Windermere, Cumbria LA23 1HU
Telephone: 01539 448551
Email: eunicemcmullen@totalise.co.uk
Web Site: http://www.eunicemcmullen.co.uk

Specialization: children's books (fiction only) for all ages including picture books for co-edition market and early teen fiction. No unsolicited MSS.

4064

ANDREW MANN LTD
1 Old Compton Street, London W1D 5JA
Telephone: (020) 7734 4751
Fax: (020) 7287 9264
Email: info@andrewmann.co.uk
Web Site: http://www.andrewmann.co.uk

Directors: Anne Dewe
Tina Betts

All MSS except poetry.

Specialization: fiction, general non-fiction & film/TV/radio scripts. No unsolicited MSS. Preliminary letter, synopsis - first 30 pages and SAE essential. No reading fee. No e-mail submissions, synopses only.

Rights Representative in UK for:
USA: Richard McDonough, Irvine, CA

Overseas Representation:
China (Mainland): Big Apple Tuttle-Mori Agency Inc, Shanghai
France: VVV Agency, Paris
Germany: Thomas Schlück Literary Agency, Garbsen
Hungary: Kàtai & Bolza Literary Agents, Budapest
Israel: Deborah Harris Agency, Jerusalem
Italy: Living Literary Agency, Milan
Japan: Tuttle-Mori Agency Inc, Tokyo
Korea: Shin Won Agency, Seoul
Poland, Bulgaria, Czech Republic & Slovakia: Andrew Nurnberg Associates, London
Romania: Simona Kessler International Copyright Agency Ltd, Bucharest
Russia: Author Rights Agency
Spain, Scandinavia, Portugal & Brazil: Sane Töregård Agency, Karlshamn
Taiwan: Big Apple Tuttle-Mori Associates, Shin-Juang
Thailand: Silk Road Agency, Bangkok
Turkey: Asli Karasuil Agency, Istanbul
USA: Jonathan Lyons, New York, NY

4065

SARAH MANSON LITERARY AGENT
6 Totnes Walk, London N2 0AD
Telephone: (020) 8442 0396
Email: info@sarahmanson.com
Web Site: http://www.sarahmanson.com

Proprietor: Sarah Manson

All MSS except poetry and picture books.

Specialization: fiction for children and young adults. List of clients includes both well-established writers and promising new talent.

4066

*MARJACQ SCRIPTS
34 Devonshire Place, London W1G 6JW
Telephone: (020) 7935 9499
Fax: (020) 7935 9115
Email: enquiries@marjacq.com
Web Site: http://www.marjacq.com

Agents: Philip Patterson (Literary)
Luke Speed (Film)

All MSS except poetry or stage plays.

Specialization: literary and commercial fiction, crime, thrillers, science fiction and women's fiction, and general non-fiction. Please submit three sample chapters and synopsis in first instance. SAE essential for return of MS.

Overseas Representation:
Austria, Germany, Switzerland & parts of Eastern Europe: Transnet Contracts Ltd, Vienna
France: VVV Agency, Paris
Hungary: Kàtai & Bolza Literary Agents, Budapest
Israel: Ilana Pikarski Literary Agency, Tel Aviv
Italy: Agenzia Piergiorgio Nicolazzini, Milan
Japan: The English Agency Japan Ltd, Tokyo
Poland: Graal Ltd, Warsaw
Russia: Prava i Prevodi RAO, Moscow
Scandinavia, Netherlands, Spain & Portugal: Lennart Sane Agency, Karlshamn

Turkey: Nurcihan Kesim Literary & Merchandising Agency, Istanbul

4067

THE MARSH AGENCY LTD
50 Albemarle Street, London W1S 4BD
Telephone: (020) 7493 4361
Fax: (020) 7495 8961
Email: enquiries@marsh-agency.co.uk
Web Site: http://www.marsh-agency.co.uk

Managing Director: Paul Marsh
Manager: Camilla Ferrier (Foreign Rights)
Agents: Geraldine Cooke
Jessica Woollard
Caroline Hardman

All MSS except children's, poetry, drama, TV, film & radio.

Specialization: selling of rights in the work of English-language writers throughout the world, representing a number of British and American agencies and publishers.

Parent Company:
UK: Campbell Thomson & McLaughlin Ltd

Associated Companies:
UK: Paterson Marsh Ltd

Rights Representative in UK for:
Worldwide: see Website for full list

4068

BLANCHE MARVIN
21a St Johns Wood High Street, London NW8 7NG
Telephone: (020) 7722 2313
Fax: (020) 7722 2313

Director: Blanche Marvin

Specialization: theatre, film, TV, radio & publishing for UK & USA. MSS from published authors only.

4069

MBA LITERARY AGENTS
62 Grafton Way, London W1T 5DW
Telephone: (020) 7387 2076
Fax: (020) 7387 2042
Email: firstname@mbalit.co.uk
Web Site: http://www.mbalit.co.uk

Directors: Diana Tyler (Managing)
John Richard Parker
Meg Davis
Timothy Webb (Financial)
Laura Longrigg

All MSS except poetry, short stories.

Specialization: fiction and non-fiction. Also scripts for film, TV, radio & theatre.

Rights Representative in UK for:
USA: Beacon Artists, New York, NY; Frances Collin Agency, New York, NY; Jabberwocky (Joshua Bilmes), Sunnyside, NY; Donald Maass Agency, New York, NY; Martha Millard Literary Agency, New York, NY

Overseas Representation:
Brazil: Tassy Barham, London
Eastern Europe: Prava i Prevodi, Belgrade
France: Lora Fountain Associates, Paris
Germany: Mohrbooks Literary Agency, Zurich; Thomas Schlück Literary Agency, Garbsen
Israel: I. Pikarski Literary Agency, Tel Aviv
Italy: Vicki Satlow Literary Agency, Milan
Japan: Tuttle-Mori Agency Inc, Tokyo
Netherlands: Caroline Van Gelderen Literary Agency, Hilversum
Russia: Prava i Prevodi RAO, Moscow
Scandinavia: Licht & Burr Literary Agency, Copenhagen

Spain: Carmen Balcells Agencia Literaria SA, Barcelona

4070

THE CATHY MILLER FOREIGN RIGHTS AGENCY
18 The Quadrangle, 49 Atalanta Street, London SW6 6TU
Telephone: (020) 7386 5473
Fax: (020) 7385 1774
Email: cathy@millerrightsagency.com

Principal: Cathy Miller

All MSS except poetry & educational.

Specialization: foreign rights; acting as consultants to publishers on sales of foreign rights of non-fiction titles (psychoanalysis, medical, business & management, esoteric, health & general trade books); handling market research for lists or one-off projects; helping to set up rights departments; advising on all matters concerning translation rights and negotiations with foreign publishers.

Rights Representative in UK for:
Canada: Mark Fisher; Golden Globe Publishing, Notre Dame-de-l'Ile Perrot, PQ; Fletcher Peacock
UK: Artemis Music Publishing; Foulsham Publishers; Free Association Books; Ann Henning-Jocelyn, Countess of Roden; Karnac Books; Open Gate Press; Phantom Genius Ltd; Shepheard-Walwyn; Thorogood Publishing Ltd; White Ladder Press / Crimson Publishing
USA: Christofer Foster

Overseas Representation:
China: Mei Yao, New York, NY
Greece: Read n Right Agency, Cahlkida
Japan: The English Agency Japan Ltd, Tokyo
Korea: EYA, Seoul
Poland: Graal Ltd, Warsaw
Russia: Alexander Korzhenevski Literary Agency, Moscow
Spain: Julio F Yañez Literary Agency, Barcelona

4071

NEW AUTHORS SHOWCASE
Rivendell, Kingsgate Close, Torquay TQ2 8QA
Telephone: 01803 326617
Email: mail@newauthors.org.uk
Web Site: http://www.newauthors.org.uk

Proprietor: Barrie James

Specialization: the UK's first Internet site for displaying new authors and poets to publishers. Most genres included. Established in August 1997 it now has in excess of 500 writers.

4072

THE MAGGIE NOACH LITERARY AGENCY
8 Peacock Yard, Iliffe Street, London SE17 3LH
Telephone: 07506 717726
Email: info@mnla.co.uk

All MSS except short stories, poetry, plays, screenplays, cookery, gardening, mind/body/spirit, illustrated children's, scientific/academic/specialist non-fiction. Absolutely no illustrated books.

Specialization: fiction, general non-fiction and children's books. No unsolicited manuscripts – submissions by arrangements only. Home 15%, USA & translation 20%.

Overseas Representation:
Worldwide: Jill Hughes, Aubourn, Lincs

4073

ANDREW NURNBERG ASSOCIATES LTD
45-47 Clerkenwell Green, London
EC1R 0QX
Telephone: (020) 7417 8800
Fax: (020) 7417 8812
Email: contact@nurnberg.co.uk
Web Site: http://www.andrewnurnberg.com

Directors: Andrew Nurnberg (Managing)
Sarah Nundy
Vicky Mark

Specialization: representing leading British & American agents & authors, as well as sale of translation rights throughout the world.

Associated Companies:
Bulgaria: Andrew Nurnberg Associates, Sofia
Czech Republic: Andrew Nurnberg Associates, Prague
Hungary: Andrew Nurnberg Associates, Budapest
Latvia: Andrew Nurnberg Associates, Baltic
P. R. of China: Andrew Nurnberg Literary Agency, Beijing
Poland: Andrew Nurnberg Associates, Warsaw
Russia: Andrew Nurnberg Literary Agency, Moscow
Taiwan: Andrew Nurnberg Literary Agency, Taipei

4074

ALEXANDRA NYE, LITERARY AGENT
6 Kinnoull Avenue, Dunblane, Perthshire
FK15 9JG
Telephone: 01786 825114

Literary Agent: Alexandra Nye

All MSS except poetry, plays, TV scripts or biographies.

Specialization: all types of fiction, with special interest in literary fiction, Scottish history, upmarket thrillers. Children's fiction age range 9–12, and some non-fiction also considered (home 19%, overseas 29%, translation 15%). New authors without previous publishing experience considered. Unsolicited MSS welcome with sae for return, but preliminary letter with synopsis preferred. Reading fee for supply of detailed report on MSS. Founded 1991.

4075

DEBORAH OWEN LTD
78 Narrow Street, Limehouse, London
E14 8BP
Telephone: (020) 7987 5119 & 5441
Fax: (020) 7538 4004
Email: do@deborahowen.co.uk

Literary Agent: Deborah Owen

Specialization: small agency representing Amos Oz and Delia Smith. No new authors.

4076

PATERSON MARSH LTD
50 Albemarle Street, London W1S 4BD
Telephone: (020) 7493 4361
Fax: (020) 7495 8961
Email: paterson@patersonmarsh.co.uk
Web Site: http://www.patersonmarsh.co.uk

Managing Director: Paul Marsh
Consultant: Mark Paterson
Agent: Stephanie Ebdon

All MSS except fiction, children's, poetry, drama, TV, film & radio.

Specialization: professional psychology, psychoanalysis, psychotherapy, general non-fiction. Preliminary letter and return postage required.

Associated Companies:
UK: Sigmund Freud Copyrights

Rights Representative in UK for:
UK: Sigmund Freud Copyrights, London; Hammersmith Press, London; New Library of Psychoanalysis, London
USA: The Analytic Press, New York, NY; Brunner-Routledge US, New York, NY; International Universities Press, Madison, CT; Other Press LLC, New York, NY; Pitchstone Publishing, Los Angeles, CA; Zeig, Tucker & Theisen Inc, Redding, CT

4077

JOHN PAWSEY
60 High Street, Tarring, Worthing,
West Sussex BN14 7NR
Telephone: 01903 205167
Fax: 01903 205167

Sole Proprietor: John Pawsey

All MSS except poetry, short stories, journalism, children's, original film & stage scripts, science fiction, fantasy & horror.

Specialization: sport, popular culture, crime, fiction.

Rights Representative in UK for:
USA: Alison J. Picard, Cotuit, MA; Bobbe Siegel, New York, NY

Overseas Representation:
France: Lora Fountain Associates, Paris
Germany: Thomas Schlück Literary Agency, Garbsen
Hungary: Lex Copyright, Budapest
Italy: Living Literary Agency, Milan
Japan: The English Agency Japan Ltd, Tokyo
Korea: Korea Copyright Center, Seoul
Netherlands: International Literatur Bureau BV, Hilversum
Russia: Prava i Prevodi RAO, Moscow
Scandinavia: Sane Töregård Agency, Karlshamn
Spain & South America: International Editors Co, Barcelona
USA: Alison J. Picard, Cotuit, MA
Yugoslav States: Prava i Prevodi, Belgrade

4078

*MAGGIE PEARLSTINE ASSOCIATES LTD
31 Ashley Gardens, Ambrosden Avenue,
Westminster, London SW1P 1QE
Telephone: (020) 7828 4212
Fax: (020) 7834 5546

Translation Rights:
Aitken Alexander Associates Ltd,
29 Fernshaw Road, London SW10 0TG
Telephone: (020) 7351 7561
Fax: (020) 7376 3594
Email: sally@gillonaitken.co.uk

Director: Maggie Pearlstine

Specialization: history, current affairs, biography and health. Member of Association of Authors' Agents. No new clients. No submissions accepted by fax, e-mail or from abroad.

4079

POLLINGER LTD AUTHORS' AGENTS
9 Staple Inn, Holborn, London WC1V 7QH
Telephone: (020) 7404 0342
Fax: (020) 7242 5737
Email: info@pollingerltd.com
Web Site: http://www.pollingerltd.com

Directors: Lesley Pollinger (Managing)
Leigh Pollinger
Literary Agents: Joanna Devereux
Tim Bates
Film & TV Agent: Ruth Needham
Company Secretary: John Furzer
Editor: Joan Deitch

All MSS except poetry & articles – see website for submission details.

Specialization: adult fiction and non-fiction, children's and literary estates.

Associated Companies:
Laurence Pollinger Ltd

Rights Representative in UK for:
UK: Accent Press; Wallflower Press, London
UK (dramatic rights): Summersdale
USA: New Directions Publishing Corporation, New York, NY

Overseas Representation:
China: Big Apple Tuttle-Mori Agency, Taipei
Denmark, Finland, Norway & Sweden: Licht & Burr Literary Agency, Copenhagen
France: Michelle Lapautre Agency, Paris
Germany & Switzerland: Mohrbooks Literary Agency, Zurich
Greece: Read n Right Agency, Cahlkida
Hungary: Lex Copyright, Budapest
Israel: The Book Publishers Association of Israel, Tel Aviv
Japan: Tuttle-Mori Agency Inc, Tokyo
Korea: The Eric Yang Agency, Seoul
Portugal & Brazil: Ilidio da Fonseca Matos, Lisbon
Spain & South America: Carmen Balcells Agencia Literaria SA, Barcelona
Turkey: ONK Agency Ltd, Istanbul
Yugoslav States, Bulgaria, Poland, Czech/Slovak Rep., Russia & Romania: Prava i Prevodi, Belgrade

4080

SHELLEY POWER LITERARY AGENCY LTD
13 rue du Pré Saint Gervais, 75019 Paris,
France
Telephone: +33 1 42 38 36 49
Fax: +33 1 40 40 70 08
Email: shelley.power@wanadoo.fr

Director, Literary Agent: Shelley Power

All MSS except children's books, poetry, plays or film scripts. No horror, science fiction or fantasy.

Specialization: literary agency.

Rights Representative in UK for:
USA: The Feminist Press, New York, NY

Overseas Representation:
China: Big Apple Tuttle-Mori Agency, Taipei; Big Apple Tuttle-Mori Agency Inc, Shanghai
Czech Republic: Transnet Contracts
France: VVV Agency, Paris
Germany: Liepman AG
Greece: JLM Literary Agency, Athens
Hungary: Kàtai & Bolza Literary Agents, Budapest
Israel: Ilana Pikarski Literary Agency, Tel Aviv
Italy: Natoli, Stefan & Oliva Agenzia Letteraria, Milan
Japan: The English Agency Japan Ltd, Tokyo
Korea: The Eric Yang Agency, Seoul
Poland: Graal Ltd, Warsaw
Romania: Simona Kessler International Copyright Agency Ltd, Bucharest
Scandinavia: Licht & Burr Literary Agency, Copenhagen
Spain: Julio F Yañez Literary Agency, Barcelona

4081

PRESSBOOKSPRINT / TVMYWORLD.COM
14 Dean Street, London W1D 3RS
Telephone: (020) 7437 4188
Email: malcolm.rasala@realcreatives.com
Web Site: http://www.tvmyworld.com

Chief Executive Officer: M. Rasala
COO: M. Maco

Specialization: literary agency for books; film agent for motion pictures (recognized agent in Hollywood); TV agent for TV programmes worldwide; advertiser - supply TV programme agents; agent representing 200 professionals (directors, producers, creatives, etc.) in the motion picture, TV and advertising industries, 120 professors (Harvard, Yale, MIT, Stanford, Oxford, etc.).

Associated Companies:
USA: www.tvmyworld.com

Overseas Representation:
France: Serge Simon, Paris
Italy: Marco Fichera, Rome

4082

*REDHAMMER MANAGEMENT LTD
186 Bickenhall Mansions, London
W1U 6BX
Fax: (020) 7000 1249
Web Site: http://www.redhammer.info

Chief Executive Officer: Peter Cox

Specialization: rights representation, including literary and publishing, film and TV; merchandising. The company has a small number of successful clients who wish to accelerate the momentum of their success. Currently published writers can visit our website if they would like more information; if you have not yet been published, your submission will be considered if you follow the Submissions Procedure.

4083

ROBINSON LITERARY AGENCY LTD
Block A511, The Jam Factory,
27 Green Walk, London SE1 4TT
Telephone: (020) 7096 1460
Email: info@rlabooks.co.uk
Web Site: http://www.rlabooks.co.uk

Managing Director: Peter Robinson
Agent: Sam Copeland

All MSS except lifestyle, cookery or gardening titles.

Specialization: all areas of fiction (general, crime, literary and children's), general non-fiction (history, biography, travel, current affairs, popular culture and humour). Aims to offer a bespoke service to clients across all media. In addition to handling book rights in all languages and territories, the agency also handles TV documentary rights and presenters, film rights and merchandising. It believes in establishing long-term relations with clients and nurturing writers' careers over many years. It will offer editorial advice where appropriate and is active in seeking out new talent. Represents a broad range of authors and clients from internationally bestselling novelists to academic historians and award-winning children's writers. Works in association with specialist film agents, Sayle Screen Ltd, for the handling of film and theatre rights. Commission: 15% home, 20% overseas. Established in 2005.

Overseas Representation:
All translation markets: Rogers, Coleridge & White Ltd, London

USA: Fletcher & Parry, New York, NY;
Inkwell Management, New York, NY

4084

ROGERS, COLERIDGE & WHITE LTD
20 Powis Mews, London W11 1JN
Telephone: (020) 7221 3717
Fax: (020) 7229 9084

Agents: Deborah Rogers *(Chairman)*
Peter Straus *(Managing Director)*
Gill Coleridge *(Director)*
Patricia White *(Director)*
David Miller *(Director)*
Laurence Laluyaux *(Foreign Rights)*
Stephen Edwards *(Foreign Rights)*
Zoe Waldie
Hannah Westland
Catherine Pellegrino *(Children's)*

All MSS except screenplays, plays or technical books. No unsolicited MSS, please and no submissions by e-mail.

Specialization: handles fiction, non-fiction and children's books. Literary agency. Founded 1967. Rights representative in UK and translation for several New York agents. Commission: Home 10%; US & translation 20%.

Associated Companies:
USA: Melanie Jackson Agency

4085

*SARA (THE SUSIE ADAMS RIGHTS AGENCY)
8 Sullivan Road, London SE11 4UH
Telephone: (020) 7582 6765
Fax: (020) 7582 6765
Email: SusieARA@aol.com

Agent: Susie Adams

Specialization: subsidiary rights agent – foreign language, USA, co-editions, permissions, serial and book club, merchandise, etc.

4086

*THE SAYLE LITERARY AGENCY
1 Petersfield, Cambridge CB1 1BB
Telephone: 01223 303035
Fax: 01223 301638
Web Site: http://www.sayleliteraryagency.com

Proprietor: Rachel Calder

All MSS except children's, poetry, technical.

Specialization: fiction (literary & crime), biography, history, current affairs, travel, social issues.

Rights Representative in UK for:
USA: Darhansoff Verrill Feldman Literary Agency, New York, NY; Anne Edelstein Literary Agency, New York, NY; New England Publishing Associates, CT

Overseas Representation:
Europe & Rest of the World: The Marsh Agency, London
USA: Dunow, Carlson & Lerner Agency, New York, NY

4087

CAROLINE SHELDON LITERARY AGENCY
Thorley Manor Farm, Thorley, Yarmouth PO41 0SJ
Telephone: 01983 760205
Fax: 01983 760206

Email:
carolinesheldon@carolinesheldon.co.uk & pennyholroyde@carolinesheldon.co.uk
Web Site: http://www.carolinesheldon.co.uk & http://www.carolinesheldonillustrators.co.uk

London Office:
70–75 Cowcross Street, London EC1M 6EJ
Telephone: (020) 7336 6550
Web Site: http://www.carolinesheldon.co.uk & http://www.carolinesheldonillustrators.co.uk

Literary Agents: Caroline Sheldon
Penny Holroyde

All MSS except short stories.

Specialization: fiction, women's fiction & children's books, human interest non-fiction.

4088

DORIE SIMMONDS LITERARY AGENCY
Riverbank House,
1 Putney Bridge Approach, London SW6 3JD
Telephone: (020) 7736 0002
Fax: (020) 7736 0010
Email: dhsimmonds@aol.com

Proprietor: Dorie Simmonds
Rights Executive: Frances Lubbe

All MSS except plays, poetry or short stories.

Specialization: commercial fiction and non-fiction in both the adult and children's markets.

4089

JEFFREY SIMMONS
15 Penn House, Mallory Street, London NW8 8SX
Telephone: (020) 7224 8917
Email: jasimmons@unicombox.co.uk

All MSS except children's books, cookery, science-fiction, romances & some specialist subjects.

Specialization: biography & memoirs; cinema, drama & the arts; general fiction; history; law & crime; literature; politics & world affairs.

Overseas Representation:
Germany: Michael Meller Literary Agency, Munich
Japan: The English Agency Japan Ltd, Tokyo; Japan Uni Agency, Tokyo
Spain: Julio F Yañez Literary Agency, Barcelona

4090

SINCLAIR-STEVENSON
3 South Terrace, London SW7 2TB
Telephone: (020) 7581 2550
Fax: (020) 7581 2550

Translation Rights:
c/o David Higham Associates Ltd,
5–8 Lower John Street, Golden Square, London W1F 9HA

All MSS except children's books, science fiction, science, fantasy, film or play scripts.

Specialization: non-fiction – biography and autobiography, the arts, politics and current affairs, travel, history; and fiction.

Rights Representative in UK for:
USA: T. C. Wallace Ltd, New York, NY

Overseas Representation:
USA: T. C. Wallace Ltd, New York, NY

4091

ROBERT SMITH LITERARY AGENCY LTD
12 Bridge Wharf, 156 Caledonian Road, London N1 9UU
Telephone: (020) 7278 2444
Fax: (020) 7833 5680
Email:
robertsmith.literaryagency@virgin.net

Directors: Robert Smith *(Managing)*
Anne Smith

All MSS except fiction, poetry, children's books or reference. Writers may submit synopses but no unsolicited manuscripts.

Specialization: the agency sells books, series and articles to book publishers, newspapers and magazines across the world. It operates only in non-fiction. Main areas are autobiography and biography, show business, hot topics, history, health, lifestyle and true crime.

Overseas Representation:
Germany: Thomas Schlück Literary Agency, Garbsen
Italy: Natoli, Stefan & Oliva Agenzia Letteraria, Milan
Spain: RDC Agencia Literaria, Madrid

4092

SHIRLEY STEWART LITERARY AGENCY
3rd Floor, 4a Nelson Road, London SE10 9JB
Telephone: (020) 8293 3000

Director: Shirley Stewart

All MSS except children's books, poetry, plays, science fiction and fantasy.

Specialization: full-length MSS only. Fiction and non-fiction (home 10–15%, overseas 20%). No reading fee but preliminary letter and return postage essential.

Rights Representative in UK for:
USA: Curtis Brown Ltd, New York, NY

4093

THE SUSIJN AGENCY LTD
3rd Floor, 64 Great Titchfield Street, London W1W 7QH
Telephone: (020) 7580 6341
Fax: (020) 7580 8626
Email: info@thesusijnagency.com
Web Site: http://www.thesusijnagency.com

Literary Agents: Laura Susijn
Nicola Barr

All MSS except children's books, sci-fi, romantic fiction, fantasy, sagas, self-help, business, military and computer books.

Specialization: selling rights world-wide in literary fiction and non-fiction. Also represents non-English language publishers and authors for UK, US and translation rights world-wide. Particularly interested in literature from mixed cultural background. Deals direct, using sub-agent in Eastern Europe, Israel and the Far East. Preliminary letter, synopsis and first two chapters preferred. No reading fee.

4094

THE TENNYSON AGENCY
10 Cleveland Avenue, London SW20 9EW
Telephone: (020) 8543 5939
Email: submissions@tenagy.co.uk
Web Site: http://www.tenagy.co.uk

Partner: Adam Sheldon

All MSS except poetry, short stories, science fiction, popular romantic and historical fiction, children's books and non-fiction unrelated to the arts.

Specialization: writing for the theatre, TV, radio and film. Related subjects and literary fiction are considered on an ad hoc basis. Commission rates: literature: 12.5%, drama: 15%, overseas: 20%. Submissions by post, on invitation, following introductory letter. Full details on the agency's website.

4095

J. M. THURLEY MANAGEMENT
Archery House, 33 Archery Square, Walmer, Deal CT14 7AY
Telephone: 01304 371721
Fax: 01304 371416
Email: jmthurley@aol.com
Web Site: http://www.thecuttingedge.biz

Contacts: Jon Thurley
Patricia Preece

All MSS except short stories & poetry.

Specialization: will give editorial help by arrangement on all types of projects.

4096

LAVINIA TREVOR
29 Addison Place, London W11 4RJ
Telephone: (020) 7603 5254
Fax: 0870 129 0838
Web Site: http://www.laviniatrevor.co.uk

Agent: Lavinia Trevor

All MSS except unsolicited material.

4097

JANE TURNBULL
58 Elgin Crescent, London W11 2JJ
Telephone: (020) 7727 9409

Mailing Address:
Barn Cottage, Veryan, Truro, Cornwall TR2 5QA
Telephone: 01872 501317
Email: jane.turnbull@btinternet.com

Proprietor: Jane Turnbull

All MSS except science or romantic fiction, children's fiction, poetry or plays.

Specialization: literary fiction, current affairs, biography, design, lifestyle, health, TV tie-ins, humour, natural history. Initial letter essential; no unsolicited MSS. Commission 10% home sales, 20% US, 20% translation, 15% radio/TV/film. Founded 1986, member of the Association of Authors' Agents.

Overseas Representation:
Worldwide: Aitken Alexander Associates, London

4098

ED VICTOR LTD
6 Bayley Street, Bedford Square, London WC1B 3HE
Telephone: (020) 7304 4100
Fax: (020) 7304 4111
Email: mary@edvictor.com

Directors: Ed Victor *(Executive Chairman)*
Margaret Phillips *(Joint Managing)*
Sophie Hicks *(Foreign Rights & Joint Managing)*
Leon Morgan
Carol Ryan
Graham Greene CBE
Hitesh Shah

All MSS except short stories; poetry; technical.

Specialization: fiction, non-fiction, biography, children's books.

4099

WADE & DOHERTY LITERARY AGENCY LTD
33 Cormorant Lodge, Thomas More Street, London E1W 1AU
Telephone: (020) 7488 4171
Fax: (020) 7488 4172
Email: rw@rwla.com
Web Site: http://www.rwla.com

Partner: Broo Doherty

All MSS except scripts, poetry, plays or short stories.

Specialization: handles general fiction and non-fiction including children's books. Send detailed synopsis and first 10,000 words by e-mail. No reading fee. Commission: home 10%, overseas and translation 20% (fees negotiable if a contract has already been offered). Founded 2001.

4100

WATSON, LITTLE LTD
48–56 Bayham Place, London NW1 0EU
Telephone: (020) 7388 7529
Fax: (020) 7388 8501
Email: office@watsonlittle.com
Web Site: http://www.watsonlittle.com

Managing Director: Mandy Little
Senior Agent: James Wills

All MSS except short stories, plays, poetry, works for very small children & articles (except by established columnists).

Specialization: literary and commercial fiction, serious non-fiction, psychology, self-help, popular culture, celebrity, health, sport, humour, children's.

Rights Representative in UK for:
USA (children's): The Chudney Agency, New York, NY

Overseas Representation:
USA (adult): Howard Morhaim Literary Agency, New York, NY
USA (children's): The Chudney Agency, New York, NY
Worldwide: The Marsh Agency, London
Worldwide (film & TV associates): MBA Literary Agents, London; The Sharland Organisation, Raunds, Northants

4101

A. P. WATT LTD
20 John Street, London WC1N 2DR
Telephone: (020) 7405 6774
Fax: (020) 7831 2154
Email: apw@apwatt.co.uk
Web Site: http://www.apwatt.co.uk

Directors: Caradoc King
Linda Shaughnessy
Derek Johns
Georgia Garrett
Natasha Fairweather
Sheila Crowley
Rob Kraitt *(Associate)*

All MSS except poetry.

Specialization: general fiction and non-fiction. No unsolicited manuscripts.

4102

JOSEF WEINBERGER PLAYS LTD
[formerly Warner/Chappell Plays Ltd]
12–14 Mortimer Street, London W1T 3JJ
Telephone: (020) 7580 2827
Fax: (020) 7436 9616
Email: general.info@jwmail.co.uk
Web Site: http://www.josef-weinberger.com

Manager: Michael Callahan

Specialization: stage plays. Works in conjunction with overseas agents. No unsolicited manuscripts, preliminary letter essential.

Parent Company:
UK: Josef Weinberger Ltd

Rights Representative in UK for:
USA: Dramatists Play Service Inc, New York, NY

Overseas Representation:
Australia: Hal Leonard (Australia) Ltd, Melbourne, Vic
Canada & USA: Dramatists Play Service Inc, New York, NY
New Zealand: Play Bureau (NZ) Ltd, New Plymouth
South Africa: Dalro (Pty) Ltd, Johannesburg
Zimbabwe: National Theatre Organization, Harare

4103

JOHN WELCH LITERARY CONSULTANT & AGENT
Mill Cottage, Calf Lane, Chipping Campden, Glos GL55 6JQ
Telephone: 01386 840237
Fax: 01386 840568

Proprietor: John Welch

All MSS except fiction, children's books, poetry, plays, film & TV scripts.

Specialization: military & naval history, aviation, biography & history. Preliminary letter required.

4104

EVE WHITE LITERARY AGENT
1a High Street, Kintbury, Berks RG17 9TJ
Telephone: 01488 657656
Fax: 01488 657656
Email: eve@evewhite.co.uk
Web Site: http://www.evewhite.co.uk

Director: Eve White

Specialization: UK agency representing internationally published authors of commercial and literary fiction and non-fiction, children's fiction and picture books. The company does not represent poets and screen writers. Foreign rights handled in conjunction with Diana Mackay at Melcombe International Ltd. Authors should refer to our website for submission requirements. Clients include: Rae Earl, Tim Clark, Tabitha Suzuma, Alexander Stobbs, Ruth Saberton, Vijay Medtia & Shanta Everington. Children's authors: Andy Stanton, Jimmy Docherty, Susannah Corbett, Gillian Rogerson, David Flavell, Kate Maryon, Carolyn Ching & Rachael Mortimer.

Overseas Representation:
Commonwealth countries & USA: Eve White, Kintbury
Worldwide (excluding Commonwealth countries & USA): Melcombe International, Somerset

4105

*DINAH WIENER LTD
12 Cornwall Grove, London W4 2LB
Telephone: (020) 8994 6011
Fax: (020) 8994 6044

Directors: Dinah Wiener
D. P. Wiener
B. M. Wiener

All MSS except juvenile, plays, film scripts, poetry & short stories.

Specialization: general fiction and non-fiction.

4106

JONATHAN WILLIAMS LITERARY AGENCY
Rosney Mews, Upper Glenageary Road, Glenageary, Co Dublin, Republic of Ireland
Telephone: +353 (01) 280 3482
Fax: +353 (01) 280 3482

Director: Jonathan Williams

All MSS except plays or film scripts. Return postage and packing is appreciated. Irish postage stamps or international postal coupons, please.

Specialization: typescripts of Irish interest.

Overseas Representation:
France: Lora Fountain Associates, Paris
Italy: Agenzia Piergiorgio Nicolazzini, Milan
Japan: Tuttle-Mori Agency Inc, Tokyo
Netherlands & Germany: International Literatuur Bureau, Amsterdam
Spain & Spanish-speaking Latin America: Antonia Kerrigan Literary Agency, Barcelona

5 Trade & Allied Associations

5.1 INTERNATIONAL

5001

ENGLISH-SPEAKING UNION OF THE COMMONWEALTH
37 Charles Street, London W1J 5ED
Telephone: (020) 7529 1550
Fax: (020) 7495 6108
Email: library@esu.org
Web Site: http://www.esu.org

President: HRH The Duke of Edinburgh KG, KT, OM
Chairman: The Lord Hunt of the Wirral MBE, PC
Director General: Mrs Valerie Mitchell OBE

The English-Speaking Union is an international organization with headquarters in London and in New York. It is a voluntary body and registered charity existing to promote international friendship and understanding through a variety of educational and cultural programmes.

The ESU runs several awards: the Duke of Edinburgh English Language Book Award, the President's Award for the best non-book language materials, the Marsh Biography Award and the Marsh Children's Literature in Translation Award.

5002

FEDERATION OF EUROPEAN PUBLISHERS
31 rue Montoyer, Box 8, 1000 Brussels, Belgium
Telephone: +32 (02) 770 11 10
Fax: +32 (02) 771 20 71
Email: info@fep-fee.eu
Web Site: http://www.fep-fee.eu

Director: Ms Anne Bergman-Tahon
Legal Advisor: Ms Olga Martin Sancho

Lobbying European institutions on behalf of the European publishing community.

5003

IBBY – INTERNATIONAL BOARD ON BOOKS FOR YOUNG PEOPLE
Nonnenweg 12, Postfach, 4003 Basel, Switzerland
Telephone: +41 ((0)61) 272 29 17
Fax: +41 ((0)61) 272 27 57
Email: forest.zhang@ibby.org
Web Site: http://www.ibby.org

Director Member Services, Communications & New Projects: Elizabeth Page
President of the Executive Committee: Patricia Aldama
Deputy Director of Administration: Forest Zhang

Promotion of children's books and reading worldwide.

5004

PRIVATE LIBRARIES ASSOCIATION
Ravelston, South View Road, Pinner, Middx HA5 3YD
Email: dchambrs@aol.com
Web Site: http://www.plabooks.org

Hon President: Keith Fletcher
Hon Secretary: Stan Brett
Hon Editor & Hon Publications Secretary: David Chambers
Hon Treasurer: Dean A. Sewell

An international society of book collectors, run on a voluntary basis. Publications include a quarterly journal and *The Exchange List*, which circulate among member collectors throughout the world, *Private Press Books*, an annual bibliography, and other books concerned with book collecting.

5.2 UNITED KINGDOM & REPUBLIC OF IRELAND

5005

YR ACADEMI GYMREIG
Mount Stuart House, Mount Stuart Square, Cardiff CF10 5FQ
Telephone: (029) 2047 2266
Fax: (029) 2049 2930
Email: post@academi.org
Web Site: http://www.academi.org

Glyn Jones Centre for Writers:
Wales Millennium Centre, Bute Place, Cardiff CF10 5AL
Telephone: (as above)
Fax: (029) 2047 0691
Email: (as above)
Web Site: (as above)

Chief Executive: Peter Finch
Deputy: Lleucu Siencyn

Founded in 1959, Yr Academi Gymreig / The Welsh Academy is the national society which promotes the writers and literatures of Wales. The Academi runs courses, competitions (including the Cardiff International Poetry Competition), conferences, tours by authors, international exchanges, events for schools, readings, literary performances and festivals. The Academi also offers advice to authors, a writers' critical and mentoring service and financial bursaries, and runs the annual Book of the Year Award. It works in partnership with Tŷ Newydd, the Cricieth-based residential writers' centre.

Publications include *A470*; *Taliesin*, a quarterly literary journal in the Welsh language; *The Oxford Companion to the Literature of Wales*; *The Welsh Academy English-Welsh Dictionary*; *The Welsh Academy Encyclopaedia of Wales* published with the support of the Lottery, and a variety of translated works.

In 2004 Academi became a resident at the Wales Millennium Centre. The Glyn Jones Centre for Writers opened in 2005.

5006

ACADEMIC AND PROFESSIONAL DIVISION OF THE PUBLISHERS ASSOCIATION
29B Montague Street, London WC1B 5BW
Telephone: (020) 7691 9191
Fax: (020) 7691 9199

Email: gtaylor@publishers.org.uk
Web Site: http://www.publishers.org.uk

Director: Graham Taylor

Parent Company:
UK: The Publishers Association

The Academic and Professional Division of The Publishers Association represents the interests of publishers serving higher education, scholarly communication and the professional and commercial market. Collective activities are organized on their behalf. Membership is open to any publisher in membership of the Publishers Association who produces books, journals or similar published material for these markets.

5007

ALLIANCE OF LITERARY SOCIETIES (ALS)
59 Bryony Road, Selly Oak, Birmingham B29 4BY
Telephone: 0121 475 1805
Email: l.j.curry@bham.ac.uk
Web Site: http://www.allianceofliterarysocieties.org.uk

Chair: Linda J. Curry
Hon Treasurer / Membership Secretary: Julie Shorland

The ALS is an umbrella organization for literary societies/groups within the UK. The AGM is hosted by different member societies each year, with accompanying talks etc covering a weekend (usually in April or May). Members of affiliated societies are welcome to attend but only the delegate of the affiliated society may have a vote. Details are on the website – including subscription rates. An annual journal (*ALSo...*) is also produced. This is freely available to member societies but can be purchased by non-members.

5008

ARTS COUNCIL ENGLAND
14 Great Peter Street, London SW1P 3NQ
Telephone: 0845 300 6200
Fax: (020) 7973 6590
Email: enquiries@artscouncil.org.uk
Web Site: http://www.artscouncil.org.uk

Chair: Prof Sir Christopher Frayling
Chief Executive: Alan Davey

Arts Council England is the national development agency for the arts in England, distributing public money from government and the national lottery.

Arts Council England's main funding programme is Grants for the Arts. It is open to individuals, art organizations, national touring and other people who use the arts in their work. The grants are for activities that benefit people in England or that help artists and arts organizations from England to carry out their work.

Arts Council England has one national and nine regional offices. Founded in 1946.

5009

ASSOCIATION OF AUTHORS' AGENTS
c/o Caroline Sheldon Literary Agency,
70–75 Cowcross Street, London EC1M 6FI
Email: pennyholroyde@carolinesheldon.co.uk
Web Site: http://www.agentsassoc.co.uk

President: Philippa Milnes-Smith
Vice-President: Anthony Goff
Treasurer: Sheila Crowley
Secretary: Penny Holroyde

Founded in 1974 to institute and maintain a code of professional behaviour, to discuss matters of common professional interest and to provide a vehicle for representing the view of authors' agents in discussions on matters of common interest with other professional bodies.

5010

ASSOCIATION OF FREELANCE EDITORS, PROOFREADERS & INDEXERS (IRELAND)
11 Clonard Road, Sandyford, Dublin 16, Republic of Ireland
Telephone: +353 (0)58 48458 & (0)1 295 2194
Email: powerediting@eircom.net & Brenda@ohanlonmediaservices.com
Web Site: http://www.afepi.ie

Co-Chair: Winifred Power
Brenda O'Hanlon

The AFEPI was established to provide information to publishers on Irish freelancers working in this field, and to protect the interests of those freelancers. Membership is restricted to freelancers with experience and/or references, but skills of members are not tested or evaluated.

5011

ASSOCIATION OF ILLUSTRATORS
2nd Floor Back Building, 150 Curtain Road, London EC2A 3AR
Telephone: (020) 7613 4328
Fax: (020) 7613 4417
Web Site: http://www.theaoi.com

Managers: Derek Brazell
Ian Veacock *(Finance Officer)*
Bethany King *(Events & Marketing Co-ordinator)*
Nicolette Hamilton *(Membership Co-ordinator)*

Established in 1973 to advance and protect illustrators' rights, the AOI is a non-profit making trade association dedicated to its members' professional interest and the promotion of illustration.
Corporate members (agents and clients) receive free copy of the *Images Annual*, discounts on events, publications and our Images competition entry, plus *Varoom* – the journal of illustration and made images, published three times per year.

5012

*ASSOCIATION OF LEARNED & PROFESSIONAL SOCIETY PUBLISHERS
c/o Chief Executive ALPSP, Bluebell Lodge, 8 Rickford Road, Nailsea, Bristol BS48 4PY
Telephone: 01275 856444
Fax: 0870 706 0332
Email: ian.russell@alpsp.org
Web Site: http://www.alpsp.org

Chief Operating Officer:
Nick Evans, 9 Stanbridge Road, Putney, London SW15 1DX
Telephone: (020) 8789 2394
Fax: (020) 8789 2394
Email: nick.evans@alpsp.org
Web Site: http://www.alpsp.org

Chief Executive: Ian Russell
Managers: Nick Evans *(Chief Operating Officer)*
Ian Hunter *(Finance & Administration)*
Co-ordinators: Lesley Ogg *(Events)*
Amanda Whiting *(Training)*
Suzy Fotheringham *(Marketing & Membership)*
Dee French *(Administration)*
Editor: Sally Morris *(Editor-in-Chief, Learned Publishing)*

ALPSP is an international trade association for the community of not-for-profit publishers and those who work with them to disseminate academic and professional information; it was founded in 1972, and currently has over 350 members in more than 40 countries. ALPSP carries out research and other projects, monitors national and international issues and represents members' interests to the wider world. The Association provides co-operative services such as the ALPSP Learned Journals Collection. It also offers an extensive programme of courses and seminars, an informative website (http://www.alpsp.org), a quarterly journal, *Learned Publishing*, and a monthly electronic newsletter, *ALPSP Alert*.

5013

ASSOCIATION OF ONLINE PUBLISHERS (AOP)
Queens House, 28 Kingsway, London WC2B 6JR
Telephone: (020) 7400 7510
Fax: (020) 7404 4167
Email: info@ukaop.org.uk
Web Site: http://www.ukaop.org.uk

Directors: Ruth Brownlee
Rebecca Winfied *(Finance – Periodical Publishers Association)*
Communications & Events Manager: Ron Nussey
Project Co-ordinator: Telly Martin
Head of Operations: Liz Somerville

Parent Company:
UK: Periodical Publishers Association

The UK Association of Online Publishers (AOP) is an industry body representing online publishing companies that create original, branded, quality content. AOP champions the interests of approximately 160 publishing companies from diverse backgrounds including newspaper and magazine publishing, TV and radio broadcasting, and pure online media.
AOP presents a unified voice to industry and Government, specifically to address issues and concerns relating to all areas of online publishing. AOP publishes original research and hosts forums, awards and conferences, covering a range of topics from paid-for-content, subscription models and data protection, through to copyright, content management, new technologies and audience measurement.
The primary mission of UK AOP is to drive standards and revenue across all areas of online publishing to raise the credibility and profile of the industry.

5014

ASSOCIATION OF SUBSCRIPTION AGENTS AND INTERMEDIARIES
10 Lime Avenue, High Wycombe HP11 1DP
Telephone: 01494 534778
Email: rollo.turner@dsl.pipex.com
Web Site: http://www.subscription-agents.org

Chief Executive Officer: Rollo Turner *(Secretary General)*

Represents the interests of subscription agents and intermediaries who supply periodicals and related material in both paper and electronic form to libraries, companies and individuals worldwide.

5015

AUDIOBOOK PUBLISHING ASSOCIATION
[formerly SWPA]
Telephone: 07971 280788
Email: info@theapa.net
Web Site: http://www.theapa.net

Administrator: Charlotte McCandlish
Chair: Alison Muirden
Vice-Chair: Zoe Howes

The UK association for the audiobook industry, formerly the Spoken Word Publishing Association. Its broad membership covers all those involved in spoken word audio, one of the fastest-growing areas in publishing.

5016

AUTHORS' FOUNDATION
84 Drayton Gardens, London SW10 9SB
Telephone: (020) 7373 6642
Fax: (020) 7373 5768
Email: info@societyofauthors.org
Web Site: http://www.societyofauthors.org

Trustees: Lady Antonia Fraser
Michael Holroyd
Simon Brett
Secretary: Mark Le Fanu

Founded in 1984 to mark the centenary of the Society of Authors, the Foundation offers grants to published writers who need additional funding for research, travel, etc. Open to fiction, poetry and non-fiction. The Foundation incorporates the Phoenix Trust. Closing dates for applications: 30 April and 30 September.

5017

*AUTHORS' LICENSING & COLLECTING SOCIETY (ALCS)
The Writers' House, 13 Haydon Street, London EC3N 1DB
Telephone: (020) 7264 5700
Email: alcs@alcs.co.uk
Web Site: http://www.alcs.co.uk

Chief Executive: Owen Atkinson
Deputy Chief Executive: Barbara Hayes
Communications Officer: Alison Baxter

The Authors' Licensing & Collecting Society is the UK collective rights management society for writers of all genres. Members grant to the Society the right to administer on their behalf those rights which an author is unable to exercise as an individual or which are best handled on a collective basis. These include photocopying, rental and lending right, off-air and private recording, electronic rights, broadcast rights for BBC Prime and BBC World Service TV, cable retransmission and rights for the public reception of broadcasts. Membership costs a one-off lifetime fee of £25. Please contact the Society for further information. The ALCS administers these rights in the UK and Northern Ireland. Under reciprocal arrangements with foreign collecting societies other territories are also covered. Distributions to members are made quarterly. For advice and further information please contact the ALCS office.

5018

BAPLA (BRITISH ASSOCIATION OF PICTURE LIBRARIES AND AGENCIES)
18 Vine Hill, London EC1R 5DZ
Telephone: (020) 7713 1780
Fax: (020) 7713 1211
Email: enquiries@bapla.org.uk
Web Site: http://www.bapla.org.uk

Picture Buyers' Fair:
18 Vine Hill, London EC1R 5DZ
Telephone: (020) 7713 1780
Fax: (020) 7713 1211
Email: pbf@bapla.org.uk
Web Site: http://www.pbf.org.uk

Chief Executive Officer: Linda Royles
Association Administrator: Damalie Nakalema
Online Editor: Pauline Shakespeare

BAPLA celebrates over 30 years in the business and represents over 420 picture library and agency members. BAPLA organizes its annual Picture Buyers' Fair, and offers a range of services and seminars for image buyers and image libraries and agencies. Please see website for details.

5019

THE BIBLIOGRAPHICAL SOCIETY
c/o Institute of English Studies, Senate House, Malet Street, London WC1E 7HU
Telephone: (020) 7862 8679
Fax: (020) 7862 8720
Email: admin@bibsoc.org.uk
Web Site: http://www.bibsoc.org.uk

Hon Secretary: Margaret Ford

The Bibliographical Society promotes the study of historical, analytical, descriptive and textual bibliography. It publishes its own journal, *The Library*, and supports a publishing programme of books and monographs on bibliographical subjects.

5020

BOOK AID INTERNATIONAL
39–41 Coldharbour Lane, Camberwell, London SE5 9NR
Telephone: (020) 7733 3577
Fax: (020) 7978 8006

Email: info@bookaid.org
Web Site: http://www.bookaid.org

Patron: HRH The Duke of Edinburgh KG, KT, OM
Chair (acting): Helen Meixner
Director: Clive Nettleton

Book Aid International is the major UK support for libraries in sub-Saharan Africa. It is a cost-effective agency that believes in people's potential for self-development and transformation through learning – and that the development of human capacity is essential for escaping poverty. Support for the long-term development of the local book trade is a high priority. The aim is that locally produced and culturally relevant books should be made available for readers in Africa and elsewhere.

Book Aid International works with partners that give the widest possible access to books and information, including public library services, community resource centres, universities, colleges, schools and non-governmental organizations. Carefully selected materials are made available to these organizations in 18 developing countries – most resources are targeted in 17 countries in sub-Saharan Africa; other programmes focus on Palestine.

Currently two-thirds of all donations come from UK publishers, taking advantage of the wealth of surplus runs, superseded editions and returns that exist in the publishing industry. The rest are given by schools, colleges, libraries and individuals.

For more information about how you can help Book Aid International please contact the Book Acquisitions Officer.

5021

BOOK INDUSTRY COMMUNICATION
39–41 North Road, London N7 9DP
Telephone: (020) 7607 0021
Fax: (020) 7607 0415
Email: info@bic.org.uk
Web Site: http://www.bic.org.uk

Chairman: Michael Holdsworth
Managing Agent: Peter Kilborn

Book Industry Communication (BIC) was set up in 1991 by the Publishers Association, Booksellers Association, Library Association and the British Library to promote standards for the format and transmission of bibliographic information and electronic commerce transactions and increase efficiency within the supply chain. Its subscribers include most of the UK's major publishers and booksellers as well as bibliographic agencies and systems suppliers.

5022

BOOKSELLERS ASSOCIATION OF THE UNITED KINGDOM & IRELAND LTD
Minster House, 272 Vauxhall Bridge Road, London SW1V 1BA
Telephone: (020) 7802 0802
Fax: (020) 7802 0803
Email: mail@booksellers.org.uk
Web Site: http://www.booksellers.org.uk

President: Graham Rand
Chief Executive: Tim Godfray

Associated Companies:
UK: Batch.co.uk Ltd; Book Industry Communication Ltd; Book Tokens Ltd; Word Book Day Ltd

Founded in 1895. Represents over 4400 outlets. Promotes and looks after the interests of booksellers, helps booksellers become more efficient, fights for better distribution in the trade, helps booksellers increase sales and reduce costs and gives advice on opening and running a bookshop. Among other services, the Association produces catalogues for distribution throughout the retail trade at Christmas and directories of members, publishers and services.

5023

BOOKTRUST
Book House, 45 East Hill, London SW18 2QZ
Telephone: (020) 8516 2977
Fax: (020) 8516 2978
Email: query@booktrust.org.uk
Web Site: http://www.booktrust.org.uk

Patron: HRH the Prince Philip, Duke of Edinburgh
Chief Executive: Viv Bird

Booktrust is an independent national charity that encourages people of all ages and cultures to discover and enjoy reading.

5024

BRITISH ASSOCIATION OF COMMUNICATORS IN BUSINESS
Suite GA2, Oak House, Woodlands Business Park, Linford Wood, Milton Keynes MK14 6EY
Telephone: 01908 313755
Fax: 01908 313661
Email: enquiries@cib.uk.com
Web Site: http://www.cib.uk.com

Chief Executive: Kathie Jones

The Association aims to be the market leader for those involved in internal and corporate communications by providing professional, authoritative, dynamic, supportive and innovative services.

Membership is open to all individuals engaged in corporate communications. Major activities include the annual Communicators in Business Awards competition, an annual conference and a regular programme of educational and training events. Publications include *Communicators* magazine and *CiBNews*.

5025

BRITISH CENTRE FOR LITERARY TRANSLATION (BCLT)
University of East Anglia, Norwich NR4 7TJ
Telephone: 01603 592785
Fax: 01603 592737
Email: bclt@uea.ac.uk
Web Site: http://www.uea.ac.uk/bclt

Director: Amanda Hopkinson
Co-ordinator: Catherine Fuller

Parent Company:
UK: University of East Anglia

Raises the profile of literary translation and the professional development of literary translators. Organizes events, readings, workshops aimed at translators, professionals in arts and publishing and the general public.

5026

BRITISH FANTASY SOCIETY
56 Leyton Road, Birmingham B21 9EE
Telephone: 07845 897760
Email: secretary@britishfantasysociety.org
Web Site: http://www.britishfantasysociety.org

President: Ramsey Campbell
Chairman: Marie O'Regan
Secretary & Treasurer: Vicky Cook
Editors: Stephen Theaker *(Dark Horizons)*
Lee Harris *(Newsletter)*
Andrew Hook *(New Horizons)*

Formed for devotees of fantasy, horror and related fields in literature, art and the cinema. Publications include *Prism* (quarterly), featuring news and reviews, and *Dark Horizons* and *New Horizons* (every six months alternating), featuring fiction and articles from new and established authors, plus other more occasional publications listing fiction and nonfiction of interest. There is a small press library and an annual convention, 'FantasyCon', which features the British Fantasy Awards sponsored by the Society. Please visit our website for full information. Membership fees: UK £30 (£45 joint); Europe £40 (£60 joint); Rest of World £55 (£80 joint).

5027

*THE BRITISH GUILD OF TRAVEL WRITERS
51b Askew Crescent, London W12 9DN
Telephone: (020) 8749 1128
Fax: (020) 8181 6663
Web Site: http://www.bgtw.org

Chair: Mary Anne Evans

The Guild has a membership of around 230, all professional journalists, broadcasters and photographers who derive the majority of their earnings from travel writing or broadcasting. Monthly meetings are devoted to discussion of travel topics, usually with outside speakers, and take place at a variety of venues. There is a monthly *Newsletter* for members. An annual year book giving full details of all members together with comprehensive lists of PRs and other contacts in the travel trade is available for purchase.

5028

BSI BUSINESS INFORMATION
389 Chiswick High Road, London W4 4AL
Telephone: (020) 8996 9000
Fax: (020) 8996 7400
Web Site: http://www.bsigroup.com

Chairman: Sir David John
Directors: Clive Mosey *(Financial)*
Vincent Cassidy *(Commercial)*
Peter McKay *(Publishing)*
Shirley Bailey-Wood *(Operations)*

Parent Company:
UK: BSI Group

Associated Companies:
UK: British Standards Publishing Ltd (BSPL)

BSI Business Information is a division of the BSI Group. BSI Business Information has a range of products and services (from guide books to online products) centred on standards (45,000 international standards), standardization and codes of practice for all industries, systems and technologies. BSI Business Information also offers customers translation services, a full range of training products, international technical assistance, private standardization services. Customers can also benefit from state-of-the-art print and production facilities.

5029

BTBS THE BOOK TRADE CHARITY
[also known as The Book Trade Benevolent Society]
The Foyle Centre, The Retreat, Kings Langley, Herts WD4 8LT
Telephone: 01923 263128
Fax: 01923 270732
Email: btbs@booktradecharity.demon.co.uk & david@btbs.org
Web Site: http://www.booktradecharity.demon.co.uk

Chairman: Jo Henry
Manager, The Retreat: Jackie Bright
Chief Executive: David Hicks
Treasurer: Nigel Batt

The welfare charity of the book trade, offering support to colleagues in difficult personal circumstances.

BTBS gives direct financial support, regular and one-off, to individuals, to help with a wide range of problems.

Accommodation at The Retreat, Kings Langley, offers pre-retirement and retirement housing.

The book trade helpline (freephone 0808 100 2304) provides sympathetic, confidential help.

Anyone who has worked in the book trade (publishing, distribution, bookselling, etc. for more than one year, employed, self-employed or freelance) is eligible to apply for assistance.

5030

CHARTERED INSTITUTE OF JOURNALISTS
2 Dock Offices, Surrey Quays Road, London SE16 2XU
Telephone: (020) 7252 1187
Fax: (020) 7232 2302
Email: memberservices@cioj.co.uk
Web Site: http://www.cioj.co.uk

President: John Thorpe
Vice-President: Macer Hall
Treasurer: Norman Bartlett
General Secretary: Dominic Cooper

The senior professional society of journalists worldwide. Incorporated by Royal Charter in 1890, it had its origin in the National Association of Journalists, which was founded in 1884 and converted into the Institute in 1889. Its primary object is 'the promotion by all reasonable means of the interests of journalists and journalism'. Representing the profession as a whole, it is a completely independent body free of political partiality. It gives equal rights of membership to all members of the profession, including radio and television journalists, press photographers and public relations officers with journalistic qualifications. Trade union representation is provided by the IOJ (TU), an independent certificated trade union.

5031

THE CHARTERED INSTITUTE OF LINGUISTS
Saxon House, 48 Southwark Street, London SE1 1UN
Telephone: (020) 7940 3100
Fax: (020) 7940 3125
Email: info@iol.org.uk
Web Site: http://www.iol.org.uk

Chief Executive: John Hammond
Director of Communications: Cetty Zambrano

The Chartered Institute of Linguists (IoL) is an international professional membership organization. It promotes proficiency in modern languages worldwide amongst professional linguists, including translators, interpreters and educationalists, as well as those in the public and private sectors for whom languages are an important skill.

Through its wholly-owned subsidiary IoL Language Services Ltd (LSL) it offers translation, production and recruitment services, validation of language qualifications and assessments as well as training courses. The IoL Educational Trust, an associated charity, is an accredited awarding body offering high-level exams. The Institute helps to ensure equal access for all to the public services (law, health, local government) by providing interpreting qualifications in most of the languages spoken in the UK, and running the National Register of Public Service Interpreters (NRPSI Ltd).

The Linguist is the bi-monthly publication of the Chartered Institute of Linguists (published six times per year). It is free to all members, non-members can receive it on subscription.

5032

CHILDREN'S BOOKS IRELAND
17 North Great George's Street, Dublin 1, Republic of Ireland
Telephone: +353 (0)1 872 7475
Fax: +353 (0)1 872 7476
Email: info@childrensbooksireland.com
Web Site: http://www.childrensbooksireland.com

Director: Mags Walsh
Programme Officer: Tom Donegan
Administrator: Jenny Murray
Editors – Inis Magazine: Patricia Kennon
  Caitriona Magner

Children's Books Ireland is the national children's book organization of Ireland. The aim of Children's Books Ireland is to promote quality children's books and reading. CBI runs an annual nationwide Children's Book Festival, the Bisto/CBI Book of the Year awards, publishes *Inis*, a quarterly magazine, which carries a wide range of articles about children's books in Ireland and abroad as well as an extensive review section, and hosts an annual Children's Books conference.

CBI is a resource and support organization for teachers, pupils, writers, publishers, booksellers, librarians as well as an imaginative programmer of events for young readers.

5033

CHILDREN'S WRITERS & ILLUSTRATORS GROUP
The Society of Authors, 84 Drayton Gardens, London SW10 9SB
Telephone: (020) 7373 6642
Fax: (020) 7373 5768
Email: jmccrum@societyofauthors.org
Web Site: http://www.societyofauthors.org

Secretary: Jo McCrum

Parent Company:
UK: The Society of Authors

The Children's Writers and Illustrators Group is an organization, founded in 1963, for writers and illustrators of children's books, who are members of the Society of Authors. Meetings are held regularly, with opportunities for members to meet each other, as well as to hear talks or discussions on various aspects of their work.

5034

CILIP (CHARTERED INSTITUTE OF LIBRARY AND INFORMATION PROFESSIONALS)
7 Ridgmount Street, London WC1E 7AE
Telephone: (020) 7255 0500 & (020) 7255 0505 (textphone)
Fax: (020) 7255 0501
Email: info@cilip.org.uk
Web Site: http://www.cilip.org.uk

Chief Executive: Bob McKee
Managing Director, CILIP Enterprises: John Woolley
Publishing Director, Facet Publishing: Helen Carley

CILIP (Chartered Institute of Library and Information Professionals) was formed in April 2002 following the unification of the Institute of Information Scientists and The Library Association (founded in 1877). It has some 23,500 members working in all sectors of the information community. It is committed to enabling its members to achieve and maintain the highest professional standards and deliver or promote high quality library and information services. The Library Association's Royal Charter, granted in 1898, recognizes CILIP's work in promoting standards and enables the Institute to award Chartered status to members fulfilling the professional criteria. The Institute's publishing arm, Facet Publishing, is one of the largest publishers worldwide of library and information science titles, with over 150 titles in print.

5035

COMHAIRLE NAN LEABHRAICHEAN / THE GAELIC BOOKS COUNCIL
22 Mansfield Street, Glasgow G11 5QP
Telephone: 0141 337 6211
Fax: 0141 341 0515
Email: brath@gaelicbooks.net
Web Site: http://www.gaelicbooks.net

Chair: Prof Roibeard Ó Maolalaigh
Director: Ian MacDonald

The Council was set up in 1968 to administer the Gaelic Books Grant awarded by the Scottish Education Department, and its purpose is to stimulate Gaelic publishing. It normally has about ten members as its board, and a paid staff of four. In April 1983 the Scottish Arts Council became its main funding body, and its Assessor attends meetings. The Council became a charitable company in July 1996.

It provides financial assistance in the form of publication grants (paid to the publisher) for individual Gaelic books, and also commission grants for authors. Editorial advice is available, and a word-processing and proof-reading service.

In 2003 it launched the highly successful Ùr-Sgeul imprint for prose work in Gaelic, with the associated books, CDs and DVDs being issued by the publisher Clàr.

As a retailer, the Council stocks all Gaelic and Gaelic-related works in print, regular lists of these being published in its catalogue, *Leabhraichean Gàidhlig*, and on its website. It has its own shop at the address above, and also does mail order and mobile selling at selected events, as well as running a book club (A' Chiste Leabhraichean).

5036

COPYRIGHT TRIBUNAL
Rm 2G31, Concept House, Cardiff Road, Newport NP10 8QQ
Telephone: 01633 811035
Fax: 01633 811175
Email: copyright.tribunal@ipo.gov.uk
Web Site: http://www.ipo.gov.uk/copy/tribunal/index.htm

Chairman: Judge Fysh QC
Secretary: Sally Howls

The main function of the Tribunal is to decide, where the parties cannot agree between themselves, the terms and conditions of licences offered by, or licensing schemes operated by, collective licensing bodies in the copyright and related rights area. It has the statutory task of conclusively establishing the facts of a case and of coming to a decision which is reasonable in the light of those facts. Its decisions are appealable to the High Court only on points of law. (Appeals on a point of law against decisions of the Tribunal in Scotland are to the Court of Session.)

Broadly, the Tribunal's jurisdiction is such that anyone who has unreasonably been refused a licence by a collecting society or considers the terms of an offered licence to be unreasonable may refer the matter to the Tribunal. The Tribunal also has the power to decide some matters even though collecting societies are not involved. For example, it can settle disputes over the royalties payable by publishers of TV programme listings to broadcasting organizations.

5037

*THE CRITICS' CIRCLE
c/o 69 Marylebone Lane, London W1U 2PH
Telephone: (020) 7224 1410
Web Site: http://www.criticscircle.org.uk

President: Marianne Gray
Honorary General Secretary: Denise Silvester-Carr

Founded in 1913 by J. T. Grein, S. R. Littlewood and John Parker. Aims to promote the art of criticism and to uphold its integrity in practice; to foster and safeguard the professional interests of its members and to provide opportunities for social intercourse among them and to support the advancement of the arts. Membership is only by invitation of the Council and is confined to persons engaged professionally, regularly and substantially in the writing or broadcasting of criticism of theatre, music, film, dance and art and architecture. There is no literary section *per se*.

5038

DATA PUBLISHERS ASSOCIATION (DPA)
Queen's House, 28 Kingsway, London WC2B 6JR
Telephone: (020) 7405 0836
Fax: (020) 7404 4167
Email: sarah.gooch@dpa.org.uk
Web Site: http://www.dpa.org.uk

Executive Director: Jerry Gosney
Marketing Co-ordinator: Sarah Gooch

The Data Publishers Association (DPA) is the industry body representing data and directory publishers in the UK. Its role is to protect and promote the interests of the industry, both in print and online.

5039

DESIGN AND ARTISTS COPYRIGHT SOCIETY
33 Great Sutton Street, London EC1V 0DX
Telephone: (020) 7336 8811
Fax: (020) 7336 8822
Email: info@dacs.org.uk
Web Site: http://www.dacs.org.uk

Chief Executive: Joanna Cave
Directors: John Robinson *(Legal & International)*
  Tania Spriggens *(Communications)*
  Jane Sandeman *(Finance)*
  Jeremy Stein *(Services)*

Founded in 1984 by artists for artists. DACS is a not-for-profit organization established to administer and protect the rights of artists in the UK, including copyright and Artist's Resale Right.

Membership is open to any artist of any discipline and to the estate of an artist still in copyright.

DACS represents over 52,000 artists, including Picasso, Dali, Matisse, Wadsworth, Hamilton, Spencer and Lichtenstein.

Any publisher wishing to reproduce works of art in copyright should contact DACS in the first instance to obtain clearance prior to publication.

5040

DOI AGENCY
3rd Floor, Midas House, 62 Goldsworth Road, Woking, Surrey GU21 6LQ
Telephone: 0870 777 8712
Fax: 0870 777 8714
Email: doi.agency@nielsen.com
Web Site: http://www.doi.nielsenbookdata.co.uk

Managers: Julian Sowa *(Senior)*
  Diana Williams

Parent Company:
UK: Nielsen Book
USA: The Nielsen Company

DOIs, Digital Object Identifiers, are used to uniquely identify files or other resources on the internet. The DOI Agency is responsible for issuing DOI prefixes and numbers and can provide help and advice on maintaining DOI. Nielsen Book also runs the ISBN and SAN agencies.

5041

EDUCATIONAL PUBLISHERS COUNCIL
[Schools Division of The Publishers Association]
The Publishers Association, 29B Montague Street, London
WC1B 5BW
Telephone: (020) 7691 9191
Fax: (020) 7691 9199
Email: gtaylor@publishers.org.uk
Web Site: http://www.publishers.org.uk

Director: Graham Taylor

Parent Company:
UK: The Publishers Association

The Educational Publishers Council is particularly concerned with making known, both to the educational system and to the general public, the nature and importance of educational publishers' work. It is charged with assessing and putting forward the co-ordinated views of educational publishers. Membership is open to any firm which is in membership of The Publishers Association and gives proof of a *bona fide* interest in publishing or producing books or other permanent forms of instruction intended for classroom use.

5042

EDUCATIONAL WRITERS GROUP
The Society of Authors, 84 Drayton Gardens, London
SW10 9SB
Telephone: (020) 7373 6642
Fax: (020) 7244 0743
Email: info@societyofauthors.org
Web Site: http://www.societyofauthors.org

Secretary: Elizabeth Haylett

The Educational Writers Group is a subsidiary group of the Society of Authors. Its purpose is to advise members on their publishing problems etc, to study the conditions peculiar to the market at home and overseas, to watch developments in teaching as they affect the educational writer, and to hold meetings at which experience can be pooled, and matters of mutual interest discussed.

5043

ENGLISH ASSOCIATION
University of Leicester, University Road, Leicester LE1 7RH
Telephone: 0116 252 3982
Fax: 0116 252 2301
Email: engassoc@le.ac.uk
Web Site: http://www.le.ac.uk/engassoc

Chief Executive: Helen Lucas
Assistant: Julia Hughes

Founded in 1906 to promote the knowledge, enjoyment and study of the English language and its literatures.

The Year's Work in English Studies – the annual qualitative narrative bibliographical overview of scholarly work on English language and literature written in English. Published annually in December.

The Year's Work in Critical and Cultural Theory – companion volume to YWES, providing a narrative bibliography of work in the field of critical and cultural theory.

Order from: Julia Hughes.

5044

THE FEDERATION OF CHILDREN'S BOOK GROUPS
2 Bridge Wood View, Horsforth, Leeds LS18 5PE
Telephone: 0113 258 8910
Email: info@fcbg.org.uk
Web Site: http://www.fcbg.org.uk

A national, voluntary organization concerned with children and their books. The Federation's aim is to promote enjoyment and interest in children's books and reading, and to encourage the availability of a range of literature for all ages, from pre-school to teenage. The Federation liaises with schools, playgroups, publishers, libraries and other official bodies.
 National activities include:
  – organizes, annually, The Red House Children's Book Award
  – promotes National Share-a-Story Month in May
  – organizes an annual conference each spring.

 Members are able to receive Federation publications, including the *Federation Newsletter*, the annual *Red House Children's Book Award 'Pick of the Year' Top Fifty Booklist*, and information about National Share-a-Story Month.

5045

GAY AUTHORS WORKSHOP
BM Box 5700, London WC1N 3XX
Email: eandk2@btinternet.com

Secretary: Kathryn Byrd

Associated Companies:
UK: Gay Authors Self-Publishing Society

Gay Authors Workshop is an association of lesbians, gay men and bisexuals who are creative writers - poets, dramatists, fiction writers. Its aim is to raise the standard of gay literature by providing opportunities for gay writers to meet, read, discuss and criticize their work in a constructive way. Monthly meetings are held at different places in the London area for that purpose, and to share information about publishing outlets and competitions. Although London-based, it is a national organization. The quarterly newsletter (print and tape) keeps members in touch with activities. Membership is open to all gay writers, beginners as well as published authors. The subscription is £7 a year, £3 unwaged.

5046

GIBB MEMORIAL TRUST
2 Penarth Place, Cambridge CB3 9LU
Telephone: 01223 566630
Email: PRBligh@ntlworld.com
Web Site: http://www.gibbtrust.org

Secretary to the Trustees: P. R. Bligh *(Finance & Administration)*

The Trust is a registered charity whose aim is to support the publication of works of scholarly research within the areas of the history, literature, philosophy and religion of the Persians, Turks and Arabs. Its activities are in financing and organizing the production and publication of books, and in marketing the published works. The books are distributed by Oxbow Books in Oxford, UK, and Oakville, USA.

5047

*GUILD OF FOOD WRITERS
255 Kent House Road, Beckenham, Kent BR3 1JQ
Telephone: (020) 8659 0422
Email: gfw@gfw.co.uk
Web Site: http://www.gfw.co.uk

The Guild of Food Writers is the professional association of food writers and broadcasters in the UK. Established in 1984, it now has 350 authors, columnists, freelance journalists and broadcasters amongst its members.
 The objectives of the Guild as set out in its constitution are as follows:
 To bring together professional food writers..., to print and issue an annual list of members, to extend the range of members' knowledge and experience..., and to encourage the development of new writers by every means including competitions and awards. To contribute to the growth of public interest in, and knowledge of, the subject of food and to campaign for improvements in the quality of food.
 The Guild is a self-supporting body that offers its members a busy calendar that includes an annual lecture dinner and AGM, annual awards, monthly workshops and occasional professional and social events. It also publishes a monthly newsletter and comprehensive and detailed annual directory of members.
 The Guild offers professional support and guidance to its members. In the public forum it campaigns with authority for improvements in the awareness and quality of food in every sector of society.

5048

INDEPENDENT PUBLISHERS GUILD (IPG)
PO Box 12, Llain, Whitland SA34 0WU
Telephone: 01437 563335
Email: info@ipg.uk.com
Web Site: http://www.ipg.uk.com

Chief Executive: Bridget Shine

The Independent Publishers Guild (IPG) actively represents the interests of independent publishers in the UK and is represented on many committees and forums, which form the strategy for the UK book trade. The IPG helps publishers to do better business, somewhere they can find advice, ideas and information.
 With over 450 members and steadily growing with combined revenues of over £500M, the IPG provides a vibrant networking base. Members receive regular e-newsletters, training courses and seminars covering important areas. It also organizes an annual conference.
 The IPG runs a collective stand for members at leading international book fairs including Frankfurt and London.

5049

INFORMATION COMMISSIONER'S OFFICE
Wycliffe House, Water Lane, Wilmslow, Cheshire SK9 5AF
Telephone: 0845 630 6060
Fax: 01625 524510
Email: mail@ico.gsi.gov.uk
Web Site: http://www.ico.gov.uk

Information Commissioner: Richard Thomas

The Information Commissioner's Office is the UK's independent public body set up to promote access to official information and to protect personal information.
 It regulates and enforces the Data Protection Act, the Freedom of Information Act, the Privacy and Electronic Communications Regulations and the Environmental Information Regulations.
 The ICO provides guidance to organizations and individuals. It rules on eligible complaints and can take action when the law is broken.
 Reporting directly to Parliament, the Commissioner's powers include the ability to order compliance, using enforcement and decision notices, and prosecution.

5050

INSTITUTE OF SCIENTIFIC AND TECHNICAL COMMUNICATORS (ISTC)
Airport House, Purley Way, Croydon CR0 0XZ
Telephone: 020 8253 4506
Fax: 020 8253 4510
Email: istc@istc.org.uk
Web Site: http://www.istc.org.uk

President: Simon Butler
Treasurer: Peter Fountain
Editor: Marian Newell *(Communicator – ISTC Journal)*
Administration: Elaine Cole
Marketing Director: Paul Ballard

Formed in 1972 as a result of the amalgamation of the Presentation of Technical Information Group (1948), the Institution of Technical Authors and Illustrators (originally the Technical Publications Association), formed in 1953, and the Institute of Technical Publicity and Publications (1963).
 The Institute aims to establish and maintain professional codes of practice for those employed in all branches of scientific and technical communication. It provides a forum for the exchange of views between its members, and aims to further their expectations and interests. The membership embodies a wide range of specialist knowledge of the principles and modern practices of effective communication of scientific and technical information. Through its publications and meetings, the Institute disseminates this experience to a growing profession and to those who employ the services of its members.
 The Institute represents Great Britain on the International Council for Technical Communication (INTECOM).
 Publications: *The Communicator* (UK subscription: £37 per year).

5051

INSTITUTE OF TRANSLATION & INTERPRETING
Fortuna House, South Fifth Street, Milton Keynes MK9 2EU
Telephone: 01908 325250
Fax: 01908 325259
Email: info@iti.org.uk
Web Site: http://www.iti.org.uk

Chairman: Catherine Greensmith
General Secretary: Alan Wheatley

The Institute of Translation and Interpreting (ITI) is the UK's main professional association for translators and interpreters and aims to promote the highest standards in translating and interpreting. It has a strong corporate membership and runs professional development courses and conferences, sometimes in conjunction with its language, regional and subject networks. Membership is open to those with a genuine and proven involvement in translation and interpreting. As a full and active member of the International Federation of Translators, it maintains good contacts with translators and interpreters worldwide. ITI's bi-monthly bulletin is available on subscription through the ITI office in Milton Keynes.

ITI's directory of translators and interpreters may be accessed from the website at http://www.iti.org.uk.

5052

IP3 (INSTITUTE OF PAPER, PRINTING & PUBLISHING)
Runnymede House, off Hummer Road, Egham, Surrey TW20 9BD
Telephone: 0870 330 8625
Fax: 0870 330 8615
Email: info@ip3.org.uk
Web Site: http://www.ip3.org.uk

Also at:
Colin Walsh, Director, IP3, 25–27 High Street, Chesterton, Cambridge CB4 1ND
Telephone: 01223 352790
Fax: 01223 460718
Email: csw@bpccam.co.uk

Directors: Tim Feest
Colin Walsh
David Pryke

Fostering excellence in publishing through:
 – the promotion, support and endorsement of a programme of educational training, research and development
 – the introduction of a code of practice
 – the development of standards of occupational competence
 – the publication of bulletins, handbooks, reports and research designed to assist in the improvement of individual performance
 – the development of professional publishing qualifications
 – meetings, seminars and conferences.
 The Institute will offer individuals:
 – membership of an active community of people working in publishing
 – the opportunity to participate in and influence the direction of a body that has their best interests at heart
 – a community that can raise professional standards and, as a consequence, individual and collective status
 – opportunities to network, seek advice, guidance and career counselling
 – access to career, education and training information
 – a range of cost-saving services and activities.
 The Institute of Publishing will be a forum providing opportunities for individuals in publishing to develop themselves and progress in their careers and to meet the challenges of an increasingly competitive business.

5053

IRISH BOOK PUBLISHERS ASSOCIATION (CLÉ)
25 Denzille Lane, Dublin 2, Republic of Ireland
Telephone: +353 (01) 639 4868
Email: info@publishingireland.com
Web Site: http://www.publishingireland.com

President: Seán Ó Cearnaigh (Publisher, CoisLife)
Project Manager: Jolly Ronan
Administrator: Karen Kenny

The Irish Book Publishers Association (CLÉ) promotes the publication, distribution, sale and publicity of books at home and abroad. There are 80 members of the association. CLÉ is a member of the Federation of European Publishers and of the International Publishers Association.

5054

IRISH EDUCATIONAL PUBLISHERS ASSOCIATION
c/o Gill & Macmillan Ltd, Hume Avenue, Park West, Dublin 12, Republic of Ireland
Telephone: +353 (01) 500 9509
Fax: +353 (01) 500 9598
Email: hmahony@gllmacmillan.ie

Secretary: Anthony Murray

Contact the Association for information about activities and membership.

5055

ISBN AGENCY - UK AND IRISH REPUBLIC
3rd Floor, Midas House, 62 Goldsworth Road, Woking GU21 6LQ
Telephone: 0870 777 8712
Fax: 0870 777 8714
Email: isbn.agency@nielsen.com
Web Site: http://www.isbn.nielsenbookdata.co.uk

Senior Manager: Julian Sowa
Manager: Diana Williams

Associated Companies:
UK: Nielsen Book
USA: The Nielsen Company

The UK International Standard Book Numbering Agency is responsible for assigning ISBN prefixes to publishers based in the UK or the Irish Republic.
 The UK ISBN Agency cannot assign ISBNs to publishers based in other countries.
 The Agency:
 – allocates ISBN publisher prefixes to eligible publishers based on the information provided by the publisher;
 – advises publishers on the correct and proper implementation of the ISBN system;
 – maintains a database of publishers and their prefixes for inclusion in the *Publishers' International ISBN Directory*;
 – encourages and promotes the use of the Bookland EAN bar code format;
 – encourages and promotes the importance of the ISBN for a proper listing of titles with bibliographical agencies;
 – provides technical advice and assistance to publishers and the booktrade on all aspects of ISBN usage.
 Any new publishers wishing to apply for an allocation of ISBNs should contact the ISBN Agency for an application pack. A registration fee is payable.

5056

ISSN UK CENTRE
The British Library, Boston Spa, Wetherby, West Yorkshire LS23 7BQ
Telephone: 01937 546959
Fax: 01937 546562
Email: issn-uk@bl.uk
Web Site: http://www.bl.uk/issn

Assigns ISSN (International Standard Serial Numbers) to serial titles published in the UK.

5057

MEDICAL WRITERS GROUP
The Society of Authors, 84 Drayton Gardens, London SW10 9SB
Telephone: (020) 7373 6642
Fax: (020) 7373 5768
Email: info@societyofauthors.org & sbaxter@societyofauthors.org
Web Site: http://www.societyofauthors.org

Secretary: Sarah Baxter

The Medical Writers Group, established in 1979, is a group within the Society of Authors. Its principal objects are to represent its members in all matters affecting their interests as medical writers; to hold meetings from time to time for the discussion of matters of common interest; and to provide, through the Society, advice to members on the special problems of medical authorship. Authors who have had a book accepted for publication, but not yet published, can join the Society and obtain advice. The Group also administers the Medical Book Awards, which it co-sponsors with the Royal Society of Medicine.

5058

MUSIC PUBLISHERS ASSOCIATION
6th Floor, British Music House, 26 Berners Street, London W1T 3LR
Telephone: (020) 7580 0126
Fax: (020) 7637 3929
Email: info@mpaonline.org.uk
Web Site: http://www.mpaonline.org.uk

Chief Executive: Stephen Navin
Editor, MPA Catalogue: David Butler

Associated Companies:
UK: MCPS Ltd

The Music Publishers Association (MPA) was established in 1881 and is governed by an elected Board. The MPA exists to safeguard the interests of music publishers and the writers signed to them. It provides them with a forum and a collective voice, and aims to inform and to educate the wider public in the importance and value of copyright.
 The MPA offers a range of services and publications to those interested in music publishing and participates in education and information initiatives across the music industry.

5059

*NATIONAL ACQUISITIONS GROUP
27 Belgrave Mount, Wakefield WF1 3SB
Telephone: 01924 383010
Fax: 01924 383010
Email: nag@btconnect.com
Web Site: http://www.nag.org.uk

Chair: Maggie Sumner
Hon. Secretary: Eileen Hiller
Hon. Treasurer: Peter Longden
Administrator: Jane Butler
Publications Officer: Mark Merrill

Established in 1986, NAG is a broadly based organization which stimulates, co-ordinates and publicizes developments in library acquisitions and the book trade. The membership includes individuals and organizations within publishing, bookselling and systems supply, as well as librarians responsible for choosing and buying books for academic, public, national, government and special institutions.
 NAG has two main aims:
 – to bring together all those in any way concerned with library acquisitions, to assist them in exchanging information and comment and to promote understanding and good practice between them;
 – to seek to influence other organizations and individuals to adopt its opinions and standards.
 NAG's objectives are to:
 – provide a forum for discussion and the exchange of information;
 – extend knowledge and understanding of technological developments;
 – promote the dissemination of information about library acquisitions;
 – develop the awareness of producers, suppliers and librarians;
 – act as a channel of communication with Government and other bodies.

5060

NATIONAL ASSOCIATION FOR THE TEACHING OF ENGLISH
50 Broadfield Road, Sheffield S8 0XJ
Telephone: 0114 555 419
Fax: 0114 555 296
Email: info@nate.org.uk
Web Site: http://www.nate.org.uk

Development & Communications Director: Ian McNeilly
Publications Manager: Anne Fairhall
Company Secretary: Lyn Fairfax

NATE is the UK subject association for all aspects of English teaching from pre-school to university. NATE publishes its own and distributes other titles covering:
 – *classroom resources:* primary, secondary, post 16
 – *teaching English:* theoretical titles including: language, literacy, literature, speaking and listening, media, drama, information and communications technologies, assessment, theory, equal opportunities
 – *management & staff development:* curriculum, planning, managing the English department, whole school issues relating to English teaching.
 The Association publishes four periodicals: *English in Education*, *NATE News*, *English Drama Media* and *Classroom*.

5061

*NATIONAL LITERACY TRUST
Swire House, 59 Buckingham Gate, London SW1E 6AJ
Telephone: (020) 7828 2435
Fax: (020) 7931 9986
Email: contact@literacytrust.org.uk
Web Site: http://www.literacytrust.org.uk

National Literacy Trust:
National Reading Campaign; Reading Champions; Reading Connects; Reading Is Fundamental, UK; Reading The

Game; Talk To Your Baby

The National Literacy Trust is a registered charity (no. 1116260) dedicated to building a society in which literacy is a valued part of everybody's life and all have the reading, writing and communication skills required to support their goals. It is the only UK organization that promotes literacy development across all ages and sectors.

The Trust has an extensive website – http://www.literacytrust.org.uk – with literacy news, summaries of key issues, research and examples of practice nationwide. It also runs the National Reading Campaign on behalf of the Government, which provides information on promoting reading for pleasure to people of all ages, in schools, libraries and the wider community – see http://www.readon.org.uk.

The National Literacy Trust organizes an annual conference, courses and seminars; and runs a range of initiatives that turn promising ideas into effective action. Initiatives include Reading Is Fundamental, UK, which provides free books to children through generous publisher discounts; Reading The Game, involving the professional football community; and the Talk To Your Baby campaign, promoting the importance of parental support for early language development.

5062

NEW WRITING NORTH
Culture Lab, Newcastle University, Newcastle-upon-Tyne NE1 7RU
Telephone: 0191 222 1332
Fax: 0191 222 1372
Email: claire@newwritingnorth.com
Web Site: http://www.newwritingnorth.com

Directors: Cath Robson *(Finance)*
　Anna Disley *(Deputy)*
Projects & Marketing Officer: Olivia Mantle

New Writing North is the literature development agency for the north-east of England.

5063

NIELSEN BOOKDATA
3rd Floor, Midas House, 62 Goldsworth Road, Woking, Surrey GU21 6LQ
Telephone: 0870 777 8710
Fax: 0870 777 8711
Email: info.bookdate@nielsen.com
Web Site: http://www.nielsenbookdata.co.uk

Directors: Ann Betts *(Commercial)*
　Simon Skinner *(Sales)*
Head of Marketing: Mo Siewcharran
Head of Data Sales: Paul Dibble
Publisher Subscriptions Manager: Vesna Nall

Parent Company:
UK: Nielsen Book
USA: The Nielsen Company

Nielsen BookData is a book information provider worldwide. The company has a range of products and services which provide content-rich, accurate and timely book information for English-language titles published internationally. These services are sold to booksellers, libraries and publishers in over 110 countries, including the UK, Ireland, Europe, Australia, New Zealand, South Africa and the USA.

5064

PERIODICAL PUBLISHERS ASSOCIATION
Queens House, 28 Kingsway, London WC2B 6JR
Telephone: (020) 7404 4166
Fax: (020) 7404 4167
Email: info1@ppa.co.uk
Web Site: http://www.ppa.co.uk

Chief Executive: Jonathan Shephard
Executive Director: Nick Mazur

Associated Companies:
Republic of Ireland: Periodical Publishers Association Ireland
UK: Association of Publishing Agencies; Periodical Publishers Association Scotland; Periodicals Training Council; PPA Interactive; Teenage Magazine Arbitration Panel (TMAP)

Trade association representing publishers of consumer, business-to-business and customer magazines.

5065

THE POETRY SOCIETY
22 Betterton Street, London WC2H 9BX
Telephone: (020) 7420 9880
Fax: (020) 7240 4818
Email: info@poetrysociety.org.uk
Web Site: http://www.poetrysociety.org.uk

Director: Jules Mann
Editor, Poetry Review: Fiona Sampson

The Society's principal activities include: the quarterly publication of the UK's world-class poetry magazine, *Poetry Review*; an Advice and Information Service; the Society's newsletter, *Poetry News*; the National Poetry Competition which awards over £7000 in prizes each year and has brought many poets to national attention; the annual Foyle Young Poets of the Year Award (11–17 year olds). The Poetry Society also produces a range of publications including *The Poetry Book for Primary Schools* and *Jumpstart: Poetry in the Secondary School* as well as books exploring the links between poetry and pop, poetry and gardens, and poetry and personal development. Other resources include *poetryclass*, an invaluable teacher-training resource for both primary and secondary school teachers, free National Poetry Day materials, display materials (including Poems on the Underground posters) and The Library Poetry Pack, an information pack available with membership.

5066

PUBLIC LENDING RIGHT
Richard House, Sorbonne Close, Stockton-on-Tees TS17 6DA
Telephone: 01642 604699
Fax: 01642 615641
Email: susan.ridge@plr.uk.com
Web Site: http://www.plr.uk.com

Registrar: Jim Parker

Public Lending Right (PLR) exists to make payments to authors for the borrowing of their books from public libraries. PLR is funded by the Department for Culture, Media and Sport, and is headed by a Registrar. To qualify, authors must register their books with the PLR office. Payment calculations are based on book loans from a representative sample of public libraries. Payments are made annually. No author may receive more than £6600.

5067

THE PUBLISHERS ASSOCIATION
29B Montague Street, London WC1B 5BW
Telephone: (020) 7691 9191
Fax: (020) 7691 9199
Email: mail@publishers.org.uk
Web Site: http://www.publishers.org.uk

Chief Executive: Simon Juden
Directors: Graham Taylor *(Educational, Academic & Professional Publishing)*
　Simon Bell *(International)*

The Publishers Association is a trade organization serving book, journal and electronic publishers in the UK. It brings publishers together to discuss the main issues facing the industry and to define the practical policies that will take the industry forward. The aim of The Publishers Association is to serve and promote by all lawful means the interest of book, journal and electronic publishers and to protect their interests.

5068

*PUBLISHERS LICENSING SOCIETY LTD
37–41 Gower Street, London WC1E 6HH
Telephone: (020) 7299 7730
Fax: (020) 7299 7780
Email: pls@pls.org.uk
Web Site: http://www.pls.org.uk

Chairman: Christopher Collins
Managers: Caroline Elmslie *(Operations)*
　Lydia Murray *(Finance)*
　David Bishop *(Licensing & Communications)*
Consultant: Mark Bide
Chief Executive: Alicia Wise

The Publishers Licensing Society (PLS) obtains mandates from publishers which grant PLS the authority to license photocopying and digitization of pages from published works. PLS also consults with publishers on the development of licences.

PLS aims to maximize revenue from licences for mandating publishers and to expand the range and repertoire of mandated publishers available to licence holders. It supports the Copyright Licensing Agency (CLA) in its efforts to increase the number of legitimate users through the issuing of licences and pursues any infringements of copyright works belonging to rights holders.

5069

PUBLISHERS PUBLICITY CIRCLE
65 Airedale Avenue, London W4 2NN
Telephone: (020) 8994 1881
Email: ppc-@lineone.net
Web Site: http://www.publisherspublicitycircle.co.uk

Secretary/Treasurer: Heather White

For over 50 years, the Publishers Publicity Circle has enabled book publicists - both from publishing houses and freelance PR agencies - to meet and share information regularly. Representatives of the media are invited to speak about the ways in which they can feature authors and their books, and how book publicists can provide most effectively the information and material needed.

Annual prizes are awarded for the best publicity campaigns of the year.

A directory of the PPC membership is published each year and distributed to over 2500 media contacts, providing the names of publicity staff, their fax and telephone numbers, and email addresses.

5070

PUBLISHING SCOTLAND
Scottish Book Centre, 137 Dundee Street, Edinburgh EH11 1BG
Telephone: 0131 228 6866
Fax: 0131 228 3220
Email: enquiries@publishingscotland.org
Web Site: http://www.publishingscotland.org

Chief Executive: Marion Sinclair
Member Services & Marketing Manager: Liz Small
Administrators: Carol Lothian *(Finance & Office)*
　John-Mark Glover *(Administrative Assistant)*
　Joan Lyle *(Information & Training)*

Publishing Scotland has grown from the work of the Scottish Publishers Association (SPA), a trade association in existence for over 30 years, representing over 75 book and journal publishers. It now offers a network membership of the organization.

Publishing Scotland is a new organization with responsibility for support and development of the publishing sector in Scotland. The remit is to work with companies, organizations and individuals in the industry, and to co-ordinate joint initiatives and partnerships. Publishing Scotland provides a forum for discussions, events and for linking services and skills to needs and opportunities. Publishing Scotland provides all the services for publishers that were previously the work of the SPA.

Publishing Scotland represents its members' interests in a number of capacities, in co-operative promotion and marketing of their books, attendance at international book fairs, joint catalogue mailings, export services and training.

5071

ROMANTIC NOVELISTS ASSOCIATION
3 Griffin Road, Thame, Oxon OX9 3LB
Telephone: 01844 213947
Email: ianandcatherinejones@btinternet.com
Web Site: http://www.rna-uk.org

Chair: Catherine Jones

The Association aims to raise the prestige of good quality romantic fiction and makes annual awards for the best romantic (including historical) novel, and for the best first novel by a hitherto unpublished writer accepted for publication. A new annual award for Category Romance was made in 2003.

5072

ROYAL SOCIETY OF LITERATURE
Somerset House, Strand, London WC2R 1LA
Telephone: (020) 7845 4676

Fax: (020) 7845 4679
Email: info@rslit.org
Web Site: http://www.rslit.org

President: Sir Michael Holroyd CBE, FRHistS, FRSL
Chair: Maggie Gee FRSL
Secretary: Maggie Fergusson FRSL
Deputy Secretary: Julia Abel Smith

The Society's purpose is to sustain all that is best, whether traditional or experimental, in English Letters, and to encourage a catholic appreciation of literature. Lectures and poetry readings take place monthly at Somerset House. The Society administers a number of trusts for the advancement of Letters. The Royal Society of Literature Award under the Heinemann bequest is presented annually to one or more writers on the strength of a published work of high literary merit. The V. S. Pritchett Memorial Prize is a new prize for a previously unpublished short story. The Royal Society of Literature Ondaatje Prize was launched in 2003. The £10,000 prize will be awarded annually to the book of the highest literary merit, fiction or non-fiction, which evokes the spirit of a place.

5073

*RSA (THE ROYAL SOCIETY FOR THE ENCOURAGEMENT OF ARTS, MANUFACTURES AND COMMERCE)

8 John Adam Street, London WC2N 6EZ
Telephone: (020) 7451 6902
Fax: (020) 7839 5805
Email: editor@rsa.org.uk
Web Site: http://www.theRSA.org

Publisher:
Wardour Publishing & Design, Elsley Court,
20–22 Great Titchfield Street, London W1W 8BE
Telephone: (020) 7016 2555
Web Site: http://www.wardour.co.uk

Chairman: Gerry Acher
Directors: Stephen King *(Finance)*
  Carrie Walsh *(Commercial)*
  Stephen Farrant *(Fellowship & Marketing)*
  Matthew Taylor *(Chief Executive)*
Editor, RSA Journal: Alex Perchard

Publishes bi-monthly *RSA Journal* and reports, conference papers and occasional books.

5074

SAN AGENCY – UK & IRISH REPUBLIC

3rd Floor, Midas House, 62 Goldsworth Road, Woking, Surrey GU21 6LQ
Telephone: 0870 777 8712
Fax: 0870 777 8714
Email: san.agency@nielsen.com
Web Site: http://www.san.nielsenbookdata.co.uk

Managers: Julian Sowa *(Senior)*
  Diana Williams

Parent Company:
UK: Nielsen Book
USA: The Nielsen Company

SANs, Standard Address Numbers, are unique for geographical locations and can be assigned to the addresses of organizations involved in the bookselling or publishing industries. The SAN Agency is responsible for managing the scheme on behalf of book industry communication in the UK and Republic of Ireland. Nielsen Book also runs the ISBN and DOI agencies.

5075

SCBWI (SOCIETY OF CHILDREN'S BOOK WRITERS & ILLUSTRATORS (BRITISH ISLES REGION))

36 Mackenzie Road, Beckenham, Kent BR3 4RU
Telephone: (020) 8249 9716
Email: ra@britishscbwi.org
Web Site: http://www.britishscbwi.org

Regional Advisor (Chair): Natascha Biebow
Newsletter Editor: Eileen Ramchandran
Illustrator Co-ordinator: Anne-Marie Perks

Parent Company:
USA: SCBWI

The SCBWI is an international professional organization for writers and illustrators of children's books. It is a network for the exchange of knowledge between writers, illustrators, editors, publishers, agents, librarians, educators, booksellers and others involved with literature for young people. There are currently more than 18,000 members worldwide, in over 70 regions.

The SCBWI International sponsors three annual conferences on writing and illustrating books and multimedia, one in New York in February, one in Bologna, Italy, and one in Los Angeles in the summer, as well as dozens of regional conferences and events throughout the world. It also publishers a bi-monthly newsletter, *The Bulletin*, awards grants for works in progress, and provides many informational publications on the art and business of writing and selling written, illustrated and electronic material. The SCBWI also presents numerous grants and awards, including the Golden Kite Award for the best fiction and non-fiction books.

The SCBWI British Isles (SCBWI-BI) region meets bi-monthly, usually in London, for a speaker or workshop event. It also sponsors local critique groups and regional networks events, and publishes a quarterly newsletter, *Words and Pictures*, which includes up-to-date events and marketing information, and articles on the craft of children's writing and illustrating. It also runs a yearly Writer's Day and Illustrator's Day with hands-on workshops on improving your craft and the opportunity to meet publishing professionals and find out what they are looking for.

SCBWI is open to both published and unpublished writers and illustrators.

Full membership is open to those whose work for children's books, illustrations or photographs, films, electronic media, articles, poems or stories has been published or produced.

Associate membership is open to all those with an interest in children's literature or media, whether or not they have published.

To join, see our web site http://www.britishscbwi.org

5076

SCHOOL LIBRARY ASSOCIATION

Unit 2, Lotmead Business Village, Lotmead Farm, Wanborough, Swindon SN4 0UY
Telephone: 01793 791787
Fax: 01793 791786
Email: info@SLA.org.uk
Web Site: http://www.SLA.org.uk

Editor: Steve Hird
Review Editor: Chris Brown
Production Editor: Richard Leveridge

The School Library Association is an independent organization working to promote the development of school libraries, primary and secondary. Services to members include advice and information, publications at reduced prices, *The School Librarian*, a quarterly journal of articles and reviews, training courses and a network of area branches. Membership includes schools, colleges, local education authorities, public libraries, publishers and individuals in the United Kingdom and overseas. Membership costs £69.50 p.a.

5077

SCOTTISH BOOK TRUST

Sandeman House, Trunks Close, 55 High Street, Edinburgh EH1 1SR
Telephone: 0131 524 0160
Fax: 0131 524 0161
Email: info@scottishbooktrust.com
Web Site: http://www.scottishbooktrust.com

Chief Executive Officer: Marc Lambert
Managers: Jeanette Harris *(General)*
  Sophie Moxon *(Head of Programme)*
  Marion Boyrbouze *(Marketing & Audience Development)*

Scottish Book Trust is an independent educational charity partly supported by the Scottish Arts Council to promote reading, writing and books. It offers a comprehensive information service and publishes a range of resources to support readership and reading campaigns.

Scottish Book Trust runs the Words on Wheels project and the 'Live Literature Scotland' scheme; the latter supports over 2000 writers' visits annually, providing 50% of the author's fee and all their expenses.

Scottish Book Trust also administers National Poetry Day in Scotland, and World Book Day in Scotland.

5078

SOCIETY FOR EDITORS & PROOFREADERS

Erico House, 93–99 Upper Richmond Road, London SW15 2TG
Telephone: (020) 8785 5617
Fax: (020) 8785 5618
Email: admin@sfep.org.uk
Web Site: http://www.sfep.org.uk

Chair: Penny Williams
Finance Director: Sarah Price

Founded in 1988 with the twin aims of promoting high editorial standards and achieving recognition of its members' professional status, the Society works to disseminate information and training, foster good relations between members and their clients, and combat the isolation often experienced by freelances. It supports recognized standards of training and accreditation for editors and proofreaders, and is establishing recognized standards for its own members. Membership in 2005 was approximately 1400.

Benefits of membership include: annual directory of members seeking work; free regular newsletter; local groups throughout the country; online discussion group; annual conference; meetings and training sessions in several centres, covering aspects of current professional practice and business matters; legal helpline; discounts on selected products and services.

5079

SOCIETY OF ARCHIVISTS

Prioryfield House, 20 Canon Street, Taunton, Somerset TA1 1SW
Telephone: 01823 327030 & 327077
Fax: 01823 271719
Email: societyofarchivists@archives.org.uk
Web Site: http://www.archives.org.uk

Executive Director: John Chambers
Membership Administrator: Lorraine Logan

Publication of texts/periodicals on archives and records management. Conferences and training courses.

5080

SOCIETY OF AUTHORS

84 Drayton Gardens, London SW10 9SB
Telephone: (020) 7373 6642
Fax: (020) 7373 5768
Email: info@societyofauthors.org
Web Site: http://www.societyofauthors.org

Chairman: Tracy Chevalier
General Secretary: Mark Le Fanu

An independent trade union for authors. Its purpose is to further the interests of its 8500 members through individual advice and general campaigning. It is controlled by an elected Committee of Management and administered by a staff with long experience in the business and legal aspects of authorship. Members have access to a comprehensive advisory service and may seek advice on all forms of contracts. The Society also serves the interests of specialist writers through a number of subsidiary groups – viz the Broadcasting Group, the Translators Association, Children's Writers and Illustrators, Educational Writers, Academic Writers and Medical Writers Groups. It makes representations to government departments and promotes campaigns on behalf of the profession as a whole (eg public lending right, tax concessions for authors, etc). It also administers literary estates, publishes a quarterly journal, *The Author*, issues numerous *Quick Guides* to its members and manages a variety of awards and trust funds for authors.

5081

*SOCIETY OF AUTHORS PENSION FUND

84 Drayton Gardens, London SW10 9SB
Telephone: (020) 7373 6642
Fax: (020) 7373 5768
Email: info@societyofauthors.org
Web Site: http://www.societyofauthors.org

Secretary: Mark Le Fanu

A small number of pensions is granted by the Pension Fund Committee to authors over the age of 60 who have been members of the Society for 10 years. Pensions are normally £1700 per annum.

5082

SOCIETY OF EDITORS
University Centre, Granta Place, Cambridge CB2 1RU
Telephone: 01223 304080
Fax: 01223 304090
Email: info@societyofeditors.org
Web Site: http://www.societyofeditors.org

Executive Director: Bob Satchwell

The Society of Editors has more than 400 members in national, regional and local newspapers, magazines, broadcasting and new media, journalism, education and media law.

It campaigns for media freedom, self-regulation, the public's right to know and the maintenance of standards in journalism.

5083

SOCIETY OF INDEXERS
Woodbourn Business Centre, 10 Jessell Street, Sheffield S9 3HY
Telephone: 0114 244 9561 or 07757 813134
Fax: 0114 244 9563
Email: admin@indexers.org.uk
Web Site: http://www.indexers.org.uk

Secretary: Mrs Ann Kingdom
Treasurer: Ms Cate Allwood

Founded 1957 to raise the standards of indexing of books, periodicals and documents by holding meetings, courses and conferences and to issue a journal, *The Indexer*, and regular newsletters. Publishes and runs an open-learning course 'Training in Indexing'. The Society publishes a directory of members (*Indexers Available*) competent to do indexing in a wide range of both simple and specialized subject fields. Copies may be obtained from the Society's office, or be viewed on its website. Minimum scales of payment are recommended by the Society for use by members as a basis for negotiation with publishers. The Society wishes to impress on both publishers and authors the need for adequate and competent indexes in non-fiction works.

5084

SOCIETY OF MEDICAL WRITERS
Ashlett House, 24 Rochester Way, Sudbury, Essex CO10 1LP
Telephone: 01787 374879
Email: raymond.hume@btinternet.com
Web Site: http://www.somw.org.uk

Chairman: Dr Raymond Hume
Finance Officer: Dr Richard Cutler
Editor: Dr Michael Lasserson

Membership of the Society of Medical Writers is open to anyone who publishes or aspires to publish their work of whatever nature – medical or non-medical, fact or fiction, prose or poetry. It is intended that the association should be enjoyable, stimulating and educational so that writing from medical practice, including general practice, is improved and encouraged.

The aims of the Society are therefore to:
- improve standards of writing by medical practitioners;
- encourage literacy whether in scientific papers, review articles, historical or anecdotal essays;
- provide meetings for practitioners interested in writing, for the exchange of views, skills and ideas;
- provide education on the preparation, presentation and submission of written material for publication;
- act as a means of introduction between practitioners and suitable publishers and editors;
- maintain a register of members of the SOMW, available to commissioning editors and others;
- advise on sources of assistance with regard to technical, legal and financial aspects of writing;
- consider questions of ethics relating to writing and publication;
- further developments in the art of writing and to facilitate access to educational opportunities for those motivated to become better writers.

5085

TRANSLATORS ASSOCIATION
84 Drayton Gardens, London SW10 9SB
Telephone: (020) 7373 6642
Fax: (020) 7373 5768
Email: info@societyofauthors.org & sbaxter@societyofauthors.org
Web Site: http://www.societyofauthors.org

Secretary: Sarah Baxter

The Translators Association is a subsidiary of the Society of Authors and advises literary translators on such matters as contracts and fees. Publishers seeking book translators can search the online database.

5086

*TRAVELLING SCHOLARSHIP FUND
Society of Authors, 84 Drayton Gardens, London SW10 9SB
Telephone: (020) 7373 6642
Fax: (020) 7373 5768
Email: info@societyofauthors.org
Web Site: http://www.societyofauthors.org

Secretary: Mark Le Fanu

Founded in 1944 by an anonymous donor, to enable British creative writers to travel and to keep in touch with their colleagues abroad. A special committee annually reviews the field of contemporary literature before making its awards, which are not for open candidature, and are normally made to established writers of over 30 years of age. The Fund is administered by the Society of Authors.

5087

WATCH (WRITERS ARTISTS & THEIR COPYRIGHT HOLDERS)
The Library, University of Reading, PO Box 223, Whiteknights, Reading RG6 6AE
Telephone: 0118 378 8783
Fax: 0118 378 6636
Email: d.c.sutton@reading.ac.uk
Web Site: http://www.watch-file.com

Director: Dr D. Sutton

WATCH provides a free online database of information about the copyright holders of literary authors, artists and prominent persons. The database is in the form of an open-access public website, jointly maintained by the Universities of Texas and Reading.

5088

WELSH BOOKS COUNCIL / CYNGOR LLYFRAU CYMRU
Castell Brychan, Aberystwyth, Ceredigion, Wales SY23 2JB
Telephone: 01970 624151
Fax: 01970 625385
Email: castellbrychan@cllc.org.uk
Web Site: http://www.cllc.org.uk & http://www.gwales.com

Director: Gwerfyl Pierce Jones
Head of Department: Sion Ilar *(Design)*
   Marian Beech Hughes *(Editorial)*
   D. Philip Davies *(Information Services)*
   Menna Lloyd Williams *(Children's Books)*
   Dafydd Charles Jones *(Distribution)*
   Arwyn Roderick *(Finance)*
   Elwyn Jones *(Administration & Public Relations)*
   Helgard Krause *(Sales & Marketing)*

The Welsh Books Council is a national organization with charitable status funded by the Welsh Assembly Government. Established in 1961, it is responsible for promoting all sectors of the publishing industry in Wales, in both languages, in conjunction with publishers, booksellers, libraries and schools. The Council is also responsible for distributing publishing grants for Welsh-language publishing and Welsh writing in English. Its Wholesale Distribution Centre stocks the vast majority of Welsh-interest titles currently available. www.gwales.com, the Council's on-line information and ordering service, is a one-stop shop for titles of relevance to Wales.

5089

WORSHIPFUL COMPANY OF STATIONERS AND NEWSPAPER MAKERS
Stationers' Hall, Ave Maria Lane, London EC4M 7DD
Telephone: (020) 7248 2934
Fax: (020) 7489 1975
Email: admin@stationers.org
Web Site: http://www.stationers.org

Master: N. H. Osborne
Clerk: Brigadier D. G. Sharp AFC

The Worshipful Company of Stationers had its beginnings in a Guild dating back at least to 1403; the original Charter was granted in 1557. The Company was expanded in modern times (1933) to include the Newspaper Makers. For nearly four centuries it was essential for the protection of copyright to register books at Stationers' Hall; since 1924 an extensively used system of voluntary registration has been in force. This was discontinued in February 2000.

The Company's object has always been to promote the interests of the printing and allied trades, among them publishing and bookbinding. Its activities at the present day include the binding of apprentices and the award of scholarships to young men and women in these trades and the provision of pensions and financial help for tradesmen and their widows. The Company also plays a full part in the life of the City of London.

The Stationers' Hall may be hired for functions.

6 Trade & Allied Services

6.1 EDITORIAL SERVICES

6001

AESOP (ALL EDITORIAL SERVICES ONLINE FOR PUBLISHERS & AUTHORS)
28 Abberbury Road, Iffley, Oxford OX4 4ES
Telephone: 01865 429563
Fax: 08700 635449
Email: mart@copyedit.co.uk
Web Site: http://www.copyedit.co.uk

Owner/Editor: Martin Noble

AESOP provides the following editorial services to publishers, authors, academics and businesses: copy-editing; proof-reading; structural editing; rewriting; co-writing; ghost-writing; thesis and dissertation editing and printing; improving use of English of non-native English writers of academic reports and books; indexing; editorial reports and reviews; advice to publishers, authors and literary agents; novelization; research; fact-checking; bibliographical research; CRC (camera ready copy) in Word format; text capture; scanning/OCR; e-book production on CD-ROM or online; keying in MSS; audio transcription; tagging. Specializes in fiction, literature, poetry, media, music, performing arts, humour, biography, memoirs, travel, education, economics, psychology, history, alternative health, new age, esoteric and spiritual subjects, special needs.

6002

ASGARD PUBLISHING SERVICES
75 Woodside View, Leeds LS4 2QS
Telephone: 0113 274 1037
Fax: 0113 274 1037
Email: andrew.shackleton@asgardpublishing.co.uk
Web Site: http://www.asgardpublishing.co.uk

Also at:
Allan Scott
Telephone: 01449 741747
Fax: 01449 740118
Email: allanscott@compuserve.com

Personnel: Philip Gardner
Michael Scott Rohan
Allan Scott
Andrew Shackleton

Established in 1984. Full editorial service, including writing and re-writing, translating, copy-editing, proof-reading, indexing, design and layout. Projects can be taken from manuscript to film, or to Quark XPress files. Extensive experience with DTP, computer-based multimedia projects (including video production) and electronic publishing. Reference material is a speciality.

6003

*ASTERISK DESIGN & EDITORIAL SOLUTIONS
8 Carnyorth Terrace, Carnyorth, St Just, Cornwall TR19 7QE
Telephone: 01736 788202
Email: yvonnebristow@blue-earth.co.uk

Directors: Roger Bristow (Art)
Yvonne McFarlane (Editorial)

Offers research, copywriting/rewriting, editing, graphic design, art direction and the commissioning of original illustrations, photographs and maps. Will also draft and negotiate book contracts and can research and write copy on subjects ranging from food and drink (including recipes, recipe testing and restaurant reviews) to crafts, history, reference, travel and practical and fine art.

6004

BBR SOLUTIONS LTD
12 Cutthorpe Road, Chesterfield S42 7AE
Telephone: 01246 271662
Fax: 01246 271662
Email: solutions@bbr-online.com
Web Site: http://www.bbr-online.com/solutions

Directors: Chris Reed
Amanda Thompson

Associated Companies:
UK: BBR Distribution

BBR Solutions is an editorial and design consultancy with over 20 years' experience in publishing. It proofs and edits manuscripts for publication, and creates clean typography-led designs for books and journals. Please take a look at the company's website for some examples.

6005

BLACK ACE BOOK PRODUCTION
PO Box 7547, Perth PH2 1AU
Telephone: 01821 642822
Fax: 01821 642101
Web Site: http://www.blackacebooks.com

Directors: Hunter Steele
Boo Wood

Book production and text processing, including text capture (or scanning), editing, proofing to camera-ready/film, printing and binding, jacket artwork and design. Delivery of finished books; can sometimes help with distribution.

6006

BOOK CREATION LTD
20 Lochaline Street, London W6 9SH
Telephone: (020) 8626 1852
Fax: (020) 8626 1851
Email: hal@bookcreation.com
Web Site: http://www.bookcreation.com

Managing Director: Hal Robinson

Associated Companies:
UK: Librios Ltd

Book Creation provides editorial, translation, design and packaging/repackaging services, using Mac and PC technology, to text and layouts or final film, primarily in illustrated non-fiction, partworks, dictionaries and general reference, often involving re-use of existing illustrative or text resources.

Its sister company, Librios, provides comprehensive, XML-based electronic publishing and content management services.

6007

CHAMELEON HH PUBLISHING LTD
The Quarry House, East End, Witney, Oxon OX29 6QA
Telephone: 01993 880223
Email: chameleon@chameleonhh.co.uk
Web Site: http://www.chameleonhh.co.uk

Directors: Marion Hebblethwaite (Managing)
Robert White (Editorial)
Company Secretary: Helen Hazzledine

Editorial services for self-publishers, electronic publishing services, training in MS Word / Adobe for press quality files.

6008

COPYTRAIN
Pitts, Great Milton, Oxford OX44 7NF
Telephone: 01844 279345
Fax: 01844 279345
Email: rbalkwill@aol.com

Proprietor: Richard Balkwill

Copytrain provides a consultancy and advisory service to publishers in the training and copyright fields.
Training: Publishing Training Centre lecturer in editorial management, financial planning and copyright. Seminars in contracts, copyright and rights. Courses in all aspects of publishing and management.
Copyright: Advice to publishers on rights and copyright matters. Review of authors' and suppliers' contracts and agreements. Associate of Rightscom.
Clients include CAB International, the British Council and the Publishers Licensing Society.
Copytrain provides 'work-for-hire' writing commissions, especially in the children's reference area (non-fiction, history, railways).

6009

*EDITION
PO Box 1, Moffat, Dumfriesshire DG10 9SU
Telephone: 01683 220808
Fax: 01683 220012
Email: edition@cameronbooks.co.uk

Directors: Jill Hollis
Ian Cameron

In association with Cameron Books, Edition offers a complete range of services up to delivery of finished books. Services include: editing, proofreading, indexing, in-house typesetting, photography, picture research, design, production. Edition is able to offer an editing, design and production package including whatever ancillary services a particular title demands, and is an experienced producer of museum and exhibition catalogues and educational books as well as titles for general trade distribution.

6010

***THE EDITMASTER COMPANY**
28 Langham Place, Northampton NN2 6AA
Telephone: 01604 715915
Email: info@editmaster.co.uk
Web Site: http://www.editmaster.co.uk

Editorial Director: Christopher Long
Company Secretary: Nina Long

Associated Companies:
Germany: Cadmos Verlag GmbH

Editmaster is a project management and editorial services consultancy providing a comprehensive range of services to publishers and others producing books, reports and other printed materials.

Editmaster offers expertise in the following areas: research, report-writing, translation, editing, proof-reading, indexing, design, picture research and project management.

6011

FIRST EDITION TRANSLATIONS LTD
6 Wellington Court, Wellington Street, Cambridge CB1 1HZ
Telephone: 01223 356733
Fax: 01223 316232
Email: info@firstedit.co.uk
Web Site: http://www.firstedit.co.uk

Contact: Sheila Waller

First Edition offers complete and specialized editorial and translation services, including all necessary liaison: translation, research, editing, Americanization, proofreading, indexing, desktop publishing, print ready PDF or CD output. Assessment of foreign language books for the market.

6012

GEO GROUP & ASSOCIATES
4 Christian Fields, London SW16 3JZ
Telephone: (020) 8764 6292
Fax: 0115 981 9418
Email: Nyala.publishing@geo-group.co.uk
Web Site: http://www.geo-group.co.uk

Also at:
Nyala Publishing, 97 Rivermead, West Bridgford, Nottingham NG2 7RF
Telephone: 0115 981 9418
Email: (as above)
Web Site: (as above)

Director: John Douglas

Associated Companies:
UK: Nyala Publishing

Publishing services: pre-press, editing, design, proofreading, reading.

6013

CHRISTOPHER PICK
41 Chestnut Road, London SE27 9EZ
Telephone: (020) 8761 2585
Fax: (020) 8761 6388
Email: christopher@the-picks.co.uk

Publications Consultant: Christopher Pick

I research, write, edit and produce information materials for public- and voluntary-sector agencies and for the corporate sector. I specialize in producing documents (e.g. policy and research reports, annual reports, handbooks) that are accessible and clearly written and that meet the needs of the target audience/readership. I also write and produce 'popular' histories of organizations, companies, etc.

6014

DAVID PRICE
[trading as Acupuntuation Ltd]
4 Harbidges Lane, Long Buckby, Northampton NN6 7QL
Telephone: 01327 844119
Fax: 01327 844119
Email: acuedit@fireflyuk.net
Web Site: http://www.acuedit.co.uk

Contact: David Price

Associated Companies:
UK: Acupuntuation Ltd

Writing, rewriting, editing, proofreading.
Special interests:
– Fine Art (particularly Modern Art);
– Music (particularly operettas and musicals, pop and rock music);
– Travel Guides;
– Modern European History and Politics (particularly Eastern Europe and the former Soviet Union);
– Social and Cultural History.

6015

THE PUZZLE HOUSE
Ivy Cottage, Battlesea Green, Stradbroke, Suffolk IP21 5NE
Telephone: 01379 384656
Fax: 01379 384656
Email: puzzlehouse@btinternet.com
Web Site: http://www.thepuzzlehouse.co.uk

Partners: Roy Preston
Sue Preston

The Puzzle House supplies crossword, quiz and puzzle material for books and magazines. Full editorial service is offered on projects ranging from a one-off puzzle to full CRC book. All subject areas and age ranges catered for. Specialist interest and experience in the children's activity market. Established 1988. Puzzles available for syndication.

6016

RONNE RANDALL
26 Oak Tree Avenue, Radcliffe-on-Trent, Nottingham NG12 1AD
Telephone: 0115 933 5804
Fax: 0115 910 1630
Email: ronnerandall@aol.com

Proprietor: Ronne Randall

Accurate Americanization by a native of the USA, as well as editorial services including editing, copy editing, writing, rewriting/adaptation, and proofreading. Special interest and experience in children's books (including licensed characters). Clients include Ladybird, Macmillan, Hodder Children's Books, Templar and Parragon.

6017

READING AND RIGHTING
[Robert Lambolle Services]
618b Finchley Road, London NW11 7RR
Telephone: (020) 8455 4564
Email: lambhorn@gmail.com
Web Site: http://readingandrighting.netfirms.com

Managing Director: Robert Lambolle *(Literary/Script Consultant)*

Established in 1987, Reading & Righting is an independent script consultancy providing evaluation and editing services, based on wide-ranging agency and publishing experience. Detailed assessment, analysis of prospects and next-step guidelines for fiction, non-fiction, screenplays, plays and poetry, plus full editing service, one-to-one tutorials, mentoring, lectures, creative writing courses, and research. Prospective clients should consult website or request leaflet outlining procedure and terms.

Specialist interests include cinema, the performing arts, popular culture, psychotherapy and current affairs.

6018

SANDHURST EDITORIAL
36 Albion Road, Sandhurst, Berks GU47 9BP
Telephone: 01252 877645
Fax: 01252 890508
Email: lionel.browne@sfep.net
Web Site: http://www.sandhurst-editorial.co.uk

Proprietor: Lionel Browne

Current clients include:
UK: CAPDM; Edinburgh Business School; Fluor Ltd; HIS BRE Press; London Business School; Oxford Diocesan Publications; Oxford University Press; Palgrave Publishers; Pearson Education; Publishing Training Centre; RIBA Enterprises; Thomas Telford; Wiley Blackwell

Sandhurst Editorial provides a complete editorial service for clients inside and outside the UK, both private sector and public sector: academic and educational publishers, research associations, commercial clients, and government departments. The skills on offer include editorial development and consultancy, project management, writing, rewriting, copy-editing and proofreading.

The company specializes in science and technology, but has handled projects as diverse as bibles, biography, travel guides and corporate reports.

6019

SUNRISE SETTING LTD
12a Fore Street, St Marychurch, Torquay, Devon TQ1 4NE
Telephone: 01803 322635
Fax: 01803 323565
Email: enquiries@sunrise-setting.co.uk
Web Site: http://www.sunrise-setting.co.uk

Directors: Jessica Stock *(Finance & Marketing)*
Alistair Smith *(Technical)*

Sunrise Setting Ltd has over 20 years' experience of providing a high-quality typesetting, editorial and project management service to STM publishers, including copyediting, a full XML workflow, graphics manipulation, project management of conference proceedings, books and journals, and the writing of LaTex class files and author support.

6020

*WORDS4PROFIT
19 Albemarle Road, Gorleston-on-Sea, Norfolk NR31 7AR
Telephone: 01493 444556
Email: eldo@words4profit.com
Web Site: http://www.words4profit.com

Web Copywriter, Website Editor: Eldo Barkhuizen

Associated Companies:
UK: words4profit

Web copywriting, website editing. Established 2005.

6021

HANS ZELL PUBLISHING CONSULTANTS
Glais Bheinn, Lochcarron, Ross-shire IV54 8YB
Telephone: 01520 722951
Fax: 01520 722953
Email: hanszell@hanszell.co.uk
Web Site: http://www.hanszell.co.uk/

Proprietor: Hans M. Zell

Associated Companies:
UK: Hans Zell Publishing

Consultancy service to publishers and academic institutions, in particular providing advisory services and individual project management for publishers, research institutes, and the book community in Africa and in other developing countries.

Specialization:
– scholarly publishing, especially university press publishing, and publishing by research institutions and NGOs, including editorial and financial management, administration, marketing and promotion, pricing and distribution, general publishing management, and dealing with author and publisher contracts
– journals publishing management, including subscription management and fulfilment, financial control, journals promotion, and market assessments
– reference book publishing, particularly for reference resources focusing on Africa and the developing world, including research, project evaluations, editorial services, and market assessments
– training – in-house or through workshops and seminars – in editorial and production management, financial planning, and all areas of marketing
– marketing and distribution of books on African and development studies, and African literature and culture – providing a range of specialist mailing list services in this area, full details available on request.
– Internet training for the book professions in developing countries.

Also publisher of information resources (print and online) on Africa, African studies and African publishing.

6.2 DESIGN & PRODUCTION SERVICES

6022

BOOK PRODUCTION CONSULTANTS LTD
25–27 High Street, Chesterton, Cambridge CB4 1ND
Telephone: 01223 352790
Fax: 01223 460718
Email: bpc@bpccam.co.uk
Web Site: http://www.bpccam.co.uk

Also at:
The Baltic Exchange, St Mary Axe, London EC3A 8EX
Telephone: (020) 7623 2308
Fax: (020) 7623 2309
Email: bpc@bpccam.co.uk
Web Site: http://www.bpccam.co.uk

Managing Director: Colin Walsh
Managers: Jo Littlechild *(Marketing)*
　Susan Buck *(Accounts)*
　Jo'e Coleby *(Editorial Project)*

Associated Companies:
UK: Book Connections; Granta Editions

A totally comprehensive publishing service including editing, sub-editing, designing, technical mark-up, illustrating, technical drawing, estimating, paper buying, typesetting and origination. BPC arranges the printing and binding of black-and-white or colour publications in the UK or overseas and supervises quality control and delivery schedules; also computer software packs including design of packaging and manufacture of boxes, tapes and discs. Other specialities include the design and production of illustrated books, music and foreign language setting projects, academic journals and institutional publications, producing company sponsored books and company histories. Electronic publishing and CD-ROM origination, particularly as joint ventures, form part of current expansion. Specialist divisions include business histories (providing authors, archivists and picture researchers), contract magazine production and company literature.

6023

BOOKCRAFT LTD
18 Kendrick Street, Stroud, Glos GL5 1AA
Telephone: 0870 1601900
Fax: 0870 1601901
Email: information@bookcraft.co.uk
Web Site: http://www.bookcraft.co.uk

Director: John Button *(Publishing)*

Clients include:
UK: Collector's Library; Pearson; Taylor & Francis

Bookcraft provides publishers with a wide range of editorial, design, technical and training services.
　Main areas of activity are:
　– publishing consultancy
　– publishing software training
　– design services
　– editorial and proofreading services
　– project management.

6024

CHASE PUBLISHING SERVICES LTD
'Mead', Fortescue Road, Sidmouth, Devon EX10 9QG
Telephone: 01395 514709
Fax: 01395 514709
Email: r.addicott@chase-publishing.co.uk

Director: Ray Addicott

Chase offers a complete editorial and production service to authors and publishers – from copy-editing of the author's typescript to finished books at the delivery point. It specializes in academic books but can also work in most areas of book publishing by linking with other specialists. Founded in 1989.

6025

***DISCRIPT LTD**
24 Bedfordbury, Covent Garden, London WC2N 4BN
Telephone: (020) 7240 3196
Fax: (020) 7379 8559
Email: info@discript.com
Web Site: http://www.discript.com

Directors: Richard Bates *(Managing)*
　F. R. Bates *(Finance)*

Discript can provide editorial, proofreading, production, book design and typography, including text keyboarding, OCR capture and indexing. Whether a large technical document, illustrated book or colour leaflet is required, Discript can provide a fast efficient service. It also helps authors to self-publish.

6026

FOTOLIBRA
22 Mount View Road, London N4 4HX
Telephone: (020) 8348 1234
Email: professionals@fotoLibra.com
Web Site: http://www.fotoLibra.com

Directors: Gwyn Headley
　Yvonne Seeley

Associated Companies:
USA: Idea Logical Company Inc

Organizations who have used fotoLibra's services include:
UK: Bemrose; Carlton Books; Compendium; Hodder Headline; Macmillan; Pearson; Penguin; Quarto; Random House

fotoLibra is a picture library set up by publishers for publishers. The company has 18,000+ photographers in over 150 countries to take the required image if it is not already in the library – and there's no obligation to buy. Over 250,000 images on line.

6027

GRAHAM-CAMERON ILLUSTRATION
The Studio, 23 Holt Road, Sheringham, Norfolk NR26 8NB
Telephone: 01263 821333
Fax: 01263 821334
Email: enquiry@graham-cameron-illustration.com
Web Site: http://www.graham-cameron-illustration.com

Sales & Marketing:
Duncan Graham-Cameron, 59 Hertford Road, Brighton BN1 7GG
Telephone: 01273 385890 (mobile: 07773 523587)
Email: forename@graham-cameron-illustration.com
Web Site: (as above)

Partners: Mike Graham-Cameron *(Finance)*
　Helen Graham-Cameron *(Art)*
　Duncan Graham-Cameron *(Sales & Marketing)*

Parent Company:
UK: Graham-Cameron Publishing

Associated Companies:
UK: Helen Herbert, Fine Art

This agency has some 37 qualified professional illustrators who have a wide range of techniques, media and artistic skills. GCI specializes in pictures for educational and children's books, ELT and for general information publications.

6028

HOLBROOK DESIGN OXFORD LTD
Holbrook House, 105 Rose Hill, Oxford OX4 4HT
Telephone: 01865 459000
Email: info@holbrook-design.co.uk
Web Site: http://www.holbrook-design.co.uk

Directors: Peter Tucker *(Design)*
　Alex Tucker *(Production)*

Holbrook Design Oxford Ltd was founded as PGT Design in 1974. It offers the following services: typography, editorial design and art direction, photography; from concept through dummies, mark-up and typesetting, page layouts to artwork, in consultation with photographers, illustrators and printers. Clients include many national and international publishers. Holbrook Design has particular experience in educational and general publishing; subject areas covered range from science to religion, cookery to history and first readers to A-level.

6029

HOLBROOK HOSTING
Holbrook House, 105 Rose Hill, Oxford OX4 4HT
Telephone: 01865 459000
Email: info@holbrookhosting.com
Web Site: http://www.holbrookhosting.com

Partner: Peter Tucker *(Consultant)*

Design Systems is a consultancy providing both technical and design expertise in the implementation and use of both Macs and PCs in graphics and publishing industries. Agents include Adobe, Quark, Ventura Software, Monotype, Linotype and other associated companies. Affiliated to Holbrook Design Oxford Ltd, for many years designers in publishing and print.

6030

HYBERT DESIGN LTD
Suite 3, Maple Court, Grove Park, White Waltham, Berks SL6 3LW
Telephone: 01628 822700
Fax: 01628 822288
Email: info@hybertdesign.com
Web Site: http://www.hybertdesign.com

Also at:
Buterud P1 8722, 464 91 Dals Rostock, Sweden
Telephone: +46 (0)530 30084

Director: Tom Hybert
Company Secretary: Kate Hybert
Senior Designer: Linda Elliott

Established in 1975, Hybert Design specializes in marketing, promotion and cover design for publishers in all areas, including education, science and technology, journal and business publishing.

6031

***IMAGO PUBLISHING LTD**
Albury Court, Albury, Thame, Oxon OX9 2LP
Telephone: 01844 337000
Fax: 01844 339935
Email: reception@imago.co.uk
Web Site: http://www.imago.co.uk

Directors: Colin Risk *(Managing)*
　Jim Allpass *(Finance)*
　Angela Young
　Debbie Knight
　Cherry Jaquet *(Production)*
　Martina Scheible

Offers production consultancy, print broking and training to the publishing industry. With offices in the UK, Paris, Hong Kong, Singapore, Sydney, New York, Chicago and California, the group is able to locate and control sources of manufacture on a world-wide basis. The group works with a wide range of customers, and can offer its extensive expertise in many ways, from running all the production needs for small publishers/packagers, to sourcing and arranging for the manufacture of individual projects on a competitive brokerage basis. All types of work are handled, including colour separation, children's books, novelty products, short- and long-run general books and magazines. Training courses in colour, toy safety, paper, assessing digital images and CTP run regularly.

6032

***LEGASTAT COPYING & SCANNING**
57 Carey Street, London WC2A 2JB
Telephone: (020) 7405 9178
Fax: (020) 7405 3877
Email: services@legastat.co.uk

Proprietor: John Eddowes *(Customer Relations)*
Manager: David Collings

Legastat is a copying and scanning service in central London, specializing in the rapid xeroxing of manuscripts, advance information sheets, publicity information, etc for publishers and literary agents. The reproduction of galleys, camera-ready artwork, and large charts, roughs and posters, by xerographic machinery, is also undertaken. OHTs and high-resolution colour pix produced: also colour copies from trannies and large format colour. Printing-out and copying from disc/email. Free collection and delivery in central London to ensure rapid turnround (Legastat is open 24 hours). Clients include many of the major publishers.

Legastat's scanning operation will put typescripts onto computer and return them on any media, either as straight image or OCR/PDF documents.

6033

MY WORD!
PO Box 4575, Rugby, Warwickshire CV21 9EH
Telephone: 01788 571294
Fax: 01788 550957
Email: enquiries@myword.co.uk
Web Site: http://www.myword.co.uk

Partners: Roderick Grant
Janet Grant
DTP Operator: Sally Stow

My Word! is a family business which specializes in typesetting of materials for both printing and the Internet.

Its range includes magazines, books, newsletters, newspapers, brochures, conference and sales materials, leaflets, posters and stationery.

Clients come from both the charity and commercial sectors.

6034

SMALL PRINT
The Old School House, 74 High Street, Swavesey, Cambridge CB24 4QU
Telephone: 01954 231713 (mobile: 07760 430206)
Fax: 01954 205061
Email: info@smallprint.co.uk
Web Site: http://www.smallprint.co.uk

French Fotos:
(as above)
Telephone: (as above)
Fax: (as above)
Email: frenchfotos@aol.com
Web Site: http://www.frenchfotos.co.uk

Proprietor: Naomi Laredo
Photographer: Louise John

A flexible publishing and translation resource for publishers and businesses producing educational, training and information material.

Project management and production service includes research, copywriting, editing and proofreading, design and layout for web or print, audio and video production.

Translation and language-checking service covers most European and Asian languages.

French Fotos offers up-to-date images of France and the French, from stock or taken to order.

Clients to date include ACCA, Berlitz, Cambridge University Press, Channel 4 Learning, Dorling Kindersley, Henley Management College, Nelson Thornes.

6.3 ELECTRONIC PUBLISHING SERVICES

6035

*ELECTRONIC PUBLISHING SERVICES LTD
7–15 Rosebery Avenue, London EC1R 4SP
Telephone: (020) 7837 3345
Fax: (020) 7837 8901
Email: eps@epsltd.com
Web Site: http://www.outsellinc.com

Senior Personnel: David R. Worlock (Sales)
David J. Powell (Rights)
Jo McShea (Research Manager)
Kate Worlock

Parent Company:
UK: Outsell Inc

Consultancy and market research concerning the use of electronic media for the delivery of information products and services. Publishing – industry analysis, reports and multi-client studies.

6036

KOALA PUBLISHING LTD
Downend House, 112 North Street, Downend, Bristol BS16 5SE
Telephone: 0117 910 9111
Fax: 0117 910 9222
Email: sales@koalapub.co.uk
Web Site: http://www.koalapub.co.uk

Directors: Gordon Dennis (Commercial)
Vivienne Willoughby-Ellis (Managing)
Marketing Manager: Robin Shobbrook

Koala helps suppliers of complex products and services who need to:
– create straightforward, easy to use documentation and get it to their customers in the most effective way possible – from PDAs to printer manuals;
– efficiently organize, write and deliver their technical manuals, policies and procedures;
– reduce the cost and time constraints on professional staff of providing information to their customers, and reduce the long-term risks of litigation caused by faulty documentation.

Koala provides software products for publishing technical documentation including manuals, training materials, catalogues, directories and listings. Services include project management and control; analysis and design; bespoke programming; data format conversion; and full training and support.

6037

MMT
Glaston Hall, Spring Lane, Glaston, Oakham, Rutland LE15 9BZ
Telephone: 01572 822278
Fax: 01572 820213
Email: info@mmtdigital.co.uk
Web Site: http://www.mmtdigital.co.uk

London Office:
6–18 Northumberland Street, London N1 2HY
Telephone: (as above)
Fax: (as above)
Email: (as above)
Web Site: (as above)

Directors: Peter Cannings (Managing & Finance)
Ben Rudman (Marketing)
James Cannings (Production)

Currently working with Hodder on their e-titles.

6038

NIELSEN BOOKNET
3rd Floor, Midas House, 62 Goldsworth Road, Woking, Surrey GU21 6LQ
Telephone: 0870 777 8710
Fax: 0870 777 8711
Email: sales.booknet@nielsen.com
Web Site: http://www.nielsenbooknet.co.uk

Directors: Jonathan Nowell (President)
Simon Skinner (Sales)
Head of BookNet Sales: Stephen Long
Head of Marketing: Mo Siewcharran
Transaction Services Sales Manager: Mark Hunt

Parent Company:
UK: Nielsen Book
USA: The Nielsen Company

Nielsen BookNet provides a range of e-commerce services that allow electronic trading between booksellers, distributors, publishers, libraries and other suppliers, regardless of their size and location. Services include BookNet Web for booksellers and publishers/distributors, TeleOrdering and EDI. Nielsen BookNet is uniquely placed in the book trade to be the trading hub for orders, invoices, delivery notes and other EDI messaging.

6039

*ODS BUSINESS SERVICES LTD
Frankland Road, Blagrove, Swindon SN5 8YG
Telephone: 01793 421300
Email: sales@ods-businessservices.com
Web Site: http://www.ods-businessservices.com

Also at:
ODS Business Services London, Hatfield House, 52–54 Stamford Street, London SE1 9LX
Telephone: (020) 7960 4100
Email: sales.london@ods-businessservices.com
Web Site: (as above)

Also at:
ODS Business Services Scotland, 4 Woodside Terrace, Glasgow G3 7UY
Telephone: 0141 354 0050
Fax: 0141 354 0051
Email: sales.scotland@ods-businessservices.com
Web Site: (as above)

Directors: Ray Wheeler (Managing)
Franky Marulanda (Commercial)
Managers: Phil Doran (Operations)
Dean Watkins (Sales)
Pat Harris (Customer Services)
Marc Hendrickse (Head of Technology)
David Neve (Finance)

Associated Companies:
Germany: ODS Optical Disc Service GmbH

ODS Business Services offers:
– Data management
– Content management
– CD & DVD authoring & development
– CD & DVD express duplication
– CD & DVD replication
– Artwork design
– Print management
– Contract packaging
– Fulfilment & logistics
– Secure disposal & recycling
– Branded products & accessories

6040

*THOMAS TECHNOLOGY
Lee House, 109 Hammersmith Road, London W14 0QH
Telephone: (020) 7070 7550
Fax: (020) 7070 7551
Email: pcamilleri@thomastech.co.uk
Web Site: http://www.thomastechsolutions.com

Also at:
One Progress Drive, Horsham, PA 19044, USA
Telephone: +1 (215) 682 5000

Managing Director: Peter Camilleri

Parent Company:
Worldwide: Thomas Publishing Co Inc

Thomas Technology provides electronic publishing services to publishers, database producers, libraries and corporations. These services include data conversion, data capture, database creation, web sites, Internet publishing and CD-ROM development.

6041

*TRILOGY GROUP
Aries House, 43 Selkirk Street, Cheltenham, Glos GL52 2HJ
Telephone: 01242 222132
Fax: 01242 235103
Email: john_llewellyn@trilogygroup.com
Web Site: http://www.trilogygroup.com

Directors: Alex Dare (Managing)
Simon Gough (IT)
Mike Ribbins (Group Chairman)
Operations Manager: Ian Harris

The Trilogy Group specializes in software for the specialist publisher, especially those requiring a totally integrated business solution to handle publishing management, administration, direct and distribution sales together with active marketing. Our software, which uses Microsoft SQL Server technology, offers:
– title management
– customer management with profiles and buying history
– active marketing facilities
– direct mail management with optional integration to MailSort
– subscriptions management

- royalties
- integration to accounting systems
- vast range of 'real time' management reports
- real-time stock management
- warehouse and despatch management
- integrated on-line shopping facilities with web hosting
- multi-site management
- EPOS
- production control, scheduling and job costing.

6042

VISTA
[a division of Publishing Technology]
Link House, 19 Colonial Way, Watford, Herts WD24 4JL
Telephone: 01923 830200
Fax: 01923 238789
Email: solutions@vistacomp.com
Web Site: http://www.vistacomp.com

Director: Colin Bottle *(Managing)*
Managers: Morayea Pindziak *(International Marketing)*
John Lawson *(UK Business Development)*

Parent Company:
UK: Publishing Technology Plc

Associated Companies:
Australia: Vista
USA: Vista Inc

A worldwide provider of print and online software solutions and services for the publishing industry. Vista's author2reader™ enterprise-wide applications framework is designed to meet the unique demands of the publishing industry at all stages of the publishing process. The framework provides a modular approach that allows Vista to assemble software components that meet the needs of individual publishers from a standard set of applications. The applications are supported by an array of specialized services, from data conversion and system integration to implementation to consulting to applications hosting.
Solutions include:
– fulfilment and distribution for books and journals
– warehouse management
– web-based customer service
– title and bibliographic data management
– production management
– business intelligence
– rights and royalties
– digital asset management
– online digital solutions
– off-shore development and support services
– content delivery and web sites.

6.4 TRANSLATION SERVICES

6043

AMERICAN PIE
179 Kings Cross Road, London WC1X 9BZ
Telephone: (020) 7278 9490
Fax: (020) 7278 2447
Email: bacon@americanization.com
Web Site: http://www.langservice.com

Also at:
215 West Red Oak #I, Sunnyvale, CA 94086-6632, USA
Email: DHenderson@aol.com
Web Site: http://www.americanization.com

Directors: Josephine Bacon *(Managing)*
Dan Henderson
Secretary: Azmi Jbeily

Parent Company:
USA: American Eyes Ltd

Associated Companies:
UK: Tamr Translations Ltd

American Pie is a company of translators, book packagers and designers, specializing in publishing work and foreign language typesetting. American Pie, with offices in London and Sunnyvale, California, translates between British and American English.

6044

BRITISH CENTRE FOR LITERARY TRANSLATION (BCLT)
University of East Anglia, Norwich NR4 7TJ
Telephone: 01603 592785
Fax: 01603 592737
Email: bclt@uea.ac.uk
Web Site: http://www.uea.ac.uk

Director: Amanda Hopkinson
Co-ordinator: Catherine Fuller

Parent Company:
UK: University of East Anglia

Raises the profile of literary translation and the professional development of literary translators. Organizes events, readings, workshops aimed at translators, professionals in arts and publishing and the general public.

6045

FIRST EDITION TRANSLATIONS LTD
6 Wellington Court, Wellington Street, Cambridge CB1 1HZ
Telephone: 01223 356733
Fax: 01223 316232
Email: info@firstedit.co.uk
Web Site: http://www.firstedit.co.uk

Contact: Sheila Waller

Translations – commercial, technical, academic and of any length – undertaken in any language according to publisher's requirements. Editing, proofreading, Americanization, indexing, typesetting/desktop publishing. Output to print ready PDF or CD. Quotations given without obligation.

6046

SATRAP PUBLISHING & TRANSLATION
Suite 21, London House, 271 King Street, Hammersmith, London W6 9LZ
Telephone: (020) 8748 9397
Fax: (020) 8748 9394
Email: satrap@btconnect.com
Web Site: http://www.satrap.co.uk

Managing Director: Alex Vahdat
Manager: Mrs Homa Lohrasb *(Technical)*

Satrap Publishing is a UK-based international company, specializing in the fields of translation, typesetting and print services in Oriental and East European languages.
The company produces promotional literature, exhibition catalogues, information pamphlets, books, reports, manuals, business stationery, product labels, diaries etc for Western European companies, trade centres and various organizations which have foreign language requirements for their overseas trade links.
The human resources and advanced technical facilities available are ideal for those clients who wish to target ethnic minorities for their social, cultural and educational programmes. Satrap Publishing offers a complete package of expert translation, typesetting, professional graphic design as well as printing. Production of exclusive greeting cards and wedding stationery in non-European languages are among other services from Satrap Publishing.

6047

*SERVICES FOR EXPORT AND LANGUAGE (SEL)
Maxwell Building, University of Salford, Manchester M5 4WT
Telephone: 0161 745 7480
Fax: 0161 295 5110
Email: sales@sel-uk.com
Web Site: http://www.sel-uk.com

Translations Manager: Patrick Murphy

SEL provides translations, simultaneous and consecutive interpreters and can arrange voice-overs in most sectors, in over 30 languages. All work to ISO 9001:2000.
SEL also provides language training and country briefing. Clients include a number of advertising agencies.

6048

*SWEDISH-ENGLISH LITERARY TRANSLATORS ASSOCIATION (SELTA)
3 Roseacre Close, London W13 8DG
Telephone: (020) 8997 1218
Web Site: http://www.swedishbookreview.com

Hon Secretary: Peter Linton
Editor, Swedish Book Review: Sarah Death

SELTA aims to promote the publication of Swedish literature in English and to represent the interests of those involved in its translation. Publishes *Swedish Book Review* (**ISSN:** 0265 8119): biannual, £15 p.a.

6049

UPS TRANSLATIONS
111 Baker Street, London W1U 6RR
Telephone: (020) 7224 1220
Fax: (020) 7486 3272
Email: info@upstranslations.com
Web Site: http://www.upstranslations.com

Chairman & Managing Director: Bernard Silver
Company Secretary: Denise McKenzie
Sales Director: Justin Silver
Marketing Manager: Becky McLaughlin

Parent Company:
UK: United Publicity Services Plc

Translation of books from manuscript to final film, into and from all the languages of the world, and Americanization.

6050

SALLY WALKER LANGUAGE SERVICES
43 St Nicholas Street, Bristol BS1 1TP
Telephone: 0117 929 1594
Fax: 0117 929 0633
Email: translations@sallywalker.co.uk
Web Site: http://www.sallywalker.co.uk

Also at:
Perch Buildings, 9 Mount Stuart Square, Cardiff CF10 5EE
Telephone: (029) 2048 0747
Fax: (029) 2048 8736
Email: languages@sallywalker.co.uk
Web Site: http://www.sallywalker.co.uk

Directors: Sally Walker
David Poole *(Sales & Marketing)*

Established in 1969 Sally Walker Language Services provides a 70 language capability. Languages include all European and major Middle Eastern and Far Eastern. Additionally most Indian and African languages are offered.

6051

WESSEX TRANSLATIONS LTD
Unit A1, Premier Centre, Abbey Park Industrial Estate, Romsey, Southampton SO51 9DG
Telephone: 0870 1669 300
Fax: 0870 1669 299
Email: sales@wt-lm.com
Web Site: http://www.wt-lm.com

Directors: Jonathan Nater
Robin Weber

Associated Companies:
France: Wessex Traductions

In addition to translation our services include interpreting, typesetting, DTP and artwork, editing and proofreading, copywriting, software localization, language training, audio and video transcription, voice-overs and website translations.
Translators always work into their mother tongue, and all translations are double-checked, and then re-worked, DTPed if required and checked again before despatch. The final text is sent by email with hard copy if required to meet clients' individual software requirements, ready to print wherever possible.
A special urgent Tender Translation Service is also offered.

6.5 SALES & MARKETING SERVICES

6052

BERTOLI MITCHELL LLP
53 Chandos Place, Covent Garden, London WC2N 4HS
Telephone: (020) 7812 6416
Fax: (020) 7812 6677
Email: nb@bertolimitchell.co.uk
Web Site: http://www.bertolimitchell.co.uk

Partners: William Mitchell (Managing)
Natalina Bertoli
Senior Associate: Paul Mitton

Bertoli Mitchell LLP is a specialist mergers and acquisitions advisory firm in the publishing and information industries.
The partnership offers corporate finance services for mergers, acquisitions and divestitures including:
- sell-side advisory representation to sellers of privately held businesses and corporate clients seeking to divest business units or assets
 - buy-side advisory services and representation
 - commercial and contracts due diligence
 - valuations
Since Bertoli Mitchell was founded in 1994 it has advised successfully on over 80 transactions.
Bertoli Mitchell also undertakes strategic research and consultancy. Activities include:
- profiling, analysis, forecasting and recommendations for clients considering entry into specific markets or sectors
- benchmarking, cost audits and development of financial targets
 - development of business plans
Clients range from large fully listed international companies to shareholders of small and medium-sized private businesses.

6053

BEST MAILING SERVICES LTD
Merlin Way, North Weald, Epping, Essex CM16 6HR
Telephone: 01992 524343
Fax: 01992 524552
Email: sales@bestmailing.co.uk
Web Site: http://www.bestmailing.co.uk

Directors: Mrs Lyn Reed (Managing)
Peter Cook (Client Services)

BMS offers a complete direct mail production facility.
Comprehensive services include database management, data capture, laser printing, mail order fulfilment, subscription management, machine and hand enclosing, bulk despatch, overseas and UK postal discounts.
BMS also provides high volume digital printing and on demand publishing, backed up with a professional finishing service which includes booklet making and collating.

6054

THE BOOK DEPOT
111 Woodcote Avenue, London NW7 2PD
Telephone: (020) 8906 3708
Email: conrad@adword.fsnet.co.uk

Proprietor: Conrad Wiberg

Sales, marketing, promotion campaigns, special sales service, out of print and antiquarian bookfinding service.

6055

BOOKLINK
43 Maycock Grove, Northwood, Middx HA6 3PU
Telephone: 01923 828612
Fax: 01923 828455
Email: info@booklink.co.uk
Web Site: http://www.booklink.co.uk

Managing Director: Evelyne Duval (Agent)

Associated Companies:
UK: Musketeer Books Ltd

An international connection for foreign rights sales and consultancy. Representing French, English and American publishers/packagers.

6056

BOOKPLATE
12 Hids Copse Road, Oxford OX2 9JJ
Telephone: 01865 861669
Email: sue.miller@oxfordcreative.com
Web Site: http://www.bookplate.org.uk

Yale Representation:
47 Bedford Square, London WC1B 3DP
Telephone: (020) 7079 4900

Marketing: Sue Miller
Sales: Kate Pocock
Andrew Jarmain
Distribution: John Holloran

Bookplate brings together Yale Representation, Oxford Creative Marketing and Marston – to provide a one-stop sales, marketing and distribution package for publishers.
Working with Bookplate, publishers benefit from:
– individual marketing for each publisher ensuring maximum visibility and profile raising
– wide-ranging, flexible services customized for each publisher
– direct access to the individual sales, marketing and distribution companies
– total transparency in reporting on customers and sales
– 24/7 access to all sales and customer information – fully downloadable
– a pre-agreed fee encompassing the costs and services of all three companies payable as a percentage of net sales.
Contact Sue Miller at Oxford Creative Marketing for more information or meet us at the London and Frankfurt Book Fairs, and at BEA.

6057

BOOKS ON MUSIC
3 Kendal Green, Kendal, Cumbria LA9 5PN
Telephone: 01539 740049
Fax: 01539 737744
Email: (via website)
Web Site: http://www.booksonmusic.co.uk

Manager: Rosemary Dooley

European distributor for:
USA: Pendragon (books on music)

World distributor for:
UK: The British Journal for Ethnomusicology; Royal Musical Association Research Chronicle (journal)

Books on Music runs collaborative publishers' exhibitions at academic music conferences. Specialization in music.

6058

BROOKSIDE PUBLISHING SERVICES LTD
2 Brookside, Dundrum Road, Dublin 14, Republic of Ireland
Telephone: +353 (01) 298 9937
Fax: +353 (01) 298 2783
Email: sales@brookside.ie

Managing Director: Edwin Higel
Sales & Marketing Manager: Conor Graham
Senior Academic Sales Rep: Michael Darcy
Sales & Marketing Co-ordinator: Mariel Deegan

Agents for various imprints in Ireland including:
Cambridge University Press; Clarus Press; Continuum; A & A Farmar; First Law; Gazelle Academic; Nick Hern; Houghton Mifflin; Institute of Chartered Accountants in Ireland; Irish Academic Press; Irish Theatre Handbook; Jessica Kingsley; Learning Matters; Pharmaceutical Press; Pluto; Radcliffe Medical; Routledge / Taylor & Francis; Special Stories Publishing; Taxation Advice Bureau Guide; Tottel Publishing

Represents both trade and academic publishers.

6059

THE CENTRE FOR INTERFIRM COMPARISON
32 St Thomas Street, Winchester, Hants SO23 9HJ
Telephone: 01962 844144
Fax: 01962 843180
Email: mikebayliss@cifc.co.uk
Web Site: http://www.cifc.co.uk

Director: M. J. Bayliss

An independent organization established in 1959 by the British Institute of Management and the British Productivity Council specifically to meet the demand for a neutral specialist body to conduct interfirm comparisons (IFCs) and benchmarking projects on a confidential basis as a service to management.
In 1965, in conjunction with the Publishers Association, the Centre began a series of IFCs specifically designed for book publishers. These comparisons provide objective yardsticks for assessing how overall performance compares; where and why it differs; and lines of action for improvement. The comparisons are based on information supplied confidentially, in depth, and using carefully defined definitions, by participating firms.
The Centre is also a leading organization in the conduct of benchmarking projects for firms and organizations of all kinds and is currently carrying out projects for learned journal publishers and magazine publishers.

6060

COLMAN GETTY LTD
28 Windmill Street, London W1T 2JJ
Telephone: (020) 7631 2666
Fax: (020) 7631 2699
Email: info@colmangetty.co.uk
Web Site: http://www.colmangetty.co.uk

Also at:
5 Gayfield Square, Edinburgh EH1 3NW

Chief Executive: Dotti Irving
Directors: Liz Sich (Managing)
Mark Hutchinson

Colman Getty PR is a London- and Edinburgh-based consumer PR consultancy, founded in 1987 and headed by Dotti Irving, formerly Publicity Director of Penguin Books. The agency specializes in book publishing and issues-related PR and has an established reputation for handling complex, high-profile campaigns, individual promotions, literary awards and longer term consultancies. As well as offering a wide-based expertise in marketing, PR and publicity, Colman Getty can also handle every aspect of marketing projects – from copywriting and print production to sales promotion and advertising. Client list includes The Man Booker Prize for Fiction, the Gulbenkian Prize for Best Museum of the Year, National Poetry Day, the Guardian Hay Festival, World Book Day and a number of individual writers such as J. K. Rowling, Nigella Lawson and Patricia Cornwell. Other clients include Ceridian Centrefile, the Association of Graduate Recruiters and Management Today.

6061

COMPASS DSA LTD
13 Progress Business Park, Whittle Parkway, Slough SL1 6DQ
Telephone: 01628 559500
Fax: 01628 663876
Email: alan@compass-dsa.co.uk
Web Site: http://www.compass-dsa.co.uk

Directors: Alan Jessop (Joint Managing)
Derek Searle (Joint Managing)
Bob Cripps
June Searle

Associated Companies:
UK: Compass Academic Ltd

Client publishers:
Republic of Ireland: The Collins Press; New Island Books Ltd; The O'Brien Press Ltd
UK: Absolute Press; Allison & Busby Ltd; Birlinn Ltd; CAMRA Books; Carcanet Press; Carlton Books Ltd; Tim Coates; English Heritage; Little Books; Polygon Ltd; Serpent's Tail; Tempus Publishing Group; Which; Neil Wilson Publishing Ltd

Compass DSA is one of the leading independent sales companies, providing sales and marketing services for publishers to both the traditional and non-traditional markets across the UK and Ireland.

6062

DAVENPORT PUBLISHING SERVICES – SALES & MARKETING
11 Silbury Rise, Keynsham, Bristol BS31 1JP
Telephone: 0117 986 2914

Fax: 0117 986 2074
Email: anne@annedavenport.demon.co.uk

Proprietor & Consultant: Anne Davenport

Davenport Publishing Services offers consultancy in marketing, promotion, sales and distribution for academic, STM and society publishers.

Projects successfully completed include marketing planning and market research, promotion planning, sales advice, sourcing of overseas agents, representatives and distributors, and lapsed subscriber chasing. Davenport Publishing Services offers a full service from consultancy to implementation of marketing campaigns. Long-term or short-term projects are welcome. Clients include society publishers, university presses and independent institutions with publishing interests.

6063

DURNELL MARKETING LTD – PUBLISHERS EUROPEAN MARKETING AGENCY
2 Linden Close, Tunbridge Wells TN4 8HH
Telephone: 01892 544272
Fax: 01892 511152
Email: admin@durnell.co.uk & orders@durnell.co.uk
Web Site: http://www.durnell.co.uk

Proprietors: Andrew Durnell
Julia Lippiatt

Sales and marketing organization specializing in the sale and promotion of English-language academic and professional publications to Eastern and Western Europe (including the Republic of Ireland) & Scandinavia. Coverage includes extensive and regular academic institute and book-trade calling. Team of representatives visit individual teaching staff to promote potential textbooks, visit European booksellers to sell and promote clients' new and existing lists and arrange exhibitions and other promotional events. All academic and professional subjects covered.

6064

EDUCATION DIRECT
Riverside House, Sir Thomas Longley Road, Rochester, Kent ME2 4FN
Telephone: 01634 291122
Fax: 01634 720269
Email: info@education.co.uk
Web Site: http://www.education.co.uk

Directors: Jason Gould *(Managing)*
David Edwards *(Operations)*
Tim Roger *(Finance)*
Company Secretary: Martin Thorpe

Education Direct provides a complete range of services for companies promoting their products and services to schools, colleges and universities, including:
– a list of educational establishments and contact names;
– award-winning marketing software;
– direct mail services to the education sector;
– project management;
– dedicated telesales and customer services department.

6065

GAZELLE ACADEMIC
White Cross Mills, Hightown, Lancaster LA1 4XS
Telephone: 01524 68765
Fax: 01524 63232
Email: sales@gazellebooks.co.uk
Web Site: http://www.gazellebookservices.co.uk

Directors: Trevor Witcher *(Managing)*
Brian Haywood *(Finance)*
Mark Trotter *(Sales & Distribution)*

Parent Company:
UK: Gazelle Book Services Ltd

Clients:
Australia: FHA Publishing & Communication
Belgium: EuroComment
Canada: Calgary University Press; Canadian Humanist Publications; Wilfrid Laurier University Press; Museum of New Mexico Press; New Society Publishers
Denmark: Aarhus University Press; Museum Tusculanum Press
Finland: Finnish Literature Society; PG-Team Oy; Sophi Academic Press
Germany: Ontos-verlag.de
Israel: Yad Ben Zvi
Netherlands: Aspekt Uitgeverij BV; Nova Vista Publishing; VU University Press
Norway: Tapir Academic Press
Sweden: International Idea; Nordic Academic Press; Student Litteratur
Switzerland: INU Press
UK: Arabian Publishing; Boulevard Books; Clinical Press – Europe; Elector Electronics; William Harvey Press Ltd; Institute of Economic Affairs; Merit Publishing (Medical); Sponsorship Unit; Sussex Academic Press; TFM Publishing Ltd (Medical); World Council of Churches
USA: Ariadne Press; Colorado University Press; Current Clinical Strategies Publishing; Darwin Press; Duquesne University Press; Encounter Books; Feminist Press; Hackett Publishing Co; Harlan Davidson Inc; Ibex Publishers; J & S Publishing Co Inc; Liberty Fund; Mage Publishers; MediPress; Nova Science Publishers Inc; Scientific Publishing Co; Truman State University Press; University of Alberta Press; University of New Mexico Press; Woodbine House Inc

Gazelle Academic is now a division of Gazelle Book Services.

6066

GLOBAL BOOK MARKETING LTD
99B Wallis Road, London E9 5LN
Telephone: (020) 8533 5800
Fax: (020) 8533 5800
Email: info@globalbookmarketing.co.uk

Managing Director: A. Zurbrugg
Managers: A. Howe *(Sales)*
A. Hanson *(IT)*

European agents for:
Canada: Between the Lines; Fernwood Publishing
France: Cacimbo Editions
Germany: Bayreuth African Studies; Barbara Budrich; LIT Verlag
Jamaica: Ian Randle Publishers; Universities of the Caribbean Press
Kenya: Camerapix
South Africa: Blue Weaver Marketing; Fernwood Press; Human & Rousseau; Jacana Education; Kwela Books; Pharos; David Philip / Spearhead / New Africa Books Consortium; Tafelberg
Sweden: Nordic Africa Institute
Switzerland: Basler Afrika Bibliografien
Tanzania: Blue Mango Publishing
UK: African Rights; Battlebridge; Eastern Arts / Saffron; Horniman Museum Publications
USA: Human Rights Watch; International Publishers (New York)
Zimbabwe: African Publishing Group

Agents and representatives. Many publishers are distributed by Central Books Ltd.

6067

HAWKINS PUBLISHING SERVICES
12 Parkview Cottages, Crowhurst Lane End, Oxted, Surrey RH8 9NT
Telephone: 01342 893029
Fax: 01342 893316
Email: gill.hawkins@virgin.net

Director: Gillian Hawkins

Distributor for:
UK: James Clarke; Green Umbrella Publishing; Lutterworth Press; The National Archive; Shepheard Walwyn

Sales, marketing, publicity, rights and distribution.

6068

HUMPHRYS ROBERTS ASSOCIATES
24 High Street, London E11 2AQ
Telephone: (020) 8530 5028
Fax: (020) 8530 7870
Email: humph4hra@aol.com

Also at:
Terry Roberts, Humphrys Roberts Associates,
Caixa Postal 801, Agencia Jardim da Gloria,
06700-990 Cotia SP, Brazil
Telephone: +55 (11) 4702 4496 & 4702 6997
Fax: +55 (11) 4702 6896
Email: hrabrasil@intercall.com.br

Also at:
Christopher Humphrys, Humphrys Roberts Associates,
Apartado 83, Calle Teodoro de Molina 9, 29480 Gaucin,
Malaga, Spain
Telephone: +34 (952) 151462
Fax: +34 (952) 151463
Email: humph4hra@gmail.com

Joint Managing Directors: Christopher Humphrys
Terry Roberts

Publishers' agents and representatives, representing UK and US publishers in South America, Central America, Mexico, the Caribbean, Spain, Portugal and Gibraltar.

6069

BRIAN INNS BOOKSALES & SERVICES
9 Ashley Crescent, Warwick CV34 6QH
Telephone: 01926 498428
Fax: 01926 498428
Email: brian.inns@btinternet.com

Managing Director: Brian Inns

Specialization: general non-fiction and technical books.
Services: consultancy and solutions for publishers. Development of business with multiple bookselling groups and key accounts handled personally by Brian Inns. Specialist at improving market penetration. Representation in UK. Distribution arranged.

6070

CHRIS LLOYD SALES & MARKETING SERVICES
50a Willis Way, Poole, Dorset BH15 3SY
Telephone: 01202 649930
Fax: 01202 649950
Email: chrlloyd@globalnet.co.uk
Web Site: http://www.chrislloydsales.co.uk

Distribution:
Orca Book Services
Telephone: 01202 665432

Proprietor: Christopher Lloyd

Publishers & Imprints represented include:
Belgium: Tectum
Canada: Annick Press; Boston Mills Press; Firefly Books; Master Point Press; Robert Rose
France: Heimdal Editions; Herrisey Editions; Histoire & Collections
Netherlands: Miller Books
New Zealand: Ventura Publications
Spain: Andrea Press; Udyat Books
UK: Amateur Winemaker Books; Argus Books; Bromley Books; D & B Publishing; Finesse Bridge Books; Galago Books; Herridge & Sons; Jaguar Daimler Heritage Trust; Key Books; Know the Score; LDA (Learning Development Aids); Mindsports; Mushroom Model Publications; Raceform; Special Interest Model Books *(formerly Nexus Special Interests)*; Veloce Publishing
USA: Black Dog & Leventhal; Cycling Resources / van der Plas Publications; Meadowbrook Press; Mikaya; Potomac Books *(formerly Brasseys Inc)*

An independent sales and marketing agency for small and medium sized publishers.

6071

THE MANNING PARTNERSHIP LTD
6 The Old Dairy, Melcombe Road, Oldfield Park, Bath BA2 3LR
Telephone: 01225 478444
Fax: 01225 478440
Email: karen@manning-partnership.co.uk
Web Site: http://www.manning-partnership.co.uk

Joint Managing Directors: Garry Manning
Roger Hibbert
Managers: James Wheeler *(Sales)*
Karen Twissell *(Office)*
Office Assistant: Jo Hughes

Associated Companies:
UK: Brown Dog Books; Nightingale Press

UK Distributor for:
UK: Anness; Brimax; Carroll & Brown; Five Mile Press; Flair; Interpet Publishing; Oval Books; Peter Pauper; Powerfresh; Mathew Price; Search Press; Sourcebooks

The Manning Partnership Ltd offers a total sales, marketing and distribution solution for publishers both in the UK and in English-language export markets. Formed in March 1997. Traditional and non-traditional markets are serviced.

6072

MARKETABILITY (UK) LTD
12 Sandy Lane, Teddington, Middx TW11 0DR
Telephone: (020) 8977 2741
Fax: (020) 8977 2741
Email: rachel@marketability.info
Web Site: http://www.marketability.info

Director: Rachel Maund

Current and recent clients include:
Canada: B. C. Decker
China: Higher Education Press
Republic of Ireland: New Island
Singapore: National Book Development Council; Taylor & Francis; World Scientific
UK: BBC Active; bfi Publishing; Bradt Travel Guides; Brilliant Publications; Cambridge University Press; Centre for Alternative Technology; Church House Publishing; Compass Maps and Guides; Continuum; Dundee University Press; Elsevier; HarperCollins Publishers; Hodder Education; Lonely Planet; Macmillan; McGraw Hill; Natural History Museum Publications; NCVO (National Council for Voluntary Organisations); Nelson Thornes; nfer Nelson; Oxford University Press; Palgrave Macmillan; Paperless Proofs; Pearson Education; Pen and Sword Books; Pluto Press; ProQuest; Royal Society; Sage Publications; Taylor & Francis Group; University of Wales Press; Wiley-Blackwell Publishing; World Scientific

Marketability is a group of experienced publishing consultants, all ex-publishers, providing complete support to publishers' marketing departments, from campaigns to consultancy. It supplies resources when needed: to manage catalogue or direct marketing campaigns, devise and conduct market research, or provide consultancy and advice on strategic and practical issues. Its experience is across all publishing sectors, and with both small and large organizations.

Also provides in-company and external training courses – see our separate entry under Training.

6073

MIDAS PUBLIC RELATIONS LTD
7–8 Kendrick Mews, London SW7 3HG
Telephone: (020) 7584 7474
Fax: (020) 7584 7123
Email: info@midaspr.co.uk
Web Site: http://www.midaspr.co.uk

Chairman: Tony Mulliken
Directors: Steven Williams *(Managing)*
Jacks Thomas *(Managing)*
Emma Draude *(Deputy Managing)*
Dinah Irvine *(Finance)*

Midas has established a reputation as one of the leading PR agencies for the book, magazine and publishing industry, through its work with major publishing houses, high profile authors, corporate communications, trade and consumer events and awards, and the Direct Marketing Industry. Originally formed in 1990 to service the publishing industry, its areas of expertise now span related sectors including the arts, awards, media, home entertainment, music, children's and the direct marketing industry. A fully accredited member of the PRCA.

6074

MOMENTA PUBLISHING LTD
2 Moorlands Close, Hindhead, Surrey GU26 6SY
Telephone: 01428 606339
Fax: 01428 606339
Email: roblmomenta@compuserve.com

Director: Robert Leech
Company Secretary: Mahara Collier

Founded 1972. Momenta represents various publishing houses, mainly specializing in academic, scholastic, technical, architectural, scientific and medical books, located in continental Europe and the USA as well as the UK.

Momenta offers the following services:
full sales representation in the UK and Western Europe;
visits to bookshops, sci-tech, academic and medical centres, universities, libraries;
medical and sci-tech lecturers and personnel;
participation in book fairs, congresses and exhibitions;
detailed visit reports containing comments, impressions and recommendations;
market research;
contact with overdue debtors;
book distribution if required.

Momenta is a dynamic company with a wide experience in book sale and promotion.

6075

NIELSEN BOOKSCAN
3rd Floor, Midas House, 62 Goldsworth Road, Woking GU21 6LQ
Telephone: 01483 712222
Fax: 01483 712220
Email: info.bookscan@nielsen.com
Web Site: http://www.nielsenbookscan.co.uk

Head of Research, Development & Servicing: Jeremy Neate
Head of Marketing: Mo Siewcharran
Commercial Director: Ann Betts
UK Business Director: Julie Meynink
Managers: Reeta Windsor *(Publisher Account)*
Carol Brownlee *(Retail Account)*

Parent Company:
UK: Nielsen Book
USA: The Nielsen Company

Nielsen BookScan is a continuous book sales tracking service operating in the UK, Ireland, Australia, the USA, South Africa, Italy, New Zealand, Denmark and Spain. BookScan collects total transaction data at the point of sale directly from tills and dispatch systems of all major book retailers. This ensures that detailed and highly accurate sales information on what books are selling, and at what price, is available to the book trade.

6076

OXFORD CREATIVE MARKETING
12 Hids Copse Road, Oxford OX2 9JJ
Telephone: 01865 861669
Email: info@oxfordcreative.com
Web Site: http://www.oxfordcreative.com

Managing Director: Sue Miller

Oxford Creative Marketing provides wide-ranging marketing, publicity and consultancy serevices for academic and trade publishers.

Services include: marketing planning and new strategy advice; copywriting for corporate material, catalogues, fliers, newsletters, etc.; direct mail campaigns; and publicity campaigns for trade and academic books.

As well as handling one-off projects, the company works with some US publishers on an on-going basis.

In conjunction with Yale Representation and Marston, OCM is a partner in a venture called Bookplate, providing a one-stop, combined sales, marketing and distribution service for publishers.

6077

OXFORD PUBLICITY PARTNERSHIP LTD
5 Victoria House, 138 Watling Street East, Towcester NN12 6BT
Telephone: 01327 357770
Fax: 01327 359572
Email: info@oppuk.co.uk
Web Site: http://www.oppuk.co.uk

Director: Gary Hall

Launched in 1989, the Oxford Publicity Partnership provides a comprehensive range of sales and marketing services for general non-fiction, academic and professional publishers on an on-going or freelance basis.

OPP acts as the UK and European sales and marketing office for a number of British and North American publishers and its focus is on the development of their presence in these markets to achieve wider recognition and enhanced sales.

OPP's team of experienced marketing staff work with clients to achieve the best combination of publicity and PR, direct mail, electronic marketing, advertising, and exhibition participation. It also has close links with reps, distributors, and the book trade.

6078

PARKER ASSOCIATES
Cedar House, 35 Chichele Road, Oxted, Surrey RH8 0AE
Telephone: 01883 730207
Fax: 01883 730188
Email: 101341.1235@compuserve.com

Managing Director: Adrian Parker

Representing:
UK: Saraband; Sheldrake Press

Sales and marketing group for publishers. Selling to the UK and Ireland book trade and also to the European book trade. Eight representatives sell to the UK book trade and two to the Irish book trade. Four representatives sell to the European book trade.

6079

PUBLISHING SERVICES
9 Curwen Road, London W12 9AF
Telephone: (020) 8222 6800
Fax: (020) 8222 6799
Email: susanne@publishing-services.co.uk
Web Site: http://www.publishing-services.co.uk

Sales Force:
Signature Book Services, 20 Castlegate, York YO1 9RP
Telephone: 01904 633633
Fax: 01904 675445
Email: sales@signaturebooks.co.uk
Web Site: http://www.signaturebooks.co.uk

Clients include:
UK: Peter Lang Ltd; Lucas Publications; The Tagman Press

Publishing Services offers smaller publishers and media-friendly authors everything from third-party sales and distribution to editing, production and marketing. Our main areas are general fiction/non-fiction and trade niche areas.

It works in association with Signature Books Services and Central Books for UK sales and distribution respectively.

Core marketing services include:
– preparing sales & marketing material in association with the author and publisher
– preparing marketing plans
– implementing publicity campaigns
– liaising with the repforce about dues, sales and publicity

Publishing Services is currently running a series of seminars on grassroots marketing for the Society of Authors.

Other services vary according to the needs of the publisher and include:
– rights submissions
– website advice
– feedback on cover and inside-page design, editing, format, price and timing
– setting up systems – e.g. costings, production schedules, contracts
– special sales

Publishing Services maintains a 'virtual' office of assistants and third-party suppliers, whose services are available to clients at cost, as well as a database of independent bookshops.

6080

*JOHN RULE, PUBLISHERS SALES AGENT
40 Voltaire Road, London SW4 6DH
Telephone: (020) 7498 0115
Email: johnrule@johnrule.co.uk

Manager: John Rule

6081

SEOL LTD
West Newington House, 10 Newington Road, Edinburgh EH9 1QS
Telephone: 0131 668 1456
Fax: 0131 668 4466
Email: info@seol.ltd.uk

Joint Managing Directors: Hugh Andrew
Carol Crawford

Harry Ward
Carole Hamilton
Managers: Rona Stewart *(Financial)*
Helen Stanton *(Sales Administration)*

Clients include:
UK: Appletree Press Ltd; Argyll Publishing; Atelier; Birlinn Ltd; CILIPS (Chartered Institute of Library and Information Professionals in Scotland); Clan Books; John Donald; Fort Publishing; Goblinshead; Hallewell Publications; House of Lochar; Polygon; Rutland Press; Saltire Society; Shetland Times; Tuckwell Press; Usborne; Whittles Publishing

A sales representation agency to the trade and non-traditional outlets in Scotland.

6082

WILLIAM SNYDER PUBLISHING ASSOCIATES
5 Five Mile Drive, Oxford OX2 8HT
Telephone: 01865 513186
Fax: 01865 513186
Email: snyderpub@aol.com
Web Site: http://www.hoovers-europe.com

Managing Director: W. A. Snyder

Publishers represented include:
Belgium: Euroconfidentiel
Canada: Canadian Almanac & Directory
Germany: Germany's Top 500
UK: ELC International
USA: Bernan Press; Grey House Publishing; Hoover's Business Press; Omnigraphics; Peachtree Publishers

A specialist provider of business information on companies, people and regions. The company has formed links with several US and Canadian producers of information in reference book form, journals and in electronic formats.
  In addition, a consultancy service for organizations interested in international publishing and marketing is provided.

6083

UNIVERSITY PRESSES MARKETING
The Tobacco Factory, Raleigh Road, Southville, Bristol BS3 1TF
Telephone: 0117 902 0275
Fax: 0117 902 0294
Email: sales@universitypressesmarketing.co.uk
Web Site: http://www.universitypressesmarketing.co.uk

Chief Executive Officer: Andrew Gilman
Managers: Paul Skinner *(Office)*
Helena Svojsikova *(Area)*

Sales agent for (mainly) American university presses in the UK and Europe.

6084

THE UNIVERSITY PRESSES OF CALIFORNIA, COLUMBIA & PRINCETON LTD
John Wiley & Sons Ltd, Distribution Centre,
1 Oldlands Way, Bognor Regis, West Sussex PO22 9SA
Telephone: 01243 842165
Fax: 01243 842167
Email: lois@upccp.demon.co.uk

Managing Director: Andrew Brewer
Business Manager: Lois Edwards

6085

*PETER WARD BOOK EXPORTS
Unit 3, Taylors Yard, 67 Alderbrook Road, London SW12 8AD
Telephone: (020) 8772 3300
Fax: (020) 8772 3309
Email: peter@pwbx.com & richard@pwbx.com
Web Site: http://www.pwbx.com

Senior Partner: Peter Ward
Partner: Richard Ward

Publishers' sales representatives in Middle East, North Africa, Cyprus, Turkey, Malta, Greece and Israel.

6086

JOHN WILSON (BOOKSALES) LTD
1 High Street, Princes Risborough, Bucks HP27 0AG
Telephone: 01844 275927
Fax: 01844 274402
Email: sales@jwbs.co.uk

Directors: John S. Wilson *(Managing)*
Pat Wilson *(Administration)*

An exclusive sales and marketing organization providing comprehensive sales coverage to all types of bookselling outlets, with 8 representatives in the UK and Ireland, and overseas agents retained where required. Strong working contacts with most major distributors and publicity houses.

6.6 DISTRIBUTORS

6087

ACTIVAIR LTD
Action Court, Ashford Road, Ashford, Middx TW15 1XS
Telephone: 01784 890005
Fax: 01784 890013
Email: paul.barrett@activair.com
Web Site: http://www.activair.com

Directors: Paul Barrett *(Sales)*
Steve Lai *(Financial)*
Matt Evans *(Managing)*

Freight forwarder to the publishing industry, providing efficient cost-effective services specifically designed for the worldwide movement of trade and academic books. Services offered are by air, sea and road between publisher's warehouse and bookshop door. Sponsor of the British Book Awards.

6088

AFRICAN BOOKS COLLECTIVE
PO Box 721, Oxford OX1 9EN
Telephone: 01869 349110
Fax: 01869 349110
Email: orders@africanbookscollective.com
Web Site: http://www.africanbookscollective.com

Head: Mary Jay
Sales & Marketing: Justin Cox

Participating publishers include:
Benin: Centre Panafricain de Prospective Sociale / Pan-African Social Prospects Centre
Botswana: Lightbooks Publishers; Pyramid Publishing
Cameroon: University of Buea
Eritrea: Hdri Publishers
Ethiopia: Development Policy Management Forum (DPMF); Forum for Social Studies; Organisation for Social Science Research in Eastern and Southern Africa (OSSREA)
Ghana: Afram Publications (Ghana) Ltd; Africa Christian Press; Association of African Universities Press; Blackmask; Freedom Publishers; Ghana Universities Press; Sedco Publishing; SEM Financial Training Centre Ltd; Sub-Saharan Publishers; Third World Network Africa; Woeli Publishing Services; Women's Health Action Research Centre
Kenya: Academy Science Publishers; East African Educational Publishers; Focus Books; Kwani Trust; LawAfrica; Nairobi University Press
Lesotho: Institute of Southern African Studies, National University of Lesotho; Law Society of Lesotho
Malawi: Central Africana; Chancellor College Publishers; Kachere Series
Namibia: Reader in Namibian Sociology; University of Namibia Press
Nigeria: African Heritage Press; College Press Publishers; CSS Ltd; Enicrownfit Publishers; Fourth Dimension Publishing Co Ltd; Heinemann Educational Books (Nigeria); Ibadan Cultural Studies Group; Ibadan University Press; Kraft Books; Maiyati Chambers; Malthouse Press Ltd; New Horn Press Ltd; Obafemi Awolowo University Press; Onyoma Research Publications; Saros International Publishers; Spectrum Books Ltd; University of Lagos Press; University Press Ltd
Senegal: African Renaissance; Council for the Development of Social Science Research in Africa (CODESRIA)
Sierra Leone: PenPoint Publishers
South Africa: Africa Institute of South Africa; Brenthurst Collection / Frank Horley Books; Ikhwezi Afrika Publishers; Mail and Guardian Books; UNISA Press
Swaziland: JAN Publishing Centre
Tanzania: Centre for Energy, Environment, Science & Technology (CEEST); Dar es Salaam University Press; E & D Ltd; Mkuki na Nyota Publishers; Tanzania Publishing House
Uganda: Femrite (Uganda Women Writers' Association); Fountain Publishers
Zambia: Bookworld Publishers; Multimedia Zambia; University of Zambia; Zambia Women Writers' Association
Zimbabwe: Africa Community Publishing & Development Trust; Baobab Books; Kimaathi Publishing House; Mambo Press; Southern African Printing and Publishing House / SAPES Trust; University of Zimbabwe Publications; Weaver Press Ltd; Women and Law in South Africa Research Trust; Zimbabwe International Book Fair Trust; Zimbabwe Publishing House Ltd

African Books Collective is a major initiative to promote African-published books in Europe, North America, and in Commonwealth countries outside Africa. It is owned by the founding publishers, and is non-profit making on its own behalf. Centralized billing and shipping is provided from Oxford; and for North America by Michigan State University Press. The greater part of the list is available print-on-demand. A range of joint catalogues and other promotional material is mailed to libraries and other book buyers. English-language material is stocked, with an emphasis on scholarly, literature and children's titles. A small number of titles in French and children's titles in Swahili are also stocked. Standing order / blanket order plans are available and can be geared to meet libraries' specific requirements or acquisitions profiles. Trading started in May 1990.

6089

THE ANGLO-AMERICAN BOOK CO LTD
Crown Buildings, Bancyfelin, Carmarthen SA33 5ND
Telephone: 01267 211880
Fax: 01267 211882
Email: books@anglo-american.co.uk
Web Site: http://www.anglo-american.co.uk

Directors: Mr D. Bowman *(Managing)*
Mrs C. Lenton *(Marketing)*

UK Distributor/Representative for:
USA: American Guidance Service; Center Press; Milton H. Erickson Foundation Press; Free Spirit Publishing; Genesis II; International Society of Neuro-Semantics; Kagan & Kagan; Kendall/Hunt; Leading Edge Communications; The Melissa Institute; Meta Publications; Network 3000 Publishing; NLP Comprehensive; Science and Behavior Books; Success Strategies; Teacher Created Materials; Transforming Press; Westwood Publishing; Wood & Barnes Publishing

The Anglo-American Book Co is a stockholding distributor of British and American books with particular expertise in the NLP, personal growth, hypnotherapy, accelerated learning and psychotherapy fields. Stock book orders received by 2.30 pm are dispatched the same day.
  Order Department opening times: 9–5 Monday to Friday.

6090

ART BOOKS INTERNATIONAL LTD
The Old Mill House, Mill Lane, Uckfield, East Sussex TN22 5AA
Telephone: 01825 767396
Fax: 01825 765649
Email: sales@art-bks.com
Web Site: http://www.art-bks.com

Directors: Richard Squibb *(Managing)*
Frank McNamara *(Sales)*
Marketing Officer: Anne Tolstoy
General Manager: Sophie Armfield
Administration: Julie McCarron

UK distributor/representative for:
France: ACR Editions; Ars Latina; L'Arca Editions
Germany: Hatje Cantz; Feierabend; Jovis Verlag; Kehrer Verlag; Vitra Design Museum
India: India Book House; Mapin Publishers
Italy: Electa Mondadori; Silvana Editoriale
Republic of Ireland: Irish Museum of Modern Art
UK: Dan Giles Ltd; Immprint; Whitechapel

Specialist distributor and publisher of books on fine art, architecture, design and photography.

6091

ATLANTIC BOOKS
The Bookhouse, 18 Great Footway, Tunbridge Wells, Kent TN3 0DT
Telephone: 01892 864949
Fax: 01892 864950
Email: esther@atlanticbooks.co.uk
Web Site: http://www.atlanticbooks.co.uk

Managers: Esther Matthews *(Proprietor)*
Andy Ackerley *(Sales & Marketing)*
Jayne Robinson *(Customer Service)*
Joe Ackerley *(Warehouse)*

Supplier of all US published material; any American title.

6092

AVANTIBOOKS LTD
Unit 9, The io Centre, Whittle Way, Arlington Business Park, Stevenage SG1 2BD
Telephone: 01438 747000
Fax: 01438 741131
Email: orders@avantibooks.com
Web Site: http://www.avantibooks.com

Directors: Hilary Rosenberg
Sue Ravitz

UK distributor/representative for:
Australia: ARIS
South Africa: Natal Centre for Adult Education; Viva Books
UK: Brown & Brown Publishing; Gatehouse Media; LLU+; Newleaf Books; Suffolk Family Learning
USA: New Readers Press; Peppercorn Books & Press

Mail order bookshop, specializing in educational titles for basic skills teaching and ESOL/ELT.

6093

BBR DISTRIBUTION
12 Cutthorpe Road, Chesterfield S42 7AE
Telephone: 01246 271662
Fax: 01246 271662
Email: distribution@bbr-online.com
Web Site: http://www.bbr-online.com/catalogue

Director: Chris Reed

Parent Company:
UK: BBR Solutions Ltd

UK distributor for:
Australia: Aurealis; Chimaera Publications
Canada: Tesseract Books
Republic of Ireland: Aeon Press; Albedo One
UK: Bowland Press; British Association for Korean Studies (BAKS); EAHMH Publications; Endcliffe Press; European Association for the History of Medicine and Health Publications; Hilltop Press
USA: Automatism Press; Cambrian Publications; Cyber-Psycho's A.O.D.; Dreams and Nightmares; Fairwood Press; Jazz Police Books; New York Review of S.F.; Not One of Us; Nova Express; Ocean View Books; Permeable Press; Space & Time; Talebones; Wordcraft of Oregon

BBR is a mail order distributor of independent literary, speculative fiction and fringe interest publications, serving customers throughout the world.

6094

*BEBC DISTRIBUTION
Albion Close, Parkstone, Poole, Dorset BH12 3LL
Telephone: 01202 715555
Fax: 01202 715556
Email: bebc@bebc.co.uk
Web Site: http://www.bebcdistribution.co.uk

Managing Director: John Walsh
Managers: Charles Kipping *(Marketing)*
Rosy Jones *(Operations)*

Parent Company:
UK: The Bournemouth English Book Centre Ltd

UK Distributor/Representative for:
UK: Academic Book Collection; Accelerated Learning Centre; Actual Enterprises; Adams & Austen Press; Anglo-American Book Company; John Benjamins; Boyer Education; Brilliant Publications; Brookemead ELT; Catt Publishing; Chancerel; College of Law Publishing; Insearch Publications; Learning Matters; Lexden Publishing; Listen & Speak Publications; NCELTR; Oxfam; Ransom Publishing; Smile Mathematics; Step Forward Publishing; TP Publications; White Adder; York Associates

Distribution of publishers involved with business books, law books, English language teaching, ICT books, human rights and conservation.

6095

BETTER BOOKS
3 Paganel Drive, Dudley DY1 4AZ
Telephone: 01384 253276
Fax: 0871 715 0236
Email: sales@betterbooks.com
Web Site: http://www.betterbooks.com

Proprietor: P. J. Wilkes

UK distributor/representative for:
USA: Educators Publishing Service

Mail order distributor of books relating to dyslexia and other special educational needs.

6096

*THE BOOK SERVICE LTD
Colchester Road, Frating Green, Colchester, Essex CO7 7DW
Telephone: 01206 256000 (orders: 255678)
Fax: 01206 255715 (orders: 255930)
Email: sales@tbs-ltd.co.uk
Web Site: http://www.TheBookService.co.uk

Transworld Distribution Centre:
Sanders Road, Finedon Road Industrial Estate, Wellingborough NN8 4NL
Telephone: 01933 225761

Directors: M. Williams *(Managing)*
John Williams *(Operations)*
Colin James *(IT – Business Systems)*
Alan Henderson *(IT – Network Services)*
Justin Smith *(Finance)*

Parent Company:
UK: The Random House Group Ltd

Associated Companies:
UK: Grantham Book Services

Distribution services offered to:
AA Publishing; Andersen Press; Nicholas Brealey; Constable & Robinson; Faber & Faber; Little Brown Book Group; Mainstream Publishing; Methuen Publishing; Parragon Disney; Profile Books; Random House Group; Transworld International; Virgin Books

Distribution covers order receipt, by telephone, post, EDI and teleordering, telesales, year-round hotline service, cyclical invoicing, despatch via Parceline, Countrywide, post and own vehicles. Also included is a full sales ledger and cash collection service. Sales and stock information and royalties are offered. Debt and stock insurance available. Ancillary work such as mailing, shrink-wrapping, repricing, dump-bin and counterpack make up is also available.

6097

BOOK SYSTEMS PLUS LTD
BSP House, Station Road, Linton, Cambs CB21 4NW
Telephone: 01223 894870
Fax: 01223 894871
Email: bsp2b@aol.com
Web Site: http://www.booksystemsplus.com

Managing Director: George J. Papa
Marketing & New Business: Shirley Greenall

Publishers represented:
Australia: Bookbiz International
Canada: The Althouse Press; The Charlton Press; Detselig Enterprises Ltd; Great Escapes.com
Germany: Chateaux & Manoirs
Netherlands: Mo' Media
UK: Aardvark Publishing; Caister Academic Press; Chakula Press Ltd; Classic Locations; Cobwebs Brentwood; Cracking It; EFL Ltd; Fantom Films; Fitzwarren Publishing; Focus Publications Ltd; Gudrun Publishing / Edda UK; Hiller Airguns; Hoopoe Books; Idlewild Publishers; Institute for Psychophysical Research; Oxford Forum; Pathfinder Audio; Porpoise Books; UK International Ceramics; Vista Consulting Team Ltd; Whittet Books Ltd; Wild Boar Trading
USA: John F. Blair, Publisher

Book Systems Plus provides full distribution, invoicing and customer services to publishers from the UK and overseas. It also offers bookshop representation and marketing support. It has particular marketing expertise with travel guides and books on antiques and collectables. It acts as the UK sole agent for publishers in North America and Europe.

6098

BOOKMART LTD
Blaby Road, Wigston, Leicester LE18 4SE
Telephone: 0116 275 9060
Fax: 0116 275 9090
Email: books@bookmart.co.uk
Web Site: http://www.bookmart.co.uk

Directors: P. E. Parkin *(Managing)*
A. J. Painter *(Finance)*
D. I. Button *(Purchasing)*
L. Williams *(Rights)*
R. J. Parkin *(Sales (Books/ Distribution/ Stationery))*

Promotional books, publisher and distributor.

6099

BOOKPOINT LTD
130 Milton Park, Abingdon, Oxon OX14 4SB
Telephone: 01235 400400
Fax: 01235 832068
Web Site: http://www.bookpoint.co.uk

Directors: M. Evans *(Managing, Hachette Livre UK IT & Logistics)*
Martyn Burchall *(Operations)*
Ian Butterfield *(Finance)*
Alison Rennie *(Customer Service)*
Graham Money *(General Manager)*

Parent Company:
UK: Hachette Livre UK

Distributor for:
UK: Ashgate/Gower Publishing; Black Library; Debretts; Facet Publishing *(formerly Library Association)*; Greenhill Books; Hachette Children's; Headline Book Publishing; Hodder & Stoughton; Hodder Education; Hodder Gibson; Hodder Religious; In Easy Steps; Frances Lincoln; John Murray; Pedigree Books; Plexus Publishing; Souvenir Press; Taylor & Francis

Bookpoint services encompass a number of industry leading initiatives, plus a full suite of EDI applications, order processing, accounting, royalty maintenance, management reporting, warehousing, despatch and ancillary functions. Bookpoint also operate a Premier Next Day Service, and offer PUBEASY to booksellers.

6100

BOOKSOURCE
50 Cambuslang Road, Cambuslang, Glasgow G32 8NB
Telephone: 0845 370 0063
Fax: 0845 370 0064
Email: info@booksource.net
Web Site: http://www.booksource.net

Directors: Davinder Bedi *(Managing)*
Lorraine Fannin
Mike Miller
Christian Mclean
Dr Keith Whittles
Managers: Louise Wilson *(Client Services)*
David Warnock *(Systems & Facilities)*
Lavinia Drew *(Credit Controller)*
Derek Withers *(Customer Service)*
Jim O'Donnell *(Distribution)*

Distribution on behalf of:
Germany: Sotok Press
UK: Acair Ltd; Appletree Press; Argyll Publishing; Association for Scottish Literary Studies; Atelier Books; B

& W Publishing; Balnakeil Press; Benchmark Books; BILD Publications; Birlinn Ltd; Black & White Publishing; Blue Cow Books; Carnegie Publishing; Cicerone Press; Clairview Books; Clan Publishers; John Donald; R. R. Donnelley *(for the Scottish Executive)*; Richard Drew Ltd; Dundee University Press; Floris Books; Geddes & Grosset Ltd; Gullane Children's Books; Hawthorn Press; House of Lochar; IPC Media; Librario Publishing; Meadowside Children's Books; Mercat Press; Moonlight Publishing; New Iona Press; NMS Enterprises Ltd Publishing; Pastime Publications; Polygon; Publishing Scotland; Real Reads; Rider French Incorporation of Architects in Scotland; Rucksack Readers; Saltire Society; Sandstone Press; Saraband; Steve Savage Publishing; Scottish Society for Northern Studies; Scottish Society of Medievalists; Scottish Text Society; Shetland Times Ltd; Starlet; Rudolf Steiner Press; Strident Publishing; Sunday Herald Books; Temple Lodge Publishing; Tuckwell Press; Two Ravens Press; Waverley Press; Whittles Publishing; Wild Goose Publications; Neil Wilson Publishing; Windhorse Publications; Word Power Books
USA: Studio 9 Books and Music

Established in 1995, BookSource offers warehousing and worldwide distribution services to book trade publishers, charities and funded institutions, and other commercial enterprises.

6101

BUSHWOOD BOOKS LTD
6 Marksbury Avenue, Kew Gardens, Surrey TW9 4JF
Telephone: (020) 8392 8585
Fax: (020) 8392 9876
Email: info@bushwoodbooks.co.uk
Web Site: http://www.bushwoodbooks.co.uk

Director: Richard Hansen
PA: Victoria Hansen
Sales: Ian McLellan

Exclusive distributor for:
USA: Schiffer *(Mind, Body, Spirit titles)*; Schiffer Collectibles Arts & Crafts; Schiffer Publishing Ltd *(Military Aviation)*

The company also carries in stock hundreds of titles on antiques and collectibles, predominantly horology, jewellery, ceramics and glass. It specializes in providing a service for UK customers to purchase from North American publishers.
Bushwood Books is one of the leading UK distributors of German World War II titles in English, and also carries the Schiffer Mind, Body, Spirit list.

6102

CENGAGE LEARNING SERVICES
[a division of Cengage Learning]
Cheriton House, North Way, Andover, Hants SP10 5BE
Telephone: 01264 332424
Fax: 01264 342787
Web Site: http://cls.cengage.co.uk

Directors: Barry Hinchmore *(Managing)*
Aris Kassimatis *(Finance)*
Carrie Willicome *(Operations)*

Distributors for:
UK: Cengage Learning *(selected imprints)*; Evans Publishing Group; Janes; Sweet & Maxwell [S&M Ltd, W. Green & Sons, Gee Publishing]

6103

*CENTRAL BOOKS
99 Wallis Road, London E9 5LN
Telephone: 0845 458 9911
Fax: 0845 458 9912
Email: orders@centralbooks.com
Web Site: http://www.centralbooks.com

Directors: William Norris *(Managing)*
Mark Chilver *(Sales)*
Managers: Bob Moheebob *(Accountant)*
Chris Tordoff *(Marketing)*
Eric McCorkle *(Warehouse)*
Indy Kaur Naura *(Customer Services)*
Karen Short *(Human Resources)*
Mike Drabble *(Mail Order)*
Sasha Simic *(Magazine Sales Rep)*

Distribution for:
Australia: Fremantle Arts Centre Press
Canada: Black Rose Books; Fernwood Press
France: Zulma
Germany: European Photography
Greece: Intrac
Italy: Giancarlo Politi Editore
Jamaica: Ian Randle
Kenya: Camerapix
Netherlands: CEDLA; Get Lost Publishing; International Books; Thesis
Republic of Ireland: Dedalus Press; A & A Farmer; Galway University Press; The Lilliput Press Ltd; Oishin Publishing; Salmon Publishing Ltd; University College Dublin Press
Scandinavia: Nordic Institute of Asian Studies; Nordiska Afrikainstitutet (Scandinavian Institute of Africa)
South Africa: Cape Town University Press; Fernwood Press; Kwela; Londolozi Publishers; David Philip; Ravan Press; University of Capetown Press; University of Natal Press; Witwatersrand University Press
Switzerland: Parkett Verlag
UK: 21; Absolute Press; Accent Press; Agraphia Press; Ambit Books; Amnesty Publications; Anthem Press; Archetype; Argyll Publishing; Aurora Books; Aurora Metro; Auteur; Battlebridge; Birmingham University Press; Blue Island Publishing; Bowerdean Publishing Co Ltd; Marion Boyars Publishers; British Council for Archaeology; British Film Institute; Broadcast Books; Cadmos; CAF (Charities Aid Foundation); Calouste Gulbenkian Foundation; Jon Carpenter Publishing; Catalyst Press; Centre for Policy on Ageing; The Children's Society; CILT; Comerford & Miller; Corvo Books; CPAG (Child Poverty Action Group); Dedalus; Demos; Directory of Social Change; Disability Alliance; English Heritage; Enitharmon Press; Five Leaves Publications; Flambard; Floodlight; Flowers East; Foreign Policy Centre; Format Publishing; Fostering Network; Friction Press; Friends of the Earth; Gambit; Gibson Square Press; Golgonooza; Green Books; Green Guide Publishing; Greenprint; Greenwich Exchange; Harbord Publishing; Heretic Books Ltd *(formerly GMP Publishers Ltd)*; Holo Books; Hood Hood Books; Human Givens; Human Rights Watch; Hyphen Press; Imprint Academic; Inclusion *(formerly Unemployment Unit)*; Institute for Public Policy Research; Latin America Bureau; Lawrence & Wishart; Libris Ltd; Loki Books; London Art & Artists; LSE Books; Lucas Publications Ltd; Mares Nest; Menard Press; Merlin Press; Middlesex University Press; Minority Rights Group; Muslim Academic Trust; National Autistic Society (NAS); New Clarion Press; New Economics Foundation; New European Publications Ltd; NIACE (National Institute for Adult Continuing Education); Northway; Oberon Books; Open Gate Press; Peter Owen Ltd; Peepal Tree Books; Pomona Books; Prospect Books; Pushkin Press; Quill; Quilliam; Redstone Press; Refugee Council; Resource Publications; Right Angle Publishing; Route; Runnymede Trust; Seafarer; Seren; Serif; Smith / Doorstep; Smith Institute; Social Market Foundation; Stacey International; Tartarus; Totterdown Books; University of Hertfordshire Press; Vegan Society; Wallflower Press; Josef Weinberger Ltd; Weston Publishing; Westworld International; Windgather Press; Wooden Books; WorldView; Yorkshire Art Circus Ltd
USA: Bootstrap & Apex Press; CIT Books; Grand Street; International Publishers NY; McPherson & Co; Monthly Review; Pamphleteer's Press

The main activity and purpose of Central Books is to assist independent publishers to reach the widest possible audience for their books. Central Books offer warehousing, distribution, representation and some help with marketing and promotion. It supplies booksellers and library suppliers throughout the world. The company is one of Europe's leading distributors of magazines and journals to the book trade.

6104

*THE COLUMBA BOOKSERVICE
55A Spruce Avenue, Stillorgan Industrial Park, Blackrock, Co Dublin, Republic of Ireland
Telephone: +353 (01) 294 2556
Fax: +353 (01) 294 2564
Email: info@columba.ie
Web Site: http://www.columba.ie

Directors: Séan O Boyle *(Managing)*
Cecilia West *(Sales)*

UK distributor/representative for:
Australia: Australian Theological Forum (ATF)
Canada: Novalis
Republic of Ireland: The Columba Press
USA: Church Publishing; Michael Glazier Books; The Liturgical Press; Loyola Press; Paraclete Press; Paulist Press; Pueblo Books; Resource Publications; St Mary's Press; Twenty-third Publications

The Columba Bookservice provides trade representation, sales and marketing services and distribution for a number of religious publishers.

6105

COMBINED ACADEMIC PUBLISHERS LTD
15a Lewins Yard, East Street, Chesham, Bucks HP5 1HQ
Telephone: 01494 581601
Fax: 01494 581602
Email: nickesson@combinedacademic.co.uk
Web Site: http://www.combinedacademic.co.uk

Managing Director: Nicholas Esson
Managers: Ms Julia Monk *(Marketing)*
Ms Denise Martin *(Accounts)*
Representative: Keith Woods

UK & European distributor for:
Canada: McGill-Queen's University Press
UK: John Libbey Publishing
USA: Duke University Press; Indiana University Press; Temple University Press; University of Illinois Press; University of Nebraska Press; University of Texas Press; University of Washington Press

Combined Academic Publishers, in association with Marston Book Services, is a professional representation and distribution agency for academic and university presses.
UK and Republic of Ireland field sales are handled by our own representative and a team of experienced commisson agents, while agents are active in five continental European territories – Scandinavia; the Netherlands and Belgium; Southern Europe; Germany, Austria and Switzerland; Central and Eastern Europe – as well as the Middle East and Africa.
CAP has a pro-active marketing department offering direct mail campaigns, space advertising and review copy distribution.

6106

COMBINED BOOK SERVICES LTD
Units I/K, Paddock Wood Distribution Centre,
Paddock Wood, Tonbridge, Kent TN12 6UU
Telephone: 01892 837171
Fax: 01892 837272
Email: info@combook.co.uk
Web Site: http://www.combook.co.uk

Directors: Keith Neale *(Distribution)*
Allan Smith *(Customer Services)*

Distributors for:
Italy: LEM Art Group
UK: A Jot Publishing; J. A. Allen *(Equestrian)*; Anshan Publishers; John Calder; Claerhout Publishing; Discovery Books; Eddington Hook; Encyclopaedia Britannica; European Library; Freehand Publishing; Robert Hale; Hammersmith Press; Highworth Research; Hoberman Collection; Korero Books; Lotus Publishing; Management Books 2000; Momenta Publishing; NAG Publishers; Northcote House Publishers; Oblique; Oneworld Classics; Phoenix Publishers; Pocket Issue; Pushkin Press; Thomas Telford Ltd *(Institute of Civil Engineers)*; Woodhead Publishing

Combined Book Services provides full distribution services for publishers of trade, academic and professional books. The service includes invoicing and cash collection together with a comprehensive range of management reports. CBS also distributes calendars and stationery products.

6107

CONTOUR MANAGEMENT SERVICES (CMS)
PO Box 3042, New Milton, Hants BH25 7XG
Telephone: 01425 620532
Fax: 01425 620532
Email: mikecms@btinternet.com
Web Site: http://www.contourmanagementservices.com

Partners: Mike Cranidge *(Managing)*
Sue Cranidge

Agent and distributor for:
Australia: Meridian Maps
Baltic States: Jāna Sēta Map Publishers
Portugal: Turinta
USA: Hedberg Maps Inc; Map Link

6108 / TRADE & ALLIED SERVICES: DISTRIBUTORS

Importers and distributors of maps with a difference.

6108

CORNERHOUSE PUBLICATIONS
70 Oxford Street, Manchester M1 5NH
Telephone: 0161 200 1503
Fax: 0161 200 1504
Email: Publications@Cornerhouse.org
Web Site: http://www.Cornerhouse.org/books

Head of Publications: Paul Daniels
Administrator: Debbie Fielding
Publications Officer: Suzanne Davies

Clients include:
Germany: Walther König
Switzerland: JRP / Ringier
UK: British Council Visual Arts; Hayward Gallery; ICA; Ikon; Modern Art Oxford; Saatchi Gallery

Distributor of visual arts and photography books for publishers, museums amd galleries world-wide. A full list of publishers we distribute is available in our catalogue or at our web site: http://www.Cornerhouse.org/books.

6109

COUNTER CULTURE
The Long Barn, Sutton Mallet, Somerset TA7 9AR
Telephone: 01278 722888
Fax: 01278 722565
Email: info@counterculture-books.co.uk
Web Site: http://www.counterculture-books.co.uk

Owner: Peter Gotto

Associated Companies:
UK: Green Magic

Distributors for:
UK: Aeon Press; Ariadne Publications; Avalon; Avalonia; Blackstone; Bluestone Press; Bossiney Books; Caine Books; Capall Bann; Chalice Well; Compassbooks; Connections; Jonathon Cope; Crescent Books; Cygnus Books; Dilston Press; Sheridan Douglas; Druid Ways; Edfu; Eric; Glennie Kindred; Godsfield Press; Gothic Image; Green Books; Green Magic; Robert Hale; Hay House; Heart of Albion Press; Hermitage Publishing; Ignotus Press; Kindred Books; Kindred Press; Knockabout Comics; Lear Books; Living Wood; Mandrake; Meym Mamvro; Mythos; Neptune; Pan Dimensional; Pendragon Press; Penwith Press; Permanent Publications; Points Press; Poppy Palin; Scandinavian Yoga & Meditation School; Speaking Tree; Tagman Press; Thoth Publications; Wessex Books; Whitaker Publishing; Wild Spirit; Wooden Books
USA: Abramelin Press; Adventures Unlimited; Ash Tree Publishing; Blue Water Publishing; Book Publishing Company; Citadel Press; Crossing Press; Eaglewing; Earth Love; Mara Freeman; Granite Publishing; Hanford Mead; Heart of the Sun; Heaven and Earth Publishing; Hulogosi Press; Llewellyn; Moosewood; New Page Books; New Trends; Perelandra; Raw Family; Red Wheel/Weiser Books; Shelter; Swan Raven & Co; Ultra; US Games; Vision; Wild Flower; Witches Almanac

Book distribution and worldwide sales.

6110

DEEP BOOKS LTD
Unit 3, Goose Green Trading Estate, 47 East Dulwich Road, London SE22 9BN
Telephone: (020) 8693 0234
Fax: (020) 8693 1400
Email: sales@deep-books.co.uk
Web Site: http://www.deep-books.co.uk

Managing Director: Chris Custance
Managers: Linda Doolin *(Sales)*
 Alan Ritchie *(Marketing)*
 Paul Woodfield

Client Publishers include:
Australia: Michelle Anderson Publishing [formerly Hill of Content Publishing]; Finch Publishing; Barry Long Books (Australia); Milne Books; Women's Health Advisory Service
Austria: Ennsthaler Publishing House
Israel: Astrolog Publishing House
Italy: Lo Scarabeo
Netherlands: Binkey Kok Publications
Singapore: Lotus Bloom Publishing
UK: Findhorn Press; From Within; Khaniqahi Nimatullahi Publications (KNP); KNP London; Barry Long Books (Britain); Polair Publishing
USA: Alliance Book Company; ARE Press; Ariel Press; Avery/Penguin USA; Basic Health Publications; Bear & Co; Bear Cub Books; Berkley Publishing Group; Bindu Books; Blue Dolphin Publishing Inc; Bluestar Communications; Boys Town Press; Career Press; Chiron Publications; Alan Cohen Publishing; Crystal Clarity Publishers; Dawn Publications; Dawnhorse Publications; De Vorss & Co; Destiny Audio Books; Destiny Books; Dragonhawk Publishing; Dutton / Penguin USA; Earth Magic Productions Inc; Enthea Press; Golden Sufi Center; Gotham Books / Penguin USA; Hampton Roads Publishing; Nicolas Hays; Healing Arts Press; Himalayan Institute Press; Hunter House Inc; Ibis Press; Inner Traditions International; Inner Travel Books; Integral Yoga Publications; Jewish Light Publishing; JZK Publishing; Kali Press; Veronica Lane Books; Lantern Books; Music Design; New Page Books; Oral Traditions; Original Publications; Park St Press; Perigee/Penguin; Power Press; Riverhead Books / Penguin USA; Self Realization Fellowship; Skylight Paths; Squareone Publishers; Synergetic Press; Jeremy P. Tarcher / Penguin USA; Threshold Books; Timeless Books; Vital Health Publishing; Words of Wizdom; World Wisdom Books

Specialist mind body spirit distributors. Deep Books handles publishers lists from the UK, the USA and Australia. It provides sales and distribution for these publishers throughout the UK, Republic of Ireland, mainland Europe and Scandinavia and acts as their exclusive agents in that territory.

6111

EUROPEAN SCHOOLBOOKS LTD
Ashville Trading Estate, The Runnings, Cheltenham GL51 9PQ
Telephone: 01242 245252
Fax: 01242 224137
Email: direct@esb.co.uk
Web Site: http://www.eurobooks.co.uk

Managing Director: Frank Preiss
Marketing: Ruth Trippett

Distributor for:
Brazil: Pontes Editores
Denmark: Grafisk Forlag
France: 10/18; Assimil; Bordas; Casterman; CLE International; Armand Colin; Didier; Ecole des loisirs; Editions du Fallois; Editions du Seuil; Flammarion; Folio; Foucher; Gallimard; Garnier Flammarion; Gault Millau; Hachette; Hatier; J'ai lu; Larousse; Livres de poche; Minuit; Nathan; Presses de la cité; Presses Pocket; Presses Universitaires de France; Presses Universitaires de Grenoble; Le Robert
Germany: Arena; Bibliographisches Institut Mannheim; Brockhaus; Carlsen; Cornelsen; Deutscher Taschenbuch Verlag; Diogenes; Duden; Fischer; Gilde Buchhandlung; Goldmann; Heyne; Max Hueber Verlag; Insel; Kiepenheuer & Witsch; Knaur; Langenscheidt; Luchterhand; Reclam; Rowohlt; Suhrkamp; Ullstein; Verlag Dürr & Kessler; Verlag für Deutsch; Verlag Moritz Diesterweg
Italy: Alma Edizioni; Bonacci Editore; Edilingua; Einaudi; European Language Institute; Fabbri-Bompiani; Feltrinelli; Garzanti; Giunti; Guerra; Mondadori; Le Monnier; Oscar; Piemme; Rizzoli; Rux; La Spiga; Zanichelli
Netherlands: Intertaal
Portugal: Dinapress; Lidel Edições Técnicas; Porto Editora Lda; Public. Europa-America
Spain: Alfaguara; Alianza; Anaya; Anaya ELE; Austral; Catedra; Colegio de España; Destino; Difusión; EDELSA; Ediciones Edhasa; Ediciones Edinumen; Ediciones Molino; Ediciones SM; Espasa-Calpe; Everest; Grijalbo; Juventud; Mondadori España; Planeta; Plaza & Janes; Santillana; Seix Barral; SGEL; Sopena; Javier Vergara
UK: European Schoolbooks Publishing Ltd; Understanding Global Issues

Distributors of some 18,000 titles in the main European languages on behalf of over 100 publishers. Large-scale promotion in all sectors of the foreign languages educational market. Suppliers of foreign-published stock to academic and general bookshops. General wholesale service for non-stock titles.

6112

THE EUROSPAN GROUP
3 Henrietta Street, Covent Garden, London WC2E 8LU
Telephone: (020) 7240 0856
Fax: (020) 7379 0609
Email: info@eurospangroup.com
Web Site: http://www.eurospanbookstore.com

Directors: Michael Geelan *(Chief Executive Officer)*
 Kate Fraser *(Operations & Publisher Services)*
 Stephen Lustig *(Sales & Marketing)*

A complete list of publishers and subsidiary imprints distributed by Eurospan is available on request.

6113

FREELANCE MARKET NEWS
Sevendale House, 7 Dale Street, Manchester M1 1JB
Telephone: 0161 228 2362
Fax: 0161 228 3533
Email: fmn@writersbureau.com
Web Site: http://www.freelancemarketnews.com

Managing Editor: Miss Angela Cox

Parent Company:
UK: The Writers Bureau Ltd

Distributor for:
USA: Writer's Digest Books *(books on writing)*

6114

GAZELLE BOOK SERVICES LTD
White Cross Mills, Hightown, Lancaster LA1 4XS
Telephone: 01524 68765
Fax: 01524 63232
Email: sales@gazellebooks.co.uk
Web Site: http://www.gazellebooks.co.uk

Directors: Trevor Witcher *(Managing)*
 Brian Haywood *(Company Secretary & Finance)*
 Mark Trotter *(Distribution & Sales)*
Managers: Mick Nicholls *(Warehouse)*
 Lee Hodgkiss *(Marketing & Exhibitions)*
 Ian Waterhouse *(Customer Service)*
 Melanie Warren *(Sales & Marketing)*
Bookkeeper: Analyn Dixon

Gazelle Book Services handles both trade and academic lists and covers the whole of the UK and Europe. It provides:
 fast order turn-round;
 comprehensive stock and regular stock replenishment;
 efficient reporting and information service to customers;
 regular sales calling and regular liaison with booksellers in connection with promotion, exhibitions, special events, etc;
 following through;
 friendly, helpful service;
 regular and adaptable reporting to publishers;
 flexibility and co-operation.
 Complete list of client publishers is available on request.

6115

GRANTHAM BOOK SERVICES
Trent Road, Grantham, Lincs NG31 7XQ
Telephone: 01476 541000 (orders: 541080)
Fax: 01476 541060 (orders: 541061)
Email: orders@gbs.tbs-ltd.co.uk
Web Site: http://www.granthambookservices.co.uk

Directors: Mark Williams *(Joint Managing)*
 Rob Phillips *(Joint Managing)*
 Justin Smith *(Finance)*
Managers: David Goodere *(Customer Services)*
 Colleen McMorran *(Client Services)*
 Simon Goldstein *(Head of Operations, Grantham)*
Duty Managers: Steve McMonigle *(Operations)*
 Simon Hancox *(Logistics)*

Parent Company:
UK: Random House UK

Clients include:
France: La Martiniere
UK: AA Special Sales; Alma Books; Anness Publishing; Bounce Sales & Marketing; Chronicle; Compass Maps; Thomas Cook; Crown House; The Crowood Press; Duckworth; Footprint Handbooks; Geocentre International UK Ltd; Harbour Books; Hay House; Nick

Hern Books; Hesperus; How To Books; Kraken; Landmark Publishing; Lerner; Lonely Planet; Manning Partnership; Melia Publishing Services; National Archives; National Portrait Gallery; New Holland; One World; Osprey Publishing; Oval Books; Perseus Books; PGUK; Piatkus Books; Piccadilly Press; Quiller; Reaktion Books; Rotovision; Severn House Publishers; Sound Entertainment; Templar Publishing; Teneues; Timber Press; Titan Books
USA: Everyman; MBI; Rockport; Workman Publishing

Grantham Book Services provides a very fast and efficient distribution service for publishers. Service includes order receipt by post, fax, telephone and teleordering; invoicing and despatch. A next day delivery service, from receipt of order to delivery of books, is provided to the UK trade. Also sales ledger and cash collection service. Comprehensive range of computer reports; plus all the usual ancillary work such as shrinkwrapping, repricing, dumpbin and counter-pack make up.

6116

KUPERARD PUBLISHERS & DISTRIBUTORS
59 Hutton Grove, London N12 8DS
Telephone: (020) 8446 2440
Fax: (020) 8446 2441
Email: enquiries@kuperard.co.uk
Web Site: http://www.kuperard.co.uk

Also at:
Orca Book Services, Fleet Road, Poole, Dorset BH15 3AJ
Telephone: 01202 665432

Chief Executive: Joshua Kuperard
Managers: Martin Kaye *(Sales & Marketing)*
 Linda Tenenbaum *(Special Sales)*
 Caroline Eden *(Marketing & Publicity)*

Publishers of:
Chic Guides; Culture Smart! Guides; Customs & Etiquette; FHG Guides; Kuperard Books; NFT Guides; Simple Guides

Distributor for Religious books:
USA: HarperCollins; Lerner Books; Penguin; Random House; Schocken Books / Random House; Simon & Schuster

Distributor for classic literature:
USA: The Modern Library (Random House)

Distributor for Montessori books:
USA: Penguin; Schocken Books

Distributor for Self-Study Language Courses:
USA: Living Language (Random House)

Kuperard, a division and imprint of Bravo Ltd, acts as publishers, co-publishers and distributors, handling marketing and representation. Kuperard handle over 30 UK and overseas publishers. Stocklists, catalogues and brochures are available upon request.
 Travel subjects include leisure guides covering a wide variety of destinations and markets. Kuperard publishes cross-cultural guides for business people and travellers. Religion subjects covered include art, cookery, the Holy Land, history, language, mysticism, holocaust, faith and spirituality.

6117

LITTLEHAMPTON BOOK SERVICES LTD
Faraday Close, Durrington, Worthing, West Sussex BN13 3RB
Telephone: 01903 828500
Fax: 01903 828625
Email: ...@lbsltd.co.uk
Web Site: http://www.lbsltd.co.uk

Directors: Peter Roche *(Chairman)*
 Martin Evans *(Managing)*
 Basil May *(Finance)*
 Lesley Morgan *(Group IT)*
 Bridget Radnedge *(Publishing Services)*
 Graham Money *(Operations)*
 Alan Rakes *(Inventory)*

Parent Company:
UK: Orion Publishing Group

Clients include:
3C Publishing (Columbia Marketing Ltd); Ian Allan; Anvil Poetry Press; Aurum Press, Apple & JR Books; Automobile Association; Barefoot Books; John Blake Publishing; Bloodaxe; Carcanet; Crombie Jardine Publishing; Cyan; DAAB; Express Newspapers; Eye Books Ltd; Gibson Square Publishing; Gloucester Publishers [formerly Everyman]; The Good Hotel Guide Ltd; The Greatest in the World; Grub Street; Haus Publishing; Highdown Publishing; Infinite Ideas Co; Interact Publishing Ltd; Kogan Page; Kyle Cathie; Little Books; Make Believe Ideas Ltd; Marshall Cavendish; Myrmidon Books; Michael O'Mara Books; Octopus Publishing Group; Old St Publishing; Orion Group; PC Publishing; Pennant Books Ltd; Pitch Publishing Ltd; Private Eye; Alan Rogers' Guides Ltd; Serpent's Tail; Snowbooks Ltd; Sport Media; Summersdale; Tantor Media Inc; Taschen; Vertigo Communications LLB; Vision; Visit Britain; Which? The Consumer Association

Littlehampton Book Services provides publishers with full warehouse management and distribution services that include credit control and trust accounting, sophisticated management reporting, telesales, customer service and royalty accounting.

6118

B. McCALL BARBOUR
28 George IV Bridge, Edinburgh EH1 1ES
Telephone: 0131 225 4816
Fax: 0131 225 4816
Web Site: http://www.mccallbarbour.co.uk

Managing Partner: Rev Dr T. C. Danson-Smith
Despatch Manager: Miss G. A. Danson-Smith

USA companies represented:
USA: AMG Publishers; Chick Publications; Dake Bible Sales; Discovery House; Kirkbride Bible Co; Living Stories Inc; Thomas Nelson & Sons; Oxford University Press [Bibles]; John Peterson Music; Rainbow Study Bibles; Schoettle Publishing House; Singspiration Inc; Sword of the Lord Publishers; Zondervan Corporation

Distributor of Bibles, Christian books and greeting cards, also videos, DVDs, gifts.

6119

MACMILLAN DISTRIBUTION (MDL)
Brunel Road, Houndmills, Basingstoke, Hants RG21 6XS
Telephone: 01256 302840
Fax: 01256 841426
Email: www-mdl@macmillan.co.uk
Web Site: http://www.macmillandistribution.co.uk

Directors: David Smith *(Managing)*
 Andrew May-Miller *(Information Services)*
 Micheline Jebb *(Commercial)*
 Guy Browning *(Distribution)*

Parent Company:
UK: Macmillan Ltd

Macmillan Publishers:
Boxtree; W. H. Freeman & Worth Publishers; Macmillan Children's Books; Macmillan Digital Audio; Macmillan Education; Nature Publishing Group; Office for National Statistics (ONS); Palgrave; Pan Macmillan; Picador; Priddy Books; Sinauer Associates; University Science Books

Client Publishers:
Accent Press Ltd; Arcturus Publishing Ltd; Barrington Stoke; A. & C. Black; Bloomsbury Publishing Plc; Camra; Cico Books; Class Publishing (London) Ltd; CRW Publishing Ltd; Earthscan / James & James; First Second Editions; W. Foulsham & Co Ltd; Guinness World Records Ltd; Hayden Publishing; Innovative Kids; Jones & Bartlett; Miles Kelly Publishing; Kingfisher Publications Plc; Jessica Kingsley Publishers; Little Hare Books; Little Tiger Press (Magi); Macmillan English Campus; Macmillan New Writing; Methuen Drama; Murdoch Books (UK) Ltd; Panini Books; Persephone Book Ltd; Pinwheel Ltd; Prestel Publishing Ltd; Quadrille Publishing Ltd; Revolver Books; Rising Stars UK Ltd; Rodale; Ryland Peters & Small; Spy Publishing Ltd; I. B. Tauris; Think Books; Tokyopop; Emma Treehouse Ltd; V & A Publications; Walker Books Ltd; John Wisden & Co Ltd

Macmillan Distribution (MDL) provides an efficient and cost-effective service to the Macmillan Group and a list of over 40 third party publishers. Its award winning service embraces all aspects of order fulfilment, cash collection, and data and information provision. For the use of its customers MDL has pioneered transparent delivery information and all forms of electronic ordering, payment and returns.

6120

MARSTON BOOK SERVICES LTD
160 Milton Park, Abingdon, Oxon OX14 4SD
Telephone: 01235 465604
Fax: 01235 465655
Email: monica.harding@marston.co.uk
Web Site: http://www.marston.co.uk

Chairman: John Holloran
Directors: Ross Clayton *(Managing)*
 Graham Cooper *(Financial)*
Managers: Melanie Khosa *(Customer Service)*
 Donna Green *(Trade)*
 Monica Harding *(Client Development & Service)*

Clients represented:
Belgium: Brepols Publishing; Harvey Miller Publishers
Denmark: Copenhagen Business School Press
Germany: Berghahn; Boerm Bruckmeier Verlag GmbH
Italy: Damiani Editore
Netherlands: Asian Studies Book Services
Republic of Ireland: Cork University Press / Attic Press
Singapore: World Scientific Publishing
UK: Acumen Publishing; Adamson Publishing; Alban Books; Alpha Science International Ltd; Arts Council of England; Atrium Group; The Barbirolli Society; Bennett & Bloom; Bibles for Children; Black Dog Publishing Ltd; Bonnier Books; Burke Publishing; Church House Publishing; CIPAC; Clinical Publishing; Combined Academic Publishers Ltd; James Currey Publishers; Edinburgh University Press; Editions Assouline; Edward Elgar Publishing Ltd; Equinox; Flame Tree Publishing; Die Gestalten Verlag UK; Gibraltar Research; Harriman House Ltd; Haworth Press; Houghton Mifflin Co Inc; Hurst & Co (Publishers) Ltd; ICSA; Institute of Physics *(education only)*; Jessica Kingsley Publishers Ltd; Peter Lang Ltd; Library Reference; Lion Hudson Plc; Liverpool University Press; Manchester University Press; Manticore Books Ltd; Mapin; Merrell Publishers Ltd; The Monacelli Press; Multilingual Matters Ltd / Channel View Publications; Now Publishing; Oberon; Orthodox Christian Books Ltd; Permillion; Pluto Press; The Policy Press; Princeton Architectural Press; Public Catalogue Foundation; Research Studies Press; The Royal Society of Medicine Press Ltd; John Rule Sales & Marketing; Saint Andrew Press; Saqi; Scottish Council for Law Reporting; Society for Promoting Christian Knowledge; Terra Publishing; Third Millennium Publishing Ltd; Thorogood Publishing; Tottel Publishing; Unicorn Press; Verso; The Voltaire Foundation; John Wilson Booksales
USA: CQ Press; Enisen Publishing; Keyahoff; National Academies Press; Rizzoli International Publications

Provides fulfilment services to the publishing world.
 Services available include: order processing; customer service; credit control; management reporting; production of royalty statements; pick, pack and despatch (automated warehouse management system); digital print facility; journal fulfilment; ancillary work; exhibition services; EDI; IT support and development.

6121

MDS BOOK SALES
128 Pikes Lane, Glossop, Derbys SK13 8EH
Telephone: 01457 861508
Fax: 01457 868332
Email: mdsbooksales@aol.com
Web Site: http://www.mdsbooks.co.uk

Proprietor: Mark Senior

Associated Companies:
UK: Venture Publications Ltd

Distributor for:
UK: Birmingham Transport Historical Group; DTS Sales; John Hambley Books; Senior Publications; Venture Publications Ltd; Peter Watts Publishing

Book wholesalers and distributors specializing in transport related lists.

6122

MELIA PUBLISHING SERVICES LTD
The White House, 2A Meadrow, Godalming, Surrey GU7 3HN

Telephone: 01483 869839
Fax: 01483 869845
Email: melia@melia.co.uk

Directors: Terry Melia *(Managing)*
Billy Adair *(Sales)*
Cleve Vine *(Finance)*
Managers: Joanna Melia *(Sales)*
Linda West *(Accounts)*

Distributor for:
France: Fitway
UK: Connections; Ivy Press; Psychology News; Snake River Press; Worth Press Ltd
USA: Algonquin; Artisan; Filipacchi; Harcourt Trade Books; Kensington Publishing Corporation; Newmarket Press; Rodale; Silverback Books; St Martins Press; Storey Books; Time Inc Home Entertainment; Toby Press LLC; Workman Publishing

Sales and distribution for English language publishers.

6123

MK BOOK SERVICE
7 East Street, Hartford Road, Huntingdon PE29 1WZ
Telephone: 01480 353710
Fax: 01480 431703
Email: mkbooks@tiscali.co.uk

Owner: M. R. King

UK distributor/representative for clients including:
Argentina: Del Nuevo Extremo; Lola
Australia: Academic English Press; Gary Allen Pty Ltd NSW; Art Media; Ausmed; Australian Medical Publications; Blue Cat Books; E. J. Bowles; Coffee School Melbourne; Corkwood Press; Crossing Press; Ken Duncan Panographs; Eagles Nest Golf Guides; Golden Point Press; Haese & Harris; Hobby Investment; IBID Press; Indo Lingo Surf; JB Books; Linford; Melting Pot Press; Mitchell Wordsmith; Parrot Books; Perfect Potion; Piscean Books; Slouch Hat Publications; Wizard Study Guides; Woodmore
Bangladesh: University Press Dhaka
Canada: Creative Newfoundland; Empty Mirror Press; Fitzhenry & Whiteside
Estonia: Periodika
France: Editions Pelisser
Germany: ADAC
Iceland: Forglaid; Iceland Review; Mimir
India: Aditya Prakashan; Allied Publications; Anmol; Asa; Ashish/APH; Asia Bookclub; Atlantic Publishing; Authors Press; Best Books Kolkata; Biotech; Book Enclave; Concord Press; Daya; Deep & Deep; Diamond Pocket Books; DK Printworld Pty Ltd; Galaxy; Gene-Tech Books; Indus; Intellectual Book Corner; ISPCK; Kaushal; Low Price Publications; Mahaveer & Sons; Minerva Associates; Modern Publishers; National Book Trust; Papyrus; Rajesh; South Asian Publications; Vine Press
Israel: Beit Yochmann; Ben Zvi Press; Bible Lands Museum; Carta; Francisian Printing Press; Gefen; Israel Academy of Sciences; Israel Exploration Society; Magnes Press; Rubin Mass Publishing Jerusalem; Yad Vaschem
Italy: Biblico Pontificio; Palombi *(English language titles only)*
Latvia: Avots
Mexico: Funentes
New Zealand: Catt Publishing; Craig Printing; Jenn Falconer Books; Holst Ltd; Kingsley Wood; Look Around Design; Manaaki Whenuka Press; Photo Image; SPSS Ashburton; Wises Publications
Pakistan: Iqbal Institute; Sang-e-meel
Philippines: Asia Type
Portugal: Quinta do Pinhal; Vista Iberica
Russia: Raduga
Russian Federation: Literatura
South Africa: Galago Books; Tortoise Press
Taiwan: Far East Book Co; SMC Publishing
Thailand: Dragondance; White Lotus
UK: John Bell Training; Hakedes; Pelican Publishing; Popular Publications; George Thompson Brake; Willingham Press
Uruguay: Editions Trilice
USA: American Historical Press; Eisenbrauns; Floating Gallery Press; Global Health Solutions; Learning Unlimited; Nova Books; Tusitlal Publishing
Zimbabwe: Argosy Press; Modus Publications

Distributor for overseas publishers; importer from overseas, for whom we are not agents; distributor for selected UK publishers; library supply; booksearch for out of print UK books.

6124

MOTILAL (UK) – BOOKS OF INDIA
367 High Street, London Colney, St Albans, Herts AL2 1EA
Telephone: 01727 761677
Fax: 01727 761357
Email: info@mlbduk.com

Managing Director: R. J. McLennan
Finance: Ms Ann Moister
Customer Services: Richard Neil

Associated Companies:
UK: Ahimsa Books

Distributor for:
Australia: Chakra Press
India: Bhaktivedanta Book Trust; Motilal Banarsidass
UK: Ahimsa Books
USA: Bhaktivedanta Book Trust; Govardhan Hill; World Relief Network

Indian publishers represented include:
India: Abhinav Publications; Ahana Books; Akashdeep Publishing House; Amexfel Publishers; Anmol Publications; Aravali Books International; Aryan Books International; Asiatic Publishing House; Banjara Academy; Bihar School of Yoga; Bookwell Publications; BPB Publications; BPI (India) Pvt Ltd; Brijbasi Art Press; Centre for Studies in Civilizations; Commonwealth Youth Programme; Cosmo Publications; Deep & Deep; DK Printworld; Excel Books; Full Circle; Gemini Books; Gulshan Publications; Hind Pocket Books; Indian Book Centre; Indiana Publishing House; Indica; Indus Publishing; Institute for Human Development; International Scientific Publishing Academy; B. Jain Publishers; Jaya Books; Ben Johnston Publishing; Kalpaz Publications; Katha; KSK Publishers; Low Price Publications; Malhotra Publishing; Manas; Manohar Publishers; Motilal Banarsidass; New Age Books; Orient Paperbacks; Paljor Publications; Penguin (India); Pentagon Press; Pilgrim Press & Book Faith India; Pragati; Sundeep Prakashan; Puffin Books; Pustak Mahal; Readworthy; Regency Publications; Sahasrara Publications; Samskriti; Sanskrit Religious Institute; Shubhi Publications; Spectrum Publications; Sura Books; Tibetan Medical & Astro Institute; Torchlight Publishing; Unisun Publications; Universal Law Publishing; Vanity Books International; Wordspeak; Worldview

Distributor of books and other materials dealing with the philosophies, religions and cultures of India. Specializes in Buddhism, Hinduism, Vegetarian, Ayurvedic and Reincarnation titles.

In November 1998 we took over Motilal Books, who are the European distributors for Motilal Banarsidass Ltd (MLBD) of New Delhi. MLBD are the foremost publishers for the academic market on the topics of Hinduism, Buddhism, Jainism and all titles from India. We supply all markets with titles in all fields, books from India in general, representing all major Indian publishers.

6125

NMD TRADING CO
[trading as Northern Map Distributors]
9 Orgreave Close, Sheffield S13 9NP
Telephone: 0114 288 9522
Fax: 0114 269 1499
Email: sales@northernmap.co.uk

Directors: David N. Smith *(Managing)*
Andrew Smith

Supply bookshops and other trade outlets through the Midlands and Northern England with maps and guides and local book product. Specialize in walking and outdoor activity books. Four representatives call regularly throughout the year. Main suppliers are Ordnance Survey, George Philips, Collins, Geographers A-Z Map Co and Estate. Provide a service for small publishers into the multiple chains, e.g. W. H. Smith, Waterstone's, and a map merchandising service to garage forecourts for multiple station groups.

Sole supplier of LAM-fold maps. Also supply laminated flat maps and other special product, such as library supply. Also provide a specialist service for mounted maps.

6126

ORCA BOOK SERVICES LTD
Unit A3, Fleets Corner, Poole, Dorset BH17 0HL
Telephone: 01202 665432
Fax: 01202 666219
Email: orders@orcabookservices.co.uk
Web Site: http://www.orcabookservices.co.uk

Directors: Martyn Chapman *(Commercial)*
Colin Smith *(IT)*
Ian Whyte *(Logistics)*
Manager: Denise Shonfeld *(Finance)*
Customer Services: Trisha Clapp
Credit Control: Maggie Johnson

Parent Company:
UK: The Continuum International Publishing Group Ltd

UK distributor for:
Age Concern; Ammo Books; Arris Publishing; Duncan Baird Publishers; Berg Publishers; Black Dog & Leventhal; The Book Foundation; Burns & Oates; Compendium; Continuum International Publishing Group; CSA Word; Evans Mitchell Books; Family Doctor Publications; Firefly Books; Francis Frith Book Co; Global Oriental; GMB Publishing; Guild of Master Craftsman Publications; Histoires et Collections; John Hunt Publishing; Industrial Press; IPC Books; Islamic Texts; Know the Score Books; Kuperard Publishers; Lark Books; Learning Development Aids; Lifetime Careers Publishing; O Books; Palazzo Editions; Parkstone Press; Peerless Editions; Pepin Press; A. K. Peters; Potomac Books; Raceform Publications; Ravette Publishing; Reynolds & Hearn; Roundhouse Publishing; SEP Editrice; Special Interest Model Books; Sterling Publishing; Taunton Press; Thalamus Publishing; Ticktock Media; Van der Plas Publications; Veloce Publishing; Watkins Publishing; White Star Publishers

Orca Book Services provides a full distribution service to general, academic and specialist publishers. A comprehensive package of management reports comes as standard, and this can be tailored to the individual publisher's requirements if necessary. Royalty accounting is also available as well as representation through the various sales agencies with which we have arrangements.

6127

ORTHODOX CHRISTIAN BOOKS LTD
Studio 3, Unit 5, Silverdale Enterprise Park, Kents Lane, Newcastle-under-Lyme, Staffs ST5 6SR
Telephone: 01782 444561
Fax: 01782 624106
Email: orthbook@aol.com
Web Site: http://www.orthodoxbooks.co.uk

Managing Director: Nicholas Chapman

UK distributor for:
Greece: EN PLO Editions; Denise Harvey; Uncut Mountain Publishers
USA: Antiochian Archdiocese Publications Department; Conciliar Press; Holy Cross Press; Holy Trinity Monastery; St Herman of Alaska Press; St Nectarios Press; St Nikodemos Orthodox Publication Society; St Tikhon's Seminary Press; St Vladimir's Seminary Press

Specialist distributor, wholesaler and retailer of books and other items pertaining to the faith, life and worship of the Orthodox Christian Churches. For some publishers it has exclusive distribution rights for the UK, European Union and British Commonwealth.

6128

POMEGRANATE EUROPE LTD
Unit 1, Hurlbutt Road, Heathcote Business Centre, Warwick CV34 6TD
Telephone: 01926 430111
Fax: 01926 430888
Email: sales@pomeurope.co.uk
Web Site: http://www.pomegranate.com

Directors: Thomas Burke *(Managing)*
Ley S. Bricknell *(Sales)*
Katie Burke *(Publisher)*

Associated Companies:
USA: Pomegranate Communications Inc

UK Distributor for:
USA: Pomegranate

Pomegranate (Europe) Ltd represent, distribute and publish a high-quality range of fine art and photographic calendars, posters, cards, diaries, books of days, postcards, books and much more.

6129

REARDON PUBLISHING
PO Box 919, Cheltenham, Glos GL50 9AN
Telephone: 01242 231800
Email: reardon@bigfoot.com
Web Site: http://www.reardon.co.uk & http://www.cotswoldbookshop.com

Director: Nicholas Reardon

UK distributor for:
UK: Cassell *(selected publications)*; Cicerone *(selected publications)*; Cordee *(selected publications)*; Corinium Publications; Estate Publications; Flukes UK *(illustrated maps)*; The Gloucestershire Ramblers Association; Harvey Maps *(all maps)*; Ordnance Survey *(all maps)*; Orion *(selected publications)*; Philips Maps; Video Ex *(selected titles)*

Reardon Publishing offers a wide range of Costwold books, maps, videos, CDs and postcards and prints mostly in the specialized areas of walking, cycling, driving, folklore, leisure and tourism in both the Cotswold and associated counties, plus a new range of books on Antarctica and Antarctic heroes.

6130

JOHN RITCHIE LTD
40 Beansburn, Kilmarnock, Ayrshire KA3 1RL
Telephone: 01563 536394
Fax: 01563 571191
Email: sales@johnritchie.co.uk
Web Site: http://www.johnritchie.co.uk

Directors: Kenneth Munro *(Managing)*
Edwin Taylor

UK distributor for:
Canada: Lawson Falle
UK: Cambridge Bibles; John Ritchie Ltd Publications
USA: AMG Publications; Broadman & Holman; Gospel Folio Press; Thomas Nelson (Nashville TN); Standard Publishing

Publishing and distributing Christian, i.e. religious books, magazines, etc. Providing wholesale supply to Christian bookshops for major UK and US publishers.

6131

SCANDINAVIA CONNECTION
26 Woodsford Square, London W14 8DP
Telephone: (020) 7602 0657
Fax: (020) 7602 8556
Email: books@scandinavia-connection.co.uk
Web Site: http://www.scandinavia-connection.co.uk

Chairman: Max Morgan-Witts

Parent Company:
UK: Max Morgan-Witts Productions Ltd

UK distributor for:
Denmark: Aschehoug; Borgen; Nyt Nordisk
Finland: Otava
Iceland: JPV
Norway: Cappelen; Index; KOM; Normann's; Wennergren-Cappelen
Sweden: Atlantis; ICA; J-P Lahall
USA: Pelican *(for Norway B&B Book)*

Sole UK supplier for various Scandinavian publishers of non-fiction English edition Scandinavian books, maps, videos and CD-ROMs; UK book distributor for non-fiction English editions by Norwegian, Finnish, Icelandic, Danish and Swedish publishers.

6132

SQUADRON SIGNAL / POCKETBOND LTD
PO Box 80, Welwyn, Herts AL6 0ND
Telephone: 01707 391509
Fax: 01707 327466
Email: sales@pocketbond.co.uk

Director: Phillip Brook
Manager: Neil Fraser

Pocketbond Ltd is the UK importer of Squadron Signal Publications and Detail & Scale Publications, USA. These lists are sold and distributed in the UK and the Republic of Ireland to bookshops, book wholesalers, etc.

6133

TRADE COUNTER DISTRIBUTION
Mendlesham Industrial Estate, Norwich Road, Mendlesham, Norfolk IP14 5NA
Telephone: 01449 766629
Fax: 01449 767122
Email: patrick.curran@tradecounter.co.uk
Web Site: http://www.tradecounter.co.uk

Managing Director: Patrick Curran
General Manager: Martin Leigh
Chairman: Brian Barron

Storage, packing and distribution of books for publishers.

6134

TRANSATLANTIC PUBLISHERS GROUP LTD
Unit 242, 235 Earls Court Road, London SW5 9FE
Telephone: (020) 7373 2515
Fax: (020) 7244 1018
Email: Richard@TPGLtd.co.uk
Web Site: http://www.TransatlanticPublishers.com

Directors: Richard Williamson *(Managing)*
Mark Chaloner *(Sales & Marketing)*

UK distributor for:
Australia: Advanced Knowledge International
India: Hindustan Book Co
USA: American Institute of Mathematical Sciences; American Society of Health Systems Pharmacists (ASHP); Demos Medical Publishers; Destech Publishers; ESRI Press; Franklin Beedle & Associates; Industrial Press; Infinity Science Press; Lexicomp Inc; A. K. Peters; Potomac Books; Zero to Three Press

Distributors and agents for academic publishers in the UK, Europe and the Middle East.

6135

TURNAROUND PUBLISHER SERVICES LTD
Unit 3, Olympia Trading Estate, Coburg Road, London N22 6TZ
Telephone: (020) 8829 3000
Fax: (020) 8881 5088
Email: sales@turnaround-uk.com
Web Site: http://www.turnaround-uk.com

Directors: Bill Godber *(Managing & Sales)*
Claire Thompson *(Marketing & Company Secretary)*
Sue Gregg *(Finance)*
Andy Webb *(UK Sales)*

Clients include:
Australia: Ocean; Power Publications (Australia)
Belgium: Secret Magazine
Canada: Arsenal Pulp Press; ECW Press
Germany: Bruno Gmunder; Goliath
India: One and Only
Republic of Ireland: Brandon Books; Mount Eagle Publications
UK: Atlas Press; Beautiful Books; Bitter Lemon; Cheeky Guides; Cherry Red; Chrome Dreams; Creation Books; Device; Easyway Guide; Fab Press; Head Press; Headhunters; Kimani Press; Knockabout; Dewi Lewis Publishing; Milo Books; No Exit Press; Oldcastle Books; Paddleless Press; Panini UK / Marvel; Pocket Essentials; Rebellion / 2000 AD; Shelter Publications; Tindal St Press; Turnaround; Vision Sports Publishing; The X Press
USA: Africa World Press Inc; Akashic; Alyson; Amok Books; Arcadia; Bantam *(select stock holdings only)*; Berkley Boulvard *(select stock holdings only)*; Bookmarks; Circlet Press; Cleis Press; Dalkey Archive Press; Disinformation; Disney Editions *(select stock holdings only)*; Fantagraphics; Feral House; Graywolf Books; Greenery Press; HarperCollins US *(select stock holdings only)*; Hyperion *(select stock holdings only)*; Kensington; Milet; NBM; The Overlook Press; Powerhouse Books; Quick American; Seven Stories Press; Soft Skull Press; Soho Press; Speck Press; Starbooks Press; Steerforth Press; Umbrage; Verse Chorus Press; Warner Books *(select stock holdings only)*

Distribution only:
UK: Allison & Busby

Sales only:
Canada: Black Rose Books (Central Books)
UK: Anvil Books; Marion Boyars; Duckworth/Overlook; Maia Press; Serif

Turnaround provides a sales, marketing and distribution service for a range of UK, US and Irish publishers in the UK and Europe.

6136

TURPIN DISTRIBUTION
Pegasus Drive, Stratton Business Park, Biggleswade, Beds SG18 8TQ
Telephone: 01767 604868
Fax: 01767 604949
Email: neil.castle@turpin-distribution.com

Also at:
Turpin North America, The Bleachery, 143 West Street, New Milford, CT 06778, USA
Telephone: +1 (860) 350 0041
Fax: +1 (860) 350 0039

Managing Director: Lorna Summers
Company Accountant: Richard Stroud
Head Customer Relations / Sales: Neil Castle

Parent Company:
UK: Eurospan

Clients include:
France: Organisation for Economic Cooperation and Development (OECD); SaS-Lavoisier
Germany: Dechema
Greece: Adcotec
Japan: Japanese Society for Analytical Chemistry
Netherlands: Brill Academic Publishers; Kluwer Law International; New in Chess
Russia: Turpin-Moscow
UK: Abington Publishing; Adcotec; Philip Allan Updates *(magazines)*; Association of Learned and Professional Society Publishers (ALPSP); The Association of Project Managers; Beech Tree Publishing; Berg Publishing; The Bodleian Library; The British Library; The British Psychological Society; Chandos Publishers; Dunedin Academic Press; Equinox Publishing; Euromoney PLC; The Eurospan Group; Fiscal Publications; Global Oriental; John Harper Publishing; Institute of Cast Metal Engineers; Intellect Journals; Internet Archaeology; IP Publishing; Journal of Transport & Economic Policy; Logos Journal; Millennium / London School of Economics; NIACE; Pharmaceutical Press; Pickering & Chatto; Pion Publishers; Royal College of Obstetricians and Gynaecologists; Royal College of Psychiatrists; Sapiens; Science & Technology Letters; Society of Chemical Industry; Spiramus; The Way; White Horse Press; Wrightson Biomedical
USA: American Association Cancer Research; American School of Classical Studies; Aspen Publishers Inc; Berghahn Journals; Greenwood *(journals)*; Idea Group Inc. Journals; Nova Science Publishers *(journals)*; United Nations

Turpin specializes in worldwide distribution of learned and academic book and journal publications. It sends out renewals/invoices etc. in the publisher's name with their logo and trading terms. It bills and collects in multiple currencies and provides multilingual customer care. Publishers' sales and financial reports are delivered via secure internet access. Turpin can handle both print and online products. Customer care and warehousing in the UK and the USA.

6137

VINE HOUSE DISTRIBUTION LTD
Waldenbury, North Chailey, East Sussex BN8 4DR
Telephone: 01825 723398
Fax: 01825 724188
Email: richard@vinehouseuk.co.uk
Web Site: http://www.vinehouseuk.co.uk

Customer Services:
The Old Mill House, Mill Lane, Uckfield, East Sussex TN22 5AA
Telephone: 01825 767396
Fax: 01825 765649
Email: sales@vinehouseuk.co.uk
Web Site: http://www.vinehouseuk.co.uk

Directors: Richard Squibb
　Sarah Squibb
　Tara Horwood
Managers: Sally Pulling *(Customer Services)*
　Pauline Gosden *(Customer Services)*
　Sophie Armfield *(Publicity)*

Associated Companies:
UK: Vine House Book Promotion

Clients include:
Australia: 20/21 Design; Clockwork Media; Epic Guides; Inn Australia
Italy: Mediane
Monaco: Christian Philippsen
New Zealand: Travelwise
Norway: Knud Robberstad
Russia: Link of Times Foundation
Spain: Editorial Moll
Sweden: JAC International; MagDig Media
Switzerland: Chronosports; Editions J. R. Piccard
UK: Ashgrove Publishing; Assess4care; Association of Illustrators; At Heart Publishing; Bearmondsey Publishing; Boleyn Books; The Book Guild; British Institute of Radiology; Creative Monochrome; Dance Books; Delancey Press *(imprint of The Book Guild)*; Dove Publishing; Fitzjames Press; Football World; Good Life Press; Haldane Mason; Hochland Communications; Martin Holmes Rallying; Honeyglen Publishing; Horse's Mouth Publications; Immel Publishing; Sheila Markham Rare Books; Andrew Martin International; Masquerade Publications; Motor Racing Publications; Oxbridge Applications; Picnic Publishing; Julian Richer Publishing; Royal Academy of Dancing; Safety House; Saxon Books; Shadowline Publishing; R. D. & A. S. Shepherd Partnership; Silent But Deadly Publications; Silver Moon Books; Superbrands; Tartarus Press; Temple House Books; Tiger Books; Touchstone Books; Troubador Publishing; John van Weenen; Who Works Publications; Wooden Dragon Press
USA: Aslan Publishing; Dance Horizons; Jagrand Publishing; Millennium Advertising; Princeton Book Co; Wine Appreciation Guild

Vine House Distribution provides a comprehensive range of services for small and medium sized book publishers, including representation, distribution, marketing, publicity and promotion, and mail order fulfilment.

6138

VIRTUE BOOKS LTD
Edward House, Tenter Street, Rotherham S60 1LB
Telephone: 01709 365005
Fax: 01709 829982
Email: info@virtue.co.uk
Web Site: http://www.virtue.co.uk

Directors: Richard Russum *(Commercial)*
　Peter Russum *(Managing)*

Parent Company:
UK: E. Russum & Sons Ltd

Specialist distributor, concentrating almost exclusively on books on cookery, food and drink. Virtue holds stocks of over 300 titles and supplies mainly to professional and domestic kitchen shops, cook shops, food shops, delicatessens, etc. Some of the titles on its list are exclusive to Virtue, but the majority are sourced from British, American and some continental publishers.

6139

WINDSOR BOOKS INTERNATIONAL
5 Castle End Park, Castle End Road, Ruscombe, Berks RG10 9XQ
Telephone: 0118 934 6367
Fax: 0118 934 6368
Email: geoffcowen@windsorbooks.co.uk
Web Site: http://www.windsorbooks.co.uk

Managing Director: Geoff Cowen
Managers: Angela Prysor-Jones *(Publicity)*
　Eileen Johnson *(Credit Control)*

UK Distributor/Representative for:
Australia: Atoll Editions; Explore Australia Pty Ltd; Watermark Press
France: Editions Sisyphe; Petit Futé Guides
Germany: Meyer & Meyer Verlag
Italy: Bonechi Edizioni 'Il Turismo' SRL
Mexico: AM Editores
Republic of Ireland: Georgina Campbell's Guides to Ireland
Sweden: Arvinius Forlag
UK: Bill Brandt Archive; WRTH Publications Ltd
USA: Allworth Press; Breckling Press; C & T Publishing; Creative Homeowner; Getty Publications; Hunter Publishing; Landauer Books; Open Road Publishing; Portland Press; Vanguard Productions; Westholme Publishing

Windsor Books International, a division of the Roundhouse Group, provides distribution combined with sales representation and marketing in the UK and European markets, linked to Orca Distribution Services Ltd. The Windsor sales team consists of six representatives in the UK and Republic of Ireland and six covering West and Eastern Europe.

6.7 REMAINDER MERCHANTS

6140

AB BOOKS
21 Chalice Court, Hedge End, Southampton SO30 4TA
Telephone: 01489 799082
Fax: 01489 799082
Email: abbooks@tiscali.co.uk

Proprietor: A. C. Butler

Remainder and bargain book sales.

6141

BOOKMARK REMAINDERS LTD
Rivendell, Illand, Launceston, Cornwall PL15 7LS
Telephone: 01566 782728
Fax: 01566 782059
Email: andrew-rattray@book-bargains.co.uk
Web Site: http://www.book-bargains.co.uk

Directors: Andrew Rattray
　Carol Rattray

A wide range of genuine remainders and bargain books. Prompt payment to publishers, authors for surplus stocks.

6142

FANSHAW BOOKS LTD
Unit 7, Lysander Mews, Lysander Grove, London N19 3QP
Telephone: (020) 7281 9387
Fax: (020) 7561 3502
Email: info@roybloom.com
Web Site: http://www.roybloom.com

Managing Director: Adam Bloom
Chairman: Roy Bloom

New remainder company specializing in real publishers' editions, mainly non-fiction, art, military, etc.

6143

OCTAGON BOOKS (WHOLESALE) LTD
The Old Exchange, New Pond Road, Holmer Green, High Wycombe, Bucks HP15 6SU
Telephone: 01494 711717 (mobile: 07718 364857)
Fax: 01494 711176
Email: ronive@lineone.net

Director: Ron Ive

All types of remainders and promotional reprints.

6144

JIM OLDROYD BOOKS
14–18 London Road, Sevenoaks, Kent TN13 1AJ
Telephone: 01732 463356
Fax: 01732 464486
Email: jim@oldroyd.co.uk & paula@oldroyd.co.uk
Web Site: http://www.oldroyd.co.uk

Directors: Jim Oldroyd
　Paula Ireland
Manager: Niki Oldroyd *(Buyer)*

Remainders, bargain books and overstocks of adult and children's books. All ages and all interests.

6145

PR BOOKS LTD
Unit 2, Mealbank Trading Estate, Mealbank, Kendal, Cumbria LA8 9DL
Telephone: 01539 733332
Fax: 01539 733375
Email: info@prbooks.com
Web Site: http://www.prbooks.co.uk

Joint Managing Directors: Paul Farrar
　Ruth Farrar
Regional Sales: Thomas Seddon
General Manager: Mark Farrar

PR Books Ltd is an international trader in remainder books and distributes an extensive range of books and CDs worldwide. It has over 3500 remainder titles including educational, children's (books and activity packs), natural history, military history, cookery, travel, art & craft, social stationery, reference and a broad range of budget CDs, videos and DVDs.

6146

SANDERSON BOOKS LTD
Front Street, Klondyke, Cramlington, Northumberland NE23 6RF
Telephone: 01670 735855
Fax: 01670 730974
Email: sales@sandersonbooks.com
Web Site: http://www.sandersonbooks.com

Director: John Sanderson
Manager: Anne Pearson

6147

SANDPIPER BOOKS LTD
24 Langroyd Road, London SW17 7PL
Telephone: (020) 8767 7421
Fax: (020) 8682 0280
Email: enquiries@sandpiper.co.uk
Web Site: http://www.sandpiper.co.uk

Managing Director: Robert Collie

Hardback reprints of Oxford University Press monographs in classical and mediaeval studies, philosophy and history, retailing at paperback prices and retaining the OUP imprint. These OUP books are exclusive to Sandpiper. The company also buys remainders exclusively from university presses and the scholarly divisions of major publishers as well as from smaller companies, and supplies an extensive network of trade and non-trade outlets both in the UK and overseas.

6.8 MAIN WHOLESALERS

6148

AQUAPRESS
25 Farriers Way, Temple Farm Industrial Estate, Southend-on-Sea, Essex SS2 5RY
Telephone: 0870 830 8120
Fax: 0870 830 8280
Email: info@aquapress.co.uk
Web Site: http://www.aquapress.co.uk

Registered Office:
9 Nelson Street, Southend-on-Sea, Essex SS1 1EH

Proprietor: Chris Davey
Sales Manager: Angela Davey
Marketing: Magdalena Strzyminska

UK distributor for:
USA: Best Publishing; Cornell Maritime Press; Gary Gentile Productions; Watersport Publishing Inc

AquaPress is a specialist publisher and distributor for diving and medical books, and also specializes in printing waterproof manuals and books. AquaPress supplies wholesale to the diving and medical industry both UK and overseas as well as the general book trade.

6149

ARGOSY LIBRARIES LTD
Unit 12, North Park, North Road, Finglas, Dublin 11, Republic of Ireland
Telephone: +353 (01) 823 9500
Fax: +353 (01) 823 9599
Email: info@argosybooks.ie
Web Site: http://www.argosybooks.ie

Managing Director: Fergal Stanley
Managers: Eddie Walsh (General)
  Ronan Richmond (Sales)
  Mary Healy (Buyer)

Trade book wholesaler specializing in books of Irish interest and maps and guides to Ireland. Export service available.

6150

BAKER & TAYLOR UK LTD
Charbridge Way, Bicester, Oxon OX26 4ST
Telephone: 01869 363500
Fax: 01869 363555

Directors: Diane White (Buying)
  Annette Burgess (Commercial)
  Gareth Powell (Managing)

Parent Company:
USA: Baker & Taylor

Baker & Taylor offers book distribution and merchandising service. A full-time sales force covers the entire UK and Northern Ireland, supported by five senior managers.
  Operating from its computerized distribution centre at Bicester, Baker & Taylor offers over 10,000 titles from stock totally geared to the specialist markets it services, delivered fast. Baker & Taylor's range extends to gardening, DIY and the home, cookery, natural history, travel and leisure, illustrated stationery, gift books and children's books. It supplies books mainly to garden centres, home and DIY outlets, department stores, the natural history / heritage markets and the gift sector, and offers a specialist service to non-traditional children's book outlets and club warehouses.

6151

BOOKSPEED
16 Salamander Yards, Edinburgh EH6 7DD
Telephone: 0131 467 8100
Fax: 0131 467 8008
Email: sales@bookspeed.com
Web Site: http://www.bookspeed.com

Director: Kingsley Dawson
Sales Manager: Fiona Stout
Buyer: Matthew Perren

Parent Company:
UK: Rhodawn Ltd

Consultants and suppliers of books to specialist retailers in the gift, leisure and heritage markets.

6152

*BOOKWORLD WHOLESALE LTD
Unit 10, Hodfar Road, Sandy Lane Industrial Estate, Stourport-on-Severn, Worcs DY13 9QB
Telephone: 01299 823330
Fax: 01299 829970
Email: info@bookworldws.co.uk
Web Site: http://www.bookworldws.co.uk

Director: Justin Gainham (Sales)
Manager: Andrea Gainham (Warehouse)

Transport, military and modelling book specialist distributor, now selling craft, doll and martial arts books, mainly to the UK; some export sales to Europe and the USA.
  Minimum order one book, full trade terms given but postage added to orders under £50 in value. Teleordering mnemonic BK WORLD.
  Range of distribution whole of UK. Number of publishers for whom we distribute is in excess of 70.

6153

GARDNERS BOOKS LTD
1 Whittle Drive, Eastbourne, East Sussex BN23 6QH
Telephone: 01323 521555
Fax: 01323 521666
Email: sales@gardners.com
Web Site: http://www.gardners.com

Chairman: Alan Little
Directors: Jonathan Little (Managing)
  Jean Little
  Andrew Little (Technical)
  Bob Jackson (Commercial)
  Simon Morley (Buying)
  Nicky Little (Finance)
  David O'Reilly (Warehouse)
Managers: Phil Edwards (Senior Buying)
  Gail Harbour (Buying)
  David Brewster (Customer Care)
  Gary Sheppard (Marketing)

From local bookshops to non-traditional outlets, multinational companies and e-commerce concerns, Gardners Books are a UK-based book wholesaler who specializes in meeting the needs of booksellers and retailers around the world.
  Gardners have a physical stockholding in excess of 850,000 titles from over 4000 publishers available from their custom-built 350,000 square foot office and distribution centre, which is now complemented by their digital warehouse featuring thousands of eBooks, audio downloads and digital marketing materials.
  Orders can be placed 24 hours a day via their account holders' website, Gardlink electronic ordering system, Gardcall automated telephone enquiry service, fax and EDI. Their customer care team are available from Monday to Saturday between 9am and 6pm to take orders and assist customers.
  Their website www.gardners.com is free to account holders and features data on over 1.2 million British books in print, as well as real-time stock figures, invoices, back-orders and promotional offers. Information on additional services Gardners offer such as B2B and B2C home delivery fulfilment to marketing materials, distribution services and print-on-demand can also be found on the site. BA member.

6154

SHOGUN INTERNATIONAL LTD
87 Gayford Road, London W12 9BY
Telephone: (020) 8749 2022
Fax: (020) 8740 1086

Manager: G. Blanc

Sole UK agent for:
Hong Kong: Leung Ting Publications
Sweden: Japanska
USA: Dragon Books Publishing Corp; Ohara Publications (Black Belt Communications Inc); Unique Publications

Shogun International deals exclusively with wholesaling of martial arts goods and related sports books.

6.9 MAIN LIBRARY SUPPLIERS

6155

THE HOLT JACKSON BOOK CO LTD
Preston Road, Lytham, Lancs FY8 5AX
Telephone: 01253 737464
Fax: 01253 733361
Email: info@holtjackson.co.uk
Web Site: http://www.holtjackson.co.uk

Chairman: Yvette Stafford
Directors: Kathryn Pattinson (Managing)
  J. K. Holden
Senior Managers: C. Southall (Production)
  Mrs J. Holborn (Customer Care)
  Mrs L. Cairns (Human Resources)

Parent Company:
UK: The Little Group Ltd

Associated Companies:
UK: Cawdor Book Services Ltd; Lawrence Book Co Ltd

Booksellers.

6156

STEVEN SIMPSON BOOKS
5 Hardingham Road, Hingham, Norwich NR9 4LX
Telephone: 01953 850471
Fax: 01953 850471
Email: info@aquariumatlas.co.uk
Web Site: http://www.aquariumatlas.co.uk

Proprietor: S. J. Simpson

UK distributor for:
Germany: Hans A. Baenasch / Mergus Verlag GmbH (exclusive); Birgit Schmettkamp Verlag (exclusive); Verlag ACS Aqualog GmbH (exclusive); Verlag Eugen Ulmer KG (exclusive)
Italy: Aquapress Publishers (exclusive); FAO (Food & Agriculture Organization of the United Nations)
Nepal: T. K. Shrestha (exclusive)

Distributor to the trade for overseas publishers in the field of natural history.

6157

STARKMANN LTD
6 Broadley Street, London NW8 8AE
Telephone: (020) 7724 5335
Fax: (020) 7724 9863
Email: orders@starkmann.co.uk
Web Site: http://www.starkmann.com

Delivery Address:
6 Plympton Place, London NW8 8AD

Managing Director: Bernard Starkmann
Managers: Kishor Chandarana (Accountant)
  Dr Bernard Starkmann (Sales)
  Moira Bowyer (Operations)
  Rodney Latham (IT)

Suppliers of academic and scientific books and ebooks to university, college, industrial and research libraries in Europe. Customers and potential customers receive frequent and accurate new book information. Distribution of the main line publishers from UK, USA, Netherlands, Germany and Switzerland. Supplies made at publisher's list price. Fast airfreight service of US books. Comprehensive website featuring bibliographic database, online ordering, order tracking, new title alert service and special offers.

6158

ROY YATES BOOKS
Smallfields Cottage, Cox Green, Rudgwick, Horsham, West Sussex RH12 3DE
Telephone: 01403 822299
Fax: 01403 823012
Email: roy@royyatesbooks.fsnet.co.uk

Managing Director: Roy Yates

Specialist supplier of children's books to schools and libraries; distributes multilingual books; distributes foreign-language books.

6.10 BOOK CLUBS

6159

ARTISTS' CHOICE LTD
The Old Post Office, Bythorn, Huntingdon, Cambs PE28 0QN
Telephone: 01832 710201
Fax: 01832 710488
Email: henry@artists-choice.co.uk
Web Site: http://www.artists-choice.co.uk & http://www.acaward.com

Managing Director: Henry Malt

Book club aimed at the amateur artist.

6160

BIBLIOPHILE BOOKS
Unit 5 Datapoint Business Centre, 6 South Crescent, London E16 4TL
Telephone: (020) 7474 2474
Fax: (020) 7474 8589

6161

Email: orders@bibliophilebooks.com
Web Site: http://www.bibliophilebooks.com

General Manager: Jackie McDaid
Distribution: Steven Lee
Director: Anne Quigley

Produces 10 catalogues a year, offering books at bargain prices to private buyers. Range: general, eg biography, history, travel, handicrafts, humour, literature.

6161

LETTERBOX LIBRARY
71–73 Allen Road, Stoke Newington, London N16 8RY
Telephone: (020) 7503 4801
Fax: (020) 7503 4800
Email: info@letterboxlibrary.com
Web Site: http://www.letterboxlibrary.com

Contacts: Kerry Mason
  Maikim Stern
  Fen Coles

Letterbox Library is a children's bookseller specializing in children's books which celebrate equality and diversity. Quarterly catalogues are produced with up to 50 new titles, offered at discounts to members. Books are multicultural and non-sexist, and also show groups of people traditionally under-represented in children's books, e.g. different faith groups, disabled children, refugees. All books are approved by an independent team of reviewers. Subscription is £5 a year and entitles members to discounts. Non-members can buy books at the retail price. Letterbox Library also provides book displays for schools and libraries and attends exhibitions. Letterbox Library is a social enterprise.

6162

POETRY BOOK SOCIETY
4th Floor, 2 Tavistock Place, London WC1H 9RA
Telephone: (020) 7833 9247
Fax: (020) 7833 5990
Email: info@poetrybooks.co.uk
Web Site: http://www.poetrybooks.co.uk & http://www.poetrybookshoponline.com

Director: Chris Holifield

Publicly funded charity, membership organization, mail order book club promoting contemporary poetry titles to an international readership. Quarterly publication of *Bulletin* magazine featuring selected new poetry titles. Also has Children's Poetry Bookshelf, relaunched 2005 with new website (http://www.childrenspoetrybookshelf.co.uk) and parent and library memberships. The Society also acts as sole distributor for The Poetry Archive CDs.
  Membership from £12 p.a.
  Also runs http://www.poetrybookshoponline.com, selling a wide range of poetry and SoundBlast performance poets' CDs.

6.11 LITERARY & TRADE EVENTS

6163

BOOKSELLERS ASSOCIATION ANNUAL CONFERENCE
Minster House, 272 Vauxhall Bridge Road, London SW1V 1BA
Telephone: (020) 7802 0802
Fax: (020) 7802 0803
Email: naomi.gane@booksellers.org.uk
Web Site: http://www.booksellers.org.uk

Chief Executive: Tim Godfray
Conference Organizer: Naomi Gane
Head of Marketing & Events: Alan Staton

Major UK book trade event. The Conference provides opportunity for those supplying or serving the retail book trade to meet trade customers and for both to learn from business programme. **Details from:** above address.

6164

THE TIMES CHELTENHAM LITERATURE FESTIVAL
Cheltenham Festivals Ltd, 109 Bath Road, Cheltenham, Glos GL53 7LS
Telephone: 01242 774400
Fax: 01242 256457
Email: clair.greenaway@cheltenhamfestivals.com
Web Site: http://www.cheltenhamfestivals.com

Chief Executive: Donna Renney
Artistic Director: Sarah Smyth
Executive Director: Clair Greenaway

Annual in October. Promoted by Cheltenham Festivals Ltd. Performances, poetry readings, talks and discussions by literary personalities. Includes Book It! Festival for Children, Voices Off Fringe Festival and Write Away creative writing workshops.
  Details from: Artistic Director: Sarah Smyth or Executive Director: Clair Greenaway.

6165

CHILDREN'S BOOK WEEK
Booktrust, Book House, 45 East Hill, Wandsworth, London SW18 2QZ
Telephone: (020) 8516 2976
Fax: (020) 8516 2992
Email: education@booktrust.org.uk
Web Site: http://www.booktrust.org.uk

Patron: HRH The Prince Philip Duke of Edinburgh
Executive Director: Chris Meade
Chairman: Kimberley Reynolds
Resources Manager: Kelly Harris

Children's Book Week is an annual event which takes place every October. It is a national event promoting the idea that reading and books are fun!
  Promotional resource materials are available for schools, libraries, bookshops and book groups throughout the UK.

6166

CIANA LTD
24 Langroyd Road, London SW17 7PL
Telephone: (020) 8682 1969
Fax: (020) 8682 1997
Email: enquiries@ciana.co.uk
Web Site: http://www.ciana.co.uk

Directors: Robert Collie
  Sarah Weedon

Organizers of two annual trade fairs for the remainder, overstock and promotional book market. Over 100,000 discounted books, stationery items, CDs and DVDs. The September Fair is held in London Islington. The January Fair is in the Barbican in the City of London.

6167

EDINBURGH INTERNATIONAL BOOK FESTIVAL
5A Charlotte Square, Edinburgh EH2 4DR
Telephone: 0131 718 5666
Fax: 0131 226 5335
Email: admin@edbookfest.co.uk
Web Site: http://www.edbookfest.co.uk

Directors: Catherine Lockerbie
  Sara Grady *(Children & Education Programme)*
Managers: Kath Mainland *(General)*
  Amanda Barry *(Marketing)*
  Lois Wolffe *(Sponsorship & Development)*

The Edinburgh International Book Festival began in 1983 and is now an annual event. It exists to promote books and reading to all ages and is primarily for the public.
  The festival runs its own, independent book sales operation on the site – a tented village in Edinburgh's Charlotte Square Gardens.
  More than 700 events take place over 17 days in August, representing both adult and children's literature.

6168

FRANKFURT BOOK FAIR
Reineckstrasse 3, 60313 Frankfurt am Main, Germany
Telephone: +49 69 2102 0
Fax: +49 69 2102 227 & 277
Email: info@book-fair.com
Web Site: http://www.book-fair.com

Chief Executive Officer: Juergen Boos
Director, Marketing & Sales: Thomas Minkus

Parent Company:
Germany: Börsenverein des Deutschen Buchhandels

The Frankfurt Book Fair is the largest event of its kind in the world. Annual participation stands at 7400 exhibitors from 108 countries and 290,000 visitors. The Multimedia area at the Frankfurt Book Fair is a showcase for the latest electronic media innovations.
  Open exclusively to the trade for three days and to the public for two days it attracts publishers, booksellers, authors, distributors, art dealers, artists and the whole range of multimedia companies.

6169

GÖTEBORG BOOK FAIR
412 94 Göteborg, Sweden
Telephone: +46 (031) 708 8400
Fax: +46 (031) 209103
Email: info@goteborg-bookfair.com
Web Site: http://www.goteborg-bookfair.com

Public Relations Manager: Birgitta Jacobsson Ekblom
Managing Director: Anna Falck

Göteborg Book Fair is one of the biggest bookfairs in northern Europe; 100,000 visits in four days, 800 exhibitors, 450 seminars and more than 1000 journalists covering the fair.
  Göteborg Book Fair is arranged annually in September.

6170

INTERNATIONAL BOOK EXHIBITIONS & FAIRS: GENERAL DIRECTORATE
Malaya Dmitrovka Street 16, Moscow 127006, Russia
Telephone: +7 (495) 699 4034, 699 9790 & 699 3466
Fax: +7 (495) 699 2539 & 299 1110
Email: mibf@mibf.ru & vBelov@mibf.ru
Web Site: http://www.mibf.ru

General Director: Nikolay Ph. Ovsyannikov
Head of Foreign Relations Department: Nina Sudjina
Project Manager: Valery Belov

Organization of annual Moscow International and Russian National Book Fairs, as well as collective and national book stands of Russian publishers at the international book fairs.

6171

LEIPZIG BOOK FAIR
Leipziger Messe GmbH, Messe-Allee 1, 04356 Leipzig, Germany
Telephone: +49 (0)341 678 8240
Fax: +49 (0)341 678 8242
Email: info@leipziger-buchmesse.de
Web Site: http://www.leipziger-buchmesse.de

Exhibition Director: Oliver Zille

The Leipzig Book Fair is an independent, general book fair concentrating on the German-speaking countries of Europe (Germany, Austria and Switzerland). It also features international book art and is additionally characterized by general themes (e.g. audio books, travelling) which change from year to year and which are highlighted by special events relating to these themes. The commercial aspect of the Leipzig Book Fair is accompanied by a wide range of fringe events, including a section for antique books and prints.
  Visitors to the Leipzig Book Fair are mainly made up of representatives from publishers, the book trade, libraries, the newer media, the printing industry, and all other areas connected with the production of books, including book illustrators and graphic designers.
  2009 dates: 12–15 March.

6172

LONDON BOOK FAIR
Oriel House, 26 The Quadrant, Richmond, Surrey TW9 1DL
Telephone: (020) 8910 7815
Fax: (020) 8910 7930
Email: emma.lowe@reedexpo.co.uk
Web Site: http://www.londonbookfair.co.uk

Group Exhibition Director: Alistair Burtenshaw

Managers: Sarah Hicks (Marketing)
  Emma House (Exhibition)
  Emma Lowe (Sales)
  Matt Colgan (Sales)
  Vibeke Burke (Marketing)
Executive: Rachel Jones (Sales)
Exhibition Administrator: Erin Dowling

The London Book Fair is a spring forum for booksellers, publishers, librarians and book production services worldwide. Timed to provide a concentrated three-day trading and educational platform offering access to the world's books, real business contacts and shared knowledge.

2009 Fair: 20–22 April at Earls Court, London. For further information, please visit our website http://www.london-bookfair.co.uk

6173

THE LONDON LITERARY MAFIA
618b Finchley Road, London NW11 7RR
Telephone: (020) 8455 4564
Email: lambhorn@gmail.com
Web Site: http://www.phantomcaptain.netfirms.com

Director: Neil Hornick (Artistic)

Parent Company:
UK: The Phantom Captain

'Are You Reading Me?' – Established in 1997, The London Literary Mafia (a.k.a. The Phantom Captain Literary Lions) is a performance company specializing in entertainments, talks and readings devised to brighten up literature festivals, conferences, book launches, award ceremonies, promotions, luncheons and dinners, book fairs, writing courses and related writer/reader-themed events. Activities draw on the extensive experience of Neil Hornick, artistic director of the company, as writer-director-actor and (under a pen-name) as a professional literary consultant. Events can be commissioned and designed for specific occasions.

6174

*MILIA – THE WORLD'S INTERACTIVE CONTENT MARKETPLACE
Reed Midem, 11 rue du Colonel Pierre Avia, BP 572, 75726 Paris Cedex 15, France
Telephone: +33 1 41 90 45 80
Fax: +33 1 41 90 45 70
Email: ted.baracos@reedmidem.com
Web Site: http://www.milia.com

Also at:
Reed Midem UK, Walmar House, 296 Regent Street, London W1B 3AB
Telephone: (020) 7528 0086
Fax: (020) 7895 0949
Email: elizabeth.delaney@reedmidem.com
Web Site: http://www.miptu.com

Executive Director: Ted Baracos
Sales Manager: Elizabeth Delaney

Next: 7–11 April 2008; Palais des Festivals, Cannes, France.

6175

SALON DU LIVRE DE MONTREAL
300 rue St-Sacrement, Bureau 430, Montreal, PQ, Canada H2Y 1X4
Telephone: +1 (514) 845 2365
Fax: +1 (514) 845 7119
Email: slm.info@videotron.ca
Web Site: http://www.salondulivredemontreal.com

General Manager: Francine Bois

The Salon du Livre de Montréal is a public book fair which aims to promote reading.

6176

TOKYO INTERNATIONAL BOOK FAIR
Reed Exhibitions Japan Ltd, 18F Shinjuku Nomura Building, 1-26-2 Nishi-Shinjuku, Shinjuku-ku, Tokyo 163-0570, Japan
Telephone: +81 3 3349 8507
Fax: +81 3 3345 7929
Email: tibf-eng@reedexpo.co.jp
Web Site: http://www.bookfair.jp/english

International Sales Director: Kaoru Iwata
International Sales Manager: Janet Or
Show Director: Keisuke Amano

Parent Company:
UK: Reed Exhibition Companies

Tokyo International Book Fair (TIBF) represents the world's second largest single publishing market - Japan. TIBF has built its success upon the full support of its joint organization committee comprising the seven most influential Japanese publishing trade associations.

TIBF offers exhibitors opportunities to meet major book publishers, literary agents, distributors and booksellers from all over Japan and neighbouring countries such as Korea, Taiwan, Hong Kong and China, and develop extensive business opportunities including:
  – international rights negotiation
  – joint publishing projects
  – direct book exports.

2009 Fair: 9–13 July at Tokyo Big Sight.

For more information, please contact Reed Exhibitions in Tokyo.

6177

WORLD BOOK DAY
c/o Booksellers' Association, 272–274 Vauxhall Bridge Road, London SW1V 1BA
Telephone: (020) 7802 0802
Email: cathy.schofield@blueyonder.co.uk
Web Site: http://www.worldbookday.com

Word Book Day Co-ordinator: Cathy Schofield

One of the UK's biggest celebrations of books and reading, held on the first Thursday in March. It is a partnership of publishers, booksellers and interested parties who work together to promote books and reading for the personal enrichment and enjoyment of all. One of the main aims of World Book Day is to encourage children to explore the pleasures of reading by providing them with the opportunity to have a book of their own. Thanks to the generosity of National Book Tokens and participating booksellers, schoolchildren are entitled to receive a World Book Day £1 book token, which can be exchanged for one of the specially published £1 books or is redeemable against a book or audiobook of their choice.

6.12 PUBLISHING REFERENCE BOOKS & PERIODICALS

6178

THE AUTHOR
84 Drayton Gardens, London SW10 9SB
Telephone: (020) 7373 6642
Fax: (020) 7373 5768
Email: TheAuthor@societyofauthors.org
Web Site: http://www.societyofauthors.org

Editor: Andrew Rosenheim
Manager: Kate Pool

Parent Company:
UK: The Society of Authors

Free to members. £12, post free, per copy for others. Annual subscription: £30, post free.

The quarterly journal of the Society of Authors. Articles on the legal, commercial and technical side of authorship.

6179

BOOKS FOR KEEPS
1 Effingham Road, London SE12 8NZ
Telephone: (020) 8852 4953
Fax: (020) 8318 7580
Email: enquiries@booksforkeeps.co.uk
Web Site: http://www.booksforkeeps.co.uk

Managing Director: Richard Hill
Editor: Rosemary Stones

ISSN: 0143-909X

6 issues pa. Annual subscription: £25.50 (UK), £28.50 (Europe), £31.50 (worldwide: airmail only).

Reviews all children's books and carries articles/features about authors, publishing, education, etc. Main readership - teachers, librarians and parents.

6180

BOOKS IN PRINT 2007–2008
Bowker (UK) Ltd, 1st Floor, Medway House, Cantelupe Road, East Grinstead, West Sussex RH19 3BJ
Telephone: 01342 310450
Fax: 01342 310486
Email: sales@bowker.co.uk
Web Site: http://www.bowker.co.uk

Directors: Doug McMillan (Managing)
  Pam Roud (Sales)
Marketing Manager: Jo Grange

Associated Companies:
USA: R. R. Bowker LLC; Cambridge Information Group

ISBN: 978 0 8352 4863 1

Published August 2007, 7 volumes, hbk, £595.

Full bibliographic and ordering information for over two million titles published or distributed in the USA. There are 164,000 titles new to this edition.

6181

THE BOOKSELLER
5th Floor, Endeavour House, 189 Shaftesbury Avenue, London WC2H 8TJ
Telephone: (020) 7420 6006
Fax: (020) 7420 6103
Email: letters-to-editor@bookseller.co.uk
Web Site: http://www.theBookseller.com

Directors: Nigel Roby (Managing)
  David Wright (Advertising)
Editor-in-Chief: Neill Denny

Parent Company:
USA: Nielsen Entertainment Media

ISSN: 0006-7539

Weekly £4.40. Annual subscription: £170 (UK: book retailers and public libraries), £179 (UK: all other businesses), £185/€270 (Europe – airmail), £185/$296 (rest of world – surface mail), £257/$411 (rest of world – airmail), Aus$658.

The weekly newspaper of the book trade, offering in the course of a year over 7000 pages of news, analysis, features, letters, advertising and lists of books published in the UK. Major national and international events reported, regular authoritative articles on matters of trade, special features, book features and rights, stock market, legal and financial pages. Twice a year a six-month special issue of nearly 900 pages provides the best reference source for British publishers' publishing plans. Regular supplements in specialist areas.

6182

BOOKSELLER & PUBLISHER
Thorpe-Bowker, PO Box 6509, St Kilda Road Central, Vic, Australia 8008
Telephone: +61 (03) 8517 8333
Fax: +61 (03) 8517 8399
Email: tim.coronel@thorpe.com.au
Web Site: http://www.booksellerandpublisher.com.au

General Manager: Gary Pengelly
Publisher: Tim Coronel
Advertising Manager: Robert Hamilton-Jones
Production & Design: Ran Schuman

Parent Company:
USA: R. R. Bowker LLC

6183

CHILDREN'S BOOKS IN PRINT 2008
Bowker (UK) Ltd, 1st Floor, Medway House, Cantelupe Road, East Grinstead, West Sussex RH19 3BJ
Telephone: 01342 310450
Fax: 01342 310486

Email: marketing@bowker.co.uk
Web Site: http://www.bowker.co.uk

Directors: Doug McMillan *(Managing)*
Pam Roud *(Sales)*
Marketing Manager: Jo Grange

Associated Companies:
USA: R. R. Bowker LLC; Cambridge Information Group

ISBN: 978 0 8352 4891 4

Published December 2007, 2-volume set, hbk, £175.

Most complete list of currently available children's books published in the USA.

6184

CHILDREN'S WRITERS' & ARTISTS' YEARBOOK
A. & C. Black Publishers Ltd, 38 Soho Square, London W1D 3HB
Telephone: (020) 7758 0201
Fax: (020) 7758 0222
Email: wayb@acblack.com
Web Site: http://www.acblack.com & http://www.writersandartists.co.uk

Directors: Jill Coleman *(Managing)*
Jonathan Glasspool *(Deputy Managing)*

Parent Company:
UK: Bloomsbury Publishing Plc

ISBN: 978 14 081 0 3777

Annual. 2009 edition, published August 2008, £12.99.

A comprehensive guide to markets in all areas of children's media. Contains articles and information on a wide range of topics written by well-known authors and illustrators, best-selling publishers and editors, leading figures in TV and radio and other children's media experts. Also contains market contacts including book publishers and packagers, literary and art agents, magazines, TV and radio, festivals, courses and bookshops.

6185

THE COMPLETE DIRECTORY OF LARGE PRINT BOOKS AND SERIALS 2008
Bowker (UK) Ltd, 1st Floor, Medway House, Cantelupe Road, East Grinstead, West Sussex RH19 3BJ
Telephone: 01342 310450
Fax: 01342 310486
Email: marketing@bowker.co.uk
Web Site: http://www.bowker.co.uk

Directors: Doug McMillan *(Managing)*
Pam Roud *(Sales)*
Marketing Manager: Jo Grange

Associated Companies:
USA: R. R. Bowker LLC; Cambridge Information Group

ISBN: 978 0 8352 4941 6

Published January 2008. Imprint: R. R. Bowker, 1 volume, pbk, £205.

Bigger than ever, this invaluable guide covers the large print field like no other resource. Inside you'll discover current, accurate bookfinding and ordering information on some 22,500 titles.

6186

DIRECTORY OF UK & IRISH BOOK PUBLISHERS
The Booksellers Association of UK & Ireland, 272 Vauxhall Bridge Road, London SW1V 1BA
Telephone: (020) 7802 0802
Fax: (020) 7802 0803
Email: mail@booksellers.org.uk
Web Site: http://www.booksellers.org.uk

Chief Executive: Tim Godfray

ISBN: 978 0 9552233 5 8

Annual. 2008 edition, £79.31 (plus P&P overseas), £61.69 (BA members).

Contains addresses and comprehensive information (including personnel, e-mail and www sites) about UK and Irish publishers, sales agents, remainder dealers, distributors and book wholesalers, including distribution arrangements in the UK for overseas publications. Also includes trade terms and returns information, details of product specialization such as audio books, electronic publishing and maps, plus a subject specialization index and ISBN prefixes.

The *Directory of UK & Irish Book Publishers* – jointly published by the Booksellers Association and Nielsen BookData – combines and replaces the old BA *Directory of UK & Irish Book Publishers* and BookData's *The Red Book: Directory of Publishers*.

There is a more detailed listing available simultaneously as an online searchable database at http://www.ukpublishers.net. Purchasers of the book will automatically have access to the online service for the subscription period of one year. The online Directory also includes additional information and 6000+ entries not included in the print version and will be updated with new entries and amendments throughout the year.

6187

DIY: BOOKFINDING AND BOOKSELLING
Magna Graecia's Publishers, PO Box 342, Oxford OX2 7YF
Telephone: 01865 553653
Fax: 01865 553653
Email: info@magnagraeciaspublishers.co.uk
Web Site: http://www.magnagraeciaspublishers.co.uk

Director: Luigi Gigliotti *(Research Editor)*

Single parts: £29.95 each, except Volume 5: £19.95. Complete set: £229.60 plus p&p.

List of titles reported wanted by our members, clients in the UK and worldwide. The Register is updated daily. It is available on-line or in print format.

Set of eight parts: Volume One (3 parts) by authors; Volume Two (2 parts) by titles; Volume Three (1 part) by categories; Volume Four (1 part) by subjects; Volume Five (1 part) by subjects.

6188

GLOBAL BOOKS IN PRINT ON DISC
Bowker (UK) Ltd, 1st Floor, Medway House, Cantelupe Road, East Grinstead, West Sussex RH19 3BJ
Telephone: 01342 310450
Fax: 01342 310486
Email: marketing@bowker.co.uk
Web Site: http://www.bowker.co.uk

Directors: Doug McMillan *(Managing)*
Pam Roud *(Sales)*
Marketing Manager: Jo Grange

Associated Companies:
USA: R. R. Bowker LLC; Cambridge Information Group

Annual subscription: from £2220.

Monthly CD-ROM of over 2.7 million records of English-language titles. Single most complete listing of English language titles. Also available on the web – http://www.globalbooksinprint.com.

6189

THE NEW WALFORD: GUIDE TO REFERENCE RESOURCES
Facet Publishing, 7 Ridgmount Street, London WC1E 7AE
Telephone: (020) 7255 0597
Fax: (020) 7255 0591
Email: info@facetpublishing.co.uk
Web Site: http://www.facetpublishing.co.uk

Managing Director: John Woolley
Managers: Lena Stuart *(Marketing)*
Rohini Ramachandran *(Sales)*
Publisher: Helen Carley
Production: Kathryn Beecroft
Commissioning Editor: Louise Le Bas
Desk Editor: Lin Franklin

In three volumes. Vol. 1: Science, Technology and Medicine (**ISBN:** 978 1 85604 495 5, June 2005, 800 pp, hbk, £149.95). Vol. 2: The Social Sciences (**ISBN:** 978 1 85604 498 1, 2007, 800 pp, hbk, £159.95). Vol. 3: Arts, Humanities and General Reference (**ISBN:** 978 1 85604 499 8, 2009, 800 pp, hbk, £159.95).

6190

NEW WELSH REVIEW
PO Box 170, Aberystwyth, Ceredigion SY23 1WZ
Telephone: 01970 628410
Fax: 01970 628410
Email: admin@newwelshreview.com
Web Site: http://www.newwelshreview.com

Editor: Francesca Rhydderch
Development Manager: Sue Fisher

New Welsh Review is a quarterly magazine which brings its readers a selection of new writing from Wales and the UK. Each issue includes a range of critical articles, book reviews, fiction and poetry. While the magazine's focus is on Welsh writing in English, its outlook is deliberately eclectic, encompassing broader European and international literary contexts.

6191

PUBLISHING, BOOKS & READING IN SUB-SAHARAN AFRICA: A CRITICAL BIBLIOGRAPHY
Hans Zell Publishing Consultants, Glais Bheinn, Lochcarron, Ross-shire IV54 8YB
Telephone: 01520 722951
Fax: 01520 722953
Email: hanszell@hanszell.co.uk
Web Site: http://www.africanpublishingcompanion.com

Editor: Hans Zell

ISBN: 978 0 9541029 5 1

Published September 2008, 672 pp, cased, £130/€195/$260.

A completely revised and fully updated edition, covering both print and online resources. *Publishing, Books & Reading in Sub-Saharan Africa: A Critical Bibliography* charts the growth of publishing and book development in the countries of Africa south of the Sahara, as well as including a very large number of entries on many other topics as they relate to books and reading in Africa. It is a detailed documentation resource on the current state of the book on the African continent.

6192

PUBLISHING NEWS
Publishing News Ltd, 7 John Street, London WC1N 2ES
Telephone: (020) 7405 2500
Fax: 0870 870 0385
Email: mailbox@publishingnews.co.uk
Web Site: http://www.publishingnews.co.uk

Managing Director: Jo Henry
Editors: Liz Thomson
Roger Tagholm *(Deputy)*

Associated Companies:
UK: BML Ltd; British Book Awards; British Book Industry Awards

Weekly. £110 a year (UK only), £125 (Europe), £140 (elsewhere).

Weekly newspaper of the book trade. Hardback and paperback reviews and extensive listings of new paperbacks. Interviews with leading personalities in the trade, authors, agents and features on specialist book areas. Full international coverage.

6193

SHEPPARD'S DIRECTORIES
Richard Joseph Publishers Ltd, PO Box 15, Torrington, Devon EX38 8ZJ
Telephone: 01805 625750
Email: office@sheppardsworld.co.uk
Web Site: http://www.sheppardsworld.co.uk

Managing Director: Richard Joseph

Sheppard's Directories are a comprehensive set of reference books available for the secondhand and antiquarian book trades. Information is presented in the same format for each directory; the principal section gives full details of dealerships, arranged geographically; an Alphabetical Business Index, Proprietor's index and a detailed Speciality Index. Valuable information is also given in the introductory pages.

Volumes include: British Isles, Europe, North America, Australia and New Zealand, Latin America and Southern Africa, International Print and Map Sellers and International Ephemera Dealers. Sheppard's Directories are sold to dealers throughout the world. Now available for online searches.

6194

THE TIMES LITERARY SUPPLEMENT
Times House, 1 Pennington Street, London E98 1BS
Telephone: (020) 7782 5000
Fax: (020) 7782 4966
Email: letters@the-tls.co.uk
Web Site: http://www.the-tls.co.uk

Editors: Sir Peter Stothard
 Alan Jenkins (Deputy)
 David Horspool (Managing)

The TLS is a weekly literary review, which carries notices by leading authorities on up to 3000 books a year on literature and language, history, politics, philosophy, the arts and music, social studies, economics, natural history and many other subjects. It also reviews exhibitions and performing arts, carries articles of general interest, publishes poetry and has a letters page which is the principal forum for literary debate. It is essential reading for librarians, booksellers and academics, and also for its broad, worldwide general readership.

6195

WRITERS' & ARTISTS' YEARBOOK
A. & C. Black Publishers Ltd, 38 Soho Square, London W1D 3HB
Telephone: (020) 7758 0201
Fax: (020) 7758 0222
Email: wayb@acblack.com
Web Site: http://www.acblack.com & http://www.writersandartists.co.uk

Directors: Jill Coleman (Managing)
 Jonathan Glasspool (Deputy Managing)

Parent Company:
UK: Bloomsbury Publishing Plc

ISBN: 978 1 4081 026 4

Annual. 2009 edition, published June 2008, £14.99.

A guide for freelance writers and artists. Details of English-language periodicals; of British, American and Commonwealth publishers; of British, American and Continental literary agents; and of press, art and photographic agencies. Practical information on such topics as copyright, libel and income tax; and on the Internet. Articles on writing for newspapers and the periodical press, on films, television, radio, artists, and markets for verse and drama.

6196

WRITERS' FORUM
PO Box 6337, Bournemouth BH1 9EH
Telephone: 01202 586848
Email: editorial@writers-forum.com
Web Site: http://www.writers-forum.com

Advertisement & PR Manager:
Wendy O'Brien, 4 Endsleigh Crescent, Clyst Honiton, Exeter EX5 2AW
Telephone: 01392 367962
Fax: 01392 360701
Email: wendy.obrien@virgin.net

Publisher: Tim Harris
Editor: Carl Styants
Advertising & PR Manager: Wendy O'Brien
Subscriptions Manager: Chris Wigg

11 issues a year. Subscription: UK £33; Worldwide £46.

Welcomes articles on any aspect of the craft and business of writing. Length: 800–2000 words. Payment: by arrangement. Administrators of Short Story Competition, plus poetry and short story competitions for subscribers in each issue. Founded 1993.

6.13 TRAINING

6197

THE CENTRE FOR PUBLISHING STUDIES
University of Stirling, Stirling FK9 4LA
Telephone: 01786 467510
Fax: 01786 466210
Email: ajmw1@stir.ac.uk
Web Site: http://www.pubstud.co.uk

Directors: Prof Andrew Wheatcroft
 James McCall (Deputy)
Lecturers: Ewan Murray
 Helen Sun
 Frances Sessford
 Scott Russell

The Centre specializes in the study of and teaching about the publishing industry internationally. Centre staff have experience in North America, Africa, East Asia (especially China and Malaysia) and other areas, are engaged in editorial and marketing consultancy, and are active in publishing, training, and cultural organizations. There is current work on international book publishing.
 The Centre runs a well-established one year full-time Mlitt course in Publishing Studies, with three main taught elements: contemporary publishing – publishing business, industry structure, authors, bookselling, marketing, financial, intellectual property (IP), group projects; editorial function – varieties of editing, practical skills in copy editing, proofreading; production – overview of manufacturing, design, desktop publishing, Internet Web pages, practical projects; handprinting, papermaking facilities; students research 20,000-word dissertations on individual topics; there are visiting trade speakers. Most students go into editorial or marketing jobs. There are also PhD research students. The Centre also offers short courses for businesses and organizations.
 A new specialist course, the MSc in International Publishing Management, began in January 2006.

6198

CENTRE FOR PUBLISHING, UNIVERSITY COLLEGE LONDON
SLAIS, UCL, Gower Street, London WC1E 6BT
Telephone: (020) 7679 2473
Fax: (020) 7383 0557
Email: mapublishing@ucl.ac.uk
Web Site: http://www.publishing.ucl.ac.uk

Directors: Prof Iain Stevenson (Teaching)
 Prof David Nicholas
 Dr Ian Rowlands (Research)
Industry Liaison: Prof Anthony Watkinson
Administrator: Ms Kerstin Michaels
Administration Secretary: Ms Lucy Lyons
Electronic Publishing: Dr Clayre Warwick

Research and education in publishing. Offers a taught MA in Publishing and Electronic Communication & Publishing. Also MPhil and PhD research in publishing.

6199

CITY UNIVERSITY
Department of Journalism and Publishing, Northampton Square, London EC1V 0HB
Telephone: (020) 7040 0100
Fax: (020) 7040 8594
Email: maryann.kernan.l@city.ac.uk
Web Site: http://www.city.ac.uk/journalism

Programme Director: Mary Ann Kernan
Visiting Lecturers: Max Adam
 Richard Balkwill
 Neil Dunnicliffe
 Brenda Stones
 Dominic Vaughan

Offers a full-time one year Master's Degree (MA) in Publishing Studies to prepare entrants and re-entrants to the industry. Comprises nine taught units, a 5–6 week industrial placement and a dissertation. The department has close industry links and the course is supervised by leading industry professionals.
 Also conducts research into publishing and supervises research students.
 The MSc in Electronic Publishing offers a practical introduction to digital media, information management and multi-media production. Please contact Dr Vesna Brujic-Okretic in the Department of Infomatics: (020) 7040 8551 or v.brujic-okretic@city.ac.uk.

6200

GERMAN TUITION – BARBARA CLASSEN
2 Blackall Street, London EC2A 4AD
Telephone: (020) 7613 3177
Email: barbara@germantuition.com
Web Site: http://www.germantuition.com

Director/Tutor: Barbara Classen
Co-Tutors: Nicole Nagel
 Itamar Groisman
 Eva Friedrich
 Marina de Quay
 Janka Troeber

The company offers lively German tuition at all levels and specializes in German for the book trade. Students can choose between one-to-one tuition or small groups of 4–6. German Tuition also offers short-term tailor-made intensive courses.
 Tutors are professional, experienced native speakers and offer free consultations with trial lesson. Students may work towards one of many recognized exams.
 Clients include publishers, booksellers, journalists and other professionals.
 Classes are held in the central London German Tuition office or in client's office/home 7 days a week.
 German Tuition London has a small branch in Freiburg, Germany, offering tailor-made German language holidays and Business German courses for the book trade, usually over one week.

6201

LONDON COLLEGE OF COMMUNICATION
Elephant & Castle, London SE1 6SB
Telephone: (020) 7514 6569
Fax: (020) 7514 2035
Email: info@lcc.arts.ac.uk
Web Site: http://www.lcc.arts.ac.uk

Head of College: Marilyn McMenemy
Marketing Manager: Anne Nicholls (Head of Marketing & Communications)

Parent Company:
UK: University of the Arts, London

MA, BA Hons Publishing, Postgrad Dip/Cert Publishing.

LCC offers a range of full and part-time courses in publishing, printing and media. These include postgraduate, undergraduate and Further Education courses.
 A range of short courses and part-time programmes is also offered. These cover almost every aspect of the printing and publishing industry.

6202

MARKETABILITY (UK) LTD
12 Sandy Lane, Teddington, Middx TW11 0DR
Telephone: (020) 8977 2741
Fax: (020) 8977 2741
Email: rachel@marketability.info
Web Site: http://www.marketability.info

Director: Rachel Maund

Current and recent clients for training include:
Australia: Australian Publishers Association; Victorian Law Foundation
China: Elsevier; Higher Education Press
Mexico: CANIEM (Mexican Publishers' Association)
Republic of Ireland: CLÉ (Irish Book Publishers Association)
Russia: Guild of Book Dealers
Singapore: National Book Development Council; Taylor & Francis; Wiley Asia; World Scientific
UK: ALPSP; Ashgate Publishing; Birlinn; A & C Black; Blackwell's UK; CABI Publishing; Cambridge University Press; Centre for Alternative Technology; City University; Continuum; Crown House Publishing; Edinburgh University Press; Elsevier; Granada Learning; HarperCollins Publishers; Institute of Physics; Learning Matters; Little, Brown Book Group; London College of Communications; Lonely Planet; Macmillan; McGraw Hill; NCVO (National Council for Voluntary

Organisations); Nelson Thornes; Osprey Publishing; Oxford Brookes University; Oxford University Press; Palgrave Macmillan; Pavilion Publishing; Pearson Education; Primal Pictures; Publishing Scotland; Publishing Training Centre; Sage Publications; Specialist Schools and Academies Trust; Taylor & Francis Group; University College London; Welsh Books Council; John Wiley & Sons; Wiley-Blackwell

Marketability provides practical training to publishers, both through its small-group open workshop programme and through tailored in-house training. These flexible courses can be devised to cover a wide range of publishing issues. All tutors are actively working for publishers in the areas they are training in.

The open course programme includes: academic marketing, e-marketing, copywriting, copywriting for the web, schools marketing, direct mail, marketing to the book trade, marketing planning, introduction to marketing in publishing, publicity, essential editorial skills, profitable commissioning. There are numerous in-house course options including market research, working with authors, grammar and proofreading.

Also provides marketing support and consultancy. See separate entry under Sales and Marketing Services.

6203

NAPIER UNIVERSITY, SCHOOL OF CREATIVE INDUSTRIES
Craighouse Campus, Craighouse Road, Edinburgh EH10 5LG
Telephone: 0131 455 6133
Fax: 0131 455 6193
Email: de.allan@napier.ac.uk
Web Site: http://www.napier.ac.uk\sci

BA and MSc Publishing. Higher education full and part-time qualifications.

6204

OXFORD INTERNATIONAL CENTRE FOR PUBLISHING STUDIES
Oxford Brookes University, Buckley Building, Gipsy Lane, Headington, Oxford OX3 0BP
Telephone: 01865 484967
Fax: 01865 484082
Email: angus.phillips@brookes.ac.uk
Web Site: http://www.brookes.ac.uk/publishing

Director: Angus Phillips

The Centre for Publishing Studies offers a BA in Publishing and MAs in Publishing, International Publishing, Publishing and Language, and Digital Publishing. In addition, it provides evening and daytime short courses and bespoke training and consultancy for publishing companies and other organizations involved in publishing.

6205

OXFORD PUBLISHING CONSULTANCY
27 Forelands Field Road, Bembridge, Isle of Wight PO35 5TR
Telephone: 01983 872304
Fax: 01983 872304
Email: Bembridge27@aol.com

Managing Director: Paul Richardson

The Oxford Publishing Consultancy offers strategic management consultancy and training to book publishers nationally and internationally. It has particular expertise in China, Russia and Central and Eastern Europe.

6206

THE PUBLISHING TRAINING CENTRE AT BOOK HOUSE
45 East Hill, Wandsworth, London SW18 2QZ
Telephone: (020) 8874 2718
Fax: (020) 8870 8985
Email: publishing.training@bookhouse.co.uk
Web Site: http://www.train4publishing.co.uk

Chief Executive: John Whitley
Managers: Orna O'Brien (Course Administration)
Alex Painter (Marketing)

The Publishing Training Centre was set up in 1979 as an educational charity for book and journal publishers.

It offers over 60 different courses, most of which are run several times a year. Courses are between one and five days long and cover a wide range of publishing and management skills.

Most courses are held at The Publishing Training Centre's London premises, though some are residential, and are based mainly in the Oxford area.

In addition, The Publishing Training Centre offers:
– in-company courses in the UK and overseas;
– distance learning courses in proofreading, editing, picture research, editorial project management and copywriting;
  – consultancy service;
  – training needs analysis;
  – books.

The Publishing Training Centre is responsible for the development and updating of the industry-agreed standards for each job function specific to publishing.

6207

SOCIETY FOR EDITORS AND PROOFREADERS
Erico House, 93–99 Upper Richmond Road, London SW15 2TG
Telephone: (020) 8785 5617
Fax: (020) 8785 5618
Email: admin@sfep.org.uk
Web Site: http://www.sfep.org.uk

Chair: Penny Williams
Company Secretary: Justina Utuka

One of the major aims of the Society for Editors and Proofreaders is to help editorial freelances and staff to improve and update their skills. It is gradually building up a wide range of one-day courses, from 'Introduction to Proofreading' to 'Project Management' and 'On-Screen Editing', as well as more specialized courses. Most of its courses are run in London. About twice a year, two or three courses are run in Edinburgh, York and Bristol. Discounts are offered to members of the SFEP and to SI and NUJ members. Current details can be found on our website.

7 Appendices

7.1 PUBLISHERS CLASSIFIED BY FIELDS OF ACTIVITY

The categories shown below are those in which the publishers listed have declared their interest. The list is intended to be neither exclusive nor comprehensive.

Packagers are shown in *italic* print.

ACADEMIC & SCHOLARLY

Acumen Publishing Ltd
Adam Matthew Publications Ltd
Age Concern Books
Akros Publications
Al-Furqan Islamic Heritage Foundation
Alban Books Ltd
Alpha Science International Ltd
American Psychiatric Publishing Inc
Amnesty International International Secretariat
Amolibros
Peter Andrew Publishing Co Ltd
Anglo-Saxon Books
Anshan Ltd
Apex Publishing Ltd
Archetype Publications Ltd
Archive Editions Ltd
Arena Books (Publishers)
Ashgate Publishing Ltd
Ashmolean Museum Publications
Association for Learning Technology
Association for Scottish Literary Studies
Audio-Forum - The Language Source
Aurora Metro Publications Ltd
Austin & Macauley Publishers Ltd
Authentic Media
B & D Publishing
B Squared
Bedford Freeman Worth (BFW)
Berg Publishers
Berghahn Books
Joseph Biddulph Publisher
Black Ace Books
Blackhall Publishing
Blackstaff Press
Bodleian Library Publishing
Book Marketing Ltd
BookPower
Borthwick Publications
Bowker (UK) Ltd
Boydell & Brewer Ltd
Bridgewater Book Co
British Association for Adoption & Fostering
British Library
British Museum Press
Burns & Oates
Business Education Publishers
CABI
Calypso Publications

Cambridge Publishing Management Ltd
Cambridge University Press
Canopus Publishing Ltd
Carnegie Publishing Ltd
Jon Carpenter Publishing
Cengage Learning EMEA
Centre for Economic Policy Research
Centre for Policy on Ageing
Chalksoft Ltd
Channel View Publications Ltd
Chartered Institute of Personnel & Development
Christian Education
The Chrysalis Press
Church of Ireland Publishing
CILT, the National Centre for Languages
T. & T. Clark
James Clarke & Co
Coachwise Ltd
Coastal Publishing
Cois Life
Commonwealth Secretariat
Construction Industry Research & Information Association (CIRIA)
The Continuum International Publishing Group Ltd
Coordination Group Publications Ltd (CGP Ltd)
Cork University Press
CQ Press
Crescent Moon Publishing
Crossbow Education Ltd
James Currey Publishers
Dance Books Ltd
Darton, Longman & Todd Ltd
The Davenant Press
Richard Dennis Publications
J M Dent
Ashley Drake Publishing Ltd
Gerald Duckworth & Co Ltd
Dunedin Academic Press
Earthscan
Economic & Social Research Institute
Edinburgh University Press
Edward Elgar Publishing Ltd
Elsevier Ltd
Emerald Group Publishing Ltd
Energy Institute
English Heritage
Equinox Publishing Ltd
The Erskine Press
Ethics International Press Ltd
Evangelical Press & Services Ltd
Everyman's Library
Fabian Society
Facet Publishing
Feather Books
Five Leaves Publications
Floris Books
Four Courts Press
Free Association Books
Friends of the Earth

Garnet Publishing Ltd
GeoCenter International Ltd
Geography Publications
Geological Society Publishing House
Gill & Macmillan Ltd
Global Oriental Ltd
Global Professional Publishing
Glyndwr Publishing
The Goldsmith Press Ltd
Gracewing Publishing
Granta Editions
Greenleaf Publishing
Greenwood Publishing Group
Guildhall Press
Gwasg Gwenffrwd
Hachette Livre UK Ltd
Hambledon Continuum Ltd
Hart McLeod Ltd
Hart Publishing
Harvard University Press
Hawthorn Press
Roger Heavens
Helion & Co Ltd
Hobnob Press
Hodder Education
Hodder Gibson
Holo Books
Human Kinetics Europe Ltd
C. Hurst & Co (Publishers) Ltd
Hypatia Publications
Icon Books Ltd
Immunisation Information
Imperial College Press
Imprint Academic
Institute for Fiscal Studies
Institute of Acoustics
Institute of Development Studies
Institute of Education (Publications), University of London
Institute of Employment Rights
Institution of Engineering and Technology (IET)
Intellect Ltd
Interactyx
International Medical Press
International Network for the Availability of Scientific Publications (INASP)
The Islamic Texts Society
Ithaca Press
IVP
IWA Publishing
James & James (Publishers) Ltd
Janus Publishing Co Ltd
Jarndyce Booksellers
Richard Kay Publications
Kegan Paul Ltd
Kew Publishing
Jessica Kingsley Publishers
Kogan Page Ltd
Kube Publishing Ltd
Peter Lang Ltd
Learning Matters Ltd
Libris Ltd

The Lilliput Press Ltd
The Littman Library of Jewish Civilization
Liverpool University Press
Living Time® Media International
Lund Humphries
The Lutterworth Press
M & K Update
McGraw-Hill Education
McGraw-Hill Publishing Company
Maney Publishing
Melisende Publishing Ltd
Mentor Books
Mercier Press Ltd
The Merlin Press Ltd
Merlin Publishing/Wolfhound Press
Merrell Publishers Ltd
Merton Priory Press Ltd
Methodist Publishing House
Microform Academic Publishers
The MIT Press Ltd
Multi Science Publishing Co Ltd
Myriad Editions
NATE (National Association for the Teaching of English)
The National Academies Press
National Children's Bureau
National Gallery Co Ltd
National Portrait Gallery Publications
The National Trust
The National Youth Agency
Natural History Museum Publishing
Network Continuum Education Ltd
NMS Enterprises Limited - Publishing
Oak Tree Press
OICA International (UK) Ltd
On Stream Publications Ltd
Oneworld Publications
Onlywomen Press Ltd
Open Gate Press
Open University Worldwide
Orchard Publishing
Oxbow Books
Oxfam Publishing
Oxford University Press
Packard Publishing Ltd
Palgrave Macmillan
Panaf Books
Paragon Publishing
Pathfinder Books
Pavilion Publishing (Brighton) Ltd
PCCS Books Ltd
Pearson Education Ltd
The Penguin Group (UK) Ltd
Phaidon Press Ltd
The Pharmaceutical Press
Pickering & Chatto (Publishers) Ltd
Pluto Books Ltd
The Policy Press
Polity Press
Portland Press Ltd

Princeton University Press
Professional Engineering Publishing
ProQuest
Rand Publications
The Richmond Publishing Co
Risk Books
Robinswood Press Ltd
Round Hall Ltd
Roundhouse Publishing Ltd
Routledge-Cavendish
Joseph Rowntree Foundation
Royal Collection Publications
Royal College of General Practitioners
Royal College of Psychiatrists
Royal Geographical Society (with Institute of British Geographers)
Royal Irish Academy
The Royal Society of Chemistry
Russell House Publishing Ltd
Sage Publications Ltd
Saint Albert's Press
St Jerome Publishing Ltd
Sandstone Press Ltd
Saqi Books
Save the Children
Schott Music Ltd
Scion Publishing Ltd
SCM-Canterbury Press Ltd
Scottish Text Society
SEDA Publications
Shaw & Sons Ltd
Shepheard-Walwyn (Publishers) Ltd
Sigel Press
Slightly Foxed
SLS Legal Publications (NI)
Smith Settle Printing & Bookbinding Ltd
Colin Smythe Ltd
Social Affairs Unit
The Society for Promoting Christian Knowledge (SPCK)
Society of Antiquaries of Scotland
The Society of Metaphysicians Ltd
Souvenir Press Ltd
Springer Verlag London
Stacey International
Stainer & Bell Ltd
Stott's Correspondence College
Studymates Ltd
Sussex Academic Press
Sussex Publications
The Swedenborg Society
Symposium Publications Literary & Art
I. B. Tauris & Co Ltd
Taylor & Francis
Taylor Graham Publishing
Thames & Hudson Ltd
Trentham Books
Troubador Publishing Ltd
TSO (The Stationery Office Ltd)
UCAS

University College Dublin Press
University of Exeter Press
University of Hertfordshire Press
University of Wales Press
Vallentine Mitchell Publishers
Veritas Publications
Victoria & Albert Museum Publishing
Voltaire Foundation Ltd
Wallflower Press
Warburg Institute
Waterside Press
Waterside Press
Paul Watkins Publishing
Whiting & Birch Ltd
Whittles Publishing
John Wiley & Sons Ltd
WIT Press
Wolters Kluwer Health (P & E) Ltd
World Microfilms
XPL Publishing
Yale University Press London
Zed Books Ltd
Zeticula

ACCOUNTANCY & TAXATION

Age Concern Books
Peter Andrew Publishing Co Ltd
Blackhall Publishing
BookPower
Cambridge University Press
The Chartered Institute of Public Finance & Accountancy
Corpus Publishing Ltd
Emerald Group Publishing Ltd
W. Foulsham & Co Ltd
Global Professional Publishing
Gower Publishing Co Ltd
Granta Editions
Hodder Education
How To Books Ltd
In Easy Steps Ltd
Institute for Fiscal Studies
Jordan Publishing Ltd
Kogan Page Ltd
McGraw-Hill Education
National Housing Federation
Nelson Thornes Ltd
Oak Tree Press
Palgrave Macmillan
ProQuest
Round Hall Ltd
Sigel Press
Adam Smith Institute
Thorogood Publishing Ltd
Tru-Est Ltd
TSO (The Stationery Office Ltd)
Which? Books
John Wiley & Sons Ltd
XPL Publishing

AGRICULTURE

Blackstaff Press
CABI
Cambridge University Press
Carnegie Publishing Ltd
Commonwealth Secretariat
The Crowood Press Ltd
Earthscan
Eco-logic Books
Edward Elgar Publishing Ltd
Food Trade Press Ltd
Granta Editions
Institute of Development Studies
Manson Publishing Ltd
The National Academies Press
The National Trust
Old Pond Publishing
Oxfam Publishing
Packard Publishing Ltd
ProQuest
Smith Settle Printing & Bookbinding Ltd
Merlin Unwin Books Ltd
Whittet Books Ltd
John Wiley & Sons Ltd

ANIMAL CARE & BREEDING

Amber Books Ltd
Amolibros
Austin & Macauley Publishers Ltd
BookPower
CABI
Calypso Publications
Capall Bann Publishing
Carroll & Brown Ltd
Chalksoft Ltd
Collins & Brown
Corpus Publishing Ltd
The Crowood Press Ltd
D & N Publishing
The Davenant Press
David & Charles Ltd
Findhorn Press Ltd
Focus Publishing (Sevenoaks) Ltd
Robert Hale Ltd
HarperCollins Publishers Ltd
Haynes Publishing
Hodder Education
Manson Publishing Ltd
The National Academies Press
Octopus Publishing Group
Quiller Publishing Ltd
Souvenir Press Ltd
Whittet Books Ltd
John Wiley & Sons Ltd

ANTIQUES & COLLECTING

Antique Collectors' Club Ltd
Austin & Macauley Publishers Ltd
BLA Publishing Ltd
Bodleian Library Publishing
British Museum Press
Cameron Books
Cameron & Hollis
Carlton Publishing Group
Caxton Publishing Group Ltd
Conran Octopus
The Crowood Press Ltd
D & N Publishing
David & Charles Ltd
Richard Dennis Publications
W. Foulsham & Co Ltd
Granta Editions
Greenlight Publishing
Robert Hale Ltd
HarperCollins Publishers Ltd
Hilmarton Manor Press
Hodder Education
How To Books Ltd
Kegan Paul Ltd
Lund Humphries
The Lutterworth Press
Milestone Publications
Miller's
Mitchell Beazley
The National Trust
Newpro UK Ltd
NMS Enterprises Limited - Publishing
Octopus Publishing Group
The Orion Publishing Group Ltd
The Penguin Group (UK) Ltd
Prestel Publishing Ltd
Quantum Publishing
Quiller Publishing Ltd
Royal Collection Publications
Scala Publishers Ltd
Shire Publications Ltd
Souvenir Press Ltd
Stenlake Publishing Ltd
Tartarus Press
Thames & Hudson Ltd
Third Millennium Publishing Ltd
Unicorn Press
Victoria & Albert Museum Publishing
John Wiley & Sons Ltd
Philip Wilson Publishers

ARCHAEOLOGY

Archetype Publications Ltd
Ashmolean Museum Publications
Batsford
Blackstaff Press
Borthwick Publications
Boydell & Brewer Ltd
British Museum Press
Brown & Whittaker Publishing
Cambridge Publishing Management Ltd
Cambridge University Press
Capall Bann Publishing
Carnegie Publishing Ltd
Construction Industry Research & Information Association (CIRIA)
Cork University Press
Cornwall Editions Ltd
Council for British Archaeology
James Currey Publishers
The Davenant Press
Gerald Duckworth & Co Ltd
Edinburgh University Press
Emerald Group Publishing Ltd
English Heritage
Equinox Publishing Ltd
Evangelical Press & Services Ltd
Ex Libris Press
Four Courts Press
Geography Publications
Glasgow Museums
Green Magic
Greenlight Publishing
Halsgrove
Hambledon Continuum Ltd
Heart of Albion Press
Hobnob Press
Hodder Education
Holo Books
Kegan Paul Ltd
The King's England Press
Logaston Press
Maney Publishing
Melisende Publishing Ltd
Mercier Press Ltd
Mercury Books
Merton Priory Press Ltd
Mitchell Beazley
The National Trust
Natural History Museum Publishing
NMS Enterprises Limited - Publishing
North York Moors National Park
The Orion Publishing Group Ltd
Oxbow Books
The Penguin Group (UK) Ltd
Prestel Publishing Ltd
Quantum Publishing
Reardon Publishing
Royal Irish Academy
Scottish Children's Press
Scottish Cultural Press
Sessions of York
Shire Publications Ltd
Smith Settle Printing & Bookbinding Ltd
Society of Antiquaries of Scotland
Souvenir Press Ltd
Stacey International
Sussex Academic Press
I. B. Tauris & Co Ltd
Taylor & Francis
Thames & Hudson Ltd
Twelveheads Press
University of Exeter Press
University of Wales Press
Warburg Institute
John Wiley & Sons Ltd
WIT Press
Yale University Press London

ARCHITECTURE & DESIGN

Antique Collectors' Club Ltd
Architectural Association Publications
Ashgate Publishing Ltd
Aurum Press
AVA Publishing (UK) Ltd
Duncan Baird Publishers
Batsford
Berg Publishers
Joseph Biddulph Publisher
A. & C. Black (Publishers) Ltd
Black Dog Publishing Ltd
Bodleian Library Publishing
Bridgewater Book Co
Cambridge Publishing Management Ltd
Cambridge University Press
Cameron Books
Cameron & Hollis
Carlton Publishing Group
Caxton Publishing Group Ltd
Centre for Alternative Technology Publications
Conran Octopus
Construction Industry Research & Information Association (CIRIA)
Cork University Press
Richard Dennis Publications
Donhead Publishing Ltd
Earthscan
Eco-logic Books
English Heritage
Garnet Publishing Ltd
GeoCenter International Ltd
Gower Publishing Co Ltd
Gracewing Publishing
Graffeg
Graham-Cameron Publishing & Illustration
Green Books
Hambledon Continuum Ltd
HarperCollins Publishers Ltd
Haynes Publishing
Hayward Publishing
The Herbert Press
Hilmarton Manor Press
Historical Publications Ltd
Intellect Ltd
Kegan Paul Ltd
Laurence King Publishing Ltd
Dewi Lewis Publishing
Liberties Press
The Lilliput Press Ltd
Frances Lincoln Ltd
Liverpool University Press
Logaston Press
Lund Humphries
The Lutterworth Press
McGraw-Hill Education
Maney Publishing
Melisende Publishing Ltd
Merrell Publishers Ltd
The MIT Press Ltd
Mitchell Beazley
Multi Science Publishing Co Ltd
The National Trust
NMS Enterprises Limited - Publishing
W. W. Norton & Company Ltd
The O'Brien Press Ltd
Octopus Publishing Group
Ovolo Publishing Ltd
Packard Publishing Ltd
Pallas Athene
Papadakis Publisher
Paragon Publishing
Pavilion
Phaidon Press Ltd
Prestel Publishing Ltd
Quantum Publishing
Redcliffe Press Ltd
Regency House Publishing Ltd
RotoVision SA
Roundhouse Publishing Ltd
Joseph Rowntree Foundation
Royal Collection Publications
Sansom & Co Ltd
Saqi Books
Scala Publishers Ltd
Sheldrake Press
Shire Publications Ltd
Stacey International
I. B. Tauris & Co Ltd
Taylor & Francis
Thomas Telford Ltd
Teneues Publishing UK Ltd
Thames & Hudson Ltd
Toucan Books Ltd
Tyne Bridge Publishing
Unicorn Press
Victoria & Albert Museum Publishing
Warburg Institute
Paul Watkins Publishing
David West Children's Books
John Wiley & Sons Ltd
Philip Wilson Publishers
WIT Press
World Microfilms

Cameron Books
Cameron & Hollis
Carlton Publishing Group
Caxton Publishing Group Ltd
Worth Press Ltd
Yale University Press London

ATLASES & MAPS

AA Publishing
Ian Allan Publishing Ltd
Amber Books Ltd
The Belmont Press
Bridgewater Book Co
British Geological Survey
Carel Press
Caxton Publishing Group Ltd
Collins Geo
Cork University Press
G. L. Crowther
Discovery Walking Guides Ltd
Earthscan
Encyclopaedia Britannica (UK) Ltd
Express Newspapers
Folens Ltd
Geddes & Grosset
GeoCenter International Ltd
The Geographical Association
Geography Publications
Alan Godfrey Maps
HarperCollins Publishers Ltd
Harvey Map Services Ltd
Haynes Publishing
Hodder Education
Instant-Books UK Ltd
Macmillan Education
Mercury Books
Michelin Maps & Guides
Monkey Puzzle Media Ltd
Myriad Editions
New Internationalist Publications Ltd
Octopus Publishing Group
Old House Books
The Penguin Group (UK) Ltd
Philip's
Quantum Publishing
Reardon Publishing
Roundhouse Publishing Ltd
Royal Irish Academy
Tarquin Publications
Toucan Books Ltd
John Wiley & Sons Ltd

AUDIO BOOKS

Ashgrove Publishing
Austin & Macauley Publishers Ltd
Barefoot Books
BBC Audiobooks Ltd
Beautiful Books Ltd
John Blake Publishing Ltd
Bloomsbury Publishing Plc
British Library, Publishing Office
Cló Iar-Chonnachta
Coachwise Ltd
CSA Word
Dref Wen Cyf/Ltd
Feather Books
Gatehouse Media Ltd
Hachette Children's Books
HarperCollins Publishers Ltd
Hodder Education
Hodder & Stoughton General
ISIS Publishing Ltd
Kube Publishing Ltd
Little, Brown Book Group
Little People Books
Macmillan Children's Books Ltd
Magna Large Print Books
Naxos Audiobooks
The Orion Publishing Group Ltd
The Penguin Group (UK) Ltd
Reardon Publishing
Scottish Cultural Press
Sigel Press
Simon & Schuster (UK) Ltd
Studymates Ltd
Summersdale Publishers Ltd
Sussex Publications
Topical Resources
Transworld Publishers Ltd
Witherby Seamanship International

PUBLISHERS CLASSIFIED BY FIELDS OF ACTIVITY / 145

AVIATION

Air-Britain (Historians) Ltd
Ian Allan Publishing Ltd
Amber Books Ltd
Ashgate Publishing Ltd
BLA Publishing Ltd
Bridge Books
Brooklands Books Ltd
Caxton Publishing Group Ltd
Conway
Countryside Books
Crécy Publishing Ltd
The Crowood Press Ltd
D & N Publishing
Focus Publishing (Sevenoaks) Ltd
Granta Editions
Greenhill Books / Lionel Leventhal Ltd
Grub Street
Halsgrove
Haynes Publishing
Hodder Education
Icon Books Ltd
Jane's Information Group Ltd
McGraw-Hill Education
Multi Science Publishing Co Ltd
Osprey Publishing Ltd
Professional Engineering Publishing
Quantum Publishing
Regency House Publishing Ltd
Special Interest Model Books Ltd
Stenlake Publishing Ltd
Truran
TSO (The Stationery Office Ltd)
John Wiley & Sons Ltd
Worth Press Ltd

BIBLIOGRAPHY & LIBRARY SCIENCE

Akros Publications
Ashgate Publishing Ltd
Bowker (UK) Ltd
British Library
British Library, Publishing Office
Cambridge University Press
James Clarke & Co
The Continuum International Publishing Group Ltd
James Currey Publishers
Facet Publishing
Galactic Central Publications
Greenwood Publishing Group
Gwasg Gwenffrwd
Hypatia Publications
Institute of Development Studies
International Network for the Availability of Scientific Publications (INASP)
Jarndyce Booksellers
Kegan Paul Ltd
Jay Landesman
LISU
The MIT Press Ltd
Nielsen Book
ProQuest
Sage Publications Ltd
Colin Smythe Ltd
Sussex Academic Press
Taylor Graham Publishing
Voltaire Foundation Ltd
Warburg Institute
Zeticula

BIOGRAPHY & AUTOBIOGRAPHY

Accent Press Ltd
Acumen Publishing Ltd
Ian Allan Publishing Ltd
Allison & Busby
Alma Books Ltd
Amolibros
Apex Publishing Ltd
Appletree Press Ltd
Arcadia Books Ltd
Argyll Publishing
Atlantic Books
Attic Press
Aureus Publishing Ltd
Aurum Press
Austin & Macauley Publishers Ltd
Authentic Media
Authorhouse UK Ltd
Back-In-Print Books Ltd
Barny Books
Bene Factum Publishing Ltd
Berghahn Books
Black Ace Books
Black Spring Press Ltd
Blackstaff Press
John Blake Publishing Ltd
Bloomsbury Publishing Plc
Bodleian Library Publishing
Book Castle Publishing Ltd
Marion Boyars Publishers Ltd
Brandon/Mount Eagle Publications
Nicholas Brealey Publishing
Breedon Books Publishing Co Ltd
Brewin Books Ltd
British Library
British Library, Publishing Office
Brown & Whittaker Publishing
Business Education Publishers
Cambridge Publishing Management Ltd
Cambridge University Press
Canongate Books
The Catholic Truth Society
Christian Focus Publications
The Chrysalis Press
James Clarke & Co
Cló Iar-Chonnachta
Constable & Robinson Ltd
The Continuum International Publishing Group Ltd
Countyvise Ltd
Crescent Moon Publishing
Crimson Publishing
Cualann Press Ltd
Currach Press
Darton, Longman & Todd Ltd
The Davenant Press
Day One Publications
Richard Dennis Publications
Denor Press Ltd
J M Dent
Ashley Drake Publishing Ltd
Dreamcatcher Publishing Ltd
Gerald Duckworth & Co Ltd
Equinox Publishing Ltd
The Erskine Press
Essential Works Ltd
Evangelical Press & Services Ltd
Ex Libris Press
Express Newspapers
Eye Books Ltd
Faber & Faber Ltd
Family Publications
Flambard Press
Geography Publications
Gibson Square
Gill & Macmillan Ltd
Global Oriental Ltd
Glyndwr Publishing
The Goldsmith Press Ltd
Gomer
Gothic Image Publications
Gracewing Publishing
Granta Books
Granta Editions
Green Books
Greenwood Publishing Group
Guildhall Press
Gwasg Gwenffrwd
Gwasg Gwynedd
Halban Publishers
Robert Hale Ltd
Halsgrove
HarperCollins Publishers Ltd
Harvard University Press
Haynes Publishing
Highland Books
Hodder & Stoughton Faith
Hodder & Stoughton General
Alison Hodge Publishers
Holo Books
Honno (Welsh Women's Press)
Hypatia Publications
Icon Books Ltd
ISIS Publishing Ltd
Janus Publishing Co Ltd
Richard Kay Publications
Kegan Paul Ltd
Kingsway Publications
Jay Landesman
Libris Ltd
The Lilliput Press Ltd
Lion Hudson Plc
Little, Brown Book Group
The Littman Library of Jewish Civilization
Living Time® Media International
Luath Press Ltd
The Lutterworth Press
Mainstream Publishing Co (Edinburgh) Ltd
Maverick House Publishers
Mentor Books
Mercier Press Ltd
The Merlin Press Ltd
Merlin Publishing/Wolfhound Press
Merton Priory Press Ltd
Microform Academic Publishers
The MIT Press Ltd
Motor Racing Publications Ltd
Murdoch Books UK Ltd
John Murray Publishers
National Portrait Gallery Publications
The National Trust
Natural History Museum Publishing
New Island Books Ltd
NMS Enterprises Limited - Publishing
The O'Brien Press Ltd
Octagon Press Ltd
The Oleander Press
Omnibus Press
On Stream Publications Ltd
Onlywomen Press Ltd
Orion Books Ltd
The Orion Publishing Group Ltd
Peter Owen Publishers
Oxbow Books
Pan Macmillan
Panaf Books
Pavilion
Pen Press Publishers Ltd
The Penguin Group (UK) Ltd
Piatkus Books
Pipers' Ash Ltd
Piquant Editions
Plowright Press
Portobello Books Ltd
Profile Books
Quartet Books
Quiller Publishing Ltd
The Radcliffe Press
Robson Books
Roundhouse Publishing Ltd
Route Publishing Ltd
Royal Collection Publications
St Pauls Publishing
Salt Publishing Ltd
Sandstone Press Ltd
Saqi Books
SCM-Canterbury Press Ltd
Scottish Children's Press
Scottish Cultural Press
Seren
Sessions of York
Shepheard-Walwyn (Publishers) Ltd
The Shetland Times Ltd
Shire Publications Ltd
Short Books Ltd
Simon & Schuster (UK) Ltd
Slightly Foxed
Smith Settle Printing & Bookbinding Ltd
Colin Smythe Ltd
Souvenir Press Ltd
Stacey International
Stainer & Bell Ltd
Rudolf Steiner Press
Strong Oak Press
Sussex Academic Press
Tabb House
I. B. Tauris & Co Ltd
Telegram
Thames & Hudson Ltd
Thorogood Publishing Ltd
F. A. Thorpe Publishing
Thoth Publications
Transworld Publishers Ltd
Troubador Publishing Ltd
Truran
Tyne Bridge Publishing
Unicorn Press
United Writers Publications Ltd
University of Wales Press
Merlin Unwin Books Ltd
Upfront Publishing
Vallentine Mitchell Publishers
Veloce Publishing Ltd
Veritas Publications
Vertical Editions
Victoria & Albert Museum Publishing
Virgin Books Ltd
Vision
Voltaire Foundation Ltd
Warburg Institute
Waterside Press
Waterside Press
Weidenfeld & Nicolson
Whittles Publishing
John Wiley & Sons Ltd
Neil Wilson Publishing Ltd
Windhorse Publications
The Women's Press
Y Lolfa Cyf
Yale University Press London
Zeticula
Zymurgy Publishing

BIOLOGY & ZOOLOGY

Austin & Macauley Publishers Ltd
Bedford Freeman Worth (BFW)
Bender Richardson White
BLA Publishing Ltd
BookPower
Brown & Whittaker Publishing
CABI
Calypso Publications
Cambridge University Press
D & N Publishing
Earthscan
Focus Publishing (Sevenoaks) Ltd
HarperCollins Publishers Ltd
Harvard University Press
Hodder Education
Imperial College Press
Jones & Bartlett International
Kew Publishing
Letts and Lonsdale
McGraw-Hill Education
Manson Publishing Ltd
Mentor Books
The MIT Press Ltd
The National Academies Press
Natural History Museum Publishing
Nelson Thornes Ltd
NMS Enterprises Limited - Publishing
North York Moors National Park
W. W. Norton & Company Ltd
OICA International (UK) Ltd
Open University Worldwide
Packard Publishing Ltd
Palgrave Macmillan
Portland Press Ltd
ProQuest
The Richmond Publishing Co
Royal Irish Academy
Scion Publishing Ltd
Studymates Ltd
Taylor & Francis
Think Books
Ward Lock Educational Co Ltd
Whittet Books Ltd
John Wiley & Sons Ltd
WIT Press

CHEMISTRY

Anshan Ltd
Atlantic Europe Publishing Co Ltd
BBC Active
Bedford Freeman Worth (BFW)
BLA Publishing Ltd
Cambridge University Press
Elsevier Ltd
Energy Institute
Food Trade Press Ltd
HarperCollins Publishers Ltd
Hodder Education
Icon Books Ltd
Imperial College Press
Jones & Bartlett International
Letts and Lonsdale
McGraw-Hill Education
The National Academies Press
Nelson Thornes Ltd
W. W. Norton & Company Ltd
OICA International (UK) Ltd
Open University Worldwide
Palgrave Macmillan
The Royal Society of Chemistry
Scion Publishing Ltd
Studymates Ltd
Taylor & Francis
Ward Lock Educational Co Ltd
John Wiley & Sons Ltd

CHILDREN'S BOOKS

A.M.S. Educational Ltd
AA Publishing
Acair Ltd
Accent Press Ltd
Aladdin Books Ltd
Alban Books Ltd
Albion Press Ltd
Allied Mouse Ltd
Alligator Books Ltd
Amnesty International UK
Amolibros
Andersen Press Ltd
Ann Arbor Publishers Ltd
Antique Collectors' Club Ltd
Apex Publishing Ltd
Arcturus Publishing Ltd
Atlantic Europe Publishing Co Ltd
Aurora Metro Publications Ltd
Austin & Macauley Publishers Ltd
Australian Consolidated Press UK
Authentic Media
Authorhouse UK Ltd
Award Publications Ltd
b small publishing ltd
Barefoot Books
Barny Books
Nicola Baxter Ltd
BBC Active
Bender Richardson White
Bene Factum Publishing Ltd
Bible Reading Fellowship
BLA Publishing Ltd
A. & C. Black (Publishers) Ltd
Bloomsbury Publishing Plc
Bodleian Library Publishing
Book Marketing Ltd
Book Street Ltd
Marion Boyars Publishers Ltd
Bridgewater Book Co
British Association for Adoption & Fostering
British Museum Press
Brown Dog Books
Brown Wells & Jacobs Ltd
Cambridge Publishing Management Ltd
Cambridge University Press
Carlton Publishing Group
The Catholic Truth Society
Catnip Publishing Ltd
Caxton Publishing Group Ltd
Chalksoft Ltd
Chicken House Publishing Ltd
Child's Play (International) Ltd
Christian Education
Christian Focus Publications
Classical Comics Ltd
Cló Iar-Chonnachta
Coachwise Ltd
Cois Life
Constable & Robinson Ltd
Cornwall Editions Ltd
Corpus Publishing Ltd
Cowley Robinson Publishing Ltd
CRW Publishing Ltd

Cyhoeddiadau'r Gair
Day One Publications
Delancey Press Ltd
J M Dent
Ashley Drake Publishing Ltd
Dramatic Lines
Dreamcatcher Publishing Ltd
Dref Wen Cyf/Ltd
Eddison Sadd Editions Ltd
Egmont UK Ltd
Elliott & Thompson
Elm Grove Books Ltd
Emma Treehouse Ltd
Encyclopaedia Britannica (UK) Ltd
English Heritage
Evans Publishing Group
Everyman's Library
Faber & Faber Ltd
Feather Books
Five Leaves Publications
Floris Books
The Fostering Network
W. Foulsham & Co Ltd
Galore Park Publishing Ltd
Geddes & Grosset
Gill & Macmillan Ltd
Glowworm Books & Gifts Ltd
Gomer
Graham-Cameron Publishing & Illustration
W. F. Graham (Northampton) Ltd
Guildhall Press
Gwasg Gwenffrwd
Gwasg Gwynedd
Hachette Children's Books
Hachette Livre UK Ltd
Peter Haddock Publishing
Haldane Mason Ltd
HarperCollins Publishers Ltd
Hawthorn Press
Haynes Publishing
Highland Books
Holland Publishing Plc
John Hunt Publishing Ltd
Icon Books Ltd
Janus Publishing Co Ltd
The King's England Press
Jessica Kingsley Publishers
Kingsway Publications
Kube Publishing Ltd
Lagoon Books
LDA
Letterland International Ltd
Letts and Lonsdale
Frances Lincoln Ltd
Lion Hudson Plc
Little People Books
Little Tiger Press
Living Time® Media International
Lomond Books Ltd
Luath Press Ltd
The Lutterworth Press
McCrimmon Publishing Co Ltd
Macmillan Children's Books Ltd
Macmillan Education
Mandrake of Oxford
Meadowside Children's Books
The Medici Society Ltd
Mercier Press Ltd
Mercury Junior
Merlin Publishing/Wolfhound Press
Milet Publishing Ltd
Monkey Puzzle Media Ltd
Moonlight Publishing Ltd
MW Educational
National Gallery Co Ltd
The National Trust
Natural History Museum Publishing
Nelson Thornes Ltd
NMS Enterprises Limited - Publishing
North York Moors National Park
The O'Brien Press Ltd
Onlywomen Press Ltd
Orion Books Ltd
The Orion Publishing Group Ltd
Orpheus Books Ltd
Oxfam Publishing
Oxford University Press
Pan Macmillan

Pavilion
Pavilion Children's Books
Pen Press Publishers Ltd
The Penguin Group (UK) Ltd
Phaidon Press Ltd
Piccadilly Press
Pipers' Ash Ltd
Playne Books Ltd
Porthill Publishers
Positive Press Ltd
Tony Potter Publishing
Prestel Publishing Ltd
Mathew Price Ltd
Quantum Publishing
Random House Children's Books
Random House UK Ltd
Ransom Publishing Ltd
Ravette Publishing Ltd
Reader's Digest Children's Publishing Ltd
Reardon Publishing
Regency House Publishing Ltd
Ripley Publishing Ltd
Rising Stars UK Ltd
Robinswood Press Ltd
Roundhouse Publishing Ltd
Save the Children
Scala Publishers Ltd
Scholastic UK Ltd
Scottish Children's Press
Scripture Union Publishing
Search Press Ltd
Seasquirt Publications
Sessions of York
SGC Books
Sheldrake Press
Short Books Ltd
Sigel Press
Simon & Schuster (UK) Ltd
Slightly Foxed
Solidus
Speechmark Publishing Ltd
Stacey International
Symposium Publications Literary & Art
Ta Ha Publishers Ltd
Tabb House
Tamarind Ltd
Tangerine Designs Ltd
Tangerine Designs Ltd
Tarquin Publications
Tate Publishing
Templar Publishing
Think Books
Titan Publishing Group
Top That! Publishing Plc
Topical Resources
Toucan Books Ltd
Troubador Publishing Ltd
Tucker Slingsby Ltd
United Writers Publications Ltd
Usborne Publishing Ltd
Veritas Publications
David West Children's Books
John Wiley & Sons Ltd
Wordsworth Editions Ltd
Y Lolfa Cyf
Zero to Ten

CINEMA, VIDEO, TV & RADIO

Aurora Metro Publications Ltd
Aurum Press
Austin & Macauley Publishers Ltd
Berg Publishers
Berghahn Books
Black Dog Publishing Ltd
Black Spring Press Ltd
Blackstaff Press
Bloomsbury Publishing Plc
Marion Boyars Publishers Ltd
Bridgewater Book Co
Cambridge Publishing Management Ltd
Cameron Books
Cameron & Hollis
Carlton Publishing Group
The Continuum International Publishing Group Ltd
Crescent Moon Publishing
Currach Press
Essential Works Ltd

Faber & Faber Ltd
Gibson Square
Greenwood Publishing Group
Robert Hale Ltd
HarperCollins Publishers Ltd
Harvard University Press
Nick Hern Books
Hodder Education
Hodder & Stoughton General
Intellect Ltd
Living Time® Media International
Luath Press Ltd
Mainstream Publishing Co (Edinburgh) Ltd
Mentor Books
Merlin Publishing/Wolfhound Press
W. W. Norton & Company Ltd
Oldcastle Books Ltd
The Orion Publishing Group Ltd
Peter Owen Publishers
Pan Macmillan
Pavilion
The Penguin Group (UK) Ltd
Phaidon Press Ltd
Pluto Books Ltd
Polity Press
Prestel Publishing Ltd
Reardon Publishing
Robson Books
RotoVision SA
Roundhouse Publishing Ltd
Charles Skilton Ltd
Stenlake Publishing Ltd
Sussex Publications
I. B. Tauris & Co Ltd
Telos Publishing Ltd
Titan Publishing Group
Transworld Publishers Ltd
United Writers Publications Ltd
University of Exeter Press
Virgin Books Ltd
Wallflower Press
David West Children's Books
World Microfilms

COMPUTER SCIENCE

Age Concern Books
Anshan Ltd
Austin & Macauley Publishers Ltd
Bernard Babani (Publishing) Ltd
BBC Active
BLA Publishing Ltd
BookPower
Business Education Publishers
Cambridge University Press
Carlton Publishing Group
Emerald Group Publishing Ltd
Free Association Books
Global Professional Publishing
Haynes Publishing
Hodder Education
Imperial College Press
In Easy Steps Ltd
Institution of Engineering and Technology (IET)
Intellect Ltd
IOP Publishing
Jones & Bartlett International
Lawpack Publishing Ltd
McGraw-Hill Education
Market House Books Ltd
The MIT Press Ltd
Multi Science Publishing Co Ltd
Nelson Thornes Ltd
W. W. Norton & Company Ltd
Open University Worldwide
O'Reilly UK Ltd
Palgrave Macmillan
Paragon Publishing
Professional Engineering Publishing
Taylor Graham Publishing
TSO (The Stationery Office Ltd)
Usborne Publishing Ltd
John Wiley & Sons Ltd
WIT Press

COOKERY, WINES & SPIRITS

Absolute Press

Accent Press Ltd
Appletree Press Ltd
Arcturus Publishing Ltd
Ashgrove Publishing
Attic Press
Aurora Metro Publications Ltd
Aurum Press
Austin & Macauley Publishers Ltd
Australian Consolidated Press UK
Authorhouse UK Ltd
Duncan Baird Publishers
Blackstaff Press
John Blake Publishing Ltd
Bloomsbury Publishing Plc
Bossiney Books Ltd
Bridgewater Book Co
Brown & Whittaker Publishing
Cambridge Publishing Management Ltd
Cameron Books
Camra Books
Capall Bann Publishing
Carlton Publishing Group
Jon Carpenter Publishing
Carroll & Brown Ltd
Caxton Publishing Group Ltd
Collins & Brown
Conran Octopus
Copper Beech Publishing Ltd
Currach Press
David & Charles Ltd
Dedalus Ltd
Ashley Drake Publishing Ltd
Eddison Sadd Editions Ltd
Equinox Publishing Ltd
Essential Works Ltd
Ex Libris Press
Faber & Faber Ltd
A. & A. Farmar
Findhorn Press Ltd
Focus Publishing (Sevenoaks) Ltd
W. Foulsham & Co Ltd
Garnet Publishing Ltd
Geddes & Grosset
GeoCenter International Ltd
Gill & Macmillan Ltd
The Goldsmith Press Ltd
Graffeg
Granta Editions
Grub Street
Haldane Mason Ltd
HarperCollins Publishers Ltd
Ian Henry Publications Ltd
Hodder Education
Hodder & Stoughton General
Alison Hodge Publishers
Kegan Paul Ltd
Lagoon Books
Liberties Press
Frances Lincoln Ltd
Little, Brown Book Group
Lomond Books Ltd
Luath Press Ltd
Mainstream Publishing Co (Edinburgh) Ltd
Merlin Publishing/Wolfhound Press
Mitchell Beazley
Murdoch Books UK Ltd
National Gallery Co Ltd
The National Trust
Need2Know
New Internationalist Publications Ltd
NMS Enterprises Limited - Publishing
W. W. Norton & Company Ltd
The O'Brien Press Ltd
Octopus Publishing Group
On Stream Publications Ltd
The Orion Publishing Group Ltd
Papadakis Publisher
Pavilion
Pen Press Publishers Ltd
The Penguin Group (UK) Ltd
Phaidon Press Ltd
Piatkus Books
Prospect Books
Quadrille Publishing Ltd
Quantum Publishing
Quiller Publishing Ltd
Robson Books

Roundhouse Publishing Ltd
Saqi Books
Scottish Children's Press
Scottish Cultural Press
Sheldrake Press
Simon & Schuster (UK) Ltd
Charles Skilton Ltd
Snowbooks
Special Interest Model Books Ltd
Summersdale Publishers Ltd
Top That! Publishing Plc
Transworld Publishers Ltd
Troubador Publishing Ltd
Truran
Tucker Slingsby Ltd
Merlin Unwin Books Ltd
White Ladder Press
John Wiley & Sons Ltd
Neil Wilson Publishing Ltd
Y Lolfa Cyf
Zymurgy Publishing

CRAFTS & HOBBIES

Accent Press Ltd
Amber Books Ltd
Apex Publishing Ltd
Arcturus Publishing Ltd
Aurum Press
Australian Consolidated Press UK
Bernard Babani (Publishing) Ltd
Batsford
A. & C. Black (Publishers) Ltd
Book Street Ltd
Bridgewater Book Co
Brown Wells & Jacobs Ltd
Calypso Publications
Cambridge Publishing Management Ltd
Capall Bann Publishing
Carlton Publishing Group
Carroll & Brown Ltd
Caxton Publishing Group Ltd
Collins & Brown
Conran Octopus
The Crowood Press Ltd
D & N Publishing
David & Charles Ltd
Eco-logic Books
Essential Works Ltd
Floris Books
Focus Publishing (Sevenoaks) Ltd
W. Foulsham & Co Ltd
Greenlight Publishing
Haldane Mason Ltd
HarperCollins Publishers Ltd
Hawthorn Press
Haynes Publishing
The Herbert Press
Hodder Education
The Ilex Press Ltd
In Easy Steps Ltd
The Ivy Press Ltd
Kegan Paul Ltd
Lomond Books Ltd
The Lutterworth Press
Melisende Publishing Ltd
Mitchell Beazley
Murdoch Books UK Ltd
Octopus Publishing Group
Old House Books
The Orion Publishing Group Ltd
The Penguin Group (UK) Ltd
Quadrille Publishing Ltd
Quantum Publishing
Quiller Publishing Ltd
Regency House Publishing Ltd
Roundhouse Publishing Ltd
Search Press Ltd
Sigma Press
Snowbooks
Souvenir Press Ltd
Special Interest Model Books Ltd
Stenlake Publishing Ltd
Stobart Davies Ltd
Stott's Correspondence College
Summersdale Publishers Ltd
Tarquin Publications
Thames & Hudson Ltd
Top That! Publishing Plc
Toucan Books Ltd

Tucker Slingsby Ltd
Usborne Publishing Ltd
David West Children's Books
Willow Island Editions

CRIME

Accent Press Ltd
Allison & Busby
Alma Books Ltd
Amber Books Ltd
Apex Publishing Ltd
Arcadia Books Ltd
Arcturus Publishing Ltd
Atlantic Books
Austin & Macauley Publishers Ltd
Authorhouse UK Ltd
Back-In-Print Books Ltd
Bitter Lemon Press
Blackstaff Press
John Blake Publishing Ltd
Canongate Books
Carlton Publishing Group
Caxton Publishing Group Ltd
CBD Research Ltd
Constable & Robinson Ltd
Countyvise Ltd
Essential Works Ltd
Express Newspapers
Feather Books
Five Leaves Publications
Flambard Press
Focus Publishing (Sevenoaks) Ltd
W. Foulsham & Co Ltd
Guildhall Press
Robert Hale Ltd
HarperCollins Publishers Ltd
Hodder & Stoughton General
Icon Books Ltd
ISIS Publishing Ltd
Janus Publishing Co Ltd
Little, Brown Book Group
Living Time® Media International
Luath Press Ltd
Mainstream Publishing Co
 (Edinburgh) Ltd
Mandrake of Oxford
Maverick House Publishers
Mentor Books
Merlin Publishing/Wolfhound
 Press
New Island Books Ltd
Onlywomen Press Ltd
The Orion Publishing Group Ltd
Pen Press Publishers Ltd
The Penguin Group (UK) Ltd
Piatkus Books
Robson Books
Sandstone Press Ltd
Severn House Publishers Ltd
Simon & Schuster (UK) Ltd
Snowbooks
Social Affairs Unit
Telos Publishing Ltd
Transworld Publishers Ltd
Troubador Publishing Ltd
Vision
Waterside Press
Waterside Press
Neil Wilson Publishing Ltd
The Women's Press
Zymurgy Publishing

DO-IT-YOURSELF

Bridgewater Book Co
Caxton Publishing Group Ltd
Centre for Alternative Technology
 Publications
Collins & Brown
Conran Octopus
The Crowood Press Ltd
D & N Publishing
David & Charles Ltd
Essential Works Ltd
Express Newspapers
Focus Publishing (Sevenoaks) Ltd
Granta Editions
Green Books
HarperCollins Publishers Ltd
Haynes Publishing
Hodder Education
Janus Publishing Co Ltd
Lawpack Publishing Ltd
Murdoch Books UK Ltd
Octopus Publishing Group
Ovolo Publishing Ltd
Pen Press Publishers Ltd
The Penguin Group (UK) Ltd
Quadrille Publishing Ltd
Quantum Publishing
Search Press Ltd
Stobart Davies Ltd
Summersdale Publishers Ltd
John Wiley & Sons Ltd

ECONOMICS

Adam Matthew Publications Ltd
Peter Andrew Publishing Co Ltd
Arena Books (Publishers)
Ashgate Publishing Ltd
Atlantic Books
Berghahn Books
Blackhall Publishing
BookPower
Nicholas Brealey Publishing
Cambridge University Press
Jon Carpenter Publishing
Centre for Economic Policy
 Research
The Chartered Institute of Public
 Finance & Accountancy
Commonwealth Secretariat
The Continuum International
 Publishing Group Ltd
Council of Mortgage Lenders
James Currey Publishers
J M Dent
Earthscan
Economic & Social Research
 Institute
Edward Elgar Publishing Ltd
Emerald Group Publishing Ltd
Euromonitor International Plc
Fabian Society
Free Association Books
Garnet Publishing Ltd
Gill & Macmillan Ltd
Global Professional Publishing
Green Books
Greenwood Publishing Group
HarperCollins Publishers Ltd
Harvard University Press
Hodder Education
C. Hurst & Co (Publishers) Ltd
Icon Books Ltd
Imperial College Press
Institute for Fiscal Studies
Institute of Development Studies
Institute of Employment Rights
Ithaca Press
Janus Publishing Co Ltd
Jarndyce Booksellers
Kegan Paul Ltd
Kube Publishing Ltd
McGraw-Hill Education
Mehring Books
Mentor Books
The Merlin Press Ltd
Microform Academic Publishers
The MIT Press Ltd
Nelson Thornes Ltd
W. W. Norton & Company Ltd
Open University Worldwide
Oxfam Publishing
Palgrave Macmillan
Pathfinder Books
Pickering & Chatto (Publishers) Ltd
Pluto Books Ltd
The Policy Press
Princeton University Press
ProQuest
Rand Publications
Joseph Rowntree Foundation
Sage Publications Ltd
Shepheard-Walwyn (Publishers)
 Ltd
Adam Smith Institute
Social Affairs Unit
Spokesman
Sussex Academic Press
Taylor & Francis
Troubador Publishing Ltd
Tru-Est Ltd
TSO (The Stationery Office Ltd)
John Wiley & Sons Ltd
Yale University Press London
Zed Books Ltd

EDUCATIONAL & TEXTBOOKS

A.M.S. Educational Ltd
Acair Ltd
Accent Press Ltd
Acumen Publishing Ltd
Adamson Publishing Ltd
Age Concern Books
Aladdin Books Ltd
Alban Books Ltd
Philip Allan Publishers Ltd
American Psychiatric Publishing
 Inc
Amnesty International UK
Anglo-Saxon Books
Ann Arbor Publishers Ltd
Anshan Ltd
Arcturus Publishing Ltd
Ashgate Publishing Ltd
Association for Scottish Literary
 Studies
Atlantic Europe Publishing Co Ltd
Aurora Metro Publications Ltd
Austin & Macauley Publishers Ltd
AVA Publishing (UK) Ltd
B & D Publishing
B Squared
Bernard Babani (Publishing) Ltd
Back-In-Print Books Ltd
Badger Publishing Ltd
Nicola Baxter Ltd
BBC Active
BEAM Education
Bender Richardson White
Berg Publishers
Bible Reading Fellowship
A. & C. Black (Publishers) Ltd
Book Marketing Ltd
BookPower
Borthwick Publications
Bridgewater Book Co
Brilliant Publications
Business Education Publishers
Butterfingers Books
Calypso Publications
*Cambridge Publishing
 Management Ltd*
Cambridge University Press
Capall Bann Publishing
Careers Europe
Carel Press
The Catholic Truth Society
John Catt Educational Ltd
Cengage Learning EMEA
Centre for Alternative Technology
 Publications
Chalksoft Ltd
Channel View Publications Ltd
Chartered Institute of Personnel &
 Development
Chemcord Ltd
Christian Education
Christian Focus Publications
CILT, the National Centre for
 Languages
Claire Publications
Classical Comics Ltd
Cló Iar-Chonnachta
Coachwise Ltd
Cois Life
Collins Geo
Colourpoint Books
The Continuum International
 Publishing Group Ltd
CQ Press
Crimson Publishing
Crossbow Education Ltd
Darton, Longman & Todd Ltd
The Davenant Press
Diagram Visual Information Ltd
Dramatic Lines
Dreamcatcher Publishing Ltd
Dref Wen Cyf/Ltd
Earthscan
Economic & Social Research
 Institute
Edinburgh University Press
Educational Planning Books Ltd
Edward Elgar Publishing Ltd
Elm Publications
Elsevier Ltd
Emerald Group Publishing Ltd
English Heritage
Equinox Publishing Ltd
Ethics International Press Ltd
Evans Publishing Group
Exley Publications Ltd
Facet Publishing
First & Best in Education Ltd
Folens Ltd
The Fostering Network
W. Foulsham & Co Ltd
Freelance Market News
Friends of the Earth
Galore Park Publishing Ltd
Gatehouse Media Ltd
The Geographical Association
Geography Publications
Gill & Macmillan Ltd
Global Professional Publishing
Gower Publishing Co Ltd
*Graham-Cameron Publishing &
 Illustration*
Granada Learning
Granta Editions
Greenleaf Publishing
Greenwood Publishing Group
Guildhall Press
Gwasg Gwenffrwd
Hachette Children's Books
Hachette Livre UK Ltd
Haldane Mason Ltd
HarperCollins Publishers Ltd
Hart McLeod Ltd
Hawthorn Press
Ian Henry Publications Ltd
Hinton House Publishers
Hodder Education
Hodder Gibson
Holland Publishing Plc
Hopscotch Educational Publishing
How To Books Ltd
Human Kinetics Europe Ltd
Hypatia Publications
Icon Books Ltd
Immunisation Information
In Easy Steps Ltd
Institute of Development Studies
Institute of Education
 (Publications), University of
 London
Intellect Ltd
Janus Publishing Co Ltd
Jolly Learning Ltd
Jones & Bartlett International
Hilda King Educational
Jessica Kingsley Publishers
Chris Kington Publishing
Kogan Page Ltd
Kube Publishing Ltd
LDA
Learning Matters Ltd
Learning Together
Letterland International Ltd
Letts and Lonsdale
Lexus Ltd
Lion Hudson Plc
Little People Books
The Littman Library of Jewish
 Civilization
Liverpool University Press
Living Time® Media International
The Lutterworth Press
McCrimmon Publishing Co Ltd
McGraw-Hill Education
McGraw-Hill Publishing Company
Macmillan Education
Management Pocketbooks Ltd
Marshall Cavendish Partworks Ltd
Kevin Mayhew Ltd
Mentor Books
Merlin Publishing/Wolfhound
 Press
Methodist Publishing House
Monkey Puzzle Media Ltd
MW Educational
NATE (National Association for the
 Teaching of English)
The National Academies Press
The National Autistic Society
 (NAS)
National Children's Bureau
National Extension College Trust
 Ltd
National Housing Federation
The National Youth Agency
Natural History Museum
 Publishing
Nelson Thornes Ltd
Network Continuum Education
 Ltd
NMS Enterprises Limited -
 Publishing
North York Moors National Park
Northcote House Publishers Ltd
Norwood Publishers Ltd
Oak Tree Press
OICA International (UK) Ltd
Open University Worldwide
Optimus Professional Publishing
Orchard Publishing
Oxfam Publishing
Oxford University Press
Packard Publishing Ltd
Palgrave Macmillan
Paragon Publishing
Pavilion Publishing (Brighton) Ltd
Pearson Education Ltd
Pearson Education Oxford
Pen Press Publishers Ltd
Philip's
The Policy Press
Polity Press
Portland Press Ltd
Positive Press Ltd
Radcliffe Publishing Ltd
Rand Publications
Ransom Publishing Ltd
The Richmond Publishing Co
Rising Stars UK Ltd
Robinswood Press Ltd
Round Hall Ltd
Routledge-Cavendish
The Royal Society of Chemistry
Russell House Publishing Ltd
Sage Publications Ltd
Save the Children
Scholastic UK Ltd
SchoolPlay Productions Ltd
SCM-Canterbury Press Ltd
Scripture Union Publishing
Shaw & Sons Ltd
Sigel Press
Social Affairs Unit
The Society of Metaphysicians Ltd
Southgate Publishers
Speechmark Publishing Ltd
Stacey International
Rudolf Steiner Press
Step Forward Publishing Ltd
Stokesby House Publications
STRI (Sports Turf Research
 Institute)
Studymates Ltd
Supportive Learning Publications
 (SLP)
Sussex Academic Press
Symposium Publications Literary &
 Art
Tamarind Ltd
Tarquin Publications
Taylor & Francis
Teachit (UK) Ltd
Thames & Hudson Ltd
Third Millennium Publishing Ltd
THRASS (UK) Ltd
Topical Resources
Trentham Books
Trotman Publishing
Trust for the Study of Adolescence
TSO (The Stationery Office Ltd)
UCAS
United Writers Publications Ltd
University of Hertfordshire Press
University of Wales Press
Veritas Publications
Ward Lock Educational Co Ltd
Waterside Press
Waterside Press
Whittles Publishing

148 / PUBLISHERS CLASSIFIED BY FIELDS OF ACTIVITY

John Wiley & Sons Ltd
Witherby Seamanship International
Zeticula

ELECTRONIC (EDUCATIONAL)

Adam Matthew Digital Ltd
Atlantic Europe Publishing Co Ltd
AVA Publishing (UK) Ltd
Bernard Babani (Publishing) Ltd
BBC Active
Bowker (UK) Ltd
British Library, Publishing Office
Cambridge University Press
Carel Press
Chalksoft Ltd
Coachwise Ltd
Collins Geo
Commonwealth Secretariat
The Continuum International Publishing Group Ltd
Dreamcatcher Publishing Ltd
Elm Publications
Emerald Group Publishing Ltd
Encyclopaedia Britannica (UK) Ltd
Ethics International Press Ltd
First & Best in Education Ltd
Folens Ltd
The Geographical Association
Global Professional Publishing
HarperCollins Publishers Ltd
Haynes Publishing
Heart of Albion Press
Hodder Education
Human Kinetics Europe Ltd
Imperial College Press
Intellect Ltd
Jolly Learning Ltd
Kogan Page Ltd
Lagoon Books
Letterland International Ltd
McCrimmon Publishing Co Ltd
McGraw-Hill Education
National Extension College Trust Ltd
National Gallery Co Ltd
Nelson Thornes Ltd
New Internationalist Publications Ltd
Open University Worldwide
Optimus Professional Publishing
Oxfam Publishing
Palgrave Macmillan
Paragon Publishing
ProQuest
Radcliffe Publishing Ltd
Ransom Publishing Ltd
Rising Stars UK Ltd
Robinswood Press Ltd
Royal Geographical Society (with Institute of British Geographers)
The Royal Society of Chemistry
Sage Publications Ltd
The Society of Metaphysicians Ltd
Studymates Ltd
Summersdale Publishers Ltd
THRASS (UK) Ltd
John Wiley & Sons Ltd

ELECTRONIC (ENTERTAINMENT)

Bernard Babani (Publishing) Ltd
The Ilex Press Ltd
Lagoon Books
Summersdale Publishers Ltd
Tangerine Designs Ltd

ELECTRONIC (PROFESSIONAL & ACADEMIC)

Adam Matthew Digital Ltd
Ashgate Publishing Ltd
Bernard Babani (Publishing) Ltd
Berghahn Books
Bowker (UK) Ltd
Cambridge University Press
Centre for Policy on Ageing
The Continuum International Publishing Group Ltd

Earthscan
Emerald Group Publishing Ltd
Energy Institute
Equinox Publishing Ltd
Ethics International Press Ltd
Facet Publishing
Garnet Publishing Ltd
Global Professional Publishing
Gwasg Gwenffrwd
Hachette Livre UK Ltd
Harlequin Mills & Boon Ltd
HarperCollins Publishers Ltd
Hodder Education
Human Kinetics Europe Ltd
Imperial College Press
In Easy Steps Ltd
Institution of Engineering and Technology (IET)
Intellect Ltd
International Medical Press
International Network for the Availability of Scientific Publications (INASP)
IOP Publishing
IWA Publishing
Jane's Information Group Ltd
Jordan Publishing Ltd
Chris Kington Publishing
Kogan Page Ltd
McGraw-Hill Education
Maney Publishing
Methodist Publishing House
Multi Science Publishing Co Ltd
Myriad Editions
National Children's Bureau
National Gallery Co Ltd
Network Continuum Education Ltd
Outsell Inc / EPS
Oxford University Press
Paragon Publishing
Pavilion Publishing (Brighton) Ltd
Pearson Education Ltd
Pearson Education Oxford
The Pharmaceutical Press
Portland Press Ltd
ProQuest
Radcliffe Publishing Ltd
Round Hall Ltd
Routledge-Cavendish
Royal College of General Practitioners
Royal Geographical Society (with Institute of British Geographers)
The Royal Society of Chemistry
St Jerome Publishing Ltd
Summersdale Publishers Ltd
Taylor & Francis
Teachit (UK) Ltd
TSO (The Stationery Office Ltd)
Voltaire Foundation Ltd
John Wiley & Sons Ltd
WIT Press
Witherby Seamanship International
Wolters Kluwer Health (P & E) Ltd
Woodhead Publishing Ltd

ENGINEERING

Peter Andrew Publishing Co Ltd
Anshan Ltd
Bernard Babani (Publishing) Ltd
BookPower
Cambridge University Press
Construction Industry Research & Information Association (CIRIA)
Conway
Earthscan
Emerald Group Publishing Ltd
Energy Institute
Geological Society Publishing House
Gower Publishing Co Ltd
IChemE
Imperial College Press
Institute of Physics & Engineering in Medicine
Institution of Engineering and Technology (IET)
IWA Publishing

McGraw-Hill Education
Maney Publishing
Multi Science Publishing Co Ltd
The National Academies Press
Nelson Thornes Ltd
Open University Worldwide
Palgrave Macmillan
Professional Engineering Publishing
Special Interest Model Books Ltd
Taylor & Francis
Thomas Telford Ltd
TSO (The Stationery Office Ltd)
Tyne Bridge Publishing
Whittles Publishing
John Wiley & Sons Ltd
WIT Press
Woodhead Publishing Ltd

ENGLISH AS A FOREIGN LANGUAGE

Austin & Macauley Publishers Ltd
BBC Active
Cambridge Publishing Management Ltd
Cambridge University Press
Cengage Learning EMEA
Folens Ltd
Gatehouse Media Ltd
The Goldsmith Press Ltd
Graham-Cameron Publishing & Illustration
HarperCollins Publishers Ltd
Hodder Education
Letterland International Ltd
Living Time® Media International
McGraw-Hill Education
Macmillan Education
Milet Publishing Ltd
New Island Books Ltd
Open University Worldwide
Paragon Publishing
Robinswood Press Ltd
Sandstone Press Ltd
Speechmark Publishing Ltd
Studymates Ltd
Symposium Publications Literary & Art

ENVIRONMENT & DEVELOPMENT STUDIES

Anshan Ltd
Ashgate Publishing Ltd
Atlantic Europe Publishing Co Ltd
Austin & Macauley Publishers Ltd
Berghahn Books
CABI
Cambridge University Press
Cameron Books
Capall Bann Publishing
Jon Carpenter Publishing
Centre for Alternative Technology Publications
Channel View Publications Ltd
Commonwealth Secretariat
The Continuum International Publishing Group Ltd
Cork University Press
CQ Press
James Currey Publishers
Darton, Longman & Todd Ltd
Earthscan
Eco-logic Books
Economic & Social Research Institute
Edward Elgar Publishing Ltd
Emerald Group Publishing Ltd
Energy Institute
Ethics International Press Ltd
Fabian Society
Friends of the Earth
Geological Society Publishing House
Granta Editions
Green Books
Greenleaf Publishing
Hodder Education
Imperial College Press

Institute of Development Studies
Intellect Ltd
Kegan Paul Ltd
Macmillan Education
The MIT Press Ltd
Multi Science Publishing Co Ltd
Myriad Editions
The National Academies Press
Nelson Thornes Ltd
New Internationalist Publications Ltd
North York Moors National Park
Octagon Press Ltd
On Stream Publications Ltd
Open Gate Press
Open University Worldwide
Oxfam Publishing
Packard Publishing Ltd
Palgrave Macmillan
Paragon Publishing
Plowright Press
Pluto Books Ltd
Routledge-Cavendish
Royal Geographical Society (with Institute of British Geographers)
Sandstone Press Ltd
Alastair Sawday Publishing
Scottish Cultural Press
Sigel Press
Social Affairs Unit
The Society of Metaphysicians Ltd
Southgate Publishers
Stokesby House Publications
STRI (Sports Turf Research Institute)
Sussex Academic Press
Taylor & Francis
Thames & Hudson Ltd
Think Books
John Wiley & Sons Ltd
WIT Press
Woodhead Publishing Ltd
Zed Books Ltd
Zeticula

FASHION & COSTUME

Amber Books Ltd
Aurum Press
Austin & Macauley Publishers Ltd
AVA Publishing (UK) Ltd
Batsford
Berg Publishers
A. & C. Black (Publishers) Ltd
Black Dog Publishing Ltd
Bridgewater Book Co
Carlton Publishing Group
Collins & Brown
Copper Beech Publishing Ltd
D & N Publishing
Essential Works Ltd
Glasgow Museums
Global Oriental Ltd
Granta Editions
The Herbert Press
The Ivy Press Ltd
Janus Publishing Co Ltd
Kegan Paul Ltd
Laurence King Publishing Ltd
Maney Publishing
Mitchell Beazley
National Portrait Gallery Publications
The National Trust
Nelson Thornes Ltd
The Orion Publishing Group Ltd
Peter Owen Publishers
Oxbow Books
Papadakis Publisher
Pavilion
Phaidon Press Ltd
Prestel Publishing Ltd
Quadrille Publishing Ltd
Quantum Publishing
RotoVision SA
Charles Skilton Ltd
Stott's Correspondence College
Thames & Hudson Ltd
Unicorn Press

Victoria & Albert Museum Publishing
David West Children's Books
Yale University Press London

FICTION

Acair Ltd
Accent Press Ltd
Albyn Press
Allison & Busby
Alma Books Ltd
Amolibros
Apex Publishing Ltd
Arcadia Books Ltd
Arena Books (Publishers)
Argyll Publishing
Ashgrove Publishing
Atlantic Books
Aurora Metro Publications Ltd
Austin & Macauley Publishers Ltd
Authorhouse UK Ltd
Back-In-Print Books Ltd
Barny Books
Beautiful Books Ltd
Birlinn Ltd
Bitter Lemon Press
Black Ace Books
Black Spring Press Ltd
Blackstaff Press
Bloomsbury Publishing Plc
Blue Sky Press
Marion Boyars Publishers Ltd
Brandon/Mount Eagle Publications
Canongate Books
Capuchin Classics
Caxton Publishing Group Ltd
The Chrysalis Press
Classical Comics Ltd
Cló Iar-Chonnachta
Cois Life
Collins & Brown
Colourpoint Books
Constable & Robinson Ltd
Cornwall Editions Ltd
CRW Publishing Ltd
Dedalus Ltd
Delancey Press Ltd
Denor Press Ltd
J M Dent
Dreamcatcher Publishing Ltd
Dref Wen Cyf/Ltd
Gerald Duckworth & Co Ltd
Elliott & Thompson
Enitharmon Press
Everyman's Library
Faber & Faber Ltd
Feather Books
Five Leaves Publications
Flambard Press
Freelance Market News
The Gallery Press
Garnet Publishing Ltd
Victor Gollancz Ltd
Granta Books
Guildhall Press
Hachette Children's Books
Halban Publishers
Robert Hale Ltd
HarperCollins Publishers Ltd
Ian Henry Publications Ltd
Hodder & Stoughton General
Honno (Welsh Women's Press)
House of Lochar
Icon Books Ltd
ISIS Publishing Ltd
Ithaca Press
Janus Publishing Co Ltd
Jarndyce Booksellers
Kegan Paul Ltd
Kingsway Publications
Legend Press
Libris Ltd
The Lilliput Press Ltd
Little, Brown Book Group
Living Time® Media International
Luath Press Ltd
Magna Large Print Books
The Maia Press Ltd
Mandrake of Oxford
Mentor Books

Mercier Press Ltd
Merlin Publishing/Wolfhound Press
Milet Publishing Ltd
John Murray Publishers
Myriad Editions
Myrmidon Books Ltd
New Internationalist Publications Ltd
New Island Books Ltd
Oldcastle Books Ltd
Oneworld Classics
Onlywomen Press Ltd
Orion Books Ltd
The Orion Publishing Group Ltd
Peter Owen Publishers
Pan Macmillan
Paragon Publishing
Pen Press Publishers Ltd
The Penguin Group (UK) Ltd
Piatkus Books
Pipers' Ash Ltd
Portobello Books Ltd
Profile Books
Publishing House
Quartet Books
Rising Stars UK Ltd
Robinswood Press Ltd
Route Publishing Ltd
Salt Publishing Ltd
Sandstone Press Ltd
Saqi Books
Scottish Children's Press
Seren
Severn House Publishers Ltd
Short Books Ltd
Sigel Press
Silver Moon Books
Simon & Schuster (UK) Ltd
Charles Skilton Ltd
Slightly Foxed
Snowbooks
Solidus
Spokesman
Sportsbooks Ltd
Tabb House
Tartarus Press
Telegram
Telos Publishing Ltd
Templar Publishing
F. A. Thorpe Publishing
Tindal Street Press
Transita Ltd
Transworld Publishers Ltd
Troubador Publishing Ltd
Truran
United Writers Publications Ltd
Upfront Publishing
Usborne Publishing Ltd
Voltaire Foundation Ltd
Waterside Press
Weidenfeld & Nicolson
Whittles Publishing
The Women's Press
Wordsworth Editions Ltd
Worth Press Ltd
Y Lolfa Cyf
Zeticula

FINE ART & ART HISTORY

Akros Publications
Albyn Press
Antique Collectors' Club Ltd
Apex Publishing Ltd
Archetype Publications Ltd
Arcturus Publishing Ltd
Ashgate Publishing Ltd
Ashmolean Museum Publications
Duncan Baird Publishers
A. & C. Black (Publishers) Ltd
Black Dog Publishing Ltd
Blackthorn Press
Bodleian Library Publishing
Bridgewater Book Co
British Library
British Library, Publishing Office
British Museum Press
Cambridge Publishing Management Ltd
Cambridge University Press
Cameron Books

Cameron & Hollis
Canongate Books
Caxton Publishing Group Ltd
Chaucer Press
Cork University Press
Crescent Moon Publishing
D & N Publishing
Richard Dennis Publications
Gerald Duckworth & Co Ltd
Elliott & Thompson
Essential Works Ltd
Four Courts Press
Gibson Square
Glasgow Museums
The Goldsmith Press Ltd
Gomer
Gothic Image Publications
Granta Editions
Green Books
Hachette Children's Books
Halsgrove
Hambledon Continuum Ltd
HarperCollins Publishers Ltd
Harvard University Press
Hayward Publishing
The Herbert Press
Hilmarton Manor Press
Alison Hodge Publishers
Hypatia Publications
The Ilex Press Ltd
Janus Publishing Co Ltd
Kegan Paul Ltd
Kew Publishing
Laurence King Publishing Ltd
Dewi Lewis Publishing
The Lilliput Press Ltd
Frances Lincoln Ltd
The Littman Library of Jewish Civilization
Liverpool University Press
Logaston Press
Lund Humphries
The Lutterworth Press
Mainstream Publishing Co (Edinburgh) Ltd
Mandrake of Oxford
The Medici Society Ltd
Melisende Publishing Ltd
Merlin Publishing/Wolfhound Press
Merrell Publishers Ltd
The MIT Press Ltd
Mitchell Beazley
Monkey Puzzle Media Ltd
John Murray Publishers
National Galleries of Scotland
National Gallery Co Ltd
National Gallery of Ireland
National Portrait Gallery Publications
The National Trust
Natural History Museum Publishing
NMS Enterprises Limited - Publishing
W. W. Norton & Company Ltd
Octopus Publishing Group
Open University Worldwide
The Orion Publishing Group Ltd
Pallas Athene
Phaidon Press Ltd
Porthill Publishers
Prestel Publishing Ltd
Quantum Publishing
Quiller Publishing Ltd
Redcliffe Press Ltd
RotoVision SA
Roundhouse Publishing Ltd
Royal Collection Publications
Sansom & Co Ltd
Saqi Books
Scala Publishers Ltd
Seren
Charles Skilton Ltd
Stacey International
Rudolf Steiner Press
Strong Oak Press
Sussex Academic Press
Sussex Publications
Symposium Publications Literary & Art
Tate Publishing

I. B. Tauris & Co Ltd
Thames & Hudson Ltd
Third Millennium Publishing Ltd
Toucan Books Ltd
Truran
Tyne Bridge Publishing
Unicorn Press
Victoria & Albert Museum Publishing
Warburg Institute
Paul Watkins Publishing
Philip Wilson Publishers
Yale University Press London

GARDENING

Absolute Press
Age Concern Books
Amolibros
Antique Collectors' Club Ltd
Arcturus Publishing Ltd
Aurum Press
Austin & Macauley Publishers Ltd
Batsford
Bene Factum Publishing Ltd
Bridgewater Book Co
Burall Floraprint
Cambridge Publishing Management Ltd
Capall Bann Publishing
Caxton Publishing Group Ltd
Centre for Alternative Technology Publications
Chalksoft Ltd
Conran Octopus
Copper Beech Publishing Ltd
Crescent Moon Publishing
The Crowood Press Ltd
D & N Publishing
Dedalus Ltd
J M Dent
Eco-logic Books
Ex Libris Press
Express Newspapers
Floris Books
Focus Publishing (Sevenoaks) Ltd
W. Foulsham & Co Ltd
Friends of the Earth
GeoCenter International Ltd
Graffeg
Green Books
HarperCollins Publishers Ltd
Hawthorn Press
Haynes Publishing
Hodder Education
Alison Hodge Publishers
How To Books Ltd
Kegan Paul Ltd
Frances Lincoln Ltd
Luath Press Ltd
Mitchell Beazley
Murdoch Books UK Ltd
The National Trust
New Island Books Ltd
W. W. Norton & Company Ltd
Octopus Publishing Group
The Orion Publishing Group Ltd
Packard Publishing Ltd
Pallas Athene
Pan Macmillan
Papadakis Publisher
Pavilion
The Penguin Group (UK) Ltd
Prestel Publishing Ltd
Quadrille Publishing Ltd
Quantum Publishing
Quiller Publishing Ltd
Search Press Ltd
SGC Books
Shire Publications Ltd
Slightly Foxed
Souvenir Press Ltd
Thames & Hudson Ltd
Think Books
Top That! Publishing Plc
Toucan Books Ltd
Transworld Publishers Ltd
Truran
Tucker Slingsby Ltd
White Ladder Press
Whittet Books Ltd
John Wiley & Sons Ltd

Willow Island Editions

GAY & LESBIAN STUDIES

Amnesty International UK
Arcadia Books Ltd
Aurora Metro Publications Ltd
Austin & Macauley Publishers Ltd
Cló Iar-Chonnachta
The Continuum International Publishing Group Ltd
Cork University Press
Gibson Square
Guildhall Press
The MIT Press Ltd
Onlywomen Press Ltd
Peter Owen Publishers
Pen Press Publishers Ltd
Routledge-Cavendish
Silver Moon Books
Charles Skilton Ltd
Taylor & Francis
Thames & Hudson Ltd
Virgin Books Ltd
Vision
The Women's Press

GENDER STUDIES

Adam Matthew Publications Ltd
Amnesty International UK
Arcadia Books Ltd
Ashgate Publishing Ltd
Attic Press
Aurora Metro Publications Ltd
Berghahn Books
Black Dog Publishing Ltd
Cambridge University Press
Capall Bann Publishing
Commonwealth Secretariat
The Continuum International Publishing Group Ltd
Cork University Press
Crescent Moon Publishing
James Currey Publishers
Economic & Social Research Institute
Edinburgh University Press
Equinox Publishing Ltd
Garnet Publishing Ltd
Global Oriental Ltd
Greenwood Publishing Group
HarperCollins Publishers Ltd
Harvard University Press
Hawthorn Press
Hodder Education
Holo Books
C. Hurst & Co (Publishers) Ltd
Icon Books Ltd
Institute of Development Studies
Intellect Ltd
Ithaca Press
Karnac Books Ltd
The Merlin Press Ltd
Merlin Publishing/Wolfhound Press
The MIT Press Ltd
Myriad Editions
National Portrait Gallery Publications
W. W. Norton & Company Ltd
Onlywomen Press Ltd
Oxfam Publishing
Palgrave Macmillan
Pathfinder Books
PCCS Books Ltd
Piatkus Books
Plowright Press
Pluto Books Ltd
The Policy Press
Polity Press
Routledge-Cavendish
Sage Publications Ltd
Saqi Books
SCM-Canterbury Press Ltd
Sheldon Press
Souvenir Press Ltd
Sussex Academic Press
I. B. Tauris & Co Ltd
Taylor & Francis
Trentham Books
University of Wales Press

Vision
The Women's Press
Word for Life Trust
Yale University Press London
Zed Books Ltd

GEOGRAPHY & GEOLOGY

Albyn Press
Amolibros
Ashgate Publishing Ltd
Atlantic Europe Publishing Co Ltd
BBC Active
Bedford Freeman Worth (BFW)
Blackstaff Press
British Geological Survey
Cambridge University Press
Chalksoft Ltd
G. L. Crowther
James Currey Publishers
D & N Publishing
Diagram Visual Information Ltd
Dunedin Academic Press
Earthscan
Ex Libris Press
Focus Publishing (Sevenoaks) Ltd
The Geographical Association
Geography Publications
Geological Society Publishing House
Global Oriental Ltd
Graffeg
HarperCollins Publishers Ltd
Hodder Education
Icon Books Ltd
Imray Laurie Norie & Wilson Ltd
Jones & Bartlett International
Kegan Paul Ltd
Letts and Lonsdale
Luath Press Ltd
McGraw-Hill Education
Maney Publishing
Manson Publishing Ltd
Mentor Books
Mercury Books
Monkey Puzzle Media Ltd
The National Academies Press
Natural History Museum Publishing
Nelson Thornes Ltd
NMS Enterprises Limited - Publishing
North York Moors National Park
W. W. Norton & Company Ltd
Old House Books
Open University Worldwide
Optimus Professional Publishing
Packard Publishing Ltd
Palgrave Macmillan
Ransom Publishing Ltd
Roadmaster Publishing
Royal Geographical Society (with Institute of British Geographers)
Scottish Cultural Press
Stacey International
Supportive Learning Publications (SLP)
Sussex Academic Press
I. B. Tauris & Co Ltd
Taylor & Francis
Trans-Pennine Publishing Ltd
Truran
TSO (The Stationery Office Ltd)
Ward Lock Educational Co Ltd
David West Children's Books
Whittles Publishing
John Wiley & Sons Ltd
WIT Press
Zeticula

GUIDE BOOKS

AA Publishing
Absolute Press
Accent Press Ltd
Age Concern Books
Akros Publications
Albyn Press
Apex Publishing Ltd
Appletree Press Ltd
Argyll Publishing

150 / PUBLISHERS CLASSIFIED BY FIELDS OF ACTIVITY

Arris Publishing Ltd
Back-In-Print Books Ltd
Birlinn Ltd
Blackstaff Press
Bossiney Books Ltd
Bradt Travel Guides Ltd
Bridgewater Book Co
British Geological Survey
Brown & Whittaker Publishing
Camra Books
Canongate Books
Capall Bann Publishing
The Catholic Truth Society
Cicerone Press Ltd
Collins Geo
Countryside Books
Crimson Publishing
D & N Publishing
Day One Publications
Discovery Walking Guides Ltd
English Heritage
Everyman's Library
Ex Libris Press
Express Newspapers
FHG Guides Ltd
Findhorn Press Ltd
Footprint Handbooks
W. Foulsham & Co Ltd
Garnet Publishing Ltd
GeoCenter International Ltd
The Geographical Association
Gill & Macmillan Ltd
Gothic Image Publications
Gracewing Publishing
Graffeg
Granta Editions
Green Books
Guildhall Press
Halsgrove
Harden's Ltd
HarperCollins Publishers Ltd
Haynes Publishing
Heart of Albion Press
Hobnob Press
Holo Books
How To Books Ltd
Instant-Books UK Ltd
Kegan Paul Ltd
Frances Lincoln Ltd
Logaston Press
Lomond Books Ltd
Luath Press Ltd
Mainstream Publishing Co (Edinburgh) Ltd
Mentor Books
Merlin Publishing/Wolfhound Press
Michelin Maps & Guides
National Gallery Co Ltd
The National Trust
New Island Books Ltd
NMS Enterprises Limited - Publishing
North York Moors National Park
The O'Brien Press Ltd
Old House Books
The Orion Publishing Group Ltd
Pallas Athene
Pan Macmillan
The Penguin Group (UK) Ltd
Prestel Publishing Ltd
Reardon Publishing
Roadmaster Publishing
Roundhouse Publishing Ltd
Royal Collection Publications
S. B. Publications
Alastair Sawday Publishing
Scala Publishers Ltd
Sheldrake Press
The Shetland Times Ltd
Shire Publications Ltd
Sigma Press
Simon & Schuster (UK) Ltd
Charles Skilton Ltd
Stacey International
Summersdale Publishers Ltd
I. B. Tauris & Co Ltd
Thames & Hudson Ltd
Think Books
Third Millennium Publishing Ltd
Top That! Publishing Plc
Travel Publishing Ltd

Troubador Publishing Ltd
Truran
Twelveheads Press
Which? Books
John Wiley & Sons Ltd
Willow Island Editions
Neil Wilson Publishing Ltd
Y Lolfa Cyf

HEALTH & BEAUTY

Age Concern Books
Amberwood Publishing Ltd
Peter Andrew Publishing Co Ltd
Apex Publishing Ltd
Argyll Publishing
Ashgrove Publishing
Aurum Press
Austin & Macauley Publishers Ltd
Duncan Baird Publishers
A. & C. Black (Publishers) Ltd
Blackstaff Press
Bloomsbury Publishing Plc
Bridgewater Book Co
Capall Bann Publishing
Carlton Publishing Group
Carroll & Brown Ltd
Class Publishing
Collins & Brown
Constable & Robinson Ltd
Paul H. Crompton Ltd
Diagram Visual Information Ltd
Eddison Sadd Editions Ltd
Essential Works Ltd
Express Newspapers
Findhorn Press Ltd
Floris Books
W. Foulsham & Co Ltd
Granta Editions
Green Books
Haldane Mason Ltd
HarperCollins Publishers Ltd
Harvard University Press
Hawker Publications
Haynes Publishing
Hodder Education
Human Kinetics Europe Ltd
Icon Books Ltd
The Ivy Press Ltd
Kegan Paul Ltd
Jessica Kingsley Publishers
Liberties Press
Frances Lincoln Ltd
Mainstream Publishing Co (Edinburgh) Ltd
Mentor Books
Merlin Publishing/Wolfhound Press
Mitchell Beazley
Monkey Puzzle Media Ltd
Murdoch Books UK Ltd
Need2Know
Nelson Thornes Ltd
Octopus Publishing Group
OICA International (UK) Ltd
On Stream Publications Ltd
The Orion Publishing Group Ltd
Pan Macmillan
Pavilion
Pen Press Publishers Ltd
The Penguin Group (UK) Ltd
Piatkus Books
Quadrille Publishing Ltd
Quantum Publishing
Robson Books
Roundhouse Publishing Ltd
SGC Books
Sheldon Press
Simon & Schuster (UK) Ltd
Souvenir Press Ltd
Speechmark Publishing Ltd
Stott's Correspondence College
Temple Lodge Publishing
Top That! Publishing Plc
Transworld Publishers Ltd
Tucker Slingsby Ltd
Virgin Books Ltd
White Ladder Press
John Wiley & Sons Ltd
The Women's Press

HISTORY & ANTIQUARIAN

Acair Ltd
Acumen Publishing Ltd
Adam Matthew Publications Ltd
Akros Publications
Al-Furqan Islamic Heritage Foundation
Albyn Press
Ian Allan Publishing Ltd
Allison & Busby
Amber Books Ltd
Amolibros
Anglo-Saxon Books
Appletree Press Ltd
Archive Editions Ltd
Arcturus Publishing Ltd
Arena Books (Publishers)
Arris Publishing Ltd
Ashgate Publishing Ltd
Ashmolean Museum Publications
Atlantic Books
Atlantic Europe Publishing Co Ltd
Barny Books
Batsford
BBC Active
The Belmont Press
Bene Factum Publishing Ltd
Berghahn Books
Birlinn Ltd
Black Ace Books
Black Dog Publishing Ltd
Blackstaff Press
Blackthorn Press
Bodleian Library Publishing
Book Castle Publishing Ltd
Borthwick Publications
Bossiney Books Ltd
Boydell & Brewer Ltd
Brewin Books Ltd
Bridge Books
Bridgewater Book Co
British Library
British Library, Publishing Office
Brown & Whittaker Publishing
Business Education Publishers
Cambridge University Press
Canongate Books
Capall Bann Publishing
Carlton Publishing Group
Carnegie Publishing Ltd
Jon Carpenter Publishing
The Catholic Truth Society
Christian Focus Publications
The Chrysalis Press
Church of Ireland Publishing
James Clarke & Co
Cló Iar-Chonnachta
Colourpoint Books
Columba
The Continuum International Publishing Group Ltd
Conway
Copper Beech Publishing Ltd
Cork University Press
Cornwall Editions Ltd
Countryside Books
Countyvise Ltd
Crécy Publishing Ltd
Cualann Press Ltd
Currach Press
James Currey Publishers
D & N Publishing
The Davenant Press
Richard Dennis Publications
J M Dent
Ashley Drake Publishing Ltd
Dramatic Lines
Gerald Duckworth & Co Ltd
Dunedin Academic Press
Edinburgh University Press
Elliott & Thompson
English Heritage
Equinox Publishing Ltd
The Erskine Press
Evangelical Press & Services Ltd
Ex Libris Press
A. & A. Farmar
Five Leaves Publications
Four Courts Press
Free Association Books
Garnet Publishing Ltd

Geddes & Grosset
Geography Publications
Gibson Square
Gill & Macmillan Ltd
Glasgow Museums
Global Oriental Ltd
Glyndwr Publishing
Alan Godfrey Maps
Gomer
Gracewing Publishing
Greenhill Books / Lionel Leventhal Ltd
Greenwood Publishing Group
Gresham Books Ltd
Guildhall Press
Gwasg Gwenfrwd
Halban Publishers
Halsgrove
Hambledon Continuum Ltd
HarperCollins Publishers Ltd
Harvard University Press
Heart of Albion Press
Helion & Co Ltd
Ian Henry Publications Ltd
Historical Publications Ltd
Hobnob Press
Hodder Education
Hodder & Stoughton General
Holo Books
House of Lochar
Icon Books Ltd
Intellect Ltd
Ithaca Press
James & James (Publishers) Ltd
Janus Publishing Co Ltd
Richard Kay Publications
Kegan Paul Ltd
The King's England Press
Landmark Publishing Ltd
Letts and Lonsdale
Liberties Press
The Lilliput Press Ltd
Little, Brown Book Group
The Littman Library of Jewish Civilization
Liverpool University Press
Logaston Press
Lomond Books Ltd
Luath Press Ltd
The Lutterworth Press
Mainstream Publishing Co (Edinburgh) Ltd
Maney Publishing
Mehring Books
Melisende Publishing Ltd
Mentor Books
Mercier Press Ltd
Mercury Books
The Merlin Press Ltd
Merlin Publishing/Wolfhound Press
Merton Priory Press Ltd
Meyrick Marketing Ltd
Microform Academic Publishers
Mitchell Beazley
Monkey Puzzle Media Ltd
Murdoch Books UK Ltd
John Murray Publishers
National Archives of Scotland
National Portrait Gallery Publications
The National Trust
Nelson Thornes Ltd
NMS Enterprises Limited - Publishing
North York Moors National Park
W. W. Norton & Company Ltd
The Nostalgia Collection
Octopus Publishing Group
Old House Books
Oldcastle Books Ltd
The Oleander Press
Oneworld Publications
Open University Worldwide
Optimus Professional Publishing
The Orion Publishing Group Ltd
Osprey Publishing Ltd
Peter Owen Publishers
Oxbow Books
Palgrave Macmillan
Pan Macmillan
Pathfinder Books

The Penguin Group (UK) Ltd
Piatkus Books
Pickering & Chatto (Publishers) Ltd
Playne Books Ltd
Plowright Press
Polity Press
Portobello Books Ltd
Profile Books
ProQuest
Quantum Publishing
Quartet Books
The Radcliffe Press
Reardon Publishing
Redcliffe Press Ltd
Reflections of a Bygone Age
Roundhouse Publishing Ltd
Royal Collection Publications
Royal Irish Academy
S. B. Publications
Saint Albert's Press
Saqi Books
Scottish Children's Press
Scottish Cultural Press
Scottish Text Society
Sessions of York
Sheaf Publishing
Sheldrake Press
Shepheard-Walwyn (Publishers) Ltd
Shire Publications Ltd
Short Books Ltd
Slightly Foxed
Smith Settle Printing & Bookbinding Ltd
Society of Antiquaries of Scotland
Society of Genealogists Enterprises Ltd
Spokesman
Sportsbooks Ltd
Stacey International
Stainer & Bell Ltd
Stenlake Publishing Ltd
Strong Oak Press
Studymates Ltd
Summersdale Publishers Ltd
Supportive Learning Publications (SLP)
Sussex Academic Press
Sussex Publications
I. B. Tauris & Co Ltd
Taylor & Francis
Tentmaker Publications
Thames & Hudson Ltd
Toucan Books Ltd
Trans-Pennine Publishing Ltd
Transworld Publishers Ltd
Troubador Publishing Ltd
Truran
Twelveheads Press
Tyne Bridge Publishing
Unicorn Press
University of Exeter Press
University of Hertfordshire Press
University of Wales Press
Vallentine Mitchell Publishers
Voltaire Foundation Ltd
Warburg Institute
Waterside Press
Waterside Press
Paul Watkins Publishing
David West Children's Books
John Wiley & Sons Ltd
Neil Wilson Publishing Ltd
World Microfilms
Yale University Press London
Zeticula

HUMOUR

Accent Press Ltd
Allison & Busby
Alma Books Ltd
Antique Collectors' Club Ltd
Apex Publishing Ltd
Appletree Press Ltd
Arcturus Publishing Ltd
Atlantic Books
Aurora Metro Publications Ltd
Aurum Press
Austin & Macauley Publishers Ltd
Authorhouse UK Ltd
Barny Books

PUBLISHERS CLASSIFIED BY FIELDS OF ACTIVITY / 151

Beautiful Books Ltd
Birlinn Ltd
Blackstaff Press
John Blake Publishing Ltd
Bodleian Library Publishing
Bridgewater Book Co
Brown Dog Books
Canongate Books
Carlton Publishing Group
Constable & Robinson Ltd
Countryside Books
Countyvise Ltd
CRW Publishing Ltd
David & Charles Ltd
Delancey Press Ltd
Gerald Duckworth & Co Ltd
Elliott & Thompson
Essential Works Ltd
Exley Publications Ltd
Express Newspapers
Eye Books Ltd
Feather Books
W. Foulsham & Co Ltd
Gibson Square
Gill & Macmillan Ltd
Gothic Image Publications
Guildhall Press
Robert Hale Ltd
HarperCollins Publishers Ltd
Ian Henry Publications Ltd
Hodder & Stoughton Faith
Hodder & Stoughton General
Holo Books
Icon Books Ltd
ISIS Publishing Ltd
Janus Publishing Co Ltd
Kingsway Publications
Lagoon Books
Jay Landesman
Little, Brown Book Group
Lomond Books Ltd
Luath Press Ltd
Mainstream Publishing Co (Edinburgh) Ltd
Maverick House Publishers
Mentor Books
Mercier Press Ltd
Merlin Publishing/Wolfhound Press
John Murray Publishers
The National Trust
New Island Books Ltd
The O'Brien Press Ltd
Octagon Press Ltd
The Oleander Press
The Orion Publishing Group Ltd
Pen Press Publishers Ltd
The Penguin Group (UK) Ltd
Piatkus Books
Porthill Publishers
Portico
Tony Potter Publishing
Quadrille Publishing Ltd
Quiller Publishing Ltd
Ravette Publishing Ltd
Reardon Publishing
Robson Books
Sandstone Press Ltd
Saqi Books
Sheldrake Press
Short Books Ltd
Simon & Schuster (UK) Ltd
Snowbooks
Souvenir Press Ltd
Summersdale Publishers Ltd
Supportive Learning Publications (SLP)
Think Books
Top That! Publishing Plc
Transworld Publishers Ltd
Troubador Publishing Ltd
Tucker Slingsby Ltd
United Writers Publications Ltd
Merlin Unwin Books Ltd
Weidenfeld & Nicolson
John Wiley & Sons Ltd
Neil Wilson Publishing Ltd
Y Lolfa Cyf
Zeticula
Zymurgy Publishing

ILLUSTRATED & FINE EDITIONS

Absolute Press
Albyn Press
Ashgate Publishing Ltd
Birlinn Ltd
Blackstaff Press
Bridgewater Book Co
British Library
British Library, Publishing Office
Canongate Books
Richard Dennis Publications
Enitharmon Press
The Erskine Press
Essential Works Ltd
Everyman's Library
Express Newspapers
Global Oriental Ltd
Granta Editions
Halsgrove
HarperCollins Publishers Ltd
The Herbert Press
The Ivy Press Ltd
Kegan Paul Ltd
Dewi Lewis Publishing
The Lilliput Press Ltd
Frances Lincoln Ltd
Lomond Books Ltd
The Lutterworth Press
Mainstream Publishing Co (Edinburgh) Ltd
Maney Publishing
Melisende Publishing Ltd
Merrell Publishers Ltd
Mitchell Beazley
National Portrait Gallery Publications
The Old Stile Press
The Orion Publishing Group Ltd
Phaidon Press Ltd
Piquant Editions
Quiller Publishing Ltd
Royal Collection Publications
Sandstone Press Ltd
Scala Publishers Ltd
Shepheard-Walwyn (Publishers) Ltd
Charles Skilton Ltd
Slightly Foxed
Smith Settle Printing & Bookbinding Ltd
Snowbooks
The Society for Promoting Christian Knowledge (SPCK)
Stacey International
Tartarus Press
Thames & Hudson Ltd
Think Books
University of Wales Press
Merlin Unwin Books Ltd
Veloce Publishing Ltd
Virgin Books Ltd
Weidenfeld & Nicolson
Whittet Books Ltd
Yale University Press London
Zymurgy Publishing

INDUSTRY, BUSINESS & MANAGEMENT

Accent Press Ltd
Amnesty International UK
Peter Andrew Publishing Co Ltd
Arena Books (Publishers)
Ashgate Publishing Ltd
Atlantic Books
Aurelian Information Ltd
AVA Publishing (UK) Ltd
Barny Books
BCR Publishing Ltd
Bene Factum Publishing Ltd
Blackhall Publishing
BookPower
Nicholas Brealey Publishing
Business Education Publishers
Cambridge Publishing Management Ltd
Cambridge University Press
Carnegie Publishing Ltd
Cengage Learning EMEA
Centre for Economic Policy Research
Chartered Institute of Personnel & Development
Commonwealth Secretariat
Construction Industry Research & Information Association (CIRIA)
Crimson Publishing
Earthscan
Edward Elgar Publishing Ltd
Elm Publications
Emerald Group Publishing Ltd
Energy Institute
Ethics International Press Ltd
Euromonitor International Plc
Executive Grapevine International Ltd
W. Foulsham & Co Ltd
Gower Publishing Co Ltd
Greenleaf Publishing
Greenwood Publishing Group
HarperCollins Publishers Ltd
Hawthorn Press
Hodder Education
How To Books Ltd
ICSA Information & Training Ltd
The Ilex Press Ltd
Imperial College Press
Institute for Employment Studies
Institute of Development Studies
IWA Publishing
James & James (Publishers) Ltd
Jane's Information Group Ltd
Jordan Publishing Ltd
Kogan Page Ltd
McGraw-Hill Education
Management Pocketbooks Ltd
Market House Books Ltd
Mentor Books
The MIT Press Ltd
The National Academies Press
Nelson Thornes Ltd
Oak Tree Press
OICA International (UK) Ltd
Open University Worldwide
Palgrave Macmillan
Pen Press Publishers Ltd
The Penguin Group (UK) Ltd
Piatkus Books
Princeton University Press
Profile Books
Radcliffe Publishing Ltd
Round Hall Ltd
Roundhouse Publishing Ltd
Sage Publications Ltd
Sessions of York
Sherwood Publishing
Simon & Schuster (UK) Ltd
Social Affairs Unit
Souvenir Press Ltd
Studymates Ltd
Sussex Academic Press
Taylor & Francis
Thorogood Publishing Ltd
Trotman Publishing
Troubador Publishing Ltd
Tru-Est Ltd
TSO (The Stationery Office) Ltd)
United Writers Publications Ltd
Weidenfeld & Nicolson
John Wiley & Sons Ltd
WIT Press
Witherby Seamanship International
Woodhead Publishing Ltd
XPL Publishing
Zambezi Publishing Ltd

LANGUAGES & LINGUISTICS

Anglo-Saxon Books
Appletree Press Ltd
Association for Scottish Literary Studies
Audio-Forum - The Language Source
b small publishing ltd
BBC Active
Berghahn Books
Joseph Biddulph Publisher
Brilliant Publications
Cambridge University Press
Carel Press
Channel View Publications Ltd
CILT, the National Centre for Languages
Cló Iar-Chonnachta
Cois Life
The Continuum International Publishing Group Ltd
Ashley Drake Publishing Ltd
Edinburgh University Press
Emerald Group Publishing Ltd
Equinox Publishing Ltd
GeoCenter International Ltd
Geography Publications
Global Oriental Ltd
Gomer
Gwasg Gwenffrwd
HarperCollins Publishers Ltd
Hodder Education
How To Books Ltd
Icon Books Ltd
Intellect Ltd
Ithaca Press
Jarndyce Booksellers
Kegan Paul Ltd
Letts and Lonsdale
Lexus Ltd
Libris Ltd
Liverpool University Press
Luath Press Ltd
Macmillan Education
Maney Publishing
Mentor Books
Milet Publishing Ltd
The MIT Press Ltd
National Extension College Trust Ltd
Nelson Thornes Ltd
The Oleander Press
Open University Worldwide
Packard Publishing Ltd
Palgrave Macmillan
Paragon Publishing
Portico
Royal Irish Academy
Scottish Children's Press
Scottish Cultural Press
Speechmark Publishing Ltd
Stacey International
Studymates Ltd
Ta Ha Publishers Ltd
Taigh na Teud Music Publishers
Taylor & Francis
Troubador Publishing Ltd
Truran
University of Wales Press
Laurence Urdang Inc
Usborne Publishing Ltd
Voltaire Foundation Ltd
Waterside Press
Paul Watkins Publishing
John Wiley & Sons Ltd
Y Lolfa Cyf
Yale University Press London

LAW

Amnesty International International Secretariat
Amnesty International UK
Peter Andrew Publishing Co Ltd
Ashgate Publishing Ltd
Atlantic Books
Bartsky Ltd
Bene Factum Publishing Ltd
Joseph Biddulph Publisher
Blackhall Publishing
Borthwick Publications
Business Education Publishers
Cambridge University Press
Class Publishing
Commonwealth Secretariat
Delta Alpha Publishing Ltd
J M Dent
Earthscan
Edinburgh University Press
Edward Elgar Publishing Ltd
Four Courts Press
Global Professional Publishing
Gower Publishing Co Ltd
Granta Editions
W. Green The Scottish Law Publisher
Greenwood Publishing Group
Hachette Livre UK Ltd
Hart Publishing
Harvard University Press
Hodder Education
Holo Books
How To Books Ltd
Incorporated Council of Law Reporting for England and Wales
Institute for Fiscal Studies
Institute of Employment Rights
The Islamic Texts Society
Ithaca Press
Jones & Bartlett International
Jordan Publishing Ltd
Kegan Paul Ltd
Jessica Kingsley Publishers
Kube Publishing Ltd
Law Society Publishing
Lawpack Publishing Ltd
Leatherhead Food International
Legal Action Group
McGraw-Hill Education
Market House Books Ltd
Merlin Publishing/Wolfhound Press
National Extension College Trust Ltd
National Housing Federation
Oak Tree Press
Oxford University Press
Palgrave Macmillan
Pearson Education Ltd
Pluto Books Ltd
Round Hall Ltd
Routledge-Cavendish
Russell House Publishing Ltd
Shaw & Sons Ltd
SLS Legal Publications (NI)
Studymates Ltd
Summersdale Publishers Ltd
Sussex Academic Press
Taylor & Francis
Thomson International Legal & Regulatory
Thorogood Publishing Ltd
Trentham Books
Tru-Est Ltd
TSO (The Stationery Office Ltd)
Waterside Press
Waterside Press
Weidenfeld & Nicolson
Which? Books
Witherby Seamanship International
Woodhead Publishing Ltd
XPL Publishing

LITERATURE & CRITICISM

Adam Matthew Publications Ltd
Akros Publications
Albyn Press
Allison & Busby
Amolibros
Appletree Press Ltd
Arena Books (Publishers)
Ashgate Publishing Ltd
Association for Scottish Literary Studies
Atlantic Books
Austin & Macauley Publishers Ltd
Back-In-Print Books Ltd
Beautiful Books Ltd
Berghahn Books
Blackstaff Press
Blackthorn Press
Bloodaxe Books Ltd
Bodleian Library Publishing
Marion Boyars Publishers Ltd
Boydell & Brewer Ltd
Brandon/Mount Eagle Publications
Cambridge University Press
Canongate Books
Carel Press
Chaucer Press
The Chrysalis Press
Classical Comics Ltd
Cló Iar-Chonnachta
Cois Life

The Continuum International
 Publishing Group Ltd
Cork University Press
Crescent Moon Publishing
James Currey Publishers
Dedalus Ltd
J M Dent
Dionysia Press Ltd
Ashley Drake Publishing Ltd
Gerald Duckworth & Co Ltd
Edinburgh University Press
Elliott & Thompson
Enitharmon Press
Everyman's Library
Faber & Faber Ltd
Feather Books
Freelance Market News
Garnet Publishing Ltd
Gill & Macmillan Ltd
Global Oriental Ltd
The Goldsmith Press Ltd
Gomer
Green Books
Greenwood Publishing Group
Guildhall Press
Gwasg Gwenffrwd
Halban Publishers
HarperCollins Publishers Ltd
Harvard University Press
Hippopotamus Press
Hobnob Press
Hodder Education
How To Books Ltd
Icon Books Ltd
Intellect Ltd
Ithaca Press
Janus Publishing Co Ltd
Jarndyce Booksellers
Jay Landesman
Liberties Press
Libris Ltd
The Lilliput Press Ltd
Little, Brown Book Group
The Littman Library of Jewish
 Civilization
Liverpool University Press
Living Time® Media International
Luath Press Ltd
The Lutterworth Press
Mainstream Publishing Co
 (Edinburgh) Ltd
Mandrake of Oxford
Maney Publishing
Mehring Books
Mercier Press Ltd
Mercury Books
Merlin Publishing/Wolfhound
 Press
Microform Academic Publishers
NATE (National Association for the
 Teaching of English)
National Portrait Gallery
 Publications
Nelson Thornes Ltd
New Island Books Ltd
Northcote House Publishers Ltd
W. W. Norton & Company Ltd
Oldcastle Books Ltd
The Oleander Press
Oneworld Classics
Oneworld Publications
Onlywomen Press Ltd
Open University Worldwide
Peter Owen Publishers
Oxbow Books
Palgrave Macmillan
Pan Macmillan
Pen Press Publishers Ltd
The Penguin Group (UK) Ltd
Pickering & Chatto (Publishers) Ltd
Pipers' Ash Ltd
Pluto Books Ltd
Polity Press
ProQuest
Redcliffe Press Ltd
Roundhouse Publishing Ltd
Salt Publishing Ltd
Sandstone Press Ltd
Sansom & Co Ltd
Saqi Books
Scottish Cultural Press
Scottish Text Society

Seren
Charles Skilton Ltd
Colin Smythe Ltd
Souvenir Press Ltd
Stenlake Publishing Ltd
Studymates Ltd
Sussex Academic Press
Sussex Publications
The Swedenborg Society
Symposium Publications Literary &
 Art
Tabb House
Tartarus Press
Taylor & Francis
Thames & Hudson Ltd
Troubador Publishing Ltd
University of Exeter Press
University of Hertfordshire Press
University of Wales Press
Voltaire Foundation Ltd
Waterside Press
John Wiley & Sons Ltd
The Women's Press
Wordsworth Editions Ltd

MAGIC & THE OCCULT

Amolibros
Arcturus Publishing Ltd
Austin & Macauley Publishers Ltd
Duncan Baird Publishers
The Banton Press
Blue Beyond Books
Bossiney Books Ltd
Bridgewater Book Co
Capall Bann Publishing
Caxton Publishing Group Ltd
Collins & Brown
Crescent Moon Publishing
Eddison Sadd Editions Ltd
Focus Publishing (Sevenoaks) Ltd
W. Foulsham & Co Ltd
Geddes & Grosset
Godsfield Press Ltd
Gothic Image Publications
Green Magic
Robert Hale Ltd
HarperCollins Publishers Ltd
Heart of Albion Press
John Hunt Publishing Ltd
Janus Publishing Co Ltd
Kegan Paul Ltd
Luath Press Ltd
Mandrake of Oxford
Octagon Press Ltd
Pen Press Publishers Ltd
Piatkus Books
Quadrille Publishing Ltd
Quantum Publishing
Reardon Publishing
Regency House Publishing Ltd
The Society of Metaphysicians Ltd
Souvenir Press Ltd
Rudolf Steiner Press
Temple Lodge Publishing
Thames & Hudson Ltd
Thoth Publications
Troubador Publishing Ltd
Warburg Institute
John Wiley & Sons Ltd
Word for Life Trust
Zambezi Publishing Ltd

MATHEMATICS & STATISTICS

Al-Furqan Islamic Heritage
 Foundation
Amnesty International UK
Anshan Ltd
Atlantic Books
Atlantic Europe Publishing Co Ltd
Bernard Babani (Publishing) Ltd
BBC Active
BEAM Education
Bedford Freeman Worth (BFW)
Blackstaff Press
Cambridge University Press
Carel Press
Chalksoft Ltd
Claire Publications
Economic & Social Research
 Institute

Focus Publishing (Sevenoaks) Ltd
Global Professional Publishing
Hodder Education
Icon Books Ltd
Imperial College Press
The Institute of Mathematics and
 its Applications
IOP Publishing
Jones & Bartlett International
S. Karger AG
Letts and Lonsdale
McGraw-Hill Education
Mentor Books
The National Academies Press
National Extension College Trust
 Ltd
Nelson Thornes Ltd
W. W. Norton & Company Ltd
Open University Worldwide
Palgrave Macmillan
ProQuest
Sage Publications Ltd
Studymates Ltd
Supportive Learning Publications
 (SLP)
Tarquin Publications
Taylor & Francis
TSO (The Stationery Office Ltd)
University of Hertfordshire Press
Ward Lock Educational Co Ltd
John Wiley & Sons Ltd
WIT Press

**MEDICAL (INCL. SELF HELP &
ALTERNATIVE MEDICINE)**

Accent Press Ltd
Age Concern Books
Amberwood Publishing Ltd
American Psychiatric Publishing
 Inc
Anshan Ltd
Apex Publishing Ltd
Arcturus Publishing Ltd
Argyll Publishing
Ashgrove Publishing
Austin & Macauley Publishers Ltd
Duncan Baird Publishers
Barny Books
Bartsky Ltd
Bene Factum Publishing Ltd
BLA Publishing Ltd
Blackhall Publishing
Blackstaff Press
BookPower
Bridgewater Book Co
CABI
*Cambridge Publishing
 Management Ltd*
Cambridge University Press
Capall Bann Publishing
Jon Carpenter Publishing
Carroll & Brown Ltd
Caxton Publishing Group Ltd
Class Publishing
Collins & Brown
Columba
Constable & Robinson Ltd
Corpus Publishing Ltd
Paul H. Crompton Ltd
D & N Publishing
Denor Press Ltd
Economic & Social Research
 Institute
Eddison Sadd Editions Ltd
Elsevier Ltd
The Erskine Press
Essential Works Ltd
Findhorn Press Ltd
Floris Books
Focus Publishing (Sevenoaks) Ltd
W. Foulsham & Co Ltd
Free Association Books
Geddes & Grosset
Godsfield Press Ltd
Granta Editions
Green Magic
Greenwood Publishing Group
Hachette Livre UK Ltd
Haldane Mason Ltd
HarperCollins Publishers Ltd
Hawker Publications

Haynes Publishing
Ian Henry Publications Ltd
Hodder Education
Hodder & Stoughton Faith
How To Books Ltd
Human Kinetics Europe Ltd
Immunisation Information
Imperial College Press
Institute of Physics & Engineering
 in Medicine
International Medical Press
Janus Publishing Co Ltd
Jones & Bartlett International
S. Karger AG
Richard Kay Publications
Kegan Paul Ltd
Jessica Kingsley Publishers
Kingsway Publications
Little, Brown Book Group
Luath Press Ltd
McGraw-Hill Education
Mainstream Publishing Co
 (Edinburgh) Ltd
Mandrake of Oxford
Maney Publishing
Manson Publishing Ltd
Market House Books Ltd
Mitchell Beazley
The National Academies Press
National Extension College Trust
 Ltd
Need2Know
Nelson Thornes Ltd
OICA International (UK) Ltd
Open University Worldwide
Oxford University Press
Palgrave Macmillan
Pavilion Publishing (Brighton) Ltd
PCCS Books Ltd
Pen Press Publishers Ltd
The Penguin Group (UK) Ltd
The Pharmaceutical Press
Piatkus Books
Portland Press Ltd
Professional Engineering
 Publishing
ProQuest
Publishing House
Quadrille Publishing Ltd
Quantum Publishing
Quintessence Publishing Co Ltd
Radcliffe Publishing Ltd
Round Hall Ltd
Roundhouse Publishing Ltd
Routledge-Cavendish
Royal College of General
 Practitioners
Royal College of Psychiatrists
Royal Society of Medicine Press
 Ltd
Scion Publishing Ltd
Sheldon Press
Simon & Schuster (UK) Ltd
Social Affairs Unit
The Society for Promoting
 Christian Knowledge (SPCK)
The Society of Metaphysicians Ltd
Souvenir Press Ltd
Speechmark Publishing Ltd
Springer Verlag London
Rudolf Steiner Press
Stokesby House Publications
Studymates Ltd
Taylor & Francis
Temple Lodge Publishing
Troubador Publishing Ltd
TSO (The Stationery Office Ltd)
Merlin Unwin Books Ltd
Whiting & Birch Ltd
John Wiley & Sons Ltd
WIT Press
Wolters Kluwer Health (P & E) Ltd
Word for Life Trust
XPL Publishing
Zambezi Publishing Ltd

MILITARY & WAR

A.M.S. Educational Ltd
Air-Britain (Historians) Ltd
Ian Allan Publishing Ltd
Amber Books Ltd

Amnesty International UK
Anglo-Saxon Books
Apex Publishing Ltd
Appletree Press Ltd
Arcturus Publishing Ltd
Ashgate Publishing Ltd
Atlantic Books
Aurum Press
Austin & Macauley Publishers Ltd
Back-In-Print Books Ltd
Barny Books
Bene Factum Publishing Ltd
Berghahn Books
Birlinn Ltd
BLA Publishing Ltd
Blackstaff Press
Bodleian Library Publishing
Boydell & Brewer Ltd
Brewin Books Ltd
Bridge Books
Brooklands Books Ltd
Business Education Publishers
*Cambridge Publishing
 Management Ltd*
Carlton Publishing Group
Caxton Publishing Group Ltd
Chatham Publishing
Constable & Robinson Ltd
Conway
Crécy Publishing Ltd
The Crowood Press Ltd
Cualann Press Ltd
D & N Publishing
David & Charles Ltd
Elliott & Thompson
English Heritage
The Erskine Press
Essential Works Ltd
Eye Books Ltd
Focus Publishing (Sevenoaks) Ltd
W. Foulsham & Co Ltd
Glyndwr Publishing
*Graham-Cameron Publishing &
 Illustration*
Greenhill Books / Lionel Leventhal
 Ltd
Greenwood Publishing Group
Grub Street
Robert Hale Ltd
Halsgrove
Hambledon Continuum Ltd
HarperCollins Publishers Ltd
Harvard University Press
Haynes Publishing
Helion & Co Ltd
Hodder & Stoughton General
Icon Books Ltd
Jane's Information Group Ltd
Janus Publishing Co Ltd
Richard Kay Publications
Little, Brown Book Group
Luath Press Ltd
The Lutterworth Press
Mainstream Publishing Co
 (Edinburgh) Ltd
Maritime Books
Maverick House Publishers
Mercury Books
Microform Academic Publishers
Middleton Press
John Murray Publishers
Myriad Editions
NMS Enterprises Limited -
 Publishing
W. W. Norton & Company Ltd
The Nostalgia Collection
Oneworld Publications
The Orion Publishing Group Ltd
Osprey Publishing Ltd
Pathfinder Books
Pen Press Publishers Ltd
The Penguin Group (UK) Ltd
Piatkus Books
Quantum Publishing
Quiller Publishing Ltd
The Radcliffe Press
Rand Publications
Reardon Publishing
Regency House Publishing Ltd
Ripping Yarns.com
Roundhouse Publishing Ltd
Scottish Cultural Press

PUBLISHERS CLASSIFIED BY FIELDS OF ACTIVITY / 153

Shire Publications Ltd
Sigel Press
Charles Skilton Ltd
Souvenir Press Ltd
Spokesman
Stacey International
Strong Oak Press
Studymates Ltd
Sussex Academic Press
I. B. Tauris & Co Ltd
Taylor & Francis
Thames & Hudson Ltd
Third Millennium Publishing Ltd
Thorogood Publishing Ltd
Trans-Pennine Publishing Ltd
Transworld Publishers Ltd
Troubador Publishing Ltd
Truran
Tyne Bridge Publishing
Unicorn Press
United Writers Publications Ltd
University of Wales Press
Merlin Unwin Books Ltd
Virgin Books Ltd
Vision
David West Children's Books
Whittles Publishing
John Wiley & Sons Ltd
Neil Wilson Publishing Ltd
Worth Press Ltd
Yale University Press London
Zeticula

MUSIC

Amolibros
Appletree Press Ltd
Arc Publications Ltd
Arcturus Publishing Ltd
Ashgate Publishing Ltd
Atlantic Books
Attic Press
Aureus Publishing Ltd
Aurum Press
Beautiful Books Ltd
BLA Publishing Ltd
A. & C. Black (Publishers) Ltd
Black Dog Publishing Ltd
Black Spring Press Ltd
Blackstaff Press
John Blake Publishing Ltd
Blue Beyond Books
Blue Sky Press
Marion Boyars Publishers Ltd
Boydell & Brewer Ltd
Bridgewater Book Co
British Library, Publishing Office
Cambridge University Press
Canongate Books
Capall Bann Publishing
Carlton Publishing Group
Chalksoft Ltd
Cló Iar-Chonnachta
Collins & Brown
The Continuum International Publishing Group Ltd
Cork University Press
Crescent Moon Publishing
Currach Press
Dance Books Ltd
J M Dent
Dunedin Academic Press
Elliott & Thompson
Equinox Publishing Ltd
Essential Works Ltd
Faber & Faber Ltd
Feather Books
Focus Publishing (Sevenoaks) Ltd
GeoCenter International Ltd
Granta Editions
Greenwood Publishing Group
Gresham Books Ltd
Guildhall Press
Robert Hale Ltd
Harvard University Press
Hawthorn Press
Haynes Publishing
Jay Landesman
Libris Ltd
The Lilliput Press Ltd
Little, Brown Book Group

The Littman Library of Jewish Civilization
Luath Press Ltd
McCrimmon Publishing Co Ltd
Mainstream Publishing Co (Edinburgh) Ltd
Market House Books Ltd
Kevin Mayhew Ltd
Merlin Publishing/Wolfhound Press
The MIT Press Ltd
Mitchell Beazley
Moorley's Print & Publishing Ltd
W. W. Norton & Company Ltd
Oldcastle Books Ltd
Omnibus Press
Ovolo Publishing Ltd
Peter Owen Publishers
Packard Publishing Ltd
Pavilion
PC Publishing
Pen Press Publishers Ltd
The Penguin Group (UK) Ltd
Phaidon Press
Piatkus Books
Portico
Prestel Publishing Ltd
ProQuest
Quantum Publishing
Quartet Books
Robson Books
RotoVision SA
Roundhouse Publishing Ltd
SchoolPlay Productions Ltd
Schott Music Ltd
SCM-Canterbury Press Ltd
Scripture Union Publishing
The Shetland Times Ltd
Simon & Schuster (UK) Ltd
Souvenir Press Ltd
Spartan Press Music Publishers Ltd
Stainer & Bell Ltd
Rudolf Steiner Press
Sussex Academic Press
Sussex Publications
Taigh na Teud Music Publishers
Taylor & Francis
Thames & Hudson Ltd
Transworld Publishers Ltd
University of Wales Press
Usborne Publishing Ltd
Virgin Books Ltd
Ward Lock Educational Co Ltd
David West Children's Books
Wild Goose Publications
John Wiley & Sons Ltd
Neil Wilson Publishing Ltd
Y Lolfa Cyf
Yale University Press London

NATURAL HISTORY

AA Publishing
Antique Collectors' Club Ltd
Arcturus Publishing Ltd
Argyll Publishing
Arris Publishing Ltd
Atlantic Books
Aurum Press
Austin & Macauley Publishers Ltd
Duncan Baird Publishers
Bender Richardson White
BLA Publishing Ltd
A. & C. Black (Publishers) Ltd
Blackstaff Press
Bridgewater Book Co
British Library, Publishing Office
British Museum Press
Brown & Whittaker Publishing
Calypso Publications
Cambridge Publishing Management Ltd
Cambridge University Press
Cameron Books
Capall Bann Publishing
Carlton Publishing Group
Carnegie Publishing Ltd
Caxton Publishing Group Ltd
Chalksoft Ltd
Cornwall Editions Ltd
Countyvise Ltd
The Crowood Press Ltd

D & N Publishing
David & Charles Ltd
The Erskine Press
Ex Libris Press
Focus Publishing (Sevenoaks) Ltd
Graffeg
Graham-Cameron Publishing & Illustration
Granta Editions
Green Books
Haldane Mason Ltd
Robert Hale Ltd
Halsgrove
HarperCollins Publishers Ltd
Harvard University Press
Hodder Education
Alison Hodge Publishers
Icon Books Ltd
Kegan Paul Ltd
Logaston Press
Lomond Books Ltd
Luath Press Ltd
The Lutterworth Press
The MIT Press Ltd
Mitchell Beazley
Monkey Puzzle Media Ltd
The National Academies Press
The National Trust
Natural History Museum Publishing
Newpro UK Ltd
NMS Enterprises Limited - Publishing
North York Moors National Park
W. W. Norton & Company Ltd
Octopus Publishing Group
Old House Books
Open University Worldwide
Optimus Professional Publishing
The Orion Publishing Group Ltd
Oxbow Books
Packard Publishing Ltd
Papadakis Publisher
The Penguin Group (UK) Ltd
Philip's
Quantum Publishing
Quiller Publishing Ltd
Reardon Publishing
The Richmond Publishing Co
Roundhouse Publishing Ltd
Royal Collection Publications
S. B. Publications
Scottish Children's Press
Scottish Cultural Press
Sessions of York
SGC Books
The Shetland Times Ltd
Shire Publications Ltd
Souvenir Press Ltd
Stacey International
Stobart Davies Ltd
Thames & Hudson Ltd
Think Books
Top That! Publishing Plc
Toucan Books Ltd
Troubador Publishing Ltd
Truran
Merlin Unwin Books Ltd
Usborne Publishing Ltd
David West Children's Books
White Ladder Press
Whittet Books Ltd
Whittles Publishing
John Wiley & Sons Ltd
Willow Island Editions
Yale University Press London
Zymurgy Publishing

NAUTICAL

Adlard Coles Nautical
Ian Allan Publishing Ltd
Amber Books Ltd
Amolibros
Austin & Macauley Publishers Ltd
The Belmont Press
BLA Publishing Ltd
A. & C. Black (Publishers) Ltd
Brown, Son & Ferguson, Ltd
Chatham Publishing
Conway
Crécy Publishing Ltd

The Crowood Press Ltd
Ex Libris Press
Focus Publishing (Sevenoaks) Ltd
Glyndwr Publishing
Granta Editions
Haynes Publishing
Imray Laurie Norie & Wilson Ltd
Jane's Information Group Ltd
Janus Publishing Co Ltd
Middleton Press
The National Academies Press
W. W. Norton & Company Ltd
The Nostalgia Collection
The Orion Publishing Group Ltd
Oxbow Books
Professional Engineering Publishing
Quantum Publishing
Quiller Publishing Ltd
Reardon Publishing
Roadmaster Publishing
Scottish Cultural Press
Special Interest Model Books Ltd
Stenlake Publishing Ltd
Truran
TSO (The Stationery Office Ltd)
Twelveheads Press
Tyne Bridge Publishing
Unicorn Press
United Writers Publications Ltd
Paul Watkins Publishing
Whittles Publishing
Neil Wilson Publishing Ltd
Witherby Seamanship International

PHILOSOPHY

Acumen Publishing Ltd
Alban Books Ltd
Amolibros
Apex Publishing Ltd
Arcturus Publishing Ltd
Arena Books (Publishers)
Ashgate Publishing Ltd
Atlantic Books
Austin & Macauley Publishers Ltd
Duncan Baird Publishers
Black Ace Books
Black Dog Publishing Ltd
Blue Beyond Books
Marion Boyars Publishers Ltd
Boydell & Brewer Ltd
Cambridge University Press
Canongate Books
Capall Bann Publishing
Jon Carpenter Publishing
T. & T. Clark
James Clarke & Co
The Continuum International Publishing Group Ltd
Cork University Press
Crescent Moon Publishing
Darton, Longman & Todd Ltd
Dunedin Academic Press
Edinburgh University Press
Emerald Group Publishing Ltd
Equinox Publishing Ltd
Everyman's Library
Fabian Society
Floris Books
Four Courts Press
Free Association Books
Gibson Square
Global Oriental Ltd
Gothic Image Publications
Gracewing Publishing
Green Books
Greenwood Publishing Group
Halban Publishers
Harvard University Press
Heart of Albion Press
Hodder Education
John Hunt Publishing Ltd
Icon Books Ltd
Imprint Academic
Intellect Ltd
Janus Publishing Co Ltd
Kegan Paul Ltd
Letts and Lonsdale
The Littman Library of Jewish Civilization

Living Time® Media International
The Lutterworth Press
McGraw-Hill Education
Mandrake of Oxford
The MIT Press Ltd
W. W. Norton & Company Ltd
Octagon Press Ltd
Oneworld Publications
Open Gate Press
The Orion Publishing Group Ltd
Palgrave Macmillan
Pathfinder Books
Pen Press Publishers Ltd
The Penguin Group (UK) Ltd
Pipers' Ash Ltd
Pluto Books Ltd
Polity Press
Mathew Price Ltd
Princeton University Press
Roundhouse Publishing Ltd
Routledge-Cavendish
St Pauls Publishing
Saqi Books
SCM-Canterbury Press Ltd
Shepheard-Walwyn (Publishers) Ltd
Short Books Ltd
The Society of Metaphysicians Ltd
Souvenir Press Ltd
Spokesman
Rudolf Steiner Press
Sussex Academic Press
Taylor & Francis
Temple Lodge Publishing
Thames & Hudson Ltd
Troubador Publishing Ltd
University of Wales Press
Merlin Unwin Books Ltd
Veritas Publications
Voltaire Foundation Ltd
Warburg Institute
Weidenfeld & Nicolson
John Wiley & Sons Ltd
Windhorse Publications
Yale University Press London

PHOTOGRAPHY

Akros Publications
Arcadia Books Ltd
Aurum Press
AVA Publishing (UK) Ltd
Black Dog Publishing Ltd
Blackstaff Press
Bridgewater Book Co
Cló Iar-Chonnachta
Collins & Brown
Cork University Press
Crescent Moon Publishing
Currach Press
D & N Publishing
David & Charles Ltd
Essential Works Ltd
Eye Books Ltd
Flambard Press
Focus Publishing (Sevenoaks) Ltd
Freelance Market News
Garnet Publishing Ltd
GeoCenter International Ltd
Gomer
Gothic Image Publications
Graffeg
Guildhall Press
Robert Hale Ltd
HarperCollins Publishers Ltd
Haynes Publishing
Hayward Publishing
Alison Hodge Publishers
The Ilex Press Ltd
In Easy Steps Ltd
Dewi Lewis Publishing
Libris Ltd
The Lilliput Press Ltd
Luath Press Ltd
Lund Humphries
Mainstream Publishing Co (Edinburgh) Ltd
Mentor Books
Merlin Publishing/Wolfhound Press
Merrell Publishers Ltd
Meyrick Marketing Ltd

154 / PUBLISHERS CLASSIFIED BY FIELDS OF ACTIVITY

The MIT Press Ltd
Mitchell Beazley
National Galleries of Scotland
National Portrait Gallery
 Publications
New Internationalist Publications
 Ltd
Newpro UK Ltd
Papadakis Publisher
Pavilion
The Penguin Group (UK) Ltd
Phaidon Press Ltd
Prestel Publishing Ltd
Quadrille Publishing Ltd
Quantum Publishing
RotoVision SA
Roundhouse Publishing Ltd
Royal Collection Publications
Saqi Books
Stacey International
Tate Publishing
Teneues Publishing UK Ltd
Thames & Hudson Ltd
Third Millennium Publishing Ltd
Truran
Unicorn Press
Merlin Unwin Books Ltd
Victoria & Albert Museum
 Publishing
Weidenfeld & Nicolson
John Wiley & Sons Ltd
Neil Wilson Publishing Ltd
Yale University Press London
Zymurgy Publishing

PHYSICS

Anshan Ltd
Atlantic Europe Publishing Co Ltd
BBC Active
Bedford Freeman Worth (BFW)
BLA Publishing Ltd
Cambridge University Press
Canopus Publishing Ltd
HarperCollins Publishers Ltd
Hodder Education
Icon Books Ltd
Imperial College Press
Institute of Physics & Engineering
 in Medicine
IOP Publishing
Jones & Bartlett International
Letts and Lonsdale
McGraw-Hill Education
Multi Science Publishing Co Ltd
The National Academies Press
National Extension College Trust
 Ltd
Nelson Thornes Ltd
W. W. Norton & Company Ltd
Open University Worldwide
Palgrave Macmillan
ProQuest
Studymates Ltd
Taylor & Francis
Ward Lock Educational Co Ltd
John Wiley & Sons Ltd

POETRY

Acair Ltd
Accent Press Ltd
Akros Publications
Albyn Press
Amolibros
Anglo-Saxon Books
Anvil Press Poetry Ltd
Apex Publishing Ltd
Arc Publications Ltd
Arcturus Publishing Ltd
Association for Scottish Literary
 Studies
Atlantic Books
Authorhouse UK Ltd
Barddas
Joseph Biddulph Publisher
Blackstaff Press
Bloodaxe Books Ltd
Blue Beyond Books
Blue Sky Press
Brown & Whittaker Publishing
Canongate Books

Cló Iar-Chonnachta
Cois Life
Countyvise Ltd
Crescent Moon Publishing
Dreamcatcher Publishing Ltd
Elliott & Thompson
Enitharmon Press
Ex Libris Press
Express Newspapers
Faber & Faber Ltd
Feather Books
Five Leaves Publications
Flambard Press
W. Foulsham & Co Ltd
Freelance Market News
The Gallery Press
The Goldsmith Press Ltd
Gomer
Guildhall Press
Gwasg Gwenffrwd
Hachette Children's Books
HarperCollins Publishers Ltd
Hippopotamus Press
Icon Books Ltd
ISIS Publishing Ltd
Janus Publishing Co Ltd
Jarndyce Booksellers
Kegan Paul Ltd
The King's England Press
Jay Landesman
Libris Ltd
Little, Brown Book Group
Living Time® Media International
Luath Press Ltd
Macmillan Children's Books Ltd
Mandrake of Oxford
Mentor Books
Mercier Press Ltd
Merlin Publishing/Wolfhound
 Press
Methodist Publishing House
Moorley's Print & Publishing Ltd
New Island Books Ltd
NMS Enterprises Limited -
 Publishing
W. W. Norton & Company Ltd
Octagon Press Ltd
The Old Stile Press
The Oleander Press
Oneworld Classics
Paragon Publishing
Pen Press Publishers Ltd
The Penguin Group (UK) Ltd
Pentathol Publishing
Pipers' Ash Ltd
ProQuest
Redcliffe Press Ltd
Route Publishing Ltd
Saint Albert's Press
Salt Publishing Ltd
Saqi Books
Scottish Children's Press
Scottish Cultural Press
Scottish Text Society
Seren
Sessions of York
Charles Skilton Ltd
Spokesman
Stenlake Publishing Ltd
Studymates Ltd
Summer Palace Press
Symposium Publications Literary &
 Art
Tabb House
Triumph House
Troubador Publishing Ltd
University of Wales Press
Upfront Publishing
John Wiley & Sons Ltd
Wordsworth Editions Ltd

POLITICS & WORLD AFFAIRS

Acumen Publishing Ltd
Amnesty International
 International Secretariat
Amnesty International UK
Amolibros
Apex Publishing Ltd
Appletree Press Ltd
Arcadia Books Ltd
Archive Editions Ltd

Arena Books (Publishers)
Arris Publishing Ltd
Ashgate Publishing Ltd
Atlantic Books
Attic Press
Austin & Macauley Publishers Ltd
Berghahn Books
Blackstaff Press
Bloomsbury Publishing Plc
Brandon/Mount Eagle
 Publications
Cambridge University Press
Canongate Books
Jon Carpenter Publishing
Centre for Economic Policy
 Research
Commonwealth Secretariat
The Continuum International
 Publishing Group Ltd
Conway
CQ Press
James Currey Publishers
Ashley Drake Publishing Ltd
Gerald Duckworth & Co Ltd
Dunedin Academic Press
Earthscan
Edinburgh University Press
Ethics International Press Ltd
Faber & Faber Ltd
Fabian Society
Garnet Publishing Ltd
Gibson Square
Gill & Macmillan Ltd
Global Oriental Ltd
Gothic Image Publications
Granta Books
Green Books
Greenwood Publishing Group
Guildhall Press
Gwasg Gwenffrwd
Halban Publishers
Robert Hale Ltd
Hambledon Continuum Ltd
HarperCollins Publishers Ltd
Harvard University Press
Hodder Education
Hodder & Stoughton General
C. Hurst & Co (Publishers) Ltd
Icon Books Ltd
Imprint Academic
Institute of Development Studies
Institute of Employment Rights
Ithaca Press
Jane's Information Group Ltd
Janus Publishing Co Ltd
Richard Kay Publications
Kegan Paul Ltd
Liberties Press
Little, Brown Book Group
The Littman Library of Jewish
 Civilization
Liverpool University Press
Luath Press Ltd
The Lutterworth Press
McGraw-Hill Education
Mainstream Publishing Co
 (Edinburgh) Ltd
Maverick House Publishers
Mehring Books
Melisende Publishing Ltd
Mentor Books
Mercier Press Ltd
The Merlin Press Ltd
Merlin Publishing/Wolfhound
 Press
Microform Academic Publishers
The MIT Press Ltd
Monkey Puzzle Media Ltd
Myriad Editions
Nelson Thornes Ltd
New Internationalist Publications
 Ltd
New Island Books Ltd
W. W. Norton & Company Ltd
The O'Brien Press Ltd
Oneworld Publications
Open Gate Press
Open University Worldwide
The Orion Publishing Group Ltd
Oxfam Publishing
Palgrave Macmillan
Panaf Books

Pathfinder Books
Pen Press Publishers Ltd
The Penguin Group (UK) Ltd
Pluto Books Ltd
The Policy Press
Polity Press
Portobello Books Ltd
Princeton University Press
Profile Books
ProQuest
Publishing House
The Radcliffe Press
Rand Publications
Roundhouse Publishing Ltd
Routledge-Cavendish
Joseph Rowntree Foundation
Sage Publications Ltd
Sandstone Press Ltd
Saqi Books
Save the Children
Seren
Sessions of York
Shepheard-Walwyn (Publishers)
 Ltd
Simon & Schuster (UK) Ltd
Adam Smith Institute
Social Affairs Unit
Spokesman
Stacey International
Rudolf Steiner Press
Studymates Ltd
Sussex Academic Press
I. B. Tauris & Co Ltd
Taylor & Francis
Temple Lodge Publishing
Transworld Publishers Ltd
Trentham Books
Troubador Publishing Ltd
TSO (The Stationery Office Ltd)
University of Wales Press
Vallentine Mitchell Publishers
Vision
Weidenfeld & Nicolson
John Wiley & Sons Ltd
The Women's Press
Y Lolfa Cyf
Yale University Press London
Zed Books Ltd

PSYCHOLOGY & PSYCHIATRY

American Psychiatric Publishing
 Inc
Ann Arbor Publishers Ltd
Anshan Ltd
Ashgrove Publishing
Atlantic Books
Austin & Macauley Publishers Ltd
Beautiful Books Ltd
Bedford Freeman Worth (BFW)
Blackhall Publishing
Nicholas Brealey Publishing
British Association for Adoption &
 Fostering
Cambridge University Press
Capall Bann Publishing
Channel View Publications Ltd
Columba
Constable & Robinson Ltd
Darton, Longman & Todd Ltd
Delancey Press Ltd
Ashley Drake Publishing Ltd
Emerald Group Publishing Ltd
The Fostering Network
Free Association Books
Gill & Macmillan Ltd
Global Oriental Ltd
Gothic Image Publications
Greenwood Publishing Group
HarperCollins Publishers Ltd
Harvard University Press
Hawthorn Press
Heart of Albion Press
Hodder Education
Human Kinetics Europe Ltd
Icon Books Ltd
Imprint Academic
Jones & Bartlett International
S. Karger AG
Karnac Books Ltd
Jessica Kingsley Publishers
Letts and Lonsdale

Little, Brown Book Group
Living Time® Media International
McGraw-Hill Education
Market House Books Ltd
The MIT Press Ltd
The National Academies Press
The National Autistic Society
 (NAS)
National Extension College Trust
 Ltd
Nelson Thornes Ltd
W. W. Norton & Company Ltd
Octagon Press Ltd
Oneworld Publications
Open Gate Press
Open University Worldwide
Palgrave Macmillan
Pavilion Publishing (Brighton) Ltd
PCCS Books Ltd
The Penguin Group (UK) Ltd
Piatkus Books
Pipers' Ash Ltd
ProQuest
Royal College of General
 Practitioners
Royal College of Psychiatrists
Russell House Publishing Ltd
Sage Publications Ltd
Sheldon Press
Sherwood Publishing
The Society for Promoting
 Christian Knowledge (SPCK)
Souvenir Press Ltd
Speechmark Publishing Ltd
Sussex Academic Press
Taylor & Francis
Troubador Publishing Ltd
United Writers Publications Ltd
University of Hertfordshire Press
Whiting & Birch Ltd
John Wiley & Sons Ltd
The Women's Press

**REFERENCE BOOKS,
DIRECTORIES & DICTIONARIES**

Adam Matthew Publications Ltd
Adamson Publishing Ltd
Age Concern Books
Alban Books Ltd
Albyn Press
Ian Allan Publishing Ltd
Alligator Books Ltd
Amber Books Ltd
American Psychiatric Publishing
 Inc
Anglo-Saxon Books
Antique Collectors' Club Ltd
AP Information Services Ltd
Apex Publishing Ltd
Appletree Press Ltd
Arcturus Publishing Ltd
Ashgate Publishing Ltd
Atlantic Books
Atlantic Europe Publishing Co Ltd
Aurelian Information Ltd
Aurora Metro Publications Ltd
AVA Publishing (UK) Ltd
Duncan Baird Publishers
Bender Richardson White
Bene Factum Publishing Ltd
Joseph Biddulph Publisher
BLA Publishing Ltd
A. & C. Black (Publishers) Ltd
Blackstaff Press
Bodleian Library Publishing
Bowker (UK) Ltd
Boydell & Brewer Ltd
Bridgewater Book Co
British Association for Adoption &
 Fostering
British Library, Publishing Office
British Museum Press
Burns & Oates
Calypso Publications
*Cambridge Publishing
 Management Ltd*
Cambridge University Press
Camra Books
Canopus Publishing Ltd
Carel Press
Caxton Publishing Group Ltd

PUBLISHERS CLASSIFIED BY FIELDS OF ACTIVITY / 155

CBD Research Ltd
Chambers Harrap Publishers Ltd
Christian Research Association
Church House Publishing
T. & T. Clark
James Clarke & Co
Collins & Brown
Commonwealth Secretariat
The Continuum International Publishing Group Ltd
Countryside Books
CQ Press
Crimson Publishing
D & N Publishing
Delta Alpha Publishing Ltd
J M Dent
Diagram Visual Information Ltd
Earthscan
Edinburgh University Press
Edward Elgar Publishing Ltd
Elm Grove Books Ltd
Encyclopaedia Britannica (UK) Ltd
Energy Institute
Equinox Publishing Ltd
Essential Works Ltd
Euromonitor International Plc
Evangelical Press & Services Ltd
Executive Grapevine International Ltd
Express Newspapers
Facet Publishing
Folens Ltd
Food Trade Press Ltd
W. Foulsham & Co Ltd
Friends of the Earth
Geddes & Grosset
GeoCenter International Ltd
Geography Publications
Gill & Macmillan Ltd
Global Professional Publishing
Glyndwr Publishing
Gomer
Granta Editions
Green Books
Greenwood Publishing Group
Gwasg Gwenffrwd
Hachette Children's Books
Peter Haddock Publishing
Hambledon Continuum Ltd
Harden's Ltd
HarperCollins Publishers Ltd
Harvard University Press
Haynes Publishing
Hemming Information Services
Hilmarton Manor Press
Hodder Education
How To Books Ltd
Icon Books Ltd
In Easy Steps Ltd
International Network for the Availability of Scientific Publications (INASP)
IVP
IWA Publishing
Jane's Information Group Ltd
Jarndyce Booksellers
Richard Joseph Publishers Ltd
Richard Kay Publications
Kegan Paul Ltd
Kogan Page Ltd
Lawpack Publishing Ltd
Letts and Lonsdale
Dewi Lewis Publishing
Lexus Ltd
The Lilliput Press Ltd
LISU
Logaston Press
Lomond Books Ltd
The Lutterworth Press
McGraw-Hill Education
Macmillan Education
Market House Books Ltd
Mentor Books
Mercury Books
Merlin Publishing/Wolfhound Press
Milet Publishing Ltd
The MIT Press Ltd
Mitchell Beazley
Multi Science Publishing Co Ltd
National Children's Bureau
National Housing Federation

The National Trust
Natural History Museum Publishing
Network Continuum Education Ltd
New Internationalist Publications Ltd
OICA International (UK) Ltd
Old House Books
The Oleander Press
On Stream Publications Ltd
The Orion Publishing Group Ltd
Packard Publishing Ltd
Palgrave Macmillan
Pen Press Publishers Ltd
The Penguin Group (UK) Ltd
Philip's
Portico
Portland Press Ltd
ProQuest
Quiller Publishing Ltd
Radcliffe Publishing Ltd
RotoVision SA
Round Hall Ltd
Roundhouse Publishing Ltd
Royal Irish Academy
The Royal Society of Chemistry
Sage Publications Ltd
SCM-Canterbury Press Ltd
Scottish Cultural Press
Shaw & Sons Ltd
Social Affairs Unit
Stacey International
Stainer & Bell Ltd
STRI (Sports Turf Research Institute)
Tartarus Press
I. B. Tauris & Co Ltd
Taylor & Francis
Thames & Hudson Ltd
Think Books
Top That! Publishing Plc
Toucan Books Ltd
Trotman Publishing
Tru-Est Ltd
Truran
TSO (The Stationery Office Ltd)
UCAS
Unicorn Press
University of Wales Press
Merlin Unwin Books Ltd
Laurence Urdang Inc
Usborne Publishing Ltd
Veloce Publishing Ltd
Virgin Books Ltd
Voltaire Foundation Ltd
Waterside Press
Waterside Press
Which? Books
John Wiley & Sons Ltd
Witherby Seamanship International
The Women's Press
Word for Life Trust
Wordsworth Editions Ltd
Zeticula

RELIGION & THEOLOGY

Al-Furqan Islamic Heritage Foundation
Alban Books Ltd
R. L. Allan & Son Publishers
Apex Publishing Ltd
Arcturus Publishing Ltd
Arena Books (Publishers)
Ashgate Publishing Ltd
Atlantic Books
Atlantic Europe Publishing Co Ltd
Austin & Macauley Publishers Ltd
Authentic Media
Authorhouse UK Ltd
Duncan Baird Publishers
The Banner of Truth Trust
The Banton Press
BBC Active
Bender Richardson White
Berghahn Books
Bible Reading Fellowship
BLA Publishing Ltd
Blackstaff Press
Blue Beyond Books

Book Marketing Ltd
Borthwick Publications
Bridgewater Book Co
Bryntirion Press
Burns & Oates
Cambridge Publishing Management Ltd
Cambridge University Press
Capall Bann Publishing
The Catholic Truth Society
Christian Education
Christian Focus Publications
Christian Research Association
Church House Publishing
Church of Ireland Publishing
T. & T. Clark
James Clarke & Co
Columba
The Continuum International Publishing Group Ltd
Countyvise Ltd
Crescent Moon Publishing
Paul H. Crompton Ltd
James Currey Publishers
Cyhoeddiadau'r Gair
Darton, Longman & Todd Ltd
The Davenant Press
Day One Publications
Gerald Duckworth & Co Ltd
Dunedin Academic Press
Eagle Publishing Ltd
Edinburgh University Press
Equinox Publishing Ltd
Evangelical Press & Services Ltd
Family Publications
Feather Books
Findhorn Press Ltd
Floris Books
W. Foulsham & Co Ltd
Four Courts Press
Free Association Books
Garnet Publishing Ltd
Global Oriental Ltd
Godsfield Press Ltd
Gothic Image Publications
Gracewing Publishing
Green Magic
Greenwood Publishing Group
Gresham Books Ltd
Gwasg Gwenffrwd
Hachette Livre UK Ltd
Halban Publishers
HarperCollins Publishers Ltd
Harvard University Press
Hawthorn Press
Heart of Albion Press
Highland Books
Hodder Education
Hodder & Stoughton Faith
John Hunt Publishing Ltd
C. Hurst & Co (Publishers) Ltd
Icon Books Ltd
Imprint Academic
The Islamic Texts Society
Ithaca Press
IVP
Janus Publishing Co Ltd
Kegan Paul Ltd
Jessica Kingsley Publishers
Kingsway Publications
Kube Publishing Ltd
Liberties Press
Frances Lincoln Ltd
Lion Hudson Plc
The Littman Library of Jewish Civilization
The Lutterworth Press
McCrimmon Publishing Co Ltd
Mandrake of Oxford
Kevin Mayhew Ltd
Melisende Publishing Ltd
Mercier Press Ltd
Merlin Publishing/Wolfhound Press
Methodist Publishing House
Microform Academic Publishers
Moorley's Print & Publishing Ltd
National Extension College Trust Ltd
Nelson Thornes Ltd
Octagon Press Ltd
Oneworld Publications

The Open Bible Trust
Open Gate Press
Open University Worldwide
Oxford University Press
Palgrave Macmillan
Paragon Publishing
PCCS Books Ltd
Pen Press Publishers Ltd
The Penguin Group (UK) Ltd
Pickering & Chatto (Publishers) Ltd
Pipers' Ash Ltd
Piquant Editions
ProQuest
Redemptorist Publications
Roundhouse Publishing Ltd
Sage Publications Ltd
Saint Albert's Press
St Pauls Publishing
Saqi Books
SCM-Canterbury Press Ltd
Scottish Children's Press
Scottish Cultural Press
Scripture Union Publishing
Sessions of York
Shepheard-Walwyn (Publishers) Ltd
The Society for Promoting Christian Knowledge (SPCK)
Souvenir Press Ltd
Stacey International
Stainer & Bell Ltd
Rudolf Steiner Press
Studymates Ltd
Sussex Academic Press
The Swedenborg Society
Ta Ha Publishers Ltd
I. B. Tauris & Co Ltd
Taylor & Francis
Temple Lodge Publishing
Tentmaker Publications
Thames & Hudson Ltd
Tharpa Publications
Thoth Publications
Trinitarian Bible Society
Triumph House
University of Wales Press
Vallentine Mitchell Publishers
Veritas Publications
Voltaire Foundation Ltd
Warburg Institute
Ward Lock Educational Co Ltd
Wild Goose Publications
John Wiley & Sons Ltd
Windhorse Publications
Word for Life Trust
Worth Press Ltd
Yale University Press London
Zeticula

SCIENCE FICTION

Apex Publishing Ltd
Atlantic Books
Austin & Macauley Publishers Ltd
Authorhouse UK Ltd
Carlton Publishing Group
Constable & Robinson Ltd
Dreamcatcher Publishing Ltd
Gerald Duckworth & Co Ltd
Victor Gollancz Ltd
Greenwood Publishing Group
HarperCollins Publishers Ltd
Hodder & Stoughton General
Icon Books Ltd
ISIS Publishing Ltd
Janus Publishing Co Ltd
Little, Brown Book Group
Liverpool University Press
Living Time® Media International
Orion Books Ltd
The Orion Publishing Group Ltd
Pan Macmillan
Paragon Publishing
Pen Press Publishers Ltd
Pipers' Ash Ltd
Sandstone Press Ltd
Severn House Publishers Ltd
Sigel Press
Simon & Schuster (UK) Ltd
Snowbooks
Transworld Publishers Ltd
Troubador Publishing Ltd

United Writers Publications Ltd

SCIENTIFIC & TECHNICAL

Anshan Ltd
Archetype Publications Ltd
Atlantic Europe Publishing Co Ltd
Bernard Babani (Publishing) Ltd
BookPower
British Geological Survey
CABI
Calypso Publications
Cambridge University Press
Canopus Publishing Ltd
Chalksoft Ltd
Commonwealth Secretariat
Construction Industry Research & Information Association (CIRIA)
J M Dent
Donhead Publishing Ltd
Earthscan
Elsevier Ltd
Energy Institute
English Heritage
Forensic Science Society
Free Association Books
Geological Society Publishing House
Granta Editions
Greenleaf Publishing
HarperCollins Publishers Ltd
Haynes Publishing
Hodder Education
Human Kinetics Europe Ltd
IChemE
Icon Books Ltd
Imperial College Press
Imprint Academic
In Easy Steps Ltd
Institute of Acoustics
Institute of Clinical Research
Institute of Food Science & Technology
Institute of Physics & Engineering in Medicine
Institution of Engineering and Technology (IET)
Intellect Ltd
IOP Publishing
IWA Publishing
Jones & Bartlett International
Kew Publishing
Leatherhead Food International
Letts and Lonsdale
McGraw-Hill Education
Maney Publishing
Manson Publishing Ltd
Market House Books Ltd
Mentor Books
The MIT Press Ltd
Monkey Puzzle Media Ltd
Multi Science Publishing Co Ltd
The National Academies Press
Natural History Museum Publishing
Nelson Thornes Ltd
NMS Enterprises Limited - Publishing
OICA International (UK) Ltd
Oneworld Publications
Open University Worldwide
Packard Publishing Ltd
Palgrave Macmillan
Paragon Publishing
PC Publishing
The Pharmaceutical Press
Pickering & Chatto (Publishers) Ltd
Portland Press Ltd
Professional Engineering Publishing
ProQuest
Radcliffe Publishing Ltd
The Richmond Publishing Co
The Royal Society of Chemistry
Sage Publications Ltd
Scion Publishing Ltd
The Society of Metaphysicians Ltd
Stobart Davies Ltd
STRI (Sports Turf Research Institute)
Studymates Ltd
Taylor & Francis

Taylor Graham Publishing
Thomas Telford Ltd
TSO (The Stationery Office Ltd)
University of Hertfordshire Press
Usborne Publishing Ltd
David West Children's Books
Whittles Publishing
John Wiley & Sons Ltd
WIT Press
Witherby Seamanship International
Woodhead Publishing Ltd

SOCIOLOGY & ANTHROPOLOGY

Acumen Publishing Ltd
Age Concern Books
Arena Books (Publishers)
Ashgate Publishing Ltd
Austin & Macauley Publishers Ltd
Berg Publishers
Berghahn Books
Blackhall Publishing
British Association for Adoption & Fostering
British Museum Press
Cambridge University Press
Jon Carpenter Publishing
Centre for Policy on Ageing
Channel View Publications Ltd
The Continuum International Publishing Group Ltd
Crescent Moon Publishing
James Currey Publishers
Dunedin Academic Press
Earthscan
Economic & Social Research Institute
Edinburgh University Press
Emerald Group Publishing Ltd
Equinox Publishing Ltd
The Fostering Network
Garnet Publishing Ltd
Global Oriental Ltd
Greenwood Publishing Group
Gwasg Gwenffrwd
Harvard University Press
Heart of Albion Press
Hodder Education
C. Hurst & Co (Publishers) Ltd
Icon Books Ltd
Imprint Academic
Institute of Development Studies
Institute of Education (Publications), University of London
Intellect Ltd
Ithaca Press
Janus Publishing Co Ltd
Jarndyce Booksellers
Kegan Paul Ltd
Jessica Kingsley Publishers
Learning Matters Ltd
Letts and Lonsdale
The Littman Library of Jewish Civilization
Liverpool University Press
McGraw-Hill Education
Mandrake of Oxford
The Merlin Press Ltd
Microform Academic Publishers
National Extension College Trust Ltd
Nelson Thornes Ltd
NMS Enterprises Limited - Publishing
Octagon Press Ltd
Oneworld Publications
Open University Worldwide
Oxbow Books
Palgrave Macmillan
Panaf Books
Pathfinder Books
Pavilion Publishing (Brighton) Ltd
Piatkus Books
Plowright Press
Pluto Books Ltd
The Policy Press
Polity Press
Princeton University Press
Joseph Rowntree Foundation

Russell House Publishing Ltd
Sage Publications Ltd
Saqi Books
Save the Children
Scottish Cultural Press
Shire Publications Ltd
Social Affairs Unit
Souvenir Press Ltd
Spokesman
Rudolf Steiner Press
Studymates Ltd
Sussex Academic Press
I. B. Tauris & Co Ltd
Taylor & Francis
Thames & Hudson Ltd
University of Hertfordshire Press
University of Wales Press
Vision
Waterside Press
Waterside Press
Whiting & Birch Ltd
John Wiley & Sons Ltd
Zed Books Ltd

SPORTS & GAMES

Absolute Press
Ian Allan Publishing Ltd
Amber Books Ltd
Amolibros
Peter Andrew Publishing Co Ltd
Apex Publishing Ltd
Appletree Press Ltd
Arcturus Publishing Ltd
Aureus Publishing Ltd
Aurum Press
Austin & Macauley Publishers Ltd
A. & C. Black (Publishers) Ltd
Blackstaff Press
John Blake Publishing Ltd
Breedon Books Publishing Co Ltd
Bridgewater Book Co
Brown Dog Books
Butterfingers Books
Cambridge Publishing Management Ltd
Carel Press
Carlton Publishing Group
Christian Focus Publications
Cicerone Press Ltd
Coachwise Ltd
Collins & Brown
Copper Beech Publishing Ltd
Corpus Publishing Ltd
Countyvise Ltd
Paul H. Crompton Ltd
The Crowood Press Ltd
Cualann Press Ltd
Currach Press
D & N Publishing
David & Charles Ltd
Diagram Visual Information Ltd
Ashley Drake Publishing Ltd
Essential Works Ltd
Express Newspapers
FHG Guides Ltd
Focus Publishing (Sevenoaks) Ltd
Footprint Handbooks
Gomer
Granta Editions
Greenwood Publishing Group
Haldane Mason Ltd
HarperCollins Publishers Ltd
Hart McLeod Ltd
Harvey Map Services Ltd
Haynes Publishing
Roger Heavens
Hodder Education
Hodder & Stoughton General
Alison Hodge Publishers
Human Kinetics Europe Ltd
Icon Books Ltd
Imray Laurie Norie & Wilson Ltd
Janus Publishing Co Ltd
Jones & Bartlett International
Jessica Kingsley Publishers
Lagoon Books
Letts and Lonsdale
Liberties Press
Frances Lincoln Ltd
Little, Brown Book Group
Luath Press Ltd

The Lutterworth Press
Mainstream Publishing Co (Edinburgh) Ltd
Maverick House Publishers
Mentor Books
Merlin Publishing/Wolfhound Press
Mitchell Beazley
Monkey Puzzle Media Ltd
Motor Racing Publications Ltd
Multi Science Publishing Co Ltd
Nelson Thornes Ltd
W. W. Norton & Company Ltd
The O'Brien Press Ltd
Octopus Publishing Group
Old House Books
Oldcastle Books Ltd
The Oleander Press
The Orion Publishing Group Ltd
Packard Publishing Ltd
Pan Macmillan
Paragon Publishing
Pen Press Publishers Ltd
Pipers' Ash Ltd
Portico
Prestel Publishing Ltd
Quantum Publishing
Quiller Publishing Ltd
Raceform Ltd
Ripping Yarns.com
Robson Books
Roundhouse Publishing Ltd
Russell House Publishing Ltd
Sandstone Press Ltd
Scottish Children's Press
Short Books Ltd
Sigma Press
Simon & Schuster (UK) Ltd
Smith Settle Printing & Bookbinding Ltd
Snowbooks
Soccer Books Ltd
Souvenir Press Ltd
Sportsbooks Ltd
STRI (Sports Turf Research Institute)
Summersdale Publishers Ltd
Supportive Learning Publications (SLP)
Sussex Academic Press
Taylor & Francis
Transworld Publishers Ltd
United Writers Publications Ltd
University of Wales Press
Merlin Unwin Books Ltd
Usborne Publishing Ltd
Veloce Publishing Ltd
Vertical Editions
Virgin Books Ltd
Weidenfeld & Nicolson
David West Children's Books
John Wiley & Sons Ltd
Y Lolfa Cyf
Yore Publications

THEATRE, DRAMA & DANCE

Amolibros
Peter Andrew Publishing Co Ltd
Ashgate Publishing Ltd
Association for Scottish Literary Studies
Aurora Metro Publications Ltd
Austin & Macauley Publishers Ltd
Berghahn Books
A. & C. Black (Publishers) Ltd
Black Dog Publishing Ltd
Blackstaff Press
Marion Boyars Publishers Ltd
Bridgewater Book Co
Brown, Son & Ferguson, Ltd
Cambridge University Press
Capall Bann Publishing
Carel Press
Classical Comics Ltd
Cló Iar-Chonnachta
Cois Life
Collins & Brown
The Continuum International Publishing Group Ltd
Crescent Moon Publishing
Cressrelles Publishing Co Ltd

The Crowood Press Ltd
D & N Publishing
Dance Books Ltd
Ashley Drake Publishing Ltd
Dramatic Lines
Essential Works Ltd
Faber & Faber Ltd
Feather Books
Five Leaves Publications
Focus Publishing (Sevenoaks) Ltd
Samuel French Ltd
The Gallery Press
Granta Editions
Greenwood Publishing Group
Guildhall Press
Hanbury Plays
Ian Henry Publications Ltd
Nick Hern Books
Human Kinetics Europe Ltd
Intellect Ltd
Kenyon-Deane
Kingsway Publications
Jay Landesman
The Littman Library of Jewish Civilization
Luath Press Ltd
Market House Books Ltd
Mercier Press Ltd
J. Garnet Miller
Moorley's Print & Publishing Ltd
NATE (National Association for the Teaching of English)
Nelson Thornes Ltd
New Island Books Ltd
New Playwrights' Network
Northcote House Publishers Ltd
W. W. Norton & Company Ltd
Open University Worldwide
Peter Owen Publishers
Palgrave Macmillan
Paragon Publishing
Pavilion
Pen Press Publishers Ltd
Pipers' Ash Ltd
Playne Books Ltd
The Playwrights Publishing Co
Prestel Publishing Ltd
ProQuest
Robson Books
RotoVision SA
Roundhouse Publishing Ltd
SchoolPlay Productions Ltd
Scottish Cultural Press
Seren
Charles Skilton Ltd
Colin Smythe Ltd
Souvenir Press Ltd
Spokesman
Stainer & Bell Ltd
Rudolf Steiner Press
Studymates Ltd
Supportive Learning Publications (SLP)
Sussex Academic Press
Taylor & Francis
Thames & Hudson Ltd
Trentham Books
Troubador Publishing Ltd
University of Exeter Press
University of Hertfordshire Press
Victoria & Albert Museum Publishing
Waterside Press
Waterside Press
Joseph Weinberger Ltd
Yale University Press London

TRANSPORT

AA Publishing
Albyn Press
Ian Allan Publishing Ltd
Amber Books Ltd
Ashgate Publishing Ltd
Atlantic Books
Barny Books
The Belmont Press
Black Dog Publishing Ltd
Breedon Books Publishing Co Ltd
Brewin Books Ltd
Brooklands Books Ltd
Capital Transport Publishing

Carlton Publishing Group
Caxton Publishing Group Ltd
Chatham Publishing
Colourpoint Books
Conway
Copper Beech Publishing Ltd
Countyvise Ltd
Crécy Publishing Ltd
The Crowood Press Ltd
G. L. Crowther
Currach Press
D & N Publishing
Earthscan
Edward Elgar Publishing Ltd
Elm Publications
Essential Works Ltd
Ex Libris Press
Express Newspapers
Focus Publishing (Sevenoaks) Ltd
Friends of the Earth
GeoCenter International Ltd
Glasgow Museums
Gomer
Haynes Publishing
Ian Henry Publications Ltd
House of Lochar
Imray Laurie Norie & Wilson Ltd
Irwell Press Ltd
Jane's Information Group Ltd
Kogan Page Ltd
Landmark Publishing Ltd
McGraw-Hill Education
Maritime Books
Merton Priory Press Ltd
Middleton Press
Motor Racing Publications Ltd
NMS Enterprises Limited - Publishing
The Nostalgia Collection
Old House Books
Old Pond Publishing
Professional Engineering Publishing
Quantum Publishing
Quiller Publishing Ltd
Reflections of a Bygone Age
Roadmaster Publishing
Sheaf Publishing
Sheldrake Press
Shire Publications Ltd
Charles Skilton Ltd
Snowbooks
Soccer Books Ltd
Special Interest Model Books Ltd
Stenlake Publishing Ltd
Tentmaker Publications
Trans-Pennine Publishing Ltd
Troubador Publishing Ltd
TSO (The Stationery Office Ltd)
Twelveheads Press
Veloce Publishing Ltd
David West Children's Books
WIT Press
Witherby Seamanship International
Zeticula

TRAVEL & TOPOGRAPHY

AA Publishing
Absolute Press
Amolibros
Chris Andrews Publications Ltd
Appletree Press Ltd
Arcadia Books Ltd
Arena Books (Publishers)
Arris Publishing Ltd
Aurora Metro Publications Ltd
Aurum Press
Austin & Macauley Publishers Ltd
Beautiful Books Ltd
The Belmont Press
Berghahn Books
Black Dog Publishing Ltd
Blackstaff Press
Book Castle Publishing Ltd
Boydell & Brewer Ltd
Bradt Travel Guides Ltd
Brandon/Mount Eagle Publications
Nicholas Brealey Publishing
Bridge Books

PUBLISHERS CLASSIFIED BY FIELDS OF ACTIVITY / 157

Bridgewater Book Co
Calypso Publications
Cambridge Publishing Management Ltd
Camra Books
Centre for Alternative Technology Publications
Channel View Publications Ltd
The Chrysalis Press
Cicerone Press Ltd
Cló Iar-Chonnachta
Collins Geo
Constable & Robinson Ltd
Countryside Books
Crescent Moon Publishing
Crimson Publishing
Cualann Press Ltd
Currach Press
D & N Publishing
Day One Publications
Discovery Walking Guides Ltd
Gerald Duckworth & Co Ltd
Eland Publishing Ltd
Elliott & Thompson
Elm Publications
English Heritage
The Erskine Press
Everyman's Library
Ex Libris Press
Express Newspapers
Eye Books Ltd
Footprint Handbooks
W. Foulsham & Co Ltd
Garnet Publishing Ltd
GeoCenter International Ltd
The Geographical Association
Gibson Square
Gill & Macmillan Ltd
Global Oriental Ltd
Gothic Image Publications
Graffeg
Granta Books
Granta Editions
Green Books
Green Magic
Gwasg Gwenffrwd
Robert Hale Ltd
Halsgrove
HarperCollins Publishers Ltd
Haynes Publishing
Historical Publications Ltd
Hobnob Press
Alison Hodge Publishers
Holo Books
House of Lochar
How To Books Ltd
Imray Laurie Norie & Wilson Ltd
Instant-Books UK Ltd
Kegan Paul Ltd
The King's England Press
Landmark Publishing Ltd
Libris Ltd
Frances Lincoln Ltd
Little, Brown Book Group
Luath Press Ltd
Melisende Publishing Ltd
Mentor Books
Merlin Publishing/Wolfhound Press
Meyrick Marketing Ltd
Michelin Maps & Guides
Mitchell Beazley
Monkey Puzzle Media Ltd
Murdoch Books UK Ltd
John Murray Publishers
The National Trust
The O'Brien Press Ltd
Octagon Press Ltd
Old House Books
The Oleander Press
The Orion Publishing Group Ltd
Pallas Athene
Pan Macmillan
Pavilion
Pen Press Publishers Ltd
The Penguin Group (UK) Ltd
Playne Books Ltd
Portobello Books Ltd
Prestel Publishing Ltd
Punk Publishing Ltd
Quiller Publishing Ltd
The Radcliffe Press
Reardon Publishing
Ripping Yarns.com
Roadmaster Publishing
Robson Books
Alan Rogers Guides Ltd
Roundhouse Publishing Ltd
S. B. Publications
Alastair Sawday Publishing
Scala Publishers Ltd
SCM-Canterbury Press Ltd
Sheldrake Press
Shire Publications Ltd
Sigma Press
Simon & Schuster (UK) Ltd
Charles Skilton Ltd
Slightly Foxed
Smith Settle Printing & Bookbinding Ltd
Souvenir Press Ltd
Stacey International
Strong Oak Press
Summersdale Publishers Ltd
Sunflower Books
Teneues Publishing UK Ltd
Thames & Hudson Ltd
Thorogood Publishing Ltd
F. A. Thorpe Publishing
Trans-Pennine Publishing Ltd
Transworld Publishers Ltd
Travel Publishing Ltd
Trotman Publishing
Troubador Publishing Ltd
United Writers Publications Ltd
Weidenfeld & Nicolson
White Ladder Press
John Wiley & Sons Ltd
Willow Island Editions
Neil Wilson Publishing Ltd
Zeticula
Zymurgy Publishing

VETERINARY SCIENCE

BookPower
CABI
Luath Press Ltd
Manson Publishing Ltd
The National Academies Press
Old Pond Publishing
The Pharmaceutical Press
Quiller Publishing Ltd
Souvenir Press Ltd
TSO (The Stationery Office Ltd)
Whittet Books Ltd
John Wiley & Sons Ltd

VOCATIONAL TRAINING & CAREERS

Austin & Macauley Publishers Ltd
Bene Factum Publishing Ltd
BookPower
Nicholas Brealey Publishing
Cambridge Publishing Management Ltd
Cengage Learning EMEA
CILT, the National Centre for Languages
The Continuum International Publishing Group Ltd
Crimson Publishing
Emerald Group Publishing Ltd
Ethics International Press Ltd
The Fostering Network
Gower Publishing Co Ltd
Hawker Publications
Hodder Education
How To Books Ltd
In Easy Steps Ltd
Jones & Bartlett International
Jessica Kingsley Publishers
Kogan Page Ltd
Lawpack Publishing Ltd
Letts and Lonsdale
McGraw-Hill Education
National Extension College Trust Ltd
National Housing Federation
Need2Know
Nelson Thornes Ltd
Optimus Professional Publishing
Palgrave Macmillan
Radcliffe Publishing Ltd
Royal College of General Practitioners
Russell House Publishing Ltd
Southgate Publishers
Trotman Publishing
UCAS
Which? Books
John Wiley & Sons Ltd

7.2 INDEX OF ISBN PREFIXES

978 0 00 360 **2191**	978 0 571 **2272**	978 0 7278 **2691**	978 0 85131 **2019, 2342**	978 0 85953 **2172**	978 0 87140 **2549**
978 0 00 447 **2191**	978 0 572 **2289**	978 0 7294 **2814**	978 0 85151 **2075**	978 0 85956 **2211**	978 0 87187 **2208**
978 0 07 **2473**	978 0 573 **2292**	978 0 7360 **2380**	978 0 85162 **2679**	978 0 85964 **2622**	978 0 87289 **2208**
978 0 08 **2254**	978 0 575 **2314, 2574**	978 0 7432 **2706**	978 0 85174 **2131**	978 0 85967 **2050**	978 0 87322 **2380**
978 0 09 1014 **2731**	978 0 576 **2050**	978 0 7434 **2706**	978 0 85177 **2009, 2199**	978 0 85969 **2696, 2716**	978 0 87348 **2588**
978 0 09 4 **2196**	978 0 582 9 **2198**	978 0 7435 **2706**	978 0 85186 **2662**	978 0 85976 **2095**	978 0 87879 **2034**
978 0 09 540 **2616**	978 0 593 **2782**	978 0 7444 **2471**	978 0 85197 **2345**	978 0 85979 **2209**	978 0 88010 **2731**
978 0 09 545 **2616**	978 0 596 **2572**	978 0 7453 **2609**	978 0 85198 **2138**	978 0 85989 **2800**	978 0 88011 **2380**
978 0 10 **2791**	978 0 600 **2555**	978 0 7456 **2611**	978 0 85199 **2138**	978 0 85991 **2116**	978 0 88150 **2549**
978 0 11 **2791**	978 0 603 5 **2249**	978 0 7459 **2093, 2460, 2716**	978 0 85224 **2247**	978 0 86003 **2017, 2369**	978 0 89207 **2767**
978 0 12 **2254**	978 0 631 **2464**		978 0 85229 **2256**	978 0 86012 **2135**	978 0 89381 **2767**
978 0 14 **2597**	978 0 642 **2767**	978 0 7460 **2806**	978 0 85231 **2640**	978 0 86017 **2197**	978 0 89391 **2406**
978 0 17 **2539**	978 0 646 **2669**	978 0 7463 **2548**	978 0 85234 **2264**	978 0 86020 **2806**	978 0 89789 **2330**
978 0 225 **2198**	978 0 670 **2597**	978 0 7470 **2100**	978 0 85242 **2724**	978 0 86025 **2360**	978 0 89930 **2330**
978 0 227 **2183**	978 0 671 **2706**	978 0 7475 **2107**	978 0 85244 **2318**	978 0 86037 **2439**	978 0 900001 **2568**
978 0 230 **2585**	978 0 674 **2350**	978 0 7478 **2701**	978 0 85249 **2730**	978 0 86065 **2436**	978 0 900002 **2211**
978 0 232 **2224**	978 0 684 **2706**	978 0 7486 **2095, 2247**	978 0 85255 **2221**	978 0 86071 **2515**	978 0 900036 **2012**
978 0 233 **2150**	978 0 689 8 **2706**	978 0 7487 **2539**	978 0 85263 **2701**	978 0 86072 **2627**	978 0 900090 **2052**
978 0 237 **2265, 2848**	978 0 691 **2619**	978 0 7490 **2022**	978 0 85272 **2125**	978 0 86074 **2336**	978 0 900162 **2071**
978 0 241 **2597**	978 0 7020 **2254**	978 0 7492 **2569**	978 0 85288 **2391**	978 0 86078 **2050**	978 0 900246 **2158**
978 0 245 **2164, 2369**	978 0 7028 **2191**	978 0 7494 **2438**	978 0 85290 **2119**	978 0 86082 **2528**	978 0 900274 **2681**
978 0 262 **2511**	978 0 7043 **2836**	978 0 7495 **2001**	978 0 85292 **2166**	978 0 86093 **2016**	978 0 900379 **2285**
978 0 264 **2198**	978 0 7045 **2050**	978 0 7496 **3001**	978 0 85293 **2257**	978 0 86104 **2609**	978 0 900395 **2301**
978 0 275 **2330**	978 0 7062 **2817**	978 0 7497 **2249**	978 0 85295 **2384**	978 0 86140 **2712**	978 0 900458 **2801**
978 0 281 **2716**	978 0 7070 **2246**	978 0 7499 **2462, 2602**	978 0 85296 **2405**	978 0 86142 **2012**	978 0 900549 **2516**
978 0 283 **2585**	978 0 7078 **2534**	978 0 7505 **2479**	978 0 85299 **2167**	978 0 86145 **2001**	978 0 900550 **2354**
978 0 284 **2015, 2707**	978 0 7079 **2359**	978 0 7512 **2050**	978 0 85303 **2807**	978 0 86152 **2003**	978 0 900662 **2700**
978 0 285 **2722**	978 0 7083 **2802**	978 0 7515 **2462**	978 0 85308 **2424**	978 0 86155 **2535**	978 0 900675 **2712**
978 0 291 **2050**	978 0 7089 **2773**	978 0 7518 **2125**	978 0 85318 **2016**	978 0 86163 **2068**	978 0 900680 **2719**
978 0 297 **2574, 2820**	978 0 7090 **2342**	978 0 7528 **2574**	978 0 85323 **2465**	978 0 86188 **2602**	978 0 900751 **2286**
978 0 300 **2844**	978 0 7091 **2342**	978 0 7531 **2412**	978 0 85331 **2050, 2317, 2470**	978 0 86201 **2685**	978 0 900768 **2802**
978 0 304 **2198, 2574**	978 0 7103 **2429**	978 0 7534 **2475**		978 0 86208 **2489**	978 0 900841 **2724**
978 0 309 **2524**	978 0 7105 **2339**	978 0 7538 **2574**	978 0 85342 **2495**	978 0 86209 **2489**	978 0 900860 **2554**
978 0 313 **2330**	978 0 7106 **2419**	978 0 7546 **2050, 2317**	978 0 85343 **2211**	978 0 86210 **2027, 2028**	978 0 900886 **2834**
978 0 316 **2462**	978 0 7110 **2016**	978 0 7619 **2665**	978 0 85365 **2274**	978 0 86217 **2809**	978 0 900891 **2561**
978 0 325 **2330**	978 0 7112 **2459**	978 0 7637 **2423**	978 0 85369 **2600**	978 0 86232 **2847**	978 0 900898 **2133**
978 0 330 **2475, 2585**	978 0 7119 **2562**	978 0 7847 63 **2767**	978 0 85389 **2709**	978 0 86239 **2436**	978 0 900946 **2767**
978 0 333 **2475, 2476, 2583, 2585**	978 0 7123 **2126, 2127**	978 0 8039 **2665**	978 0 85390 **2809**	978 0 86241 **2143**	978 0 900977 **2037**
	978 0 7131 **2369**	978 0 8058 **2757**	978 0 85404 **2662**	978 0 86242 **2010**	978 0 901072 **2712**
978 0 334 **2681**	978 0 7134 **2081, 2291**	978 0 8212 **2462**	978 0 85421 **2685**	978 0 86243 **2843**	978 0 901205 **2212**
978 0 337 **2791**	978 0 7136 **2009, 2100, 2198, 2361**	978 0 8213 **2791**	978 0 85429 **2354**	978 0 86264 **2030**	978 0 901223 **2405**
978 0 340 **2337, 2369, 2370, 2371, 2372**		978 0 8222 **2821**	978 0 85439 **2668**	978 0 86278 **2553**	978 0 901286 **2484**
	978 0 7141 **2128, 2767**	978 0 8247 **2757**	978 0 85440 **2731**	978 0 86281 **2040**	978 0 901291 **2523**
978 0 349 **2462**	978 0 7145 **2115, 2564**	978 0 8264 **2198**	978 0 85442 **2734**	978 0 86297 **2532**	978 0 901366 **2628**
978 0 352 **2812**	978 0 7148 **2599**	978 0 8330 **2633**	978 0 85476 **2436**	978 0 86304 **2554**	978 0 901495 **2515**
978 0 385 **2782**	978 0 7151 **2177**	978 0 8352 **2114**	978 0 85481 **2816**	978 0 86315 **2283**	978 0 901714 **2661**
978 0 393 **2549**	978 0 7153 **2226**	978 0 8371 **2330**	978 0 85491 **2436**	978 0 86319 **2543**	978 0 901764 **2213**
978 0 414 **2326**	978 0 7155 **2211, 2430**	978 0 8416 5 **2300**	978 0 85496 **2091**	978 0 86322 **2118**	978 0 901787 **2586**
978 0 415 **2757**	978 0 7156 **2241**	978 0 8424 8 **2618**	978 0 85503 **2491**	978 0 86327 **2499**	978 0 901791 **2530**
978 0 416 **2249**	978 0 7162 04 **2502**	978 0 8493 **2757**	978 0 85532 **2686**	978 0 86338 **2263**	978 0 901938 **2679**
978 0 443 **2254**	978 0 7163 **2273**	978 0 85000 **2065**	978 0 85533 **2510, 2512**	978 0 86341 **2405**	978 0 901976 **2798**
978 0 460 **2233, 2574**	978 0 7167 **2088**	978 0 85031 **2022**	978 0 85546 **2642**	978 0 86343 **2544**	978 0 902028 **2036**
978 0 470 **2828**	978 0 7169 **2369, 2370**	978 0 85036 **2498**	978 0 85596 **2240**	978 0 86347 **2243**	978 0 902088 **2436**
978 0 471 **2828**	978 0 7171 **2305**	978 0 85045 **2575**	978 0 85597 **2472**	978 0 86356 **2672**	978 0 902197 **2386**
978 0 485 **2198**	978 0 7181 **2597**	978 0 85054 **2311**	978 0 85598 **2580**	978 0 86368 **2206**	978 0 902241 **2659**
978 0 485 19 **2091**	978 0 7185 **2198**	978 0 85059 **2354**	978 0 85640 **2102**	978 0 86369 **2812**	978 0 902280 **2354**
978 0 500 **2767**	978 0 7188 **2471**	978 0 85079 **2270**	978 0 85646 **2037**	978 0 86372 **2415**	978 0 902363 **2179**
978 0 521 **2140**	978 0 7195 **2369, 2519**	978 0 85084 **2658**	978 0 85648 **2460**	978 0 86381 **2334**	978 0 902548 **2227**
978 0 540 **2601**	978 0 7198 **2342**	978 0 85088 **2315**	978 0 85660 **2787**	978 0 86383 **2315**	978 0 902561 **2202**
978 0 550 **2164, 2369**	978 0 7201 **2198**	978 0 85092 **2194**	978 0 85667 **2831**	978 0 86388 **2725**	978 0 902662 **2428**
978 0 552 **2782**	978 0 7206 **2578**	978 0 85105 **2712**	978 0 85668 **2579**	978 0 86565 **2767**	978 0 902664 **2849**
978 0 553 **2782**	978 0 7219 **2694**	978 0 85110 **2416**	978 0 85676 **2821**	978 0 86569 **2330**	978 0 902675 **2561**
978 0 563 **2082, 2083**	978 0 7220 **2198**	978 0 85111 **2416**	978 0 85683 **2698**	978 0 86709 **2330**	978 0 902752 **2306**
978 0 565 **2536**	978 0 7230 **2191**	978 0 85115 **2116**	978 0 85684 **2416**	978 0 86715 **2629**	978 0 902771 **2041**
978 0 566 **2050, 2317**	978 0 7243 **2254**	978 0 85124 **2726**	978 0 85696 **2354**	978 0 86729 **2423**	978 0 902817 **2527**
978 0 567 **2182, 2198**	978 0 7277 **2761**	978 0 85130 **2011**	978 0 85934 **2071**	978 0 87070 **2767**	978 0 902992 **2396**

INDEX OF ISBN PREFIXES / 159

978 0 902996 **2295**
978 0 903001 **2134**
978 0 903102 **2223**
978 0 903148 **2529**
978 0 903162 **2531**
978 0 903317 **2303**
978 0 903354 **2399**
978 0 903534 **2124**
978 0 903540 **2283**
978 0 903598 **2529**
978 0 903685 **2231**
978 0 903715 **2399**
978 0 903729 **2415**
978 0 903857 **2112**
978 0 903903 **2717**
978 0 903962 **2285**
978 0 903983 **2382**
978 0 904011 **2295**
978 0 904017 **2533**
978 0 904139 **2162**
978 0 904179 **2366**
978 0 904498 **2614**
978 0 904572 **2181**
978 0 904651 **2040**
978 0 904693 **2764**
978 0 904709 **2523**
978 0 904722 **2364**
978 0 904766 **2832**
978 0 904849 **2666**
978 0 904864 **2843**
978 0 905005 **2755**
978 0 905028 **2165**
978 0 905091 **2403**
978 0 905099 **2450**
978 0 905104 **2704**
978 0 905114 **2446**
978 0 905140 **2553**
978 0 905150 **2441**
978 0 905209 **2811**
978 0 905249 **2279**
978 0 905272 **2745**
978 0 905366 **2089**
978 0 905367 **2402**
978 0 905392 **2206**
978 0 905418 **2331**
978 0 905451 **2833**
978 0 905478 **2030**
978 0 905483 **2825**
978 0 905715 **2712**
978 0 905743 **2729**
978 0 905748 **2449**
978 0 905762 **2847**
978 0 905838 **2382**
978 0 906048 **2405**
978 0 906127 **2290**
978 0 906155 **2283**
978 0 906183 **2767**
978 0 906212 **2753**
978 0 906290 **2797**
978 0 906294 **2793**
978 0 906301 **2139**
978 0 906362 **2316**
978 0 906391 **2481**
978 0 906427 **2106**
978 0 906447 **2544**
978 0 906500 **2566**
978 0 906506 **2141, 3014**
978 0 906517 **2711**
978 0 906520 **2506**
978 0 906522 **2517**
978 0 906527 **2582**
978 0 906551 **2343**
978 0 906554 **2471**
978 0 906602 **2302**
978 0 906672 **2561**
978 0 906690 **2343**
978 0 906720 **2373**
978 0 906731 **2174**
978 0 906782 **2323**
978 0 906798 **2051**
978 0 906938 **2048**
978 0 906969 **2361**
978 0 907018 **2749**
978 0 907115 **2226**
978 0 907123 **2281**
978 0 907345 **2452**
978 0 907383 **2244, 2418**
978 0 907461 **2748**
978 0 907462 **2036**
978 0 907476 **2689**
978 0 907480 **2547**
978 0 907526 **2732**
978 0 907547 **2681**
978 0 907554 **2311**
978 0 907566 **2790**
978 0 907579 **2209**
978 0 907590 **2738**
978 0 907621 **2628**
978 0 907628 **2344**
978 0 907631 **2715**
978 0 907638 **2212**
978 0 907664 **2559**
978 0 907679 **2136**
978 0 907768 **2207**
978 0 907771 **2486**
978 0 907845 **2390**
978 0 907849 **2052**
978 0 907861 **2785**
978 0 907871 **2250**
978 0 907895 **2608**
978 0 907926 **2345**
978 0 907969 **2120**
978 0 918438 **2380**
978 0 929087 **2492**
978 0 930448 **2679**
978 0 930454 **2805**
978 0 931250 **2380**
978 0 931421 **2034**
978 0 936756 **2511**
978 0 942299 **2511**
978 0 946015 **2288**
978 0 946095 **2331**
978 0 946139 **2253**
978 0 946211 **2057**
978 0 946245 **2641**
978 0 946284 **2215**
978 0 946407 **2041**
978 0 946418 **2368**
978 0 946439 **2427**
978 0 946451 **2333**
978 0 946462 **2264**
978 0 946487 **2469**
978 0 946535 **2679**
978 0 946551 **2305**
978 0 946590 **2755**
978 0 946609 **2354**
978 0 946616 **2363**
978 0 946621 **2413**
978 0 946626 **2228**
978 0 946640 **2458**
978 0 946796 **2031**
978 0 946897 **2579**
978 0 946947 **2029**
978 0 946960 **2291**
978 0 946962 **2240**
978 0 947548 **2494**
978 0 947554 **2209**
978 0 947568 **2758**
978 0 947645 **2530**
978 0 947672 **3025**
978 0 947697 **2175**
978 0 947718 **2277**
978 0 947731 **2121**
978 0 947778 **2567**
978 0 94778 **2468**
978 0 94788 **2284**
978 0 947971 **2551**
978 0 947981 **2516**
978 0 947988 **2827**
978 0 948006 **2768**
978 0 948080 **2784**
978 0 948107 **2811**
978 0 948183 **2193**
978 0 948204 **2079**
978 0 948230 **2002**
978 0 948238 **2099**
978 0 948253 **2628**
978 0 948285 **2261**
978 0 948353 **2560**
978 0 948358 **2516**
978 0 948512 **2301**
978 0 948513 **2742**
978 0 948543 **2008**
978 0 948565 **2094**
978 0 948578 **2267**
978 0 948636 **2546**
978 0 948643 **2018**
978 0 948667 **2367**
978 0 948690 **2582**
978 0 948691 **2834**
978 0 948817 **2332**
978 0 948848 **2461**
978 0 948867 **2618**
978 0 948877 **2054**
978 0 9500508 **2364**
978 0 9501861 **2335**
978 0 9502121 **2331**
978 0 9502686 **2133**
978 0 9503527 **2624**
978 0 9503647 **2737**
978 0 9505458 **2695**
978 0 9505570 **2121**
978 0 9505828 **2253**
978 0 9506431 **2790**
978 0 9506563 **2267**
978 0 9506882 **2344**
978 0 9507735 **2784**
978 0 9508285 **2122**
978 0 9508674 **2638**
978 0 9509643 **2032**
978 0 9509773 **2110**
978 0 9510242 **2467**
978 0 9513240 **2137**
978 0 9513492 **2020**
978 0 9514490 **2735**
978 0 9515877 **2061**
978 0 9516129 **2207**
978 0 9516295 **2201**
978 0 9517723 **2025**
978 0 9521492 **2624**
978 0 9521964 **2699**
978 0 9522351 **2084**
978 0 9522754 **2090**
978 0 9524749 **2747**
978 0 9526056 **2232**
978 0 9527302 **2324**
978 0 9528428 **2132**
978 0 9529986 **2584**
978 0 9530575 **2271**
978 0 9532775 **2132**
978 0 9533478 **2846**
978 0 9533651 **2558**
978 0 9535036 **2219**
978 0 9535353 **2057**
978 0 9535895 **2776**
978 0 9535912 **2740**
978 0 9536631 **2325**
978 0 9536757 **2061**
978 0 9536768 **2439**
978 0 9538460 **2047**
978 0 9539119 **2229**
978 0 9539852 **2699**
978 0 9539877 **2084**
978 0 9540331 **2032**
978 0 9540499 **2541**
978 0 9540535 **2103**
978 0 9541303 **2776**
978 0 9541544 **2727**
978 0 9541794 **2644**
978 0 9542079 **2617**
978 0 9542189 **2801**
978 0 9542330 **2061**
978 0 9542813 **2767**
978 0 9542945 **2488**
978 0 9542963 **2325**
978 0 9543161 **2047**
978 0 9543781 **2401**
978 0 9543855 **2661**
978 0 9543914 **2823**
978 0 9544075 **2095**
978 0 9544334 **2319**
978 0 9544416 **2219**
978 0 9544619 **2239**
978 0 9544752 **2740**
978 0 9545335 **2456**
978 0 9545575 **2579**
978 0 9545870 **2053**
978 0 9546894 **2767**
978 0 9546912 **2061**
978 0 9547230 **2325**
978 0 9547757 **2747**
978 0 9547913 **2776**
978 0 9548219 **2823**
978 0 9548707 **2488**
978 0 9548708 **2488**
978 0 9548790 **2768**
978 0 9549345 **2398**
978 0 9549727 **2152**
978 0 9549846 **2144**
978 0 9551032 **2451**
978 0 9551384 **2776**
978 0 9551566 **2061**
978 0 9551795 **2401**
978 0 9552036 **2625**
978 0 9552122 **2740**
978 0 9553741 **2231**
978 0 9554273 **2219**
978 0 9554514 **2158**
978 0 9554992 **2239**
978 0 9556055 **2047**
978 0 9556476 **2776**
978 0 9668946 **2230**
978 1 4039 **2583**
978 1 4052 **2249**
978 1 4055 **2462**
978 1 4066 **2082**
978 1 4087 **2462**
978 1 4129 **2665**
978 1 4165 **2706**
978 1 4169 **2706**
978 1 4208 **2066**
978 1 4259 **2066**
978 1 4343 **2066**
978 1 56338 **2198**
978 1 56592 **2572**
978 1 56643 **2208**
978 1 56720 **2330**
978 1 56750 **2330, 2406**
978 1 56802 **2208**
978 1 57027 **2511**
978 1 57113 **2116**
978 1 57181 **2092**
978 1 57356 **2330**
978 1 58435 **2511**
978 1 59339 **2256**
978 1 59604 **3001**
978 1 59711 **2767**
978 1 74045 **2518**
978 1 74196 **2518**
978 1 84000 **2510, 2512**
978 1 84003 **2489**
978 1 84011 **2763**
978 1 84014 **2050**
978 1 84017 **2683**
978 1 84018 **2481**
978 1 84022 **2839**
978 1 84024 **2741**
978 1 84033 **2732**
978 1 84037 **2628**
978 1 84046 **2385**
978 1 84059 **2508**
978 1 84064 **2251**
978 1 84067 **2157**
978 1 84076 **2485**
978 1 84078 **2392**
978 1 84085 **2453**
978 1 84089 **2265, 2848**
978 1 84091 **2195**
978 1 84097 **2045**
978 1 84101 **2093**
978 1 84103 **2710**
978 1 84113 **2349**
978 1 84114 **2343**
978 1 84119 **2196**
978 1 84127 **2182, 2198**
978 1 84135 **2068**
978 1 84138 **2590**
978 1 84146 **2200**
978 1 84148 **2078**
978 1 84149 **2462**
978 1 84150 **2406**
978 1 84151 **2311**
978 1 84158 **2095**
978 1 84161 **2637**
978 1 84162 **2117**
978 1 84163 **2284**
978 1 84167 **2636**
978 1 84175 **2277**
978 1 84176 **2575**
978 1 84181 **2312**
978 1 84183 **2095**
978 1 84186 **2157**
978 1 84187 **2673**
978 1 84191 **2284**
978 1 84193 **2046**
978 1 84195 **2143**
978 1 84196 **2591**
978 1 84200 **2748**
978 1 84204 **2468**
978 1 84210 **2494**
978 1 84212 **2574**
978 1 84217 **2579**
978 1 84218 **2101**
978 1 84222 **2150**
978 1 84227 **2065**
978 1 84229 **2778**
978 1 84231 **2298**
978 1 84234 **2265, 2848**
978 1 84239 **2021**
978 1 84243 **2560**
978 1 84246 **2431**
978 1 84255 **2573, 2574**
978 1 84262 **2479**
978 1 84264 **2263**
978 1 84270 **2030**
978 1 84277 **2847**
978 1 84282 **2469**
978 1 84285 **2739**
978 1 84291 **2436**
978 1 84298 **2381**
978 1 84303 **2284**
978 1 84306 **2442**
978 1 84310 **2435**
978 1 84315 **2453**
978 1 84323 **2315**
978 1 84339 **2417**
978 1 84340 **2190**
978 1 84341 **2095**
978 1 84344 **2560**
978 1 84347 **2590**
978 1 84351 **2458**
978 1 84354 **2055**
978 1 84358 **2105**
978 1 84361 **2795**
978 1 84365 **2590**
978 1 84368 **2584**
978 1 84371 **2198**
978 1 84376 **2251**
978 1 84377 **2301**
978 1 84395 **2773**
978 1 84398 **2166**
978 1 84400 **2626**
978 1 84407 **2244**
978 1 84408 **2462**
978 1 84409 **2279**
978 1 84414 **2422**
978 1 84417 **2489**
978 1 84424 **2073**
978 1 84425 **2354**
978 1 84426 **2804**
978 1 84437 **2049**
978 1 84445 **2447**
978 1 84447 **2157**
978 1 84448 **2686**
978 1 84454 **2105**
978 1 84455 **2787**
978 1 84458 **2590**
978 1 84465 **2005**
978 1 84471 **2669**
978 1 84474 **2416**
978 1 84483 **2074**
978 1 84486 **2199**
978 1 84489 **2017, 2369**
978 1 84490 **2822**
978 1 84494 **2122**
978 1 84506 **2463**
978 1 84507 **2459**
978 1 84508 **2167**
978 1 84511 **2631, 2756**
978 1 84513 **2062**
978 1 84519 **2744**
978 1 84520 **2091**
978 1 84524 **2334**
978 1 84525 **2769**
978 1 84527 **2334**
978 1 84528 **2379**
978 1 84529 **2196**
978 1 84533 **2510**
978 1 84539 **2490**
978 1 84540 **2390**
978 1 84541 **2165**
978 1 84542 **2251**
978 1 84545 **2092**
978 1 84550 **2174**
978 1 84553 **2260**
978 1 84559 **2412**
978 1 84560 **2496, 2497**
978 1 84564 **2833**
978 1 84569 **2837**
978 1 84576 **2777**
978 1 84583 **2762**
978 1 84584 **2808**
978 1 84589 **2503**
978 1 84593 **2138**
978 1 84596 **2481**
978 1 84603 **2575**
978 1 84609 **2562**
978 1 84617 **2773**
978 1 84619 **2632**
978 1 84621 **2552**
978 1 84622 **2849**
978 1 84623 **2391**
978 1 84625 **2227**
978 1 84627 **2615**
978 1 84631 **2465**
978 1 84634 **2269**
978 1 84643 **2172**
978 1 84645 **2330**
978 1 84647 **2155**
978 1 84659 **2760**
978 1 84680 **2645**
978 1 84686 **2078**
978 1 84688 **2023**
978 1 84689 **2628**
978 1 84691 **2073**
978 1 84697 **2095**
978 1 84709 **2716**
978 1 84714 **2198**
978 1 84715 **2463**
978 1 84717 **2553**
978 1 84720 **2251**
978 1 84725 **2198**
978 1 84730 **2809**
978 1 84737 **2706**
978 1 84738 **2706**
978 1 84739 **2706**
978 1 84744 **2462**
978 1 84749 **2564**
978 1 84751 **2691**
978 1 84762 **2200**
978 1 84769 **2165**
978 1 84772 **2562**
978 1 84774 **2439**
978 1 84782 **2773**
978 1 84784 **2311**
978 1 84788 **2091**
978 1 84797 **2215**
978 1 84802 **2258**
978 1 84812 **2603**
978 1 84813 **2847**
978 1 84819 **2435**
978 1 84829 **2035**
978 1 84831 **2385**
978 1 84834 **2394**
978 1 84844 **2251**
978 1 84859 **2194**
978 1 84880 **3036**
978 1 85008 **2284**
978 1 85010 **2354**
978 1 85015 **2269**
978 1 85022 **2790**
978 1 85029 **2195**
978 1 85035 **2840**
978 1 85038 **2374**
978 1 85043 **2631, 2756**
978 1 85048 **2695**
978 1 85049 **2133, 2264**
978 1 85055 **2278**
978 1 85058 **2704**
978 1 85065 **2382**
978 1 85072 **2690**
978 1 85074 **2258**
978 1 85075 **2182, 2198**
978 1 85078 **2065**
978 1 85089 **2412**
978 1 85097 **2629**
978 1 85116 **2163, 2692**
978 1 85124 **2109**
978 1 85128 **2320**
978 1 85137 **2351**
978 1 85145 **2590**
978 1 85149 **2036**
978 1 85153 **2642**
978 1 85158 **2481**
978 1 85168 **2565**
978 1 85172 **2609**
978 1 85175 **2681**
978 1 85177 **2811**
978 1 85182 **2290**
978 1 85184 **2395**
978 1 85196 **2604**
978 1 85200 **2798**
978 1 85205 **2345**
978 1 85207 **2045**
978 1 85223 **2215**
978 1 85224 **2106**
978 1 85227 **2812**
978 1 85228 **2719**
978 1 85235 **2295**
978 1 85249 **2142**
978 1 85260 **2354**
978 1 85265 **2507**

160 / INDEX OF ISBN PREFIXES

978 1 85273 **2223**
978 1 85276 **2284**
978 1 85278 **2251**
978 1 85284 **2179, 2498**
978 1 85285 **2344**
978 1 85297 **2261**
978 1 85302 **2435**
978 1 85304 **2637**
978 1 85306 **2206**
978 1 85310 **2628**
978 1 85311 **2681**
978 1 85312 **2833**
978 1 85315 **2663**
978 1 85321 **2175**
978 1 85326 **2839**
978 1 85328 **2444**
978 1 85331 **2247**
978 1 85332 **2355**
978 1 85340 **2603**
978 1 85341 **2582**
978 1 85343 **2291**
978 1 85356 **2528**
978 1 85359 **2165**
978 1 85361 **3037**
978 1 85364 **2065**
978 1 85375 **2150**
978 1 85381 **2462**
978 1 85383 **2244**
978 1 85390 **2809**
978 1 85398 **2051**
978 1 85399 **2241**
978 1 85410 **2062**
978 1 85411 **2689**
978 1 85414 **2146**
978 1 85418 **2386, 2772**
978 1 85424 **2460**
978 1 85430 **2463**
978 1 85437 **2755**
978 1 85444 **2052**
978 1 85450 **2253**
978 1 85455 **2206**
978 1 85458 **2212**
978 1 85459 **2362**
978 1 85486 **2724**
978 1 85487 **2196**
978 1 85503 **2446**
978 1 85506 **2198**
978 1 85509 **2354**
978 1 85514 **2533**
978 1 85520 **2129**
978 1 85521 **2050**
978 1 85532 **2575**
978 1 85534 **2299**
978 1 85539 **2198, 2540**
978 1 85549 **2083**
978 1 85557 **2106**
978 1 85561 **2590**
978 1 85566 **2116**
978 1 85573 **2837**
978 1 85575 **2427**
978 1 85576 **3021**
978 1 85578 **2614**
978 1 85584 **2731**
978 1 85594 **2057**
978 1 85602 **2590**
978 1 85604 **2274**
978 1 85607 **2193, 2220**
978 1 85609 **2834**
978 1 85615 **2216**
978 1 85628 **2050**
978 1 85635 **2495**
978 1 85649 **2847**
978 1 85651 **2335**
978 1 85652 **2076**
978 1 85669 **2767**
978 1 85691 **2742**
978 1 85695 **2412**
978 1 85703 **2379**
978 1 85709 **2530**
978 1 85710 **2653**
978 1 85711 **2007**
978 1 85723 **2462**
978 1 85724 **3036**
978 1 85732 **2510, 2512**
978 1 85741 **2721**
978 1 85742 **2050**
978 1 85750 **2293**
978 1 85753 **2199**
978 1 85756 **2420**
978 1 85757 **2323**
978 1 85758 **2453**
978 1 85759 **2676**
978 1 85770 **2675**
978 1 85775 **2632**
978 1 85780 **2016**
978 1 85782 **2105**
978 1 85788 **2119**
978 1 85792 **2174**
978 1 85793 **2590**
978 1 85794 **2551**
978 1 85795 **2794**
978 1 85797 **2573, 2574**
978 1 85798 **2573, 2574**
978 1 85799 **2573**
978 1 85800 **2652**
978 1 85805 **2453**
978 1 85810 **2719**
978 1 85811 **2842**
978 1 85852 **2502**
978 1 85856 **2784**
978 1 85858 **2121**
978 1 85860 **2305**
978 1 85864 **2399**
978 1 85868 **2150**
978 1 85880 **2073**
978 1 85881 **2573, 2574**
978 1 85894 **2500**
978 1 85895 **2551**
978 1 85898 **2251**
978 1 85902 **2315**
978 1 85903 **2479**
978 1 85904 **2050**
978 1 85918 **2202**
978 1 85928 **2050**
978 1 85936 **2151**
978 1 85937 **2503**
978 1 85941 **2655**
978 1 85944 **2225**
978 1 85959 **2184**
978 1 85960 **2354**
978 1 85964 **2297**
978 1 85972 **2050**
978 1 85973 **2091**
978 1 85983 **2120**
978 1 85985 **2460**
978 1 85994 **2222**
978 1 86013 **2058, 2745**
978 1 86023 **2495**
978 1 86024 **2065**
978 1 86029 **2029**
978 1 86034 **2307**
978 1 86049 **2462**
978 1 86057 **2237**
978 1 86064 **2631, 2756**
978 1 86071 **2038**
978 1 86072 **2386**
978 1 86076 **2552**
978 1 86082 **2154**
978 1 86089 **2652**
978 1 86094 **2389**
978 1 86105 **2649**
978 1 86126 **2215**
978 1 86134 **2610**
978 1 86144 **2538**
978 1 86154 **2767**
978 1 86161 **2786**
978 1 86163 **2145**
978 1 86171 **2210**
978 1 86176 **2168**
978 1 86177 **2824**
978 1 86187 **2269**
978 1 86197 **2621**
978 1 86202 **2284**
978 1 86205 **2589, 2590**
978 1 86207 **2322**
978 1 86209 **2452**
978 1 86214 **2056**
978 1 86223 **2714**
978 1 86228 **2785**
978 1 86239 **2303**
978 1 86396 **2064**
978 1 869847 **2541**
978 1 869860 **2056**
978 1 869890 **2353**
978 1 869928 **2483**
978 1 869981 **2648**
978 1 870015 **2340**
978 1 870098 **2324**
978 1 870109 **2711**
978 1 870206 **2376**
978 1 870322 **2673**
978 1 870325 **2826**
978 1 870352 **2457**
978 1 870450 **2774**
978 1 870471 **2482**
978 1 870491 **2313**
978 1 870516 **2751**
978 1 870612 **2259**
978 1 870673 **2036**
978 1 870727 **2580**
978 1 870732 **2612**
978 1 870775 **2592**
978 1 870874 **2525**
978 1 870890 **2044**
978 1 870905 **2632**
978 1 870946 **2422**
978 1 870985 **2527**
978 1 871048 **2738**
978 1 871133 **2294**
978 1 871177 **2824**
978 1 871199 **2110**
978 1 871201 **2207**
978 1 871217 **2275**
978 1 871504 **3040**
978 1 871512 **2309**
978 1 871516 **2406**
978 1 871569 **2100, 2361**
978 1 871585 **2743**
978 1 871608 **2411**
978 1 871615 **2819**
978 1 871676 **2174**
978 1 871814 **2647**
978 1 871846 **2210**
978 1 871871 **2568**
978 1 871891 **2262**
978 1 871931 **2750**
978 1 872074 **2732**
978 1 872082 **2628**
978 1 872119 **2628**
978 1 872229 **2383**
978 1 872362 **2184**
978 1 872365 **2149**
978 1 872423 **2205**
978 1 872424 **2122**
978 1 872438 **2434**
978 1 872475 **2678**
978 1 872621 **2754**
978 1 872642 **2705**
978 1 872699 **2425**
978 1 872758 **2607**
978 1 872853 **2552**
978 1 872870 **2818, 3042**
978 1 872883 **2356**
978 1 872977 **2779**
978 1 872988 **2097**
978 1 873045 **2492**
978 1 873130 **2607**
978 1 873132 **2043**
978 1 873150 **2165**
978 1 873226 **2282**
978 1 873245 **2207**
978 1 873271 **2401**
978 1 873328 **2028**
978 1 873329 **2697**
978 1 873357 **2396**
978 1 873385 **2448**
978 1 873394 **2236**
978 1 873429 **2584**
978 1 873431 **2737**
978 1 873475 **2741**
978 1 873533 **2432**
978 1 873580 **2825**
978 1 873590 **2557**
978 1 873592 **2258**
978 1 873600 **2735**
978 1 873626 **2120**
978 1 873674 **2803**
978 1 873712 **2711**
978 1 873721 **2346**
978 1 873784 **2550**
978 1 873793 **2506**
978 1 873827 **2467**
978 1 873829 **3012**
978 1 873859 **2218**
978 1 873868 **2124**
978 1 873877 **2638**
978 1 873936 **2244**
978 1 873938 **2297**
978 1 873951 **2749**
978 1 873982 **2228**
978 1 873992 **2013**
978 1 873994 **2080**
978 1 874016 **2180**
978 1 874029 **2392**
978 1 874045 **2661**
978 1 874061 **2560**
978 1 874099 **2086**
978 1 874105 **2808**
978 1 874181 **2151**
978 1 874192 **2638**
978 1 874241 **2655**
978 1 874250 **2213**
978 1 874267 **2307**
978 1 874312 **2237**
978 1 874427 **2845**
978 1 874545 **2485**
978 1 874579 **2527**
978 1 874597 **2542**
978 1 874622 **2358**
978 1 874640 **2048**
978 1 874675 **2458**
978 1 874700 **2186**
978 1 874719 **2328**
978 1 874735 **2069**
978 1 874744 **2095**
978 1 874774 **2464**
978 1 874783 **2209**
978 1 874790 **2352**
978 1 876213 **2655**
978 1 876857 **2669**
978 1 877864 **2119**
978 1 890951 **2511**
978 1 897675 **2123**
978 1 897685 **2563**
978 1 897738 **2329**
978 1 897765 **2176**
978 1 897766 **2152**
978 1 897784 **2830**
978 1 897799 **2303**
978 1 897913 **2363**
978 1 897940 **2748**
978 1 897976 **2684**
978 1 897999 **2094**
978 1 898000 **2078**
978 1 898049 **2160**
978 1 898059 **2593**
978 1 898128 **2161**
978 1 898146 **2624**
978 1 898217 **2445**
978 1 898218 **2683**
978 1 898281 **2033**
978 1 898283 **2210**
978 1 898307 **2145**
978 1 898323 **2117**
978 1 898392 **2192**
978 1 898543 **2801**
978 1 898591 **2137**
978 1 898595 **2744**
978 1 898617 **2201**
978 1 898697 **2332**
978 1 898723 **2744**
978 1 898784 **2763**
978 1 898852 **2700**
978 1 898924 **2664**
978 1 898937 **2501**
978 1 898947 **2624**
978 1 899003 **2766**
978 1 899047 **2276**
978 1 899085 **2301**
978 1 899120 **2673**
978 1 899171 **2279**
978 1 899233 **2245**
978 1 899235 **2454**
978 1 899247 **2059**
978 1 899248 **2155**
978 1 899280 **2526**
978 1 899293 **2788**
978 1 899308 **2025**
978 1 899383 **2113**
978 1 899434 **2312**
978 1 899483 **2148**
978 1 899573 **3028**
978 1 899579 **2832**
978 1 899618 **2753**
978 1 899726 **2624**
978 1 899738 **2652**
978 1 899750 **2060**
978 1 899807 **2727**
978 1 899820 **3032**
978 1 899827 **2682, 2683**
978 1 899857 **2570**
978 1 899863 **2378**
978 1 899869 **2237**
978 1 899870 **2516**
978 1 899877 **2237**
978 1 899929 **2029**
978 1 899988 **2626**
978 1 900072 **2041**
978 1 900127 **2636**
978 1 900138 **2641**
978 1 900178 **2639, 2671**
978 1 900188 **2579**
978 1 900222 **2417**
978 1 900289 **2819**
978 1 900322 **2324**
978 1 900369 **2849**
978 1 900437 **2077**
978 1 900506 **2034**
978 1 900564 **2259**
978 1 900592 **2357**
978 1 900621 **2799**
978 1 900639 **2116**
978 1 900693 **2186**
978 1 900718 **2421**
978 1 900796 **2596**
978 1 900826 **2767**
978 1 900828 **2767**
978 1 900850 **2042**
978 1 900891 **2214**
978 1 900899 **2029**
978 1 900949 **2286**
978 1 900988 **2729**
978 1 900990 **2527**
978 1 901033 **2098**
978 1 901092 **2587**
978 1 901097 **2162**
978 1 901146 **2520**
978 1 901176 **2189**
978 1 901223 **2078**
978 1 901231 **2207**
978 1 901242 **2659**
978 1 901250 **2813**
978 1 901295 **2808**
978 1 901323 **3031**
978 1 901362 **2349**
978 1 901557 **2827**
978 1 901577 **2156**
978 1 901657 **2101**
978 1 901663 **2546**
978 1 901670 **2766**
978 1 901706 **2506**
978 1 901764 **2493**
978 1 901768 **2218**
978 1 901786 **2461**
978 1 901846 **2707**
978 1 901866 **2458**
978 1 901888 **2136**
978 1 901903 **2307**
978 1 901927 **2654**
978 1 901970 **2674**
978 1 901982 **2560**
978 1 902007 **2783**
978 1 902011 **2118**
978 1 902031 **2180**
978 1 902109 **2209**
978 1 902163 **2657, 2767**
978 1 902175 **2160**
978 1 902202 **2038**
978 1 902210 **2744**
978 1 902239 **2377**
978 1 902272 **3041**
978 1 902279 **2152**
978 1 902283 **2078**
978 1 902304 **2332**
978 1 902420 **2186**
978 1 902438 **2733**
978 1 902455 **2679**
978 1 902463 **2341**
978 1 902467 **2829**
978 1 902472 **2678**
978 1 902523 **2187**
978 1 902538 **2062**
978 1 902586 **2494**
978 1 902602 **2542**
978 1 902628 **2605**
978 1 902636 **2764**
978 1 902646 **2445**
978 1 902653 **2484**
978 1 902683 **2005**
978 1 902686 **2767**
978 1 902694 **2696, 2716**
978 1 902719 **2237**
978 1 902737 **2711**
978 1 902751 **2029**
978 1 902757 **2626**
978 1 902771 **2204**
978 1 902788 **2139**
978 1 902806 **2801**
978 1 902813 **2440**
978 1 902831 **2048**
978 1 902859 **2567**
978 1 902882 **2428**
978 1 902902 **2044**
978 1 902915 **2069**
978 1 902916 **2244**
978 1 902928 **2409**
978 1 902930 **2247**
978 1 902932 **2297**
978 1 902973 **2778**
978 1 902984 **2296**
978 1 903016 **2780**
978 1 903025 **2841**
978 1 903042 **2560**
978 1 903056 **2130**
978 1 903063 **2556**
978 1 90306501 **2846**
978 1 9030700 **2271**
978 1 9030701 **2271**
978 1 9030702 **2271**
978 1 9030703 **2271**
978 1 9030704 **2271**
978 1 903071 **2090**
978 1 903087 **2227**
978 1 903142 **2086**
978 1 903171 **2234**
978 1 903172 **2079**
978 1 903174 **2590**
978 1 903185 **2729**
978 1 903207 **2155**
978 1 903221 **2062**
978 1 903222 **2130**
978 1 903223 **2016**
978 1 903238 **2830**
978 1 903266 **2411**
978 1 903278 **2529**
978 1 903285 **2155**
978 1 903300 **2447**
978 1 903307 **2450**
978 1 903313 **2033**
978 1 903331 **2466**
978 1 903333 **3015**
978 1 903337 **2447**
978 1 903341 **2267**
978 1 903364 **2815**
978 1 903366 **2558**
978 1 903370 **2590**
978 1 903434 **2171**
978 1 903448 **2301**
978 1 903458 **2353**
978 1 903462 **2718**
978 1 903471 **2286**
978 1 903506 **2850**
978 1 903517 **2228**
978 1 903529 **2310**
978 1 903530 **2268**
978 1 903532 **2237**
978 1 903550 **2268**
978 1 903552 **2072**
978 1 903577 **2838**
978 1 903582 **2499**
978 1 903613 **2404**
978 1 903619 **2422**
978 1 903682 **2413**
978 1 903689 **2606**
978 1 903699 **2124**
978 1 903706 **2808**
978 1 903747 **2110**
978 1 903765 **2242**
978 1 90377 **2064**
978 1 903776 **2482**
978 1 903816 **2381**
978 1 903845 **2626**
978 1 903852 **2507**
978 1 903853 **2123**
978 1 903855 **2664**
978 1 903889 **2762**
978 1 903900 **2744**
978 1 903933 **2304**
978 1 903942 **2770**
978 1 903954 **2590**
978 1 903973 **2767**
978 1 903975 **2686**
978 1 903998 **2324**
978 1 904001 **2624**
978 1 904007 **2449**
978 1 904010 **2332**
978 1 904018 **2596**
978 1 904024 **2173**
978 1 904027 **2252**
978 1 904048 **2560**
978 1 904053 **2445**
978 1 904057 **2628**

INDEX OF ISBN PREFIXES / 161

978 1 904091 **2810**	978 1 904633 **2217**	978 1 905175 **2781**	978 1 905646 **2356**	978 1 906353 **2276**	978 3 7658 **2617**
978 1 904095 **2702**	978 1 904634 **2259**	978 1 905203 **2596**	978 1 905664 **2124**	978 1 906358 **2039**	978 3 7913 **2617**
978 1 904113 **2464**	978 1 904668 **2157,**	978 1 905207 **2670**	978 1 905674 **2815**	978 1 906359 **2799**	978 3 7931 **2679**
978 1 904132 **2813**	**2496, 2497**	978 1 905214 **2049**	978 1 905686 **2657**	978 1 906474 **2113**	978 3 7957 **2679**
978 1 904233 **2462**	978 1 904675 **2800**	978 1 905222 **2469**	978 1 905693 **2628**	978 1 906476 **2830**	978 3 8055 **2426**
978 1 904242 **2192**	978 1 904677 **2570**	978 1 905224 **2449**	978 1 905710 **2069**	978 1 906502 **2332**	978 3 8238 **2765**
978 1 904243 **2180**	978 1 904687 **3003**	978 1 905236 **2078**	978 1 905712 **2767**	978 1 906509 **2797**	978 3 8327 **2765**
978 1 904244 **2151**	978 1 904705 **2387, 2767**	978 1 905237 **2788**	978 1 905716 **2217**	978 1 906510 **2788**	978 3 8331 **2300**
978 1 904301 **2542**	978 1 904724 **2156**	978 1 905238 **2398**	978 1 905722 **2526**	978 1 906517 **2570**	978 3 85604 **2642**
978 1 904307 **2377**	978 1 904737 **2455**	978 1 905246 **2307**	978 1 905740 **2035**	978 1 906523 **2541**	978 3 86521 **2767**
978 1 904317 **2630**	978 1 904744 **2788**	978 1 905257 **2205**	978 1 905745 **2813**	978 1 906534 **3042**	978 3 87090 **2679**
978 1 904339 **2646**	978 1 904746 **2700**	978 1 905261 **2445**	978 1 905756 **2358**	978 1 906542 **2079**	978 3 87624 **2767**
978 1 904353 **2132**	978 1 904754 **2596**	978 1 905267 **2546**	978 1 905780 **2123**	978 1 906558 **2451**	978 3 87632 **2629**
978 1 904380 **2818, 3042**	978 1 904764 **2815**	978 1 905286 **2367**	978 1 905802 **2522**	978 1 906562 **2708**	978 3 88243 **2767**
978 1 904396 **2467**	978 1 904768 **2260**	978 1 905288 **3034**	978 1 905816 **2800**	978 1 906570 **2041**	978 3 88618 **2300**
978 1 904434 **2783**	978 1 904772 **2098**	978 1 905294 **2171**	978 1 905820 **2466**	978 1 906578 **2192**	978 3 901974 **2679**
978 1 904439 **3015**	978 1 904777 **2286**	978 1 905313 **2801**	978 1 905886 **2788**	978 1 906582 **2061**	978 3 905509 **2767**
978 1 904442 **2171**	978 1 904787 **2527**	978 1 905339 **2341**	978 1 905893 **2173**	978 1 906601 **2282**	978 3 920030 **2679**
978 1 904444 **2039**	978 1 904788 **2808**	978 1 905366 **2038**	978 1 905941 **2703**	978 1 906632 **2110**	978 3 920045 **2679**
978 1 904445 **2826**	978 1 904798 **2035**	978 1 905379 **2488**	978 1 906005 **2592**	978 1 906641 **2267**	978 3 920201 **2679**
978 1 904449 **2157, 2169**	978 1 904842 **2680**	978 1 905385 **2032**	978 1 906008 **2506**	978 1 906663 **2467**	978 3 920468 **2679**
978 1 904456 **2541**	978 1 904863 **2715**	978 1 905390 **2377**	978 1 906013 **3034**	978 1 906710 **2596**	978 3 923051 **2679**
978 1 904459 **2486**	978 1 904880 **2203**	978 1 905408 **2641**	978 1 906021 **2702**	978 1 906727 **2713**	978 3 931141 **2767**
978 1 904466 **2644**	978 1 904884 **2178**	978 1 905410 **2823**	978 1 906033 **2358**	978 1 931788 **2767**	978 3 932398 **2679**
978 1 904474 **2506**	978 1 904887 **2552**	978 1 905472 **2151**	978 1 906053 **2648**	978 1 932799 **3001**	978 3 937315 **2679**
978 1 904494 **2605**	978 1 904912 **2775**	978 1 905473 **3031**	978 1 906067 **2152**	978 1 933116 **2208**	978 3 938780 **2767**
978 1 904513 **2763**	978 1 904919 **2217**	978 1 905483 **2456**	978 1 906093 **2328**	978 1 934772 **2617**	978 4 87417 **2629**
978 1 904516 **2590**	978 1 904943 **2332**	978 1 905494 **2542**	978 1 906098 **2286**	978 1 94738 **2096**	978 8 88118 **2767**
978 1 904529 **2720**	978 1 904946 **2235**	978 1 905496 **2363**	978 1 906134 **2048**	978 2 06 **2504**	978 8 88491 **2767**
978 1 904537 **2639, 2671**	978 1 904977 **2702**	978 1 905499 **2461**	978 1 906136 **2674**	978 2 0801 **2767**	978 9 544983 **2108**
978 1 904550 **2172**	978 1 904982 **2043**	978 1 905509 **2779**	978 1 906142 **2304**	978 2 0803 **2767**	978 9 748225 **2767**
978 1 904558 **2799**	978 1 904999 **2849**	978 1 905512 **2281**	978 1 906147 **2218**	978 2 8315 **2300**	978 9 749863 **2767**
978 1 904559 **2480**	978 1 905005 **2713**	978 1 905523 **2558**	978 1 906155 **2098**	978 2 88046 **2651**	978 90 3258 **2153**
978 1 904563 **2617**	978 1 905010 **2827**	978 1 905538 **2570**	978 1 906205 **2207**	978 2 88479 **2067**	978 90 4760 **2153**
978 1 904575 **2733**	978 1 905021 **2849**	978 1 905540 **2187**	978 1 906206 **2596**	978 2 884790 **2767**	978 962 421 **2300**
978 1 904587 **2454**	978 1 905022 **2849**	978 1 905541 **2664**	978 1 906215 **2650**	978 2 940373 **2067, 2767**	978 962 593 **2300**
978 1 904598 **2095**	978 1 905056 **2645**	978 1 905559 **2340**	978 1 906221 **2788**	978 2 940411 **2067**	978 962 634 **2537**
978 1 904605 **2218**	978 1 905117 **2155**	978 1 905560 **2186**	978 1 906224 **2086**	978 3 03911 **2443**	978 981 234 **2300**
978 1 904607 **2095**	978 1 905119 **2579**	978 1 905582 **2319**	978 1 906254 **2593**	978 3 254 **2679**	978 981 246 **2300**
978 1 904609 **2237**	978 1 905147 **2042**	978 1 905600 **2149**	978 1 906295 **2775**	978 3 468 **2300**	978 981 258 **2300**
978 1 904614 **2041**	978 1 905153 **2630**	978 1 905624 **2258**	978 1 906307 **2469**	978 3 570 91 **2765**	
978 1 904622 **2547**	978 1 905156 **2630**	978 1 905636 **2087**	978 1 906332 **2185**	978 3 575 **2300**	

7.3 INDEX OF PERSONAL NAMES

Damien Abbott **2230**
Vivienne Abbott **2313**
Claire Abel **2247**
Julia Abel Smith **5072**
Jacqueline Abromet **2596**
Khalil Abu Shawareb **2415**
Gerry Acher **5073**
Andy Ackerley **6091**
Joe Ackerley **6091**
Beverley Acreman **2757**
Billy Adair **6122**
Max Adam **6199**
Colin Adams **2100, 2107**
Janis Adams **2529**
Michael Adams **2290**
Susie Adams **4085**
Stephen Adamson **2008**
Ray Addicott **6024**
Michael Addison **2681**
David Ahier **2156**
Mari Ahlfeld-Smith **2651**
Haris Ahmad **2439**
Gillon Aitken **4001**
Amanda Aknai **2730**
S. C. Albert **2058, 2736, 2745, 2840**
Michael Alcock **4049**
Patricia Aldama **5003**
Linda Alderson **2359**
Angela Aldretsch **2469**
Clare Alexander **4001**
Huw Alexander **2665**
Dr Jean Alexander **2125**
Rachel Alexander **2272**
Thomas Allain-Chapman **2177**
David Allan **2016**
Gordon Allan **2309**
Katrena Allan **2309**
Kevin Allard **2681**
Richard K. Allday **2428**
Diane Allen **2479**
Liz Allen **2597**
Mark Allen **2733**
Simon Allen **2473**
Stephanie Allen **2708**
Keith Allen-Jones **2269**
Katherine Allenby **2177**
Edward Allhusen **2557**
Hilary Allom **3021**
Yoram Allon **2815**
Jim Allpass **6031**
Ms Cate Allwood **5083**
Charmian Allwright **2337**
Isabelle Almeida **2180**
Keisuke Amano **6176**
Frances Ambler **2811**
Irene Amore **2098**
Alexander Anandam **2668**
Nele Andersch **2469**
Barry Anderson **2662**
Darley Anderson **4003**
J. Anderson **2789**
Kathleen Anderson **2143**
Lindsay Anderson **2166**
Sue Anderson **2205, 2472**

Hugh Andrew **2095, 6081**
Adrian Andrews **2196**
Chris Andrews **2032**
Ella Andrews **4003**
Peter Andrews **2245**
Virginia Andrews **2032**
Dawn Angel **2303**
Helen Anjomshoaa **2117**
Juliet Annan **2597**
Donna Anton **2383**
Bill Antrobus **2379, 2781**
Myrddin ap Dafydd **2334**
Catrina Appleby **2204**
Matt Applewhite **2362**
Steven Apps **2738**
Myles Archbald **2348**
Sophie Armfield **6090, 6137**
Jackie Arrowsmith **2206**
Inger Arthur **2686**
Okezie I. Aruoma **2556**
Lynn Ashman **2596**
Audrey Ashton **2838**
Jo Ashworth **2318**
Louise Ashworth **2142**
Martin Ashworth **2631, 2756**
Rory Aspell **2380**
Ivon Asquith **2247**
Neil Astley **2106**
Richard Astor **2080**
David Atkins **2761**
Jonathan Atkins **2706**
Owen Atkinson **5017**
Will Atkinson **2272**
James Attlee **2755**
Susan Attwood **2774**
Tony Attwood **2280**
Au Bak Ling **2817, 3007**
Cormac Austin **2102**
Meg Avent **2002**
Alan Avery **2103**
Felicity Awdry **2433**
Linda Ayres **2064**
Pete Ayrton **2621**
Fatima Azzam **2413**

Michael H. Babani **2071**
Suzanne Baboneau **2706**
Josephine Bacon **6043**
Elinor Bagenal **2171**
Paul Baggaley **2348**
Richard Baggaley **2619**
Iradj Bagherzade **2756**
C. Baile de Laperriere **2364**
S. Baile de Laperriere **2364**
David Bailey **3021**
Gill Bailey **2602**
Nicola Bailey **2500**
Roberta Bailey **2046**
Sarah Bailey **2191**
Shirley Bailey-Wood **5028**
Duncan Baird **2074**
Liz Baird **3034**
Robin Baird-Smith **2135, 2182, 2198, 2344**

Simon Baker **2800**
W. Baker **2678**
Robert Baldock **2844**
David Baldwin **2163, 2692**
Gillian Baldwin **2163, 2692**
Sue Bale **2476**
Richard Balkwill **6008, 6199**
Alan Ball **2493**
K. M. Ball **2806**
Paul Ballard **5050**
Sara Ballard **3003**
Laura Bamford **2064**
Nikole Bamford **2440**
Ian Bannerman **2757**
Ted Baracos **6174**
Laura Barber **2615**
R. W. Barber **2116**
Jennifer Barclay **2741**
Sheena Barclay **2191**
Dean Bargh **2328**
Christine Barham **3021**
Tassy Barham **4007**
Dan Raymond Barker **2541**
Graham Barker **2086**
Joanne Barker **3026**
Eldo Barkhuizen **6020**
Geoff Barlow **2603**
Tony Barlow **4020**
Geoff Barnard **2399**
Emma Barnes **2713**
Jan Barnes **2201**
Samantha Barnett **2205**
Pete Barnsley **2065**
Victoria Barnsley **2348**
Alison Barr **2716**
Nicola Barr **4093**
Stephen Barr **2665**
Aoife Barrett **2499**
Helen Barrett **2268**
Paul Barrett **6087**
Brian Barron **6133**
Nikki Barrow **2519**
Amanda Barry **6167**
Jean Barry **2295**
Susan Barry **2337**
Oliver Barter **2617**
Jason Bartholomew **2372, 2519**
Norman Bartlett **5030**
Ian Bartley **2767**
Ben Barton **2645**
Richard Batchelor **2213**
Denise Bates **2348**
F. R. Bates **6025**
Richard Bates **6025**
Tim Bates **4079**
Ailsa Bathgate **2481**
Nigel Batt **5029**
Nicholas Battle **2206**
Suzanne Battle **2206**
Claire Baumforth **2444**
Andrew Bax **2632**
Alison Baxter **5017**
Duncan Baxter **2468**

Nicola Baxter **3005**
Sarah Baxter **5057, 5085**
Dennis Baylis **2397**
M. J. Bayliss **6059**
Ros Baynes **2381, 2482**
John Beaton **2628**
Karen Beaulah **3013**
Claire Beaumont **2621**
Felicia Beder **2232**
Davinder Bedi **6100**
Anne Beech **2609**
Diana Beech **2704**
Graham Beech **2704**
Marian Beech Hughes **5088**
Kathryn Beecroft **2274, 6189**
Elsepth Beidas **2117**
Mary Bekhait **4056**
Barry Belasco **2289**
Jim Belben **2369**
Heather Bell **2779**
Peter Bell **2779**
Richard Bell **2829**
Simon Bell **2465, 5067**
Lorella Belli **4008**
Valery Belov **6170**
Lionel Bender **3006**
Robert Benewick **2521**
Ian Bennett **2397**
Lizzie Bennett **2389**
Ron Bennett **2140**
Guy Bentham **2194**
Marion Berghahn **2092**
Ms Anne Bergman-Tahon **5002**
Johan Bergström-Allen **2666**
Grant Berry **2534**
Natalina Bertoli **6052**
Marguerita Best **2398**
Richard Beswick **2462**
Alan Bett **2326**
Ann Betts **2545, 5063, 6075**
Martin Betts **2187**
Tina Betts **4064**
Monty Bhatia **2463**
Nikhil Bhoopal **2847**
Michael Bickers **2084**
K. Bickmore **2749**
Mark Bicknell **2676**
Joseph Biddulph **2094**
Mark Bide **5068**
Natascha Biebow **5075**
Carol Bignell **2315**
Anne Bihan **2844**
Ashley Biles **2672, 2760**
Patricia A. Billings **2508**
Derek Bingham **2156**
Valerie Bingham **2681**
Adrian Binsted **2285**
Diana Birch **2824**
Jane Birch **2312**
Viv Bird **5023**
Sarah Birdsey **2706**

David Birkett **2847**
Eleanor Birne **2519**
James Birney **2157**
Yahya Birt **2439**
Auriol Bishop **2372**
Bridget Bishop **2674**
David Bishop **5068**
Gillian Bissell **2803**
Charlotte Black **2700**
James Black **2043**
Rita Black **2106**
Kate Blackadder **2546**
Simon Blackett **2444**
Carole Blake **4009**
Caroline Blake **2822**
Deborah Blake **2241**
John Blake **2105**
Suzanne Blake **2191**
David Blakeley **2307**
G. Blanc **6154**
Terry Bland **4038**
Clare Blick **2258**
P. R. Bligh **5046**
Claudia Bloch **2533**
Adam Bloom **6142**
Roy Bloom **6142**
Robin Bloxsidge **2465**
Andrea Blue **2166**
Richard Blundell **2396**
John Blunsden **2516**
Vickie Boff **2812**
Debbie Bogard **2657**
Thierry Bogliolo **2279**
Carlo Boi **2154**
Francine Bois **6175**
Camilla Bolton **4003**
Anna Bond **2585**
Graham Bond **2359**
John Bond **2348**
Steve Bonner **2632**
Luigi Bonomi **4010**
Alun Boore **2240**
Anne Boore **2240**
Gwilym Boore **2240**
Rhys Boore **2240**
Roger Boore **2240**
Juergen Boos **6168**
Robin Booth **2362**
James Booth-Clibborn **2599**
Ian Borthwick **2837**
Sara Borthwick **2459**
Rosanna Bortoli **2100**
Wendy Bosberry-Scott **2156**
Suzanne Bosman **2530**
Achim Bosse **2424**
Colin Bottle **6042**
Christopher Boughton **2140**
Emma Bourne **2539**
Stephen R. R. Bourne **2140**
Sue Bourner **2674**
Anna Bowen **2030**
Mike Bowen **2083**

Paul Bowes **2110**
Mr D. Bowman **6089**
Jayney Bown **2328**
Peter Bowron **2597**
Moira Bowyer **6157**
Jenny Boyce **2777**
Brian Boyd **2176**
Carrie Boyes **2518**
Marion Boyrbouze **5077**
Lee Brackstone **2272**
Adam Bradbury **2293**
Emma Bradford **3002**
Rosemary Bradley **2128**
Ross Bradshaw **2281**
Tina Brand **2420**
Trudy Brannan **2536**
Alex Bratt **2098**
David Brawn **2235, 2348, 2394**
Ros Brawn **2235, 2394**
Michael Bray **2410**
Denis Brazell **2838**
Derek Brazell **5011**
Nicholas Brealey **2119**
Prof. C. A. Brebbia **2833**
Jessica Breen **2290**
Liz Breeze **2607**
Tony Breeze **2607**
Elizabeth Brennan **2101**
Michael Brennan **2220**
Simon Brett **5016**
Stan Brett **5004**
T. Breverton **2310**
Andrew Brewer **6084**
John Brewer **2503**
Alan Brewin **2121**
Alistair Brewin **2121**
Julie Brewin **2121**
David Brewster **6153**
Ley S. Bricknell **6128**
Peter Bridgewater **2387, 3011, 3027**
Dr Peter Brierley **2175**
Dee Brigham **2435**
Jackie Bright **2039, 5029**
Katharine Bright-Holmes **2115**
Adrian Brink **2183, 2471**
Roger Bristow **6003**
Isabel Britten **2259**
Catherine Britton **2126, 2127**
Alan Brodie **4011**
Tom Bromley **2613, 2649**
Phillip Brook **6132**
Joan Brookbank **2500**
Rosalie Brookhouse **2213**
Judith Brooks **2808**
Jenny Broom **3012**
Stephen Brough **2621**
Andrew Brown **2140**
Cameron Brown **2217**
Chris Brown **5076**
David Brown **2525, 2579**
Graham Brown **3009, 3012**

INDEX OF PERSONAL NAMES / 163

Jackie Brown **2468**
Jean Brown **2040**
Jenny Brown **4012**
Julian Brown **2630**
Kate Brown **2531**
Lesley Brown **2022**
Luke Brown **2776**
Mark Brown **2076**
Olive Brown **2132**
Richard Brown **2154**
T. Nigel Brown **2131**
Terence Brown **2458**
Trevor E. Brown **2291**
Alison Browne **2665**
Lionel Browne **6018**
Guy Browning **6119**
Carol Brownlee **6075**
Fiona Brownlee **2481**
Ruth Brownlee **5013**
Ken Bruce **2091**
Laura Brudenell **2190, 2589**
Claire Brumham **2425**
Charlotte Bruton **4016**
Catherine Bruzzone **2069**
Felicity Bryan **4013**
Clive Bryant **2185**
Douglas Buchanan **2170**
Pat Buchanan **2170**
Lance Bucharov **2389**
Jason Buck **2503**
John Buck **2503**
Stuart Buck **2778**
Susan Buck **2323, 6022**
Edwin Buckhalter **2691**
Marlene Buckland **2721**
B. R. Buckley **2176**
Howard Buckley **2140**
Jane Buckley **2176**
Mike Buckley **2475**
Patrick Buckley **2661**
Jessica Buckman **4014**
Peter Buckman **4002**
Rosemarie Buckman **4014**
David Bucknor **2463**
Dr Phil Budden **2383**
Belinda Budge **2348**
Jan Budkowski **2846**
Sam Bufton **2300**
D. Bull **2583**
Penny Bull **2183, 2471**
Judith Bullent **2511**
Anjali Bulley **2811**
Jonathan Bunce **2539**
Mette Bundgaard **2443**
James Bunkum **2354**
Laura Bunney **2837**
Martyn Burchall **6099**
Joel Burden **2770**
Neil Burden **2172**
Jo Burges **2050**
Annette Burgess **6150**
Donal Burke **2844**
Katie Burke **6128**
Michael Burke **2468**
Sinead Burke **2166**
Thomas Burke **6128**
Vibeke Burke **6172**
Brie Burkeman **4015**
B. Burkett **2001**
Molly Burkett **2079**
R. Burleigh **2837**
Piers Burnett **2062**
Donna Burridge **2300**
S. Burridge **2583**
Sarah Burrows **2663**
David Burt **2770**
Alistair Burtenshaw **6172**
Brian J. Burton **2345**
Mike Burton **2359**
Peter Burton **2284**
Tim Burton **2528**
Kate Burvill **2767**
S. Bush **2486**
Madeleine Buston **4003**
Sue Buswell **2348**
Alan Butcher **2016**
A. C. Butler **6140**
David Butler **5058**
Dr Eamonn Butler **2711**
Jane Butler **5059**
Simon Butler **2343, 5050**
Ian Butterfield **6099**
D. I. Button **6098**
John Button **6023**
Jamie Byng **2143**
Kathryn Byrd **5045**
Kevin Byrne **2378**
Mary Byrne **2603**
Brenda Byrom **2070**

Tom Cabot **2815**
Mrs L. Cairns **6155**
Liz Calder **2107**
Rachel Calder **4086**
Helen Calderon **2117**
Paul Callaghan **2136**
Michael Callahan **2821, 4102**
T. Callan **2246**
David Calvert **2063**
Ben Cameron **2590**
Graham Cameron **2572**
Ian Cameron **2141, 3014, 6009**
Jacci Cameron **2351**
Louise Cameron **2438**
R. A. Cameron **2549**
Peter Camilleri **6040**
Jane Camillin **2164**
Alastair Campbell **2387**
Alison Campbell **2663**
Bianca Campbell **2405**
Bill Campbell **2481**
Cassandra Campbell **2019**
David Campbell **2266, 2676**
Eric Campbell **2018**
Mary Campbell **2837**
Ramsey Campbell **5026**
Stephen Campbell **2154**
Jamie Camplin **2767**
Andreas Campomar **2196**
James Cannings **6037**
Peter Cannings **6037**
Steve Cannon **2419**
Nick Canty **2405**
V. Capstick **2583**
Anwar Cara **2439**
Miss Rufeedah Cara **2439**
Gloria Carey **2666**
Michael Carey **2148**
Helen Carley **2274, 5034, 6189**
Louise Carlin **2393**
Suzanne Carnell **2475**
Jane Caron **2120**
Stephen Caron **2120**
Aurea Carpenter **2702**
Fiona Carpenter **2585**
Jon Carpenter **2152**
Andrea Carr **2645**
Robert Carr-Archer **2533**
Amy Carroll **2153**
Ms Lorraine Carter **2833**
Phil Carter **2380**
Giorgio Casarotto **4017**
Jenne Casarotto **4017**
Andy Casey **2300**
Stewart Cass **2807**
Vincent Cassidy **5028**
Amanda Castle **2419**
Neil Castle **6136**
Alison Cathie **2626**
Charles Catton **3003**
Joanna Cave **5039**
Anastasia Cavouras **3035**
J. Cawley **2394**
Roger Cazalet **2462**
Flavio Centofanti **2476**
Tom Chalmers **2451**
Mark Chaloner **6134**
David Chambers **5004**
Geeta Chambers **2772**
John Chambers **5079**
Jan Chamier **2196**
Laurent Chaminade **2389**
Alexia Chan **2369**
Kishor Chandarana **6157**
Claire Chandler **2500**
John Chandler **2368**
Graham Chapman **2393**
Ian Stewart Chapman **2706**
Jennifer Chapman **4018**
Martyn Chapman **6126**
Melissa Chapman **2184**
Nicholas Chapman **6127**
Paul Chapman **2665**
Philip Chapman **2592**
Sîan Chapman **2802**
Simon Chappell **2572**
Richard Charkin **2107**
Chris Charlesworth **2562**
Dr C. Chatfield **2011**
Mark Chatterton **2520**
Joan Checkley **2031**
Philip Checkley **2031**
Anna Cheifetz **2589**
Paul Cherry **2017**
Christoph Chesher **2757**
Jo Cheshire **2384**
Katie Chester **2686**
Vivian Cheung **2777**
Tracy Chevalier **5080**
Mark Chilver **6103**
Gill Chitty **2204**
Mr Chok **2046**
Jane Cholmeley **2705**
Robert Chote **2396**
Sue Christelow **2725**
Jo Christian **2459**
Tirzah Christian **2213**
Ed Christie **2782**
Jennifer Christie **4035**
Jonathan Christie **2195**
Marus Clapham **2217**
Trisha Clapp **6126**
Adrian Clark **4009**
Anne Clark **2603**
Bridget Clark **2765**
Tim Clark **2676**
Catherine Clarke **4013**
Julie Clarke **2652**
Tom Clarke **2774**
Vanessa Clarke **2475**
Barbara Classen **6200**
Jorgen Clausen **2528**
Ross Clayton **2159, 6120**
Celia Clear **2755**
Nigel Clements **2354**
Mary Clemmey **4019**
B. Cleveland **2129**
Mary Clewer **2318**
P. Clifford **2116**
Paul Clifford **2460**
Terry Clutterham **2685**
Ken Coates **2726**
John Cobbett **2393**
Elspeth Cochrane **4020**
Anne Cockburn **2280**
Adrian Cockell **2284**
Beka Cohen **2533**
Jeannie Cohen **2568**
Denis Cole **2460**
Elaine Cole **5050**
Susan Cole **3019**
Jo'e Coleby **2323, 6022**
Beryl L. Coleman **2544**
Christopher J. Coleman **2544**
Jill Coleman **2009, 2100, 2361, 6184, 6195**
Gill Coleridge **4084**
Fen Coles **6161**
Thomas Coles **2445**
Matt Colgan **6172**
L. H. R. Collard **2137**
Robert Collie **6147, 6166**
Mahara Collier **6074**
Polly Collingridge **2143**
David Collings **6032**
Christopher Collins **5068**
Mike Collins **2057, 2202**
Jacky Colliss Harvey **2657**
Simon Colverson **2602**
Terry Compton **2788**
Sue Concill **2779**
Anthony Cond **2465**
Amanda Conlon-McKenna **2809**
Eamonn Connelly **2809**
S. Connolly **2648**
Steve Connolly **2369**
Margaret Conroy **2337**
Peter Constable **2172**
Jean Constantine **2073**
John Conway **3022**
Jane Conway-Gordon **4022**
Michael Coogan **2205**
Debbie Cook **2249**
Graham Cook **2354**
Peter Cook **6053**
Vicky Cook **5026**
D. C. S. Cooke **2785**
Daniel Cooke **2066**
Geraldine Cooke **4067**
Rachel Cooke **2337**
Thomas Cooney **2542**
Charlie Cooper **2046**
Dominic Cooper **5030**
Graham Cooper **6120**
Imogen Cooper **2171**
Jason Cooper **2272**
P. Cooper **2264**
Philip Cooper **2433**
Sara Cooper **2380**
T. Cooper **2695**
Kath Cope **2779**
Kim Cope **2500**
Sam Copeland **4083**
Richard Copsey **2666**
Hannah Corbett **2706**
Heather Corbett **2790**
Ivan Corbett **2790**
Robert Corfe **2047**
Russell Corfe **2047**
Andy Cork **2804**
David Corkill **4005**
Clive Cornelius **2685**
Robert Cornford **2580**
Tim Coronel **6182**
Lore Cortis **2092**
Adela Cory **2074**
Graham Coster **2062**
Peter Cotton **2462**
Simon Couchman **2778**
Nelly Coudoa **3008**
Katie Cowan **2190**
Richard Coward **2791**
Athol E. Cowen **2598**
Geoff Cowen **6139**
Jerry Cowhig **2410**
Belle Cowie **2628**
Stewart Cowley **3016**
Chris Cowlin **2039**
Miss Angela Cox **3024, 6113**
Beth Cox **2172**
Justin Cox **6088**
Peter Cox **4082**
Matthew Crabbe **2646**
David Crabtree **2092**
Ludo Craddock **2464**
Alan Craig **2055**
Mike Cranidge **6107**
Sue Cranidge **6107**
Oliver Craske **2676**
Carol Crawford **6081**
Claire Creaser **2461**
Elfreda Crehan **2455**
Jacqueline Cressey **2384**
F. Rupert Crew **4024**
Sophie Cringle **2204**
Bob Cripps **6061**
Denise Cripps **2677**
Henry Crisp **2025**
June Crisp **2025**
M. Critchley **2486**
Jon Croft **2002**
Paul Crompton **2213**
Alastair Cronin **2440**
Dr Nicholas Cronk **2814**
Lester Crook **2631**
Gillian Crosby **2162**
Guy Croton **3023**
Patrick Crowley **2495**
Roz Crowley **2563**
Sheila Crowley **4101, 5009**
G. L. Crowther **2216**
Leila Cruickshank **2469**
Margaret Crush **2751**
D. Cumberland **2719**
Sioux Cumming **2409**
Barry Cunningham **2171**
Patrick Curran **6133**
James Currey **2221**
Susan Currie **2562**
Linda J. Curry **5007**
B. D. Curtin **2305**
Becky Curtis **2412**
Sharon Curtis **2723**
Hazel Cushion **2004**
Robert Cushion **2004**
Chris Custance **6110**
Amanda Cuthbert **2324**
Dr Richard Cutler **5084**
Gillian Cutress **2072**

Rosalind Dace **2686**
Paul Dack **2656**
Lara Dafert **2022**
Dr John Daintith **3029**
Andrew Dalby **2268**
Ian Daley **2654**
Danny Daly **2265**
Teresa Daly **2220**
Tracey Daly **2710**
Penny Daniel **2621**
Paul Daniels **6108**
Miss G. A. Danson-Smith **6118**
Rev Dr T. C. Danson-Smith **6118**
Edouard d'Araille **2466**
Michael Darcy **6058**
Alex Dare **6041**
J. Dargan **2600**
Anne Davenport **6062**
Alan Davey **5008**
Angela Davey **6148**
Chris Davey **6148**
Gillian Davidson **2246**
Ian Davidson **2247**
Julian Davidson **2343**
Robert Davidson **2670**
Mrs S. J. Davie **2642**
Alan Davies **2775**
Aled Davies **2222**
D. Philip Davies **5088**
Gill Davies **3033**
Hilary Davies **2775**
John Davies **2332**
Martin Davies **2369**
Nick Davies **2143**
Ray Davies **2241**
Suzanne Davies **6108**
Tim Davies **2066**
Paul Davighi **2631, 2756**
Clare Davis **2811**
Meg Davis **4069**
Peter Davis **2768**
Peter Davison **2140**
Tom Davy **2159**
Victoria Dawbarn **2601**
Kingsley Dawson **6151**
Patrick Dawson **2286**
Richard Dawson **2472**
Stuart Dawson **2757**
Chris Day **2783**
John Day **2614**
Jon Day **2145**
Julia Day **2145**
Crispin de Boos **2261**
Lesley de Boos **2261**
Daniela de Groote **2042**
Caroline de la Bédoyère **2686**
Martin de la Bédoyère **2686**
Valerie de la Rochette **2082**
Marina de Quay **6200**
Sheila de Vallee **2587**
Caroline de Wolfe **4026**
Sophie Dean **2696, 2716**
Sarah Death **6048**
Mariel Deegan **2542, 6058**
Joan Deitch **4079**
Elizabeth Delaney **6174**
Michael Dell **2419**
Richard Dell **2791**
Paul Dempsey **2083**
James M. Dening **2045**
Buchan Dennis **2231**
Gordon Dennis **6036**
John Dennis **2215**
Kate Dennis **2014**
Magnus Dennis **2231**
Richard Dennis **2231**
Neill Denny **6181**
Yolande Denny **2463**
Phil Denvir **2665**
Chris Derby **2025**
Graeme Derby **2491**
Joanna Devereux **4079**
Sheena Dewan **2813**
Anne Dewe **4064**
Paul Dibble **2545, 5063**
Roger Dickens **2166**
Lorraine Dickey **2195**
John Dickinson **2380**
C. J. Dicks **2828**
David Dickson **2458**
James Dickson **2579**
Keith Didcock **2625**
Jeremy Dieguez **2476**
John Dilger **2154**
Marion Dill **2086**
Jacqui Dilley **2284**
Anna Disley **5062**
Analyn Dixon **6114**
Isobel Dixon **4009**
Eric Dobby **2308**
Jackie Dobbyne **3013**
Julie Dobson **2499**
Francis Dodds **2837**
Richard Dodman **2226**
Elizabeth Dodsworth **2138**
Sue Doggett **2093**
Broo Doherty **4099**
Donna Doherty **2809**
Miriam Doherty **2436**
Anne Dolamore **2332**
Catherine Dolan **2652**
Sara Domville **2226**
Tom Donegan **5032**
Jim Donnelly **2370**
Jim Donohue **2254**
Walter Donohue **2272**
Paulette Dooler **2757**
Rosemary Dooley **6057**
Linda Doolin **6110**
Novin Doostdar **2565**
Phil Doran **6039**
Leonie Dorkins **2545**
Tasja Dorkofikis **2615**
Richard Dorrance **2123**
John Douglas **6012**
Nicky Douglas **2741**
Anne-Marie Doulton **4002**
Michael Dover **2820**
Francesca Dow **2597**
I. Dowdeswell **2129**
Claire Dowling **2078**
Erin Dowling **6172**
Richard Dowling **2050, 2317**
Leanne Down **3016**
Malcolm Down **2065**
Lorna Downing **2423**
Jackie Downs **2815**
Jane Doyle **2561**
Ursula Doyle **2585**
Mike Drabble **6103**
Ashley Drake **2237, 2802**
Clare Drake **2197**
Melanie Drake **2187**
Siwan Drake **2237**
Emma Draude **6073**
Michelle Draycott **2500**
Lavinia Drew **6100**
Lynne Drew **2348**
Jacquie Drewe **4025**
Julian Drinkall **2476, 2478**
Alison Dry **2035**
Chris Dry **2795**
Lorna Dubose **2412**
Miss M. Dudley **2709**
Robert Dudley **4028**
Sarah Dudman **2475**
Gilly Duff **2609**
Michelle Duff **2691**
Valerie Duff **2055**
Geoff Duffield **2585**
Karen Duffy **2055**
Anne Duggan **2295**
Amanda Dula **2643**
Jonathan Dunbar **2174**
Pete Duncan **2196**
Emma Dunford **2602**

164 / INDEX OF PERSONAL NAMES

Susie Dunlop **2022**
Andrew Dunn **2459**
Michael Dunn **2417**
Neil Dunnicliffe **6199**
Kirsty Dunseath **2820**
Ellen Dupont **3039**
Andrew Durnell **6063**
P. W. Durrance **2030**
Evelyne Duval **6055**
Michael Dwyer **2382**

Douglas Eadie **2778**
Graham Eames **2062**
Sam Eardley **2369**
Jonathan Earl **2767**
Kathryn Earle **2091**
Alan Earnshaw **2780**
Helena Earnshaw **2376**
Larraine Earnshaw **2780**
Peter Earnshaw **2780**
Sheila Ebbutt **2086**
Stephanie Ebdon **4076**
Shaun Ebelthite **4046**
Nick Eddison **3019**
John Eddowes **6032**
Caroline Eden **6116**
Carolyn Eden **2466**
Sam Edenborough **4047**
HRH The Duke of Edinburgh KG, KT, OM **5001, 5020, 5023, 6165**
Jane Edmonds **2280**
Steven Edney **2195, 2312, 2510, 2512, 2555, 2601**
Judy Edrich **2397**
Clive Edwards **2681**
David Edwards **6064**
Elwyn Edwards **2077**
Gary Edwards **2399**
Helen Edwards **2782**
Lois Edwards **6084**
Malcolm Edwards **2574, 2820**
Margot Edwards **2603**
Penny Edwards **2107**
Phil Edwards **6153**
Ros Edwards **4029**
Stephen Edwards **4084**
John Elford **2324**
Edward Elgar **2251**
Sandy Elgar **2251**
Valerie Eliot **2272**
Alwyn Elis **2336**
Nan Elis **2336**
Frances Ellery **2673**
Charles Elliott **4037**
David Elliott **2627, 2836**
Linda Elliott **6030**
Mark Elliott **2040**
Helen Ellis **2348**
Martin Ellis **2850**
W. Ellis **2116**
Karen Ellison **2763**
Caroline Elmslie **5068**
Sarah Elvins **2801**
Cliff Elwell **2837**
Hugh Elwes **3020**
Susie Elwes **3020**
Camilla Elworthy **2585**
Stephen Embrey **2767**
Leon F. Embry **2292**
Jean Emmerson **2207**
John Emmerson **2207**
Paul Emmett **2476**
Zoe Engert **2447**
Helen English **2367**
Breda Ennis **2313**
Tom Erhardt **4017**
Jenny Ertle **2636**
Mary Esdaile **4047**
Nicholas Esson **6105**
Jamie Etherington **2632**
Nicole Ettinger **2631, 2756**
Ms Alex Evans **2265**
Christine Evans **2156**
Jane Evans **2734**
Janet Evans **2277**
Jonathan Evans **2156**
Jude Evans **2463**
M. Evans **6099**
Martin Evans **2574, 6117**
Mary Anne Evans **5027**
Matt Evans **6087**
Nick Evans **5012**
Nigel Evans **2734**
Paul Evans **2277**
Sam Evans **2196**
Val Eve **2297**
Debbie Everson **2117**
Helen M. Exley **2269**
Lincoln Exley **2269**
Richard A. Exley **2269**
Nigel Eyre **2757**

Sarah Fabiny **2475**
Chris Facey **2100**
Christopher Fagg **2770**
Lyn Fairfax **2523, 5060**
Anne Fairhall **2523, 5060**
Suzanne Fairless-Aitken **2106**
Melissa Fairley **2475**
Natasha Fairweather **4101**
Rob Fakes **2760**
Anna Falck **6169**
Peter Fallon **2295**
Lorraine Fannin **6100**
Martin Fanning **2290**
Samuel Fanous **2109**
Lotta Farley **2256**
Anne Farlow **2665**
Anna Farmar **2276**
Tony Farmar **2276**
Stephen Farrant **5073**
Mark Farrar **6145**
Nigel Farrar **2138**
Paul Farrar **6145**
Ruth Farrar **6145**
Antony Farrell **2458**
Emma Farrell **2797**
James Farrell **2047**
Ms Helen Farrelly **2658**
W. H. Farries **2478**
Nigel Farrow **2050, 2317, 2470**
Kathleen Farrul **2107**
Ed Faulkner **2812**
Clodagh Feehan **2495**
Mary Feehan **2495**
Tim Feest **5052**
Jonathan Feinmesser **2599**
Mick Felton **2689**
Rebecca Fenton **2218**
Sasha Fenton **2846**
Trevor Fenwick **2263**
Christopher Ferguson **2767**
Maggie Fergusson FRSL **5072**
Joaquim Fernandes **4001**
Camilla Ferrier **4067**
Samantha Ferris **4053**
Stewart Ferris **2741**
Richard Fidczuk **2665**
D. Fidler **2620**
Debbie Fielding **6108**
Jennifer Fifield **3036**
Barry Finch **2716**
Peter Finch **5005**
Frances Fineran **2353**
Stuart Finglass **2105**
Larry Finlay **2782**
Najma Finlay **2385**
Mark Finnie **2065**
R. Firth **2001**
R. Fisher **2093**
Richard Fisher **2140**
Sara Fisher **4040**
Steve Fisher **4003**
Sue Fisher **6190**
Peter Fishpool **2173**
J. D. Fitz Gerald **2246**
Ken Fleet **2726**
C. E. Fleming **2478**
P. Fleming **3016**
Clare Fletcher **2814**
Jo Fletcher **2314**
Keith Fletcher **5004**
Louise Fletcher **2128**
Margaret Fletcher **2015, 2707**
Tracy Florance **2475**
Anna Flowers **2794**
Sally Floyer **2597**
Klaus Flugge **2030**
Simon Flynn **2385**
Martin Fojt **2255**
Dirk Folens **2284**
Paul Folland **2802**
Rebecca Folland **4048**
Anthony Forbes Watson **2585**
Margaret Ford **5019**
Rachel Ford **2778**
Melanie Forder **2073**
Lorne Forsyth **2252**
Moira Forsyth **2670**
Linda Foster **2177**
Lisa Foster **4011**
Paul Foster **2599**
Suzy Fotheringham **5012**
Mervin Foulds **2398**
Sarah Foulkes **2444**
Peter Fountain **5050**
Chelsey Fox **4031**
Nicola Frame **2822**
Ms Sydney Francis **2341**
Teresa Francis **2128**
Lara Frankena **2672**
Andrew Franklin **2621**
Lin Franklin **6189**
Sarah Franklin **2101**
Lady Antonia Fraser **5016**
Helen Fraser **2597**
Kate Fraser **6112**
Lindsey Fraser **4032**
Neil Fraser **6132**
Paul Fraser **2590**
Prof Sir Christopher Frayling **5008**
Christian Frederking **2767**
Michael Freedman **2763**
A. Freeman **2390**
Dee French **5012**
Julian Friedmann **4009**
Eva Friedrich **6200**
Natalie Friend **2296**
Liz Friend Smith **2631**
Sue Frost **2016**
Ann Fry **2449**
C. Fry **2600**
Helenka Fuglewicz **4029**
Katie Fulford **2348**
Catherine Fuller **5025, 6044**
Julia Fuller **2788**
Gina Fullerlove **2431**
Lydia Furlong **2531**
Andrew Furlow **2385**
John Furzer **4079**
Alexander Fyjis-Walker **2584**
Judge Fysh QC **5036**

Jacqueline Gabbitas **2259**
Jüri Gabriel **2228, 4033**
Oliver Gadsby **2135, 2182, 2198, 2344, 2540**
Susan Gaigher **2101**
Helen Gainford **2254**
Andrea Gainham **6152**
Justin Gainham **6152**
James Gaisford **2226**
Kelsang Gakyi **2768**
Isabel Galan **2654**
Maureen Gallagher **2082**
Alessandro Gallenzi **2023, 2564**
Michael Gallico **2484**
Mrs S. Gamble **2709**
Sally Gaminara **2782**
Naomi Gane **6163**
Josette Garcia **2572**
Roberto Garcia **2679**
Jean Gardiner **2064**
Brenda Gardner **2603**
John Gardner **2022**
Leslie Gardner **4006**
Philip Gardner **6002**
Wendy Gardner **2247**
G. N. S. Garner **2248**
P. Garnett **2486**
Georgia Garrett **4101**
Oliver Garrett **2534**
Lea Garton **2603**
André Gaspard **2672, 2760**
Lynn Gaspard **2760**
Pat Gauntlett **2205**
Suzanne Gaved **2078**
Linda Gawley **2314, 2574**
David Gaylard **2601**
Karen Geary **2372**
Maggie Gee FRSL **5072**
Michael Geelan **6112**
Jonny Geller **4025**
Jamie George **2316**
Deborah Gerrard **2117**
Steven Gerrard **2005**
Paul Gerrish **2172**
Kate Gibbard **2538**
Catherine Gibbs **2702**
Sarah Gibbs **2303**
Alex Gibson **2818**
Bryan Gibson **2818, 3042**
Chris Gibson **2585**
Gilbert Gibson **4005**
Nichole Gibson **2662**
Anthony Giddens **2611**
Jon Gifford **2561**
Luigi Gigliotti **6187**
C. Gilbert **2442**
Andrew Gilfillan **2140**
Kathy Gilfillan **2458**
Lewis Gill **2433**
M. H. Gill **2305**
Peter Gill **2319**
Richard Gill **2301**
Miss C. Gillett **2675**
Rebecca Gillieron **2115**
Isabel Gillies **2386**
Andrew Gilman **6083**
Dr Simon Gilmour **2717**
Janine Giovanni **2782**
Tessa Girvan **4047**
Jonathan Glasspool **2100, 6184, 6195**
Duncan Glen **2012**
Margaret Glen **2012**
Kerry Glencourse **4034**
Stephanie Glencross **4038**
Anne Glenn **2475**
Christopher Glennie **2453**
Ben Glover **2438**
John-Mark Glover **5070**
Aisling Glynn **2542**
Stasz Gnych **3003**
Bill Godber **6135**
Anna Goddard **2151**
Mark Goddard **2723**
Pat Goddard **2723**
Roger Goddard-Coote **3030**
Janet Godden **2814**
Tim Godfray **5022, 6163, 6186**
Alan Godfrey **2311**
Hannah Godfrey **2443**
Mark Godfrey **2737**
Celso Godilano **2668**
David Godwin **4034**
Heather Godwin **4034**
Alison Goff **2555**
Anthony Goff **5009**
Alan Golbourn **2329**
Daniel Golbourn **2329**
S. Gold **2001**
Simon Goldstein **6115**
Sarah Gooch **5038**
S. Good **2390**
Bill Goodall **2435**
M. Goodall **2404**
David Goodere **6115**
Josephine Gooderham **2317**
Lennie Goodings **2462**
J. Goodman **2150**
Vivien Goodwin **2292**
Alan Goodworth **2653**
Matt Goodworth **2653**
Helen Gordon **2191**
Iain Gordon **2670**
Caroline Gorham **2143**
Ed Gorman **2038**
Stephanie Gorton **2143**
Pauline Gosden **6137**
A. L. Gosling **2264**
Jerry Gosney **5038**
Peter Gotto **2325, 6109**
Simon Gough **6041**
Jason Gould **6064**
Mervin Gould **2719**
Lesley Gowers **2628**
Brenda Gowley **2665**
Sara Grady **6167**
Conor Graham **6058**
Daniel Graham **2778**
David Graham **2615**
Neil Graham **2481**
Noel Graham **2181**
Tim Graham **2320**
Duncan Graham-Cameron **3025, 6027**
Helen Graham-Cameron **3025, 6027**
Mike Graham-Cameron **3025, 6027**
Jane Graham Maw **4035**
Anita Grahame **2744**
Anthony Grahame **2744**
Michelle Grainger **2120**
Rod Grainger **2808**
Laura Grandi **2459**
Jo Grange **2114, 6180, 6183, 6185, 6188**
Dr Douglas Grant **2242**
Mrs Gilly Grant **2326**
Ian Grant **2203, 2256**
Janet Grant **6033**
Lucy Grant **2562**
Nick Grant **2016**
Roderick Grant **6033**
Sandra Grant **2723**
James Graves **2191, 2348**
Avril Gray **2682, 2683**
Marianne Gray **5037**
Melanie Gray **2626**
Nicholas Gray **2018**
Rebecca Gray **2621**
Wendy Gray **2018**
Barry Graystone **2753**
Annette Green **4004**
David Green **2757**
Donna Green **6120**
J. Green **2530**
Jane Green **2818**
Joe Green **2674**
Krystyna Green **2196**
Shirley Greenall **6097**
Clair Greenaway **6164**
Graham Greene CBE **4098**
J. Greenhough **2150**
Sonya Greenhough **2269**
Catherine Greensmith **5051**
Ann Greenwood **2045**
Steven Greer **2491**
Sue Gregg **6135**
Dave Greggor **2778**
Jane Gregory **4038**
Donald Greig **2117**
Chris Gribble **2423**
Andrew Griffin **2753, 2842**
Kate Griffin **2621**
Christina Griffiths **2022**
Tamsin Griffiths **2087**
R. Grimes **2620**
Wendy Grisham **2371**
Clare Grist Taylor **2386**
Itamar Groisman **6200**
Ron Grosset **2299**
Jane Grounsell **2014**
Mike Grover **2165**
T. Grover **2165**
Anna Groves **2534**
Garmon Gruffudd **2843**
Lefi Gruffudd **2843**
David Grundy **2277**
David Gudgin **2263**
Vivienne Guinness **2458**
Mudasir Gul **2183, 2471**
Sevak E. Gulbekian **2731, 2764**
Allan Guthrie **4012**
Philip Gwyn Jones **2615**

Sara Hackwood **2167**
David Haddock **2339**
Inka Hagen **2542**
Pat Haines **2723**
Martine Halban **2340**
Peter Halban **2340**
John Hale **2342**
Lucy Hale **2372**
Robert Hale **2342**
Susan Hale **2342**
Vicky Hales-Dutton **3023**
Ben Hall **4025**
Chris Hall **2236**
D. Hall **2390**
Gary Hall **2026, 2524, 2633, 6077**
Mrs Hazel Hall **2805**
Isobel Hall **2503**
Macer Hall **5030**
Simon Hall **2142**
Valerie Hall **2260**
Elizabeth Hallett **2371, 2372**
Karen Halliday **2452**
Chrysandra Halstead **2256**
Margaret Halton **2585**
Maggie Hamand **2480**
Carole Hamilton **6081**
Cynthia Hamilton **2177**
Nicolette Hamilton **5011**
William Hamilton **4040**
Chris Hamilton-Emery **2669**
Jennifer Hamilton-Emery **2669**
Robert Hamilton-Jones **6182**
John Hammond **5031**
Tom Hampson **2273**
Liz Hancock **2814**
Terry Hancock **2067**
Simon Hancox **6115**
Ed Handyside **2522**
Priscilla Hannaford **2123**
Andrew Hansen **2617**
Richard Hansen **6101**
Victoria Hansen **6101**
A. Hanson **6066**
Jackie Harbor **2757**
Gail Harbour **6153**
Rupert Harbour **2490**
Peter Harden **2346**
Richard Harden **2346**
Becky Hardie **2196**
Dr Melissa Hardie **2383**
Diane Harding **2422**
Monica Harding **6120**
Caroline Hardman **4067**
David Hardstaff **2491**
June Hardy **2047**
John Hargreaves **2466**
Katie Harker **3001**
Allison Harper **2212**
Leonie Harries **2375**
Sarah Harrigan **2510, 2512**
Jean Harrington **2488**
R. Harrington **2549**
Ian Harris **6041**
Jeanette Harris **5077**
John Harris **2431**
Jonathan Harris **2447**
Katie Harris **2844**
Kelly Harris **6165**
Lee Harris **5026**
Linden Harris **2539**
Matthew Harris **2772**
Nathan Harris **2166**
Nicholas Harris **3031**
Nick Harris **2256**
Pat Harris **6039**
Tim Harris **6196**
Toby Harris **2807**
David Harrison **2140**
Leonard Harrow **2493**
Graham Hart **3026**
Richard Hart **2349**
D. Harte **2806**
R. H. Hartgill **2583**
James Hartley **2466**
Lee Hartley **2491**
Sarah Hartley **3031**
Claire Harvey **2580**
Fran Harvey **2541**

INDEX OF PERSONAL NAMES / 165

Susan Harvey **2351**
Antony Harwood **4039**
Robert Hastings **2099**
Ken Hathaway **2215**
Niamh Hatton **2495**
Niki Haunch **2255**
Jane Havell **2480**
D. Hawcock **3016**
Jennie Hawden **2251**
Chris Hawkins **2411**
Frances Hawkins **2838**
Gillian Hawkins **6067**
Jackie Hawkins **2224**
Keith Hawkins **2010, 2838**
Dr R. Hawkins **2352**
Rebecca Haworth **2377, 2733**
Mrs Julie Hay **2699**
Barbara Hayes **5017**
Ben Hayes **2344**
Gary Hayes **2086**
Tony Hayes **2499**
Elizabeth Haylett **5042**
J. Haynes **2354**
Andrew Hayward **2196**
Elaine Hayward **2181**
Juan Hayward **2686**
Brian Haywood **6065, 6114**
L. Haywood **2695**
Helen Hazzledine **6007**
Gwyn Headley **6026**
Martin Healy **2290**
Mary Healy **6149**
Duncan Heath **2385**
Jonathan Heath **2628**
Nova Jayne Heath **2196**
Robert Heath **2821**
Kat Heathcote **2834**
Carol Heaton **4037**
David Heaton **2604**
Roger Heavens **2357**
Sally Heavens **2357**
Clive Hebard **2105**
Marion Hebblethwaite **6007**
Ernest Hecht **2722**
Pat Hegarty **3034**
Ruth Hegarty **2661**
Margret Heilegenstadt **3021**
Oscar Heini **2100**
David Held **2611**
C. Hellawell **2210**
Jane Helps **2256**
Alan Henderson **6096**
Anna Henderson **2800**
Barrie Henderson **2778**
Dan Henderson **6043**
Mark Hendle **2030**
Rt Rev Paul Hendricks **2154**
Marc Hendrickse **6039**
Stewart Heney **2834**
Jo Henry **5029, 6192**
Donald Henson **2204**
C. Herisson **2806**
Richard Herkes **2436**
Nick Hern **2362**
Andrew Herne **2528**
Julia Heron **2239**
Brid Hetherington **2219**
Leon Heward-Mills **2761**
Margaret Hewinson **2088, 2583**
Anne Hewitt **2398**
Andrew Hewson **4049**
Anne Hext **2214**
Robert Hext **2214**
Michael Heyworth **2204**
Roger Hibbert **2130, 6071**
Jason Hickey **2339**
Rachel Hickman **2171**
David Hicks **5029**
Sarah Hicks **6172**
Simon Hicks **2689**
Sophie Hicks **4098**
Edwin Higel **2542, 6058**
Martin Higgins **2782**
Lisa Highton **2372**
Tristan Hilderley **2016**
Catherine Hill **2449**
Richard Hill **6179**
Eileen Hiller **5059**
Angharad Hills **2303**
Barry Hinchmore **6102**
Vanessa Hinkley **2221**
Paul Hippsley **2333**
Julie Hird **2201**
Steve Hird **5076**
Amruta Hiremath **2795**
Rebecca Hirst **2184**
D. Hiscocks **2271**
W. B. Hiscocks **2271**
Tony Histed **2665**
Vanessa Histon **2794**
Ms Hita **3008**
Shaun Hobbs **2138**
Victoria Hobbs **4040**
Georgina Hobhouse **2378**
Wendy Hobson **2289**
Angela Hockley **2422**
Jamie Hodder-Williams **2372**
Alison Hodge **2373**
Alistair Hodge **2151**
Lee Hodgkiss **6114**
Antonia Hodgson **2462**
Christine Hodgson **2256**
Rebecca Hodkinson **2106**
Adrian Hodnett **2318**
Susanna Hoe **2375**
Andrew Hogbin **2703**
Mrs J. Holborn **6155**
J. K. Holden **6155**
Leonard Holdsworth **2015, 2707**
Michael Holdsworth **5021**
Chris Holifield **6162**
J. W. Holland **2374**
Richard Holland **2223**
Mrs S. M. Holland **2374**
Jill Hollis **2141, 3014, 6009**
Leo Hollis **2196**
John Holloran **6056, 6120**
Jane Holloway **2266**
Sara Holloway **2322**
Tim Holman **2462**
David Holmes **2124**
Jim Holmes **2227**
Sir Michael Holroyd CBE, FRHistS, FRSL **5016, 5072**
Nick Holroyd **2297, 2415**
Rachel Holroyd **4017**
Penny Holroyde **4087, 5009**
Brenda Holyoake **2173**
Julian Honer **2500**
Stephen Honey **2444**
Susan Hood **2178**
Andrew Hook **5026**
Jeremy Hook **2791**
Eleanor Hooker **2579**
Caroline Hooper **2239**
Clare Hooper **2465**
Peter Hooper **2010**
Emma Hopkin **2475, 2585**
Peter Hopkins **2429**
Amanda Hopkinson **5025, 6044**
Andy Hopkinson **2535**
Tony Hopwood **2528**
Kate Hordern **4042**
Chris Horn **2777**
Camilla Hornby **4025**
Pat Hornby **2339**
Pauline Horne **2412**
Neil Hornick **6173**
David Horspool **6194**
Diane Horton **2173**
Patricia Horton **2102**
Roger Horton **2757**
Tara Horwood **6137**
Julian Hosie **2847**
Valerie Hoskins **4043**
Sylvia Hotchin **2184**
Petra Hourd **2300**
Emma House **6172**
Jane Housham **2801**
Charlotte Howard **4031**
Emma Howard **2147**
Frances Howard-Gordon **2316**
Peter Howcroft **2213**
C. Howden **2675**
Adrian Howe **2498, 6066**
David J. Howe **2762**
Ms E. Howe **2675**
Susan Howe **2574**
Matt Howells **2757**
Zoe Howes **5015**
Sally Howls **5036**
Alison Hubert **2476**
Ruth Huddleston **2763**
John Hudson **2258**
Anstice Hughes **2173**
C. Hughes **2210**
Cory Hughes **2004**
Dr H. G. A. Hughes **2335**
James Hughes **2015, 2707**
Jo Hughes **6071**
Julia Hughes **5043**
Mark Hughes **2354**
Meuryn Hughes **2060**
Siobhan Hughes **2462**
Sonia Hughes **2843**
Dan Hull **2204**
Mark Hull **2484**
Brian Hulme **2548**
Dr Raymond Hume **5084**
Eryl Humphrey Jones **2196**
Christopher Humphrys **6068**
Adrian Hunt **2482**
Elaine Hunt **2763**
John Hunt **2381**
L. Hunt **2806**
Mark Hunt **6038**
The Lord Hunt of the Wirral MBE, PC **5001**
Mrs Debbie Hunter **2117**
Ian Hunter **5012**
Alan Hurcombe **2677**
Philippa Hurd **2617**
Sinead Hurley **2081**
Vincent Hurley **2458**
M. Hutchinson **2640**
Mark Hutchinson **6060**
Victoria Huxley **2049**
Kate Hybert **6030**
Tom Hybert **6030**
David Hyde **2706**
Elaine Hyde **2765**
Maura Hyland **2809**
Emma Hyman **2396**
Jane Hyne **2530**
Mrs Jill Hyslop **2326**

Sion Ilar **5088**
Michael Illingworth **2269**
S. C. Inchcombe **2478**
Christopher Ind **2147**
Fiona Inglis **4025**
Karen Ingram **2380**
L. Ingram-Brown **2131**
D. Inman **2150**
Brian Inns **6069**
Matt Inwood **2002**
Paula Ireland **6144**
Dinah Irvine **6073**
I. Irvine **2695**
Dotti Irving **6060**
Helen Irwin **2038**
Patsy Irwin **2782**
Robert Irwin **2228**
Han Ismail **2812**
Ron Ive **6143**
Kaoru Iwata **6176**

Bob Jackson **6153**
Carol Jackson **4025**
Chris Jackson **2436**
Gill Jackson **2342**
Ian Jackson **3019**
Katherine Jackson **2665**
Michael D. Jackson **2770**
Zoë Jackson **2286**
N. M. Jacobs **2457**
Nina Jacobson **2811**
Birgitta Jacobsson Ekblom **6169**
Jo Jacomb **2212**
Clémence Jacquinet **2266**
Dave Jago **2659**
Tom Jaine **2623**
Barrie James **4071**
Colin James **6096**
Katy James **2446**
Meinir James **2315**
Richard James **2395**
Yvonne James **2025**
David Jamieson **2073**
Patrick Janson-Smith **4057**
Peter Janson-Smith **4002**
Cherry Jaquet **6031**
Andrew Jarmain **2844, 6056**
Angela Jarman **2041**
Bob Jarrett **2690**
Heather Jarrold **2558**
Alan Jarvis **2757**
Eric Jarvis **2502**
Mary Jay **6088**
Peter Jay **2037, 2117**
Roni Jay **2823**
Azmi Jbeily **6043**
Micheline Jebb **6119**
Aidan Jenkins **2061**
Alan Jenkins **6194**
Ceri Jenkins **2017**
Rachel Jenkins **2353**
G. H. Jennings **2139**
Grant Jessé **3028**
Alan Jessop **6061**
Caroline Jestaz **2832**
Darin Jewell **4046**
Pelle Johansson **2214**
Ruth Johansson **2214**
Sir David John **5028**
Louise John **6034**
R. John **2366**
Susan John-Richards **2013**
Derek Johns **4101**
Ruth Johns **2608**
Alan Johnson **2172**
Andy Johnson **2467**
Douglas H. Johnson **2221**
Eileen Johnson **6139**
Frances Johnson **2555**
Jane Johnson **2348**
Maggie Johnson **6126**
Maralyn Johnson **2140**
Marlene Johnson **2337**
Pete Johnson **2173**
Treena Johnson **2401**
Andrew Johnston **2628**
Ms Elaine Johnston **2125**
Malcolm Johnston **2192**
Norman Johnston **2192**
Pamela Johnston **2044**
Sheila Johnston **2192**
Stuart Johnston **2849**
Wesley Johnston **2192**
Drummond Johnstone **2721**
Celia Joicey **2533**
Mike Jolley **2763**
E. Jolliffe **2052**
Christopher Jolly **2422**
Bethan Jones **2106**
Brian Jones **2265**
Carolyn Jones **2401**
Catherine Jones **5071**
Dafydd Charles Jones **5088**
Diana Jones **2782**
Duncan Jones **2054**
Elwyn Jones **5088**
Gordon Jones **2334**
Haydn Jones **2196**
Ian Jones **2663**
Jackie Jones **2247**
Kate Jones **4044**
Kathie Jones **5024**
Martin Jones **2664**
Michelle Jones **2417**
Mike Jones **2706**
Nicholas Jones **2460**
R. Jones **2806**
Rachel Jones **6172**
Rob Jones **2713**
Roger Jones **2267**
Rosy Jones **6094**
Steve Jones **2296**
Rupert Jones-Parry **2092**
J. M. Jordan **2116**
Richard Joseph **2425, 6193**
Katherine Josselyn **2087**
Janet Joyce **2260**
Louisa Joyner **2812**
Lucy Juckes **4012**
Jane C. Judd **4050**
Simon Juden **5067**
Andrius Juknys **2098**
Gary June **2597**

Constance Kaine **2767**
E. R. Kakembo **2586**
S. S. Kakembo **2586**
Satnam Kanvar **2259**
Dr Thomas Karger **2426**
Aris Kassimatis **6102**
Sunder Katwala **2273**
Julia Kaufmann OBE **2059**
Indy Kaur Naura **6103**
Ian Kay **2419**
Leslie Kay **2224**
Martin Kaye **6116**
Jean Kazan **2210**
Antony Kearns **2730**
Paul Keegan **2272**
L. Keelan **2583**
Moyna Keenan **2255**
Charlotte Kelly **4017**
Frances Kelly **4052**
Nicole Kemble **2651**
Karen Kendall **2502**
Fiona Kennedy **2573**
Joanna Kennedy **2105**
Nicki Kennedy **4047**
Ruth Kennedy **2809**
Anna Kenning **2617**
Patricia Kennon **5032**
Karen Kenny **5053**
David Kent **2462**
Stephen Kent **2844**
Mel Kenyon **4017**
Chenile Keogh **2499**
Mary Ann Kernan **6199**
Siobhan Kerry **2348**
Sophie Kersey **2686**
Scott Key **2419**
Victoria Keys **2029**
Irene Khan **2027**
J. Khawam **2504**
Melanie Khosa **6120**
Susan Kidby **2039**
Andrew Kidd **4001**
Ed Kielbasiewicz **2348**
Robert Kiernan **2549**
Peter Kilborn **5021**
Vanessa Kilcoyne **2319**
Catheryn Kilgarriff **2115**
Ruth Killick **2621**
Tracy Killick **2312**
Anthony Kinahan **2242**
Bethany King **5011**
Caradoc King **4101**
David King **2068**
Hilda King **2432**
Jannet King **2521**
Jonathan King **2016**
Julia King **2082**
Laurence King **2433**
M. R. King **6123**
R. E. King **2432**
S. King **2549**
Stephen King **5073**
Zoë King **4003**
Mrs Ann Kingdom **5083**
Jemima Kingsley **2435**
Jessica Kingsley **2435**
Claire Kingsnorth **2393**
Simon Kingston **2716**
Fiona Kinnear **2655**
Huw Kinsey **2133**
Charles Kipping **6094**
Andrew Kirk **2465**
Lloyd Kirton **2431**
P. Kisray **2828**
Graham Kitchen **2289**
Alan Kittridge **2793**
S. A. Kitzinger **2457**
Gillian Klein **2784**
Dr B. J. Knapp **2056**
Andrew Knight **4053**
Caroline Knight **2055**
D. J. G. Knight **2478, 2583**
Debbie Knight **6031**
Jonathan Knight **2625**
Peter Knight **4053**
Richard Knight **2545**
Katherine Knowler **2601**
John Knox **2230**
Helen Kogan **2438**
Philip Kogan **2438**
Helena Korjonen **2398**
Jo Koster **2369**
Harshad Kotecha **2392**
Sevanti Kotecha **2392**
Rob Kraitt **4101**
Sandra Kramer **2827**
Helgard Krause **5088**
Joshua Kuperard **6116**
Elria Kwant **2606**
Pieter Kwant **2606**
Robert Kynaston **2342**

Candida Lacey **2521**
Tony Lacey **2597**
Jessica Lagan **2045**
Steve Lai **6087**
Karen Laister **2093**
Brian Lake **2421**
Ruth Lake **2166**
Laurence Laluyaux **4084**
David Lamb **2512**
Mrs M. Lamb **2637**
R. Lamb **2637**
Susan Lamb **2573, 2574**
Val Lamb **2579**
David Lambert **2301**
Linda Lambert **2361**
Marc Lambert **5077**
Robert Lambolle **6017**
Wendy Lampa **2679**
Rupert Lancaster **2372**
Nick Landau **2777**
Brian Landers **2597**
Jay Landesman **2441**
Andrew Lane **2640**
Eric Lane **2228**
Liz Lane **2725**
Roger Lane **2226**
Sally Lansdell **2119**
Naomi Laredo **6034**
Judy Large **2353**
Martin Large **2353**
Kay Larkin **2159**
M. Larkin **2806**
D. Larlham **2785**
Gillian Laskier **2249**
Dr Michael Lasserson **5084**
Rodney Latham **6157**
Tony Latham **2562**
Clare Lattin **2626**
Peter D. Laverack **2034**
Maria Laverty **3001**
Peter Lavery **2585**
Aude Lavielle **2463**
John Lawes **2089**
Mark Lawes **2089**
Graham Lawler **2739**
Judith Lawler **2739**
Juliet Lawler **2348**
Julie Lawrence **2547**
S. R. Lawrence **2549**
John Lawson **6042**
Andy Lay **2782**
Louise Le Bas **2274, 6189**
Mark Le Fanu **5016, 5080, 5081, 5086**
Nigel Le Page **2505**
Penny Le Tissier **2530**
Dr Geoffrey Leader **2232**
Lucille Leader **2232**
Alison Lee **4011**
Caroline Lee **2472**
John Lee **2199**
Steven Lee **6160**
T. A. Lee **2001**
T. K. Lee **2224**
Thomas Lee **2787**
V. J. Lee **2566**
Robert Leech **6074**
Tracy Leeming **2083**
Sheril Leich **2837**
Martin Leigh **6133**
Paula Leigh **2206**

166 / INDEX OF PERSONAL NAMES

Mrs C. Lenton **6089**
Gundhild Lenz-Mulligan **4054**
David Leonard **2223**
Kath Leonard **2187**
Julie Leppard **2251**
David Lester **2212, 2787**
J. A. Leung **2420**
Lionel Leventhal **2168, 2327**
Richard Leveridge **5076**
Darrel Lewis **3008**
Dewi Lewis **2454**
G. Lewis **2806**
Giles Lewis **2379, 2781**
Helen Lewis **2626**
Isabelle Lewis **2521**
J. H. Lewis **2315**
Jonathan Lewis **2315**
Julia Lewis **2656**
Luke Lewis **2606**
Margaret Lewis **2282**
Mary Lewis **2331**
Paul Lewis **2331**
Peter Lewis **2282**
Sarah Lewis **2802**
Simon Liebesny **2609**
Geoffrey Lill **2603**
Angela Lilley **2476**
Ken Lillywhite **2410**
Fiona Lindsay **4056**
Lynda Lines **3030**
Richard Lines **2746**
Claire L'Infant **2757**
Benn Linfield **2135, 2182, 2198, 2344, 2540**
Margaret Ling **2847**
Tony Linsell **2033**
Rebecca Linssen **2733**
Peter Linton **6048**
Julia Lippiatt **6063**
Paul Litherland **2337**
Clare Litt **2579**
Alan Little **6153**
Andrew Little **6153**
Christopher Little **4057**
Jean Little **6153**
Jonathan Little **6153**
Mandy Little **4100**
Nicky Little **6153**
Peter Little **2065**
Jo Littlechild **2323, 6022**
Colette Littman **2464**
Robert Littman **2464**
Francesca Liversidge **2782**
Chrissie Lloyd **2153**
Christopher Lloyd **2724, 6070**
Deborah Lloyd **2230**
Jonathan Lloyd **4025**
Linda Lloyd **2596**
Rick Lloyd **2532**
Menna Lloyd Williams **5088**
Alan Llwyd **2077**
Judith Ann Loades **2225**
Catherine Lockerbie **6167**
Lynn Lockett **3043**
Nick Lockett **2308**
Katy Lockwood-Holmes **2283**
Azhar Lodhi **2173**
Tif Loehnis **4048**
Lorraine Logan **5079**
Ruth Logan **2107**
Mrs Homa Lohrasb **6046**
Christopher Long **6010**
Nina Long **6010**
Stephen Long **2545, 6038**
Peter Longden **5059**
Tom Longford **2318**
Annette Longman **2063**
Helen Longmate **2435**
Laura Longrigg **4069**
Julian Loose **2272**
Alan Lord **2353**
Georgina Lord **2224**
M. Lord **2620**
Jose Lorenzo **2078**
Ros Loten **2379, 2781**
Carol Lothian **5070**
Krystina Lotoczko **2644**
Odile Louis-Sidney **2763**
Jane Lovell **2579**
Emma Lowe **6172**
Andrew Lownie **4059**
Frances Lubbe **4088**
Helen Lucas **5043**
J. R. Lucas **2678**
G. Luciano **2549**
Dr John Ludden **2125**
Dorothy Lumley **4027**
Brian Lund **2641**
F. Mary Lund **2641**
Stephen Lustig **6112**
Sarah Lutyens **4060**
Angela Luxton **2555**
Joan Lyle **5070**
Rachel Lynch **2050, 2317**
Shelly Lynds **2484**
Claire Lynes **2120**
John Lyon **2301**
Ms Lucy Lyons **6198**

Juliet Mabey **2565**
Catherine McAllister **2725**
Kevin Macan-Lind **2397**
Paul McAvoy **2040**
Rev Denis McBride **2640**
Finbarr McCabe **2157, 2169, 2496, 2497**
Phelim MacCafferty **2401**
James McCall **6197**
Karen McCall **2803**
Heather McCallum **2844**
Charlotte McCandlish **5015**
Martin McCann **2652**
Julie McCarron **6090**
D. McCarthy **2052**
Daniel C. McCarthy **2494**
Jane McClean **2502**
Roy McCloughry **2460**
Janet McConkey **2448**
Stephen McConkey **2448**
David McConnell **2288**
Eric McCorkle **6103**
W. J. McCreadie **2062**
Don McCrimmon **2472**
Joan McCrimmon **2472**
Jo McCrum **5033**
Ruth McCurry **2716**
Jackie McDaid **6160**
Chani McDain **2469**
Jemma McDonagh **4038**
Alexandra McDonald **2765**
Ian MacDonald **2300, 5035**
James MacDonald Lockhart **4039**
Jonathan McDonnell **2756**
Terri McDonnell **2652**
Steve MacDonogh **2118**
Gavin MacDougall **2469**
Frances McDowall **2559**
Nicolas McDowall **2559**
Diane McEntee **2300**
Tag McEntegart **2409**
Rosalie MacFarlane **2462**
Yvonne McFarlane **6003**
Marie McFeely **2531**
W. D. McFeely **2549**
Kunak McGann **2553**
Hamish MacGibbon **2418**
Margaret McGillen **2273**
Jason McGovern **2265**
Christine Macgregor **2106**
Patrick McGuire **2256**
Fiona McIntosh **2574**
Judith Mackay **2521**
Peter McKay **5028**
Bob McKee **5034**
Catherine Mackenzie **2174**
Denise McKenzie **6049**
George P. MacKenzie **2525**
Kate Mackenzie **2475**
Peter MacKenzie **2481**
Rebecca Mackenzie **2247**
Ursula Mackenzie **2462**
William MacKenzie **2174**
Willie Mackenzie **2174**
Margaret McKeown **2632**
Maggie McKernan **4062**
Stephen Mackey **2176**
Amanda Mackie **2153**
Will Mackie **2282**
Dr Gordon McKillop **2737**
Ellen McKinlay **2847**
Jenny McKinley **2676**
Kirsty McLachlan **4034**
Becky McLaughlin **6049**
John McLaughlin **4016**
Christian Maclean **2283**
Christian Mclean **6100**
Diana Macleash **2316**
Ian McLellan **2046, 6101**
R. J. McLennan **6124**
Brigid Macleod **2322, 2615**
Chris McLeod **3026**
Margaret Anne Macleod **2003**
Neil MacLeod **2837**
Norma Macleod **2003**
Sheila McMacken **2809**
Paula McMahon **2527**
Marilyn McMenemy **6201**
Rob McMenemy **2249**
Andrew Macmillan **2265, 2848**
Caroline MacMillan **2069**
Doug McMillan **2114, 6180, 6183, 6185, 6188**
Heather McMillan **3023**
Steve McMonigle **6115**
Colleen McMorran **6115**
Murdo McNab **2768**
Sarah McNair **4011**
Rebecca McNally **2475**
Ms Caroline McNamara **2138**
Frank McNamara **6090**
Dr Robert McNamee **2814**
Anne McNeil **2337**
Iain Macneil **2834**
Ian McNeilly **2523, 5060**
Stephen McNeilly **2746**
M. Maco **4081**
Sue Macpherson **2673**
Elaine McQuade **2677**
Joe McQuilling **2136**
Jo McShea **6035**
Jenny McVeigh **4048**
Louise Madden **2472**
Philip Magee **2174**
Steven Maginn **2476**
Caitriona Magner **5032**
Alan Mahar **2776**
Tim Mahar **2369**
Trevor Maher **2468**
Kath Mainland **6167**
Steven Mair **2405**
Mark Majurey **2757**
John Makinson **2597**
Roopi Makkar **2084**
Ian Malcolm **2619**
Ross Malik **2063**
Gillian Malpass **2844**
Henry Malt **6159**
Gina Mance **2244**
Patrick Mancini **2515**
Dallas Manderson **2314, 2574**
Geoffrey Mann **2664**
Jules Mann **5065**
Garry Manning **2130, 6071**
J. Manning **2305**
Robert Manser **2462, 2602**
Michael Manson **2485**
Sarah Manson **4065**
Jenny Manstead **3011**
Roy Mantel **2289**
Olivia Mantle **5062**
Monica Manwaring **2318**
Khalid Manzoor **2439**
Sally Mapstone **2684**
Ziyad Marar **2665**
Anne Marimuthu **2337**
Sue Mariscal **2801**
Vicky Mark **4073**
Charlotte Markey **2269**
Emma Markey **2446**
Bev Markham **2532**
Robert Markless **2396**
Cfyn Markwick-Day **2108**
Vivian Marr **2164**
Margaret Marriott **2166**
Neal Marriott **2303**
Bob Marsh **2135, 2182, 2198, 2344, 2540**
Nigel Marsh **2272**
Paul Marsh **4016, 4067, 4076**
Adam Marshall **2614**
Alison Marshall **2123**
Anne Marshall **2643**
C. J. Marshall **2648**
Fiona Marshall **2696, 2716**
Ian Marshall **2573**
S. M. Marshall **2648**
Nick Marston **4025**
W. Marston **2789**
Will Marston **2561**
Alan Martin **2473**
Alasdair Martin **2750**
Alison Martin **2782**
Anna Martin **2366**
Christine Martin **2750**
Denise Martin **2192**
Ms Denise Martin **6105**
Elizabeth Martin **3029**
Fergal Martin **2154**
Gaby Martin **4053**
Judy Martin **2203**
Margaret Martin **2003**
Telly Martin **5013**
Ms Olga Martin Sancho **5002**
Louise Martine **2296**
Ms Britta Martins-Simon **2265**
Franky Marulanda **6039**
Blanche Marvin **4068**
Colin Mason **2275**
Kerry Mason **6161**
Paul Mason **3030**
Rebecca Mason **2527**
Simon Mason **2330**
Alex Massey **2427**
Nicola Mather **2679**
Peter Mathews **2545**
Annabel Matthews **2032**
Belinda Matthews **2272**
Esther Matthews **6091**
Kara Matthews **2845**
Sally Matthews **4045**
Steven Matthews **2795**
Kit Maude **2115, 2578**
Liz Maude **2030**
Rachel Maund **6072, 6202**
Anne Maxfield **2541**
John Maxwell **2169**
Basil May **6117**
Julie May **2117**
Sylvia May **2348**
Andrew May-Miller **6119**
Peter Mayer **2241**
Kevin Mayhew **2489**
Sadie Mayne **2521**
Carolyn Mays **2372**
Nick Mazur **5064**
Chris Meade **6165**
Peter Meades **2767**
David Meads **2046**
Brenda Medhurst **2681**
Lynne Medhurst **2484**
Sue Medlicott **2599**
Brian Meek **2767**
David Meggs **2068**
Helen Meixner **5020**
Mrs L. A. Melech **2747**
Simon Melhuish **2440**
Joanna Melia **6122**
Terry Melia **6122**
David Mellin **2479**
Jim Melrose **2170**
Barbara Mennell **2799**
Cathy Mercer **2526**
Hugh Merrell **2500**
Mark Merrill **5059**
Michael Messenger **2793**
Tracey Messenger **2177**
Tim Messinger **2489**
Ian Metcalfe **2371, 2585**
Alexandra Mew **3001**
Julie Meynink **2545, 6075**
Ms Kerstin Michaels **6198**
Colin Midson **2107**
Becky Miles **2643**
Helen Miles **2720**
R. C. A. Miles **2001**
Edward Milford **2244**
Jacqui Millar **2539**
Cathy Miller **4070**
David Miller **4084**
Helen Miller **2801**
Judith Miller **2510**
Mike Miller **2299, 6100**
Steven Miller **2140**
Sue Miller **2208, 6056, 6076**
Sara Miller McCune **2665**
Lynn Millhouse **2536**
Margaret Milligan **2018**
Claire Milloy **2010**
Ion Mills **2560**
J. Milne **2586**
Philippa Milnes-Smith **5009**
Nicky Milsted **2204**
Lisa Milton **2314, 2573, 2574**
Elisabetta Minervini **2023, 2564**
Pamela Minett **2735**
Thomas Minkus **6168**
Matthew Minter **2354**
Ravi Mirchandoni **2055**
John Misselbrook **2614**
Alex Mitchell **2074**
Catriona Mitchell **2491**
Dr J. C. V. Mitchell **2506**
John Mitchell **2369, 2370**
Mike Mitchell **2228**
Stephen Mitchell **2393**
Mrs Valerie Mitchell OBE **5001**
William Mitchell **6052**
Paul Mitton **6052**
Bob Moheebob **6103**
L. Mohin **2566**
Neville Moir **2095**
Ms Ann Moister **6124**
Carsten Moller **2249**
Sarah Molloy **4040**
Erin Monahan **2777**
Graham Money **6099, 6117**
Ms Julia Monk **6105**
Caroline Montgomery **4024**
Doreen Montgomery **4024**
A. F. Moon **2254**
Tracey Mooney **2465**
Jamie Moore **2191**
Louise Moore **2597**
Susannah Moore **3034**
Anna Moores **2117**
Nim Moorlhy **2450**
Ruben Mootoosamy **2847**
Noelle Moran **2799**
Jennie Morant **2580**
Alan Mordue **2696, 2716**
Elizabeth Moreira **2201**
Gaby Morgan **2475**
Gwyneth Morgan **2545**
Ian Morgan **2417**
Kim Morgan **2483**
Leon Morgan **4098**
Lesley Morgan **6117**
Mogg Morgan **2483**
Tom Morgan **2533**
Max Morgan-Witts **6131**
Joanna Moriarty **2696, 2716**
Georgina Morley **2585**
Simon Morley **6153**
Kirsten Morphet **2044**
Brian Morris **2067**
Claire Morris **4038**
Heather Morris **2130**
Mary Morris **2241**
Michael Morris **3009**
Sally Morris **5012**
Anthony Mortimer **2718**
Julia Mortimer **2610**
Michael Mosbacher **2715**
Jane Moseley **3022**
Clive Mosey **5028**
Jenny Mosley **2616**
Robert Mossop **2472**
Gregory Moxon **2632**
Sophie Moxon **5077**
Lisa Moylett **4023**
Ray Mudie **2105**
Alison Muirden **5015**
J. Mulholland **2600**
Ben Mullane **2444**
Ruth Müller-Wirth **2533**
Tony Mulliken **6073**
Keith Mullock **2348**
Ms Jenny Mulvanny **2265**
Toby Mundy **2055**
Kenneth Munro **6130**
Oli Munson **4009**
Alan Murphy **2286**
Andrea Murphy **2136**
Anna Murphy **2554**
Janet Murphy **2009, 2100**
John Murphy **2040**
Kate Murphy **2386**
Patrick Murphy **6047**
Anthony Murray **2305, 5054**
Bonnie Murray **2770**
Catriona Murray **2247**
Ewan Murray **6197**
I. Murray **2504**
Jenny Murray **5032**
Judith Murray **4037**
Lydia Murray **5068**
P. Murray Hill **2150**
Jamie Musialek **2239**
Lucy Myers **2050, 2470**

Nicole Nagel **6200**
Thom Nairn **2234**
Jackie Naish **2229**
Damalie Nakalema **5018**
Vesna Nall **2545, 5063**
E. Nani-Kofi **2586**
Howard Nash **2011**
Julia Nash **2209**
Janet Nassau **2421**
Jonathan Nater **6051**
Anna Navidski **2252**
Stephen Navin **5058**
Trevor Naylor **2767**
Keith Neale **6106**
Patrick Neale **4002**
Jeremy Neate **6075**
Ruth Needham **4079**
Mark Neeter **2577**
Richard Neil **6124**
R. W. Neilson **2404**
Terry Nemko **2664**
Clive Nettleton **5020**
Johanna Neurath **2767**
Thomas Neurath **2767**
David Neve **6039**
Adam Nevill **2812**
Anthony Nevill **2466**
Peter R. Newberry **2515**
Mrs Susan Newbury **2629**
Marian Newell **5050**
Catherine Newman **2337**
Sam Newman **2083**
Joan Newmann **2740**
Kate Newmann **2740**
Angela Newton **2822**
Guy Newton **2055**
Nigel Newton **2100, 2107, 2361**
Tim Newton **3013**
Caitriona Ní Bhaoill **2186**
Deirdre Ní Thuathail **2186**
Niamh Nic Daéid **2287**
C. Nic Pháidín **2189**
Charles V. Nicholas **3001**
Prof David Nicholas **6198**
John Nicholas **2238**
Roland Nicholas **2539**
Anne Nicholls **6201**
Mick Nicholls **6114**
Jeanne Nicholson **2078**
Victoria Nickerson **2802**
Douglas Nicoll **2481**
John Nicoll **2459**
Rebecca Nicolson **2702**
Gillian Nineham **2632**
C. Nobbs **2828**

INDEX OF PERSONAL NAMES / 167

Janet Noble **2444**
Martin Noble **6001**
Chantal Noel **2597**
Anne Nolan **2050**
Deirdre Nolan **2542**
William Nolan **2302**
Thomas Nold **2426**
Rodney Noon **2339**
Paul Norbury **2307**
Jonathan Norman **2050, 2317**
Shirley Norrie **2527**
William Norris **6103**
Jeremy North **2757**
Rosemary North **2685**
Randall Northam **2727**
Veronica Northam **2727**
Alison Norwood **2399**
Anthony Nott **2087**
Arnaud Nourry **2574**
Jonathan Nowell **2545, 6038**
Sarah Nundy **4073**
Dan Nunn **2297, 2415**
Debbie Nunn **2434**
Andrew Nurnberg **4073**
Ron Nussey **5013**
Alexandra Nye **4074**

Tom Oakes **2046**
Caroline Oakley **2160, 2376**
Amanda O'Boyle **2815**
Séan O Boyle **2193, 6104**
Eileen O'Brien **2101**
Ivan O'Brien **2553**
John O'Brien **2223**
Michael O'Brien **2553**
Orna O'Brien **6206**
Wendy O'Brien **6196**
S. Ó Cearnaigh **2189**
Seán Ó Cearnaigh **5053**
Dan Och **2847**
Micheal Ó Conghaile **2186**
Michael O'Connell **2578**
P. O'Connell **2246**
Peter O'Connell **2456**
Gerard O'Connor **2101**
Kaori O'Connor **2429**
Rebecca O'Connor **2760**
Sarah Odedina **2107**
Jim O'Donnell **6100**
Jo O'Donoghue **2220**
Moria O'Donovan **2202**
Sharon O'Donovan **2495**
M. D. O'Dwyer **2305**
Christine Oelschlaeger **2166**
Martin Oestreicher **2459**
Karen O'Flaherty **2410**
Lesley Ogg **5012**
Brenda O'Hanlon **5010**
Brian O'Kane **2552**
Rita O'Kane **2552**
M. O'Keeffe **2305**
Sean O'Keeffe **2456**
Richard Oldershaw **2761**
Brian Oldman **2128**
Jo Oldridge **2491**
Jim Oldroyd **6144**
Niki Oldroyd **6144**
Rhonda Oliver **2614**
Peter Olver **2204**
Conor O'Mahony **2101**
Prof Roibeard Ó Maolalaigh **5035**
Alex O'Neill **2827**
Ann O'Neill **2809**
John O'Nions **2460**
Janet Or **6176**
Marie O'Regan **5026**
David O'Reilly **6153**
Tamsine O'Riordan **2847**
I. Orton **2789**
Giselle Osborne **2355**
N. H. Osborne **5089**
Erin Osborne-Martin **2717**
Jane O'Shea **2626**
Francine O'Sullivan **2251**
Janetta Otter-Barry **2459**
Nicholas Oulton **2296**

Antoaneta Ouzuonova **2183, 2471**
Nikolay Ph. Ovsyannikov **6170**
Alwena Owen **2336**
Antonia Owen **2578**
Bill Owen **2436**
David Owen **3019**
Deborah Owen **4075**
Kate Owen **2657**
Peter Owen **2578**

Susan Pacitti **2306**
Michael Packard **2582**
Roger Packham **2357**
John Paculabo **2436**
Elizabeth Page **5003**
Stephen Page **2272**
Georgina Paget **4043**
A. J. Painter **6098**
Alex Painter **6206**
Sarah Pakenham **2030**
Neil Palfreyman **2767**
Irene Palko **2238**
C. L. Palmer **2116**
Tristan Palmer **2091**
Judith Pamplin **2549**
Bob Pannell **2205**
Brian Pannhausen **2339**
Gabriele Pantucci **4006**
George J. Papa **6097**
Alexandra Papadakis **2587**
Andreas Papadakis **2587**
M. Pargitter **2366**
Cheryl Park **2140**
Adele Parker **2757**
Adrian Parker **6078**
Jane Parker **2349**
Jim Parker **5066**
John Richard Parker **4069**
Nicky Parker **2028**
Robert Parker **2662**
Rosalie Parker **2754**
P. E. Parkin **6098**
R. J. Parkin **6098**
Nigel Parkinson **2014**
Miss I. Parris **2637**
Clive Parry **2665**
Robin Parry **2065**
Dave Parsons **2685**
Eileen Parsons **2817, 3007**
Jayne Parsons **2100**
Elaine Partington **3019**
Sian Partridge **2380**
Rebecca Pash **2636**
Aude Pasquier **2224**
Nigel Passmore **2016**
Komal Patel **2081, 2199**
Millie Patel **2444**
Claire Paterson **4048**
Jan Paterson **2083**
Jennie Paterson **2708**
Maggie Paterson **2028**
Mark Paterson **4076**
Melissa Patey **2603**
Melanie Patrick **2609**
Philip Patterson **4066**
Kathryn Pattinson **6155**
Stephen Paul **2387, 3011, 3027**
Elisabeth Pavey **2291**
Stephen Pawley **2265**
John Pawsey **4077**
Neil Paynter **2827**
Mal Peachey **3022**
Helena Peacock **2597**
John W. Peacock **2476, 2583**
Lucy Peake **2288**
Jill Pearce **2236**
Sharon Pearce **2231**
Tim Pearce **2645**
Corinne Pearlman **2521**
Maggie Pearlstine **4078**
Anne Pearson **6146**
Nick Pearson **2348, 2578**
Jonny Pegg **4025**
Catherine Pellegrino **4084**
Gary Pengelly **6182**
Michael Penny **2567**
Sylvia Penny **2567**
Alex Perchard **5073**

Lucia Perez **2183, 2471**
Victor Perfitt **2025**
Nick Perkins **2399**
Anne-Marie Perks **5075**
Rebecca Perks **2393**
Matthew Perren **6151**
Nick Perren **2433**
June Perrin **2718**
Tina Persaud **2081**
John Peters **2255**
Elisabeth Petersdorff **2568**
Simon Petherick **2087**
P. Petker **2352**
David Pettigrew **2732**
Paul Petzold **2059**
Neil Philip **3002**
HRH The Prince Philip Duke of Edinburgh (*see under* Edinburgh)
Alan Philipp **2038**
Gail Philipp **2038**
Roland Philipps **2519**
Adrian Phillips **2117**
Angus Phillips **6204**
Margaret Phillips **4098**
Rob Phillips **6115**
Tracy Phillips **2475**
Les Phipps **2337**
Prof K. K. Phua **2389**
Christopher Pick **6013**
Brian Pickles **2070**
Dale Pickles **2070**
William Pidduck **2006, 2007**
L. Pierce **2254**
Gwerfyl Pierce Jones **5088**
Clare Pierotti **2812**
Hanri Pieterse **2140**
Arabella Pike **2348**
Janet Pilch **2433**
Esther Pilger **2450**
Morayea Pindziak **6042**
Lynda Pine **2507**
B. Pinker **2134**
Sarah Piper **2548**
Dr Madsen Pirie **2711**
Gail Pirkis **2708**
Anna Pisani **2064**
Mike Pitts **2204**
Julian Platt **2770**
David Playne **3033**
Sean Plunkett **2348**
Kate Pocock **2844, 6056**
Mark Pollard **2604**
Leigh Pollinger **4079**
Lesley Pollinger **4079**
Sabrina Ponte **2268**
Helen Ponting **2613, 2649**
Kate Pool **6178**
David Poole **6050**
Cally Poplak **2249**
C. L. M. Porter **2442**
Helen Porter **2224**
R. Porter **2150**
S. Porter **2442**
Joanne Potter **2803**
Sally Potter **2348**
Simon Potter **2804**
Dr Tony Potter **3034**
Ms Andrea Powell **2138**
David J. Powell **6035**
Gareth Powell **6150**
J. Powell **2129**
James Powell **2604**
Richard Powell **3021**
Anna Power **4049**
Cathy Power **2752, 3038**
Deborah C. Power **2355**
Shelley Power **4080**
Winifred Power **5010**
Martin Powter **2476**
G. Pratt **2278**
Jeremy M. Pratt **2209**
Patricia Preece **4095**
Frank Preiss **6111**
Amanda Preston **4010**
Graham Preston **2160**
Roy Preston **6015**
Sue Preston **6015**
Eugene Priante **2668**
Andrew Price **2599**
David Price **6014**

Mathew Price **2618**
Sarah Price **5078**
Stephen Price **2460**
Sue Price **2436**
Terry Price **2169**
Trevor Price **2224**
David Price-Goodfellow **3017**
Namrita Price-Goodfellow **3017**
Caroline Priday **2619**
Alexandra Pringle **2107**
Mark Prior **2314, 2574**
Chiara Priorelli **2022**
Kathryn Pritchard **2177**
Sara Pritchard **4017**
B. Privett **2833**
Rossella Proscia **2159**
Simon Prosser **2597**
Leila Proud **2148**
D. H. Provan **2131**
David Pryke **5052**
Mairwen Prys Jones **2315**
Angela Prysor-Jones **6139**
Brian Pugh **2682, 2683**
Peter Pugh **2385**
Steven Pugsley **2343**
Trish Pugsley **2752, 3038**
Vicky Pulley **2460**
John Pullin **2620**
Sally Pulling **6137**
Gary Pulsifer **2042**
Eoin Purcell **2495**
Libby Putman **2078**
Penelope Putnikovich **2612**
Radomir Putnikovich **2612**

Mrs D. Quick **2675**
Anne Quigley **6160**
Hilary Quinn **2251**
Toner Quinn **2186**
Kathryn Quinton **2526**

Bridget Radnedge **6117**
Grace Rafael **2596**
Dr J. U. N. Rafai **2748**
Ron Ragsdale **2140**
T. C. Railton **2374**
Alan Rakes **6117**
Philip Ralli **2363**
Rohini Ramachandran **2274, 6189**
Eileen Ramchandran **5075**
David Rametta **2491**
Maria Ranauro **2530**
Graham Rand **5022**
Ronne Randall **6016**
M. Rasala **4081**
Oliver Rathbone **2427**
Andrew Rattray **6141**
Carol Rattray **6141**
Sue Ravitz **6092**
James Rawes **2789**
John Rawlinson **2075**
Dr Jonathan Ray **2680**
Jim Rayner **2125**
Nikki Read **2379, 2781**
Simon Read **2140**
Nicholas Reardon **2638, 6129**
Tony Reavill **2277**
Andrea Reece **2155**
Chris Reed **6004, 6093**
Mrs Lyn Reed **6053**
Robin Rees **2144**
Lord Rees-Mogg **2604**
George Reeve **2411**
Rosanne Reeves **2376**
Brendan Reid **2652**
Elaine Reid **2014**
Margaret Reid **2014**
Maria Rejt **2585**
Donna Renney **6164**
Jill Renney **2547**
Alison Rennie **6099**
Amanda Renshaw **2599**
Clive Reynard **2217**
Kimberley Reynolds **6165**
Nick Reynolds **2443**
Ken Rhodes **2135, 2182, 2198, 2344, 2540**

Francesca Rhydderch **6190**
Mike Ribbins **6041**
Louise Rice **2530**
Michael Graham Rice **2011**
Suzannah Rich **2241**
Carole Richards **2353**
M. J. Richards **2116**
Susan Richards **2386**
Bryony Richardson **2780**
Gill Richardson **2209**
John Richardson **2367**
Julia Richardson **2674**
Kim Richardson **3006**
Matthew Richardson **2780**
Paul Richardson **6205**
Peter Richardson **2663**
Rob Richardson **2674**
Ronan Richmond **6149**
Stephen Rickard **2636**
Andy Riddle **2286**
Philip Riden **2501**
Peter Ridley **2046**
Amanda Ridout **2348**
Rosie Ries **2105**
Roger Rigge **2697**
Simon Rigge **2697**
David Riley **2249**
Jane Riley **2827**
Sally Riley **4001**
Lee Ripley **2433**
Ian Rippington **2391**
Jon Rippon **2459**
Michelle Ripton **2181**
Colin Risk **6031**
Alan Ritchie **6110**
Duncan Ritchie **2253**
Sheila Ritchie **2253**
David Riviere **2660**
G. Robbins-Cherry **2394**
N. Robbins-Cherry **2394**
Margaret Robe **2128**
John Roberts **2227**
Joy Roberts **2766**
Lyn Roberts **2814**
Mared Roberts **2843**
Mark Roberts **2227**
Michael Roberts **2640**
Phil Roberts **2743, 2766**
Sarah Roberts **2459**
Terry Roberts **6068**
Bruce Robertson **3018**
Charlotte Robertson **2706**
Elinor Robertson **2165**
Ian Robertson **2644**
Stuart Robertson **2105**
Andrew Robinson **2159**
Hal Robinson **6006**
Jayne Robinson **6091**
Jeremy Robinson **2210**
John Robinson **2714, 5039**
Michael Robinson **2714**
Nick Robinson **2196**
Peter Robinson **2783, 4083**
T. Robinson **2622**
Annabel Robson **2668**
Cath Robson **5062**
Cheryl Robson **2061**
Elizabeth Robson **2342**
Steve Robson **2061**
Nigel Roby **6181**
Aimee Roche **2585**
Peter Roche **2574, 6117**
Katie Roden **2369**
Anna Roderick **2165**
Arwyn Roderick **5088**
Derek Rodger **2048**
Sally Rodohan **2038**
Derek Roebuck **2375**
Tim Roger **6064**
Deborah Rogers **4084**
Duncan Rogers **2358**
Emma Rogers **2570**
Juliet Rogers **2518**
Sarah Rogers **2755**
Stephen Rogers **2681**
Wilfrid Rogers **2358**
Brian Ronan **2495**
Jolly Ronan **5053**
Sarah Rooney **3019**
Angela Rose **2322**

Tessa Rose **2046**
Hilary Rosenberg **6092**
Andrew Rosenheim **6178**
Simon Rosenheim **2490**
Liz Rosindale **2484**
Alyssum Ross **2369**
Jamie Ross **2445**
Kathryn Ross **4032**
Neill Ross **2772**
Nick Ross **2462**
Simon Ross **2140**
Sue Ross **2701**
Susan Ross **2082**
Victoria Ross **4023**
Nina Rossey **2772**
Angeline Rothermundt **2042**
Pam Roud **2114, 6180, 6183, 6185, 6188**
D. P. Rowland **2785**
Jane Rowland **2788**
Dr Ian Rowlands **6198**
Kate Rowlandson **2381**
Pru Rowlandson **2322, 2615**
Emma Rowley **3001**
Russell Roworth **2445**
Nicola Royan **2684**
Fran Royle **2301**
Linda Royles **5018**
Prof. F. Ruane **2246**
Felicity Rubinstein **4060**
Steve Rudd **2434**
Khal Rudin **2006, 2007**
Ben Rudman **6037**
Georgina Rudman **2142**
John Rule **6080**
George Russell **2416**
Gillie Russell **2348**
Ian Russell **5012**
R. B. Russell **2754**
Scott Russell **6197**
Peter Russum **6138**
Richard Russum **6138**
Jan Rutherford **2095**
Amanda Rutherfurd **2229**
Carol Ryan **4098**
Sarah Ryan **2832**
Martin Rynja **2304**

Emma Sabin **2359**
Robert Sackville-West **3039**
John Sadler **2812**
Anna Sainaghi **3016**
Sally Salvesen **2844**
Darryl Samaraweera **4006**
Marion Samler **2053**
Fiona Sampson **5065**
Alan Samson **2820**
Ron Samuel **2341**
Micky Sandell **2663**
Jane Sandeman **5039**
Maureen Sanders **2809**
Michael Sanders **2551**
Peter J. Sanders **2593**
John Sanderson **6146**
Mark Sanderson **2663**
April Sankey **2651**
Julie Sankey **2215**
A. N. Sansom **2639, 2671**
Clara Sansom **2639, 2671**
John Sansom **2639, 2671**
Mario Santos **2348**
Peter Sapsed **3029**
Bob Satchwell **5082**
Davida Saunders **2530**
Deborah Saunders **2424**
Alastair Sawday **2674**
Bob Saxton **2074**
Anja Scaife **2778**
Martina Scheible **6031**
Elizabeth Scheinkman **4025**
Seb Schmoller **2053**
Cathy Schofield **6177**
Don Schofield **2011**
John Schofield **2821**
Melisa Schulman **2078**
Ran Schuman **6182**
Vivienne Schuster **4025**
Erica Sciolti **2257**

168 / INDEX OF PERSONAL NAMES

Allan Scott **6002**
Daniel Scott **2055**
Heather Scott **2686**
Ian Scott **2164**
Mark Scott **2537**
Max Scott **2147, 2729**
Bill Scott-Kerr **2782**
Michael Scott Rohan **6002**
Robert Scriven **2348**
Richard Scrivener **2763**
Derek Searle **6061**
June Searle **6061**
Mark Searle **2769**
John Seccombe **2742**
Thomas Seddon **6145**
Yvonne Seeley **6026**
Veruschka Selbach **2091, 2244**
Ingrid Selberg **2706**
John F. Selby **4055**
Rona Selby **2030**
John Sellers **3015**
J. Selwood **2523**
Mark Senior **6121**
Robert Senior **2263**
Anya Serota **2143**
Frances Sessford **6197**
W. Mark Sessions **2690**
Shikha Sethi **2760**
Dean A. Sewell **5004**
Ann Sexsmith **2350, 2511**
Andrew Shackleton **6002**
Hitesh Shah **4098**
Shaila Shah **2124**
Pauline Shakespeare **5018**
Anil Shamdasani **2161**
Fiona Shand **2532**
Adrian Shanks **2050**
Joanna Sharland **2575**
Andrew Sharp **2337**
Brigadier D. G. Sharp AFC **5089**
Margaret Sharp **2029**
Stan Sharp **2029**
Jo Sharrocks **2591**
Linda Shaughnessy **4101**
Alison Shaw **2610**
Angela Shaw **2377, 2733**
C. P. Shaw **2369**
Carol Shaw **2279**
Lesley Shaw **4001**
Adam Sheldon **4094**
Caroline Sheldon **4087**
Alexandra Shelly **2229**
Pete Shemilt **2140**
Jonathan Shephard **5064**
Allan Shepherd **2160**
Rodney Shepherd **2460**
Gary Sheppard **6153**
M. Sheppard **2798**
Jodi Shields **4017**
Annie Shillito **2674**
Bridget Shine **5048**
Robin Shobbrook **6036**
Denise Shonfeld **6126**
Julie Shorland **5007**
Karen Short **6103**
Liz Short **2095**
Vanessa Shorten **2036**
Liz Sich **6060**
A. Siddiqui **2748**
Dr Abia A. Siddiqui **2748**
Sally Siddons **2110**
Nick Sidle **2020**
Delia Siedle **2663**
Lleucu Siencyn **5005**
Mo Siewcharran **2545, 5063, 6038, 6075**
Thomas Sigel **2703**
Michelle Signore **2105**
J. Silberman **2588**
Bernard Silver **6049**
Justin Silver **6049**
Denise Silvester-Carr **5037**
Sasha Simic **6103**
Dorie Simmonds **4088**
Andrew Simmons **2095**
Mark Simon **2484**
David Simpson **2529**
S. J. Simpson **6156**
Tony Simpson **2726**
Blaise Simqu **2665**
Darren Sims **2547**
Marion Sinclair **5070**
Jonathan Sinclair Wilson **2244**
A. Singleton **2620**
Sitakumari **2020**
Rob Sitton **2837**
Anna Skinner **2247**
Carole Skinner **2086**
Julia Skinner **2503**
Paul Skinner **6083**
Simon Skinner **2545, 5063, 6038**
Cathy Slater **2518**
Janet Slingsby **3041**
Sara Slinn **2112**
Tony Sloggett **2330**
Liz Small **5070**
Karen Smart **2004**
Rebecca Smart **2575, 2701**
Susie Smart **2650**
John Smedley **2050**
Alderson Smith **2466**
Alistair Smith **6019**
Allan Smith **6106**
Amanda Smith **2292**
Andrew Smith **6125**
Anne Smith **4091**
Bob Smith **2095**
Cathy Smith **2476**
Christine Smith **2681**
Clare Smith **2348**
Colin Smith **6126**
David Smith **4004, 6119**
David N. Smith **6125**
Denise Smith **2234**
Dorcas Smith **2181**
Eve Smith **2234**
Geoffrey Smith **2049**
James Smith **2036**
Jane Smith **2555**
Janice Smith **2102**
Jennifer Smith **2173**
Justin Smith **6096, 6115**
L. G. Smith **2543**
Leslie Smith **2211, 2430, 2509**
Lucy Smith **2212**
Marcus Smith **2204**
Michael Smith **2438**
R. H. Smith **2694**
Robert Smith **4091**
Roger Smith **2558**
S. Smith **2828**
Simon Smith (Colwall) **2211, 2430, 2509**
Simon Smith (London) **2578**
Vincent Smith **2626**
Kirsty Smy **2166**
Sarah Smye **2036**
Maura Smyth **2652**
Sarah Smyth **6164**
Colin Smythe **2712**
Nick Snode **2472**
Robert Snuggs **2155, 2603**
W. A. Snyder **6082**
Nicolas Soames **2537**
Liz Somerville **5013**
Paul Somerville **2591**
Tracy Somorjay **2177**
Richard South **2791**
C. Southall **6155**
Julian Sowa **5040, 5055, 5074**
James Spackman **2519**
Angela Spall **2772**
Simon Spanton **2314**
Mrs B. M. Sparkes **2678**
Marilyn Sparrow **2044**
Graham Speake **2443**
Luke Speed **4066**
Lara Speicher **2126**
Ms Spence **3008**
Piers Spence **2651**
Jessica Spencer **2787**
M. Spencer **2620**
Sharon Spencer **2786**
Martin Spettigue **3008**
Tom Spicer **2144**
Diane Spivey **2462**
Tania Spriggens **5039**
John Sprinks **2518**
Richard Squibb **6090, 6137**
Sarah Squibb **6137**
Melanie Stacey **2767**
T. C. G. Stacey **2729**
John Stachiewicz **2534**
Geoff Staff **2140**
Charlotte Stafford **2844**
Peter Stafford **2453**
Yvette Stafford **6155**
Clive Stanhope **2218**
Fergal Stanley **6149**
Stephanie Stansbie **2463**
Helen Stanton **2095, 6081**
Mark Stanton **2092, 4012**
Naomi Starkey **2093**
Dr Bernard Starkmann **6157**
Alan Staton **6163**
Diana Steel **2036**
Hunter Steele **2097, 6005**
Isabella Steer **2631, 2756**
Jeremy Stein **5039**
John Stengelhofen **2793**
Richard Stenlake **2732**
Heather Stephens **2238**
Phil Stephensen-Payne **2294**
Maikim Stern **6161**
Norman Steven **2242**
Mrs Sue Steven **2826**
Suzie Stevens **2822**
Prof Iain Stevenson **6198**
Ian Stevenson **2723**
Amanda Stewart **2691**
Rona Stewart **2095, 6081**
Shirley Stewart **4092**
Anne Stibbs **3029**
Lee Stinton **2789**
Molly Stirling **4010**
Jessica Stock **6019**
John Stoddart **2433**
Alison Stokes **2004**
Victoria Stone **2108**
Brenda Stones **6199**
Rosemary Stones **6179**
Derek Stordahl **2473**
Mary Rose Storey **2441**
Sir Peter Stothard **6194**
Fiona Stout **6151**
Karen Stout **2467**
Sally Stow **6033**
Irina Stoyanova **2055**
Jackie Strachan **3022**
Androula Stratton **2422**
Peter Straus **4084**
Mark Streatfeild **2314, 2574**
Rolf Stricker **2072**
Tessa Strickland **2078**
Scipio Stringer **2767**
Richard Stroud **6136**
Magdalena Strzyminska **6148**
John Stuart **2328**
Lena Stuart **2274, 6189**
Paul E. Stuart **3036**
Stephen Stuart-Smith **2259**
Liz Stuckey **2631, 2756**
Philip Sturrock **2575**
Carl Styants **6196**
Nina Sudjina **6170**
Andrew Sugden **2545**
Robert Sulley **2369**
T. Sully **2798**
Lorna Summers **6136**
Maggie Sumner **5059**
Helen Sun **6197**
Laura Susijn **4093**
Deborah Susman **2109**
J. K. B. Sutherland **2390**
K. A. Sutherland **2390**
Dr D. Sutton **5087**
Karolina Sutton **4044**
Lorna Rae Sutton **2827**
Helena Svojsikova **6083**
Paul Swallow **2813**
Ms Su Swallow **2265**
Amy Swann **2660**
Janice Swanson **4025**
David Swarbick **2348**
Andrew Sweeney **2177**
Christine Swift **2752, 3038**
Amanda Synnott **2541**

Tri Ta **2827**
Danka Tadd **2616**
Roger Tagholm **6192**
Angie Tainsh **2119**
Pamela Tamburini **2668**
Silvana Tann **2078**
Robert Tapsfield **2288**
Louise Tarn **2780**
Jane Tatam **3004**
Anya Tatyanchenko **2084**
Clare Taylor **2811**
Edwin Taylor **6130**
Graham Taylor **5006, 5041, 5067**
Imogen Taylor **2585**
J. Taylor **2622**
Jonathan Taylor **2348**
Lesley A. Taylor **2546**
Lynn Taylor **2221**
Matthew Taylor **5073**
Paul Taylor **2292**
Peter J. Taylor **2758**
Robin Taylor **2258**
Susan Taylor **2597**
Maggie Taylor-Sanders **2593**
Rosemary Taylorson **2847**
Valerie Teague **3010**
David Tebbutt **2272**
Hugh Tempest-Radford **2797**
Linda Tenenbaum **6116**
Hendrik Teneues **2765**
Emilia Terragni **2599**
Peter Terrell **2455**
Vivien Tesseras **2603**
Stephen Theaker **5026**
P. A. Thew **2305**
Christine Thirkell **2640**
Robert Thirlby **2412, 2479, 2773**
Nansi Thirsk **2106**
Simon Thirsk **2106**
Dr A. Thomas **2478**
Annette Thomas **2583, 2585**
Christopher Thomas **2262**
Diane Thomas **2159**
Guy Thomas **2679**
Jacks Thomas **6073**
Julian Thomas **2348**
Lindsay Thomas **2228**
Mark Thomas **3008**
Neil Thomas **2772**
Penny Thomas **2689**
Richard Thomas **5049**
Dr Rosamund Thomas **2262**
Moritz Thommen **2426**
Amanda Thompson **6004**
Brad Thompson **2051, 2252**
Christine Thompson **2529**
Claire Thompson **6135**
Ian Thompson **2174**
Jayne Thompson **2079**
Jeremy Thompson **2788**
John Thompson **2611**
Peter Thompson **3003**
Emma Thomson **2117**
Jan Thomson **2247**
Liz Thomson **6192**
Michelle Thorn **2577**
Carolyn Thorne **2812**
Sarah Thorne **2527**
Euan Thorneycroft **4040**
Derek Thornhill **2153**
Peter Thornton **2339**
Roger Thorp **2755**
John Thorpe **5030**
Martin Thorpe **6064**
Jon Thurley **4095**
Sara Ticci **2767**
Anthony Tierney **2290**
Nikki Tilbury **3027**
S. Tilley **2622**
Clare Tillyer **2105**
Chris Tinsley **2575**
Teresa Tinsley **2180**
Jenni Tinson **2807**
F. M. Tobin **2305**
Jenny Todd **2143**
Janice Tolan **2369**
Anne Tolstoy **6090**
Daniel Tomkins **2659**
John Tomlin **2197**
P. Tomlinson **2394**
Morgan Tomos **2843**
Helen Tookey **2465**
Antony Topping **4037**
Anna Torborg **2713**
Chris Tordoff **2209, 6103**
Frances Townsend **2551**
Peter Townsend **2551**
Nancy Traversy **2078**
Helen Trayler **2839**
Howard Trent **2536**
Jeremy Trevathan **2585**
Lavinia Trevor **4096**
Elisabeth Tribe **2369**
Ryan Tring **2074**
Ruth Trippett **6111**
Annabel Trodd **3037**
B. H. Trodd **3037**
Miss N. Trodd **3037**
Janka Troeber **6200**
Andrew Troszok **2450**
Mark Trotter **6065, 6114**
R. N. Trubshaw **2356**
Kevin Tubridy **2753**
Alex Tucker **6028**
Alison Tucker **2303**
Del Tucker **3041**
Fiona Tucker **2270**
Peter Tucker **6028, 6029**
Sarah Tucker **2755**
Sedat Turhan **2508**
Jane Turnbull **4097**
A. Turner **2052**
Dorcas Turner **2301**
Richard Turner **2492**
Rollo Turner **5014**
Sarah Turner **2067**
Steven Tweed **2476**
Catherine Twibill **2495**
Adriana Twinn **2172**
Ann Twiselton **2511**
Karen Twissell **2130, 6071**
Dave Twydell **2845**
Fay Twydell **2845**
Shaun Tyas **2819**
Alex Tyla **2526**
David Tyler **2006, 2007**
Diana Tyler **4069**
J. Tyler **2806**
A. Tyson **2605**
Mrs A. M. Tyson **2605**

Pat Underwood **2742**
Julia Unwin CBE **2656**
Merlin Unwin **2803**
Andrew Upton **2586**
Laurence Urdang **2805**
T. P. Usborne **2806**
Justina Utuka **6207**

Pallavi Vadhia **2533**
Alex Vahdat **6046**
M. van de Weijer **2539**
Aidan van de Weyer **2183, 2471**
Mark van Harmelen **2053**
Juliet van Oss **4023**
Danie van Straaten **2174**
Roger Van Zwanenberg **2609**
Lucy Vanderbilt **2348**
Caroline Vandridge-Ames **2424**
E. Vartto **2317**
Roderic Vassie **2505**
Dominic Vaughan **2681, 6199**
Ian Veacock **5011**
Marianne Velmans **2782**
Ed Victor **4098**
Marco Vinaccia **2410**
Nicola Vinall **2291**
Gilly Vincent **4018**
Cleve Vine **6122**
Hermann Vonlanthen **2426**
Ann-Marie Vowles **2424**
Joanne Voysey **2795**
Ajda Vucicevic **4010**

Amy Wack **2689**
Karl Waddicor **2810**
Anna Waddington-Feather **2277**
Revd John Waddington-Feather **2277**
Sheila Waddington-Feather **2277**
L. Waite **2254**
Carol Wakefield **2730**
Keith Wakefield **2730**
Susan Walby **2128**
Zoe Waldie **4084**
Safiya Waley **2098**
Julie Walker **2409**
Lynne Walker **2204**
Sally Walker **6050**
Stephen James Walker **2762**
Simon Wallace **2441**
Esther Waller **2171**
Sheila Waller **6011, 6045**
Helen Wallis **3028**
Caroline Walmsley **2067**
Aoife Walsh **2290**
Brendan Walsh **2224**
Carrie Walsh **5073**
Colin Walsh **2323, 5052, 6022**
Eddie Walsh **6149**
John Walsh **6094**
Mags Walsh **5032**
David Walshaw **2551**
Philip Walters **2369**
Roger Walton **2074**
Dean Wanless **2359**
Claire Ward **2782**
David Ward **2107**
Harry Ward **6081**
Nigel Ward **2348**
Pauline Ward **2652**
Peter Ward **6085**
Richard Ward **6085**
Sue Ward **2624**
Tony Ward **2041**
Vivien Ward **2198, 2540**
Andrew Ware **2453**
Caroline Warhurst **2454**
Richard Warner **2184, 2423**
David Warnock **6100**
Melanie Warren **6114**
Stephen Warren **2604**
Dr Clayre Warwick **6198**
Sarah Wasley **2322**
D. Watchus **2001**
Ian Waterhouse **6114**
Anne Waters **2652**
Donald Waters **2710**
Nigel Waters **2782**
Pat Waters-Marsh **2547**
Heather Watherston **2440**
Dean Watkins **6039**
Simon Watkins **2680**
Prof Anthony Watkinson **6198**
C. Watling **2600**
Caroline Watson **3023**
Jonathan Watson **2075**
Louise Watson **2022**
Natalie Watson **2681**
Rebecca Watson **4043**
Samantha Watson **2545**
Sophie Watson **2202**
Susan Watt **2348**
Gordon Watts **2438**
Helen Watts **2128**
Simonne Waud **2153**
Peter Waverly **2383**
David Wavre **2243**
David Way **2126, 2127**
Mary Web **2553**
Andy Webb **6135**
Debbie Webb **2507**
Judith Webb **2679**

INDEX OF PERSONAL NAMES

Ken Webb **2217, 2841**
M. L. Webb **2116**
Mark Webb **3032**
Michael Webb **2354**
Robert Webb **2609**
Rowena Webb **2372**
Rupert Webb **2841**
Timothy Webb **4069**
Charlene Webber **4046**
Connie Webber **2464**
Peter Webber **2011**
Robin Weber **6051**
Thomas Webster **2191**
Sarah Weedon **6166**
Sabine Weeke **2279**
Jose Wehnes **2254**
Lord Weidenfeld **2574**
Stuart Weir **2631, 2756**
Carole Welch **2372**
John Welch **4103**
Michael Welch **2685**
Tracie Welch **2231**
Anthony Weldon **2090**
Tom Weldon **2597**
Andrew Welham **2510, 2512, 2555**
P. J. Weller **2600**
Julia Wells **2272**
Troth Wells **2541**
Mrs C. S. Wenden **2678**
Jonathan Wendon **2452**
Mark Wendon **2452**
Robert Wendover **2460**
Anthony R. A. Werner **2698**
Alison West **2528**
Bee West **2324**
Cecilia West **2193, 6104**
David West **3043**
Ian West **2626**
Linda West **6122**
M. West **2155**
Anne Westgarth **2522**
Hannah Westland **4084**

Anna Weston **2268**
Caroline Wetherilt **2355**
Tim Whale **2777**
Prof Andrew Wheatcroft **6197**
Alan Wheatley **5051**
Suzanne Wheatley **2330**
James Wheeler **2130, 6071**
Jo Wheeler **2185**
Ray Wheeler **6039**
J. Wheeler-Melech **2747**
B. Whelan **2246**
C. T. Whelan **2246**
Carolyn Whitaker **4058**
Andrew White **2035**
Ben White **3006**
Caroline White **2749**
Catherine White **2298**
Chas White **2149**
Diane White **6150**
Elizabeth White **2135, 2198, 2344, 2540**
Eve White **4104**
Heather White **5069**
Isabel White **4015**
Jane White **2113**
Jonathan White **2590**
Maria White **2095**
Mark White **2298**
Patricia White **4084**
Patrick White **2164, 2369**
Paul White **2113**
Robert White **6007**
Shân White **2035**
Susan White **2317**
Amanda Whiting **5012**
David Whiting **2824**
James Whiting **2146**
John Whitley **6206**
Hayley Whitlock **2300**
Jean Whitnall **2371**
Mrs E. Whittaker **3001**
Jean Whittaker **2132**

Annabel Whittet **2825**
Dr Keith Whittles **2826, 6100**
A. Whitton **2150**
Paul Whitton **2460**
Sarah Whitworth **2837**
Kevin Whomes **2489**
Ian Whyte **6126**
Conrad Wiberg **6054**
Kathryn Wickett **2837**
Jacqueline Wieczovek **2253**
B. M. Wiener **4105**
D. P. Wiener **4105**
Dinah Wiener **4105**
Chris Wigg **6196**
Barbara Wiggins **2784**
David Wightman **2009, 2100**
Sarah Wilbourne **2027**
Helen Wild **2402**
Katy Wild **2777**
M. Wiley **2246**
Ian Wilkes **2360**
P. J. Wilkes **6095**
Stephen Wilkins **2167**
Verna Wilkins **2751**
Anna Wilkinson **2068**
Martin Wilkinson **2379, 2781**
Adrian Willard **2436**
Alastair Williams **2741**
Andy Williams **2140**
Conrad Williams **4009**
Crispin Williams **2694**
Diana Williams **5040, 5055, 5074**
J. Williams **2246**
John Williams **6096**
Jonathan Williams **2179, 4106**
Kath Williams **2065**
L. Williams **6098**
Lesley Williams **2179**

Liz Williams **2065**
M. Williams **6096**
Mark Williams **6115**
Nicholas Williams **2730**
Paul Williams **2620, 2843**
Penny Williams **5078, 6207**
Peter Williams **2620**
Robert Williams **2166, 2393**
Ruth Williams **2603**
Sarah Williams **2165**
Steven Williams **6073**
Susan A. Williams **2122**
Victoria Williams **2218**
W. Alister Williams **2122**
A. Williamson **2264**
Dr J. J. Williamson **2719**
Richard Williamson **6134**
Carrie Willicome **6102**
Laura Willis **2767**
Robert Willis **2262**
Vivienne Willoughby-Ellis **6036**
Howard Willows **2545**
James Wills **4100**
Adam Wilson **2450**
Anna Wilson **2672, 2760**
Anne Wilson **2737**
Brian Wilson **2416**
Mrs E. N. Wilson **2391**
Ed Wilson **4049**
Graham Wilson **2380**
Ian Wilson **2320**
J. Wilson **2600**
John S. Wilson **6086**
Kate Wilson **2677**
Louise Wilson **6100**
Maggie Wilson **2546**
Neil Wilson **2830**
Pat Wilson **6086**
Patricia Wilson **2640**
Tatiana Wilson **2229**
William Wilson **2391**

Angela Winchester **2402**
Caroline Windle **2166**
Tom Windross **2530**
Reeta Windsor **6075**
Jon Windus **2545**
Rebecca Winfied **5013**
James Wisdom **2688**
Julia Wisdom **2348**
Alicia Wise **5068**
Darren Wise **2050, 2317**
Gordon Wise **4025**
Judith Wise **2184**
Robert Wise **2562**
E. Witchell **2816**
Trevor Witcher **6065, 6114**
Derek Withers **6100**
K. Wodehouse **2052**
Mrs A. M. Wolfenden **2550**
M. H. Wolfenden **2550**
Lois Wolffe **6167**
Kit Yee Wong **2037**
Amanda Wood **2763**
Boo Wood **2097, 6005**
Dawn Wood **2166**
Dinah Wood **2272**
Hazel Wood **2708**
Jeanette Wood **2045**
Jon Wood **2573**
Emma Woodfield **2391**
Paul Woodfield **6110**
Martin Woodhead **2837**
Keith Woods **6105**
Mrs L. S. Woods **2675**
Lindsay Woods **2675**
Rachel Woodward **2775**
Gill Woolcott **2812**
Sarah Wooldridge **4045**
Kevin Woolf **2777**
Philip Woolfson **2232**
Jessica Woollard **4067**
John Woolley **2274, 5034, 6189**
David R. Worlock **6035**

Kate Worlock **6035**
Chris Wright **2444**
David Wright **6181**
Derek Wright **2839**
E. Wright **2806**
Helen Wright **2102**
Jennifer Wright **2676**
Julie Wright **2706**
Malcolm Wright **2647**
Nicholas Wright **2701**
Patrick Wright **2549**
Timothy Wright **2247**
Fiona Wyatt **2350**
Suella Wynne **2295**

May Yao **2406**
Helen Yates **2393**
John Yates **2159**
Roy Yates **6158**
Jeremy Yates-Round **2354**
Masoud Yazdani **2406**
Stephen Yeo **2161**
June York **2274**
Michael York **2541**
David Youdan **2403**
Alex F. Young **2732**
Angela Young **6031**
Claire Young **2530**
Ms C. Yuen **2719**

Cetty Zambrano **5031**
Hans M. Zell **6021, 6191**
Forest Zhang **5003**
Colin Ziegler **2536**
Richard Ziemacki **2140**
Oliver Zille **6171**
Anthony Zurbrugg **2498, 6066**
Rolf Zurlinden **2426**

7.4 INDEX OF COMPANIES & IMPRINTS

Bold figures indicate a principal entry in the Directory; other figures refer to citations within principal entries.

10/18 6111
11:9 2830
20/21 Design 6137
21 6103
321 Go! 2636
3C Publishing (Columbia Marketing Ltd) 6117

A Jot Publishing 6106
A piacere 2679
The A Plus Series of 11+ Practice Papers 2520
AA Publishing **2001**, 6096
AA Special Sales 6115
AAA Road Maps of USA, Canada, Mexico 2001
Aardvark Publishing 6097
Aarhus University Press 6065
AB Books **6140**
Abacus 2462
Abbey Press 2640
Aber-Torchlight Books 2739
Abhinav Publications 6124
Abingdon Press 2014
Abington Publishing 2837, 6136
Ablex Publishing 2330
Abramelin Press 6109
Absolute Press **2002**, 6061, 6103
Yr Academi Gymreig **5005**
Academic and Professional Division of The Publishers Association **5006**
Academic Book Collection 6094
Academic English Press 6123
Academic Press 2254
Academic Therapy Publications 2034
The Academy of the 3rd Millennium 2466
Academy Science Publishers 6088
Acair Ltd **2003**, 6100
Acanthus Press 2036
ACC Books 2036
Accelerated Learning Centre 6094
Accent Press Ltd **2004**, 6103, 6119
Ace Publications Ltd 2329
Acora 2681
Acorn Editions 2471
ACP Publishing Pty Ltd 2064
ACR Editions 2364, 6090
Actinic Press 2211
Activair Ltd **6087**
Actual Enterprises 6094
Acumen Publishing Ltd **2005**, 6120
Acupuncturist Ltd 6014
ADAC 6123
Adam Matthew Digital Ltd **2006**, 2007
Adam Matthew Publications Ltd 2006, **2007**
Adams & Austen Press 6094
Adams Media 2226
Adamson Publishing Ltd **2008**, 6120
Adcotec 6136
Henri Addor & Associates 2364
ADEC 2364

Adelson Galleries 2036
Aditya Prakashan 6123
Adlard Coles Nautical **2009**, 2100
Adler Planetarium and Astronomy 2036
Advanced Knowledge International 6134
Advanced Pathfinder 2180
Advances in Art & Urban Futures 2406
Advances in Human Computer Interaction 2406
The Advantage Series of SATs Practice Papers 2520
Adventures in Art Series 2617
Adventures Unlimited 6109
Aegis Consulting/Aberjona Press 2358
Aeon Press 6093, 6109
Aerofax 2016
AESOP (All Editorial Services Online for Publishers & Authors) **6001**
Afram Publications (Ghana) Ltd 6088
Africa Book Centre Ltd 2498
Africa Christian Press 6088
Africa Community Publishing & Development Trust 6088
Africa Institute of South Africa 6088
Africa World Press Inc 6135
African Books Collective **6088**
African Heritage Press 6088
African Publishing Group 6066
African Renaissance 6088
African Rights 6066
Afterall 2511
afterschoolclub.net 2538, 2786
Age Concern Books **2010**, 6126
Agraphia Press 6103
Ahana Books 6124
Ahimsa Books 6124
Air-Britain (Historians) Ltd **2011**
Air Research Publications 2209
Airdata Publications 2209
Airplan Flight Equipment Ltd 2209
Airtime Publishing 2209
Aitken Alexander Associates **4001**
Akacia 2686
Akanthina 2579
Akashdeep Publishing House 6124
Akashic 6135
Akros Publications **2012**
Al-Furqan Islamic Heritage Foundation **2013**
Al-Ghazali Series 2413
Al Madad Foundation 2252
Aladdin Books Ltd 2337, **3001**
Aladdin/Watts 2337, 3001
Alastair Sawday's Special Places to Stay 2674
Alba House 2668
Alban Books Ltd **2014**, 6120
Albedo One 6093
Albion Press Ltd **3002**
Albyn Press **2015**
Alcemi 2843
Alfaguara 6111
Algonquin 6122
Alianza 6111
Ian Allan Publishing Ltd **2016**, 6117

Philip Allan Publishers Ltd **2017**, 2338, 2369
Philip Allan Updates 2017, 6136
R. L. Allan & Son Publishers **2018**
Allcloud Ltd 3016
Umberto Allemandi 2036
Allen Lane 2597
Allen & Unwin 2459, 2653
Gary Allen Pty Ltd NSW 6123
J. A. Allen **2019**, 2342, 6106
Mark Allen Group 2377, 2733
Alliance Book Company 6110
Alliance of Literary Societies (ALS) **5007**
Allied Mouse Ltd **2020**
Allied Publications 6123
Alligator Books Ltd **2021**, 2752, 3038
Allison & Busby **2022**, 6061, 6135
Alloway Publishing 2732
Allworth Press 2653, 6139
Alma Books Ltd **2023**, 6115
Alma Edizioni 6111
Almenach de Gotha 2116
The Alpha Press 2744
Alpha Science International Ltd **2024**, 6120
ALPSP 6202
Altajir World of Islam Trust 2493
Alternative Albion 2356
The Althouse Press 6097
Alton Douglas Books 2121
Alyson 6135
AM Editores 2653, 6139
Amacom 2473
Amadeus 2679
Amateur Winemaker Books 2724, 6070
Amazing Baby 2763
Amber Books Ltd **3003**
Amberwood Publishing Ltd **2025**
Ambit Books 6103
AMC Maps & Atlases 2300
American Association Cancer Research 6136
American Association for Artificial Intelligence Press 2511
American Association of Cereal Chemists 2285
American Association of Petroleum Geologists 2303
American Eyes Ltd 6043
American Guidance Service 6089
American Historical Press 6123
American Institute of Baking 2285
American Institute of Mathematical Sciences 6134
American Numismatic Society 2579
American Pie **6043**
American Psychiatric Publishing Inc **2026**
American School of Classical Studies 6136
American School of Classical Studies in Athens 2579
American School of Prehistoric Research 2579
American Schools of Oriental Research 2579
American Society of Health Systems Pharmacists (ASHP) 6134

American Society of Papyrologists 2579
Amexfel Publishers 6124
AMG Publications 6118, 6130
Ammo Books 6126
Amnesty International International Secretariat **2027**, 2028
Amnesty International UK **2028**
Amnesty Publications 6103
Amok Books 6135
Amolibros **3004**
The Ampersand Agency Ltd **4002**
A.M.S. Educational Ltd **2029**
Anaya 6111
Anaya ELE 6111
Anchor Books 2538, 2786
Anchorage Press 2211, 2430
Andersen Artists (greetings cards) 2030
Andersen Press Ltd **2030**, 6096
Andersen Young Readers' Library 2030
Darley Anderson Literary, TV & Film Agency **4003**
Michelle Anderson Publishing 6110
Andrea Press 6070
Peter Andrew Publishing Co Ltd **2031**
Andrews McMeel 2706
Chris Andrews Publications Ltd **2032**
The Angel's Share 2830
Anglican Book Centre 2681
Anglicanshop.com 2489
The Anglo-American Book Co Ltd **6089**, 6094
Anglo-Saxon Books **2033**
Animal Ark Series 2337
Anmol 6123, 6124
Ann Arbor Publishers Ltd **2034**
Anness 6071, 6115
Annette Green Authors' Agency **4004**
Annick Press 6070
Anova Books 2081, 2190, 2534, 2589, 2590, 2613, 2649
Anshan Ltd **2035**, 6106
Anthem Press 6103
Anthroposophic Press 2731
Antiochian Archdiocese Publications Department 6127
Antique Collectors' Club Ltd **2036**
Antiquity Publications 2579, 2614
Anvil Editions 2037, 6135
Anvil Press Poetry Ltd **2037**, 6117
ANWB 2391
AP Information Services Ltd **2038**
Apa Guides 2300
Aperture 2767
Apex One 2427
Apex Publishing Ltd **2039**
Apollo-Verlag Paul Lincke GmbH 2679
Apollos 2416
Appin Press 2207
Applause Books 2653
Appletree Press Ltd **2040**, 6081, 6100
AquaPress **6148**, 6156
Aquarius Collection Ltd **4005**
Aquarius Library **4005**
Arabian Publishing 6065
Aravali Books International 6124
Arbeiterpresse Verlag 2492

INDEX OF COMPANIES & IMPRINTS / 171

The Arbitration Press 2375
Arc Publications Ltd **2041**
Arc Theatre Co 2149
Arcadia Books Ltd **2042**, 6135
Archaeological Institute of America 2579
Archaeology of York 2204
The Archbishops' Council 2177
Archetype Publications Ltd **2043**, 6103
Archipelago Press 2653
Architectura & Natura 2036
Architectural Association Publications **2044**
Architecture & Urbanism (Serial books) 2098
Archival Facsimiles 2261
Archive Editions Ltd **2045**
Archon Press Ltd 3001
Arcturus Publishing Ltd **2046**, 2289, 6119
Arden Shakespeare 2159
Ardis 2241
ARE Press 6110
Arena Books (Publishers) **2047**, 2050, 6111
Argosy Libraries Ltd **6149**
Argosy Press 6123
Argus Books 2724, 6070
Argyll Publishing **2048**, 6081, 6100, 6103
Ariadne Press 6065, 6109
Ariel Press 6110
ARIS 6092
Aris & Phillips 2579
Arkana 2597
Arkivia Books 2653
Armatura Press 2579
Arnold 2369
Edward Arnold Ltd 2371
Arnoldsche Verlagsanstalt 2036
Arris Publishing Ltd **2049**, 6126
Arrow 2635
Ars Latina 6090
Ars Obscura 2719
Ars-Viva-Verlag 2679
Arsenal Pulp Press 6135
Arsenale Editrice 2036
Art Address Verlag 2364
Art & Antiques Editions 2364
Art Books International Ltd **6090**
Art Dictionaries Ltd 2639, 2671
Art Gallery of NSW 2767
Art in Close-Up Series 2210
Art Media 6123
Art Rom 2778
Art Trade Press 2364
Art Tricks 2778
Artellus Ltd **4006**
Artisan 6122
Artists' Choice Ltd **6159**
Arts Council England 2784, **5008**, 6120
Arvinius Forlag 6139
Aryan Books International 6124
Asa 6123
Ascension Press 2275
Aschehoug 6131
Asgard Publishing Services **6002**
Ash Tree Publishing 6109
Ashby & Woolsey 2686
Ashgate Publishing Ltd **2050**, 2317, 2470, 6202
Ashgate/Gower Publishing 6099
Ashgrove Publishing **2051**, 6137
Ashish/APH 6123
Ashmolean Museum Publications **2052**
ASI (Research) Ltd 2711
Asia Bookclub 6123
Asia Type 6123
Asian Studies Book Services 6120
Asiatic Publishing House 6124
Aslan 2460, 6137
ASLS Annual Volumes (series) 2054
Aspects of Tourism 2165
Aspekt Uitgeverij BV 6065
Aspire Publications Ltd 2038, 6136
Assess4care 6137
Assimil 6111
Association for Learning Technology **2053**
The Association for Physical Education 2187
Association for Scottish Literary Studies **2054**, 6100
Association for Study of Travel in Egypt & the Near East 2579
Association of African Universities Press 6088

Association of Authors' Agents **5009**
Association of Christian Teachers of Wales 2133
Association of Freelance Editors, Proofreaders & Indexers (Ireland) **5010**
Association of Illustrators **5011**, 6137
Association of Learned and Professional Society Publishers (ALPSP) **5012**, 6136
Association of Online Publishers (AOP) **5013**
The Association of Project Managers 6136
Association of Publishing Agencies 5064
Association of Subscription Agents and Intermediaries **5014**
Asterisk Design & Editorial Solutions **6003**
Astrolog Publishing House 6110
At Heart Publishing 6137
Atelier 6081, 6100
Athelney 2033
Athlone 2198
Atlantic Books **2055, 6091**
Atlantic Europe Publishing Co Ltd **2056**
Atlantic Publishing 6123
Atlantis 6131
Atlantis-Musikbuch-Verlag 2679
Atlas Press 6135
Atoll Editions 6139
Atom 2462
Atria 2706
Atrium 2202, 6120
Attic Press **2057**, 2202
Attwood & Binsted Ltd 2285
Auburn House 2330
Audio 2479
Audio Books 2462
Audio-Forum - The Language Source **2058**
Audiobook Publishing Association **5015**
Carl Auer International 2427
Augener 2730
Augsburg Fortress Publishers 2014
Aum Publications 3008
Aurealis 6093
Aurelian Information Ltd **2059**
Aureus Publishing Ltd **2060**
Aurora Books 6103
Aurora Metro Publications Ltd **2061**, 6103
Aurum Press **2062**
Aurum Press, Apple & JR Books 6117
Ausmed 6123
Austin & Macauley Publishers Ltd **2063**
Austral 6111
Australian Centre for Egyptology 2579
Australian Consolidated Press UK **2064**
Australian Medical Publications 6123
Australian Publishers Association 6202
Australian Theological Forum 2681, 6104
Australian Women's Weekly Home Library 2064
Auteur 6103
Authentic Bibles 2065
Authentic Lifestyle 2065
Authentic Media **2065**
Authentic US Lifestyle 2065
Authentik Guides 2286
The Author **6178**
Author Solutions Inc 2066
Authorhouse UK Ltd **2066**
Authors' Foundation **5016**
Authors' Licensing & Collecting Society (ALCS) **5017**
Authors Press 6123
Automatism Press 6093
Automobile Association 2001, 6117
Autonomedia 2609
AVA Publishing (UK) Ltd **2067**, 2767
Avalon 6109
Avalonia 6109
avantibooks ltd **6092**
Ave Maria Press 2014
Avebury 2050
Avery/Penguin USA 6110
Aviation Publications Inc 2209
Avots 6123
Awa Press 2653
Award Publications Ltd **2068**
The Azur Corporation 2036
Azure Books 2696, 2716

B & D Publishing **2085**
b small publishing ltd **2069**
B Squared **2070**
B & W Publishing 6100

Babani Press 2071
Bernard Babani (Publishing) Ltd **2071**
Back-In-Print Books Ltd **2072**
Back to Front 2720
Backpacking Guide Series 2117
Backstreet 2636
Badger Publishing Ltd **2073**
Hans A. Baenasch / Mergus Verlag GmbH 6156
Duncan Baird Publishers **2074**, 2706, 6126
W. G. Baird (Holdings) Ltd 2102
Baker Book House 2264
Baker & Taylor UK Ltd **6150**
Balintore Holdings 2174
Balnakeil Press 6100
Banjara Academy 6124
The Banner of Truth Trust **2075**
Bantam 2782, 6135
The Banton Press **2076**
Baobab Books 6088
BAPLA (British Association of Picture Libraries and Agencies) **5018**
The Barbirolli Society 6120
Barbour 2436
Barddas **2077**
Bardic Edition 2679
Barefoot Books **2078**, 6117
Tassy Barham Associates **4007**
Baring & Rogerson 2250
Barn Owl Books Ltd 2459
Barnabas 2093
Barny Books **2079**
Barrington Stoke 6119
Bartholomew 2191
Bartok Records 2679
Bartsky Ltd **2080**
Basic Health Publications 6110
Basler Afrika Bibliografien 6066
Batch.co.uk Ltd 5022
Batsford **2081**
Battlebridge 6066, 6103
Mark Batty Publisher 2767
Baylor University Press 2014
Bayreuth African Studies 6066
BBC Active **2082**, 6072
BBC Audiobooks Ltd **2083**
BBC Paperbacks 2597
BBC Worldwide 2083
BBR Distribution 6004, **6093**
BBR Solutions Ltd **6004**, 6093
BCR Publishing Ltd **2084**
BDS 2545
BEAM Education **2086**
Bear & Co 6110
Bear Creek Books 2375
Bear Cub Books 6110
Bearmondsey Publishing 6137
Beautiful Books Ltd **2087**, 6135
BEBC Distribution **6094**
Bedford 2583
Bedford Freeman Worth (BFW) **2088**, 2478
Bedfordshire Historical Record Society 2116
Beech Tree Publishing 6136
Chris Beetles 2036
Beginner's Guide to Needlecrafts 2686
Beit Yochmann 6123
Beknap 2350
Belair Publications 2284
Belitha Press 2590
John Bell Training 6123
Lorella Belli Literary Agency (LBLA) **4008**
The Belmont Press **2089**
Bemrose 6026
Ben Zvi Press 6123
Bender Richardson White **3006**
Bene Factum Publishing Ltd **2090**
Anton J. Benjamin GmbH 2679
John Benjamins 6094
Bennett & Bloom 6120
David Bennett Books 2590
Robert Bentley Publishers 2129
Berg Publishers **2091**, 6126, 6136
Berghahn Books **2092**, 6120
Berghahn Journals 6136
Bergin & Garvey 2330
Berith Publications 2766
Berkley Boulvard 6135
Berkley Publishing Group 6110
Berlin Verlag 2107

Berlitz 2300
Bernan Press 2791, 6082
Bernards (Publishers) Ltd 2071
Berrett-Koehler 2473
Bertoli Mitchell LLP **6052**
Best Books Kolkata 6123
Best Mailing Services Ltd **6053**
Best Publishing 6148
Beta Plus 2036
Bethlehem Books 2275
Better Books **6095**
Better Care Guides 2352
Better Yourself Books 2668
Between the Lines 6066
Beuth (The German Standards Institute) 2837
Beyond Control (Research Proceeding) 2053
bfi Publishing 6072
Bhaktivedanta Book Trust 6124
Bible Lands Museum 6123
Bible Reading Fellowship **2093**
Bible Search Publications Inc 2567
Bible Society 2416
Bibles for Children 6120
Biblico Pontificio 6123
The Bibliographical Society **5019**
Bibliographisches Institut Mannheim 6111
Bibliography of British Newspapers 2126
Bibliophile Books **6160**
Bibliotheque des Arts 2364
Joseph Biddulph Publisher **2094**
Big Fish 2590
Big Time 2339
Bihar School of Yoga 6124
BILD Publications 6100
Bilingual Education & Bilingualism 2165
Bindu Books 6110
Binkey Kok Publications 6110
Binsted Frères SA 2285
The Biochemical Society 2614
Biographies 2605
Bioscientifica Ltd 2614
Biotech 6123
Birkbeck Law Press 2655
Birlinn Ltd **2095**, 6061, 6081, 6100, 6202
Birmingham Transport Historical Group 6121
Birmingham University Press 6103
Bitter Lemon Press **2096**, 6135
BL Publishing 2706
BLA Publishing Ltd 2817, **3007**
Black Ace Book Production **6005**
Black Ace Books **2097**
Black Amber 2042
Black Dog & Leventhal 6070, 6126
Black Dog Publishing Ltd **2098**, 6120
Black Lace (heteroerotic fiction by women) 2812
Black Library 6099
Black Rose Books 6103
Black Rose Books (Central Books) 6135
Black Sparrow Press 2653
Black Spring Press Ltd **2099**
Black Swan 2782
Black & White Publishing 6100
A. & C. Black (New Testament Commentaries) 2198
A. & C. Black (Publishers) Ltd 2009, **2100**, 2107, 2361, 6119, 6202
Blackhall Publishing **2101**
Blackmask 6088
Blackstaff Press **2102**
Blackstone 6109
Blackthorn Press **2103**
Blackwell Publishing **2104**
Blackwell's UK 6202
John F. Blair, Publisher 6097
Blake Friedmann Literary Agency Ltd **4009**
John Blake Publishing Ltd **2105**, 6117
Bliss Books 2042
Bloodaxe Books Ltd **2106**, 6117
Bloody Books 2087
Bloomberg Press 2438
Bloomsbury Publishing Plc **2107**, 2361, 6119, 6184, 6195
Blue Beyond Books **3008**
Blue Books 2624
Blue Cat Books 6123
Blue Cow Books 6100
Blue Dolphin Publishing Inc 6110
Blue Island Publishing 6103

Blue Mango Publishing 6066
Mr Blue Sky Ltd 2108
Blue Sky Press **2108**
Blue Water Publishing 6109
Blue Weaver Marketing 6066
Bluestar Communications 6110
Bluestone Press 6109
BML Ltd 6192
BMM 2727
Bodleian Library Publishing **2109**, 6136
Boerm Bruckmeier Verlag GmbH 6120
Boffin Boy 2636
Boleyn Books 6137
Bonacci Editore 6111
Bonechi Edizioni 'Il Turismo' SRL 6139
Bonnier Books 6120
Luigi Bonomi Associates Ltd **4010**
Book Aid International **5020**
Book Blocks 2217
Book Castle (Deltastar Ltd) 2110
Book Castle Publishing Ltd **2110**
Book Connections 2323, 6022
Book Creation Ltd **6006**
The Book Depot **6054**
Book Enclave 6123
The Book Foundation 6126
The Book Guild 6137
Book Industry Communication **5021**, 5022
Book Marketing Ltd **2111**
Book Production Consultants Ltd 2323, **6022**
Book Publishing Company 6109
The Book Service Ltd **6096**
Book Street Ltd **3009**
Book Systems Plus Ltd **6097**
Book Tokens Ltd 5022
Bookbiz International 6097
Bookcraft Ltd **6023**
Bookinabox 3019
Booklink **6055**
Bookmark Remainders Ltd **6141**
Bookmarks 6135
Bookmart Ltd **6098**
Bookplate **6056**
Bookpoint Ltd **6099**
BookPower **3010**
Books for Keeps **6179**
Books in Print 2007–2008 **6180**
Books on Music **6057**
The Bookseller **6181**
Bookseller Publications 2545
Bookseller & Publisher **6182**
Booksellers Association Annual Conference **6163**
Booksellers Association of the United Kingdom & Ireland Ltd **5022**
BookSource **6100**
Bookspeed **6151**
Booktrust **5023**
Bookwell Publications 6124
Bookworld Publishers 6088
Bookworld Wholesale Ltd **6152**
Boosey & Hawkes Music Publishers Ltd 2679
Chris Boot 2767
Booth-Clibborn 2767
Bootstrap & Apex Press 6103
Bordas 6111
Borgen 6131
Born to Shop 2637
Börsenverein des Deutschen Buchhandels 6168
Borthwick Publications **2112**
Bossiney Books Ltd **2113**, 6109
Boston Mills Press 6070
Bote & Bock GmbH & Co KG 2679
Boulevard Books 6065
Bounce Sales & Marketing 6115
The Bournemouth English Book Centre Ltd 6094
Bowerdean Publishing Co Ltd 4028, 6103
Bowker (UK) Ltd **2114**
R. R. Bowker LLC 6180, 6182, 6183, 6185, 6188
Bowland Press 6093
E. J. Bowles 6123
Boxer Books 2459
Boxtree 2478, 2585, 6119
Marion Boyars Publishers Ltd **2115**, 6103, 6135
Boydell & Brewer Ltd **2116**
Boydell Press 2116

Boyds Mills Press 2653
Boyer Education 6094
Boynton/Cook 2330
Boys Town Press 6110
BPB Publications 6124
BPI (India) Pvt Ltd 6124
Bradford Books 2511
Henry Bradshaw Society 2116
Bradt Travel Guides Ltd **2117**, 6072
Brandon/Mount Eagle Publications **2118**, 6135
Bill Brandt Archive 6139
Brassey's (UK) 2199
Braun Verlagshaus 2767
George Braziller 2036
Nicholas Brealey Publishing **2119**, 6096
Breckling Press 2653, 6139
Breedon Books Publishing Co Ltd **2120**
Brenthurst Collection / Frank Horley Books 6088
Brepols Publishing 6120
D. S. Brewer 2116
Brewin Books Ltd **2121**
Bridge Books **2122**
Bridge Reports 2399
Bridgewater Book Co **3011**
Brijbasi Art Press 6124
Brill Academic Publishers 6136
Brilliant Publications **2123**, 6072, 6094
Brimax 2130, 6071
Brioni Books 2036
Bristol Classical Press 2241
Bristol Phoenix Press 2800
British Academic Press 2756
British Academy 2579
British and Irish Archaeological Bibliography 2204
British Artists Series 2755
British Association for Adoption & Fostering **2124**
British Association for Korean Studies (BAKS) 6093
British Association of Communicators in Business **5024**
British Book Awards 6192
British Book Industry Awards 6192
British Centre for Literary Translation (BCLT) **5025**, 6044
British Council for Archaeology 6103
British Council Visual Arts 6108
British Fantasy Society **5026**
British Film Institute 6103
British Geological Survey **2125**
British Geotechnical Society 2761
The British Guild of Travel Writers **5027**
British Institute in East Africa 2579
The British Institute of Archaeology at Ankara 2579
British Institute of Radiology 6137
The British Journal for Ethnomusicology 6057
British Library **2126**, 6136
British Library, Publishing Office **2127**
The British Library Studies in Medieval Culture 2126
The British Library Studies in the History of the Book 2126
British Museum Press **2128**, 2579, 2767
British Poets Series 2210
The British Psychological Society 6136
British Railways in Colour 2780
British Records Relating to America in Microform (BRRAM) (series) 2505
The British School at Rome 2579
British School of Archaeology in Iraq 2579
British Standards Publishing Ltd (BSPL) 5028
Broadcast Books 6103
Broadman & Holman 6130
Brockhampton Press 2157
Brockhaus 6111
Alan Brodie Representation Ltd **4011**
Andrew Brodie Publications 2100
Bromley Books 6070
Brookemead ELT 6094
Brookers 2652
Brooklands Books Ltd **2129**
Brooks/Cole 2159
Brookside Publishing Services Ltd **6058**
Brown & Benchmark 2473
Brown & Brown Publishing 6092
Brown Dog Books **2130**, 6071

Brown, Son & Ferguson, Ltd **2131**
Brown Wells & Jacobs Ltd **3012**
Brown & Whittaker Publishing **2132**
Jenny Brown Associates **4012**
Wm. C. Brown 2473
Felicity Bryan **4013**
Bryntirion Press **2133**, 2264
BSI Business Information **5028**
BTBS The Book Trade Charity **5029**
Bucher 2617
The Buckman Agency **4014**
Barbara Budrich 6066
Bulfinch 2462
David Bull Publishing 2354
Bulletin 2399
Burall Floraprint **2134**
Burke Publishing 6120
Brie Burkeman **4015**
Burke's Peerage 2116
Burning House 2087
Burns & Oates **2135**, 2198, 6126
Buses in Colour 2780
Bushwood Books Ltd **6101**
Business Education Publishers **2136**
Butterfingers Books **2137**

C-Licence 2653
C & T Publications 2653, 6139
CAB International 2138
CABI **2138**, 6202
Cacimbo Editions 6066
Cadmos 6010, 6103
Caedmon of Whitby 2819
CAF (Charities Aid Foundation) 6103
Caine Books 6109
Francis Cairns Publications 2579
Caister Academic Press 6097
Calder Publications 2564
John Calder 6106
Calgary University Press 6065
California University Press 2828
Calouste Gulbenkian Foundation 6103
Calvary Press 2264
The Calypso Organization 2139
Calypso Publications **2139**
Camber Publications Ltd 2209
Cambrian Publications 6093
Cambridge Bibles 6130
Cambridge Global Grid for Learning 2140
Cambridge Hitachisoft Educational Solutions PLC 2140
Cambridge Information Group 2114, 6180, 6183, 6185, 6188
Cambridge Knowledge (China) Ltd 2140
Cambridge Philological Society 2579
Cambridge Printing Services Ltd 2140
Cambridge Publishing Management Ltd **3013**
Cambridge University Press **2140**, 6058, 6072, 6202
Camden House 2116
Camden Music 2723
Camerapix 6066, 6103
Cameron Books 2141, **3014**
Cameron & Hollis **2141**, 3014
Campaign for Learning 2721
Campaign for Real Ale Ltd 2142
Campbell 2475, 2478, 2585
Campbell Thomson & McLaughlin Ltd **4016**, 4067
Georgina Campbell 2653
Georgina Campbell's Guides to Ireland 6139
Campden & Chorleywood Research Association 2285
Camra Books **2142**, 6061, 6119
Can do computing 2010
Canadian Almanac & Directory 6082
Canadian Humanist Publications 6065
Candle 2460
CANIEM (Mexican Publishers' Association) 6202
Canongate Books **2143**
Canopus Publishing Ltd **2144**
Canterbury Press, Norwich 2681
Canterbury & York Society 2116
Hatje Cantz 6090
Capall Bann Publishing **2145**, 6109
CAPDM 6018
Cape Town University Press 6103
Jonathan Cape 2635
Capella 2046

Capital History 2146
Capital Transport Publishing **2146**
Cappelen 6131
Capstone 2653, 2828
Capuchin Classics **2147**
Carcanet 6061, 6117
Career Press 6110
Careers Bradford Ltd 2148
Careers Europe **2148**
Carel Press **2149**
Carey Publications 2264
Carlsen 6111
Carlton Publishing Group **2150**, 6026, 6061
Carmelite Charitable Trust 2666
Carmelite Institute 2666
The Carmelite Press 2666
Carnegie Publishing 6100
Carnegie Publishing Ltd **2151**, 6100
Carolina Biological Supply Co Inc 2582
Jon Carpenter Publishing **2152**, 6103
Carroll & Brown Ltd 2130, **2153**, 6071
Carswell 2652
Carta 6123
Cartech 2129
Cartographica Press 3035
Casarotto Ramsay & Associates Ltd **4017**
Cassell 2574, 6129
Cassell Academic 2198
Cassell Illustrated 2555
Cassell Reference 2198
Casterman 6111
Catalyst Press 6103
Catedra 6111
The Catholic Truth Society **2154**
Catnip Publishing Ltd **2155**
Catt Publishing 6094, 6123
John Catt Educational Ltd **2156**
Caversham Communications Ltd 2707
Cawdor Book Services Ltd 6155
Caxton Publishing Group Ltd **2157**, 2169, 2496, 2497
CBA Research Reports 2204
CBD Research Ltd **2158**
CEDLA 6103
Celtic Studies Publications 2579
Cengage Learning EMEA **2159**, 6102
Cengage Learning Services **6102**
Centaur 2568, 2577
Centennial Photo Service 2544
Center for Old World Archaeology & Art 2579
Center Press 6089
Central Africana 6088
Central Books **6103**
Centre for Albanian Archaeology 2579
Centre for Alternative Technology Publications **2160**, 6072, 6202
Centre for Economic Policy Research **2161**
Centre for Energy, Environment, Science & Technology (CEEST) 6088
The Centre for Interfirm Comparison **6059**
Centre for Policy on Ageing **2162**, 6103
The Centre for Publishing Studies **6197**
Centre for Publishing, University College London **6198**
Centre for Studies in Civilizations 6124
Centre Panafricain de Prospective Sociale / Pan-African Social Prospects Centre 6088
Centro Di 2036
Century 2635
CGP Study 2200
Chakra Press 6124
Chakula Press Ltd 6097
Chalice Well 6109
Chalksoft Ltd **2163**, 2692
Chambers Harrap Publishers Ltd **2164**, 2338, 2369
Chameleon HH Publishing Ltd **6007**
Chancellor College Publishers 6088
Chancerel 6094
Chancery House Press 2158
Chandos Publishers 6136
Channel 4 Books 2782
Channel View Publications Ltd **2165**, 2614
Chapman & Vincent **4018**
Geoffrey Chapman 2198
Paul Chapman Publishing Ltd 2665
Chapter House Ltd 2018
Charisma House 2436
The Charlton Press 6097

INDEX OF COMPANIES & IMPRINTS / 173

Charnwood Hardback Series 2773
Chartered Institute of Journalists **5030**
The Chartered Institute of Linguists **5031**
Chartered Institute of Loss Adjustors 2834
Chartered Institute of Personnel & Development **2166**
The Chartered Institute of Public Finance & Accountancy **2167**
Chase Publishing Services Ltd **6024**
Chastleton Travel 2049
Chateaux & Manoirs 6097
Chatham Publishing **2168**
Chatto & Windus 2635
Chaucer Press 2157, **2169**
Cheeky Guides 6135
Chelsea Green Publishing Co 2324
Cheltenham Tourism 2638
The Times Cheltenham Literature Festival **6164**
Chemcord Ltd **2170**
Chemical Publishing Co Inc 2285
Cherry Red 6135
Cherrytree 2265, 2848
Chic Guides 6116
Chick Publications 6118
Chicken House Publishing Ltd **2171**, 2677
Child Language and Child Development 2165
Children in Charge 2435
Children's Book Week **6165**
Children's Books in Print 2008 **6183**
Children's Books Ireland **5032**
Childrens Corner Ltd 2051
Children's Crafts 2686
Children's Libraries 2605
Children's Picture Books 2030
The Children's Society 6103
Children's Writers' & Artists' Yearbook **6184**
Children's Writers & Illustrators Group **5033**
Child's Play (International) Ltd **2172**
Chilton Designs 2624
Chimaera Publications 6093
Chinese Classroom 2455
The Chippendale Society 2036
Chiriotti Editori Srl 2285
Chiron Publications 6110
Chrismar Inc 2351
Christchurch Publishers Ltd 2015, 2707
Christian Education **2173**
Christian Focus Publications **2174**
Christian Heritage 2174
Christian Medical Fellowship 2416
Christian Research Association **2175**
Christianity & Literature Series 2277
Christie's Books 2036
Christmas is Fun 2374
Chrome Dreams 6135
Chronicle 6115
Chronosports 6137
Chrysalis Children's Books 2590
The Chrysalis Press **2176**
Chuoshuppan-Sha 2668
Church House Publishing **2177**, 6072, 6120
Church of England Record Society 2116
Church of Ireland Publishing **2178**
Church Publishing 6104
Churchill-Livingstone 2254
Ciana Ltd **6166**
Cicerone Press Ltd **2179**, 2638, 6100, 6129
Cico Books 6119
CILIP (Chartered Institute of Library and Information Professionals) 2274, **5034**
CILIPS (Chartered Institute of Library and Information Professionals in Scotland) 6081
CILT, the National Centre for Languages **2180**, 6103
CIPAC 6120
Circlet Press 6135
Circusstuff 2137
CIRIA Publications 2197
CIT Books 6103
Citadel Press 6109
Citeaux 2579
City & Council of Newcastle upon Tyne 2794
City of Birmingham Libraries 2121
City University **6199**, 6202

Claerhout Publishing 6106
Claire Publications 2029, **2181**
Clairview Books 6100
Clan Books 6081
Clan Publishers 6100
Clar 2095
Claridge Press 2198
Robin Clark 2627
T. & T. Clark **2182**
James Clarke & Co **2183**, 2471, 2681, 6067
Clarus Press 6058
Class Publishing **2184**, 6119
Classic Collection 2544
Classic Locations 6097
Classic Marques 2780
Classic Pathfinder 2180
Classic Publications 2016
Classic Reading 2523
Classical Comics Ltd **2185**
Classical Press of Wales 2579
Classical Spectrum 2679
CLE International 6111
CLÉ (Irish Book Publishers Association) 6202
Cleis Press 6135
Mary Clemmey Literary Agency **4019**
Clever Books (Pty) Ltd 2478
Cliff College Publishing 2515
Clinical Press – Europe 6065
Clinical Publishing 6120
Clive Bingley 2274
Cló Iar-Chonnachta **2186**
Clockwork Media 6137
Clunie Press 2427
Coachwise Ltd **2187**
Coastal Publishing **2188**
Tim Coates 6061
Cobwebs Brentwood 6097
Elspeth Cochrane Personal Management **4020**
Coffee School Melbourne 6123
Alan Cohen Publishing 6110
Cois Life **2189**
Cold Spring Harbor Laboratory Press 2680
Colegio de España 6111
Armand Colin 6111
Rosica Colin Ltd **4021**
Collector's Library **2217**, 6023
College of Law Publishing 6094
College Press Publishers 2478, 6088
Collins & Brown **2190**
Collins Cartographic 2191
Collins Classics 2348
Collins Crime 2348
Collins Dictionaries COBUILD 2348
Collins Geo **2191**
Collins Longman 2191
Collins New Naturalist Library 2348
The Collins Press 6061
Collins Teacher 2348
Collins/Times Maps & Atlases 2348
CollinsEducation 2348
CollinsGems 2348
J R Collis Publications 2260
Colman Getty Ltd **6060**
Colne Edition 2723
Colorado University Press 6065
ColorCards 2725
Colouring is Fun 2374
Colourpoint Books **2192**
Columba **2193**
The Columba Bookservice 2220, **6104**
The Columba Press 2193, 6104
Columbia University Press 2828
Combined Academic Publishers Ltd **6105**, 6120
Combined Book Services Ltd **6106**
Comerford & Miller 6103
Comhairle nan Leabhraichean / The Gaelic Books Council **5035**
Commentary 2396
Commission for Racial Equality 2784
Common Ground 2245
Commonwealth Secretariat **2194**
Commonwealth Youth Programme 6124
Communication Disorders Across Languages 2165
Community, Culture and Change 2435
Companion Guides 2116
Compass Academic Ltd 6061
Compass DSA Ltd **6061**

Compass Maps and Guides 6072, 6109, 6115
Compendium 6026, 6126
The Complete Directory of Large Print Books and Serials 2008 **6185**
Complete Guides 2392
Complete Results & Line-ups (Series) 2714
Completion Press 2731
Compukort 2351
Computational Mechanics International Ltd 2833
Conciliar Press 6127
Concord Press 6123
Condor Books 2722
Conflict & Peace Building 2353
Connections 6109, 6122
Connections Book Publishing 3019
Conran Octopus **2195**, 2555
Conspiracy Books Ltd 3022
Constable & Robinson Ltd **2196**, 6096
Construction Industry Publications 2791
Construction Industry Research & Information Association (CIRIA) **2197**
Contact Pastoral Trust 2260
Contemporary Drama Service 2345
The Continuum International Publishing Group Ltd 2135, 2182, **2198**, 2344, 2540, 6058, 6072, 6126, 6202
Contour Management Services (CMS) **6107**
Controversies and Dilemmas Series 2663
Conway **2199**
Jane Conway-Gordon Ltd **4022**
Conway Maritime Press 2199
David C. Cook 2436
Thomas Cook 6115
Cool Kits 2778
Coombs Moylett Literary Agency **4023**
Coordination Group Publications Ltd (CGP Ltd) **2200**
Jonathon Cope 6109
Copenhagen Business School Press 6120
Copper Beech Publishing Ltd **2201**
Copyright Tribunal **5036**
Copytrain **6008**
Cordee 2638, 6129
Corgi 2782
Corinium Publications 2638, 6129
Cork Publishing Ltd 2552
Cork University Press 2057, **2202**
Cork University Press / Attic Press 6120
Corkwood Press 6123
Cornell Maritime Press 6148
Cornelsen 6111
Cornerhouse Publications **6108**
Cornish Classics 2790
Cornucopia 2605
Cornwall Editions Ltd **2203**
Corpus of British Medieval Library Catalogues 2126
Corpus Publishing Ltd **3015**
Correspondance complète de Françoise de Graffigny 2814
Correspondance complète de Jean Jacques Rousseau 2814
Correspondance complète de Pierre Bayle 2814
Correspondance générale de La Beaumelle 2814
Corvo Books 6103
Corwin Press Inc 2665
Cosmo Publications 6124
Cotsen Institute of Archaeology at UCLA 2579
Council for British Archaeology **2204**
Council for British Research in the Levant 2579
Council for the Development of Social Science Research in Africa (CODESRIA) 6088
Council of Europe 2791
Council of Mortgage Lenders **2205**
Counter Culture **6109**
Country Bumpkins 2686
Country Living Rural Guides 2783
Country Pubs & Inns 2783
Countryman Press 2549
Countryside Books **2206**
The County Gardens Guides Inspirations Series 2373
Countyvise Ltd **2207**
Covenanters Press 2849

Cover to Cover Cassettes (Audio Cassettes & CDs) 2083
Cowley Robinson Publishing Ltd **3016**
CPAG (Child Poverty Action Group) 6103
CQ Press **2208**, 6120
Cracking It 6097
Cracking KS3 Scripts 2523
Craig Printing 6123
Cranz GmbH 2679
CRC 2757, 2837
Creation Books 6135
Creative Colouring 2374
Creative Communications 2640
Creative Company/Stargazer 3001
Creative Homeowner 2653, 6139
Creative Monochrome 6137
Creative Newfoundland 6123
Crécy Publishing Ltd **2209**
Crescent Books 6109
Crescent Moon Publishing **2210**
Cressrelles Publishing Co Ltd **2211**, 2430, 2509
Rupert Crew Ltd **4024**
Crime Express 2281
Crimson Publishing **2212**, 2787
Critical Language and Literary Studies 2165
Critical Psychology Division (Series) 2593
Critical Reading at post 16 2523
The Critics' Circle **5037**
Crombie Jardine Publishing 6117
Paul H. Crompton Ltd **2213**
Crossbow Education Ltd **2214**
Crossing Press 6109, 6123
Crossway Books 2416
Crown House 6115, 6202
The Crowood Press Ltd **2215**, 6115
G. L. Crowther **2216**
Crucial 2447
Crucible Books 2151
Cruising Guide Publications 2391
CRW Publishing Ltd **2217**, 6119
Crystal Clarity Publishers 6110
CSA Word **2218**, 6126
CSS Ltd 6088
CTI Publications Inc 2285
CTS Publications 2154
Cualann Press Ltd **2219**
Cube Publications Ltd 2206
Culture Smart! Guides 6116
Culture & Sport Glasgow 2306
Cumberland House 2653
Cumbria Heritage 2780
Currach Press 2193, **2220**
Current Clinical Strategies Publishing 6065
Current Law Publishers 2771
James Currey Publishers **2221**, 6120
Curriculum Concepts UK 2004
Curtis Brown **4025**
Customs & Etiquette 6116
Cutting Edge 2636
Cyan 6117
Cyber-Psycho's A.O.D. 6093
Cycling Resources / van der Plas Publications 6070
Cygnus Books 6109
Cyhoeddiadau'r Gair **2222**
Czech Institute of Archaeology 2579

D & B Publishing 6070
D & N Publishing **3017**
DAAB 6117
Dake Bible Sales 6118
Dakini 2767
Dalkey Archive Press 6135
Damiani Editore 6120
Dance Books Ltd **2223**, 6137
Dance Horizons 2223, 6137
Dar Al Saqi Sarl 2672
Dar es Salaam University Press 6088
Darby Publications 2515
Dark Man 2636
Dartmouth 2050
Darton, Longman & Todd Ltd **2224**
Darwin Press 6065
Data Publishers Association (DPA) **5038**
The Davenant Press **2225**
Davenport Publishing Services – Sales & Marketing **6062**
David & Charles Ltd **2226**
Dawn Publications 6110
Dawnhorse Publications 6110

Day by Day with God 2093
Day One Christian Ministries 2227
Day One Publications **2227**
Daya 6123
Y Ddraig Fach 2237
-De, -Dis, -Ex 2098
Alain de Gourcuff Editeur 2036
De la Mare Publishing Ltd 2272
De Vorss & Co 6110
Felix de Wolfe Ltd **4026**
Dean 2249
Deben Gallery 2036
Debretts 6099
Dechema 6136
B. C. Decker 2473, 6072
Dedalus Ltd **2228**, 6103
Deep Books Ltd **6110**
Deep & Deep 6123, 6124
Dekker 2757
Del Nuevo Extremo 6123
Delancey Press Ltd **2229**, 6137
Delius Trust 2679
Delmar Learning 2159
Delta Alpha Publishing Ltd **2230**
Demos 6103, 6134
Richard Dennis Publications **2231**
Denor Press Ltd **2232**
J M Dent **2233**, 2574
DEO Publishing 2681
Design and Artists Copyright Society **5039**
Design and Technology Association 2784
Design Handbooks 2361
Design Source Books 2686
Desktop Publications 2029
Destech Publishers 6134
Destino 6111
Destiny Books 6110
Detselig Enterprises Ltd 6097
Andre Deutsch 2150
Deutscher Apotheker Verlag 2791
Deutscher Taschenbuch Verlag 6111
Development Bibliographies 2399
Development Policy Management Forum (DPMF) 6088
Device 6135
Diagram Visual Information Ltd **3018**
Diamond Pocket Books 6123
Didier 6111
Difusión 6111
Dilston Press 6109
Dimension Books 2640
Dinapress 6111
Dinas 2843
Diogenes 6111
Dionysia Press Ltd **2234**
Directory of Social Change 6103
Directory of UK & Irish Book Publishers **6186**
Disability Alliance 6103
Discovery Books 6106
Discovery House 6118
Discovery Walking Guides Ltd **2235**
Discript Ltd **6025**
Discussion Papers 2399
Disinformation 6135
Disney Editions 6135
DIY: Bookfinding and Bookselling **6187**
DK Printworld 6123, 6124
DNA Press 2680
Tom Doherty Associates LLC 2478
DOI Agency **5040**
Dolmen Press 2712
John Donald 2095, 6081, 6100
Donhead Publishing Ltd **2236**
R. R. Donnelley 6100
Doodle Design 2374
Dorian Literary Agency **4027**
Dorling Kindersley Ltd 2597
Dorling Kindersley Religious 2416
Doubleday 2782
Douglas Press 2048
Sheridan Douglas 6109
Dove Publishing 6137
The Dovecote Press 2206
Dover Books 2226, 2562
Dragon Books Publishing Corp 6154
Dragondance 6123
Dragonhawk Publishing 6110
Ashley Drake Publishing Ltd **2237**
Drama Book Publishers 2362
Dramatic Lines **2238**
Dramatists Play Service Inc 2821

Draw Books 2100
Dreamcatcher Publishing Ltd **2239**
Dreams and Nightmares 6093
Dref Wen Cyf/Ltd **2240**
Richard Drew Ltd 6100
Drive! Touring Maps 2235
Driveabout Series 2638
Druid Ways 6109
DSCH 2679
DTS Sales 6121
Brian Dubé Inc 2137
Gerald Duckworth & Co Ltd **2241**, 6115
Duckworth/Overlook 6135
Duden 6111
Robert Dudley Agency **4028**
Duke University Press 6105
Duke Video 2354
Ken Duncan Panographs 6123
Dundee University Press 6072, 6100
Dunedin Academic Press **2242**, 6136
Duquesne University Press 6065
Durham County Council 2125
Durkheim Press 2092
Durnell Marketing Ltd – Publishers European Marketing Agency **6063**
Dutton / Penguin USA 6110

E & D Ltd 6088
Eagle Publishing Ltd **2243**, 2358, 2416
Eagles Nest Golf Guides 6123
Eaglewing 6109
EAHMH Publications 6093
Early English Church Music 2730
Early English Text Society 2116
Early Years 2353
Earth Love 6109
Earth Magic Productions Inc 6110
Earthscan **2244**, 2614
Earthscan / James & James 6119
East African Educational Publishers 6088
Eastern Arts / Saffron 6066
Easyway Guide 6135
Ebiz Guides 2653
Ebury 2635
Eccentric Series 2117
Ecclesiastical History Society 2116
Eco-logic Books **2245**
Ecole des loisirs 6111
Economic & Social Research Institute **2246**
The Economist Books 2621
ECS Publishing Co 2730
ECW Press 6135
Eddington Hook 6106
Eddison Sadd Editions Ltd **3019**
EDELSA 6111
Eden Project 2782
Edfu 6109
Ediciones Castillo SA de CV 2478
Ediciones Edhasa 6111
Ediciones Edinumen 6111
Ediciones Molino 6111
Ediciones San Pablo 2668
Ediciones SM 6111
Edições San Pablo 2668
Edilingua 6111
Edinburgh Business School 6018
Edinburgh International Book Festival **6167**
Edinburgh University, Dept of Archaeology 2579
Edinburgh University Press **2247**, 6120, 6202
Edition **6009**
Edition de l' Amateur 2364
Edition HH 2679
Editions Acatos 2364
Editions Assouline 6120
Editions de l'Echelle de Jacob 2364
Editions du Briel 2391
Editions du Fallois 6111
Les Editions du Mont Tonnerre 2286
Editions du Seuil 6111
Editions J. R. Piccard 6137
Editions l'Octogone 2653
Editions Mediaspaul 2668
Editions Pelisser 6123
Editions Scala 2676
Editions Sisyphe 6139
Editions Thames & Hudson sarl 2767
Editions Trilice 6123
Editions Vagnon 2391
Editions Van Wilder 2364
Editions Vausor 2036

Editions Vial 2364
The Editmaster Company **6010**
Editorial Estrada SA 2478
Editorial Macmillan de Mexico SA de CV 2478
Editorial Moll 6137
Editorial Prensa Iberica SA 2022
Editorial Puerto de Palos SA 2478
Editoriale Shopping Italia srl 2072
Editrice Reflex 2544
Edizioni Carmelitane 2666
Edizioni San Paolo 2668
Education Direct **6064**
Educational Company of Ireland 2073
Educational Fun Factory 2029
Educational Planning Books Ltd **2248**
Educational Publishers Council **5041**
Educational Writers Group **5042**
Educators Publishing Service 6095
Edwards Fuglewicz **4029**
Wm B. Eerdmans Publishing Co 2014
EFL Ltd 6097
Egmont UK Ltd **2249**
Egypt Exploration Society 2579
Einaudi 6111
Eisenbrauns 6123
Ekdotike Athenon 2579
Eland Publishing Ltd **2250**
ELC International 6082
Electa Architecture 2599
Electa Mondadori 6090
Elector Electronics 6065
Electric Word PLC 2570, 2725
Electronic Publishing Services Ltd **6035**
Edward Elgar Publishing Ltd **2251**, 6120
Eliot Werner Publications 2579
Elliott & Thompson **2252**
Elm Bank Publications 2406
Elm Consulting Ltd 2253
Elm Grove Books Ltd **3020**
Elm Publications **2253**
Elsevier 6072, 6202
Elsevier Ltd **2254**, 6072, 6202
ELSP (Ex Libris Self Publishing) 2267
ELST (Educational Low-Priced Sponsored Textbooks) 3010
ELT Press 2712
ELT Trading SA de CV 2140
Emerald Group Publishing Ltd **2255**
The Emirates Center for Strategic Studies & Research 2756
Emma Treehouse Ltd **3021**
Empire of the Senses 2228
Empiricus Books 2420
Empty Mirror Press 6123
EN PLO Editions 6127
Encounter Books 6065
Encyclopaedia Britannica (UK) Ltd **2256**, 6106
Encyclopaedia Universalis 2256
Endcliffe Press 6093
Energy Institute **2257**, 2614
Engin 2508
English Association **5043**
English Eccentricities 2201
English Heritage **2258**, 2791, 6061, 6103
English Place-Name Society 2819
English-Speaking Union of the Commonwealth **5001**
Enicrownfit Publishers 6088
Enigma Publishing 2089
Enisen Publishing 6120
Enitharmon Press **2259**, 6103
Ennsthaler Publishing House 6110
Enthea Press 6110
Envirobook Pty 2152
Epic Guides 6137
Eponymists in Medicine Series 2663
Epworth 2502, 2681
Equinox Publishing Ltd **2260**, 6120, 6136
Eric 6109
Milton H. Erickson Foundation Press 6089
Lawrence Erlbaum Associates 2757
The Erskine Press **2261**
ESC Publishing 2771
Espasa-Calpe 6111
ESRI Press 6134
Essential Artists Series 2755
Essential Works Ltd **3022**
Estate Publications 2638, 6129
Ethics International Press Ltd **2262**
The Etiquette Collection 2201

Ernst Eulenburg Ltd 2679
Euro Crime 2042
EuroComment 6065
Euroconfidentiel 6082
Euromapping 2391
Euromoney PLC 6136
Euromonitor International Plc **2263**
Europe 1992–2010 2228
European American Music Distributors LLC 2679
European Association for the History of Medicine and Health Publications 6093
European Communities/Union 2791
European Institute of Education & Social Policy 2784
European Language Institute 6111
European Library 6106
European Medical Journal 2624
European Music Centre 2723
European Pharmacopoeia Commission 2791
European Photography 6103
European Respiratory Society 2484
European Schoolbooks Ltd **6111**
European Studies Series 2406
European Writers Series 2210
Europresse SARL 2264
The Eurospan Group **6112**, 6136
Evangelical Library (London) 2133
Evangelical Library of Wales 2133
Evangelical Movement of Wales 2133
Evangelical Press of Wales 2133
Evangelical Press & Services Ltd **2264**
Evans Brothers 2265, 2848
Evans Mitchell Books 6126
Evans Publishing Group **2265**, 6102
Faith Evans Associates **4030**
Events, People to be Remembered (Joseph Banks – Sir John Hawrins) 2079
Everest 6111
Everyman 2635, 2266, 6115
Everyman Paperbacks 2233, 2574
Everyman's Library **2266**
Ex Libris Press **2267**, 2368
Excel Books 6124
Executive Grapevine International Ltd **2268**
The Exeter Press Ltd 2800
Exley Publications Ltd **2269**
Expert Gardening Books 2782
Expert Information 2614
Explorasaws 2778
Explore Australia 2653, 6139
Explore Books 2356
Express Newspapers **2270**, 6117
Eye Books Ltd **2271**, 6117

F & W Publications 2226
Fab Press 6135
Fabbri-Bompiani 6111
Faber & Faber Ltd **2272**, 6096
Fabian Pamphlet 2273
Fabian Society **2273**
Facet Publishing **2274**, 6099
Facts & Comparisons 2791
Fairview Press 2653
Fairwood Press 6093
Falconbury Ltd 2772
Jenn Falconer Books 6123
Falconwood Series 2029
Family Activities & Crafts 2353
Family Doctor Publications 6126
Family First Ltd 2608
Family Law 2424
Family Publications **2275**
Famous Fleets 2780
Fanshaw Books Ltd **6142**
Fantagraphics 6135
Fantom Films 6097
FAO (Food & Agriculture Organization of the United Nations) 6156
Far East Book Co 6123
Fare Stage 2780
A. & A. Farmar **2276**, 6058, 6103
Farrar, Straus & Giroux LLC 2478
Feather Books **2277**
Featherstone Education 2100
The Federation of Children's Book Groups **5044**
Federation of European Publishers **5002**
Feierabend 6090
Felicity Wishes range 2337
Feltrinelli 6111

INDEX OF COMPANIES & IMPRINTS / 175

Feminist Press 6065
Femrite (Uganda Women Writers' Association) 6088
Fennica Gehrmann 2679
Feral House 6135
Fernwood Press 6066, 6103
FHA Publishing & Communication 6065
FHG Guides Ltd **2278**, 6116
Field Day Essays 2202
Field Studies Council 2642
file-online.com 2778
Filipacchi 6122
Finch.Publishing 6110
Findel Education 2446
Findhorn Press Ltd **2279**, 6110
Fine Arts Museum of San Francisco 2036
Fine Arts Society 2036
Finesse Bridge Books 6070
Finesse Press 2137
Finnish Literature Society 6065
Finzi Trust 2679
Fire and Blood series 2606
Firefly Books 6070, 6126
Fireside 2706
First & Best in Education Ltd **2280**
First Edition Translations Ltd **6011, 6045**
First Law 6058
First Second Editions 6119
First Stone Publishing 3015
First Time Authors Fiction 2574
Fiscal Publications 6136
Fischer 6111
Carl Fischer Music 2679
Fiske & Freeman 2036
Fitway 6122
Fitzhenry & Whiteside 6123
The Fitzjames Press 2516, 6137
Fitzwarren Publishing 6097
Five Leaves Publications **2281**, 6103
Five Mile Press 2130, 6071
Flair 6071
Flambard Press **2282**, 6103
Flame Tree Publishing 6120
Flammarion SA 2767, 6111
Floating Gallery Press 6123
Floodlight 6103
Floramedia 2134
Floraprint 2134
Floris Books **2283**, 6100
Flowers East 6103
Flukes UK 2638, 6129
Fluor Ltd 6018
Focus 6088, 6097
Focus Publishing (Sevenoaks) Ltd **3023**
Folens Ltd **2284**
Folio 6111
Folio (Salt) 2669
Fono 2508
Food and Agriculture Organisation of the United Nations 2791
Food & Nutrition Press Inc 2285
Food Processors Institute 2285
Food Trade Press Ltd **2285**
Football In (Series) 2714
Football World 6137
Footprint Handbooks 2001, **2286**, 6115
Foreign Policy Centre 6103
Forensic Focus 2435
Forensic Science Society **2287**
Forglaid 6123
Format Publishing 6103
Fort Publishing 6081
Forté Uitgevers 2686
Fortune Street® 2466
Forum for Social Studies 6088
Forward Press Ltd 2538, 2786
The Fostering Network **2288**, 6103
fotoLibra **6026**
Foucher 6111
G. T. Foulis 2354
W. Foulsham & Co Ltd **2289**, 6119
Foundation for Islamic Knowledge 2439
Fountain 2544, 6088
Four Courts Press **2290**
Fourth Dimension Publishing Co Ltd 6088
Fourth Estate 2348
Fox & Howard Literary Agency **4031**
Fragile Earth 2674
Francisian Printing Press 6123
Frankfurt Book Fair **6168**
Franklin Beedle & Associates 6134
Franklin Watts 2337

Fraser Ross Associates **4032**
Free Association Books **2291**
Free Presbyterian Publishing 2264
Free Press 2706
Free Spirit 2653, 6089
Freedom Publishers 6088
Freehand Publishing 6106
Freelance Market News **3024, 6113**
Mara Freeman 6109
W. H. Freeman 2088, 2583
W. H. Freeman & Worth Publishers 6119
Fremantle Arts Centre Press 6103
Samuel French Ltd **2292**
Sigmund Freud Copyrights 4076
Friction Press 6103
Friends of the Earth **2293**, 6103
Frieze 2767
Francis Frith Book Co 6126
From Within 6110
Fry Art Gallery 2036
Full Circle 6124
Fun Kits 2778
Fundamental Rights & Liberties Series: Principles & Applications 2413
Funentes 6123
Funkkia 2752, 3038
Fusion Press 2813

G. S. Music 2723
Jüri Gabriel **4033**
Gaia 2555
Galactic Central Publications **2294**
Galago Books 6070, 6123
Galaxy 6123
Gale 2159
The Gallery Press **2295**
Galliard 2730
Gallimard 6111
Galore Park Publishing Ltd **2296**
Galway University Press 6103
Gambero Rosso 2036
Gambit 6103
Gamsberg Macmillan Publishers (Pty) Ltd 2478
Garden Art Press 2036
Gardners Books Ltd **6153**
Garfield 2637
Garland Science 2757
Garnet Publishing Ltd **2297**, 2415
J. Garnet Miller 2211
Garnier Flammarion 6111
Garzanti 6111
Gaskell 2659
Gatehouse Books **2298**
Gatehouse Media Ltd **2298**, 6092
Gateway 2305
Gault Millau 6111
Gay Authors Self-Publishing Society 5045
Gay Authors Workshop **5045**
Gazelle Academic 6058, **6065**
Gazelle Book Services Ltd 6065, **6114**
Geddes & Grosset **2299**, 6100
Gee Publishing 2771
Gefen 6123
Gemini Books 6124
Gene-Tech Books 6123
Genesis II 6089
Grant Jessé 3028
Ian Grant Publishers 2203
Gary Gentile Productions 6148
Geo Group & Associates **6012**
GeoCenter International Ltd **2300**, 6115
The Geographical Association **2301**
Geography Publications **2302**
Geological Society Publishing House **2303**
German Tuition – Barbara Classen **6200**
Germany's Top 500 6082
Die Gestalten Verlag UK 6120
Get Lost Publishing 6103
Get Through Series 2663
Getty Publications 2653, 6139
Ghana Universities Press 6088
Gibb Memorial Trust 2579, **5046**
Gibraltar Research 6120
Gibson Square **2304**, 6103, 6117
Bryan Gibson Publications 3042
Robert Gibson & Sons 2370
Gilde Buchhandlung 6111
Dan Giles Ltd 6090
Gill & Macmillan Ltd **2305**, 2478
Ginn 2595
Giunti 6111
The Glamorgan County History Trust 2802
Glasgow Museums **2306**

The Glasshouse Press 2655
Michael Glazier Books 6104
Glennie Kindred 6109
Global Book Marketing Ltd **6066**
Global Books in Print on Disc **6188**
Global Exchange 2653
Global Health Solutions 6123
Global Oriental Ltd **2307**, 6126, 6136
Global Professional Publishing **2308**
Globe Pequot Press 2286
Gloucester Publishers 6117
The Gloucestershire Ramblers Association 6129
Glowworm Books & Gifts Ltd **2309**
Glyndwr Publishing **2310**
GMB Publishing 2438, 6126
GML Publishing 2036
Bruno Gmunder 6135
Goal! 2636
Goblinshead 6081
Alan Godfrey Maps **2311**
David R. Godine 2653
Godsfield Press Ltd **2312**, 2555, 6109
David Godwin Associates **4034**
Gold Editions 2252
Golden Dawn 2483
Golden Handshake 2441
Golden Point Press 6123
Golden Sufi Center 6110
Goldmann 6111
The Goldsmith Press Ltd **2313**
Golfers Guides 2783
Golgonooza 6103
Goliath 6135
Victor Gollancz Ltd **2314**, 2573, 2574
Gomer **2315**
Good Book Company 2416
The Good Food Guide 2822
The Good Hotel Guide Ltd 6117
Good Life Press 6137
Goodall Publications 2209
Gorgias Press 2579
Gorilla Guides 2729
Gospel Folio Press 6130
Gospel Standard Publications 2264
Goss & Crested China Ltd 2507
Göteborg Book Fair **6169**
Gotham Books / Penguin USA 6110
Gothic Image Publications **2316**, 6109
Govardhan Hill 6124
Gower Publishing Co Ltd 2050, **2317**
GPC Books 2802
Grace Publications 2264
Gracewing Publishing **2318**
Graffeg **2319**
Grafiche Vianello 2036
Grafisk Forlag 6111
Graham-Cameron Illustration 3025, **6027**
Graham-Cameron Publishing & Illustration **3025**, 6027
Graham Maw Christie **4035**
W. F. Graham (Northampton) Ltd **2320**
Granada Learning **2321**, 6202
Grand Street 6103
Granite Publishing 6109
Granta Books **2322**, 2615
Granta Editions **2323**, 6022
Granta Magazine 2322
Grantham Book Services 6096, **6115**
Graphic Arts Center 2653
Graywolf Books 6135
Great Escapes.com 6097
Great Fiction 2624
Great Ideas 2436
The Greatest in the World 6117
Green Books **2324**, 6103, 6109
Green Books & Resurgence Books 2324
Green Earth Books 2324
Green Fuse 2004
Green Guide Publishing 6103
The Green Guide Series 2504
Green Magic **2325**, 6109
Green Print 2498
Green Umbrella Publishing 6067
Green Volunteers 2212
W. Green The Scottish Law Publisher **2326**, 2771
Louise Greenberg Books Ltd **4036**
Greene & Heaton Ltd **4037**
Greenery Press 6135

Greenhill Books / Lionel Leventhal Ltd **2327**, 6099
Greenleaf Publishing **2328**
Greenlight Publishing **2329**
Greenprint 6103
Greenwich Exchange 6103
Greenwich Medical Media Ltd 2140
Greenwood Publishing Group **2330**, 6136
Gregg International 2050
Gregg Revivals 2050
Gregory & Company Authors' Agents **4038**
The Jane Gregory Agency 4038
Gresham Books Ltd **2331**, 2837
Grey House Publishing 6082
Richard Griffin (1820) Ltd 2753, 2842
Griffith Institute of Oxford University 2579
Grijalbo 6111
The Grimsay Press 2849
Grove Atlantic Inc 2055
Grub Street **2332**, 6117
GRUND 2364
Gryphon House 2653
Guardian Books 2100
Gudrun Publishing / Edda UK 6097
Guerra 6111
Guggenheim Museum Publications 2767
Guide to Series 2117
Guided Reading Packs 2523
Guidelines 2093
Guidelines for Research in Parapsychology 2801
Guild of Book Dealers 6202
Guild of Food Writers **5047**
Guild of Master Craftsman Publications 6126
Guildford Press 2757
Guildhall Press **2333**
Guinness World Records Ltd 6119
Gullane Children's Books 6100
Gulshan Publishers 6124
Gwasg Addysgol Cymru 2237
Gwasg Carreg Gwalch **2334**
Gwasg Gwenffrwd **2335**
Gwasg Gwynedd **2336**
Gwasg Prifysgol Cymru 2802

Hachette Children's Books **2337**, 2338, 6099
Hachette Livre UK Ltd 2164, 2337, **2338**, 2371, 2372, 2462, 2510, 2519, 2574, 2602, 6099, 6111
Hackett Publishing Co 6065
Hackman 2637
Peter Haddock Publishing **2339**
Haese & Harris 6123
Hakedes 6123
Halban Publishers **2340**, 2574
Haldane Mason Ltd **2341**, 6137
Hale & Iremonger 2653
Robert Hale Ltd 2019, **2342**, 6106, 6109
Half Halt Press 2628
Halgo 2579
Hallewell Publications 6081
Halloween is Fun 2374
Halsgrove **2343**
Halstar **2343**
Hambledon Continuum Ltd 2198, **2344**
John Hambley Books 6121
Hamish Hamilton 2597
Hamlyn 2555
Hammersmith Press 6106
Mark Hammerton Group 2650
Hampton Roads Publishing 6110
Hanbury Plays **2345**
Hanford Mead 6109
Hanfrageo Holdings Ltd 2006, 2007
Happy Cat Books 2155
Harbord Publishing 6103
Harbour Books 6115
Harcourt Brace & Co 2472
Harcourt Publishers Ltd 2254
Harcourt Religion Publishers (RE division) 2472
Harcourt Trade Books 6122
Harden's Ltd **2346**
Hardie Grant Books 2653
Patrick Hardy 2471
Thomas Hardy Studies Series 2210
Harlan Davidson Inc 6065
Harlequin Mills & Boon Ltd **2347**
Harper Perennial 2348

INDEX OF COMPANIES & IMPRINTS

Harper Sport 2348
Harper Thorsons/Harper Element 2348
John Harper Publishing 6136
HarperCollins Publishers Ltd 2191, **2348**, 2640, 6072, 6116, 6202
HarperCollins US 6135
Harrap 2164, 2369
Harriman House Ltd 6120
Harrison House 2436
Hart McLeod Ltd **3026**
Hart Publishing **2349**
Alan & Simone Hartman 2036
Harvard Business School Press 2473
Harvard University Press **2350**, 2828
Harvey Map Services Ltd **2351**, 2638, 6129
Harvey Miller Publishers 6120
Denise Harvey 6127
William Harvey Press Ltd 6065
Harvill Secker 2635
Antony Harwood Ltd **4039**
Hatier 6111
Haus Publishing 6117
Havering Museum 2360
Hawker Publications **2352**
Hawkins Publishing Services **6067**
Haworth Press 6120
Hawthorn Press **2353**, 6100
Hay House 6109, 6115
Hayden Publishing 6119
Haynes Publishing **2354**
Nicolas Hays 6110
Hayward Gallery 6108
Hayward Publishing **2355**
R. Hazell & Co 2694
Hdri Publishers 6088
Head Press 6135
Headhunters 6135
Headline Book Publishing Ltd 2369, 2371, 2372, 6099
Healing Arts Press 6110
Health Directions 2653
Health Research 2719
Heart of Albion Press **2356**, 6109
Heart of the Sun 6109
A. M. Heath & Co Ltd **4040**
Heaven and Earth Publishing 6109
Roger Heavens **2357**
Hedberg Maps Inc 6107
Heel Verlag 2036
Heimdal Editions 6070
Heinemann 2595, 2635
Heinemann Educational Books (Nigeria) 6088
Heinemann USA 2330
Heinle 2159
Helion & Co Ltd **2358**
Christopher Helm (incorporating Pica Press) 2100
Helping Children with Feelings 2725
Hemming Information Services **2359**
Hendricksen Publishers 2014, 2264
G. Henle Verlag 2679
Ian Henry Publications Ltd **2360**
Joseph Henry Press 2524
The Herbert History of Art & Architecture 2361
The Herbert Press 2100, **2361**
Helen Herbert, Fine Art 6027
Hereford County Council 2121
Heretic Books Ltd 6103
Hermitage Publishing 6109
Nick Hern Books **2362**, 6058, 6115
Herridge & Sons 6070
Herrisey Editions 6070
Hertfordshire Publications 2801
Hesperus 6115
Heyne 6111
Hidden Inns 2783
Hidden Places 2783
High Noon Books 2034
High Stakes Gambling Books 2560
David Higham Associates **4041**
Highdown Books 2630, 6117
Higher Education Press 6072, 6202
Highland Books **2363**
Highworth Research 6106
Hikoki Publications 2209
Hiller Airguns 6097
Hilltop Press 6093
Hilmarton Manor Press **2364**
Himalayan Institute Press 6110
Hind Pocket Books 6124

Hindustan Book Co 6134
Hinton House Publishers **2365**
Hippopotamus Press **2366**
HIS 2419
HIS BRE Press 6018
Hisarlik Press 2237
Histoires et Collections 6070, 6126
Historical Publications Ltd **2367**
History-into-Print 2121
History of Boston Project 2428
History & Society Series 2302
HNH International 2537
Hobby Investment 6123
Hoberman Collection 6106
Hobnob Press **2368**
Hochland Communications 6137
Hodder 2370
Hodder Arnold 2369
Hodder Children's Books 2337
Hodder Christian Books 2371
Hodder Education 2017, 2338, **2369**, 6072, 6099
Hodder Gibson 2369, **2370**, 6099
Hodder Headline 2370, 6026
Hodder Headline Plc/Hachette Livre 2369
Hodder Home Learning Series 2337
Hodder Murray 2369
Hodder Religious 6099
Hodder & Stoughton 2338, 2369, 2371, 2372, 6099
Hodder & Stoughton Ed SA (Pty) Ltd 2478
Hodder & Stoughton Educational 2369
Hodder & Stoughton Faith **2371**
Hodder & Stoughton General **2372**
Hodder Wayland 2337
Alison Hodge Publishers **2373**
Matth. Hohner AG 2679
Holbrook Design Oxford Ltd **6028**
Holbrook Hosting **6029**
Holland Publishing Plc **2374**
Hollydata Publishers Ltd 2051
Martin Holmes Rallying 6137
Holmgren Design Services 2245
Holo Books **2375**, 6103
Holst Ltd 6123
The Holt Jackson Book Co Ltd **6155**
Henry Holt and Co LLC 2478
Holtzbrinck Publishers LLC 2478
Holy Cross Press 6127
Holy Trinity Monastery 6127
Home Planners 2653
Homer Kitabevi 2579
Honeyglen Publishing 6137
Honno (Welsh Women's Press) **2376**
Honor 2436
Hood Hood Books 6103
Alan C. Hood & Co Inc 2245
Hoopoe Books 6097
Hoover's Business Press 6082
Hopscotch Educational Publishing **2377**
Kate Hordern Literary Agency **4042**
Horniman Museum Publications 6066
Horse's Mouth Publications 6137
Valerie Hoskins Associates **4043**
Houghton Mifflin 6058, 6120
Houghton Mifflin Harcourt 2330
House of Lochar **2378**, 6081, 6100
Hove Foto Books 2544
How To Books Ltd **2379**, 2781, 6115
Hudson Hills Press LLC 2036
Max Hueber Verlag 6111
Hughes Massie Ltd 4001
Hulogosi Press 6109
Human Givens 6103
Human Horizons 2722
Human Kinetics Europe Ltd **2380**
Human Rights Watch 6066, 6103
Human & Rousseau 6066
humming earth 2849
Humphrys Roberts Associates **6068**
Hunt Edition 2723
Hunt End Books 2121
John Hunt Publishing Ltd **2381**, 6126
Hunter House Inc 6110
Hunter Publishing 2653, 6139
C. Hurst & Co (Publishers) Ltd **2382**, 6120
Hutchinson 2635
Hybert Design Ltd **6030**
Hydrographic Office 2391
Hymns Ancient & Modern 2681
Hypatia Publications **2383**
Hyperion 2679, 6135

Hyphen Press 6103

I-Quiz 2778
Ibadan Cultural Studies Group 6088
Ibadan University Press 6088
IBBY – International Board on Books for Young People **5003**
Ibex Publishers 6065
IBID Press 6123
Ibis Press 6110
IBS-STL UK 2065
ICA 6108, 6131
Iceland Review 6123
IChemE **2384**
ICM Books **4044**
Icon Books Ltd **2385**
ICS Publications 2640
ICSA Information & Training Ltd **2386**, 6120
ID Publishing 2654
Idea Group Inc. Journals 6136
Idea Logical Company Inc 6026
Idealist Studies 2390
Ides et Calendes 2364
Idlewild Publishers 6097
IDS Commisioned Studies 2399
IES Report Series 2395
Ignatius Press 2275
Ignotus Press 6109
Ikhwezi Afrika Publishers 6088
Ikon 6108
The Ilex Press Ltd **2387**, 2767, 3011
Illuminata Publishers 2579
Images 2036
Imago Publishing Ltd **6031**
IMG UK Ltd **4045**
Immel Publishing 6137
Immprint 6090
Immunisation Information **2388**
IMP 2562
Imperial College Press **2389**
Imprint Academic **2390**, 6103
Imprint Art 2390
Imray Laurie Norie & Wilson Ltd **2391**
In Easy Steps Ltd **2392**, 6099
The In Pinn 2830
In Practice Series 2663
Inclusion 6103
Incomplete Guides (Series) 2593
Incorporated Council of Law Reporting for England and Wales **2393**
Independent Books 2209
Independent Publishers Guild (IPG) **5048**
Index 6131
India Book House 6090
Indian Book Centre 6124
Indiana Publishing House 6124
Indiana University Press 6105
Indica 6124
Indo Lingo Surf 6123
Indus 6123, 6124
Industrial Press 6126, 6134
Industrial Society 2119
Infinite Ideas Co 6117
Infinity Science Press 6134
Info Tech 2180
Informa Plc 2757
Information Commissioner's Office **5049**
Information for Industry 2771
Inkubook 2066
Inkubuzz 2066
Inn Australia 6137
Inner Traditions International 6110
Inner Travel Books 6110
Innovative Kids 6119
Brian Inns Booksales & Services **6069**
Inpharm-Internet Services Ltd 2828
Insearch Publications 6094
Insel 6111
Insiders' Guides 2286
Insight Guides 2300
INSPEC Inc 2405
The Inspira Group **4046**
Inspire 2502
Instant-Books UK Ltd **2394**
Institute for Aegean Prehistory Academic Press 2579
Institute for Archaeo-Metallurgical Studies 2767
Institute for Cultural Research 2554
Institute for Employment Studies **2395**
Institute for Fiscal Studies **2396**

Institute for Human Development 6124
Institute for Mesoamerican Studies 2579
Institute for Philosophical Research 2579
Institute for Psychophysical Research 6097
Institute for Public Policy Research 6103
Institute of Acoustics **2397**
Institute of Cast Metal Engineers 6136
Institute of Chartered Accountants in Ireland 6058
Institute of Chartered Shipbrokers 2834
Institute of Classical Archaeology 2579
Institute of Clinical Research **2398**
Institute of Development Studies **2399**
Institute of Economic Affairs 6065
Institute of Education (Publications), University of London **2400**
Institute of Employment Rights **2401**
Institute of Food Science & Technology **2402**
Institute of Islamic Thought 2439
The Institute of Mathematics and its Applications **2403**
The Institute of Physics **2410**, 6120, 6202
Institute of Physics & Engineering in Medicine **2404**
Institute of Policy Studies 2439
Institute of Psycho-Analysis, London 2427
Institute of Risk Management 2834
Institute of Scientific and Technical Communicators (ISTC) **5050**
Institute of Southern African Studies, National University of Lesotho 6088
Institute of Translation & Interpreting **5051**
Institution of Civil Engineers 2761
Institution of Engineering and Technology (IET) **2405**
Institution of Mechanical Engineers 2620
Integral Yoga Publications 6110
Intellect Journals 6136
Intellect Ltd **2406**
Intellect Play Series 2406
Intellectual Book Corner 6123
Interact Publishing Ltd 6117
Interactyx **2407**
Intercargo 2834
Intercontinental Literary Agency **4047**
Intercultural Press 2119
The Interface Collection 2801
Interlink Publishing 2653
International Association of Classification Societies 2834
International Atomic Energy Agency 2791
International Bible Reading Association 2173
International Book Distributors 2734
International Book Exhibitions & Fairs: General Directorate **6170**
International Books 6103
International Chamber of Shipping 2834
International Congress and Symposium Series 2663
International Creative Management Inc **4044**
International Food Information Service 2138
International Greetings PLC Group 2021
International Idea 6065
International Labour Organisation 2791
International Library of African Studies 2756
International Library of Historical Studies 2756
International Library of Human Geography 2756
International Library of Political Studies 2756
International Medical Press **2408**
International Monetary Fund 2791
International Monographs in Prehistory 2579
International Network for the Availability of Scientific Publications (INASP) **2409**
International Organisations 2791
International Publishers (New York) 6066, 6103
International Scientific Publishing Academy 6124
International Society of Neuro-Semantics 6089
International Tanker Owners' Pollution Federation 2834
International Thomson Corporation 2326

INDEX OF COMPANIES & IMPRINTS / 177

International Water Association 2417, 2614
Internet Archaeology 6136
Interpet Publishing 2130, 6071
Intersentia 2349
Intertaal 6111
INTERTANKO 2834
Interweave Press 2686
Into Print 3032
Intrac 6103
INU Press 6065
The Iona Community 2827
IOP Publishing **2410**
IP Publishing 6136
IP3 (Institute of Paper, Printing & Publishing) **5052**
IPC Books 6126
IPC Media 6100
IPEM Report Series 2404
Iqbal Institute 6123
Irish Academic Press 6058
Irish Book Publishers Association (CLÉ) **5053**
Irish Cruising Club 2391
Irish Educational Publishers Association **5054**
Irish Museum of Modern Art 6090
Irish Narratives 2202
Irish Theatre Handbook 6058
Irwell Press Ltd **2411**
Irwin 2473
ISBN Agency - UK and Irish Republic **5055**
Iseb Publications 2296
ISIS Publishing Ltd **2412**, 2773
Islamic Book Publishers 2439
Islamic Foundation 2439
The Islamic Texts Society **2413**, 6126
Isma'ili Heritage Series 2756
ISMN: 57 999 2723
ISPCK 6123
Israel Academy of Sciences 6123
Israel Antiquities Authority 2579
Israel Exploration Society 6123
ISSN UK Centre **5056**
Iste Ltd **2414**
Istituto Italiano di Ricerche Metafisiche 2719
Italian Studies 2788
Itchy Fingers Publications 2679
Ithaca Press 2297, **2415**
iUniverse 2066
IVP **2416**
The Ivy Press Ltd 3011, **3027**, 6122
IWA Publishing **2417**

J & S Publishing Co Inc 6065
JAC International 6137
Jacana Education 6066
Jacana Media 2351
jack afrika Publishing Ltd 2261
Melanie Jackson Agency 4084
Jagrand Publishing 6137
Jaguar Daimler Heritage Trust 6070
J'ai lu 6111
B. Jain Publishers 6124
James & James (Publishers) Ltd 2244, **2418**
Jamieson Library 2383
JAN Publishing Centre 6088
Jāna Sēta Map Publishers 6107
Jane's Information Group Ltd 2348, **2419**, 6102
Janklow & Nesbit (UK) Ltd **4048**
Peter Janson-Smith Ltd 4016
Janus Books 2420
Janus Publishing Co Ltd **2420**
Japanese Pharmacopoeia 2791
Japanese Society for Analytical Chemistry 6136
Japanska 6154
Jarndyce Booksellers **2421**
Jaya Books 6124
Jazz Police Books 6093
JB Books 6123
Jewish Light Publishing 6110
Joe's Press 2210
Johns Hopkins University Press 2828
Johnson & Alcock Ltd **4049**
Ben Johnston Publishing 6124
Jolly Learning Ltd **2422**
Jones & Bartlett International **2423**, 6119
Die Jonglerie 2137
Jordan Publishing Ltd **2424**

Jordans 2424
Michael Joseph 2597
Richard Joseph Publishers Ltd **2425**
Joshua Press 2264
Journal of Juristic Papyrology 2579
Journal of Mines & Minerals 2125
Journal of Transport & Economic Policy 6136
Journeyman Press 2609
Jovis Verlag 6090
JPV 6131
JRP / Ringier 6108
Jane Judd Literary Agency **4050**
Edward E. Judge & Sons 2285
Juicy Lucy 2637
Junction Books Ltd 2420
JurisPrudent 2080
Juventud 6111
JZK Publishing 6110

K & M Books 2766
Kabushiki Kaisha Phoenic 2140
Kachere Series 6088
Kagan & Kagan 6089
Kali Press 6110
Kalpaz Publications 6124
Kangaroo Press 2686
Karavadra: Multimedia 3028
S. Karger AG **2426**
Karnac Books Ltd **2427**
Michelle Kass Associates **4051**
Katha 6124
Kaushal 6123
Richard Kay Publications **2428**
Keele University Press 2247
Kegan Paul Ltd **2429**
Kehrer Verlag 6090
The Frances Kelly Agency **4052**
Miles Kelly Publishing 6119
Kelsey Museum of Archaeology 2579
Kendall/Hunt 6089
Kenilworth Press 2628
Kennedy & Boyd 2849
Kensington 6122, 6135
Kent County Council 2206
Kenyon-Deane 2211, **2430**
Kew Publishing 2036, **2431**
Key Advances Series 2663
Key Books 6070
Key Paper Conferences Series 2663
Key Porter Books 2653
Keyahoff 6120
The Khalili Collection 2756, 2579
Khaniqahi Nimatullahi Publications (KNP) 6110
Kickstarters 2605
Kiepenheuer & Witsch 6111
Kimaathi Publishing House 6088
Kimani Press 6135
KinderKlub 3032
Kindred Books 6109
Hilda King Educational **2432**
Laurence King Publishing Ltd **2433**, 2767
Kingfisher **2475**, 6119
The King's England Press **2434**
Kingscourt / McGraw-Hill 2474
Kingsley Wood 6123
Jessica Kingsley Publishers **2435**, 6058, 6119, 6120
Kingsway Publications **2436**
Chris Kington Publishing **2437**
Kipper range 2337
Kirkbride Bible Co 6118
Kluwer Law 2791, 6136
Knaur 6111
Knight Features **4053**
Knight Paperbacks 2157
Knock Knock Books 2653
Knockabout 6109, 6135
Alfred A. Knopf 2266
Know How Know Why 2778
Know the Game 2100
Know the Score 6070, 6126
Knox Press 2264
KNP London 6110
Koala Publishing Ltd **6036**
Kogan Page Ltd **2438**, 6117
KOM 6131
Walther König 6108
Korero Books 6106
Kraft Books 6088
Kraken 6115

Krause Publications 2226
KRB (formerly Kestrel Railway Books) 2016
KSK Publishers 6124
Kube Publishing Ltd **2439**
Kudos 2778
Kuperard Publishers & Distributors 2278, **6116**, 6126
Kwani Trust 6088
Kwela 6066, 6103
Kyle Cathie 6117

Labels Unlimited 2098
Ladybird 2597
Lagoon Books **2440**
J-P Lahall 6131
Landauer 2653, 6139
Jay Landesman **2441**
Landmark Publishing Ltd **2442**, 6115
Landscapes Series 2742
Veronica Lane Books 6110
Peter Lang Ltd **2443**, 6079, 6120
Langenscheidt 2300, 6111
Language & Education Library 2165
Language Planning and Policy 2165
Languages for Intercultural Communication and Education 2165
Languages Information Centre 2094
Lannoo/Terra Publishers 2036
Lantern Books 6110
L'Arca Editions 6090
Large Print 2479
Lark Books 6126
Larousse 6111
Latin America Bureau 6103
Wilfrid Laurier University Press 6065
Law Society of Lesotho 6088
Law Society Publishing **2444**
LawAfrica 6088
Lawpack Publishing Ltd **2445**
Lawrence Book Co Ltd 6155
Lawrence & Wishart 6103
Lawson Falle 6130
Laynforah 2036
LBC 2652
LDA **2446**, 6070
Leading Edge Communications 6089
Lear Books 6109
Learning Development Aids 6126
Learning Factory 3001
Learning is Fun 2374
Learning Matters Ltd **2447**, 6058, 6094, 6202
Learning Through Landscapes Trust 2721
Learning Together **2448**, 2653
Learning Unlimited 6123
Learning World 2590
Leatherhead Food International **2449**
Leatherhead Food Research Association 2285
Leckie & Leckie 2453
Legal Action Group **2450**
Legal Information Resources 2771
Legastat Copying & Scanning **6032**
Legend Press **2451**
Legenda 2484, 2579
Leicester University Press 2198
Leipzig Book Fair **6171**
Leisure Arts 2686
LEM Art Group 6106
Lenz-Mulligan Rights & Co-editions **4054**
Hal Leonard Corporation 2679
Leopard Learning 2029
Lerner 6115, 6116
Let's Explore **2469**
Letterbox Library **6161**
Letterland International Ltd **2452**
The Letters of Marsilio Ficino 2698
Letts and Lonsdale **2453**
Leung Ting Publications 6154
Lionel Leventhal Ltd 2168
Barbara Levy Literary Agency **4055**
Lewis 2016
Lewis Masonic 2016
Dewi Lewis Publishing **2454**, 6135
J. D. Lewis & Sons Ltd 2315
Lexden Publishing 6094
Lexicomp Inc 6134
Lexus Ltd **2455**
John Libbey Publishing 6105
Liberties Media Ltd **2456**
Liberties Press **2456**
Liberty Fund 6065

Librairie du Liban 2582
Librario Publishing 6100
Library Association Publishing 2274
Library of Analytical Psychology 2427
Library of International Relations 2756
Library of Middle East History 2756
Library of Modern Middle East Studies 2756
Library of Ottoman Studies 2756
Library Reference 6120
Libri Publications 2756
Librios Ltd 6006
Libris Ltd **2457**, 6103
Libros McGraw-Hill de Mexico SA de CV 2473
Lidel Edições Técnicas 6111
Life Journey 2436
Lifetime Careers Publishing 6126
Lifeway, Broodman & Holmon 2436
Lightbooks Publishers 6088
Liguori/Triumph 2640
The Lilliput Press Ltd **2458**, 6103
Limelight Management **4056**
Lincoln Records Society 2116
Frances Lincoln Ltd **2459**, 6099
Linden Press 2568
Lindisfarne Press 2283
Linford 2773, 6123
Ling Kee (UK) Ltd 2817, 3007
Linguistic Diversity & Language Rights 2165
Link of Times Foundation 6137
Lion Hudson Plc **2460**, 6120
Listen & Live 2653
Listen & Speak Publications 6094
LISU **2461**
LIT Verlag 6066
Literatura 6123
Little Books 6061, 6117
Little, Brown Book Group 2338, **2462**, 2602, 6096, 6202
The Little Group Ltd 6155
Little Hare Books 6119
Little People Books **3028**
Little Tiger Press 2100, **2463**
Little Tiger Press (Magi) 6119
Christopher Little Literary Agency **4057**
Littlehampton Book Services Ltd 2574, **6117**
The Littman Library of Jewish Civilization **2464**
The Liturgical Press 6104
Liver Press 2207
Liveright 2549
Liverpool University Press **2465**, 6120
Livewire Books for Young Adults 2836
Living Language (Random House) 6116
Living Stories Inc 6118
Living Time® Media International **2466**
Living Wood 6109
Living Word Series 2838
Livres de poche 6111
Llewellyn 6109
Chris Lloyd Sales & Marketing Services **6070**
LLU+ 6092
Local Map Series 2504
Loeb Classical Library 2350, 2828
Logaston Press **2467**
Logos Journal 6136
Loki Books 6103
Lola 6123
Lomond Books Ltd **2468**
Londolozi Publishers 6103
London Art & Artists 6103
London Book Fair **6172**
London Business School 6018
London College of Communication **6201**, 6202
London Independent Books **4058**
The London Literary Mafia **6173**
Lonely Planet 6072, 6115, 6202
Long Barn Books 2706
Barry Long Books 6110
Look Around Design 6123
Lorenz 2130
Lotus Bloom Publishing 6110
Lotus Publishing 6106
Loughborough University 2461
Low Price Publications 6123, 6124
Andrew Lownie Literary Agency Ltd **4059**
Loyola Press 2640, 6104

178 / INDEX OF COMPANIES & IMPRINTS

LPPHA (London Police Pensioner Housing Association) 2803
LSE Books 6103
LTP Publications 2472
Luath Press Ltd **2469**
Lucas Publications 6079, 6103
Luchterhand 6111
Lund Humphries 2050, 2317, **2470**
The Lutterworth Press 2183, **2471**, 2681, 6067
Lutyens & Rubinstein **4060**
Luxor Press 2707
Lynx Communication 2716

M & K Update **2513**
Duncan McAra **4061**
B. McCall Barbour **6118**
McCrimmon Publishing Co Ltd **2472**
McDonald Institute for Archaeological Research 2579
McGill-Queen's University Press 6105
McGraw-Hill Education **2473**, 6072, 6202
McGraw-Hill International Book Co 2473
McGraw-Hill Publishing Company **2474**
McKeever Publishing 3008
McKeown's Price Guides 2544
The McKernan Literary Agency & Consultancy **4062**
Maclean Press 2095
Macmillan Academic Publishing Inc 2478
Macmillan Aidan Ltd 2478
Macmillan Armenia CJS 2478
Macmillan Art Publishers 2579
Macmillan Boleswa Publishers Pty Ltd 2478
Macmillan Botswana Publishing Co (Pty) Ltd 2478
Macmillan Children's Books Ltd **2475**, 2476, 2478, 2583, 2585, 6119
Macmillan Digital Audio 6119
Macmillan Distribution (MDL) 2478, 3021, **6119**
Macmillan do Brasil 2478
Macmillan Education 2475, **2476**, 2478, 2583, 2585, 6119
Macmillan English Campus 6119
Macmillan Heinemann ELT 2476
Macmillan Hellas SA 2478
Macmillan Iberia SA 2478
Macmillan India Ltd 2478
Macmillan Kenya (Publishers) Ltd 2478
Macmillan Korea Publishers Ltd 2478
Macmillan Language House Ltd 2478
Macmillan Ltd 2475, 2476, 2478, 2583, 2585, 6026, 6072, 6119, 6202
Macmillan Malawi Ltd 2478
Macmillan Mozambique Lda 2478
Macmillan New Asia Publishers Ltd 2478
Macmillan New Writing 6119
Macmillan Nigeria Publishers Ltd 2478
Macmillan Polska Sp.Z.O.O. 2478
Macmillan Press Ltd **2477**
Macmillan Publishers Australia Pty Ltd 2478
Macmillan Publishers Cameroon Ltd 2478
Macmillan Publishers (China) Ltd 2478
Macmillan Publishers Egypt Ltd 2478
Macmillan Publishers Inc 2478
Macmillan Publishers Ltd 2475, 2476, **2478**, 2583, 2585
Macmillan Publishers New Zealand Ltd 2478
Macmillan Publishers SA 2478
Macmillan Publishers (Zambia) Ltd 2478
Macmillan Romania SRL 2478
Macmillan Rwanda Publishers Ltd 2478
Macmillan South Africa Publishers (Pty) Ltd 2478
Macmillan Swaziland National Publishing Co (Pty) Ltd 2478
Macmillan Uganda Ltd 2478
Eunice McMullen Ltd **4063**
McPherson & Co 6103
MCPS Ltd 5058
Macquarie Library Pty Ltd 2478
Macquarie Online Pty Ltd 2478
Maelor Interactive Publishing 2122
MagDig Media 6137
Mage Publishers 6065
Magi Publications 2463
Magic Bookshop Bears 2778
Magna Large Print Books **2479**, 2773
Magnes Press 6123

Magpie Books 2196
Mahaveer & Sons 6123
The Maia Press Ltd **2480**, 6135
Mail and Guardian Books 6088
Mainstream 2635, 6096
Mainstream Baptists for Life & Growth 2515
Mainstream Publishing Co (Edinburgh) Ltd **2481**
Maiyati Chambers 6088
Make Believe Ideas Ltd 6117
Malhotra Publishing 6124
Malthouse Press Ltd 6088
Mambo Press 6088
Mammoth 2249
Manaaki Whenuka Press 6123
Management Books 2000 6106
Management Pocketbooks Ltd **2482**
Manas 6124
Manchester University Press 6120
Mandragora 2036
Mandrake of Oxford **2483**, 6109
Maney Publishing **2484**, 2579
Andrew Mann Ltd **4064**
The Manning Partnership Ltd 2130, **6071**, 6115
Manohar Publishers 6124
Mansell 2198
Mansion Field 2849
Manson Publishing Ltd **2485**
Sarah Manson Literary Agent 4036, **4065**
Manticore Books Ltd 6120
Manufacture Française des Pneumatiques Michelin 2504
Map Link 6107
MAP (Model & Allied Publications) 2724
Mapin 6090, 6120
Mares Nest 6103
Maresfield Library 2427
Marg Publications 2653
Marino Books 2495
Maritime Books **2486**
Marjacq Scripts **4066**
Market House Books Ltd **3029**
Marketability (UK) Ltd **6072, 6202**
Sheila Markham Rare Books 6137
Marling Menu Masters 2544
The Marsh Agency Ltd **4067**
Marshall Cavendish 6117
Marshall Cavendish Partworks Ltd **2487**
Marsilio Ficino's Commentaries on Plato's Writings 2698
Marston Book Services Ltd **6120**
Andrew Martin International 6137
Martingale & Co 2653
La Martiniere 6115
Blanche Marvin **4068**
Masquerade Publications 6137
Master Point Press 6070
Matador 2788
Matthias Media 2416
Maverick House Publishers **2488**
Mayer Edition 2364
Kevin Mayhew Ltd **2489**
MBA Literary Agents **4069**
MBI 6115
MDS Book Sales **6121**
Meadowbrook Press 6070
Meadowside Children's Books **2490**, 6100
Mediane 6137
Medias Paul 2668
Medical Partners Publishing 2680
Medical Writers Group **5057**
The Medici Society Ltd **2491**
MediPress 6065
Megatastic 2778
Meher Baba Books 2618
Mehring Books **2492**
Melia Publishing Services Ltd 6115, **6122**
Melisende Publishing Ltd **2493**
The Melissa Institute 6089
Melting Pot Press 6123
Memorycatcher Books 2239
Menard Press 6103
Mentor Books 2174, **2494**
Mercantila Publishing AS 2285
Mercat 2095, 6100
Mercer University Press 2318
Mercier Press Ltd **2495**
Mercury Arts Publications 2731
Mercury Books 2157, **2496**
Mercury Junior **2497**

Meridian Books 2206
Meridian Maps 6107
Merit Publishing (Medical) 6065
Merlin Media Ltd 2499
The Merlin Press Ltd **2498**, 6103
Merlin Publishing/Wolfhound Press **2499**
Merrell Publishers Ltd **2500**, 6120
Merrick & Day 2036
Merseyside Port Folios 2207
Merton Priory Press Ltd **2501**
David Messum 2036
Met Specials 2515
Meta Publications 6089
Metaphysical Research Group 2719
Methodist Publishing House **2502**
Methuen 2249, 6096
Methuen Drama 6119
Metro Books 2105
Meyer & Meyer 2653, 6139
Meym Mamvro 6109
Meyrick Marketing Ltd **2503**
Michelin Maps & Guides **2504**
Microform Academic Publishers **2505**
Midas Public Relations Ltd **6073**
Middlesex University Press 6103
Middleton Press **2506**
Midland Publishing 2016
Mikaya 6070
Milestone Publications **2507**
Milet Publishing Ltd **2508**, 6135
Milia – The World's Interactive Content Marketplace **6174**
Millennium / London School of Economics 6136
Millennium Advertising 6137
Miller Books 6070
The Cathy Miller Foreign Rights Agency **4070**
J. Garnet Miller **2509**
Miller's **2510**
Mills & Boon Large Print 2479
Millstream 2016
Milne Books 6110
Sally Milner Publishing 2686
Milo Books 6135
Mimir 6123
MIMO Distribution 2192
Mindsports 6070
Minerva Associates 6123
Mini Guide Series 2117
Mini Maestro 2778
Minority Rights Group 6103
Minuit 6111
The MIT Press Ltd **2511**, 2828
Mitchell Beazley 2510, **2512**, 2555
Mitchell Wordsmith 6123
MK Book Service **6123**
Mkuki na Nyota Publishers 6088
MMT **6037**
Mo' Media 6097
Mobius 2372
Modern Art Oxford 6108
Modern Artists Series 2755
Modern English Fiction 2228
Modern Humanities Research Association 2484
Modern Languages in Practice 2165
The Modern Library (Random House) 6116
Modern Publishers 6123
Modus Publications 6123
Mole Publishing Co 2245
Momenta Publishing Ltd **6074**, 6106
The Monacelli Press 6120
Monarch 2460
Monastic Research Bulletin 2112
Mondadori 6111
Monkey Puzzle Media Ltd **3030**
Le Monnier 6111
Montagud Editores SA 2285
Monthly Review 6103
Monuments in the Landscape Series 2467
Moonlight Publishing Ltd **2514**, 6100
Moorley's Print & Publishing Ltd **2515**
Moorside Words & Music 2277
Moosewood 6109
Morgan Hill 2771
Morgan Publishing 2237
Max Morgan-Witts Productions Ltd 6131
Mosaic Educational Publications 2721
Mosby 2254
Möseler Verlag 2679
Motilal Banarsidass 6124

Motilal (UK) – Books of India **6124**
Motor Racing Publications Ltd **2516**, 6137
Mount Eagle 2118, 6135
Movements in Modern Art Series 2755
Mowbray 2198
MPS Technologies Ltd 2478
MRP Publishing 2516
Multi Science Publishing Co Ltd **2517**
Multilingual Matters 2165
Multilingual Matters Ltd / Channel View Publications 6120
Multimedia Zambia 6088
James Munro & Co 2131
Murdoch Books UK Ltd **2518**, 6119
John Murray Publishers 2388, 2369, **2519**, 6099
Museum of Fine Arts, Boston 2579
Museum of London Archaeology Service 2579
Museum of Modern Art, New York 2767
Museum of New Mexico Press 6065
Museum Tusculanum Press 6065
Mushroom Model Publications 6070
Music Design 6110
Music for London Entertainment 2730
Music Publishers Association **5058**
Music Sales 2562
Music Technology Books Ltd 2592
Musica Britannica 2730
Musica Russica 2679
Musikverlag Doblinger 2679
Musikverlag Zimmermann 2679
Musketeer Books Ltd 6055
Muslim Academic Trust 6103
Múzicas Editions 2723
MW Educational **2520**
My Word! **6033**
Mykologia Lucerne 2642
Myriad Editions **2521**
Myrmidon Books Ltd **2522**, 6117
Mythos 6109
Myths 2143

Giorgio Nada Editore 2354
NAG 2342, 6106
Nairobi University Press 6088
Namara Group 2627
Napier University, School of Creative Industries **6203**
Natal Centre for Adult Education 6092
NATE (National Association for the Teaching of English) **2523**
Nathan 6111
The National Academies Press **2524**, 6120
National Acquisitions Group **5059**
National Archives 6067, 6115
National Archives of Scotland **2525**
National Association for the Teaching of English **5060**
The National Autistic Society (NAS) **2526**, 6103
National Book Development Council 6072, 6202
National Book Trust 6123
National Charities Database 2059
National Children's Bureau **2527**
The National Coaching Foundation 2187
National Extension College Trust Ltd **2528**
National Galleries of Scotland 2036, **2529**
National Gallery Co Ltd **2530**
National Gallery of Australia 2767
National Gallery of Ireland **2531**
National Gallery of Victoria 2653
The National Gallery Trust 2530
National Heritage Board of Sweden 2579
National Housing Federation **2532**
National Literacy Trust **5061**
National Map Series 2504
National Museums Scotland 2546
National Portrait Gallery Publications **2533**, 6115
National Reading Campaign 5061
National Series of Waterway Tramway and Railway Atlases 2216
The National Trust **2534**
The National Youth Agency **2535**
Natural Environment Research Council 2125
Natural History Museum Publishing **2536**, 6072
Natural Wonders Press 2036
Nature America Inc 2478

Nature Japan KK 2478
Nature Publishing Group Ltd 2478, 6119
Navicarte 2391
Navigator series of maps 2089
Naxos Audiobooks **2537**
NBM 6135
NCELTR 6094
NCLC Publishers Ltd 2273
NCVO (National Council for Voluntary Organisations) 6072, 6202
Need2Know **2538**, 2786
Nelles Maps 2300
Nelson Thornes Ltd 2086, **2539**, 6072, 6202
Thomas Nelson (Nashville TN) 6130
Thomas Nelson & Sons 6118
Nene Valley Publishing 2163, 2692
Neptune 6109
Net 2508
Network 3000 Publishing 6089
Network Continuum Education Ltd 2198, **2540**
New Age Books 6124
New Architecture 2587
New Authors Showcase **4071**
New Cavendish Books 2036
New Clarion Press 6103
New Daylight 2093
New Directions Publishing Corporation 2549
New Economics Foundation 6103
New Education Press (N.E.P.) 2029
New European Publications Ltd 6103
New Fiction 2538, 2786
New Futures 2160
New Holland 6115
New Horn Press Ltd 6088
New in Chess 2653, 6136
New International Version 2371
New Internationalist Publications Ltd **2541**
New Iona Press 6100
New Island Books Ltd **2542**, 6061, 6072
New Kadampa Tradition 2768
New Knowledge Books 2731
New Leaf Press 2436
New Light Bibles 2371
New Mermaids 2100
New Multilingual Matters 2165
New Page Books 6109, 6110
New Pathfinder 2180
New Perspectives on Language and Education 2165
New Playwrights' Network 2211, **2543**
New Readers Press 6092
New Society Publishers 6065
New Trends 6109
The New Walford: Guide to Reference Resources **6189**
New Welsh Review **6190**
New Writing North **5062**
New Writing Scotland (series) 2054
New York Review of S.F. 6093
Newark Museum 2036
Newcastle Libraries and Information Service 2794
Newleaf 2305, 6092
Newman House 2318
Newmarket Press 6122
Newpro UK Ltd **2544**
News Corporation 2348
Nexgen 2436
Nexus (heteroerotic fiction) 2812
Nexus Special Interest Books 2724
nfer Nelson 6072
NFT Guides 6116
NIACE (National Institute for Adult Continuing Education) 6103, 6136
Nicholas Enterprises Ltd 3001
Nicholson 2191
Nielsen Book **2545**, 5040, 5055, 5063, 5074, 6038, 6075
Nielsen BookData **5063**
Nielsen BookData Asia Pacific 2545
Nielsen BookNet 2545, **6038**
Nielsen BookScan 2545, **6075**
The Nielsen Company 2545, 5040, 5055, 5063, 5074, 6038, 6075
Nielsen Entertainment Media 6181
Nightingale Press 2130, 6071
Nimbus Press 2515
Niyogi Books 2831
NLP Comprehensive 6089

NMD Trading Co **6125**
NMS Enterprises Limited - Publishing **2546**, 6100
No Exit Press (Crime & Noir Fiction) 2560, 6135
No-Nonsense Series 2541
The Maggie Noach Literary Agency **4072**
Non-Parliamentary Publications 2791
Non Writing Viewpoints 2165
Noodle Books 2016
Nordic Academic Press 6065
Nordic Africa Institute 6066
Nordic Institute of Asian Studies 6103
Nordiska Afrikainstitutet (Scandinavian Institute of Africa) 6103
Normann's 6131
North York Moors National Park **2547**
Northcote House Publishers Ltd **2548**, 6106
Northern and Shell Media 2270
Northern Ireland Publications 2791
Northern Nigerian Publishing Co Ltd 2478
Northern Universities Press 2484
Northway 6103
Norton 2549
Jeffrey Norton Publishing 2058
W. W. Norton & Company Ltd **2549**, 2828
Norwood Publishers Ltd **2550**
The Nostalgia Collection **2551**
Nostalgia Road 2647, 2780
Not One of Us 6093
Notes on English Literature 2225
Notes on History 2225
Notes on Politics 2225
Nova Books 6123
Nova Express 6093
Nova Music 2723
Nova Science Publishers 6065, 6136
Nova Vista Publishing 6065
Novalis 6104
Now Publishing 6120
Andrew Nurnberg Associates Ltd **4073**
Nyala Publishing 6012
Alexandra Nye, Literary Agent **4074**
Nyt Nordisk 6131

O-Books 2381, 2653, 6126
Oak Tree Press **2552**
Oasis Design 2245
Obafemi Awolowo University Press 6088
Oberon 6103, 6120
Oblique 6106
The O'Brien Press Ltd **2553**, 6061
Ocarina Books 2579
Ocean 6135
Ocean View Books 6093
Oceana 3035
Octagon Books (Wholesale) Ltd **6143**
Octagon Press Ltd **2554**
Octopus Publishing Group 2195, 2312, 2338, 2510, 2512, **2555**, 2601, 6117
The Odd Squad 2637
Odd Streak 2637
ODS Business Services Ltd **6039**
ODS Optical Disc Service GmbH 6039
ODT Inc (Maps) 2149
Œuvres complètes de Montesquieu 2814
Œuvres complètes de Voltaire 2814
Of Islands and Women Series 2375
Off the Motorway 2783
Office for National Statistics (ONS) 6119
Ohara Publications (Black Belt Communications Inc) 6154
OICA International (UK) Ltd **2556**
Oil Companies International Marine Forum 2834
Oishin Publishing 6103
Old House Books **2557**
Old Pond Publishing **2558**
Old Sausage Publishers 2209
Old St Publishing 6117
The Old Stile Press **2559**
Oldcastle Books Ltd **2560**, 6135
Jim Oldroyd Books **6144**
The Oleander Press **2561**
Michael O'Mara Books 6117
Omnibus Press **2562**
Omnigraphics 6082
On Stream Publications Ltd **2563**
On the Trail of 2469
Once upon a Wartime (Series) 2079
Oncoweb Publishing 2140

One and Only 6135
One Page Book Co 2149
Oneworld Classics **2564**, 6106, 6115
Oneworld Publications **2565**
Onlywomen Press Ltd **2566**
Ontos-verlag.de 6065
Onyoma Research Publications 6088
OPC 2016
Open Air 2290
The Open Bible Trust **2567**
Open Gate Press **2568**, 6103
Open Road 2653, 6139
Open University Worldwide 2473, 2474, **2569**, 2784
Optimus Professional Publishing **2570**
Oral Traditions 6110
Orbis Books 2014
Orbit 2462
Orca Book Services Ltd **6126**
Orcadian Books 2579
Orchard Books 2337
Orchard Publishing **2571**
'Ordinary' Lives Series 2608
Ordnance Survey 2391, 6129
O'Reilly UK Ltd **2572**, 2828
Organisation for Economic Cooperation and Development (OECD) 2791, 6136
Organisation for Social Science Research in Eastern and Southern Africa (OSSREA) 6088
Oriel 2574
Orient Paperbacks 6124
Oriental Institute Chicago 2579
Original Publications 6110
Orion Books Ltd **2573**, 2574, 6117, 6129
The Orion Publishing Group Ltd 2233, 2314, 2338, 2573, **2574**, 2820, 6117
Orpheus Books Ltd **3031**
Orthodox Christian Books Ltd 6120, **6127**
Oryx Press 2330
OS Maps 2638
Osborne/McGraw-Hill 2473
Oscar 6111
Osprey Publishing Ltd **2575**, 6115, 6202
Osservatore Romano 2154
OSV 2318
Otava 6131
Outsell Inc / EPS **2576**, 6035
Oval Books 6071, 6115
Over the Moon 3034
The Overlook Press 6135
Ovolo Publishing Ltd **2577**
Owen Wells Publishing 2694
Deborah Owen Ltd **4075**
Peter Owen Publishers **2578**, 6103
Oxbow Books **2579**
Oxbridge Applications 6137
Oxfam Publishing **2580**, 6094
Oxford Archaeology 2579
Oxford Brookes University 6202
Oxford Centre for Maritime Archaeology 2579
Oxford Creative Marketing **6076**
Oxford Diocesan Publications 6018
Oxford Forum 6097
Oxford Illustrated Press 2354
Oxford International Centre for Publishing Studies **6204**
Oxford International Publishers Ltd 2091
Oxford Publicity Partnership Ltd **6077**
Oxford Publishing Consultancy **6205**
Oxford University Press **2581**, 6018, 6072, 6118, 6202
Oxford University School of Archaeology 2579

P. I. E. – Peter Lang SA 2443
P. I. Global 2036
P & R Publishing 2264
Pacific Century 2209
Packard Publishing Ltd **2582**
Paddleless Press 6135
Painters Series 2210
Palace Editions 2036
Palatine Books 2151
Palazzo Editions 6135
Palgrave Macmillan 2088, 2475, 2476, 2478, **2583**, 2585, 6072, 6202
Palgrave Publishers 6018, 6119
Paljor Publications 6124
Pallas Athene **2584**
G. J. Palmer & Sons Ltd 2681

Palombi 6123
Pamphleteer's Press 6103
Pan Dimensional 6109
Pan Educational Music 2723
Pan Macmillan 2475, 2476, 2478, 2583, **2585**, 2769, 6119
Pan Macmillan Australia Pty Ltd 2478
Pan Macmillan South Africa Publishers (Pty) Ltd 2478
Panaf Books **2586**
Pandon Press 2106
Pandora 2036
Panini Books 6119
Panini UK / Marvel 6135
The Panizzi Lectures 2126
Panton 2679
Papadakis Publisher **2587**
Paper Magic 2778
Paperless Proofs 6072
Papyrus 6123
PAR 2034
Paraclete Press 6104
Paradigm Publishers 2609
Paragon House 2653
Paragon Publishing **3032**
Pardoe Blacker Design 2770
Parenting & Relationships 2353
Parents' and Teachers' Guides 2165
Park St Press 6110
Parker 2849
Parker Associates **6078**
Parker Mead Ltd 2562
Parkett Verlag 6135
Parkstone Press 6126
Parliamentary Publications 2791
Parragon Disney 6096
Parrot Books 6123
Pasold Research Fund 2484
Past & Present Publishing Ltd 2551
Pastime Publications 6100
Angela Patchell Books 2653
Paternoster 2065
Paterson Marsh Ltd 4067, **4076**
Pathfinder Audio 6097
Pathfinder Books 2180, **2588**
Patten Press 2383
The Jim Pattison Group 2643
Paulist Press 6104
Pavilion **2589**
Pavilion Children's Books **2590**
Pavilion Publishing (Brighton) Ltd **2591**, 6202
John Pawsey **4077**
Payne-Gallway 2595
PC Publishing **2592**, 6117
PCCS Books Ltd **2593**
Peachtree Publishers 6082
Peanuts 2637
Maggie Pearlstine Associates Ltd **4078**
Pearson 6023, 6026
Pearson Assessments 2034
Pearson Education Ltd 2082, **2594**, 6018, 6072, 6202
Pearson Education Oxford **2595**
Pearson Group 2594, 2595
J. M. Pearson & Sons 2391
Pedigree Books 6099
Peel Productions 2686
Peepal Tree Books 6103
Peerless Editions 6126
Pegasus Series 2617
Pelican Publishing 2310, 2653, 6123, 6131
Pen and Sword Books 6127
Pen Press Publishers Ltd **2596**
Pendragon 2016, 6057, 6109
The Penguin Group (UK) Ltd **2597**, 6026, 6116
Penguin (India) 6124
Penguin Putnam Inc 2597
Peninsula Production & Distribution Ltd 2478
Pennant Books Ltd 6117
PenPoint Publishers 6088
Pensions Research 2771
Pentagon Press 6124
Pentathol Publishing **2598**
Penwith Press 6109
People's Bible Commentary Series 2093
Pepin Press 6126
Peppercorn Books & Press 6092
Peter Peregrinus Ltd 2405

Perelandra 6109
Perfect Potion 6123
Pergamon 2254
Perigee/Penguin 6110
Periodical Publishers Association 5013, **5064**
Periodicals Training Council 5064
Periodika 6123
Periplus Editions 2300
Periscope Publishing Ltd 2617
Permanent Publications 6109
Permeable Press 6093
Permillion 6120
Persephone Book Ltd 6119
Perseus Books 6115
Person-Centred Approach & Client-Centred Therapy Essential Readers (Series) 2593
Perspectives in Education 2523
A. K. Peters 6126, 6134
John Peterson Music 6118
Petit Futé Guides 2653, 6139
Pevensey Press 2226
PG-Team Oy 6065
PGL – Autobiographies & Biographies Series 2586
PGUK 6115
Phaidon Press Ltd **2599**
The Phantom Captain 6173
The Pharmaceutical Press **2600**, 6058, 6136
Pharos 6066
Philadelphia Museum of Art 2036
David Philip / Spearhead / New Africa Books Consortium 6066, 6103
Christian Philippsen 6137
Philip's 2555, **2601**
Philips Maps 2638, 6129
Phoenix 2342, 2523, 2573, 2574, 6106
Phonics is Fun 2374
Photo Image 6123
Piatkus Books 2338, 2462, **2602**, 6115
Picador 2585, 6119
Piccadilly Press **2603**, 6115
Christopher Pick **6013**
Pickering & Chatto (Publishers) Ltd **2604**, 6136
Picnic Publishing 6137
Picton Press (Liverpool) 2207
Pictorial Presentations Ltd 2722
Piemme 6111
Pier 9 2518
Pilgrim Press & Book Faith India 6124
Pilgrim Publications 2264
Pimlico 2635
Pine Forge Press Inc 2665
Pinter 2198
Pinwheel Ltd 6119
Pion Publishers 6136
Pioneer Drama Service 2345
Pipers' Ash Ltd **2605**
Piquant Editions 2416, **2606**
Piscean Books 6123
Pitch Publishing Ltd 6117
Plan it! (series) 2010
Planeta 6111
Play Pals 2778
Playne Books Ltd **3033**
Playwrights Press Canada 2362
The Playwrights Publishing Co **2607**
Plaza & Janes 6111
Plexus Publishing 6099
Plowright Press **2608**
Plumbago Books 2116
Pluto Books Ltd **2609**, 6058, 6072, 6120
Pocket 2706
Pocket Cornwall 2373
Pocket Essentials 2560, 6135
Pocket Issue 6106
Pocket Money Press 2778
Poetica 2037
Poetry Book Society **6162**
Poetry Now 2538, 2786
The Poetry Society **5065**
Poetry Wales Press Ltd 2689
Pointed Leaf Press 2036
Points Press 6109
Polair Publishing 6110
The Policy Press **2610**, 2614, 6120
Polin Series 2464
Giancarlo Politi Editore 6103
Polity Press **2611**
Pollinger Ltd Authors' Agents **4079**

Polygon 2016, 2095, 6061, 6081, 6100
Polygon @ Edinburgh 2247
Polytantric Press 2441
Pomegranate Europe Ltd **6128**
Pomona Books 6103
Pond View 2538, 2786
Pont (English language publications for children) 2315
Pontes Editores 6111
Pop Universal Ltd 2722
Poppy Palin 6109
Popular Publications 6123
Porpoise Books 6097
David Porteous Editions 2686
Portfolio (series) 2433
Porthill Publishers **2612**
Portico **2613**
Portland Press Ltd **2614**, 2653, 6139
Porto Editora Lda 6111
Portobello Books 12 **2615**
Portrait Books 2602
Positive Press Ltd **2616**
Post Carbon Publishing 2245
Postcards from... 2109
Potomac Books 6070, 6126, 6134
Tony Potter Publishing **3034**
Power Press 6110
Power Publications 2206
Power Publications (Australia) 6135
Shelley Power Literary Agency Ltd **4080**
Powerfresh 2130, 6071
Powerhouse Books 6135
Powerhouse Museum 2470
John Cowper Powys Studies Series 2210
T & AD Poyser 2100
PPA Interactive 5064
PPP Co 2653
PR Books Ltd **6145**
Practical Action Publishing 2614
Practical Handbooks in Archaeology 2204
Practice Tests In Series 2448
Praeger Publishers 2330
Pragati 6124
Sundeep Prakashan 6124
Pressbooksprint / Tvmyworld.com **4081**
Theodore Presser Company 2679
Presses de la cité 6111
Presses Pocket 6111
Presses Universitaires de France 6111
Presses Universitaires de Grenoble 6111
Prestel Publishing Ltd **2617**, 6119
David Price **6014**
Mathew Price Ltd 2130, **2618**, 6071
Priddy Books 6119
Prim-Ed Publishing 2029
Primal Pictures 6202
Primary Modern Language 3032
Primers Series 2593
Princeton Architectural Press 6120
Princeton Book Co 2223, 6137
Princeton Selling Group Inc 2384
Princeton University Press **2619**, 2828
Print on Demand – Worldwide 2804
Printery House Inc 2472
Prion 2150
Private Eye 6117
Private Libraries Association **5004**
Pro Calima Foundation 2579
Professional Engineering Publishing 2614, **2620**
Professional Interpreting in the Real World 2165
Professional Publishing 2771
Profile Books **2621**, 6096
Progress in Neural Networks 2406
Propagator Press 2029
ProQuest **2622**, 6072
Prospect Books **2623**, 6103
Protection Publications 2741
Providence Press 2185
Psychology News 6122
Psychology Press 2757
Psychology & Self Help 2353
Public Catalogue Foundation 6120
Public Lending Right **5066**
Public. Europa-America 6111
The Publishers Association 5006, 5041, **5067**
Publishers Licensing Society Ltd **5068**
Publishers Publicity Circle **5069**
Publishing, Books & Reading in Sub-Saharan Africa: A Critical Bibliography **6191**

Publishing House **2624**
Publishing News **6192**
Publishing Scotland **5070**, 6100, 6202
Publishing Services **6079**
Publishing Technology Plc 6042
The Publishing Training Centre at Book House 6018, 6202, **6206**
Pueblo Books 6104
Puffin 2597, 6124
Punk Publishing Ltd **2625**
Pushkin Press 6103, 6106
Pustak Mahal 6124
Pustaka Sufes SDN BHD 2515
Putnam Aeronautical Books 2199
The Puzzle House **6015**
Puzzle Zone 2374, 2778
PWM 2679
Pyramid Publishing 6088

Quadrille Publishing Ltd **2626**, 6119
Quality Medical Pub. 2653
Quantum Publishing 2289, **3035**
Quartet Books **2627**
Quarto 2062, 2651, 3035, 6026
Queen's Temple Publications 2723
The Quest for 2469
Quick American 6135
Quiet Spaces 2093
Quill 6103
Quiller Publishing Ltd **2628**, 6115
Quilliam 6103
Quinta do Pinhal 6123
Quintessence Publishing Co Ltd **2629**
Quintessenz Verlag 2629
Quorum Books 2330

R & D Books 2473
Raceform Ltd **2630**, 6070, 6126
Racing Post 2630
Radcliffe Medical 6058
The Radcliffe Press **2631**, 2756
Radcliffe Publishing Ltd **2632**
Radio Collection (Audio Cassettes, CDs & MP3 CDs) 2083
Raduga 6123
Rail Guide Series 2117
Railway Preservation 2780
Rainbow Magic 2337
Rainbow Study Bibles 6118
Raintree 2595
Rajesh 6123
Rambler Association 2638
Rand Publications **2633**
Randall International 2036
Ronne Randall **6016**
Ian Randle 6066, 6103
Random House 2030, 6026, 6116
Random House Australia Pty Ltd 2782
Random House Children's Books **2634**, 2782
Random House Group 2635, 6096
Random House Inc 2782
Random House New Zealand Ltd 2782
Random House of Canada Ltd 2782
Random House (Pty) Ltd 2782
Random House UK Ltd 2481, **2635**, 2782, 6115
Ransom Publishing Ltd **2636**, 6094
Ravan Press 6103
Ravette Publishing Ltd **2637**, 6126
Raw Family 6109
The Ray Society 2680
RCC Pilotage Foundation 2391
RCL (Resources for Christian Living) 2640
RCPsych Publications 2659
RDR Books 2653
RE Today Services 2173
Reader in Namibian Sociology 6088
The Reader's Digest Association Inc 3036
Reader's Digest Books 2226
Reader's Digest Children's Publishing Ltd **3036**
Reading and Righting **6017**
Reading Champions 5061
Reading Connects 5061
Reading Is Fundamental, UK 5061
Reading The Game 5061
Readworthy 6124
Reaktion Books 6115
Real Reads 6100
Reardon Publishing **2638**, **6129**
Rebellion / 2000 AD 6135

Rebus Press 2427
Recent Advances Series 2663
Reclam 6111
Records of the Raj (series) 2505
The Red Guide Series 2504
Red Kite 2016, 2341
Red Wheel/Weiser Books 6109
Redcliffe Press Ltd **2639**, 2671
Redemptorist Publications **2640**
Redhammer Management Ltd **4082**
Redhouse/Sev 2508
Redstone Press 6103
Reed Exhibition Companies 6176
Thomas Reed Publications 2009
Reeds Almanac 2009
Reflections of a Bygone Age **2641**
Reflections on Practice 2180
Reformation Heritage Books 2264
Reformation Trust 2264
Refugee Council 6103
Regal 2436
Regatta Press 2579
Regency House Publishing Ltd **3037**
Regency Publications 6124
Regina Press (Malhame) 2640
Regional and Local History 2801
Regional Map Series 2504
Religious and Moral Education Press 2681
Remus Publishing 2089
Renegade Juggling 2137
Report 2396
Research Highlights in Social Work 2435
Research Reports 2399
Research Series 2246
Research Studies Press 6120
Resource File 2180
Resource Publications 6103, 6104
Resources in Education 2548
Resurrection Press 2640
Retail Entertainment Data 2562
Revisions 2098
Revival 2439
Revolver Books 6119
Reynolds & Hearn 6126
RGS-IBG Book Series 2660
RH Business Books 2357
Rhodawn Ltd 6151
RIBA Enterprises 6018
Richard III and Yorkist History Trust 2819
Julian Richer Publishing 6137
The Richmond Publishing Co **2642**
Rideabout Series 2638
Rider 2635
Rider French Publications 6100
Ries & Erler 2679
Rigby 2595
Right Angle Publishing 6103
Riksantikvarieambetet 2579
Rimal Publications 2493
Ripley Publishing Ltd **2643**
Ripping Yarns.com **2644**
RiRá 2305
Rising Stars UK Ltd **2645**, 6119
Risk Books **2646**
John Ritchie Ltd **6130**
Ritika 2036
River Books 2767
Riverhead Books / Penguin USA 6110
Riveroak 2436
Riverside Book Company 2036
Rizzoli 6111, 6120
Roadmaster Publishing **2647**
Knud Robberstad 6137
Le Robert 6111
Roberts & Co 2680
Robins Lane Press 2653
Robinson 2196
Robinson Literary Agency Ltd **4083**
Robinswood Press Ltd **2648**
Robson Books **2649**
Rockbuy Ltd 2644
Rockpool Children's Books 2752, 3038
Rockport 6115
Rodale 6119, 6122
Rogan House 2562
Rogers, Coleridge & White Ltd **4084**
Rogers' Therapeutic Conditions Series (Vols 1–4) 2593
Alan Rogers Guides Ltd **2650**, 6117
Romantic Novelists Association **5071**
Robert Rose 6070
J Ross Publishing 2653

INDEX OF COMPANIES & IMPRINTS / 181

Norman Ross Publishing Inc 2840
RotoVision SA **2651**, 6115
Rough Guides 2597
Round Hall Ltd **2652**
Round Table Series 2663
Roundabout Books 2653
Roundhouse Publications (Asia) 2375
Roundhouse Publishing Ltd **2653**, 6126
Roundtrip Travel 2653
Route Publishing Ltd **2654**, 6103
Routledge / Taylor & Francis 6058
Routledge-Cavendish **2655**, 2757
Routledge India Office 2757
Joseph Rowntree Foundation **2656**
Rowohlt 6111
The Royal Academy of Arts 2767
Royal Academy of Dancing 6137
Royal Botanic Gardens 2431
Royal Collection Publications **2657**, 2767
Royal College of General Practitioners **2658**
Royal College of Obstetricians and Gynaecologists 6136
Royal College of Psychiatrists **2659**, 6136
Royal Geographical Society (with Institute of British Geographers) **2660**
Royal Incorporation of Architects in Scotland 6100
Royal Irish Academy **2661**
Royal Musical Association Research Chronicle 6057
Royal Ontario Museum 2036
Royal Pavilion Libraries & Museums 2036
The Royal Pharmaceutical Society of Great Britain 2600
The Royal Society 2614, 6072
The Royal Society of Chemistry 2614, **2662**
Royal Society of Edinburgh 2138
Royal Society of Literature 2116, **5072**
Royal Society of Medicine Press Ltd 2614, **2663**, 6120
RSA (The Royal Society for the encouragement of Arts, Manufactures and Commerce) **5073**
Rubicon Press 2729
Rubin Mass Publishing Jerusalem 6123
Rucksack Readers 6100
John Rule, Publishers Sales Agent **6080**
John Rule Sales & Marketing 6120
Runnymede Trust 6103
Runpast 2016
Rural Railways 2780
Russell House Publishing Ltd **2664**
Bertrand Russell Peace Foundation Ltd 2726
Russian Music Publishing 2679
E. Russum & Sons Ltd 6138
Ruth's Archive 2608
Rutland Press 6081
Rux 6111
RV Verlag 2300
Ryelands 2343
Ryland Peters & Small 6119
Rylands 2343
Ryukyu Imports 2213

S. B. Publications **2675**
S.C.P. Childrens Ltd 2683
S.C.P. Publishers Ltd 2682
SA Design 2129
Saatchi Gallery 6108
William H. Sadlier Inc 2275
Safety House 6137
Sage Publications Ltd **2665**, 6072, 6202
Sahasrara Publications 6124
Saint Albert's Press **2666**
Saint Andrew Press 6120
St Anthony Messenger Press/Franciscan Catholic Book Publishing Co 2640
St Bedes 2318
St David's Press (formerly Ashley Drake Publishing) 2237
St George's Chapel, Windsor 2579
St Herman of Alaska Press 6127
St Ives Artists Series 2755
St Jerome Publishing Ltd **2667**
St Martins Press 2478, 6122
St Mary's Press 6104
St Nectarios Press 6127
St Nikodemos Orthodox Publication Society 6127
St Pauls Publishing **2668**

St Tikhon's Seminary Press 6127
St Vladimir's Seminary Press 6127
Salmon Publishing Ltd 6103
Salon du Livre de Montreal **6175**
Salt Publishing Ltd **2669**
Saltire Society 6081, 6100
Samskriti 6124
SAN Agency – UK & Irish Republic **5074**
Sanctuary 2272, 2562
Sanderson Books Ltd **6146**
Sandhurst Editorial **6018**
Sandpiper Books Ltd **6147**
Sandstone Press Ltd **2670**, 6100
Sang-e-meel 6123
Sangam Books Ltd 2493
Sanskrit Religious Institute 6124
Sansom & Co Ltd 2639, **2671**
Santana Books 2653
Santillana 6111
Sapiens 6136
Saqi Books **2672**, 2760, 6120
SARA (The Susie Adams Rights Agency) **4085**
Saraband 6078, 6100
Saros International Publishers 6088
SaS-Lavoisier 6136
Satin Publications Ltd 2813
Satrap Publishing & Translation **6046**
W. B. Saunders 2254
Steve Savage Publishing 6100
Save the Children **2673**
Alastair Sawday Publishing **2674**
Saxon Books 6137
The Sayle Literary Agency **4086**
Scala Publishers Ltd 2036, **2676**
Scandinavia Connection **6131**
Scandinavian Academic Press 2237
Scandinavian Yoga & Meditation School 6109
Lo Scarabeo 6110
SCBWI (Society of Children's Book Writers & Illustrators (British Isles Region)) **5075**
Sceptre 2372
Margit Schaleck Agency 3001
Schiffer 6101
Schirmer Books 2562
Birgit Schmettkamp Verlag 6156
Schocken Books / Random House 6116
Schoettle Publishing House 6118
Scholastic UK Ltd 2171, **2677**
School Garden Co 2163
School Library Association **5076**
School of Colour Publishing 2686
SchoolPlay Productions Ltd **2678**
Schott Music Ltd **2679**
Science and Behavior Books 6089
Science & Technology Letters 6136
Scientific Publishing Co 6065
Scion Publishing Ltd **2680**
SCM-Canterbury Press Ltd **2681**
Scolar Fine Art Ltd 2050
Scolar Press 2050
Scotforth Books 2151
Scotnotes (series) 2054
Scots in 2469
Scottish Book Trust **5077**
Scottish Children's Press **2682**, 2683
Scottish Council for Law Reporting 6120
Scottish Cultural Press **2683**
Scottish Society for Northern Studies 6100
Scottish Society of Medievalists 6100
Scottish Text Society **2684**, 6100
Scottish Tourist Board 2001
SCR Publishing 2614
Scrapbook Storytelling 2686
Screenpress Publishing 2272
Scribner 2706
Scriptum 2767
Scripture Union Publishing **2685**
Sculptors Series 2210
Scutari Press 2254
Seafarer 6103
Seaflower Books 2267
Search Press Ltd 2130, **2686**, 6071
Seasquirt Publications 2653, **2687**
Second Language Acquisition 2165
Secret Magazine 6135
SEDA Publications **2688**
Sedco Publishing 6088
Seix Barral 6111
Self-Counsel Press 2653
Self Realization Fellowship 6110

SEM Financial Training Centre Ltd 6088
Semiotext(e) 2511
Senior Publications 6121
Senter Series 2029
SEOL Ltd **6081**
SEP Editrice 6126
SEPM 2303
Seren **2689**, 6103
Serial Books Design 2098
Serif 6103, 6135
Serpent's Tail 2621, 6061, 6117
Servant Publications 2640
Servedit-Acatos 2364
Serveonline Ltd 2739
Services for Export and Language (SEL) **6047**
Sessions of York **2690**
William Sessions Holdings Ltd 2690
Seven Locks Press 2653
Seven Stories Press 6135
Severn House Publishers Ltd **2691**, 6115
SGC Books 2163, **2692**
SGEL 6111
Shadowline Publishing 6137
Sharon House Publishing **2693**
Shaw & Sons Ltd **2694**
Sheaf Publishing **2695**
Sheed & Ward 2198
Sheffield Academic Press 2198
Sheldon Press **2696**, 2716
Caroline Sheldon Literary Agency **4087**
Sheldrake Press **2697**, 6078
Shelter 6109, 6135
Shepheard-Walwyn (Publishers) Ltd **2698**, 6067
R. D. & A. S. Shepherd Partnership 6137
Sheppard 2425
Sheppard's Directories **6193**
Sherwood Publishing **2699**
The Shetland Times Ltd **2700**, 6081, 6100
Shire Publications Ltd **2701**
The Shoe String Book Co 2036
Shogun International Ltd **6154**
Short Books Ltd **2702**
T. K. Shrestha 6156
Shubhi Publications 6124
Sickle Moon Books 2250
Sidgwick & Jackson Ltd 2478, 2585
Sigel Press **2703**
Sigma Press **2704**
Signal Books 2382
Sikorski 2679
Silent But Deadly Publications 6137
Silvana Editoriale 6090
Silver Link Publishing Ltd 2551
Silver Moon Books **2705**, 6137
Silverback Books 6122
Dorie Simmonds Literary Agency **4088**
Jeffrey Simmons **4089**
Simon & Schuster (UK) Ltd **2706**, 6116
Simple Guides 6116
Steven Simpson Books **6156**
Sinauer Associates 2088, 2583, 6119
Sinclair-Stevenson 2653, **4090**
Singing Dragon 2435
Singspiration Inc 6118
Sisyphe Editions 2653
Siti's Sisters 2636
Sitric Books Ltd 2458
Charles Skilton Ltd 2015, **2707**
Skira Editore 2767
Skylight Paths 6110
SLG Press 2681
Slightly Foxed **2708**
Slouch Hat Publications 6123
SLS Legal Publications (NI) **2709**
Small Print **6034**
SMC Publishing 6123
Smile Mathematics 6094
Smiling Tiger Publications 2213
Smith / Doorstep 6103
Smith Gryphon Publishers Ltd 2105
Smith Institute 6103
Smith Settle Printing & Bookbinding Ltd **2710**
Adam Smith Institute **2711**
J. & C. Smith 2036
Ken Smith Publishing Ltd 2710
Robert Smith Literary Agency Ltd **4091**
Smyth & Helwys 2318
Colin Smythe Ltd **2712**
Snake River Press 6122

Snowbooks **2713**, 6117
William Snyder Publishing Associates **6082**
Soccer Books Ltd **2714**
Social Affairs Unit **2715**
Social Market Foundation 6103
Social Science Press 2092
Social Work Christian Fellowship 2515
Socialist Renewal 2726
Sociedad de Metafisica Inglesa 2719
Societas 2390
Societas Archaeologica Upsaliensis 2579
Society for Editors and Proofreaders **5078, 6207**
The Society for Endocrinology 2614
Society for Italian Studies 2484
Society for Medieval Archaeology 2484
Society for Name Studies in Britain and Ireland 2819
The Society for Promoting Christian Knowledge (SPCK) 2696, **2716**, 6120
Society of Antiquaries of London 2579
Society of Antiquaries of Scotland **2717**
Society of Archivists **5079**
Society of Authors 5033, **5080**, 6178
Society of Authors Pension Fund **5081**
Society of Chemical Industry 6136
The Society of Consulting Marine Engineers and Ship Surveyors 2834
Society of Editors **5082**
Society of Genealogists Enterprises Ltd **2718**
Society of Indexers **5083**
Society of International Gas Tanker & Terminal Operators 2834
Society of Medical Writers **5084**
The Society of Metaphysicians Ltd **2719**
Soft Skull Press 6135
Soho Press 6135
Solid Ground Publications 2264
Solidus **2720**
Sopena 6111
Sophi Academic Press 6065
Sophia Books 2731
Sophia Institute 2640
Sotheby's NY 2036
Sotok Press 6100
Sound Entertainment 6115
Sound View Press 2364
Soundings Audio Books 2773
Soundprints 2653
Sourcebooks 6071
South Asian Publications 6123
South Street Press 2297
South Western 2159
Southern African Printing and Publishing House / SAPES Trust 6088
Southgate Publishers **2721**
Southwater 2130
Souvenir Press Ltd **2722**, 6099
Sovereign Publications 2264
Spa Books 2738
Space & Time 6093
Spartan Press Music Publishers Ltd **2723**
SPCK 2716
Speaking Tree 6109
Special Interest Model Books Ltd **2724**, 6070, 6126
Special Publications (Warburg) 2816
Special Stories Publishing 6058
Specialist Schools and Academies Trust 6202
Specialty Press 2016
Speck Press 6135
Spectrum 2583, 6088, 6124
Speechmark Publishing Ltd **2725**
Sphere 2462
La Spiga 6111
Spinfolds 3033
Spiral Guides 2001
Spiramus 6136
Spire Books 2579
Spitfire 2252
Spokesman **2726**
Sponsorship Unit 6065
Sport Media 6117
Sportsbooks Ltd **2727**
The Sportsman's Press 2628
Spotlight Poets 2786
Springer Verlag London **2728**
SPSS Ashburton 6123
Spy Publishing Ltd 6119
Squadron Signal / Pocketbond Ltd **6132**

182 / INDEX OF COMPANIES & IMPRINTS

Squareone Publishers 6110
Stacey Arts Ltd 2147, 2729
Stacey International **2729**, 6103
Stackpole Books 2628
Stadium & Arena 3032
Stagecraft 2605
Stahleisen (The German Iron & Steel Institute) 2837
Stainer & Bell Ltd **2730**
Standard Publishing 6130
Stanfords Charts 2391
Starbooks Press 6135
Starchasers 2636
Starkmann Ltd **6157**
Starlet 6100
Starting Out... 2548
The Stationery Office 2354
Steerforth Press 6135
Steidl 2767
Rudolf Steiner Education 2353
Rudolf Steiner Press **2731**, 6100
Stenlake Publishing Ltd **2732**
Step Forward Publishing Ltd **2733**, 6094
Patrick Stephens Ltd 2354
Steps in Counselling Series 2593
Sterling Publishing 6126
Stern Portfolios 2765
Steven & Sons 2771
Shirley Stewart Literary Agency **4092**
Stichting Kunstboek 2036
Stickertastic 2778
Stipes Publishing LLC 2582
Stobart Davies Ltd **2734**
Stockton Press Ltd 2478, 2583
Stokesby House Publications **2735**
Storey Books 6122
Storm King 2036
Storycatcher Books / children's fiction 2239
Stott's Correspondence College **2736**
Richard Strauss GmbH & Co KG 2679
STRI (Sports Turf Research Institute) **2737**
Strident Publishing 6100
Stripes Publishing 2463
Strokes International 2653
Strong Oak Press **2738**
Student Litteratur 6065
Studies of the Warburg Institute 2816
Studio 9 Books and Music 6100
Studymates Ltd **2739**
Sub-Saharan Publishers 6088
Success Strategies 6089
Suffolk Family Learning 6092
Suffolk Records Society 2116
Suhrkamp 6111
John Sullivan 2016
Summer Palace Press **2740**
Summersdale Publishers Ltd **2741**, 6117
Sun Books Pty Ltd 2478
Sun Chalice 2774
Sun-Pacific Music (London) Ltd 4005
Sunday Herald Books 6100
Sunflower Books **2742**
Sunrise Setting Ltd **6019**
Sunshine Music Co 2723
Superbrands 6137
Supporters' Guide (Series) 2714
Supportive Learning Publications (SLP) **2743**
Sura Books 6124
Surtees Society 2116
Survivor 2436
The Susijn Agency Ltd **4093**
Sussex Academic Press **2744**, 6065
Sussex Publications 2058, **2745**
with Sussex Pubs 2058
SVEC (Studies on Voltaire and the Eighteenth Century) 2814
Swan Hill Press 2628
Swan Raven & Co 6109
The Swedenborg Society **2746**
Swedish-English Literary Translators Association (SELTA) **6048**
Swedish Pharmaceutical Press 2757
Sweet & Maxwell 2652, 2771, 6102
Sword of the Lord Publishers 6118
Sybex International Corp 2828
Sympo Sunrise (Children's Stories) **2747**
Symposium Brush-Up Shakespeare Series **2747**
Symposium Gem Art Series **2747**
Symposium Publications Literary & Art **2747**

Synergetic Press 6110
Systemic Thinking Theory & Practice Series 2427

T & H Holdings Ltd 2767
T2 2788
Ta Ha Publishers Ltd **2748**
Tabb House **2749**
Tafelberg 6066
The Tagman Press 6079, 6109
Taigh na Teud Music Publishers **2750**
Talebones 6093
Talk To Your Baby 5061
Tallis Press 2015
Tamar Books 2113
Tamarind Ltd 2459, **2751**
Tamesis 2116
Tamr Translations Ltd 6043
Tangerine Designs Ltd **2752**, 3038
Tanker Structure Co-operative Forum 2834
Tantor Media Inc 6117
Tanzania Publishing House 6088
Tapir Academic Press 6065
Tara Publishing 2459
Jeremy P. Tarcher / Penguin USA 6110
Tardy 2364
Tarquin Publications **2753**
Tartarus Press **2754**, 6103, 6137
Taschen 2117
Tata-McGraw-Hill Publishing Co Ltd 2473
Tate Publishing **2755**
Taunton Press 6126
I. B. Tauris & Co Ltd **2756**, 6119
Tavistock Institute of Marital Studies 2427
Taxation Advice Bureau Guide 6058
Taylor & Francis 2655, **2757**, 6023, 6072, 6099, 6202
Taylor Graham Publishing **2758**
Teach Yourself 2369
Teacher Created Materials 6089
Teachers Pets 2778
Teachers' Pocketbooks 2482
Teaching Ethics (Book series) 2262
Teachit (UK) Ltd **2759**
Teapot Press 3034
Tectum 6070
Teenage Magazine Arbitration Panel (TMAP) 5064
Telegram **2760**
Thomas Telford Ltd **2761**, 6018, 6106
Telos Publishing Ltd **2762**
Templar Publishing **2763**, 6115
Temple House Books 6137
Temple Lodge Publishing **2764**, 6100
Temple University Press 6105
Templegate 2318
Templeton Foundation Press 2014
Tempus Publishing 2534, 6061
Teneues Publishing UK Ltd **2765**, 6115
The Tennyson Agency **4094**
Tentmaker Publications **2766**
Terra Publishing 6120
Tesseract Books 6093
Text Publishing 2143
TFM Publishing Ltd (Medical) 6065
Thalamus Publishing 2653, 6126
Thames Head 3007
Thames & Hudson 2767
Thames & Hudson Ltd **2767**
Tharpa Publications **2768**
Theatre Communications Group 2362
Themis Books 2324
Thesis 6103
G. Thieme Verlag 2791
Think Books **2769**, 6119
Think Publishing 2769
Third Millennium Information Ltd 2418
Third Millennium Publishing Ltd **2770**, 6120
Third World Network Africa 6088
Thirsty Books 2048
Thoemmes Continuum 2198
Thomas Publishing Co Inc 6040
Thomas Reeds 2100
Thomas Technology **6040**
George Thompson Brake 6123
Thomson Corp 2652
Thomson International Legal & Regulatory **2771**
Thomson Round Hall 2652
Thomson Tax 2771
D. C. Thomson & Co Ltd 2299, 2339, 2490

Thorogood Publishing Ltd **2772**, 6120
F. A. Thorpe Publishing **2773**
Thoth Publications **2774**, 6109
THRASS (UK) Ltd **2775**
Threshold Books 6110
J. M. Thurley Management **4095**
Tibetan Medical & Astro Institute 6124
Ticktock Media 6126
Tide Mill Press 2778
Tiger Books 6137
Timber Press 6115
Time Inc Home Entertainment 6122
Timeless Books 6110
TimeLife 2157
Times Books 2191, 2348
The Times Literary Supplement **6194**
Tindal Street Press **2776**, 6135
Tir Eolas 2712
Titan Publishing Group **2777**, 6115
Toby Press LLC 6122
Tokyo International Book Fair **6176**
Tokyopop 6119
Tolkien 2348
Top That! Publishing Plc **2778**
Topical Resources **2779**
Topics in Translation 2165
Tor 2585
Torchlight Publishing 6124
Tortoise Press 6123
Tottel Publishing 6058, 6120
Totterdown Books 6103
Toucan Books Ltd **3039**
Touchstone 2706, 6137
Tour & Trail Maps 2235, 2394
Tourism & Cultural Change 2165
TP Publications 6094
Trade Counter Distribution **6133**
Trade Paperbacks 2691
Trailblazers 2636
M. T. Train 2036
Trans-Pennine Publishing Ltd 2647, **2780**
Transatlantic Publishers Group Ltd **6134**
Transforming Press 6089
Transita Ltd **2781**
Translating Europe 2165
Translators Association **5085**
Transworld Publishers Ltd **2782**, 6096
Traplet Publications 2686
Travel Publishing Ltd **2783**
Travel Series 2001
Traveller's Guide Series 2316
Travellers Handbook 2286
Travelling Scholarship Fund **5086**
Travelmates 2455
Travelwise 6137
Treasures of the Bodleian Library 2109
Treehouse Children's Books 3021
Emma Treehouse Ltd 6119
Trends in Functional Programming 2406
Trentham Books **2784**
Trentham Print Design Ltd 2784
Lavinia Trevor **4096**
Triangle Books 2716
Trilogy Group **6041**
Trinitarian Bible Society **2785**
Trinity Collections 2605
Trinity Press International 2198, 2681
Triumph Books 2653
Triumph House 2538, **2786**
Trolley 2617
Trotman Publishing 2212, **2787**
Troubador Publishing Ltd **2788**, 6137
Tru-Est Ltd **2789**
Trucking Turtle Publishing 2245
Truedata Computer Services 2515
Truman State University Press 6065
Truran **2790**
Trust for the Study of Adolescence **3040**
TSO (The Stationery Office Ltd) **2791**
TTS Group **2792**
Tucker Slingsby Ltd **3041**
Tuckwell Press 6081, 6100
Tufton Books 2681
Turinta 6107
A. Turizm 2508
Turnaround Publisher Services Ltd **6135**
Jane Turnbull **4097**
Turpin Distribution **6136**
Turpion-Moscow 6136
Tusitlal Publishing 6123
Twelveheads Press **2793**
Twenty-third Publications 6104

Two Ravens Press 6100
Shaun Tyas 2819
Tyne Bridge Publishing **2794**

UCAS **2795**
UCL Press 2655
Udyat Books 6070
UK DOI Agency 2545
UK International Ceramics 6097
UK ISBN Agency 2545
UK SAN Agency 2545
Ullmann 2300
Ullstein 6111
Ultra 6109
Ulverscroft Large Print Books Ltd 2412, 2479, 2773, **2796**
Ulysses Travel Guides 2653
Umbrage 6135
Uncut Mountain Publishers 6127
Yr Undeb Cristnogol 2133
Undercurrents 2202
Understanding Global Issues 6111
P. A. Underwood Ltd 2742
UNESCO Institute for Educational Planning 2784
Unicorn Press **2797**, 6120
Unimax Macmillan Ltd 2478
Unique Publications 2213, 6154
UNISA Press 6088
Unisun Publications 6124
United Kingdom Hydrographic Office 2391
United Nations 2791, 6136
United Publicity Services Plc 6049
United Publishers Services Ltd 2140
United Writers Publications Ltd **2798**
Universal Edition Ltd 2679
Universal Law Publishing 6124
Universities of the Caribbean Press 6066
University College Dublin Press **2799**, 6103
University College London 6202
University of Alberta Press 6065
University of Bristol 2610
University of Buea 6088
University of Capetown Press 6103
The University of Chicago Press 2828
University of East Anglia 5025, 6044
University of Edinburgh 2247
University of Exeter Press **2800**
University of Hawaii Press 2391
University of Hertfordshire Press **2801**, 6103
University of Iceland Press 2579
University of Illinois Press 6105
University of Lagos Press 6088
University of Namibia Press 6088
University of Natal Press 6103
University of Nebraska Press 6105
University of New Mexico Press 6065
University of Oxford 2109, 2814
University of Queensland Press 2653
University of Rochester Press 2116
University of Salzburg Press 2366
University of Texas Press 6105
University of the Arts, London 6201
University of Wales Press **2802**, 6072
University of Washington Press 6105
University of York 2112
University of Zambia 6088
University of Zimbabwe Publications 6088
University Press Dhaka 6123
University Press Ltd 6088
University Press of Mississippi 2653
University Presses Marketing **6083**
The University Presses of California, Columbia & Princeton Ltd **6084**
University Science Books 2088, 2583, 6119
Unveiled Publishing 2358
Merlin Unwin Books Ltd **2803**
Upfront Publishing **2804**
UPS Translations **6049**
Laurence Urdang Inc **2805**
US Games 6109
US Pharmacopoeia Convention 2791
Usborne Publishing Ltd **2806**, 6081
Useful Music 2723
Usharp 2363

V & A Publications 2100, 6119
Vacation Work 2212
Vallentine Mitchell Publishers **2807**
Van der Plas Publications 6126

Van Duren 2712
Van Hasbroeck 2544
John van Weenen 6137
Vanguard Press 2653
Vanguard Productions 6139
Vanity Books International 6124
Vanwell Publishing 2358
Variorum 2050
Vathek Publishing 2614
VDI (The Association of German Engineers) 2837
Vegan Society 6103
Veloce Publishing Ltd **2808**, 6070, 6126
Vendome 2767
Venton 2406
Ventura Publishing Ltd 2597, 6070
Venture Publications Ltd 6121
Ventus Books 2607
Verba Volant 2036
Verbatim Books 2805
Verey & von Kanitz Rural Classics 2245
Javier Vergara 6111
Veritas Communications 2809
Veritas Publications **2809**
Verlag ACS Aqualog GmbH 6156
Verlag Dürr & Kessler 6111
Verlag Eugen Ulmer KG 6156
Verlag für Deutsch 6111
Verlag Moritz Diesterweg 6111
Vermilion 2635
Verse Chorus Press 6135
Verso 6120
Vertical Editions **2810**
Vertigo Communications LLB 6117
The Veterinary Press Ltd 2485
VGSF 2314
Victor 2436
Ed Victor Ltd **4098**
Victoria & Albert Museum Publishing **2811**
Victoria County History 2116
Victorian Law Foundation 6202
Video Ex 2638, 6129
Viewpoints 2469
Vif Une nouvelle collection en livre de poche 2814
Viking 2597
Viking Ship Museum, Roskilde 2579
Vine House Distribution Ltd **6137**
Vine Press 6123
Vintage 2635
Violette Editions 2767
Virago 2462
Virgin Books Ltd **2812**, 6096
Virtue Books Ltd **6138**
Visibilia series 2606
Vision **2813**, 6109, 6117
Vision Sports Publishing 6135
Visit Britain 6117
Vista **6042**
Vista Consulting Team Ltd 6097
Vista Iberica 6123
Vista Inc 6042
Vital Health Publishing 6110
The Vital Spark 2830
Vitra Design Museum 6090
Viva Books 6092
VIZ Media 2706
Voltaire Foundation Ltd **2814**, 6120
Georg von Holtzbrinck GmbH 2478
Voyager 2348
VU University Press 6065

W & N Illustrated 2574
Waanders Publishers 2036
Wade & Doherty Literary Agency Ltd **4099**
Wadsworth 2159
Wales Books - Glyndwr Publishing 2310
Walk & Eat Series 2742

Walk with Luath 2469
Walk! Guide Books 2235, 2394
Walkabout Series 2638
Walkcards (series) 2638
Walker Books Ltd 6119
Sally Walker Language Services **6050**
W.H. Walker & Bros 2089
Wallflower Press **2815**, 6103
The Walters Art Museum 2036
Warburg Institute **2816**
Ward Lock Educational Co Ltd **2817**, 3007
Peter Ward Book Exports **6085**
Frederick Warne 2597
Warner Books 6135
WATCH (Writers Artists & Their Copyright Holders) **5087**
William Waterman Publications 2738
Watermark Press 2653, 6139
Waterside Press **2818**, **3042**
Watersport Publishing Inc 6148
Waterway Books 2089
Waterways World Books 2577
Watkins Publishing 2074, 6126
Paul Watkins Publishing **2819**
Watson, Little Ltd **4100**
A. P. Watt Ltd **4101**
Peter Watts Publishing 6121
Waverley Books Ltd 2299
Waverley Press 6100
The Way 6136
Wealth Management Information Services Ltd 2789
Weaver Press Ltd 6088
Wedding Bible Co 2004
Weekes 2730
WEF Publishing 2614
Weidenfeld & Nicolson 2574, **2820**
Josef Weinberger Plays Ltd 2821, **4102**
Joseph Weinberger Ltd **2821**, 4102, 6103
John Welch Literary Consultant & Agent **4103**
Welsh Academic Press 2237
Welsh Books Council / Cyngor Llyfrau Cymru **5088**, 6202
Welsh Sunday School Council 2222
Wennergren-Cappelen 6131
Wessex Archaeology 2579
Wessex Books 6109
Wessex Translations Ltd **6051**
West Dunbartonshire Libraries & Museums 2048
West Group 2652
West Highland Series (Walking Booklets) 2378
West of England Trust 2424
David West Children's Books **3043**
Westbury 2710
Western Academic & Specialist Press 2579
Westholme 2653, 6139
Westlaw UK 2771
Westminster John Knox Press 2014
Weston Publishing 6103
Westwood Publishing 6089
Westworld International 6103
We've Made It Easy 2010
Wexas International 2286
Which? Books 2597, **2822**, 6061
Which? The Consumer Association 6117
Whitaker Publishing 6109
Whitaker's Almanacks 2100
White Adder 6094
White Horse Press 6136
White Ladder Press 2212, **2823**
White Lotus 6123
White Star Publishers 6126
Eve White Literary Agent **4104**
Whitechapel 6090
Whitefriars Press 2666

Whiting & Birch Ltd **2824**
Whittet Books Ltd **2825**, 6097
Whittles Publishing **2826**, 6081, 6100
Who Works Publications 6137
Who's Who in British History series 2698
Whurr Publishers Ltd 2828
Dinah Wiener Ltd **4105**
Michael Wilcox School of Colour 2653
Wild Boar Trading 6097
Wild Flower 6109
Wild Goose Publications **2827**, 6100
Wild Lives 2469
Wild Spirit 6109
Wildlife Series 2117
Wildwood House 2050
Wiley-Blackwell Ltd 2828, 6018, 6072, 6202
John Wiley & Sons Ltd **2828**
Jonathan Williams Literary Agency **4106**
Joseph Williams 2730
Willingham Press 6123
Willow Island Editions **2829**
John Wilson (Booksales) Ltd **6086**, 6120
Neil Wilson Publishing Ltd **2830**, 6061, 6100
Philip Wilson Publishers 2756, **2831**
Robert Wilson Designs 2089
Wiltshire Buildings Record 2368
Wiltshire Record Society 2368
Windgather Press 2579, 6103
Windhorse Publications **2832**, 6100
Windsor Books International 2653, **6139**
Wine Appreciation Guild 6137
Winnicott Studies (Series) 2427
Wisden 2100, 2597, 6119
Wise Publications 2562, 6123
WIT Press **2833**
Witches Almanac 6109
Witherby Seamanship International **2834**
Witwatersrand University Press 6103
Wizard Books 2385
Wizard Study Guides 6123
Woeli Publishing Services 6088
Wolfhound Press 2499
Wolters Kluwer Health (P & E) Ltd **2835**
Wolters Kluwer NV 2539
Women and Law in South Africa Research Trust 6088
Women's Health Action Research Centre 6088
Women's Health Advisory Service 6110
The Women's History Press 2375
The Women's Press 2627, **2836**
Wood & Barnes Publishing 6089
Woodbine House Inc 6065
The Woodbridge Co Ltd 2419
Wooden Books 6103, 6109
Wooden Dragon Press 6137
Woodhead Publishing Ltd **2837**, 6106
Woodmore 6123
Woodstock Books Ltd 2710
Word Book Day Ltd 5022
Word for Life Trust **2838**
Word for Word (Audio Cassettes & CDs) 2083
Word Power Books 6100
Wordclay 2066
Wordcraft of Oregon 6093
Words of Wizdom 6110
words4profit **6020**
Wordspeak 6124
Wordsworth Editions Ltd **2839**
Working Papers 2396, 2399
Working Waterways series 2089
Workman Publishing 6115, 6122
Workshop Practice Series 2724
World Bank 2791
World Book Day **6177**

World Council of Churches 6065
World Health Organisation 2791
World Microfilms 2058, **2840**
World Relief Network 6124
World Scientific 2389, 6072, 6120, 6202
World Tourism Organisation 2791
World Trade Organisation 2791
World Trade Press 2791
World Wisdom Books 6110
WorldView 6103, 6124
Worshipful Company of Stationers and Newspaper Makers **5089**
Worth Books 2653
Worth Press Ltd **2841**, 6122
Worth Publishers 2088, 2583
Wrightson Biomedical 6136
Writers and Their Work 2548
Writers' & Artists' Yearbook **6195**
Writers' Bookshop 2538, 2786
The Writers Bureau Ltd 3024, 6113
Writer's Digest Books 6113
Writers' Forum **6196**
Writings of Mary Baker Eddy 2653
WRTH Publications Ltd 6139
WWF United Kingdom 2642
www.tvmyworld.com 4081
Wychwood Press 2152

The X Press 6135
Xcite Books 2004
XPL Publishing **2842**
XRX Books 2686

Y Lolfa Cyf **2843**
Yad Ben Zvi 6065
Yad Vashem 2092, 6123
Yale Egyptological Seminar 2579
Yale Representation Ltd 2844
Yale University Press London 2828, **2844**
Roy Yates Books **6158**
Yellow Jersey 2635
YMAA 2213
Yore Publications **2845**
York Associates 6094
York University, Dept of Archaeology 2579
Yorke Edition 2723
Yorkshire Archaeological Society 2116
Yorkshire Art Circus Ltd 6103
Young Pathfinder 2180
Young Picador 2475
Young Spitfire 2252
Young Writers 2538, 2786
Your Rights (series) 2010
Youthworks 2416

Zagat 2706
Zambezi Publishing Ltd **2846**
Zambia Women Writers' Association 6088
Zanichelli 6111
Zed Books Ltd **2847**
Zeig Tucker & Co 2427
Hans Zell Publishing Consultants 2221, **6021**
Zen On Music Company 2679
Zena Publications 2802
Zero to Ten 2265, **2848**
Zero to Three Press 6134
Zeticula **2849**
Zigzag 2590
Zimbabwe International Book Fair Trust 6088
Zimbabwe Publishing House Ltd 6088
Zondervan Corporation 6118
Zone Books (Urzone Publishing Ltd) 2511
Zoom Map Series 2504
Zulma 6103
Zymurgy Publishing **2850**

7.5 UK PUBLISHERS BY POSTCODE

LONDON & SOUTH-EAST ENGLAND

Brighton
BN1 1WZ **3040**
BN1 9RE **2399**
BN1 9RF **2395**
BN2 1GJ **2596**
BN2 3RL **2591**
BN3 1DD **2651**
BN3 1FL **2521**
BN7 2NZ **2387, 3011, 3027**
BN11 1BE **2067**
BN23 6NT **2436**
BN24 9BP **2744**
BN25 2UB **2675**
BN41 1WR **2653**
Bromley
BR2 9JF **2084**
BR3 5JS **2158**
Canterbury
CT20 2WP **2307**
Croydon
CR5 2YH **2419**
CR9 5YP **2516**
Dartford
DA1 4BZ **2694**
Guildford
GU3 1LP **2728**
GU7 2EP **2363**
GU9 7HS **2572**
GU11 3HR **2050, 2317, 2470**
GU21 6LQ **2545**
GU29 9AZ **2506**
GU34 1HG **2223**
GU34 3HQ **2640**
GU47 9DD **2070**
Harrow
HA3 5ZH **2146**
HA3 8RU **2089**
HA6 1UN **2751**
HA8 7BJ **2807**
HA9 9EA **2612**
Hemel Hempstead
HP10 8EU **2432**
HP17 8NT **2284**
HP18 0DQ **2805**
HP20 2NQ **3029**
Ilford
IG7 6DL **2422**
IG8 8HD **2374**
Kingston-upon-Thames
KT3 3AB **2629**
KT5 9SP **2762**
KT11 1LG **2129**
KT12 4RG **2016**
KT14 7ZF **2765**
KT22 7RY **2449**
London
E1 6JJ **2098**
E1M 5QL **2418**
E2 6DG **2588**
E8 3BH **2480**
E9 5LN **2498**

E14 4JD **2761**
E14 4JP **2195, 2312, 2510, 2512, 2555, 2601**
E14 5LB **2063**
EC1A 9PN **2681**
EC1M 4AR **2673**
EC1M 5NP **2451**
EC1M 5QL **2770**
EC1M 5UX **2263**
EC1M 6BF **2241**
EC1M 6PE **3039**
EC1M 7BA **2718**
EC1N 8FN **2487**
EC1N 8QU **2493**
EC1N 8RT **2806**
EC1N 8TS **2124**
EC1N 8XA **2244**
EC1R 0HT **2019, 2342**
EC1R 0JH **2621, 2702**
EC1R 4QB **2119**
EC1R 4QL **2250**
EC1R 4SX **2576**
EC1V 0AT **2266, 2676**
EC1V 0BB **2437, 2570**
EC1V 0DG **2161**
EC1V 1LR **2433**
EC1V 1NG **2526**
EC1V 3QP **2162**
EC1V 4JX **2708**
EC1V 7QE **2527**
EC1V 9BP **2197**
EC1Y 1SP **2665**
EC2A 3AR **2099**
EC2A 3DU **2772**
EC2A 3EA **2028**
EC3R 5DD **2408**
EC3R 6AE **2270**
EC4A 2HS **2490**
EC4Y 0DY **2462, 2602**
N1 1EW **2304**
N1 2LZ **2230**
N1 3JT **2086**
N1 6ND **2831**
N1 7JQ **2293**
N1 8BZ **2441**
N1 9JB **2435**
N1 9JF **2847**
N1 9JN **2438, 2713, 3010**
N1 9LQ **2155**
N1 9PA **2599**
N1 9PF **3003**
N1 9RR **2475, 2585**
N1 9UN **2450**
N1 9XW **2478**
N3 1DZ **2730**
N3 2JU **2021**
N3 2UU **2038**
N6 5AA **2609**
N7 8PL **2367**
N7 9BH **3035**
N7 9DP **2385**
N12 8ZR **2232**
N19 4PT **2139**
N22 6TZ **2508**

NW1 0ND **2062**
NW1 1DB **2677**
NW1 2DB **2126, 2127**
NW1 3BH **2337, 2338, 2369, 2371, 2372, 2519**
NW1 4DF **2822**
NW1 8PR **2603**
NW1 9PT **3022**
NW3 3PF **2771**
NW3 5HT **2427**
NW5 1AP **2584**
NW5 2DU **2259**
NW5 2JU **3018**
NW5 2RZ **2459**
NW5 2XL **2457**
NW6 1DZ **2568**
NW6 1LU **2059**
NW6 3HR **2705**
NW6 6RD **2153**
NW7 2XU **2291**
NW8 6WD **2058, 2736, 2745, 2840**
NW9 6JZ **2491**
NW10 3YB **2341**
NW11 7DL **2485**
SE1 0BL **2797**
SE1 0HX **2500**
SE1 0JF **2813**
SE1 0UP **2777**
SE1 2BH **2256**
SE1 2EJ **2046**
SE1 3AW **2445**
SE1 3RS **2586**
SE1 6LH **2388**
SE1 7JN **2600**
SE1 7NX **2135, 2182, 2198, 2344, 2540**
SE1 8HA **2288**
SE1 8RD **2835**
SE1 8XX **2355**
SE9 2TZ **2175**
SE10 8RF **2037**
SE11 5AY **2154**
SE11 5SD **2625**
SE14 5DB **2556**
SE17 3LH **2271**
SE19 3RY **3009, 3012**
SE23 3HZ **2824**
SE24 0PB **2377, 2733**
SW1A 1BQ **2657**
SW1E 6LB **2789**
SW1H 0QS **2417**
SW1H 9BN **2273**
SW1H 9JJ **2620**
SW1P 3AZ **2177**
SW1P 3BL **2711**
SW1P 4RG **2755**
SW1P 4ST **2696, 2716**
SW1V 2SA **2030, 2635, 2812**
SW1V 2SS **2359**
SW1X 7DL **2453**
SW1X 8PG **2659**
SW1Y 4RX **2646**
SW1Y 5HX **2194**

SW3 4AH **2015, 2707**
SW5 0RE **2578**
SW6 1RU **2426**
SW6 6AW **2463**
SW7 1PU **2658**
SW7 2AR **2660**
SW7 2RL **2811**
SW7 3HG **2742**
SW7 5BD **2536**
SW8 5WZ **2090**
SW9 0BB **2748**
SW11 2JW **2260**
SW11 3AS **2668**
SW11 5DH **2352**
SW11 6SS **2332**
SW12 0DA **2697**
SW13 9JJ **2440**
SW14 8ER **2698**
SW15 1AZ **3043**
SW15 1DQ **2213**
SW15 1NL **2115**
SW15 2PE **2218**
SW15 2TG **2518**
SW16 4ER **2010**
SW18 1YW **2072**
SW18 4JJ **2224**
SW19 1JQ **2166**
SW19 3NN **2785**
SW19 5EF **2013**
W1B 1AH **2386**
W1B 5DL **2087**
W1B 5SA **2715**
W1D 3HB **2009, 2361**
W1D 3QY **2107**
W1D 3QZ **2100**
W1F 7BB **2679**
W1F 9JW **2340**
W1G 0AE **2663**
W1G 7AR **2257**
W1G 8DH **2080**
W1H 1PD **2554**
W1J 6HE **2229**
W1J 7PG **2587**
W1S 4EX **2645**
W1T 2LD **2627, 2836**
W1T 3JJ **2821**
W1T 3JW **2150**
W1T 3LJ **2562**
W1T 3QT **2549**
W1T 4EJ **2022**
W1T 5DX **2414**
W1T 5HJ **2043**
W1T 5JR **2292**
W1T 6DF **3001**
W1U 6BY **2420**
W1U 6NR **2265**
W1W 7AB **2042**
W1W 8AF **2815**
W1Y 0RA **2590**
W2 4BU **2631, 2756**
W2 5BP **2747**
W2 5RH **2672, 2760**
W4 5TF **2321**
W5 5SA **2634, 2782**
W6 7NF **2071**
W6 7NJ **2402**

W6 7PA **2184, 2423**
W6 8JB **2348**
W6 9ER **2196**
W8 4BH **2147, 2729**
W8 6SA **2249**
W10 5ST **2566**
W10 6BL **2769**
W11 2LW **2096**
W11 4QR **2322, 2615**
W12 8QP **2362**
W14 0RA **2081, 2190, 2199, 2589, 2613, 2649**
W14 9PB **2105**
WC1A 2QA **2617**
WC1A 2TH **2604, 2746**
WC1B 3DP **2844**
WC1B 3ES **2044**
WC1B 3JH **2157, 2169, 2496, 2497**
WC1B 3PA **2421, 2722**
WC1B 3PL **2382**
WC1B 3QQ **2128**
WC1B 3SW **2429**
WC1E 7AE **2274, 2396**
WC1E 7EY **2350, 2511**
WC1H 0AB **2816**
WC1H 0AL **2400**
WC1H 9HF **2688**
WC1N 2BX **2051, 2252**
WC1N 2ES **2111**
WC1N 3AU **2272**
WC1N 3JZ **2055**
WC1R 4LR **2159**
WC1V 6NY **2532**
WC1V 7QX **2767**
WC1X 0DW **2027**
WC1X 8HB **2706**
WC1X 9DH **3019**
WC2A 1PL **2444**
WC2A 1PP **2393**
WC2B 4PJ **2205**
WC2H 0HE **2533**
WC2H 0LS **2626**
WC2H 7HH **2530**
WC2H 9EA **2233, 2314, 2573, 2574, 2820**
WC2H 9HE **2389**
WC2N 4LB **2180**
WC2N 6DF **2346**
WC2N 6RL **2167**
WC2R 0RL **2082, 2597**
Luton
LU5 4RU **2110**
LU6 2ES **2123**
Medway
ME2 4HN **2025**
ME5 9AQ **2647**
ME14 5XU **2210**
Portsmouth
PO8 9JL **2507**
PO14 1BU **2108**
PO19 1RP **2741**
PO19 7DN **2582**
PO19 8SQ **2828**

Reading
RG1 4QS **2297, 2415**
RG8 8LU **2567**
RG9 4PG **2056**
RG14 5DS **2206**
RG17 7RU **3017**
RG20 6NL **2630**
RG21 4EA **2001**
RG21 6XS **2088, 2583**
RG21 6YR **2300**
RG27 0JG **2818, 3042**
Redhill
RH4 1DN **2763**
RH10 7WD **2738**
RH13 8RA **2637**
RH17 5PA **3034**
RH18 5ES **2731, 2764**
RH19 3BJ **2114**
RH19 3BT **2817, 3007**
RH19 4FS **2201**
Romford
RM1 4LH **2360**
Slough
SL1 5AP **2289**
SL2 3PQ **2045**
SL2 3RS **2642**
SL6 2QL **2473, 2474**
SL8 5YS **2398**
SL9 8XA **2712**
SL9 9QE **2117**
Southall
UB9 5NX **3006**
UB9 6AT **2845**
Southampton
SO23 8RY **2074**
SO23 9EH **2636**
SO24 0BE **2381**
SO24 9JH **2482**
SO40 7AA **2833**
Southend
SS1 1EF **2403**
SS3 0EQ **2472**
SS9 2LB **2520**
St Albans
AL1 2HA **2268**
AL1 3BN **2397**
AL1 4EG **2842**
AL1 4JL **2753**
AL1 4LW **2142**
AL5 1EQ **2560**
AL6 9EQ **2537**
AL10 9AB **2801**
Sutton (Surrey)
SM1 1DF **2691**
Tonbridge
TN2 3DR **2686**
TN4 9AT **2035**
TN11 8HL **2011**
TN13 3AJ **3023**
TN16 1BZ **2285**
TN17 1HE **2650**
TN18 5AD **2308**
TN30 6BW **2296**
TN35 4PG **2719**
Twickenham
TW1 3QS **3041**

UK PUBLISHERS BY POSTCODE / 185

TW1 4HX **2061**
TW2 5RQ **2238**
TW7 6NH **2848**
TW9 1SR **2347**
TW9 2LL **2023, 2564**
TW9 2ND **2212, 2787**
TW9 3AE **2431**
TW9 3HA **2069**
Watford
  WD6 3PW **2168, 2327**
  WD17 1JA **2504**
  WD19 4BG **2269**

SOUTH-WEST ENGLAND

Bath
  BA1 2BT **2002**
  BA1 3JN **2303**
  BA1 5BG **2078, 3036**
  BA1 5DZ **3016**
  BA2 3AF **2245**
  BA2 3BH **2083**
  BA2 3DZ **2286**
  BA2 3LR **2130**
  BA2 4JT **2759**
  BA2 7WE **2752, 3038**
  BA6 8XR **2316**
  BA8 0TQ **3020**
  BA11 1DS **2171**
  BA11 4EL **2366**
  BA11 4LW **3021**
  BA14 0AA **2616**
  BA22 7JJ **2354**
Bournemouth
  BH15 3SY **2724**
  BH20 6AE **2188**
Bristol
  BS1 4ND **2144**
  BS1 6BE **2410**
  BS1 6JS **2424**
  BS8 1QU **2610**
  BS8 3EA **2639, 2671**
  BS21 7HH **2165**
  BS26 2JU **2137**
  BS41 9LR **2674**
  BS99 1DE **2406**
Dorchester
  DT1 1TT **2808**
  DT7 3LS **2664**
  DT9 4HP **2618**
Exeter
  EX1 1NX **2447**
  EX4 4QR **2800**
  EX5 5HY **2390**
  EX17 4LW **2721**
  EX32 9HG **2624**
  EX38 8ZJ **2425**
Jersey
  JE2 3LD **2267**
Plymouth
  PL2 2EQ **2846**
  PL6 7PP **2783**
  PL14 4EL **2486**
  PL15 8LD **2113**
  PL19 9NQ **2548**
  PL23 1EQ **2203**
  PL28 8BG **2749**
Salisbury
  SP3 5QP **2503**
  SP3 6FA **2368**
  SP7 9LY **2236**
Swindon
  SN2 2GZ **2258**
  SN2 2NA **2534**
  SN5 7YD **2172**
  SN7 7DS **2544**
  SN8 2AA **2006, 2007**
  SN8 2HR **2215**
  SN11 8SB **2364**
  SN11 8YE **2825**
  SN12 8SB **2243**
  SN15 4BW **2605**
Taunton
  TA4 1NE **2145**
  TA4 1QF **3004**
  TA7 9AR **2325**

TA19 0LE **2231**
TA21 9PZ **2343**
Torquay
  TQ9 6EB **2324**
  TQ9 7DL **2623**
  TQ12 4PU **2226**
  TQ12 5UL **2823**
  TQ13 8PA **2557**
Truro
  TR4 8EE **2790**
  TR4 8ZJ **2793**
  TR18 4AW **2383**
  TR20 8BG **2798**
  TR20 8XA **2373**

MIDLANDS

Birmingham
  B9 4AA **2776**
  B29 6LB **2173**
  B80 7LG **2121**
  B91 1UE **2358**
Coventry
  CV8 2GN **2176**
  CV21 3HQ **2384**
  CV34 4XE **2608**
  CV37 1EP **2085**
  CV47 0FB **2392**
Derby
  DE6 1EJ **2442**
  DE7 5DA **2515**
  DE21 4SZ **2120**
Dudley
  DY8 3XY **2648**
Gloucester
  GL5 1BJ **2353**
  GL6 7RL **2720**
  GL7 3QB **2217**
  GL15 6YD **3015**
  GL16 7NS **2838**
  GL50 1UA **2251**
  GL50 2JR **2727**
  GL50 9AN **2638**
  GL52 3LZ **2795**
  GL53 7TH **2539**
  GL56 0YN **2049**
Hereford
  HR3 6QH **2467**
  HR3 8QU **2550**
  HR6 0QF **2318**
  HR6 8NZ **2227**
  HR9 5LA **2593**
Leicester
  LE1 7FW **2788**
  LE5 3GJ **2535**
  LE7 7FU **2773, 2796**
  LE11 1UD **2687**
  LE11 3TU **2461**
  LE11 5DN **2774**
  LE12 6UJ **2356**
  LE67 9SY **2439**
Milton Keynes
  MK2 2EB **2685**
  MK7 6AA **2569**
  MK9 2BE **2066**
  MK13 9HG **2725**
  MK45 4BE **2411**
Northampton
  NN3 6AP **2064**
  NN3 6RT **2320**
  NN5 7HJ **2235, 2394**
  NN7 3JB **3032**
  NN12 6BT **2026, 2524, 2633**
  NN12 9AR **2185**
  NN13 7BE **2365**
  NN14 4BW **2551**
  NN17 4HH **2280**
Nottingham
  NG1 9AW **2281**
  NG6 0BT **2726**
  NG7 2RD **2684**
  NG7 3HR **2416**
  NG12 5GG **2125**
  NG12 5HT **2641**
  NG14 5AL **2607**

NG17 2HU **2792**
NG32 2BB **2079**
Oxford
  OX1 1AP **2483**
  OX1 1ST **2409**
  OX1 2EW **2579**
  OX1 2JW **2349**
  OX1 2PH **2052**
  OX1 3BG **2109**
  OX1 3HJ **2375**
  OX1 5RP **2275**
  OX2 0BS **2221**
  OX2 0ES **2412**
  OX2 0LX **2032**
  OX2 0PH **2575, 2701**
  OX2 0UJ **2464**
  OX2 6DP **2581**
  OX2 6JX **2814**
  OX2 7AR **2565**
  OX2 7DR **2460**
  OX2 7QD **2331**
  OX2 8DP **2330**
  OX2 8EJ **2595**
  OX2 9RU **2208**
  OX3 0BP **2053**
  OX4 1AW **2091**
  OX4 1BW **2541**
  OX4 1RE **2092**
  OX4 2JY **2580**
  OX4 2JZ **2024**
  OX4 3PP **2476**
  OX5 1GB **2254**
  OX5 1RX **2379, 2781**
  OX7 3PH **2152**
  OX7 6RU **3002**
  OX10 8DE **2138**
  OX12 8JY **2514**
  OX14 1AA **2632**
  OX14 3FE **2093**
  OX14 4RN **2655, 2757**
  OX15 0SE **2017**
  OX15 4FF **2680**
  OX18 4XN **2225**
  OX20 1TW **2619**
  OX28 4AW **3031**
  OX29 8SZ **2443**
Shrewsbury
  SY3 0WN **2277**
  SY4 1JA **2628**
  SY4 5JX **2466**
  SY8 1DB **2803**
Stoke-on-Trent
  ST4 5NP **2784**
  ST4 7LU **2766**
  ST17 0TE **2214**
Worcester
  WR9 7EE **2345**
  WR9 7RP **2031**
  WR13 6RN **2211, 2430, 2509, 2543**

EAST ANGLIA

Cambridge
  CB1 1JE **2413**
  CB1 1JT **2561**
  CB1 2NT **2183, 2471**
  CB1 5JX **2669**
  CB2 1UR **2611**
  CB2 8HN **2528**
  CB2 8RU **2140**
  CB3 7NU **3013**
  CB3 9ND **2571**
  CB4 0WF **2662**
  CB4 1ND **2323**
  CB4 3BW **2703**
  CB5 8DT **2832**
  CB5 8SW **2622**
  CB5 9HP **3026**
  CB21 6AH **2837**
  CB23 1HJ **2357**
  CB23 7AY **2452**
Chelmsford
  CM6 2PP **2239**
  CM7 4SL **2643**
  CM8 1WF **2329**

CM15 9TB **2517**
CM20 2JE **2594**
Colchester
  CO2 8HP **2614**
  CO3 3HU **2678**
  CO6 1JE **2181**
  CO15 5WN **2039**
Ipswich
  IP1 3RP **3008**
  IP1 5LT **2558**
  IP12 1AP **2778**
  IP12 2QW **3030**
  IP12 3DF **2116**
  IP12 4SD **2036**
  IP14 3BW **2489**
  IP17 2HD **2156**
  IP25 6QH **2592**
  IP33 2BL **2047**
  IP33 3PH **2262**
Norwich
  NR3 1PD **2791**
  NR3 3AX **2008**
  NR14 7UR **3005**
  NR16 2PB **2261**
  NR26 8NB **3025**
  NR29 3ET **2735**
Peterborough
  PE2 6XP **2804**
  PE2 9JX **2538, 2786**
  PE4 6ZP **2502**
  PE11 1NZ **2163, 2692**
  PE11 4TA **2819**
  PE13 2TH **2134**
  PE21 8EU **2428**
  PE27 5BT **2391**
  PE28 0AE **2577**
  PE28 2NJ **2253**
  PE28 5XE **2228**
  PE37 7XG **2033**
Stevenage
  SG1 2AY **2405**
  SG1 4QX **3037**
  SG1 4SU **2073**
  SG8 5NJ **2841**
  SG12 9HJ **2839**
  SG14 2JA **2699**

NORTH-EAST ENGLAND

Bradford
  BD1 3PT **2148**
  BD16 1AU **2737**
  BD16 1WA **2255**
  BD23 4DT **2810**
  BD23 4ND **2479**
Darlington
  DL3 0PH **2264**
  DL8 4AY **2754**
Doncaster
  DN35 8HU **2714**
Durham
  DH4 5QY **2136**
  DH8 7PW **2311**
Harrogate
  HG1 1BX **2287**
Leeds
  LS3 1AB **2484**
  LS6 4NB **2029**
  LS8 2SP **2294**
  LS12 4HP **2187**
  LS19 7XY **2710**
  LS28 6AT **2380**
Newcastle-upon-Tyne
  NE1 3DY **2522**
  NE6 2HL **2850**
  NE43 7TN **2005**
  NE47 5DX **2282**
  NE48 1RP **2106**
  NE70 7JX **2034**
  NE99 1DX **2794**
Sheffield
  S1 2BS **2492**
  S1 4BF **2301**
  S3 7WL **2695**
  S3 8GG **2328**
  S8 0XJ **2523**

S32 1DJ **2248**
S41 0FR **2501**
S63 9BL **2434**
S80 3LR **2068**
Wakefield
  WF3 2AP **2505**
  WF4 4PX **2829**
  WF5 9AQ **2693**
  WF8 4WW **2654**
York
  YO10 5DD **2112**
  YO10 5DX **2666**
  YO16 6BT **2339**
  YO18 8AL **2103**
  YO24 1ES **2404**
  YO30 6WP **2656**
  YO30 7BZ **2204**
  YO31 9HS **2690**
  YO62 5BP **2547**

NORTH-WEST ENGLAND

Carlisle
  CA2 5AU **2149**
  CA3 9HZ **2606**
  CA12 5AS **2513**
  CA16 6FA **2780**
Chester
  CH3 8JF **2775**
  CH41 9HH **2207**
Lancaster
  LA1 4SL **2151**
  LA7 7PY **2179**
  LA12 9QQ **2768**
  LA20 6HH **2200**
Liverpool
  L3 5SD **2401**
  L69 7ZU **2465**
Manchester
  M1 1JB **3024**
  M22 5LH **2209**
  M23 9HH **2667**
Oldham
  OL14 6DA **2041**
Preston
  PR1 8JP **2216**
  PR3 5LE **2779**
  PR9 0QT **2758**
Stockport
  SK4 4ND **2454**
  SK9 5DY **2704**
  SK14 4SH **2446**
Warrington
  WA4 9DE **2298**

WALES

Cardiff
  CF5 1GZ **2319**
  CF10 4UP **2802**
  CF14 2EA **2240**
  CF14 7ZY **2237**
  CF31 3AE **2689**
  CF31 4DX **2133**
  CF32 0TN **2060**
  CF37 5PB **2094**
  CF46 6SA **2004**
  CF71 9AY **2310**
Llandudno
  LL12 7AW **2122**
  LL13 7NS **2598**
  LL14 5HL **2743**
  LL18 9AY **2739**
  LL21 9WZ **2335**
  LL26 0EH **2334**
  LL53 6SH **2222**
  LL55 2BD **2336**
Mid-Wales
  LD7 1UP **3028**
  SY20 9AZ **2160**
  SY23 1JH **2376**
  SY24 5HE **2843**
Newport (Gwent)
  NP25 4TN **2559**
Swansea
  SA6 6AE **2077**

SA18 3HP **2734**
SA44 4JL **2315**
SA62 5AU **3033**

SCOTLAND

Aberdeen
  AB12 3RT **2644**
  AB34 5LP **2407**
Dumfries
  DG10 9SU **2141, 3014**
Edinburgh
  EH1 1JF **2546**
  EH1 1TE **2143**
  EH1 2ND **2469**
  EH1 3QB **2242**
  EH1 3UG **2481**
  EH1 3YY **2525**
  EH1 4JF **2717**
  EH2 4PS **2326**
  EH4 3BL **2014**
  EH4 3DS **2529**
  EH7 4AY **2164**
  EH8 9LF **2247**
  EH9 1QS **2095**
  EH11 1SH **2283**
  EH12 6EL **2075**
  EH15 1JG **2234**
  EH22 3LJ **2682, 2683**
  EH52 5LH **2309**
  EH52 5NF **2468**
  EH54 8SB **2834**
Falkirk
  FK16 6BJ **2351**
Glasgow
  G2 3DH **2827**
  G2 6TS **2018**
  G3 8NQ **2849**
  G4 0PX **2306**
  G12 8QH **2054**
  G13 1BQ **2830**
  G40 2AB **2455**
  G41 2SD **2131**
  G64 2QT **2191**
  G74 2JZ **2170**
Inverness
  IV15 9SS **2020**
  IV15 9WJ **2670**
  IV20 1TW **2174**
  IV36 3TE **2279**
  IV42 8PY **2750**
Kilmarnock
  KA5 6RD **2732**
  KA27 8SB **2076**
Kirkcaldy
  KY1 2AW **2012**
  KY12 7XG **2219**
Motherwell
  ML11 9DJ **2299**
Orkney
  KW6 6EY **2826**
Paisley & Isles
  HS1 2QN **2003**
  PA1 1NB **2370**
  PA1 1TJ **2278**
  PA22 3AE **2048**
  PA61 7YR **2378**
  PA75 6PR **2132**
Perth
  PH2 1AU **2097**
  PH20 1BU **2723**
Shetland
  ZE1 0PX **2700**

NORTHERN IRELAND

Belfast
  BT3 9LE **2102**
  BT5 6NW **2448**
  BT7 1AP **2040**
  BT9 5AU **2740**
  BT9 5BS **2709**
  BT23 4YH **2192**
  BT48 0LZ **2333**